Arguing About Political Philosophy

Arguing About Political Philosophy is an engaging survey of political philosophy that is perfect for beginning and advanced undergraduates. Selections cover classic philosophical sources such as Rousseau and Locke, as well as contemporary writers such as Nozick and Dworkin. In addition, this text includes a number of readings drawn from economics, literature, and sociology, which serve to introduce philosophical questions about politics in novel and intriguing ways. As well as standard topics such as political authority and distributive justice, special attention is given to global issues that have become especially pressing in recent years, such as the right of individuals or groups to secede, the nature of global distributive justice, the morality of immigration, and the moral status of war and terrorism.

The volume is divided into three parts—Foundational Concepts; Government, the Economy, and Morality; and Global Justice—helping students get to grips with classic and core arguments and emerging debates in:

- Political authority
- Rights
- Justice
- Political economy
- Property rights
- Distributive justice
- Freedom
- Equality
- Immigration
- War, humanitarianism, torture

Matt Zwolinski provides lucid and engaging introductions to each section, giving an overview of the debate and outlining the arguments of each section's readings. *Arguing About Political Philosophy* is an exciting introduction for students new to political philosophy.

Matt Zwolinski is an Assistant Professor of Philosophy at the University of San Diego, and a co-director of USD's Institute for Law and Philosophy. He has published on issues of exploitation and market exchange, and on the nature and value of liberty in political philosophy.

Arguing About Philosophy

This exciting and lively series introduces key subjects in philosophy with the help of a vibrant set of readings. In contrast to many standard anthologies which often reprint the same technical and remote extracts, each volume in the *Arguing About Philosophy* series is built around essential but fresher philosophical readings, designed to attract the curiosity of students coming to the subject for the first time. A key feature of the series is the inclusion of well-known yet often neglected readings from related fields, such as popular science, film and fiction. Each volume is edited by leading figures in their chosen field and each section carefully introduced and set in context, making the series an exciting starting point for those looking to get to grips with philosophy.

Arguing About Knowledge
Edited by Duncan Pritchard and Ram Neta

Arguing About Law
Edited by John Oberdiek and Aileen
Kanvanagh

Arguing About Metaethics
Edited by Andrew Fisher and Simon Kirchin

Arguing About the Mind
Edited by Brie Gertler and Lawrence Shapiro

Arguing About Art 3rd Edition
Edited by Alex Neill and Aaron Ridley

Arguing About Metaphysics
Edited by Michael Rea

Arguing About Political Philosophy
Edited by Matt Zwolinski

Arguing About Religion
Edited by Kevin Timpe

Forthcoming:
Arguing About Language
Edited by Darragh Byrne and Max Kolbel

Arguing About Political Philosophy

Edited by
Matt Zwolinski

Routledge
Taylor & Francis Group

NEW YORK AND LONDON

First published 2009
by Routledge
270 Madison Ave, New York, NY 10016

Simultaneously published in the UK
by Routledge
2 Park Square, Milton Park, Abingdon, Oxon OX14 4RN

Routledge is an imprint of the Taylor & Francis Group, an informa business

Typeset in Joanna by
RefineCatch Limited, Bungay, Suffolk
Printed and bound in the United States of America on acid-free paper by
Edwards Brothers, Inc.

Library of Congress Cataloging-in-Publication Data
Arguing about political philosophy / Matt Zwolinski, editor.
p. cm. – (Arguing about philosophy)
1. Political science–Philosophy. I. Zwolinski, Matt.
JA71.A74 2009
320.01–dc22
2008027005

ISBN-10: 0–415–99078–5 (hbk)
ISBN-10: 0–415–99079–3 (pbk)

ISBN-13: 978–0–415–99078–3 (hbk)
ISBN-13: 978–0–415–99079–0 (pbk)

Dedication

For Jen, with gratitude for all you've shared with me, and hope for all that's yet to come.

Contents

Acknowledgements   xi
General Introduction   xv
What's Your Political Philosophy?   xix

PART 1
Foundational Concepts   1

1a.   POLITICAL AUTHORITY   3

    i. Life Without a State   7

1   *Thomas Hobbes* The State of Nature as a State of War
    (*Leviathan* chapters 11, 13, 15)   7

2   *John Locke* The State of Nature and the Law of Nature
    (*Second Treatise* chapters 2, 3, 9)   13

3   *Robert Axelrod* The Evolution of Cooperation   20

4   *Murray N. Rothbard* Society Without a State   36

    ii. The Social Contract   46

5   *Thomas Hobbes* From Contract to Leviathan
    (*Leviathan* chapters 14, 17)   46

6   *John Locke* Social Contract and the State as Agent
    (*Second Treatise* chapter 8)   52

7   *Jean-Jacques Rousseau* The Social Contract   55

8   *David Hume* Of the Original Contract   71

9   *Charles Tilly* War Making and State Making as
    Organized Crime   78

    iii. Democratic Authority   90

10 *Amy Gutmann and Dennis Thompson*
    Moral Disagreement in a Democracy   90

11   *Gerald F. Gaus* Public Justification and
Democratic Adjudication   106

1b.   RIGHTS   123

12   *United Nations* Universal Declaration of Human Rights   127

13   *Ronald Dworkin* Taking Rights Seriously   132

14   *Joel Feinberg* The Nature and Value of Rights   148

15   *Robert Nozick* Libertarian Rights   159

1c.   JUSTICE   165

16   *David Hume* Justice as Convention   169

17   *John Stuart Mill* Justice and Utility   178

18   *John Rawls* A Theory of Justice   194

19   *Michael J. Sandel* The Procedural Republic and the
Unencumbered Self   219

PART 2
Government, the Economy, and Morality   229

2a.   POLITICAL ECONOMY   231

20   *Karl Marx and Frederick Engels* The Communist
Manifesto and Critique of the Gotha Program   235

21   *Frédéric Bastiat* What is Seen and What is Not Seen   256

22   *Charles Wolf, Jr.* Market Failure   262

23   *William C. Mitchell and Randy T. Simmons*
Pathological Politics: The Anatomy of Government
Failure   269

2b.   PROPERTY RIGHTS   281

24   *John Locke* Property (*Second Treatise* chapter 5)   285

25   *Henry George* The Injustice of Private Property in
Land (1882)   294

26   *David Schmidtz* The Institution of Property   308

27   *G.A. Cohen* Marx and Locke on Land and Labour   320

2c.   DISTRIBUTIVE JUSTICE   339

28   *Barbara Ehrenreich* Nickel and Dimed   343

29   *Robert Nozick* The Entitlement Theory of Justice   358

30   *F. A. Hayek* The Atavism of Social Justice   371

31   *Bruce A. Ackerman* On Getting What We Don't Deserve   379

32   *Kai Nielsen* A Moral Case for Socialism   387

2d.   FREEDOM   395

33   *John Stuart Mill* On Liberty   399

34   *Isaiah Berlin* Two Concepts of Liberty   415

35   *Franklin Delano Roosevelt* The Four Freedoms:
     Annual Message to Congress, January 6, 1941   437

36   *George Fitzhugh* Capitalism as Slavery   439

2e.   EQUALITY   451

37   *Jean-Jacques Rousseau* Discourse on the Origins of
     Inequality   455

38   *Harry Frankfurt* Equality as a Moral Ideal   466

39   *Kurt Vonnegut* Harrison Bergeron   478

40   *Richard J. Arneson* Equality and Equal Opportunity
     for Welfare   482

41   *David Schmidtz* Equal Respect and Equal Shares   495

PART 3
Global Justice   515

3a. IMMIGRATION   517

42   *Chandran Kukathas* The Case for Open Immigration   521

43   *David Miller* Immigration: The Case for Limits   533

3b. GLOBAL DISTRIBUTIVE JUSTICE   545

44   *Peter Singer* Famine, Affluence, and Morality   549

45   *Thomas Pogge* World Poverty and Human Rights   558

46   *Chandran Kukathas* The Mirage of Global Justice   565

3c. SECESSION   585

47   *Herbert Spencer* The Right to Ignore the State   589

48   *Allen Buchanan* Secession and Nationalism   595

3d. WAR, HUMANITARIANISM, AND TORTURE   605

49   *Randolph Bourne* War is the Health of the State   609

50   *Fernando R. Tesón* The Liberal Case for Humanitarian
     Intervention   626

51   *David Luban* Liberalism, Torture, and the Ticking Bomb   647

     Glossary   664
     Index   667

Acknowledgements

It has been my tremendous pleasure to have Kate Ahl at Routledge as an editor on this project. I couldn't have hoped for a more responsive and supportive individual with whom to have worked. My great thanks go to her and to her assistant, Mike Andrews, for all they have done to make this book a reality.

I am also extremely grateful to Kevin Timpe, who helped get this project off the ground by putting me in touch with Routledge, and who has been a great source of help on everything from introductions to cover art since. Many individuals provided me with helpful suggestions regarding the readings for this volume, especially Gerald Gaus, Jason Brennan, Chris Callaway, Eric Rovie, Mark LeBar, Aeon Skoble, and the bloggers and commentators at PEA Soup.

The editor and publishers wish to thank the following for permission to use copyrighted material:

Basic Books, a member of Perseus Books Group, for Robert Axelrod, material from *The Evolution of Cooperation*, copyright © 1984 by Robert Axelrod; and Robert Nozick, "Liberation Rights" from *Anarchy, State, and Utopia*, copyright © 1974 by Basic Books Inc.

Blackwell Publishing for Chandran Kukathas, "The Case for Open Immigration" in *Contemporary Debates in Applied Ethics*, eds. Andrew I. Cohen and Christopher Heath Wellman (2005) pp. 193–205; David Miller, "Immigration: The Case for Limits" in *Contemporary Debates in Applied Ethics*, eds. Andrew I. Cohen and Christopher Heath Wellman (2005) pp. 207–219; Peter Singer, "Famine, Affluence, and Morality" in *Philosophy and Public Affairs* 1:3 (Spring 1972) pp. 229–243; Allen Buchanan, "Secession and Nationalism" in *A Companion to Contemporary Political Philosophy*, eds. Robert Goodin and Philip Petit (1993) pp. 586–96; and Thomas Pogge, "World Poverty and Human Rights" in *Ethics and International Affairs* 19:1 (2005) pp. 1–7.

The British Academy for G.A. Cohen, "Marx and Locke on Land and Labour" in *Proceedings of the British Academy* LXXI (1985). Copyright © 1986 The British Academy.

Cambridge University Press for Charles Tilly, excerpts from "War Making and State Making as Organized Crime" in *Bringing the State Back In*, eds. Peter Evans, Dietrich Rueschmeyer, and Theda Skocpol (1985) pp. 169–177, 181–186, © 1975 Cambridge University Press; Amy Gutmann and Dennis Thompson, "Moral Disagreement in a Democracy" in *Social Philosophy and Policy* 12:1 (1995) pp. 87–110, © 1995 Social Philosophy & Policy Foundation; Bruce A. Ackerman,

"On Getting What We Don't Deserve" in *Social Philosophy and Policy* 1:1 (1983) pp. 60–70, © 1983 Social Philosophy & Policy Foundation; David Schmidtz, "Equal Respect and Equal Shares" in *Social Philosophy and Policy* 19:1 (2002) pp. 244–274, © 2002 Social Philosophy & Policy Foundation; Chandran Kukathas, "The Mirage of Global Justice" in *Social Philosophy and Policy* 23:1 (January 2006) pp. 1–28, © 2006 Social Philosophy & Policy Foundation; and Fernando R. Tesón, "The Liberal Case for Humanitarian Intervention" from *Humanitarian Intervention: Ethical, Legal, and Political Dilemmas*, ed. J. L. Holzgrefe and Robert O. Keohane (2003) pp. 93–129, © 2003 Cambridge University Press.

The *Critical Review* and Kai Nielsen for "A Moral Case for Socialism" in *Critical Review*, vol. 3 (Summer/Fall 1989) pp. 542–552.

Curtis Brown Group Ltd. for Isaiah Berlin, excerpts from "Two Concepts of Liberty" in *Liberty*, ed. Henry Hardy (Oxford University Press, 2002) pp. 168–200, 207–208, 212–217.

Dell Publishing, a division of Random House, Inc., for Kurt Vonnegut, "Harrison Bergeron" from *Welcome to the Monkey House*. Copyright © 1961 by Kurt Vonnegut, Jr.

The Foundation for Economic Education for Frédéric Bastiat, "What is Seen and What is Not Seen" in *Selected Essays on Political Economy, 1848*, trans. Seymour Cain, ed. George B. de Huszar (1995). Foundation for Economic Education, Irvington-on-Hudson, NY 10533, www.fee.org. All rights reserved.

Harvard University Press for Ronald Dworkin, material from *Taking Rights Seriously*, pp. 184–205, copyright © 1977, 1978 by Ronald Dworkin; and John Rawls, material from *Theory of Justice* (1971). Copyright © 1971 by the President and Fellows of Harvard College.

Henry Holt and Company, LLC, for excerpts from *Nickel and Dimed: On (Not) Getting By in America* by Barbara Ehrenreich. Copyright © 2001 by Barbara Ehrenreich.

The Mises Institute for Murray N. Rothbard, "Society Without a State," in the *Libertarian Forum*, vol. VII, no. 1 (January 1975) pp. 3–7.

MIT Press for Charles Wolf, Jr., "Market Failure" from *Markets or Governments: Choosing between Imperfect Alternatives*, pp. 17–29. Copyright © 1993 Massachusetts Institute of Technology.

Oxford University Press, Inc. for David Schmidtz, "The Institution of Property" in *Environmental Ethics: What Really Matters, What Really Works*, ed. David Schmidtz and Elizabeth Willott (2002).

Sage Publications for Michael J. Sandel, "The Procedural Republic and the Unencumbered Self" in *Political Theory* 12:1 (February 1984) pp. 81–96. Copyright © 1984 Sage Publications, Inc.

Springer Science+Business Media for Joel Feinberg, "The Nature and Value of Rights" in the *Journal of Value Inquiry* 4 (1970) pp. 243–257; Gerald F. Gaus, "Public Justification and Democratic Adjudication" in *Constitutional Political Economy*, Vol. 2, No. 3 (1991) pp. 251–281; and Richard J. Arneson, "Equality and Equal Opportunity for Welfare" in *Philosophical Studies*, Vol. 55 (1989) pp. 229–241, © 1989 Kluwer Academic Publishers.

The United Nations for the "Universal Declaration of Human Rights."

University of Chicago Press for F. A. Hayek, "The Atavism of Social Justice" from *New Studies in Philosophy, Politics, Economics, and the History of Ideas* (1978) pp. 57–68, © F. A. Hayek; and Harry Frankfurt, "Equality as a Moral Ideal" in *Ethics*, Vol. 98, No. 1 (October 1987) pp. 21–43, © 1987 The University of Chicago Press.

The *Virginia Law Review* for David Luban, "Liberalism, Torture, and the Ticking Bomb" in the *Virginia Law Review* Vol. 91 (2005), pp. 1425–1461.

Westview Press, a member of Perseus Books Group, for William C. Mitchell and Randy T. Simmons, "Pathalogical Politics" from *Beyond Politics: Markets, Welfare, and the Failure of Bureaucracy*, pp. 66–81. Copyright © 1994 by The Independent Institute.

Every effort has been made to contact copyright holders for their permission to reprint material in this book. The publishers would be grateful to hear from any copyright holder who is not here acknowledged and will undertake to rectify any errors or omissions in future editions of this book.

GENERAL INTRODUCTION

WHETHER WE LIKE IT OR NOT, politics pervades our lives. Political rules control what kinds of foods are available to us from our grocer and at what cost, what sorts of drugs we can consume for medicinal or recreational purposes, how fast we can drive, who we can sleep with, the kind of education we can or must provide for our children, what and where we may speak in public, and how we may practice our religion, to give just the beginning of a very long list. We can choose—and many people do—not to think about politics in any kind of systematic and rigorous way. But we cannot choose to isolate ourselves from its effects.

This is a book for people who want to think seriously about politics. It is, to be more specific, a book about political philosophy. Philosophy, of course, is not the only way of thinking seriously about politics. Most obviously, one could also choose to study the subject through the methodology of political science. Psychologists, sociologists, historians, and even economists also provide intellectual tools with which to think critically about political issues. What, then, differentiates the philosophic approach from these others?

The first important difference between philosophical analysis and other approaches is that philosophy is at its core a *non-empirical* approach. To study politics empirically is to be concerned with observation and measurement. Political scientists engage in empirical research, for instance, when they look at the voting patterns of different ethnic or religious groups, or when they attempt to measure the effects of certain public policies on crime rates. Philosophical research, on the other hand, tends to look very different. For philosophers, the primary tools of inquiry are logical argument and conceptual analysis. Conceptual analysis involves trying to clearly define or characterize abstract concepts such as justice or the state, and to distinguish them from other closely related subjects such as equality or society. Logical argument involves discerning and evaluating the internal structure of the reasons people give to support their claims, and trying to ensure that the claims we ourselves make follow from our premises.

What does the use of these tools look like in practice? Suppose someone claims that the primary function of the state is to provide security for its citizens, and that therefore we ought to have an extremely restrictive immigration policy in order to protect ourselves from foreign threats. As philosophers, we can respond to this claim by, first, using the method of conceptual analysis to scrutinize the claim about the nature of statehood. Is the primary function of the state really protection of citizens? Protection from what? What if the promotion of security conflicts with the preservation of liberty? Surely security isn't the *only* thing we care about, so can we come up with a conception of statehood that better responds to the plurality of values we hold? Even if we accept the idea that the function of statehood is to provide security, however, we can still ask whether it follows logically from this definition that a restrictive immigration policy is warranted. Strictly speaking, of course, it only follows *if* a restrictive immigration policy turns out to be a good way of promoting security. So that's one assumption that needs to be flagged and set aside for closer scrutiny. Are there any other hidden assumptions embedded in the argument? By deploying the tools of logic we can help to uncover such assumptions and thereby discern the validity or invalidity of political arguments. (Philosophy can't do all the work though—a philosopher can tell you that your argument tacitly assumes a certain claim about the effects of a public policy, but it is up to economists, sociologists, or political scientists to tell us whether that claim is *as an empirical matter* true or false.)

The second important difference between the philosophical approach to politics and the approaches taken by other disciplines is that philosophy is often explicitly *normative* in its approach. To approach a subject from a normative perspective is to make claims about *values,* or about what *ought* to be the case. Normative approaches are to be distinguished from *descriptive* approaches, which merely purport to tell us the way things *are* (and not whether the way things are is good or bad). It is important to recognize that not *all* of philosophy is normative. Claims about the nature of certain concepts, for instance, are not necessarily normative, even (and this is tricky!) if the concepts themselves *are* normative concepts. "Justice," for instance, is clearly a normative concept in the sense that calling something just or unjust involves making a kind of value claim. But a philosopher who proposes to define justice as giving each person his or her due, for instance, is not necessarily making a value claim. They might simply be trying to issue a report on the way a word is used by a certain community. Often, however, philosophers *will* be making value claims—and sometimes they will do so in the context of providing a definition. So, for instance, if I were to define justice as treating people according to what their actions merit, and I defended this definition by saying that this is the only way of understanding justice that captures what is *truly important and valuable* about justice, then I would be making a normative claim. My definition of the word "justice" is based on my belief that some value is more important or significant than others, and that is a quintessentially normative belief.

Sometimes it can be difficult to tell whether a philosopher is making a normative claim or whether they are simply trying to provide a value-neutral definition or description of how things are. Making this determination will require careful attention on your part as a reader. At other times, however, value claims—such as the claim that torture is degrading and ought not to be practiced—will be front and center in a philosopher's argument. This would be seen as unscientific and uncalled for in strictly empirical approaches to politics. But philosophy, as a partially normative discipline, calls upon us to think about, scrutinize, and argumentatively defend our values and their application to the political realm.

Political discussion will not be productive if we are not clear on what the words we use mean. Nor will we get very far unless we have some idea of where we want to go—what values we are trying to promote. Philosophy, then, is an indispensable tool for thinking about politics. But philosophy by itself—since it refrains from empirical investigation regarding how the world actually works—cannot get us very far either.

Philosophical analysis must be supplemented by empirical research from other disciplines. Some of that research is presented in this book. Axelrod's essay on game theory, Tilly's essay on the history of the state, and Ehrenreich's journalistic account of working-class America, for instance, are all essentially empirical approaches to politics. I have included them in this volume because they provide us with some data with which to pursue our philosophical analysis, and because they demonstrate quite nicely how philosophical questions arise even in the course of non-philosophical investigation. Part of your development as a budding political philosopher will be learning how to adjust your philosophical worldview in light of empirical evidence, while simultaneously scrutinizing the philosophical assumptions underlying those empirical claims. This is a difficult task, but given the importance of the subject, it is also a crucial one. My hope is that the readings in this book will make it a challenging and exciting one as well.

Further Reading

The following are good introductions to the subject of political philosophy:

Hampton, J. (1997). *Political Philosophy*. Boulder, CO: Westview.
Kymlicka, W. (2002). *Contemporary Political Philosophy: An Introduction* (2nd edn.). Oxford: Oxford University Press.
Narveson, J. (2008). *You and the State: A Short Introduction to Political Philosophy*. Lanham, MD: Rowman and Littlefield.

WHAT'S YOUR POLITICAL PHILOSOPHY?

This survey provides a way for readers to see where they stand on a variety of the issues covered in this book. Instructors might find it useful to administer this survey on the first day of class, both to get a sense of where students stand and to provoke some initial discussion. Later, you can ask students to return to the various parts of the survey after the corresponding readings have been covered in the course to see what changes, if any, those readings have produced in students' beliefs.

For each item, indicate the degree to which you agree with the statement.

Political Authority

1.   It is never morally justifiable to break the law.

Strongly Disagree   Disagree   Neither agree nor disagree   Agree   Strongly Agree

2.   If the law tells me to do/not do something, then this gives me *some* reason to do/not do that thing.

Strongly Disagree   Disagree   Neither agree nor disagree   Agree   Strongly Agree

3.   Political authority is justified because it derives from the consent of the governed.

Strongly Disagree   Disagree   Neither agree nor disagree   Agree   Strongly Agree

4.   In the absence of government, life would be very bad for people in general.

Strongly Disagree   Disagree   Neither agree nor disagree   Agree   Strongly Agree

5.   Democracy is the best way of settling disagreements among free and equal citizens.

Strongly Disagree   Disagree   Neither agree nor disagree   Agree   Strongly Agree

6.   If the majority of citizens vote in support of a law, then government is morally justified in enforcing that law.

Strongly Disagree   Disagree   Neither agree nor disagree   Agree   Strongly Agree

Rights

7.   All human beings have natural rights which exist prior to and independent of government.

Strongly Disagree   Disagree   Neither agree nor disagree   Agree   Strongly Agree

8. If someone has a right not to have X done to them, then it is in all circumstances absolutely morally unjustifiable to do X to them.

Strongly Disagree   Disagree   Neither agree nor disagree   Agree   Strongly Agree

9. If we are in desperate need through no fault of our own, we have a right for others or for the government to provide us with aid.

Strongly Disagree   Disagree   Neither agree nor disagree   Agree   Strongly Agree

10. The only right we have is the right to be free from the initiation of aggression by others.

Strongly Disagree   Disagree   Neither agree nor disagree   Agree   Strongly Agree

Justice

11. We should do what justice requires no matter how bad the consequences might be.

Strongly Disagree   Disagree   Neither agree nor disagree   Agree   Strongly Agree

12. What is just is a function of what produces good consequences for society in the long run.

Strongly Disagree   Disagree   Neither agree nor disagree   Agree   Strongly Agree

13. The laws of my country are mostly just.

Strongly Disagree   Disagree   Neither agree nor disagree   Agree   Strongly Agree

14. The requirements of justice do not vary from culture to culture or across time.

Strongly Disagree   Disagree   Neither agree nor disagree   Agree   Strongly Agree

Political Economy

15. Capitalism exploits the working class.

Strongly Disagree   Disagree   Neither agree nor disagree   Agree   Strongly Agree

16. Even if they serve no other purpose, military bases help the economy by providing jobs for people.

Strongly Disagree   Disagree   Neither agree nor disagree   Agree   Strongly Agree

17. Relatively unregulated capitalism does a better job at making people well-off than any other system.

Strongly Disagree   Disagree   Neither agree nor disagree   Agree   Strongly Agree

18. Market failures like monopolies are best addressed by government regulation.

Strongly Disagree   Disagree   Neither agree nor disagree   Agree   Strongly Agree

Property Rights

19.   All private ownership of land is unjust.

Strongly Disagree   Disagree   Neither agree nor disagree   Agree   Strongly Agree

20.   Most private property as it exists in the world today came about unjustly.

Strongly Disagree   Disagree   Neither agree nor disagree   Agree   Strongly Agree

21.   Private property in the means of production should be abolished.

Strongly Disagree   Disagree   Neither agree nor disagree   Agree   Strongly Agree

22.   Government taxation is a violation of property rights.

Strongly Disagree   Disagree   Neither agree nor disagree   Agree   Strongly Agree

Distributive Justice

23.   The fact that the rich in a country like the United States have so much more wealth than the poor is unjust.

Strongly Disagree   Disagree   Neither agree nor disagree   Agree   Strongly Agree

24.   Inequality of wealth is unjust regardless of how it came about.

Strongly Disagree   Disagree   Neither agree nor disagree   Agree   Strongly Agree

25.   Socialism is superior to capitalism in terms of producing a just distribution of wealth.

Strongly Disagree   Disagree   Neither agree nor disagree   Agree   Strongly Agree

26.   Government should try to make sure that people get the wealth or income that they deserve.

Strongly Disagree   Disagree   Neither agree nor disagree   Agree   Strongly Agree

Freedom

27.   The promotion of individual freedom is one of the most important purposes of government.

Strongly Disagree   Disagree   Neither agree nor disagree   Agree   Strongly Agree

28.   A person is free to the extent that that person is not interfered with by others.

Strongly Disagree   Disagree   Neither agree nor disagree   Agree   Strongly Agree

29.   True freedom requires the ability and material resources to achieve one's goals.

Strongly Disagree   Disagree   Neither agree nor disagree   Agree   Strongly Agree

30.   Capitalism is the best economic system for promoting individual freedom.

Strongly Disagree   Disagree   Neither agree nor disagree   Agree   Strongly Agree

Equality

31. All human beings are equal, morally speaking.

Strongly Disagree   Disagree   Neither agree nor disagree   Agree   Strongly Agree

32. Government should try to promote economic equality through its laws and regulations.

Strongly Disagree   Disagree   Neither agree nor disagree   Agree   Strongly Agree

33. Government should promote equality of opportunity, rather than equality of outcome.

Strongly Disagree   Disagree   Neither agree nor disagree   Agree   Strongly Agree

34. A large amount of material inequality is compatible with the moral equality of persons.

Strongly Disagree   Disagree   Neither agree nor disagree   Agree   Strongly Agree

Immigration

35. My country currently allows too much immigration.

Strongly Disagree   Disagree   Neither agree nor disagree   Agree   Strongly Agree

36. Illegal immigrants who are just trying to improve their lives are not doing anything morally wrong.

Strongly Disagree   Disagree   Neither agree nor disagree   Agree   Strongly Agree

37. The most moral immigration policy is one where borders are completely or almost completely open.

Strongly Disagree   Disagree   Neither agree nor disagree   Agree   Strongly Agree

38. Governments ought to discriminate among potential immigrants and admit only those who will promote the country's national interest.

Strongly Disagree   Disagree   Neither agree nor disagree   Agree   Strongly Agree

Global Distributive Justice

39. It is unfair that some people are born into countries struggling with desperate poverty, while others are born into luxury.

Strongly Disagree   Disagree   Neither agree nor disagree   Agree   Strongly Agree

40. It is morally wrong for individuals in wealthy countries like the United States to spend money on luxuries while others starve.

Strongly Disagree   Disagree   Neither agree nor disagree   Agree   Strongly Agree

41. Justice requires a radical transformation of the global political and economic order.

Strongly Disagree   Disagree   Neither agree nor disagree   Agree   Strongly Agree

42. More capitalism, and less government, will promote global justice.

Strongly Disagree   Disagree   Neither agree nor disagree   Agree   Strongly Agree

Secession

43. It is sometimes permissible for cultural and ethnic groups to secede from their larger political unit.

Strongly Disagree   Disagree   Neither agree nor disagree   Agree   Strongly Agree

44. It would be unfair for a wealthy group to secede from a country in order to avoid paying taxes to support the poor.

Strongly Disagree   Disagree   Neither agree nor disagree   Agree   Strongly Agree

45. Any group or even individual should be able to secede from the state and become an autonomous political unit.

Strongly Disagree   Disagree   Neither agree nor disagree   Agree   Strongly Agree

War, Humanitarian Intervention, and Torture

46. War is never morally justified.

Strongly Disagree   Disagree   Neither agree nor disagree   Agree   Strongly Agree

47. The only moral war is a defensive war.

Strongly Disagree   Disagree   Neither agree nor disagree   Agree   Strongly Agree

48. It is sometimes true that State A is morally justified in going to war with State B to protect citizens of State B from their own government.

Strongly Disagree   Disagree   Neither agree nor disagree   Agree   Strongly Agree

49. Torture is under no circumstances morally permissible.

Strongly Disagree   Disagree   Neither agree nor disagree   Agree   Strongly Agree

50. Governments should never permit their agents to torture under any circumstances.

Strongly Disagree   Disagree   Neither agree nor disagree   Agree   Strongly Agree

PART 1

Foundational Concepts

1a. POLITICAL AUTHORITY

GOVERNMENTS CLAIM, and are usually assumed to have, a kind of moral authority to do things that no other individual or group of individuals may do. Governments can take your money without your permission and spend it on things they think are important—whether or not you agree. Governments can tell you what sorts of drugs you may or may not consume, what kinds of things you may or may not say in public, and what kinds of goods and services you may or may not sell to others. Governments can even force you to be a part of their army, where they will not only tell you what to eat, wear and say, but also who to kill. And if you disobey any of your government's directives, it can forcibly round you up and lock you away in a small concrete room for as long as it likes—or possibly it will even kill you.

What gives governments the right to do these things? Or *does* government have the right to do them? Are there any limits on what government may legitimately do and, if so, where do these limits come from?

The readings in this section explore these questions by looking at the issue of political authority. Specifically, we will be exploring political authority as a *normative* notion. A government may have authority in a *de facto* sense if it rules effectively, and perhaps if a sufficient portion of the population believes that it is a proper authority. But to have authority in a normative sense requires more than this, even if what exactly it requires is a matter of some controversy. Some hold that the essence of legitimate authority is the ability to coerce subjects in a way that is morally justified. Others hold that it is the ability to impose duties on subjects through laws. And still others hold that legitimate authority is essentially concerned with the right to rule. Note how these conceptions come apart—A might have a right to rule over B, for instance, without B having a corresponding duty to obey A. However the details are fleshed out, what normative conceptions of political authority have in common is that they make a *moral* claim about governments' commands and/or citizens' responses to those commands.

Historically, some of the most popular accounts of authority have been based on the idea of individual consent and the *social contract*. The idea behind such accounts is that political authority is legitimate when it is consented to by those who are subject to it. If, then, we can look back to a time when individuals lived without a common government—when they lived in what is generally referred to as a *state of nature*—we can see what the conditions in such a state would be like, and thereby see both what reasons such individuals would have to consent to a government (and hence to extricate themselves from the state of nature), and what *kind* of government they would have reason to consent to.

Hobbes, Locke, and Rousseau present three different accounts of the state of nature, and three correspondingly different accounts of the social contract by which government is first instituted. Each of their accounts is rich in detail and raises numerous questions of philosophic interest. But a brief comparison of one of the many aspects on which Hobbes and Locke differ can provide some insight as to how theories of the state of nature and theories of political authority are related. For Locke, the state of nature is governed by a law of nature by which individuals are forbidden from harming one another in their life, liberty or estate. Not all individuals follow this law in all circumstances, and even when individuals act in good faith, there sometimes arise understandable disagreements regarding who did what to whom and whether or not what was done was actually a breach of nature's law. But war and conflict are not the normal condition of the state of nature, and all that is necessary to remedy the "inconveniences" of this state is a limited government with adjudicative and policing powers. For Hobbes, on the other hand, the state of nature is a state of perpetual war of every man against every man, and the life of man in such a state is "solitary, poor, nasty, brutish and short." As long as individuals are left in such a state to rely on their own judgment and power, this state of war will continue. For Hobbes, then, the solution to the problem of the state of nature requires a much more powerful form of government—one which will supplant individuals' reliance on their own judgment by replacing it with authoritative law, and which will back up that law with awe-inspiring force.

As compelling as these stories about the social contract may be, they face several serious difficulties. First, as will be made clear in the essay by Charles Tilly, it is not clear that governments arose in a way that had anything to do with individual consent at all. But if there never was any social contract, then how can the contract be used to justify any of the governments we actually have? Second, even if a contract could bind the people who signed on to it and thereby originally established a government, it is not clear how future generations could be bound to it. Must each person born into the society sign on to the contract as well? Or do we look instead (as Locke does) for signs of some form of "tacit," rather than explicit, consent? And finally, as David Hume points out, the claim that a social contract could legitimate government authority only works if we assume that people have a moral obligation to keep their promises. But it is not clear why we should take *this* duty to be fundamental and self-evident. Both justice and fidelity to promises, Hume argues, are "artificial" virtues, and so we make no real explanatory progress by justifying one in terms of the other. *Both* promise-keeping and obedience to the law must be explained in terms of some more fundamental moral fact, and for Hume this is simply that both are necessary in order for society to subsist.

Social contract theorists often respond to the first problem by claiming that their theories are not meant to provide a *historical* account of what was actually consented to, but rather a *hypothetical* account of what individuals would *have reason to consent to*, given certain assumptions about their circumstances. Stories about the state of nature and the social contract are not meant to be accurate accounts of some actual event that occurred in the distant past. Rather, they are meant to be heuristics for thinking about certain enduring and significant aspects of human nature and social relations, and the way in which those facts give us reason to endorse certain forms of government. Whether we *actually* consented to those forms of government, then, is not really the issue. What matters is that we would have *reason* to do so, and this fact can help us answer the question of whether or not our current government is one which we ought to view as legitimate. As we will see later in the book, John Rawls is explicit in describing his social contract account as a hypothetical one. But all of the accounts in this section will probably strike contemporary readers as more plausible if read in this way.

Still, even hypothetical social contract accounts have their problems. Those who think that there is something important about *actual* consent, for instance, will be disturbed by the move from thinking about *actual* contracts justifying states, to *hypothetical* ones doing so. After all, in many contexts this substitution would surely be inappropriate. If you actually agree to sell me your car for $5,000, then it is permissible for me to take your car in exchange for giving you my money. But in the absence of any explicit agreement, I cannot simply leave a check on your porch and drive off in your car, no matter how convinced I am that you *would* have agreed to the bargain if I had asked you.

Partly, this is because it is very difficult for me to have any confidence in what you *would have* agreed to without your actually telling me. And this is why we find so much disagreement among social contract theorists. Different theorists make different assumptions about the social conditions that individuals would find themselves in, in the absence of a common government, and about the goals and desires those individuals would have. Some, like Murray Rothbard, even conclude that individuals would get along just fine in a state of nature, and would have no reason to consent to any government at all! Given that there exists so much disagreement regarding what individuals would have reason to consent to, how can we hope to use social contract theories as a way of justifying legitimate political authority?

The problem of enduring disagreement between reasonable people on pressing questions of moral and political theory has led some theorists to look to democratic theory as an alternative way of justifying legitimate authority. Democracy can provide both a forum for citizens to deliberate about their values and a procedure for resolving disputes and settling on a policy that is acceptable to the community as a whole. The last few readings in this section, then, survey different conceptions of and justifications for democratic rule as an alternative method for justifying political authority.

Further Reading

Edmundson, W. (1998). *Three Anarchical Fallacies*. Cambridge: Cambridge University Press.

Green, L. (1988). *The Authority of the State*. Oxford: Oxford University Press.

Klosko, G. (2004). *The Principle of Fairness and Political Obligation* (2nd edn.). Lanham, MD: Rowman & Littlefield.

Klosko, G. (2005). *Political Obligations*. Oxford: Oxford University Press.

Pitkin, H. (1965). Obligation and Consent: Part One. *American Political Science Review, 59,* 990–999.

Pitkin, H. (1966). Obligation and Consent: Part Two. *American Political Science Review, 60,* 39–52.

Rawls, J. (1964). Legal Obligation and the Duty of Fair Play. In S. Hook (Ed.), *Law and Philosophy*. New York: New York University Press.

Raz, J. (1979). *The Authority of Law*. Oxford: Oxford University Press.

Sanders, J. T., & Narveson, J. (1996). *For and Against the State: New Essays*. Lanham, MD: Rowman & Littlefield.

Simmons, A. J. (1979). *Moral Principles and Political Obligations*: Princeton, NJ: Princeton University Press.

Simmons, A. J. (2001). *Justification and Legitimacy: Essays on Rights and Obligations*. Cambridge: Cambridge University Press.

Smith, M. B. E. (1973). Is There a Prima Facie Obligation to Obey the Law? *Yale Law Journal, 82,* 950–976.

Wellman, C. H., & Simmons, A. J. (2005). *Is There a Duty to Obey the Law?* Cambridge: Cambridge University Press.

Wolff, R. P. (1970). *In Defense of Anarchism* (3rd edn.). Berkeley, CA: University of California Press.

i. Life Without a State

Chapter 1

Thomas Hobbes

THE STATE OF NATURE AS A STATE OF WAR

Thomas Hobbes (1588–1679) was an English philosopher whose major work, *Leviathan*, was published in 1651 to great controversy amidst the English Civil War, and later went on to become one of the most influential works in the social contract tradition of political philosophy. In these excerpts, Hobbes gives us his thoughts on what life would be like in a "state of nature"—a state where human beings lived without the protection of any government. He also begins his description of the moral "law of nature" to which people are subject in this state, and argues that under certain special circumstances, people have reason to act justly.

Of the Difference of Manners

By Manners, I mean not here, Decency of behaviour; as how one man should salute another, or how a man should wash his mouth, or pick his teeth before company, and such other points of the *Small Moralls*; But those qualities of man-kind, that concern their living together in Peace, and Unity. To which end we are to consider, that the Felicity of this life, consisteth not in the repose of a mind satisfied. For there is no such *Finis ultimus*, (utmost ayme,) nor *Summum Bonum*, (greatest Good,) as is spoken of in the Books of the old Morall Philosophers. Nor can a man any more live, whose Desires are at an end, than he, whose Senses and Imaginations are at a stand. Felicity is a continuall progresse of the desire, from one object to another; the attaining of the former, being still but the way to the later. The cause whereof is, That the object of mans desire, is not to enjoy once onely, and for one instant of time; but to assure for ever, the way of his future desire. And therefore the voluntary actions, and inclinations of all men, tend, not only to the procuring, but also to the assuring of a contented life; and differ onely in the way: which ariseth partly from the diversity of passions, in divers men; and partly from the difference of the knowledge, or opinion each one has of the causes, which produce the effect desired.

So that in the first place, I put for a generall inclination of all mankind, a perpetuall and restlesse desire of Power after power, that ceaseth onely in Death. And the cause of this, is not alwayes that a man hopes for a more intensive delight, than he has already attained to; or that he cannot be content with a moderate power: but because he cannot assure the power and means to live well, which he hath present, without the acquisition of more. And from hence it is, that Kings, whose power is greatest, turn their endeavours to the assuring it at home by Lawes, or abroad by Wars: and when that is done, there succeedeth a new desire; in some, of Fame from new Conquest; in others, of ease and sensuall pleasure; in others, of admiration, or being flattered for excellence in some art, or other ability of the mind. [. . .]

Of the *Naturall Condition* of Mankind, as Concerning their Felicity, and Misery

Nature hath made men so equall, in the faculties of body, and mind; as that though there bee found one man sometimes manifestly stronger in body, or of quicker mind then another; yet when all is reckoned together, the difference between man, and man, is not so considerable, as that one man can thereupon claim to himselfe any benefit, to which another may not pretend, as well as he. For as to the strength of body, the weakest has strength enough to kill the strongest, either by secret machination, or by confederacy with others, that are in the same danger with himselfe.

And as to the faculties of the mind, (setting aside the arts grounded upon words, and especially that skill of proceeding upon generall, and infallible rules, called Science; which very few have, and but in few things; as being not a native faculty, born with us; nor attained, (as Prudence,) while we look after somewhat els,) I find yet a greater equality amongst men, than that of strength. For Prudence, is but Experience; which equall time, equally bestowes on all men, in those things they equally apply themselves unto. That which may perhaps make such equality incredible, is but a vain conceipt of ones owne wisdome, which almost all men think they have in a greater degree, than the Vulgar; that is, than all men but themselves, and a few others, whom by Fame, or for concurring with themselves, they approve. For such is the nature of men, that howsoever they may acknowledge many others to be more witty, or more eloquent, or more learned; Yet they will hardly believe there be many so wise as themselves: For they see their own wit at hand, and other mens at a distance. But this proveth rather that men are in that point

equall, than unequall. For there is not ordinarily a greater signe of the equall distribution of any thing, than that every man is contented with his share.

From this equality of ability, ariseth equality of hope in the attaining of our Ends. And therefore if any two men desire the same thing, which neverthelesse they cannot both enjoy, they become enemies; and in the way to their End, (which is principally their owne conservation, and sometimes their delectation only,) endeavour to destroy, or subdue one an other. And from hence it comes to passe, that where an Invader hath no more to feare, than an other mans single power; if one plant, sow, build, or possesse a convenient Seat, others may probably be expected to come prepared with forces united, to dispossesse, and deprive him, not only of the fruit of his labour, but also of his life, or liberty. And the Invader again is in the like danger of another.

And from this diffidence of one another, there is no way for any man to secure himselfe, so reasonable, as Anticipation; that is, by force, or wiles, to master the persons of all men he can, so long, till he see no other power great enough to endanger him: And this is no more than his own conservation requireth, and is generally allowed. Also because there be some, that taking pleasure in contemplating their own power in the acts of conquest, which they pursue farther than their security requires; if others, that otherwise would be glad to be at ease within modest bounds, should not by invasion increase their power, they would not be able, long time, by standing only on their defence, to subsist. And by consequence, such augmentation of dominion over men, being necessary to a mans conservation, it ought to be allowed him.

Againe, men have no pleasure, (but on the contrary a great deale of griefe) in keeping company, where there is no power able to over-awe them all. For every man looketh that his companion should value him, at the same rate he sets upon himselfe: And upon all signes of contempt, or undervaluing, naturally endeavours, as far as he dares (which amongst them that have no common power, to keep them in quiet, is far enough to make them destroy each other,) to extort a greater value from his contemners, by dommage; and from others, by the example.

So that in the nature of man, we find three principall causes of quarrell. First, Competition; Secondly, Diffidence; Thirdly, Glory.

The first, maketh men invade for Gain; the second, for Safety; and the third, for Reputation. The first use Violence, to make themselves Masters of other mens persons, wives, children, and cattell; the second, to defend them; the third, for trifles, as a word, a smile, a different opinion, and any other signe of undervalue, either direct in their Persons, or by reflexion in their Kindred, their Friends, their Nation, their Profession, or their Name.

Hereby it is manifest, that during the time men live without a common Power to keep them all in awe, they are in that condition which is called Warre; and such a warre, as is of every man, against every man. For WARRE, consisteth not in Battell onely, or the act of fighting; but in a tract of time, wherein the Will to contend by Battell is sufficiently known: and therefore the notion of Time, is to be considered in the nature of Warre; as it is in the nature of Weather. For as the nature of Foule weather, lyeth not in a showre or two of rain; but in an inclination thereto of many dayes together: So the nature of War, consisteth not in actuall fighting; but in the known disposition thereto, during all the time there is no assurance to the contrary. All other time is PEACE.

Whatsoever therefore is consequent to a time of Warre, where every man is Enemy to every man; the same is consequent to the time, wherein men live without other security, than what their own strength, and their own invention shall furnish them withall. In such condition, there is no place for Industry; because the fruit thereof is uncertain: and consequently no Culture of the Earth; no Navigation, nor use of the commod-ities that may be imported by Sea; no commodious Building; no Instruments of moving, and removing such things as require much force; no Knowledge of the face of the Earth; no account of Time; no Arts; no Letters; no Society; and which is worst of all, continuall feare, and danger of violent death; And the life of man, solitary, poore, nasty, brutish, and short.

It may seem strange to some man, that has not well weighed these things; that Nature should thus dissociate, and render men apt to invade, and destroy one another: and he may therefore, not trusting to this Inference, made from the Passions, desire perhaps to have the same confirmed by Experience. Let him therefore consider with himselfe, when taking a journey, he armes himselfe, and seeks to go well accompanied; when going to sleep, he locks his dores; when even in his house he locks his chests; and this when he knows there bee Lawes, and publike Officers, armed, to revenge all injuries shall bee done him; what opinion he has of his fellow subjects, when he rides armed; of his fellow Citizens, when he locks his dores; and of his children, and servants, when he locks his chests. Does he not there as much accuse mankind by his actions, as I do by my words? But neither of us accuse mans nature in it. The Desires, and other Passions of man, are in themselves no Sin. No more are the Actions, that proceed from those Passions, till they know a Law that forbids them: which till Lawes be made they cannot know: nor can any Law be made, till they have agreed upon the Person that shall make it.

It may peradventure be thought, there was never such a time, nor condition of warre as this; and I believe it was never generally so, over all the world: but there are many places, where they live so now. For the savage people in many places of *America*, except the government of small Families, the concord whereof dependeth on naturall lust, have no government at all; and live at this day in that brutish manner, as I said before. Howsoever, it may be perceived what manner of life there would be, where there were no common Power to feare; by the manner of life, which men that have formerly lived under a peacefull government, use to degenerate into, in a civill Warre.

But though there had never been any time, wherein particular men were in a condition of warre one against another; yet in all times, Kings, and Persons of Soveraigne authority, because of their Independency, are in continuall jealousies, and in the state and posture of Gladiators; having their weapons pointing, and their eyes fixed on one another; that is, their Forts, Garrisons, and Guns upon the Frontiers of their Kingdomes; and continually Spyes upon their neighbours; which is a posture of War. But because they uphold thereby, the Industry of their Subjects; there does not follow from it, that misery, which accompanies the Liberty of particular men.

To this warre of every man against every man, this also is consequent; that nothing can be Unjust. The notions of Right and Wrong, Justice and Injustice have there no place. Where there is no common Power, there is no Law: where no Law, no Injustice. Force, and Fraud, are in warre the two Cardinall vertues. Justice, and Injustice are none of the Faculties neither of the Body, nor Mind. If they were, they might be in a man that were alone in the world, as well as his Senses, and Passions. They are Qualities, that relate to men in Society, not in Solitude. It is consequent also to the same condition, that there be no Propriety, no Dominion, no Mine and Thine distinct; but onely that to be every mans that he can get; and for so long, as he can keep it. And thus much for the ill condition, which man by meer Nature is actually placed in; though with a possibility to come out of it, consisting partly in the Passions, partly in his Reason.

The Passions that encline men to Peace, are Feare of Death; Desire of such things as are necessary to commodious living; and a Hope by their Industry to obtain them. And Reason suggesteth convenient Articles of Peace, upon which men may be drawn to agreement. These Articles, are they, which otherwise are called the Lawes of Nature.

Of Other Lawes of Nature

From that law of Nature, by which we are obliged to transferre to another, such Rights, as being retained, hinder the peace of Mankind, there followeth a Third; which is this, *That men performe their Covenants made*: without which, Covenants are in vain, and but Empty words; and the Right of all men to all things remaining, wee are still in the condition of Warre.

And in this law of Nature, consisteth the Fountain and Originall of JUSTICE. For where no Covenant hath preceded, there hath no Right been transferred, and every man has right to every thing; and consequently, no action can be Unjust. But when a Covenant is made, then to break it is Unjust: And the definition of INJUSTICE, is no other than *the not Performance of Covenant*. And whatsoever is not Unjust, is Just.

But because Covenants of mutuall trust, where there is a feare of not performance on either part, are invalid; though the Originall of Justice be the making of Covenants; yet Injustice actually there can be none, till the cause of such feare be taken away; which while men are in the naturall condition of Warre, cannot be done. Therefore before the names of Just, and Unjust can have place, there must be some coercive Power, to compell men equally to the performance of their Covenants, by the terrour of some punishment, greater than the benefit they expect by the breach of their Covenant; and to make good that Propriety, which by mutuall Contract men acquire, in recompence of the universall Right they abandon: and such power there is none before the erection of a Commonwealth. And this is also to be gathered out of the ordinary definition of Justice in the Schooles: For they say, that *Justice is the constant Will of giving to every man his own*. And therefore where there is no *Own*, that is, no Propriety, there is no Injustice; and where there is no coërceive Power erected, that is, where there is no

Common-wealth, there is no Propriety; all men having Right to all things: Therefore where there is no Common-wealth, there nothing is Unjust. So that the nature of Justice, consisteth in keeping of valid Covenants: but the Validity of Covenants begins not but with the Constitution of a Civil Power, sufficient to compell men to keep them: And then it is also that Propriety begins.

The Foole hath sayd in his heart, there is no such thing as Justice; and sometimes also with his tongue; seriously alleaging, that every mans conservation, and contentment, being committed to his own care, there could be no reason, why every man might not do what he thought conduced thereunto: and therefore also to make, or not make; keep, or not keep Covenants, was not against Reason, when it conduced to ones benefit. He does not therein deny, that there be Covenants; and that they are sometimes broken, sometimes kept; and that such breach of them may be called Injustice, and the observance of them Justice: but he questioneth, whether Injustice, taking away the feare of God, (for the same Foole hath said in his heart there is no God,) may not sometimes stand with that Reason, which dictateth to every man his own good; and particularly then, when it conduceth to such a benefit, as shall put a man in a condition, to neglect not onely the dispraise, and revilings, but also the power of other men. The Kingdome of God is gotten by violence: but what if it could be gotten by unjust violence? were it against Reason so to get it, when it is impossible to receive hurt by it? and if it be not against Reason, it is not against Justice: or else Justice is not to be approved for good. From such reasoning as this, Succesfull wickedness hath obtained the name of Vertue: and some that in all other things have disallowed the violation of Faith; yet have allowed it, when it is for the getting of a Kingdome. And the Heathen that believed, that *Saturn* was deposed by his son *Jupiter*, believed nevertheless the same *Jupiter* to be the avenger of Injustice: Somewhat like to a piece of Law in *Cokes* Commentaries on *Litleton*; where

he sayes, If the right Heire of the Crown be attainted of Treason; yet the Crown shall descend to him, and *eo instante* the Atteynder be voyd: From which instances a man will be very prone to inferre; that when the Heire apparent of a Kingdome, shall kill him that is in possession, though his father; you may call it Injustice, or by what other name you will; yet it can never be against Reason, seeing all the voluntary actions of men tend to the benefit of themselves; and those actions are most Reasonable, that conduce most to their ends. This specious reasoning is neverthelesse false.

For the question is not of promises mutuall, where there is no security of performance on either side; as when there is no Civil Power erected over the parties promising; for such promises are no Covenants: But either where one of the parties has performed already; or where there is a Power to make him performe; there is the question whether it be against reason, that is, against the benefit of the other to performe, or not. And I say it is not against reason. For the manifestation whereof, we are to consider; First, that when a man doth a thing, which notwithstanding any thing can be foreseen, and reckoned on, tendeth to his own destruction, howsoever some accident which he could not expect, arriving may turne it to his benefit; yet such events do not make it reasonably or wisely done. Secondly, that in a condition of Warre, wherein every man to every man, for want of a common Power to keep them all in awe, is an Enemy, there is no man can hope by his own strength, or wit, to defend himselfe from destruction without the help of Confederates; where every one expects the same defence by the Confederation, that any one else does: and therefore he which declares he thinks it reason to deceive those that help him, can in reason expect no other means of safety, than what can be had from his own single Power. He therefore that breaketh his Covenant, and consequently declareth that he thinks he may with reason do so, cannot be received into any

Society, that unite themselves for Peace and Defence, but by the errour of them that receive him; nor when he is received, be retayned in it, without seeing the danger of their errour; which errours a man cannot reasonably reckon upon as the means of his security: and therefore if he be left, or cast out of Society, he perisheth; and if he live in Society, it is by the errours of other men, which he could not foresee, nor reckon upon; and consequently against the reason of his preservation; and so, as all men that contribute not to his destruction, forbear him onely out of ignorance of what is good for themselves. [. . .]

Chapter 2

John Locke

THE STATE OF NATURE AND THE LAW OF NATURE

John Locke (1632–1704) was an English philosopher and revolutionary who was an influential supporter of the Glorious Revolution wherein King James II was overthrown and the relative balance of power swung toward Parliament. His *Second Treatise of Civil Government* (published in 1698) was an extended critique of authoritarianism and a defense of limited, representative government. In these excerpts, Locke argues that the state of nature is not *necessarily* a state of war, as Hobbes had believed. It is governed by a law of nature which people can come to know through reason and use to secure a mostly peaceful existence, though it will still be plagued by serious inconveniences that can only be rectified by the establishment of a government.

Of the State of Nature

4. To understand Political Power right, and derive it from its Original, we must consider what State all Men are naturally in, and that is, a *State of perfect Freedom* to order their Actions, and dispose of their Possessions, and Persons as they think fit, within the bounds of the Law of Nature, without asking leave, or depending upon the Will of any other Man.

A *State* also of *Equality*, wherein all the Power and Jurisdiction is reciprocal, no one having more than another: there being nothing more evident, than that Creatures of the same species and rank promiscuously born to all the same advantages of Nature, and the use of the same faculties, should also be equal one amongst another without Subordination or Subjection, unless the Lord and Master of them all, should by any manifest Declaration of his Will set one above another, and confer on him by an evident and clear appointment an undoubted Right to Dominion and Sovereignty.

5. This *equality* of Men by Nature, the Judicious Hooker looks upon as so evident in it self, and beyond all question, that he makes it the Foundation of that Obligation to mutual Love amongst Men, on which he Builds the Duties they own one another, and from whence he derives the great Maxims of Justice and Charity. His words are;

The like natural inducement, hath brought Men to know that it is no less their Duty, to Love others than themselves, for seeing those things which are equal, must needs all have one measure; If I cannot but wish to receive good, even as much at every Man's hands, as any Man can wish unto his own Soul, how should I look to have any part of my desire herein satisfied, unless my self be careful to satisfie the like desire, which is undoubtedly in other Men, being of one and the same *nature? to have any thing offered them repugnant to this desire, must needs in all respects grieve them as much as me, so that if I do harm, I must look to suffer, there being no reason that others should shew greater measure of love to me, than they have by me, shewed unto them; my desire therefore to be lov'd of my equals in nature, as much as possible may be, imposeth upon me a natural Duty of bearing to themward, fully the like affection; From which relation of equality between our selves and them, that are as our selves, what several Rules and Canons, natural reason hath drawn for direction of Life, no Man is ignorant. Eccl. Pol. Lib. 1.*

6. But though this be a *State of Liberty*, yet it is not a *State of Licence*, though Man in that State have an uncontroleable Liberty, to dispose of his Person or Possessions, yet he has not Liberty to destroy himself, or so much as any Creature in his Possession, but where some nobler use, than its bare Preservation calls for it. The *State of Nature* has a Law of Nature to govern it, which obliges every one: And Reason, which is that Law, teaches all Mankind, who will but consult it, that being all equal and independent, no one ought to harm another in his Life, Health, Liberty, or Possessions. For Men being all the Workmanship of one Omnipotent, and infinitely wise Maker; All the Servants of one Sovereign Master, sent into the World by his order and about his business, they are his Property, whose Workmanship they are, made to last during his, not one anothers Pleasure. And being furnished with like Faculties, sharing all in one Community of Nature, there cannot be supposed any such *Subordination* among us, that may Authorize us to destroy one another, as if we were made for one anothers uses, as the inferior ranks of Creatures are for ours. Every one as he is *bound to preserve himself*, and not to quit his Station wilfully; so by the like reason when his own Preservation comes not in competition, ought he, as much as he can, *to preserve the rest of Mankind*, and may not unless it be to do Justice on an Offender, take away, or impair the life, or what tends to the Preservation of the Life, Liberty, Health, Limb or Goods of another.

7. And that all Men may be restrained from invading others Rights, and from doing hurt to one another, and the Law of Nature be observed, which willeth the Peace and *Preservation of all Mankind*, the *Execution* of the Law of Nature is in that State, put into every Mans hands, whereby every one has a right to punish the transgressors of that Law to such a Degree, as may hinder its Violation. For the *Law of Nature* would, as all other Laws that concern Men in this World, be in vain, if there were no body that in the State of Nature, had a *Power to Execute* that Law, and thereby preserve the innocent and restrain offenders, and if any one in the State of Nature may punish another, for any evil he has done, every one may do so. For in that *State of perfect Equality*, where naturally there is no superiority or jurisdiction of one, over another, what any may do in Prosecution of that Law, every one must needs have a Right to do.

8. And thus in the State of Nature, *one Man comes by a Power over another*; but yet no Absolute or Arbitrary Power, to use a Criminal when he has got him in his hands, according to the passionate heats, or boundless extravagancy of his own Will, but only to retribute to him, so far as calm reason and conscience dictates, what is proportionate to his Transgression, which is so much as may serve for *Reparation* and *Restraint*. For these two are the only reasons, why one Man may lawfully do harm to another, which is that we call *punishment*. In transgressing the Law of Nature, the Offender declares himself to live by another Rule, than that of *reason* and common Equity, which is that measure God has set to the actions of Men, for their mutual security: and so he becomes dangerous to Mankind, the tye, which is to secure them from injury and violence, being slighted and broken by him. Which being a trespass against the whole Species, and the Peace and Safety of it, provided for by the Law of Nature, every man upon this score, by the Right he hath to preserve Mankind in general, may restrain, or where it is necessary, destroy things noxious to

them, and so may bring such evil on any one, who hath transgressed that Law, as may make him repent the doing of it, and thereby deter him, and by his Example others, from doing the like mischief. And in this case, and upon this ground, every *Man hath a Right to punish the Offender, and be Executioner of the Law of Nature.*

9. I doubt not but this will seem a very strange Doctrine to some Men: but before they condemn it, I desire them to resolve me, by what Right any Prince or State can put to death, or *punish an Alien*, for any Crime he commits in their Country. 'Tis certain their Laws by vertue of any Sanction they receive from the promulgated Will of the Legislative, reach not a Stranger. They speak not to him, nor if they did, is he bound to hearken to them. The Legislative Authority, by which they are in Force over the Subjects of that Common-wealth, hath no Power over him. Those who have the Supream Power of making Laws in *England, France* or *Holland*, are to an *Indian*, but like the rest of the World, Men without Authority: And therefore if by the Law of Nature, every Man hath not a Power to punish Offences against it, as he soberly judges the Case to require, I see not how the Magistrates of any Community, can *punish an Alien* of another Country, since in reference to him, they can have no more Power, than what every Man naturally may have over another.

10. Besides the Crime which consists in violating the Law, and varying from the right Rule of Reason, whereby a Man so far becomes degenerate, and declares himself to quit the Principles of Human Nature, and to be a noxious Creature, there is commonly *injury* done to some Person or other, and some other Man receives damage by his Transgression, in which Case he who hath received any damage, has besides the right of punishment common to him with other Men, a particular Right to seek *Reparation* from him that has done it. And any other Person who finds it just, may also joyn with him that is

injur'd, and assist him in recovering from the Offender, so much as may make satisfaction for the harm he has suffer'd.

11. From these *two distinct Rights*, the one of *Punishing the Crime for restraint,* and preventing the like Offence, which right of punishing is in every body; the other of taking *reparation,* which belongs only to the injured party, comes it to pass that the Magistrate, who by being Magistrate, hath the common right of punishing put into his hands, can often, where the publick good demands not the execution of the Law, *remit* the punishment of Criminal Offences by his own Authority, but yet cannot *remit* the satisfaction due to any private Man, for the damage he has received. That, he who has suffered the damage has a Right to demand in his own name, and he alone can *remit*: The damnified Person has this Power of appropriating to himself, the Goods or Service of the Offender, by *Right of Self-preservation,* as every Man has a Power to punish the Crime, to prevent its being committed again, *by the Right he has of Preserving all Mankind,* and doing all reasonable things he can in order to that end: And thus it is, that every Man in the State of Nature, has a Power to kill a Murderer, both to deter others from doing the like Injury, which no Reparation can compensate, by the Example of the punishment that attends it from every body, and also *to secure* Men from the attempts of a Criminal, who having renounced Reason, the common Rule and Measure, God hath given to Mankind, hath by the unjust Violence and Slaughter he hath committed upon one, declared War against all Mankind, and therefore may be destroyed as a *Lyon* or a *Tyger,* one of those wild Savage Beasts, with whom Men can have no Society nor Security: And upon this is grounded the great Law of Nature, *Who so sheddeth Mans Blood, by Man shall his Blood be shed.* And *Cain* was so fully convinced, that every one had a Right to destroy such a Criminal, that after the Murther of his Brother, he cries out, *Every one that findeth me, shall slay me;* so plain was it writ in the Hearts of all Mankind.

12. By the same reason, may a Man in the State of Nature *punish the lesser breaches* of that Law. It will perhaps be demanded, with death? I answer, Each Transgression may be *punished* to that *degree*, and with so much *Severity* as will suffice to make it an ill bargain to the Offender, give him cause to repent, and terrifie others from doing the like. Every Offence that can be committed in the State of Nature, may in the State of Nature be also punished, equally, and as far forth as it may, in a Common-wealth; for though it would be besides my present purpose, to enter here into the particulars of the Law of Nature, or its *measures of punishment*: yet, it is certain there is such a Law, and that too, as intelligible and plain to a rational Creature, and a Studier of that Law, as the positive Laws of Common-wealths, nay possibly plainer; As much as Reason is easier to be understood, than the Phansies and intricate Contrivances of Men, following contrary and hidden interests put into Words; For so truly are a great part of the *Municipal Laws* of Countries, which are only so far right, as they are founded on the Law of Nature, by which they are to be regulated and interpreted.

13. To this strange Doctrine, viz. That *in the State of Nature, every one has the Executive Power* of the Law of Nature, I doubt not but it will be objected, That it is unreasonable for Men to be Judges in their own Cases, that Self-love will make Men partial to themselves and their Friends. And on the other side, that Ill Nature, Passion and Revenge will carry them too far in punishing others. And hence nothing but Confusion and Disorder will follow, and that therefore God hath certainly appointed Government to restrain the partiality and violence of Men. I easily grant, that *Civil Government* is the proper Remedy for the Inconveniences of the State of Nature, which must certainly be Great, where Men may be Judges in their own Case, since 'tis easily to be imagined, that he who was so unjust as to do his Brother an Injury, will scarce be so just as to condemn himself for it: But I shall desire those who make this Objection, to remember that *Absolute Monarchs* are but Men, and if Government is to be the Remedy of those Evils, which necessarily follow from Mens being Judges in their own Cases, and the State of Nature is therefore not to be endured, I desire to know what kind of Government that is, and how much better it is than the State of Nature, where one Man commanding a multitude, has the Liberty to be Judge in his own Case, and may do to all his Subjects whatever he pleases, without the least liberty to any one to question or controle those who Execute his Pleasure? And in whatsoever he doth, whether led by Reason, Mistake or Passion, must be submitted to? Much better it is in the State of Nature wherein Men are not bound to submit to the unjust will of another: And if he that judges, judges amiss in his own, or any other Case, he is answerable for it to the rest of Mankind.

14. 'Tis often asked as a mighty Objection, *Where are,* or ever were, there any *Men in such a State of Nature?* To which it may suffice as an answer at present; That since all *Princes* and Rulers of *Independent* Governments all through the World, are in a State of Nature, 'tis plain the World never was, nor ever will be, without Numbers of Men in that State. I have named all Governors of *Independent* Communities, whether they are, or are not, in League with others: For 'tis not every Compact that puts an end to the State of Nature between Men, but only this one of agreeing together mutually to enter into one Community, and make one Body Politick; other Promises and Compacts, Men may make one with another, and yet still be in the State of Nature. The Promises and Bargains for Truck, &c. between the two Men in the Desert Island, mentioned by *Garcilasso De la vega,* in his History of *Peru,* or between a *Swiss* and an *Indian,* in the Woods of *America,* are binding to them, though they are perfectly in a State of Nature, in reference to one another. For Truth and keeping of Faith belongs to Men, as Men, and not as Members of Society.

15. To those that say, There were never any Men in the State of Nature; I will not only oppose the Authority of the Judicious Hooker, *Eccl. Pol. Lib. I. Sect.* 10. where he says, *The Laws which have been hitherto mentioned, i.e. the Laws of Nature, do bind Men, although they have never any settled fellowship, never any Solemn Agreement amongst themselves what to do or not to do, but for as much as we are not by our selves sufficient to furnish our selves with competent store of things, needful for such a Life, as our Nature doth desire, a Life, fit for the Dignity of Man; therefore to supply those Defects and Imperfections which are in us, as living singly and solely by our serves, we are naturally induced to seek Communion and Fellowship with others, this was the Cause of Mens uniting themselves, at first in Politick Societies.* But I moreover affirm, That all Men are naturally in that State, and remain so, till by their own Consents they make themselves Members of some Politick Society; And I doubt not in the Sequel of this Discourse, to make it very clear.

Of the State of War

16. The *State of War* is a State of Enmity and Destruction; And therefore declaring by Word or Action, not a passionate and hasty, but a sedate settled Design, upon another Mans Life, *puts him in a State of War* with him against whom he has declared such an Intention, and so has exposed his Life to the others Power to be taken away by him, or any one that joyns with him in his Defence, and espouses his Quarrel: it being reasonable and just I should have a Right to destroy that which threatens me with Destruction. For by the *Fundamental Law of Nature, Man being to be preserved,* as much as possible, when all cannot be preserv'd, the safety of the Innocent is to be preferred: And one may destroy a Man who makes War upon him, or has discovered an Enmity to his being, for the same Reason, that he may kill a *Wolf* or a *Lyon;* because such Men are not under the ties of the Common Law of Reason, have no other Rule, but that of Force and Violence, and so may be treated as Beasts of Prey, those dangerous and noxious Creatures, that will be sure to destroy him, whenever he falls into their Power.

17. And hence it is, that he who attempts to get another Man into his Absolute Power, does thereby put *himself into a State of War* with him; It being to be understood as a Declaration of a Design upon his Life. For I have reason to conclude, that he who would get me into his Power without my consent, would use me as he pleased, when he had got me there, and destroy me too when he had a fancy to it: for no body can desire to *have me in his Absolute Power,* unless it be to compel me by force to that, which is against the Right of my Freedom, i.e. make me a Slave. To be free from such force is the only security of my Preservation: and reason bids me look on him, as an Enemy to my Preservation, who would take away that *Freedom,* which is the Fence to it: so that he who makes an *attempt to enslave* me, thereby puts himself into a State of War with me. He that in the State of Nature, *would take away the Freedom,* that belongs to any one in that State, must necessarily be supposed to have a design to take away every thing else, that *Freedom* being the Foundation of all the rest: As he that in the State of Society, would take away the *Freedom* belonging to those of that Society or Common-wealth, must be supposed to design to take away from them every thing else, and so be looked on as in *a State of War.*

18. This makes it Lawful for a Man to kill *a Thief,* who has not in the least hurt him, nor declared any design upon his Life, any farther than by the use of Force, so to get him in his Power, as to take away his Money, or what he pleases from him: because using force, where he has no Right, to get me into his Power, let his pretence be what it will, I have no reason to suppose, that he, who would *take away my Liberty,* would not when he had me in his Power, take away every thing else. And therefore it is Lawful for me to treat him, as one who has put *himself into a State of War* with me, *i.e.* kill him if I can; for to that hazard does

he justly expose himself, whoever introduces a State of War, and is *aggressor* in it.

19.   And here we have the plain *difference between the State of Nature, and the State of War*, which however some Men have confounded, are as far distant, as a State of Peace, Good Will, Mutual Assistance, and Preservation, and a State of Enmity, Malice, Violence, and Mutual Destruction are one from another. Men living together according to reason, without a common Superior on Earth, with Authority to judge between them, is *properly the State of Nature*. But force, or a declared design of force upon the Person of another, where there is no common Superior on Earth to appeal to for relief, *is the State of War*: And 'tis the want of such an appeal gives a Man the Right of War even against an *aggressor*, though he be in Society and a fellow Subject. Thus a *Thief*, whom I cannot harm but by appeal to the Law, for having stolen all that I am worth, I may kill, when he sets on me to rob me, but of my Horse or Coat: because the Law, which was made for my Preservation, where it cannot interpose to secure my Life from present force, which if lost, is capable of no reparation, permits me my own Defence, and the Right of War, a liberty to kill the aggressor, because the aggressor allows not time to appeal to our common Judge, nor the decision of the Law, for remedy in a Case, where the mischief may be irreparable. *Want of a common Judge with Authority, puts all Men in a State of Nature: Force without Right, upon a Man's Person, makes a State of War*, both where there is, and is not, a common Judge.

20.   But when the actual force is over, the *State of War* ceases between those that are in Society, and are equally on both sides Subjected to the fair determination of the Law; because then there lies open the remedy of appeal for the past injury, and to prevent future harm: but where no such appeal is, as in the State of Nature, for want of positive Laws, and Judges with Authority to appeal to, the *State of War once begun, continues,* with a right to the innocent Party, to destroy the other

whenever he can, until the aggressor offers Peace, and desires reconciliation on such Terms, as may repair any wrongs he has already done, and secure the innocent for the future: nay where an appeal to the Law, and constituted Judges lies open, but the remedy is deny'd by a manifest perverting of Justice, and a barefaced wresting of the Laws, to protect or indemnifie the violence or injuries of some Men, or Party of Men, *there* it *is* hard to imagine any thing but *a State of War.* For wherever violence is used, and injury done, though by hands appointed to administer Justice, it is still violence and injury, however colour'd with the Name, Pretences, or Forms of Law, the end whereof being to protect and redress the innocent, by an unbiassed application of it, to all who are under it; wherever that is not *bona fide* done, *War is made* upon the Sufferers, who having no appeal on Earth to right them, they are left to the only remedy in such Cases, an appeal to Heaven.

21.   To avoid this State of War (wherein there is no appeal but to Heaven, and wherein every the least difference is apt to end, where there is no Authority to decide between the Contenders) is one great *reason of Mens putting themselves into Society,* and quitting the State of Nature. For where there is an Authority, a Power on Earth, from which relief can be had by *appeal,* there the continuance of the State of War is excluded, and the Controversie is decided by that Power. Had there been any such Court, any superior Jurisdiction on Earth, to determine the right between *Jephtha* and the *Ammonites,* they had never come to a State of War, but we see he was forced to appeal to *Heaven. The Lord the Judge* (says he) *be Judge this day between the Children of Israel, and the Children of Ammon, Judg.* 11. 27. and then Prosecuting, and relying on his *appeal,* he leads out his Army to Battle: And therefore in such Controversies, where the question is put, *who shall be Judge?* It cannot be meant, who shall decide the Controversie; every one knows what *Jephtha* here tells us, that *the Lord the Judge,* shall judge. Where there is no Judge on Earth, the

Appeal lies to God in Heaven. That Question then cannot mean, who shall judge? whether another hath put himself in a State of War with me, and whether I may as *Jephtha* did, appeal to Heaven in it? Of that I my self can only be Judge in my own Conscience, as I will answer it at the great Day, to the Supream Judge of all Men. [. . .]

Of the Ends of Political Society and Government

123. If Man in the State of Nature be so free, as has been said; If he be absolute Lord of his own Person and Possessions, equal to the greatest, and subject to no Body, why will he part with his Freedom? Why will he give up this Empire, and subject himself to the Dominion and Controul of any other Power? To which 'tis obvious to Answer, that though in the state of Nature he hath such a right, yet the Enjoyment of it is very uncertain, and constantly exposed to the Invasion of others. For all being Kings as much as he, every Man his Equal, and the greater part no strict Observers of Equity and Justice, the enjoyment of the property he has in this state is very unsafe, very unsecure. This makes him willing to quit a Condition, which however free, is full of fears and continual dangers: And 'tis not without reason, that he seeks out, and is willing to joyn in Society with others who are already united, or have a mind to unite for the mutual *Preservation* of their Lives, Liberties and Estates, which I call by the general Name, *Property*.

124. The great and *chief end* therefore, of Mens uniting into Commonwealths, and putting themselves under Government, *is the Preservation of their Property*. To which in the state of Nature there are many things wanting.

First, There wants an *establish'd*, settled, known *Law*, received and allowed by common consent to be the Standard of Right and Wrong, and the common measure to decide all Controversies between them. For though the Law of Nature be plain and intelligible to all rational Creatures; yet Men being biassed by their Interest, as well as ignorant for want of study of it, are not apt to allow of it as a Law binding to them in the application of it to their particular Cases.

125. *Secondly*, In the State of Nature there wants a *known and indifferent Judge*, with Authority to determine all differences according to the established Law. For every one in that state being both Judge and Executioner of the Law of Nature, Men being partial to themselves, Passion and Revenge is very apt to carry them too far, and with too much heat, in their own Cases; as well as negligence, and unconcernedness, to make them too remiss, in other Mens.

126. *Thirdly*, In the state of Nature there often wants *Power* to back and support the Sentence when right, and to *give* it due *Execution*. They who by any Injustice offended, will seldom fail, where they are able, by force to make good their Injustice: such resistance many times makes the punishment dangerous, and frequently destructive, to those who attempt it.

127. Thus Mankind, notwithstanding all the Priviledges of the state of Nature, being but in an ill condition, while they remain in it, are quickly driven into Society. Hence it comes to pass, that we seldom find any number of Men live any time together in this State. The inconveniencies, that they are therein exposed to, by the irregular and uncertain exercise of the Power every Man has of punishing the transgressions of others, make them take Sanctuary under the establish'd Laws of Government, and therein seek *the preservation of their Property*. 'Tis this makes them so willingly give up every one his single power of punishing to be exercised by such alone as shall be appointed to it amongst them; and by such Rules as the Community, or those authorised by them to that purpose, shall agree on. And in this we have the original *right and rise* of both *the Legislative and Executive Power*, as well as of the Governments and Societies themselves. [. . .]

Chapter 3

Robert Axelrod

THE EVOLUTION OF COOPERATION

Robert Axelrod (1943–   ) is a Professor of Political Science and Public Policy at
the University of Michigan. He is best known for his work on game theory and
cooperation in *The Evolution of Cooperation* (1984). In that work, excerpts from
which are reproduced here, he explores the problem of the "prisoner's dilemma," a
type of game which is thought to model a wide variety of situations in which rational
self-interested persons interact with each other. He argues, drawing on the results of a
computer tournament, that cooperation can be rational in a prisoner's dilemma as
long as there is a chance that the parties will meet each other again.

The Problem of Cooperation

Under what conditions will cooperation
emerge in a world of egoists without
central authority? This question has intrigued
people for a long time. And for good reason. We
all know that people are not angels, and that they
tend to look after themselves and their own first.
Yet we also know that cooperation does occur
and that our civilization is based upon it. But, in
situations where each individual has an incentive
to be selfish, how can cooperation ever develop?

The answer each of us gives to this question
has a fundamental effect on how we think and
act in our social, political, and economic relations with others. And the answers that others
give have a great effect on how ready they will be
to cooperate with us.

The most famous answer was given over three
hundred years ago by Thomas Hobbes. It was
pessimistic. He argued that before governments
existed, the state of nature was dominated by the
problem of selfish individuals who competed
on such ruthless terms that life was "solitary,
poor, nasty, brutish, and short". In his view,
cooperation could not develop without a central
authority, and consequently a strong government was necessary. Ever since, arguments about
the proper scope of government have often
focused on whether one could, or could not,
expect cooperation to emerge in a particular
domain if there were not an authority to police
the situation. [. . .]

This basic problem occurs when the pursuit
of self-interest by each leads to a poor outcome
for all. To make headway in understanding the
vast array of specific situations which have this
property, a way is needed to represent what is
common to these situations without becoming
bogged down in the details unique to each. Fortunately, there is such a representation available:
the famous *Prisoner's Dilemma* game.

In the Prisoner's Dilemma game, there are
two players. Each has two choices, namely

cooperate or defect. Each must make the choice without knowing what the other will do. No matter what the other does, defection yields a higher payoff than cooperation. The dilemma is that if both defect, both do worse than if both had cooperated. This simple game will provide the basis for the entire analysis used in this essay.

The way the game works is shown in figure 3.1. One player chooses a row, either cooperating or defecting. The other player simultaneously chooses a column, either cooperating or defecting. Together, these choices result in one of the four possible outcomes shown in that matrix. If both players cooperate, both do fairly well. Both get R, the *reward for mutual cooperation*. In the concrete illustration of figure 3.1 the reward is 3 points. This number might, for example, be a payoff in dollars that each player gets for that outcome. If one player cooperates but the other defects, the defecting player gets the *temptation to defect*, while the cooperating player gets the *sucker's payoff*. In the example, these are 5 points and 0 points respectively. If both defect, both get 1 point, the *punishment for mutual defection*.

What should you do in such a game? Suppose you are the row player, and you think the column player will cooperate. This means that you will get one of the two outcomes in the first column of figure 3.1. You have a choice. You can cooperate as well, getting the 3 points of the reward for mutual cooperation. Or you can defect, getting the 5 points of the temptation payoff. So it pays to defect if you think the other player will cooperate. But now suppose that you

think the other player will defect. Now you are in the second column of figure 3.1, and you have a choice between cooperating, which would make you a sucker and give you 0 points, and defecting, which would result in, mutual punishment giving you 1 point. So it pays to defect if you think the other player will defect. This means that it is better to defect if you think the other player will cooperate, *and* it is better to defect if you think the other player will defect. So no matter what the other player does, it pays for you to defect.

So far, so good. But the same logic holds for the other player too. Therefore, the other player should defect no matter what you are expected to do. So you should both defect. But then you both get 1 point which is worse than the 3 points of the reward that you both could have gotten had you both cooperated. Individual rationality leads to a worse outcome for both than is possible. Hence the dilemma.

The Prisoner's Dilemma is simply an abstract formulation of some very common and very interesting situations in which what is best for each person individually leads to mutual defection, whereas everyone would have been better off with mutual cooperation. The definition of Prisoner's Dilemma requires that several relationships hold among the four different potential outcomes. The first relationship specifies the order of the four payoffs. The best a player can do is get T, the temptation to defect when the other player cooperates. The worst a player can do is get S, the sucker's payoff for cooperating while

		Column Player	
		Cooperate	Defect
Row Player	Cooperate	R = 3, R = 3 Reward for mutual cooperation	S = 0, T = 5 Sucker's payoff, and temptation to defect
	Defect	T = 5, S = 0 Temptation to defect and sucker's payoff	P = 1, P = 1 Punishment for mutual defection

NOTE: The payoffs to the row chooser are listed first.

Figure 3.1 The Prisoner's Dilemma.

the other player defects. In ordering the other two outcomes, R, the reward for mutual cooperation, is assumed to be better than P, the punishment for mutual defection. This leads to a preference ranking of the four payoffs from best to worst as T, R, P, and S.

The second part of the definition of the Prisoner's Dilemma is that the players cannot get out of their dilemma by taking turns exploiting each other. This assumption means that an even chance of exploitation and being exploited is not as good an outcome for a player as mutual cooperation. It is therefore assumed that the reward for mutual cooperation is greater than the average of the temptation and the sucker's payoff. This assumption, together with the rank ordering of the four payoffs, defines the Prisoner's Dilemma.

Thus two egoists playing the game *once* will both choose their dominant choice, defection, and each will get less than they both could have gotten if they had cooperated. If the game is played a known finite number of times, the players still have no incentive to cooperate. This is certainly true on the last move since there is no future to influence. On the next-to-last move neither player will have an incentive to cooperate since they can both anticipate a defection by the other player on the very last move. Such a line of reasoning implies that the game will unravel all the way back to mutual defection on the first move of any sequence of plays that is of known finite length. This reasoning does not apply if the players will interact an indefinite number of times. And in most realistic settings, the players cannot be sure when the last interaction between them will take place. As will be shown later, with an indefinite number of interactions, cooperation can emerge. The issue then becomes the discovery of the precise conditions that are necessary and sufficient for cooperation to emerge.

In this essay I will examine interactions between just two players at a time. A single player may be interacting with many others, but the player is assumed to be interacting with them one at a time. The player is also assumed to recognize another player and to remember how the two of them have interacted so far. This ability to recognize and remember allows the history of the particular interaction to be taken into account by a player's strategy.

A variety of ways to resolve the Prisoner's Dilemma have been developed. Each involves allowing some additional activity that alters the strategic interaction in such a way as to fundamentally change the nature of the problem. The original problem remains, however, because there are many situations in which these remedies are not available. Therefore, the problem will be considered in its fundamental form, without these alterations.

1   There is no mechanism available to the players to make enforceable threats or commitments. Since the players cannot commit themselves to a particular strategy, each must take into account all possible strategies that might be used by the other player. Moreover the players have all possible strategies available to themselves.

2   There is no way to be sure what the other player will do on a given move. This eliminates the possibility of metagame analysis which allows such options as "make the same choice as the other is about to make." It also eliminates the possibility of reliable reputations such as might be based on watching the other player interact with third parties. Thus the only information available to the players about each other is the history of their interaction so far.

3   There is no way to eliminate the other player or run away from the interaction. Therefore each player retains the ability to cooperate or defect on each move.

4   There is no way to change the other player's payoffs. The payoffs already include whatever consideration each player has for the interests of the other.

Under these conditions, words not backed by actions are so cheap as to be meaningless. The players can communicate with each other only through the sequence of their own behavior. This is the problem of the Prisoner's Dilemma in its fundamental form.

What makes it possible for cooperation to emerge is the fact that the players might meet again. This possibility means that the choices made today not only determine the outcome of this move, but can also influence the later choices of the players. The future can therefore cast a shadow back upon the present and thereby affect the current strategic situation.

But the future is less important than the present—for two reasons. The first is that players tend to value payoffs less as the time of their obtainment recedes into the future. The second is that there is always some chance that the players will not meet again. An ongoing relationship may end when one or the other player moves away, changes jobs, dies, or goes bankrupt.

For these reasons, the payoff of the next move always counts less than the payoff of the current move. A natural way to take this into account is to cumulate payoffs over time in such a way that the next move is worth some fraction of the current move. The *weight* (or importance) of the next move relative to the current move will be called w. It represents the degree to which the payoff of each move is discounted relative to the previous move, and is therefore a *discount parameter*.

The discount parameter can be used to determine the payoff for a whole sequence. To take a simple example, suppose that each move is only half as important as the previous move, making $w = \frac{1}{2}$. Then a whole string of mutual defections worth one point each move would have a value of 1 on the first move, $\frac{1}{2}$ on the second move, $\frac{1}{4}$ on the third move, and so on. The cumulative value of the sequence would be $1 + \frac{1}{2} + \frac{1}{4} + \frac{1}{8} \ldots$ which would sum to exactly 2. In general, getting one point on each move would be worth $1 + w + w^2 + w^3 \ldots$. A very useful fact is that the sum of this infinite

series for any w greater than zero and less than one is simply $1/(1 - w)$. To take another case, if each move is worth 90 percent of the previous move, a string of 1's would be worth ten points because $1/(1 - w) = 1/(1 - .9) = 1/.1 = 10$. Similarly, with w still equal to .9, a string of 3 point mutual rewards would be worth three times this, or 30 points.

Now consider an example of two players interacting. Suppose one player is following the policy of always defecting (ALL D), and the other player is following the policy of TIT FOR TAT. TIT FOR TAT is the policy of cooperating on the first move and then doing whatever the other player did on the previous move. This policy means that TIT FOR TAT will defect once after each defection of the other player. When the other player is using TIT FOR TAT, a player who always defects will get T on the first move, and P on all subsequent moves. The *value* (or *score*) to someone using ALL D when playing with someone using TIT FOR TAT is thus the sum of T for the first move, wP for the second move, w^2P for the third move, and so on.

Both ALL D and TIT FOR TAT are strategies. In general, a *strategy* (or *decision rule*) is a specification of what to do in any situation that might arise. The situation itself depends upon the history of the game so far. Therefore, a strategy might cooperate after some patterns of interaction and defect after others. Moreover, a strategy may use probabilities, as in the example of a rule which is entirely random with equal probabilities of cooperation and defection on each move. A strategy can also be quite sophisticated in its use of the pattern of outcomes in the game so far to determine what to do next. An example is one which, on each move, models the behavior of the other player using a complex procedure (such as a Markov process), and then uses a fancy method of statistical inference (such as Bayesian analysis) to select what seems the best choice for the long run. Or it may be some intricate combination of other strategies.

The first question you are tempted to ask is,

"What is the best strategy?" In other words, what strategy will yield a player the highest possible score? This is a good question, but as will be shown later, no best rule exists independently of the strategy being used by the other player. In this sense, the iterated Prisoner's Dilemma is completely different from a game like chess. A chess master can safely use the assumption that the other player will make the most feared move. This assumption provides a basis for planning in a game like chess, where the interests of the players are completely antagonistic. But the situations represented by the Prisoner's Dilemma game are quite different. The interests of the players are not in total conflict. Both players can do well by getting the reward, R, for mutual cooperation or both can do poorly by getting the punishment, P, for mutual defection. Using the assumption that the other player will always make the move you fear most will lead you to expect that the other will never cooperate, which in turn will lead you to defect, causing unending punishment. So unlike chess, in the Prisoner's Dilemma it is not safe to assume that the other player is out to get you.

In fact, in the Prisoner's Dilemma, the strategy that works best depends directly on what strategy the other player is using and, in particular, on whether this strategy leaves room for the development of mutual cooperation. This principle is based on the weight of the next move relative to the current move being sufficiently large to make the future important. In other words, the discount parameter, w, must be large enough to make the future loom large in the calculation of total payoffs. After all, if you are unlikely to meet the other person again, or if you care little about future payoffs, then you might as well defect now and not worry about the consequences for the future.

This leads to the first formal proposition. It is the sad news that if the future is important, there is no one best strategy.

Proposition 1.   If the discount parameter, w, is

sufficiently high, there is no best strategy independent of the strategy used by the other player.

The proof itself is not hard. Suppose that the other player is using ALL D, the strategy of always defecting. If the other player will never cooperate, the best you can do is always to defect yourself. Now suppose, on the other hand, that the other player is using a strategy of "permanent retaliation." This is the strategy of cooperating until you defect and then always defecting after that. In that case, your best strategy is never to defect, provided that the temptation to defect on the first move will eventually be more than compensated for by the long-term disadvantage of getting nothing but the punishment, P, rather than the reward, R, on future moves. This will be true whenever the discount parameter, w, is sufficiently great. Thus, whether or not you should cooperate, even on the first move, depends on the strategy being used by the other player. Therefore, if w is sufficiently large, there is no one best strategy. [. . .]

The Success of TIT FOR TAT in Computer Tournaments

Since the Prisoner's Dilemma is so common in everything from personal relations to international relations, it would be useful to know how best to act when in this type of setting. However, the proposition of the previous section demonstrates that there is no one best strategy to use. What is best depends in part on what the other player is likely to be doing. Further, what the other is likely to be doing may well depend on what the player expects *you* to do.

To get out of this tangle, help can be sought by combing the research already done concerning the Prisoner's Dilemma for useful advice. Fortunately, a great deal of research has been done in this area. [. . .]

Unfortunately, none of this research on the

Prisoner's Dilemma reveals very much about how to play the game well. [. . .]

To learn more about how to choose effectively in an iterated Prisoner's Dilemma, a new approach is needed. Such an approach would have to draw on people who have a rich understanding of the strategic possibilities inherent in a non-zero-sum setting, a situation in which the interests of the participants partially coincide and partially conflict. Two important facts about non-zero-sum settings would have to be taken into account. First, the proposition of the previous section demonstrates that what is effective depends not only upon the characteristics of a particular strategy, but also upon the nature of the other strategies with which it must interact. The second point follows directly from the first. An effective strategy must be able at any point to take into account the history of the interaction as it has developed so far.

A computer tournament for the study of effective choice in the iterated Prisoner's Dilemma meets these needs. In a computer tournament, each entrant writes a program that embodies a rule to select the cooperative or non-cooperative choice on each move. The program has available to it the history of the game so far, and may use this history in making a choice. If the participants are recruited primarily from those who are familiar with the Prisoner's Dilemma, the entrants can be assured that their decision rule will be facing rules of other informed entrants. Such recruitment would also guarantee that the state of the art is represented in the tournament.

Wanting to find out what would happen, I invited professional game theorists to send in entries to just such a computer tournament. It was structured as a round robin, meaning that each entry was paired with each other entry. As announced in the rules of the tournament, each entry was also paired with its own twin and with RANDOM, a program that randomly cooperates and defects with equal probability. Each game consisted of exactly two hundred moves. The payoff matrix for each move was the familiar one described in the previous section. It awarded both players 3 points for mutual cooperation, and 1 point for mutual defection. If one player defected while the other player cooperated, the defecting player received 5 points and the cooperating player received 0 points.

No entry was disqualified for exceeding the allotted time. In fact, the entire round robin tournament was run five times to get a more stable estimate of the scores for each pair of players. In all, there were 120,000 moves, making for 240,000 separate choices.

The fourteen submitted entries came from five disciplines: psychology, economics, political science, mathematics, and sociology. [. . .]

One remarkable aspect of the tournament was that it allowed people from different disciplines to interact with each other in a common format and language. Most of the entrants were recruited from those who had published articles on game theory in general or the Prisoner's Dilemma in particular.

TIT FOR TAT, submitted by Professor Anatol Rapoport of the University of Toronto, won the tournament. This was the simplest of all submitted programs and it turned out to be the best!

TIT FOR TAT, of course, starts with a cooperative choice, and thereafter does what the other player did on the previous move. This decision rule is probably the most widely known and most discussed rule for playing the Prisoner's Dilemma. It is easily understood and easily programmed. It is known to elicit a good degree of cooperation when played with humans. As an entry in a computer tournament, it has the desirable properties that it is not very exploitable and that it does well with its own twin. It has the disadvantage that it is too generous with the RANDOM rule, which was known by the participants to be entered in the tournament.

In addition, TIT FOR TAT was known to be a powerful competitor. In a preliminary tournament, TIT FOR TAT scored second place;

and in a variant of that preliminary tournament, TIT FOR TAT won first place. All of these facts were known to most of the people designing programs for the Computer Prisoner's Dilemma Tournament, because they were sent copies of a description of the preliminary tournament. Not surprisingly, many of them used the TIT FOR TAT principle and tried to improve upon it.

The striking fact is that *none* of the more complex programs submitted was able to perform as well as the original, simple TIT FOR TAT. [. . .]

Analysis of the results showed that neither the discipline of the author, the brevity of the program—nor its *length*—accounts for a rule's relative success. What does?

Before answering this question, a remark on the interpretation of numerical scores is in order. In a game of 200 moves, a useful benchmark for very good performance is 600 points, which is equivalent to the score attained by a player when both sides always cooperate with each other. A useful benchmark for very poor performance is 200 points, which is equivalent to the score attained by a player when both sides never cooperate with each other. Most scores range between 200 and 600 points, although scores from 0 to 1000 points are possible. The winner, TIT FOR TAT, averaged 504 points per game.

Surprisingly, there is a single property which distinguishes the relatively high-scoring entries from the relatively low-scoring entries. This is the property of being *nice*, which is to say never being the first to defect. (For the sake of analyzing this tournament, the definition of a nice rule will be relaxed to include rules which will not be the first to defect before the last few moves, say before move 199.)

Each of the eight top-ranking entires (or rules) is nice. None of the other entries is. There is even a substantial gap in the score between the nice entries and the others. The nice entries received tournament averages between 472 and 504, while the best of the entries that were not nice received only 401 points. Thus, not being

the first to defect, at least until virtually the end of the game, was a property which, all by itself, separated the more successful rules from the less successful rules in this Computer Prisoner's Dilemma Tournament.

Each of the nice rules got about 600 points with each of the other seven nice rules and with its own twin. This is because when two nice rules play, they are sure to cooperate with each other until virtually the end of the game. Actually the minor variations in end-game tactics did not account for much variation in the scores.

Since the nice rules all got within a few points of 600 with each other, the thing that distinguished the relative rankings among the nice rules was their scores with the rules which are not nice. This much is obvious. What is not obvious is that the relative ranking of the eight top rules was largely determined by just two of the other seven rules. These two rules are *kingmakers* because they do not do very well for themselves, but they largely determine the rankings among the top contenders.

The most important kingmaker was based on an "outcome maximization" principle originally developed as a possible interpretation of what human subjects do in the Prisoner's Dilemma laboratory experiments. This rule, called DOWNING, is a particularly interesting rule in its own right. It is well worth studying as an example of a decision rule which is based upon a quite sophisticated idea. Unlike most of the others, its logic is not just a variant of TIT FOR TAT. Instead it is based on a deliberate attempt to understand the other player and then to make the choice that will yield the best long-term score based upon this understanding. The idea is that if the other player does not seem responsive to what DOWNING is doing, DOWNING will try to get away with whatever it can by defecting. On the other hand, if the other player does seem responsive, DOWNING will cooperate. To judge the other's responsiveness, DOWNING estimates the probability that the other player cooperates after it (DOWNING) cooperates, and also the probability that the other player cooperates after DOWNING defects. For each move, it updates its estimate of these two conditional probabilities and then selects the choice which will maximize its own long-term payoff under the assumption that it has correctly modeled the other player. If the two conditional probabilities have similar values, DOWNING determines that it pays to defect, since the other player seems to be doing the same thing whether DOWNING cooperates or not. Conversely, if the other player tends to cooperate after a cooperation but not after a defection by DOWNING, then the other player seems responsive, and DOWNING will calculate that the best thing to do with a responsive player is to cooperate. Under certain circumstances, DOWNING will even determine that the best strategy is to alternate cooperation and defection.

At the start of a game, DOWNING does not know the values of these conditional probabilities for the other players. It assumes that they are both .5, but gives no weight to this estimate when information actually does come in during the play of the game.

This is a fairly sophisticated decision rule, but its implementation does have one flaw. By initially assuming that the other player is unresponsive, DOWNING is doomed to defect on the first two moves. These first two defections led many other rules to punish DOWNING, so things usually got off to a bad start. But this is precisely why DOWNING served so well as a kingmaker. First-ranking TIT FOR TAT and second-ranking TIDEMAN AND CHIERUZZI both reacted in such a way that DOWNING learned to expect that defection does not pay but that cooperation does. All of the other nice rules went downhill with DOWNING.

The nice rules did well in the tournament largely because they did so well with each other, and because there were enough of them to raise substantially each other's average score. As long as the other player did not defect, each of the nice rules was certain to continue cooperating until virtually the end of the game. But what happened if there was a defection? Different rules responded quite differently, and their response was important in determining their overall success. A key concept in this regard is the forgiveness of a decision rule. *Forgiveness* of a rule can be informally described as its propensity to cooperate in the moves after the other player has defected.

Of all the nice rules, the one that scored lowest was also the one that was least forgiving. This is FRIEDMAN, a totally unforgiving rule that employs permanent retaliation. It is never the first to defect, but once the other defects even once, FRIEDMAN defects from then on. In contrast, the winner, TIT FOR TAT, is unforgiving for one move, but thereafter is totally forgiving of that defection. After one punishment, it lets bygones be bygones.

One of the main reasons why the rules that are not nice did not do well in the tournament is that most of the rules in the tournament were not very forgiving. A concrete illustration will help. Consider the case of JOSS, a sneaky rule that tries to get away with an occasional defection. This decision rule is a variation of TIT FOR TAT. Like TIT FOR TAT, it always defects immediately after the other player defects. But instead of always cooperating after the other player cooperates, 10 percent of the time it defects after the other player cooperates. Thus it tries to sneak in an occasional exploitation of the other player.

This decision rule seems like a fairly small variation of TIT FOR TAT, but in fact its overall performance was much worse, and it is interesting to see exactly why. Table 3.1 shows the move-by-move history of a game between JOSS and TIT FOR TAT. At first both players cooperated, but on the sixth move, JOSS selected one of its probabilistic defections. On the next move JOSS cooperated again, but TIT FOR TAT defected in response to JOSS's previous defection. Then JOSS defected in response to TIT FOR TAT's defection. In effect, the single defection of

Table 3.1 Illustrative Game Between TIT FOR TAT and
JOSS

moves	1–20	11111	23232	32323	23232
moves	21–40	32324	44444	44444	44444
moves	41–60	44444	44444	44444	44444
moves	61–80	44444	44444	44444	44444
moves	81–100	44444	44444	44444	44444
moves	101–120	44444	44444	44444	44444
moves	121–140	44444	44444	44444	44444
moves	141–160	44444	44444	44444	44444
moves	161–180	44444	44444	44444	44444
moves	181–200	44444	44444	44444	44444

Score in this game: TIT FOR TAT 236; JOSS 241.

Legend: 1 both cooperated
2 TIT FOR TAT only cooperated
3 JOSS only cooperated
4 neither cooperated

JOSS on the sixth move created an *echo* back and forth between JOSS and TIT FOR TAT. This echo resulted in JOSS defecting on all the subsequent even numbered moves and TIT FOR TAT defecting on all the subsequent odd numbered moves.

On the twenty-fifth move, JOSS selected another of its probabilistic defections. Of course, TIT FOR TAT defected on the very next move and another reverberating echo began. This echo had JOSS defecting on the odd numbered moves. Together these two echoes resulted in both players defecting on every move after move 25. This string of mutual defections meant that for the rest of the game they both got only one point per turn. The final score of this game was 236 for TIT FOR TAT and 241 for JOSS. Notice that while JOSS did a little better than TIT FOR TAT, both did poorly.

The problem was a combination of an occasional defection after the other's cooperation by JOSS, combined with a short-term lack of forgiveness by both sides. The moral is that if both sides retaliate in the way that JOSS and TIT FOR TAT did, it does not pay to be as greedy as JOSS was.

A major lesson of this tournament is the importance of minimizing echo effects in an environment of mutual power. When a single defection can set off a long string of recriminations and counterrecriminations, both sides suffer. A sophisticated analysis of choice must go at least three levels deep to take account of these echo effects. The first level of analysis is the direct effect of a choice. This is easy, since a defection always earns more than a cooperation. The second level considers the indirect effects, taking into account that the other side may or may not punish a defection. This much of the analysis was certainly appreciated by many of the entrants. But the third level goes deeper and takes into account the fact that in responding to the defections of the other side, one may be repeating or even amplifying one's own previous exploitative choice. Thus a single defection may be successful when analyzed for its direct effects, and perhaps even when its secondary effects are taken into account. But the real costs may be in the tertiary effects when one's own isolated defections turn into unending mutual recriminations. Without their realizing it, many of these rules actually would up punishing themselves. With the other player serving as a mechanism to delay the self-punishment by a few moves, this aspect of self-punishment was not picked up by many of the decision rules.

Despite the fact that none of the attempts at more or less sophisticated decision rules was an improvement on TIT FOR TAT, it was easy to find several rules that would have performed substantially better than TIT FOR TAT in the environment of the tournament. The existence of these rules should serve as a warning against the facile belief that an eye for an eye is necessarily the best strategy. There are at least three rules that would have won the tournament if submitted.

The sample program sent to prospective contestants to show them how to make a submission would in fact have won the tournament if anyone had simply clipped it and mailed it in! But no one did. The sample program defects only if the other player defected on the previous two moves. It is a more forgiving version of TIT FOR TAT in that it does not punish isolated defections. The excellent performance of this TIT FOR TWO TATS rule highlights the fact that a common error of the contestants was to expect that gains could be made from being relatively less forgiving than TIT FOR TAT, whereas in fact there were big gains to be made from being even more forgiving. The implication of this finding is striking, since it suggests that even expert strategists do not give sufficient weight to the importance of forgiveness.

Another rule which would have won the tournament was also available to most of the contestants. This was the rule which won the preliminary tournament, a report of which was used in recruiting the contestants. Called LOOK AHEAD, it was inspired by techniques used in artificial intelligence programs to play chess. It is interesting that artificial intelligence techniques could have inspired a rule which was in fact better than any of the rules designed by game theorists specifically for the Prisoner's Dilemma.

A third rule which would have won the tournament was a slight modification of DOWNING. If DOWNING had started with initial assumptions that the other players would be responsive rather than unresponsive, it too would have won and won by a large margin. A kingmaker could have been king. DOWNING's initial assumptions about the other players were pessimistic. It turned out that optimism about their responsiveness would not only have been more accurate but would also have led to more successful performance. It would have resulted in first place rather than tenth place.

These results from supplementary rules reinforce a theme from the analysis of the tournament entries themselves: the entries were too competitive for their own good. In the first place, many of them defected early in the game without provocation, a characteristic which was very costly in the long run. In the second place, the optimal amount of forgiveness was considerably greater than displayed by any of the entries (except possibly DOWNING). And in the third place, the entry that was most different from the others, DOWNING, floundered on its own misplaced pessimism regarding the initial responsiveness of the others.

The analysis of the tournament results indicate that there is a lot to be learned about coping in an environment of mutual power. Even expert strategists from political science, sociology, economics, psychology, and mathematics made the systematic errors of being too competitive for their own good, not being forgiving enough, and being too pessimistic about the responsiveness of the other side.

The effectiveness of a particular strategy depends not only on its own characteristics, but also on the nature of the other strategies with which it must interact. For this reason, the results of a single tournament are not definitive. Therefore, a second round of the tournament was conducted.

The results of the second round provide substantially better grounds for insight into the nature of effective choice in the Prisoner's Dilemma. The reason is that the entrants to the second round were all given the detailed analysis of the first round, including a discussion of the supplemental rules that would have done very well in the environment of the first round. Thus they were aware not only of the outcome of the first round, but also of the concepts used to analyze success, and the strategic pitfalls that were discovered. Moreover, they each knew that the others knew these things. Therefore, the second round presumably began at a much higher level of sophistication than the first round, and its results could be expected to be that much more valuable as a guide to effective choice in the Prisoner's Dilemma.

The second round was also a dramatic improvement over the first round in sheer size of the tournament. The response was far greater than anticipated. There was a total of sixty-two entries from six countries. The contestants were largely recruited through announcements in journals for users of small computers. The game theorists who participated in the first round of the tournament were also invited to try again. The contestants ranged from a ten-year-old computer hobbyist to professors of computer science, physics, economics, psychology, mathematics, sociology, political science, and evolutionary biology. The countries represented were the United States, Canada, Great Britain, Norway, Switzerland, and New Zealand.

The second round provided a chance both to test the validity of the themes developed in the analysis of the first round and to develop new concepts to explain successes and failures. The entrants also drew their own lessons from the experience of the first round. But different people drew different lessons. What is particularly illuminating in the second round in the way the entries based on different lessons actually interact.

TIT FOR TAT was the simplest program submitted in the first round, and it won the first round. It was the simplest submission in the second round, and it won the second round. Even though all the entrants to the second round knew that TIT FOR TAT had won the first round, no one was able to design an entry that did any better.

This decision rule was known to all of the entrants to the second round because they all had the report of the earlier round, showing that TIT FOR TAT was the most successful rule so far. They had read the arguments about how it was known to elicit a good degree of cooperation when played with humans, how it is not very exploitable, how it did well in the preliminary tournament, and how it won the first round. The report on the first round also explained some of the reasons for its success, pointing in particular to its property of never being the first to defect ("niceness") and its propensity to cooperate after the other player defected ("forgiveness" with the exception of a single punishment).

Even though an explicit tournament rule allowed anyone to submit any program, even one authored by someone else, only one person submitted TIT FOR TAT. This was Anatol Rapoport, who submitted it the first time.

The second round of the tournament was conducted in the same manner as the first round, except that minor end-game effects were eliminated. As announced in the rules, the length of the games was determined probabilistically with a 0.00346 chance of ending with each given move. This is equivalent to setting $w = .99654$. Since no one knew exactly when the last move would come, end-game effects were successfully avoided in the second round.

Once again, none of the personal attributes of the contestants correlated significantly with the performance of the rules. The professors did not do significantly better than the others, nor did the Americans. Those who wrote in FORTRAN rather than BASIC did not do significantly better either, even though the use of FORTRAN would usually indicate access to something more than a bottom-of-the-line microcomputer.. [. . .]

On average, short programs did not do significantly better than long programs, despite the victory of TIT FOR TAT. But on the other hand, neither did long programs (with their greater complexity) do any better than short programs.

The determination of what does account for success in the second round is not easy because there were 3969 ways the 63 rules (including RANDOM) were paired in the round robin tournament. . . . In all, there were over a million moves in the second round.

As in the first round, it paid to be nice. Being the first to defect was usually quite costly. More than half of the entries were nice, so obviously most of the contestants got the message from the first round that it did not pay to be the first to defect.

In the second round, there was once again a substantial correlation between whether a rule was nice and how well it did. Of the top fifteen rules, all but one were nice (and that one ranked eighth). Of the bottom fifteen rules, all but one were not nice. The overall correlation between whether a rule was nice and its tournament score was a substantial .58.

A property that distinguishes well among the nice rules themselves is how promptly and how reliably they responded to a challenge by the other player. A rule can be called *retaliatory* if it immediately defects after an "uncalled for" defection from the other. Exactly what is meant by "uncalled for" is not precisely determined. The point, however, is that unless a strategy is incited to an immediate response by a challenge from the other player, the other player may simply take more and more frequent advantage of such an easygoing strategy.

There were a number of rules in the second round of the tournament that deliberately used controlled numbers of defections to see what they could get away with. To a large extent, what determined the actual rankings of the nice rules was how well they were able to cope with these challengers. The two challengers that were especially important in this regard I shall called TESTER and TRANQUILIZER.

TESTER was submitted by David Gladstein

and came in forty-sixth in the tournament. It is designed to look for softies, but is prepared to back off if the other player shows it won't be exploited. The rule is unusual in that it defects on the very first move in order to test the other's response. If the other player ever defects, it apologizes by cooperating and playing tit-for-tat for the rest of the game. Otherwise, it cooperates on the second and third moves but defects every other move after that. TESTER did a good job of exploiting several supplementary rules that would have done quite well in the environment of the first round of the tournament. For example, TIT FOR TWO TATS defects only after the other player defects on the preceding two moves. But TESTER never does defect twice in a row. So TIT FOR TWO TATS always cooperates with TESTER, and gets badly exploited for its generosity. Notice that TESTER itself did not do particularly well in the tournament. It did, however, provide low scores for some of the more easygoing rules.

As another example of how TESTER causes problems for some rules which had done well in the first round, consider the three variants of Leslie Downing's outcome maximization principle. There were two separate submissions of the REVISED DOWNING program, based on DOWNING, which looked so promising in round one. These came from Stanley F. Quayle and Leslie Downing himself. A slightly modified version came from a youthful competitor, eleven-year-old Steve Newman. However, all three were exploited by TESTER since they all calculated that the best thing to do with a program that cooperated just over half the time after one's own cooperation was to keep on cooperating. Actually they would have been better off doing what TIT FOR TAT and many other high-ranking programs did, which was to defect immediately on the second move in response to TESTER's defection on the first move. This would have elicited TESTER's apology and things would have gone better thereafter.

TRANQUILIZER illustrates a more subtle way

of taking advantage of many rules, and hence a more subtle challenge. It first seeks to establish a mutually rewarding relationship with the other player, and only then does it cautiously try to see if it will be allowed to get away with something. TRANQUILIZER was submitted by Craig Feathers and came in twenty-seventh in the tournament. The rule normally cooperates but is ready to defect if the other player defects too often. Thus the rule tends to cooperate for the first dozen or two dozen moves if the other player is cooperating. Only then does it throw in an unprovoked defection. By waiting until a pattern of mutual cooperation has been developed, it hopes to lull the other side into being forgiving of occasional defections. If the other player continues to cooperate, then defections become more frequent. But as long as TRANQUILIZER is maintaining an average payoff of at least 2.25 points per move, it does not defect twice in succession, and it does not defect more than one-quarter of the time. It tries to avoid pressing its luck too far.

What it takes to do well with challenging rules like TESTER and TRANQUILIZER is to be ready to retaliate after an "uncalled for" defection from the other. So while it pays to be nice, it also pays to be retaliatory. TIT FOR TAT combines these desirable properties. It is nice, forgiving, and retaliatory. It is never the first to defect; it forgives an isolated defection after a single response; but it is always incited by a defection no matter how good the interaction has been so far.

The lessons of the first round of the tournament affected the environment of the second round, since the contestants were familiar with the results. The report on the first round of the Computer Prisoner's Dilemma Tournament concluded that it paid to be not only nice but also forgiving. The contestants in the second round knew that such forgiving decision rules as TIT FOR TWO TATS and REVISED DOWNING would have done even better than TIT FOR TAT in the environment of the first round.

In the second round, many contestants apparently hoped that these conclusions would still be relevant. Of the sixty-two entries, thirty-nine were nice, and nearly all of them were at least somewhat forgiving. TIT FOR TWO TATS itself was submitted by an evolutionary biologist from the United Kingdom, John Maynard Smith. But it came in only twenty-fourth. As mentioned earlier, REVISED DOWNING was submitted twice. But in the second round, it was in the bottom half of the tournament.

What seems to have happened is an interesting interaction between people who drew one lesson and people who drew another from the first round. Lesson One was: "Be nice and forgiving." Lesson Two was more exploitative: "If others are going to be nice and forgiving, it pays to try to take advantage of them." The people who drew Lesson One suffered in the second round from those who drew Lesson Two. Rules like TRANQUILIZER and TESTER were effective at exploiting rules which were too easygoing. But the people who drew Lesson Two did not themselves do very well either. The reason is that in trying to exploit other rules, they often eventually got punished enough to make the whole game less rewarding for both players than pure mutual cooperation would have been. For example, TRANQUILIZER and TESTER themselves achieved only twenty-seventh and forty-sixth place, respectively. Each surpassed TIT FOR TAT's score with fewer than one-third of the rules. None of the other entries that tried to apply the exploitative conclusion of Lesson Two ranked near the top either.

While the use of Lesson Two tended to invalidate Lesson One, no entrants were able to benefit more than they were hurt in the tournament by their attempt to exploit the easygoing rules. The most successful entries tended to be relatively small variations on TIT FOR TAT which were designed to recognize and give up on a seemingly RANDOM player or a very uncooperative player. But the implementations of these ideas did not do better than the pure form of TIT

FOR TAT. So TIT FOR TAT, which got along with almost everyone, won the second round of the tournament just as it had won the first round.

Would the results of the second round have been much different if the distribution of entries had been substantially different? Put another way, does TIT FOR TAT do well in a wide variety of environments? That is to say, is it *robust*?

A good way to examine this question is to construct a series of hypothetical tournaments, each with a very different distribution of the types of rules participating. . . . The results were that TIT FOR TAT won five of the six major variants of the tournament, and came in second in the sixth. This is a strong test of how robust the success of TIT FOR TAT really is.

Another way to examine the robustness of the results is to construct a whole sequence of hypothetical future rounds of the tournament. Some of the rules were so unsuccessful that they would be unlikely to be tried again in future tournaments, while others were successful enough that their continued presence in later tournaments would be likely. For this reason, it would be helpful to analyze what would happen over a series of tournaments if the more successful rules became a larger part of the environment for each rule, and the less successful rules were met less often. This analysis would be a strong test of a rule's performance, because continued success would require a rule to do well with other successful rules.

Evolutionary biology provides a useful way to think about this dynamic problem. Imagine that there are many animals of a single species which interact with each other quite often. Suppose the interactions take the form of a Prisoner's Dilemma. When two animals meet, they can cooperate with each other, not cooperate with each other, or one animal could exploit the other. Suppose further that each animal can recognize individuals it has already interacted with and can remember salient aspects of their interaction, such as whether the other has usually cooperated. A round of the tournament can then be

regarded as a simulation of a single generation of such animals, with each decision rule being employed by large numbers of individuals. One convenient implication of this interpretation is that a given animal can interact with another animal using its own decision rule, just as it can run into an animal using some other rule.

The value of this analogy is that it allows a simulation of future generations of a tournament. The idea is that the more successful entries are more likely to be submitted in the next round, and the less successful entries are less likely to be submitted again. To make this precise, we can say that the number of copies (or offspring) of a given entry will be proportional to that entry's tournament score. We simply have to interpret the average payoff received by an individual as proportional to the individual's expected number of offspring. For example, if one rule gets twice as high a tournament score in the initial round as another rule, then it will be twice as well-represented in the next round. Thus, RANDOM, for example, will be less important in the second generation, whereas TIT FOR TAT and the other high-ranking rules will be better represented.

In human terms, a rule which was not scoring well might be less likely to appear in the future for several different reasons. One possibility is that a player will try different strategies over time, and then stick with what seems to work best. Another possibility is that a person using a rule sees that other strategies are more successful and therefore switches to one of those strategies. Still another possibility is that a person occupying a key role, such as a member of Congress or the manager of a business, would be removed from that role if the strategy being followed was not very successful. Thus, learning, imitation, and selection can all operate in human affairs to produce a process which makes relatively unsuccessful strategies less likely to appear later.

The simulation of this process for the Prisoner's Dilemma tournament is actually quite straightforward. The tournament matrix gives the score each strategy gets with each of the other strategies. Starting with the proportions of each type in a given generation, it is only necessary to calculate the proportions which will exist in the next generation. The better a strategy does, the more its representation will grow.

The results provide an interesting story. The first thing that happens is that the lowest-ranking eleven entries fall to half their initial size by the fifth generation while the middle-ranking entries tend to hold their own and the top-ranking entries slowly grow in size. By the fiftieth generation, the rules that ranked in the bottom third of the tournament have virtually disappeared, while most of those in the middle third have started to shrink, and those in the top third are continuing to grow (see figure 3.2).

This process simulates survival of the fittest. A rule that is successful on average with the current distribution of rules in the population will become an even larger proportion of the environment of the other rules in the next generation. At first, a rule that is successful with

all sorts of rules will proliferate, but later as the unsuccessful rules disappear, success requires good performance with other successful rules.

This simulation provides an ecological perspective because there are no new rules of behavior introduced. It differs from an evolutionary perspective, which would allow mutations to introduce new strategies into the environment. In the ecological perspective there is a changing distribution of given types of rules. The less successful rules become less common and the more successful rules proliferate. The statistical distribution of types of individuals changes in each generation, and this changes the environment with which each of the individual types has to interact.

At first, poor programs and good programs are represented in equal proportions. But as time passes, the poorer ones begin to drop out and the good ones thrive. Success breeds more success, provided that the success derives from interactions with other successful rules. If, on the other hand, a decision rule's success derives from its ability to exploit other rules, then as these exploited rules die out, the exploiter's base of support becomes eroded and the exploiter suffers a similar fate.

A good example of ecological extinction is provided by HARRINGTON, the only non-nice rule among the top fifteen finishers in the second round. In the first two hundred or so generations of the ecological tournament, as TIT FOR TAT and the other successful nice programs were increasing their percentage of the population, HARRINGTON was also increasing its percentage. This was because of HARRINGTON's exploitative strategy. By the two hundredth generation or so, things began to take a noticeable turn. Less successful programs were becoming extinct, which meant that there were fewer and fewer prey for HARRINGTON to exploit. Soon HARRINGTON could not keep up with the successful nice rules, and by the one thousandth generation HARRINGTON was as extinct as the exploitable rules on which it preyed.

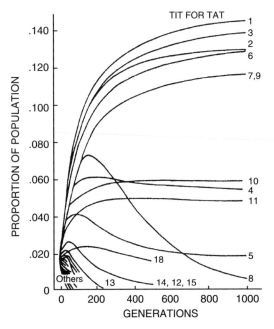

Figure 3.2 Simulated Ecological Success of the Decision Rules

The ecological analysis shows that doing well with rules that do not score well themselves is eventually a self-defeating process. Not being nice may look promising at first, but in the long run it can destroy the very environment it needs for its own success.

The results also provide yet another victory for TIT FOR TAT. TIT FOR TAT had a very slight lead in the original tournament, and never lost this lead in simulated generations. By the one-thousandth generation it was the most successful rule and still growing at a faster rate than any other rule.

The overall record of TIT FOR TAT is very impressive. To recapitulate, in the second round, TIT FOR TAT achieved the highest average score of the sixty-two entries in the tournament. It also achieved the highest score in five of the six hypothetical tournaments which were constructed by magnifying the effects of different types of rules from the second round. And in the sixth hypothetical tournament it came in second. Finally, TIT FOR TAT never lost its first-place standing in a simulation of future generations of the tournament. Added to its victory in the first round of the tournament, and its fairly good performance in laboratory experiments with human subjects, TIT FOR TAT is clearly a very successful strategy.

Proposition 1 says that there is no absolutely best rule independent of the environment. What can be said for the empirical successes of TIT FOR TAT is that it is a very robust rule: it does very well over a wide range of environments. Part of its success might be that other rules anticipate its presence and are designed to do well with it. Doing well with TIT FOR TAT requires cooperating with it, and this in turn helps TIT FOR TAT. Even rules like TESTER that were designed to see what they could get away with, quickly apologize to TIT FOR TAT. Any rule

which tries to take advantage of TIT FOR TAT will simply hurt itself. TIT FOR TAT benefits from its own nonexploitability because three conditions are satisfied:

1. The possibility of encountering TIT FOR TAT is salient.
2. Once encountered, TIT FOR TAT is easy to recognize.
3. Once recognized, TIT FOR TAT's nonexploitability is easy to appreciate.

Thus TIT FOR TAT benefits from its own clarity.

On the other hand, TIT FOR TAT foregoes the possibility of exploiting other rules. While such exploitation is occasionally fruitful, over a wide range of environments the problems with trying to exploit others are manifold. In the first place, if a rule defects to see what it can get away with, it risks retaliation from the rules that are provocable. In the second place, once mutual recriminations set in, it can be difficult to extract oneself. And, finally, the attempt to identify and give up on unresponsive rules (such as RANDOM or excessively uncooperative rules) often mistakenly led to giving up on rules which were in fact salvageable by a more patient rule like TIT FOR TAT. Being able to exploit the exploitable without paying too high a cost with the others is a task which was not successfully accomplished by any of the entries in round two of the tournament.

What accounts for TIT FOR TAT's robust success is its combination of being nice, retaliatory, forgiving, and clear. Its niceness prevents it from getting into unnecessary trouble. Its retaliation discourages the other side from persisting whenever defection is tried. Its forgiveness helps restore mutual cooperation. And its clarity makes it intelligible to the other player, thereby eliciting long-term cooperation.

Chapter 4

Murray N. Rothbard

SOCIETY WITHOUT A STATE

Murray Rothbard (1926–1995) was an economist of the Austrian School who wrote widely both in economics and in history and philosophy as well. He was a libertarian best known for his defense of anarcho-capitalism: the view that respect for individual rights requires that government be abolished entirely, and that the defensive and legal services it now provides be provided by a free market instead. This reading (published in 1975) describes the anarcho-capitalist vision and defends it against some common objections.

I

In attempting to outline how a "society without a State"—i.e. an anarchist society—might function successfully, I would first like to defuse two common but mistaken criticisms of this approach. First, is the argument that in providing for such defense or protection services as courts, police, or even law itself, I am simply smuggling the State back into society in another form, and that therefore the system I am both analyzing and advocating is not "really" anarchism. This sort of criticism can only involve us in an endless and arid dispute over semantics. Let me say from the beginning that I define the State as that institution which possesses one or both (almost always both) of the following properties: (1) it acquires its income by the physical coercion known as "taxation"; and (2) it asserts and usually obtains a coerced monopoly of the provision of defense service (police and courts) over a given territorial area. Any institution, not possessing either of these properties is not and

cannot be, in accordance with my definition, a "State". On the other hand, I define anarchist society as one where there is no legal possibility for coercive aggression against the person or property of any individual. Anarchists oppose the State because it has its very being in such aggression, namely, the expropriation of private property through taxation, the coercive exclusion of other providers of defense service from its territory, and all of the other depredations and coercions that are built upon these twin foci of invasions of individual rights.

Nor is our definition of the State arbitrary, for these two characteristics have been possessed by what is generally acknowledged to be "States" throughout recorded history. The State, by its use of physical coercion, has arrogated to itself a compulsory monopoly of defense services over its territorial jurisdiction. But it is certainly conceptually possible for such services to be supplied by private, non-State institutions, and indeed such services have historically been supplied by other organizations than the State. To be opposed to the State is then not necessarily to be opposed to services that have often been linked with it; to be opposed to the State does not necessarily imply that we must be opposed to police protection, courts, arbitration, the minting of money, postal service, or roads and highways. Some anarchists have indeed been opposed to police and to all physical coercion in defense of person and property, but this is not inherent in and is fundamentally irrelevant to the anarchist position, which is precisely marked by opposition to all physical coercion invasive of, or aggressing against, person and property.

The crucial role of taxation may be seen in the fact that the State is the only institution or organization in society which regularly and systematically acquires its income through the use of physical coercion. All other individuals or organizations acquire their income voluntarily, either (a) through the voluntary sale of goods and services to consumers on the market, or (b) through voluntary gifts or donations by members or other donors. If I cease or refrain from purchasing Wheaties on the market, the Wheaties producers do not come after me with a gun or prison to force me to purchase; if I fail to join the American Philosophical Association, the association may not force me to join or prevent me from giving up my membership. Only the State can do so; only the State can confiscate my property or put me in jail if I do not pay its tax-tribute. Therefore, only the State regularly exists and has its very being by means of coercive depredations on private property.

Neither is it legitimate to challenge this sort of analysis by claiming that in some other sense, the purchase of Wheaties or membership in the A.P.A. is in some way "coercive"; there again, we can only be trapped in an endless semantic dispute. Apart from other rebuttals which cannot be considered here, I would simply say that anarchists are interested in the abolition of this type of action e.g. aggressive physical violence against person and property, and that this is how we define "coercion". Anyone who is still unhappy with this use of the term "coercion" can simply eliminate the word from this discussion, and substitute for it "physical violence or the threat thereof", with the only loss being in literary style rather than in the substance of the argument. What anarchism proposes to do, then, is to abolish the State, i.e. to abolish the regularized institution of aggressive coercion.

It need hardly be added that the State habitually builds upon its coercive source of income by adding a host of other aggressions upon society: ranging from economic controls to the prohibition of pornography to the compelling of religious observance to the mass murder of civilians in organized warfare. In short, that the State, in the words of Albert Jay Nock, "claims and exercises a monopoly of crime" over its territorial area.

The second criticism I would like to defuse before beginning the main body of the paper is the common charge that anarchists "assume that all people are good", and that without the State no crime would be committed. In short, that anarchism assumes that with the abolition of the State a New Anarchist Man will emerge, cooperative, humane, and benevolent, so that no problem of crime will then plague the society. I confess that I do not understand the basis for this charge. Whatever other schools of anarchism profess—and I do not believe that they are open to this charge—I certainly do not adopt this view. I assume with most observers that mankind is a mixture of good and evil, of cooperative and criminal tendencies. In my view, the anarchist society is one which maximizes the tendencies for the good and the cooperative, while it minimizes both the opportunity and the moral legitimacy of the evil and the criminal. If the anarchist view is correct, and the State is indeed the great legalized and socially legitimated channel for all manner of anti-social crime—theft, oppression, mass murder—on a massive scale, then surely the abolition of such an engine of crime can do nothing but favor the good in man and discourage the bad.

A further point: in a profound sense, no social system, whether anarchist or statist, can work at all unless most people are "good" in the sense that they are not all hell-bent upon assaulting and robbing their neighbors. If everyone were so disposed, no amount of protection, whether State or private, could succeed in staving off chaos. Furthermore, the more that people are disposed to be peaceful and not aggress against their neighbors, the more successfully any social system will work, and the fewer resources will need to be devoted to police protection. The anarchist view holds that, given the "nature of man", given the degree of goodness or badness at any point of time, anarchism will maximize the opportunities for good and minimize the channels for the bad. The rest depends on the values held by the individual members of society. The only further point that need be made is that by eliminating the living example and the social legitimacy of the massive legalized crime of the State, anarchism will to a large extent promote peaceful values in the minds of the public.

We cannot of course deal here with the numerous arguments in favor of anarchism or against the State, moral, political, and economic. Nor can we take up the various goods and services now provided by the State, and show how private individuals and groups will be able to supply them far more efficiently on the free market. Here we can only deal with perhaps the most difficult area, the area where it is almost universally assumed that the State must exist and act, even if it is only a "necessary evil" instead of a positive good: the vital realm of defense or protection of person and property against aggression. Surely, it is universally asserted, the State is at least vitally necessary to provide police protection, the judicial resolution of disputes and enforcement of contracts, and the creation of the law itself that is to be enforced. My contention is that all of these admittedly necessary services of protection can be satisfactorily and efficiently supplied by private persons and institutions on the free market.

One important caveat before we begin the body of this paper: new proposals such as anarchism are almost always gauged against the implicit assumption that the present, or statist, system works to perfection. Any lacunae or difficulties with the picture of the anarchist society are considered net liabilities, and enough to dismiss anarchism out of hand. It is, in short, implicitly assumed that the State is doing its self-assumed job of protecting person and property to perfection. We cannot here go into the reasons why the State is bound to suffer inherently from grave flaws and inefficiencies in such a task. All we need do now is to point to the black and unprecedented record of the State through history: no combination of private marauders can possibly begin to match the State's unremitting record of theft, confiscation, oppression, and mass murder. No collection of Mafia or private bank robbers can begin to compare with all the Hiroshimas, Dresdens, and Lidices and their analogs through the history of mankind.

This point can be made more philosophically: it is illegitimate to compare the merits of anarchism and statism by starting with the present system as the implicit given and then critically examining only the anarchist alternative. What we must do is to begin at the zero point and then critically examine both suggested alternatives. Suppose, for example, that we were all suddenly dropped down on the earth *de novo*, and that we were all then confronted with the question of what societal arrangements to adopt. And suppose then that someone suggested: "We are all bound to suffer from those of us who wish to aggress against their fellow men. Let us than solve this problem of crime by handing all of our weapons to the Jones family, over there, by giving all of our ultimate power to settle disputes to that family. It that way, with their monopoly of coercion and of ultimate decision making, the Jones family will be able to protect each of us from each other." I submit that this proposal would get very short shrift, except perhaps from the Jones family themselves. And yet this is precisely the common argument for the existence of the State. When we start from the zero point, as in the case of the Jones family, the question of "who will guard the guardians?" becomes not simply an abiding lacuna in the theory of the State but an overwhelming barrier to its existence.

A final caveat: the anarchist is always at a disadvantage in attempting to forecast the shape of the future anarchist society. For it is impossible for observers to predict voluntary social arrangements, including the provision of goods and services, on the free market. Suppose, for example, that this were the year 1874, and someone predicted that eventually there would be a radio manufacturing industry. To be able to make such a forecast successfully, does he have to be challenged to state immediately how many radio manufacturers there would be a century hence, how big they would be, where they would be located, what technology and marketing techniques they would use, etc.? Obviously, such a challenge would make no sense, and in a profound sense the same is true of those who demand a precise portrayal of the pattern of protection activities on the market. Anarchism advocates the dissolution of the State into social and market arrangements, and these arrangements are far more flexible and less predictable than political institutions. The most that we can do, then, is to offer broad guidelines and perspectives on the shape of a projected anarchist society.

One important point to make here is that the advance of modern technology makes anarchistic arrangements increasingly feasible. Take, for example, the case of lighthouses, where it is often charged that it is unfeasible for private lighthouse operators to row out to each ship to charge it for use of the light. Apart from the fact that this argument ignores the successful existence of private lighthouses in earlier days, e.g. in England in the eighteenth century, another vital consideration is that modern electronic technology makes charging each ship for the light far more feasible. Thus, the ship would have to have paid for an electronically controlled beam which could then be automatically turned on for those ships which had paid for the service.

II

Let us now turn to the problem of how disputes —in particular, disputes over alleged violations of person and property—would be resolved in an anarchist society. First, it should be noted that all disputes involve two parties: the plaintiff, the alleged victim of the crime or tort, and the defendant, the alleged aggressor. In many cases of broken contract, of course, each of the two parties alleging that the other is the culprit is at the same time a plaintiff and a defendant.

An important point to remember is that any society, be it statist or anarchist, has to have some way of resolving disputes that will gain a majority consensus in society. There would be no need for courts or arbitrators if everyone were omniscient, and knew instantaneously which persons were guilty of any given crime or violation of contract. Since none of us are omniscient, there has to be some method of deciding who is the criminal or lawbreaker which will gain legitimacy, in short whose decision will be accepted by the great majority of the public.

In the first place, a dispute may be resolved voluntarily between the two parties themselves, either unaided or with the help of a third mediator. This poses no problem, and will automatically be accepted by society at large. It is so accepted even now, much less in a society imbued with the anarchistic values of peaceful cooperation and agreement. Secondly and similarly, the two parties, unable to reach agreement, may decide to submit voluntarily to the decision of an arbitrator. This agreement may arise either after a dispute has arisen, or be provided for in advance in the original contract. Again, there is no problem in such an arrangement gaining legitimacy. Even in the present statist era, the notorious inefficiency and coercive and cumbersome procedures of the politically run government courts have led increasing numbers of citizens to turn to voluntary and expert arbitration for a speedy and harmonious setting of disputes.

Thus, William C. Wooldridge has written that

"arbitration has grown to proportions that make the courts a secondary recourse in many areas and completely superfluous in others. The ancient fear of the courts that arbitration would 'oust' them of their jurisdiction has been fulfilled with a vengeance the common-law judges probably never anticipated. Insurance companies adjust over fifty thousand claims a year among themselves through arbitration, and the American Arbitration Association (AAA), with headquarters in New York and twenty-five regional offices across the country, last year conducted over twenty-two thousand arbitrations. Its twenty-three thousand associates available to serve as arbitrators may outnumber the total number of judicial personnel . . . in the United States . . . Add to this the unknown number of individuals who arbitrate disputes within particular industries or in particular localities, without formal AAA affiliation, and the quantitatively secondary role of official courts begins to be apparent."

Wooldridge adds the important point that, in addition to the speed of arbitration procedures vis a vis the courts, the arbitrators can proceed as experts in disregard of the official government law; in a profound sense, then, they serve to create a voluntary body of private law. "In other words," states Wooldridge, "the system of extra-legal, voluntary courts has progressed hand in hand with a body of private law; the rules of the state are circumvented by the same process that circumvents the forums established for the settlement of disputes over those rules . . . In short, a private agreement between two people, a bilateral 'law', has supplanted the official law.

The writ of the sovereign has ceased to run, and for it is substituted a rule tacitly or explicitly agreed to by the parties." Wooldridge concludes that "if an arbitrator can choose to ignore a penal damage rule or the statute of limitations applicable to the claim before him (and it is generally conceded that he has that power), arbitration can be viewed as a practically revolutionary instrument for self-liberation from the law . . ."

It may be objected that arbitration only works successfully because the courts enforce the award of the arbitrator. Wooldridge points out, however, that arbitration was unenforceable in the American courts before 1920, but that this did not prevent voluntary arbitration from being successful and expanding in the United States and in England. He points, furthermore, to the successful operations of merchant courts since the Middle Ages, those courts which successfully developed the entire body of the law merchant. None of those courts possessed the power of enforcement. He might have added the private courts of shippers which developed the body of admiralty law in a similar way.

How then did these private, "anarchistic", and voluntary courts insure the acceptance of their decisions? By the method of social ostracism, and the refusal to deal any further with the offending merchant. This method of voluntary "enforcement", indeed, proved highly successful. Wooldridge writes that "the merchants' courts were voluntary, and if a man ignored their judgment, he could not be sent to jail . . . Nevertheless, it is apparent that . . . (their) decisions were generally respected even by the losers; otherwise people would never have used them in the first place . . . Merchants made their courts work simply by agreeing to abide by the results. The merchant who broke the understanding would not be sent to jail, to be sure, but neither would he long continue to be a merchant, for the compliance exacted by his fellows . . . proved if anything more effective than physical coercion." Nor did this voluntary method fail to work in modern times. Wooldridge writes that it was precisely in the years before 1920, when arbitration awards could not be enforced in the courts,

"that arbitration caught on and developed a following in the American mercantile community. Its popularity, gained at a time when abiding by an agreement to arbitrate had to be as voluntary as the agreement itself, casts doubt on whether legal coercion was an essential adjunct to the settlement of most disputes. Cases of refusal to abide by an arbitrator's award were rare; one founder of the American Arbitration Association could not recall a single example. Like their medieval forerunners, merchants in the Americas did not have to rely on any sanctions other than those they could collectively impose on each other. One who refused to pay up might find access to his association's tribunal cut off in the future, or his name released to the membership of his trade association; these penalties were far more fearsome than the cost of the award with which he disagreed. Voluntary and private adjudications were voluntarily and privately adhered to, if not out of honor, out of the self-interest of businessmen who knew that the arbitral mode of dispute settlement would cease to be available to them very quickly if they ignored an award."

It should also be pointed out that modern technology makes even more feasible the collection and dissemination of information about people's credit ratings and records of keeping or violating their contracts or arbitration agreements. Presumably, an anarchist society would see the expansion of this sort of dissemination of data and thereby facilitate the ostracism or boycotting of contract and arbitration violators.

How would arbitrators be selected in an anarchist society? In the same way as they are chosen now, and as they were chosen in the days of strictly voluntary arbitration: the arbitrators with the best reputation for efficiency and probity would be chosen by the various parties on the market. As in other processes of the market, the arbitrators with the best record in settling disputes will come to gain an increasing amount of business, and those with poor records will no longer enjoy clients, and have to shift to another line of endeavor. Here it must be emphasized that parties in dispute will seek out those arbitrators with the best reputation for both expertise and impartiality, and that inefficient or biased arbitrators will rapidly have to find another occupation.

Thus, the Tannehills emphasize:

"the advocates of government see initiated force (the legal force of government) as the only solution to social disputes. According to them, if everyone in society were not forced to use the same court system . . . disputes would be insoluble. Apparently it doesn't occur to them that disputing parties are capable of freely choosing their own arbiters . . . They have not realized that disputants would, in fact, be far better off if they could choose among competing arbitration agencies so that they could reap the benefits of competition and specialization. It should be obvious that a court system which has a monopoly guaranteed by the force of statutory law will not give as good quality service as will free-market arbitration agencies which must compete for their customers . . .

Perhaps the least tenable argument for government arbitration of disputes is the one which holds that governmental judges are more impartial because they operate outside the market and so have no vested interests . . . owing political allegiance to government is certainly no guarantee of impartiality! A governmental judge is always impelled to be partial—in favor of the government, from whom he gets his pay and his power! On the other hand, an arbiter who sells his services in a free market knows that he must be as scrupulously honest, fair, and impartial as possible or no pair of disputants will buy his services to arbitrate their dispute. A free-market arbiter depends for his livelihood on his skill and fairness at settling disputes. A governmental judge depends on political pull."

If desired, furthermore, the contracting parties could provide in advance for a series of arbitrators:

"It would be more economical and in most cases quite sufficient to have only one arbitration agency to hear the case. But if the parties felt that a further appeal might be necessary and were willing to risk the extra expense, they could provide for a succession of two or even more arbitration agencies. The names of these agencies would be written into the contract in order from the 'first court of appeal' to the 'last court of appeal'. It would be neither necessary nor desirable to have one single, final court of appeal for every person in the society, as we have today in the United States Supreme Court."

Arbitration, then poses little difficulty for a portrayal of the free society. But what of torts or crimes of aggression where there has been no contract? Or suppose that the breaker of a contract defies the arbitration award? Is ostracism enough? In short, how can courts develop in the free-market, anarchist society which will have the power to enforce judgments against criminals or contract-breakers?

In the wide sense, defense service consists of guards or police who use force in defending person and property against attack, and judges or courts whose role is to use socially accepted procedures to determine who the criminals or tortfeasors are, as well as to enforce judicial awards, such as damages or the keeping of contracts. On the free market, many scenarios are possible on the relationship between the private courts and the police; they may be "vertically

integrated", for example, or their services may be supplied by separate firms. Furthermore, it seems likely that police service will be supplied by insurance companies who will provide crime-insurance to their clients. In that case, insurance companies will pay off the victims of crime or the breaking of contracts or arbitration awards, and then pursue the aggressors in court to recoup their losses. There is a natural market connection between insurance companies and defense service, since they need pay out less benefits in proportion as they are able to keep down the rate of crime.

Courts might either charge fees for their services, with the losers of cases obliged to pay court costs, or else they may subsist on monthly or yearly premiums by their clients, who may be either individuals or the police or insurance agencies. Suppose, for example, that Smith is an aggrieved party, either because he has been assaulted or robbed, or because an arbitration award in his favor has not been honored. Smith believes that Jones is the party guilty of the crime. Smith then goes to a court, Court A, of which he is a client, and brings charges against Jones as a defendant. In my view, the hallmark of an anarchist society is one where no man may legally compel someone who is not a convicted criminal to do anything, since that would be aggression against an innocent man's person or property. Therefore, Court A can only invite rather than subpoena Jones to attend his trial. Of course, if Jones refuses to appear or send a representative, his side of the case will not be heard. The trial of Jones proceeds. Suppose that Court A finds Jones innocent. In my view, part of the generally accepted Law Code of the anarchist society (on which see further below), is that this must end the matter, unless Smith can prove charges of gross incompetence or bias on the part of the court.

Suppose, next, that Court A finds Jones guilty. Jones might accept the verdict, either because he too is a client of the same court, because he knows he is guilty, or for some other reason. In that case, Court A proceeds to exercise judgment against Jones. Neither of these instances pose very difficult problems for our picture of the anarchist society. But suppose, instead, that Jones contests the decision; he, then, goes to his court, Court B, and the case is retried there. Suppose that Court B, too, finds Jones guilty. Again, it seems to me that the accepted Law Code of the anarchist society will assert that this ends the matter; both parties have had their say in courts which each has selected, and the decision for guilt is unanimous.

Suppose, however, the most difficult case: That Court B finds Jones innocent. The two courts, each subscribed to by one of the two parties, have split their verdicts. In that case, the two courts will submit the case to an appeals court, or arbitrator, which the two courts agree upon. There seems to be no real difficulty about the concept of an appeals court. As in the case of arbitration contracts, it seems very likely that the various private courts in the society will have prior agreements to submit their disputes to a particular appeals court. How will the appeals judges be chosen? Again, as in the case of arbitrators or of the first judges on the free market, they will be chosen for their expertise and reputation for efficiency, honesty and integrity. Obviously, appeals judges who are inefficient or biased will scarcely be chosen by courts who will have a dispute. The point here is that there is no need for a legally established or institutionalized single, monopoly appeals court system, as States now provide. There is no reason why there cannot arise a multitude of efficient and honest appeals judges who will be selected by the disputant courts, just as there are numerous private arbitrators on the market today. The appeals court renders its decision, and the courts proceed to enforce it if, in our example, Jones is considered guilty—unless, of course, Jones can prove bias in some other court proceedings.

No society can have unlimited judicial appeals, for in that case there would be no point to having judges or courts at all. Therefore, every society, whether statist or anarchist, will have to have some socially accepted cut-off point for trials and appeals. My suggestion is the rule that the agreement of any two courts be decisive. "Two" is not an arbitrary figure, for it reflects the fact that there are two parties, the plaintiff and the defendant, to any alleged crime or contract dispute.

If the courts are to be empowered to enforce decisions against guilty parties, does this not bring back the State in another form and thereby negate anarchism? No, for at the beginning of this paper I explicitly defined anarchism in such a way as not to rule out the use of defensive force—force in defense of person and property—by privately supported agencies. In the same way, it is not bringing back the State to allow persons to use force to defend themselves against aggression, or to hire guards or police agencies to defend them.

It should be noted, however, that in the anarchist society there will be no "district attorney" to press charges on behalf of "society". Only the victims will press charges as the plaintiffs. If, then, these victims should happen to be absolute pacifists who are opposed even to defensive force, then they will simply not press charges in the courts or otherwise retaliate against those who have aggressed against them. In a free society that would be their right. If the victim should suffer from murder, then his heir would have the right to press the charges.

What of the Hatfield-and-McCoy problem? Suppose that a Hatfield kills a McCoy, and that McCoy's heir does not belong to a private insurance, police agency, or court, and decides to retaliate himself? Since, under anarchism there can be no coercion of the non-criminal, McCoy would have the perfect right to do so. No one may be compelled to bring his case to a court. Indeed, since the right to hire police or courts flows from the right of self-defense against aggression, it would be inconsistent and in contradiction to the very basis of the free society to institute such compulsion. Suppose, then, that the surviving McCoy finds what he believes to be the guilty Hatfield and kills him in turn? What then? This is fine, except that McCoy may have to worry about charges being brought against him by a surviving Hatfield. Here it must be emphasized that in the law of the anarchist society based on defense against aggression, the courts would not be able to proceed against McCoy if in fact he killed the right Hatfield. His problem would arise if the courts should find that he made a grievous mistake, and killed the wrong man; in that case, he in turn would be found guilty of murder. Surely, in most instances, individuals will wish to obviate such problems by taking their case to a court and thereby gain social acceptability for their defensive retaliation—not for the act of retaliation but for the correctness of deciding who the criminal in any given case might be. The purpose of the judicial process, indeed, is to find a way of general agreement on who might be the criminal or contract-breaker in any given case. The judicial process is not a good in itself; thus, in the case of an assassination, such as Jack Ruby's murder of Oswald, on public television, there is no need for a complex judicial process since the name of the murderer is evident to all.

Will not the possibility exist of a private court that may turn venal and dishonest, or of a private police force that turns criminal and extorts money by coercion? Of course such an event may occur, given the propensities of human nature. Anarchism is not a moral cure-all. But the important point is that market forces exist to place severe checks on such possibilities, especially in contrast to a society where a State exists. For, in the first place, judges, like arbitrators, will prosper on the market in proportion to their reputation for efficiency and impartiality. Secondly, on the free market important checks and balances exist against venal courts or criminal police forces. Namely, that there are competing courts and police agencies to whom the victims may turn for redress. If the "Prudential Police Agency" should turn outlaw and

extract revenue from victims by coercion, the latter would have the option of turning to the "Mutual" or "Equitable" Police Agency for defense and for pressing charges against Prudential. These are the genuine "checks and balances" of the free market, genuine in contrast to the phony checks and balances of a State system, where all the alleged "balancing" agencies are in the hands of one monopoly government. Indeed, given the monopoly "protection service" of a State, what is there to prevent a State from using its monopoly channels of coercion to extort money from the public? What are the checks and limits of the State? None, except for the extremely difficult course of revolution against a Power with all of the guns in its hands. In fact, the State provides an easy, legitimated channel for crime and aggression, since it has its very being in the crime of tax-theft, and the coerced monopoly of "protection." It is the State, indeed, that functions as a mighty "protection racket" on a giant and massive scale. It is the State that says: "Pay us for your 'protection' or else." In the light of the massive and inherent activities of the State, the danger of a "protection racket" emerging from one or more private police agencies is relatively small indeed.

Moreover, it must be emphasized that a crucial element in the power of the State is its legitimacy in the eyes of the majority of the public, the fact that after centuries of propaganda, the depredations of the State are looked upon rather as benevolent services. Taxation is generally not seen as theft, nor war as mass murder, nor conscription as slavery. Should a private police agency turn outlaw, should "Prudential" become a protection racket, it would then lack the social legitimacy which the State has managed to accrue to itself over the centuries. "Prudential" would be seen by all as bandits, rather than as legitimate or divinely appointed "sovereigns", bent on promoting the "common good" or the "general welfare". And lacking such legitimacy, Prudential would have to face the wrath of the public and the defense and retaliation of the other private defense agencies, the police and courts, on the free market. Given these inherent checks and limits, a successful transformation from a free society to bandit rule becomes most unlikely. Indeed, historically, it has been very difficult for a State to arise to supplant a stateless society; usually, it has come about through external conquest rather than by evolution from within a society.

Within the anarchist camp, there has been much dispute on whether the private courts would have to be bound by a basic, common Law Code. Ingenious attempts have been made to work out a system where the laws or standards of decision-making by the courts would differ completely from one to another. But in my view all would have to abide by the basic Law Code, in particular, prohibition of aggression against person and property, in order to fulfill our definition of anarchism as a system which provides no legal sanction for such aggression. Suppose, for example, that one group of people in society hold that all redheads are demons who deserve to be shot on sight. Suppose that Jones, one of this group, shoots Smith, a redhead. Suppose that Smith or his heir presses charges in a court, but that Jones' court, in philosophic agreement with Jones, finds him innocent therefore. It seems to me that in order to be considered legitimate, any court would have to follow the basic libertarian law code of the inviolate right of person and property. For otherwise, courts might legally subscribe to a code which sanctions such aggression in various cases, and which to that extent would violate the definition of anarchism and introduce, if not the State, then a strong element of statishness or legalized aggression into the society.

But again I see no insuperable difficulties here. For in that case, anarchists, in agitating for their creed, will simply include in their agitation the idea of a general libertarian Law Code as part and parcel of the anarchist creed of abolition of legalized aggression against person or property in the society.

In contrast to the general law code, other aspects of court decisions could legitimately vary in accordance with the market or the wishes of the clients e.g., the language the cases will be conducted in, the number of judges to be involved, etc.

There are other problems of the basic Law Code which there is no time to go into here: for example, the definition of just property titles or the question of legitimate punishment of convicted offenders—though the latter problem of course exists in statist legal systems as well. The basic point, however, is that the State is not needed to arrive at legal principles or their elaboration: indeed, much of the common law, the law merchant, admiralty law, and private law in general, grew up apart from the State, by judges not making the law but finding it on the basis of agreed upon principles derived either from custom or reason. The idea that the State is needed to make law is as much a myth as that the State is needed to supply postal or police service.

Enough has been said here, I believe, to indicate that an anarchist system for settling disputes would be both viable and self-subsistent: that once adopted, it could work and continue indefinitely. How to arrive at that system is of course a very different problem, but certainly at the very least it will not likely come about unless people are convinced of its workability, are convinced, in short, that the State is not a necessary evil.

Chapter 5

Thomas Hobbes

FROM CONTRACT TO LEVIATHAN

Thomas Hobbes (1588–1679) was an English philosopher whose major work, *Leviathan,* was published in 1651 to great controversy amidst the English Civil War, and later went on to become one of the most influential works in the social contract tradition of political philosophy. In these excerpts, Hobbes discusses the moral imperative that persons are under to remove themselves from the state of nature, and the contract amongst each other by which they do so.

Of the First and Second *Naturall Lawes,* and of *Contracts*

The Right Of Nature, which Writers commonly call *Jus Naturale,* is the Liberty each man hath, to use his own power, as he will himselfe, for the preservation of his own Nature; that is to say, of his own Life; and consequently, of doing any thing, which in his own Judgement, and Reason, hee shall conceive to be the aptest means thereunto.

By LIBERTY, is understood, according to the proper signification of the word, the absence of externall Impediments: which Impediments, may oft take away part of a mans power to do what hee would; but cannot hinder him from using the power left him, according as his judgement, and reason shall dictate to him.

A LAW OF NATURE, (*Lex Naturalis,*) is a Precept, or generall Rule, found out by Reason, by which a man is forbidden to do, that, which is destructive of his life, or taketh away the means of preserving the same; and to omit, that, by which he thinketh it may be best preserved. For though

they that speak of this subject, use to confound *Jus,* and *Lex, Right* and *Law;* yet they ought to be distinguished; because RIGHT, consisteth in liberty to do, or to forbeare; Whereas LAW, determineth, and bindeth to one of them: so that Law, and Right, differ as much, as Obligation, and Liberty; which in one and the same matter are inconsistent.

And because the condition of Man, (as hath been declared in the precedent Chapter) is a condition of Warre of every one against every one; in which case every one is governed by his own Reason; and there is nothing he can make use of, that may not be a help unto him, in preserving his life against his enemyes; It followeth, that in such a condition, every man has a Right to every thing; even to one anothers body. And therefore, as long as this naturall Right of every man to every thing endureth, there can be no security to any man, (how strong or wise soever he be,) of living out the time, which Nature ordinarily alloweth men to live. And consequently it is a precept, or generall rule of Reason, *That every man, ought to endeavour Peace, as farre as he has* hope of obtaining it; *and when he cannot obtain it, that he may seek, and use, all helps, and advantages of Warre*. The first branch of which Rule, containeth the first, and Fundamentall Law of Nature; which is, *to seek Peace, and follow it*. The Second, the summe of the Right of Nature; which is, *By all means we can, to defend our selves*.

From this Fundamentall Law of Nature, by which men are commanded to endeavour Peace, is derived this second Law; *That a man be willing, when others are so too, as farre-forth, as for Peace, and defence of himselfe he shall think it necessary, to lay down this right to all things; and be contented with so much liberty against other men, as he would allow other men against himselfe*. For as long as every man holdeth this Right, of doing any thing he liketh; so long are all men in the condition of Warre. But if other men will not lay down their Right, as well as he; then there is no Reason for any one, to devest himself of his: For that were to expose himselfe to Prey, (which no man is bound to) rather than to dispose himselfe to Peace. This is that Law of the Gospell; *Whatsoever you require that others should do to you, that do ye to them*. And that Law of all men, *Quod tibi fieri non vis, alteri ne feceris*. [. . .]

Whensoever a man Transferreth his Right, or Renounceth it; it is either in consideration of some Right reciprocally transferred to himselfe; or for some other good he hopeth for thereby. For it is a voluntary act: and of the voluntary acts of every man, the object is some *Good to himself*. And therefore there be some Rights, which no man can be understood by any words, or other signes, to have abandoned, or transferred. As first a man cannot lay down the right of resisting them, that assault him by force, to take away his life; because he cannot be understood to ayme thereby, at any Good to himselfe. The same may be sayd of Wounds, and Chayns, and Imprisonment; both because there is no benefit consequent to such patience; as there is to the patience of suffering another to be wounded, or imprisoned: as also because a man cannot tell, when he seeth men proceed against him by violence, whether they intend his death or not.

And lastly the motive, and end for which this renouncing, and transferring of Right is introduced, is nothing else but the security of a mans person, in his life, and in the means of so preserving life, as not to be weary of it. And therefore if a man by words, or other signes, seem to despoyle himselfe of the End, for which those signes were intended; he is not to be understood as if he meant it, or that it was his will; but that he was ignorant of how such words and actions were to be interpreted.

The mutuall transferring of Right, is that which men call CONTRACT.

There is difference, between transferring of Right to the Thing; and transferring, or tradition, that is, delivery of the Thing it selfe. For the Thing may be delivered together with the Translation of the Right; as in buying and selling with ready mony; or exchange of goods, or lands: and it may be delivered some time after.

Again, one of the Contractors, may deliver the Thing contracted for on his part, and leave the other to perform his part at some determinate time after, and in the mean time be trusted; and then the Contract on his part, is called PACT, or COVENANT: Or both parts may contract now, to performe hereafter: in which cases, he that is to performe in time to come, being trusted, his performance is called *Keeping of Promise*, or Faith; and the fayling of performance (if it be voluntary) *Violation of Faith*. [. . .]

If a Covenant be made, wherein neither of the parties performe presently, but trust one another; in the condition of meer Nature, (which is a condition of Warre of every man against every man,) upon any reasonable suspition, it is Voyd: But if there be a common Power set over them both, with right and force sufficient to compell performance; it is not Voyd. For he that performeth first, has no assurance the other will performe after; because the bonds of words are too weak to bridle mens ambition, avarice, anger, and other Passions, without the feare of some coerceive Power; which in the condition of meer Nature, where all men are equall, and judges of the justnesse of their own fears cannot possibly be supposed. And therefore he which performeth first, does but betray himselfe to his enemy; contrary to the Right (he can never abandon) of defending his life, and means of living.

But in a civil estate, where there is a Power set up to constrain those that would otherwise violate their faith, that feare is no more reasonable; and for that cause, he which by the Covenant is to perform first, is obliged so to do.

The cause of feare, which maketh such a Covenant invalid, must be always something arising after the Covenant made; as some new fact, or other signe of the Will not to performe: else it cannot make the Covenant voyd. For that which could not hinder a man from promising, ought not to be admitted as a hindrance of performing. [. . .]

Covenants entred into by fear, in the condition of meer Nature, are obligatory. For example, if I Covenant to pay a ransome, or service for my life, to an enemy; I am bound by it. For it is a Contract, wherein one receiveth the benefit of life; the other is to receive mony, or service for it; and consequently, where no other Law (as in the condition, of meer Nature) forbiddeth the performance, the Covenant is valid. Therefore Prisoners of warre, if trusted with the payment of their Ransome, are obliged to pay it: And if a weaker Prince, make a disadvantageous peace with a stronger, for feare; he is bound to keep it; unlesse (as hath been sayd before) there ariseth some new, and just cause of feare, to renew the war. And even in Common-wealths, if I be forced to redeem my selfe from a Theefe by promising him mony, I am bound to pay it, till the Civill Law discharge me. For whatsoever I may lawfully do without Obligation, the same I may lawfully Covenant to do through feare: and what I lawfully Covenant, I cannot lawfully break. [. . .]

A Covenant not to defend my selfe from force, by force, is always voyd. For (as I have shewed before) no man can transferre, or lay down his Right to save himselfe from Death, Wounds, and Imprisonment, (the avoyding whereof is the onely End of laying down any Right, and therefore the promise of not resisting force, in no Covenant transferreth any right; nor is obliging. For though a man may Covenant thus, *Unlesse I do so, or so, kill me*; he cannot Covenant thus, *Unlesse I do so, or so, I will not resist you, when you come to kill me*. For man by nature chooseth the lesser evill, which is danger of death in resisting; rather than the greater, which is certain and present death in not resisting. And this is granted to be true by all men, in that they lead Criminals to Execution, and Prison, with armed men, notwithstanding that such Criminals have consented to the Law, by which they are condemned. [. . .]

Of the Causes, Generation, and Definition of a *Common-Wealth*

The finall Cause, End, or Designe of men, (who naturally love Liberty, and Dominion over others), in the introduction of that restraint upon themselves, (in which wee see them live in Common-wealths,) is the foresight of their own preservation, and of a more contented life thereby; that is to say, of getting themselves out from that miserable condition of Warre, which is necessarily consequent (as hath been shewn) to the naturall Passions of men, when there is no visible Power to keep them in awe, and tye them by feare of punishment to the performance of their Covenants, and observation of those Lawes of Nature set down in the fourteenth and fifteenth Chapters.

For the Lawes of Nature (as *Justice, Equity, Modesty, Mercy,* and (in summe) *doing to others, as wee would be done to,*) of themselves, without the terrour of some Power, to cause them to be observed, are contrary to our naturall Passions, that carry us to Partiality, Pride, Revenge, and the like. And Covenants, without the Sword, are but Words, and of no strength to secure a man at all. Therefore notwithstanding the Lawes of Nature, (which every one hath then kept, when he has the will to keep them, when he can do it safely,) if there be no Power erected, or not great enough for our security; every man will and may lawfully rely on his own strength and art, for caution against all other men. And in all places, where men have lived by small Families, to robbe and spoyle one another, has been a Trade, and so farre from being reputed against the Law of Nature, that the greater spoyles they gained, the greater was their honour; and men observed no other Lawes therein, but the Lawes of Honour; that is, to abstain from cruelty, leaving to men their lives, and instruments of husbandry. And as small Familyes did then; so now do Cities and Kingdomes which are but greater Families (for their own security) enlarge their Dominions, upon all pretences of danger, and fear of Invasion, or assistance that may be given to Invaders, endeavour as much as they can, to subdue, or weaken their neighbours, by open force, and secret arts, for want of other Caution, justly; and are remembered for it in after ages with honour.

Nor is it the joyning together of a small number of men, that gives them this security; because in small numbers, small additions on the one side or the other, make the advantage of strength so great, as is sufficient to carry the Victory; and therefore gives encouragement to an Invasion. The Multitude sufficient to confide in for our Security, is not determined by any certain number, but by comparison with the Enemy we feare; and is then sufficient, when the odds of the Enemy is not of so visible and conspicuous moment, to determine the event of warre, as to move him to attempt.

And be there never so great a Multitude; yet if their actions be directed according to their particular judgements, and particular appetites, they can expect thereby no defence, nor protection, neither against a Common enemy, nor against the injuries of one another. For being distracted in opinions concerning the best use and application of their strength, they do not help, but hinder one another; and reduce their strength by

mutuall opposition to nothing: whereby they are easily, not onely subdued by a very few that agree together; but also when there is no common enemy, they make warre upon each other, for their particular interests. For if we could suppose a great Multitude of men to consent in the observation of Justice, and other Lawes of Nature, without a common Power to keep them all in awe; we might as well suppose all Mankind to do the same; and then there neither would be, nor need to be any Civil Government, or Common-wealth at all; because there would be Peace without subjection.

Nor is it enough for the security, which men desire should last all the time of their life, that they be governed, and directed by one judgement, for a limited time; as in one Battell, or one Warre. For though they obtain a Victory by their unanimous endeavour against a forraign enemy; yet afterwards, when either they have no common enemy, or he that by one part is held for an enemy, is by another part held for a friend, they must needs by the difference of their interests dissolve, and fall again into a Warre amongst themselves.

It is true, that certain living creatures, as Bees, and Ants, live sociably one with another, (which are therefore by *Aristotle* numbred amongst Politicall creatures;) and yet have no other direction, than their particular judgements and appetites; nor speech, whereby one of them can signifie to another, what he thinks expedient for the common benefit: and therefore some man may perhaps desire to know, why Man-kind cannot do the same. To which I answer,

First, that men are continually in competition for Honour and Dignity, which these creatures are not; and consequently amongst men there ariseth on that ground, Envy and Hatred, and finally Warre; but amongst these not so.

Secondly, that amongst these creatures, the Common good differeth not from the Private; and being by nature enclined to their private, they procure thereby the common benefit. But man, whose Joy consisteth in comparing himselfe with other men, can relish nothing but what is eminent.

Thirdly, that these creatures, having not (as man) the use of reason, do not see, nor think they see any fault, in the administration of their common businesse: whereas amongst men, there are very many, that thinke themselves wiser, and abler to govern the Publique, better than the rest; and these strive to reforme and innovate, one this way, another that way; and thereby bring it into Distraction and Civill warre.

Fourthly, that these creatures, though they have some use of voice, in making knowne to one another their desires, and other affections; yet they want that art of words, by which some men can represent to others, that which is Good, in the likenesse of Evill; and Evill, in the likenesse of Good; and augment, or diminish the apparent greatnesse of Good and Evill; discontenting men, and troubling their Peace at their pleasure.

Fiftly, irrationall creatures cannot distinguish betweene *Injury*, and *Dammage*; and therefore as long as they be at ease, they are not offended with their fellowes: whereas Man is then most troublesome, when he is most at ease: for then it is that he loves to shew his Wisdome, and controule the Actions of them that governe the Common-wealth.

Lastly, the agreement of these creatures is Naturall; that of men, is by Covenant only, which is Artificiall: and therefore it is no wonder if there be somewhat else required (besides Covenant) to make their Agreement constant and lasting; which is a Common Power, to keep them in awe, and to direct their actions to the Common Benefit.

The only way to erect such a Common Power, as may be able to defend them from the invasion of Forraigners, and the injuries of one another, and thereby to secure them in such sort, as that by their owne industrie, and by the fruites of the Earth, they may nourish themselves and live contentedly; is, to conferre all their power and strength upon one Man, or upon one Assembly of men, that may reduce all their Wills, by plurality of voices, unto one Will: which is as much as to say, to appoint one man, or Assembly of men, to beare their Person; and every one to owne, and acknowledge himself to be Author of whatsoever he that so beareth their Person, shall Act, or cause to be Acted, in those things which concerne the Common Peace and Safetie; and therein to submit their Wills, every one to his Will, and their Judgements, to his Judgment. This is more than Consent, or Concord; it is a reall Unitie of them all, in one and the same Person, made by Covenant of every man with every man, in such manner, as if every man should say to every man, *I Authorise and give up my Right of Governing my selfe, to this Man, or to this Assembly of men, on this condition, that thou give up thy Right to him, and Authorise all his Actions in like manner.* This done, the Multitude so united in one Person, is called a COMMON-WEALTH, in latine CIVITAS. This is the Generation of that great LEVIATHAN, or rather (to speake more reverently) of that *Mortall God,* to which wee owe under the *Immortall God,* our peace and defence. For by this Authoritie, given him by every particular man in the Common-Wealth, he hath the use of so much Power and Strength conferred on him, that by terror thereof, he is inabled to forme the wills of them all, to Peace at home, and mutuall ayd against their enemies abroad. And in him consisteth the Essence of the Common-wealth; which (to define it,) is *One Person, of whose Acts a great Multitude, by mutuall Covenants one with another, have made themselves every one the Author, to the end he may use the strength and means of them all, as he shall think expedient, for their Peace and Common Defence.*

And he that carryeth this Person, is called SOVERAIGNE, and said to have *Soveraigne Power;* and every one besides, his SUBJECT.

The attaining to this Soveraigne Power, is by two wayes. One, by Naturall force; as when a man maketh his children, to submit themselves, and their children to his government, as being able to destroy them if they refuse; or by Warre subdueth his enemies to his will, giving them their lives on that condition. The other, is when men agree amongst themselves, to submit to some Man, or Assembly of men, voluntarily, on confidence to be protected by him against all others. This later, may be called a Politicall Common-wealth or Commonwealth by *Institution*; and the former, a Commonwealth by *Acquisition*.

Chapter 6

John Locke

SOCIAL CONTRACT AND THE STATE AS AGENT

John Locke (1632–1704) was an English philosopher and revolutionary who was an influential supporter of the Glorious Revolution wherein King James II was over-thrown and the relative balance of power swung toward Parliament. In this excerpt from his *Second Treatise* (1698), Locke discusses his version of the social contract by which government is created, and the role of both express and tacit consent in justifying that government.

Of the Beginning of Political Societies

95. Men being, as has been said, by Nature, all free, equal and independent, no one can be put out of this Estate, and subjected to the Political Power of another, without his own Consent. The only way whereby any one devests himself of his Natural Liberty, and puts on the bonds of Civil Society is by agreeing with other Men to joyn and unite into a Community, for their comfortable, safe, and peaceable living one amongst another, in a secure Enjoyment of their Properties, and a greater Security against any that are not of it. This any number of Men may do, because it injures not the Freedom of the rest; they are left as they were in the Liberty of the State of Nature. When any number of Men have so consented to make one Community or Government, they are thereby pres-ently incorporated, and make one Body Politick, wherein the Majority have a Right to act and con-clude the rest.

96. For when any number of Men have, by the consent of every individual, made a Community, they have thereby made that Community one Body, with a Power to Act as one Body, which is only by the will and determination of the majority. For that which acts any Community, being only the consent of the individuals of it, and it being necessary to that which is one body to move one way; it is necessary the Body should move that way whither the greater force carries it, which is the consent of the majority: or else it is impossible it should act or continue one Body, one Community, which the consent of every individual that united into it, agreed that it should; and so every one is bound by that consent to be concluded by the majority. And therefore we see that in Assemblies impowered to act by positive Laws where no number is set by that positive Law which impowers them, the act of the Majority passes for the act of the whole, and of course determines, as having by the Law of Nature and Reason, the power of the whole.

97. And thus every Man, by consenting with others to make one Body Politick under one Government, puts himself under an Obligation

to every one of that Society, to submit to the determination of the majority, and to be concluded by it; or else this *original Compact*, whereby he with others incorporates into *one Society*, would signifie nothing, and be no Compact, if he be left free, and under no other ties, than he was in before in the State of Nature. For what appearance would there be of any Compact? What new Engagement if he were no farther tied by any Decrees of the Society, than he himself thought fit, and did actually consent to? This would be still as great a liberty, as he himself had before his Compact, or any one else in the State of Nature hath, who may submit himself and consent to any acts of it if he thinks fit.

98. For if *the consent of the majority* shall not in reason, be received, *as the act of the whole*, and conclude every individual; nothing but the consent of every individual can make any thing to be the act of the whole: But such a consent is next impossible ever to be had, if we consider the Infirmities of Health, and Avocations of Business, which in a number, though much less than that of a Common-wealth, will necessarily keep many away from the publick Assembly. To which if we add the variety of Opinions, and contrariety of Interests, which unavoidably happen in all Collections of Men, the coming into Society upon such terms, would be only like Cato's coming into the Theatre, only to go out again. Such a Constitution as this would make the mighty *Leviathan* of a shorter duration, than the feeblest Creatures; and not let it outlast the day it was born in: which cannot be suppos'd till we can think, that Rational Creatures should desire and constitute Societies only to be dissolved. For where the *majority* cannot conclude the rest, there they cannot act as one Body, and consequently will be immediately dissolved again.

99. Whosoever therefore out of a state of Nature unite into a *Community*, must be understood to give up all the power, necessary to the ends for which they unite into Society, to the majority of the Community, unless they expressly agreed in any number greater than the majority. And this is done by barely agreeing to *unite into one Political Society*, which is *all the Compact that is*, or needs be, between the Individuals, that enter into, or make up a *Common-wealth*. And thus that, which begins and actually *constitutes any Political Society*, is nothing but the consent of any number of Freemen capable of a majority to unite and incorporate into such a Society. And this is that, and that only, which did, or could give *beginning* to any *lawful Government* in the World. [. . .]

119. *Every Man* being, as has been shewed, *naturally free*, and nothing being able to put him into subjection to any Earthly Power, but only his own Consent; it is to be considered, what shall be understood to be *a sufficient Declaration of a Mans Consent, to make him subject* to the Laws of any Government. There is a common distinction of an express and a tacit consent, which will concern our present Case. No body doubts but an *express Consent*, of any Man, entring into any Society, makes him a perfect Member of that Society, a Subject of that Government. The difficulty is, what ought to be look'd upon as a *tacit Consent*, and how far it binds, i.e. how far any one shall be looked on to have consented, and thereby submitted to any Government, where he has made no Expressions of it at all. And to this I say, that every Man, that hath any Possession, or Enjoyment, of any part of the Dominions of any Government, doth thereby give his *tacit Consent*, and is as far forth obliged to Obedience to the Laws of that Government, during such Enjoyment, as any one under it; whether this his Possession be of Land, to him and his Heirs for ever, or a Lodging only for a Week; or whether it be barely travelling freely on the Highway; and in Effect, it reaches as far as the very being of any one within the Territories of that Government.

120. To understand this the better, it is fit to consider, that every Man, when he, at first, incorporates himself into any Commonwealth,

he, by his uniting himself thereunto, annexed also, and submits to the Community those Possessions, which he has, or shall acquire, that do not already belong to any other Government. For it would be a direct Contradiction, for any one, to enter into Society with others for the securing and regulating of Property: And yet to suppose his Land, whose Property is to be regulated by the Laws of the Society, should be exempt from the Jurisdiction of that Government, to which he himself the Proprietor of the Land, is a Subject. By the same Act therefore, whereby any one unites his Person, which was before free, to any Commonwealth; by the same he unites his Possessions, which were before free, to it also; and they become, both of them, Person and Possession, subject to the Government and Dominion of that Commonwealth, as long as it hath a being. *Whoever* therefore, from thenceforth, by Inheritance, Purchase, Permission, or otherways *enjoys any part of the Land*, so annext to, and under the Government of *that Commonwealth, must take it with the Condition* it is under; that is, *of submitting to the Government of the Commonwealth*, under whose Jurisdiction it is, as far forth, as any Subject of it.

121. But since the Government has a direct Jurisdiction only over the Land, and reaches the Possessor of it, (before he has actually incorporated himself in the Society) only as he dwells upon, and enjoys that: *The Obligation* any one is under, by Virtue of such Enjoyment, *to submit to the Government, begins and ends with the Enjoyment*; so that whenever the Owner, who has given nothing but such a *tacit Consent* to the Government, will, by Donation, Sale, or otherwise, quit the said Possession, he is at liberty to go and incorporate himself into any other Commonwealth, or to agree with others to begin a new one, *in vacuis locis*, in any part of the World, they can find free and unpossessed: Whereas he, that has once, by actual Agreement, and any *express* Declaration, given his *Consent* to be of any Commonweal, is perpetually and indispensably obliged to be and remain unalterably a Subject to it, and can never be again in the liberty of the state of Nature; unless by any Calamity, the Government, he was under, comes to be dissolved; or else by some publick Act cuts him off from being any longer a Member of it.

122. But submitting to the Laws of any Country, living quietly, and enjoying Priviledges and Protection under them, *makes not a Man a Member of that Society*: This is only a local Protection and Homage due to, and from all those, who, not being in a state of War, come within the Territories belonging to any Government, to all parts whereof the force of its Law extends. But this no more *makes a Man a Member of that Society*, a perpetual Subject of that Commonwealth, than it would make a Man a Subject to another in whose Family he found it convenient to abide for some time; though, whilst he continued in it, he were obliged to comply with the Laws, and submit to the Government he found there. And thus we see, that *Foreigners*, by living all their Lives under another Government, and enjoying the Priviledges and Protection of it, though they are bound, even in Conscience, to submit to its Administration, as far forth as any Denison; yet do not thereby come to be *Subjects or Members of that Commonwealth*. Nothing can make any Man so, but his actually entering into it by positive Engagement, and express Promise and Compact. This is that, which I think, concerning the beginning of Political Societies, and that *Consent which makes any one a Member* of any Commonwealth.

Chapter 7

Jean-Jacques Rousseau

THE SOCIAL CONTRACT
Or Principles of Political Right

Jean-Jacques Rousseau (1712–1778), was a philosopher of the French Enlightenment who was influential both on Kant's development of his ethical theory and on the French Revolution. In this excerpt from his *Social Contract* (1762), Rousseau argues that legitimate political authority will be based on what he calls the General Will. Because the General Will is constituted by the wills of all the individuals who make up society, Rousseau's notion of political authority is one in which the people is sovereign over itself.

1. Subject of the First Book

Man is born free; and everywhere he is in chains. One thinks himself the master of others, and still remains a greater slave than they. How did this change come about? I do not know. What can make it legitimate? That question I think I can answer.

If I took into account only force, and the effects derived from it, I should say: "As long as a people is compelled to obey, and obeys, it does well; as soon as it can shake off the yoke, and shakes it off, it does still better; for, regaining its liberty by the same right as took it away, either it is justified in resuming it, or there was no justification for those who took it away." But the social order is a sacred right which is the basis of all other rights. Nevertheless, this right does not come from nature, and must therefore be founded on conventions. Before coming to that, I have to prove what I have just asserted.

2. The First Societies

The most ancient of all societies, and the only one that is natural, is the family: and even so the children remain attached to the father only so long as they need him for their preservation. As soon as this need ceases, the natural bond is dissolved. The children, released from the obedience they owed to the father, and the father, released from the care he owed his children, return equally to independence. If they remain united, they continue so no longer naturally, but voluntarily; and the family itself is then maintained only by convention.

This common liberty results from the nature of man. His first law is to provide for his own preservation, his first cares are those which he owes to himself; and, as soon as he reaches years of discretion, he is the sole judge of the proper means of preserving himself, and consequently becomes his own master.

The family then may be called the first model of political societies: the ruler corresponds to the father, and the people to the children; and all, being born free and equal, alienate their liberty only for their own advantage. The whole difference is that, in the family, the love of the father for his children repays him for the care he takes of them, while, in the State, the pleasure of commanding takes the place of the love which the chief cannot have for the peoples under him.

Grotius denies that all human power is established in favour of the governed, and quotes slavery as an example. His usual method of reasoning is constantly to establish right by fact. It would be possible to employ a more logical method, but none could be more favourable to tyrants.

It is then, according to Grotius, doubtful whether the human race belongs to a hundred men, or that hundred men to the human race: and, throughout his book, he seems to incline to the former alternative, which is also the view of Hobbes. On this showing, the human species is divided into so many herds of cattle, each with its ruler, who keeps guard over them for the purpose of devouring them.

As a shepherd is of a nature superior to that of his flock, the shepherds of men, i.e., their rulers, are of a nature superior to that of the peoples under them. Thus, Philo tells us, the Emperor Caligula reasoned, concluding equally well either that kings were gods, or that men were beasts.

The reasoning of Caligula agrees with that of Hobbes and Grotius. Aristotle, before any of them, had said that men are by no means equal naturally, but that some are born for slavery, and others for dominion.

Aristotle was right; but he took the effect for the cause. Nothing can be more certain than that every man born in slavery is born for slavery. Slaves lose everything in their chains, even the desire of escaping from them: they love their servitude, as the comrades of Ulysses loved their brutish condition. If then there are slaves by nature, it is because there have been slaves against nature. Force made the first slaves, and their cowardice perpetuated the condition. [. . .]

3. The Right of the Strongest

The strongest is never strong enough to be always the master, unless he transforms strength into right, and obedience into duty. Hence the right of the strongest, which, though to all seeming meant ironically, is really laid down as a fundamental principle. But are we never to have an explanation of this phrase? Force is a physical power, and I fail to see what moral effect it can have. To yield to force is an act of necessity, not of will—at the most, an act of prudence. In what sense can it be a duty?

Suppose for a moment that this so-called "right" exists. I maintain that the sole result is a mass of inexplicable nonsense. For, if force creates right, the effect changes with the cause: every force that is greater than the first succeeds to its right. As soon as it is possible to disobey with impunity, disobedience is legitimate; and, the strongest being always in the right, the only thing that matters is to act so as to become the strongest. But what kind of right is that which perishes when force fails? If we must obey perforce, there is no need to obey because we ought; and if we are not forced to obey, we are under no obligation to do so. Clearly, the word "right" adds nothing to force: in this connection, it means absolutely nothing.

Obey the powers that be. If this means yield to force, it is a good precept, but superfluous: I can answer for its never being violated. All power comes from God, I admit; but so does all sickness: does that mean that we are forbidden to call in the doctor? A brigand surprises me at the edge of a wood: must I not merely surrender my purse on compulsion; but, even if I could withhold it, am I in conscience bound to give it up? For certainly the pistol he holds is also a power.

Let us then admit that force does not create right, and that we are obliged to obey only legitimate powers. In that case, my original question recurs.

4. Slavery

Since no man has a natural authority over his fellow, and force creates no right, we must conclude that conventions form the basis of all legitimate authority among men.

If an individual, says Grotius, can alienate his liberty and make himself the slave of a master, why could not a whole people do the same and make itself subject to a king? There are in this passage plenty of ambiguous words which would need explaining; but let us confine ourselves to the word *alienate*. To alienate is to give or to sell. Now, a man who becomes the slave of another does not give himself; he sells himself, at the least for his subsistence: but for what does a people sell itself? A king is so far from furnishing his subjects with their subsistence that he gets his own only from them; and, according to Rabelais, kings do not live on nothing. Do subjects then give their persons on condition that the king takes their goods also? I fail to see what they have left to preserve.

It will be said that the despot assures his subjects civil tranquillity. Granted; but what do they gain, if the wars his ambition brings down upon them, his insatiable avidity, and the vexations conduct of his ministers press harder on them than their own dissensions would have done? What do they gain, if the very tranquillity they enjoy is one of their miseries? Tranquillity is found also in dungeons; but is that enough to make them desirable places to live in? The Greeks imprisoned in the cave of the Cyclops lived there very tranquilly, while they were awaiting their turn to be devoured.

To say that a man gives himself gratuitously, is to say what is absurd and inconceivable; such an act is null and illegitimate, from the mere fact that he who does it is out of his mind. To say the same of a whole people is to suppose a people of madmen; and madness creates no right.

Even if each man could alienate himself, he could not alienate his children: they are born men and free; their liberty belongs to them, and no one but they has the right to dispose of it. Before they come to years of discretion, the father can, in their name, lay down conditions for their preservation and well-being, but he cannot give them irrevocably and without conditions: such a gift is contrary to the ends of nature, and exceeds the rights of paternity. It would therefore be necessary, in order to legitimise an arbitrary government, that in every generation the people should be in a position to accept or reject it; but, were this so, the government would be no longer arbitrary.

To renounce liberty is to renounce being a man, to surrender the rights of humanity and even its duties. For him who renounces everything no indemnity is possible. Such a renunciation is incompatible with man's nature; to remove all liberty from his will is to remove all morality from his acts. Finally, it is an empty and contradictory convention that sets up, on the one side, absolute authority, and, on the other, unlimited obedience. Is it not clear that we can be under no obligation to a person from whom we have the right to exact everything? Does not this condition alone, in the absence of equivalence or exchange, in itself involve the nullity of the act? For what right can my slave have against me, when all that he has belongs to me, and, his right being mine, this right of mine against myself is a phrase devoid of meaning?

Grotius and the rest find in war another origin for the so-called right of slavery. The victor having, as they hold, the right of killing the vanquished, the latter can buy back his life at the price of his liberty; and this convention is the more legitimate because it is to the advantage of both parties.

But it is clear that this supposed right to kill the conquered is by no means deducible from the state of war. Men, from the mere fact that, while they are living in their primitive independence, they have no mutual relations stable enough to constitute either the state of peace or the state of war, cannot be naturally enemies. War is constituted by a relation between things, and not between persons; and, as the state of war cannot arise out of simple personal relations, but only out of real relations, private war, or war of man with man, can exist neither in the state of nature, where there is no constant property, nor in the social state, where everything is under the authority of the laws.

Individual combats, duels and encounters, are acts which cannot constitute a state; while the private wars, authorised by the Establishments of Louis IX, King of France, and suspended by the Peace of God, are abuses of feudalism, in itself an absurd system if ever there was one, and contrary to the principles of natural right and to all good polity.

War then is a relation, not between man and man, but between State and State, and individuals are enemies only accidentally, not as men, nor even as citizens, but as soldiers; not as members of their country, but as its defenders. Finally, each State can have for enemies only other States, and not men; for between things disparate in nature there can be no real relation. [. . .]

The right of conquest has no foundation other than the right of the strongest. If war does not give the conqueror the right to massacre the conquered peoples, the right to enslave them cannot be based upon a right which does not exist. No one has a right to kill an enemy except when he cannot make him a slave, and the right to enslave him cannot therefore be derived from the right to kill him. It is accordingly an unfair exchange to make him buy at the price of his liberty his life, over which the victor holds no right. Is it not clear that there is a vicious circle in founding the right of life and death on the right of slavery, and the right of slavery on the right of life and death?

Even if we assume this terrible right to kill everybody, I maintain that a slave made in war, or a conquered people, is under no obligation to a master, except to obey him as far as he is compelled to do so. By taking an equivalent for his life, the victor has not done him a favour; instead of killing him without profit, he has killed him usefully. So far then is he from acquiring over him any authority in addition to that of force, that the state of war continues to subsist between them: their mutual relation is the effect of it, and the usage of the right of war does not imply a treaty of peace. A convention has indeed been made; but this convention, so far from destroying the state of war, presupposes its continuance.

So, from whatever aspect we regard the question, the right of slavery is null and void, not only as being illegitimate, but also because it is absurd and meaningless. The words *slave* and *right* contradict each other, and are mutually exclusive. It will always be equally foolish for a man to say to a man or to a people: "I make with you a convention wholly at your expense and wholly to my advantage; I shall keep it as long as I like, and you will keep it as long as I like."

5. That We Must Always go Back to a First Convention

Even if I granted all that I have been refuting, the friends of despotism would be no better off. There will always be a great difference between subduing a multitude and ruling a society. Even if scattered individuals were successively enslaved by one man, however numerous they might be, I still see no more than a master and his slaves, and certainly not a people and its ruler; I see what may be termed an aggregation, but not an association; there is as yet neither public good nor body politic. The man in question, even if he has enslaved half the world, is still only an individual; his interest, apart from that of others, is still a purely private interest. If this same man comes to die, his empire, after him, remains scattered and without unity, as an oak falls and dissolves into a heap of ashes when the fire has consumed it.

A people, says Grotius, can give itself to a king.

Then, according to Grotius, a people is a people before it gives itself. The gift is itself a civil act, and implies public deliberation. It would be better, before examining the act by which a people gives itself to a king, to examine that by which it has become a people; for this act, being necessarily prior to the other, is the true foundation of society.

Indeed, if there were no prior convention, where, unless the election were unanimous, would be the obligation on the minority to submit to the choice of the majority? How have a hundred men who wish for a master the right to vote on behalf of ten who do not? The law of majority voting is itself something established by convention, and presupposes unanimity, on one occasion at least.

6. The Social Compact

I Suppose men to have reached the point at which the obstacles in the way of their preservation in the state of nature show their power of resistance to be greater than the resources at the disposal of each individual for his maintenance in that state. That primitive condition can then subsist no longer; and the human race would perish unless it changed its manner of existence.

But, as men cannot engender new forces, but only unite and direct existing ones, they have no other means of preserving themselves than the formation, by aggregation, of a sum of forces great enough to overcome the resistance. These they have to bring into play by means of a single motive power, and cause to act in concert.

This sum of forces can arise only where several persons come together: but, as the force and liberty of each man are the chief instruments of his self-preservation, how can he pledge them without harming his own interests, and neglecting the care he owes to himself? This difficulty, in its bearing on my present subject, may be stated in the following terms:

The problem is to find a form of association which will defend and protect with the whole common force the person and goods of each associate, and in which each, while uniting himself with all, may still obey himself alone, and remain as free as before.

This is the fundamental problem of which the *Social Contract* provides the solution.

The clauses of this contract are so determined by the nature of the act that the slightest modification would make them vain and ineffective; so that, although they have perhaps never been formally set forth, they are everywhere the same and everywhere tacitly admitted and recognised, until, on the violation of the social compact, each regains his original rights and resumes his natural liberty, while losing the conventional liberty in favour of which he renounced it.

These clauses, properly understood, may be reduced to one—the total alienation of each associate, together with all his rights, to the whole community; for, in the first place, as each gives himself absolutely, the conditions are the same for all; and, this being so, no one has any interest in making them burdensome to others.

Moreover, the alienation being without reserve, the union is as perfect as it can be, and no associate has anything more to demand: for, if the individuals retained certain rights, as there would be no common superior to decide between them and the public, each, being on one point his own judge, would ask to be so on all; the state of nature would thus continue, and the association would necessarily become inoperative or tyrannical.

Finally, each man, in giving himself to all, gives himself to nobody; and as there is no associate over whom he does not acquire the same right as he yields others over himself, he gains an equivalent for everything he loses, and an increase of force for the preservation of what he has.

If then we discard from the social compact what is not of its essence, we shall find that it reduces itself to the following terms:

Each of us puts his person and all his power in common under the supreme direction of the general will, and, in our corporate capacity, we receive each member as an indivisible part of the whole.

At once, in place of the individual personality of each contracting party, this act of association creates a moral and collective body, composed of as many members as the assembly contains votes, and receiving from this act its unity, its common identity, its life and its will. This public person, so formed by the union of all other persons formerly took the name of *city*, and now takes that of *Republic* or *body politic*; it is called by its members *State* when passive. *Sovereign* when active, and *Power* when compared with others like itself. Those who are associated in it take collectively the name of *people*, and severally are called *citizens*, as sharing in the sovereign power, and *subjects*, as being under the laws of the State. But these terms are often confused and taken one for another: it is enough to know how to distinguish them when they are being used with precision.

7. The Sovereign

This formula shows us that the act of association comprises a mutual undertaking between the public and the individuals, and that each individual, in making a contract, as we may say, with himself, is bound in a double capacity; as a member of the Sovereign he is bound to the individuals, and as a member of the State to the Sovereign. But the maxim of civil right, that no one is bound by undertakings made to himself, does not apply in this case; for there is a great difference between incurring an obligation to yourself and incurring one to a whole of which you form a part.

Attention must further be called to the fact that public deliberation, while competent to bind all the subjects to the Sovereign, because of the two different capacities in which each of them may be regarded, cannot, for the opposite reason, bind the Sovereign to itself; and that it is consequently against the nature of the body politic for the Sovereign to impose on itself a law which it cannot infringe. Being able to regard itself in only one capacity, it is in the position of an individual who makes a contract with himself; and this makes it clear that there neither is nor can be any kind of fundamental law binding on the body of the people—not even the social contract itself. This does not mean that the body politic cannot enter into undertakings with others, provided the contract is not infringed by them; for in relation to what is external to it, it becomes a simple being, an individual.

But the body politic or the Sovereign, drawing its being wholly from the sanctity of the contract, can never bind itself, even to an outsider, to do anything derogatory to the original act, for instance, to alienate any part of itself, or to submit to another Sovereign. Violation of the act by which it exists would be self-annihilation; and that which is itself nothing can create nothing.

As soon as this multitude is so united in one body, it is impossible to offend against one of the members without attacking the body, and still more to offend against the body without the members resenting it. Duty and interest therefore equally oblige the two contracting parties to give each other help; and the same men should seek to combine, in their double capacity, all the advantages dependent upon that capacity.

Again, the Sovereign, being formed wholly of the individuals who compose it, neither has nor can have any interest contrary to theirs; and consequently the sovereign power need give no guarantee to its subjects, because it is impossible for the body to wish to hurt all its members. We shall also see later on that it cannot hurt any in particular. The Sovereign, merely by virtue of what it is, is always what it should be.

This, however, is not the case with the relation of the subjects to the Sovereign, which, despite the common interest, would have no security that they would fulfil their undertakings, unless it found means to assure itself of their fidelity.

In fact, each individual, as a man, may have a particular will contrary or dissimilar to the general will which he has as a citizen. His particular interest may speak to him quite differently from the common interest: his absolute and naturally independent existence may make him look upon what he owes to the common cause as a gratuitous contribution, the loss of which will do less harm to others than the payment of it is burdensome to himself; and, regarding the moral person which constitutes the State as a *persona ficta*, because not a man, he may wish to enjoy the rights of citizenship without being ready to fulfil the duties of a subject. The continuance of such an injustice could not but prove the undoing of the body politic.

In order then that the social compact may not be an empty formula, it tacitly includes the undertaking, which alone can give force to the rest, that whoever refuses to obey the general will shall be compelled to do so by the whole body. This means nothing less than that he will be forced to be free; for this is the condition which, by giving each citizen to his country, secures him against all personal dependence. In this lies the key to the working of the political machine; this alone legitimises civil undertakings, which, without it, would be absurd, tyrannical, and liable to the most frightful abuses.

8. The Civil State

The passage from the state of nature to the civil state produces a very remarkable change in man, by substituting justice for instinct in his conduct, and giving his actions the morality they had formerly lacked. Then only, when the voice of duty takes the place of physical impulses and right of appetite, does man, who so far had considered only himself, find that he is forced to act on different principles, and to consult his reason before listening to his inclinations. Although, in this state, he deprives himself of some advantages which he got from nature, he gains in return others so great, his faculties are so stimulated and developed, his ideas so extended, his feelings so ennobled, and his whole soul so uplifted, that, did not the abuses of this new condition often degrade him below that which he left, he would be bound to bless continually the happy moment which took him from it for ever, and, instead of a stupid and unimaginative animal, made him an intelligent being and a man.

Let us draw up the whole account in terms easily commensurable. What man loses by the social contract is his natural liberty and an unlimited right to everything he tries to get and succeeds in getting; what he gains is civil liberty and the proprietorship of all he possesses. If we are to avoid mistake in weighing one against the other, we must clearly distinguish natural liberty, which is bounded only by the strength of the individual, from civil liberty, which is limited by the general will; and possession, which is merely the effect of force or the right of the first occupier, from property, which can be founded only on a positive title.

We might, over and above all this, add, to what man acquires in the civil state, moral liberty, which alone makes him truly master of himself; for the mere impulse of appetite is slavery, while obedience to a law which we prescribe to ourselves is liberty. But I have already said too much on this head, and the philosophical meaning of the word liberty does not now concern us.

9. Real Property

Each member of the community gives himself to it, at the moment of its foundation, just as he is, with all the resources at his command, including the goods he possesses. This act does not make possession, in changing hands, change its nature, and become property in the hands of the Sovereign; but, as the forces of the city are incomparably greater than those of an individual, public possession is also, in fact, stronger and more irrevocable, without being any more legitimate, at any rate from the point of view of foreigners. For the State, in relation to its members, is master of all their goods by the social contract, which, within the State, is the basis of all rights; but, in relation to other powers, it is so only by the right of the first occupier, which it holds from its members.

The right of the first occupier, though more real than the right of the strongest, becomes a real right only when the right of property has already been established. Every man has naturally a right to everything he needs; but the positive act which makes him proprietor of one thing excludes him from everything else. Having his share, he ought to keep to it, and can have no further right against the community. This is why the right of the first occupier, which in the state of nature is so weak, claims the respect of every man in civil society. In this right we are respecting not so much what belongs to another as what does not belong to ourselves.

In general, to establish the right of the first occupier over a plot of ground, the following conditions are necessary: first, the land must not yet be inhabited; secondly, a man must occupy only the amount he needs for his subsistence; and, in the third place, possession must be taken, not by an empty ceremony, but by labour and cultivation, the only sign of proprietorship that should be respected by others, in default of a legal title.

In granting the right of first occupancy to necessity and labour, are we not really stretching it as far as it can go? Is it possible to leave such a right unlimited? Is it to be enough to set foot on a plot of common ground, in order to be able to call yourself at once the master of it? Is it to be enough that a man has the strength to expel others for a moment, in order to establish his right to prevent them from ever returning? How can a man or a people seize an immense territory and keep it from the rest of the world except by a punishable usurpation, since all others are being robbed, by such an act, of the place of habitation and the means of subsistence which nature gave

them in common? When Nunez Balboa, standing on the sea-shore, took possession of the South Seas and the whole of South America in the name of the crown of Castile, was that enough to dispossess all their actual inhabitants, and to shut out from them all the princes of the world? On such a showing, these ceremonies are idly multiplied, and the Catholic King need only take possession all at once, from his apartment, of the whole universe, merely making a subsequent reservation about what was already in the possession of other princes.

We can imagine how the lands of individuals, where they were contiguous and came to be united, became the public territory, and how the right of Sovereignty, extending from the subjects over the lands they held, became at once real and personal. The possessors were thus made more dependent, and the forces at their command used to guarantee their fidelity. The advantage of this does not seem to have been felt by ancient monarchs, who called themselves Kings of the Persians, Scythians, or Macedonians, and seemed to regard themselves more as rulers of men than as masters of a country. Those of the present day more cleverly call themselves Kings of France, Spain, England, etc.: thus holding the land, they are quite confident of holding the inhabitants.

The peculiar fact about this alienation is that, in taking over the goods of individuals, the community, so far from despoiling them, only assures them legitimate possession, and changes usurpation into a true right and enjoyment into proprietorship. Thus the possessors, being regarded as depositaries of the public good, and having their rights respected by all the members of the State and maintained against foreign aggression by all its forces, have, by a cession which benefits both the public and still more themselves, acquired, so to speak, all that they gave up. This paradox may easily be explained by the distinction between the rights which the Sovereign and the proprietor have over the same estate, as we shall see later on.

It may also happen that men begin to unite

one with another before they possess anything, and that, subsequently occupying a tract of country which is enough for all, they enjoy it in common, or share it out among themselves, either equally or according to a scale fixed by the Sovereign. However the acquisition be made, the right which each individual has to his own estate is always subordinate to the right which the community has over all: without this, there would be neither stability in the social tie, nor real force in the exercise of Sovereignty.

I shall end this chapter and this book by remarking on a fact on which the whole social system should rest: i.e., that, instead of destroying natural inequality, the fundamental compact substitutes, for such physical inequality as nature may have set up between men, an equality that is moral and legitimate, and that men, who may be unequal in strength or intelligence, become every one equal by convention and legal right.

BOOK II

1. That Sovereignty is Inalienable

The first and most important deduction from the principles we have so far laid down is that the general will alone can direct the State according to the object for which it was instituted, i.e., the common good: for if the clashing of particular interests made the establishment of societies necessary, the agreement of these very interests made it possible. The common element in these different interests is what forms the social tie; and, were there no point of agreement between them all, no society could exist. It is solely on the basis of this common interest that every society should be governed.

I hold then that Sovereignty, being nothing less than the exercise of the general will, can never be alienated, and that the Sovereign, who is no less than a collective being, cannot be represented except by himself: the power indeed may be transmitted, but not the will.

In reality, if it is not impossible for a particular will to agree on some point with the general will, it is at least impossible for the agreement to be lasting and constant; for the particular will tends, by its very nature, to partiality, while the general will tends to equality. It is even more impossible to have any guarantee of this agreement; for even if it should always exist, it would be the effect not of art, but of chance. The Sovereign may indeed say: "I now will actually what this man wills, or at least what he says he wills"; but it cannot say: "What he wills tomorrow, I too shall will" because it is absurd for the will to bind itself for the future, nor is it incumbent on any will to consent to anything that is not for the good of the being who wills. If then the people promises simply to obey, by that very act it dissolves itself and loses what makes it a people; the moment a master exists, there is no longer a Sovereign, and from that moment the body politic has ceased to exist.

This does not mean that the commands of the rulers cannot pass for general wills, so long as the Sovereign, being free to oppose them, offers no opposition. In such a case, universal silence is taken to imply the consent of the people. This will be explained later on. [. . .]

3. Whether the General Will is Fallible

It follows from what has gone before that the general will is always right and tends to the public advantage; but it does not follow that the deliberations of the people are always equally correct. Our will is always for our own good, but we do not always see what that is; the people is never corrupted, but it is often deceived, and on such occasions only does it seem to will what is bad.

There is often a great deal of difference between the will of all and the general will; the latter considers only the common interest, while the former takes private interest into account, and is no more than a sum of particular wills: but take away from these same wills the pluses and minuses that cancel one another, and the general will remains as the sum of the differences.

If, when the people, being furnished with adequate information, held its deliberations, the citizens had no communication one with another, the grand total of the small differences would always give the general will, and the decision would always be good. But when factions arise, and partial associations are formed at the expense of the great association, the will of each of these associations becomes general in relation to its members, while it remains particular in relation to the State: it may then be said that there are no longer as many votes as there are men, but only as many as there are associations. The differences become less numerous and give a less general result. Lastly, when one of these associations is so great as to prevail over all the rest, the result is no longer a sum of small differences, but a single difference; in this case there is no longer a general will, and the opinion which prevails is purely particular.

It is therefore essential, if the general will is to be able to express itself, that there should be no partial society within the State, and that each citizen should think only his own thoughts: which was indeed the sublime and unique system established by the great Lycurgus. But if there are partial societies, it is best to have as many as possible and to prevent them from being unequal, as was done by Solon, Numa and Servius. These precautions are the only ones that can guarantee that the general will shall be always enlightened, and that the people shall in no way deceive itself.

4. The Limits of the Sovereign Power

If the State is a moral person whose life is in the union of its members, and if the most important of its cares is the care for its own preservation, it must have a universal and compelling force, in order to move and dispose each part as may be most advantageous to the whole. As nature gives each man absolute power over all his members, the social compact gives the body politic absolute power over all its members also; and it is this power which, under the direction of the general will, bears, as I have said, the name of Sovereignty.

But, besides the public person, we have to consider the private persons composing it, whose life and liberty are naturally independent of it. We are bound then to distinguish clearly between the respective rights of the citizens and the Sovereign, and between the duties the former have to fulfil as subjects, and the natural rights they should enjoy as men.

Each man alienates, I admit, by the social compact, only such part of his powers, goods and liberty as it is important for the community to control; but it must also be granted that the Sovereign is sole judge of what is important.

Every service a citizen can render the State he ought to render as soon as the Sovereign demands it; but the Sovereign, for its part, cannot impose upon its subjects any fetters that are useless to the community, nor can it even wish to do so; for no more by the law of reason than by the law of nature can anything occur without a cause.

The undertakings which bind us to the social body are obligatory only because they are mutual; and their nature is such that in fulfilling them we cannot work for others without working for ourselves. Why is it that the general will is always in the right, and that all continually will the happiness of each one, unless it is because there is not a man who does not think of "each" as meaning him, and consider himself in voting for all? This proves that equality of rights and the idea of justice which such equality creates originate in the preference each man gives to himself, and accordingly in the very nature of man. It proves that the general will, to be really such, must be general in its object as well as its essence; that it must both come from all and apply to all; and that it loses its natural rectitude when it is directed to some particular and determinate object, because in such a case we are judging of something foreign to us, and have no true principle of equity to guide us.

Indeed, as soon as a question of particular fact or right arises on a point not previously regulated by a general convention, the matter becomes contentious. It is a case in which the individuals concerned are one party, and the public the other, but in which I can see neither the law that ought to be followed nor the judge who ought to give the decision. In such a case, it would be absurd to propose to refer the question to an express decision of the general will, which can be only the conclusion reached by one of the parties and in consequence will be, for the other party, merely an external and particular will, inclined on this occasion to injustice and subject to error. Thus, just as a particular will cannot stand for the general will, the general will, in turn, changes its nature, when its object is particular, and, as general, cannot pronounce on a man or a fact. When, for instance, the people of Athens nominated or displaced its rulers, decreed honours to one, and imposed penalties on another, and, by a multitude of particular decrees, exercised all the functions of government indiscriminately, it had in such cases no longer a general will in the strict sense; it was acting no longer as Sovereign, but as magistrate. This will seem contrary to current views; but I must be given time to expound my own.

It should be seen from the foregoing that what makes the will general is less the number of voters than the common interest uniting them; for, under this system, each necessarily submits to the conditions he imposes on others: and this admirable agreement between interest and justice gives to the common deliberations an equitable character which at once vanishes when any particular question is discussed, in the absence of a common interest to unite and identify the ruling of the judge with that of the party.

From whatever side we approach our principle, we reach the same conclusion, that the social compact sets up among the citizens an equality of such a kind, that they all bind themselves to observe the same conditions and should therefore all enjoy the same rights. Thus, from the very nature of the compact, every act of Sovereignty, i.e., every authentic act of the general will, binds or favours all the citizens equally; so that the Sovereign recognises only the body of the nation, and draws no distinctions between those of whom it is made up. What, then, strictly speaking, is an act of Sovereignty? It is not a convention between a superior and an inferior, but a convention between the body and each of its members. It is legitimate, because based on the social contract, and equitable, because common to all; useful, because it can have no other object than the general good, and stable, because guaranteed by the public force and the supreme power. So long as the subjects have to submit only to conventions of this sort, they obey no-one but their own will; and to ask how far the respective rights of the Sovereign and the citizens extend, is to ask up to what point the latter can enter into undertakings with themselves, each with all, and all with each.

We can see from this that the sovereign power, absolute, sacred and inviolable as it is, does not and cannot exceed the limits of general conventions, and that every man may dispose at will of such goods and liberty as these conventions leave him; so that the Sovereign never has a right to lay more charges on one subject than on another, because, in that case, the question becomes particular, and ceases to be within its competency.

When these distinctions have once been admitted, it is seen to be so untrue that there is, in the social contract, any real renunciation on the part of the individuals, that the position in which they find themselves as a result of the contract is really preferable to that in which they were before. Instead of a renunciation, they have made an advantageous exchange: instead of an uncertain and precarious way of living they have got one that is better and more secure; instead of natural independence they have got liberty, instead of the power to harm others security for themselves, and instead of their strength, which others might overcome, a right which social union makes invincible. Their very life, which they have devoted to the State, is by it constantly protected; and when they risk it in the State's defence, what more are they doing than giving back what they have received from it? What are they doing that they would not do more often and with greater danger in the state of nature, in which they would inevitably have to fight battles at the peril of their lives in defence of that which is the means of their preservation? All have indeed to fight when their country needs them; but then no one has ever to fight for himself. Do we not gain something by running, on behalf of what gives us our security, only some of the risks we should have to run for ourselves, as soon as we lost it? [. . .]

7. The Legislator

In order to discover the rules of society best suited to nations, a superior intelligence beholding all the passions of men without experiencing any of them would be needed. This intelligence would have to be wholly unrelated to our nature, while knowing it through and through; its happiness would have to be independent of us, and yet ready to occupy itself with ours; and lastly, it would have, in the march of time, to look forward to a distant glory, and, working in one century, to be able to enjoy in the next. It would take gods to give men laws.

What Caligula argued from the facts, Plato, in the dialogue called the *Politicus*, argued in defining the civil or kingly man, on the basis of right. But if great princes are rare, how much more so are great legislators? The former have only to follow the pattern which the latter have to lay down. The legislator is the engineer who invents the machine, the prince merely the mechanic who sets it up and makes it go. "At the birth of societies," says Montesquieu, "the rulers of Republics establish institutions, and afterwards the institutions mould the rulers."

He who dares to undertake the making of a people's institutions ought to feel himself capable, so to speak, of changing human nature, of transforming each individual, who is by himself a complete and solitary whole, into part of a greater whole from which he in a manner receives his life and being; of altering man's constitution for the purpose of strengthening it; and of substituting a partial and moral existence for the physical and independent existence nature has conferred on us all. He must, in a word, take away from man his own resources and give him instead new ones alien to him, and incapable of being made use of without the help of other men. The more completely these natural resources are annihilated, the greater and the more lasting are those which he acquires, and the more stable and perfect the new institutions; so that if each citizen is nothing and can do nothing without the rest, and the resources acquired by the whole are equal or superior to the aggregate of the resources of all the individuals, it may be said that legislation is at the highest possible point of perfection.

The legislator occupies in every respect an extraordinary position in the State. If he should do so by reason of his genius, he does so no less by reason of his office, which is neither magistracy, nor Sovereignty. This office, which sets up the Republic, nowhere enters into its constitution; it is an individual and superior function, which has nothing in common with human empire; for if he who holds command over men ought not to have command over the laws, he who has command over the laws ought not any more to have it over men; or else his laws would be the ministers of his passions and would often merely serve to perpetuate his injustices: his private aims would inevitably mar the sanctity of his work.

When Lycurgus gave laws to his country, he began by resigning the throne. It was the custom of most Greek towns to entrust the establishment of their laws to foreigners. The Republics of modern Italy in many cases followed this example; Geneva did the same and profited by it. Rome, when it was most prosperous, suffered a revival of all the crimes of tyranny, and was brought to the verge of destruction, because it put the legislative authority and the sovereign power into the same hands.

Nevertheless, the decemvirs themselves never claimed the right to pass any law merely on their own authority. "Nothing we propose to you," they said to the people, "can pass into law without your consent. Romans, be yourselves the authors of the laws which are to make you happy."

He, therefore, who draws up the laws has, or should have, no right of legislation, and the people cannot, even if it wishes, deprive itself of this incommunicable right, because, according to the fundamental compact, only the general will can bind the individuals, and there can be no assurance that a particular will is in conformity with the general will, until it has been put to the free vote of the people. This I have said already; but it is worth while to repeat it.

Thus in the task of legislation we find together two things which appear to be incompatible: an enterprise too difficult for human powers, and, for its execution, an authority that is no authority.

There is a further difficulty that deserves attention. Wise men, if they try to speak their language to the common herd instead of its own, cannot possibly make themselves understood. There are a thousand kinds of ideas which it is impossible to translate into popular language. Conceptions that are too general and objects that are too remote are equally out of its range: each individual, having no taste for any other plan of government than that which suits his particular interest, finds it difficult to realise the advantages he might hope to draw from the continual privations good laws impose. For a young people to be able to relish sound principles of political theory and follow the fundamental rules of statecraft, the effect would have to become the cause; the social spirit, which should be created

by these institutions, would have to preside over their very foundation; and men would have to be before law what they should become by means of law. The legislator therefore, being unable to appeal to either force or reason, must have recourse to an authority of a different order, capable of constraining without violence and persuading without convincing.

This is what has, in all ages, compelled the fathers of nations to have recourse to divine intervention and credit the gods with their own wisdom, in order that the peoples, submitting to the laws of the State as to those of nature, and recognising the same power in the formation of the city as in that of man, might obey freely, and bear with docility the yoke of the public happiness.

This sublime reason, far above the range of the common herd, is that whose decisions the legislator puts into the mouth of the immortals, in order to constrain by divine authority those whom human prudence could not move. But it is not anybody who can make the gods speak, or get himself believed when he proclaims himself their interpreter. The great soul of the legislator is the only miracle that can prove his mission. Any man may grave tablets of stone, or buy an oracle, or feign secret intercourse with some divinity, or train a bird to whisper in his ear, or find other vulgar ways of imposing on the people. He whose knowledge goes no further may perhaps gather round him a band of fools; but he will never found an empire, and his extravagances will quickly perish with him. Idle tricks form a passing tie; only wisdom can make it lasting. The Judaic law, which still subsists, and that of the child of Ishmael, which, for ten centuries, has ruled half the world, still proclaim the great men who laid them down; and, while the pride of philosophy or the blind spirit of faction sees in them no more than lucky impostures, the true political theorist admires, in the institutions they set up, the great and powerful genius which presides over things made to endure.

We should not, with Warburton, conclude

from this that politics and religion have among us a common object, but that, in the first periods of nations, the one is used as an instrument for the other. [. . .]

BOOK IV

1. That the General Will is Indestructible

As long as several men in assembly regard themselves as a single body, they have only a single will which is concerned with their common preservation and general well-being. In this case, all the springs of the State are vigorous and simple and its rules clear and luminous; there are no embroilments or conflicts of interests; the common good is everywhere clearly apparent, and only good sense is needed to perceive it. Peace, unity and equality are the enemies of political subtleties. Men who are upright and simple are difficult to deceive because of their simplicity; lures and ingenious pretexts fail to impose upon them, and they are not even subtle enough to be dupes. When, among the happiest people in the world, bands of peasants are seen regulating affairs of State under an oak, and always acting wisely, can we help scorning the ingenious methods of other nations, which make themselves illustrious and wretched with so much art and mystery?

A State so governed needs very few laws; and, as it becomes necessary to issue new ones, the necessity is universally seen. The first man to propose them merely says what all have already felt, and there is no question of factions or intrigues or eloquence in order to secure the passage into law of what every one has already decided to do, as soon as he is sure that the rest will act with him.

Theorists are led into error because, seeing only States that have been from the beginning wrongly constituted, they are struck by the impossibility of applying such a policy to them.

They make great game of all the absurdities a clever rascal or an insinuating speaker might get the people of Paris or London to believe. They do not know that Cromwell would have been put to "the bells" by the people of Berne, and the Duc de Beaufort on the treadmill by the Genevese.

But when the social bond begins to be relaxed and the State to grow weak, when particular interests begin to make themselves felt and the smaller societies to exercise an influence over the larger, the common interest changes and finds opponents: opinion is no longer unanimous; the general will ceases to be the will of all; contradictory views and debates arise; and the best advice is not taken without question.

Finally, when the State, on the eve of ruin, maintains only a vain, illusory and formal existence, when in every heart the social bond is broken, and the meanest interest brazenly lays hold of the sacred name of "public good," the general will becomes mute: all men, guided by secret motives, no more give their views as citizens than if the State had never been; and iniquitous decrees directed solely to private interest get passed under the name of laws.

Does it follow from this that the general will is exterminated or corrupted? Not at all: it is always constant, unalterable and pure; but it is subordinated to other wills which encroach upon its sphere. Each man, in detaching his interest from the common interest, sees clearly that he cannot entirely separate them; but his share in the public mishaps seems to him negligible beside the exclusive good he aims at making his own. Apart from this particular good, he wills the general good in his own interest, as strongly as any one else. Even in selling his vote for money, he does not extinguish in himself the general will, but only eludes it. The fault he commits is that of changing the state of the question, and answering something different from what he is asked. Instead of saying, by his vote, "It is to the advantage of the State," he says, "It is of advantage to this or that man or party that this or that view should prevail." Thus the law of public order in assemblies is not so much to maintain in them the general will as to secure that the question be always put to it, and the answer always given by it.

I could here set down many reflections on the simple right of voting in every act of Sovereignty—a right which no one can take from the citizens—and also on the right of stating views, making proposals, dividing and discussing, which the government is always most careful to leave solely to its members, but this important subject would need a treatise to itself, and it is impossible to say everything in a single work.

2. Voting

It may be seen, from the last chapter, that the way in which general business is managed may give a clear enough indication of the actual state of morals and the health of the body politic. The more concert reigns in the assemblies, that is, the nearer opinion approaches unanimity, the greater is the dominance of the general will. On the other hand, long debates, dissensions and tumult proclaim the ascendancy of particular interests and the decline of the State.

This seems less clear when two or more orders enter into the constitution, as patricians and plebeians did at Rome; for quarrels between these two orders often disturbed the comitia, even in the best days of the Republic. But the exception is rather apparent than real; for then, through the defect that is inherent in the body politic, there were, so to speak, two States in one, and what is not true of the two together is true of either separately. Indeed, even in the most stormy times, the plebiscita of the people, when the Senate did not interfere with them, always went through quietly and by large majorities. The citizens having but one interest, the people had but a single will.

At the other extremity of the circle, unanimity recurs; this is the case when the citizens, having fallen into servitude, have lost both liberty and will. Fear and flattery then change votes into acclamation; deliberation ceases, and only worship or malediction is left. Such was the vile manner in which the senate expressed its views under the Emperors. It did so sometimes with absurd precautions. Tacitus observes that, under Otho, the senators, while they heaped curses on Vitellius, contrived at the same time to make a deafening noise, in order that, should he ever become their master, he might not know what each of them had said.

On these various considerations depend the rules by which the methods of counting votes and comparing opinions should be regulated, according as the general will is more or less easy to discover, and the State more or less in its decline.

There is but one law which, from its nature, needs unanimous consent. This is the social compact; for civil association is the most voluntary of all acts. Every man being born free and his own master, no one, under any pretext whatsoever, can make any man subject without his consent. To decide that the son of a slave is born a slave is to decide that he is not born a man.

If then there are opponents when the social compact is made, their opposition does not invalidate the contract, but merely prevents them from being included in it. They are foreigners among citizens. When the State is instituted, residence constitutes consent; to dwell within its territory is to submit to the Sovereign.

Apart from this primitive contract, the vote of the majority always binds all the rest. This follows from the contract itself. But it is asked how a man can be both free and forced to conform to wills that are not his own. How are the opponents at once free and subject to laws they have not agreed to?

I retort that the question is wrongly put. The citizen gives his consent to all the laws, including those which are passed in spite of his opposition, and even those which punish him when he dares to break any of them. The constant will of all the members of the State is the general will; by virtue of it they are citizens and free. When in the popular assembly a law is proposed, what the people is asked is not exactly whether it approves or rejects the proposal, but whether it is in conformity with the general will, which is their will. Each man, in giving his vote, states his opinion on that point; and the general will is found by counting votes. When therefore the opinion that is contrary to my own prevails, this proves neither more nor less than that I was mistaken, and that what I thought to be the general will was not so. If my particular opinion had carried the day I should have achieved the opposite of what was my will; and it is in that case that I should not have been free.

This presupposes, indeed, that all the qualities of the general will still reside in the majority: when they cease to do so, whatever side a man may take, liberty is no longer possible.

In my earlier demonstration of how particular wills are substituted for the general will in public deliberation, I have adequately pointed out the practicable methods of avoiding this abuse; and I shall have more to say of them later on. I have also given the principles for determining the proportional number of votes for declaring that will. A difference of one vote destroys equality; a single opponent destroys unanimity; but between equality and unanimity, there are several grades of unequal division, at each of which this proportion may be fixed in accordance with the condition and the needs of the body politic.

There are two general rules that may serve to regulate this relation. First, the more grave and important the questions discussed, the nearer should the opinion that is to prevail approach unanimity. Secondly, the more the matter in hand calls for speed, the smaller the prescribed difference in the numbers of votes may be allowed to become: where an instant decision has to be reached, a majority of one vote should be enough. The first of these two rules seems more in harmony with the laws, and the second with practical affairs. In any case, it is the combination of them that gives the best proportions for determining the majority necessary.

Chapter 8

David Hume

OF THE ORIGINAL CONTRACT

David Hume (1711–1776) was a Scottish philosopher who wrote widely in metaphysics, ethics, history, politics, and almost everything else. His writings often express a skepticism regarding established doctrines, and in the current selection (1748) Hume casts doubt on the notion of a social contract as a significant justification of present-day political authority. Not only did such a contract never exist, Hume argues, but it is not clear why it would be *necessary* to create obligations to obey, since it already presupposes that people are subject to at least one obligation to which they did *not* consent—namely, the obligation to do what they promise to do. We should instead hold, Hume thinks, that both the duty to keep promises and the duty to obey governments are grounded in the same consideration—they are necessary for the promotion of the general interests or necessities of society.

As no party, in the present age, can well support itself, without a philosophical or speculative system of principles, annexed to its political or practical one; we accordingly find, that each of the factions, into which this nation is divided, has reared up a fabric of the former kind, in order to protect and cover that scheme of actions, which it pursues.

The people being commonly very rude builders, especially in this speculative way, and more especially still, when actuated by party-zeal; it is natural to imagine, that their workmanship must be a little unshapely, and discover evident marks of that violence and hurry, in which it was raised. The one party, by tracing up government to the DEITY, endeavour to render it so sacred and inviolate, that it must be little less than sacrilege, however tyrannical it may become, to touch or invade it, in the smallest article. The other party, by founding government altogether on the consent of the PEOPLE, suppose that there is a kind of *original contract*, by which the subjects have tacitly reserved the power of resisting their sovereign, whenever they find themselves aggrieved by that authority, with which they have, for certain purposes, voluntarily entrusted him. These are the speculative principles of the two parties; and these too are the practical consequences deduced from them.

I shall venture to affirm, *That both these systems of speculative principles are just; though not in the sense, intended by the parties: And, That both the schemes of practical consequences are prudent; though not in the extremes, to which each party, in opposition to the other, has commonly endeavoured to carry them.* [. . .]

When we consider how nearly equal all men are in their bodily force, and even in their mental powers and faculties, till cultivated by education;

we must necessarily allow, that nothing but their own consent could, at first, associate them together, and subject them to any authority. The people, if we trace government to its first origin in the woods and desarts, are the source of all power and jurisdiction, and voluntarily, for the sake of peace and order, abandoned their native liberty, and received laws from their equal and companion. The conditions, upon which they were willing to submit; were either expressed, or were so clear and obvious, that it might well be esteemed superfluous to express them. If this, then, be meant by the *original contract*, it cannot be denied, that all government is, at first, founded on a contract, and that the most ancient rude combinations of mankind were formed chiefly by that principle. In vain, are we asked in what records this charter of our liberties is registered. It was not written on parchment, nor yet on leaves or barks of trees. It preceded the use of writing and all the other civilized arts of life. But we trace it plainly in the nature of man, and in the equality, or something approaching equality, which we find in all the individuals of that species. The force, which now prevails, and which is founded on fleets and armies, is plainly political, and derived from authority, the effect of established government. A man's natural force consists only in the vigour of his limbs, and the firmness of his courage; which could never subject multitudes to the command of one. Nothing but their own consent, and their sense of the advantages resulting from peace and order, could have had that influence.

Yet even this consent was long very imperfect, and could not be the basis of a regular administration. The chieftain, who had probably acquired his influence during the continuance of war, ruled more by persuasion than command; and till he could employ force to reduce the refractory and disobedient, the society could scarcely be said to have attained a state of civil government. No compact or agreement, it is evident, was expressly formed for general submission; an idea far beyond the comprehension of savages: Each exertion of authority in the chieftain must have been particular, and called forth by the present exigencies of the case: The sensible utility, resulting from his interposition, made these exertions become daily more frequent; and their frequency gradually produced an habitual, and, if you please to call it so, a voluntary, and therefore precarious, acquiescence in the people.

But philosophers, who have embraced a party (if that be not a contradiction in terms) are not contented with these concessions. They assert, not only that government in its earliest infancy arose from consent or rather the voluntary acquiescence of the people; but also, that, even at present, when it has attained full maturity, it rests on no other foundation. They affirm, that all men are still born equal, and owe allegiance to no prince or government, unless bound by the obligation and sanction of a *promise*. And as no man, without some equivalent, would forego the advantages of his native liberty, and subject himself to the will of another; this promise is always understood to be conditional, and imposes on him no obligation, unless he meet with justice and protection from his sovereign. These advantages the sovereign promises him in return; and if he fail in the execution, he has broken, on his part, the articles of engagement, and has thereby freed his subject from all obligations to allegiance. Such, according to these philosophers, is the foundation of authority in every government; and such the right of resistance, possessed by every subject.

But would these reasoners look abroad into the world, they would meet with nothing that, in the least, corresponds to their ideas, or can warrant so refined and philosophical a system. On the contrary, we find, every where, princes, who claim their subjects as their property, and assert their independent right of sovereignty, from conquest or succession. We find also, every where, subjects, who acknowledge this right in their prince, and suppose themselves born under obligations of obedience to a certain sovereign, as much as under the ties of reverence and duty to certain parents. These connexions are always conceived to be equally independent of our consent, in PERSIA and CHINA; in FRANCE and SPAIN; and even in HOLLAND and ENGLAND, wherever the doctrines above-mentioned have not been carefully inculcated. Obedience or subjection becomes so familiar, that most men never make any enquiry about its origin or cause, more than about the principle of gravity, resistance, or the most universal laws of nature. Or if curiosity ever move them; as soon as they learn, that they themselves and their ancestors have, for several ages, or from time immemorial, been subject to such a form of government or such a family; they immediately acquiesce, and acknowledge their obligation to allegiance. Were you to preach, in most parts of the world, that political connexions are founded altogether on voluntary consent or a mutual promise, the magistrate would soon imprison you, as seditious, for loosening the ties of obedience; if your friends did not before shut you up as delirious, for advancing such absurdities. It is strange, that an act of the mind, which every individual is supposed to have formed, and after he came to the use of reason too, otherwise it could have no authority; that this act, I say, should be so much unknown to all of them, that, over the face of the whole earth, there scarcely remain any traces or memory of it.

But the contract, on which government is founded, is said to be the *original contract*; and consequently may be supposed too old to fall under the knowledge of the present generation. If the agreement, by which savage men first associated and conjoined their force, be here meant, this is acknowledged to be real; but being so ancient, and being obliterated by a thousand changes of government and princes, it cannot now be supposed to retain any authority. If we would say any thing to the purpose, we must assert, that every particular government, which is lawful, and which imposes any duty of allegiance on the subject, was, at first, founded on consent

and a voluntary compact. But besides that this supposes the consent of the fathers to bind the children, even to the most remote generations, (which republican writers will never allow) besides this, I say, it is not justified by history or experience, in any age or country of the world.

Almost all the governments, which exist at present, or of which there remains any record in story, have been founded originally, either on usurpation or conquest, or both, without any pretence of a fair consent, or voluntary subjection of the people. When an artful and bold man is placed at the head of an army or faction, it is often easy for him, by employing, sometimes violence, sometimes false pretences, to establish his dominion over a people a hundred times more numerous than his partizans. He allows no such open communication, that his enemies can know, with certainty, their number or force. He gives them no leisure to assemble together in a body to oppose him. Even all those, who are the instruments of his usurpation, may wish his fall; but their ignorance of each other's intention keeps them in awe, and is the sole cause of his security. By such arts as these, many governments have been established; and this is all the *original contract*, which they have to boast of.

The face of the earth is continually changing, by the encrease of small kingdoms into great empires, by the dissolution of great empires into smaller kingdoms, by the planting of colonies, by the migration of tribes. Is there any thing discoverable in all these events, but force and violence? Where is the mutual agreement or voluntary association so much talked of?

Even the smoothest way, by which a nation may receive a foreign master, by marriage or a will, is not extremely honourable for the people; but supposes them to be disposed of, like a dowry or a legacy, according to the pleasure or interest of their rulers.

But where no force interposes, and election takes place; what is this election so highly vaunted? It is either the combination of a few great men, who decide for the whole, and will allow of no opposition: Or it is the fury of a multitude, that follow a seditious ringleader, who is not known, perhaps, to a dozen among them, and who owes his advancement merely to his own impudence, or to the momentary caprice of his fellows.

Are these disorderly elections, which are rare too, of such mighty authority, as to be the only lawful foundation of all government and allegiance?

In reality, there is not a more terrible event, than a total dissolution of government, which gives liberty to the multitude, and makes the determination or choice of a new establishment depend upon a number, which nearly approaches to that of the body of the people: For it never comes entirely to the whole body of them. Every wise man, then, wishes to see, at the head of a powerful and obedient army, a general, who may speedily seize the prize, and give to the people a master, which they are so unfit to chuse for themselves. So little correspondent is fact and reality to those philosophical notions. [. . .]

It is in vain to say, that all governments are or should be, at first, founded on popular consent, as much as the necessity of human affairs will admit. This favours entirely my pretension. I maintain, that human affairs will never admit of this consent; seldom of the appearance of it. But that conquest or usurpation, that is, in plain terms, force, by dissolving the ancient governments, is the origin of almost all the new ones, which were ever established in the world. And that in the few cases, where consent may seem to have taken place, it was commonly so irregular, so confined, or so much intermixed either with fraud or violence, that it cannot have any great authority.

My intention here is not to exclude the consent of the people from being one just foundation of government where it has place. It is surely the best and most sacred of any. I only pretend, that it has very seldom had place in any degree, and never almost in its full extent. And that

therefore some other foundation of government must also be admitted.

Were all men possessed of so inflexible a regard to justice, that, of themselves, they would totally abstain from the properties of others; they had for ever remained in a state of absolute liberty, without subjection to any magistrate or political society: But this is a state of perfection, of which human nature is justly deemed incapable. Again; were all men possessed of so perfect an understanding, as always to know their own interests, no form of government had ever been submitted to, but what was established on consent, and was fully canvassed by every member of the society: But this state of perfection is likewise much superior to human nature. Reason, history, and experience shew us, that all political societies have had an origin much less accurate and regular; and were one to choose a period of time, when the people's consent was the least regarded in public transactions, it would be precisely on the establishment of a new government. In a settled constitution, their inclinations are often consulted; but during the fury of revolutions, conquests, and public convulsions, military force or political craft usually decides the controversy.

When a new government is established, by whatever means, the people are commonly dissatisfied with it, and pay obedience more from fear and necessity, than from any idea of allegiance or of moral obligation. The prince is watchful and jealous, and must carefully guard against every beginning or appearance of insurrection. Time, by degrees, removes all these difficulties, and accustoms the nation to regard, as their lawful or native princes, that family, which, at first, they considered as usurpers or foreign conquerors. In order to found this opinion, they have no recourse to any notion of voluntary consent or promise, which, they know, never was, in this case, either expected or demanded. The original establishment was formed by violence, and submitted to from necessity. The subsequent administration is also supported by power, and acquiesced in by the people, not as a matter of choice, but of obligation. They imagine not, that their consent gives their prince a title: But they willingly consent, because they think, that, from long possession, he has acquired a title, independent of their choice or inclination.

Should it be said, that, by living under the dominion of a prince, which one might leave, every individual has given a *tacit* consent to his authority, and promised him obedience; it may be answered, that such an implied consent can only have place, where a man imagines, that the matter depends on his choice. But where he thinks (as all mankind do who are born under established governments) that by his birth he owes allegiance to a certain prince or certain form of government; it would be absurd to infer a consent or choice, which he expressly, in this case, renounces and disclaims.

Can we seriously say, that a poor peasant or artizan has a free choice to leave his country, when he knows no foreign language or manners, and lives from day to day, by the small wages which he acquires? We may as well assert, that a man, by remaining in a vessel, freely consents to the dominion of the master; though he was carried on board while asleep, and must leap into the ocean, and perish, the moment he leaves her. [. . .]

A company of men, who should leave their native country, in order to people some uninhabited region, might dream of recovering their native freedom; but they would soon find, that their prince still laid claim to them, and called them his subjects, even in their new settlement. And in this he would but act conformably to the common ideas of mankind.

The truest *tacit* consent of this kind, that is ever observed, is when a foreigner settles in any country, and is beforehand acquainted with the prince, and government, and laws, to which he must submit: Yet is his allegiance, though more voluntary, much less expected or depended on, than that of a natural born subject. On the contrary, his native prince still asserts a claim to him. And if he punish not the renegade, when he seizes him in war with his new prince's commission; this clemency is not founded on the municipal law, which in all countries condemns the prisoner; but on the consent of princes, who have agreed to this indulgence, in order to prevent reprisals. [. . .]

Suppose, that an usurper, after having banished his lawful prince and royal family, should establish his dominion for ten or a dozen years in any country, and should preserve so exact a discipline in his troops, and so regular a disposition in his garrisons, that no insurrection had ever been raised, or even murmur heard, against his administration: Can it be asserted, that the people, who in their hearts abhor his treason, have tacitly consented to his authority, and promised him allegiance, merely because, from necessity, they live under his dominion? Suppose again their native prince restored, by means of an army, which he levies in foreign countries: They receive him with joy and exultation, and shew plainly with what reluctance they had submitted to any other yoke. I may now ask, upon what foundation the prince's title stands? Not on popular consent surely: For though the people willingly acquiesce in his authority, they never imagine, that their consent made him sovereign. They consent; because they apprehend him to be already, by birth, their lawful sovereign. And as to that tacit consent, which may now be inferred from their living under his dominion, this is no more than what they formerly gave to the tyrant and usurper. [. . .]

But would we have a more regular, at least a more philosophical, refutation of this principle of an original contract or popular consent; perhaps, the following observations may suffice.

All *moral* duties may be divided into two kinds. The first are those, to which men are impelled by a natural instinct or immediate propensity, which operates on them, independent of all ideas of obligation, and of all views, either to public or private utility. Of this nature are, love of children, gratitude to benefactors, pity to the unfortunate. When we reflect on the advantage, which results to society from such humane instincts, we pay them the just tribute of moral approbation and esteem: But the person, actuated by them, feels their power and influence, antecedent to any such reflection.

The *second* kind of moral duties are such as are not supported by any original instinct of nature, but are performed entirely from a sense of obligation, when we consider the necessities of human society, and the impossibility of supporting it, if these duties were neglected. It is thus *justice* or a regard to the property of others, *fidelity* or the observance of promises, become obligatory, and acquire an authority over mankind. For as it is evident, that every man loves himself better than any other person, he is naturally impelled to extend his acquisitions as much as possible; and nothing can restrain him in this propensity, but reflection and experience, by which he learns the pernicious effects of that licence, and the total dissolution of society which must ensue from it. His original inclination, therefore, or instinct, is here checked and restrained by a subsequent judgment or observation.

The case is precisely the same with the political or civil duty of *allegiance*, as with the natural duties of justice and fidelity. Our primary instincts lead us, either to indulge ourselves in unlimited freedom, or to seek dominion over others: And it is reflection only, which engages us to sacrifice such strong passions to the interests of peace and public order. A small degree of experience and observation suffices to teach us, that society cannot possibly be maintained without the authority of magistrates, and that this authority must soon fall into contempt, where exact obedience is not payed to it. The observation of these general and obvious interests is the source of all allegiance, and of that moral obligation, which we attribute to it.

What necessity, therefore, is there to found the duty of *allegiance* or obedience to magistrates on that of *fidelity* or a regard to promises, and to

suppose, that it is the consent of each individual, which subjects him to government; when it appears, that both allegiance and fidelity stand precisely on the same foundation, and are both submitted to by mankind, on account of the apparent interests and necessities of human society? We are bound to obey our sovereign, it is said; because we have given a tacit promise to that purpose. But why are we bound to observe our promise? It must here be asserted, that the commerce and intercourse of mankind, which are of such mighty advantage, can have no security where men pay no regard to their engagements. In like manner, may it be said, that men could not live at all in society, at least in a civilized society, without laws and magistrates and judges, to prevent the encroachments of the strong upon the weak, of the violent upon the just and equitable. The obligation to allegiance being of like force and authority with the obligation to fidelity, we gain nothing by resolving the one into the other. The general interests or necessities of society are sufficient to establish both.

If the reason be asked of that obedience, which we are bound to pay to government, I readily answer, *because society could not otherwise subsist*: And this answer is clear and intelligible to all mankind. Your answer is, *because we should keep our word*. But besides, that no body, till trained in a philosophical system, can either comprehend or relish this answer: Besides this, I say, you find yourself embarrassed, when it is asked, *why we are bound to keep our word?* Nor can you give any answer, but what would, immediately, without any circuit, have accounted for our obligation to allegiance. [. . .]

We shall only observe, before we conclude, that, though an appeal to general opinion may justly, in the speculative sciences of metaphysics, natural philosophy, or astronomy, be deemed unfair and inconclusive, yet in all questions with regard to morals, as well as criticism, there is really no other standard, by which any controversy can ever be decided. And nothing is a clearer proof, that a theory of this kind is erroneous, than to find, that it leads to paradoxes, repugnant to the common sentiments of mankind, and to the practice and opinion of all nations and all ages. The doctrine, which founds all lawful government on an *original contract*, or consent of the people, is plainly of this kind; nor has the most noted of its partizans, in prosecution of it, scrupled to affirm, *that absolute monarchy is inconsistent with civil society, and so can be no form of civil government at all; and that the supreme power in a state cannot take from any man, by taxes and impositions, any part of his property, without his own consent or that of his representatives.* What authority any moral reasoning can have, which leads into opinions so wide of the general practice of mankind, in every place but this single kingdom, it is easy to determine.

The only passage I meet with in antiquity, where the obligation of obedience to government is ascribed to a promise, is in PLATO's *Crito*: where SOCRATES refuses to escape from prison, because he had tacitly promised to obey the laws. Thus he builds a *tory* consequence of passive obedience, on a *whig* foundation of the original contract.

New discoveries are not to be expected in these matters. If scarce any man, till very lately, ever imagined that government was founded on compact, it is certain, that it cannot, in general, have any such foundation.

The crime of rebellion among the ancients was commonly expressed by the terms νεωτερίζειν, *novas res moliri.*

Note

* Both terms mean to make innovations, especially political changes.

Chapter 9

Charles Tilly

WAR MAKING AND STATE MAKING AS ORGANIZED CRIME

Charles Tilly (1929–2008) was an American sociologist whose work also drew on and developed the fields of history and political science. In this essay (published in 1985), Tilly surveys the historical evidence on the actual origin of states to reveal a picture much more violent than that suggested by the social contract theories of Hobbes, Locke, and Rousseau. Tilly argues that states arise as a form of protection racket—offering defense to their subjects, but often from threats that they themselves have created.

Warning

If protection rackets represent organized crime at its smoothest, then war making and state making—quintessential protection rackets with the advantage of legitimacy—qualify as our largest examples of organized crime. Without branding all generals and statesmen as murderers or thieves, I want to urge the value of that analogy. At least for the European experience of the past few centuries, a portrait of war makers and state makers as coercive and self-seeking entrepreneurs bears a far greater resemblance to the facts than do its chief alternatives: the idea of a social contract, the idea of an open market in which operators of armies and states offer services to willing consumers, the idea of a society whose shared norms and expectations call forth a certain kind of government.

The reflections that follow merely illustrate the analogy of war making and state making with organized crime from a few hundred years of European experience and offer tentative arguments concerning principles of change and variation underlying the experience. My reflections grow from contemporary concerns: worries about the increasing destructiveness of war, the expanding role of great powers as suppliers of arms and military organization to poor countries, and the growing importance of military rule in those same countries. They spring from the hope that the European experience, properly understood, will help us to grasp what is happening today, perhaps even to do something about it.

The Third World of the twentieth century does not greatly resemble Europe of the sixteenth or seventeenth century. In no simple sense can we read the future of Third World countries from the pasts of European countries. Yet a thoughtful exploration of European experience will serve us well. It will show us that coercive exploitation played a large part in the creation of the European states. It will show us that popular resistance to coercive exploitation forced would-be power holders to concede protection and constraints on their own action. It will therefore help us to eliminate faulty implicit comparisons between today's Third World and yesterday's Europe. That clarification will make it easier to understand exactly how today's world is different and what we therefore have to explain. It may even help us to explain the current looming presence of military organization and action throughout the world. Although that result would delight me, I do not promise anything so grand.

This essay, then, concerns the place of organized means of violence in the growth and change of those peculiar forms of government we call national states: relatively centralized, differentiated organizations the officials of which more or less successfully claim control over the chief concentrated means of violence within a population inhabiting a large, contiguous territory. The argument grows from historical work on the formation of national states in Western Europe, especially on the growth of the French state from 1600 onward. But it takes several deliberate steps away from that work, wheels, and stares hard at it from theoretical ground. The argument brings with it few illustrations and no evidence worthy of the name.

Just as one repacks a hastily filled rucksack after a few days on the trail—throwing out the waste, putting things in order of importance, and balancing the load—I have repacked my theoretical baggage for the climb to come; the real test of the new packing arrives only with the next stretch of the trail. The trimmed-down argument stresses the interdependence of war making and state making and the analogy between both of those processes and what, when less successful and smaller in scale, we call organized crime. War makes states, I shall claim. Banditry, piracy, gangland rivalry, policing, and war making all belong on the same continuum—that I shall claim as well. For the historically limited period in which national states were becoming the dominant organizations in Western countries, I shall also claim that mercantile capitalism and state making reinforced each other.

Double-Edged Protection

In contemporary American parlance, the word "protection" sounds two contrasting tones. One is comforting, the other ominous. With one tone, "protection" calls up images of the shelter against danger provided by a powerful friend, a large insurance policy, or a sturdy roof. With the other, it evokes the racket in which a local strong man forces merchants to pay tribute in order to avoid damage—damage the strong man himself threatens to deliver. The difference, to be sure, is a matter of degree: A hell-and-damnation priest is likely to collect contributions from his parishioners only to the extent that they believe his predictions of brimstone for infidels; our neighborhood mobster may actually be, as he claims to be, a brothel's best guarantee of operation free of police interference.

Which image the word "protection" brings to mind depends mainly on our assessment of the reality and externality of the threat. Someone who produces both the danger and, at a price, the shield against it is a racketeer. Someone who provides a needed shield but has little control over the danger's appearance qualifies as a legitimate protector, especially if his price is no higher than his competitors'. Someone who supplies reliable, low-priced shielding both from local racketeers and from outside marauders makes the best offer of all.

Apologists for particular governments and for government in general commonly argue, precisely, that they offer protection from local and external violence. They claim that the prices they charge barely cover the costs of protection. They call people who complain about the price of protection "anarchists," "subversives," or both at once. But consider the definition of a racketeer as someone who creates a threat and then charges for its reduction. Governments' provision of protection, by this standard, often qualifies as racketeering. To the extent that the threats against which a given government protects its citizens are imaginary or are consequences of its own activities, the government has organized a protection racket. Since governments themselves commonly simulate, stimulate, or even fabricate threats of external war and since the repressive and extractive activities of governments often constitute the largest current threats to the livelihoods of their own citizens, many governments operate in essentially the same ways as racketeers. There is, of course, a difference: Racketeers, by the conventional definition, operate without the sanctity of governments.

How do racketeer governments themselves acquire authority? As a question of fact and of ethics, that is one of the oldest conundrums of political analysis. Back to Machiavelli and Hobbes, nevertheless, political observers have recognized that, whatever else they do, governments organize and, wherever possible, monopolize violence. It matters little whether we take violence in a narrow sense, such as damage to persons and objects, or in a broad sense, such as violation of people's desires and interests; by either criterion, governments stand out from other organizations by their tendency to monopolize the concentrated means of violence. The distinction between "legitimate" and "illegitimate" force, furthermore, makes no difference to the fact. If we take legitimacy to depend on conformity to an abstract principle or on the assent of the governed (or both at once), these conditions may serve to justify, perhaps even to explain, the tendency to monopolize force; they do not contradict the fact.

In any case, Arthur Stinchcombe's agreeably cynical treatment of legitimacy serves the purposes of political analysis much more efficiently. Legitimacy, according to Stinchcombe, depends rather little on abstract principle or assent of the governed: "The person *over whom power is exercised* is not usually as important as *other power-holders.*" Legitimacy is the probability that other authorities will act to confirm the decisions of a given authority. Other authorities, I would add, are much more likely to confirm the decisions of a challenged authority that controls substantial

force; not only fear of retaliation, but also desire to maintain a stable environment recommend that general rule. The rule underscores the importance of the authority's monopoly of force. A tendency to monopolize the means of violence makes a government's claim to provide protection, in either the comforting or the ominous sense of the word, more credible and more difficult to resist.

Frank recognition of the central place of force in governmental activity does not require us to believe that governmental authority rests "only" or "ultimately" on the threat of violence. Nor does it entail the assumption that a government's only service is protection. Even when a government's use of force imposes a large cost, some people may well decide that the government's other services outbalance the costs of acceding to its monopoly of violence. Recognition of the centrality of force opens the way to an understanding of the growth and change of governmental forms.

Here is a preview of the most general argument: Power holders' pursuit of war involved them willy-nilly in the extraction of resources for war making from the populations over which they had control and in the promotion of capital accumulation by those who could help them borrow and buy. War making, extraction, and capital accumulation interacted to shape European state making. Power holders did not undertake those three momentous activities with the intention of creating national states—centralized, differentiated, autonomous, extensive political organizations. Nor did they ordinarily foresee that national states would emerge from war making, extraction, and capital accumulation.

Instead, the people who controlled European states and states in the making warred in order to check or overcome their competitors and thus to enjoy the advantages of power within a secure or expanding territory. To make more effective war, they attempted to locate more capital. In the short run, they might acquire that capital by conquest, by selling off their assets, or by coercing or dispossessing accumulators of capital. In the long run, the quest inevitably involved them in establishing regular access to capitalists who could supply and arrange credit and in imposing one form of regular taxation or another on the people and activities within their spheres of control.

As the process continued, state makers developed a durable interest in promoting the accumulation of capital, sometimes in the guise of direct return to their own enterprises. Variations in the difficulty of collecting taxes, in the expense of the particular kind of armed force adopted, in the amount of war making required to hold off competitors, and so on resulted in the principal variations in the forms of European states. It all began with the effort to monopolize the means of violence within a delimited territory adjacent to a power holder's base.

Violence and Government

What distinguished the violence produced by states from the violence delivered by anyone else? In the long run, enough to make the division between "legitimate" and "illegitimate" force credible. Eventually, the personnel of states purveyed violence on a larger scale, more effectively, more efficiently, with wider assent from their subject populations, and with readier collaboration from neighboring authorities than did the personnel of other organizations. But it took a long time for that series of distinctions to become established. Early in the state-making process, many parties shared the right to use violence, the practice of using it routinely to accomplish their ends, or both at once. The continuum ran from bandits and pirates to kings via tax collectors, regional power holders, and professional soldiers.

The uncertain, elastic line between "legitimate" and "illegitimate" violence appeared in the upper reaches of power. Early in the state-making process, many parties shared the right to use violence, its actual employment, or both at once. The long love–hate affair between aspiring state makers and pirates or bandits illustrates the division. "Behind piracy on the seas acted cities and city-states," writes Fernand Braudel of the sixteenth century. "Behind banditry, that terrestrial piracy, appeared the continual aid of lords." In times of war, indeed, the managers of full-fledged states often commissioned privateers, hired sometime bandits to raid their enemies, and encouraged their regular troops to take booty. In royal service, soldiers and sailors were often expected to provide for themselves by preying on the civilian population: commandeering, raping, looting, taking prizes. When demobilized, they commonly continued the same practices, but without the same royal protection; demobilized ships became pirate vessels, demobilized troops bandits.

It also worked the other way: A king's best source of armed supporters was sometimes the world of outlaws. Robin Hood's conversion to royal archer may be a myth, but the myth records a practice. The distinctions between "legitimate" and "illegitimate" users of violence came clear only very slowly, in the process during which the state's armed forces became relatively unified and permanent.

Up to that point, as Braudel says, maritime cities and terrestrial lords commonly offered protection, or even sponsorship, to freebooters. Many lords who did not pretend to be kings, furthermore, successfully claimed the right to levy troops and maintain their own armed retainers. Without calling on some of those lords to bring their armies with them, no king could fight a war; yet the same armed lords constituted the king's rivals and opponents, his enemies' potential allies. For that reason, before the seventeenth century, regencies for child sovereigns reliably produced civil wars. For the same reason, disarming the great stood high on the agenda of every would-be state maker.

The Tudors, for example, accomplished that

agenda through most of England. "The greatest triumph of the Tudors," writes Lawrence Stone,

> was the ultimately successful assertion of a royal monopoly of violence both public and private, an achievement which profoundly altered not only the nature of politics but also the quality of daily life. There occurred a change in English habits that can only be compared with the further step taken in the nineteenth century, when the growth of a police force finally consolidated the monopoly and made it effective in the greatest cities and the smallest villages.

Tudor demilitarization of the great lords entailed four complementary campaigns: eliminating their great personal bands of armed retainers, razing their fortresses, taming their habitual resort to violence for the settlement of disputes, and discouraging the cooperation of their dependents and tenants. In the Marches of England and Scotland, the task was more delicate, for the Percys and Dacres, who kept armies and castles along the border, threatened the Crown but also provided a buffer against Scottish invaders. Yet they, too, eventually fell into line.

In France, Richelieu began the great disarmament in the 1620s. With Richelieu's advice, Louis XIII systematically destroyed the castles of the great rebel lords, Protestant and Catholic, against whom his forces battled incessantly. He began to condemn dueling, the carrying of lethal weapons, and the maintenance of private armies. By the later 1620s, Richelieu was declaring the royal monopoly of force as doctrine. The doctrine took another half-century to become effective:

> Once more the conflicts of the Fronde had witnessed armies assembled by the "grands." Only the last of the regencies, the one after the death of Louis XIV, did not lead to armed uprisings. By that time Richelieu's principle

had become a reality. Likewise in the Empire after the Thirty Years' War only the territorial princes had the right of levying troops and of maintaining fortresses. . . . Everywhere the razing of castles, the high cost of artillery, the attraction of court life, and the ensuing domestication of the nobility had its share in this development.

By the later eighteenth century, through most of Europe, monarchs controlled permanent, professional military forces that rivaled those of their neighbors and far exceeded any other organized armed force within their own territories. The state's monopoly of large-scale violence was turning from theory to reality.

The elimination of local rivals, however, posed a serious problem. Beyond the scale of a small city-state, no monarch could govern a population with his armed force alone, nor could any monarch afford to create a professional staff large and strong enough to reach from him to the ordinary citizen. Before quite recently, no European government approached the completeness of articulation from top to bottom achieved by imperial China. Even the Roman Empire did not come close. In one way or another, every European government before the French Revolution relied on indirect rule via local magnates. The magnates collaborated with the government without becoming officials in any strong sense of the term, had some access to government-backed force, and exercised wide discretion within their own territories: junkers, justices of the peace, lords. Yet the same magnates were potential rivals, possible allies of a rebellious people.

Eventually, European governments reduced their reliance on indirect rule by means of two expensive but effective strategies: (a) extending their officialdom to the local community and (b) encouraging the creation of police forces that were subordinate to the government rather than to individual patrons, distinct from war-making forces, and therefore less useful as the tools of dissident magnates. In between, however, the builders of national power all played a mixed strategy: eliminating, subjugating, dividing, conquering, cajoling, buying as the occasions presented themselves. The buying manifested itself in exemptions from taxation, creations of honorific offices, the establishment of claims on the national treasury, and a variety of other devices that made a magnate's welfare dependent on the maintenance of the existing structure of power. In the long run, it all came down to massive pacification and monopolization of the means of coercion.

Protection as Business

In retrospect, the pacification, cooptation, or elimination of fractious rivals to the sovereign seems an awesome, noble, prescient enterprise, destined to bring peace to a people; yet it followed almost ineluctably from the logic of expanding power. If a power holder was to gain from the provision of protection, his competitors had to yield. As economic historian Frederic Lane put it twenty-five years ago, governments are in the business of selling protection . . . whether people want it or not. Lane argued that the very activity of producing and controlling violence favored monopoly, because competition within that realm generally raised costs, instead of lowering them. The production of violence, he suggested, enjoyed large economies of scale.

Working from there, Lane distinguished between (a) the monopoly profit, or *tribute*, coming to owners of the means of producing violence as a result of the difference between production costs and the price exacted from "customers" and (b) the *protection rent* accruing to those customers—for example, merchants—who drew effective protection against outside competitors. Lane, a superbly attentive historian of Venice, allowed specifically for the case of a government that generates protection rents for its merchants by deliberately attacking their competitors. In

their adaptation of Lane's scheme, furthermore, Edward Ames and Richard Rapp substitute the apt word "extortion" for Lane's "tribute." In this model, predation, coercion, piracy, banditry, and racketeering share a home with their upright cousins in responsible government.

This is how Lane's model worked: If a prince could create a sufficient armed force to hold off his and his subjects' external enemies and to keep the subjects in line for 50 megapounds but was able to extract 75 mega-pounds in taxes from those subjects for that purpose, he gained a tribute of $(75 - 50 =)$ 25 megapounds. If the 10-pound share of those taxes paid by one of the prince's merchant-subjects gave him assured access to world markets at less than the 15-pound shares paid by the merchant's foreign competitors to their princes, the merchant also gained a protection rent of $(15 - 10 =)$ 5 pounds by virtue of his prince's greater efficiency. That reasoning differs only in degree and in scale from the reasoning of violence-wielding criminals and their clients. Labor racketeering (in which, for example, a ship owner holds off trouble from longshoremen by means of a timely payment to the local union boss) works on exactly the same principle: The union boss receives tribute for his no-strike pressure on the longshoremen, while the ship owner avoids the strikes and slowdowns longshoremen impose on his competitors.

Lane pointed out the different behavior we might expect of the managers of a protection-providing government owned by

1. Citizens in general
2. A single self-interested monarch
3. The managers themselves

If citizens in general exercised effective ownership of the government—O distant ideal!—we might expect the managers to minimize protection costs and tribute, thus maximizing protection rent. A single self-interested monarch, in contrast, would maximize tribute, set costs so as to accomplish that maximization of tribute, and be indifferent to the level of protection rent. If the managers owned the government, they would tend to keep costs high by maximizing their own wages, to maximize tribute over and above those costs by exacting a high price from their subjects, and likewise to be indifferent to the level of protection rent. The first model approximates a Jeffersonian democracy, the second a petty despotism, the third a military junta.

Lane did not discuss the obvious fourth category of owner: a dominant class. If he had, his scheme would have yielded interesting empirical criteria for evaluating claims that a given government was "relatively autonomous" or strictly subordinate to the interests of a dominant class. Presumably, a subordinate government would tend to maximize monopoly profits—returns to the dominant class resulting from the difference between the costs of protection and the price received for it—as well as tuning protection rents nicely to the economic interests of the dominant class. An autonomous government, in contrast, would tend to maximize managers' wages and its own size as well and would be indifferent to protection rents. Lane's analysis immediately suggests fresh propositions and ways of testing them.

Lane also speculated that the logic of the situation produced four successive stages in the general history of capitalism:

1. A period of anarchy and plunder
2. A stage in which tribute takers attracted customers and established their monopolies by struggling to create exclusive, substantial states
3. A stage in which merchants and landlords began to gain more from protection rents than governors did from tribute
4. A period (fairly recent) in which technological changes surpassed protection rents as sources of profit for entrepreneurs

In their new economic history of the Western world, Douglass North and Robert Paul Thomas

make stages 2 and 3—those in which state makers created their monopolies of force and established property rights that permitted individuals to capture much of the return from their own growth-generating innovations—the pivotal moment for sustained economic growth. Protection, at this point, overwhelms tribute. If we recognize that the protected property rights were mainly those of capital and that the development of capitalism also facilitated the accumulation of the wherewithal to operate massive states, that extension of Lane's analysis provides a good deal of insight into the coincidence of war making, state making, and capital accumulation.

Unfortunately, Lane did not take full advantage of his own insight. Wanting to contain his analysis neatly within the neoclassical theory of industrial organization, Lane cramped his treatment of protection: treating all taxpayers as "customers" for the "service" provided by protection-manufacturing governments, brushing aside the objections to the idea of a forced sale by insisting that the "customer" always had the choice of not paying and taking the consequences of nonpayment, minimizing the problems of divisibility created by the public-goods character of protection, and deliberately neglecting the distinction between the costs of producing the means of violence in general and the costs of giving "customers" protection by means of that violence. Lane's ideas suffocate inside the neoclassical box and breathe easily outside it. Nevertheless, inside or outside, they properly draw the economic analysis of government back to the chief activities that real governments have carried on historically: war, repression, protection, adjudication. [. . .]

What Do States Do?

As should now be clear, Lane's analysis of protection fails to distinguish among several different uses of state-controlled violence. Under the general heading of organized violence, the agents of states characteristically carry on four different activities:

1. War making: Eliminating or neutralizing their own rivals outside the territories in which they have clear and continuous priority as wielders of force
2. State making: Eliminating or neutralizing their rivals inside those territories
3. Protection: Eliminating or neutralizing the enemies of their clients
4. Extraction: Acquiring the means of carrying out the first three activities—war making, state making, and protection

The third item corresponds to protection as analyzed by Lane, but the other three also involve the application of force. They overlap incompletely and to various degrees; for example, war making against the commercial rivals of the local bourgeoisie delivers protection to that bourgeoisie. To the extent that a population is divided into enemy classes and the state extends its favors partially to one class or another, state making actually reduces the protection given some classes.

War making, state making, protection, and extraction each take a number of forms. Extraction, for instance, ranges from outright plunder to regular tribute to bureaucratized taxation. Yet all four depend on the state's tendency to monopolize the concentrated means of coercion. From the perspectives of those who dominate the state, each of them—if carried on effectively—generally reinforces the others. Thus, a state that successfully eradicates its internal rivals strengthens its ability to extract resources, to wage war, and to protect its chief supporters. In the earlier European experience, broadly speaking, those supporters were typically landlords, armed retainers of the monarch, and churchmen.

Each of the major uses of violence produced characteristic forms of organization. War making

yielded armies, navies, and supporting services. State making produced durable instruments of surveillance and control within the territory. Protection relied on the organization of war making and state making but added to it an apparatus by which the protected called forth the protection that was their due, notably through courts and representative assemblies. Extraction brought fiscal and accounting structures into being. The organization and deployment of violence themselves account for much of the characteristic structure of European states.

The general rule seems to have operated like this: The more costly the activity, all other things being equal, the greater was the organizational residue. To the extent, for example, that a given government invested in large standing armies—a very costly, if effective, means of war making—the bureaucracy created to service the army was likely to become bulky. Furthermore, a government building a standing army while controlling a small population was likely to incur greater costs, and therefore to build a bulkier structure, than a government within a populous country. Brandenburg–Prussia was the classic case of high cost for available resources. The Prussian effort to build an army matching those of its larger Continental neighbors created an immense structure; it militarized and bureaucratized much of German social life.

In the case of extraction, the smaller the pool of resources and the less commercialized the economy, other things being equal, the more difficult was the work of extracting resources to sustain war and other governmental activities; hence, the more extensive was the fiscal apparatus. England illustrated the corollary of that proposition, with a relatively large and commercialized pool of resources drawn on by a relatively small fiscal apparatus. As Gabriel Ardant has argued, the choice of fiscal strategy probably made an additional difference. On the whole, taxes on land were expensive to collect as compared with taxes on trade, especially large flows of trade past easily controlled checkpoints. Its position astride the entrance to the Baltic gave Denmark an extraordinary opportunity to profit from customs revenues.

With respect to state making (in the narrow sense of eliminating or neutralizing the local rivals of the people who controlled the state), a territory populated by great landlords or by distinct religious groups generally imposed larger costs on a conqueror than one of fragmented power or homogeneous culture. This time, fragmented and homogeneous Sweden, with its relatively small but effective apparatus of control, illustrates the corollary.

Finally, the cost of protection (in the sense of eliminating or neutralizing the enemies of the state makers' clients) mounted with the range over which that protection extended. Portugal's effort to bar the Mediterranean to its merchants' competitors in the spice trade provides a textbook case of an unsuccessful protection effort that nonetheless built up a massive structure.

Thus, the sheer size of the government varied directly with the effort devoted to extraction, state making, protection, and, especially, war making but inversely with the commercialization of the economy and the extent of the resource base. What is more, the relative bulk of different features of the government varied with the cost/resource ratios of extraction, state making, protection, and war making. In Spain we see hypertrophy of Court and courts as the outcome of centuries of effort at subduing internal enemies, whereas in Holland we are amazed to see how small a fiscal apparatus grows up with high taxes within a rich, commercialized economy.

Clearly, war making, extraction, state making, and protection were interdependent. Speaking very, very generally, the classic European statemaking experience followed this causal pattern:

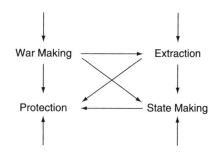

In an idealized sequence, a great lord made war so effectively as to become dominant in a substantial territory, but that war making led to increased extraction of the means of war—men, arms, food, lodging, transportation, supplies, and/or the money to buy them—from the population within that territory. The building up of war-making capacity likewise increased the capacity to extract. The very activity of extraction, if successful, entailed the elimination, neutralization, or cooptation of the great lord's local rivals; thus, it led to state making. As a by-product, it created organization in the form of tax-collection agencies, police forces, courts, exchequers, account keepers; thus it again led to state making. To a lesser extent, war making likewise led to state making through the expansion of military organization itself, as a standing army, war industries, supporting bureaucracies, and (rather later) schools grew up within the state apparatus. All of these structures checked potential rivals and opponents. In the course of making war, extracting resources, and building up the state apparatus, the managers of states formed alliances with specific social classes. The members of those classes loaned resources, provided technical services, or helped ensure the compliance of the rest of the population, all in return for a measure of protection against their own rivals and enemies. As a result of these multiple strategic choices, a distinctive state apparatus grew up within each major section of Europe.

How States Formed

This analysis, if correct, has two strong implications for the development of national states. First, popular resistance to war making and state making made a difference. When ordinary people resisted vigorously, authorities made concessions: guarantees of rights, representative institutions, courts of appeal. Those concessions, in their turn, constrained the later paths of war making and state making. To be sure, alliances with fragments of the ruling class greatly increased the effects of popular action; the broad mobilization of gentry against Charles I helped give the English Revolution of 1640 a far greater impact on political institutions than did any of the multiple rebellions during the Tudor era.

Second, the relative balance among war making, protection, extraction, and state making significantly affected the organization of the states that emerged from the four activities. To the extent that war making went on with relatively little extraction, protection, and state making, for example, military forces ended up playing a larger and more autonomous part in national politics. Spain is perhaps the best European example. To the extent that protection, as in Venice or Holland, prevailed over war making, extraction, and state making, oligarchies of the protected classes tended to dominate subsequent national politics. From the relative predominance of state making sprang the disproportionate elaboration of policing and surveillance; the Papal States illustrate that extreme. Before the twentieth century, the range of viable imbalances was fairly small. Any state that failed to put considerable effort into war making was likely to disappear. As the twentieth century wore on, however, it became increasingly common for one state to lend, give, or sell war-making means to another; in those cases, the recipient state could put a disproportionate effort into extraction, protection, and/or state making and yet survive. In our own time, clients of the United States and the Soviet Union provide numerous examples.

This simplified model, however, neglects the external relations that shaped every national state. Early in the process, the distinction between "internal" and "external" remained as unclear as the distinction between state power and the power accruing to lords allied with the state. Later, three interlocking influences connected any given national state to the European network of states. First, there were the flows of resources in the form of loans and supplies, especially loans and supplies devoted to war making. Second, there was the competition among states for hegemony in disputed territories, which stimulated war making and temporarily erased the distinctions among war making, state making, and extraction. Third, there was the intermittent creation of coalitions of states that temporarily combined their efforts to force a given state into a certain form and position within the international network. The war-making coalition is one example, but the peace-making coalition played an even more crucial part: From 1648, if not before, at the ends of wars all effective European states coalesced temporarily to bargain over the boundaries and rulers of the recent belligerents. From that point on, periods of major reorganization of the European state system came in spurts, at the settlement of widespread wars. From each large war, in general, emerged fewer national states than had entered it.

War as International Relations

In these circumstances, war became the normal condition of the international system of states and the normal means of defending or enhancing a position within the system. Why war? No simple answer will do; war as a potent means served more than one end. But surely part of the answer goes back to the central mechanisms of state making: The very logic by which a local lord extended or defended the perimeter within which he monopolized the means of violence, and thereby increased his return from tribute, continued on a larger scale into the logic of war. Early in the process, external and internal rivals overlapped to a large degree. Only the establishment of large perimeters of control within which great lords had checked their rivals sharpened the line between internal and external. George Modelski sums up the competitive logic cogently:

Global power . . . strengthened those states that attained it relatively to all other political and other organizations. What is more, other states competing in the global power game developed similar organizational forms and similar hardiness: they too became nation-states—in a defensive reaction, because forced to take issue with or to confront a global power, as France confronted Spain and later Britain, or in imitation of its obvious success and effectiveness, as Germany followed the example of Britain in Weltmacht, or as earlier Peter the Great had rebuilt Russia on Dutch precepts and examples. Thus not only Portugal, the Netherlands, Britain and the United States became nation-states, but also Spain, France, Germany, Russia and Japan. The short, and the most parsimonious, answer to the question of why these succeeded where "most of the European efforts to build states failed" is that they were either global powers or successfully fought with or against them.

This logic of international state making acts out on a large scale the logic of local aggrandizement. The external complements the internal.

If we allow that fragile distinction between "internal" and "external" state-making processes, then we might schematize the history of European state making as three stages: (*a*) The differential success of some power holders in "external" struggles establishes the difference between an "internal" and an "external" arena for the deployment of force; (*b*) "external" competition generates "internal" state making; (*c*) "external" compacts among states influence the form and locus of particular states ever more

powerfully. In this perspective, state-certifying organizations such as the League of Nations and the United Nations simply extended the European-based process to the world as a whole. Whether forced or voluntary, bloody or peaceful, decolonization simply completed that process by which existing states leagued to create new ones.

The extension of the Europe-based state-making process to the rest of the world, however, did not result in the creation of states in the strict European image. Broadly speaking, internal struggles such as the checking of great regional lords and the imposition of taxation on peasant villages produced important organizational features of European states: the relative subordination of military power to civilian control, the extensive bureaucracy of fiscal surveillance, the representation of wronged interests via petition and parliament. On the whole, states elsewhere developed differently. The most telling feature of that difference appears in military organization. European states built up their military apparatuses through sustained struggles with their subject populations and by means of selective extension of protection to different classes within those populations. The agreements on protection constrained the rulers themselves, making them vulnerable to courts, to assemblies, to withdrawals of credit, services, and expertise.

To a larger degree, states that have come into being recently through decolonization or through reallocations of territory by dominant states have acquired their military organization from outside, without the same internal forging of mutual constraints between rulers and ruled. To the extent that outside states continue to supply military goods and expertise in return for commodities, military alliance or both, the new states harbor powerful, unconstrained organizations that easily overshadow all other organizations within their territories. To the extent that outside states guarantee their boundaries, the managers of those military organizations exercise extraordinary power within them. The advantages of military power become enormous, the incentives to seize power over the state as a whole by means of that advantage very strong. Despite the great place that war making occupied in the making of European states, the old national states of Europe almost never experienced the great disproportion between military organization and all others forms of organization that seems the fate of client states throughout the contemporary world. A century ago, Europeans might have congratulated themselves on the spread of civil government throughout the world. In our own time, the analogy between war making and state making, on the one hand, and organized crime, on the other, is becoming tragically apt.

Chapter 10

Amy Gutmann and Dennis Thompson

MORAL DISAGREEMENT IN A DEMOCRACY

Amy Gutmann (1949–) is a political theorist and currently President of the University of Pennsylvania. Dennis Thompson (1940–) is a professor of political philosophy at Harvard's Kennedy School of Government. In this essay, they argue that deep disagreement about significant moral issues is an intractable feature of our society, and that majority rule democracy provides the fairest way of dealing with these disagreements.

Moral disagreement about public policies —issues such as abortion, affirmative action, and health care—is a prominent feature of contemporary American democracy. Yet it is not a central concern of the leading theories of democracy. The two dominant democratic approaches in our time—procedural democracy and constitutional democracy—fail to offer adequate responses to the problem of moral disagreement. Both suggest some elements that are necessary in any adequate response, but neither one alone nor both together are sufficient. We argue here that an adequate conception of democracy must make moral deliberation an essential part of the political process. What we call "deliberative democracy" adds an important dimension to the theory and practice of politics that the leading conceptions of democracy neglect.

I. The Problem of Moral Disagreement

What makes a disagreement moral? No doubt there is disagreement about what should count

as moral disagreement itself, and this disagreement also has a place in deliberative democracy. It is nevertheless possible to identify some general features of morality, three characteristics that moral claims typically have in politics, which citizens and theorists of many different moral positions can acknowledge and to which any adequate conception of democracy should respond.

First, although they are sometimes expressed as personal complaints, moral arguments are general rather than particular in form. They apply to anyone who is similarly situated in the morally relevant respect. The poor woman who seeks an abortion, the white male job applicant who opposes affirmative action, and the mother who needs prenatal care do not assert merely that they, or even only their friends, family, and associates, should receive the benefit; they maintain that all citizens, similarly situated, should receive it. The form of their claims, if fully developed, would impute rights and wrongs, or ascribe virtue and vice, to anyone who is similar in the respects that the argument assumes to be morally significant.

Second, the content of the argument reaches beyond the moral concerns of its maker. It appeals to values or principles that are shared or could be shared by fellow citizens. In politics, if not in morality in general, we try to base our claims on values or principles that no one, whatever his or her status, could reasonably reject. Reaching in these ways for a common perspective, or at least for some shared standards, is of course not always successful. But it is a feature of moral argument that is especially important in politics. It enables us, for example, to recognize an argument as a moral one even if we disagree with its conclusions.

Third, moral arguments also take place in context: they implicitly rely on assumptions about matters of fact, common estimates of risks, suppositions about feasibility, and general beliefs about human nature and social processes. The assumptions may or may not be universally true, but whether they are does not usually affect a particular argument. Citizens who make the claims would not be moved if they learned that their moral claim would not be understood, let alone accepted, if they tried to make it in some remote village in Asia or among the Ick in Uganda. Even those who rely on what they regard as universal moral principles do not presume that their practical conclusions are independent of facts about the society in which they live. The arguments begin from where we are, and appeal to those with whom we now live. This is why moral relativism is seldom an issue in practical political ethics.

These characteristics suggest correctly that moral claims seek some common ground. The claimants reach out to find principles or perspectives that others can accept. But even when the moral claimants seem to find some common principles, the disagreement persists. Citizens and officials who disagree with other citizens and officials, or who expect others to disagree with them, seek to justify or criticize political decisions and public policies or political actions more generally. The disagreements are often deep. If they were not, there would be no need for argument. If they were too deep, there would be no point in argument. The disagreement lies in the range between simple misunderstanding and immutable irreconcilability.

What are these deeper sources of moral disagreement? This too may be a controversial question, but again we need to provide some general indication of those sources so that we can later assess how various forms of democracy respond to such disagreement. The temptation to try to turn moral disagreements into some simpler kind of conflict is great, especially in politics. Moral conflict seems slightly mysterious, dangerously subjective, and at once naive and complex. In a kind of reverse transmutation, some theorists attempt to reduce moral claims to self-interest and group interests.

Moral disagreements, these theorists assume, simply reflect the conflicting interests of individuals or groups. This familiar view has been around for a long time—finding its most systematic political statement in the theory of Thomas Hobbes. On this view, moral disagreements cannot properly be understood on their own terms. Moral terms are "inconstant names," referring to "things which please and displease us," which vary depending on what an individual sees to be in his or her interest. The reduction of morality to self-interest cannot be sustained. We may disagree about precisely what is at stake in the debate over whether and when abortion should be legal, but even Hobbes, who thought his own birth traumatic, would not have supposed that the abortion controversy is best understood as a battle between the self-interest of women and fetuses.

It is of course possible to define self-interest so expansively that it subsumes all the interests citizens might have in fulfilling legitimate expectations, upholding rights, rewarding desert, and seeking fair treatment for themselves and people they care about. But only someone in the grip of a single-valued theory would try to do so. Such an expansive concept is misleading: it elides the distinction between interests exclusively in one-self and interests in other people and impersonal values. To criticize someone for being self-interested makes sense only if self-interest is understood as having interests only in oneself, and failing to demonstrate sufficient regard for the interests of others. If all human action is assumed to be a reflection of self-interest, the charge of self-interest loses its critical content, and the claim that moral disagreements can be reduced to conflicts of self-interest becomes a tautology.

Even if moral conflict cannot be meaningfully reduced to self-interest, some theorists insist that it can be reduced to a clash of group interests, another kind of nonmoral conflict. The effort to reduce moral conflict to group interest, exemplified in some Marxist theories and in a somewhat different way in pluralist political science, encounters problems analogous to those of the self-interest approach. Consider the issue of distributing health care in the United States. Disagreements about what constitutes a just health-care policy abound, but they do not simply mirror the differences among groups, defined by income, age, ethnicity, gender, or profession. (Even when there is a correlation between certain group differences and political positions on health-care policy, there remains considerable moral disagreement within groups. The moral disagreement tends to be greater, moreover, before members of the group make any deliberative attempt to reach a consensus for political purposes.) Furthermore, if society were to become more egalitarian, moral conflict over the distribution of health care might shift its focus to different health-care issues, but it would surely not disappear.

Hume's account of the sources of moral conflict (or, as it has come to be known, the circumstances of justice) begins to explain why we should not expect moral conflict to disappear with a more egalitarian society, even if the issues that create the most conflict change significantly over time. Moral conflicts of the kind in which

we are interested arise in conditions of scarcity and limited generosity. Hume is surely right that moral conflict is rooted not primarily in certain kinds of societies, but in more fundamental and more nearly universal features of societies. Hume is also convincing when he claims that among those features are scarcity of resources and the limited generosity of human nature. But Hume's account does not go far enough. There are at least two other sources of moral conflict that he ignores, and they make the problem of moral disagreement both more complex and more challenging than he implies.

Even totally benevolent individuals trying to decide on the morally best standards to govern a society of abundance would not be able to reconcile some moral conflicts. They would still face, for example, the problem of abortion. Nor is abortion a unique case. Similar moral conflicts characterize some aspects of the controversies over legalizing violent pornography, capital punishment, surrogate parenting, and many other contemporary issues over which moral opinion divides. These moral conflicts can be understood and experienced by one person taking a moral point of view, appreciating the competing claims of more than one fundamental value, and therefore struggling internally to resolve the conflict. The sources of moral disagreement lie partly within morality itself.

The other circumstance we should add to Hume's account is incomplete understanding. Even if everyone were completely benevolent, some may reasonably give different weight to the many complex factors, moral and empirical, that affect the choice of public policies. Recognizing this human limitation does not imply moral skepticism, and is even compatible with believing that there are moral truths. It simply expresses a recognition that, at any particular moment in history, we cannot collectively resolve some moral dilemmas on their own terms.

If moral disagreement is so pervasive, how can we ever hope to resolve it? Some basis for hope of achieving some modest kind of resolution is to be found in the nature of moral claims themselves. Just as the problem of disagreement lies partly within morality itself, so does the basis for its resolution. The two primary characteristics of moral claims in politics—that they apply to everyone similarly situated and that they appeal to values each is assumed to share—support the possibility of resolution. If citizens make claims that they expect others would not reasonably reject, they are already engaged in a process of finding some common ground on which to resolve their conflicts.

In an important sense, however, we should not expect finally to resolve moral conflicts. The problem of moral disagreement should be considered a condition with which we must learn to live rather than an obstacle to be overcome on the way to a just society. We may reach some resolutions, but they are partial and tentative. They do not stand outside the process of moral argument, prior to it or protected from its provocations. We do not begin with a common morality, a substantial set of the principles or values that we assume we share, and then apply it to decisions and policies. Nor for that matter do we end with such a morality. Rather, the principles and values with which we live are provisional, formed and continually revised in the process of making and responding to moral claims in public life.

In its political aspect, this process embodies some form of democracy. Democracy seems a natural and reasonable way of coping with moral disagreement, since it is a conception of government that, at least in theory, accords equal respect to the moral claims of each citizen, and is therefore morally justifiable from the perspective of each citizen. If we have to morally disagree over matters of justice, it is better to do so in a democracy that as far as possible respects the moral status of each of us.

The leading conceptions of democracy may be divided into two types: procedural and constitutional. Both in effect accept the goal of finding a common perspective for resolving moral disagreement: decisions and policies should in principle be acceptable to the people who are bound by them. Moral disagreements that are rooted in incomplete understanding, for example, should not be resolved by adopting policies or passing laws whose rationale citizens cannot reasonably accept. In this way, both forms of democracy seek a common perspective that is comprehensible to, and cannot reasonably be rejected by, the people bound by it. To what extent do they succeed?

II. The Response of Procedural Democracy

Procedural democracy defends popular rule as the fairest way of resolving moral conflicts. The simplest form of popular rule is majoritarianism: members of a sovereign society agree to be governed by the will of a majority or their accountable representatives. The decision of a majority at any particular time is provisional, since it may always be revised by subsequent majorities; but what the majority decides resolves the moral conflict as a matter of law and policy at any particular time.

In the face of moral conflict (including disagreement about conceptions of democracy), majoritarianism commends itself as the default solution. It institutionalizes the premise, shared by all democrats, that each citizen should be respected as a political equal. If citizens cannot agree on the moral substance of policies and decisions, and no representative can be relied on to resolve substantive moral conflicts, then the claims or each citizen should be weighed equally, and the greatest number should prevail. Majority rule institutionalizes the idea that the claims of every person count equally in deciding which way the political community of which they are each a part should move. The alternative is to impose the claims of the minority on the majority, and this assumes that the moral convictions of some citizens count for more than those of others. Such an assumption cannot be justified to people who consider themselves political equals.

Procedural democrats would argue that this rationale provides the common perspective we are seeking. The members of the losing minority, even if their position is morally correct, should not reasonably reject majoritarianism. Majority rule does not substantively resolve a moral conflict; it yields only a provisional procedural resolution. Majorities may of course believe that their view is right, but procedural democracy does not claim the majority's decision is morally right, only that the majority has the right to decide. Numerical might does not make moral right. Majorities have a right to govern only because minorities do not.

Some procedural democrats deny that there are any correct substantive moral conclusions in politics; there are no "fundamental values" that should be shared by all citizens. But the moral skepticism that these denials imply is not required by procedural democracy, and in fact would undermine it. If there is no reason to believe that any moral claim is valid, then there is no reason to count any claim at all, and no reason therefore to defer to the claims of the greatest number. Stronger justifications for majoritarianism do not rest on moral skepticism. They assume only that citizens cannot collectively agree, and should not be reasonably expected to do so, on the solutions to many moral conflicts. At the basis of this assumption lies a substantive moral value—political equality. The very basis for saying that the disagreement cannot be resolved (that citizens can reasonably reject its resolution) presumes that the (reasonable) moral claims of *each* citizen deserve respect.

Yet as soon as we recognize that proceduralism presumes this substantive value, we can ask whether majority rule adequately protects it. The answer, a simple example will make clear, is that it does not. Proceduralists, we shall see, need to qualify their majoritarianism in ways that move procedural democracy in the direction of constitutional democracy.

Imagine five people who find themselves together in a railway car, some of whom wish to smoke and some of whom object to others smoking in their presence. None of them can leave, and the car is not designated either smoking or nonsmoking. The passengers do not agree on any substantive principle such as "Everyone has a basic interest or right to smoke in each other's presence," or "Everyone has a basic interest or right not to inhale unwanted fumes." How should the conflict be resolved?

Brian Barry, who first described this hypothetical example, explains the appeal of letting majority preference determine the outcome:

> [Q]uite persuasive arguments can be made for saying that the decision should not simply reflect the number of people who want to smoke as against the number who dislike being in the presence of smokers. But, since opposing principles can be advanced, the existence of relevant principles does not seem to offer a sound basis for resistance to a majority decision.

Barry imagines the Archbishop of Canterbury among the five passengers, claiming "the right to decide the smoking question on the basis either of his social position or on the basis of his presumptive expertise in casuistry." If the Archbishop's claim is accepted by all the other passengers, no decision-making problem arises, because there is agreement. If some of the passengers reject his claim, it again is difficult to see how the question can be settled except by a vote. If the Archbishop finds himself in the minority, it must be because he has failed to convince enough of his fellow passengers that he is right, or at least that he has the right to decide. He may continue to insist that his view should have been accepted, just as a believer in the natural right to smoke may continue to maintain that the others should have accepted his claim. But, in the face of actual rejection of the minority views, the case for deferring to the majority decision looks strong.

But the case looks different if we vary the example. Suppose that two of the passengers argue: "Nonsmokers should not be subject to the substantial health risks of passive smoking, and smokers are also harming themselves by smoking. So it is in no one's interest to smoke in this railway car." The vote is taken, and the two health-minded passengers lose, three to two. Does the case for deferring to the majority look as strong as before? Surely whether it does depends on the nature of the health risks. If we assume that the health risks are minor and uncertain, the case for majority rule still looks strong, though less so than it would be if there were no health risks at all. If we assume that the risks are likely to be great, however, the case weakens. Our confidence in the majority principle seems to decline as the health risks increase in severity and likelihood.

This simple example reveals that the appeal of majority rule depends on certain background assumptions, conditions that we implicitly take for granted in accepting it as the best way to deal with moral conflict. In the complex world of politics, these conditions can be quite complex and are rarely satisfied. When they are spelled out, majoritarianism looks less compelling, and proceduralism less satisfactory, as a way of resolving moral conflict.

Two conditions are most relevant for the moral conflicts in politics. One is that the participants should have roughly equal chances of constituting the majority. As far as we could tell, none of the passengers in the railway car had any special relationships or history of prior associations; there were no voting blocs or ethnic or racial alliances that would interfere with a decision on the merits of the issue. Majority rule loses its moral appeal when there are "discrete and insular minorities" in a democracy, citizens who systematically find themselves in the minority on most important decisions because of the prejudices or distinctly different interests of majorities. In these circumstances, majoritarianism often works unfairly to the disadvantage

of minorities, especially on issues of critical importance to them. Because the inspiration of procedural democracy is the ideal of citizens ruling themselves on equal terms rather than being ruled by an external power, the presence of discrete and insular minorities who consistently lose out undermines the moral appeal of majoritarian procedures. It is reasonable for discrete and insular minorities to reject majoritarianism on issues of critical importance to them if there is a procedural alternative that would better protect their legitimate interests.

Another condition qualifies the majority principle still further: the majority must not infringe the vital interests of individuals. If one of the passengers in the railway car is likely to suffer a severe asthma attack if he breathes tobacco smoke, he is surely not bound by a majority decision in favor of smoking. More generally, we should want to say that decisions that violate the vital interests of any citizen cannot be justified simply by virtue of the fact that they result from a majoritarian or any other generally acceptable procedure. Decisions that do not protect each citizen's basic liberty, as far as possible, can reasonably be rejected. Thus, even an otherwise acceptable procedural principle does not alone vindicate some substantive decisions.

Most procedural democrats accept that procedures should be constrained by some substantive values, but they try to restrict those values to those that are necessary to preserve the democratic process itself. They agree that the majority must respect politically relevant rights such as freedom of speech, press, and association, the rule of law, and universal adult suffrage. But if our aim is to find a common perspective to resolve moral conflict, why limit ourselves to these procedural constraints? We have already seen that some decisions consistent with these procedural constraints—imposing life-threatening health risks on a few people for the sake of enhancing the pleasure of a greater number of people—cannot be justified. We have seen that the substance of the moral conflict may affect the justifiability of the procedure. If majoritarianism must be constrained by values internal to the democratic process, then it would seem that it should also be limited by values external to the process, such as those we have called vital interests. Indeed, some of these may also be necessary conditions of a fair democratic process. Procedure and substance are too intertwined to serve as markers for a distinction between constraints that should be part of a common perspective and those that should not. Neither kind of limit on majoritarianism can reasonably be rejected in general without considering the context of particular decisions and policies.

Acknowledging these limits of majority rule does not deny proceduralism a place in a common perspective for resolving moral conflicts. Some procedures are necessary for peacefully resolving moral conflicts, and no one has yet proposed a definitive decision-making procedure that is generally more justified than majority rule. Majoritarianism should not be dismissed, because, as Robert Dahl reminds us, "all the [procedural] alternatives to majority rule are also seriously flawed."

Yet procedural democracy can never provide a completely adequate common perspective for resolving moral conflicts. In the absence of ideal conditions (such as those we identified in the example of the railway car), procedural democracy is incomplete in three respects.

First, it is indeterminate with respect to what it should know best—procedures. Under some conditions (for example, permanent minorities), majority rule is not the uniquely right procedure for resolving moral conflicts. To decide whether majority rule or some other procedure is justified, we have to attend to the substantive values that are at stake in political decisions. Proceduralists therefore need to incorporate moral deliberation as a precondition for adequately resolving many political disputes. This need undermines the original aim of proceduralism: to avoid substantive moral

disagreement by less controversial procedural means. There is no way of realizing this aim without putting moral substance back into the procedure itself. This is one way in which deliberative democracy significantly revises proceduralism. Procedural indeterminacy opens the door for moral conflicts over procedures as well as substantive outcomes, and these conflicts cannot be resolved by invoking majority rule, interest-group bargaining, or any other procedural principle. There is no substitute for substantive moral deliberation in resolving conflicts over procedures.

Even when it determines a correct procedure, procedural democracy remains incomplete in further ways, which also point to the need for deliberative democracy. One way is evident from our discussion of the modified railway-car example: even when otherwise justified, majority rule may not overrule vital interests (for example, serious and avoidable risks to health). The other way in which procedural democracy is incomplete can be brought out by modifying the example yet again. Suppose that one of the five passengers has specialized knowledge, gained by years of study, about the health risks of smoking. Another passenger, who has no strong views about whether smoking should be permitted in the car, wants to hear more about the pros and cons of the issue before she votes. No one objects to majority rule as the ultimate decision-making rule, but these two passengers object to the idea of simply taking a vote. They think it essential to discuss the substance of the question before anyone casts a vote.

This final variation of the example reminds us that any simple procedural principle such as majority rule is usually silent about an aspect of decision making that is of critical moral importance—the nature of the moral claims that are made before the vote is taken. To assess the justifiability of the procedure in particular instances, we need to know what kind of discussion took place, who participated, what arguments they presented, and how each responded to the claims of others. This is the moral deliberation that, we shall argue, is an essential part of any democratic process that seeks to resolve moral disagreement.

Procedural democracy does not so much reject as ignore deliberation. Proceduralists seek to resolve moral disagreement mainly by avoiding it: they make do with few substantive moral constraints, and they make little room for substantive moral discussion. Their silence about the content of political claims often accompanies a view of politics as the aggregation of individual or group interests. All claims come into the political process as expressions of preferences or interests. It is irrelevant, by proceduralist standards, whether these claims are supported by moral reasons or whether they can stand the test of public deliberation, as long as they are aggregated by the right procedure. The proceduralist view therefore naturally supports, and is in turn supported by, the well-known model of politics as interest-group bargaining, where the relative power of groups and their ability to take advantage of political procedures determines the outcome.

This model is inadequate as a moral understanding of politics for reasons that parallel the three ways in which proceduralism is incomplete. First, the procedures by which interest groups bargain are themselves not usually a product of interest-group bargaining. Nor should they be. Justifying procedures, as we have seen, requires attention to moral considerations. Second, interest-group bargaining cannot be justified if it violates the vital interests of individuals. Interest groups can constrain their own political demands by respect for the vital interests of others, but such self-constraint does not come naturally, nor is it guaranteed by any political procedure. To protect individual rights, a process of interest-group bargaining requires either self-constraint by interest groups or external constraints. In either case, protecting the vital interests of individuals adds a missing nonprocedural element to the interest-group bargaining model. Third, at its best, interest-group bargaining is not well described as a process of merely asserting and aggregating interests. It is also a process of creating and modifying understandings of interests through collective discussion. Before they bargain, interest groups first deliberate internally to develop a morally defensible conception of their interests. In addition to bargaining with other groups, they also often appeal on moral grounds for public support.

Even at its best, however, interest-group bargaining cannot completely satisfy the demands of a common perspective. In every democratic society, some citizens are excluded from interest groups or included only in relatively weak ones, which cannot effectively represent the interests of their members. But even in an ideal society where interest groups had equal power, the three problems of proceduralism discussed above would still not be overcome. We have seen that even under the ideal conditions that proceduralists typically describe to justify interest-group bargaining, they find themselves under pressure to acknowledge more moral constraints and admit more moral discussion. Proceduralists are thus driven first in the direction of constitutional democracy and ultimately back toward deliberative democracy.

III. The Response of Constitutional Democracy

The critical difference between constitutional and procedural democrats is not that the former protect individual rights against majority rule, and the latter do not. Procedural democrats recognize two kinds of rights that limit majoritarianism: (1) rights such as voting equality that are *integral* to democratic procedures; and (2) rights such as a guaranteed minimum income that, though *external* to the democratic process, are *necessary* for its fair functioning. They take notice of a third kind of right but deny it priority over majority rule: (3) rights that are *external* to the democratic process and *not necessary* for its fair functioning. The view that this third kind of right should constrain any democratic procedure is what distinguishes constitutional from procedural democrats.

We have already seen the intuitive appeal of constitutional democracy: some majority decisions are not acceptable because they violate vital or basic interests of individuals—for example, by posing serious health risks. From considering cases of this kind, we come to accept a general principle that holds that any legitimate decision-making procedure must respect a set of individual rights that protect the vital interests of individuals against the claims of majorities, pluralities, or minorities. A common perspective for resolving moral conflicts thus must make room for moral judgments not only of procedures but of their results. Constitutional democracy broadens the search for substantive values that can be included in a common perspective to resolve moral disagreements.

Broadening the search in this way, however, creates difficulties for constitutional democrats, parallel to the difficulties faced by procedural democrats. One difficulty is the same for both proceduralists and constitutionalists. Constitutional democrats insist, no less than procedural democrats, that citizens need morally justified processes for arriving at politically binding decisions. John Rawls, whose theory we take as a paradigm of constitutional democracy, writes "that some form of majority rule is justified as the best available way of insuring just and effective legislation. It is compatible with equal liberty . . . and possesses a certain naturalness; for if minority rule is allowed, there is no obvious criterion to select which one is to decide and equality is violated." Like proceduralists, constitutionalists also confront the problem of deciding what form of majority rule, if any, is the most justifiable way of securing just legislation.

Constitutional democrats face a further difficulty. Because they go further than procedural democrats in constraining democratic processes by substantive standards, the common perspective they propose becomes even more contestable. The substantive standards they offer seem compelling when stated abstractly: who would deny that majorities should not violate the vital interests of their fellow citizens? But the abstraction purchases reasonable agreement on the principles at the price of reasonable disagreement about their interpretation. The more abstract the constitutional standards, the more contestable their interpretation. For the purpose of assessing and resolving moral conflict in political life, the interpretation matters just as much as the principle. We must have a way of dealing with these interpretative disagreements before constitutional standards can establish a common perspective to inform not only the theory but also the practice of democratic politics.

To illustrate this problem of interpretation, consider Rawls's principle of equal liberty. Among the basic freedoms on Rawls's list are "the liberty and integrity of the person." What does this liberty require in practice? Recall the railway car: would a majority decision to permit smoking count as a violation of basic liberty? More generally, would public policies permitting environmental pollution, or policies prohibiting it, contravene a basic liberty? The problem is not that we need more facts about the risks and the consequences: even with perfect information, we would still have to decide what risks to impose, and to what extent they violate this basic liberty. Giving priority to liberty in our common perspective, as constitutional democrats propose, scarcely begins to answer any of the specific questions that shape moral conflicts in everyday politics.

Constitutionalizing liberty still leaves wide differences of reasonable opinion about many important issues concerning individual liberty, such as legalizing violent pornography, prostitution, and abortion. Rawls does not, of course, offer his theory as a solution to such conflicts; he hopes that by focusing on the basic structure of society, he can avoid the indeterminacy of the conflicts posed by public policy. Perhaps a theory of justice is warranted in trying to avoid such conflicts, but theoretically informed practice that seeks a common perspective to resolve such conflicts is not.

Similar difficulties plague the constitutionalists' search for principles to govern social and economic inequalities. What policies would satisfy, for example, Rawls's principle of "fair equality of opportunity" or his "difference principle"? (The difference principle requires that social and economic inequalities "be to the greatest benefit of the least advantaged members of society.") Does fair equality of opportunity demand, or permit, preferential hiring for African Americans, Native Americans, Hispanics, and women? Does the difference principle require universal access to health care? Constitutional democrats who insist on using these principles to constrain the democratic process have to provide answers to such questions, and at a level of specificity sufficient to resolve the conflicts they express. This seems more than a Herculean task.

In his more recent writing, Rawls in effect addresses this difficulty by suggesting that fair equality of opportunity and the difference principle should not be included among the elements of what we are calling a common perspective. "These matters are nearly always open to wide differences of reasonable opinion," he writes, and they "rest on complicated inferences and intuitive judgments that require us to assess complex social and economic information about topics poorly understood." He concludes that "freedom of movement and free choice of occupation and a social minimum covering citizens' basic needs count as constitutional essentials while the principle of fair opportunity and the difference principle do not."

In this way Rawls escapes the problem of interpretation that plagues some constitutional democrats, at least as far as principles dealing with equal opportunity and social inequalities

are concerned. But many, perhaps most, of the large questions of public policy fall within the territory that would be governed by the principles of fair equality of opportunity and the difference principle. The question therefore persists: on what basis should conflicts about these issues be resolved? Rawls relies on "established political procedures [being] reasonably regarded as fair" to resolve these substantive disagreements. It appears that we have returned to proceduralism. The problem of resolving moral conflicts over social and economic inequalities becomes again the problem of justifying a set of political procedures. Yet, as we have seen, neither constitutional nor procedural democrats suggest how this can be done, or why we should even think it possible to resolve the remaining substantive disagreements over social and economic inequalities merely by procedural means.

Constitutional democrats do not ignore the importance of the democratic process. Rawls himself argues cogently for the value of citizenship and participation in politics. In the spirit of John Stuart Mill, he writes that democratic self-government enhances "the sense of political competence of the average citizen." Citizens are expected to vote and therefore "to have political opinions." He echoes Mill in declaring that the democratic citizen is "called upon to weigh interests other than his own, and to be guided by some conception of justice and the public good rather than by his own inclinations." Citizens must "appeal to principles that others can accept." Political liberty "is not solely a means," but also a valued way of life for citizens. All of this suggests a morally robust political process.

Yet like other constitutional democrats, Rawls stops short of suggesting that a well-ordered democracy requires ordinary citizens and public officials to engage in extensive moral deliberation to resolve their moral disagreements. This is puzzling. One would think that if democratic citizens are to value political liberty not merely as a means, if they are to weigh the interests of others, and to be guided in their actions by a sense of justice, then democratic governments should encourage moral discussion about controversial political issues. Forums for moral deliberation should abound, and citizens and their representatives should continually confront their moral conflicts together. The lack of these forums both in theory and practice—what we might call the deliberative deficit—should be a matter of considerable concern to constitutional democrats.

.When Rawls considers how to make the two principles of justice more specific, he does not propose that citizens discuss their disagreements in the public forum. Rather, he suggests that each of us alone perform an extended and intricate thought-experiment, a kind of private deliberation, incorporating a veil of ignorance that obscures our own personal interests and compels us to judge on a more impersonal basis. This process of reflection may be seen as a philosophical analogue of judicial deliberation. For some constitutional democrats, the U.S. Supreme Court performs the same function.

Here is how the solitary deliberation might go, as each of us alone tries to develop the common perspective by making the principles more specific. Having agreed on the two principles of justice, we first enter a constitutional mode of thinking. We imagine ourselves as delegates at a constitutional convention trying to design institutions and procedures that will yield results in accord with the principles of justice. Having created the best possible constitution for our social circumstances, we recognize that it does not address most of the important issues of public policy, such as environmental pollution or preferential hiring. Lifting the veil of ignorance further so that we can know more about the current circumstances of society, we move to a legislative mode of thinking and try to decide what laws and policies would be just for our society. Even after we have gone through all the stages of thinking in this solitary process, we are likely to find that

this test is often indeterminate. . . . [W]hen this is so, justice is to that extent likewise indeterminate. Institutions within the permitted range are equally just, meaning that they could be chosen; they are compatible with all the constraints of the theory. . . . This indeterminacy in the theory of justice is not in itself a defect. It is what we should expect.

Rawls is surely right that we should expect considerable indeterminacy in any theory of justice. He is also certainly right to suggest that each of us should think through the principles of justice on our own as best we can. But why should the indeterminacy of justice begin just where the determinacy of our solitary philosophical reflection leaves off? It appears that for Rawls and other constitutional democrats the point at which our solitary thinking about justice becomes indeterminate also marks the point at which social justice and our ability to find a common perspective on moral disagreements in politics becomes incapacitated. We might as well check our deliberative thinking at the door to the public forum; in any case we had better keep it to ourselves.

This conclusion fits uncomfortably within a theory that requires democratic citizens to achieve a high degree of moral and political competence and to maintain a stable commitment to principles of justice. The necessary competence and commitment are not likely to be sustained unless citizens consider together in public forums the meaning of constitutional principles and their implications for specific decisions and policies of government. Furthermore, it is premature to conclude that these principles are indeterminate over such a wide range of public policies. Just because we cannot in advance philosophically establish principles specific enough to constrain public policy, we should not conclude that we could not discover such principles through discussion with our fellow citizens in a process informed by the facts of political life, and inspired by the ideals of moral deliberation.

IV. The Need for Moral Deliberation

How far do procedural and constitutional democracy move toward a common moral perspective for resolving moral disagreements in politics? Both procedural and constitutional democrats rightly agree that the fundamental values of democratic institutions, such as equal political liberty, must be justified by moral arguments. They seek to show that democratic institutions protect the equal right of all citizens to participate in political processes and to enjoy basic freedoms. The justifications typically appeal to a moral conception of the person as a free and equal autonomous agent. At the foundation of democratic institutions, according to both proceduralists and constitutionalists, lie fundamental moral ideals that are or should be widely shared.

Procedural and constitutional democrats also agree that democratic institutions are not justified unless they generally produce morally acceptable results. Democratic institutions that produce policies that deprive some citizens of freedom of speech or religion, or deny others reasonable opportunities to live a decent life, would be rejected by both procedural and constitutional democrats. The precise content of the criticisms that proceduralists and constitutionalists make against such results may differ, but both have at their disposal the resources for a substantial moral appraisal of the laws and policies that emerge at the end of any democratic process.

Moral argument—justification from a common perspective—thus plays an important role in warranting both its foundations and its conclusions. It makes its appearance at both the beginning and the end of the democratic process. What role should it play within the ongoing processes of everyday politics—in what we might call "middle democracy"? If a common perspective for resolving moral disagreements must rely on moral arguments to justify the foundations and results of democracy, then should it not also require moral arguments within the ongoing processes of democracy? Yet on this question, on the place of moral argument within democratic politics, procedural and constitutional democrats are surprisingly silent. This is puzzling in a way that has not been sufficiently appreciated. If democracy must be moral in its structure and its outcomes, how can it remain amoral within its internal processes?

Middle democracy is the land of everyday politics, where legislators, executives, administrators, and judges make and apply policies and laws, sometimes arguing among themselves, sometimes explaining themselves to citizens. It is here that much of the moral life of a democracy, for good or for evil, is to be found. It is a land that democrats seeking a common moral perspective on democracy can scarcely afford to bypass. A democratic theory that is to remain faithful to its moral premises and aspirations for justice must take seriously the possibility of moral argument within these processes.

Given the limited generosity and incomplete understanding of both officials and citizens, what goes on in these processes generally falls far short of any moral ideal. Perhaps that is why so many democratic theorists seem to want to ignore the possibility of principled moral argument here. The everyday operation of the democratic process is imperfect, to be sure, but so are its structures and results. It is hard to see how we gain anything, morally speaking, by limiting ourselves to only some of its imperfect parts. It is more likely that neglecting the possibility of moral argument in any part will only multiply the imperfections in the whole. Amorality is rarely the weapon of choice in the battle against immorality. The amorality of a political process is surely more troubling than its imperfection. Imperfection is endemic to the human condition; amorality is not.

Many constitutional democrats recognize the importance of extensive moral deliberation within one of our democratic institutions—the Supreme Court. They argue that judges cannot interpret constitutional principles without engaging in moral deliberation at least in order to fashion a coherent view from the many moral values that our constitutional tradition expresses. The fact that this process itself is imperfect—that judges disagree morally, even about the relevance of morality in the process—is not thought to be a reason to diminish the role of deliberation. On the contrary: the failures of moral argument in the judicial process are thought to make the quest for successes all the more urgent. Why is the same not true for the rest of the democratic process?

Moral argument is at least as important and no less frequent in other democratic institutions. Legislators, for example, make moral arguments regularly, and often quite capably, taking into account the conditions under which they work. Consider the way the U.S. Congress discussed the controversial issue of federal subsidies for abortion. In 1976, Congress adopted the so-called Hyde Amendment to the Medicaid provisions of the Social Security Act. The Medicaid provisions subsidize health care for citizens below the poverty line, and the amendment prohibited federal subsidies for Medicaid abortions except to save the life of the mother. A year later, rape and incest were added as exceptions. In 1980, the Supreme Court in a five-to-four decision upheld the constitutionality of the Hyde Amendment. Congress recurrently debated the issue at length, while the Court has considered the case only once so far.

The controversy over subsidizing abortion for poor women has many of the features of the many moral disagreements that make their way through our imperfect legislative and judicial processes. The sources of the controversy include not only scarcity of resources and the limited generosity of citizens, but also incompatible values and incomplete understanding of how best to weigh the many factors that would help decide among the values. The issue is undeniably one in which moral principles are at stake, not merely personal preferences or group interests. Citizens and officials on both sides of the issue credibly invoke basic constitutional principles, in effect supporting the claim of constitutional democrats that decisions about fundamental moral values should be reviewed by authorities standing outside the ordinary political process, specifically the judiciary. But the controversy also provides evidence against the view that courts are the forum of principle in our democratic system, and that the legislatures are incapable, or demonstrably less capable, of considering moral principles in the making of law. Congressional debates over the Hyde Amendment have been replete with (good and bad) principled arguments—indeed, on this issue, more so than the opinions of the Supreme Court.

Even if moral deliberation in the wider democratic process is possible, it may not be desirable. We think that Congress reached the wrong conclusion on the question of subsidizing abortion. We cannot therefore locate the value of deliberation wholly in the justice of the policies it produces. (Those who agree with Congress on this issue should have no trouble in finding another case that would test their commitment to deliberation in the face of outcomes with which they disagree.) Extending the domain of deliberation may have other risks, too. Once the moral sensibilities of citizens and officials are engaged, they may be less willing to compromise. Issues come to be seen as matters of principle, creating occasions for high-minded statements, unyielding stands, and no-holds-barred opposition. Furthermore, once the forum admits reasonable moral claims, it cannot easily exclude the unreasonable ones. There are moral fanatics as well as moral sages, and in politics the former are likely to be more vocal than the latter.

These are real risks. It should be clear that no political process can avoid them completely, but more widespread deliberation is likely to decrease them. It is a hollow hope that any one institution, even the Supreme Court, could be relied on to reach the right conclusions, were it to do all our deliberating. Moral sensitivity, it is true, may sometimes make necessary political compromises more difficult, but its absence also makes unjustifiable ones more common. Moral argument can arouse moral fanatics, but it also combats their claims on their own terms. Furthermore, there is no reason to believe that the chief alternative to deliberation—bargaining among interests—protects us any better from moral extremism. The extremists in the abortion debate neither deliberate nor bargain: they turn to violence outside the political process.

However we weigh these risks, we should also consider the positive value of moral deliberation in politics. The case for deliberation is best made by looking at specific issues of policy, noticing how it works in practice and how it might work better. But four general reasons—paralleling the four sources of moral disagreement—are worth emphasizing in general terms. Together they provide a compelling case on democratic grounds for extending the domain of deliberation within the democratic process, for granting it authority to deal with the moral conflicts that procedural and constitutional democracy fail to resolve.

The first reason concerns the contribution that deliberation makes to the legitimacy of decisions and policies. Given scarce resources, some citizens will not get what they want, or even what they need, and sometimes none will. The hard choices that governments make in these circumstances should be more acceptable even to those who receive less than they deserve, if their claims have been considered on their merits, rather than on the basis of relative wealth, status, or power. Even among policies with which we disagree, we should take a different attitude toward those that are adopted after consideration of the relevant conflicting moral claims, and those that are adopted after only calculation of the relative strength of the competing political interests. Moral justifications do not, of course, make up for the material resources that we fail to receive. But they help sustain the

political legitimacy that makes possible our collective efforts to secure more of those resources in the future, and to live with each other civilly in the meantime.

Second, deliberation responds to our limited generosity by creating forums in which we are encouraged to take a broader perspective on questions of public policy. John Stuart Mill presented one of the earliest and still most cogent accounts of such a process. Mill argued that when participating in political discussion, a citizen is

> called upon . . . to weigh interests not his own; to be guided, in case of conflicting claims, by another rule than his private partialities; to apply, at every turn, principles and maxims which have for their reason of existence the common good. . . .

We do not need to make the optimistic assumption that most citizens will suddenly become public-spirited when they find themselves deliberating in the public forum. Much depends on the background conditions: the level of political competence (how well informed citizens are), the distribution of resources (how equally situated they are), and the nature of the political culture (what kind of arguments are taken seriously). All we need to assume is that citizens and their representatives are more likely to take a broader view of issues, to consider the claims of more of their fellow citizens, in a process in which moral arguments are taken seriously than in a process in which assertions of political power prevail.

The third reason for encouraging deliberation is that it can clarify the nature of a moral conflict. We are more likely to recognize what is morally at stake in a dispute if we employ moral reasoning in trying to resolve it. Deliberation helps sort out the self-interested from the public-spirited claims, and among the latter helps identify those that have greater weight. Through this kind of deliberative process, we can begin to isolate those conflicts that embody genuinely incompatible values. Those that do not may then turn out to be more easily resolvable: we might discover that they are the result of misunderstanding or lack of information, or we might now see ways to settle them by ordinary political processes of negotiation and compromise. For those conflicts that persist, those that represent moral conflict for which there is no reasonable resolution at present, deliberation can help citizens better understand the moral seriousness of the views they oppose, and better cooperate with their fellow citizens who hold these views. This potential for mutual respect is part of the common perspective that we seek.

In some situations, making democratic government more deliberative may increase political tensions and conflict, at least in the short run. Creating more deliberative forums may bring previously excluded voices into politics, and these voices are not likely to sing in harmony. We should count this as a virtue of deliberative democracy in bringing to light legitimate moral conflicts that are suppressed by political processes that are not sufficiently deliberative. The aim of deliberative democracy is not consensus per se but a morally justified consensus. Deliberative democracy strives for consensus not for its own sake but for the sake of finding a genuinely common perspective. No conception of democracy can justify the suppression of moral voices for the sake of producing political consensus in the short run. Deliberative democracy decreases the risk of suppressing such conflict at the same time as it increases the chances of clarifying the values at stake in all our conflicts.

Finally, deliberation takes seriously the incomplete understanding that characterizes moral conflict. More than other kinds of political processes, it contains the means of its own correction. Through the give-and-take of argument citizens can learn from each other, come to recognize their individual and collective mistakes, and develop new views and policies that are more widely justifiable. When interest groups

bargain and negotiate without deliberating, they may learn how better to get what they want, but they are not likely to learn that they should not try to get what they want. The main source of movement in this kind of politics is shifts in power, not changes of mind. Power shifts may bring improvement, but only accidentally. Changes of mind are responsive to reasons that at least direct our attention to improvement. When majorities are obligated to offer reasons to dissenting minorities, they expose their position to criticism and give minorities their most effective and fairest chance of persuading majorities of the justice of their position. We may even hope, encouraged by Aristotle, that views better than those held by either the majority or the minority will emerge from such a process. But even when deliberation fails to produce a satisfactory resolution of a moral conflict at any particular time, its self-correcting capacity remains our best hope—and our only democratic hope—for discovering such a resolution in the future.

For all these reasons, we should try to press deliberation beyond the boundaries that procedural and constitutional democracy now set. Both proceduralists and constitutionalists tend to neglect the importance of deliberation within the democratic process. Nevertheless, extending deliberation is consistent with the moral aspirations of constitutional and procedural democrats, and may even be required by them. As we have seen, procedural and constitutional democracy are indeterminate in a critical respect: both need, but neither provides, a way of arriving at provisionally justifiable resolutions of moral conflicts with sufficient specificity.

Furthermore, the conflict between these forms of democracy itself is not likely to be resolved without giving greater scope to deliberation in the political process than either now recognizes. Constitutional democrats tend to regard procedural democracy as dangerously amoral, and look to the judiciary for moral protection. Procedural democrats rightly point out that judicial processes, like legislative ones, are imperfect, and cannot be relied on for reaching morally right conclusions. Proceduralists ask: Why then make judges the arbiters of our fundamental moral conflicts? As long as procedural democrats neglect the need for deliberation, constitutional democrats have a powerful answer: An imperfectly deliberative judicial process is better than a consistently unprincipled legislative process. With all its imperfections, judicial deliberation comes closer to serving the ideal of a common perspective than does the interest-group bargaining to which the proceduralists give license.

We need not choose between proceduralism and constitutionalism, however, if we recognize the alternative of deliberative democracy, develop its principles, and pursue their practical implications. Our discussion has focused on developing a conception of deliberative democracy, an alternative to proceduralism and constitutionalism. That is, we believe, the most important step in restoring deliberation to its proper place in democracy.

Once we understand the conception of deliberative democracy, we can better develop the institutions that will realize it. Various forms of democratic government—including direct, participatory, and representative democracy—can all be designed in a way that is conducive to deliberation. The point of a conception of deliberative democracy is not to elevate one institutional form of democracy above the others, but rather to find ways of making each form more deliberative. Nor should deliberative democracy rely on one "master" deliberative forum, such as a judicial system, to convert power politics into a principled politics. Not only courts and legislatures, but administrative agencies, city councils, and local boards of education can and should deliberate. The practical task of deliberative democrats is to consider how each

political institution can be designed to facilitate deliberation.

Some changes in political institutions will certainly be necessary. Deliberation requires, for example, that officials justify their actions in public, and that the reasons they give be accessible to citizens. This requirement may force some changes in the role of experts in policy making; at the least, they will have to find better ways to explain their recommendations in public forums. The requirement would also rule out some secret or confidential processes of policy making that now take place. Also, deliberative democracy would give preference to forums in which citizens with different moral perspectives could talk to each other, rather than the kind of forums that are now more common, in which citizens merely express their views to government. Congressional hearings, for example, would consist not merely of a procession of interest-group representatives giving testimony, but also of panels of citizens debating among themselves.

Deliberative democracy has implications for reform of not only political but also social institutions. Schools and other institutions of civic education, for example, must teach future citizens the skills and virtues of public deliberation. Similarly, the many institutions in which citizens work and with which they interact— corporations, hospitals, the media—should provide opportunities for constructively engaging moral disagreement.

If all democratic institutions including judicial processes are imperfect, and all democratic institutions including legislative processes depend on the give-and-take of moral argument to correct their mistakes, then procedural and constitutional democrats can find some common ground. They can find it if each pays greater attention to the need for moral deliberation within all democratic forums.

Chapter 11

Gerald F. Gaus

PUBLIC JUSTIFICATION AND DEMOCRATIC ADJUDICATION

Gerald Gaus (1952–   ) is a professor of philosophy at the University of Arizona who has written widely on liberalism and the public justification of coercion. In this reading (published in 1991), Gaus starts from a problem of disagreement similar to that discussed by Gutmann and Thompson and uses it to argue for an "umpire model of political authority," embodied in a constitutional representative democracy.

I. Two Liberal Contractual Strategies

Two deep commitments shape liberal moral and political theory. First, liberals embrace some variant of value pluralism. The liberal world is populated by individuals who are deeply committed to disparate values, aims and projects; and while a person's values and projects shape his own life, they do not in themselves provide others with reasons to do anything. Hence the fundamental question of liberal theory: under what terms are such individuals, each committed to his own particular goals, to live together? The second commitment constrains the sorts of answers that liberals can put forward. Liberals insist that moral and political principles are justified if and only if each member of the community has good reason to embrace them. Liberals thus stress *public justification*: moral and political principles must be justified to each and every member of the public. Taken together, these two commitments constitute a demanding justificatory project: moral and/or political principles must be acceptable to each and every member of the community, yet each person evaluates the principles in the light of his own aims and commitments.

Contractualist theories carry out this project by envisaging these diverse individuals making a pact that defines the terms of their association: if all can embrace the pact from their many perspectives, it is publicly justified. But the contractualist pact takes two rather different forms. The agreement defining the terms of association may be essentially *procedural and political*. On this view, the ends of citizens are deeply pluralistic, and so all that can be hoped for are political procedures that give each a reasonable chance of pursuing his interests (or perhaps procedures that structure the pursuit of private interests such that all benefit from each person's self-interested action). Some liberals advocate democratic procedures on precisely this ground: i.e. that they provide each citizen a fair opportunity to advance his interests. To be sure, public choice theory insists that, because unconstrained democratic rule encourages some to gain at the expense of others, it is not publicly justified. Not all rational citizens would consent to it. Consequently, public choice theorists have investigated what sorts of constitutional orders could be publicly justified. But despite this disagreement, the democratic pluralist and the constitutional economist agree that the political order is to be understood as a mechanism operated by individuals devoted to their own ends.

Contrast to this the second type of contractual pact, which articulates a *substantive and moral bargain*. On this approach, individuals devoted to their own ends agree on a set of substantive moral principles, which may be understood as a fair bargain about the division of the fruits of social life, or a reasonable compromise that advances the values of everyone. As Rawls says, the principles of justice are the "result of a fair agreement or bargain" and articulate "a pact reconciliation." Once such moral principles have been publicly justified, the task of the political order is to implement them. Whereas the political-procedural strategy conceives of politics as directly mediating the conflicts among individuals engendered by their diverse ends, this strategy identifies moral principles as the direct mediators; only insofar as political institutions articulate the demands of the moral contract do they serve this mediating function. This leads to a very different conception of political life. For political-procedural contractualists such as Buchanan and Tullock, the aim is "to construct political institutions in such a fashion that individuals acting in pursuit of their own interests will be led, by the institutional structure in which such action takes place, to further the interests of their fellow members in the political group." In contrast, the substantive-moral contractualist seeks political institutions that best implement the substantive articles of association; and, typically at least, such contractualists doubt that this can be achieved via a politics in which each single-mindedly advances his own private ends. Rawls, for example, insists that "political parties be autonomous with respect to private demands, that is, demands not expressed in the public forum and argued openly by reference to a conception of the public good."

My concern in this paper is with this substantive-moral contractualism. In contrast to the procedural-political strategy—which has given rise to the field of constitutional economics—the moral contract's implication for the selection of social choice rules has been inadequately explored. I begin in sections II and III by examining the nature of political authority for the moral-substantive contractualist. Having understood the point of political authority for such contractualists, I then (section IV) sketch a procedure for the choice of decision-making rules. Representative democracy, I shall argue, is a publicly justified procedure for resolving disputes about the demands of the moral contract. Politics, we might say, is the continuation of ethics by other means.

II. Public Justification and Its Contestability

1. *Teleological and Deontological Justifications*

The contractualist, then, seeks to show that each and every member of the community has good reason to embrace some set of moral principles. How might this be done? Contractualists have employed two broad types of arguments: deontological and what might be called constrained teleological arguments.

Consider the latter. The most common justificatory strategy of contractualists is to show that each person's aims or values are advanced by some set of moral principles. David Gauthier's theory is an exemplar of this approach. He writes:

If social institutions and practices can benefit all, then some set of social arrangements should be acceptable to all as a co-operative venture. Each person's concern to fulfil her own interests should ensure her willingness to join her fellows in a venture assuring her an expectation of increased fulfillment. She may of course reject some proposed venture as insufficiently advantageous to her when she considers both the distribution of benefits that it affords, and the availability of alternatives. Affording mutual advantage is a necessary condition for the acceptability of a set of social arrangements as a co-operative venture, not a sufficient condition. But we may suppose that some set affording mutual advantage will also be mutually acceptable; a contractarian theory must set out conditions for sufficiency.

Gauthier, then, argues that social institutions are justified only if they advance the good (i.e. benefit) of all. Note that this is essentially a teleological argument: the right (what is justified) is that which advances the good. What distinguishes such a contractual argument from our usual understanding of teleology is that, in contrast to, say, Benthamite utilitarianism, the good is different for different people. That is, whereas a Benthamite holds that (i) the right advances the good and (ii) we all should adopt the same view of the ultimate good (i.e. pleasure in itself is good), the teleological contractualist holds (i) but rejects (ii). We each have different notions of the good. Let us call such a contractualist justification a *constrained teleology*: it is teleological insofar as the justification shows that the good (or value) is advanced, but the teleological nature of the argument is constrained because what is of value differs from person to person, and the justification must show that an arrangement advances what is of value from each of these perspectives. It is unlikely that any arrangement will maximize the promotion of value from every perspective: individuals may have to compromise on arrangements that promote the values of all to a reasonable extent, but do not maximally promote anyone's values. It is in this sense that the teleological character of the justification is constrained: it advances, but does not necessarily maximize, what is of value from each perspective.

Constrained teleological arguments do not exhaust the possibility of contractual justifications: *deontological* arguments seek to demonstrate that all members of the community share a moral belief or commitment. Rawls, for example, writes:

> Our hope is that there is a common desire for agreement, as well as a sufficient sharing of certain underlying notions and implicitly held principles, so that the effort to reach an understanding has some foothold. The aim of political philosophy, when it presents itself in the public culture of a democratic society, is to articulate and make explicit those shared notions and principles thought to be already latent in common sense; or, as is often the case, if common sense is hesitant and uncertain, and doesn't know what to think, to propose to it certain conceptions and principles congenial to its most essential convictions and historical traditions. To justify a Kantian conception within a democratic society. . . . is to discover and formulate the deeper bases of agreement which one hopes are embedded in common sense. . . .

Understood in this way, contractual justification is the search for shared commitment to certain moral principles. Principles are accepted by all not because they advance everyone's values, but because everyone shares the convictions that the principles articulate. This sheds light on the contractualist project. According to John Gray, "[c]ontractarian agreement presupposes a vast background of shared understandings without which the contractarian method yields nothing." Gray takes this as a definitive critique of contractualism, but it is not. Insofar as the contractualist is endeavoring to publicly justify a set of moral principles—that is, to show that all citizens have good reason to embrace them—it is neither surprising nor upsetting that contractualist argument draws on the shared moral beliefs and understandings of the public.

It would seem that an adequate contractualism will employ both types of arguments. Some set of principles can be justified to all on the grounds that (i) they articulate our basic shared intuitions and convictions and (ii) they reasonably advance the values of each. Prima facie, it is difficult to see why either justificatory strategy should be excluded: both are relevant to showing what principles agents entertaining diverse values have good reason to embrace. And, after all, showing that is the aim of contractualism.

2. The Rational Contestability of Liberal Public Morality

This is a demanding goal. No doubt to many it is fantastically demanding. But even if it is not plausible to expect contractualism to provide a publicly justified detailed moral code, it is, I venture, reasonable to suppose that it can help in two other ways. First, contractualist arguments seem able to proffer public justifications of general principles, such as those upholding rights to basic liberties (e.g. equal freedom of speech, association, occupation), private property and at least minimal welfare provision. Secondly, contractualist philosophy can provide guidance as to the types of arguments and general political positions that are favored in public justification. For example, contractualism can provide a principled defense of certain compromise arrangements as most likely to provide everyone with good reasons for embracing policies. Nevertheless, because of the nature of both deontological and constrained teleological justification, once the contractualist argument proceeds beyond abstract basic principles its claim to have provided a public justification will be increasingly contested—and rationally so.

As we have seen, deontological arguments appeal to shared moral judgments and self-understandings. This places each person in something of a privileged position in evaluating them: it is open to each to determine whether he or she really is committed to the considered judgment or shared understanding. This places the individual citizen in a special position to accept or reject the conclusions reached by the contractualist philosopher. As Rawls makes very clear, ultimately any account of our public morality must be assessed from the perspective of "you and me"—each reader-citizen must judge "how well the view meshes with and articulates our more firm moral convictions. . . ." This does not imply, however, that each person has an actual veto over every proposed moral code. Not everyone embraces principles that she has good reason to accept; some, for instance, may be irrational and refuse to acknowledge the publicly justified morality. The aim of public justification is to provide everyone with good reasons for embracing principles and policies, it does not require that everyone actually accepts them. Still, we must admit that each person is in a privileged—if not unchallengeable—position about just what are her commitments and intuitions.

In contrast to deontological justification, constrained teleological justification seeks to show that everyone's values are reasonably advanced by certain arrangements. About such matters bargaining theory is apt to have much to tell us: given certain configurations of values, it can provide assistance as to what constitutes a reasonable compromise. But, once again, the ultimate claim of the constrained teleological argument is that each person's values are being reasonably advanced by the arrangement. Here too each person seems to be in a privileged position insofar as one usually best understands just what are one's values and takes a special care in evaluating whether those values are doing well or ill under various arrangements. Hence ordinary citizens are apt to contest claims that their values are being reasonably promoted. And, while once again, they might be wrong about this, their intimacy with their own values, and care in evaluating how they are doing, will often provide them with a sound basis for contesting the claim that an arrangement is publicly justified.

III. The Basis of Liberal Authority

1. *Rational Belief and Disagreement*

Individuals, all devoted to the ideal of a publicly justified morality, will thus find themselves engaged in controversies about the content of this morality. For example, Alf may insist that, though the liberal contract must make some provision for private property rights, such rights are only justified given significant redistribution. In contrast, Betty may maintain that, while some minimalist welfare measures are justified, the liberal contract gives little scope for redistribution. What are they to do?

Well first, of course, they may—and hopefully do—argue with each other. Since, after all, public justification is a matter of providing reasons, both should have reasons to support their position. At this point they have an *epistemological* dispute that requires adjudication. They both believe that (i) there is a fact to the matter—either mandatory large-scale redistribution can or cannot be publicly justified, (ii) they both cannot be right, (iii) they both have reason to embrace the position that is publicly justified and reject the other. Yet, once we appreciate the sources of the rational contestability of liberal morality, we will not expect consensus. In the absence of agreement, what is Alf to do?

If Alf believes that his view is publicly justified, he may be tempted to simply impose it on Betty. A commitment to public justification is a commitment to a morality that can be justified to all. Alf, though, believes that his moral views *are* justified to all, even though Betty disagrees; so why not just go ahead and impose them on Betty if he can? If his evidence is good enough for him reasonably to believe that redistribution is required, why isn't it good enough to justify redistributing from Betty to Charlie, regardless of what Betty thinks? Consider a parallel problem in science. One research group has evidence in favor of their theory, and they believe their

theory; a competing group has been working on a competing theory, which their evidence leads them to embrace. The two groups, then, have competing beliefs; and they both, say, acknowledge that these are competing. In the public discourse that is science, neither has yet been able to prevail: the evidence does not speak unequivocally. The scientific community is still split among proponents of each theory. In this case, it seems neither group can be shown to be rationally defective for holding their theory. Although each group has a reasonable belief that their theory is correct, neither has been able to show that acceptance of their theory is rationally demanded. Let us say in such a case that it is reasonable to believe that p, but also reasonable to believe that $\sim p$; a group that reasonably believes that p aims to show that it is *not* reasonable to believe that $\sim p$.

Alf, then, is in the position of reasonably believing that p (large-scale redistribution is publicly justified), but he has not yet been able to show that it is unreasonable to hold $\sim p$. (It is crucial to keep in mind here that he is not simply asserting that he likes p, or even that p promotes his values—those would not constitute public justificatory arguments at all. Alf's claim must be that, on the basis of either a deontological or a constrained teleological argument, p is publicly justified.) In this case, however, Alf admits that his public justificatory argument does not fall "into the category of arguments with which it is impossible responsibly to disagree." If so, it seems that Alf fails to publicly justify p. Both in science and in morals, to justify to others that reason requires they embrace p is a far more demanding task than reasonably believing that p. And if it is reasonable to believe that p but it is also reasonable to believe that $\sim p$, on what grounds does Alf impose p on Betty, who believes that $\sim p$? Her belief too is reasonable, so she would be equally justified in imposing $\sim p$ on him.

2. Two Simple Types of Authority

In science the epistemological dispute can continue until one side wins, i.e. belief that p or belief that $\sim p$ is shown to be unreasonable. But in morals the dispute is not only epistemological, it is practical too. Alf and Betty not only disagree about (i) whether extensive mandatory redistribution is part of the publicly justified morality but also (ii) whether, right here and now, the holdings of some are to be transferred to others. They not only have an epistemological dispute about what is publicly justified, they are endorsing competing policies which lead them into conflict. And if, as we are supposing, they are committed to justifying their demands on each other, they cannot rely on mere force (either force of arms, or force of sheer numbers of supporters). The resolution of the dispute must be publicly justified. How?

One possibility is that they will go to a sage: someone who has superior access to the moral truth, and whose practical judgments more closely track the moral truth than do their own. We could say that such a person is an authority on morals. The sage, priest, elder or moral philosopher is, on this view, taken to have superior epistemological insight, and this is taken to give him superior practical wisdom. And surely we sometimes do seek the counsel of those with such insight and wisdom. But for this option to be a genuine solution to Alf and Betty's difficulty, three requirements must be met:

(a)   There must exist some people who possess superior moral insight.

(b)   The selection of some rather than others as moral authorities must be publicly justified.

(c)   Those who are publicly recognized as moral authorities must exhibit significantly more convergence in their opinions than does the public at large.

We can grant (a): the problems arise with (b)

and (c). It would seem that the dispute about who are the proper moral authorities would be just as rationally intractable as the initial disagreement about what is to be done. Alf, supporting redistribution, suggests we let his priest decide; Betty believes that a libertarian philosopher would provide sounder advice. If, *ex hypothesi*, neither is able to show the other's substantive views to be unreasonable, it seems doubtful that it will be any easier to show the other's preferred moral authority to be unreasonable. Jointly, (b) and (c) are very demanding requirements: if we meet one, it practically ensures that we won't be able to satisfy the other. Say, for instance, we adopt a very loose test of who is an expert on public morality, e.g. anyone who has taken introduction to ethics in college. *Perhaps* we could publicly justify that criterion; but then surely we have no hope of meeting (c)'s requirement of significant convergence of opinion. The only way to meet (c) is to have a very exacting test of expertise, and that will make it impossible to meet condition (b).

Jan Narveson thus is quite right: the liberal recognizes "no high priests of morals." But Alf and Betty may conclude that this is no real loss. After all, what is really necessary is that they resolve their practical dispute about what to do: maybe they need not attempt to adjudicate their epistemological controversy at all. As in scientific discourse, perhaps they can leave the matter open, hoping that in time a clear public justification will be forthcoming. In terms of Richard B. Friedman's analysis, Alf and Betty may well conclude that they do not need *an* authority on morals; they require only that someone be *in* authority to end the practical dispute. According to Friedman, to be *an* authority is to have superior knowledge such that others are warranted in accepting your judgments. He writes:

> . . . the basic purpose of this sort of authority is to substitute the knowledge of one person for the ignorance or lesser knowledge of another person, although what the person

who defers thereby comes to possess as a surrogate for his ignorance is not knowledge, but "true belief" in the sense of belief that is indeed justified, though the believer knows not why.

Friedman contrasts this conception of authority to a second, which he calls being "*in* authority." The key to being *in* authority is that others recognize your judgments as reasons for them to act, even if they do not accept them as reasons to believe. As Friedman puts it, instead of acting on one's "private judgment" one who follows such authority acts on the will of another—even if it conflicts with one's own private judgement. On this matter the person in authority will decide what is to be done: his decision replaces yours about what you are to do. Particularly important in this regard is that your obedience to the directives of the authority does not depend on you agreeing with their wisdom. As Friedman says:

> The idea being conveyed by such notions as the surrender of private judgment or individual judgment is that in obeying, say, a command simply because it comes from someone accorded the right to rule, the subject does not make his obedience conditional on his own personal examination of the thing he is being asked to do. Rather, he accepts as a sufficient reason for following a prescription the fact that it is prescribed by someone acknowledged by him as entitled to rule. The man who accepts authority is thus said to surrender his private or individual judgment because he does not insist that reasons be given that he can grasp and that satisfy him, as a condition of his obedience.

Consider, then, a practical authority entirely divorced from any claim to being *an* epistemological authority. In such a case the authority would instruct Alf and Betty to ϕ, without making any claim that, on its understanding of the liberal public morality, ϕ is the morally required

act or policy. Certainly such authority is possible: it is the authority of a pure coordinator. If Alf and Betty are in a coordination game, it matters little to them what they do as long as they both do the same thing. The by now hackneyed example is rules of the road: Alf and Betty desire coordination such that they drive on the same side, and they are indifferent as to which side it is. Hence, the authority can solve the practical dispute by simply issuing a directive, with no claim that it is based on an examination of the relative merits of driving on the right or the left. In this case the authority makes no claim to resolve the underlying epistemological dispute because there really is no such dispute: the problem is purely practical. But surely this does not correspond to the dispute we have been examining. In our case, because Alf and Betty's practical controversy is indeed based on an epistemological dispute, it seems doubtful they would be satisfied with a dispute resolution procedure that makes no attempt to track the underlying epistemological issue. After all, they conceive of themselves as disagreeing about *what to do* because they disagree about *what is right*; to resolve the former without reference to the latter treats their moral dispute as if it were no more than a conflict of preferences.

3. The Umpire Model of Authority

Alf and Betty appear trapped in a dilemma. They reject the purely practical account of authority because it makes no attempt to relate the resolution of the practical controversy to the proper solution of the epistemological disagreement. But they rejected the sage account of political authority because they seem unable to identify an authority that could resolve their epistemological controversy. Locke, I want to suggest, points the way out of the dilemma. Recall Locke's proposal that, in order to escape the inconveniences of each relying on his own moral judgment, we appoint an "Umpire". Let us then consider more carefully the idea of an umpire in a game. Players require an umpire because they have practical disputes based on their different views on how the rules of the game apply to particular situations. Often the dispute is simply about matters of fact such as whether or not Betty hit the ball in foul territory. But not all the time. When a player is charged with unsportsmanlike conduct, the dispute is not simply about what was done, but whether it constituted the prohibited conduct. Neither in law nor in sporting matches do rules apply themselves: they need to be interpreted, and the application requires practical judgment. The umpire, then, makes his practical determinations on the basis of his epistemological judgments concerning the rules of the game. This makes the umpire appear to be something of a sage. But players typically do not, and nothing about accepting an umpire requires that they must, see the umpire as a sage. Players certainly may, but usually do not, take the umpire's decisions as reasons to believe: quite often they do not acknowledge him to be *an* authority in the sense that they defer to his judgments about what to believe. Players often enough continue to believe what they did before the umpire decided—they accept his judgment as a resolution of the practical dispute though not the epistemological dispute. Yet the participants expect the umpire to deliberate about what to do on the basis of the rules and the facts. Although the problem is essentially a practical one, the umpire's resolution is to be based on his determinations concerning the facts and the rules of the games, both epistemological matters.

Umpireship, then, constitutes a complicated mix of epistemological and practical concerns. The umpire's aim is to produce practical determinations that best track what the rules require. Yet players need only conceive of him as a practical authority (they see him as being *in* authority, not *an* authority). Indeed, it follows that players are committed to accepting the umpire's practical authority even when they are confident his decision is wrong. Unless players were prepared to do so they could not proceed

with the game. For situations will arise when players reasonably disagree about what is the appropriate thing to do. Unless they are prepared to follow the umpire's decisions in these cases, the umpire could not do his job. To be sure, there are limits. At some point we say things like "These just are not even reasonable calls. This fellow is either blind or has been paid off." Even when we disagree with an umpire we can usually grasp how someone seeking to apply the rules of the game would make that decision. But if an umpire consistently acts in ways that, as far as we can tell, have nothing to do with the rules of the game, we will sooner or later conclude that he is either incompetent or corrupt. We can say, then, that the players only accept the practical authority of the umpire for decisions within some range of reasonable decisions, R.

IV. The Justification of Democratic Adjudication

The umpire model of political authority yields two requirements for any decision procedure for resolving moral disputes:

(i)   It generally must be practically decisive;
(ii) It must yield decisions that are typically within R.

The first criterion follows from the practical necessity to resolve disputes: we turn to an umpire to resolve the practical dispute about what is to be done. But the umpire model of political authority also requires that the umpire's decisions be within range R—i.e. that we can reasonably interpret them as decisions about what is publicly justified. If people are to resolve their disputes by resorting to an umpire, it must be the case, firstly, that there is at least one procedure that meets these two requirements. Secondly, if more than one procedure does, people must be able to resolve their dispute about which to adopt.

I believe that both conditions can be met:

citizens can justify to each other an adjudicative procedure for resolving their disputes about what policies liberal morality requires. Moreover, I believe that this adjudicative procedure is a form of representative democracy. The support of this claim takes the form of a four-stage justificatory argument. At each point citizens seek to narrow the field of acceptable adjudicative procedures: if the argument succeeds, by the end of the fourth stage only one procedure (or, rather, family of procedures) remains.

1. The First Stage: The Constitution as Social Contract

Recall once again Alf and Betty's problem: within some range of possible decisions, R, both acknowledge that each is unable to show that the other's judgments about liberal morality are unreasonable. It is decisions within this range that each is committed to adjudicating. In contrast, Alf believes that issues outside this range are settled: the true liberal position on these matters, he believes, has been demonstrated. So the first task in publicly justifying an adjudication procedure is to identify those liberal principles and policies that have been publicly justified. The result will be a constitution—or, rather parts of a constitution, for as yet it will say nothing about the workings of government, only a statement of the basic principles of the liberal polity. Such a constitution can be understood—as many American jurists did understand state constitutions in the eighteenth century—as specifications of the social contract. Presumably it would include statements of liberal principles that are definitively publicly justified—e.g. freedom of speech—as well as prohibitions on umpiring some disputes—e.g. religion. We can thus understand such a constitution as a statement of the basic consensus on fundamental principles, which is to guide the umpire (and which will itself require further interpretation). Although the constitution as social contract clearly implies that the umpiring procedure is not omnicompe-

tent or omnipotent, in itself it does not imply any limitation of, say, legislative supremacy. Whether or not judicial review is justified, and just what such review amounts to, are separate questions. It is entirely consistent to conceive of the constitution as specifying the social contract and to deem the legislature as the supreme interpreter of that contract. In any event, I shall leave aside here the vexed question of whether the primary adjudication mechanism should be supplemented by a review mechanism, instead focusing on the choice of the primary umpiring procedure.

2. The Second Stage: Excluding the Unreliable and the Indecisive

Suppose our contractors have specified those liberal principles that are publicly justified. They then will seek an adjudication procedure whose outcomes best conform to these principles. In the words of Blackstone, they aim at procedures that minimize "unreasonable" legislation. This requirement is clearly fundamental: the disputants seek an umpire whose practical decisions track the requirements of liberal public morality. Consequently, an umpire who makes decisions that are generally recognized as unreasonable will not perform the required task. We must, then, reject any proposed method of adjudication that typically yields decisions outside R. This points to deep difficulties with random devices, such as a toss of the coin, as they generate incentives to formulate proposals that are outside R. In a random system Alf might advance, with some chance of acceptance, the opinion that public morality requires that he be supported in luxury by the state—not a proposal apt to be seriously entertained by a procedure that pays some attention to the merits of a case. This is particularly worrisome to the contractualist, according to whom each individual is devoted to his own values and aims. At this point we are examining ways to adjudicate disputes about what policy is publicly justified—citizens, we suppose, have divergent opinions on this moral question. But there is always a danger for moral-substantive contractualists that this moral dispute will dissolve into nothing more than each individual asserting the primacy of his own values, transforming moral discourse into a simple clash of values. Random devices encourage precisely this transformation, as they hold out equal hope to all proposals, no matter how self-interested.

Thoroughly random devices would be rejected on another ground: they are indecisive. Given a choice to be made among N options, a purely random procedure, giving each a chance of 1/N, could select one option. And thus it would seem decisive. But on closer examination its decisiveness evaporates, as defeated options could be immediately resubmitted for reconsideration, each still having a 1/N chance of success. This ongoing possibility for losers to reopen every issue could well produce instability that, by comparison, makes Condorcet cycles seem a minor irritation. To be sure, the random procedure could be hedged by various *ad hoc* rules, forbidding reconsideration of an issue for a specified period, but then the problem of individuating an "issue" would arise. (If a proposal prohibiting a certain type of pollution is rejected, is a proposal to tax those polluters at very high rates reasserting a defeated proposal or opening a new issue?)

3. The Third Stage: Preferring the More Reliable

Weak and Strong Epistemological Claims

Suppose that we have excluded all proposals that can be shown to be unreliable, i.e. ways of adjudicating disputes that do not reliably yield decisions that can be understood as reasonable interpretations of the public morality. Now it is certain that many decision procedures remain in contention, including, no doubt, the following:

Direct democracy
Representative democracy
Functional representation (as in Guild socialism)
Corporatism
Weak guardianship (extra influence to the more politically competent as in Mill's plural voting scheme)
Strong guardianship (rule by only the exceptionally qualified).

In the third stage of justification we try to narrow the set of possible decision procedures by showing that some are more reliable than others or more decisive. It needs to be stressed that Alf and Betty wish not only to resolve their practical dispute, but to do so in a way that best tracks liberal morality. Hence, in the context of publicly justifying an umpire, they both have conclusive reason to employ the most reliable decision procedure. So any demonstration of the superior reliability of one over another would be conclusive reason to reject the latter. At this stage each proposal can advance both a strong and a weak claim. A strong claim contends that a procedure is epistemologically superior to all others, and hence merits selection; the weak claim is that no procedure has been shown superior to it, and so it has not been eliminated.

Mill's Strong Epistemological Claim for Political Inequality

At this point John Stuart Mill's case for political inequality is apt to be pressed. If our regulative concern is to obtain high-quality decisions, it is reasonable to suppose that we ought to seek out political wisdom and give it special weight. Indeed, Mill believes that all reasonable people would acknowledge that the political judgment of some is superior to that of others. "No one but a fool, and only a fool of a peculiar description, feels offended by the acknowledgment that there are others whose opinion, and even whose wish, is entitled to greater consideration than his." Mill, then, suggests that our common aim of securing the most reliable procedure would lead us to reject political equality—hence his plural voting scheme, which awards varying numbers of votes on the basis of occupation. If we accept Mill's argument, it would seem that proposals based on one person, one vote (i.e. democracy) would not survive this third stage.

If Mill could provide a public justification identifying a certain class as those possessing superior knowledge, the case for a democracy based on political equality would surely be undermined. Shirley Robin Letwin asks a good question and gives a good answer:

> Would we want democracy if we had access to indisputable knowledge of what ought to be done? The answer is, of course, no. Whether such knowledge were derived from God, history, science, or nature, it would be folly if not sacrilege to let the ignorant decide. Any reasonable person would want to hand over all public discussion to the sages or technicians who knew the truth . . . We would be obliged to agree with Nietzsche that only a blind, mean refusal to acknowledge our superiors can sustain a preference for democracy.

But our problem is that, given any proposal identifying a sage, it is reasonable to reject that sage in favor of another. Mill might believe that the university educated have the requisite superior insight, but it seems reasonable for workers to question whether such people have adequate insight into the values of the working class and the way their values fare under various proposals. Mill's strong epistemological claim for procedural inequality thus fails.

In these thoroughly democratic times, I suppose that this is all that really needs to be said. After all, most of us don't feel the pull of Mill's argument for political inequality; it is more of a theoretical possibility than a real option. But we would be gravely mistaken to take Mill's challenge too lightly. He is surely correct about one thing: it must be wrong to claim, as does Bruce A. Ackerman, that ". . . each liberal statesmen's [i.e. citizen's] opinion is at least as good as any others [sic]." Some *are* wiser than others, some *do* understand public morality and politics better than others. If the democratic response to Mill's argument for political inequality required this false claim about equal wisdom, democracy is in deep trouble. Recall, however, that I did not reject the claim that there are moral authorities; what I disputed is the assertion that the selection of some rather then others as authorities can be publicly justified. However, if we take Mill's point seriously, we must consider whether we can draw on these authorities without making this unjustifiable selection. Mill rightly perceived that some possess special moral and practical knowledge, but he was unable to provide a public justification for selecting a particular group. An epistemologically superior umpiring procedure would seek to draw on this expertise. Is there any way to?

Mill suggests an answer. Although his plural voting scheme is sometimes taken as the most important expression of his concern with competence, we should remember that Mill's fundamental aim was to justify *representative* government. For Mill, representative democracy acknowledges that citizens will always disagree about who is competent, yet it still allows the competent to possess special influence. He writes:

> . . . [I]t is so important that the electors should choose as their representatives wiser men than themselves, and should consent to be governed according to their superior wisdom, while it is impossible that conformity to their own opinions, when they have opinions, should not enter largely into their judgment as to who possesses the wisdom, and how far its presumed possessor has verified the presumption by his conduct . . .

On Mill's vision, representative democracy is not a "second-best" approximation to "real," direct, democracy. It is an ideal in itself, and one which does not suppose that the opinions of all citizens are equally sound; indeed, it allows citizens to draw on superior judgment without having to agree on a class of political superiors.

The rejection of strong guardianship

Mill's strong inegalitarian claim fails: he cannot show that his plural voting scheme is epistemologically superior. This is not to claim, though, that the scheme has been eliminated: the failure to establish the strong epistemological claim does not entail the rejection of the weak claim that no procedure has been shown superior to Mill's proposal. However, Mill points to another consideration which really does seem decisive against some proposals:

> . . . the rights and interests of every or any person are only secure from being disregarded, when the interested person is himself able, and habitually disposed, to stand up for them. . . .
> . . . [H]uman beings are only secure from evil at the hands of others in proportion as they have the power of being, and are, self-protecting. . . .

Following Mill, modern democrats have insisted that the chief benefit of democratic government is that the rights of all citizens are more likely to be protected against incursion by those holding power. Such responsive government, it is claimed, is more apt to yield decisions that track liberal morality than are procedures that vest political power in an "enlightened few." If this argument is sound—and given the history of elite rule, it is hard to deny its soundness—it indicates that strong guardianships (i.e where political power is restricted to a small class) cannot make out their weak epistemological claim: as umpires of liberal morality, they are inferior to more inclusive procedures. But modern Millians stress another point. Representative government, they claim, "tends to produce

morally acceptable laws and policies. At least it tends to produce laws and policies within the bounds of the permissible as determined by reasonable moral standards." This is not simply a consequence of self-protection: the responsiveness of representative government "encourages both citizens and representatives to think of legislation and policy-making in terms of what can be justified; and it leads them to formulate principles and conceptions of the common good in terms of which they can carry out the process of justification."

Admittedly, these considerations do not demonstrate in a deductive manner that unresponsive regimes are inferior to more inclusive procedures (such as standard representative democracy, functional representative regimes and Millian representative government) as ways to resolve disputes about liberal morality. But the record of narrowly-based elite regimes as arbiters of liberal morality is unambiguously dismal; neither the Party nor technocrats have given us any reason to doubt Mill's case for significant responsiveness as a condition of a reasonably competent umpire of liberal morality.

The Rejection of Direct Democracy

The case for rejecting highly exclusionary elite regimes would seem to lead to a case for the most highly responsive procedures—i.e. those which make extensive direct appeal to the populace to adjudicate policy disputes. But pretty obviously, as even those attracted to them typically acknowledge, the costs of employing such direct procedures in even moderately sized groups are horrendous. Individual citizens would have to spend an enormous amount of time studying the implications of complex policy proposals if direct democracy is to make any claim to reasonably track liberal morality. And these costs are much more troublesome for a direct democracy that claims to umpire disputes about public morality than one which seeks simply to express the popular will. If all a citizen is supposed to do is express his or her preferences so that the popular will can be ascertained, it is not necessary that citizens think a great deal about the issues. But if the citizen's task is to render a judgment about the demands of the public morality as it relates to some policy issue, then the unlikelihood that citizens will devote much time studying the problem is a grave objection to the procedure. So to say that direct democracy entails high costs for citizens is not just to claim, say, that we would have to forgo some luxuries in order to achieve it. It is to cast severe doubts on whether it could properly function: if it requires such devotion from citizens—who, we are supposing, entertain a wide variety of values and are not solely devoted to politicking—we must conclude that it is unlikely to work, i.e. produce reasonable decisions.

Confronted with the daunting problems of widespread direct democracy, many of those who are drawn to it advocate modified versions, which seek to somehow employ delegates without giving them real political authority. I shall not comment on the schemes here; suffice it to say that they have great difficulty avoiding collapsing into some form of representative government, giving the representatives significant political authority over the citizens. The reason for this is not obscure; in large organizations hierarchical authority is efficient. That is, hierarchical authority reduces the transaction costs necessary to arrive at decisions; and systems that are very costly to run are, as I have indicated, not likely to deliver the goods. Because of this, it seems most unlikely that any extensive and relatively pure system of direct democracy would survive this justificatory stage.

Weak vs. Strong Epistemological Claims for Representative Democracy

The family of procedures that can be described as constitutional representative democracy, I have suggested, will survive this stage of the justificatory argument. This does not imply the strong claim that they can be shown to be the best adjudicative procedures; it only implies the weaker claim that no other procedures can be demonstrated to be more reliable. This difference between these two claims is fundamental. It is most doubtful that any specific form of democracy, or indeed any social decision procedure, can be shown to yield the "best results." Perhaps the most imposing barrier to any such demonstration is presented by social choice theory. As William Riker stresses, in all voting procedures the method of counting the votes partially determines the outcome. Under different plausible systems, the same configuration of individual preferences yields different outcomes. To some extent the outcome will always be independent of the citizens' evaluations of the merits of the dispute and an artefact of the way the votes are counted. This leads Riker to conclude that "[t]he claim that voting produces a fair and accurate outcome simply cannot be sustained when the method of counting partially determines the outcome of voting."

Riker is certainly correct this far: we must reject the claim of any voting system that it yields the uniquely correct summation of voters' preferences. And if we conceive of voters' preferences as judgments, then we must also conclude that no system of voting can rightfully claim that it necessarily and uniquely generates the correct social answer given the configuration of citizen judgments. But, given the account of democratic adjudication developed here, it does not follow, as Riker believes it does, that this ambiguity helps to show that ". . . the social amalgamation of individual values are . . . often inadequate—indeed meaningless—interpretations of public opinion." Riker's conclusion supposes that a necessary condition for meaningfulness is that, for any given configuration of citizen preferences, there must be a unique social decision. But the umpire model of political authority makes no such presupposition: given the same configuration of individual opinions, two different rulings may both be acceptable. To be sure, both cannot be correct, but we have already rejected the sage account of political authority which ties rational compliance to the supposition that the authority's judgment is always correct.

4. The Fourth Stage: From Consequentialism to Proceduralism

I have indicated that those procedures that are the least responsive to the judgments of the populace, as well as those that are the most responsive, will be rejected on epistemological grounds. However, we have by no means resolved our dispute about what umpiring procedure to adopt: both democratic and non-democratic procedures remain in contention after the first three stages of justification. How are we to decide among these? By the end of the third stage all epistemological arguments have been exhausted; *ex hypothesi* none can be demonstrated to be more reliable than the others. It seems, then, that we must turn to some other considerations as we cannot afford to accept an indeterminate solution to our disputes. We require a decisive way to resolve our disagreements about the nature of public morality. Moreover, we need to keep in mind that the selected procedure must be justified to all. It is not enough to insist that, since your procedure is within the remaining set you can justifiably impose it upon others: for they too have their preferred procedures within the set, and there is no reason why they should defer to you.

Why Contractors will not Employ Value-Promoting Arguments

It may seem that at this point contractors will decide among the remaining proposals by considering which best promotes their values. Having exhausted arguments in terms of tracking the public morality, Alf might begin deliberating in terms of what best promotes his own values. For instance, suppose Alf's values are pretty strongly conservative; he puts a premium on preserving the social order as it stands. In the light of these values, Alf may opt for decision procedures that render change difficult. Umpiring procedures that require extraordinary majorities to change the status quo may be very attractive to him. To be sure, others have conflicting values, and so will prefer other procedures. Betty, strongly devoted to environmental values in a society that presently does little for such values, is apt to favor very different procedures. This depiction of their justificatory problem would appear to point towards a bargaining solution: each would have to compromise on a system that adequately promotes the values of all. Recall that this is the method of constrained teleological justification (II.1). But this approach to the justification of adjudicative procedures is inappropriate. It confuses (i) the justification of public morality with (ii) the justification of procedures for adjudicating disputes about this morality. As I stressed earlier, according to the substantive contractual strategy, when justifying a public morality it is entirely appropriate for contractors to employ constrained teleological and deontological arguments. Presumably, all have tried to do that, and each citizen has arrived at some judgment as to what policies follow from such considerations. Now the question is a different one: how are we to adjudicate our differences about what policies are appropriate? To once again bring in value-promoting arguments would be to misunderstand the nature of disagreement on this justificatory level. At this level of justificatory discourse the salient characteristic of the contractors is that they have divergent opinions about the demands of liberal morality, not (directly, at any rate) that they entertain different conceptions of the good.

The Principle of Political Equality

Throughout the argument I have been supposing that each contractor C rationally prefers acting on his own judgment (or some wise person he nominates as sage) about what morality requires to being coerced into following an umpire whose judgment C believes to be less reliable than is C's own or some wise person nominated by C. This is a modest supposition. It does not imply that individuals refuse ever to be coerced into following an umpire with whom they disagree or whom they believe to be less competent then are they; it only assumes that they prefer not to be. Nor does it imply that a person always feels most confident of his own opinion; Alf may sometimes defer to others whom he believes are wiser. But free deference will not achieve agreement, since citizens nominate a wide variety of sages. And some reasonably believe that they can do as well themselves as any sage could do. Given this, no proposal nominating particular sages will be accepted; some citizen will reasonably object to the sage on the grounds that the sage's judgments are not as reliable as his own or the person's own favorite sage (recall here the sources of contestability in II.2).

Contractors with this rational preference will only accept procedures characterized by the principle of political equality, according to which no citizen's political judgment is publicly recognized as superior to any other citizen's, and so is not institutionally accorded more weight on the basis of such superiority. To grasp why contractors are committed to political equality at this stage of justification consider Betty's proposal denying it. Betty proposes that there is some person (herself) whose judgments about what is morally required are to be accorded more institutional weight than are Alf's. Can this proposal be justified to Alf—i.e. can Alf be provided with reasons to embrace it? At this point in the justificatory process Betty has exhausted all claims that her judgment is better. More generally, she cannot show that this procedure will lead to better results. So Alf demands to know why he should acquiesce in having a lesser voice when he cannot be shown that this will lead to better decisions. Peter Singer argues that in

this case Alf and Betty should compromise on political equality:

> When the merits of incompatible claims cannot be ascertained, or when agreement on the merits of such claims cannot be reached, a procedure like tossing a coin or dividing what is in dispute equally, is the fairest course that can be taken . . .
>
> . . . [A] society which disagrees fundamentally over the kind of decision procedure it should have is in a state appropriate for fair compromise. The various incompatible claims that are being made cannot be settled by rational argument, nor is it likely that they can be settled by any decision-procedure, since it is precisely the decision-procedure that is in dispute.

According to Singer, the fair compromise is one which "gives no advantage to any parties to the dispute"—and this, he believes, is "one person, one vote." Singer, I think, is right that the case for political equality can be understood as a compromise or bargain between those who would claim complete authority for themselves; in this case a reasonable compromise does indeed point to a "50–50" split of authority—equal authority. However, the case for political equality need not employ formal bargaining models. The point is given (i) that all contractors are committed to the public justification of some umpiring procedure and (ii) the failure of all arguments demonstrating the superior epistemological insights of some group, (iii) that contractors do not appeal directly to their values, but instead their regulative concern is the acceptance of the procedure that best tracks liberal morality and (iv) that contractors prefer acting on their own judgments, or their nominated sage's, to judgments they believe are wrong, citizen-contractors have no reason to accept anything less than political equality, nor can anyone justify to others giving him more than equal say. The crucial point is that once we have eliminated all possible arguments in terms of better results, there is nothing much to say for procedural inequality.

I want to suggest, then, that arguments stressing procedural equality will be particularly attractive at this stage. Procedural equality can be understood as a series of constraints on voting systems that express the principle of political equality: viz. that no citizen's judgments are publicly recognized as superior to any other's. Consider, for example, decision rules characterized by undifferentiatedness (anonymity) and neutrality (within the acceptable range). According to undifferentiatedness, the decision procedure's results are invariant when the voters' identities are changed but the overall structure of preferences remains unaltered. Mill's plural voting would, then, be rejected as it is inconsistent with this condition: it can yield different results given the same overall preference structure depending upon who holds those preferences.

Neutrality would also seem a widely attractive feature. In this context to describe a decision procedure as neutral is to say that it should be equally easy (or, alternatively, equally difficult) for either Alf's or Betty's position to be upheld by the umpire. In short, the umpire selection process should not be biased towards some results rather than others. Such a bias would be tantamount to an admission that some views are sounder than others, but it is a feature of this fourth stage of justification that there is no public grounding for this claim. As Ackerman says, "Since neither *A* nor *B* is uncontroversially the inferior liberal . . . [position], a rational decision procedure should not make either one easier to enact than the other." Ackerman is correct so long as we are selecting umpires to adjudicate disputes within the range of reasonable differences of opinion. Recall, though, that we concluded some form of constitutionalism is justified; consequently, it is reasonable to

suppose that all citizens would embrace non-neutral procedures to alter constitutional provisions. This would serve both to avoid rigidity while allowing citizens to protect principles that are publicly justified from being ignored or overturned by faulty umpires.

I shall not proceed here to discuss other features of the preferred procedure. For now, the important point is that procedural fairness can help us to decide on adjudicative procedures when we have exhausted the arguments showing procedures to be more or less apt to yield reasonable determinations. If, within the set of reliable procedures, some are procedurally fair to all citizens, then citizens have better reasons to embrace these procedures than other reliable ones which are not. And this leads us to some version of one person, one vote representative democracy.

V. Conclusion

The ideal of public justification looms large in contemporary liberal theory. Liberals have insisted that the principles and institutions regulating our social life must be justified to all. But once we proceed past foundational principles, reasonable people of good will, committed to public justification, differ about where this commitment leads. In this paper I have sketched an account of political authority and democracy that depicts them as responses to our moral disagreements and our inability to rationally resolve them on their merits. Democratic adjudication is a way to cope with our ignorance. It is not justified because it always provides the right answers; indeed, we cannot even show that it is the "worst system except for all the rest." But constitutional democracy seems a reasonably adequate way of adjudicating our disputes; and it has the unique virtue that it can be justified to all citizens.

1b. RIGHTS

> We hold these truths to be self-evident, that all men . . . are endowed by their Creator with certain unalienable Rights, that among these are Life, Liberty and the Pursuit of Happiness . . .
> Thomas Jefferson, *U.S. Declaration of Independence*, 1776

A LAS, WHAT WAS SELF-EVIDENT to Jefferson has been anything but to political philosophers. The famous utilitarian philosopher and legal reformer Jeremy Bentham, for instance, derided the idea of natural rights as "simple nonsense." And even those who agree upon the importance of rights—as do all of the authors represented in this section—disagree sharply about the *content* and *moral justification* of those rights. Do we really have a right to the pursuit of happiness, and if so what on earth does this mean? What if I like to pursue happiness by using drugs that the government has banned? And if "Life, Liberty and the Pursuit of Happiness" are merely *among* the unalienable rights with which we have been endowed by our Creator, then what are the rest, and how are we supposed to find out?

Questions about rights are some of the most important questions in all of political philosophy. Rights are, after all, about what you can and cannot do, and about what the government can and cannot do for you or, more ominously, *to* you. Having or not having the right to vote, the right to speak freely, the right to practice your own religion, all make a tremendous practical difference in the way you live your life. It's tempting, therefore, to jump right into the fray and start any discussion on rights by debating the substantive question of which rights we do and do not have.

But this would be a mistake. For even if rights are of supreme practical importance, they are also tremendously difficult to be clear about from a philosophical perspective. Before we dive into the substantive questions, then, there are a number of philosophical distinctions which need to be made.

First, there is the difference between legal and moral rights. When we say that Joe has a right to drink alcoholic beverages, we might be saying one of two things. One thing we might be saying is that under the rules of the legal system, Joe is allowed to drink alcoholic beverages. That he can engage in this activity without fear of legal punishment is important for Joe and others like him to know, and so we can see why it would be important to have a class of people in society who are experts about exactly what legal rights we have, and who will tell us in exchange for lots and lots of money. But what are we to make of someone who, say, claimed during the period of the American prohibition of alcohol that she has a right to drink whatever she likes? It's possible that such a person simply isn't aware of what the law says—that she's simply making a *mistake*. More likely, though, such a person is not making a claim about her legal rights at all. What she is saying is that she has a *moral* right to drink, and that this moral right is something which holds *regardless* of what the law says. When she says that she has a moral right to drink, she means that it is something which she is morally free to do, and perhaps even that it is something which, morally speaking, the law *ought* to allow her to do, whether or not it actually does so. One can thus consistently claim both that one has a moral right to do something which one does not have a legal right to do (a slave in the American South during the 1850s might have the moral, but not the legal, right to escape), and that one has a legal right to do something which one does not have a moral right to do (if those who adhere to a pro-life position on abortion are right, then we have a legal but not a moral right to abort a child in the United States).

So far we have talked as though having a right simply meant that one was "free to do" something. But this needs to be made more precise. Some rights, after all, don't seem to have anything to do with *doing* something at all. My right to be free from physical assault, for instance, is more a claim about what *others* may do than what *I* may do. We can make better sense of rights by applying some distinctions first introduced by W.H. Hohfeld in the early twentieth century. According to Hohfeld, all rights are composed of some mixture of four more basic elements—privileges, claims, powers, and immunities. To have a privilege to *X* is to have no duty not to *X*. I have a privilege-right to walk down the street if I have no duty *not* to walk down the street. Claims are always claims *on* someone else; so for Alf to have a claim that Barney perform some action *X* is for Barney to have a duty to Alf to perform action *X*. Both privileges and claims are rules about what we can or cannot do. We can think of them, borrowing a term from H.L.A. Hart, as "primary rules." Powers and immunities, on the other hand, are "secondary rules"—what they have to do with is our ability to introduce, change, and alter primary rules. So Alf has a power if and only if Alf has the ability within a set of rules to alter the primary rules that apply to Alf or to some other person Barney. When, on the other hand, Alf lacks the power to alter the primary rules that apply to Barney, then Barney has an immunity against Alf in this respect. Alf has the power to waive his right to be punched in the face by Barney, and can do so by agreeing to enter into a boxing match with him. Barney, however, has an immunity against Alf waiving *Barney's* right not to be punched in the face.

Keeping clear on the various Hohfeldian elements of rights can allow us to make better sense of some of the claims we find in political philosophy. The claim that Jen has a property right to her watch, for instance, can be more precise as follows. It means that Jen has a privilege to use her watch in various ways, and that she has a claim against others using it in certain ways without her consent (which in turn entails that others have a *duty* not to use it in those ways without her consent). She also has an immunity against others altering this claim, and power to waive it herself—by granting someone else the temporary privilege to use it, or by selling the watch and thereby permanently divesting herself of her claims and privileges with regard to it. Importantly, once we start analyzing property rights in this way, we see that they need not be "all or nothing." If I have a property right in my land, I might have the privilege to do certain things with it—such as build a house or plant a garden—while lacking the privilege to do other things. If someone else has an easement through my property, then they have a claim against me to allow them free passage, and I thus have a corresponding duty to allow that passage and not to obstruct it by, say, completely enclosing my land within a brick wall. To be clear about rights, then, whether it is a property right in land or the right to "the pursuit of happiness," we need to be clear about precisely which privileges, claims, powers and immunities go into them.

One final distinction which will often prove useful in making sense of debates over rights is that between negative and positive rights. A negative right is a right against certain sorts of interference by others. It is negative insofar as all it requires of others is that they *abstain* from certain kinds of action. Rights against robbery and assault are classic instances of negative rights. Positive rights, on the other hand, require others to perform some sort of positive act—such as providing you with some kind of good or service. Rights to health care and education are examples of positive rights. Libertarians tend to believe that negative rights are the only kind of rights that exist—or, at least, that they are the only kind of rights which should be *politically enforced*. Those on the political left, on the other hand, generally believe in the existence or political enforcement of a robust set of both negative and positive rights.

The first reading in this section, the *U.N. Declaration of Human Rights*, is both an important historical document and a nice test for one's understanding of the distinctions described above. Some of the rights enumerated in this document are stated at a very high level of abstraction. What specific claims, privileges, powers and immunities do they guarantee? Does the document speak in terms of negative rights, positive rights, or both? And what underlying theory could *justify* this set of rights? In other words, what moral reasons do we have to think that all persons possess these rights, but not others? Readers are encouraged to think carefully about the idea of rights embodied in this document and how it comports with their own ideas about rights. This will lay the groundwork for the more abstract reflection on the nature of rights contained in the readings by Dworkin, Feinberg, and Nozick.

Further Reading

Hart, H. L. A. (1955). Are There Any Natural Rights? *Philosophical Review, 64*, 175–191.

Hohfeld, W. (1919). *Fundamental Legal Conceptions*. New Haven: Yale University Press.

Holmes, S., & Sunstein, S. (1999). *The Cost of Rights*. New York: W.W. Norton.

Kamm, F. (1992). Non-consequentialism, the Person as End-in-Itself, and the Significance of Status. *Philosophy and Public Affairs, 21*(4), 354–389.

Lyons, D. (1970). The Correlativity of Rights and Duties. *Nous, 4*, 45–57.

Nagel, T. (1995). Personal Rights and Public Space. *Philosophy and Public Affairs, 24*(2), 83–107.

Narveson, J. (1988). *The Libertarian Idea*. Philadelphia: Temple University Press.

Nickel, J. (2006). *Making Sense of Human Rights* (2nd ed.). Oxford: Blackwell Publishing.

Rainbolt, G. (2006). *The Concept of Rights*. Dordrecht: Springer.

Raz, J. (1986). *The Morality of Freedom*. Oxford: Oxford University Press.

Steiner, H. (1994). *An Essay on Rights*. New York: Blackwell.

Thomson, J. J. (2005). *The Realm of Rights*. Cambridge, MA: Harvard University Press.

Waldron, J. (1984). *Theories of Rights*. Oxford: Oxford University Press.

Wellman, C. (1985). *A Theory of Rights*. Totowa, NJ: Rowman & Littlefield.

Chapter 12

United Nations

UNIVERSAL DECLARATION OF HUMAN RIGHTS

This document was adopted by the United Nations on December 10, 1948, largely in response to the atrocities of World War II. Its thirty articles represent the views of the General Assembly on those rights which all persons have irrespective of their country of citizenship. It was later supplemented by the International Covenant on Economic, Social, and Cultural Rights, and the International Covenant on Civil and Political Rights.

Preamble

Whereas recognition of the inherent dignity and of the equal and inalienable rights of all members of the human family is the foundation of freedom, justice and peace in the world,

Whereas disregard and contempt for human rights have resulted in barbarous acts which have outraged the conscience of mankind, and the advent of a world in which human beings shall enjoy freedom of speech and belief and freedom from fear and want has been proclaimed as the highest aspiration of the common people,

Whereas it is essential, if man is not to be compelled to have recourse, as a last resort, to rebellion against tyranny and oppression, that human rights should be protected by the rule of law,

Whereas it is essential to promote the development of friendly relations between nations,

Whereas the peoples of the United Nations have in the Charter reaffirmed their faith in fundamental human rights, in the dignity and worth of the human person and in the equal rights of men and women and have determined to promote social progress and better standards of life in larger freedom,

Whereas Member States have pledged themselves to achieve, in co-operation with the United Nations, the promotion of universal respect for and observance of human rights and fundamental freedoms,

Whereas a common understanding of these rights and freedoms is of the greatest importance for the full realization of this pledge,

Now, Therefore THE GENERAL ASSEMBLY proclaims THIS UNIVERSAL DECLARATION OF HUMAN RIGHTS as a common standard of achievement for all peoples and all nations, to the end that every individual and every organ of society, keeping this Declaration constantly in mind, shall strive by teaching and education to promote respect for these rights and freedoms and by progressive measures, national and international, to secure their universal and effective recognition and observance, both among the peoples of Member States themselves and among the peoples of territories under their jurisdiction.

Article 1

All human beings are born free and equal in dignity and rights. They are endowed with reason and conscience and should act towards one another in a spirit of brotherhood.

Article 2

Everyone is entitled to all the rights and freedoms set forth in this Declaration, without distinction of any kind, such as race, colour, sex, language, religion, political or other opinion, national or social origin, property, birth or other status. Furthermore, no distinction shall be made on the basis of the political, jurisdictional or international status of the country or territory to which a person belongs, whether it be independent, trust, non-self-governing or under any other limitation of sovereignty.

Article 3

Everyone has the right to life, liberty and security of person.

Article 4

No one shall be held in slavery or servitude; slavery and the slave trade shall be prohibited in all their forms.

Article 5

No one shall be subjected to torture or to cruel, inhuman or degrading treatment or punishment.

Article 6

Everyone has the right to recognition everywhere as a person before the law.

Article 7

All are equal before the law and are entitled without any discrimination to equal protection of the law. All are entitled to equal protection against any discrimination in violation of this Declaration and against any incitement to such discrimination.

Article 8

Everyone has the right to an effective remedy by the competent national tribunals for acts violating the fundamental rights granted him by the constitution or by law.

Article 9

No one shall be subjected to arbitrary arrest, detention or exile.

Article 10

Everyone is entitled in full equality to a fair and public hearing by an independent and impartial tribunal, in the determination of his rights and obligations and of any criminal charge against him.

Article 11

(1) Everyone charged with a penal offence has the right to be presumed innocent until proved guilty according to law in a public trial at which he has had all the guarantees necessary for his defence.

(2) No one shall be held guilty of any penal offence on account of any act or omission which did not constitute a penal offence, under national or international law, at the time when it

was committed. Nor shall a heavier penalty be imposed than the one that was applicable at the time the penal offence was committed.

Article 12

No one shall be subjected to arbitrary interference with his privacy, family, home or correspondence, nor to attacks upon his honour and reputation. Everyone has the right to the protection of the law against such interference or attacks.

Article 13

(1) Everyone has the right to freedom of movement and residence within the borders of each state.

(2) Everyone has the right to leave any country, including his own, and to return to his country.

Article 14

(1) Everyone has the right to seek and to enjoy in other countries asylum from persecution.

(2) This right may not be invoked in the case of prosecutions genuinely arising from non-political crimes or from acts contrary to the purposes and principles of the United Nations.

Article 15

(1) Everyone has the right to a nationality.

(2) No one shall be arbitrarily deprived of his nationality nor denied the right to change his nationality.

Article 16

(1) Men and women of full age, without any limitation due to race, nationality or religion, have the right to marry and to found a family. They are entitled to equal rights as to marriage, during marriage and at its dissolution.

(2) Marriage shall be entered into only with the free and full consent of the intending spouses.

(3) The family is the natural and fundamental group unit of society and is entitled to protection by society and the State.

Article 17

(1) Everyone has the right to own property alone as well as in association with others.

(2) No one shall be arbitrarily deprived of his property.

Article 18

Everyone has the right to freedom of thought, conscience and religion; this right includes freedom to change his religion or belief, and freedom, either alone or in community with others and in public or private, to manifest his religion or belief in teaching, practice, worship and observance.

Article 19

Everyone has the right to freedom of opinion and expression; this right includes freedom to hold opinions without interference and to seek, receive and impart information and ideas through any media and regardless of frontiers.

Article 20

(1) Everyone has the right to freedom of peaceful assembly and association.

(2) No one may be compelled to belong to an association.

Article 21

(1) Everyone has the right to take part in the

government of his country, directly or through freely chosen representatives.

(2) Everyone has the right of equal access to public service in his country.

(3) The will of the people shall be the basis of the authority of government; this will shall be expressed in periodic and genuine elections which shall be by universal and equal suffrage and shall be held by secret vote or by equivalent free voting procedures.

Article 22

Everyone, as a member of society, has the right to social security and is entitled to realization, through national effort and international co-operation and in accordance with the organization and resources of each State, of the economic, social and cultural rights indispensable for his dignity and the free development of his personality.

Article 23

(1) Everyone has the right to work, to free choice of employment, to just and favourable conditions of work and to protection against unemployment.

(2) Everyone, without any discrimination, has the right to equal pay for equal work.

(3) Everyone who works has the right to just and favourable remuneration ensuring for himself and his family an existence worthy of human dignity, and supplemented, if necessary, by other means of social protection.

(4) Everyone has the right to form and to join trade unions for the protection of his interests.

Article 24

Everyone has the right to rest and leisure, includ-

ing reasonable limitation of working hours and periodic holidays with pay.

Article 25

(1) Everyone has the right to a standard of living adequate for the health and well-being of himself and of his family, including food, clothing, housing and medical care and necessary social services, and the right to security in the event of unemployment, sickness, disability, widowhood, old age or other lack of livelihood in circumstances beyond his control.

(2) Motherhood and childhood are entitled to special care and assistance. All children, whether born in or out of wedlock, shall enjoy the same social protection.

Article 26

(1) Everyone has the right to education. Education shall be free, at least in the elementary and fundamental stages. Elementary education shall be compulsory. Technical and professional education shall be made generally available and higher education shall be equally accessible to all on the basis of merit.

(2) Education shall be directed to the full development of the human personality and to the strengthening of respect for human rights and fundamental freedoms. It shall promote understanding, tolerance and friendship among all nations, racial or religious groups, and shall further the activities of the United Nations for the maintenance of peace.

(3) Parents have a prior right to choose the kind of education that shall be given to their children.

Article 27

(1) Everyone has the right freely to participate

in the cultural life of the community, to enjoy the arts and to share in scientific advancement and its benefits.

(2) Everyone has the right to the protection of the moral and material interests resulting from any scientific, literary or artistic production of which he is the author.

Article 28

Everyone is entitled to a social and international order in which the rights and freedoms set forth in this Declaration can be fully realized.

Article 29

(1) Everyone has duties to the community in which alone the free and full development of his personality is possible.

(2) In the exercise of his rights and freedoms, everyone shall be subject only to such limitations as are determined by law solely for the purpose of securing due recognition and respect for the rights and freedoms of others and of meeting the just requirements of morality, public order and the general welfare in a democratic society.

(3) These rights and freedoms may in no case be exercised contrary to the purposes and principles of the United Nations.

Article 30

Nothing in this Declaration may be interpreted as implying for any State, group or person any right to engage in any activity or to perform any act aimed at the destruction of any of the rights and freedoms set forth herein.

Chapter 13

Ronald Dworkin

TAKING RIGHTS SERIOUSLY

Ronald Dworkin (1931–) is a professor of jurisprudence at University College London and the New York University School of Law, and has written widely on both theoretical and practical philosophical issues in the law. This essay, taken from his book *Taking Rights Seriously* (1977), discusses the practical importance of rights, and explores the implications of rights theories for two questions: (1) whether citizens ever have the moral right to break the law, and (2) how a legal regime should deal with the fact that there is significant controversy regarding which rights people do and do not have.

1. The Rights of Citizens

The language of rights now dominates political debate in the United States. Does the Government respect the moral and political rights of its citizens? Or does the Government's foreign policy, or its race policy, fly in the face of these rights? Do the minorities whose rights have been violated have the right to violate the law in return? Or does the silent majority itself have rights, including the right that those who break the law be punished? It is not surprising that these questions are now prominent. The concept of rights, and particularly the concept of rights against the Government, has its most natural use when a political society is divided, and appeals to co-operation or a common goal are pointless.

The debate does not include the issue of whether citizens have *some* moral rights against their Government. It seems accepted on all sides that they do. Conventional lawyers and politi-cians take it as a point of pride that our legal system recognizes, for example, individual rights of free speech, equality, and due process. They base their claim that our law deserves respect, at least in part, on that fact, for they would not claim that totalitarian systems deserve the same loyalty.

Some philosophers, of course, reject the idea that citizens have rights apart from what the law happens to give them. Bentham thought that the idea of moral rights was 'nonsense on stilts'. But that view has never been part of our ortho-dox political theory, and politicians of both parties appeal to the rights of the people of justify a great part of what they want to do. I shall not be concerned, in this essay, to defend the thesis that citizens have moral rights against their governments; I want instead to explore the implications of that thesis for those, including the present United States Government, who profess to accept it.

It is much in dispute, of course, what *particular*

rights citizens have. Does the acknowledged right to free speech, for example, include the right to participate in nuisance demonstrations? In practice the Government will have the last word on what an individual's rights are, because its police will do what its officials and courts say. But that does not mean that the Government's view is necessarily the correct view; anyone who thinks it does must believe that men and women have only such moral rights as Government chooses to grant, which means that they have no moral rights at all.

All this is sometimes obscured in the United States by the constitutional system. The American Constitution provides a set of individual *legal* rights in the First Amendment, and in the due process, equal protection, and similar clauses. Under present legal practice the Supreme Court has the power to declare an act of Congress or of a state legislature void if the Court finds that the act offends these provisions. This practice has led some commentators to suppose that individual moral rights are fully protected by this system, but that is hardly so, nor could it be so.

The Constitution fuses legal and moral issues, by making the validity of a law depend on the answer to complex moral problems, like the problem of whether a particular statute respects the inherent equality of all men. This fusion has important consequences for the debates about civil disobedience. . . . But it leaves open two prominent questions. It does not tell us whether the Constitution, even properly interpreted, recognizes all the moral rights that citizens have, and it does not tell us whether, as many suppose, citizens would have a duty to obey the law even if it did invade their moral rights.

Both questions become crucial when some minority claims moral rights which the law denies, like the right to run its local school system, and which lawyers agree are not protected by the Constitution. The second question becomes crucial when, as now, the majority is sufficiently aroused so that Constitutional amendments to eliminate rights, like the right against self-incrimination, are seriously proposed. It is also crucial in nations, like the United Kingdom, that have no constitution of a comparable nature.

Even if the Constitution were perfect, of course, and the majority left it alone, it would not follow that the Supreme Court could guarantee the individual rights of citizens. A Supreme Court decision is still a legal decision, and it must take into account precedent and institutional considerations like relations between the Court and Congress, as well as morality. And no judicial decision is necessarily the right decision. Judges stand for different positions on controversial issues of law and morals and, as the fights over Nixon's Supreme Court nominations showed, a President is entitled to appoint judges of his own persuasion, provided that they are honest and capable.

So, though the constitutional system adds something to the protection of moral rights against the Government, it falls far short of guaranteeing these rights, or even establishing what they are. It means that, on some occasions, a department other than the legislature has the last word on these issues, which can hardly satisfy someone who thinks such a department profoundly wrong.

It is of course inevitable that some department of government will have the final say on what law will be enforced. When men disagree about moral rights, there will be no way for either side to prove its case, and some decision must stand if there is not to be anarchy. But that piece of orthodox wisdom must be the beginning and not the end of a philosophy of legislation and enforcement. If we cannot insist that the Government reach the right answers about the rights of its citizens, we can insist at least that it try. We can insist that it take rights seriously, follow a coherent theory of what these rights are, and act consistently with its own professions. I shall try to show what that means, and how it bears on the present political debates.

2. Rights and the Right to Break the Law

I shall start with the most violently argued issue. Does an American ever have the moral right to break a law? Suppose someone admits a law is valid; does he therefore have a duty to obey it? Those who try to give an answer seem to fall into two camps. The conservatives, as I shall call them, seem to disapprove of any act of disobedience; they appear satisfied when such acts are prosecuted, and disappointed when convictions are reversed. The other group, the liberals, are much more sympathetic to at least some cases of disobedience; they sometimes disapprove of prosecutions and celebrate acquittals. If we look beyond these emotional reactions, however, and pay attention to the arguments the two parties use, we discover an astounding fact. Both groups give essentially the same answer to the question of principle that supposedly divides them.

The answer that both parties give is this. In a democracy, or at least a democracy that in principle respects individual rights, each citizen has a general moral duty to obey all the laws, even though he would like some of them changed. He owes that duty to his fellow citizens, who obey laws that they do not like, to his benefit. But this general duty cannot be an absolute duty, because even a society that is in principle just may produce unjust laws and policies, and a man has duties other than his duties to the State. A man must honour his duties to his God and to his conscience, and if these conflict with his duty to the State, then he is entitled, in the end, to do what he judges to be right. If he decides that he must break the law, however, then he must submit to the judgment and punishment that the State imposes, in recognition of the fact that his duty to his fellow citizens was overwhelmed but not extinguished by his religious or moral obligation.

Of course this common answer can be elaborated in very different ways. Some would describe the duty to the State as fundamental, and picture the dissenter as a religious or moral fanatic. Others would describe the duty to the State in grudging terms, and picture those who oppose it as moral heroes. But these are differences in tone, and the position I described represents, I think, the view of most of those who find themselves arguing either for or against civil disobedience in particular cases.

I do not claim that it is everyone's view. There must be some who put the duty to the State so high that they do not grant that it can ever be overcome. There are certainly some who would deny that a man ever has a moral duty to obey the law, at least in the United States today. But these two extreme positions are the slender tails of a bell curve, and all those who fall in between hold the orthodox position I described – that men have a duty to obey the law but have the right to follow their consciences when it conflicts with that duty.

But if that is so, then we have a paradox in the fact that men who give the same answer to a question of principle should seem to disagree so much, and to divide so fiercely, in particular cases. The paradox goes even deeper, for each party, in at least some cases, takes a position that seems flatly inconsistent with the theoretical position they both accept. This position was tested, for example, when someone evaded the draft on grounds of conscience, or encouraged others to commit this crime. Conservatives argued that such men must be prosecuted, even though they are sincere. Why must they be prosecuted? Because society cannot tolerate the decline in respect for the law that their act constitutes and encourages. They must be prosecuted, in short, to discourage them and others like them from doing what they have done.

But there seems to be a monstrous contradiction here. If a man has a right to do what his conscience tells him he must, then how can the State be justified in discouraging him from doing it? Is it not wicked for a state to forbid and punish what it acknowledges that men have a right to do?

Moreover, it is not just conservatives who argue that those who break the law out of moral conviction should be prosecuted. The liberal is notoriously opposed to allowing racist school officials to go slow on desegregation, even though he acknowledges that these school officials think they have a moral right to do what the law forbids. The liberal does not often argue, it is true, that the desegregation laws must be enforced to encourage general respect for law. He argues instead that the desegregation laws must be enforced because they are right. But his position also seems inconsistent: can it be right to prosecute men for doing what their conscience requires, when we acknowledge their right to follow their conscience?

We are therefore left with two puzzles. How can two parties to an issue of principle, each of which thinks it is in profound disagreement with the other, embrace the same position on that issue? How can it be that each side urges solutions to particular problems which seem flatly to contradict the position of principle that both accept? One possible answer is that some or all of those who accept the common position are hypocrites, paying lip service to rights of conscience which in fact they do not grant.

There is some plausibility in this charge. A sort of hypocrisy must have been involved when public officials who claim to respect conscience denied Muhammad Ali the right to box in their states. If Ali, in spite of his religious scruples, had joined the Army, he would have been allowed to box even though, on the principles these officials say they honour, he would have been a worse human being for having done so. But there are few cases that seem so straightforward as this one, and even here the officials did not seem to recognize the contradiction between their acts and their principles. So we must search for some explanation beyond the truth that men often do not mean what they say.

The deeper explanation lies in a set of confusions that often embarrass arguments about rights. These confusions have clouded all the issues I mentioned at the outset and have crippled attempts to develop a coherent theory of how a government that respects rights must behave.

In order to explain this, I must call attention to the fact, familiar to philosophers, but often ignored in political debate, that the word 'right' has different force in different contexts. In most cases when we say that someone has 'right' to do something, we imply that it would be wrong to interfere with his doing it, or at least that some special grounds are needed for justifying any interference. I use this strong sense of right when I say that you have the right to spend your money gambling, if you wish, though you ought to spend it in a more worthwhile way. I mean that it would be wrong for anyone to interfere with you even though you propose to spend your money in a way that I think is wrong.

There is a clear difference between saying that someone has a right to do something in this sense and saying that it is the 'right' thing for him to do, or that he does no 'wrong' in doing it. Someone may have the right to do something that is the wrong thing for him to do, as might be the case with gambling. Conversely, something may be the right thing for him to do and yet he may have no right to do it, in the sense that it would not be wrong for someone to interfere with his trying. If our army captures an enemy soldier, we might say that the right thing for him to do is to try to escape, but it would not follow that it is wrong for us to try to stop him. We might admire him for trying to escape, and perhaps even think less of him if he did not. But there is no suggestion here that it is wrong of us to stand in his way; on the contrary, if we think our cause is just, we think it right for us to do all we can to stop him.

Ordinarily this distinction, between the issues of whether a man has a right to do something and whether it is the right thing for him to do, causes no trouble. But sometimes it does, because sometimes we say that a man has a right to do something when we mean only to deny that it is the wrong thing for him to do. Thus we say that the captured soldier has a 'right' to try to escape when we mean, not that we do wrong to stop him, but that he has no duty not to make the attempt. We use 'right' this way when we speak of someone having the 'right' to act on his own principles, or the 'right' to follow his own conscience. We mean that he does no wrong to proceed on his honest convictions, even though we disagree with these convictions, and even though, for policy or other reasons, we must force him to act contrary to them.

Suppose a man believes that welfare payments to the poor are profoundly wrong, because they sap enterprise, and so declares his full income-tax each year but declines to pay half of it. We might say that he has a right to refuse to pay, if he wishes, but that the Government has a right to proceed against him for the full tax, and to fine or jail him for late payment if that is necessary to keep the collection system working efficiently. We do not take this line in most cases; we do not say that the ordinary thief has a right to steal, if he wishes, so long as he pays the penalty. We say a man has the right to break the law, even though the State has a right to punish him, only when we think that, because of his convictions, he does no wrong in doing so.[1]

These distinctions enable us to see an ambiguity in the orthodox question: Does a man ever have a right to break the law? Does that question mean to ask whether he ever has a right to break the law in the strong sense, so that the Government would do wrong to stop him, by arresting and prosecuting him? Or does it mean to ask whether he ever does the right thing to break the law, so that we should all respect him even though the Government should jail him?

If we take the orthodox position to be an answer to the first – and most important – question, then the paradoxes I described arise. But if we take it as an answer to the second, they do not. Conservatives and liberals do agree that sometimes a man does not do the wrong thing to break a law, when his conscience so requires.

They disagree, when they do, over the different issue of what the State's response should be. Both parties do think that sometimes the State should prosecute. But this is not inconsistent with the proposition that the man prosecuted did the right thing in breaking the law.

The paradoxes seem genuine because the two questions are not usually distinguished, and the orthodox position is presented as a general solution to the problem of civil disobedience. But once the distinction is made, it is apparent that the position has been so widely accepted only because, when it is applied, it is treated as an answer to the second question but not the first. The crucial distinction is obscured by the troublesome idea of a right to conscience; this idea has been at the centre of most recent discussions of political obligation, but it is a red herring drawing us away from the crucial political questions. The state of a man's conscience may be decisive, or central, when the issue is whether he does something morally wrong in breaking the law; but it need not be decisive or even central when the issue is whether he has a right, in the strong sense of that term, to do so. A man does not have the right, in that sense, to do whatever his conscience demands, but he may have the right, in that sense, to do something even though his conscience does not demand it.

If that is true, then there has been almost no serious attempt to answer the questions that almost everyone means to ask. We can make a fresh start by stating these questions more clearly. Does an American ever have the right, in a strong sense, to do something which is against the law? If so, when? In order to answer these questions put in that way, we must try to become clearer about the implications of the idea, mentioned earlier, that citizens have at least some rights against their government.

I said that in the United States citizens are supposed to have certain fundamental rights against their Government, certain moral rights made into legal rights by the Constitution. If this idea is significant, and worth bragging about, then these rights must be rights in the strong sense I just described. The claim that citizens have a right to free speech must imply that it would be wrong for the Government to stop them from speaking, even when the Government believes that what they will say will cause more harm than good. The claim cannot mean, on the prisoner-of-war analogy, only that citizens do no wrong in speaking their minds, though the Government reserves the right to prevent them from doing so.

This is a crucial point, and I want to labour it. Of course a responsible government must be ready to justify anything it does, particularly when it limits the liberty of its citizens. But normally it is a sufficient justification, even for an act that limits liberty, that the act is calculated to increase what the philosophers call general utility – that it is calculated to produce more over-all benefit than harm. So, though the New York City government needs a justification for forbidding motorists to drive up Lexington Avenue, it is sufficient justification if the proper officials believe, on sound evidence, that the gain to the many will outweigh the inconvenience to the few. When individual citizens are said to have rights against the Government, however, like the right of free speech, that must mean that this sort of justification is not enough. Otherwise the claim would not argue that individuals have special protection against the law when their rights are in play, and that is just the point of the claim.

Not all legal rights, or even Constitutional rights, represent moral rights against the Government. I now have the legal right to drive either way on Fifty-seventh Street, but the Government would do no wrong to make that street one-way if it thought it in the general interest to do so. I have a Constitutional right to vote for a congressman every two years, but the national and state governments would do no wrong if, following the amendment procedure, they made a congressman's term four years instead of two, again on the basis of a judgment that this would be for the general good.

But those Constitutional rights that we call fundamental like the right of free speech, are supposed to represent rights against the Government in the strong sense; that is the point of the boast that our legal system respects the fundamental rights of the citizen. If citizens have a moral right of free speech, then governments would do wrong to repeal the First Amendment that guarantees it, even if they were persuaded that the majority would be better off if speech were curtailed.

I must not overstate the point. Someone who claims that citizens have a right against the Government need not go so far as to say that the State is *never* justified in overriding that right. He might say, for example, that although citizens have a right to free speech, the Government may override that right when necessary to protect the rights of others, or to prevent a catastrophe, or even to obtain a clear and major public benefit (though if he acknowledged this last as a possible justification he would be treating the right in question as not among the most important or fundamental). What he cannot do is to say that the Government is justified in overriding a right on the minimal grounds that would be sufficient if no such right existed. He cannot say that the Government is entitled to act on no more than a judgment that its act is likely to produce, overall, a benefit to the community. That admission would make his claim of a right pointless, and would show him to be using some sense of 'right' other than the strong sense necessary to give his claim the political importance it is normally taken to have.

But then the answers to our two questions about disobedience seem plain, if unorthodox. In our society a man does sometimes have the right, in the strong sense, to disobey a law. He had that right whenever that law wrongly invades his rights against the Government. If he has a moral right to free speech, that is, then he has a moral right to break any law that the Government, by virtue of his right, had no right to adopt. The right to disobey the law is not a separate right, having something thing to do with conscience, additional to other rights against the Government. It is simply a feature of these rights against the Government, and it cannot be denied in principle without denying that any such rights exist.

These answers seem obvious once we take rights against the Government to be rights in the strong sense I described. If I have a right to speak my mind on political issues, then the Government does wrong to make it illegal for me to do so, even if it thinks this is in the general interest. If, nevertheless, the Government does make my act illegal, then it does a further wrong to enforce that law against me. My right against the Government means that it is wrong for the Government to stop me from speaking; the Government cannot make it right to stop me just by taking the first step.

This does not, of course, tell us exactly what rights men do have against the Government. It does not tell us whether the right of free speech includes the right of demonstration. But it does mean that passing a law cannot affect such rights as men do have, and that is of crucial importance, because it dictates the attitude that an individual is entitled to take toward his personal decision when civil disobedience is in question.

Both conservatives and liberals suppose that in a society which is generally decent everyone has a duty to obey the law, whatever it is. That is the source of the 'general duty' clause in the orthodox position, and though liberals believe that this duty can sometimes be 'overridden', even they suppose, as the orthodox position maintains, that the duty of obedience remains in some submerged form, so that a man does well to accept punishment in recognition of that duty. But this general duty is almost incoherent in a society that recognizes rights. If a man believes he has a right to demonstrate, then he must believe that it would be wrong for the Government to stop him, with or without benefit of a law. If he is entitled to believe that, then it is silly to speak of a duty to obey the law as such, or

of a duty to accept the punishment that the State has no right to give.

Conservatives will object to the short work I have made of their point. They will argue that even if the Government was wrong to adopt some law, like a law limiting speech, there are independent reasons why the Government is justified in enforcing the law once adopted. When the law forbids demonstration, then, so they argue, some principle more important than the individual's right to speak is brought into play, namely the principle of respect for law. If a law, even a bad law, is left unenforced, then respect for law is weakened, and society as a whole suffers. So an individual loses his moral right to speak when speech is made criminal, and the Government must, for the common good and for the general benefit, enforce the law against him.

But this argument, though popular, is plausible only if we forget what it means to say that an individual has a right against the State. It is far from plain that civil disobedience lowers respect for law, but even if we suppose that it does, this fact is irrelevant. The prospect of utilitarian gains cannot justify preventing a man from doing what he has a right to do, and the supposed gains in respect for law are simply utilitarian gains. There would be no point in the boast that we respect individual rights unless that involved some sacrifice, and the sacrifice in question must be that we give up whatever marginal benefits our country would receive from overriding these rights when they prove inconvenient. So the general benefit cannot be a good ground for abridging rights, even when the benefit in question is a heightened respect for law.

But perhaps I do wrong to assume that the argument about respect for law is only an appeal to general utility. I said that a state may be justified in overriding or limiting rights on other grounds, and we must ask, before rejecting the conservative position, whether any of these apply. The most important – and least well understood – of these other grounds invokes the notion of *competing rights* that would be jeopardized if the right in question were not limited. Citizens have personal rights to the State's protection as well as personal rights to be free from the State's interference, and it may be necessary for the Government to choose between these two sorts of rights. The law of defamation, for example, limits the personal right of any man to say what he thinks, because it requires him to have good grounds for what he says. But this law is justified, even for those who think that it does invade a personal right, by the fact that it protects the right of others not to have their reputations ruined by a careless statement.

The individual rights that our society acknowledges often conflict in this way, and when they do it is the job of government to discriminate. If the Government makes the right choice, and protects the more important at the cost of the less, then it has not weakened or cheapened the notion of a right; on the contrary it would have done so had it failed to protect the more important of the two. So we must acknowledge that the Government has a reason for limiting rights if it plausibly believes that a competing right is more important.

May the conservative seize on this fact? He might argue that I did wrong to characterize his argument as one that appeals to the general benefit, because it appeals instead to competing rights, namely the moral right of the majority to have its laws enforced, or the right of society to maintain the degree of order and security it wishes. These are the rights, he would say, that must be weighed against the individual's right to do what the wrongful law prohibits.

But this new argument is confused, because it depends on yet another ambiguity in the language of rights. It is true that we speak of the 'right' of society to do what it wants, but this cannot be a 'competing right' of the sort that may justify the invasion of a right against the Government. The existence of rights against the Government would be jeopardized if the Government were able to defeat such a right by appealing to the right of a democratic majority to work its will. A right against the Government must be a right to do something even when the majority thinks it would be wrong to do it, and even when the majority would be worse off for having it done. If we now say that society has a right to do whatever is in the general benefit, or the right to preserve whatever sort of environment the majority wishes to live in, and we mean that these are the sort of rights that provide justification for overruling any rights against the Government that may conflict, then we have annihilated the latter rights.

In order to save them, we must recognize as competing rights only the rights of other members of the society as individuals. We must distinguish the 'rights' of the majority as such, which cannot count as a justification for overruling individual rights, and the personal rights of members of a majority, which might well count. The test we must use is this. Someone has a competing right to protection, which must be weighed against an individual right to act, if that person would be entitled to demand that protection from his government on his own title, as an individual, without regard to whether a majority of his fellow citizens joined in the demand.

It cannot be true, on this test, that anyone has a right to have all the laws of the nation enforced. He has a right to have enforced only those criminal laws, for example, that he would have a right to have enacted if they were not already law. The laws against personal assault may well fall into that class. If the physically vulnerable members of the community – those who need police protection against personal violence – were only a small minority, it would still seem plausible to say that they were entitled to that protection. But the laws that provide a certain level of quiet in public places, or that authorize and finance a foreign war, cannot be thought to rest on individual rights. The timid lady on the streets of Chicago is not entitled to just the degree of quiet that now obtains, nor is she entitled to have boys drafted to fight in wars she approves. There are laws – perhaps desirable laws – that provide these advantages for her, but the justification for these laws, if they can be justified at all, is the common desire of a large majority, not her personal right. If, therefore, these laws do abridge someone else's moral right to protest, or his right to personal security, she cannot urge a competing right to justify the abridgement. She has no personal right to have such laws passed, and she has no competing right to have them enforced either.

So the conservative cannot advance his argument much on the ground of competing rights, but he may want to use another ground. A government, he may argue, may be justified in abridging the personal rights of its citizens in an emergency, or when a very great loss may be prevented, or perhaps, when some major benefit can clearly be secured. If the nation is at war, a policy of censorship may be justified even though it invades the right to say what one thinks on matters of political controversy. But the emergency must be genuine. There must be what Oliver Wendell Holmes described as a clear and present danger, and the danger must be one of magnitude.

Can the conservative argue that when any law is passed, even a wrongful law, this sort of justification is available for enforcing it? His argument might be something of this sort. If the Government once acknowledges that it may be wrong – that the legislature might have adopted, the executive approved, and the courts left standing, a law that in fact abridges important rights – then this admission will lead not simply to a marginal decline in respect for law, but to a crisis of order. Citizens may decide to obey only those laws they personally approve, and that is anarchy. So the Government must insist that whatever a citizen's rights may be before a law is passed and upheld by the courts, his rights thereafter are determined by that law.

But this argument ignores the primitive distinction between what may happen and what will happen. If we allow speculation to support

the justification of emergency or decisive benefit, then, again, we have annihilated rights. We must, as Learned Hand said, discount the gravity of the evil threatened by the likelihood of reaching that evil. I know of no genuine evidence to the effect that tolerating some civil disobedience, out of respect for the moral position of its authors, will increase such disobedience, let alone crime in general. The case that it will must be based on vague assumptions about the contagion of ordinary crimes, assumptions that are themselves unproved, and that are in any event largely irrelevant. It seems at least as plausible to argue that tolerance will increase respect for officials and for the bulk of the laws they promulgate, or at least retard the rate of growing disrespect.

If the issue were simply the question whether the community would be marginally better off under strict law enforcement, then the Government would have to decide on the evidence we have, and it might not be unreasonable to decide, on balance, that it would. But since rights are at stake, the issue is the very different one of whether tolerance would destroy the community or threaten it with great harm, and it seems to me simply mindless to suppose that the evidence makes that probable or even conceivable.

The argument from emergency is confused in another way as well. It assumes that the Government must take the position either that a man never has the right to break the law, or that he always does. I said that any society that claims to recognize rights at all must abandon the notion of a general duty to obey the law that holds in all cases. This is important, because it shows that there are no short cuts to meeting a citizen's claim to right. If a citizen argues that he has a moral right not to serve in the Army, or to protest in a way he finds effective, then an official who wants to answer him, and not simply bludgeon him into obedience, must respond to the particular point he makes, and cannot point to the draft law or a Supreme Court decision as having even special, let alone decisive, weight.

Sometimes an official who considers the citizen's moral arguments in good faith will be persuaded that the citizen's claim is plausible, or even right. It does not follow, however, that he will always be persuaded or that he always should be.

I must emphasize that all these propositions concern the strong sense of right, and they therefore leave open important questions about the right thing to do. If a man believes he has the right to break the law, he must then ask whether he does the right thing to exercise that right. He must remember that reasonable men can differ about whether he has a right against the Government, and therefore the right to break the law, that he thinks he has; and therefore that reasonable men can oppose him in good faith. He must take into account the various consequences his acts will have, whether they involve violence, and such other considerations as the context makes relevant; he must not go beyond the rights he can in good faith claim, to acts that violate the rights of others.

On the other hand, if some official, like a prosecutor, believes that the citizen does *not* have the right to break the law, then *he* must ask whether he does the right thing to enforce it. . . . [C]ertain features of our legal system, and in particular the fusion of legal and moral issues in our Constitution, mean that citizens often do the right thing in exercising what they take to be moral rights to break the law, and that prosecutors often do the right thing in failing to prosecute them for it. . . . I want to ask whether the requirement that Government take its citizens' rights seriously has anything to do with the crucial question of what these rights are.

3. Controversial Rights

The argument so far has been hypothetical: if a man has a particular moral right against the Government, that right survives contrary legislation or adjudication. But this does not tell us what rights he has, and it is notorious that reasonable

men disagree about that. There is wide agreement on certain clearcut cases; almost everyone who believes in rights at all would admit, for example, that a man has a moral right to speak his mind in a non-provocative way on matters of political concern, and that this is an important right that the State must go to great pains to protect. But there is great controversy as to the limits of such paradigm rights, and the so-called 'anti-riot' law involved in the famous Chicago Seven trial of the last decade is a case in point.

The defendants were accused of conspiring to cross state lines with the intention of causing a riot. This charge is vague – perhaps unconstitutionally vague – but the law apparently defines as criminal emotional speeches which argue that violence is justified in order to secure political equality. Does the right of free speech protect this sort of speech? That, of course, is a legal issue, because it invokes the free-speech clause of the First Amendment of the Constitution. But it is also a moral issue, because, as I said, we must treat the First Amendment as an attempt to protect a moral right. It is part of the job of governing to 'define' moral rights through statutes and judicial decisions, that is, to declare officially the extent that moral rights will be taken to have in law. Congress faced this task in voting on the anti-riot bill, and the Supreme Court has faced it in countless cases. How should the different departments of government go about defining moral rights?

They should begin with a sense that whatever they decide might be wrong. History and their descendants may judge that they acted unjustly when they thought they were right. If they take their duty seriously, they must try to limit their mistakes, and they must therefore try to discover where the dangers of mistake lie.

They might choose one of two very different models for this purpose. The first model recommends striking a balance between the rights of the individual and the demands of society at large. If the Government *infringes* on a moral right (for example, by defining the right of free speech more narrowly than justice requires), then it has done the individual a wrong. On the other hand, if the Government *inflates* a right (by defining it more broadly than justice requires) then it cheats society of some general benefit, like safe streets, that there is no reason it should not have. So a mistake on one side is as serious as a mistake on the other. The course of government is to steer to the middle, to balance the general good and personal rights, giving to each its due.

When the Government, or any of its branches, defines a right, it must bear in mind, according to the first model, the social cost of different proposals and make the necessary adjustments. It must not grant the same freedom to noisy demonstrations as it grants to calm political discussion, for example, because the former causes much more trouble than the latter. Once it decides how much of a right to recognize, it must enforce its decision to the full. That means permitting an individual to act within his rights, as the Government has defined them, but not beyond, so that if anyone breaks the law, even on grounds of conscience, he must be punished. No doubt any government will make mistakes, and will regret decisions once taken. That is inevitable. But this middle policy will ensure that errors on one side will balance out errors on the other over the long run.

The first model, described in this way, has great plausibility, and most laymen and lawyers, I think, would respond to it warmly. The metaphor of balancing the public interest against personal claims is established in our political and judicial rhetoric, and this metaphor gives the model both familiarity and appeal. Nevertheless, the first model is a false one, certainly in the case of rights generally regarded as important, and the metaphor is the heart of its error.

The institution of rights against the Government is not a gift of God, or an ancient ritual, or a national sport. It is a complex and troublesome practice that makes the Government's job of securing the general benefit more difficult and more expensive, and it would be a frivolous and wrongful practice unless it served some point. Anyone who professes to take rights seriously, and who praises our Government for respecting them, must have some sense of what that point is. He must accept, at the minimum, one or both of two important ideas. The first is the vague but powerful idea of human dignity. This idea, associated with Kant, but defended by philosophers of different schools, supposes that there are ways of treating a man that are inconsistent with recognizing him as a full member of the human community, and holds that such treatment is profoundly unjust.

The second is the more familiar idea of political equality. This supposes that the weaker members of a political community are entitled to the same concern and respect of their government as the more powerful members have secured for themselves, so that if some men have freedom of decision whatever the effect on the general good, then all men must have the same freedom. I do not want to defend or elaborate these ideas here, but only to insist that anyone who claims that citizens have rights must accept ideas very close to these.

It makes sense to say that a man has a fundamental right against the Government, in the strong sense, like free speech, if that right is necessary to protect his dignity, or his standing as equally entitled to concern and respect, or some other personal value of like consequence. It does not make sense otherwise.

So if rights make sense at all, then the invasion of a relatively important right must be a very serious matter. It means treating a man as less than a man, or as less worthy of concern than other men. The institution of rights rests on the conviction that this is a grave injustice, and that it is worth paying the incremental cost in social policy or efficiency that is necessary to prevent it. But then it must be wrong to say that inflating rights is as serious as invading them. If the Government errs on the side of the individual, then it simply pays a little more in social efficiency than it has to pay; it pays a little more, that is, of the same coin that it has already decided must be spent. But if it errs against the individual it inflicts an insult upon him that, on its own reckoning, it is worth a great deal of that coin to avoid.

So the first model is indefensible. It rests, in fact, on a mistake I discussed earlier, namely the confusion of society's rights with the rights of members of society. 'Balancing' is appropriate when the Government must choose between competing claims of right – between the Southerner's claim to freedom of association, for example, and the black man's claim to an equal education. Then the Government can do nothing but estimate the merits of the competing claims, and act on its estimate. The first model assumes that the 'right' of the majority is a competing right that must be balanced in this way; but that, as I argued before, is a confusion that threatens to destroy the concept of individual rights. It is worth noticing that the community rejects the first model in that area where the stakes for the individual are highest, the criminal process. We say that it is better that a great many guilty men go free than that one innocent man be punished, and that homily rests on the choice of the second model for government.

The second model treats abridging a right as much more serious than inflating one, and its recommendations follow from that judgment. It stipulates that once a right is recognized in clear-cut cases, then the Government should act to cut off that right only when some compelling reason is presented, some reason that is consistent with the suppositions on which the original right must be based. It cannot be an argument for curtailing a right, once granted, simply that society would pay a further price for extending it. There must be something special about that further cost, or there must be some other feature of the case, that makes it sensible to say that although great social cost is warranted to protect the original right, this particular cost is not necessary. Otherwise, the Government's failure

to extend the right will show that its recognition of the right in the original case is a sham, a promise that it intends to keep only until that becomes inconvenient.

How can we show that a particular cost is not worth paying without taking back the initial recognition of a right? I can think of only three sorts of grounds that can consistently be used to limit the definition of a particular right. First, the Government might show that the values protected by the original right are not really at stake in the marginal case, or are at stake only in some attenuated form. Second, it might show that if the right is defined to include the marginal case, then some competing right, in the strong sense I described earlier, would be abridged. Third, it might show that if the right were so defined, then the cost to society would not be simply incremental, but would be of a degree far beyond the cost paid to grant the original right, a degree great enough to justify whatever assault on dignity or equality might be involved.

It is fairly easy to apply these grounds to one group of problems the Supreme Court faced, imbedded in constitutional issues. The draft law provided an exemption for conscientious objectors, but this exemption, as interpreted by the draft boards, has been limited to those who object to *all* wars on *religious* grounds. If we suppose that the exemption is justified on the ground that an individual has a moral right not to kill in violation of his own principles, then the question is raised whether it is proper to exclude those whose morality is not based on religion, or whose morality is sufficiently complex to distinguish among wars. The Court held, as a matter of Constitutional law, that the draft boards were wrong to exclude the former, but competent to exclude the latter.

None of the three grounds I listed can justify either of these exclusions as a matter of political morality. The invasion of personality in forcing men to kill when they believe killing immoral is just as great when these beliefs are based on secular grounds, or take account of the fact that wars differ in morally relevant ways, and there is no pertinent difference in competing rights or in national emergency. There are differences among the cases, of course, but they are insufficient to justify the distinction. A government that is secular on principle cannot prefer a religious to a non-religious morality as such. There are utilitarian arguments in favour of limiting the exception to religious or universal grounds – an exemption so limited may be less expensive to administer, and may allow easier discrimination between sincere and insincere applicants. But these utilitarian reasons are irrelevant, because they cannot count as grounds for limiting a right.

What about the anti-riot law, as applied in the Chicago trial? Does the law represent an improper limitation of the right to free speech, supposedly protected by the First Amendment? If we were to apply the first model for government to this issue, the argument for the anti-riot law would look strong. But if we set aside talk of balancing as inappropriate, and turn to the proper grounds for limiting a right, then the argument becomes a great deal weaker. The original right of free speech must suppose that it is an assault on human personality to stop a man from expressing what he honestly believes, particularly on issues affecting how he is governed. Surely the assault is greater, and not less, when he is stopped from expressing those principles of political morality that he holds most passionately, in the face of what he takes to be outrageous violations of these principles.

It may be said that the anti-riot law leaves him free to express these principles in a non-provocative way. But that misses the point of the connection between expression and dignity. A man cannot express himself freely when he cannot match his rhetoric to his outrage, or when he must trim his sails to protect values he counts as nothing next to those he is trying to vindicate. It is true that some political dissenters speak in ways that shock the majority, but it is arrogant for the majority to suppose that the orthodox

methods of expression are the proper ways to speak, for this is a denial of equal concern and respect. If the point of the right is to protect the dignity of dissenters, then we must make judgments about appropriate speech with the personalities of the dissenters in mind, not the personality of the 'silent' majority for whom the anti-riot law is no restraint at all.

So the argument fails, that the personal values protected by the original right are less at stake in this marginal case. We must consider whether competing rights, or some grave threat to society, nevertheless justify the anti-riot law. We can consider these two grounds together, because the only plausible competing rights are rights to be free from violence, and violence is the only plausible threat to society that the context provides.

I have no right to burn your house, or stone you or your car, or swing a bicycle chain against your skull, even if I find these to be natural means of expression. But the defendants in the Chicago trial were not accused of direct violence; the argument runs that the acts of speech they planned made it likely that others would do acts of violence, either in support of or out of hostility to what they said. Does this provide a justification?

The question would be different if we could say with any confidence how much and what sort of violence the anti-riot law might be expected to prevent. Will it save two lives a year, or two hundred, or two thousand? Two thousand dollars of property, or two hundred thousand, or two million? No one can say, not simply because prediction is next to impossible, but because we have no firm understanding of the process by which demonstration disintegrates into riot, and in particular of the part played by inflammatory speech, as distinct from poverty, police brutality, blood lust, and all the rest of human and economic failure. The Government must try, of course, to reduce the violent waste of lives and property, but it must recognize that any attempt to locate and remove a cause of riot, short of a reorganization of society, must be an exercise in speculation, trial, and error. It must make its decisions under conditions of high uncertainty, and the institution of rights, taken seriously, limits its freedom to experiment under such conditions.

It forces the Government to bear in mind that preventing a man from speaking or demonstrating offers him a certain and profound insult, in return for a speculative benefit that may in any event be achieved in other if more expensive ways. When lawyers say that rights may be limited to protect other rights, or to prevent catastrophe, they have in mind cases in which cause and effect are relatively clear, like the familiar example of a man falsely crying 'Fire!' in a crowded theater.

But the Chicago story shows how obscure the causal connections can become. Were the speeches of Hoffman or Rubin necessary conditions of the riot? Or had thousands of people come to Chicago for the purposes of rioting anyway, as the Government also argues? Were they in any case sufficient conditions? Or could the police have contained the violence if they had not been so busy contributing to it, as the staff of the President's Commission on Violence said they were?

These are not easy questions, but if rights mean anything, then the Government cannot simply assume answers that justify its conduct. If a man has a right to speak, if the reasons that support that right extend to provocative political speech, and if the effects of such speech on violence are unclear, then the Government is not entitled to make its first attack on that problem by denying that right. It may be that abridging the right to speak is the least expensive course, or the least damaging to police morale, or the most popular politically. But these are utilitarian arguments in favor of starting one place rather than another, and such arguments are ruled out by the concept of rights.

This point may be obscured by the popular belief that political activists look forward to violence and 'ask for trouble' in what they say. They can hardly complain, in the general view, if they are taken to be the authors of the violence they expect, and treated accordingly. But this repeats the confusion I tried to explain earlier between having a right and doing the right thing. The speaker's motives may be relevant in deciding whether he does the right thing in speaking passionately about issues that may inflame or enrage the audience. But if he has a right to speak, because the danger in allowing him to speak is speculative, his motives cannot count as independent evidence in the argument that justifies stopping him.

But what of the individual rights of those who will be destroyed by a riot, of the passer-by who will be killed by a sniper's bullet or the shopkeeper who will be ruined by looting? To put the issue in this way, as a question of competing rights, suggests a principle that would undercut the effect of uncertainty. Shall we say that some rights to protection are so important that the Government is justified in doing all it can to maintain them? Shall we therefore say that the Government may abridge the rights of others to act when their acts might simply increase the risk, by however slight or speculative a margin, that some person's right to life or property will be violated?

Some such principle is relied on by those who oppose the Supreme Court's recent liberal rulings on police procedure. These rulings increase the chance that a guilty man will go free, and therefore marginally increase the risk that any particular member of the community will be murdered, raped, or robbed. Some critics believe that the Court's decisions must therefore be wrong.

But no society that purports to recognize a variety of rights, on the ground that a man's dignity or equality may be invaded in a variety of ways, can accept such a principle. If forcing a man to testify against himself, or forbidding him to speak, does the damage that the rights against self-incrimination and the right of free speech assume, then it would be contemptuous for the State to tell a man that he must suffer this damage against the possibility that other men's risk of loss may be marginally reduced. If rights make sense, then the degrees of their importance cannot be so different that some count not at all when others are mentioned.

Of course the Government may discriminate and may stop a man from exercising his right to speak when there is a clear and substantial risk that his speech will do great damage to the person or property of others, and no other means of preventing this are at hand, as in the case of the man shouting 'Fire!' in a theater. But we must reject the suggested principle that the Government can simply ignore rights to speak when life and property are in question. So long as the impact of speech on these other rights remains speculative and marginal, it must look elsewhere for levers to pull.

4. Why Take Rights Seriously?

I said at the beginning of this essay that I wanted to show what a government must do that professes to recognize individual rights. It must dispense with the claim that citizens never have a right to break its law, and it must not define citizens' rights so that these are cut off for supposed reasons of the general good. Any Government's harsh treatment of civil disobedience, or campaign against vocal protest, may therefore be thought to count against its sincerity.

One might well ask, however, whether it is wise to take rights all that seriously after all. America's genius, at least in her own legend, lies in not taking any abstract doctrine to its logical extreme. It may be time to ignore abstractions, and concentrate instead on giving the majority of our citizens a new sense of their Government's concern for their welfare, and of their title to rule.

That, in any event, is what former Vice-President Agnew seemed to believe. In a policy statement on the issue of 'weirdos' and social misfits, he said that the liberals' concern for individual rights was a headwind blowing in the face of the ship of state. That is a poor metaphor, but the philosophical point it expresses is very well taken. He recognized, as many liberals do not, that the majority cannot travel as fast or as far as it would like if it recognizes the rights of individuals to do what, in the majority's terms, is the wrong thing to do.

Spiro Agnew supposed that rights are divisive, and that national unity and a new respect for law may be developed by taking them more skeptically. But he is wrong. America will continue to be divided by its social and foreign policy, and if the economy grows weaker again the divisions will become more bitter. If we want our laws and our legal institutions to provide the ground rules within which these issues will be contested then these ground rules must not be the conqueror's law that the dominant class imposes on the weaker, as Marx supposed the law of a capitalist society must be. The bulk of the law – that part which defines and implements social, economic, and foreign policy – cannot be neutral. It must state, in its greatest part, the majority's view of the common good. The institution of rights is therefore crucial, because it represents the majority's promise to the minorities that their dignity and equality will be respected. When the divisions among the groups are most violent, then this gesture, if law is to work, must be most sincere.

The institution requires an act of faith on the part of the minorities, because the scope of their rights will be controversial whenever they are important, and because the officers of the majority will act on their own notions of what these rights really are. Of course these officials will disagree with many of the claims that a minority makes. That makes it all the more important that they take their decisions gravely. They must show that they understand what rights are, and they must not cheat on the full implications of the doctrine. The Government will not re-establish respect for law without giving the law some claim to respect. It cannot do that if it neglects the one feature that distinguishes law from ordered brutality. If the Government does not take rights seriously, then it does not take law seriously either.

Note

1 It is not surprising that we sometimes use the concept of having a right to say that others must not interfere with an act and sometimes to say that the act is not the wrong thing to do. Often, when someone has *no* right to do something, like attacking another man physically, it is true *both* that it is the wrong thing to do and that others are entitled to stop it, by demand, if not by force. It is therefore natural to say that someone has a right when we mean to deny *either* of these consequences, as well as when we mean to deny both.

Chapter 14

Joel Feinberg

THE NATURE AND VALUE OF RIGHTS

Joel Feinberg (1926–2004) was one of the leading legal and political philosophers of the twentieth century, whose major work involved the development and critical evaluation of a theory of individual liberty inspired by John Stuart Mill. In this essay (published in 1970), Feinberg explores the significance of rights by asking us to imagine a world without them, and goes on to analyze rights in terms of a kind of valid claim which exists against the backdrop of some set of rules.

1

I would like to begin by conducting a thought experiment. Try to imagine Nowheresville – a world very much like our own except that no one, or hardly any one (the qualification is not important), has *rights*. If this flaw makes Nowheresville too ugly to hold very long in contemplation, we can make it as pretty as we wish in other moral respects. We can, for example, make the human beings in it as attractive and virtuous as possible without taxing our conceptions of the limits of human nature. In particular, let the virtues of moral sensibility flourish. Fill this imagined world with as much benevolence, compassion, sympathy, and pity as it will conveniently hold without strain. Now we can imagine men helping one another from compassionate motives merely, quite as much or even more than they do in our actual world from a variety of more complicated motives.

This picture, pleasant as it is in some respects, would hardly have satisfied Immanuel Kant. Benevolently motivated actions do good, Kant admitted, and therefore are better, *ceteris paribus*, than malevolently motivated actions; but no action can have supreme kind of worth – what Kant called "moral worth" – unless its whole motivating power derives from the thought that it is *required by duty*. Accordingly, let us try to make Nowheresville more appealing to Kant by introducing the idea of duty into it, and letting the sense of duty be a sufficient motive for many beneficent and honorable actions. But doesn't this bring our original thought experiment to an abortive conclusion? If duties are permitted entry into Nowheresville, are not rights necessarily smuggled in along with them?

The question is well-asked, and requires here a brief digression so that we might consider the so-called "doctrine of the logical correlativity of rights and duties." This is the doctrine that (i) all duties entail other people's rights and (ii) all rights entail other people's duties. Only the first part of the doctrine, the alleged entailment from duties to rights, need concern us here. Is this part of the doctrine correct? It should not be surprising that my answer is: "In a sense yes and in a sense no." Etymologically, the word "duty" is associated with actions that are *due* someone else, the payments of debts to creditors, the keeping of agreements with promisees, the payment of club dues, or legal fees, or tariff levies to appropriate authorities or their representatives. In this original sense of "duty," all duties are correlated with the rights of those to whom the duty is owed. On the other hand, there seem to be numerous classes of duties, both of a legal and non-legal kind, that are *not* logically correlated with the rights of other persons. This seems to be a consequence of the fact that the word "duty" has come to be used for *any* action understood to be *required*, whether by the rights of others, or by law, or by higher authority, or by conscience, or whatever. When the notion of requirement is in clear focus it is likely to seem the only element in the idea of duty that is essential, and the other component notion – that a duty is something *due* someone else – drops off. Thus, in this widespread but derivative usage, "duty" tends to be used for any action we feel we *must* (for whatever reason) do. It comes, in short, to be a term of moral modality merely; and it is no wonder that the first thesis of the logical correlativity doctrine often fails.

Let us then introduce duties into Nowheresville, but only in the sense of actions that are, or are believed to be, morally mandatory, but not in the older sense of actions that are due others and can be claimed by others as their right. Nowheresville now can have duties of the sort imposed by positive law. A legal duty is not something we are implored or advised to do merely; it is something the law, or an authority under the law, *requires* us to do whether we want to or not, under pain of penalty. When traffic lights turn red, however, there is no determinate person who can plausibly be said to claim our stopping as his due, so that the motorist owes it to *him* to stop, in the way a debtor owes it to his creditor to pay. In our own actual world, of course, we sometimes owe it to our *fellow motorists* to stop; but that kind of right-correlated duty

does not exist in Nowheresville. There, motorists "owe" obedience to the Law, but they owe nothing to one another. When they collide, no matter who is at fault, no one is morally accountable to anyone else, and no one has any sound grievance or "right to complain."

When we leave legal contexts to consider moral obligations and other extra-legal duties, a greater variety of duties-without-correlative-rights present themselves. Duties of charity, for example, require us to contribute to one or another of a large number of eligible recipients, no one of whom can claim our contribution from us as his due. Charitable contributions are more like gratuitous services, favors, and gifts than like repayments of debts or reparations; and yet we do have duties to be charitable. Many persons, moreover, in our actual world believe that they are required by their own consciences to do more than that "duty" that *can* be demanded of them by their prospective beneficiaries. I have quoted elsewhere the citation from H. B. Acton of a character in a Malraux novel who "gave all his supply of poison to his fellow prisoners to enable them by suicide to escape the burning alive which was to be their fate and his." This man, Acton adds, "probably did not think that [the others] had more of a right to the poison than he had, though he thought it his duty to give it to them." I am sure that there are many actual examples, less dramatically heroic than this fictitious one, of persons who believe, rightly or wrongly, that they *must do* something (hence the word "duty") for another person in excess of what that person can appropriately demand of him (hence the absence of "right").

Now the digression is over and we can return to Nowheresville and summarize what we have put in it thus far. We now find spontaneous benevolence in somewhat larger degree than in our actual world, and also the acknowledged existence of duties of obedience, duties of charity, and duties imposed by exacting private consciences, and also, let us suppose, a degree of conscientiousness in respect to those duties somewhat in excess of what is to be found in our actual world. I doubt that Kant would be fully satisfied with Nowheresville even now that duty and respect for law and authority have been added to it; but I feel certain that he would regard their addition at least as an improvement. I will now introduce two further moral practices into Nowheresville that will make that world very little more appealing to Kant, but will make it appear more familiar to us. These are the practices connected with the notions of *personal desert* and what I call a *sovereign monopoly of rights*.

When a person is said to deserve something good from us what is meant in part is that there would be a certain propriety in our giving that good thing to him in virtue of the kind of person he is, perhaps, or more likely, in virtue of some specific thing he has done. The propriety involved here is a much weaker kind than that which derives from our having promised him the good thing or from his having qualified for it by satisfying the well-advertised conditions of some public rule. In the latter case he could be said not merely to deserve the good thing but also to have a *right* to it, that is to be in a position to demand it as his due; and of course we will not have that sort of thing in Nowheresville. That weaker kind of propriety which is mere desert is simply a kind of *fittingness* between one party's character or action and another party's favorable response, much like that between humor and laughter, or good performance and applause.

The following seems to be the origin of the idea of deserving good or bad treatment from others: A master or lord was under no obligation to reward his servant for especially good service; still a master might naturally feel that there would be a special fittingness in giving a gratuitous reward as a grateful response to the good service (or conversely imposing a penalty for bad service). Such an act while surely fitting and proper was entirely supererogatory. The fitting response in turn from the rewarded servant should be gratitude. If the deserved reward had not been given him he should have had no complaint, since he only *deserved* the reward, as opposed to having a *right* to it, or a ground for claiming it as his due.

The idea of desert has evolved a good bit away from its beginnings by now, but nevertheless, it seems clearly to be one of those words J. L. Austin said "never entirely forget their pasts." Today servants qualify for their wages by doing their agreed upon chores, no more and no less. If their wages are not forthcoming, their contractual rights have been violated and they can make legal claim to the money that is their due. If they do less than they agreed to do, however, their employers may "dock" them, by paying them proportionately less than the agreed upon fee. This is all a matter of right. But if the servant does a splendid job, above and beyond his minimal contractual duties, the employer is under no further obligation to reward him, for this was not agreed upon, even tacitly, in advance. The additional service was all the servant's idea and done entirely on his own. Nevertheless, the morally sensitive employer may feel that it would be exceptionally appropriate for him to respond, freely on *his* own, to the servant's meritorious service, with a reward. The employee cannot demand it as his due, but he will happily accept it, with gratitude, as a fitting response to his desert.

In our age of organized labor, even this picture is now archaic; for almost every kind of exchange of service is governed by hard bargained contracts so that even bonuses can sometimes be demanded as a matter of right, and nothing is given for nothing on either side of the bargaining table. And perhaps that is a good thing; for consider an anachoronistic instance of the earlier kind of practice that survives, at least as a matter of form, in the quaint old practice of "tipping." The tip was originally conceived as a reward that has to be earned by "zealous service." It is not something to be taken for granted as a standard response to *any* service. That is to say that its payment is a "*gratuity*," not a discharge of obligation, but something given apart from, or in addition to, anything the recipient can expect as a matter of right. That is what tipping originally meant at any rate, and tips are still referred to as "gratuities" in the tax forms. But try to explain all that to a New York cab driver! If he has *earned* his gratuity, by God, he has it coming, and there had better be sufficient acknowledgement of his desert or he'll give you a piece of his mind! I'm not generally prone to defend New York cab drivers, but they do have a point here. There is the making of a paradox in the queerly unstable concept of an "earned gratuity." One can understand how "desert" in the weak sense of "propriety" or "mere fittingness" tends to generate a stronger sense in which desert is itself the ground for a claim of right.

In Nowheresville, nevertheless, we will have only the original weak kind of desert. Indeed, it will be impossible to keep this idea out if we allow such practices as teachers grading students, judges awarding prizes, and servants serving benevolent but class-conscious masters. Nowheresville is a reasonably good world in many ways, and its teachers, judges, and masters will generally try to give students, contestants, and servants the grades, prizes, and rewards they deserve. For this the recipients will be grateful; but they will never think to complain, or even feel aggrieved, when expected responses to desert fail. The masters, judges, and teachers don't *have* to do good things, after all, for *anyone*. One should be happy that they *ever* treat us well, and not grumble over their occasional lapses. Their hoped for responses, after all, are *gratuities*, and there is no wrong in the omission of what is merely gratuitous. Such is the response of persons who have no concept of *rights*, even persons who are proud of their own deserts.

Surely, one might ask, rights have to come in somewhere, if we are to have even moderately complex forms of social organization. Without rules that confer rights and impose obligations, how can we have ownership of property, bargains and deals, promises and contracts,

appointments and loans, marriages and partnerships? Very well, let us introduce all of these social and economic practices into Nowheresville, but *with one big twist*. With them I should like to introduce the curious notion of a "sovereign right-monopoly." You will recall that the subjects in Hobbes's *Leviathan* had no rights whatever against their sovereign. He could do as he liked with them, even gratuitously harm them, but this gave them no valid grievance against him. The sovereign, to be sure, had a certain duty to treat his subjects well, but this duty was owed not to the subjects directly, but to God, just as we might have a duty to a person to treat his property well, but of course no duty to the property itself but only to its owner. Thus, while the sovereign was quite capable of *harming* his subjects, he could commit no *wrong* against them that they could complain about, since they had no prior claims against his conduct. The only party *wronged* by the sovereign's mistreatment of his subjects was God, the supreme lawmaker. Thus, in repenting cruelty to his subjects, the sovereign might say to God, as David did after killing Uriah, "to Thee only have I sinned."

Even in the *Leviathan*, however, ordinary people had ordinary rights *against one another*. They played roles, occupied offices, made agreements, and signed contracts. In a genuine "sovereign right-monopoly," as I shall be using that phrase, they will do all those things too, and thus incur genuine obligations toward one another; but the obligations (here is the twist) will not be owed directly *to* promisees, creditors, parents, and the like, but rather to God alone, or to the members of some elite, or to a single sovereign under God. Hence, the rights correlative to the obligations that derive from these transactions are all owned by some "outside" authority.

As far as I know, no philosopher has ever suggested that even our role and contract obligations (in this, our actual world) are all owed directly to a divine intermediary; but some theologians have approached such extreme moral occasionalism. I have in mind the familiar phrase in certain widely distributed religious tracts that "it takes three to marry," which suggests that marital vows are not made between bride and groom directly but between each spouse and God, so that if one breaks his vow, the other cannot rightly complain of being wronged, since only God could have claimed performance of the marital duties as his *own* due; and hence God alone had a claim-right violated by nonperformance. If John breaks his vow to God, he might then properly repent in the words of David: "To Thee only have I sinned."

In our actual world, very few spouses conceive of their mutual obligations in this way; but their small children, at a certain stage in their moral upbringing, are likely to feel precisely this way toward *their* mutual obligations. If Billy kicks Bobby and is punished by Daddy, he may come to feel contrition for his naughtiness induced by his painful estrangement from the loved parent. Hy may then be happy to make amends and sincere apology *to Daddy*; but when Daddy insists that he apologize to his wronged brother, that is another story. A direct apology to Billy would be a tacit recognition of Billy's status as a right-holder against him, some one he can wrong as well as harm, and someone to whom he is directly accountable for his wrongs. This is a status Bobby will happily accord Daddy; but it would imply a respect for Billy that he does not presently feel, so he bitterly resents according it to him. On the "three-to-marry" model, the relations between each spouse and God would be like those between Bobby and Daddy; respect for the other spouse as an independent claimant would not even be necessary; and where present, of course, never sufficient.

The advocates of the "three to marry" model who conceive it either as a description of our actual institution of marriage or a recommendation of what marriage ought to be, may wish to escape this embarrassment by granting rights to spouses in capacities other than as promisees. They may wish to say, for example, that when John promises God that he will be faithful to Mary, a right is thus conferred not only on God as promisee but also on Mary herself as third-party beneficiary, just as when John contracts with an insurance company and names Mary as his intended beneficiary, she has a right to the accumulated funds after John's death, even though the insurance company made no promise to her. But this seems to be an unnecessarily cumbersome complication contributing nothing to our understanding of the marriage bond. The life insurance transaction is necessarily a three party relation, involving occupants of three distinct offices, no two of whom alone could do the whole job. The transaction, after all, is defined as the purchase by the customer (first office) from the vendor (second office) of protection for a beneficiary (third office) against the customer's untimely death. Marriage, on the other hand, in this our actual world, appears to be a binary relation between a husband and wife, and even though third parties such as children, neighbors, psychiatrists, and priests may sometimes be helpful and even causally necessary for the survival of the relation, they are not logically necessary to our *conception* of the relation, and indeed many married couples do quite well without them. Still, I am not now purporting to describe our actual world, but rather trying to contrast it with a counterpart world of the imagination. In *that* world, it takes three to make almost *any* moral relation and all rights are owned by God or some sovereign under God.

There will, of course, be delegated authorities in the imaginary world, empowered to give commands to their underlings and to punish them for their disobedience. But the commands are all given in the name of the right-monopoly who in turn are the only persons to whom obligations are owed. Hence, even intermediate superiors do not have claim-rights against their subordinates but only legal *powers* to create obligations in the subordinates *to* the monopolistic right-holders, and also the legal *privilege* to impose penalties in the name of that monopoly.

2

So much for the imaginary "world without rights." If some of the moral concepts and practices I have allowed into that world do not sit well with one another, no matter. Imagine Nowheresville with all of these practices if you can, or with any harmonious subset of them, if you prefer. The important thing is not what I've let into it, but what I have kept out. The remainder of this paper will be devoted to an analysis of what precisely a world is missing when it does not contain rights and why that absence is morally important.

The most conspicuous difference, I think, between the Nowheresvillians and ourselves has something to do with the activity of *claiming*. Nowheresvillians, even when they are discriminated against invidiously, or left without the things they need, or otherwise badly treated, do not think to leap to their feet and make righteous demands against one another, though they may not hesitate to resort to force and trickery to get what they want. They have no notion of rights, so they do not have a notion of what is their due; hence they do not claim before they take. The conceptual linkage between personal rights and claiming has long been noticed by legal writers and is reflected in the standard usage in which "claim-rights" are distinguished from the mere liberties, immunities, and powers, also sometimes called "rights," with which they are easily confused. When a person has a legal claim-right to X, it must be the case (i) that he is at liberty in respect to X, i.e., that he has no duty to refrain from or relinquish X, and also (ii) that his liberty is the ground of other people's *duties* to grant him X or not to interfere with him in respect to X. Thus, in the sense of claim-rights, it is true by definition that rights logically entail other people's duties. The paradigmatic examples of such rights are the creditor's right to be paid a debt by his debtor, and the landowner's right not to be interfered with by anyone in the exclusive occupancy of his land. The creditor's right against his debtor, for example, and the debtor's duty to his creditor, are precisely the same relation seen from two different vantage points, as inextricably linked as the two sides of the same coin.

And yet, this is not quite an accurate account of the matter, for it fails to do justice to the way claim-rights are somehow prior to, or more basic than, the duties with which they are necessarily correlated. If Nip has a claim-right against Tuck, it is because of this fact that Tuck has a duty to Nip. It is only because something from Tuck is *due* Nip (directional element) that there is something Tuck *must do* (modal element). This is a relation, moreover, in which Tuck is bound and Nip is free. Nip not only *has* a right, but he can choose whether or not to exercise it, whether to claim it, whether to register complaints upon its infringement, even whether to release Tuck from his duty, and forget the whole thing. If the personal claim-right is also backed up by criminal sanctions, however, Tuck may yet have a duty of obedience to the law from which no one, not even Nip, may release him. He would even have such duties if he lived in Nowheresville; but duties subject to acts of claiming, duties derivative from and contingent upon the personal rights of others, are unknown and undreamed of in Nowheresville.

Many philosophical writers have simply identified rights with claims. The dictionaries tend to define "claims," in turn, as "assertions of right," a dizzying piece of circularity that led one philosopher to complain – "We go in search of rights and are directed to claims, and then back again to rights in bureaucratic futility." What then is the relation between a claim and a right?

As we shall see, a right *is* a kind of claim, and a claim is "an assertion of right," so that a formal definition of either notion in terms of the other will not get us very far. Thus if a "formal definition" of the usual philosophical sort is what we are after, the game is over before it has begun, and we can say that the concept of a right is a "simple, undefinable, unanalysable primitive."

Here as elsewhere in philosophy this will have the effect of making the commonplace seem unnecessarily mysterious. We would be better advised, I think, not to attempt a formal definition of either "right" or "claim," but rather to use the idea of a claim in informal elucidation of the idea of a right. This is made possible by the fact that *claiming* is an elaborate sort of rule-governed *activity*. A claim is that which is claimed, the object of the act of claiming. There is, after all, a verb "to claim," but no verb "to right." If we concentrate on the whole activity of claiming, which is public, familiar, and open to our observation, rather than on its upshot alone, we may learn more about the generic nature of rights than we could ever hope to learn from a formal definition, even if one were possible. Moreover, certain facts about rights more easily, if not solely, expressible in the language of claims and claiming are essential to a full understanding not only of what rights are, but also why they are so vitally important.

Let us begin then by distinguishing between: (i) making claim to . . ., (ii) claiming that . . ., and (iii) having a claim. One sort of thing we may be doing when we claim is to *make claim to something*. This is "to petition or seek by virtue of supposed right; to demand as due." Sometimes this is done by an acknowledged right-holder when he serves notice that he now wants turned over to him that which has already been acknowledged to be his, something borrowed, say, or improperly taken from him. This is often done by turning in a chit, a receipt, an I.O.U., a check, an insurance policy, or a deed, that is, a *title* to something currently in the possession of someone else. On other occasions, making claim is making application for titles or rights themselves, as when a mining prospector stakes a claim to mineral rights, or a householder to a tract of land in the public domain, or an inventor to his patent rights. In the one kind of case, to make claim is to exercise rights one already has by presenting title; in the other kind of case it is to apply for the title itself, by showing that one

has satisfied the conditions specified by a rule for the ownership of title and therefore that one can demand it as one's due.

Generally speaking, only the person who has a title or who has qualified for it, or someone speaking in his name, can make claim to something as a matter of right. It is an important fact about rights (or claims), then, that they can be claimed only by those who have them. Anyone can claim, of course, *that* this umbrella is yours, but only you or your representative can actually claim the umbrella. If Smith owes Jones five dollars, only Jones can claim the five dollars as his own, though any bystander can *claim that* it belongs to Jones. One important difference then between *making legal claim to* and *claiming that* is that the former is a legal performance with direct legal consequences whereas the latter is often a mere piece of descriptive commentary with no legal force. Legally speaking, *making claim to* can itself make things happen. This sense of "claiming," then, might well be called "the performative sense." The legal power to claim (performatively) one's right or the things to which one has a right seems to be essential to the very notion of a right. A right to which one could not make claim (i.e. not even for recognition) would be a very "imperfect" right indeed!

Claiming that one has a right (what we can call "propositional claiming" as opposed to "performative claiming") is another sort of thing one can do with language, but it is not the sort of doing that characteristically has legal consequences. To claim that one has rights is to make an assertion that one has them, and to make it in such a manner as to demand or insist that they be recognized. In this sense of "claim" many things in addition to rights can be claimed, that is, many other kinds of proposition can be asserted in the claiming way. I can claim, for example, that you, he, or she has certain rights, or that Julius Caesar once had certain rights; or I can claim that certain statements are true, or that I have certain skills, or accomplishments, or virtually anything at all. I can claim that the earth is flat. What is essential to *claiming that* is the manner of assertion. One can assert without even caring very much whether any one is listening, but part of the point of propositional claiming is to *make sure* people listen. When I claim to others that I know something, for example, I am not merely asserting it, but rather "obtruding my putative knowledge upon their attention, demanding that it be recognized, that appropriate notice be taken of it by those concerned . . ." Not every truth is properly assertable, much less claimable, in every context. To claim that something is the case in circumstances that justify no more than calm assertion is to behave like a boor. (This kind of boorishness, I might add, is probably less common in Nowheresville.) But not to claim in the appropriate circumstances that one has a right is to be spiritless or foolish. A list of "appropriate circumstances" would include occasions when one is challenged, when one's possession is denied, or seems insufficiently acknowledged or appreciated; and of course even in these circumstances, the claiming should be done only with an appropriate degree of vehemence.

Even if there are conceivable circumstances in which one would admit rights diffidently, there is no doubt that their characteristic use and that for which they are distinctively well suited, is to be claimed, demanded, affirmed, insisted upon. They are especially sturdy objects to "stand upon," a most useful sort of moral furniture. Having rights, of course, makes claiming possible; but it is claiming that gives rights their special moral significance. This feature of rights is connected in a way with the customary rhetoric about what it is to be a human being. Having rights enables us to "stand up like men," to look others in the eye, and to feel in some fundamental way the equal of anyone. To think of oneself as the holder of rights is not to be unduly but properly proud, to have that minimal self-respect that is necessary to be worthy of the love and esteem of others. Indeed, respect for persons (this is an intriguing idea) may simply be respect for their rights, so that there cannot be the one

without the other; and what is called "human dignity" may simply be the recognizable capacity to assert claims. To respect a person then, or to think of him as possessed of human dignity, simply *is* to think of him as a potential maker of claims. Not all of this can be packed into a definition of "rights;" but these are *facts* about the possession of rights that argue well their supreme moral importance. More than anything else I am going to say, these facts explain what is wrong with Nowheresville.

We come now to the third interesting employment of the claiming vocabulary, that involving not the verb "to claim" but the substantive "a claim." What is it to *have a claim* and how is this related to rights? I would like to suggest that *having a claim consists in being in a position to claim, that is, to make claim to or claim that.* If this suggestion is correct it shows the primacy of the verbal over the nominative forms. It links claims to a kind of activity and obviates the temptation to think of claims as *things*, on the model of coins, pencils, and other material possessions which we can carry in our hip pockets. To be sure, we often make or establish our claims by presenting titles, and these typically have the form of receipts, tickets, certificates, and other pieces of paper or parchment. The title, however, is not the same thing as the claim; rather it is the evidence that establishes the claim as valid. On this analysis, one might have a claim without ever claiming that to which one is entitled, or without even knowing that one has the claim; for one might simply be ignorant of the fact that one is in a position to claim; or one might be unwilling to exploit that position for one reason or another, including fear that the legal machinery is broken down or corrupt and will not enforce one's claim despite its validity.

Nearly all writers maintain that there is some intimate connection between having a claim and having a right. Some identify right and claim without qualification; some define "right" as justified or justifiable claim, others as recognized claim, still others as valid claim. My own preference is for the latter definition. Some writers, however, reject the identification of rights with valid claims on the ground that all claims as such are valid, so that the expression "valid claim" is redundant. These writers, therefore, would identify rights with claims *simpliciter*. But this is a very simple confusion. All claims, to be sure, are *put forward* as justified, whether they are justified in fact or not. A claim conceded even by its maker to have no validity is not a claim at all, but a mere demand. The highwayman, for example, *demands* his victim's money; but he hardly makes claim to it as rightfully his own.

But it does not follow from this sound point that it is redundant to qualify claims as justified (or as I prefer, valid) in the definition of a right; for it remains true that not all claims put forward as valid really are valid; and only the valid ones can be acknowledged as rights.

If having a valid claim is not redundant, i.e., if it is not redundant to pronounce *another's* claim valid, there must be such a thing as having a claim that is not valid. What would this be like? One might accumulate just enough evidence to argue with relevance and cogency that one has a right (or ought to be granted a right), although one's case might not be overwhelmingly conclusive. In such a case, one might have strong enough argument to be entitled to a hearing and given fair consideration. When one is in this position, it might be said that one "has a claim" that deserves to be weighed carefully. Nevertheless, the balance of reasons may turn out to militate against recognition of the claim, so that the claim, which one admittedly had, and perhaps still does, is not a valid claim or right. "Having a claim" in this sense is an expression very much like the legal phrase "having a *prima facie* case." A plaintiff establishes a *prima facie* case for the defendant's liability when she establishes grounds that will be sufficient for liability unless outweighed by reasons of a different sort that may be offered by the defendant. Similarly, in the criminal law, a grand jury returns an indictment when it thinks that the prosecution has

sufficient evidence to be taken seriously and given a fair hearing, whatever countervailing reasons may eventually be offered on the other side. That initial evidence, serious but not conclusive, is also sometimes called a *prima facie* case. In a parallel "*prima facie* sense" of "claim," having a claim to X is not (yet) the same as having a right to X, but is rather having a case of at least minimal plausibility that one has a right to X, a case that does establish a right, not to X, but to a fair hearing and consideration. Claims, so conceived, differ in degree: some are stronger than others. Rights, on the other hand, do not differ in degree; no one right is more of a right than another.

Another reason for not identifying rights with claims *simply* is that there is a well-established usage in international law that makes a theoretically interesting distinction between claims and rights. Statesmen are sometimes led to speak of "claims" when they are concerned with the natural needs of deprived human beings in conditions of scarcity. Young orphans *need* good upbringings, balanced diets, education, and technical training everywhere in the world; but unfortunately there are many places where these goods are in such short supply that it is impossible to provision all who need them. If we persist, nevertheless, in speaking of these needs as constituting rights and not merely claims, we are committed to the conception of a right which is an entitlement *to* some good, but not a valid claim *against* any particular individual; for in conditions of scarcity there may be no determinate individuals who can plausibly be said to have a duty to provide the missing goods to those in need. J. E. S. Fawcett therefore prefers to keep the distinction between claims and rights firmly in mind. "Claims," he writes, "are needs and demands in movement, and there is a continuous transformation, as a society advances [toward greater abundance] of economic and social claims into civil and political rights . . . and not all countries or all claims are by any means at the same stage in the process." The manifesto writers on the other side who seem to identify needs, or at least basic needs, with what they call "human rights," are more properly described, I think, as urging upon the world community the moral principle that *all* basic human needs ought to be recognized as *claims* (in the customary *prima facie* sense) worthy of sympathy and serious consideration right now, even though, in many cases, they cannot yet plausibly be treated as *valid* claims, that is, as grounds of any other people's duties. This way of talking avoids the anomaly of ascribing to all human beings now, even those in pre-industrial societies, such "economic and social rights" as "periodic holidays with pay."

Still, for all of that, I have a certain sympathy with the manifesto writers, and I am even willing to speak of a special "manifesto sense" of "right," in which a right need not be correlated with another's duty. Natural needs are real claims if only upon hypothetical future beings not yet in existence. I accept the moral principle that to have an unfulfilled need is to have a kind of claim against the world, even if against no one in particular. A natural need for some good as such, like a natural desert, is always a reason in support of a claim to that good. A person in need, then, is always "in a position" to make a claim, even when there is no one in the corresponding position to do anything about it. Such claims, based on need alone, are "permanent possibilities of rights," the natural seed from which rights grow. When manifesto writers speak of them as if already actual rights, they are easily forgiven, for this is but a powerful way of expressing the conviction that they ought to be recognized by states here and now as potential rights and consequently as determinants of *present* aspirations and guides to *present* policies. That usage, I think, is a valid exercise of rhetorical licence.

I prefer to characterize rights as valid claims rather than justified ones, because I suspect that justification is rather too broad a qualification. "Validity," as I understand it, is justification of a peculiar and narrow kind, namely justification within a system of rules. A man has a legal right when the official recognition of his claim (as valid) is called for by the governing rules. This definition, of course, hardly applies to moral rights, but that is not because the genus of which moral rights are a species is something other than *claims*. A man has a moral right when he has a claim the recognition of which is called for – not (necessarily) by legal rules – but by moral principles, or the principles of an enlightened conscience.

There is one final kind of attack on the generic identification of rights with claims, and it has been launched with great spirit in a recent article by H. J. McCloskey, who holds that rights are not essentially claims at all, but rather entitlements. The springboard of his argument is his insistence that rights in their essential character are always *rights to*, not *rights against*:

My right to life is not a right against anyone. It is my right and by virtue of it, it is normally permissible for me to sustain my life in the face of obstacles. It does give rise to rights against others *in the sense* that others have or may come to have duties to refrain from killing me, but it is essentially a right of mine, not an infinite list of claims, hypothetical and actual, against an infinite number of actual, potential, and as yet nonexistent human beings ... Similarly, the right of the tennis club member to play on the club courts is a right to play, not a right against some vague group of potential or possible obstructors.

The argument seems to be that since rights are essentially rights *to*, whereas claims are essentially claims *against*, rights cannot be claims, though they can be grounds for claims. The argument is doubly defective though. First of all, contrary to McCloskey, rights (at least legal claim-rights) *are* held *against* others. McCloskey admits this in the case of *in personam* rights (what he calls "special rights") but denies it in the case of *in rem* rights (which he calls "general rights"):

> Special rights are sometimes against specific individuals or institutions – e.g. rights created by promises, contracts, etc. . . . but these differ from . . . characteristic . . . general rights where the right is simply a right to . . .

As far as I can tell, the only reason McCloskey gives for denying that *in rem* rights are against others is that those against whom they would have to hold make up an enormously multitudinous and "vague" group, including hypothetical people not yet even in existence. Many others have found this a paradoxical consequence of the notion of *in rem* rights, but I see nothing troublesome in it. If a general rule gives me a right of noninterference in a certain respect against everybody, then there are literally hundreds of millions of people who have a duty toward me in that respect; and if the same general rule gives the same right to everyone else, then it imposes on me literally hundreds of millions of duties – or duties towards hundreds of millions of people. I see nothing paradoxical about this, however. The duties, after all, are negative; and I can discharge all of them at a stroke simply by minding my own business. And if all human beings make up one moral community and there are hundreds of millions of human beings, we should expect there to be hundreds of millions of moral relations holding between them.

McCloskey's other premise is even more obviously defective. There is no good reason to think that all *claims* are "essentially" *against*, rather than *to*. Indeed most of the discussion of claims above has been of claims *to*, and as we have seen, the law finds it useful to recognize claims *to*

(or "mere claims") that are not yet qualified to be claims *against*, or rights (except in a "manifesto sense" of "rights").

Whether we are speaking of claims or rights, however, we must notice that they seem to have two dimensions, as indicated by the prepositions "to" and "against," and it is quite natural to wonder whether either of these dimensions is somehow more fundamental or essential than the other. All rights seem to merge *entitlements to* do, have, omit, or be something with *claims against* others to act or refrain from acting in certain ways. In some statements of rights the entitlement is perfectly determinate (e.g. *to* play tennis) and the claim vague (e.g. *against* "some vague group of potential or possible obstructors"); but in other cases the object of the claim is clear and determinate (e.g. *against* one's parents), and the entitlement general and indeterminate (e.g. *to* be given a proper upbringing.) If we mean by "entitlement" that *to* which one has a right and by "claim" something directed at those *against* whom the right holds (as McCloskey apparently does), then we can say that all claim-rights necessarily involve both, though in individual cases the one element or the other may be in sharper focus.

In brief conclusion: To have a right is to have a claim against someone whose recognition as valid is called for by some set of governing rules or moral principles. To have a *claim* in turn, is to have a case meriting consideration, that is, to have reasons or grounds that put one in a position to engage in performative and propositional claiming. The activity of claiming, finally, as much as any other thing, makes for self-respect and respect for others, gives a sense to the notion of personal dignity, and distinguishes this otherwise morally flawed world from the even worse world of Nowheresville.

Chapter 15

Robert Nozick

LIBERTARIAN RIGHTS

Robert Nozick (1938–2002) was a professor of philosophy at Harvard University for almost his entire professional career. He wrote widely in such areas as epistemology and decision theory, but his best-known work is *Anarchy, State, and Utopia* (1974), a book-length exploration of libertarian political theory. In this excerpt, Nozick discusses the idea of rights as side-constraints, and argues that accepting the side-constraint *form* of rights gives us reason to believe that the *content* of rights is libertarian.

Individuals have rights, and there are things no person or group may do to them (without violating their rights). So strong and far-reaching are these rights that they raise the question of what, if anything, the state and its officials may do. How much room do individual rights leave for the state? [. . .]

Our main conclusions about the state are that a minimal state, limited to the narrow functions of protection against force, theft, fraud, enforcement of contracts, and so on, is justified; that any more extensive state will violate persons' rights not to be forced to do certain things, and is unjustified; and that the minimal state is inspiring as well as right. Two noteworthy implications are that the state may not use its coercive apparatus for the purpose of getting some citizens to aid others, or in order to prohibit activities to people for their own good or protection. [. . .]

The Minimal State and the Ultraminimal State

The night-watchman state of classical liberal theory, limited to the functions of protecting all its citizens against violence, theft, and fraud, and to the enforcement of contracts, and so on, appears to be redistributive. We can imagine at least one social arrangement intermediate between the scheme of private protective associations and the night-watchman state. Since the night-watchman state is often called a minimal state, we shall call this other arrangement the *ultraminimal state*. An ultraminimal state maintains a monopoly over all use of force except that necessary in immediate self-defense, and so excludes private (or agency) retaliation for wrong and exaction of compensation; but it provides protection and enforcement services only to those who purchase its protection and enforcement policies. People who don't buy a protection contract from the monopoly don't get protected. [. . .]

A proponent of the ultraminimal state may seem to occupy an inconsistent position. . . . Greatly concerned to protect rights against violation, he makes this the sole legitimate function of the state; and he protests that all other functions are illegitimate because they themselves involve the violation of rights. Since he accords paramount place to the protection and nonviolation of rights, how can he support the ultraminimal state, which would seem to leave some persons' rights unprotected or illprotected? How can he support this *in the name of* the nonviolation of rights?

Moral Constraints and Moral Goals

This question assumes that a moral concern can function only as a moral *goal*, as an end state for some activities to achieve as their result. It may, indeed, seem to be a necessary truth that "right," "ought," "should," and so on, are to be explained in terms of what is, or is intended to be, productive of the greatest good, with all goals built into the good. Thus it is often thought that what is wrong with utilitarianism (which is of this form) is its too narrow conception of good. Utilitarianism doesn't, it is said, properly take rights and their nonviolation into account; it instead leaves them a derivative status. Many of the counterexample cases to utilitarianism fit under this objection, for example, punishing an innocent man to save a neighborhood from a vengeful rampage. But a theory may include in a primary way the nonviolation of rights, yet include it in the wrong place and the wrong manner. For suppose some condition about minimizing the total (weighted) amount of violations of rights is built into the desirable end state to be achieved. We then would have something like a "utilitarianism of rights"; violations of rights (to be *minimized*) merely would replace the total happiness as the relevant end state in the utilitarian structure. (Note that we do not hold the nonviolation of our rights as our sole greatest good or even rank it first lexicographically to

exclude trade-offs, if there is some desirable society we would choose to inhabit even though in it some rights of ours sometimes are violated, rather than move to a desert island where we could survive alone.) This still would require us to violate someone's rights when doing so minimizes the total (weighted) amount of the violation of rights in the society. For example, violating someone's rights might deflect others from their intended action of gravely violating rights, or might remove their motive for doing so, or might divert their attention, and so on. A mob rampaging through a part of town killing and burning will violate the rights of those living there. Therefore, someone might try to justify his punishing another he knows to be innocent of a crime that enraged a mob, on the grounds that punishing this innocent person would help to avoid even greater violations of rights by others, and so would lead to a minimum weighted score for rights violations in the society.

In contrast to incorporating rights into the end state to be achieved, one might place them as side constraints upon the actions to be done: don't violate constrains C. The rights of others determine the constraints upon your actions. (A *goal-directed* view with constraints added would be: among those acts available to you that don't violate constraints C, act so as to maximize goal G. Here, the rights of others would constrain your goal-directed behavior. I do not mean to imply that the correct moral view includes mandatory goals that must be pursued; even within the constraints.) This view differs from one that tries to build the side constraints C *into* the goal G. The side-constraint view forbids you to violate these moral constraints in the pursuit of your goals; whereas the view whose objective is to minimize the violation of these rights allows you to violate the rights (the constraints) in order to lessen their total violation in the society.[1]

The claim that the proponent of the ultraminimal state is inconsistent, we now can see, assumes that he is a "utilitarian of rights." It assumes that his goal is, for example, to minimize the weighted amount of the violation of rights in the society, and that he should pursue this goal even through means that themselves violate people's rights. Instead, he may place the nonviolation of rights as a constraint upon action, rather than (or in addition to) building it into the end state to be realized. The position held by this proponent of the ultraminimal state will be a consistent one if his conception of rights holds that your being *forced* to contribute to another's welfare violates your rights, whereas someone else's not providing you with things you need greatly, including things essential to the protection of your rights, does not *itself* violate your rights, even though it avoids making it more difficult for someone else to violate them. (That conception will be consistent provided it does not construe the monopoly element of the ultraminimal state as itself a violation of rights.) That it is a consistent position does not, of course, show that it is an acceptable one.

Why Side Constraints?

Isn't it *irrational* to accept a side constraint C, rather than a view that directs minimizing the violations of C? (The latter view treats C as a condition rather than a constraint.) If nonviolation of C is so important, shouldn't that be the goal? How can a concern for the nonviolation of C lead to the refusal to violate C even when this would prevent other more extensive violations of C? What is the rationale for placing the nonviolation of rights as a side constraint upon action instead of including it solely as a goal of one's actions?

Side constraints upon action reflect the underlying Kantian principle that individuals are ends and not merely means; they may not be sacrificed or used for the achieving of other ends without their consent. Individuals are inviolable. More should be said to illuminate this talk of ends and means. Consider a prime example of a means, a tool. There is no side constraint on how

we may use a tool, other than the moral constraints on how we may use it upon others. There are procedures to be followed to preserve it for future use ("don't leave it out in the rain"), and there are more and less efficient ways of using it. But there is no limit on what we may do to it to best achieve our goals. Now imagine that there was an overrideable constraint C on some tool's use. For example, the tool might have been lent to you only on the condition that C not be violated unless the gain from doing so was above a certain specified amount, or unless it was necessary to achieve a certain specified goal. Here the object is not *completely* your tool, for use according to your wish or whim. But it is a tool nevertheless, even with regard to the overrideable constraint. If we add constraints on its use that may not be overridden, then the object may not be used as a tool in *those ways. In those respects,* it is not a tool at all. Can one add enough constraints so that an object cannot be used as a tool at all, in *any* respect?

Can behavior toward a person be constrained so that he is not to be used for any end except as he chooses? This is an impossibly stringent condition if it requires everyone who provides us with a good to approve positively of every use to which we wish to put it. Even the requirement that he merely should not object to any use we plan would seriously curtail bilateral exchange, not to mention sequences of such exchanges. It is sufficient that the other party stands to gain enough from the exchange so that he is willing to go through with it, even though he objects to one or more of the uses to which you shall put the good. Under such conditions, the other party is not being used solely as a means, in that respect. Another party, however, who would not choose to interact with you if he knew of the uses to which you *intend* to put his actions or good, is being used as a means, even if he receives enough to choose (in his ignorance) to interact with you. ("All along, you were just *using* me" can be said by someone who chose to interact only because he was ignorant of another's goals and of the uses to which he himself would be put.) Is it morally incumbent upon someone to reveal his intended uses of an interaction if he has good reason to believe the other would refuse to interact if he knew? Is he *using* the other person, if he does not reveal this? And what of the cases where the other does not choose to be of use at all? In getting pleasure from seeing an attractive person go by, does one use the other solely as a means? Does someone so use an object of sexual fantasies? These and related questions raise very interesting issues for moral philosophy; but not, I think, for political philosophy.

Political philosophy is concerned only with *certain* ways that persons may not use others; primarily, physically aggressing against them. A specific side constraint upon action toward others expresses the fact that others may not be used in the specific ways the side constraint excludes. Side constraints express the inviolability of others, in the ways they specify. These modes of inviolability are expressed by the following injunction: "Don't use people in specified ways." An end-state view, on the other hand, would express the view that people are ends and not merely means (if it chooses to express this view at all), by a different injunction: "Minimize the use in specified ways of persons as means." Following this precept itself may involve using someone as a means in one of the ways specified. Had Kant held this view, he would have given the second formula of the categorical imperative as, "So act as to minimize the use of humanity simply as a means," rather than the one he actually used: "Act in such a way that you always treat humanity, whether in your own person or in the person of any other, never simply as a means, but always at the same time as an end."

Side constraints express the inviolability of other persons. But why may not one violate persons for the greater social good? Individually, we each sometimes choose to undergo some pain or sacrifice for a greater benefit or to avoid a greater harm: we go to the dentist to avoid worse suffering later; we do some unpleasant work for its

results; some persons diet to improve their health or looks; some save money to support themselves when they are older. In each case, some cost is borne for the sake of the greater overall good. Why not, *similarly*, hold that some persons have to bear some costs that benefit other persons more, for the sake of the overall social good? But there is no *social entity* with a good that undergoes some sacrifice for its own good. There are only individual people, different individual people, with their own individual lives. Using one of these people for the benefit of others, uses him and benefits the others. Nothing more. What happens is that something is done to him for the sake of others. Talk of an overall social good covers this up. (Intentionally?) To use a person in this way does not sufficiently respect and take account of the fact that he is a separate person, that his is the only life he has. He does not get some overbalancing good from his sacrifice, and no one is entitled to force this upon him—least of all a state or government that claims his allegiance (as other individuals do not) and that therefore scrupulously must be *neutral* between its citizens.

Libertarian Constraints

The moral side constraints upon what we may do, I claim, reflect the fact of our separate existences. They reflect the fact that no moral balancing act can take place among us; there is no moral outweighing of one of our lives by others so as to lead to a greater overall *social* good. There is no justified sacrifice of some of us for others. This root idea, namely, that there are different individuals with separate lives and so no one may be sacrificed for others, underlies the existence of moral side constraints, but it also, I believe, leads to a libertarian side constraint that prohibits aggression against another.

The stronger the force of an end-state maximizing view, the more powerful must be the root idea capable of resisting it that underlies the existence of moral side constraints. Hence the more seriously must be taken the existence of distinct individuals who are not resources for others. An underlying notion sufficiently powerful to support moral side constraints against the powerful intuitive force of the end-state maximizing view will suffice to derive a libertarian constraint on aggression against another. Anyone who rejects that particular side constraint has three alternatives: (1) he must reject all side constraints; (2) he must produce a different explanation of why there are moral side constraints rather than simply a goal-directed maximizing structure, an explanation that doesn't itself entail the libertarian side constraint; or (3) he must accept the strongly put root idea about the separateness of individuals and yet claim that initiating aggression against another is compatible with this root idea. Thus we have a promising sketch of an argument from moral form to moral content: the form of morality includes F (moral side constraints); the best explanation of morality's being F is p (a strong statement of the distinctness of individuals); and from p follows a particular moral content, namely, the libertarian constraint. The particular moral content gotten by this argument, which focuses upon the fact that there are distinct individuals each with his own life to lead, will not be the full libertarian constraint. It will prohibit sacrificing one person to benefit another. Further steps would be needed to reach a prohibition on paternalistic aggression: using or threatening force for the benefit of the person against whom it is wielded. For this, one must focus upon the fact that there are distinct individuals, each with his own life to lead.

A nonaggression principle is often held to be an appropriate principle to govern relations among nations. What difference is there supposed to be between sovereign individuals and sovereign nations that makes aggression permissible among individuals? Why may individuals jointly, through their government, do to someone what no nation may do to another? If anything, there is a stronger case for nonaggression among individuals; unlike nations, they do not contain as parts individuals that others legitimately might intervene to protect or defend.

I shall not pursue here the details of a principle that prohibits physical aggression, except to note that it does not prohibit the use of force in defense against another party who is a threat, even though he is innocent and deserves no retribution. An *innocent threat* is someone who innocently is a causal agent in a process such that he would be an aggressor had he chosen to become such an agent. If someone picks up a third party and throws him at you down at the bottom of a deep well, the third party is innocent and a threat; had he chosen to launch himself at you in that trajectory he would be an aggressor. Even though the falling person would survive his fall onto you, may you use your ray gun to disintegrate the falling body before it crushes and kills you? Libertarian prohibitions are usually formulated so as to forbid using violence on innocent persons. But innocent threats, I think, are another matter to which different principles must apply. Thus, a full theory in this area also must formulate the *different* constraints on response to innocent threats. Further complications concern *innocent shields of threats*, those innocent persons who themselves are nonthreats but who are so situated that they will be damaged by the only means available for stopping the threat. Innocent persons strapped onto the front of the tanks of aggressors so that the tanks cannot be hit without also hitting them are innocent shields of threats. (Some uses of force on people to get at an aggressor do not act upon innocent shields of threats; for example, an aggressor's innocent child who is tortured in order to get the aggressor to stop wasn't *shielding* the parent.) May one knowingly injure innocent shields? If one may attack an aggressor and injure an innocent shield, may the innocent shield fight back in self-defense (supposing that he cannot move against or fight the aggressor)? Do we get two persons battling each other in self-defense? Similarly, if you use force against an innocent threat to you, do you thereby become an innocent threat to him, so that he may now justifiably use additional force against you (supposing that he can do this, yet cannot prevent his original threateningness)? I tiptoe around these incredibly difficult issues here, merely noting that a view that says it makes nonaggression central must resolve them explicitly at some point.

Note

1   The question of whether these side constraints are absolute, or whether they may be violated in order to avoid catastrophic moral horror, and if the latter, what the resulting structure might look like, is one I hope largely to avoid.

1c. JUSTICE

IN APPROXIMATELY 360 BC, Plato wrote one of the first and most enduring systematic works of philosophy ever written. Its title was *The Republic*, and its subject was justice—as an attribute of individuals and of the societies in which they live. Some twenty-three hundred years later, John Rawls would write in his *Theory of Justice* that "justice is the first virtue of social institutions," and would go on to change the way philosophers thought about it forever.

What is this concept which has proved to be of such enduring philosophical interest? What does it mean to call someone or something unjust, and what implications does it have for the way we ought to behave toward one another?

All of us, I suspect, can remember some experience in which we were treated unjustly. Perhaps when we were younger, a sibling did something bad for which we were blamed. Or perhaps we were passed over for a job or a scholarship in favor of some lesser qualified candidate who happened to have an inside connection with the person making the decision. What makes such events unjust is that we were not given what we were *due*. Those in charge of meting out punishment—even parents!—are obligated to look carefully at the evidence and place blame only on those who are guilty. Those whose job it is to make hiring decisions or decisions regarding scholarships ought to award those honors on the basis of *merit*, and not on the basis of prior personal connections or other irrelevant criteria. Justice demands that people get, in a sense, "what they've got coming to them."

And, importantly, it demands that people get what's coming to them even if we don't always like the results. What is required by justice will often conflict with what is in our own self-interest, as for instance when justice requires that we return a lost wallet to its rightful owner. In cases such as these, justice seems to require us to put the interests of society or of particular other persons ahead of our own. But matters are even more complicated than this. For justice will often demand that we perform or abstain from certain actions even when this demand *undermines* the interests of society as a whole. The fact that a policy of performing involuntary medical experiments on randomly selected citizens is unjust, for instance, entails that we must not allow it even if the welfare of society would be greatly advanced by it. The fact that it would be unjust to sentence a defendant to prison with insufficient evidence means that we must let him go, *even if we know that he is guilty and that society would be better off with him behind bars!*

Justice, then, is a very demanding requirement. It requires that we act in ways which are contrary to our own interests, and even sometimes contrary to the interests of our society as a whole. But this raises a philosophical puzzle. If justice is so demanding, then why should we think ourselves bound to obey its demands? From where do the requirements of justice derive their authority?

Historically, two broad categories of answer have been given to this question. The first, expressed in this section by David Hume and John Stuart Mill, holds that the demands of justice are warranted by the beneficial consequences that adherence to them produces. It is true that *single instances* of just conduct can produce harmful consequences as, Hume notes, when "a man of merit, of beneficent disposition, restores a great fortune to a miser, or a seditious bigot." But the long-run consequences of adherence to justice *as a rule* are tremendously beneficial, and society needs fixed and stable rules so that its members can form reliable expectations of what they may and may not do without fear of punishment.

The second category of response derives from Immanuel Kant, and finds its expression in this section in the reading from John Rawls. For these thinkers, the demands of justice obligate us not because of their tendency to produce good consequences, but rather because they are necessary conditions on our treating each other with *respect*. The problem with slavery, on this view, is not that it tends to make society as a whole worse off than it would otherwise be, but that it treats the slave as an *object* instead of as a human being. Human beings are ends in themselves, and slavery treats them as though they were mere instruments to be used for the satisfaction of *other* people's ends. Whether it produces good or bad long-term effects for society as a whole is beside the point.

This question of the moral foundations of justice is of great philosophic importance. But of equal philosophic importance—and perhaps greater practical importance—are questions about the *content* of justice's demands. Even once we know that the claims of justice "trump" claims of individual or social interest, this still leaves unclear just what, exactly, justice demands that we do. Mill gives us a pluralistic answer to this question. For Mill, justice demands (among other things) that we give people what they deserve, that we not break faith with others, that we be impartial (at least when impartiality is demanded), that we respect others' rights, and that we treat them equally.

Mill's list, however, leaves many questions unanswered. When, for instance, are we required by justice to treat others impartially? Surely it is morally permissible— perhaps even morally required—for a parent to devote more time and energy to the care of her own children than she devotes to the aid of strangers. But just as surely, this permissible partiality has its limits. A judge in a criminal trial would not be permitted to allow her verdict to be influenced by the fact that the defendant is her child. The exact contour of these limits, however, is difficult to specify with any philosophical precision, just as it is difficult to say what exactly constitutes morally required equal treatment, or what people deserve.

For a consequentialist like Mill, these difficult questions can be answered by looking back to the utilitarian foundations of justice. Since the *point* of justice is to promote utility, we can resolve difficult questions about the content of justice by figuring out which rules (or which interpretations of a given rule) would be utility-maximizing. If (as seems unlikely) utility would be maximized by a rule requiring the state to enforce a constant equality of material well-being among its citizens, then *that* is the kind of equality required by justice. But if (as seems more plausible) utility would be better promoted by a rule requiring the state to enforce only equality of *opportunity* for material well-being, then *that* would be the sort of equality that justice requires.

Rawls' method of arriving at the content of justice is different, and reflects his more Kantian moral underpinnings. The starting place for Rawls' reflection is the moral arbitrariness of fortune. What we have, as individuals, is largely—perhaps entirely, in Rawls' view—the result of luck. We did nothing to deserve being born into one social class rather than another, nor did we deserve being born with a genetic propensity for health, height, and intelligence rather than their opposites. And to the extent that our success in life depends on these factors, it too is the result of luck. To allow an individual's fate to rest on luck, however, is manifestly unjust. Thus Rawls' "original position" asks us to think about what principles of justice we would choose if we wanted ones that would allow us to live good lives for ourselves but didn't know how smart, healthy, rich, and so on we were. Rawls' conclusion is that parties so situated in a fair initial bargaining position would choose principles guaranteeing each a maximum set of basic liberties, and requiring that no inequalities be permitted in society unless they can be shown to be to the benefit of the least well-off person.

Rawls' main task is to articulate principles of social and distributive justice. But in so doing he raises an important question—just how should we conceive of the people who are to be the *subject* of these principles? Is Rawls right to argue that everything about us that arose from chance is morally arbitrary and hence not something to be taken account of in the design of principles of justice? Michael Sandel is not convinced. Much of what is meaningful about our lives—our families, our religious affiliations, our nationality—is not chosen from the perspective of a purely rational and autonomous agent. Rather, he argues, we are born into a life that is already culturally embedded. In the face of such embeddedness, it is not clear that liberal theories of justice which privilege autonomy and individual rights are the best hope for realizing our values.

The readings in this section bring out some of the most important aspects of the concept of justice. But our discussion of justice will not end here. Many of the later sections of this book will be devoted to looking at the requirements of justice in specific contexts—the distribution of wealth, immigration law, etc. Readers are thus encouraged to focus their thinking for now on the nature and theoretical justification of justice, and to rest assured that more concrete questions about its content will be taken up later.

Further Reading

Aristotle, *Nicomachean Ethics,* book V.

Nussbaum, M. (2006). *Frontiers of Justice: Disability, Nationality, Species Membership.* Cambridge, MA: Belknap Press.

O'Neill, O. (2000). *Bounds of Justice.* Cambridge: Cambridge University Press.

Rawls, J. (1971). *A Theory of Justice* (1st edn). Cambridge, MA: Belknap Press.

Sandel, M. (1998). *Liberalism and the Limits of Justice.* Cambridge: Cambridge University Press.

Sandel, M. (2007). *Justice: A Reader.* Oxford: Oxford University Press.

Schmidtz, D. (2006). *Elements of Justice.* Cambridge: Cambridge University Press.

Tomasi, J. (2001). *Liberalism and the Limits of Justice.* Princeton, NJ: Princeton University Press.

Chapter 16

David Hume

JUSTICE AS CONVENTION

David Hume (1711–1776) was a Scottish philosopher who wrote widely in metaphysics, ethics, history, politics, and almost everything else. In these excerpts from his *Treatise of Human Nature* (1739–1740), Hume argues that justice is an artificial virtue in the sense that it must be established to serve the public interest and does not follow from our natural sentiments. Justice is both necessary and possible because of certain key features of the human condition—namely, scarcity in the objects of our desire, and a general selfishness combined with a limited form of benevolence toward others.

Of the Origin of Justice and Property

We now proceed to examine two questions, viz. *concerning the manner, in which the rules of justice are establish'd by the artifice of men; and concerning the reasons, which determine us to attribute to the observance or neglect of these rules a moral beauty and deform-ity.* These questions will appear afterwards to be distinct. We shall begin with the former.

Of all the animals, with which this globe is peopled, there is none towards whom nature seems, at first sight, to have exercis'd more cruelty than towards man, in the numberless wants and necessities, with which she has loaded him, and in the slender means, which she affords to the relieving these necessities. In other creatures these two particulars generally compensate each other. If we consider the lion as a voracious and carnivorous animal, we shall easily discover him to be very necessitous; but if we turn our eye to his make and temper, his agility, his courage, his arms, and his force, we shall find, that his

advantages hold proportion with his wants. The sheep and ox are depriv'd of all these advantages; but their appetites are moderate, and their food is of easy purchase. In man alone, this unnatural conjunction of infirmity, and of necessity, may be observ'd in its greatest perfection. Not only the food, which is requir'd for his sustenance, flies his search and approach, or at least requires his labour to be produc'd, but he must be possess'd of cloaths and lodging, to defend him against the injuries of the weather; tho' to consider him only in himself, he is provided neither with arms, nor force, nor other natural abilities, which are in any degree answerable to so many necessities.

'Tis by society alone he is able to supply his defects, and raise himself up to an equality with his fellow-creatures, and even acquire a superiority above them. By society all his infirmities are compensated; and tho' in that situation his wants multiply every moment upon him, yet his abilities are still more augmented, and leave him in every respect more satisfy'd and happy, than 'tis possible for him, in his savage and solitary condition, ever to become. When every individual person labours apart, and only for himself, his force is too small to execute any considerable work; his labour being employ'd in supplying all his different necessities, he never attains a perfection in any particular art; and as his force and success are not at all times equal, the least failure in either of these particulars must be attended with inevitable ruin and misery. Society provides a remedy for these *three* inconveniencies. By the conjunction of forces, our power is augmented: By the partition of employments, our ability encreases: And by mutual succour we are less expos'd to fortune and accidents. 'Tis by this additional *force*, *ability*, and *security*, that society becomes advantageous.

But in order to form society, 'tis requisite not only that it be advantageous, but also that men be sensible of its advantages; and 'tis impossible, in their wild uncultivated state, that by study and reflection alone, they shou'd ever be able to attain this knowledge. Most fortunately, therefore, there is conjoin'd to those necessities, whose remedies are remote and obscure, another necessity, which having a present and more obvious remedy, may justly be regarded as the first and original principle of human society. This necessity is no other than that natural appetite betwixt the sexes, which unites them together, and preserves their union, till a new tye takes place in their concern for their common off-spring. This new concern becomes also a principle of union betwixt the parents and offspring, and forms a more numerous society; where the parents govern by the advantage of their superior strength and wisdom, and at the same time are restrain'd in the exercise of their authority by that natural affection, which they bear their children. In a little time, custom and habit operating on the tender minds of the children, makes them sensible of the advantages, which they may reap from society, as well as fashions them by degrees for it, by rubbing off those rough cor-

ners and untoward affections, which prevent their coalition.

For it must be confest, that however the circumstances of human nature may render an union necessary, and however those passions of lust and natural affection may seem to render it unavoidable; yet there are other particulars in our *natural temper*, and in our *outward circumstances*, which are very incommodious, and are even contrary to the requisite conjunction. Among the former, we may justly esteem our *selfishness* to be the most considerable. I am sensible, that, generally speaking, the representations of this quality have been carry'd much too far; and that the descriptions, which certain philosophers delight so much to form of mankind in this particular, are as wide of nature as any accounts of monsters, which we meet with in fables and romances. So far from thinking, that men have no affection for any thing beyond themselves, I am of opinion, that tho' it be rare to meet with one, who loves any single person better than himself; yet 'tis as rare to meet with one, in whom all the kind affections, taken together, do not over-ballance all the selfish. Consult common experience: Do you not see, that tho' the whole expence of the family be generally under the direction of the master of it, yet there are few that do not bestow the largest part of their fortunes on the pleasures of their wives, and the education of their children, reserving the smallest portion for their own proper use and entertainment? This is what we may observe concerning such as have those endearing ties; and may presume, that the case wou'd be the same with others, were they plac'd in a like situation.

But tho' this generosity must be acknowledg'd to the honour of human nature, we may at the same time remark, that so noble an affection, instead of fitting men for large societies, is almost as contrary to them, as the most narrow selfishness. For while each person loves himself better than any other single person, and in his love to others bears the greatest affection to his relations and acquaintance, this must necessarily produce an opposition of passions, and a consequent opposition of actions; which cannot but be dangerous to the new-establish'd union.

'Tis however worth while to remark, that this contrariety of passions wou'd be attended with but small danger, did it not concur with a peculiarity in our *outward circumstances*, which affords it an opportunity of exerting itself. There are three different species of goods, which we are possess'd of; the internal satisfaction of our mind, the external advantages of our body, and the enjoyment of such possessions as we have acquir'd by our industry and good fortune. We are perfectly secure in the enjoyment of the first. The second may be ravish'd from us, but can be of no advantage to him who deprives us of them. The last only are both expos'd to the violence of others, and may be transferr'd without suffering any loss or alteration; while at the same time, there is not a sufficient quantity of them to supply every one's desires and necessities. As the improvement, therefore, of these goods is the chief advantage of society, so the *instability* of their possession, along with their *scarcity*, is the chief impediment.

In vain shou'd we expect to find, in *uncultivated nature*, a remedy to this inconvenience; or hope for any inartificial principle of the human mind, which might controul those partial affections, and make us overcome the temptations arising from our circumstances. The idea of justice can never serve to this purpose, or be taken for a natural principle, capable of inspiring men with an equitable conduct towards each other. That virtue, as it is now understood, wou'd never have been dream'd of among rude and savage men. For the notion of injury or injustice implies an immorality or vice committed against some other person: And as every immorality is deriv'd from some defect or unsoundness of the passions, and as this defect must be judg'd of, in a great measure, from the ordinary course of nature in the constitution of the mind; 'twill be easy to know, whether we be guilty of any immorality, with regard to others, by consider-

ing the natural, and usual force of those several affections, which are directed towards them. Now it appears, that in the original frame of our mind, our strongest attention is confin'd to ourselves; our next is extended to our relations and acquaintance; and 'tis only the weakest which reaches to strangers and indifferent persons. This partiality, then, and unequal affection, must not only have an influence on our behaviour and conduct in society, but even on our ideas of vice and virtue; so as to make us regard any remarkable transgression of such a degree of partiality, either by too great an enlargement, or contraction of the affections, as vicious and immoral. This we may observe in our common judgments concerning actions, where we blame a person, who either centers all his affections in his family, or is so regardless of them, as, in any opposition of interest, to give the preference to a stranger, or mere chance acquaintance. From all which it follows, that our natural uncultivated ideas of morality, instead of providing a remedy for the partiality of our affections, do rather conform themselves to that partiality, and give it an additional force and influence.

The remedy, then, is not deriv'd from nature, but from *artifice*; or more properly speaking, nature provides a remedy in the judgment and understanding, for what is irregular and incommodious in the affections. For when men, from their early education in society, have become sensible of the infinite advantages that result from it, and have besides acquir'd a new affection to company and conversation; and when they have observ'd, that the principal disturbance in society arises from those goods, which we call external, and from their looseness and easy transition from one person to another; they must seek for a remedy, by putting these goods, as far as possible, on the same footing with the fix'd and constant advantages of the mind and body. This can be done after no other manner, than by a convention enter'd into by all the members of the society to bestow stability on the possession of those external goods, and leave every one in the peaceable enjoyment of what he may acquire by his fortune and industry. By this means, every one knows what he may safely possess; and the passions are restrain'd in their partial and contradictory motions. Nor is such a restraint contrary to these passions; for if so, it cou'd never be enter'd into, nor maintain'd; but it is only contrary to their heedless and impetuous movement. Instead of departing from our own interest, or from that of our nearest friends, by abstaining from the possessions of others, we cannot better consult both these interests, than by such a convention; because it is by that means we maintain society, which is so necessary to their well-being and subsistence, as well as to our own.

This convention is not of the nature of a *promise*: For even promises themselves, as we shall see afterwards, arise from human conventions. It is only a general sense of common interest; which sense all the members of the society express to one another, and which induces them to regulate their conduct by certain rules. I observe, that it will be for my interest to leave another in the possession of his goods, *provided* he will act in the same manner with regard to me. He is sensible of a like interest in the regulation of his conduct. When this common sense of interest is mutually express'd, and is known to both, it produces a suitable resolution and behaviour. And this may properly enough be call'd a convention or agreement betwixt us, tho' without the interposition of a promise; since the actions of each of us have a reference to those of the other, and are perform'd upon the supposition, that something is to be perform'd on the other part. Two men, who pull the oars of a boat, do it by an agreement or convention, tho' they have never given promises to each other. Nor is the rule concerning the stability of possession the less deriv'd from human conventions, that it arises gradually, and acquires force by a slow progression, and by our repeated experience of the inconveniencies of transgressing it. On the contrary, this experience assures us still more, that the sense of interest has become common to all

our fellows, and gives us a confidence of the future regularity of their conduct: And 'tis only on the expectation of this, that our moderation and abstinence are founded. In like manner are languages gradually establish'd by human conventions without any promise. In like manner do gold and silver become the common measures of exchange, and are esteem'd sufficient payment for what is of a hundred times their value.

After this convention, concerning abstinence from the possessions of others, is enter'd into, and every one has acquir'd a stability in his possessions, there immediately arise the ideas of justice and injustice; as also those of *property, right,* and *obligation.* The latter are altogether unintelligible without first understanding the former. Our property is nothing but those goods, whose constant possession is establish'd by the laws of society; that is, by the laws of justice. Those, therefore, who make use of the words *property,* or *right,* or *obligation,* before they have explain'd the origin of justice, or even make use of them in that explication, are guilty of a very gross fallacy, and can never reason upon any solid foundation. A man's property is some object related to him. This relation is not natural, but moral, and founded on justice. 'Tis very preposterous, therefore, to imagine, that we can have any idea of property, without fully comprehending the nature of justice, and showing its origin in the artifice and contrivance of men. The origin of justice explains that of property. The same artifice gives rise to both. As our first and most natural sentiment of morals is founded on the nature of our passions, and gives the preference to ourselves and friends, above strangers; 'tis impossible there can be naturally any such thing as a fix'd right or property, while the opposite passions of men impel them in contrary directions, and are not restrain'd by any convention or agreement.

No one can doubt, that the convention for the distinction of property, and for the stability of possession, is of all circumstances the most necessary to the establishment of human society, and that after the agreement for the fixing and observing of this rule, there remains little or nothing to be done towards settling a perfect harmony and concord. All the other passions, beside this of interest, are either easily restrain'd, or are not of such pernicious consequence, when indulg'd. *Vanity* is rather to be esteem'd a social passion, and a bond of union among men. Pity and *love* are to be consider'd in the same light. And as to *envy* and *revenge*, tho' pernicious, they operate only by intervals, and are directed against particular persons, whom we consider as our superiors or enemies. This avidity alone, of acquiring goods and possessions for ourselves and our nearest friends, is insatiable, perpetual, universal, and directly destructive of society. There scarce is any one, who is not actuated by it; and there is no one, who has not reason to fear from it, when it acts without any restraint, and gives way to its first and most natural movements. So that upon the whole, we are to esteem the difficulties in the establishment of society, to be greater or less, according to those we encounter in regulating and restraining this passion.

'Tis certain, that no affection of the human mind has both a sufficient force, and a proper direction to counter-ballance the love of gain, and render men fit members of society, by making them abstain from the possessions of others. Benevolence to strangers is too weak for this purpose; and as to the other passions, they rather inflame this avidity, when we observe, that the larger our possessions are, the more ability we have of gratifying all our appetites. There is no passion, therefore, capable of controuling the interested affection, but the very affection itself, by an alteration of its direction. Now this alteration must necessarily take place upon the least reflection; since 'tis evident, that the passion is much better satisfy'd by its restraint, than by its liberty, and that by preserving society, we make much greater advances in the acquiring possessions, than by running into the solitary and forlorn condition, which must follow upon violence and an universal licence. The question,

therefore, concerning the wickedness or goodness of human nature, enters not in the least into that other question concerning the origin of society; nor is there any thing to be consider'd but the degrees of men's sagacity or folly. For whether the passion of self-interest be esteem'd vicious or virtuous, 'tis all a case; since itself alone restrains it: So that if it be virtuous, men become social by their virtue; if vicious, their vice has the same effect.

Now as 'tis by establishing the rule for the stability of possession, that this passion restrains itself; if that rule be very abstruse, and of difficult invention; society must be esteem'd, in a manner, accidental, and the effect of many ages. But if it be found, that nothing can be more simple and obvious than that rule; that every parent, in order to preserve peace among his children, must establish it; and that these first rudiments of justice must every day be improv'd, as the society enlarges: If all this appear evident, as it certainly must, we may conclude, that 'tis utterly impossible for men to remain any considerable time in that savage condition, which precedes society; but that his very first state and situation may justly be esteem'd social. This, however, hinders not, but that philosophers may, if they please, extend their reasoning to the suppos'd *state of nature*; provided they allow it to be a mere philosophical fiction, which never had, and never cou'd have any reality. Human nature being compos'd of two principal parts, which are requisite in all its actions, the affections and understanding; 'tis certain, that the blind motions of the former, without the direction of the latter, incapacitate men for society: And it may be allow'd us to consider separately the effects, that result from the separate operations of these two component parts of the mind. The same liberty may be permitted to moral, which is allow'd to natural philosophers; and 'tis very usual with the latter to consider any motion as compounded and consisting of two parts separate from each other, tho' at the same time they acknowledge it to be in itself uncompounded and inseparable.

This *state of nature*, therefore, is to be regarded as a mere fiction, not unlike that of the *golden age*, which poets have invented; only with this difference, that the former is describ'd as full of war, violence and injustice; whereas the latter is painted out to us, as the most charming and most peaceable condition, that can possibly be imagin'd. The seasons, in that first age of nature, were so temperate, if we may believe the poets, that there was no necessity for men to provide themselves with cloaths and houses as a security against the violence of heat and cold. The rivers flow'd with wine and milk: The oaks yielded honey; and nature spontaneously produc'd her greatest delicacies. Nor were these the chief advantages of that happy age. The storms and tempests were not alone remov'd from nature; but those more furious tempests were unknown to human breasts, which now cause such uproar, and engender such confusion. Avarice, ambition, cruelty, selfishness, were never heard of: Cordial affection, compassion, sympathy, were the only movements, with which the human mind was yet acquainted. Even the distinction of *mine* and *thine* was banish'd from that happy race of mortals, and carry'd with them the very notions of property and obligation, justice and injustice.

This, no doubt, is to be regarded as an idle fiction; but yet deserves our attention, because nothing can more evidently show the origin of those virtues, which are the subjects of our present enquiry. I have already observ'd, that justice takes its rise from human conventions; and that these are intended as a remedy to some inconveniencies, which proceed from the concurrence of certain *qualities* of the human mind with the *situation* of external objects. The qualities of the mind are *selfishness* and *limited generosity*: And the situation of external objects is their *easy change*, join'd to their *scarcity* in comparison of the wants and desires of men. But however philosophers may have been bewilder'd in those speculations, poets have been guided more infallibly, by a certain taste or common instinct, which in most kinds of reasoning goes farther than any of that

art and philosophy, with which we have been yet acquainted. They easily perceiv'd, if every man had a tender regard for another, or if nature supply'd abundantly all our wants and desires, that the jealousy of interest, which justice supposes, cou'd no longer have place; nor wou'd there be any occasion for those distinctions and limits of property and possession, which at present are in use among mankind. Encrease to a sufficient degree the benevolence of men, or the bounty of nature, and you render justice useless, by supplying its place with much nobler virtues, and more valuable blessings. The selfishness of men is animated by the few possessions we have, in proportion to our wants; and 'tis to restrain this selfishness, that men have been oblig'd to separate themselves from the community, and to distinguish betwixt their own goods and those of others.

Nor need we have recourse to the fictions of poets to learn this; but beside the reason of the thing, may discover the same truth by common experience and observation. 'Tis easy to remark, that a cordial affection renders all things common among friends; and that marry'd people in particular mutually lose their property, and are unacquainted with the *mine* and *thine*, which are so necessary, and yet cause such disturbance in human society. The same effect arises from any alteration in the circumstances of mankind; as when there is such a plenty of any thing as satisfies all the desires of men: In which case the distinction of property is entirely lost, and every thing remains in common. This we may observe with regard to air and water, tho' the most valuable of all external objects; and may easily conclude, that if men were supply'd with every thing in the same abundance, or if *every one* had the same affection and tender regard for *every one* as for himself; justice and injustice wou'd be equally unknown among mankind.

Here then is a proposition, which, I think may be regarded as certain, *that 'tis only from the selfishness and confin'd generosity of man, along with the scanty provision nature has made for his wants, that justice derives its origin.* If we look backward we shall find, that this proposition bestows an additional force on some of those observations, which we have already made on this subject.

First, we may conclude from it, that a regard to public interest, or a strong extensive benevolence, is not our first and original motive for the observation of the rules of justice; since 'tis allow'd, that if men were endow'd with such a benevolence, these rules you'd never have been dreamt of.

Secondly, we may conclude from the same principle, that the sense of justice is not founded on reason, or on the discovery of certain connexions and relations of ideas, which are eternal, immutable, and universally obligatory. For since it is confest, that such an alteration as that above-mention'd, in the temper and circumstances of mankind, wou'd entirely alter our duties and obligations, 'tis necessary upon the common system, *that the sense of virtue is deriv'd from reason,* to show the change which this must produce in the relations and ideas. But 'tis evident, that the only cause, why the extensive generosity of man, and the perfect abundance of every thing, wou'd destroy the very idea of justice, is because they render it useless; and that, on the other hand, his confin'd benevolence, and his necessitous condition, give rise to that virtue, only by making it requisite to the public interest, and to that of every individual. 'Twas therefore a concern for our own, and the public interest, which made us establish the laws of justice; and nothing can be more certain, than that it is not any relation of ideas, which gives us this concern, but our impressions and sentiments, without which every thing in nature is perfectly indifferent to us, and can never in the least affect us. The sense of justice, therefore, is not founded on our ideas, but on our impressions.

Thirdly, we may farther confirm the foregoing proposition, *that those impressions, which give rise to this sense of justice, are not natural to the mind of man, but arise from artifice and human conventions.* For since any considerable alteration of temper and circumstances destroys equally justice and injustice; and since such an alteration has an effect only by changing our own and the public interest; it follows, that the first establishment of the rules of justice depends on these different interests. But if men pursu'd the public interest naturally, and with a hearty affection, they wou'd never have dream'd of restraining each other by these rules; and if they pursu'd their own interest, without any precaution, they wou'd run head-long into every kind of injustice and violence. These rules, therefore, are artificial, and seek their end in an oblique and indirect manner; nor is the interest, which gives rise to them, of a kind that cou'd be pursu'd by the natural and inartificial passions of men.

To make this more evident, consider, that tho' the rules of justice are establish'd merely by interest, their connexion with interest is somewhat singular, and is different from what may be observ'd on other occasions. A single act of justice is frequently contrary to *public interest;* and were it to stand alone, without being follow'd by other acts, may, in itself, be very prejudicial to society. When a man of merit, of a beneficent disposition, restores a great fortune to a miser, or a seditious bigot, he has acted justly and laudably, but the public is a real sufferer. Nor is every single act of justice, consider'd apart, more conducive to private interest, than to public; and 'tis easily conceiv'd how a man may impoverish himself by a signal instance of integrity, and have reason to wish, that with regard to that single act, the laws of justice were for a moment suspended in the universe. But however single acts of justice may be contrary, either to public or private interest, 'tis certain, that the whole plan or scheme is highly conducive, or indeed absolutely requisite, both to the support of society, and the well-being of every individual. 'Tis impossible to separate the good from the ill. Property must be stable, and must be fix'd by general rules. Tho' in one instance the public be a sufferer, this momentary ill is amply compensated by the steady prosecution of the rule, and by the peace and order, which it establishes in society. And even every individual person must find himself a gainer, on ballancing the account; since, without justice, society must immediately dissolve, and every one must fall into that savage and solitary condition, which is infinitely worse than the worst situation that can possibly be suppos'd in society. When therefore men have had experience enough to observe, that whatever may be the consequence of any single act of justice, perform'd by a single person, yet the whole system of actions, concurr'd in by the whole society, is infinitely advantageous to the whole, and to every part; it is not long before justice and property take place. Every member of society is sensible of this interest: Every one expresses this sense to his fellows, along with the resolution he has taken of squaring his actions by it, on condition that others will do the same. No more is requisite to induce any one of them to perform an act of justice, who has the first opportunity. This becomes an example to others. And thus justice establishes itself by a kind of convention or agreement; that is, by a sense of interest, suppos'd to be common to all, and where every single act is perform'd in expectation that others are to perform the like. Without such a convention, no one wou'd ever have dream'd, that there was such a virtue as justice, or have been induc'd to conform his actions to it. Taking any single act, my justice may be pernicious in every respect; and 'tis only upon the supposition, that others are to imitate my example, that I can be induc'd to embrace that virtue; since nothing but this combination can render justice advantageous, or afford me any motives to conform my self to its rules.

We come now to the *second* question we propos'd, viz. *Why we annex the idea of virtue to justice, and of vice to injustice?* This question will not detain us long after the principles, which we have already establish'd. All we can say of it at present will be dispatch'd in a few words: And for farther satisfaction, the reader must wait till we come to the *third* part of this book. The *natural* obligation to justice, viz. Interest, has been fully explain'd; but as to the *moral* obligation, or the sentiment of right and wrong, 'twill first be requisite to examine the natural virtues, before we can give a full and satisfactory account of it.

After men have found by experience, that their selfishness and confin'd generosity, acting at their liberty, totally incapacitate them for society; and at the same time have observ'd, that society is necessary to the satisfaction of those very passions, they are naturally induc'd to lay themselves under the restraint of such rules, as may render their commerce more safe and commodious. To the imposition then, and observance of these rules, both in general, and in every particular instance, they are at first mov'd only by a regard to interest; and this motive, on the first formation of society, is sufficiently strong and forcible. But when society has become numerous, and has encreas'd to a tribe or nation, this interest is more remote; nor do men so readily perceive, that disorder and confusion follow upon every breach of these rules, as in a more narrow and contracted society. But tho' in our own actions we may frequently lose sight of that interest, which we have in maintaining order, and may follow a lesser and more present interest, we never fail to observe the prejudice we receive, either mediately or immediately, from the injustice of others; as not being in that case either blinded by passion, or byass'd by any contrary temptation. Nay when the injustice is so distant from us, as no way to affect our interest, it still displeases us; because we consider it as prejudicial to human society, and pernicious to every one that approaches the person guilty of it. We partake of their uneasiness by *sympathy*; and as every thing, which gives uneasiness in human actions, upon the general survey, is call'd *vice*, and whatever produces satisfaction, in the same manner, is denominated *virtue*; this is the reason why the sense of moral good and evil follows upon justice and injustice. And tho' this sense, in the present case, be deriv'd only from contemplating the actions of others, yet we fail not to extend it even to our own actions. The *general rule* reaches beyond those instances, from which it arose; while at the same time we naturally *sympathize* with others in the sentiments they entertain of us. Thus *self-interest* is the original motive to the *establishment* of justice: But a *sympathy* with *public* interest is the source of the *moral* approbation, which attends that virtue. This latter principle of sympathy is too weak to controul our passions; but has sufficient force to influence our taste, and give us the sentiments of approbation or blame.

Tho' this progress of the sentiments be *natural*, and even necessary, 'tis certain, that it is here forwarded by the artifice of politicians, who, in order to govern men more easily, and preserve peace in human society, have endeavour'd to produce an esteem for justice, and an abhorrence of injustice. This, no doubt, must have its effect; but nothing can be more evident, than that the matter has been carry'd too far by certain writers on morals, who seem to have employ'd their utmost efforts to extirpate all sense of virtue from among mankind. Any artifice of politicians may assist nature in the producing of those sentiments, which she suggests to us, and may even on some occasions, produce alone an approbation or esteem for any particular action; but 'tis impossible it shou'd be the sole cause of the distinction we make betwixt vice and virtue. For if nature did not aid us in this particular, 'twou'd be in vain for politicians to talk of *honourable* or *dishonourable*, *praise-worthy* or *blameable*. These words wou'd be perfectly unintelligible, and wou'd no more have any idea annex'd to them, than if they were of a tongue perfectly unknown to us. The utmost politicians can perform, is, to extend the natural sentiments beyond their original bounds; but still nature must furnish the materials, and give us some notion of moral distinctions.

As public praise and blame encrease our esteem for justice; so private education and instruction contribute to the same effect. For as parents easily observe, that a man is the more useful, both to himself and others, the greater degree of probity and honour he is endow'd with; and that those principles have greater force, when custom and education assist interest and reflection: For these reasons they are induc'd to inculcate on their children, from their earliest infancy, the principles of probity, and teach them to regard the observance of those rules, by which society is maintain'd, as worthy and honourable, and their violation as base and infamous. By this means the sentiments of honour may take root in their tender minds, and acquire such firmness and solidity, that they may fall little short of those principles, which are the most essential to our natures, and the most deeply radicated in our internal constitution.

What farther contributes to encrease their solidity, is the interest of our reputation, after the opinion, *that a merit or demerit attends justice or injustice*, is once firmly establish'd among mankind. There is nothing, which touches us more nearly than our reputation, and nothing on which our reputation more depends than our conduct, with relation to the property of others. For this reason, every one, who has any regard to his character, or who intends to live on good terms with mankind, must fix an inviolable law to himself, never, by any temptation, to be induc'd to violate those principles, which are essential to a man of probity and honour.

I shall make only one observation before I leave this subject, *viz.* That tho' I assert, that in the *state of nature*, or that imaginary state, which preceded society, there be neither justice nor injustice, yet I assert not, that it was allowable, in such a state, to violate the property of others. I only maintain, that there was no such thing as property; and consequently cou'd be no such thing as justice or injustice. I shall have occasion to make a similar reflection with regard to *promises*, when I come to treat of them; and I hope this reflection, when duly weigh'd, will suffice to remove all odium from the foregoing opinions, with regard to justice and injustice.

Chapter 17

John Stuart Mill

JUSTICE AND UTILITY

John Stuart Mill (1806–1873) was a British philosopher and, with Jeremy Bentham, one of the most historically influential proponents of the moral philosophy known as utilitarianism. In these excerpts, taken from *Utilitarianism* (1863), Mill sets forth the basic tenets of utilitarianism and shows its connection with the constraint of conduct by *rules*. He then goes on to show how utilitarianism is, contrary to what many of its critics had charged (and continue to charge), compatible with respect for justice, and indeed necessary to explain the importance of that virtue.

The creed which accepts as the foundation of morals "utility" or the "greatest happiness principle" holds that actions are right in proportion as they tend to promote happiness; wrong as they tend to produce the reverse of happiness. By happiness is intended pleasure and the absence of pain; by unhappiness, pain and the privation of pleasure. To give a clear view of the moral standard set up by the theory, much more requires to be said; in particular, what things it includes in the ideas of pain and pleasure, and to what extent this is left an open question. But these supplementary explanations do not affect the theory of life on which this theory of morality is grounded—namely, that pleasure and freedom from pain are the only things desirable as ends; and that all desirable things (which are as numerous in the utilitarian as in any other scheme) are desirable either for pleasure inherent in themselves or as means to the promotion of pleasure and the prevention of pain. [. . .]

[U]tility is often summarily stigmatized as an immoral doctrine by giving it the name of "expediency," and taking advantage of the popular use of that term to contrast it with principle. But the expedient, in the sense in which it is opposed to the right, generally means that which is expedient for the particular interest of the agent himself; as when a minister sacrifices the interests of his country to keep himself in place. When it means anything better than this, it means that which is expedient for some immediate object, some temporary purpose, but which violates a rule whose observance is expedient in a much higher degree. The expedient, in this sense, instead of being the same thing with the useful, is a branch of the hurtful. Thus it would often be expedient, for the purpose of getting over some momentary embarrassment, or attaining some object immediately useful to ourselves or others, to tell a lie. But inasmuch as the cultivation in ourselves of a sensitive feeling on the subject of veracity is one of the most useful, and the enfeeblement of that feeling one of the most hurtful, things to which our conduct can be instrumental; and inasmuch as any, even unintentional, deviation from truth does that much toward weakening the trust-worthiness of human assertion, which is not only the principal support of all present social well-being, but the insufficiency of which does more than any one thing that can be named to keep back civilization, virtue, everything on which human happiness on the largest scale depends—we feel that the violation, for a present advantage, of a rule of such transcendent expediency is not expedient, and that he who, for the sake of convenience to himself or to some other individual, does what depends on him to deprive mankind of the good, and inflict upon them the evil, involved in the greater or less reliance which they can place in each other's word, acts the part of one of their worst enemies. Yet that even this rule, sacred as it is, admits of possible exceptions is acknowledged by all moralists; the chief of which is when the withholding of some fact (as of information from a malefactor, or of bad news from a person dangerously ill) would save an individual (especially an individual other than oneself) from great and unmerited evil, and when the withholding can only be effected by denial. But in order that the exception may not extend itself beyond the need, and may have the least possible effect in weakening reliance on veracity, it ought to be recognized and, if possible, its limits defined; and, if the principle of utility is good for anything, it must be good for weighing these conflicting utilities against one another and marking out the region within which one or the other preponderates.

Again, defenders of utility often find themselves called upon to reply to such objections as this—that there is not time, previous to action, for calculating and weighing the effects of any line of conduct on the general happiness. This is exactly as if anyone were to say that it is impossible to guide our conduct by Christianity because there is not time, on every occasion on which anything has to be done, to read through the Old and New Testaments. The answer to the objection is that there has been ample time,

namely, the whole past duration of the human species. During all that time mankind have been learning by experience the tendencies of actions; on which experience all the prudence as well as all the morality of life are dependent. People talk as if the commencement of this course of experience had hitherto been put off, and as if, at the moment when some man feels tempted to meddle with the property or life of another, he had to begin considering for the first time whether murder and theft are injurious to human happiness. Even then I do not think that he would find the question very puzzling; but, at all events, the matter is now done to his hand. It is truly a whimsical supposition that, if mankind were agreed in considering utility to be the test of morality, they would remain without any agreement as to what is useful, and would take no measures for having their notions on the subject taught to the young and enforced by law and opinion. There is no difficulty in proving any ethical standard whatever to work ill if we suppose universal idiocy to be conjoined with it; but on any hypothesis short of that, mankind must by this time have acquired positive beliefs as to the effects of some actions on their happiness; and the beliefs which have thus come down are the rules of morality for the multitude, and for the philosopher until he has succeeded in finding better. That philosophers might easily do this, even now, on many subjects; that the received code of ethics is by no means of divine right; and that mankind have still much to learn as to the effects of actions on the general happiness, I admit or rather earnestly maintain. The corollaries from the principle of utility, like the precepts of every practical art, admit of indefinite improvement, and, in a progressive state of the human mind, their improvement is perpetually going on. But to consider the rules of morality as improvable is one thing; to pass over the intermediate generalization entirely and endeavor to test each individual action directly by the first principle is another. It is a strange notion that the acknowledgment of a first principle is inconsistent with the admission of secondary ones. To inform a traveler respecting the place of his ultimate destination is not to forbid the use of landmarks and direction-posts on the way. The proposition that happiness is the end and aim of morality does not mean that no road ought to be laid down to that goal, or that persons going thither should not be advised to take one direction rather than another. Men really ought to leave off talking a kind of nonsense on this subject, which they would neither talk nor listen to on other matters of practical concernment. Nobody argues that the art of navigation is not founded on astronomy because sailors cannot wait to calculate the Nautical Almanac. Being rational creatures, they go to sea with it ready calculated; and all rational creatures go out upon the sea of life with their minds made up on the common questions of right and wrong, as well as on many of the far more difficult questions of wise and foolish. And this, as long as foresight is a human quality, it is to be presumed they will continue to do. Whatever we adopt as the fundamental principle of morality, we require subordinate principles to apply it by; the impossibility of doing without them, being common to all systems, can afford no argument against any one in particular; but gravely to argue as if no such secondary principles could be had, and as if mankind had remained till now, and always must remain, without drawing any general conclusions from the experience of human life is as high a pitch, I think, as absurdity has ever reached in philosophical controversy. [. . .]

On the Connection between Justice and Utility

In all ages of speculation one of the strongest obstacles to the reception of the doctrine that utility or happiness is the criterion of right and wrong has been drawn from the idea of justice. The powerful sentiment and apparently clear perception which that word recalls with a rapidity and certainty resembling an instinct have seemed to the majority of thinkers to point to an inherent quality in things; to show that the just must have an existence in nature as something absolute, generically distinct from every variety of the expedient and, in idea, opposed to it, though (as is commonly acknowledged) never, in the long run, disjoined from it in fact.

In the case of this, as of our other moral sentiments, there is no necessary connection between the question of its origin and that of its binding force. That a feeling is bestowed on us by nature does not necessarily legitimate all its promptings. The feeling of justice might be a peculiar instinct, and might yet require, like our other instincts, to be controlled and enlightened by a higher reason. If we have intellectual instincts leading us to judge in a particular way, as well as animal instincts that prompt us to act in a particular way, there is no necessity that the former should be more infallible in their sphere than the latter in theirs; it may as well happen that wrong judgments are occasionally suggested by those, as wrong actions by these. But though it is one thing to believe that we have natural feelings of justice, and another to acknowledge them as an ultimate criterion of conduct, these two opinions are very closely connected in point of fact. Mankind are always predisposed to believe that any subjective feeling, not otherwise accounted for, is a revelation of some objective reality. Our present object is to determine whether the reality to which the feeling of justice corresponds is one which needs any such special revelation, whether the justice or injustice of an action is a thing intrinsically peculiar and distinct from all its other qualities or only a combination of certain of those qualities presented under a peculiar aspect. For the purpose of this inquiry it is practically important to consider whether the feeling itself, of justice and injustice, is *sui generis* like our sensations of color and taste or a derivative feeling formed by a combination of others. And this it is the more essential to examine, as people are in general willing enough to allow that objectively the dictates of justice coincide with a part of the field of general expediency; but inasmuch as the subjective mental feeling of justice is different from that which commonly attaches to simple expediency, and, except in the extreme cases of the latter, is far more imperative in its demands, people find it difficult to see in justice only a particular kind or branch of general utility, and think that its superior binding force requires a totally different origin.

To throw light upon this question, it is necessary to attempt to ascertain what is the distinguishing character of justice, or of injustice; what is the quality, or whether there is any quality, attributed in common to all modes of conduct designated as unjust (for justice, like many other moral attributes, is best defined by its opposite), and distinguishing them from such modes of conduct as are disapproved, but without having that particular epithet of disapprobation applied to them. If in everything which men are accustomed to characterize as just or unjust some one common attribute or collection of attributes is always present, we may judge whether this particular attribute or combination of attributes would be capable of gathering round it a sentiment of that peculiar character and intensity by virtue of the general laws of our emotional constitution, or whether the sentiment is inexplicable and requires to be regarded as a special provision of nature. If we find the former to be the case, we shall, in resolving this question, have resolved also the main problem; if the latter, we shall have to seek for some other mode of investigating it.

To find the common attributes of a variety of objects, it is necessary to begin by surveying the objects themselves in the concrete. Let us therefore advert successively to the various modes of action and arrangements of human affairs which are classed, by universal or widely spread opinion, as just or as unjust. The things well known to excite the sentiments associated with those names are of a very multifarious character. I shall pass them rapidly in review, without studying any particular arrangement.

In the first place, it is mostly considered unjust to deprive anyone of his personal liberty, his property, or any other thing which belongs to him by law. Here, therefore, is one instance of the application of the terms "just" and "unjust" in a perfectly definite sense, namely, that it is just to respect, unjust to violate, the *legal rights* of anyone. But this judgment admits of several exceptions, arising from the other forms in which the notions of justice and injustice present themselves. For example, the person who suffers the deprivation may (as the phrase is) have *forfeited* the rights which he is so deprived of—a case to which we shall return presently. But also—

Secondly, the legal rights of which he is deprived may be rights which *ought* not to have belonged to him; in other words, the law which confers on him these rights may be a bad law. When it is so or when (which is the same thing for our purpose) it is supposed to be so, opinions will differ as to the justice or injustice of infringing it. Some maintain that no law, however bad, ought to be disobeyed by an individual citizen; that his opposition to it, if shown at all, should only be shown in endeavoring to get it altered by competent authority. This opinion (which condemns many of the most illustrious benefactors of mankind, and would often protect pernicious institutions against the only weapons which, in the state of things existing at the time, have any chance of succeeding against them) is defended by those who hold it on grounds of expediency, principally on that of the importance to the common interest of mankind, of maintaining inviolate the sentiment of submission to law. Other persons, again, hold the directly contrary opinion that any law, judged to be bad, may blamelessly be disobeyed, even though it be not judged to be unjust but only inexpedient, while others would confine the license of disobedience to the case of unjust laws; but, again, some say that all laws which are inexpedient are unjust, since every law imposes some restriction on the natural liberty of mankind, which restriction is an injustice unless legitimated by tending to their good. Among these diversities of opinion it seems to be universally admitted that there may be unjust laws, and that law, consequently, is not the ultimate criterion of justice, but may give to one person a benefit, or impose on another an evil, which justice condemns. When, however, a law is thought to be unjust, it seems always to be regarded as being so in the same way in which a breach of law is unjust, namely, by infringing somebody's right, which, as it cannot in this case be a legal right, receives a different appellation and is called a moral right. We may say, therefore, that a second case of injustice consists in taking or withholding from any person that to which he has a *moral right*.

Thirdly, it is universally considered just that each person should obtain that (whether good or evil) which he *deserves*, and unjust that he should obtain a good or be made to undergo an evil which he does not deserve. This is, perhaps, the clearest and most emphatic form in which the idea of justice is conceived by the general mind. As it involves the notion of desert, the question arises what constitutes desert? Speaking in a general way, a person is understood to deserve good if he does right, evil if he does wrong; and in a more particular sense, to deserve good from those to whom he does or has done good, and evil from those to whom he does or has done evil. The precept of returning good for evil has never been regarded as a case of the fulfillment of justice, but as one in which the claims of justice are waived, in obedience to other considerations.

Fourthly, it is confessedly unjust to *break faith* with anyone: to violate an engagement, either express or implied, or disappoint expectations raised by our own conduct, at least if we have raised those expectations knowingly and voluntarily. Like the other obligations of justice already spoken of, this one is not regarded as absolute, but as capable of being over-ruled by a stronger obligation of justice on the other side, or by such conduct on the part of the person concerned as is deemed to absolve us from our obligation to him and to constitute a *forfeiture* of the benefit which he has been led to expect.

Fifthly, it is, by universal admission, inconsistent with justice to be *partial*—to show favor or preference to one person over another in matters to which favor and preference do not properly apply. Impartiality, however, does not seem to be regarded as a duty in itself, but rather as instrumental to some other duty; for it is admitted that favor and preference are not always censurable, and, indeed, the cases in which they are condemned are rather the exception than the rule. A person would be more likely to be blamed than applauded for giving his family or friends no superiority in good offices over strangers when he could do so without violating any other duty; and no one thinks it unjust to seek one person in preference to another as a friend, connection, or companion. Impartiality where rights are concerned is of course obligatory, but this is involved in the more general obligation of giving to everyone his right. A tribunal, for example, must be impartial because it is bound to award, without regard to any other consideration, a disputed object to the one of two parties who has the right to it. There are other cases in which impartiality means being solely influenced by desert, as with those who, in the capacity of judges, preceptors, or parents, administer reward and punishment as such. There are cases, again, in which it means being solely influenced by considerations for the public interest, as in making a selection among candidates for a government employment. Impartiality, in short, as an obligation of justice, may be said to mean being exclusively influenced by the considerations which it is supposed ought to influence the particular case in hand, and resisting solicitation of any motives which prompt to conduct different from what those considerations would dictate.

Nearly allied to the idea of impartiality is that of *equality*, which often enters as a component part both into the conception of justice and into the practice of it, and, in the eyes of many persons, constitutes its essence. But in this, still more than in any other case, the notion of justice varies in different persons, and always conforms in its variations to their notion of utility. Each person maintains that equality is the dictate of justice, except where he thinks that expediency requires inequality. The justice of giving equal protection to the rights of all is maintained by those who support the most outrageous inequality in the rights themselves. Even in slave countries it is theoretically admitted that the rights of the slave, such as they are, ought to be as sacred as those of the master, and that a tribunal which fails to enforce them with equal strictness is wanting in justice; while, at the same time, institutions which leave to the slave scarcely any rights to enforce are not deemed unjust because they are not deemed inexpedient. Those who think that utility requires distinctions of rank do not consider it unjust that riches and social privileges should be unequally dispensed; but those who think this inequality inexpedient think it unjust also. Whoever thinks that government is necessary sees no injustice in as much inequality as is constituted by giving to the magistrate powers not granted to other people. Even among those who hold leveling doctrines, there are differences of opinion about expediency. Some communists consider it unjust that the produce of the labor of the community should be shared on any other principle than that of exact equality; others think it just that those should receive most whose wants are greatest; while others hold that those who work harder, or who produce more, or whose services are more valuable to the community, may justly claim a larger quota in the division of the produce. And the sense of natural justice may be plausibly appealed to in behalf of every one of these opinions.

Among so many diverse applications of the term "justice," which yet is not regarded as ambiguous, it is a matter of some difficulty to seize the mental link which holds them together, and on which the moral sentiment adhering to the term essentially depends. Perhaps, in this embarrassment, some help may be derived from the history of the word, as indicated by its etymology.

In most if not all languages, the etymology of the word which corresponds to "just" points distinctly to an origin connected with the ordinances of law. *Justum* is a form of *jussum*, that which has been ordered. *Dikaion* comes directly from *dike*, a suit at law. *Recht*, from which came *right* and *righteous*, is synonymous with law. The courts of justice, the administration of justice, are the courts and the administration of law. *La justice*, in French, is the established term for judicature. I am not committing the fallacy, imputed with some show of truth to Horne Tooke, of assuming that a word must still continue to mean what it originally meant. Etymology is slight evidence of what the idea now signified is, but the very best evidence of how it spraing up. There can, I think, be no doubt that the *idée mère*, the primitive element, in the formation of the notion of justice was conformity to law. It constituted the entire idea among the Hebrews, up to the birth of Christianity; as might be expected in the case of a people whose laws attempted to embrace all subjects on which precepts were required, and who believed those laws to be a direct emanation from the Supreme Being. But other nations, and in particular the Greeks and Romans, who knew that their laws had been made originally, and still continued to be made, by men, were not afraid to admit that those men might make bad laws; might do, by law, the same things, and from the same motives, which if done by individuals without the sanction of law would be called unjust. And hence the sentiment of injustice came to be attached, not to all violations of law, but only to violations of such laws as *ought* to exist, including such as ought to exist but do not, and to laws themselves if supposed to be contrary to what ought to be law. In this manner the idea of law and of its injunctions was still predominant in the notion of justice, even when the laws actually in force ceased to be accepted as the standard of it.

It is true that mankind consider the idea of justice and its obligations as applicable to many things which neither are, nor is it desired that they should be, regulated by law. Nobody desires that laws should interfere with the whole detail of private life; yet everyone allows that in all daily conduct a person may and does show himself to be either just or unjust. But even here, the idea of the breach of what ought to be law still lingers in a modified shape. It would always give us pleasure, and chime in with our feelings of fitness, that acts which we deem unjust should be punished, though we do not always think it expedient that this should be done by the tribunals. We forego that gratification on account of incidental inconveniences. We should be glad to see just conduct enforced and injustice repressed, even in the minutest details, if we were not, with reason, afraid of trusting the magistrate with so unlimited an amount of power over individuals. When we think that a person is bound in justice to do a thing, it is an ordinary form of language to say that he ought to be compelled to do it. We should be gratified to see the obligation enforced by anybody who had the power. If we see that its enforcement by law would be inexpedient, we lament the impossibility, we consider the impunity given to injustice as an evil and strive to make amends for it by bringing a strong expression of our own and the public disapprobation to bear upon the offender. Thus the idea of legal constraint is still the generating idea of the notion of justice, though undergoing several transformations before that notion as it exists in an advanced state of society becomes complete.

The above is, I think, a true account, as far as it goes, of the origin and progressive growth of the idea of justice. But we must observe that it contains as yet nothing to distinguish that obligation from moral obligation in general. For the truth is that the idea of penal sanction, which is the essence of law, enters not only into the conception of injustice, but into that of any kind of wrong. We do not call anything wrong unless we mean to imply that a person ought to be punished in some way or other for doing it—if not by law, by the opinion of his fellow creatures; if not by opinion, by the reproaches of his own conscience. This seems the real turning point of the distinction between morality and simple expediency. It is a part of the notion of duty in every one of its forms that a person may rightfully be compelled to fulfill it. Duty is a thing which may be *exacted* from a person, as one exacts a debt. Unless we think that it may be exacted from him, we do not call it his duty. Reasons of prudence, or the interest of other people, may militate against actually exacting it, but the person himself, it is clearly understood, would not be entitled to complain. There are other things, on the contrary, which we wish that people should do, which we like or admire them for doing, perhaps dislike or despise them for not doing, but yet admit that they are not bound to do; it is not a case of moral obligation; we do not blame them, that is, we do not think that they are proper objects of punishment. How we come by these ideas of deserving and not deserving punishment will appear, perhaps, in the sequel; but I think there is no doubt that this distinction lies at the bottom of the notions of right and wrong; that we call any conduct wrong, or employ, instead, some other term of dislike or disparagement, according as we think that the person ought, or ought not, to be punished for it; and we say it would be right to do so and so, or merely that it would be desirable or laudable, according as we would wish to see the person whom it concerns compelled, or only persuaded and exhorted, to act in that manner.

This, therefore, being the characteristic difference which marks off, not justice, but morality in general from the remaining provinces of expediency and worthiness, the character is still to be sought which distinguishes justice from other branches of morality. Now it is known that ethical writers divide moral duties into two classes, denoted by the ill-chosen expressions, duties of perfect and of imperfect obligation; the latter being those in which, though the act is obligatory, the particular occasions of performing it are left to our choice, as in the case of charity or beneficence, which we are indeed bound to practice but not toward any definite person, nor at any prescribed time. In the more precise language of philosophic jurists, duties of perfect obligation are those duties in virtue of which a correlative right resides in some person or persons; duties of imperfect obligation are those moral obligations which do not give birth to any right. I think it will be found that this distinction exactly coincides with that which exists between justice and the other obligations of morality. In our survey of the various popular acceptations of justice, the term appeared generally to involve the idea of a personal right—a claim on the part of one or more individuals, like that which the law gives when it confers a proprietary or other legal right. Whether the injustice consists in depriving a person of a possession, or in breaking faith with him, or in treating him worse than he deserves, or worse than other people who have no greater claims— in each case the supposition implies two things: a wrong done, and some assignable person who is wronged. Injustice may also be done by treating a person better than others; but the wrong in this case is to his competitors, who are also assignable persons. It seems to me that this feature in the case—a right in some person, correlative to the moral obligation—constitutes the specific difference between justice and generosity or beneficence. Justice implies something which it is not only right to do, and wrong not to do, but which some individual person can claim from us as his moral right. No one has a moral right to our generosity or beneficence because we are not morally bound to practice those virtues toward any given individual. And it will be

found with respect to this as to every correct definition that the instances which seem to conflict with it are those which most confirm it. For if a moralist attempts, as some have done, to make out that mankind generally, though not any given individual, have a right to all the good we can do them, he at once, by that thesis, includes generosity and beneficence within the category of justice. He is obliged to say that our utmost exertions are *due* to our fellow creatures, thus assimilating them to a debt; or that nothing less can be a sufficient *return* for what society does for us, thus classing the case as one of gratitude; both of which are acknowledged cases of justice, and not of the virtue of beneficence; and whoever does not place the distinction between justice and morality in general, where we have now placed it, will be found to make no distinction between them at all, but to merge all morality in justice.

Having thus endeavored to determine the distinctive elements which enter into the composition of the idea of justice, we are ready to enter on the inquiry whether the feeling which accompanies the idea is attached to it by a special dispensation of nature, or whether it could have grown up, by any known laws, out of the idea itself; and, in particular, whether it can have originated in considerations of general expediency.

I conceive that the sentiment itself does not arise from anything which would commonly or correctly be termed an idea of expediency, but that, though the sentiment does not, whatever is moral in it does.

We have seen that the two essential ingredients in the sentiment of justice are the desire to punish a person who has done harm and the knowledge or belief that there is some definite individual or individuals to whom harm has been done.

Now it appears to me that the desire to punish a person who has done harm to some individual is a spontaneous outgrowth from two sentiments, both in the highest degree natural and which either are or resemble instincts: the impulse of self-defense and the feeling of sympathy.

It is natural to resent and to repel or retaliate any harm done or attempted against ourselves or against those with whom we sympathize. The origin of this sentiment it is not necessary here to discuss. Whether it be an instinct or a result of intelligence, it is, we know, common to all animal nature; for every animal tries to hurt those who have hurt, or who it thinks are about to hurt, itself or its young. Human beings, on this point, only differ from other animals in two particulars. First, in being capable of sympathizing, not solely with their offspring, or, like some of the more noble animals, with some superior animal who is kind to them, but with all human, and even with all sentient, beings; secondly, in having a more developed intelligence, which gives a wider range to the whole of their sentiments, whether self-regarding or sympathetic. By virtue of his superior intelligence, even apart from his superior range of sympathy, a human being is capable of apprehending a community of interest between himself and the human society of which he forms a part, such that any conduct which threatens the security of the society generally is threatening to his own, and calls forth his instinct (if instinct it be) of self-defense. The same superiority of intelligence joined to the power of sympathizing with human beings generally enables him to attach himself to the collective idea of his tribe, his country, or mankind in such a manner that any act hurtful to them raises his instinct of sympathy and urges him to resistance.

The sentiment of justice, in that one of its elements which consists of the desire to punish, is thus, I conceive, the natural feeling of retaliation or vengeance, rendered by intellect and sympathy applicable to those injuries, that is, to those hurts, which would us through, or in common with, society at large. This sentiment, in itself, has nothing moral in it; what is moral is the exclusive subordination of it to the social sympathies, so as to wait on and obey their call. For the natural feeling would make us resent indiscriminately whatever anyone does that is disagreeable to us; but, when moralized by the social feeling, it only acts in the directions conformable to the general good: just persons resenting a hurt to society, though not otherwise a hurt to themselves, and not resenting a hurt to themselves, however painful, unless it be of the kind which society has a common interest with them in the repression of.

It is no objection against this doctrine to say that, when we feel our sentiment of justice outraged, we are not thinking of society at large or of any collective interest, but only of the individual case. It is common enough, certainly, though the reverse of commendable, to feel resentment merely because we have suffered pain; but a person whose resentment is really a moral feeling, that is, who considers whether an act is blamable before he allows himself to resent it—such a person, though he may not say expressly to himself that he is standing up for the interest of society, certainly does feel that he is asserting a rule which is for the benefit of others as well as for his own. If he is not feeling this, if he is regarding the act solely as it affects him individually, he is not consciously just; he is not concerning himself about the justice of his actions. This is admitted even by anti-utilitarian moralists. When Kant (as before remarked) propounds as the fundamental principle of morals, "So act that thy rule of conduct might be adopted as a law by all rational beings," he virtually acknowledges that the interest of mankind collectively, or at least of mankind indiscriminately, must be in the mind of the agent when conscientiously deciding on the morality of the act. Otherwise he uses words without a meaning; for that a rule even of utter selfishness could not possibly be adopted by all rational beings— that there is any insuperable obstacle in the nature of things to its adoption—cannot be even plausibly maintained. To give any meaning to Kant's principle, the sense put upon it must be that we ought to shape our conduct by a rule which all rational beings might adopt *with benefit to their collective interest.*

To recapitulate: the idea of justice supposes two things—a rule of conduct and a sentiment which sanctions the rule. The first must be supposed common to all mankind and intended for their good. The other (the sentiment) is a desire that punishment may be suffered by those who infringe the rule. There is involved, in addition, the conception of some definite person who suffers by the infringement, whose rights (to use the expression appropriated to the case) are violated by it. And the sentiment of justice appears to me to be the animal desire to repel or retaliate a hurt or damage to oneself or to those with whom one sympathizes, widened so as to include all persons, by the human capacity of enlarged sympathy and the human conception of intelligent self-interest. From the latter elements the feeling derives its morality; from the former, its peculiar impressiveness and energy of self-assertion.

I have, throughout, treated the idea of a *right* residing in the injured person and violated by the injury, not as a separate element in the composition of the idea and sentiment, but as one of the forms in which the other two elements clothe themselves. Those elements are a hurt to some assignable person or persons, on the one hand, and a demand for punishment, on the other. An examination of our own minds, I think, will show that these two things include all that we mean when we speak of violation of a right. When we call anything a person's right, we mean that he has a valid claim on society to protect him in the possession of it, either by the force of law or by that of education and opinion. If he has what we consider a sufficient claim, on whatever account, to have something guaranteed to him by society, we say that he has a right to it. If we desire to prove that anything does not belong to him by right, we think this done as soon as it is admitted that society ought not to take measures for securing it to him, but

should leave him to chance or to his own exertions. Thus a person is said to have a right to what he can earn in fair professional competition, because society ought not to allow any other person to hinder him from endeavoring to earn in that manner as much as he can. But he has not a right to three hundred a year, though he may happen to be earning it; because society is not called on to provide that he shall earn that sum. On the contrary, if he owns ten thousand pounds three-per-cent stock, he *has* a right to three hundred a year because society has come under an obligation to provide him with an income of that amount.

To have a right, then, is, I conceive, to have something which society ought to defend me in the possession of. If the objector goes on to ask why it ought, I can give him no other reason than general utility. If that expression does not seem to convey a sufficient feeling of the strength of the obligation, nor to account for the peculiar energy of the feeling, it is because there goes to the composition of the sentiment, not a rational only but also an animal element— the thirst for retaliation; and this thirst derives its intensity, as well as its moral justification, from the extraordinarily important and impressive kind of utility which is concerned. The interest involved is that of security, to everyone's feelings the most vital of all interests. All other earthly benefits are needed by one person, not needed by another; and many of them can, if necessary, be cheerfully foregone or replaced by something else; but security no human being can possibly do without; on it we depend for all our immunity from evil and for the whole value of all and every good, beyond the passing moment, since nothing but the gratification of the instant could be of any worth to us if we could be deprived of everything the next instant by whoever was momentarily stronger than ourselves. Now this most indispensable of all necessaries, after physical nutriment cannot be had unless the machinery for providing it is kept unintermittedly in active play. Our notion, therefore, of the claim we have on our fellow creatures to join in making safe for us the very groundwork of our existence gathers feelings around it so much more intense than those concerned in any of the more common cases of utility that the difference in degree (as is often the case in psychology) becomes a real difference in kind. The claim assumes that character of absoluteness, that apparent infinity and incommensurability with all other considerations which constitute the distinction between the feeling of right and wrong and that of ordinary expediency and inexpediency. The feelings concerned are so powerful and we count so positively on finding a responsive feeling in others (all being alike interested) that *ought* and *should* grow into *must*, and recognized indispensability becomes a moral necessity, analogous to physical, and often not inferior to it in binding force.

If the preceding analysis, or something resembling it, be not the correct account of the notion of justice—if justice be totally independent of utility, and be a standard *per se*, which the mind can recognize by simple introspection of itself—it is hard to understand why that internal oracle is so ambiguous, and why so many things appear either just or unjust, according to the light in which they are regarded.

We are continually informed that utility is an uncertain standard, which every different person interprets differently, and that there is no safety but in the immutable, ineffaceable, and unmistakable dictates of justice, which carry their evidence in themselves and are independent of the fluctuations of opinion. One would suppose from this that on questions of justice there could be no controversy; that, if we take that for our rule, its application to any given case could leave us in as little doubt as a mathematical demonstration. So far is this from being the fact that there is as much difference of opinion, and as much discussion, about what is just as about what is useful to society. Not only have different nations and individuals different notions of

justice, but in the mind of one and the same individual, justice is not some one rule, principle, or maxim, but many which do not always coincide in their dictates, and, in choosing between which, he is guided either by some extraneous standard or by his own personal predilections.

For instance, there are some who say that it is unjust to punish anyone for the sake of example to others, that punishment is just only when intended for the good of the sufferer himself. Others maintain the extreme reverse, contending that to punish persons who have attained years of discretion, for their own benefit, is despotism and injustice, since, if the matter at issue is solely their own good, no one has a right to control their own judgment of it; but that they may justly be punished to prevent evil to others, this being the exercise of the legitimate right of self-defense. Mr. Owen, again, affirms that it is unjust to punish at all, for the criminal did not make his own character; his education and the circumstances which surrounded him have made him a criminal, and for these he is not responsible. All these opinions are extremely plausible; and so long as the question is argued as one of justice simply, without going down to the principles which lie under justice and are the source of its authority, I am unable to see how any of these reasoners can be refuted. For in truth every one of the three builds upon rules of justice confessedly true. The first appeals to the acknowledged injustice of singling out an individual and making him a sacrifice, without his consent, for other people's benefit. The second relies on the acknowledged justice of self-defense and the admitted injustice of forcing one person to conform to another's notions of what constitutes his good. The Owenite invokes the admitted principle that it is unjust to punish anyone for what he cannot help. Each is triumphant so long as he is not compelled to take into consideration any other maxims of justice than the one he has selected; but as soon as their several maxims are brought face to face, each disputant seems to have exactly as much to say for himself as the others. No one of them can carry out his own notion of justice without trampling upon another equally binding. These are difficulties; they have always been felt to be such; and many devices have been invented to turn rather than to overcome them. As a refuge from the last of the three, men imagined what they called the freedom of the will—fancying that they could not justify punishing a man whose will is in a thoroughly hateful state unless it be supposed to have come into that state through no influence of anterior circumstances. To escape from the other difficulties, a favorite contrivance has been the fiction of a contract whereby at some unknown period all the members of society engaged to obey the laws and consented to be punished for any disobedience to them, thereby giving to their legislators the right, which it is assumed they would not otherwise have had, of punishing them, either for their own good or for that of society. This happy thought was considered to get rid of the whole difficulty and to legitimate the infliction of punishment, in virtue of another received maxim of justice, *volenti non fit injuria*— that is not unjust which is done with the consent of the person who is supposed to be hurt by it. I need hardly remark that, even if the consent were not a mere fiction, this maxim is not superior in authority to the others which it is brought in to supersede. It is, on the contrary, an instructive specimen of the loose and irregular manner in which supposed principles of justice grow up. This particular one evidently came into use as a help to the coarse exigencies of courts of law, which are sometimes obliged to be content with very uncertain presumptions, on account of the greater evils which would often arise from any attempt on their part to cut finer. But even courts of law are not able to adhere consistently to the maxim, for they allow voluntary engagements to be set aside on the ground of fraud, and sometimes on that of mere mistake or misinformation.

Again, when the legitimacy of inflicting punishment is admitted, how many conflicting conceptions of justice come to light in discussing the proper apportionment of punishments to offenses. No rule on the subject recommends itself so strongly to the primitive and spontaneous sentiment of justice as the *lex talionis*, an eye for an eye and a tooth for a tooth. Though this principle of the Jewish and of the Mohammedan law has been generally abandoned in Europe as a practical maxim, there is, I suspect, in most minds, a secret hankering after it; and when retribution accidentally falls on an offender in that precise shape, the general feeling of satisfaction evinced bears witness how natural is the sentiment to which this repayment in kind is acceptable. With many, the test of justice in penal infliction is that the punishment should be proportioned to the offense, meaning that it should be exactly measured by the moral guilt of the culprit (whatever be their standard for measuring moral guilt), the consideration, what amount of punishment is necessary to deter from the offense having nothing to do with the question of justice, in their estimation; while there are others to whom that consideration is all in all, who maintain that it is not just, at least for man, to inflict on a fellow creature, whatever may be his offenses, any amount of suffering beyond the least that will suffice to prevent him from repeating, and others from imitating, his misconduct.

To take another example from a subject already once referred to. In co-operative industrial association, is it just or not that talent or skill should give a title to superior remuneration? On the negative side of the question it is argued that whoever does the best he can deserves equally well, and ought not in justice to be put in a position of inferiority for no fault of his own; that superior abilities have already advantages more than enough, in the admiration they excite, the personal influence they command, and the internal sources of satisfaction attending them, without adding to these a superior share of the world's goods; and that society is bound in justice rather to make compensation to the less favored for this unmerited inequality of advantages than to aggravate it. On the contrary side it is contended that society receives more from the more efficient laborer; that, his services being more useful, society owes him a larger return for them; that a greater share of the joint result is actually his work, and not to allow his claim to it is a kind of robbery; that, if he is only to receive as much as others, he can only be justly required to produce as much, and to give a smaller amount of time and exertion, proportioned to his superior efficiency. Who shall decide between these appeals to conflicting principles of justice? Justice has in this case two sides to it, which it is impossible to bring into harmony, and the two disputants have chosen opposite sides; the one looks to what it is just that the individual should receive, the other to what it is just that the community should give. Each, from his own point of view, is unanswerable; and any choice between them, on grounds of justice, must be perfectly arbitrary. Social utility alone can decide the preference.

How many, again, and how irreconcilable are the standards of justice to which reference is made in discussing the repartition of taxation. One opinion is that payment ot the state should be in numerical proportion to pecuniary means. Others think that justice dictates what they term graduated taxation—taking a higher percentage from those who have more to spare. In point of natural justice a strong case might be made for disregarding means altogether, and taking the same absolute sum (whenever it could be got) from everyone; as the subscribers to a mess or to a club all pay the same sum for the same privileges, whether they can all equally afford it or not. Since the protection (it might be said) of law and government is afforded to and is equally required by all, there is no injustice in making all by it at the same price. It is reckoned justice, not injustice, that a dealer should charge to all customers the same price for the same article, not a price varying according to their means of payment. This doctrine, as applied to taxation, finds

no advocates because it conflicts so strongly with man's feelings of humanity and of social expediency; but the principle of justice which it invokes is as true and as binding as those which can be appealed to against it. Accordingly it exerts a tacit influence on the line of defense employed for other modes of assessing taxation. People feel obliged to argue that the state does more for the rich man than for the poor, as a justification for its taking more from them, though this is in reality not true, for the rich would be far better able to protect themselves, in the absence of law or government, than the poor, and indeed would probably be successful in converting the poor into their slaves. Others, again, so far defer to the same conception of justice as to maintain that all should pay an equal capitation tax for the protection of their persons (these being of equal value to all), and an unequal tax for the protection of their property, which is unequal. To this others reply that the all of one man is as valuable to him as the all of another. From these confusions there is no other mode of extrication than the utilitarian.

Is, then, the difference between the just and the expedient a merely imaginary distinction? Have mankind been under a delusion in thinking that justice is a more sacred thing than policy, and that the latter ought only to be listened to after the former has been satisfied? By no means. The exposition we have given of the nature and origin of the sentiment recognizes a real distinction; and no one of those who profess the most sublime contempt for the consequences of actions as an element in their morality attaches more importance to the distinction than I do. While I dispute the pretensions of any theory which sets up an imaginary standard of justice not grounded on utility, I account the justice which is grounded on utility to be the chief part, and incomparably the most sacred and binding part, of all morality. Justice is a name for certain classes of moral rules which concern the essentials of human well-being more nearly, and are therefore of more absolute obligation, than any other rules for the guidance of life; and the notion which we have found to be of the essence of the idea of justice—that of a right residing in an individual—implies and testifies to this more binding obligation.

The moral rules which forbid mankind to hurt one another (in which we must never forget to include wrongful interference with each other's freedom) are more vital to human well-being than any maxims, however important, which only point out the best mode of managing some department of human affairs. They have also the peculiarity that they are the main element in determining the whole of the social feelings of mankind. It is their observance which alone preserves peace among human beings; if obedience to them were not the rule, and disobedience the exception, everyone would see in everyone else an enemy against whom he must be perpetually guarding himself. What is hardly less important, these are the precepts which mankind have the strongest and the most direct inducements for impressing upon one another. By merely giving to each other prudential instruction or exhortation, they may gain, or think they gain, nothing; in inculcating on each other the duty of positive beneficence, they have an unmistakable interest, but far less in degree; a person may possibly not need the benefits of others, but he always needs that they should not do him hurt. Thus the moralities which protect every individual from being harmed by others, either directly or by being hindered in his freedom of pursuing his own good, are at once those which he himself has most at heart and those which he has the strongest interest in publishing and enforcing by word and deed. It is by a person's observance of these that his fitness to exist as one of the fellowship of human beings is tested and decided; for on that depends his being a nuisance or not to those with whom he is in contact. Now it is these moralities primarily which compose the obligations of justice. The most marked cases of injustice, and those which give the tone to the feeling of repugnance which

characterizes the sentiment, are acts of wrongful aggression or wrongful exercise of power over someone; the next are those which consist in wrongfully withholding from him something which is his due—in both cases inflicting on him a positive hurt, either in the form of direct suffering or of the privation of some good which he had reasonable ground, either of a physical or of a social kind, for counting upon.

The same powerful motives which command the observance of these primary moralities enjoin the punishment of those who violate them; and as the impulses of self-defense, of defense of others, and of vengeance are all called forth against such persons, retribution, or evil for evil, becomes closely connected with the sentiment of justice, and is universally included in the idea. Good for good is also one of the dictates of justice; and this, though its social utility is evident, and though it carries with it a natural human feeling, has not at first sight that obvious connection with hurt or injury which, existing in the most elementary cases of just and unjust, is the source of the characteristic intensity of the sentiment. But the connection, though less obvious, is not less real. He who accepts benefits and denies a return of them when needed inflicts a real hurt by disappointing one of the most natural and reasonable of expectations, and one which he must at least tacitly have encouraged, otherwise the benefits would seldom have been conferred. The important rank, among human evils and wrongs, of the disappointment of expectation is shown in the fact that it constitutes the principal criminality of two such highly immoral acts as a breach of friendship and a breach of promise. Few hurts which human beings can sustain are greater, and none wound more, than when that on which they habitually and with full assurance relied fails them in the hour of need; and few wrongs are greater than this mere withholding of good; none excite more resentment, either in the person suffering or in a sympathizing spectator. The principle, therefore, of giving to each what they deserve, that is, good for good as well as evil for evil, is not only included within the idea of justice as we have defined it, but is a proper object of that intensity of sentiment which places the just in human estimation above the simply expedient.

Most of the maxims of justice current in the world, and commonly appealed to in its transactions, are simply instrumental to carrying into effect the principles of justice which we have now spoken of. That a person is only responsible for what he has done voluntarily, or could voluntarily have avoided, that it is unjust to condemn any person unheard; that the punishment ought to be proportioned to the offense, and the like, are maxims intended to prevent the just principle of evil for evil from being perverted to the infliction of evil without that justification. The greater part of these common maxims have come into use from the practice of courts of justice, which have been naturally led to a more complete recognition and elaboration than was likely to suggest itself to others, of the rules necessary to enable them to fulfill their double function—of inflicting punishment when due, and of awarding to each person his right.

That first of judicial virtues, impartiality, is an obligation of justice, partly for the reason last mentioned, as being a necessary condition of the fulfillment of other obligations of justice. But this is not the only source of the exalted rank, among human obligations, of those maxims of equality and impartiality, which, both in popular estimation and in that of the most enlightened, are included among the precepts of justice. In one point of view, they may be considered as corollaries from the principles already laid down. If it is a duty to do to each according to his deserts, returning good for good, as well as repressing evil by evil, it necessarily follows that we should treat all equally well (when no higher duty forbids) who have deserved equally well of us, and that society should treat all equally well who have deserved equally well of it, that is, who have deserved equally well absolutely. This is the highest abstract standard of social and distributive justice, toward which all institutions and the efforts of all virtuous citizens should be made in the utmost possible degree to converge. But this great moral duty rests upon a still deeper foundation, being a direct emanation from the first principle of morals, and not a mere logical corollary from secondary or derivative doctrines. It is involved in the very meaning of utility, or the greatest happiness principle. That principle is a mere form of words without rational signification unless one person's happiness, supposed equal in degree (with the proper allowance made for kind), is counted for exactly as much as another's. Those conditions being supplied, Bentham's dictum, "everybody to count for one, nobody for more than one," might be written under the principle of utility as an explanatory commentary. The equal claim of everybody to happiness, in the estimation of the moralist and of the legislator, involves an equal claim to all the means of happiness except in so far as the inevitable conditions of human life and the general interest in which that of every individual is included set limits to the maxim; and those limits ought to be strictly construed. As every other maxim of justice, so this is by no means applied or held applicable universally; on the contrary, as I have already remarked, it bends to every person's ideas of social expediency. But in whatever case it is deemed applicable at all, it is held to be the dictate of justice. All persons are deemed to have a *right* to equality of treatment, except when some recognized social expediency requires the reverse. And hence all social inequalities which have ceased to be considered expedient assume the character, not of simple inexpediency, but of injustice, and appear so tyrannical that people are apt to wonder how they ever could have been tolerated—forgetful that they themselves, perhaps, tolerate other inequalities under an equally mistaken notion of expediency, the correction of which would make that which they approve seem quite as monstrous as what they have at last learned to condemn. The entire history of social improvement has been a series of transitions by which one custom or institution after another, from being a supposed primary necessity of social existence, has passed into the rank of a universally stigmatized injustice and tyranny. So it has been with the distinctions of slaves and freemen, nobles and serfs, patricians and plebeians; and so it will be, and in part already is, with the aristocracies of color, race, and sex.

It appears from what has been said that justice is a name for certain moral requirements which, regarded collectively, stand higher in the scale of social utility, and are therefore of more paramount obligation, than any others, though particular cases may occur in which some other social duty is so important as to overrule any one of the general maxims of justice. Thus, to save a life, it may not only be allowable, but a duty, to steal or take by force the necessary food or medicine, or to kidnap and compel to officiate the only qualified medical practitioner. In such cases, as we do not call anything justice which is not a virtue, we usually say, not that justice must give way to some other moral principle, but that what is just in ordinary cases is, by reason of that other principle, not just in the particular case. By this useful accommodation of language, the character of indefeasibility attributed to justice is kept up, and we are saved from the necessity of maintaining that there can be laudable injustice.

The considerations which have now been adduced resolve, I conceive, the only real difficulty in the utilitarian theory of morals. It has always been evident that all cases of justice are also cases of expediency; the difference is in the peculiar sentiment which attaches to the former, as contradistinguished from the latter. If this characteristic sentiment has been sufficiently accounted for; if there is no necessity to assume for it any peculiarity of origin; if it is simply the natural feeling of resentment, moralized by being made co-existensive with the demands of social good; and if this feeling not only does but ought to exist in all the classes of cases to which the idea of justice corresponds—that idea no longer presents itself as a stumbling block to the utilitarian ethics. Justice remains the appropriate name for certain social utilities which are vastly more important, and therefore more absolute and imperative, than any others are as a class (though not more so than others may be in particular cases); and which, therefore, ought to be, as well as naturally are, guarded by a sentiment, not only different in degree, but also in kind; distinguished from the milder feeling which attaches to the mere idea of promoting human pleasure or convenience at once by the more definite nature of its commands and by the sterner character of its sanctions.

Chapter 18

John Rawls

A THEORY OF JUSTICE

John Rawls (1921–2002) was the most influential political philosopher of the twentieth century. This excerpt is from his seminal work, *A Theory of Justice* (1971). In it, he argues for two principles of justice which are to govern the "basic structure of society"—one guaranteeing equal basic liberties to all, and another ensuring that inequalities are to the advantage of the least well-off. These principles are based on a hypothetical contract made from behind a veil of ignorance—a position that Rawls argues expresses our understanding of persons as free and equal.

1. The Role of Justice

Justice is the first virtue of social institutions, as truth is of systems of thought. A theory however elegant and economical must be rejected or revised if it is untrue; likewise laws and institutions no matter how efficient and well-arranged must be reformed or abolished if they are unjust. Each person possesses an inviolability founded on justice that even the welfare of society as a whole cannot override. For this reason justice denies that the loss of freedom for some is made right by a greater good shared by others. It does not allow that the sacrifices imposed on a few are outweighed by the larger sum of advantages enjoyed by many. Therefore in a just society the liberties of equal citizenship are taken as settled; the rights secured by justice are not subject to political bargaining or to the calculus of social interests. The only thing that permits us to acquiesce in an erroneous theory is the lack of a better one; analogously, an injustice is tolerable only when it is necessary to avoid an even greater injustice. Being first virtues of human activities, truth and justice are uncompromising.

These propositions seem to express our intuitive conviction of the primacy of justice. No doubt they are expressed too strongly. In any event I wish to inquire whether these contentions or others similar to them are sound, and if so how they can be accounted for. To this end it is necessary to work out a theory of justice in the light of which these assertions can be interpreted and assessed. I shall begin by considering the role of the principles of justice. Let us assume, to fix ideas, that a society is a more or less self-sufficient association of persons who in their relations to one another recognize certain rules of conduct as binding and who for the most part act in accordance with them. Suppose further that these rules specify a system of cooperation designed to advance the good of those taking part in it. Then, although a society is a cooperative venture for mutual advantage, it is typically marked by a conflict as well as by an identity of interests. There is an identity of interests since social cooperation makes possible a better life for all than any would have if each were to live solely by his own efforts. There is a conflict of interests since persons are not indifferent as to how the greater benefits produced by their collaboration are distributed, for in order to pursue their ends they each prefer a larger to a lesser share. A set of principles is required for choosing among the various social arrangements which determine this division of advantages and for underwriting an agreement on the proper distributive shares. These principles are the principles of social justice: they provide a way of assigning rights and duties in the basic institutions of society and they define the appropriate distribution of the benefits and burdens of social cooperation. [. . .]

3. The Main Idea of the Theory of Justice

My aim is to present a conception of justice which generalizes and carries to a higher level of abstraction the familiar theory of the social contract as found, say, in Locke, Rousseau, and Kant. In order to do this we are not to think of the original contract as one to enter a particular society or to set up a particular form of government. Rather, the guiding idea is that the principles of justice or the basic structure of society are the object of the original agreement. They are the principles that free and rational persons concerned to further their own interests would accept in an initial position of equality as defining the fundamental terms of their association. These principles are to regulate all further agreements; they specify the kinds of social cooperation that can be entered into and the forms of government that can be established. This way of regarding the principles of justice I shall call justice as fairness.

Thus we are to imagine that those who engage in social cooperation choose together, in one joint act, the principles which are to assign basic rights and duties and to determine the division of social benefits. Men are to decide in advance how they are to regulate their claims against one another and what is to be the foundation charter of their society. Just as each person must decide by rational reflection what constitutes his good, that is, the system of ends which it is rational for him to pursue, so a group of persons must decide once and for all what is to count among them as just and unjust. The choice which rational men would make in this hypothetical situation of equal liberty, assuming for the present that this choice problem has a solution, determines the principles of justice.

In justice as fairness the original position of equality corresponds to the state of nature in the traditional theory of the social contract. This original position is not, of course, thought of as an actual historical state of affairs, much less as a primitive condition of culture. It is understood as a purely hypothetical situation characterized so as to lead to a certain conception of justice. Among the essential features of this situation is that no one knows his place in society, his class position or social status, nor does any one know his fortune in the distribution of natural assets and abilities, his intelligence, strength, and the like. I shall even assume that the parties do not know their conceptions of the good or their special psychological propensities. The principles of justice are chosen behind a veil of ignorance. This ensures that no one is advantaged or disadvantaged in the choice of principles by the outcome of natural chance or the contingency of social circumstances. Since all are similarly situated and no one is able to design principles to favor his particular condition, the principles of justice are the result of a fair agreement or bargain. For given the circumstances of the original position, the symmetry of everyone's relations to each other, this initial situation is fair between individuals as moral persons, that is, as rational beings with their own ends and capable, I shall assume, of a sense of justice. The original position is, one might say, the appropriate initial status quo, and thus the fundamental agreements reached in it are fair. This explains the propriety of the name "justice as fairness": it conveys the idea that the principles of justice are agreed to in an initial situation that is fair. The name does not mean that the concepts of justice and fairness are the same, any more than the phrase "poetry as metaphor" means that the concepts of poetry and metaphor are the same.

Justice as fairness begins, as I have said, with one of the most general of all choices which persons might make together, namely, with the choice of the first principles of a conception of justice which is to regulate all subsequent criticism and reform of institutions. Then, having chosen a conception of justice, we can suppose that they are to choose a constitution and a legislature to enact laws, and so on, all in accordance with the principles of justice initially agreed upon. Our social situation is just if it is such that by this sequence of hypothetical agreements we would have contracted into the general system of rules which defines it. Moreover, assuming that the original position does determine a set of principles (that is, that a particular conception of justice would be chosen), it will then be true that whenever social institutions satisfy these principles those engaged in them can say to one another that they are cooperating on terms to which they would agree if they were free and equal persons whose relations with respect to one another were fair. They could all view their arrangements as meeting the stipulations which they would acknowledge in an initial situation that embodies widely accepted and reasonable constraints on the choice of principles. The general recognition of this fact would provide the basis for a public acceptance of the corresponding principles of justice. No society can, of course, be a scheme of cooperation which men enter voluntarily in a literal sense; each person finds himself placed at birth in some particular position in some particular society, and the nature of this position materially affects his life prospects. Yet a society satisfying the principles

of justice as fairness comes as close as a society can to being a voluntary scheme, for it meets the principles which free and equal persons would assent to under circumstances that are fair. In this sense its members are autonomous and the obligations they recognize self-imposed.

One feature of justice as fairness is to think of the parties in the initial situation as rational and mutually disinterested. This does not mean that the parties are egoists, that is, individuals with only certain kinds of interests, say in wealth, prestige, and domination. But they are conceived as not taking an interest in one another's interests. They are to presume that even their spiritual aims may be opposed, in the way that the aims of those of different religions may be opposed. Moreover, the concept of rationality must be interpreted as far as possible in the narrow sense, standard in economic theory, of taking the most effective means to given ends. I shall modify this concept to some extent, as explained later (§25), but one must try to avoid introducing into it any controversial ethical elements. The initial situation must be characterized by stipulations that are widely accepted.

In working out the conception of justice as fairness one main task clearly is to determine which principles of justice would be chosen in the original position. To do this we must describe this situation in some detail and formulate with care the problem of choice which it presents. These matters I shall take up in the immediately succeeding chapters. It may be observed, however, that once the principles of justice are thought of as arising from an original agreement in a situation of equality, it is an open question whether the principle of utility would be acknowledged. Offhand it hardly seems likely that persons who view themselves as equals, entitled to press their claims upon one another, would agree to a principle which may require lesser life prospects for some simply for the sake of a greater sum of advantages enjoyed by others. Since each desires to protect his interests, his capacity to advance his conception of the good, no one has a reason to acquiesce in an enduring loss for himself in order to bring about a greater net balance of satisfaction. In the absence of strong and lasting benevolent impulses, a rational man would not accept a basic structure merely because it maximized the algebraic sum of advantages irrespective of its permanent effects on his own basic rights and interests. Thus it seems that the principle of utility is incompatible with the conception of social cooperation among equals for mutual advantage. It appears to be inconsistent with the idea of reciprocity implicit in the notion of a well-ordered society. Or, at any rate, so I shall argue.

I shall maintain instead that the persons in the initial situation would choose two rather different principles: the first requires equality in the assignment of basic rights and duties, while the second holds that social and economic inequalities, for example inequalities of wealth and authority, are just only if they result in compensating benefits for everyone, and in particular for the least advantaged members of society. These principles rule out justifying institutions on the grounds that the hardships of some are offset by a greater good in the aggregate. It may be expedient but it is not just that some should have less in order that others may prosper. But there is no injustice in the greater benefits earned by a few provided that the situation of persons not so fortunate is thereby improved. The intuitive idea is that since everyone's well-being depends upon a scheme of cooperation without which no one could have a satisfactory life, the division of advantages should be such as to draw forth the willing cooperation of everyone taking part in it, including those less well situated. Yet this can be expected only if reasonable terms are proposed. The two principles mentioned seem to be a fair agreement on the basis of which those better endowed, or more fortunate in their social position, neither of which we can be said to deserve, could expect the willing cooperation of others when some workable scheme is a necessary condition of the welfare of all. Once we decide to look for a conception of justice that nullifies the accidents of natural endowment and the contingencies of social circumstance as counters in quest for political and economic advantage, we are led to these principles. They express the result of leaving aside those aspects of the social world that seem arbitrary from a moral point of view.

The problem of the choice of principles, however, is extremely difficult. I do not expect the answer I shall suggest to be convincing to everyone. It is, therefore, worth noting from the outset that justice as fairness, like other contract views, consists of two parts: (1) an interpretation of the initial situation and of the problem of choice posed there, and (2) a set of principles which, it is argued, would be agreed to. One may accept the first part of the theory (or some variant thereof), but not the other, and conversely. The concept of the initial contractual situation may seem reasonable although the particular principles proposed are rejected. To be sure, I want to maintain that the most appropriate conception of this situation does lead to principles of justice contrary to utilitarianism and perfectionism, and therefore that the contract doctrine provides an alternative to these views. Still, one may dispute this contention even though one grants that the contractarian method is a useful way of studying ethical theories and of setting forth their underlying assumptions. [. . .]

4. The Original Position and Justification

I have said that the original position is the appropriate initial status quo which insures that the fundamental agreements reached in it are fair. This fact yields the name "justice as fairness." It is clear, then, that I want to say that one conception of justice is more reasonable than another, or justifiable with respect to it, if rational persons in the initial situation would choose its principles over those of the other for the role of justice. Conceptions of justice are to be ranked by their acceptability to persons so circumstanced. Understood in this way the question of justification is settled by working out a problem of deliberation: we have to ascertain which principles it would be rational to adopt given the contractual situation. This connects the theory of justice with the theory of rational choice.

If this view of the problem of justification is to succeed, we must, of course, describe in some detail the nature of this choice problem. A problem of rational decision has a definite answer only if we know the beliefs and interests of the parties, their relations with respect to one another, the alternatives between which they are to choose, the procedure whereby they make up their minds, and so on. As the circumstances are presented in different ways, correspondingly different principles are accepted. The concept of the original position, as I shall refer to it, is that of the most philosophically favored interpretation of this initial choice situation for the purposes of a theory of justice.

But how are we to decide what is the most favored interpretation? I assume, for one thing, that there is a broad measure of agreement that principles of justice should be chosen under certain conditions. To justify a particular description of the initial situation one shows that it incorporates these commonly shared presumptions. One argues from widely accepted but weak premises to more specific conclusions. Each of the presumptions should by itself be natural and plausible; some of them may seem innocuous or even trivial. The aim of the contract approach is to establish that taken together they impose significant bounds on acceptable principles of justice. The ideal outcome would be that these conditions determine a unique set of principles; but I shall be satisfied if they suffice to rank the main traditional conceptions of social justice.

One should not be misled, then, by the somewhat unusual conditions which characterize the original position. The idea here is simply to make vivid to ourselves the restrictions that it seems reasonable to impose on arguments for principles of justice, and therefore on these principles themselves. Thus it seems reasonable and generally acceptable that no one should be advantaged or disadvantaged by natural fortune or social circumstances in the choice of principles. It also seems widely agreed that it should be impossible to tailor principles to the circumstances of one's own case. We should insure further that particular inclinations and aspirations, and persons' conceptions of their good do not affect the principles adopted. The aim is to rule out those principles that it would be rational to propose for acceptance, however little the chance of success, only if one knew certain things that are irrelevant from the standpoint of justice. For example, if a man knew that he was wealthy, he might find it rational to advance the principle that various taxes for welfare measures be counted unjust; if he knew that he was poor, he would most likely propose the contrary principle. To represent the desired restrictions one imagines a situation in which everyone is deprived of this sort of information. One excludes the knowledge of those contingencies which sets men at odds and allows them to be guided by their prejudices. In this manner the veil of ignorance is arrived at in a natural way. This concept should cause no difficulty if we keep in mind the constraints on arguments that it is meant to express. At any time we can enter the original position, so to speak, simply by following a certain procedure, namely, by arguing for principles of justice in accordance with these restrictions.

It seems reasonable to suppose that the parties in the original position are equal. That is, all have the same rights in the procedure for choosing principles; each can make proposals, submit reasons for their acceptance, and so on. Obviously the purpose of these conditions is to represent equality between human beings as moral persons, as creatures having a conception of their good and capable of a sense of justice. The basis of equality is taken to be similarity in these two respects. Systems of ends are not ranked in value; and each man is presumed to have the requisite ability to understand and to act upon whatever principles are adopted. Together with the veil of ignorance, these conditions define the principles of justice as those which rational persons concerned to advance their interests would consent to as equals when none are known to be advantaged or disadvantaged by social and natural contingencies.

There is, however, another side to justifying a particular description of the original position. This is to see if the principles which would be chosen match our considered convictions of justice or extend them in an acceptable way. We can note whether applying these principles would lead us to make the same judgments about the basic structure of society which we now make intuitively and in which we have the greatest confidence; or whether, in cases where our present judgments are in doubt and given with hesitation, these principles offer a resolution which we can affirm on reflection. There are questions which we feel sure must be answered in a certain way. For example, we are confident that religious intolerance and racial discrimination are unjust. We think that we have examined these things with care and have reached what we believe is an impartial judgment not likely to be distorted by an excessive attention to our own interests. These convictions are provisional fixed points which we presume any conception of justice must fit. But we have much less assurance as to what is the correct distribution of wealth and authority. Here we may be looking for a way to remove our doubts. We can check an interpretation of the initial situation, then, by the capacity of its principles to accommodate our firmest convictions and to provide guidance where guidance is needed.

In searching for the most favored description of this situation we work from both ends. We begin by describing it so that it represents generally shared and preferably weak conditions. We

then see if these conditions are strong enough to yield a significant set of principles. If not, we look for further premises equally reasonable. But if so, and these principles match our considered convictions of justice, then so far well and good. But presumably there will be discrepancies. In this case we have a choice. We can either modify the account of the initial situation or we can revise our existing judgments, for even the judgments we take provisionally as fixed points are liable to revision. By going back and forth, sometimes altering the conditions of the contractual circumstances, at others withdrawing our judgments and conforming them to principle, I assume that eventually we shall find a description of the initial situation that both expresses reasonable conditions and yields principles which match our considered judgments duly pruned and adjusted. This state of affairs I refer to as reflective equilibrium. It is an equilibrium because at last our principles and judgments coincide; and it is reflective since we know to what principles our judgments conform and the premises of their derivation. At the moment everything is in order. But this equilibrium is not necessarily stable. It is liable to be upset by further examination of the conditions which should be imposed on the contractual situation and by particular cases which may lead us to revise our judgments. Yet for the time being we have done what we can to render coherent and to justify our convictions of social justice. We have reached a conception of the original position.

I shall not, of course, actually work through this process. Still, we may think of the interpretation of the original position that I shall present as the result of such a hypothetical course of reflection. It represents the attempt to accommodate within one scheme both reasonable philosophical conditions on principles as well as our considered judgments of justice. In arriving at the favored interpretation of the initial situation there is no point at which an appeal is made to self-evidence in the traditional sense either of general conceptions or particular convictions. I do not claim for the principles of justice proposed that they are necessary truths or derivable from such truths. A conception of justice cannot be deduced from self-evident premises or conditions on principles; instead, its justification is a matter of the mutual support of many considerations, of everything fitting together into one coherent view.

A final comment. We shall want to say that certain principles of justice are justified because they would be agreed to in an initial situation of equality. I have emphasized that this original position is purely hypothetical. It is natural to ask why, if this agreement is never actually entered into, we should take any interest in these principles, moral or otherwise. The answer is that the conditions embodied in the description of the original position are ones that we do in fact accept. Or if we do not, then perhaps we can be persuaded to do so by philosophical reflection. Each aspect of the contractual situation can be given supporting grounds. Thus what we shall do is to collect together into one conception a number of conditions on principles that we are ready upon due consideration to recognize as reasonable. These constraints express what we are prepared to regard as limits on fair terms of social cooperation. One way to look at the idea of the original position, therefore, is to see it as an expository device which sums up the meaning of these conditions and helps us to extract their consequences. On the other hand, this conception is also an intuitive notion that suggests its own elaboration, so that led on by it we are drawn to define more clearly the standpoint from which we can best interpret moral relationships. We need a conception that enables us to envision our objective from afar: the intuitive notion of the original position is to do this for us.

5. Classical Utilitarianism

There are many forms of utilitarianism, and the development of the theory has continued in recent years. I shall not survey these forms here, nor take account of the numerous refinements found in contemporary discussions. My aim is to work out a theory of justice that represents an alternative to utilitarian thought generally and so to all of these different versions of it. I believe that the contrast between the contract view and utilitarianism remains essentially the same in all these cases. Therefore I shall compare justice as fairness with familiar variants of intuitionism, perfectionism, and utilitarianism in order to bring out the underlying differences in the simplest way. With this end in mind, the kind of utilitarianism I shall describe here is the strict classical doctrine which receives perhaps its clearest and most accessible formulation in Sidgwick. The main idea is that society is rightly ordered, and therefore just, when its major institutions are arranged so as to achieve the greatest net balance of satisfaction summed over all the individuals belonging to it.

We may note first that there is, indeed, a way of thinking of society which makes it easy to suppose that the most rational conception of justice is utilitarian. For consider: each man in realizing his own interests is certainly free to balance his own losses against his own gains. We may impose a sacrifice on ourselves now for the sake of a greater advantage later. A person quite properly acts, at least when others are not affected, to achieve his own greatest good, to advance his rational ends as far as possible. Now why should not a society act on precisely the same principle applied to the group and therefore regard that which is rational for one man as right for an association of men? Just as the well-being of a person is constructed from the series of satisfactions that are experienced at different moments in the course of his life, so in very much the same way the well-being of society is to be constructed from the fulfillment of the systems of desires of the many individuals who belong to it. Since the principle for an individual is to advance as far as possible his own welfare, his own system of desires, the principle for society is to advance as far as possible the welfare of the group, to realize to the greatest extent the comprehensive system of desire arrived at from the desires of its members. Just as an individual balances present and future gains against present and future losses, so a society may balance satisfactions and dissatisfactions between different individuals. And so by these reflections one reaches the principle of utility in a natural way: a society is properly arranged when its institutions maximize the net balance of satisfaction. The principle of choice for an association of men is interpreted as an extension of the principle of choice for one man. Social justice is the principle of rational prudence applied to an aggregative conception of the welfare of the group.

This idea is made all the more attractive by a further consideration. The two main concepts of ethics are those of the right and the good; the concept of a morally worthy person is, I believe, derived from them. The structure of an ethical theory is, then, largely determined by how it defines and connects these two basic notions. Now it seems that the simplest way of relating them is taken by teleological theories: the good is defined independently from the right, and then the right is defined as that which maximizes the good. More precisely, those institutions and acts are right which of the available alternatives produce the most good, or at least as much good as any of the other institutions and acts open as real possibilities (a rider needed when the maximal class is not a singleton). Teleological theories have a deep intuitive appeal since they seem to embody the idea of rationality. It is natural to think that rationality is maximizing something and that in morals it must be maximizing the good. Indeed, it is tempting to suppose that it is self-evident that things should be arranged so as to lead to the most good.

It is essential to keep in mind that in a teleological theory the good is defined independently from the right. This means two things. First, the theory accounts for our considered judgments as to which things are good (our judgments of value) as a separate class of judgments intuitively distinguishable by common sense, and then proposes the hypothesis that the right is maximizing the good as already specified. Second, the theory enables one to judge the goodness of things without referring to what is right. For example, if pleasure is said to be the sole good, then presumably pleasures can be recognized and ranked in value by criteria that do not presuppose any standards of right, or what we would normally think of as such. Whereas if the distribution of goods is also counted as a good, perhaps a higher order one, and the theory directs us to produce the most good (including the good of distribution among others), we no longer have a teleological view in the classical sense. The problem of distribution falls under the concept of right as one intuitively understands it, and so the theory lacks an independent definition of the good. The clarity and simplicity of classical teleological theories derives largely from the fact that they factor our moral judgments into two classes, the one being characterized separately while the other is then connected with it by a maximizing principle.

Teleological doctrines differ, pretty clearly, according to how the conception of the good is specified. If it is taken as the realization of human excellence in the various forms of culture, we have what may be called perfectionism. This notion is found in Aristotle and Nietzsche, among others. If the good is defined as pleasure, we have hedonism; if as happiness, eudaimonism, and so on. I shall understand the principle of utility in its classical form as defining the good as the satisfaction of desire, or perhaps better, as the satisfaction of rational desire. This accords with the view in all essentials and provides, I believe, a fair interpretation of it. The appropriate terms of social cooperation are settled by whatever in the circumstances will achieve the greatest sum of satisfaction of the rational desires of individuals. It is impossible to deny the initial plausibility and attractiveness of this conception.

The striking feature of the utilitarian view of justice is that it does not matter, except indirectly, how this sum of satisfactions is distributed among individuals any more than it matters, except indirectly, how one man distributes his satisfactions over time. The correct distribution in either case is that which yields the maximum fulfillment. Society must allocate its means of satisfaction whatever these are, rights and duties, opportunities and privileges, and various forms of wealth, so as to achieve this maximum if it can. But in itself no distribution of satisfaction is better than another except that the more equal distribution is to be preferred to break ties. It is true that certain common sense precepts of justice, particularly those which concern the protection of liberties and rights, or which express the claims of desert, seem to contradict this contention. But from a utilitarian standpoint the explanation of these precepts and of their seemingly stringent character is that they are those precepts which experience shows should be strictly respected and departed from only under exceptional circumstances if the sum of advantages is to be maximized. Yet, as with all other precepts, those of justice are derivative from the one end of attaining the greatest balance of satisfaction. Thus there is no reason in principle why the greater gains of some should not compensate for the lesser losses of others; or more importantly, why the violation of the liberty of a few might not be made right by the greater good shared by many. It simply happens that under most conditions, at least in a reasonably advanced stage of civilization, the greatest sum of advantages is not attained in this way. No doubt the strictness of common sense precepts of justice has a certain usefulness in limiting men's propensities to injustice and to socially injurious actions, but the utilitarian believes that to affirm this strictness as a first principle of morals is a mistake. For just as it is rational for one man to maximize the fulfillment of his system of desires, it is right for a society to maximize the net balance of satisfaction taken over all of its members.

The most natural way, then, of arriving at utilitarianism (although not, of course, the only way of doing so) is to adopt for society as a whole the principle of rational choice for one man. Once this is recognized, the place of the impartial spectator and the emphasis on sympathy in the history of utilitarian thought is readily understood. For it is by the conception of the impartial spectator and the use of sympathetic identification in guiding our imagination that the principle for one man is applied to society. It is this spectator who is conceived as carrying out the required organization of the desires of all persons into one coherent system of desire; it is by this construction that many persons are fused into one. Endowed with ideal powers of sympathy and imagination, the impartial spectator is the perfectly rational individual who identifies with and experiences the desires of others as if these desires were his own. In this way he ascertains the intensity of these desires and assigns them their appropriate weight in the one system of desire the satisfaction of which the ideal legislator then tries to maximize by adjusting the rules of the social system. On this conception of society separate individuals are thought of as so many different lines along which rights and duties are to be assigned and scarce means of satisfaction allocated in accordance with rules so as to give the greatest fulfillment of wants. The nature of the decision made by the ideal legislator is not, therefore, materially different from that of an entrepreneur deciding how to maximize his profit by producing this or that commodity, or that of a consumer deciding how to maximize his satisfaction by the purchase of this or that collection of goods. In each case there is a single person whose system of desires determines the best allocation of limited means. The correct decision is essentially a question of efficient administration. This view of social cooperation is the consequence of extending to society the principle of choice for one man, and then, to make this extension work, conflating all persons into one through the imaginative acts of the impartial sympathetic spectator. Utilitarianism does not take seriously the distinction between persons.

6. Some Related Contrasts

It has seemed to many philosophers, and it appears to be supported by the convictions of common sense, that we distinguish as a matter of principle between the claims of liberty and right on the one hand and the desirability of increasing aggregate social welfare on the other; and that we give a certain priority, if not absolute weight, to the former. Each member of society is thought to have an inviolability founded on justice or, as some say, on natural right, which even the welfare of every one else cannot override. Justice denies that the loss of freedom for some is made right by a greater good shared by others. The reasoning which balances the gains and losses of different persons as if they were one person is excluded. Therefore in a just society the basic liberties are taken for granted and the rights secured by justice are not subject to political bargaining or to the calculus of social interests.

Justice as fairness attempts to account for these common sense convictions concerning the priority of justice by showing that they are the consequence of principles which would be chosen in the original position. These judgments reflect the rational preferences and the initial equality of the contracting parties. Although the utilitarian recognizes that, strictly speaking, his doctrine conflicts with these sentiments of justice, he maintains that common sense precepts of justice and notions of natural right have but a subordinate validity as secondary rules; they arise from the fact that under the conditions of civilized society there is great social utility in following them for the most part and in permitting violations only under exceptional circumstances. Even the excessive zeal with which we are apt to affirm these precepts and to appeal to these rights is itself granted a certain usefulness, since it counterbalances a natural human tendency to violate them in ways not sanctioned by utility. Once we understand this, the apparent disparity between the utilitarian principle and the strength of these persuasions of justice is no longer a philosophical difficulty. Thus while the contract doctrine accepts our convictions about the priority of justice as on the whole sound, utilitarianism seeks to account for them as a socially useful illusion.

A second contrast is that whereas the utilitarian extends to society the principle of choice for one man, justice as fairness, being a contract view, assumes that the principles of social choice, and so the principles of justice, are themselves the object of an original agreement. There is no reason to suppose that the principles which should regulate an association of men is simply an extension of the principle of choice for one man. On the contrary: if we assume that the correct regulative principle for anything depends on the nature of that thing, and that the plurality of distinct persons with separate systems of ends is an essential feature of human societies, we should not expect the principles of social choice to be utilitarian. To be sure, it has not been shown by anything said so far that the parties in the original position would not choose the principle of utility to define the terms of social cooperation. This is a difficult question which I shall examine later on. It is perfectly possible, from all that one knows at this point, that some form of the principle of utility would be adopted, and therefore that contract theory leads eventually to a deeper and more roundabout justification of utilitarianism. In fact a derivation of this kind is sometimes suggested by Bentham and Edgeworth, although it is not developed by them in any systematic way and to my knowledge it is not found in Sidgwick. For the present I shall simply assume that the persons in the original position would reject the utility principle and that they would adopt instead, for the kinds of reasons previously sketched, the two principles of justice already mentioned. In any case, from the standpoint of contract theory one cannot arrive at a principle of social choice merely by extending the principle of rational prudence to the system of desires constructed by the impartial spectator. To do this is not to take seriously the plurality and distinctness of individuals, nor to recognize as the basis of justice that to which men would consent. Here we may note a curious anomaly. It is customary to think of utilitarianism as individualistic, and certainly there are good reasons for this. The utilitarians were strong defenders of liberty and freedom of thought, and they held that the good of society is constituted by the advantages enjoyed by individuals. Yet utilitarianism is not individualistic, at least when arrived at by the more natural course of reflection, in that, by conflating all systems of desires, it applies to society the principle of choice for one man. And thus we see that the second contrast is related to the first, since it is this conflation, and the principle based upon it, which subjects the rights secured by justice to the calculus of social interests.

The last contrast that I shall mention now is that utilitarianism is a teleological theory whereas justice as fairness is not. By definition, then, the latter is a deontological theory, one that either does not specify the good independently from the right, or does not interpret the right as maximizing the good. (It should be noted that deontological theories are defined as non-teleological ones, not as views that characterize the rightness of institutions and acts independently from their consequences. All ethical doctrines worth our attention take consequences into account in judging rightness. One which did not would simply be irrational, crazy.) Justice as fairness is a deontological theory in the second way. For if it is assumed that the persons in the original position would choose a principle of equal liberty and restrict economic and social inequalities to those in everyone's interests, there is no reason to think that just institutions will maximize the good. (Here I suppose with utilitarianism that the good is defined as the satisfaction of rational desire.) Of course, it is

not impossible that the most good is produced but it would be a coincidence. The question of attaining the greatest net balance of satisfaction never arises in justice as fairness; this maximum principle is not used at all.

There is a further point in this connection. In utilitarianism the satisfaction of any desire has some value in itself which must be taken into account in deciding what is right. In calculating the greatest balance of satisfaction it does not matter, except indirectly, what the desires are for. We are to arrange institutions so as to obtain the greatest sum of satisfactions; we ask no questions about their source or quality but only how their satisfaction would affect the total of well-being. Social welfare depends directly and solely upon the levels of satisfaction or dissatisfaction of individuals. Thus if men take a certain pleasure in discriminating against one another, in subjecting others to a lesser liberty as a means of enhancing their self-respect, then the satisfaction of these desires must be weighed in our deliberations according to their intensity, or whatever, along with other desires. If society decides to deny them fulfillment, or to suppress them, it is because they tend to be socially destructive and a greater welfare can be achieved in other ways.

In justice as fairness, on the other hand, persons accept in advance a principle of equal liberty and they do this without a knowledge of their more particular ends. They implicitly agree, therefore, to conform their conceptions of their good to what the principles of justice require, or at least not to press claims which directly violate them. An individual who finds that he enjoys seeing others in positions of lesser liberty understands that he has no claim whatever to this enjoyment. The pleasure he takes in other's deprivations is wrong in itself: it is a satisfaction which requires the violation of a principle to which he would agree in the original position. The principles of right, and so of justice, put limits on which satisfactions have value; they impose restrictions on what are reasonable conceptions of one's good. In drawing up plans and in deciding on aspirations men are to take these constraints into account. Hence in justice as fairness one does not take men's propensities and inclinations as given, whatever they are, and then seek the best way to fulfill them. Rather, their desires and aspirations are restricted from the outset by the principles of justice which specify the boundaries that men's systems of ends must respect. We can express this by saying that in justice as fairness the concept of right is prior to that of the good. A just social system defines the scope within which individuals must develop their aims, and it provides a framework of rights and opportunities and the means of satisfaction within and by the use of which these ends may be equitably pursued. The priority of justice is accounted for, in part, by holding that the interests requiring the violation of justice have no value. Having no merit in the first place, they cannot override its claims.

This priority of the right over the good in justice as fairness turns out to be a central feature of the conception. It imposes certain criteria on the design of the basic structure as a whole; these arrangements must not tend to generate propensities and attitudes contrary to the two principles of justice (that is, to certain principles which are given from the first a definite content) and they must insure that just institutions are stable. Thus certain initial bounds are placed upon what is good and what forms of character are morally worthy, and so upon what kinds of persons men should be. Now any theory of justice will set up some limits of this kind, namely, those that are required if its first principles are to be satisfied given the circumstances. Utilitarianism excludes those desires and propensities which if encouraged or permitted would, in view of the situation, lead to a lesser net balance of satisfaction. But this restriction is largely formal, and in the absence of fairly detailed knowledge of the circumstances it does not give much indication of what these desires and propensities are. This is not, by itself, an objection to utilitarianism. It is simply a feature of utilitarian

doctrine that it relies very heavily upon the natural facts and contingencies of human life in determining what forms of moral character are to be encouraged in a just society. The moral ideal of justice as fairness is more deeply embedded in the first principles of the ethical theory. This is characteristic of natural rights views (the contractarian tradition) in comparison with the theory of utility.

In setting forth these contrasts between justice as fairness and utilitarianism, I have had in mind only the classical doctrine. This is the view of Bentham and Sidgwick and of the utilitarian economists Edgeworth and Pigou. The kind of utilitarianism espoused by Hume would not serve my purpose; indeed, it is not strictly speaking utilitarian. In his well-known arguments against Locke's contract theory, for example, Hume maintains that the principles of fidelity and allegiance both have the same foundation in utility, and therefore that nothing is gained from basing political obligation on an original contract. Locke's doctrine represents, for Hume, an unnecessary shuffle: one might as well appeal directly to utility. But all Hume seems to mean by utility is the general interests and necessities of society. The principles of fidelity and allegiance derive from utility in the sense that the maintenance of the social order is impossible unless these principles are generally respected. But then Hume assumes that each man stands to gain, as judged by his long-term advantage, when law and government conform to the precepts founded on utility. No mention is made of the gains of some outweighing the disadvantages of others. For Hume, then, utility seems to be identical with some form of the common good; institutions satisfy its demands when they are to everyone's interests, at least in the long run. Now if this interpretation of Hume is correct, there is offhand no conflict with the priority of justice and no incompatibility with Locke's contract doctrine. For the role of equal rights in Locke is precisely to ensure that the only permissible departures from the state of nature are those which respect these rights and serve the common interest. It is clear that all the transformations from the state of nature which Locke approves of satisfy this conditions and are such that rational men concerned to advance their ends could consent to them in a state of equality. Hume nowhere disputes the propriety of these constraints. His critique of Locke's contract doctrine never denies, or even seems to recognize, its fundamental contention.

The merit of the classical view as formulated by Bentham, Edgeworth, and Sidgwick is that it clearly recognizes what is at stake, namely, the relative priority of the principles of justice and of the rights derived from these principles. The question is whether the imposition of disadvantages on a few can be outweighed by a greater sum of advantages enjoyed by others; or whether the weight of justice requires an equal liberty for all and permits only those economic and social inequalities which are to each person's interests. Implicit in the contrasts between classical utilitarianism and justice as fairness is a difference in the underlying conceptions of society. In the one we think of a well-ordered society as a scheme of cooperation for reciprocal advantage regulated by principles which persons would choose in an initial situation that is fair, in the other as the efficient administration of social resources to maximize the satisfaction of the system of desire constructed by the impartial spectator from the many individual systems of desires accepted as given. The comparison with classical utilitarianism in its more natural derivation brings out this contrast. [. . .]

11. Two Principles of Justice

I shall now state in a provisional form the two principles of justice that I believe would be chosen in the original position. In this section I wish to make only the most general comments, and therefore the first formulation of these principles is tentative. As we go on I shall run through several formulations and approximate

step by step the final statement to be given much later. I believe that doing this allows the exposition to proceed in a natural way.

The first statement of the two principles reads as follows.

> First: each person is to have an equal right to the most extensive basic liberty compatible with a similar liberty for others.

> Second: social and economic inequalities are to be arranged so that they are both (a) reasonably expected to be to everyone's advantage, and (b) attached to positions and offices open to all.

There are two ambiguous phrases in the second principle, namely "everyone's advantage" and "open to to all." Determining their sense more exactly will lead to a second formulation of the principle in § 13. The final version of the two principles is given in § 46; § 39 considers the rendering of the first principle.

By way of general comment, these principles primarily apply, as I have said, to the basic structure of society. They are to govern the assignment of rights and duties and to regulate the distribution of social and economic advantages. As their formulation suggests, these principles presuppose that the social structure can be divided into two more or less distinct parts, the first principle applying to the one, the second to the other. They distinguish between those aspects of the social system that define and secure the equal liberties of citizenship and those that specify and establish social and economic inequalities. The basic liberties of citizens are, roughly speaking, political liberty (the right to vote and to be eligible for public office) together with freedom of speech and assembly; liberty of conscience and freedom of thought; freedom of the person along with the right to hold (personal) property; and freedom from arbitrary arrest and seizure as defined by the concept of the rule of law. These liberties are all required to be equal by the first principle, since citizens of a just society are to have the same basic rights.

The second principle applies, in the first approximation, to the distribution of income and wealth and to the design of organizations that make use of differences in authority and responsibility, or chains of command. While the distribution of wealth and income need not be equal, it must be to everyone's advantage, and at the same time, positions of authority and offices of command must be accessible to all. One applies the second principle by holding positions open, and then, subject to this constraint, arranges social and economic inequalities so that everyone benefits.

These principles are to be arranged in a serial order with the first principle prior to the second. This ordering means that a departure from the institutions of equal liberty required by the first principle cannot be justified by, or compensated for, by greater social and economic advantages. The distribution of wealth and income, and the hierarchies of authority, must be consistent with both the liberties of equal citizenship and equality of opportunity.

It is clear that these principles are rather specific in their content, and their acceptance rests on certain assumptions that I must eventually try to explain and justify. A theory of justice depends upon a theory of society in ways that will become evident as we proceed. For the present, it should be observed that the two principles (and this holds for all formulations) are a special case of a more general conception of justice that can be expressed as follows.

All social values—liberty and opportunity, income and wealth, and the bases of self-respect—are to be distributed equally unless an unequal distribution of any, or all, of these values is to everyone's advantage.

Injustice, then, is simply inequalities that are not to the benefit of all. Of course, this conception is extremely vague and requires interpretation.

As a first step, suppose that the basic structure of society distributes certain primary goods, that is, things that every rational man is presumed to want. These goods normally have a use whatever a person's rational plan of life. For simplicity, assume that the chief primary goods at the disposition of society are rights and liberties, powers and opportunities, income and wealth. . . . These are the social primary goods. Other primary goods such as health and vigor, intelligence and imagination, are natural goods; although their possession is influenced by the basic structure, they are not so directly under its control. Imagine, then, a hypothetical initial arrangement in which all the social primary goods are equally distributed: everyone has similar rights and duties, and income and wealth are evenly shared. This state of affairs provides a benchmark for judging improvements. If certain inequalities of wealth and organizational powers would make everyone better off than in this hypothetical starting situation, then they accord with the general conception.

Now it is possible, at least theoretically, that by giving up some of their fundamental liberties men are sufficiently compensated by the resulting social and economic gains. The general conception of justice imposes no restrictions on what sort of inequalities are permissible; it only requires that everyone's position be improved. We need not suppose anything so drastic as consenting to a condition of slavery. Imagine instead that men forego certain political rights when the economic returns are significant and their capacity to influence the course of policy by the exercise of these rights would be marginal in any case. It is this kind of exchange which the two principles as stated rule out; being arranged in serial order they do not permit exchanges between basic liberties and economic and social gains. The serial ordering of principles expresses an underlying preference among primary social goods. When this preference is rational so likewise is the choice of these principles in this order.

In developing justice as fairness I shall, for the most part, leave aside the general conception of justice and examine instead the special case of the two principles in serial order. The advantage of this procedure is that from the first the matter of priorities is recognized and an effort made to find principles to deal with it. One is led to attend throughout to the conditions under which the acknowledgment of the absolute weight of liberty with respect to social and economic advantages, as defined by the lexical order of the two principles, would be reasonable. Offhand, this ranking appears extreme and too special a case to be of much interest; but there is more justification for it than would appear at first sight. . . . Furthermore, the distinction between fundamental rights and liberties and economic and social benefits marks a difference among primary social goods that one should try to exploit. It suggests an important division in the social system. Of course, the distinctions drawn and the ordering proposed are bound to be at best only approximations. There are surely circumstances in which they fail. But it is essential to depict clearly the main lines of a reasonable conception of justice; and under many conditions anyway, the two principles in serial order may serve well enough. When necessary we can fall back on the more general conception.

The fact that the two principles apply to institutions has certain consequences. Several points illustrate this. First of all, the rights and liberties referred to by these principles are those which are defined by the public rules of the basic structure. Whether men are free is determined by the rights and duties established by the major institutions of society. Liberty is a certain pattern of social forms. The first principle simply requires that certain sorts of rules, those defining basic liberties, apply to everyone equally and that they allow the most extensive liberty compatible with a like liberty for all. The only reason for circumscribing the rights defining liberty and making men's freedom less extensive than it might otherwise be is that these equal rights as institutionally defined would interfere with one another.

Another thing to bear in mind is that when principles mention persons, or require that everyone gain from an inequality, the reference is to representative persons holding the various social positions, or offices, or whatever, established by the basic structure. Thus in applying the second principle I assume that it is possible to assign an expectation of well-being to representative individuals holding these positions. This expectation indicates their life prospects as viewed from their social station. In general, the expectations of representative persons depend upon the distribution of rights and duties throughout the basic structure. When this changes, expectations change. I assume, then, that expectations are connected: by raising the prospects of the representative man in one position we presumably increase or decrease the prospects of representative men in other positions. Since it applies to institutional forms, the second principle (or rather the first part of it) refers to the expectations of representative individuals. As I shall discuss below, neither principle applies to distributions of particular goods to particular individuals who may be identified by their proper names. The situation where someone is considering how to allocate certain commodities to needy persons who are known to him is not within the scope of the principles. They are meant to regulate basic institutional arrangements. We must not assume that there is much similarity from the standpoint of justice between an administrative allotment of goods to specific persons and the appropriate design of society. Our common sense intuitions for the former may be a poor guide to the latter.

Now the second principle insists that each person benefit from permissible inequalities in the basic structure. This means that it must be reasonable for each relevant representative man defined by this structure, when he views it as a going concern, to prefer his prospects with the inequality to his prospects without it. One is not allowed to justify differences in income or organizational powers on the ground that the disadvantages of those in one position are outweighed by the greater advantages of those in another. Much less can infringements of liberty be counterbalanced in this way. Applied to the basic structure, the principle of utility would have us maximize the sum of expectations of representative men (weighted by the number of persons they represent, on the classical view); and this would permit us to compensate for the losses of some by the gains of others. Instead, the two principles require that everyone benefit from economic and social inequalities. It is obvious, however, that there are indefinitely many ways in which all may be advantaged when the initial arrangement of equality is taken as a benchmark. How then are we to choose among these possibilities? The principles must be specified so that they yield a determinate conclusion. I now turn to this problem.

12. Interpretations of the Second Principle

I have already mentioned that since the phrases "everyone's advantage" and "equally open to all" are ambiguous, both parts of the second principle have two natural senses. Because these senses are independent of one another, the principle has four possible meanings. Assuming that the first principle of equal liberty has the same sense throughout, we then have four interpretations of the two principles. These are indicated in the table below.

I shall sketch in turn these three interpretations: the system of natural liberty, liberal equality, and democratic equality. In some respects this sequence is the more intuitive one, but the sequence via the interpretation of natural aristocracy is not without interest and I shall comment on it briefly. In working out justice as fairness, we must decide which interpretation is to be preferred. I shall adopt that of democratic equality, explaining in this chapter what this notion means. The argument for its acceptance in the original position does not begin until the next chapter.

The first interpretation (in either sequence) I shall refer to as the system of natural liberty. In this rendering the first part of the second principle is understood as the principle of efficiency adjusted so as to apply to institutions or, in this case, to the basic structure of society; and the second part is understood as an open social system in which, to use the traditional phrase, careers are open to talents. I assume in all interpretations that the first principle of equal liberty is satisfied and that the economy is roughly a free market system, although the means of production may or may not be privately owned. The system of natural liberty asserts, then, that a basic structure satisfying the principle of efficiency and in which positions are open to those able and willing to strive for them will lead to a just distribution. Assigning rights and duties in this way is thought to give a scheme which allocates wealth and income, authority and responsibility, in a fair way whatever this allocation turns out to be. The doctrine includes an important element

| "Equally open" | "Everyone's advantage" | |
	Principle of efficiency	Difference principle
Equality as careers open to talents	System of Natural Liberty	Natural Aristocracy
Equality as equality of fair opportunity	Liberal Equality	Democratic Equality

of pure procedural justice which is carried over to the other interpretations. [. . .]

The system of natural liberty selects an efficient distribution roughly as follows. Let us suppose that we know from economic theory that under the standard assumptions defining a competitive market economy, income and wealth will be distributed in an efficient way, and that the particular efficient distribution which results in any period of time is determined by the initial distribution of assets, that is, by the initial distribution of income and wealth, and of natural talents and abilities. With each initial distribution, a definite efficient outcome is arrived at. Thus it turns out that if we are to accept the outcome as just, and not merely as efficient, we must accept the basis upon which over time the initial distribution of assets is determined.

In the system of natural liberty the initial distribution is regulated by the arrangements implicit in the conception of careers open to talents (as earlier defined). These arrangements presuppose a background of equal liberty (as specified by the first principle) and a free market economy. They require a formal equality of opportunity in that all have at least the same legal rights of access to all advantaged social positions. But since there is no effort to preserve an equality, or similarity, of social conditions, except insofar as this is necessary to preserve the requisite background institutions, the initial distribution of assets for any period of time is strongly influenced by natural and social contingencies. The existing distribution of income and wealth, say, is the cumulative effect of prior distributions of natural assets—that is, natural talents and abilities—as these have been developed or left unrealized, and their use favored or disfavored over time by social circumstances and such chance contingencies as accident and good fortune. Intuitively, the most obvious injustice of the system of natural liberty is that it permits distributive shares to be improperly influenced by these factors so arbitrary from a moral point of view.

The liberal interpretation, as I shall refer to it, tries to correct for this by adding to the requirement of careers open to talents the further condition of the principle of fair equality of opportunity. The thought here is that positions are to be not only open in a formal sense, but that all should have a fair chance to attain them. Offhand it is not clear what is meant, but we might say that those with similar abilities and skills should have similar life chances. More specifically, assuming that there is a distribution of natural assets, those who are at the same level of talent and ability, and have the same willingness to use them, should have the same prospects of success regardless of their initial place in the social system, that is, irrespective of the income class into which they are born. In all sectors of society there should be roughly equal prospects of culture and achievement for everyone similarly motivated and endowed. The expectations of those with the same abilities and aspirations should not be affected by their social class.

The liberal interpretation of the two principles seeks, then, to mitigate the influence of social contingencies and natural fortune on distributive shares. To accomplish this end it is necessary to impose further basic structural conditions on the social system. Free market arrangements must be set within a framework of political and legal institutions which regulates the overall trends of economic events and preserves the social conditions necessary for fair equality of opportunity. The elements of this framework are familiar enough, though it may be worthwhile to recall the importance of preventing excessive accumulations of property and wealth and of maintaining equal opportunities of education for all. Chances to acquire cultural knowledge and skills should not depend upon one's class position, and so the school system, whether public or private, should be designed to even out class barriers.

While the liberal conception seems clearly preferable to the system of natural liberty, intuitively it still appears defective. For one thing, even if it works to perfection in eliminating the influence of social contingencies, it still permits the distribution of wealth and income to be determined by the natural distribution of abilities and talents. Within the limits allowed by the background arrangements, distributive shares are decided by the outcome of the natural lottery; and this outcome is arbitrary from a moral perspective. There is no more reason to permit the distribution of income and wealth to be settled by the distribution of natural assets than by historical and social fortune. Furthermore, the principle of fair opportunity can be only imperfectly carried out, at least as long as the institution of the family exists. The extent to which natural capacities develop and reach fruition is affected by all kinds of social conditions and class attitudes. Even the willingness to make an effort, to try, and so to be deserving in the ordinary sense is itself dependent upon happy family and social circumstances. It is impossible in practice to secure equal chances of achievement and culture for those similarly endowed, and therefore we may want to adopt a principle which recognizes this fact and also mitigates the arbitrary effects of the natural lottery itself. That the liberal conception fails to do this encourages one to look for another interpretation of the two principles of justice.

Before turning to the conception of democratic equality, we should note that of natural aristocracy. On this view no attempt is made to regulate social contingencies beyond what is required by formal equality of opportunity, but the advantages of persons with greater natural endowments are to be limited to those that further the good of the poorer sectors of society. The aristocratic ideal is applied to a system that is open, at least from a legal point of view, and the better situation of those favored by it is regarded as just only when less would be had by those below, if less were given to those above. In this way the idea of *noblesse oblige* is carried over to the conception of natural aristocracy.

Now both the liberal conception and that of natural aristocracy are unstable. For once we are troubled by the influence of either social contingencies or natural chance on the determination of distributive shares, we are bound, on reflection, to be bothered by the influence of the other. From a moral standpoint the two seem equally arbitrary. So however we move away from the system of natural liberty, we cannot be satisfied short of the democratic conception. This conception I have yet to explain. And, moreover, none of the preceding remarks are an argument for this conception, since in a contract theory all arguments, strictly speaking, are to be made in terms of what it would be rational to choose in the original position. But I am concerned here to prepare the way for the favored interpretation of the two principles so that these criteria, especially the second one, will not strike the reader as too eccentric or bizarre. I have tried to show that once we try to find a rendering of them which treats everyone equally as a moral person, and which does not weight men's share in the benefits and burdens of social cooperation according to their social fortune or their luck in the natural lottery, it is clear that the democratic interpretation is the best choice among the four alternatives. With these comments as a preface, I now turn to this conception.

13. Democratic Equality and the Difference Principle

The democratic interpretation, as the table suggests, is arrived at by combining the principle of fair equality of opportunity with the difference principle. This principle removes the indeterminateness of the principle of efficiency by singling out a particular position from which the social and economic inequalities of the basic structure are to be judged. Assuming the framework of institutions required by equal liberty and fair equality of opportunity, the higher expectations of those better situated are just if and only if they work as part of a scheme which improves the expectations of the least advantaged members of society. The intuitive idea is that the social order is not to establish and secure the more attractive prospects of those better off unless doing so is to the advantage of those less fortunate. [. . .]

17. The Tendency to Equality

I wish to conclude this discussion of the two principles by explaining the sense in which they express an egalitarian conception of justice. Also I should like to forestall the objection to the principle of fair opportunity that it leads to a callous meritocratic society. In order to prepare the way for doing this, I note several aspects of the conception of justice that I have set out.

First we may observe that the difference principle gives some weight to the considerations singled out by the principle of redress. This is the principle that undeserved inequalities call for redress; and since inequalities of birth and natural endowment are undeserved, these inequalities are to be somehow compensated for. Thus the principle holds that in order to treat all persons equally, to provide genuine equality of opportunity, society must give more attention to those with fewer native assets and to those born into the less favorable social positions. The idea is to redress the bias of contingencies in the direction of equality. In pursuit of this principle greater resources might be spent on the education of the less rather than the more intelligent, at least over a certain time of life, say the earlier years of school.

Now the principle of redress has not to my knowledge been proposed as the sole criterion of justice, as the single aim of the social order. It is plausible as most such principles are only as a prima facie principle, one that is to be weighed in the balance with others. For example, we are to weight it against the principle to improve the average standard of life, or to advance the common good. But whatever other principles we hold, the claims of redress are to be taken into

account. It is thought to represent one of the elements in our conception of justice. Now the difference principle is not of course the principle of redress. It does not require society to try to even out handicaps as if all were expected to compete on a fair basis in the same race. But the difference principle would allocate resources in education, say, so as to improve the long-term expectation of the least favored. If this end is attained by giving more attention to the better endowed, it is permissible; otherwise not. And in making this decision, the value of education should not be assessed solely in terms of economic efficiency and social welfare. Equally if not more important is the role of education in enabling a person to enjoy the culture of his society and to take part in its affairs, and in this way to provide for each individual a secure sense of his own worth.

Thus although the difference principle is not the same as that of redress, it does achieve some of the intent of the latter principle. It transforms the aims of the basic structure so that the total scheme of institutions no longer emphasizes social efficiency and technocratic values. We see then that the difference principle represents, in effect, an agreement to regard the distribution of natural talents as a common asset and to share in the benefits of this distribution whatever it turns out to be. Those who have been favored by nature, whoever they are, may gain from their good fortune only on terms that improve the situation of those who have lost out. The naturally advantaged are not to gain merely because they are more gifted, but only to cover the costs of training and education and for using their endowments in ways that help the less fortunate as well. No one deserves his greater natural capacity nor merits a more favorable starting place in society. But it does not follow that one should eliminate these distinctions. There is another way to deal with them. The basic structure can be arranged so that these contingencies work for the good of the least fortunate. Thus we are led to the difference principle if we wish to set up the social system so that no one gains or loses from his arbitrary place in the distribution of natural assets or his initial position in society without giving or receiving compensating advantages in return.

In view of these remarks we may reject the contention that the ordering of institutions is always defective because the distribution of natural talents and the contingencies of social circumstance are unjust, and this injustice must inevitably carry over to human arrangements. Occasionally this reflection is offered as an excuse for ignoring injustice, as if the refusal to acquiesce in injustice is on a par with being unable to accept death. The natural distribution is neither just nor unjust; nor is it unjust that persons are born into society at some particular position. These are simply natural facts. What is just and unjust is the way that institutions deal with these facts. Aristocratic and caste societies are unjust because they make these contingencies the ascriptive basis for belonging to more or less enclosed and privileged social classes. The basic structure of these societies incorporates the arbitrariness found in nature. But there is no necessity for men to resign themselves to these contingencies. The social system is not an unchangeable order beyond human control but a pattern of human action. In justice as fairness men agree to share one another's fate. In designing institutions they undertake to avail themselves of the accidents of nature and social circumstance only when doing so is for the common benefit. The two principles are a fair way of meeting the arbitrariness of fortune; and while no doubt imperfect in other ways, the institutions which satisfy these principles are just.

A further point is that the difference principle expresses a conception of reciprocity. It is a principle of mutual benefit. We have seen that, at least when chain connection holds, each representative man can accept the basic structure as designed to advance his interests. The social order can be justified to everyone, and in particular to those who are least favored; and in this

sense it is egalitarian. But it seems necessary to consider in an intuitive way how the condition of mutual benefit is satisfied. Consider any two representative men A and B, and let B be the one who is less favored. Actually, since we are most interested in the comparison with the least favored man, let us assume that B is this individual. Now B can accept A's being better off since A's advantages have been gained in ways that improve B's prospects. If A were not allowed his better position, B would be even worse off than he is. The difficulty is to show that A has no grounds for complaint. Perhaps he is required to have less than he might since his having more would result in some loss to B. Now what can be said to the more favored man? To begin with, it is clear that the well-being of each depends on a scheme of social cooperation without which no one could have a satisfactory life. Secondly, we can ask for the willing cooperation of everyone only if the terms of the scheme are reasonable. The difference principle, then, seems to be a fair basis on which those better endowed, or more fotunate in their social circumstances, could expect others to collaborate with them when some workable arrangement is a necessary condition of the good of all.

There is a natural inclination to object that those better situated deserve their greater advantages whether or not they are to the benefit of others. At this point it is necessary to be clear about the notion of desert. It is perfectly true that given a just system of cooperation as a scheme of public rules and the expectations set up by it, those who, with the prospect of improving their condition, have done what the system announces that it will reward are entitled to their advantages. In this sense the more fortunate have a claim to their better situation; their claims are legitimate expectations established by social institutions, and the community is obligated to meet them. But this sense of desert presupposes the existence of the cooperative scheme; it is irrelevant to the question whether in the first place the scheme is to be designed in accordance with the difference principle or some other criterion.

Perhaps some will think that the person with greater natural endowments deserves those assets and the superior character that made their development possible. Because he is more worthy in this sense, he deserves the greater advantages that he could achieve with them. This view, however, is surely incorrect. It seems to be one of the fixed points of our considered judgments that no one deserves his place in the distribution of native endowments, any more than one deserves one's initial starting place in society. The assertion that a man deserves the superior character that enables him to make the effort to cultivate his abilities is equally problematic; for his character depends in large part upon fortunate family and social circumstances for which he can claim no credit. The notion of desert seems not to apply to these cases. Thus the more advantaged representative man cannot say that he deserves and therefore has a right to a scheme of cooperation in which he is permitted to acquire benefits in ways that do not contribute to the welfare of others. There is no basis for his making this claim. From the standpoint of common sense, then, the difference principle appears to be acceptable both to the more advantaged and to the less advantaged individual. Of course, none of this is strictly speaking an argument for the principle, since in a contract theory arguments are made from the point of view of the original position. But these intuitive considerations help to clarify the nature of the principle and the sense in which it is egalitarian. [. . .]

24. The Veil of Ignorance

The idea of the original position is to set up a fair procedure so that any principles agreed to will be just. The aim is to use the notion of pure procedural justice as a basis of theory. Somehow we must nullify the effects of specific contingencies which put men at odds and tempt them to exploit social and natural circumstances to their own advantage. Now in order to do this I assume that the parties are situated behind a veil of ignorance. They do not know how the various alternatives will affect their own particular case and they are obliged to evaluate principles solely on the basis of general considerations.

It is assumed, then, that the parties do not know certain kinds of particular facts. First of all, no one knows his place in society, his class position or social status; nor does he know his fortune in the distribution of natural assets and abilities, his intelligence and strength, and the like. Nor, again, does anyone know his conception of the good, the particulars of his rational plan of life, or even the special features of his psychology such as his aversion to risk or liability to optimism or pessimism. More than this, I assume that the parties do not know the particular circumstances of their own society. That is, they do not know its economic or political situation, or the level of civilization and culture it has been able to achieve. The persons in the original position have no information as to which generation they belong. These broader restrictions on knowledge are appropriate in part because questions of social justice arise between generations as well as within them, for example, the question of the appropriate rate of capital saving and of the conservation of natural resources and the environment of nature. There is also, theoretically anyway, the question of a reasonable genetic policy. In these cases too, in order to carry through the idea of the original position, the parties must not know the contingencies that set them in opposition. They must choose principles the consequences of which they are prepared to live with whatever generation they turn out to belong to.

As far as possible, then, the only particular facts which the parties know is that their society is subject to the circumstances of justice and whatever this implies. It is taken for granted, however, that they know the general facts about human society. They understand political affairs and the principles of economic theory; they know the basis of social organization and the laws of human psychology. Indeed, the parties are presumed to know whatever general facts affect the choice of the principles of justice. There are no limitations on general information, that is, on general laws and theories, since conceptions of justice must be adjusted to the characteristics of the systems of social cooperation which they are to regulate, and there is no reason to rule out these facts. It is, for example, a consideration against a conception of justice that, in view of the laws of moral psychology, men would not acquire a desire to act upon it even when the institutions of their society satisfied it. For in this case there would be difficulty in securing the stability of social cooperation. It is an important feature of a conception of justice that it should generate its own support. That is, its principles should be such that when they are embodied in the basic structure of society men tend to acquire the corresponding sense of justice. Given the principles of moral learning, men develop a desire to act in accordance with its principles. In this case a conception of justice is stable. This kind of general information is admissible in the original position.

The notion of the veil of ignorance raises several difficulties. Some may object that the exclusion of nearly all particular information makes it difficult to grasp what is meant by the original position. Thus it may be helpful to observe that one or more persons can at any time enter this position, or perhaps, better, simulate the deliberations of this hypothetical situation, simply by reasoning in accordance with the appropriate restrictions. In arguing for a conception of justice we must be sure that it is among the permitted alternatives and satisfies the stipulated formal constraints. No considerations can be advanced in its favor unless they would be rational ones for us to urge were we to lack the kind of knowledge that is excluded. The evaluation of principles must proceed in terms of the general consequences of their public recognition and universal application, it being assumed that they

will be complied with by everyone. To say that a certain conception of justice would be chosen in the original position is equivalent to saying that rational deliberation satisfying certain conditions and restrictions would reach a certain conclusion. If necessary, the argument to this result could be set out more formally. I shall, however, speak throughout in terms of the notion of the original position. It is more economical and suggestive, and brings out certain essential features that otherwise one might easily overlook.

These remarks show that the original position is not to be thought of as a general assembly which includes at one moment everyone who will live at some time; or, much less, as an assembly of everyone who could live at some time. It is not a gathering of all actual or possible persons. To conceive of the original position in either of these ways is to stretch fantasy too far; the conception would cease to be a natural guide to intuition. In any case, it is important that the original position be interpreted so that one can at any time adopt its perspective. It must make no difference when one takes up this viewpoint, or who does so: the restrictions must be such that the same principles are always chosen. The veil of ignorance is a key condition in meeting this requirement. It insures not only that the information available is relevant, but that it is at all times the same.

It may be protested that the condition of the veil of ignorance is irrational. Surely, some may object, principles should be chosen in the light of all the knowledge available. There are various replies to this contention. Here I shall sketch those which emphasize the simplifications that need to be made if one is to have any theory at all. . . . To begin with, it is clear that since the differences among the parties are unknown to them, and everyone is equally rational and similarly situated, each is convinced by the same arguments. Therefore, we can view the choice in the original position from the standpoint of one person selected at random. If anyone after due reflection prefers a conception of justice to another, then they all do, and a unanimous agreement can be reached. We can, to make the circumstances more vivid, imagine that the parties are required to communicate with each other through a referee as intermediary, and that he is to announce which alternatives have been suggested and the reasons offered in their support. He forbids the attempt to form coalitions, and he informs the parties when they have come to an understanding. But such a referee is actually superfluous, assuming that the deliberations of the parties must be similar.

Thus there follows the very important consequence that the parties have no basis for bargaining in the usual sense. No one knows his situation in society nor his natural assets, and therefore no one is in a position to tailor principles to his advantage. We might imagine that one of the contractees threatens to hold out unless the others agree to principles favorable to him. But how does he know which principles are especially in his interests? The same holds for the formation of coalitions: if a group were to decide to band together to the disadvantage of the others, they would not know how to favor themselves in the choice of principles. Even if they could get everyone to agree to their proposal, they would have no assurance that it was to their advantage, since they cannot identify themselves either by name or description. The one case where this conclusion fails is that of saving. Since the persons in the original position know that they are contemporaries (taking the present time of entry interpretation), they can favor their generation by refusing to make any sacrifices at all for their successors; they simply acknowledge the principle that no one has a duty to save for posterity. Previous generations have saved or they have not; there is nothing the parties can now do to affect that. So in this instance the veil of ignorance fails to secure the desired result. Therefore I resolve the question of justice between generations in a different way by altering the motivation assumption. But with this adjustment no one is able to formulate principles

especially designed to advance his own cause. Whatever his temporal position, each is forced to choose for everyone.

The restrictions on particular information in the original position are, then, of fundamental importance. Without them we would not be able to work out any definite theory of justice at all. We would have to be content with a vague formula stating that justice is what would be agreed to without being able to say much, if anything, about the substance of the agreement itself. The formal constraints of the concept of right, those applying to principles directly, are not sufficient for our purpose. The veil of ignorance makes possible a unanimous choice of a particular conception of justice. Without these limitations on knowledge the bargaining problem of the original position would be hopelessly complicated. Even if theoretically a solution were to exist, we would not, at present anyway, be able to determine it.

The notion of the veil of ignorance is implicit, I think, in Kant's ethics. Nevertheless the problem of defining the knowledge of the parties and of characterizing the alternatives open to them has often been passed over, even by contract theories. Sometimes the situation definitive of moral deliberation is presented in such an indeterminate way that one cannot ascertain how it will turn out. Thus Perry's doctrine is essentially contractarian: he holds that social and personal integration must proceed by entirely different principles, the latter by rational prudence, the former by the concurrence of persons of good will. He would appear to reject utilitarianism on much the same grounds suggested earlier: namely, that it improperly extends the principle of choice for one person to choices facing society. The right course of action is characterized as that which best advances social aims as these would be formulated by reflective agreement given that the parties have full knowledge of the circumstances and are moved by a benevolent concern for one another's interests. No effort is made, however, to specify in any precise way the possible outcomes of this sort of agreement. Indeed, without a far more elaborate account, no conclusions can be drawn. I do not wish here to criticize others; rather, I want to explain the necessity for what may seem at times like so many irrelevant details.

Now the reasons for the veil of ignorance go beyond mere simplicity. We want to define the original position so that we get the desired solution. If a knowledge of particulars is allowed, then the outcome is biased by arbitrary contingencies. As already observed, to each according to his threat advantage is not a principle of justice. If the original position is to yield agreements that are just, the parties must be fairly situated and treated equally as moral persons. The arbitrariness of the world must be corrected for by adjusting the circumstances of the initial contractual situation. Moreover, if in choosing principles we required unanimity even when there is full information, only a few rather obvious cases could be decided. A conception of justice based on unanimity in these circumstances would indeed be weak and trivial. But once knowledge is excluded, the requirement of unanimity is not out of place and the fact that it can be satisfied is of great importance. It enables us to say of the preferred conception of justice that it represents a genuine reconciliation of interests. [. . .]

25. The Rationality of the Parties

[. . .] I now wish to give the final statement of the two principles of justice for institutions. For the sake of completeness, I shall give a full statement including earlier formulations.

First Principle

Each person is to have an equal right to the most extensive total system of equal basic liberties compatible with a similar system of liberty for all.

Second Principle

Social and economic inequalities are to be arranged so that they are both:

(a) to the greatest benefit of the least advantaged, consistent with the just savings principle, and

(b) attached to offices and positions open to all under conditions of fair equality of opportunity.

First Priority Rule (The Priority of Liberty)

The principles of justice are to be ranked in lexical order and therefore liberty can be restricted only for the sake of liberty. There are two cases:

(a) a less extensive liberty must strengthen the total system of liberty shared by all;

(b) a less than equal liberty must be acceptable to those with the lesser liberty.

Second Priority Rule (The Priority of Justice over Efficiency and Welfare)

The second principle of justice is lexically prior to the principle of efficiency and to that of maximizing the sum of advantages; and fair opportunity is prior to the difference principle. There are two cases:

(a) an inequality of opportunity must enhance the opportunities of those with the lesser opportunity;

(b) an excessive rate of saving must on balance mitigate the burden of those bearing this hardship.

General Conception

All social primary goods—liberty and opportunity, income and wealth, and the bases of self-respect—are to be distributed equally unless an unequal distribution of any or all of these goods is to the advantage of the least favored.

By way of comment, these principles and priority rules are no doubt incomplete. Other modifications will surely have to be made, but I shall not further complicate the statement of the principles. It suffices to observe that when we come to nonideal theory, we do not fall back straightway upon the general conception of justice. The lexical ordering of the two principles, and the valuations that this ordering implies, suggest priority rules which seem to be reasonable enough in many cases. By various examples I have tried to illustrate how these rules can be used and to indicate their plausibility. Thus the ranking of the principles of justice in ideal theory reflects back and guides the application of these principles to nonideal situations. It identifies which limitations need to be dealt with first. The drawback of the general conception of justice is that it lacks the definite structure of the two principles in serial order. In more extreme and tangled instances of nonideal theory there may be no alternative to it. At some point the priority of rules for nonideal cases will fail; and indeed, we may be able to find no satisfactory answer at all. But we must try to postpone the day of reckoning as long as possible, and try to arrange society so that it never comes.

Chapter 19

Michael J. Sandel

THE PROCEDURAL REPUBLIC AND THE UNENCUMBERED SELF

Michael Sandel (1953–   ) is a professor of political philosophy at Harvard University. He is best known as an advocate of communitarianism—a position opposed to what it perceives as the excess individualism of liberalism and one which stresses the importance of community and civil society. In this essay (published in 1984), Sandel criticizes what he sees as the Kantian/Rawlsian foundations of American liberalism, arguing that it is in some way responsible for the detachment many people feel from politics and their communities.

Political philosophy seems often to reside at a distance from the world. Principles are one thing, politics another, and even our best efforts to "live up" to our ideals typically founder on the gap between theory and practice.

But if political philosophy is unrealizable in one sense, it is unavoidable in another. This is the sense in which philosophy inhabits the world from the start; our practices and institutions are embodiments of theory. To engage in a political practice is already to stand in relation to theory. For all our uncertainties about ultimate questions of political philosophy—of justice and value and the nature of the good life—the one thing we know is that we live *some* answer all the time.

In this essay I will try to explore the answer we live now, in contemporary America. What is the political philosophy implicit in our practices and institutions? How does it stand, as philosophy? And how do tensions in the philosophy find expression in our present political condition?

It may be objected that it is a mistake to look for a single philosophy, that we live no "answer," only answers. But a plurality of answers is itself a kind of answer. And the political theory that affirms this plurality is the theory I propose to explore.

The Right and the Good

We might begin by considering a certain moral and political vision. It is a liberal vision, and like most liberal visions gives pride of place to justice, fairness, and individual rights. Its core thesis is this: a just society seeks not to promote any particular ends, but enables its citizens to pursue their own ends, consistent with a similar liberty for all; it therefore must govern by principles that do not presuppose any particular conception of the good. What justifies these regulative principles above all is not that they maximize the general welfare, or cultivate virtue, or otherwise promote the good, but rather that they conform to the concept of *right*, a moral category given prior to the good, and independent of it.

This liberalism says, in other words, that what makes the just society just is not the *telos* or purpose or end at which it aims, but precisely its refusal to choose in advance among competing purposes and ends. In its constitution and its laws, the just society seeks to provide a framework within which its citizens can pursue their own values and ends, consistent with a similar liberty for others.

The ideal I've described might be summed up in the claim that the right is prior to the good, and in two senses: The priority of the right means first, that individual rights cannot be sacrificed for the sake of the general good (in this it opposes utilitarianism), and second, that the principles of justice that specify these rights cannot be premised on any particular vision of the good life. (In this it opposes teleological conceptions in general.)

This is the liberalism of much contemporary moral and political philosophy, most fully elaborated by Rawls, and indebted to Kant for its philosophical foundations. But I am concerned here less with the lineage of this vision than with what seem to me three striking facts about it.

First, it has a deep and powerful philosophical appeal. Second, despite its philosophical force, the claim for the priority of the right over the good ultimately fails. And third, despite its philosophical failure, this liberal vision is the one by which we live. For us in late twentieth century America, it is our vision, the theory most thoroughly embodied in the practices and institutions most central to our public life. And seeing how it goes wrong as philosophy may help us to diagnose our present political condition. So first, its philosophical power; second, its philosophical failure; and third, however briefly, its uneasy embodiment in the world.

But before taking up these three claims, it is worth pointing out a central theme that connects them. And that is a certain conception of the person, of what it is to be a moral agent. Like all political theories, the liberal theory I have described is something more than a set of regulative principles. It is also a view about the way the world is, and the way we move within it. At the heart of this ethic lies a vision of the person that both inspires and undoes it. As I will try to argue now, what make this ethic so compelling, but also, finally, vulnerable, are the promise and the failure of the unencumbered self.

Kantian Foundations

The liberal ethic asserts the priority of right, and seeks principles of justice that do not presuppose any particular conception of the good. This is what Kant means by the supremacy of the moral law, and what Rawls means when he writes that "justice is the first virtue of social institutions." Justice is more than just another value. It provides the framework that *regulates* the play of competing values and ends; it must therefore have a sanction independent of those ends. But it is not obvious where such a sanction could be found.

Theories of justice, and for that matter, ethics, have typically founded their claims on one or another conception of human purposes and ends. Thus Aristotle said the measure of a *polis* is the good at which it aims, and even J.S. Mill, who in the nineteenth century called "justice the chief part, and incomparably the most binding part of all morality," made justice an instrument of utilitarian ends.

This is the solution Kant's ethic rejects. Different persons typically have different desires and ends, and so any principle derived from them can only be contingent. But the moral law needs a *categorical* foundation, not a contingent one. Even so universal a desire as happiness will not do. People still differ in what happiness consists of, and to install any particular conception as regulative would impose on some the conceptions of others, and so deny at least to some the freedom to choose their *own* conceptions. In any case, to govern ourselves in conformity with desires and inclinations, given as they are by nature or circumstance, is not really to be *self*-governing at all. It is rather a refusal of freedom, a capitulation to determinations given outside us.

According to Kant, the right is "derived entirely from the concept of freedom in the external relationships of human beings, and has nothing to do with the end which all men have by nature [i.e., the aim of achieving happiness] or with the recognized means of attaining this end." As such, it must have a basis prior to all empirical ends. Only when I am governed by principles that do not presuppose any particular ends am I free to pursue my own ends consistent with a similar freedom for all.

But this still leaves the question of what the basis of the right could possibly be. If it must be a basis prior to all purposes and ends, unconditioned even by what Kant calls "the special circumstances of human nature," where could such a basis conceivably be found? Given the stringent demands of the Kantian ethic, the moral law would seem almost to require a foundation in nothing, for any empirical precondition would undermine its priority. "Duty!" asks Kant at his most lyrical, "What origin is there worthy of thee, and where is to be found the root of thy noble descent which proudly rejects all kinship with the inclinations?"

His answer is that the basis of the moral law is to be found in the *subject*, not the object of practical reason, a subject capable of an autonomous will. No empirical end, but rather "a subject of ends, namely a rational being himself, must be made the ground for all maxims of action." Nothing other than what Kant calls "the subject of all possible ends himself" can give rise to the right, for only this subject is also the subject of an autonomous will. Only this subject could be that "something which elevates man above himself as part of the world of sense" and enables him to participate in an ideal, unconditioned realm wholly independent of our social and psychological inclinations. And only this thoroughgoing independence can afford us the detachment we need if we are ever freely to choose for ourselves, unconditioned by the vagaries of circumstance.

Who or what exactly *is* this subject? It is, in a certain sense, *us*. The moral law, after all, is a law we give *ourselves*; we don't *find* it, we *will* it. That is how it (and we) escape the reign of nature and circumstance and merely empirical ends. But what is important to see is that the "we" who do the willing are not "we" qua particular persons, you and me, each for ourselves—the moral law is not up to us as individuals—but "we" qua participants in what Kant calls "pure practical reason," "we" qua participants in a transcendental subject.

Now what is to guarantee that I *am* a subject of this kind, capable of exercising pure practical reason? Well, strictly speaking, there *is* no guarantee; the transcendental subject is only a possibility. But it is a possibility I must *presuppose* if I am to think of myself as a free moral agent. Were I wholly an empirical being, I would not be capable of freedom, for every exercise of will would be conditioned by the desire for some object. All choice would be heteronomous choice, governed by the pursuit of some end. My will could never be a first cause, only the effect of some prior cause, the instrument of one or another impulse or inclination. "When we think of ourselves as free," writes Kant, "we transfer ourselves into the intelligible world as members and recognize the autonomy of the will." And so the notion of a subject prior to and independent of experience, such as the Kantian ethic requires, appears not only possible but indispensible, a necessary presupposition of the possibility of freedom.

How does all of this come back to politics? As the subject is prior to its ends, so the right is prior to the good. Society is best arranged when it is governed by principles that do not presuppose any particular conception of the good, for any other arrangement would fail to respect persons as being capable of choice; it would treat them as objects rather than subjects, as means rather than ends in themselves.

We can see in this way how Kant's notion of the subject is bound up with the claim for the priority of right. But for those in the Anglo-American tradition, the transcendental subject will seem a strange foundation for a familiar ethic. Surely, one may think, we can take rights seriously and affirm the primacy of justice without embracing the *Critique of Pure Reason*. This, in any case, is the project of Rawls.

He wants to save the priority of right from the obscurity of the transcendental subject. Kant's idealist metaphysic, for all its moral and political advantage, cedes too much to the transcendent, and wins for justice its primacy only by denying it its human situation. "To develop a viable Kantian conception of justice," Rawls writes, "the force and content of Kant's doctrine must be detached from its background in transcendental idealism" and recast within the "canons of a reasonable empiricism." And so Rawls' project is to preserve Kant's moral and political teaching by replacing Germanic obscurities with a domesticated metaphysic more congenial to the Anglo-American temper. This is the role of the original position.

From Transcendental Subject to Unencumbered Self

The original position tries to provide what Kant's transcendental argument cannot—a foundation for the right that is prior to the good, but still situated in the world. Sparing all but essentials, the original position works like this: It invites us to imagine the principles we would choose to govern our society if we were to choose them in advance, before we knew the particular persons we would be—whether rich or poor, strong or weak, lucky or unlucky—before we knew even our interests or aims or conceptions of the good. These principles—the ones we would choose in that imaginary situation—are the principles of justice. What is more, if it works, they are principles that do not presuppose any particular ends.

What they *do* presuppose is a certain picture of the person, of the way we must be if we are beings for whom justice is the first virtue. This is the picture of the unencumbered self, a self understood as prior to and independent of purposes and ends.

Now the unencumbered self describes first of all the way we stand toward the things we have, or want, or seek. It means there is always a distinction between the values I *have* and the person I *am*. To identify any characteristics as *my* aims, ambitions, desires, and so on, is always to imply some subject "me" standing behind them, at a certain distance, and the shape of this "me" must be given prior to any of the aims or attributes I bear. One consequence of this distance is to put the self *itself* beyond the reach of its experience, to secure its identity once and for all. Or to put the point another way, it rules out the possibility of what we might call *constitutive* ends. No role or commitment could define me so completely that I could not understand myself without it. No project could be so essential that turning away from it would call into question the person I am.

For the unencumbered self, what matters above all, what is most essential to our personhood, are not the ends we choose but our capacity to choose them. The original position sums up this central claim about us. "It is not our aims that primarily reveal our nature," writes Rawls, "but rather the principles that we would acknowledge to govern the background conditions under which these aims are to be formed ... We should therefore reverse the relation between the right and the good proposed by teleological doctrines and view the right as prior."

Only if the self is prior to its ends can the right be prior to the good. Only if my identity is never tied to the aims and interests I may have at any moment can I think of myself as a free and independent agent, capable of choice.

This notion of independence carries consequences for the kind of community of which we are capable. Understood as unencumbered selves, we are of course free to join in voluntary association with others, and so are capable of community in the cooperative sense. What is denied to the unencumbered self is the possibility of membership in any community bound by moral ties antecedent to choice; he cannot belong to any community where the self *itself* could be at stake. Such a community—call it constitutive as against merely cooperative— would engage the identity as well as the interests of the participants, and so implicate its members in a citizenship more thoroughgoing than the unencumbered self can know.

For justice to be primary, then, we must be creatures of a certain kind, related to human circumstance in a certain way. We must stand to our circumstance always at a certain distance, whether as transcendental subject in the case of Kant, or as unencumbered selves in the case of Rawls. Only in this way can we view ourselves as subjects as well as objects of experience, as agents and not just instruments of the purposes we pursue.

The unencumbered self and the ethic it inspires, taken together, hold out a liberating vision. Freed from the dicates of nature and the sanction of social roles, the human subject is installed as sovereign, cast as the author of the only moral meanings there are. As participants in pure practical reason, or as parties to the original position, we are free to construct principles of justice unconstrained by an order of value antecedently given. And as actual, individual selves, we are free to choose our purposes and ends unbound by such an order, or by custom or tradition or inherited status. So long as they are not unjust, our conceptions of the good carry weight, whatever they are, simply in virtue of our having chosen them. We are, in Rawls' words, "self-originating sources of valid claims."

This is an exhilarating promise, and the liberalism it animates is perhaps the fullest expression of the Enlightenment's quest for the self-defining subject. But is it true? Can we make sense of our moral and political life by the light of the self-image it requires? I do not think we can, and I will try to show why not by arguing first within the liberal project, then beyond it.

Justice and Community

We have focused so far on the foundations of the liberal vision, on the way it derives the principles it defends. Let us turn briefly now to the substance of those principles, using Rawls as our example. Sparing all but essentials once again, Rawls' two principles of justice are these: first, equal basic liberties for all, and second, only those social and economic inequalities that benefit the least-advantaged members of society (the difference principle).

In arguing for these principles, Rawls argues against two familiar alternatives—utilitarianism and libertarianism. He argues against utilitarianism that it fails to take seriously the distinction between persons. In seeking to maximize the general welfare, the utilitarian treats society as a whole as if it were a single person; it conflates our many, diverse desires into a single system of desires, and tries to maximize. It is indifferent to the distribution of satisfactions among persons, except insofar as this may affect the overall sum. But this fails to respect our plurality and distinctness. It uses some as means to the happiness of all, and so fails to respect each as an end in himself. While utilitarians may sometimes defend individual rights, their defense must rest on the calculation that respecting those rights will serve utility in the long run. But this calculation is contingent and uncertain. So long as utility is what Mill said it is, "the ultimate appeal on all ethical questions," individual rights can never be secure. To avoid the danger that their life prospects might one day be sacrificed for the greater good of others, the parties to the original position therefore insist on certain basic liberties for all, and make those liberties prior.

If utilitarians fail to take seriously the distinctness of persons, libertarians go wrong by failing to acknowledge the arbitrariness of fortune. They define as just whatever distribution results from an efficient market economy, and oppose all redistribution on the grounds that people are entitled to whatever they get, so long as they do not cheat or steal or otherwise violate someone's rights in getting it. Rawls opposes this principle on the ground that the distribution of talents and assets and even efforts by which some get more and others get less is arbitrary from a moral point of view, a matter of good luck. To distribute the good things in life on the basis of these differences is not to do justice, but simply to carry over into human arrangements the arbitrariness of social and natural contingency. We deserve, as individuals, neither the talents our good fortune may have brought, nor the benefits that flow from them. We should therefore regard these talents as common assets, and regard one another as common beneficiaries of the rewards they bring. "Those who have been favored by nature, whoever they are, may gain from their good fortune only on terms that improve the situation of those who have lost out . . . In justice as fairness, men agree to share one another's fate."

This is the reasoning that leads to the difference principle. Notice how it reveals, in yet another guise, the logic of the unencumbered self. I cannot be said to deserve the benefits that flow from, say, my fine physique and good looks, because they are only accidental, not essential facts about me. They describe attributes I *have*, not the person I *am*, and so cannot give rise to a claim of desert. Being an unencumbered self, this is true of *everything* about me. And so I cannot, as an individual, deserve anything at all.

However jarring to our ordinary understandings this argument may be, the picture so far remains intact; the priority of right, the denial of desert, and the unencumbered self all hang impressively together.

But the difference principle requires more, and it is here that the argument comes undone. The difference principle begins with the thought,

congenial to the unencumbered self, that the assets I have are only accidentally mine. But it ends by assuming that these assets are therefore *common* assets and that society has a prior claim on the fruits of their exercise. But this assumption is without warrant. Simply because I, as an individual, do not have a privileged claim on the assets accidentally residing "here," it does not follow that everyone in the world collectively does. For there is no reason to think that their location in society's province or, for that matter, within the province of humankind, is any *less* arbitrary from a moral point of view. And if their arbitrariness within *me* makes them ineligible to serve *my* ends, there seems no obvious reason why their arbitrariness within any particular society should not make them ineligible to serve that society's ends as well.

To put the point another way, the difference principle, like utilitarianism, is a principle of sharing. As such, it must presuppose some prior moral tie among those whose assets it would deploy and whose efforts it would enlist in a common endeavor. Otherwise, it is simply a formula for using some as means to others ends, a formula this liberalism is committed to reject.

But on the cooperative vision of community alone, it is unclear what the moral basis for this sharing could be. Short of the constitutive conception, deploying an individual's assets for the sake of the common good would seem an offense against the "plurality and distinctness" of individuals this liberalism seeks above all to secure.

If those whose fate I am required to share really are, morally speaking, *others*, rather than fellow participants in a way of life with which my identity is bound, the difference principle falls prey to the same objections as utilitarianism. Its claim on me is not the claim of a constitutive community whose attachments I acknowledge, but rather the claim of a concatenated collectivity whose entanglements I confront.

What the difference principle requires, but cannot provide, is some way of identifying those *among* whom the assets I bear are properly regarded as common, some way of seeing ourselves as mutually indebted and morally engaged to begin with. But as we have seen, the constitutive aims and attachments that would save and situate the difference principle are precisely the ones denied to the liberal self; the moral encumbrances and antecedent obligations they imply would undercut the priority of right.

What, then, of those encumbrances? The point so far is that we cannot be persons for whom justice is primary, and also be persons for whom the difference principle is a principle of justice. But which must give way? Can we view ourselves as independent selves, independent in the sense that our identity is never tied to our aims and attachments?

I do not think we can, at least not without cost to those loyalties and convictions whose moral force consists partly in the fact that living by them is inseparable from understanding ourselves as the particular persons we are—as members of this family or community or nation or people, as bearers of that history, as citizens of this republic. Allegiances such as these are more than values I happen to have, and to hold, at a certain distance. They go beyond the obligations I voluntarily incur and the "natural duties" I owe to human beings as such. They allow that to some I owe more than justice requires or even permits, not by reason of agreements I have made but instead in virtue of those more or less enduring attachments and commitments that, taken together, partly define the person I am.

To imagine a person incapable of constitutive attachments such as these is not to conceive an ideally free and rational agent, but to imagine a person wholly without character, without moral depth. For to have character is to know that I move in a history I neither summon nor command, which carries consequences nonetheless for my choices and conduct. It draws me closer to some and more distant from others; it makes some aims more appropriate, others less so. As a self-interpreting being, I am able to reflect on my

history and in this sense to distance myself from it, but the distance is always precarious and provisional, the point of reflection never finally secured outside the history itself. But the liberal ethic puts the self beyond the reach of its experience, beyond deliberation and reflection. Denied the expansive self-understandings that could shape a common life, the liberal self is left to lurch between detachment on the one hand, and entanglement on the other. Such is the fate of the unencumbered self, and its liberating promise.

The Procedural Republic

But before my case can be complete, I need to consider one powerful reply. While it comes from a liberal direction, its spirit is more practical than philosophical. It says, in short, that I am asking too much. It is one thing to seek constitutive attachments in our private lives; among families and friends, and certain tightly knit groups, there may be found a common good that makes justice and rights less pressing. But with public life—at least today, and probably always—it is different. So long as the nation-state is the primary form of political association, talk of constitutive community too easily suggests a darker politics rather than a brighter one; amid echoes of the moral majority, the priority of right, for all its philosophical faults, still seems the safer hope.

This is a challenging rejoinder, and no account of political community in the twentieth century can fail to take it seriously. It is challenging not least because it calls into question the status of political philosophy and its relation to the world. For if my argument is correct, if the liberal vision we have considered is not morally self-sufficient but parasitic on a notion of community it officially rejects, then we should expect to find that the political practice that embodies this vision is not *practically* self-sufficient either—that it must draw on a sense of community it cannot supply and may even undermine. But is that so far from the circumstance we face today? Could it be that through the original position darkly, on the far side of the veil of ignorance, we may glimpse an intimation of our predicament, a refracted vision of ourselves?

How does the liberal vision—and its failure— help us make sense of our public life and its predicament? Consider, to begin, the following paradox in the citizen's relation to the modern welfare state. In many ways, we in the 1980s stand near the completion of a liberal project that has run its course from the New Deal through the Great Society and into the present. But notwithstanding the extension of the franchise and the expansion on individual rights and entitlements in recent decades, there is a widespread sense that, individually and collectively, our control over the forces that govern our lives is receding rather than increasing. This sense is deepened by what appear simultaneously as the power and the powerlessness of the nation-state. One the one hand, increasing numbers of citizens view the state as an overly intrusive presence, more likely to frustrate their purposes than advance them. And yet, despite its unprecedented role in the economy and society, the modern state seems itself disempowered, unable effectively to control the domestic economy, to respond to persisting social ills, or to work America's will in the world.

This is a paradox that has fed the appeals of recent politicians (including Carter and Reagan), even as it has frustrated their attempts to govern. To sort it out, we need to identify the public philosophy implicit in our political practice, and to reconstruct its arrival. We need to trace the advent of the procedural republic, by which I mean a public life animated by the liberal vision and self-image we've considered.

The story of the procedural republic goes back in some ways to the founding of the republic, but is central drama begins to unfold around the turn of the century. As national markets and large-scale enterprise displaced a decentralized economy, the decentralized political forms of the early, republic became outmoded as well. If democracy was to survive, the concentration of economic power would have to be met by a similar concentration of political power. But the Progressives understood, or some of them did, that the success of democracy required more than the centralization of government; it also required the nationalization of politics. The primary form of political community had to be a recast on a national scale. For Herbert Croly, writing in 1909, the "nationalizing of American political, economic, and social life" was "an essentially formative and enlightening political transformation." We would become more of a democracy only as we became "more of a nation . . . in ideas, in institutions, and in spirit."

This nationalizing project would be consummated in the New Deal, but for the democratic tradition in America, the embrace of the nation was a decisive departure. From Jefferson to the populists, the party of democracy in American political debate had been, roughly speaking, the party of the provinces, of decentralized power, of small-town and small-scale America. And against them had stood the party of the nation—first Federalists, then Whigs, then the Republicans of Lincoln—a party that spoke for the consolidation of the union. It was thus the historic achievement of the New Deal to unite, in a single party and political program, what Samuel Beer has called "liberalism and the national idea."

What matters for our purpose is that, in the twentieth century, liberalism made its peace with concentrated power. But it was understood at the start that the terms of this peace required a strong sense of national community, morally and politically to underwrite the extended involvements of a modern industrial order. If a virtuous republic of small-scale, democratic communities was no longer a possibility, a national republic seemed democracy's next best hope. This was still, in principle at least, a politics of the common good. It looked to the nation, not as a neutral framework for the play of competing interests, but rather as a formative community, concerned to shape a common life suited to the scale of modern social and economic forms.

But this project failed. By the mid- or late twentieth century, the national republic had run its course. Except for extraordinary moments, such as war, the nation proved too vast a scale across which to cultivate the shared self-understandings necessary to community in the formative, or constitutive sense. And so the gradual shift, in our practices and institutions, from a public philosophy of common purposes to one of fair procedures, from a politics of good to a politics of right, from the national republic to the procedural republic.

Our Present Predicament

A full account of this transition would take a detailed look at the changing shape of political institutions, constitutional interpretation, and the terms of political discourse in the broadest sense. But I suspect we would find in the *practice* of the procedural republic two broad tendencies foreshadowed by its philosophy: first, a tendency to crowd out democratic possibilities; second, a tendency to undercut the kind of community on which it nonetheless depends.

Where liberty in the early republic was understood as a function of democratic institutions and dispersed power, liberty in the procedural republic is defined in opposition to democracy, as an individual's guarantee against what the majority might will. I am free insofar as I am the bearer of rights, where rights are trumps. Unlike the liberty of the early republic, the modern version permits—in fact even requires—concentrated power. This has to do with the universalizing logic of rights. Insofar as I have a right, whether to free speech or a minimum income, its provision cannot be left to the vagaries of local preferences but must be assured at the most comprehensive level of political association. It cannot be one thing in New York and another in Alabama. As rights

and entitlements expand, politics is therefore displaced from smaller forms of association and relocated at the most universal form—in our case, the nation. And even as politics flows to the nation, power shifts away from democratic institutions (such as legislatures and political parties) and toward institutions designed to be insulated from democratic pressures, and hence better equipped to dispense and defend individual rights (notably the judiciary and bureaucracy).

These institutional developments may begin to account for the sense of powerlessness that the welfare state fails to address and in some ways doubtless deepens. But it seems to me a further clue to our condition recalls even more directly the predicament of the unencumbered self—lurching, as we left it, between detachment on the one hand, the entanglement on the other. For it is a striking feature of the welfare state that it offers a powerful promise of individual rights, and also demands of its citizens a high measure of mutual engagement. But the self-image that attends the rights cannot sustain the engagement.

As bearers of rights, where rights are trumps, we think of ourselves as freely choosing, individual selves, unbound by obligations antecedent to rights, or to the agreements we make. And yet, as citizens of the procedural republic that secures these rights, we find ourselves implicated willy-nilly in a formidable array of dependencies and expectations we did not choose and increasingly reject.

In our public life, we are more entangled, but less attached, than ever before. It is as though the unencumbered self presupposed by the liberal ethic had begun to come true—less liberated than disempowered, entangled in a network of obligations and involvements unassociated with any act of will, and yet unmediated by those common identifications or expansive self-definitions that would make them tolerable. As the scale of social and political organization has become more comprehensive, the terms of our collective identity have become more fragmented, and the forms of political life have outrun the common purpose needed to sustain them.

Something like this, it seems to me, has been unfolding in America for the past half-century or so. I hope I have said at least enough to suggest the shape a fuller story might take. And I hope in any case to have conveyed a certain view about politics and philosophy and the relation between them—that our practices and institutions are themselves embodiments of theory, and to unravel their predicament is, at least in part, to seek after the self-image of the age.

PART 2

Government, the Economy, and Morality

2a. POLITICAL ECONOMY

IT IS HARD TO GET FAR IN THINKING about political philosophy without running into empirical claims. This is especially true when thinking about whether and to what extent the government ought to be involved in a nation's economy. For most of us, whether the government ought to mandate a legal minimum wage, regulate foreign imports, control monopolies, or tax citizens in order to provide for roads and clean air will depend at least in part on what the *consequences* of government's following or not following these policies will be. This is obviously true for those who are moral consequentialists like Mill, but even rights-based theorists like Nozick and Rawls will give some weight to pragmatic considerations.

To address these empirical considerations in a somewhat systematic way, we turn in this section to the field of political economy. Political economy, as its name suggests, is a field devoted to the study of the intersection of politics and the economy. Its primary question is how economic production and trade should be organized by the state. Historically, political economy became a major subject of study around the time of the publication of Adam Smith's *Inquiry into the Nature and Causes of the Wealth of Nations* (1776). In this text, Smith argued against the doctrine of mercantilism, which held that nations ought to seek to enhance their own wealth by tightly restricting the importation of foreign goods, and argued in favor of free trade both within and between nations. It was in this text that Smith famously claimed that under capitalism, individuals would be led by an "invisible hand" to promote the wealth of their society, since the only way that they could enrich themselves would be to provide others with goods or services that those others valued more than their money. Social wealth, on this view, is an unintended side-effect of the individual pursuit of self-interest. This same theme of "invisibility" is discussed at length in this section by the French political economist Frédéric Bastiat, who cautions that the invisible costs of government policies will often outweigh the visible benefits, even if the former are rarely taken into account.

For Smith, the division of labor was the key for the development of a nation's wealth. By allowing individuals to specialize in a skill, to save time moving between different tasks, and to develop technology to do the same task more easily, the division of labor greatly improves the productive power of labor. Smith saw that this principle applied just as well between nations as it did within a single nation, but it would be almost forty years before that insight was formalized by the British political economist, David Ricardo. In his *Principles of Political Economy and Taxation*, Ricardo set forth the principle of comparative advantage, which demonstrates that even when one country is more productive than another in absolute terms, it will benefit both countries to specialize and trade freely. This is because even less productive countries (or individuals—the principle holds for both) can have a *comparative* advantage in certain areas of production where their opportunity costs—what they have to give up in order to engage in one activity rather than another—are lower. Thus, imagine Abe and Betty living together on an island. Suppose Betty can produce either 100 fish or 200 apples with a week's work, while Abe could only produce 50 fish or 50 apples. Even though Betty is more productive than Abe in absolute terms, Abe enjoys a comparative advantage in the production of fish, since in terms of his opportunity costs producing one fish only requires that he give up one apple, whereas for Betty to produce one fish she must give up two apples. Given that this is so, *both* Abe and Betty will be better off if each specializes in producing that good for which they enjoy the greatest comparative advantage (fish for Abe and apples for Betty), and then trades to ensure a balanced diet. Free trade will benefit not just super-productive Betty, but even moderately-productive Abe. Contemporary defenders of globalization have argued that this principle provides strong support for outsourcing and other forms of trade between not just developed countries, but between developed and developing countries alike.

Not all political economists, however, have been so sanguine about the morally beneficial effects of the pursuit of self-interest. Karl Marx, for instance, argues that capitalism, just as much as the feudalism which preceded it, is a system of class conflict. The interests of the capital-owning class require them to extract as much value as possible from laborers at the lowest cost. Workers in a capitalist system are treated as little more than machines for the production of labor, and the interest of capitalists is to get that labor out of them as cheaply as possible. This leads to a system in which workers—on whose back the productivity of an economy depends—are systematically exploited. Further, Marx paints a picture of capitalism as a ravenous beast which must consume everything in its path—traditional ways of life, the dignity of the individual, foreign nations—or else die. Contemporary critics of globalization will find Marx's writings to be a prescient critique of the current spread of that system.

Smith's doctrine of the invisible hand has been subject to less radical critiques as well. One class of problems occurs when the joint result of individual rational self-interest fails to be economically efficient. As Wolf discusses in this section, market failures such as negative externalities, public goods, and monopolies suggest that some government regulation of or intervention in the economy is necessary to promote the citizens' interests. Indeed, many economists have viewed the existence of market failures as one of the fundamental justifications for political authority. Since roads, national defense, and even arguably the law and the capitalist market itself are all public goods which cannot adequately be provided for by voluntary exchange, some coercive mechanism such as the state is required in order to provide them. Government is thus justified because it helps individuals achieve goods that they want but cannot practically produce on their own.

But even as government solves some economic problems, it creates others of its own. The field of public choice, lying at the intersection of economics and political science, applies economic tools of analysis to political institutions. And, not surprisingly, if we assume government to be populated by the same rational self-interested agents which economics supposes to populate the market, it turns out that government policies will often be aimed more at promoting the interests of politicians, rather than the interest of the public at large. In deciding upon the proper roles of government and the economy, then, we must judge an admittedly imperfect market against a government which has serious shortcomings of its own.

This section is far too brief to decisively settle the contentious issues of political economy. My hope in including it, then, is that readers will come away with an appreciation of the various ways in which the claims of political philosophers often depend on empirical matters regarding the relationship between the economy and state, and that they have an understanding of some of the more important theories that have developed from such empirical investigation.

Further Reading

Buchanan, J., & Tullock, G. (1962). *The Calculus of Consent*. Ann Arbor: University of Michigan Press.

Friedman, M. (2002). *Capitalism and Freedom* (40th Anniversary ed.). Chicago: University of Chicago Press.

Keynes, J. M. (1997). *The General Theory of Employment, Interest, and Money*. New York: Prometheus Books.

Marx, K. (1992). *Capital*. New York: Penguin.

Mill, J. S. (2004). *Principles of Political Economy with Applications to Social Philosophy*. Indianapolis: Hackett.

Mitchell, W., & Simmons, R. T. (1994). *Beyond Politics: Markets, Welfare, and the Failure of Bureaucracy*. Boulder, CO: Westview Press.

Mueller, D. C. (2003). *Public Choice III*. Cambridge: Cambridge University Press.

Ricardo, D. (2004). *On the Principles of Political Economy and Taxation*. Indianapolis: Liberty Fund.

Samuelson, P., & Nordhaus, W. (1998). *Economics*. Boston: Irwin McGraw-Hill.

Smith, A. (1982). *The Wealth of Nations*. Indianapolis: Liberty Fund.

Chapter 20

Karl Marx and Frederick Engels

THE COMMUNIST MANIFESTO

AND

CRITIQUE OF THE GOTHA PROGRAM

Karl Marx (1818–1883) and Frederick Engels (1820–1895) were German philosophers and social thinkers who were jointly responsible for the creation of the theory of communism. "The Communist Manifesto" (1848) sets out the basic tenets of communism, including its theory of class conflict and its materialist theory of history. The "Critique of the Gotha Program" (1873) is mainly directed at criticizing a rival political movement, but is also notable for its expression of the Marxist doctrine of "from each according to his ability, to each according to his needs."

THE COMMUNIST MANIFESTO

A spectre is haunting Europe—the spectre of Communism. All the Powers of old Europe have entered into a holy alliance to exorcise this spectre: Pope and Czar, Metternich and Guizot, French Radicals and German police-spies.

Where is the party in opposition that has not been decried as Communistic by its opponents in power? Where the Opposition that has not hurled back the branding reproach of Communism, against the more advanced opposition parties, as well as against its reactionary adversaries?

Two things result from this fact.

I. Communism is already acknowledged by all European Powers to be itself a Power.

II. It is high time that Communists should openly, in the face of the whole world, publish their views, their aims, their tendencies, and meet this nursery tale of the Spectre of Communism with a Manifesto of the party itself.

To this end, Communists of various nationalities have assembled in London, and sketched the following Manifesto, to be published in the English, French, German, Italian, Flemish and Danish languages.

I. Bourgeois and Proletarians

The history of all hitherto existing society is the history of class struggles.

Freeman and slave, patrician and plebeian, lord and serf, guild-master and journeyman, in a word, oppressor and oppressed, stood in constant opposition to one another, carried on an uninterrupted, now hidden, now open fight, a fight that each time ended, either in a revolutionary re-constitution of society at large, or in the common ruin of the contending classes.

In the earlier epochs of history, we find almost everywhere a complicated arrangement of society into various orders, a manifold gradation of social rank. In ancient Rome we have patricians, knights, plebeians, slaves; in the Middle Ages, feudal lords, vassals, guild-masters, journeymen, apprentices, serfs; in almost all of these classes, again, subordinate gradations.

The modern bourgeois society that has sprouted from the ruins of feudal society has not done away with class antagonisms. It has but established new classes, new conditions of oppression, new forms of struggle in place of the old ones.

Our epoch, the epoch of the bourgeoisie, possesses, however, this distinctive feature: it has simplified the class antagonisms. Society as a whole is more and more splitting up into two great hostile camps, into two great classes directly facing each other: Bourgeoisie and Proletariat.

From the serfs of the Middle Ages sprang the chartered burghers of the earliest towns. From these burgesses the first elements of the bourgeoisie were developed.

The discovery of America, the rounding of the Cape, opened up fresh ground for the rising bourgeoisie. The East-Indian and Chinese markets, the colonisation of America, trade with the colonies, the increase in the means of exchange and in commodities generally, gave to commerce, to navigation, to industry, an impulse never before known, and thereby, to the revolutionary element in the tottering feudal society, a rapid development.

The feudal system of industry, under which industrial production was monopolised by closed guilds, now no longer sufficed for the growing wants of the new markets. The manufacturing system took its place. The guild-masters were pushed on one side by the manufacturing middle class; division of labour between the different corporate guilds vanished in the face of division of labour in each single workshop.

Meantime the markets kept ever growing, the demand ever rising. Even manufacture no longer sufficed. Thereupon, steam and machinery revolutionised industrial production. The place of manufacture was taken by the giant, Modern Industry, the place of the industrial middle class, by industrial millionaires, the leaders of whole industrial armies, the modern bourgeois.

Modern industry has established the world-market, for which the discovery of America paved the way. This market has given an immense development to commerce, to navigation, to communication by land. This development has, in its turn, reacted on the extension of industry; and in proportion as industry, commerce, navigation, railways extended, in the same proportion the bourgeoisie developed, increased its capital, and pushed into the background every class handed down from the Middle Ages.

We see, therefore, how the modern bourgeoisie is itself the product of a long course of development, of a series of revolutions in the modes of production and of exchange.

Each step in the development of the bourgeoisie was accompanied by a corresponding political advance of that class. An oppressed class under the sway of the feudal nobility, an armed and self-governing association in the mediaeval commune; here independent urban republic (as in Italy and Germany), there taxable "third estate" of the monarchy (as in France), afterwards, in the period of manufacture proper, serving either the semi-feudal or the absolute monarchy as a counterpoise against the nobility, and, in fact, corner-stone of the great monarchies in general, the bourgeoisie has at last, since the establishment of Modern Industry and of the world-market, conquered for itself, in the modern representative State, exclusive political sway. The executive of the modern State is but a committee for managing the common affairs of the whole bourgeoisie.

The bourgeoisie, historically, has played a most revolutionary part.

The bourgeoisie, wherever it has got the upper hand, has put an end to all feudal, patriarchal, idyllic relations. It has pitilessly torn asunder the motley feudal ties that bound man to his "natural superiors," and has left remaining no other nexus between man and man than naked self-interest, than callous "cash payment." It has drowned the most heavenly ecstasies of religious fervour, of chivalrous enthusiasm, of philistine sentimentalism, in the icy water of egotistical calculation. It has resolved personal worth into exchange value, and in place of the numberless indefeasible chartered freedoms, has set up that single, unconscionable freedom—Free Trade. In one word, for exploitation, veiled by religious and political illusions, it has substituted naked, shameless, direct, brutal exploitation.

The bourgeoisie has stripped of its halo every occupation hitherto honoured and looked up to with reverent awe. It has converted the physician, the lawyer, the priest, the poet, the man of science, into its paid wage-labourers.

The bourgeoisie has torn away from the family its sentimental veil, and has reduced the family relation to a mere money relation.

The bourgeoisie has disclosed how it came to pass that the brutal display of vigour in the Middle Ages, which Reactionists so much admire, found its fitting complement in the most slothful indolence. It has been the first to show what man's activity can bring about. It has accomplished wonders far surpassing Egyptian pyramids, Roman aqueducts, and Gothic cathedrals; it has conducted expeditions that put in the shade all former Exoduses of nations and crusades.

The bourgeoisie cannot exist without constantly revolutionising the instruments of production, and thereby the relations of production, and with them the whole relations of society. Conservation of the old modes of production in unaltered form, was, on the contrary, the first condition of existence for all earlier industrial classes. Constant revolutionising of production,

uninterrupted disturbance of all social conditions, everlasting uncertainty and agitation distinguish the bourgeois epoch from all earlier ones. All fixed, fast-frozen relations, with their train of ancient and venerable prejudices and opinions, are swept away, all new-formed ones become antiquated before they can ossify. All that is solid melts into air, all that is holy is profaned, and man is at last compelled to face with sober senses, his real conditions of life, and his relations with his kind.

The need of a constantly expanding market for its products chases the bourgeoisie over the whole surface of the globe. It must nestle everywhere, settle everywhere, establish connexions everywhere.

The bourgeoisie has through its exploitation of the world-market given a cosmopolitan character to production and consumption in every country. To the great chargrin of Reactionists, it has drawn from under the feet of industry the national ground on which it stood. All old-established national industries have been destroyed or are daily being destroyed. They are dislodged by new industries, whose introduction becomes a life and death question for all civilised nations, by industries that no longer work up indigenous raw material, but raw material drawn from the remotest zones; industries whose products are consumed, not only at home, but in every quarter of the globe. In place of the old wants, satisfied by the productions of the country, we find new wants, requiring for their satisfaction the products of distant lands and climes. In place of the old local and national seclusion and self-sufficiency, we have intercourse in every direction, universal interdependence of nations. And as in material, so also in intellectual production. The intellectual creations of individual nations become common property. National one-sidedness and narrow-mindedness become more and more impossible, and from the numerous national and local literatures, there arises a world literature.

The bourgeoisie, by the rapid improvement

of all instruments of production, by the immensely facilitated means of communication, draws all, even the most barbarian, nations into civilisation. The cheap prices of its commodities are the heavy artillery with which it batters down all Chinese walls, with which it forces the barbarians' intensely obstinate hatred of foreigners to capitulate. It compels all nations, on pain of extinction, to adopt the bourgeois mode of production; it compels them to introduce what it calls civilisation into their midst, i.e., to become bourgeois themselves. In one word, it creates a world after its own image.

The bourgeoisie has subjected the country to the rule of the towns. It has created enormous cities, has greatly increased the urban population as compared with the rural, and has thus rescued a considerable part of the population from the idiocy of rural life. Just as it has made the country dependent on the towns, so it has made barbarian and semi-barbarian countries dependent on the civilised ones, nations of peasants on nations of bourgeois, the East on the West.

The bourgeoisie keeps more and more doing away with the scattered state of the population, of the means of production, and of property. It has agglomerated population, centralised means of production, and has concentrated property in a few hands. The necessary consequence of this was political centralisation. Independent, or but loosely connected provinces, with separate interests, laws, governments and systems of taxation, became lumped together into one nation, with one government, one code of laws, one national class-interest, one frontier and one customs-tariff.

The bourgeoisie, during its rule of scarce one hundred years, has created more massive and more colossal productive forces than have all preceding generations together. Subjection of Nature's forces to man, machinery, application of chemistry to industry and agriculture, steam-navigation, railways, electric telegraphs, clearing of whole continents for cultivation, canalisation of rivers, whole populations conjured out of the ground—what earlier century had even a presentiment that such productive forces slumbered in the lap of social labour?

We see then: the means of production and of exchange, on whose foundation the bourgeoisie built itself up, were generated in feudal society. At a certain stage in the development of these means of production and of exchange, the conditions under which feudal society produced and exchanged, the feudal organisation of agriculture and manufacturing industry, in one word, the feudal relations of property became no longer compatible with the already developed productive forces; they became so many fetters. They had to be burst asunder; they were burst asunder.

Into their place stepped free competition, accompanied by a social and political constitution adapted to it, and by the economical and political sway of the bourgeois class.

A similar movement is going on before our own eyes. Modern bourgeois society with its relations of production, of exchange and of property, a society that has conjured up such gigantic means of production and of exchange, is like the sorcerer, who is no longer able to control the powers of the nether world whom he has called up by his spells. For many a decade past the history of industry and commerce is but the history of the revolt of modern productive forces against modern conditions of production, against the property relations that are the conditions for the existence of the bourgeoisie and of its rule. It is enough to mention the commercial crises that by their periodical return put on its trial, each time more threateningly, the existence of the entire bourgeois society. In these crises a great part not only of the existing products, but also of the previously created productive forces, are periodically destroyed. In these crises there breaks out an epidemic that, in all earlier epochs, would have seemed an absurdity—the epidemic of over-production. Society suddenly finds itself put back into a state of momentary barbarism; it appears as if a famine, a universal war of devastation had cut off the supply of every means of subsistence; industry and commerce seem to be destroyed; and why? Because there is too much civilisation, too much means of subsistence, too much industry, too much commerce. The productive forces at the disposal of society no longer tend to further the development of the conditions of bourgeois property; on the contrary, they have become too powerful for these conditions, by which they are fettered, and so soon as they overcome these fetters, they bring disorder into the whole of bourgeois society, endanger the existence of bourgeois property. The conditions of bourgeois society are too narrow to comprise the wealth created by them. And how does the bourgeoisie get over these crises? On the one hand by enforced destruction of a mass of productive forces; on the other, by the conquest of new markets, and by the more thorough exploitation of the old ones. That is to say, by paving the way for more extensive and more destructive crises, and by diminishing the means whereby crises are prevented.

The weapons with which the bourgeoisie felled feudalism to the ground are now turned against the bourgeoisie itself.

But not only has the bourgeoisie forged the weapons that bring death to itself; it has also called into existence the men who are to wield those weapons—the modern working class—the proletarians.

In proportion as the bourgeoisie, i.e., capital, is developed, in the same proportion is the proletariat, the modern working class, developed —a class of labourers, who live only so long as they find work, and who find work only so long as their labour increases capital. These labourers, who must sell themselves piecemeal, are a commodity, like every other article of commerce, and are consequently exposed to all the vicissitudes of competition, to all the fluctuations of the market.

Owing to the extensive use of machinery and to division of labour, the work of the proletarians has lost all individual character, and,

consequently, all charm for the workman. He becomes an appendage of the machine, and it is only the most simple, most monotonous, and most easily acquired knack, that is required of him. Hence, the cost of production of a workman is restricted, almost entirely, to the means of subsistence that he requires for his maintenance, and for the propagation of his race. But the price of a commodity, and therefore also of labour, is equal to its cost of production. In proportion, therefore, as the repulsiveness of the work increases, the wage decreases. Nay more, in proportion as the use of machinery and division of labour increases, in the same production the burden of toil also increases, whether by prolongation of the working hours, by increase of the work exacted in a given time or by increased speed of the machinery, etc.

Modern industry has converted the little workshop of the patriarchal master into the great factory of the industrial capitalist. Masses of labourers, crowded into the factory, are organised like soliders. As privates of the industrial army they are placed under the command of a perfect hierarchy of officers and sergeants. Not only are they slaves of the bourgeois class, and of the bourgeois State; they are daily and hourly enslaved by the machine, by the overlooker, and, above all, by the individual bourgeois manufacturer himself. The more openly this despotism proclaims gain to be its end and aim, the more petty, the more hateful and the more embittering it is.

The less the skill and exertion of strength implied in manual labour, in other words, the more modern industry becomes developed, the more is the labour of men superseded by that of women. Differences of age and sex have no longer any distinctive social validity for the working class. All are instruments of labour, more or less expensive to use, according to their age and sex.

No sooner is the exploitation of the labourer by the manufacturer, so far, at an end, and he receives his wages in cash, than he is set upon by the other portions of the bourgeoisie, the landlord, the shopkeeper, the pawnbroker, etc.

The lower strata of the middle class—the small tradespeople, shopkeepers, and retired tradesmen generally, the handicraftsmen and peasants—all these sink gradually into the proletariat, partly because their diminutive capital does not suffice for the scale on which Modern Industry is carried on, and is swamped in the competition with the large capitalists, partly because their specialised skill is rendered worthless by new methods of production. Thus the proletariat is recruited from all classes of the population.

The proletariat goes through various stages of development. With its birth begins its struggle with the bourgeoisie. At first the contest is carried on by individual labourers, then by the workpeople of a factory, then by the operatives of one trade, in one locality, against the individual bourgeois who directly exploits them. They direct their attacks not against the bourgeois conditions of production, but against the instruments of production themselves; they destroy imported wares that compete with their labour, they smash to pieces machinery, they set factories ablaze, they seek to restore by force the vanished status of the workman of the Middle Ages.

At this stage the labourers still form an incoherent mass scattered over the whole country, and broken up by their mutual competition. If anywhere they unite to form more compact bodies, this is not yet the consequence of their own active union, but of the union of the bourgeoisie, which class, in order to attain its own political ends, is compelled to set the whole proletariat in motion, and is moreover yet, for a time, able to do so. At this stage, therefore, the proletarians do not fight their enemies, but the enemies of their enemies, the remnants of absolute monarchy, the landowners, the non-industrial bourgeois, the petty bourgeoisie. Thus the whole historical movement is concentrated in the hands of the bourgeoisie; every victory so obtained is a victory for the bourgeoisie.

But with the development of industry the proletariat not only increases in number; it becomes concentrated in greater masses, its strength grows, and it feels that strength more. The various interests and conditions of life within the ranks of the proletariat are more and more equalised, in proportion as machinery obliterates all distinctions of labour, and nearly everywhere reduces wages to the same low level. The growing competition among the bourgeois, and the resulting commercial crises, make the wages of the workers ever more fluctuating. The unceasing improvement of machinery, ever more rapidly developing, makes their livelihood more and more precarious; the collisions between individual workmen and individual bourgeois take more and more the character of collisions between two classes. Thereupon the workers begin to form combinations (Trades' Unions) against the bourgeois; they club together in order to keep up the rate of wages; they found permanent associations in order to make provision beforehand for these occasional revolts. Here and there the contest breaks out into riots.

Now and then the workers are victorious, but only for a time. The real fruit of their battles lies, not in the immediate result, but in the ever-expanding union of the workers. This union is helped on by the improved means of communication that are created by modern industry and that place the workers of different localities in contact with one another. It was just this contact that was needed to centralise the numerous local struggles, all of the same character, into one national struggle between classes. But every class struggle is a political struggle. And that union, to attain which the burghers of the Middle Ages, with their miserable highways, required centuries, the modern proletarians, thanks to railways, achieve in a few years.

This organisation of the proletarians into a class, and consequently into a political party, is continually being upset again by the competition between the workers themselves. But it ever rises up again, stronger, firmer, mightier. It compels legislative recognition of particular interests of the workers, by taking advantage of the divisions among the bourgeoisie itself. Thus the ten-hours' bill in England was carried.

Altogether collisions between the classes of the old society further, in many ways, the course of development of the proletariat. The bourgeoisie finds itself involved in a constant battle. At first with the aristocracy; later on, with those portions of the bourgeoisie itself, whose interests have become antagonistic to the progress of industry; at all times, with the bourgeoisie of foreign countries. In all these battles it sees itself compelled to appeal to the proletariat, to ask for its help, and thus, to drag it into the political arena. The bourgeoisie itself, therefore, supplies the proletariat with its own elements of political and general education, in other words, it furnishes the proletariat with weapons for fighting the bourgeoisie.

Further, as we have already seen, entire sections of the ruling classes are, by the advance of industry, precipitated into the proletariat, or are at least threatened in their conditions of existence. These also supply the proletariat with fresh elements of enlightenment and progress.

Finally, in times when the class struggle nears the decisive hour, the process of dissolution going on within the ruling class, in fact within the whole range of old society, assumes such a violent, glaring character, that a small section of the ruling class cuts itself adrift, and joins the revolutionary class, the class that holds the future in its hands. Just as, therefore, at an earlier period, a section of the nobility went over to the bourgeoisie, so now a portion of the bourgeoisie goes over to the proletariat, and in particular, a portion of the bourgeois ideologists, who have raised themselves to the level of comprehending theoretically the historical movement as a whole.

Of all the classes that stand face to face with the bourgeoisie today, the proletariat alone is a really revolutionary class. The other classes decay and finally disappear in the face of Modern Industry; the proletariat is its special and essential product.

The lower middle class, the small manufacturer, the shopkeeper, the artisan, the peasant, all these fight against the bourgeoisie, to save from extinction their existence as fractions of the middle class. They are therefore not revolutionary, but conservative. Nay more, they are reactionary, for they try to roll back the wheel of history. If by chance they are revolutionary, they are so only in view of their impending transfer into the proletariat, they thus defend not their present, but their future interests, they desert their own standpoint to place themselves at that of the proletariat.

The "dangerous class," the social scum, that passively rotting mass thrown off by the lowest layers of old society, may, here and there, be swept into the movement by a proletarian revolution, its conditions of life, however, prepare it far more for the part of a bribed tool of reactionary intrigue.

In the conditions of the proletariat, those of old society at large are already virtually swamped. The proletarian is without property; his relation to his wife and children has no longer anything in common with the bourgeois family-relations; modern industrial labour, modern subjection to capital, the same in England as in France, in America as in Germany, has stripped him of every trace of national character. Law, morality, religion, are to him so many bourgeois prejudices, behind which lurk in ambush just as many bourgeois interests.

All the preceding classes that got the upper hand, sought to fortify their already acquired status by subjecting society at large to their conditions of appropriation. The proletarians cannot become masters of the productive forces of society, except by abolishing their own previous mode of appropriation, and thereby also every other previous mode of appropriation. They have nothing of their own to secure and to fortify; their mission is to destroy all previous securities for, and insurances of, individual property.

All previous historical movements were movements of minorities, or in the interests of minorities. The proletarian movement is the self-conscious, independent movement of the immense majority, in the interests of the immense majority. The proletariat, the lowest stratum of our present society, cannot stir, cannot raise itself up, without the whole superincumbent strata of official society being sprung into the air.

Though not in substance, yet in form, the struggle of the proletariat with the bourgeoisie is at first a national struggle. The proletariat of each country must, of course, first of all settle matters with its own bourgeoisie.

In depicting the most general phases of the development of the proletariat, we traced the more or less veiled civil war, raging within existing society, up to the point where that war breaks out into open revolution, and where the violent overthrow of the bourgeoisie lays the foundation for the sway of the proletariat.

Hitherto, every form of society has been based, as we have already seen, on the antagonism of oppressing and oppressed classes. But in order to oppress a class, certain conditions must be assured to it under which it can, at least, continue its slavish existence. The serf, in the period of serfdom, raised himself to membership in the commune, just as the petty bourgeois, under the yoke of feudal absolutism, managed to develop into a bourgeois. The modern labourer, on the contrary, instead of rising with the progress of industry, sinks deeper and deeper below the conditions of existence of his own class. He becomes a pauper, and pauperism develops more rapidly than population and wealth. And here it becomes evident, that the bourgeoisie is unfit any longer to be the ruling class in society, and to impose its conditions of existence upon society as an over-riding law. It is unfit to rule because it is incompetent to assure an existence to its slave within his slavery, because it cannot help letting him sink into such a state, that it has to feed him, instead of being fed by him. Society can no longer live under this bourgeoisie, in other words, its existence is no longer compatible with society.

The essential condition for the existence, and for the sway of the bourgeois class, is the formation and augmentation of capital; the condition for capital is wage-labour. Wage-labour rests exclusively on competition between the labourers. The advance of industry, whose involuntary promoter is the bourgeoisie, replaces the isolation of the labourers, due to competition, by their revolutionary combination, due to association. The development of Modern Industry, therefore, cuts from under its feet the very foundation on which the bourgeoisie produces and appropriates products. What the bourgeoisie, therefore, produces, above all, is its own grave-diggers. Its fall and the victory of the proletariat are equally inevitable.

II. Proletarians and Communists

In what relation do the Communists stand to the proletarians as a whole?

The Communists do not form a separate party opposed to other working-class parties.

They have no interests separate and apart from those of the proletariat as a whole.

They do not set up any sectarian principles of their own, by which to shape and mould the proletarian movement.

The Communists are distinguished from the other working-class parties by this only:

1. In the national struggles of the proletarians of the different countries, they point out and bring to the front the common interests of the entire proletariat, independently of all nationality.

2. In the various stages of development which the struggle of the working class against the bourgeoisie has to pass through, they always and everywhere represent the interests of the movement as a whole.

The Communists, therefore, are on the one hand, practically, the most advanced and resolute section of the working-class parties of every country, that section which pushes forward all others; on the other hand, theoretically, they have over the great mass of the proletariat the advantage of clearly understanding the line of march, the conditions, and the ultimate general results of the proletarian movement.

The immediate aim of the Communists is the same as that of all the other proletarian parties: formation of the proletariat into a class, overthrow of the bourgeois supremacy, conquest of political power by the proletariat.

The theoretical conclusions of the Communists are in no way based on ideas or principles that have been invented, or discovered, by this or that would-be universal reformer.

They merely express, in general terms, actual relations springing from an existing class struggle, from a historical movement going on under our very eyes. The abolition of existing property relations is not at all a distinctive feature of Communism.

All property relations in the past have continually been subject to historical change consequent upon the change in historical conditions.

The French Revolution, for example, abolished feudal property in favour of bourgeois property.

The distinguishing feature of Communism is not the abolition of property generally, but the abolition of bourgeois property. But modern bourgeois private property is the final and most complete expression of the system of producing and appropriating products, that is based on class antagonisms, on the exploitation of the many by the few.

In this sense, the theory of the Communists may be summed up in the single sentence: Abolition of private property.

We Communists have been reproached with the desire of abolishing the right of personally acquiring property as the fruit of a man's own labour, which property is alleged to be the ground-work of all personal freedom, activity and independence.

Hard-won, self-acquired, self-earned property! Do you mean the property of the petty artisan and of the small peasant, a form of property that preceded the bourgeois form? There is no need to abolish that; the development of industry has to a great extent already destroyed it, and is still destroying it daily.

Or do you mean modern bourgeois private property?

But does wage-labour create any property for the labourer? Not a bit. It creates capital, i.e., that kind of property which exploits wage-labour, and which cannot increase except upon condition of begetting a new supply of wage-labour for fresh exploitation. Property, in its present form, is based on the antagonism of capital and wage-labour. Let us examine both sides of this antagonism.

To be a capitalist, is to have not only a purely personal, but a social *status* in production. Capital is a collective product, and only by the united action of many members, nay, in the last resort, only by the united action of all members of society, can it be set in motion.

Capital is, therefore, not a personal, it is a social power.

When, therefore, capital is converted into common property, into the property of all members of society, personal property is not thereby transformed into social property. It is only the social character of the property that is changed. It loses its class-character.

Let us now take wage-labour.

The average price of wage-labour is the minimum wage, i.e., that quantum of the means of subsistence, which is absolutely requisite to keep the labourer in bare existence as a labourer. What, therefore, the wage-labourer appropriates by means of his labour, merely suffices to prolong and reproduce a bare existence. We by no means intend to abolish this personal appropriation of the products of labour, an appropriation that is made for the maintenance and reproduction of human life, and that leaves no surplus wherewith to command the labour of others. All that we want to do away with, is the miserable character of this appropriation, under which the labourer lives merely to increase capital, and is allowed to live only in so far as the interest of the ruling class requires it.

In bourgeois society, living labour is but a means to increase accumulated labour. In Communist society, accumulated labour is but a means to widen, to enrich, to promote the existence of the labourer.

In bourgeois society, therefore, the past dominates the present; in Communist society, the present dominates the past. In bourgeois society capital is independent and has individuality, while the living person is dependent and has no individuality.

And the abolition of this state of things is called by the bourgeois, abolition of individuality and freedom! And rightly so. The abolition of bourgeois individuality, bourgeois independence, and bourgeois freedom is undoubtedly aimed at.

By freedom is meant, under the present bourgeois conditions of production, free trade, free selling and buying.

But if selling and buying disappears, free selling and buying disappears also. This talk about free selling and buying, and all the other "brave words" of our bourgeoisie about freedom in general, have a meaning, if any, only in contrast with restricted selling and buying, with the fettered traders of the Middle Ages, but have no meaning when opposed to the Communistic abolition of buying and selling, of the bourgeois conditions of production, and of the bourgeoisie itself.

You are horrified at our intending to do away with private property. But in your existing society, private property is already done away with for nine-tenths of the population; its existence for the few is solely due to its non-existence in the hands of those nine-tenths. You reproach us, therefore, with intending to do away with a form of property, the necessary condition for whose existence is the non-existence of any property for the immense majority of society.

In one word, you reproach us with intending to do away with your property. Precisely so; that is just what we intend.

From the moment when labour can no longer be converted into capital, money, or rent, into a social power capable of being monopolised, i.e., from the moment when individual property can no longer be transformed into bourgeois property, into capital, from that moment, you say, individuality vanishes.

You must, therefore, confess that by "individual" you mean no other person than the bourgeois, than the middle-class owner of property. This person must, indeed, be swept out of the way, and made impossible.

Communism deprives no man of the power to appropriate the products of society; all that it does is to deprive him of the power to subjugate the labour of others by means of such appropriation.

It has been objected that upon the abolition of private property all work will cease, and universal laziness will overtake us.

According to this, bourgeois society ought long ago to have gone to the dogs through sheer idleness; for those of its members who work, acquire nothing, and those who acquire anything, do not work. The whole of this objection is but another expression of the tautology: that there can no longer be any wage-labour when there is no longer any capital.

All objections urged against the Communistic mode of producing and appropriating material products, have, in the same way, been urged against the Communistic modes of producing and appropriating intellectual products. Just as, to the bourgeois, the disappearance of class property is the disappearance of production itself, so the disappearance of class culture is to him identical with the disappearance of all culture.

That culture, the loss of which he laments, is, for the enormous majority, a mere training to act as a machine.

But don't wrangle with us so long as you apply, to our intended abolition of bourgeois property, the standard of your bourgeois notions of freedom, culture, law, &c. Your very ideas are but the outgrowth of the conditions of your bourgeois production and bourgeois property, just as your jurisprudence is but the will of your class made into a law for all, a will, whose essential character and direction are determined by the economical conditions of existence of your class.

The selfish misconception that induces you to transform into eternal laws of nature and of reason, the social forms springing from your present mode of production and form of property—historical relations that rise and disappear in the progress of production—this misconception you share with every ruling class that has preceded you. What you see clearly in the case of ancient property, what you admit in the case of feudal property, you are of course forbidden to admit in the case of your own bourgeois form of property.

Abolition of the family! Even the most radical flare up at this infamous proposal of the Communists.

On what foundation is the present family, the bourgeois family, based? On capital, on private gain. In its completely developed form this family exists only among the bourgeoisie. But this state of things finds its complement in the practical absence of the family among the proletarians, and in public prostitution.

The bourgeois family will vanish as a matter of course when its complement vanishes, and both will vanish with the vanishing of capital.

Do you charge us with wanting to stop the exploitation of children by their parents? To this crime we plead guilty.

But, you will say, we destroy the most hallowed of relations, when we replace home education by social.

And your education! Is not that also social, and determined by the social conditions under which you educate, by the intervention, direct or indirect, of society, by means of schools, &c.? The Communists have not invented the intervention of society in education; they do but seek to alter the character of that intervention, and to rescue education from the influence of the ruling class.

The bourgeois clap-trap about the family and education, about the hallowed co-relation of parent and child, becomes all the more disgusting, the more, by the action of Modern Industry, all family ties among the proletarians are torn asunder, and their children transformed into simple articles of commerce and instruments of labour.

But you Communists would introduce community of women, screams the whole bourgeoisie in chorus.

The bourgeois sees in his wife a mere instrument of production. He hears that the instruments of production are to be exploited in common, and, naturally, can come to no other conclusion than that the lot of being common to all will likewise fall to the women.

He has not even a suspicion that the real point aimed at is to do away with the status of women as mere instruments of production.

For the rest, nothing is more ridiculous than the virtuous indignation of our bourgeois at the community of women which, they pretend, is to be openly and officially established by the Communists. The Communists have no need to introduce community of women; it has existed almost from time immemorial.

Our bourgeois, not content with having the wives and daughters of their proletarians at their disposal, not to speak of common prostitutes, take the greatest pleasure in seducing each other's wives.

Bourgeois marriage is in reality a system of wives in common and thus, at the most, what the Communists might possibly be reproached with, is that they desire to introduce, in substitution for a hypocritically concealed, an openly legal-ised community of women. For the rest, it is self-evident that the abolition of the present sys-tem of production must bring with it the aboli-tion of the community of women springing from that system, i.e., of prostitution both public and private.

The Communists are further reproached with desiring to abolish countries and nationality.

The working men have no country. We can-not take from them what they have not got. Since the proletariat must first of all acquire political supremacy, must rise to be the leading class of the nation, must constitute itself *the* nation, it is, so far, itself national, though not in the bourgeois sense of the word.

National differences and antagonisms between peoples are daily more and more vanishing, owing to the development of the bourgeoisie, to freedom of commerce, to the world-market, to uniformity in the mode of production and in the conditions of life corresponding thereto.

The supremacy of the proletariat will cause them to vanish still faster. United action, of the leading civilised countries at least, is one of the first conditions for the emancipation of the proletariat.

In proportion as the exploitation of one indi-vidual by another is put an end to, the exploit-ation of one nation by another will also be put an end to. In proportion as the antagonism between classes within the nation vanishes, the hostility of one nation to another will come to an end.

The charges against Communism made from a religious, a philosophical, and, generally, from an ideological standpoint, are not deserving of serious examination.

Does it require deep intuition to comprehend that man's ideas, views and conceptions, in one word, man's consciousness, changes with every change in the conditions of his material exist-ence, in his social relations and in his social life?

What else does the history of ideas prove, than that intellectual production changes its character in proportion as material production is changed? The ruling ideas of each age have ever been the ideas of its ruling class.

When people speak of ideas that revolutionise society, they do but express the fact, that within the old society, the elements of a new one have been created, and that the dissolution of the old ideas keeps even pace with the dissolution of the old conditions of existence.

When the ancient world was in its last throes, the ancient religions were overcome by Christi-anity. When Christian ideas succumbed in the 18th century to rationalist ideas, feudal society fought its death battle with the then revolution-ary bourgeoisie. The ideas of religious liberty and freedom of conscience merely gave expres-sion to the sway of free competition within the domain of knowledge.

"Undoubtedly," it will be said, "religious, moral, philosophical and juridical ideas have been modified in the course of historical devel-opment. But religion, morality, philosophy, political science, and law, constantly survived this change."

"There are, besides, eternal truths, such as Freedom, Justice, etc., that are common to all states of society. But Communism abolishes eternal truths, it abolishes all religion, and all morality, instead of constituting them on a new basis; it therefore acts in contradiction to all past historical experience."

What does this accusation reduce itself to? The history of all past society has consisted in the development of class antagonisms, antagonisms that assumed different forms at different epochs.

But whatever form they may have taken, one fact is common to all past ages, viz., the exploit-ation of one part of society by the other. No wonder, then, that the social consciousness of past ages, despite all the multiplicity and variety it displays, moves within certain common forms, or general ideas, which cannot completely van-ish except with the total disappearance of class antagonisms.

The Communist revolution is the most radical

rupture with traditional property relations; no wonder that its development involves the most radical rupture with traditional ideas.

But let us have done with the bourgeois objections to Communism.

We have seen above, that the first step in the revolution by the working class, is to raise the proletariat to the position of ruling class, to win the battle of democracy.

The proletariat will use its political supremacy to wrest, by degrees, all capital from the bourgeoisie, to centralise all instruments of production in the hands of the State, i.e., of the proletariat organised as the ruling class; and to increase the total of productive forces as rapidly as possible.

Of course, in the beginning, this cannot be effected except by means of despotic inroads on the rights of property, and on the conditions of bourgeois production; by means of measures, therefore, which appear economically insufficient and untenable, but which, in the course of the movement, outstrip themselves, necessitate further inroads upon the old social order, and are unavoidable as a means of entirely revolutionising the mode of production.

These measures will of course be different in different countries.

Nevertheless in the most advanced countries, the following will be pretty generally applicable.

1. Abolition of property in land and application of all rents of land to public purposes.
2. A heavy progressive or graduated income tax.
3. Abolition of all right of inheritance.
4. Confiscation of the property of all emigrants and rebels.
5. Centralisation of credit in the hands of the State, by means of a national bank with State capital and an exclusive monopoly.
6. Centralisation of the means of communication and transport in the hands of the State.
7. Extension of factories and instruments of production owned by the State; the bringing into cultivation of waste-lands, and the improvement of the soil generally in accordance with a common plan.
8. Equal liability of all to labour. Establishment of industrial armies, especially for agriculture.
9. Combination of agriculture with manufacturing industries; gradual abolition of the distinction between town and country, by a more equable distribution of the population over the country.
10. Free education for all children in public schools. Abolition of children's factory labour in its present form. Combination of education with industrial production, &c., &c.

When, in the course of development, class distinctions have disappeared, and all production has been concentrated in the hands of a vast association of the whole nation, the public power will lose its political character. Political power, properly so called, is merely the organised power of one class for oppressing another. If the proletariat during its contest with the bourgeoisie is compelled, by the force of circumstances, to organise itself as a class, if, by means of a revolution, it makes itself the ruling class, and, as such, sweeps away by force the old conditions of production, then it will, along with these conditions, have swept away the conditions for the existence of class antagonisms and of classes generally, and will thereby have abolished its own supremacy as a class.

In place of the old bourgeois society, with its classes and class antagonisms, we shall have an association, in which the free development of each is the condition for the free development of all. [. . .]

Communists everywhere support every revolutionary movement against the existing social and political order of things.

In all these movements they bring to the front, as the leading question in each, the property question, no matter what its degree of development at the time.

Finally, they labour everywhere for the union and agreement of the democratic parties of all countries.

The Communists disdain to conceal their views and aims. They openly declare that their ends can be attained only by the forcible overthrow of all existing social conditions. Let the ruling classes tremble at a Communistic revolution. The proletarians have nothing to lose but their chains. They have a world to win.

WORKING MEN OF ALL COUNTRIES, UNITE!

CRITIQUE OF THE GOTHA PROGRAM

I

1. "Labour is the source of all wealth and all culture, *and since* useful labour is possible only in society and through society, the proceeds of labour belong undiminished with equal right to all members of society."

First Part of the Paragraph: "Labour is the source of all wealth and all culture."

Labour is *not the source* of all wealth. *Nature* is just as much the source of use values (and it is surely of such that material wealth consists!) as labour, which itself is only the manifestation of a force of nature, human labour power. The above phrase is to be found in all children's primers and is correct in so far as it is *implied* that labour is performed with the appurtenant subjects and instruments. But a socialist programme cannot allow such bourgeois phrases to pass over in silence the *conditions* that alone give them meaning. And in so far as man from the beginning behaves towards nature, the primary source of all instruments and subjects of labour, as an owner, treats her as belonging to him, his labour becomes the source of use values, therefore

also of wealth. The bourgeois have very good grounds for falsely ascribing *supernatural creative power* to labour; since precisely from the fact that labour depends on nature it follows that the man who possesses no other property than his labour power must, in all conditions of society and culture, be the slave of other men who have made themselves the owners of the material conditions of labour. He can work only with their permission, hence live only with their permission.

Let us now leave the sentence as it stands, or rather limps. What would one have expected in conclusion? Obviously this:

"Since labour is the source of all wealth, no one in society can appropriate wealth except as the product of labour. Therefore, if he himself does not work, he lives by the labour of others and also acquires his culture at the expense of the labour of others."

Instead of this, by means of the verbal rivet "*and since*" a second proposition is added in order to draw a conclusion from this and not from the first one.

Second Part of the Paragraph: "Useful labour is possible only in society and through society."

According to the first proposition, labour was the source of all wealth and all culture; therefore no society is possible without labour. Now we learn, conversely, that no "useful" labour is possible without society.

One could just as well have said that only in society can useless and even socially harmful labour become a branch of gainful occupation, that only in society can one live by being idle, etc., etc.—in short, one could just as well have copied the whole of Rousseau.

And what is "useful" labour? Surely only labour which produces the intended useful result. A savage—and man was a savage after he had ceased to be an ape—who kills an animal with a stone, who collects fruits, etc., performs "useful" labour.

Thirdly. The Conclusion: "And since useful labour is possible only in society and through society, the proceeds of labour belong undiminished with equal right to all members of society."

A fine conclusion! If useful labour is possible only in society and through society, the proceeds of labour belong to society—and only so much therefrom accrues to the individual worker as is not required to maintain the "condition" of labour, society.

In fact, this proposition has at all times been made use of by the champions of the *state of society prevailing at any given time*. First come the claims of the government and everything that sticks to it, since it is the social organ for the maintenance of the social order; then come the claims of the various kinds of private property, for the various kinds of private property are the foundations of society, etc. One sees that such hollow phrases can be twisted and turned as desired.

The first and second parts of the paragraph have some intelligible connection only in the following wording:

"Labour becomes the source of wealth and culture only as social labour," or, what is the same thing, "in and through society."

This proposition is incontestably correct, for although isolated labour (its material conditions presupposed) can create use values, it can create neither wealth nor culture.

But equally incontestable is this other proposition:

"In proportion as labour develops socially, and becomes thereby a source of wealth and culture, poverty and destitution develop among the workers, and wealth and culture among the non-workers."

This is the law of all history hitherto. What, therefore, had to be done here, instead of setting down general phrases about "labour" and "society," was to prove concretely how in present capitalist society the material, etc., conditions have at last been created which enable and compel the workers to lift this social curse.

In fact, however, the whole paragraph, bungled in style and content, is only there in order to inscribe the Lassallean catchword of the "undiminished proceeds of labour" as a slogan at the top of the party banner. I shall return later to the "proceeds of labour," "equal right," etc., since the same thing recurs in a somewhat different form further on. [. . .]

3. "The emancipation of labour demands the promotion of the instruments of labour to the common property of society and the co-operative regulation of the total labour with a fair distribution of the proceeds of labour."

"Promotion of the instruments of labour to the common property" ought obviously to read their "conversion into the common property"; but this only in passing.

What are "proceeds of labour"? The product of labour or its value? And in the latter case, is it the total value of the product or only that part of the value which labour has newly added to the value of the means of production consumed?

"Proceeds of labour" is a loose notion which Lassalle has put in the place of definite economic conceptions.

What is "a fair distribution"?

Do not the bourgeois assert that the present-day distribution is "fair"? And is it not, in fact, the only "fair" distribution on the basis of the present-day mode of production? Are economic relations regulated by legal conceptions or do not, on the contrary, legal relations arise from economic ones? Have not also the socialist sectarians the most varied notions about "fair" distribution?

To understand what is implied in this connection by the phrase "fair distribution," we must take the first paragraph and this one together. The latter presupposes a society wherein "the instruments of labour are common property and the total labour is co-operatively regulated," and from the first paragraph we learn that "the proceeds of labour belong undiminished with equal right to all members of society."

"To all members of society"? To those who do not work as well? What remains then of the "undiminished proceeds of labour"? Only to those members of society who work? What remains then of the "equal right" of all members of society?

But "all members of society" and "equal right" are obviously mere phrases. The kernel consists in this, that in this communist society every worker must receive the "undiminished" Lassallean "proceeds of labour."

Let us take first of all the words "proceeds of labour" in the sense of the product of labour; then the co-operative proceeds of labour are the *total social product.*

From this must now be deducted:

First, cover for replacement of the means of production used up.

Secondly, additional portion for expansion of production.

Thirdly, reserve or insurance funds to provide against accidents, dislocations caused by natural calamities, etc.

These deductions from the "undiminished proceeds of labour" are an economic necessity and their magnitude is to be determined according to available means and forces, and partly by computation of probabilities, but they are in no way calculable by equity.

There remains the other part of the total product, intended to serve as means of consumption.

Before this is divided among the individuals, there has to be deducted again, from it:

First, the general costs of administration not belonging to production.

This part will, from the outset, be very considerably restricted in comparison with present-day society and it diminishes in proportion as the new society develops.

Secondly, that which is intended for the common satisfaction of needs, such as schools, health services, etc.

From the outset this part grows considerably in comparison with present-day society and it grows in proportion as the new society develops.

Thirdly, funds for those unable to work, etc., in short, for what is included under so-called official poor relief today.

Only now do we come to the "distribution" which the programme, under Lassallean influence, alone has in view in its narrow fashion, namely, to that part of the means of consumption which is divided among the individual producers of the co-operative society.

The "undiminished proceeds of labour" have already unnoticeably become converted into the "diminished" proceeds, although what the producer is deprived of in his capacity as a private individual benefits him directly or indirectly in his capacity as a member of society.

Just as the phrase of the "undiminished proceeds of labour" has disappeared, so now does the phrase of the "proceeds of labour" disappear altogether.

Within the co-operative society based on common ownership of the means of production, the producers do not exchange their products; just as little does the labour employed on the products appear here *as the value* of these products, as a material quality possessed by them, since now, in contrast to capitalist society, individual labour no longer exists in an indirect fashion but directly as a component part of the total labour. The phrase "proceeds of labour," objectionable also today on account of its ambiguity, thus loses all meaning.

What we have to deal with here is a communist society, not as it has *developed* on its own foundations, but, on the contrary, just as it *emerges* from capitalist society; which is thus in every respect, economically, morally and intellectually, still stamped with the birth marks of the old society from whose womb it emerges. Accordingly, the individual producer receives back from society—after the deductions have been made—exactly what he gives to it. What he has given to it is his individual quantum of labour. For example, the social working day consists of the sum of the individual hours of work; the individual labour time of the individual producer is the part of the social working day contributed by him, his share in it. He receives a certificate from society that he has furnished such and such an amount of labour (after deducting his labour for the common funds), and with this certificate he draws from the social stock of means of consumption as much as costs the same amount of labour. The same amount of labour which he has given to society in one form he receives back in another.

Here obviously the same principle prevails as that which regulates the exchange of commodities, as far as this is exchange of equal values. Content and form are changed, because under the altered circumstances no one can give anything except his labour, and because, on the other hand, nothing can pass to the ownership of individuals except individual means of consumption. But, as far as the distribution of the latter among the individual producers is concerned, the same principle prevails as in the exchange of commodity-equivalents: a given amount of labour in one form is exchanged for an equal amount of labour in another form.

Hence, *equal right* here is still in principle— *bourgeois right*, although principle and practice are no longer at loggerheads, while the exchange of equivalents in commodity exchange only exists *on the average* and not in the individual case.

In spite of this advance, this *equal right* is still constantly stigmatised by a bourgeois limitation. The right of the producers is *proportional* to the labour they supply; the equality consists in the fact that measurement is made with an *equal standard*, labour.

But one man is superior to another physically or mentally and so supplies more labour in the same time, or can labour for a longer time; and labour, to serve as a measure, must be defined by its duration or intensity, otherwise it ceases to be a standard of measurement. This *equal* right is an unequal right for unequal labour. It recognises no class differences, because everyone is only a worker like everyone else; but it tacitly recognises unequal individual endowment and thus productive capacity as natural privileges. It is, *therefore, a right of inequality, in its content, like every right.* Right by its very nature can consist only in the application of an equal standard; but unequal individuals (and they would not be different individuals if they were not unequal) are measurable only by an equal standard in so far as they are brought under an equal point of view, are taken from one *definite* side only, for instance, in the present case, are regarded *only as workers* and nothing more is seen in them, everything else being ignored. Further, one worker is married, another not; one has more children than another, and so on and so forth. Thus, with an equal performance of labour, and hence an equal share in the social consumption fund, one will in fact receive more than another, one will be richer than another, and so on. To avoid all these defects, right instead of being equal would have to be unequal.

But these defects are inevitable in the first phase of communist society as it is when it has just emerged after prolonged birth pangs from capitalist society. Right can never be higher than the economic structure of society and its cultural development conditioned thereby.

In a higher phase of communist society, after the enslaving subordination of the individual to the division of labour, and therewith also the antithesis between mental and physical labour, has vanished; after labour has become not only a means of life but life's prime want; after the productive forces have also increased with the all-round development of the individual, and all the springs of co-operative wealth flow more abundantly—only then can the narrow horizon of bourgeois right be crossed in its entirety and society inscribe on its banners: From each according to his ability, to each according to his needs!

I have dealt more at length with the "undiminished proceeds of labour," on the one hand, and with "equal right" and "fair distribution," on the other, in order to show what a crime it is to attempt, on the one hand, to force on our Party again, as dogmas, ideas which in a certain period had some meaning but have now become obsolete verbal rubbish, while again perverting, on the other, the realistic outlook, which it cost so much effort to instil into the Party but which has now taken root in it, by means of ideological nonsense about right and other trash so common among the democrats and French Socialists.

Quite apart from the analysis so far given, it was in general a mistake to make a fuss about so-called *distribution* and put the principal stress on it.

Any distribution whatever of the means of consumption is only a consequence of the distribution of the conditions of production themselves. The latter distribution, however, is a feature of the mode of production itself. The capitalist mode of production, for example, rests on the fact that the material conditions of production are in the hands of non-workers in the form of property in capital and land, while the masses are only owners of the personal condition of production, of labour power. If the elements of production are so distributed, then the present-day distribution of the means of consumption results automatically. If the material conditions of production are the co-operative property of the workers themselves, then there likewise results a distribution of the means of consumption different from the present one. Vulgar socialism (and from it in turn a section of the democracy) has taken over from the bourgeois economists the consideration and treatment of distribution as independent of the mode of production and hence the presentation of socialism as turning principally on distribution. After the real relation has long been made clear, why retrogress again? [. . .]

II

> "Starting from these basic principles, the German workers' party strives by all legal means for the *free state—and—*socialist society: the abolition of the wage system *together with* the *iron law of wages*—and—exploitation in every form; the elimination of all social and political inequality."

I shall return to the "free" state later.

So, in future, the German workers' party has got to believe in Lassalle's "iron law of wages"! That this may not be lost, the nonsense is perpetrated of speaking of the "abolition of the wage system" (it should read: system of wage labour) "*together with* the iron law of wages." If I abolish wage labour, then naturally I abolish its laws also, whether they are of "iron" or sponge. But Lassalle's attack on wage labour turns almost solely on this so-called law. In order, therefore, to prove that Lassalle's sect has conquered, the "wage system" must be abolished "*together with* the iron law of wages" and not without it.

It is well known that nothing of the "iron law of wages" is Lassalle's except the word "iron" borrowed from Goethe's "great, eternal iron laws." The word *iron* is a label by which the true believers recognise one another. But if I take the law with Lassalle's stamp on it and, consequently, in his sense, then I must also take it with his substantiation for it. And what is that? As Lange already showed, shortly after Lassalle's death, it is the Malthusian theory of population (preached by Lange himself). But if this theory is correct, then again I *cannot* abolish the law even if I abolish wage labour a hundred times over, because the law then governs not only the system of wage labour but *every* social system. Basing themselves directly on this, the economists have been proving for fifty years and more that socialism cannot abolish poverty, *which has its basis in nature*, but can only make it *general*, distribute it simultaneously over the whole surface of society!

But all this is not the main thing. *Quite apart* from the *false* Lassallean formulation of the law, the truly outrageous retrogression consists in the following:

Since Lassalle's death there has asserted itself in our Party the scientific understanding that wages are not what they *appear* to be, namely, the *value, or price, of labour*, but only a masked form for the *value, or price, of labour power*. Thereby the whole bourgeois conception of wages hitherto, as well as all the criticism hitherto directed against this conception, was thrown overboard once for all and it was made clear that the wage-worker has permission to work for his own subsistence, that is, *to live*, only in so far as he works for a certain time gratis for the capitalist (and hence also for the latter's co-consumers of surplus value); that the whole capitalist system of production turns on the increase of this gratis labour by extending the working day or by developing the productivity, that is, increasing the intensity of labour power, etc.; that, consequently, the system of wage labour is a system of slavery, and indeed of a slavery which becomes more severe in proportion as the social productive forces of labour develop, whether the worker receives better or worse payment. And after this understanding has gained more and more ground in our Party, one returns to Lassalle's dogmas although one must have known that Lassalle *did not know* what wages were, but following in the wake of the bourgeois economists took the appearance for the essence of the matter.

It is as if, among slaves who have at last got behind the secret of slavery and broken out in rebellion, a slave still in thrall to obsolete notions were to inscribe on the programme of the rebellion: Slavery must be abolished because the feeding of slaves in the system of slavery cannot exceed a certain low maximum!

Does not the mere fact that the representatives of our Party were capable of perpetrating such a monstrous attack on the understanding that has spread among the mass of our Party prove by itself with what criminal levity and with what lack of conscience they set to work in drawing up this compromise programme!

Instead of the indefinite concluding phrase of the paragraph, "the elimination of all social and political inequality," it ought to have been said that with the abolition of class distinctions all social and political inequality arising from them would disappear of itself. [. . .]

IV

I come now to the democratic section.

A. "*The free basis of the state.*"

First of all, according to II, the German workers' party strives for "the free state."

Free state—what is this?

It is by no means the aim of the workers, who have got rid of the narrow mentality of humble subjects, to set the state free. In the German Empire the "state" is almost as "free" as in Russia. Freedom consists in converting the state from an organ superimposed upon society into one completely subordinate to it, and today, too, the forms of state are more free or less free to the extent that they restrict the "freedom of the state."

The German workers' party—at least if it adopts the programme—shows that its socialist ideas are not even skin-deep; in that, instead of treating existing society (and this holds good for any future one) as the *basis* of the existing state (or of the future state in the case of future society), it treats the state rather as an independent entity that possesses its own *intellectual, ethical and libertarian bases*.

And what of the riotous misuse which the programme makes of the words "*present-day state*", "*present-day society*", and of the still more riotous misconception it creates in regard to the state to which it addresses its demands?

"Present-day society" is capitalist society, which exists in all civilised countries, more or less free from medieval admixture, more or less modified by the particular historical development of each country, more or less developed. On the other hand, the "present-day state" changes with a country's frontier. It is different in the Prusso-German Empire from what it is in Switzerland, and different in England from what it is in the United States. "The present-day state" is, therefore, a fiction.

Nevertheless, the different states of the

different civilised countries, in spite of their motley diversity of form, all have this in common, that they are based on modern bourgeois society, only one more or less capitalistically developed. They have, therefore, also certain essential characteristics in common. In this sense it is possible to speak of the "present-day states," in contrast with the future, in which its present root, bourgeois society, will have died off.

The question then arises: what transformation will the state undergo in communist society? In other words, what social functions will remain in existence there that are analogous to present state functions? This question can only be answered scientifically, and one does not get a flea-hop nearer to the problem by a thousand-fold combination of the word people with the word state.

Between capitalist and communist society lies the period of the revolutionary transformation of the one into the other. Corresponding to this is also a political transition period in which the state can be nothing but *the revolutionary dictatorship of the proletariat.*

Now the programme does not deal with this nor with the future state of communist society.

Its political demands contain nothing beyond the old democratic litany familiar to all: universal suffrage, direct legislation, popular rights, a people's militia, etc. They are a mere echo of the bourgeois People's Party, of the League of Peace and Freedom. They are all demands which, in so far as they are not exaggerated in fantastic presentation, have already been *realised.* Only the state to which they belong does not lie within the borders of the German Empire, but in Switzerland, the United States, etc. This sort of "state of the future" is a present-day state, although existing outside the "framework" of the German Empire.

But one thing has been forgotten. Since the German workers' party expressly declares that it acts within "the present-day national state," hence within *its own* state, the Prusso-German Empire—its demands would indeed otherwise

be largely meaningless, since one only demands what one has not got—it should not have forgotten the chief thing, namely, that all those pretty little gewgaws rest on the recognition of the so-called sovereignty of the people and hence are appropriate only in a *democratic republic.*

Since one has not the courage—and wisely so, for the circumstances demand caution—to demand the democratic republic, as the French workers' programmes under Louis Philippe and under Louis Napoleon did, one should not have resorted, either, to the subterfuge, neither "honest" nor decent, of demanding things which have meaning only in a democratic republic from a state which is nothing but a police-guarded military despotism, embellished with parliamentary forms, alloyed with a feudal admixture, already influenced by the bourgeoisie and bureaucratically carpentered, and then to assure this state into the bargain that one imagines one will be able to force such things upon it "by legal means."

Even vulgar democracy, which sees the millennium in the democratic republic and has no suspicion that it is precisely in this last form of state of bourgeois society that the class struggle has to be fought out to a confusion—even it towers mountains above this kind of democratism which keeps within the limits of what is permitted by the police and not permitted by logic.

That, in fact, by the word "state" is meant the government machine, or the state in so far as it forms a special organism separated from society through division of labour, is shown by the words "the German workers' party demands *as the economic basis of the state:* a single progressive income tax," etc. Taxes are the economic basis of the government machinery and of nothing else. In the state of the future, existing in Switzerland, this demand has been pretty well fulfilled. Income tax presupposes various sources of income of the various social classes, and hence capitalist society. It is, therefore, nothing remarkable that the Liverpool financial reformers, bourgeois headed by Gladstone's brother, are putting forward the same demand as the programme.

B. "The German workers' party demands as the intellectual and ethical basis of the state:

"1. Universal and *equal elementary education* by the state. Universal compulsory school attendance. Free instruction."

Equal elementary education? What idea lies behind these words? Is it believed that in present-day society (and it is only with this one has to deal) education can be *equal* for all classes? Or is it demanded that the upper classes also shall be compulsorily reduced to the modicum of education—the elementary school—that alone is compatible with the economic conditions not only of the wage-workers but of the peasants as well?

"Universal compulsory school attendance. Free instruction." The former exists even in Germany, the second in Switzerland and in the United States in the case of elementary schools. If in some states of the latter country higher educational institutions are also "free" that only means in fact defraying the cost of the education of the upper classes from the general tax receipts. Incidentally, the same holds good for "free administration of justice" demanded under A, 5. The administration of criminal justice is to be had free everywhere; that of civil justice is concerned almost exclusively with conflicts over property and hence affects almost exclusively the possessing classes. Are they to carry on their litigation at the expense of the national coffers?

The paragraph on the schools should at least have demanded technical schools (theoretical and practical) in combination with the elementary school.

"*Elementary education by the state*" is altogether objectionable. Defining by a general law the expenditures on the elementary schools, the qualifications of the teaching staff, the branches of instruction, etc., and, as is done in the United States, supervising the fulfilment of these legal specifications by state inspectors, is a very different thing from appointing the state as the educator of the people! Government and Church should rather be equally excluded from any influence on the school. Particularly, indeed, in the Prusso-German Empire (and one should not take refuge in the rotten subterfuge that one is speaking of a "state of the future"; we have seen how matters stand in this respect) the state has need, on the contrary, of a very stern education by the people.

But the whole programme, for all its democratic clang, is tainted through and through by the Lassallean sect's servile belief in the state, or, what is no better, by a democratic belief in miracles, or rather it is a compromise between these two kinds of belief in miracles, both equally remote from socialism.

"*Freedom of science*" says a paragraph of the Prussian Constitution. Why, then, here?

"*Freedom of conscience*"! If one desired at this time of the *Kulturkampf* to remind liberalism of its old catchwords, it surely could have been done only in the following form: Everyone should be able to attend to his religious as well as his bodily needs without the police sticking their noses in. But the workers' party ought at any rate in this connection to have expressed its awareness of the fact that bourgeois "freedom of conscience" is nothing but the toleration of all possible kinds of *religious freedom of conscience*, and that for its part it endeavours rather to liberate the conscience from the witchery of religion. But one chooses not to transgress the "bourgeois" level. [. . .]

Chapter 21

Frédéric Bastiat

WHAT IS SEEN AND WHAT IS NOT SEEN

Frédéric Bastiat (1801–1850) was a French political economist who, in his short life, wrote a number of influential and often witty essays defending a *laissez-faire* view of the relationship between government and the market. In this essay, Bastiat explores what economists would now refer to as opportunity costs, and argues that our tendency to ignore them in favor of more visible costs leads to wasteful and destructive public policies.

In the economic sphere an act, a habit, an institution, a law produces not only one effect, but a series of effects. Of these effects, the first alone is immediate; it appears simultaneously with its cause; *it is seen*. The other effects emerge only subsequently; *they are not seen*; we are fortunate if we *foresee* them.

There is only one difference between a bad economist and a good one: the bad economist confines himself to the *visible* effect; the good economist takes into account both the effect that can be seen and those effects that must be *foreseen*.

Yet this difference is tremendous; for it almost always happens that when the immediate consequence is favorable, the later consequences are disastrous, and vice versa. Whence it follows that the bad economist pursues a small present good that will be followed by a great evil to come, while the good economist pursues a great good to come, at the risk of a small present evil.

The same thing, of course, is true of health and morals. Often, the sweeter the first fruit of a habit, the more bitter are its later fruits: for example, debauchery, sloth, prodigality. When a man is impressed by the effect *that is seen* and has not yet learned to discern the effects *that are not seen*, he indulges in deplorable habits, not only through natural inclination, but deliberately.

This explains man's necessarily painful evolution. Ignorance surrounds him at his cradle; therefore, he regulates his acts according to their first consequences, the only ones that, in his infancy, he can see. It is only after a long time that he learns to take account of the others. Two very different masters teach him this lesson: experience and foresight. Experience teaches efficaciously but brutally. It instructs us in all the effects of an act by making us feel them, and we cannot fail to learn eventually, from having been burned ourselves, that fire burns. I should prefer, in so far as possible, to replace this rude teacher with one more gentle: foresight. For that reason I shall investigate the consequences of several economic phenomena, contrasting those *that are seen* with those *that are not seen*.

1. The Broken Window

Have you ever been witness to the fury of that solid citizen, James Goodfellow, when his incorrigible son has happened to break a pane of glass? If you have been present at this spectacle, certainly you must also have observed that the onlookers, even if there are as many as thirty of them, seem with one accord to offer the unfortunate owner the selfsame consolation: "It's an ill wind that blows nobody some good. Such accidents keep industry going. Everybody has to make a living. What would become of the glaziers if no one ever broke a window?"

Now, this formula of condolence contains a whole theory that it is a good idea for us to expose, *flagrante delicto*, in this very simple case, since it is exactly the same as that which, unfortunately, underlies most of our economic institutions.

Suppose that it will cost six francs to repair the damage. If you mean that the accident gives six francs' worth of encouragement to the aforesaid industry, I agree. I do not contest it in any way; your reasoning is correct. The glazier will come, do his job, receive six francs, congratulate himself, and bless in his heart the careless child. *That is what is seen.*

But if, by way of deduction, you conclude, as happens only too often, that it is good to break windows, that it helps to circulate money, that it results in encouraging industry in general, I am obliged to cry out: That will never do! Your theory stops at *what is seen*. It does not take account of *what is not seen.*

It *is not seen* that, since our citizen has spent six francs for one thing, he will not be able to spend them for another. It *is not seen* that if he had not had a windowpane to replace, he would have replaced, for example, his worn-out shoes or added another book to his library. In brief, he would have put his six francs to some use or other for which he will not now have them.

Let us next consider industry *in general*. The window having been broken, the glass industry gets six francs' worth of encouragement; *that is what is seen*. If the window had not been broken, the shoe industry (or some other) would have received six francs' worth of encouragement; *that is what is not seen*. And if we were to take into consideration *what is not seen*, because it is a negative factor, as well as *what is seen*, because it is a positive factor, we should understand that there is no benefit to industry *in general* or to *national employment* as a whole, whether windows are broken or not broken.

Now let us consider James Goodfellow. On the first hypothesis, that of the broken window, he spends six francs and has, neither more nor less than before, the enjoyment of one window. On the second, that in which the accident did not happen, he would have spent six francs for new shoes and would have had the enjoyment of a pair of shoes as well as of a window.

Now, if James Goodfellow is part of society, we must conclude that society, considering its labors and its enjoyments, has lost the value of the broken window. From which, by generalizing, we arrive at this unexpected conclusion: "Society loses the value of objects unnecessarily destroyed," and at this aphorism, which will make the hair of the protectionists stand on end: "To break, to destroy, to dissipate is not to encourage national employment," or more briefly: "Destruction is not profitable."

What will the *Moniteur industriel* say to this, or the disciples of the estimable M. de Saint-Chamans, who has calculated with such precision what industry would gain from the burning of Paris, because of the houses that would have to be rebuilt?

I am sorry to upset his ingenious calculations, especially since their spirit has passed into our legislation. But I beg him to begin them again, entering *what is not seen* in the ledger beside *what is seen*.

The reader must apply himself to observe that there are not only two people, but three, in the little drama that I have presented. The one, James Goodfellow, represents the consumer, reduced by destruction to one enjoyment instead of two. The other, under the figure of the glazier, shows us the producer whose industry the accident encourages. The third is the shoemaker (or any other manufacturer) whose industry is correspondingly discouraged by the same cause. It is this third person who is always in the shadow, and who, personifying *what is not seen*, is an essential element of the problem. It is he who makes us understand how absurd it is to see a profit in destruction. It is he who will soon teach us that it is equally absurd to see a profit in trade restriction, which is, after all, nothing more nor less than partial destruction. So, if you get to the bottom of all the arguments advanced in favor of restrictionist measures, you will find only a paraphrase of that common cliché: "*What would become of the glaziers if no one ever broke any windows?*"

2. The Demobilization

A nation is in the same case as a man. When a man wishes to give himself a satisfaction, he has to see whether it is worth what it costs. For a nation, security is the greatest of blessings. If, to acquire it, a hundred thousand men must be mobilized, and a hundred million francs spent, I have nothing to say. It is an enjoyment bought at the price of a sacrifice.

Let there be no misunderstanding, then, about the point I wish to make in what I have to say on this subject.

A legislator proposes to discharge a hundred thousand men, which will relieve the taxpayers of a hundred million francs in taxes.

Suppose we confine ourselves to replying to him: "These one hundred thousand men and these one hundred million francs are indispensable to our national security. It is a sacrifice; but without this sacrifice France would be torn by internal factions or invaded from without." I have no objection here to this argument, which may be true or false as the case may be, but which theoretically does not constitute any economic heresy. The heresy begins when the sacrifice itself is represented as an advantage, because it brings profit to someone.

Now, if I am not mistaken, no sooner will the author of the proposal have descended from the platform, than an orator will rush up and say:

"Discharge a hundred thousand men! What are you thinking of? What will become of them? What will they live on? On their earnings? But do you not know that there is unemployment everywhere? That all occupations are oversupplied? Do you wish to throw them on the market to increase the competition and to depress wage rates? Just at the moment when it is difficult to earn a meager living, is it not fortunate that the state is giving bread to a hundred thousand individuals? Consider further that the army consumes wine, clothes, and weapons, that it thus spreads business to the factories and the garrison towns, and that it is nothing less than a godsend to its innumerable suppliers. Do you not tremble at the idea of bringing this immense industrial activity to an end?"

This speech, we see, concludes in favor of maintaining a hundred thousand soldiers, not because of the nation's need for the services rendered by the army, but for economic reasons. It is these considerations alone that I propose to refute.

A hundred thousand men, costing the taxpayers a hundred million francs, live as well and provide as good a living for their suppliers as a hundred million francs will allow: *that is what is seen.*

But a hundred million francs, coming from the pockets of the taxpayers, ceases to provide a living for these taxpayers and their suppliers, to the extent of a hundred million francs: *that is what is not seen.* Calculate, figure, and tell me where there is any profit for the mass of the people.

I will, for my part, tell you where the *loss* is, and to simplify things, instead of speaking of a hundred thousand men and a hundred million francs, let us talk about one man and a thousand francs.

Here we are in the village of A. The recruiters make the rounds and muster one man. The tax collectors make their rounds also and raise a thousand francs. The man and the sum are transported to Metz, the one destined to keep the other alive for a year without doing anything. If you look only at Metz, yes, you are right a hundred times; the procedure is very advantageous. But if you turn your eyes to the village of A, you will judge otherwise, for, unless you are blind, you will see that this village has lost a laborer and the thousand francs that would remunerate his labor, and the business which, through the spending of these thousand francs, he would spread about him.

At first glance it seems as if the loss is compensated. What took place at the village now takes place at Metz, and that is all there is to it. But here is where the loss is. In the village a man dug and labored: he was a worker; at Metz he goes through "Right dress!" and "Left dress!": he is a soldier. The money involved and its circulation are the same in both cases: but in one there were three hundred days of productive labor; in the other there are three hundreds days of unproductive labor, on the supposition, of course, that a part of the army is not indispensable to public security.

Now comes demobilization. You point out to me a surplus of a hundred thousand workers, intensified competition and the pressure that it exerts on wage rates. That is what you see.

But here is what you do not see. You do not see that to send home a hundred thousand soldiers is not to do away with a hundred million francs, but to return that money to the taxpayers. You do not see that to throw a hundred thousand workers on the market in this way is to throw in at the same time the hundred million francs destined to pay for their labor; that, as a consequence, the same measure that increases the *supply* of workers also increases the *demand*; from which it follows that your lowering of wages is illusory. You do not see that before, as well as after, the demobilization there are a hundred million francs corresponding to the hundred thousand men; that the whole difference consists in this: that before, the country gives the hundred million francs to the hundred thousand men for doing nothing; afterwards, it

gives them the money for working. Finally, you do not see that when a taxpayer gives his money, whether to a soldier in exchange for nothing or to a worker in exchange for something, all the more remote consequences of the circulation of this money are the same in both cases: only, in the second case the taxpayer receives something; in the first he receives nothing. Result: a dead loss for the nation.

The sophism that I am attacking here cannot withstand the test of extended application, which is the touchstone of all theoretical principles. If, all things considered, there is a *national profit* in increasing the size of the army, why not call the whole male population of the country to the colors?

3. Taxes

Have you ever heard anyone say: "Taxes are the best investment; they are a life-giving dew. See how many families they keep alive, and follow in imagination their indirect effects on industry; they are infinite, as extensive as life itself."

To combat this doctrine, I am obliged to repeat the preceding refutation. Political economy knows very well that its arguments are not diverting enough for anyone to say about them: *Repetita placent*; repetition pleases. So, like Basile, political economy has "arranged" the proverb for its own use, quite convinced that, from its mouth, *Repetita docent*; repetition teaches.

The advantages that government officials enjoy in drawing their salaries are *what is seen*. The benefits that result for their suppliers are also *what is seen*. They are right under your nose. But the disadvantage that the taxpayers try to free themselves from is *what is not seen*, and the distress that results from it for the merchants who supply them is *something further that is not seen*, although it should stand out plainly enough to be seen intellectually.

When a government official spends on his own behalf one hundred sous more, this implies that a taxpayer spends on his own behalf one hundred sous the less. But the spending of the government official is *seen*, because it is done; while that of the taxpayer is *not seen*, because—alas!—he is prevented from doing it.

You compare the nation to a parched piece of land and the tax to a life-giving rain. So be it. But you should also ask yourself where this rain comes from, and whether it is not precisely the tax that draws the moisture from the soil and dries it up. You should ask yourself further whether the soil receives more of this precious water from the rain than it loses by the evaporation?

What is quite certain is that, when James Goodfellow counts out a hundred sous to the tax collector, he receives nothing in return. When, then, a government official, in spending these hundred sous, returns them to James Goodfellow, it is for an equivalent value in wheat or in labor. The final result is a loss of five francs for James Goodfellow.

It is quite true that often, nearly always if you will, the government official renders an equivalent service to James Goodfellow. In this case there is no loss on either side; there is only an exchange. Therefore, my argument is not in any way concerned with useful functions. I say this: If you wish to create a government office, prove its usefulness. Demonstrate that to James Goodfellow it is worth the equivalent of what it costs him by virtue of the services it renders him. But apart from this intrinsic utility, do not cite, as an argument in favor of opening the new bureau, the advantage that it constitutes for the bureaucrat, his family, and those who supply his needs; do not allege that it encourages employment.

When James Goodfellow gives a hundred sous to a government official for a really useful service, this is exactly the same as when he gives a hundred sous to a shoemaker for a pair of shoes. It's a case of give-and-take, and the score is even. But when James Goodfellow hands over a hundred sous to a government official to receive no service for it or even to be subjected to inconveniences, it

is as if he were to give his money to a thief. It serves no purpose to say that the official will spend these hundred sous for the great profit of our *national industry*; the more the thief can do with them, the more James Goodfellow could have done with them if he had not met on his way either the extralegal or the legal parasite.

Let us accustom ourselves, then, not to judge things solely by *what is seen*, but rather by *what is not seen*.

Last year I was on the Finance Committee, for in the Constituent Assembly the members of the opposition were not systematically excluded from all committees. In this the framers of the Constitution acted wisely. We have heard M. Thiers say: "I have spent my life fighting men of the legitimist party and of the clerical party. Since, in the face of a common danger, I have come to know them and we have had heart-to-heart talks, I see that they are not the monsters I had imagined."

Yes, enmities become exaggerated and hatreds are intensified between parties that do not mingle; and if the majority would allow a few members of the minority to penetrate into the circles of the committees, perhaps it would be recognized on both sides that their ideas are not so far apart, and above all that their intentions are not so perverse, as supposed.

However that may be, last year I was on the Finance Committee. Each time that one of our colleagues spoke of fixing at a moderate figure the salaries of the President of the Republic, of cabinet ministers, and of ambassadors, he would be told:

"For the good of the service, we must surround certain offices with an aura of prestige and dignity. That is the way to attract to them men of merit. Innumerable unfortunate people turn to the President of the Republic, and he would be in a painful position if he were always forced to refuse them help. A certain amount of ostentation in the ministerial and diplomatic salons is part of the machinery of constitutional governments, etc., etc."

Whether or not such arguments can be controverted, they certainly deserve serious scrutiny. They are based on the public interest, rightly or wrongly estimated; and, personally, I can make more of a case for them than many of our Catos, moved by a narrow spirit of niggardliness or jealousy.

But what shocks my economist's conscience, what makes me blush for the intellectual renown of my country, is when they go on from these arguments (as they never fail to do) to this absurd banality (always favorably received):

"Besides, the luxury of high officials of the government encourages the arts, industry, and employment. The Chief of State and his ministers cannot give banquets and parties without infusing life into all the veins of the body politic. To reduce their salaries would be to starve industry in Paris and, at the same time, throughout the nation."

For heaven's sake, gentlemen, at least respect arithmetic, and do not come before the National Assembly of France and say, for fear that, to its shame, it will not support you, that an addition gives a different sum depending upon whether it is added from top to bottom or from bottom to top.

Well, then, suppose I arrange to have a navvy dig me a ditch in my field for the sum of a hundred sous. Just as I conclude this agreement, the tax collector takes my hundred sous from me and has them passed on to the Minister of the Interior. My contract is broken, but the Minister will add another dish at his dinner. On what basis do you dare to affirm that this official expenditure is an addition to the national industry? Do you not see that it is only a simple *transfer* of consumption and of labor? A cabinet minister has his table more lavishly set, it is true; but a farmer has his field less well drained, and this is just as true. A Parisian caterer has gained a hundred sous, I grant you; but grant me that a provincial ditchdigger has lost five francs. All that one can say is that the official dish and the satisfied caterer are *what is seen*; the swampy field and the excavator out of work are *what is not seen*.

Good Lord! What a lot of trouble to prove in political economy that two and two make four; and if you succeed in doing so, people cry, "It is so clear that it is boring." Then they vote as if you had never proved anything at all.

Chapter 22

Charles Wolf, Jr.

MARKET FAILURE

Charles Wolf Jr. (1924–) is an economist and a senior economic adviser and corporate fellow in international economics with the RAND Corporation. This essay surveys the various kinds of market failure—cases where the market fails to provide an efficient allocation of goods and services. Such market failures are often thought to be a justification for using government policy to achieve a superior outcome.

The Inadequacies of Markets

The principal justification for public policy intervention lies in the frequent and numerous shortcomings of market outcomes. Yet this rationale is only a necessary, not a sufficient, condition for policy formulation or for government intervention. The comment made a century ago by the British economist Henry Sidgwick can hardly be improved upon: "It does not follow that whenever laissez faire falls short government interference is expedient; since the inevitable drawbacks of the latter may, in any particular case, be worse than the shortcomings of private enterprise."

Policy formulation properly requires that the realized shortcomings of market outcomes be compared with the potential shortcomings of nonmarket efforts to provide remedies. The pathology of market shortcomings or failures provides only limited help in prescribing therapies for government success.

But how are we to judge the "success" or "failure" of market outcomes? Two broad criteria are usually and properly, though sometimes ambiguously, employed: efficiency and distributional equity.

Market outcomes can be termed efficient if the same level of total benefits that they generate cannot be obtained at lower cost or, alternatively, if greater benefits cannot be generated at the same level of costs; in either case, the resulting total benefits must exceed total costs if the outcomes are to be deemed efficient. Efficiency is thus like a contest among different ways of doing a job: If the market can accomplish the job at a lower cost than can other institutional arrangements, or can do a better job for the same costs, then the market is relatively efficient. On the other hand, if other institutional arrangements can accomplish the task at lower cost, or can do it better for the same cost, then the market is, in this respect, relatively inefficient.

This criterion defines allocative, or static, efficiency. It can be extended and refined in various ways to allow for other types of efficiency. For example, dynamic efficiency—especially emphasized in the writings of Joseph Schumpeter—relates to the capability of free markets, or of other institutional arrangements, to promote new technology that lowers costs, improves product quality, or creates new and marketable products, and to promote these things at lower cost than other ways of doing them. "X-efficiency"—a term coined by Harvey Leibenstein—relates to the capability of free markets or of other institutional arrangements to lower costs and raise the productivity of any given technology by stimulating organizational improvements, increased worker and management motivation, and improvements in a wide range of business decisions, including hiring and firing, promotions, salaries and bonuses, allocation of space, furniture, telephones, parking facilities, and so on.

Whether markets are more or less able to promote these outcomes than are other institutional arrangements determines whether markets are relatively more or less dynamically efficient, or X-efficient.

Although invoking the second criterion for judging market outcomes—distributional equity—goes beyond the conventional boundaries of microeconomics, it has profound significance with respect to the formulation, evaluation, and implementation of alternative public policies. Economists are less comfortable in grappling with the murkiness of distributional issues than with the relative precision of efficiency issues. Yet the treatment of tax incidence, for example, is central to the field of public finance, and tax incidence is quintessentially distributional in character.

However, even in this instance, economists usually evaluate alternative redistributive and tax programs from the standpoint of minimizing their negative effects on economic efficiency. In the real world of public policy—whether pertaining to education, energy, housing, foreign trade, or even defense policy—distributional issues are usually more influential than efficiency ones in shaping judgments about the success or shortcomings of market outcomes. As Jacob Viner observed, extensive government intervention in the free market has come about ". . .

largely as the result of dissatisfaction with the prevailing distribution of income. . . . No modern people will have zeal for the free market unless it operates in a setting of 'distributive justice' with which they are tolerably content."

Even when the central importance of distributional equity is acknowledged, the question remains, What standard should be used to evaluate it? The answer will be very different, and often ambiguous, depending on whether equity is interpreted in the sense of equality of outcome or equality of opportunity, or in the sense of "horizontal equity" or "vertical equity," or in the Marxian sense, or in the sense of the Old Testament or the New Testament, or in the sense of assuring that the least-favored have their lot improved before any further improvements are allowed for those who are more favored.

That markets may fail to produce either economically optimal (efficient) or socially desirable (equitable) outcomes has been elaborated in a well-known and voluminous literature. Although the last word has not been written, the essential points in the accepted theory of market failure are worth summarizing as background for the subsequent discussion of nonmarket failure.

Types of Market Failure

There are four sources or types of market shortcomings or failures. I use the terms "shortcomings" and "failures" interchangeably; strictly speaking, "shortcomings" has a looser and more inclusive meaning. Most economists would confine "market failure" to departures from Pareto-efficient outcomes, thereby excluding distributional issues except to the extent that distribution affects efficiency. By contrast, many noneconomists (and even some economists) argue that distribution has, or should have, priority over efficiency, and they fault the market precisely because of its failure to accord this priority. The choice between disciplinary orthodoxy and practical relevance seems clear to me.

This essay therefore regards distributional considerations as lying within the purview of market "shortcomings" or "failures."

Externalities and Public Goods

Where economic activities create "spillovers," whether benefits or costs, that are not, respectively, appropriable by or collectible from the producer, then market outcomes will not be efficient in the allocative sense defined above. Since these external benefits or costs do not enter the calculations upon which production decisions are based, too little will tend to be produced where the externalities are (net) benefits, and too much where they are (net) costs, compared with socially efficient output levels. Education is an example of an activity that putatively yields positive externalities (benefits) for society at large in addition to the benefits directly derived by the recipient. These externalities provide a rationale for government intervention—through subsidy or direct public sector production—to compensate for the tendency of the market, if it is not prodded, to produce insufficient output.

Other instances of positive externalities are the knowledge and technology resulting from activities and expenditures devoted to research and development. To the extent these benefits are external to, and nonappropriable by, the firms that bear the associated costs, these and other firms will invest too little in R&D. Once again, the market will fail according to the criterion of allocative efficiency, unless government intervenes by subsidizing or otherwise stimulating these activities. Moreover, to the extent that dynamic efficiency—the development of new products and processes—also depends on the creation of knowledge and technology, the unfettered market will fall short on this criterion as well.

Chemical and noise emissions from aircraft or other industrial activities are examples of negative externalities (costs). Their existence provides a rationale for government intervention—

through taxing or direct regulation—to compensate for the market's tendency to produce excessive output in this instance, because the externalities are otherwise not taken into account.

"Private" goods that are associated with externalities can be distinguished from "public" goods: The former term applies where *most* of the benefits or costs associated with output are, respectively, collected or paid by the producer, although *some* are not; and the latter (public goods) applies where most of an activity's consequences consist of nonappropriable benefits (for example, national security, which is the classic example of a genuinely public good) or noncollectible costs (for example, crime, the classic public "bad").

A distinction can be made between the nonappropriable consequences (benefits or costs) associated with externalities and the joint or collective consumption associated with public goods. In the latter case, the consequences are enjoyed by or imposed on all; hence, nonappropriability is implicit in public goods.

However, the notion of public goods can also be viewed as the limiting case of a "private" good with overwhelmingly large externalities. The water pollution associated with some chemical processing plants illustrates this latter case. Viewed in this light, externalities are a more general concept than public goods.

A powerful counterargument to the market failure created by externalities has been made by Ronald Coase. Coase contends that externalities do not necessarily lead to market failure. He argues that those who are the victims of external costs (such as the external costs imposed by chemical or noise emissions) can make these costs tangible to their sources by offering to pay the latter to desist or diminish the culpable activities (for example, to refrain from or reduce the emissions). Once the offer has been made, continuance of the emissions becomes a tangible cost, because the perpetrator will lose the offered payment unless he refrains from the objectionable activity. Consequently, in an effort to eat his cake and have it, a rational, cool, and calculating source of such negative externalities will seek to diminish them. Toward this end, he will consider, for example, using different chemical processes, or following different routes, or developing appropriate new technology enabling him to continue his production activities (which accounted for the emissions in the first place), without incurring the costs that have been made tangible by the victims' offer.

Unfortunately, Coase's powerful theoretical argument runs into a serious problem of implementation. The problem lies in the difficulty of bringing about the kind of bargain or contract he envisages between the sources and the victims of the negative externalities. In practice, the difficulty (which implies costs) of accomplishing such transactions between perpetrators and victims, or between benefactors and beneficiaries, is likely to be so formidable as to preclude the bargain being struck at all. However, to the extent these formidable transaction costs can be avoided or surmounted, markets can overcome externalities and continue to function efficiently. In that event, the distribution of benefits that results from the adjusted, and now once-more efficient, market outcomes will be altered. Under the assumed bargain, the beneficiary or the victim of the prior externalities will have to part with some income in order to avoid the negative externalities or retain the positive ones, respectively. Thus, the efficiency of market outcomes will be preserved, while its distributional equity may be enhanced or diminished, depending on the equity criterion that is applied (see the discussion below on distributional equity).

Increasing Returns

Where economic activities are subject to increasing returns and decreasing marginal costs, markets will again fail to generate efficient outcomes. Under conditions of decreasing costs, the lowest cost mode of production would be achieved by a single producer. Consequently, a free market will result in monopoly. Assuming that the monopolist cannot discriminate in the prices charged to different buyers, and hence a single price prevails in the market (single-part pricing), the outcome will be inefficient, in both static and dynamic terms.

In static terms, the outcome will be inefficient because the quantity produced will be lower, and the profit-maximizing price charged by the monopolist will be higher, than warranted by the costs of production. In terms of dynamic efficiency, as defined earlier, the outcome will also leave something to be desired because incentives for innovation by a secure and unchallenged monopolist will be weaker than would likely prevail under a more competitive regime.

Where increasing returns exist, various types of government intervention may be justified to alter the market outcome: (1) through direct operation or regulation of a "natural" monopoly (for example, public utilities), through setting prices or allowable rates of return on its capital, at levels closer to those that would prevail in a competitive environment; (2) through legal protection to prevent a single-firm takeover and to encourage competition (for example, through antitrust legislation). Such types of intervention depart from a theoretically efficient outcome, although they seek to approach it.

A recent development in economics—the theory of "contestable markets"—suggests that, even in the face of increasing returns and the prevalence of monopoly, strong tendencies may persist for efficient, or nearly efficient, pricing and output decisions by monopolists, thereby avoiding or mitigating the impact of this source of market failure. The theory of contestable markets has been developed by William Baumol, and was foreshadowed several decades ago by the French economist François Perroux. Perroux suggested that, if markets are open to new entrants and there are few barriers and limited costs to entry, monopolists will be disciplined by the potential entry of competitors (the "potential rival"), who would contest the monopolized market unless profit margins are kept low and output is kept high.

Thus, where barriers to entry are low, the production of a good or provision of a service by a monopolist does not necessarily signify that he will be able to exploit monopoly power. In the case of the airline industry, for example, even monopoly suppliers of service on thinly served routes have been unable to charge monopoly prices because the existence of potential entrants and competitors has discouraged such practices by the existing monopolists. Consequently, following deregulation of the airlines, rates charged on thinly served routes have not been characterized by monopoly pricing or monopoly profits any more than have the heavily served and clearly competitive routes.

Even for the Schumpeterian criterion of dynamic efficiency, increasing returns and monopolistic market structure may not stray as far from the desirable goal of innovation and rising productivity as has usually been assumed. Here again the influence of the contestability of the market by potential entrants ("rivals") may enforce a strong discipline on monopolists, obliging them to maintain a high level of R&D and to sustain rapid innovation to protect their presently monopolized markets. Potential competition may thus have an effect similar to that of actual competition.

The recent breakup of AT&T, after lengthy litigation in which the huge corporation was found in violation of antitrust legislation, provides an interesting example of the conflict between the two preceding types of market failure: externalities and increasing returns. To remedy one source of market failure (increasing returns), the courts have perhaps created another (externalities). Perceiving a lack of effective competition in an industry subject to increasing returns (telecommunications), the courts have replaced it by a situation in which benefits from undertaking R&D and innovation, which formerly were largely "internalized" by the giant

AT&T, are now largely external to the seven or eight regional firms into which the industry has been split. Hence, incentives may be weakened for the newly competing entities in the telecommunications industry to undertake as aggressive efforts in R&D and technological improvement as did AT&T in the past. The disincentives arise because of the externalities that R&D generates: Competitors can "free ride" on the R&D expenses incurred by any one firm. By contrast, when AT&T dominated the entire market, the results of R&D and innovation were internalized by the single firm that benefited from, as well as generated, them. Hence, the "free rider" problem was avoided.

The AT&T case illustrates a frequent experience in the public policy arena. Public policy efforts motivated by the aim of remedying one type of shortcoming may well create a different one as a by-product. It remains to be seen how the balance of advantage between these two sources of market failure—externalities and increasing returns—will work out under the new market structure established in the telecommunications industry.

Market Imperfections

Where the price, information, and mobility characteristics of "perfect" markets depart significantly from those prevailing in actual markets, the outcomes resulting from those markets will not be efficient. Once again, a rationale arises for government intervention. Where prices and interest rates, for one reason or another, do not indicate relative scarcities and opportunity costs, where consumers do not have equal access to information about products and markets, where information about market opportunities and production technology is not equally available to all producers, or where factors of production are restricted in their ability to move in response to such information, market forces will not allocate efficiently and the economy will produce below its capacity. These conditions abound in the economies of less developed countries, and they are surely not unfamiliar in the economies of more developed ones. Indeed, these imperfections apply to some extent in all markets and to a greater extent in some. In such circumstances, the implication for public policy is to reduce, if not remove, these imperfections: to facilitate availability of information, to lower barriers to entry and mobility, and so on.

However, where many of the conditions required for efficient functioning of markets do not exist, improving some will not necessarily improve the efficiency of the market as a whole. Consequently, the policy implications of market imperfections may be ambiguous. Legal protection of patents provides an example of how one type of market imperfection may even contribute to market efficiency. In this case the market imperfection is the restriction of access to technological information that is created by patents. A short-run loss of efficiency results because firms that do not hold the patent are restricted in their access to improved technological information because of the price (royalty) they have to pay to obtain and to use it. Consumers are thus deprived of benefits in the short run. However, the purpose of the patent restriction is to enhance incentives for technological improvement, thereby contributing to dynamic efficiency in the long run. The presumption is that the long-run gains, due to enhancement of incentives and the resulting impetus to dynamic efficiency, will exceed the short-term losses resulting from diminished allocative efficiency.

In less developed countries, the scale and pervasiveness of market imperfections—and sometimes even the apparent absence of functioning markets—is often adduced as a rationale for government dominance and control in the economy. A "big push" by government is presumed to be needed to compensate for the inadequacies of markets.

Certainly, market imperfections abound in these countries. They are characterized by restricted access to economically relevant information, factor immobilities, price and interest rate distortions, and so on. Yet despite these characteristics, it is a striking fact that the few relatively successful developing countries—Hong Kong, Malaysia, Singapore, South Korea, and Taiwan—have greatly benefited from decisions and policies that limit the government's role in economic decisionmaking, and instead allow markets—notwithstanding their imperfections and shortcomings—to exercise a decisive role in determining resource allocations.

Distributional Equity

As already noted, most economists exclude distributional effects from judgments about the success or failure of markets. In textbook usage, the term "market failure" is usually confined to departures from competitive equilibrium and strictly efficient (Pareto-efficient) outcomes; as narrowly construed, then, "market failure" typically excludes departures from distributional equity. Nevertheless, this exclusion is usually accompanied by an acknowledgment that the distributional results of even well-functioning markets may not accord with socially accepted standards of equity, or with society's preferences for reducing excessive disparities in the distribution of income and wealth. It is also usually acknowledged that, where there is a trade-off between efficiency and equity, social consensus in democratic systems often is prepared to forgo some of the one to realize more of the other.

In welfare economics this trade-off is usually dealt with by considering the relative efficiency of various redistributive measures (for example, income taxes, excises, subsidies, unemployment relief, and income transfers) in achieving a desired redistribution (that is, minimizing the allocative distortions resulting from the income and substitution effects of redistribution).

Nevertheless, from one perspective, it is theoretically correct to consider distributional inequity as an example of market failure. From this perspective, income distribution is a particular type of public good. An "equitable" redistribution does not result from freely functioning markets because philanthropy and charity yield benefits that are external to, and not appropriable by, the donors, but are instead realized by society as a whole. Left to its own devices, the market will therefore produce less redistribution than is "efficient" (that is, socially desirable), because of the usual "free rider" problem associated with externalities, public goods, and incomplete markets.

Another perspective for viewing distributional equity is quite unrelated to market failure in the strict sense. From this perspective, the equilibrium redistribution previously referred to may be quite inequitable in terms of one or another ethical norm. Even if the market could surmount the narrow type of "failure" discussed above, its distributional outcome might still be socially and ethically unacceptable from the standpoint of one or more such norms. On these grounds, the distributional outcomes of even perfectly functioning markets can be justifiably criticized.

As noted earlier, Jacob Viner pointed out several decades ago that the decisive test of the acceptability of markets in modern democratic societies depends fundamentally on the extent to which such markets can coexist within a general setting of "distributive justice" with which the electorate is "tolerably content." Furthermore, most public policy decisions are usually even more concerned with distributional issues (namely, *who* gets the benefits and *who* pays the costs) than with efficiency issues (namely, how *large* are the benefits and costs). Since the principal aim of this book is to compare market shortcomings with the shortcomings of nonmarket remedies, distributional inequity will be included among the offenders.

Chapter 23

William C. Mitchell and Randy T. Simmons

PATHOLOGICAL POLITICS
The Anatomy of Government Failure

William Mitchell (1925–2006) was a professor of political science and a colleague of Randy Simmons (1950–   ) in the department of Political Science at Utah State University. Both of these authors wrote widely in the field of public choice—a methodological approach in which the tools of economic analysis are brought to bear on the behavior of governmental actors and institutions. In this essay, taken from their book *Beyond Politics* (1994), they discuss the concept and causes of "government failure"—cases where institutional features of government lead predictably to inefficient outcomes—in order to question the idea that government policy is the best way of addressing market failures.

In this essay we complete our analysis of government failure by showing how and why the political process is defective. We examine further whether these defects are inherent in politics or in particular institutions that might be altered and improved.

Citizen Sovereignty and Efficiency

A pathology of politics is meaningless without a normative foundation—in this case, efficiency, a much misunderstood and abused term among non-economists. Here it refers to a measure of how well society provides for the material wants of its members. This simple definition is in accord with the more precise one of Pareto, namely, that efficiency depends on whether a given policy, action, or allocation is able to improve the subjective well-being of anyone without diminishing that of others. Such a result is said to be Pareto optimal. A polity or economy producing huge quantities of unwanted goods and services even at the lowest cost would not be considered efficient. No one would be made better off, and indeed many would be worse off since the resources could be allocated for more valued uses. So, our chief concern is with *allocative* efficiency and secondarily with technical efficiency, that is, producing something at the lowest cost. We are concerned with how society meets individual preferences and whether it employs resources in their most valued uses.

Despite the importance of individual preferences in democracies, a number of otherwise attractive political features have the unhappy facility of violating Paretian optimality. The two most prominent involve redistribution of income. Redistributive gains dominate efficiency considerations in policy discussions, and democratic institutions encourage this redistributive propensity. In addition, democracy has an unfortunate but distinct penchant for enacting inefficient proposals—proposals that make some better off but at the expense of others, or even worse, that make everyone worse off in the long run. By choosing policies and rules that produce greater costs than benefits and failing to enact those having greater benefits than costs, citizens fail to achieve their highest welfare.

Sources of inefficiency in the political process may be usefully categorized in six ways: (1) perverted incentives; (2) collective provision of private wants; (3) deficient signaling mechanisms; (4) institutional myopia; (5) dynamic difficulties; and (6) electoral rules and the distortion of preferences.

Perverted Incentives

Adam Smith's greatest accomplishment was demonstrating the beneficence of the hidden hand of the market in converting self-interests into collective good. Just how the invisible hand operates has preoccupied economists for more than 200 years. The great accomplishment of modern public choice theory, and of James Buchanan and Gordon Tullock, especially, has been to demonstrate the pernicious workings of the visible hand of politics. The same decision-makers operating under market and political rules produce quite different results. Although both political and market participants are assumed to be self-interested, the incentives—objective rewards and penalties—differ profoundly. In fact, what the market and polity offer in the way of concrete rewards, encouragements, discouragements, and costs contrast so much that people who have worked in both environments are puzzled at the variations and sometimes exasperated by them. Business-people in particular find working in the public sector frustrating to say the least.

In markets, the promise of profits, fortified by the ever-present risk of loss, encourages entrepreneurs to improve their products and services while lowering the cost of doing so. The wealth of customers and entrepreneurs is increased and

the improvements spur on competitors who make their own improvements. By serving himself, the producer serves others; by serving others, he profits. It is, in short, an exchange system enabling mutual gains.

Some students of politics, including well-known economists and political scientists, see parallels and argue that politics ought also be viewed as a vast exchange system. One such economist, Roland N. McKean, has referred to the "unseen hand of bargaining" as the mechanism for converting self-interests into public good. The trouble is that politics and government do not offer a full range of profitmaking activities to their participants. In fact, the abuse of authority is feared so much that profitmaking (as distinct from self-seeking) in politics is prohibited by the imposition of extraordinary constitutional, statutory, and ethical limitations on public officials. Their discretion and even goals are carefully circumscribed. In this respect, the U.S. Constitution was designed to be a distinctly negative document. In the first place, government officials are not permitted to sell their official services or goods. And since they must offer them to all at zero or less-than-cost prices, they never learn the precise values citizens place on activities and goods. Without a market, value becomes impossible to ascertain and implement. Since everything in the market acquires a price, buyers and sellers can make comparative efficiency judgments and fairly accurate calculations about the right thing to do. Political actors have no such guidance, and without it efficient choices become, as Ludwig von Mises and Friedrich A. von Hayek argued, impossible. At best, government officials and citizens know what it costs them to purchase resources and products; they cannot determine the values consumers place on the government services produced. Thus, it is next to impossible for even the most skilled government economist to construct a valid demand curve for politically provided goods.

When choosing public policies, politicians—who wish to remain in office—must rank the vote impact higher than the efficiency impact of alternative courses of action. Their calculations are at odds with those of businesspeople, their market counterparts. Whereas the latter ask *how much* people want something, the equivalent of asking what they are willing to pay, politicians ask *how many* people want something. Politicians count majorities first and intensity of preferences and beliefs second and indirectly. A firm does not have to win majorities in order to do business; political actors do. Since a vote is weighted the same as any other vote, all votes are equal. But some buyers have more dollar-votes than others and their voices, therefore, count for more. Since equal votes and unequal dollars are fundamental facts of the political economy they provide the crucial bases for debates and conflicts over the redistribution of income, wealth, status, and power. Those who seek equality of outcomes wish to extend the realm of votes, whereas those who prefer uncertain inequality tend to favor the market domain. Ironically, extreme faith in either can lead to paradoxical results.

Separation of Costs and Benefits

Perhaps the fundamental political fact—one rent with inexpedient and untimely consequences—is the separation of cost and benefit considerations. The fact that few persons are forced to weigh them one against the other before making policy choices enables and encourages people to seek additional gains at collective expense.

As the number of entities seeking favors from government increases, the government finds itself in the difficult position of having to cater to private desires rather than providing the public goods that governments are supposed to provide. The opportunity cost of devoting more time and resources to favor-seekers is that the provision of national defense, domestic law and order, and other genuine public goods is reduced. Recognition of this disparity has led several writers to worry about "governmental

overload" or "gridlock" and the consequent frustrations engendered by failure to provide basic services. Some writers claim that much of our alleged civic malaise and even cynicism results from governments attempting to do too many things and doing none well. Such well-known neoconservatives as Irving Kristol, Samuel Huntington, Aaron Wildavsky, Richard Rose, and James Q. Wilson have made this issue a touchstone in their critiques of contemporary America. Although their point is not expressed in terms of efficiency, it is well-taken.

More economically minded analysts would point out that citizens seeking collective provision of their private wants generally seek those goods for which they would not pay in the private market. So long as the goods come free, they demand more of them and thereby misallocate scarce resources from their higher valued uses. In his personal revelations to *Atlantic Monthly* writer William Greider, David Stockman, former director of the Office of Management and Budget under President Reagan, provided a trivial but telling example of misallocation. Stockman told about two tennis courts built by the federal government with federal revenue-sharing funds near Stockman's family farm in Michigan. The local government accepted the funds and built the courts even though almost no one played tennis. It appears that the two elaborate courts were unused and the local government did not maintain them. Furthermore, local officials most certainly would not have erected the courts if they had to spend their own restricted tax monies when other projects were more needed. Local taxpayers would not have opted to increase their taxes to build the facility. But the facility was built, not only because it did not burden local tax-payers but because the expenditure of dollars from elsewhere provided a local contractor with additional work. The government might as well have used the money to build pyramids or simply to have ditches dug and then filled; the economic effects would have been the same. Virtually all vote trading or log rolling is based on a similar concentration of benefits and dispersal of costs.

The pervasiveness of this means of self-aggrandizement is saddening but understandable. How could it be otherwise when to sacrifice private goods in the public interest forces the sacrificer to pay all the costs while others enjoy the benefits? The divorce of costs from benefits not only induces a favor-seeking motive in each citizen but in the long run also turns democracy into a vast celebration of the repeal of what Milton Friedman called TANSTAAFL—"There ain't no such thing as a free lunch." The basic rule in the political process is: Free lunches are always possible in the short run. David Friedman describes the process in the following parable:

> Special interest politics is a simple game. A hundred people sit in a circle, each with his pocket full of pennies. A politician walks around the outside of the circle, taking a penny from each person. No one minds; who cares about a penny? When he has gotten all the way around the circle, the politician throws fifty cents down in front of one person, who is overjoyed at the unexpected windfall. The process is repeated, ending with a different person. After a hundred rounds, everyone is a hundred cents poorer, fifty cents richer, and happy.

And consider Henry Wallich's comment that when citizens seek government favors they become free riders:

> But when it comes to accepting benefits, citizen-taxpayers act like a group of men who sit down at a restaurant table knowing that they will split the check evenly. In this situation everybody orders generously; it adds little to one's own share of the bill and for the extravagance of his friends he will have to pay anyhow. What happens at the restaurant table explains—though it does not excuse—what happens at the public trough.

Political Signaling: Votes and Rhetoric

One of the greatest inventions is money, for it is a wonderfully convenient means enabling persons with diverse interests to communicate in simple, precise, and rapid transactions. Without a monetary system, a modern society would soon dissolve into chaos. Without money we would not be able to avoid the double contingency problem of barter, that is, finding a trading partner who wants what you have and has what you want. Barter is extraordinarily cumbersome, imprecise, and inefficient. So are the socialist substitutes for the pricing system—the surrogates that enable planners to play at market competition. Knowing these fundamental facts, however, has not dissuaded many political scientists from finding virtues in political systems that, in effect, employ barter and planning. In democracies, the chief unit of account and medium of exchange is the vote.

But consider the vote itself as an analog to money. In the first place, everyone has but one vote and that vote is indivisible. Accordingly, the vote cannot express a voter's *intensity* of preferences. Without multiple votes or a weighted voting system, voters cannot indicate to others just how much they prefer one candidate to another or one policy over another. All they can say is that they prefer whomever or whatever they vote for over the other options. The vote on the ballot can therefore convey little information and indeed, when counted on election day, votes produce considerable ambiguity. What do the individual votes mean? Both winners and losers can rationalize the outcomes. Is it a strong positive endorsement or merely a negative minimizing of a choice among bad options? As guidance to policymakers, the voting outcome is highly ambiguous. The notion of reducing the mystery and improving elections has inspired many formal theorists of public choice and others to devise intricate reforms of the ballot, electoral rules, and the like. Few of their suggestions are ever adopted.

These problems can be reduced somewhat through the use of vote trading, a form of barter that is better known in legislatures as log rolling. Although a good case can be made that vote trading offers an improvement over nontrading, the argument usually breaks down in practice because the skewed distribution of diffused costs and concentrated benefits dominates the aggregate size of those results. Vote trading will therefore favor projects in which total costs exceed total benefits. In other words, bad projects that would normally be defeated can be enacted into law when votes are traded, making all concerned worse off.

The logic of log rolling at its worst can be seen in the following example. Suppose three voters are confronted with two projects, a jail and a school, and that each project is to be voted on independently and the decision to be made by majority rule. If the voters estimated their respective costs and benefits as shown in Table 23.1, we would expect that both projects would be voted down: In the case of the jail by voters A and C while in the case of the school by voters A and B. Since both projects are inefficient, that is, total benefits are exceeded by costs, it is clear that this election would have produced the correct result.

But consider what might occur if the voters discovered and practiced log rolling. In such an event, voter B would agree to support voter C's school if C would support B's jail. As a result, the three-member polity would adopt two inefficient projects with a total loss of $200. Although B and C must help pay for each other's projects,

they would still come out as gainers; their gain, however, would have to be accomplished at the expense of A, who would have to bear $400 of the total cost of $800. We could just as easily construct further simple situations showing the opposite results, but in the real world, log rolling is more likely to confirm our blackboard illustration.

Although vote trading among ordinary voters is effectively discouraged by prohibitive transaction and monitoring costs, the politicians have managed, quite rationally, to impose a form of implicit trading on voters through the use of issue packaging. This practice occurs when individually popular proposals are combined with not-so-popular proposals in a single package—such as in party platforms or, more commonly, through nongermane amendments to bills in legislature. The less popular proposals are attached as riders so that a legislature or a president who wants to reject the dubious rider has to reject the good measures as well. Without a presidential line-item veto, many taxpayers are forced to suffer losses to support the gains of a few.

A variant on this form of vote trading is found in the strategy Anthony Downs (1957) termed a "coalition of minorities." Suppose that three issues entailing subsidies are presented to voters and that in each case 20 percent are in favor and 80 percent are opposed. One might superficially assume that political candidates would quickly announce their support of the over-whelming majorities on each issue and oppose all three subsidies. However, a politician who supported all three minority positions could garner support from 60 percent of the populace, assuming the three 20 percent minorities did not overlap. Furthermore, this majority would be much more likely to materialize and remain stable than a majority from the opposition because the gains afforded individuals are apt to have a greater impact on their voting choices than individual losses. Realistically, we should also assume that some of the taxpayers/consumers who opposed

Table 23.1 Inefficiency of Log Rolling

Project	Voter's Net Benefits		
	A	B	C
Jail	−$200	$300	−$200
School	−$200	−$200	$300
Net	−$400	$100	$100

subsidies other than their own would number among those who would gain from one or more other subsidies.

This problem does not arise in the private economy because coalitions and log rolling are irrelevant to making decisions. Each buyer and seller can and does act independently and normally without consideration of others; in fact, they compete not only across but on the same side of the market, consumer against consumer and seller against seller.

The signaling of intentions and communication more generally is conducted in polity and economy alike through the use of everyday language. The acquisition of a common language is a marvelous achievement, one that we may not fully appreciate until we visit a foreign country. But language, as English teachers know only too well, can be used with varying degrees of skill. Some people communicate better than others. Scientists and technicians, for example, are able to employ the languages of mathematics and science with extraordinary precision and economy.

Because voters are rationally ignorant (the costs of gaining particular kinds of information are greater than the benefits since one vote is essentially meaningless), politicians must employ a language designed to evoke emotion—enough emotion to motivate the right people to turn out and vote. Thus, politicians rarely speak with precise meanings, marginal calculations, or logical reasoning; instead they manipulate affect, raw emotions, group identifications, and even hatred, envy, and threats. Because premature commitment to an issue can cause one to end up in a minority position, successful politicians equivocate, hint, exaggerate, procrastinate, "straddle fences," adopt code words, and speak in *non sequiturs*. Understanding the politician is therefore extremely frustrating for those who value precise statements. But note that this problem is not the fault of the politician; it is rooted in the rational ignorance of voters, the distribution of conflicting sentiments among voters, and the nature of collective endeavor.

What all this means is clear: Political communication is rarely conducive to rational or efficient allocation of scarce resources. This does not mean that the individual politicians are irrational in their choice of language and symbolic activities. Waving the flag and kissing babies are practiced because of their tactical value in an activity that is at once a rational game and a morality play; in that conjunction lies the endless fascination and frustration of politics.

Institutional Myopia

Critics of markets often accuse them of being indifferent to the needs of future generations. This criticism has a profound appeal for many people. Since market agents are selfish and short-sighted, how could they possibly pursue conservation goals? "Cut and run" is their guiding precept. It is assumed and claimed that only the political process and governments have the incentive and the ability to serve the future. Horror stories about the exploitation of our eastern and northern woods, wanton killing of buffalo, and callous fishing of streams and ocean are cited as convincing examples and evidence of the failure.

The fact of the matter is that the historical examples are misunderstood and the capacity of governments to enact protective laws grossly overestimated. Markets are governed by persons, both buyers and sellers, constantly and necessarily engaged in comparing present and future values; if they did not make such comparisons we would have a difficult time explaining why many choose to make substantial investments during uncertain times. Profit maximizers serve themselves, but they do so by investing in uncertain future prospects. Thus, through their efforts to determine whether future generations of buyers will buy their wares, they may conserve now or invest in producing more resources for future use. In order to do this they must estimate future demands for existing goods and services and possibly for new ones. If Oregon logging firms, for example, believed that future sales of lumber products were likely to increase (for whatever reasons), they would choose to harvest fewer trees now and even plant more for future harvest; in fact, the privately owned Weyhauser Company and countless smaller tree farmers have done just that with considerable skill and investment. Private timber firms are even preserving wildlife habitat and scenic vistas because of their expected future value. And, as many close students of the oil industry have pointed out, oil companies do not pump oil twenty-four hours a day; market signals dictate the holding of vast inventories of oil in the ground. All resource holders operating in a private property, free-market context are *forced* to consider inventory policy and the future.

But what of the political possibilities? The conventional wisdom is that informed voters and dispassionate but professional public officials will be more far-sighted than corporate leaders. Deprived of making profits, officials are assumed to place higher values on the future than would entrepreneurs, but just why they should do so remains something of a mystery since future voters are either unborn or have yet to register their preferences at the polls. Common sense suggests that citizen-voters deprive themselves of a great deal in casting support for, say, conservation measures when all benefits are conferred on unknown future voters with unknown tastes. Politicians seem to understand this dilemma because historically they have not been in the forefront of ecological and environmental movements; both are only twenty or so years of age. If government is so omniscient, why did it take so long to protect our environment? Socialist countries, it seems, are even more negligent. We must not forget that for the politician a week is an eternity, especially around election time. The reason for politicians' myopia is simple; voters are also myopic. And voters are short-sighted because most public policies confer either long-run benefits with immediate costs

or immediate gains with delayed costs. In the first instance, political systems produce inaction, delay, and caution; in the second, speedy action is undertaken but it is usually ill-considered, excessive, and enacted under the strains of crisis. . . . Legislation enacted during increasing unemployment may create the illusion of action and accomplishment but always at considerable, real, long-run costs in the operation of free markets. Price controls enacted during inflation are a singular example of such illusory gains and real costs.

There seem to be no compelling reasons why voters, politicians, and bureaucrats should be more future-oriented than selfish buyers and sellers. Removing property rights and the profit motive does not enhance the future's prospects; their absence actually diminishes the time horizons of political beings.

Dynamics: Uncertainty, Innovation, and Welfare

Facing uncertainty, governments understandably behave in highly uncertain and unpredictable ways. On the one hand, bureaucracies seem lethargic; on the other, legislatures and chief executives seem all too often to bounce from inaction to hyperaction and back again. Private firms appear to be somewhat more stable in their responses. Perhaps the reason for the variances between government and private firms has to do with the existence of profit and its connection with uncertainty in markets and the absence of profit but the presence of uncertainty in politics.

Students of international politics and public planning have long observed that governments are woefully underequipped with vital information and practical theories on which to base their actions. Unlike private firms, governments do not have a single purpose or goal such as profit maximization; instead they pursue conflicting objectives and make "trade-offs." Relating conflicting ends and highly uncertain means is inherently difficult. Economists might phrase it by saying society does not have a "social welfare function" or a single "public interest." Public planners facing this dilemma react with either excessive caution or haste. There are plentiful examples of both responses. Grandiose projects have been authorized overnight without much assurance of success, while promising programs are avoided and delayed. Few reclamation programs, for instance, have positive cost-benefit ratios, yet they have been enacted with disconcerting consistency. And we should expect such misallocations as long as politicians continue to spend taxpayers' money and interest groups can gain private benefits at public expense.

Elected officials respond to changing voter preferences in predictable ways, usually in erratic over-responses, while the bureaucrats held responsible for the implementation of hastily conceived plans behave in less dramatic but equally inappropriate ways, often involving inaction and delay. Among bureaucrats, the costs of errors are thought to exceed the gains from risky choices, so excessive caution or prudence is the norm. The morass of regulation can be used to delay action, for example. Inadequate resources, due-process requirements, competing claims among clients, and fear of legislators all contribute to maximizing time wasted in performance of regulatory goals. Milton and Rose Friedman caught the paradox of inactivity and frenetic response when they wrote:

> He, the businessman, can begin small and grow. And, equally important, he can fail to grow. . . . Contrast this with the political process. To adopt some measure requires first persuading a majority before the measure can be tried. It is hard to start small, and once started, almost impossible to fail. That is why governmental intervention is at once so rigid and so unstable.

Policies, once adopted, come to have the status of sacred cows, even when they are manifestly inefficient. This paradox, like many others encountered in politics, can be easily unraveled once we understand that inefficient policies can be enacted if benefits are highly concentrated and costs widely distributed. Beneficiaries enjoying benefits have little difficulty keeping their gains because abolishing them would do great damage and confer but small gains on millions of taxpayers. So the latter do not act, while the former can be certain to mobilize enormous resources in defense of privilege. Apparently people will fight harder to keep a certain gain than they will to bring about a greater but uncertain gain. No wonder the Social Security program remains with us. No wonder all the bankrupt farm programs are not only with us but grow. No wonder other subsidies hang on, and worse, multiply and increase.

Inefficient and even destructive policies continue to exist and grow because virtually every policy can be defended as having contributed some good to someone in need. Even those most disadvantaged by a certain institution or policy are often among those who defend practices such as minimum wages, equal opportunity laws, and rent control. Ironically, efficiency reforms have few constituents even during so-called conservative administrations; in fact, one might well contend that conservatives are particularly well-suited to consolidating and legitimizing past inefficiencies as well as serving the interests of the better off. Four recent Republican presidents have not diminished the scope of the welfare state. Some wag has said "The Republican party can only promise to do what the Democrats do, only do less of it." If so, innovation in the practical political sense is largely the prerogative of the political Left, and their reforms typically consist of additions to the state's activities and power. Undoing state activities inspires few.

Once again Milton Friedman has some intriguing insights—this time into the close connection between beliefs about the role of government, time perspective, and policy innovation.

The liberal in the original sense—the person who gives primacy to freedom and believes in limited government—tends to take the long view, to put major emphasis on the ultimate and permanent consequences of policies rather than on the immediate and possible transitory consequences. The modern liberal—the person who gives primacy to welfare and believes in greater governmental control—tends to take the short view, to put primary emphasis on the immediate effects of policy measures. This connection is one of reciprocal cause and effect. The man who has a short time perspective will be impatient with the slow workings of voluntary arrangements in producing changes in institutions. He will want to achieve changes at once, which requires centralized authority that can override objections. Hence he will be disposed to favor a greater role for government. But conversely, the man who favors a greater role for government will thereby be disposed to have a shorter time perspective. Partly, he will be so disposed because centralized government can achieve changes of some kinds rapidly; hence he will feel that if the longer term consequences are adverse, he—through the government—can introduce new measures that will counter them, that he can have his cake and eat it. Partly, he will have a short time perspective because the political process demands it. In the market, an entrepreneur can experiment with a new innovation without first persuading the public. He need only have confidence that after he has made his innovation enough of the public will buy his product to make it pay. He can afford to wait until they do. Hence, he can have a long time perspective. In the political process, an entrepreneur must first get elected in order to be in a position to innovate. To get elected, he must persuade the public in advance. Hence he must look at immediate results that he can offer the public. He may not be able to take a

very long time perspective and still hope to be in power.

The future is not likely to be well served by government, not even by well-meaning members of government. Private entrepreneurs, however, can serve the future as they pursue their private interests.

Electoral Rules: Paradoxes and Impossibilities

Although we have examined numerous properties of democracy, we have ignored one of the most important—the impact of formal rules on group decisionmaking and especially rules pertaining to elections in which voters choose candidates and policies. According to such famous theorists as Kenneth Arrow, Duncan Black, Charles Plott, William H. Riker, and a host of lesser-known formal analysts, rules matter. Because their work is highly technical, accessibility is achieved only by considerable translation and oversimplification.

Much formal political theory, but hardly all, is based on the pathbreaking work of Kenneth Arrow and Duncan Black, the former a Nobel Laureate in Economics. Our discussion is based mostly on their efforts. For those who see little fault in democracy, Arrow's results are earthshaking because he proved that no democratic voting rule can satisfy five basic conditions—perfectly reasonable ones—simultaneously. One or more must be violated in the effort to arrive at collective results that are consistent with individual preferences. He also shows that majority rule does not function well when voters have more than two options. If three options are offered and each voter is asked to rank the three, it is frequently the case that no one option will win a majority of first-place rankings. And, if they were to consider their three ranked options in pairs, voters would soon learn that voting cycles had resulted, with each option defeating another and no one winning.

All this can be illustrated with the use of the following table in which we suppose there are three voters and three options, which might be policies or candidates. In any event, the voters rank their preferences as shown in the table.

Ranking	Voters		
	A	B	C
1st	a	b	c
2nd	b	c	a
3rd	c	a	b

If each option is paired or compared with each other option, *a* will beat *b*, and *b* will beat *c*, but *c* will in turn beat *a*. Thus, majority rule has some severe problems for each option can beat every other option, with no determinate winner emerging that can claim to be the majority preference. Cycling is the name of this phenomenon. Of course, there are ways out of the dilemma and ways of preventing it, and there is no necessity that cycling will occur. But it is true that as the number of options increases relative to the number of voters, the cycle will occur with increasing frequency. For our purposes it is sufficient to note that the cycle is real, and although it does not prevent our society from employing majority rule it does create difficulties that should not and cannot be ignored. Majority rule is not perfect.

If plurality enables victory we immediately run into the fact that the winning alternative may garner less than a simple majority and that the losers constitute more than a majority of 50 percent plus one. Like thirteen other presidents, Abraham Lincoln won office not with a majority but a plurality. It has also been argued that plurality rules may be affected by the existence of a third option. For example, one's choices are influenced by whether a third alternative is included. And if we employ a unanimity rule, we soon learn that everyone has a veto power. Are we willing to allow vast majorities to be over-ruled by one or a few voters? Some students of elections have advanced a variety of weighted voting schemes designed to overcome some of the difficulties of political choice, but their proposals do not solve all of them. The big problem is how to weigh the votes, for that determination will affect the totaling of the various scores. So technical ingenuity has yet to resolve all of Arrow's reservations. And we have not even mentioned the agenda problem, or the order in which options are voted upon, a problem that can be solved but only through manipulation.

Of course, American democracy does not operate by any such direct voting as suggested by Arrow's criteria; instead citizens vote directly on a few policy issues and mostly in elections to select among candidates for public office. In the latter, specific forms of electoral institutions operate that are peculiar to different democracies. For example, American presidential candidates are selected through party conventions and primary elections in which delegates to a national convention are chosen. The nominated candidates then compete in a national election consisting of fifty different state elections in which the winning candidate receives all of a state's electoral vote, whether the victory was gained by a substantial majority or by one vote; it is a winner-take-all result. As political scientists know so well, the strongest candidate in the primaries may not be the one who would be strongest in the general election; this is the case because the more committed voters who attend the party primaries tend to select the more extreme competitors. In addition, candidates for the presidency tend to devote more of their attention to states with more electoral college votes and ignore those with fewer votes.

Earlier we mentioned the problem of the geographical distribution of voters and its relationship to final policy choices. Several studies have shown that neither overall majority nor strongly held minority views will necessarily be reflected by majority voting if the legislative body is made up of members elected from separate districts with a winner-take-all rule in each district. These single-member districts can result in a legislature or convention that does not represent the voters. The overall majority position, for example, may win overwhelming majorities in less than half the districts but lose by small margins in a bare majority of districts. The result is that the majority position is in a minority in the legislature. Conversely, the overall minority position may win overwhelming majorities in a handful of districts, lose by small margins in most other districts, and end up placing few representatives in the legislature. Those who win bare majorities in the districts can therefore win a huge majority in the legislature. All this is accomplished under majority rule! It becomes clear why politicians have such fierce fights over geographical boundaries for legislative districts; their own interests are at stake and so are those of voters.

Another consequence of the U.S. electoral system is the frequent honoring of the so-called median voter, that is, politicians tend to adopt positions that converge on the preferences of median voters instead of extreme positions. The logic of seeking voters is said to drive candidates into a "tweedle-dee-tweedle-dum" situation in which they have no discernible differences. Thus, providing no choice for voters is the best choice for candidates. Of course, minority voters on the far reaches of the normal unimodal preference distribution lose because they are in the minority. At best they gain only vague rhetorical reassurances from the candidates. Since the median voter gets so much attention, it is to the advantage of concerned interest groups to shape voter preferences for one position or another. As Gordon Tullock argued, the name of the political game is shaping preferences and their distribution. That is why political advertising, including the uninformative, is such an important ingredient in the electoral process. At its worst, advertising tempts exaggeration, deception, and lies. Shaping the options and the

agenda become additional subjects of intense scrutiny among activists, for on such factors the outcomes of elections depend.

Since most voting is for candidates rather than issues, and most policy-making takes place between elections, we cannot ascribe much significance to median voters beyond their symbolic value and the few generalized constraints they place on government through elections. In our estimation it is risky to argue that the policies of the center voters prevail. Instead, both theory and empirical outcomes strongly support the notion that most of the distributive policies enacted by government would not be favored by sovereign majorities if the voters were directly confronted in referenda with issues involving tariffs, quotas, makework rules, barriers to entry, and government loans. The only way in which voters might adopt such policies would be through log rolling, but elections that allowed for this practice would be prohibitively expensive. The democratic political process is not, as Robert Dahl wrote more than thirty years ago, "a majestic march of median-voter majorities but rather the steady appeasement of minorities." If this is true, surely we have a major failure of the polity.

Even a cursory review of a vast and highly intricate, technical body of theory and empirical studies illustrates the extensive perversity of electoral institutions, the cornerstone of democracy. Even if voters, politicians, bureaucrats, and interest groups were all altruistic and informed, their individual policy preferences would be distorted through the workings of the basic rules themselves. These rules create winners and losers and seemingly have no particularly rational or consistent basis. Those who hope for pervasive market imperfections and failures to be properly handled and improved by government are apt to be disappointed. No set of rules can guarantee the achievement of fair and efficient policies. Nor should we assume that politicians and others are indifferent to manipulating the rules themselves; they cannot afford disinterest. Although generations of political theorists have often suspected these results, we could not place much confidence in their suspicions until formal public choice theory enabled us to better understand the actual mechanisms.

Justice and Redistribution

Continual reference has been made to the problem of equity or justice in the context of both markets and democracy but without any sustained analysis. We have alluded to the fact that although government in liberal societies is often expected to rectify "unjust" market distributions of wealth and income, such governments more often than not exacerbate inequalities. . . .

An efficient distribution of income and wealth may or may not be considered just or equitable. If, for example, most wealth were in the hands of a single family and a government proposed to take some away and redistribute it to the less well-off, such a proposal would have to be termed inefficient since the wealthy family would object. Whether a particular distribution is just depends on the criteria we employ in making such judgments. And there is no widespread agreement on the appropriate criteria.

Regardless of one's feelings about distributive outcomes, there remains the positive problem of determining how various political processes will, in fact, decide such issues. Many members of the Left are inclined to believe not only that greater equality should prevail but that under majority rule it will so prevail. We doubt that a good case can be made in defense of the prediction. Our reasoning is as follows:

Suppose that a simple majority of voters is required to pass a redistribution bill and that

100 voters, each of whom has a different income, participate in the decision. Under this arrangement the two median voters (income recipients) will decide the outcome. Those persons could support the choice of the wealthier 49 voters or the choice of the less well-off 49 voters. If they bargain, they may quickly surmise that they can command more of the redistribution by supporting the upper income group than by joining the poorer folk. Or they may reason that they will stand to gain more from the redistribution brought about by taxing the rich. In either case, the median voters will have the power to decide the outcome, and in this case they could exact an outcome that would maximize their share. According to this theory, first advanced independently by Stigler and Tullock, the middle class profits the most from the redistributive efforts of democratic governments. Whether or not the facts of empirical life support this theory is still in doubt because it is not easy to test; furthermore, it is complicated by the fact that much redistribution takes place within each income class. We do know that welfare programs for the poor cannot be adopted without the support of the middle class, which extracts its rewards by having benefits extended to its own members. More than one study has demonstrated this to be so in such fields as housing, education, transportation, environmental improvements, and health services. And, of course, much tax policy is designed to confer tax benefits on the middle class.

The point is this: The political process not only promotes inefficiency but is skewed to advance the interests of those who are better off. Those who do well in the marketplace also do well in the polity.

2b. PROPERTY RIGHTS

THE FACT THAT BILL GATES owns a lot of stuff has important normative implications. It means, for instance, that if I were to try to walk off with some of it without his permission, he could use a moderate level of physical violence to stop me. Or, more commonly, he could call the police who could either credibly threaten or administer such violence on his behalf. Even if the property in question is Bill's ten millionth loaf of bread and I am on the brink of starvation, the fact that I *need* the bread more than he does is irrelevant. Property rights, in this case, seem to trump other moral considerations such as need, desert, or merit.

How, then, can such property rights be justified? What kind of moral story can we tell that would legitimate someone claiming an object as *hers* and forcibly excluding all others from its use without her consent?

It might seem that it would be relatively easy to come up with such a story, at least when the object in question is something that someone has *made*. If I own two widgets, and put them together into some kind of super-widget, then my ownership claim to the super-widget simply follows from my ownership claims over its constituent parts—the two original widgets plus my labor.

But this story is *too* easy. For just as we may demand a story about how one came to legitimately own the super-widget, so can we ask a similar story about how one came to legitimately own its constituent parts. If the constituent parts were themselves made by somebody (or bought from somebody who made them), then we simply push our demand for justification back to *their* constituent parts. But eventually this story will have to stop. For eventually, everything that is made by someone is made out of things that were *not* made by anybody—the raw materials of the earth. And here we face an entirely different sort of problem. How can something which was once owned by nobody come to be owned by somebody?

Actually, not all philosophers would be happy with this way of stating the question. For it embodies an assumption that the raw materials of the earth are owned by nobody. But one might also plausibly hold that they are owned by *everybody*—that the raw materials of the earth are the collective property of humankind.

Whichever way we think of the raw materials of the earth, we face what has become known as the *problem of original appropriation*: how can one person or group of persons appropriate to themselves something which had not previously been appropriated? There are a variety of different responses one could make to this problem. One could, for instance, deny that *any* act of original appropriation is morally permissible, and that the earth that originally belonged to humankind in common still rightfully does. On this view, private property is a kind of theft—it is an instance of one person claiming for herself what rightfully belongs to everyone.

This claim seems more plausible for some types of property than for others. If I plant an apple tree on uncultivated and unoccupied land, and then harvest the apples myself, it seems implausible to suppose that I have stolen anything from the human race. *Land,* on the other hand, seems to pose a more difficult problem since it both exists in a fixed quantity and is not created by any human effort. One could conceivably then (as Henry George actually does) argue that the original appropriation of some property is justified while holding that the land itself belongs to humankind in common.

As the more attentive readers will have noticed, several of the examples I have given above are based on the implicit or explicit assumptions that individuals own their own labor, and that this can help them to establish ownership rights in those things they create with their labor. This assumption is generally held as part of a broader assumption known as the *self-ownership thesis*. The self-ownership thesis holds that individuals own themselves and, since their labor is a part of themselves, own their labor as well. The most famous proponent of a self-ownership thesis was Locke, who used it to justify private property by arguing that individuals can come to own previously unowned goods by "mixing their labor" with them, so long as certain conditions were met. The main contemporary defenders of the self-ownership thesis are libertarians and other defenders of private property such as Robert Nozick, but the claim is also sometimes endorsed by critics of private property. These critics agree that individuals own *themselves,* but deny that they can come to own external goods simply by mixing their labor with those goods. Philosophers who draw this line sometimes end up advocating a position known as *left-libertarianism* wherein individuals have a right to bodily integrity and the raw fruits of their labor, but have no correspondingly strong rights over external goods, which such theorists generally hold ought to be distributed in some egalitarian manner.

Of course, tracing current property claims back to a justified act of original appropriation is not the *only* way to justify property. One could also make the case for certain kinds of property on the grounds that such property promotes the value of freedom. Property—especially private property—allows individuals a domain in which they can make decisions without needing permission from others, and so provides them with the material goods necessary to carry out their plans of life. Or, one could justify property on utilitarian grounds, by arguing that private property provides individuals with an incentive to labor in a way which increases the wealth of society as a whole. What is important to note, though, is that the nature of the *moral justification* we give for property rights will affect the *form and content* those property rights ultimately have. If property rights are based on a kind of deontological respect for self-ownership, for instance, then criticisms of property rights based on consequentialist considerations (consider a city government that wishes to exercise the power of eminent domain to prevent a property owner from refusing to sell and thereby blocking a proposed development) will have considerably less traction, since rights are generally thought to trump consequences as a moral concern. On the other hand, if property rights are justified by the way in which they promote freedom, then those property rights will be probably limited in certain ways when they appear to conflict with freedom—as when they lead to monopolies or, arguably, the subjection of poor workers to wealthy capitalists.

Discussions about the origins of property rights might seem arcane. But they are of tremendous practical importance for several reasons. First, we sometimes have to make decisions about how to allocate property rights in previously unowned goods. Most of the land in the world has been claimed by now, but as of yet there is no private property on the moon. And property rights in the air, water, and ideas are becoming increasingly important. Second, we sometimes have to decide whether existing property arrangements came about in a just way, and if not what we should do about it. Many advocates for the poor in Latin America, for instance, argue that some policy of land reform is necessary to rectify for past injustices. Finally, we would like to know which existing or proposed government policies are compatible with a proper respect for property rights. In the United States, government can often seize private property which it views as "blighted" in order to turn it over to private industry so as to promote economic development. Does this count as an unjustifiable violation of individuals' property rights? What about zoning laws that prevent people from running certain kinds of business in certain neighborhoods? What about taxation? Is taxation, as Nozick and other libertarians have argued, morally on a par with forced labor? Given its connection to questions of governmental taxation and regulation, the issue of property rights will have important implications for our thinking about other issues of political philosophy—especially issues of distributive justice—as well.

Further Reading

Cohen, G. A. (1995). *Self-ownership, Freedom, and Equality*. Cambridge; New York [Paris, France]: Cambridge University Press; Maison des sciences de l'homme.

Ellickson, R. (1993). Property in Land. *Yale Law Journal, 102*, 1315–1400.

Gaus, G. F. (1990). Are Property Rights Problematic? *Monist. 0, 90*, 483–503.

Lomasky, L. E. (1987). *Persons, Rights, and the Moral Community*. Oxford: Oxford University Press.

Moore, A. D. (1998). Intangible Property: Privacy, Power, and Information Control. *American Philosophical Quarterly, 35*(4), 365–378.

Munzer, S. R. (1990). *A Theory of Property*. Cambridge: Cambridge University Press.

Narveson, J. (1999). Property Rights: Original Acquisition and Lockean Provisos. *Public Affairs Quarterly, 13*(3), 205–227.

Nozick, R. (1974). *Anarchy, State, and Utopia*. New York: Basic Books.

Schmidtz, D. (1990). When is Original Appropriation Required? *Monist. 0, 90*, 504–518.

Sreenivasan, G. (1995). *The Limits of Lockean Rights in Property*. Oxford: Oxford University Press.

Verhaegh, M. (2004). Kant and Property Rights. *Journal of Libertarian Studies, 18*(3), 11–32.

Waldron, J. (1991). *The Right to Private Property*. Oxford: Oxford University Press.

Chapter 24

John Locke

PROPERTY

John Locke (1632–1704) was an English philosopher and revolutionary who was an influential supporter of the Glorious Revolution wherein King James II was overthrown and the relative balance of power swung toward Parliament. His *Second Treatise of Civil Government* (published in 1698) was an extended critique of authoritarianism and a defense of limited, representative government. In this excerpt, Locke argues that human beings can come to acquire property rights in external goods by "mixing their labor" with those goods, so long as enough and as good is left for others.

25. Whether we consider natural *Reason*, which tells us that Men, being once born, have a right to their Preservation, and consequently to Meat and Drink, and such other things, as Nature affords for their Subsistence: Or *Revelation*, which gives us an account of those Grants God made of the World to *Adam*, and to *Noah*, and his Sons, 'tis very clear, that God, as King *David* says, *Psal. CXV.* xvi. *has given the Earth to the Children of Men*, given it to Mankind in common. But this being supposed, it seems to some a very great difficulty, how any one should ever come to have a *Property* in any thing: I will not content my self to answer, That if it be difficult to make out *Property*, upon a supposition, that God gave the World to *Adam* and his Posterity in common; it is impossible that any Man, but one universal Monarch, should have any *Property*, upon a supposition, that God gave the World to *Adam*, and his Heirs in Succession, exclusive of all the rest of his Posterity. But I shall endeavour to shew, how Men might come to have a property in several parts of that which God gave to Mankind in common, and that without any express Compact of all the Commoners.

26. God, who hath given the World to Men in common, hath also given them reason to make use of it to the best advantage of Life, and convenience. The Earth, and all that is therein, is given to Men for the Support and Comfort of their being. And though all the Fruits it naturally produces, and Beasts it feeds, belong to Mankind in common, as they are produced by the spontaneous hand of Nature; and no body has originally a private Dominion, exclusive of the rest of Mankind, in any of them, as they are thus in their natural state: yet being given for the use of Men, there must of necessity be a means *to appropriate* them some way or other before they can be of any use, or at all beneficial to any particular Man. The Fruit, or Venison, which nourishes the wild *Indian*, who knows no Inclosure, and is still a Tenant in common, must be his, and so his, i.e. a part of him, that another can no longer have any

right to it, before it can do him any good for the support of his Life.

27. Though the Earth, and all inferior Creatures be common to all Men, yet every Man has a *Property* in his own *Person*. This no Body has any Right to but himself. The *Labour* of his Body, and the *Work* of his Hands, we may say, are properly his. Whatsoever then he removes out of the State that Nature hath provided, and left it in, he hath mixed his *Labour* with, and joyned to it something that is his own, and thereby makes it his *Property*. It being by him removed from the common state Nature placed it in, hath by this *labour* something annexed to it, that excludes the common right of other Men. For this *Labour* being the unquestionable Property of the Labourer, no Man but he can have a right to what that is once joyned to, at least where there is enough, and as good left in common for others.

28. He that is nourished by the Acorns he pickt up under an Oak, or the Apples he gathered from the Trees in the Wood, has certainly appropriated them to himself. No Body can deny but the nourishment is his. I ask then, When did they begin to be his? When he digested? Or when he eat? Or when he boiled? Or when he brought them home? Or when he pickt them up? And 'tis plain, if the first gathering made them not his, nothing else could. That *labour* put a distinction between them and common. That added something to them more than Nature, the common Mother of all, had done; and so they became his private right. And will any one say he had no right to those Acorns or Apples he thus appropriated, because he had not the consent of all Mankind to make them his? Was it a Robbery thus to assume to himself what belonged to all in Common? If such a consent as that was necessary, Man had starved, notwithstanding the Plenty God had given him. We see in *Commons*, which remain so by Compact, that 'tis the taking any part of what is common, and removing it out of the state Nature leaves it in, which *begins the*

Property; without which the Common is of no use. And the taking of this or that part, does not depend on the express consent of all the Commoners. Thus the Grass my Horse has bit; the Turfs my Servant has cut; and the Ore I have digg'd in any place where I have a right to them in common with others, become my *Property*, without the assignation or consent of any body. The *labour* that was mine, removing them out of that common state they were in, hath *fixed* my *Property* in them.

29. By making an explicit consent of every Commoner, necessary to any ones appropriating to himself any part of what is given in common, Children or Servants could not cut the Meat which their Father or Master had provided for them in common, without assigning to every one his peculiar part. Though the Water running in the Fountain be every ones, yet who can doubt, but that in the Pitcher is his only who drew it out? His *labour* hath taken it out of the hands of Nature, where it was common, and belong'd equally to all her Children, and *hath* thereby *appropriated* it to himself.

30. Thus this Law of reason makes the Deer, that *Indian's* who hath killed it; 'tis allowed to be his goods who hath bestowed his labour upon it, though before, it was the common right of every one. And amongst those who are counted the Civiliz'd part of Mankind, who have made and multiplied positive Laws to determine Property, this original Law of Nature for the *beginning of* Property, in what was before common, still takes place; and by vertue thereof, what Fish any one catches in the Ocean, that great and still remaining Common of Mankind; or what Ambergriese any one takes up here, is *by* the *Labour* that removes it out of that common state Nature left it in, *made* his *Property* who takes that pains about it. And even amongst us the Hare that any one is Hunting, is thought his who pursues her during the Chase. For being a Beast that is still looked upon as common, and no Man's private Posses-

sion; whoever has imploy'd so much *labour* about any of that kind, as to find and pursue her, has thereby removed her from the state of Nature, wherein she was common, and hath *begun a Property*.

31. It will perhaps be objected to this, That if gathering the Acorns, or other Fruits of the Earth, &c. makes a right to them, then any one may *ingross* as much as he will. To which I Answer, Not so. The same Law of Nature, that does by this means give us Property, does also *bound that Property too. God has given us all things richly*, 1 Tim. vi. 17. is the Voice of Reason confirmed by Inspiration. But how far has he given it us? *To enjoy*. As much as any one can make use of to any advantage of life before it spoils; so much he may by his labour fix a Property in. Whatever is beyond this, is more than his share, and belongs to others. Nothing was made by God for Man to spoil or destroy. And thus considering the plenty of natural Provisions there was a long time in the World, and the few spenders, and to how small a part of that provision the industry of one Man could extend it self, and ingross it to the prejudice of others; especially keeping within the *bounds*, set by reason of what might serve for his *use*; there could be then little room for Quarrels or Contentions about Property so establish'd.

32. But the *chief matter of Property* being now not the Fruits of the Earth, and the Beasts that subsist on it, but the *Earth it self*; as that which takes in and carries with it all the rest: I think it is plain, that *Property* in that too is acquired as the former. *As much Land* as a Man Tills, Plants, Improves, Cultivates, and can use the Product of, so much is his *Property*. He by his Labour does, as it were, inclose it from the Common. Nor will it invalidate his right to say, Every body else has an equal Title to it; and therefore he cannot appropriate, he cannot inclose, without the Consent of all his Fellow-Commoners, all Mankind. God, when he gave the World in common to all Mankind, commanded Man also to labour, and the penury

of his Condition required it of him. God and his Reason commanded him to subdue the Earth, i.e. improve it for the benefit of Life, and therein lay out something upon it that was his own, his labour. He that in Obedience to this Command of God, subdued, tilled and sowed any part of it, thereby annexed to it something that was his *Property*, which another had no Title to, nor could without injury take from him.

33. Nor was this *appropriation* of any parcel of *Land*, by improving it, any prejudice to any other Man, since there was still enough, and as good left; and more than the yet unprovided could use. So that in effect, there was never the less left for others because of his inclosure for himself. For he that leaves as much as another can make use of, does as good as take nothing at all. No Body could think himself injur'd by the drinking of another Man, though he took a good Draught, who had a whole River of the same Water left him to quench his thirst. And the Case of Land and Water, where there is enough of both, is perfectly the same.

34. God gave the World to Men in Common; but since he gave it them for their benefit, and the greatest Conveniencies of Life they were capable to draw from it, it cannot be supposed he meant it should always remain common and uncultivated. He gave it to the use of the Industrious and Rational, (and *Labour* was to be *his* Title to it;) not to the Fancy or Covetousness of the Quarrelsom and Contentious. He that had as good left for his Improvement, as was already taken up, needed not complain, ought not to meddle with what was already improved by another's Labour: If he did, 'tis plain he desired the benefit of another's Pains, which he had no right to, and not the Ground which God had given him in common with others to labour on, and whereof there was as good left, as that already possessed, and more than he knew what to do with, or his Industry could reach to.

35. 'Tis true, in *Land* that is *common* in *England*, or any other Country, where there is Plenty of People under Government, who have Money and Commerce, no one can inclose or appropriate any part, without the consent of all his Fellow-Commoners: Because this is left common by Compact, *i.e.* by the Law of the Land, which is not to be violated. And though it be Common, in respect of some Men, it is not so to all Mankind; but is the joint property of this Countrey, or this Parish. Besides, the remainder, after such inclosure, would not be as good to the rest of the Commoners as the whole was, when they could all make use of the whole: whereas in the beginning and first peopling of the great Common of the World, it was quite otherwise. The Law Man was under, was rather for *appropriating*. God Commanded, and his Wants forced him to *labour*. That was his *Property* which could not be taken from him where-ever he had fixed it. And hence subduing or cultivating the Earth, and having Dominion, we see are joyned together. The one gave Title to the other. So that God, by commanding to subdue, gave Authority so far to *appropriate*. And the Condition of Humane Life, which requires Labour and Materials to work on, necessarily introduces *private Possessions*.

36. The measure of Property, Nature has well set, by the Extent of Mens *Labour, and the Conveniency of Life*: No Mans Labour could subdue, or appropriate all: nor could his Enjoyment consume more than a small part; so that it was impossible for any Man, this way, to intrench upon the right of another, or acquire, to himself, a Property, to the Prejudice of his Neighbour, who would still have room, for as good, and as large a Possession (after the other had taken out his) as before it was appropriated. This *measure* did confine every Man's *Possession*, to a very moderate Proportion, and such as he might appropriate to himself, without Injury to any Body in the first Ages of the World, when Men were more in danger to be lost, by wandering from their Company, in the then vast Wilderness of the Earth, than to be straitned for want of room to plant in. And the same *measure* may be allowed still, without prejudice to any Body, as full as the World seems. For supposing a Man, or Family, in the state they were, at first peopling of the World by the Children of *Adam*, or *Noah*; let him plant in some in-land, vacant places of *America*, we shall find that the *Possessions* he could make himself upon the *measures* we have given, would not be very large, nor, even to this day, prejudice the rest of Mankind, or give them reason to complain, or think themselves injured by this Man's Incroachment, though the Race of Men have now spread themselves to all the corners of the World, and do infinitely exceed the small number [which] was at the beginning. Nay, the extent of *Ground* is of so little value, *without labour*, that I have heard it affirmed, that in *Spain* it self, a Man may be permitted to plough, sow, and reap, without being disturbed, upon Land he has no other Title to, but only his making use of it. But, on the contrary, the Inhabitants think themselves beholden to him, who, by his Industry on neglected, and consequently waste Land, has increased the stock of Corn, which they wanted. But be this as it will, which I lay no stress on; This I dare boldly affirm, That the same *Rule of Propriety*, (viz.) that every Man should have as much as he could make use of, would hold still in the World, without straitning any body, since there is Land enough in the World to suffice double the Inhabitants had not the *Invention of Money*, and the tacit Agreement of Men to put a value on it, introduced (by Consent) larger Possessions, and a Right to them; which, how it has done, I shall, by and by, shew more at large.

37. This is certain, That in the beginning, before the desire of having more than Men needed, had altered the intrinsick value of things, which depends only on their usefulness to the Life of Man; or [Men] had *agreed, that a little piece of yellow Metal*, which would keep without wasting or decay, should be worth a great piece of Flesh, or a whole heap of Corn; though Men had a Right

to appropriate, by their Labour, each one to himself, as much of the things of Nature, as he could use: Yet this could not be much, nor to the Prejudice of others, where the same plenty was still left, to those who would use the same Industry. To which let me add, that he who appropriates land to himself by his labour, does not lessen but increase the common stock of mankind. For the provisions serving to the support of humane life, produced by one acre of inclosed and cultivated land, are (to speak much within compasse) ten times more, than those, which are yeilded by an acre of Land, of an equal richnesse, lyeing wast in common. And therefor he, that incloses Land and has a greater plenty of the conveniencys of life from ten acres, than he could have from an hundred left to Nature, may truly be said, to give ninety acres to Mankind. For his labour now supplys him with provisions out of ten acres, which were but the product of an hundred lying in common. I have here rated the improved land very low in making its product but as ten to one, when it is much nearer an hundred to one. For I aske whether in the wild woods and uncultivated wast of America left to Nature, without any improvement, tillage or husbandry, a thousand acres will yeild the needy and wretched inhabitants as many conveniencies of life as ten acres of equally fertile land doe in Devonshire where they are well cultivated?

Before the Appropriation of Land, he who gathered as much of the wild Fruit, killed, caught, or tamed, as many of the Beasts as he could; he that so employed his Pains about any of the spontaneous Products of Nature, as any way to alter them, from the state which Nature put them in, by placing any of his *Labour* on them, did thereby *acquire a Property in them*: But if they perished, in his Possession, without their due use; if the Fruits rotted, or the Venison putrified, before he could spend it, he offended against the common Law of Nature, and was liable to be punished; he invaded his Neighbour's share, for he had *no Right, farther than his Use* called for any of

them, and they might serve to afford him Conveniencies of Life.

38. The same *measures* governed the *Possession of Land* too: Whatsoever he tilled and reaped, laid up and made use of, before it spoiled, that was his peculiar Right; whatsoever he enclosed, and could feed, and make use of, the Cattle and Product was also his. But if either the Grass of his Inclosure rotted on the Ground, or the Fruit of his planting perished without gathering, and laying up, this part of the Earth, notwithstanding his Inclosure, was still to be looked on as Waste, and might be the Possession of any other. Thus, at the beginning, *Cain* might take as much Ground as he could till, and make it his own Land, and yet leave enough to *Abel's* Sheep to feed on; a few Acres would serve for both their Possessions. But as Families increased, and Industry inlarged their Stocks, their *Possessions inlarged* with the need of them; but yet it was commonly *without any fixed property in the ground* they made use of, till they incorporated, settled themselves together, and built Cities, and then, by consent, they came in time, to set out the *bounds of their distinct Territories*, and agree on limits between them and their Neighbours, and by Laws within themselves, settled the *Properties* of those of the same Society. For we see, that in that part of the World which was first inhabited, and therefore like to be best peopled, even as low down as *Abraham's* time, they wandred with their Flocks, and their Herds, which was their substance, freely up and down; and this *Abraham* did, in a Country where he was a Stranger. Whence it is plain, that at least, a great part of the *Land lay in common*; that the Inhabitants valued it not, nor claimed Property in any more than they made use of. But when there was not room enough in the same place, for their Herds to feed together, they, by consent, as *Abraham* and *Lot* did, Gen. xiii. 5. separated and inlarged their pasture, where it best liked them. And for the same Reason *Esau* went from his Father, and his Brother, and planted in *Mount Seir*, Gen. xxxvi. 6.

39. And thus, without supposing any private Dominion, and property in *Adam*, over all the World, exclusive of all other Men, which can no way be proved, nor any ones Property be made out from it; but supposing the *World* given as it was to the Children of Men *in common*, we see how *labour* could make Men distinct titles to several parcels of it, for their private uses; wherein there could be no doubt of Right, no room for quarrel.

40. Nor is it so strange, as perhaps before consideration it may appear, that the *Property of labour* should be able to over-ballance the Community of Land. For 'tis *Labour* indeed that *puts the difference of value* on every thing; and let any one consider, what the difference is between an Acre of Land planted with Tobacco, or Sugar, sown with Wheat or Barley; and an Acre of the same Land lying in common, without any Husbandry upon it, and he will find, that the improvement of *labour makes* the far greater part of *the value*. I think it will be but a very modest Computation to say, that of the *Products* of the Earth useful to the Life of Man $\frac{9}{10}$ are the *effects of labour*: nay, if we will rightly estimate things as they come to our use, and cast up the several Expenses about them, what in them is purely owing to *Nature*, and what to *labour*, we shall find, that in most of them $\frac{99}{100}$ are wholly to be put on the account of *labour*.

41. There cannot be a clearer demonstration of any thing, than several Nations of the *Americans* are of this, who are rich in Land, and poor in all the Comforts of Life; whom Nature having furnished as liberally as any other people, with the materials of Plenty, *i.e.* a fruitful Soil, apt to produce in abundance, what might serve for food, rayment, and delight; yet for want of improving it by labour, have not one hundredth part of the Conveniencies we enjoy: And a King of a large fruitful Territory there feeds, lodges, and is clad worse than a day Labourer in *England*.

42. To make this a little clearer, let us but trace some of the ordinary provisions of Life, through their several progresses, before they come to our use, and see how much they receive of their *value from Humane Industry*. Bread, Wine and Cloth, are things of daily use, and great plenty, yet notwithstanding, Acorns, Water, and Leaves, or Skins, must be our Bread, Drink and Clothing, did not labour furnish us with these more useful Commodities. For whatever *Bread* is more worth than Acorns, *Wine* than Water, and *Cloth* or *Silk* than Leaves, Skins, or Moss, that is wholly *owing to* labour and industry. The one of these being the Food and Rayment which unassisted Nature furnishes us with; the other provisions which our industry and pains prepare for us, which how much they exceed the other in value, when any one hath computed, he will then see, how much *labour makes the far greatest part of the value* of things, we enjoy in this World: And the ground which produces the materials, is scarce to be reckon'd in, as any, or at most, but a very small, part of it; So little, that even amongst us, Land that is left wholly to Nature, that hath no improvement of Pasturage, Tillage, or Planting, is called, as indeed it is, *wast*; and we shall find the benefit of it amount to little more than nothing. This shews, how much numbers of men are to be preferd to largenesse of dominions, and that the increase of lands and the right imploying of them is the great art of government. And that Prince who shall be so wise and godlike as by established laws of liberty to secure protection and incouragement to the honest industry of Mankind against the oppression of power and narrownesse of Party will quickly be too hard for his neighbours. But this bye the bye. To return to the argument in hand.

43. An Acre of Land that bears here Twenty Bushels of Wheat, and another in *America*, which, with the same Husbandry, would do the like, are without doubt, of the same natural, intrinsick Value. But yet the Benefit Mankind receives from the one, in a Year, is worth 5 *l.* and from the other

possibly not worth a Penny, if all the Profit an *Indian* received from it were to be valued, and sold here; at least, I may truly say, not $\frac{1}{1000}$. 'Tis *Labour* then which *puts the greatest part of Value upon Land*, without which it would scarcely be worth any thing: 'tis to that we owe the greatest part of all its useful Products: for all that the Straw, Bran, Bread, of that Acre of Wheat, is more worth than the Product of an Acre of as good Land, which lies wast, is all the Effect of Labour. For 'tis not barely the Plough-man's Pains, the Reaper's and Thresher's Toil, and the Bakers Sweat, is to be counted into the *Bread* we eat; the Labour of those who broke the Oxen, who digged and wrought the Iron and Stones, who felled and framed the Timber imployed about the Plough, Mill, Oven, or any other Utensils, which are a vast Number, requisite to this Corn, from its being seed to be sown to its being made Bread, must all be *charged on the* account of *Labour*, and received as an effect of that: Nature and the Earth furnished only the almost worthless Materials, as in themselves. 'Twould be a strange *Catalogue of things, that Industry provided and made use of*, about every *Loaf of Bread*, before it came to our use, if we could trace them; Iron, Wood, Leather, Bark, Timber, Stone, Bricks, Coals, Lime, Cloth, Dying-Drugs, Pitch, Tar, Masts, Ropes, and all the Materials made use of in the Ship, that brought any of the Commodities made use of by any of the Workmen, to any part of the Work, all which, 'twould be almost impossible, at least too long, to reckon up.

44. From all which it is evident, that though the things of Nature are given in common, yet Man (by being Master of himself, and *Proprietor of his own Person*, and the actions or *Labour* of it) had still in himself *the great Foundation of Property*; and that which made up the great part of what he applied to the Support or Comfort of his being, when Invention and Arts had improved the conveniencies of Life, was perfectly his own, and did not belong in common to others.

45. Thus *Labour*, in the Beginning, *gave a Right of Property*, where-ever any one was pleased to imploy it, upon what was common, which remained, a long while, the far greater part, and is yet more than Mankind makes use of. Men, at first, for the most part, contented themselves with what un-assisted Nature Offered to their Necessities: and though afterwards, in some parts of the World, (where the Increase of People and Stock, with the *Use of Money*) had made Land scarce, and so of some Value, the several *Communities* settled the Bounds of their distinct Territories, and by Laws within themselves, regulated the Properties of the private Men of their Society, and so, *by Compact and Agreement, settled the Property* which Labour and Industry began; and the Leagues that have been made between several States and Kingdoms, either expressly or tacitly disowning all Claim and Right to the Land in the others Possession, have, by common Consent, given up their Pretences to their natural common Right, which originally they had to those Countries, and so have, by *positive agreement, settled a* Property amongst themselves, in distinct Parts and parcels of the Earth: yet there are still *great Tracts of Ground* to be found, which (the Inhabitants thereof not having joyned with the rest of Mankind, in the consent of the Use of their common Money) *lie waste*, and are more than the People, who dwell on it, do, or can make use of, and so still lie in common. Tho' this can scarce happen amongst that part of Mankind, that have consented to the use of Money.

46. The greatest part of *things really useful* to the Life of Man, and such as the necessity of subsisting made the first Commoners of the World look after, as it doth the *Americans* now, *are* generally *things of short duration*; such as, if they are not consumed by use, will decay and perish of themselves: Gold, Silver, and Diamonds, are things, that Fancy or Agreement hath put the Value on, more then real Use, and the necessary Support of Life. Now of those good things which Nature hath provided in common, every one had a Right

(as hath been said) to as much as he could use, and had a Property in all that he could affect with his Labour: all that his Industry could extend to, to alter from the State Nature had put it in, was his. He that *gathered* a Hundred Bushels of Acorns or Apples, had thereby a *Property* in them; they were his Goods as soon as gathered. He was only to look that he used them before they spoiled; else he took more than his share, and robb'd others. And indeed it was a foolish thing, as well as dishonest, to hoard up more than he could make use of. If he gave away a part to any body else, so that it perished not uselesly in his Possession, these he also made use of. And if he also bartered away Plumbs that would have rotted in a Week, for Nuts that would last good for his eating a whole Year, he did no injury; he wasted not the common Stock; destroyed no part of the portion of Goods that belonged to others, so long as nothing perished uselesly in his hands. Again, if he would give us Nuts for a piece of Metal, pleased with its colour; or exchanged his Sheep for Shells, or Wool for a sparkling Pebble or a Diamond, and keep those by him all his Life, he invaded not the Right of others, he might heap up as much of these durable things as he pleased; the *exceeding of the bounds of his* just Property not lying in the largeness of his Possession, but the perishing of any thing uselesly in it.

47. And thus *came in the use of Money*, some lasting thing that Men might keep without spoiling, and that by mutual consent Men would take in exchange for the truly useful, but perishable Supports of Life.

48. And as different degrees of Industry were apt to give Men Possessions in different Proportions, so this *Invention of Money* gave them the opportunity to continue to enlarge them. For supposing an Island, separated from all possible Commerce with the rest of the World, wherein there were but a hundred Families, but there were Sheep, Horses and Cows, with other useful Animals, wholsome Fruits, and Land enough for Corn for a hundred thousand times as many, but nothing in the Island, either because of its Commonness, or Perishableness, fit to supply the place of *Money:* What reason could any one have there to enlarge his Possessions beyond the use of his Family, and a plentiful supply to its Consumption, either in what their own Industry produced, or they could barter for like perishable, useful Commodities, with others? Where there is not something both lasting and scarce, and so valuable to be hoarded up, there Men will not be apt to enlarge their *Possessions of Land*, were it never so rich, never so free for them to take. For I ask, What would a Man value Ten Thousand, or an Hundred Thousand Acres of excellent *Land*, ready cultivated, and well stocked too with Cattle, in the middle of the in-land Parts of *America*, where he had no hopes of Commerce with other Parts of the World, to draw *Money* to him by the Sale of the Product? It would not be worth the inclosing, and we should see him give up again to the wild Common of Nature, whatever was more than would supply the Conveniencies of Life to be had there for him and his Family.

49. Thus in the beginning all the World was *America*, and more so than that is now; for no such thing as *Money* was any where known. Find out something that hath the *Use and Value of Money* amongst his Neighbours, you shall see the same Man will begin presently to *enlarge* his *Possessions*.

50. But since Gold and Silver, being little useful to the Life of Man in proportion to Food, Rayment, and Carriage, has its *value* only from the consent of Men, whereof Labour yet makes, in great part, *the measure*, it is plain, that Men have agreed to disproportionate and unequal Possession of the Earth, they having by a tacit and voluntary consent found out a way, how a man may fairly possess more land than he himself can use the product of, by receiving in exchange for the overplus, Gold and Silver, which may be hoarded up without injury to any one, these metalls

not spoileing or decaying in the hands of the possessor. This partage of things, in an inequality of private possessions, men have made practicable out of the bounds of Societie, and without compact, only by putting a value on gold and silver and tacitly agreeing in the use of Money. For in Governments the Laws regulate the right of property, and the possession of land is determined by positive constitutions.

51. And thus, I think, it is very easie to conceive without any difficulty, *how Labour could at first begin a title of Property* in the common things of Nature, and how the spending it upon our uses bounded it. So that there could then be no reason of quarrelling about Title, nor any doubt about the largeness of Possession it gave. Right and conveniency went together; for as a Man had a Right to all he could imploy his Labour upon, so he had no temptation to labour for more than he could make use of. This left no room for Controversie about the Title, nor for Incroachment on the Right of others; what Portion a Man carved to himself, was easily seen; and it was useless as well as dishonest to carve himself too much, or take more than he needed.

Chapter 25

Henry George

THE INJUSTICE OF PRIVATE PROPERTY IN LAND

Henry George (1839–1897) was an American political economist best known for his support of the Single Tax (land rent) movement. In this excerpt, taken from his *Progress and Poverty* (1879), George argues that while people fully own themselves and the products of their labor, there are no just grounds for full private property in natural resources, and hence government is justified in extracting from the current holders of resources a tax to be redistributed to society as a whole.

Justice is a relation of congruity which really subsists between two things. This relation is always the same, whatever being considers it, whether it be God, or an angel, or lastly a man.

Montesquieu

The Injustice of Private Property in Land

When it is proposed to abolish private property in land the first question that will arise is that of justice. Though often warped by habit, superstition, and selfishness into the most distorted forms, the sentiment of justice is yet fundamental to the human mind, and whatever dispute arouses the passions of men, the conflict is sure to rage, not so much as to the question 'Is it wise?' as to the question 'Is it right?'

This tendency of popular discussions to take an ethical form has a cause. It springs from a law of the human mind; it rests upon a vague and instinctive recognition of what is probably the deepest truth we can grasp. That alone is wise which is just; that alone is enduring which is right. In the narrow scale of individual actions and individual life this truth may be often obscured, but in the wider field of national life it everywhere stands out.

I bow to this arbitrament, and accept this test. If our inquiry into the cause which makes low wages and pauperism the accompaniments of material progress has led us to a correct conclusion, it will bear translation from terms of political economy into terms of ethics, and as the source of social evils show a wrong. If it will not do this, it is disproved. If it will do this, it is proved by the final decision. If private property in land be just, then is the remedy I propose a false one; if, on the contrary, private property in land be unjust, then is this remedy the true one.

What constitutes the rightful basis of property? What is it that enables a man justly to say of a thing, 'It is mine!' From what springs the sentiment which acknowledges his exclusive right as against all the world? Is it not, primarily, the right of a man to himself, to the use of his own powers, to the enjoyment of the fruits of his own exertions? Is it not this individual right, which springs from and is testified to by the natural facts of individual organization – the fact that each particular pair of hands obey a particular brain and are related to a particular stomach; the fact that each man is a definite, coherent, independent whole – which alone justifies individual ownership? As a man belongs to himself, so his labor when put in concrete form belongs to him.

And for this reason, that which a man makes or produces is his own, as against all the world – to enjoy or to destroy, to use, to exchange, or to give. No one else can rightfully claim it, and his exclusive right to it involves no wrong to any one else. Thus there is to everything produced by human exertion a clear and indisputable title to exclusive possession and enjoyment, which is perfectly consistent with justice, as it descends from the original producer, in whom it vested by natural law. The pen with which I am writing is justly mine. No other human being can rightfully lay claim to it, for in me is the title of the producers who made it. It has become mine, because transferred to me by the stationer, to whom it was transferred by the importer, who obtained the exclusive right to it by transfer from the manufacturer, in whom, by the same process of purchase, vested the rights of those who dug the material from the ground and shaped it into a pen. Thus, my exclusive right of ownership in the pen springs from the natural right of the individual to the use of his own faculties.

Now, this is not only the original source from which all ideas of exclusive ownership arise – as is evident from the natural tendency of the mind to revert to it when the idea of exclusive ownership is questioned, and the manner in which social relations develop – but it is necessarily the only source. There can be to the ownership of anything no rightful title which is not derived from the title of the producer and does not rest upon the natural right of the man to himself.

There can be no other rightful title, because (1st) there is no other natural right from which any other title can be derived, and (2nd) because the recognition of any other title is inconsistent with and destructive of this.

For (1st) what other right exists from which the right to the exclusive possession of anything can be derived, save the right of a man to himself? With what other power is man by nature clothed, save the power of exerting his own faculties? How can he in any other way act upon or affect material things or other men? Paralyze the motor nerves, and your man has no more external influence or power than a log or stone. From what else, then, can the right of possessing and controlling things be derived? If it spring not from man himself, from what can it spring? Nature acknowledges no ownership or control in man save as the result of exertion. In no other way can her treasures be drawn forth, her powers directed, or her forces utilized or controlled. She makes no discriminations among men, but is to all absolutely impartial. She knows no distinction between master and slave, king and subject, saint and sinner. All men to her stand upon an equal footing and have equal rights. She recognizes no claim but that of labor, and recognizes that without respect to the claimant. If a pirate spread his sails, the wind will fill them as well as it will fill those of a peaceful merchantman or missionary bark; if a king and a common man be thrown overboard, neither can keep his head above water except by swimming; birds will not come to be shot by the proprietor of the soil any quicker than they will come to be shot by the poacher; fish will bite or will not bite at a book in utter disregard as to whether it is offered them by a good little boy who goes to Sunday school, or a bad little boy who plays truant; grain will grow only as the ground is prepared and the seed is sown; it is only at the call of labor that ore can be raised from the mine; the sun shines and the rain falls, alike upon just and unjust. The laws of nature are the decrees of the Creator. There is written in them no recognition of any right save that of labor; and in them is written broadly and clearly the equal right of all men to the use and enjoyment of nature; to apply to her by their exertions, and to receive and possess her reward. Hence, as nature gives only to labor, the exertion of labor in production is the only title to exclusive possession.

(2nd) This right of ownership that springs from labor excludes the possibility of any other right of ownership. If a man be rightfully entitled to the produce of his labor, then no one can be rightfully entitled to the ownership of anything which is not the produce of his labor, or the labor of some one else from whom the right has passed to him. If production give to the producer the right to exclusive possession and enjoyment, there can rightfully be no exclusive possession and enjoyment of anything not the production of labor, and the recognition of private property in land is a wrong. For the right to the producer of labor cannot be enjoyed without the right to the free use of the opportunities offered by nature, and to admit the right of property in these is to deny the right of property in the produce of labor. When nonproducers can claim as rent a portion of the wealth created by producers, the right of the producers to the fruits of their labor is to that extent denied.

There is no escape from this position. To affirm that a man can rightfully claim exclusive ownership in his own labor when embodied in material things, is to deny that any one can rightfully claim exclusive ownership in land. To affirm the rightfulness of property in land, is to affirm a claim which has no warrant in nature, as against a claim founded in the organization of man and the laws of the material universe.

What most prevents the realization of the injustice of private property in land is the habit of including all the things that are made the subject of ownership in one category, as property, or, if any distinction is made, drawing the line, according to the unphilosophical distinction of the lawyers, between personal property and real estate, or things movable and things immovable.

The real and natural distinction is between things which are the produce of labor and things which are the gratuitous offerings of nature; or, to adopt the terms of political economy between wealth and land.

These two classes of things are in essence and relations widely different, and to class them together as property is to confuse all thought when we come to consider the justice of the injustice, the right or the wrong of property.

A house and the lot on which it stands are alike property, as being the subject of ownership, and are alike classed by the lawyers as real estate. Yet in nature and relations they differ widely. The one is produced by human labor, and belongs to the class in political economy styled wealth. The other is a part of nature, and belongs to the class in political economy styled land.

The essential character of the one class of things is that they embody labor, are brought into being by human exertion, their existence or nonexistence, their increases or diminution, depending on man. The essential character of the other class of things is that they do not embody labor, and exist irrespective of human exertion and irrespective of man; they are the field or environment in which man finds himself; the storehouse from which his needs must be supplied, the raw material upon which and the forces with which alone his labor can act.

The moment this distinction is realized, that moment is it seen that the sanction which natural justice gives to one species of property is denied to the other; that the rightfulness which attaches to individual property in the produce of labor implies the wrongfulness of individual property in land; that, whereas the recognition of the one places all men upon equal terms, securing to each the due reward of his labor, the recognition of the other is the denial of the equal rights of men, permitting those who do not labor to take the natural reward of those who do.

Whatever may be said for the institution of

private property in land, it is therefore plain that it cannot be defended on the score of justice.

The equal right of all men to the use of land is as clear as their equal right to breathe the air – it is a right proclaimed by the fact of their existence. For we cannot suppose that some men have a right to be in this world and others no right.

If we are all here by the equal permission of the Creator, we are all here with an equal title to the enjoyment of his bounty – with an equal right to the use of all that nature so impartially offers. This is a right which is natural and inalienable; it is a right which vests in every human being as he enters the world and which during his continuance in the world can be limited only by the equal rights of others. There is in nature no such thing as a fee simple in land. There is no earth no power which can rightfully make a grant of exclusive ownership in land. If all existing men were to unite to grant away their equal rights, they could not grant away the right of those who follow them. For what are we but tenants for a day? Have we made the earth, that we should determine the rights of those who after us shall tenant it in their turn? The Almighty, who created the earth for man and man for the earth, has entailed it upon all the generations of the children of men by a decree written upon the constitution of all things – a decree which no human action can bar and no prescription determine. Let the parchments be ever so many, or possession ever so long, natural justice can recognize no right in one man to the possession and enjoyment of land that is not equally the right of all his fellows. Though his titles have been acquiesced in by generation after generation, to the landed estates of the Duke of Westminster the poorest child that is born in London today has as much right as has his eldest son. Though the sovereign people of the state of New York consent to the landed possessions of the Astors, the puniest infant that comes wailing into the world in the squalidest room of the most miserable tenement house, becomes at that moment seized of an equal right with the millionaires. And it is robbed if the right is denied.

Our previous conclusions, irresistible in themselves, thus stand approved by the highest and final test. Translated from terms of political economy into terms of ethics they show a wrong as the source of the evils which increase as material progress goes on.

The masses of men, who in the midst of abundance suffer want; who, clothed with political freedom, are condemned to the wages of slavery; to whose toil laborsaving inventions bring no relief, but rather seem to rob them of a privilege, instinctively feel that 'there is something wrong.' And they are right.

The wide spreading social evils which everywhere oppress men amid an advancing civilization spring from a great primary wrong – the appropriation, as the exclusive property of some men, of the land on which and from which all must live. From this fundamental injustice flow all the injustices which distort and endanger modern development, which condemn the producer of wealth to poverty and pamper the nonproducer in luxury, which rear the tenement house with the palace, plant the brothel behind the church, and compel us to build prisons as we open new schools.

There is nothing strange or inexplicable in the phenomena that are now perplexing the world. It is not that material progress is not in itself a good; it is not that nature has called into being children for whom she has failed to provide; it is not that the Creator has left on natural laws a taint of injustice at which even the human mind revolts, that material progress brings such bitter fruits. That amid our highest civilization men faint and die with want is not due to the niggardliness of nature, but to the injustice of man. Vice and misery; poverty and pauperism, are not the legitimate results of increase of population and industrial development; they only follow increase of population and industrial development because land is treated as private property – they are the direct and necessary results of the violation of the supreme law of justice, involved in giving to some men the exclusive possession of that which nature provides for all men.

The recognition of individual proprietorship of land is the denial of the natural rights of other individuals – it is a wrong which must show itself in the inequitable division of wealth. For as labor cannot produce without the use of land, the denial of the equal right to the use of land is necessarily the denial of the right of labor to its own produce. If one man can command the land upon which others must labor, he can appropriate the produce of their labor as the price of his permission to labor. The fundamental law of nature, that her enjoyment by man shall be consequent upon his exertion, is thus violated. The one receives without producing; the others produce without receiving. The one is unjustly relative, capability of land that determines its value. No matter what may be its intrinsic qualities, land that is no better than other land which may be had for the using can have no value. And the value of land always measures the difference between it and the best land that may be had for the using. Thus, the value of land expresses in exact and tangible form the right of the community in land held by an individual; and rent expresses the exact amount which the individual should pay to the community to satisfy the equal rights of all other members of the community. Thus, if we concede to priority of possession the undisturbed use of land, confiscating rent for the benefit of the community, we reconcile the fixity of tenure which is necessary for improvement with a full and complete recognition of the equal rights of all to the use of land.

As for the deduction of a complete and exclusive individual right to land from priority of occupation, that is, if possible, the most absurd ground on which landownership can be defended. Priority of occupation give exclusive and perpetual title to the surface of a globe on which, in the order of nature, countless generations succeed each other! Had the men of the last generation any better right to the use of this world than we of this? or the men of a hundred years ago? Or of a thousand years ago? Had the mound builders, or the cave dwellers, the contemporaries of the mastodon and the three-toed horse, or the generations still further back, who, in dim æons that we can think of only as geologic periods, followed each other on the earth we now tenant for our little day?

Has the first comer at a banquet the right to turn back all the chairs and claim that none of the other guests shall partake of the food provided, except as they make terms with him? Does the first man who presents a ticket at the door of a theater, and passes in, acquire by his priority the right to shut the doors and have the performance go on for him alone? Does the first passenger who enters a railroad car obtain the right to scatter his baggage over all the seats and compel the passengers who come in after him to stand up?

The cases are perfectly analogous. We arrive and we depart, guests at a banquet continually spread, spectators and participants in an entertainment where there is room for all who come; passengers from station to station, on an orb that whirls through space – our rights to take and possess cannot be exclusive; they must be bounded everywhere by the equal rights of others. Just as the passenger in a railroad car may spread himself and his baggage over as many seats as he pleases, until other passengers come in, so may a settler take and use as much land as he chooses, until it is needed by others—a fact which is shown by the land acquiring a value – when his right must be curtailed by the equal rights of the others, and no priority of appropriation can give a right which will bar these equal rights of others. If this were not the case, then by priority of appropriation one man could acquire and could transmit to whom he pleased, not merely the exclusive right to 160 acres, or to 640 acres, but to a whole township, a whole state, a whole continent.

And to this manifest absurdity does the recognition of individual right to land come when carried to its ultimate – that any one human being, could he concentrate in himself the individual rights to the land of any country, could expel therefrom all the rest of its inhabitants; and could he thus concentrate the individual rights to the whole surface of the globe, he alone of all the teeming population of the earth would have the right to live.

And what upon this supposition would occur is, upon a smaller scale, realized in actual fact. The territorial lords of Great Britain, to whom grants of land have given the 'white parasols and elephants mad with pride,' have over and over again expelled from large districts the native population, whose ancestors had lived on the land from immemorial times – driven them off to emigrate, to become paupers, or to starve. And on uncultivated tracts of land in the new state of California may be seen the blackened chimneys of homes from which settlers have been driven by before of laws which ignore natural right, and great stretches of land which might be populous are desolate, because the recognition of exclusive ownership has put it in the power of one human creature to forbid his fellows from using it. The comparative handful of proprietors who own the surface of the British Islands would be doing only what English law gives them full power to do, and what many of them have done on a smaller scale already, were they to exclude the millions of British people from their native islands. And such an exclusion, by which a few hundred thousand should at will banish thirty million people from their native country, while it would be more striking, would not be a whit more repugnant to natural right than the spectacle now presented, of the vast body of the British people being compelled to pay such enormous sums to a few of their number for the privilege of being permitted to live upon and use the land which they so fondly call their own; which is endeared to them by memories so tender and so glorious, and for which they are held in duty bound, if need be, to spill their blood and lay down their lives.

I refer only to the British Islands, because, landownership being more concentrated there, they afford a more striking illustration of what private property in land necessarily involves. 'To whomsoever the soil at any time belongs, to him belong the fruits of it,' is a truth that becomes more and more apparent as population becomes denser and invention and improvement add to productive power; but it is everywhere a truth – as much in our new States as in the British Islands or by the banks of the Indus.

Claim of Landowners to Compensation

The truth is, and from this truth there can be no escape, that there is and can be no just title to an exclusive possession of the soil, and that private property in land is a bold, bare, enormous wrong, like that of chattel slavery.

The majority of men in civilized communities do not recognize this, simply because the majority of men do not think. With them whatever is, is right, until its wrongfulness has been frequently pointed out, and in general they are ready to crucify whoever first attempts this.

But it is impossible for any one to study political economy, even as at present taught, or to think at all upon the production and distribution of wealth, without seeing that property in land differs essentially from property in things of human production, and that it has no warrant in abstract justice.

This is admitted, either expressly or tacitly, in every standard work on political economy, but in general merely by vague admission or omission. Attention is in general called away from the truth, as a lecturer on moral philosophy in a slaveholding community might call away attention from too close a consideration of the natural rights of men, and private property in land is accepted without comment, as an existing fact, or is assumed to be necessary to the proper use of land and the existence of the civilized state.

The examination through which we have

passed has proved conclusively that private property in land cannot be justified on the ground of utility – that, on the contrary, it is the great cause to which are to be traced the poverty, misery, and degradation, the social disease and the political weakness which are showing themselves so menacingly amid advancing civilization. Expediency, therefore, joins justice in demanding that we abolish it.

When expediency thus joins justice in demanding that we abolish an institution that has no broader base or stronger ground than a mere municipal regulation, what reason can there be for hesitation?

The consideration that seems to cause hesitation, even on the part of those who see clearly that land by right is common property, is the idea that having permitted land to be treated as private property for so long, we should in abolishing it be doing a wrong to those who have been suffered to base their calculations upon its permanence; that having permitted land to be held as rightful property, we should by the resumption of common rights be doing injustice to those who have purchased it with what was unquestionably their rightful property. Thus, it is held that if we abolish private property in land, justice requires that we should fully compensate those who now possess it, as the British Government, in abolishing the purchase and sale of military commissions, felt itself bound to compensate those who held commissions which they had purchased in the belief that they could sell them again, or as in abolishing slavery in the British West Indies $100,000,000 was paid the slaveholders.

Even Herbert Spencer, who in his 'Social Statics' has so clearly demonstrated the invalidity of every title by which the exclusive possession of land is claimed, gives countenance to this idea (though it seems to me inconsistently) by declaring that justly to estimate and liquidate the claims of the present landholders 'who have either by their own acts or by the acts of their ancestors given for their estates equivalents of honestly earned wealth,' to be 'one of the most intricate problems society will one day have to solve.'

It is this idea that suggests the proposition, which finds advocates in Great Britain, that the government shall purchase at its market price the individual proprietorship of the land of the country, and it was this idea which led John Stuart Mill, although clearly perceiving the essential injustice of private property in land, to advocate, not a full resumption of the land, but only a resumption of accuring advantages in the future. His plan was that a fair and even liberal estimate should be made of the market value of all the land in the kingdom, and that future additions to that value, not due to the improvements of the proprietor, should be taken by the state.

To say nothing of the practical difficulties which such cumbrous plans involve, in the extension of the functions of government which they would require and the corruption they would beget, their inherent and essential defect lies in the impossibility of bridging over by any compromise the radical difference between wrong and right. Just in proportion as the interests of the landholders are conserved, just in that proportion must general interests and general rights be disregarded, and if landholders are to lose nothing of their special privileges, the people at large can gain nothing. To buy up individual property rights would merely be to give the landholders in another form a claim of the same kind and amount that their possession of land now gives them; it would be to raise for them by taxation the same proportion of the earnings of labor and capital that they are now enabled to appropriate in rent. Their unjust advantage would be preserved and the unjust disadvantage of the non-landholders would be continued. To be sure there would be a gain to the people at large when the advance of rents had made the amount which the landholders would take under the present system greater than the interest upon the purchase price of the land at present rates, but this would be only a future gain, and in the meanwhile there would not only be no relief, but the burden imposed upon labor and capital for the benefit of the present landholders would be much increased. For one of the elements in the present market value of land is the expectation of future increase of value, and thus, to buy the lands at market rates and pay interest upon the purchase money would be to saddle producers not only with the payment of actual rent, but with the payment in full of speculative rent. Or to put it in another way: The land would be purchased at prices calculated upon a lower than the ordinary rate of interest (for the prospective increase in land values always makes the market price of land much greater than would be the price of anything else yielding the same present return), and interest upon the purchase money would be paid at the ordinary rate. Thus, not only all that the land yields them now would have to be paid the landowners, but a considerably larger amount. It would be, virtually, the state taking a perpetual lease from the present landholders at a considerable advance in rent over what they now receive. For the present the state would merely become the agent of the landholders in the collection of their rents, and would have to pay over to them not only what they received, but considerably more.

Mr. Mill's plan for nationalizing the future 'unearned increase in the value of land,' by fixing the present market value of all lands and appropriating to the state future increase in value, would not add to the injustice of the present distribution of wealth, but it would not remedy it. Further speculative advance of rent would cease, and in the future the people at large would gain the difference between the increase of rent and the amount at which that increase was estimated in fixing the present value of land, in which, of course, prospective, as well as present, value is an element. But it would leave, for all the future, one class in possession of the enormous advantage over others which they now have. All that can be said of this plan is, that it might be better than nothing.

Such inefficient and impracticable schemes may do to talk about, where any proposition more efficacious would not at present be entertained, and their discussion is a hopeful sign, as it shows the entrance of the thin end of the wedge of truth. Justice in men's mouths is cringingly humble when she first begins a protest against a time-honored wrong, and we of the English-speaking nations still wear the collar of the Saxon thrall, and have been educated to look upon the 'vested rights' of landowners with all the superstitious reverence that ancient Egyptians looked upon the crocodile. But when the times are ripe for them, ideas grow, even though insignificant in their first appearance. One day, the Third Estate covered their heads when the king put on his hat. A little while thereafter, and the head of a son of St. Louis rolled from the scaffold. The antislavery movement in the United States commenced with talk of compensating owners, but when four millions of slaves were emancipated, the owners got no compensation, not did they clamor for any. And by the time the people of any such country as England or the United States are sufficiently aroused to the injustice and disadvantages of individual ownership of land to induce them to attempt its nationalization, they will be sufficiently aroused to nationalize it in a much more direct and easy way than by purchase. They will not trouble themselves about compensating the proprietors of land.

Nor is it right that there should be any concern about the proprietors of land. That such a man as John Stuart Mill should have attached so much importance to the compensation of landowners as to have urged the confiscation merely of the future increase in rent, is explainable only by his acquiescence in the current doctrines that wages are drawn from capital and that population constantly tends to press upon subsistence. These blinded him as to the full effects of the private appropriation of land. He saw that 'the claim of the landholder is altogether subordinate to the general policy of the state,' and that 'when private property in land is not expedient, it is unjust,' but, entangled in the toils of the Malthusian doctrine, he attributed, as he expressly states in a paragraph I have previously quoted, the want and suffering that he saw around him to 'the niggardliness of nature, not to the injustice of man,' and thus to him the nationalization of land seemed comparatively a little thing, that could accomplish nothing toward the eradication of pauperism and the abolition of want – ends that could be reached only as men learned to repress a natural instinct. Great as he was and pure as he was – warm heart and noble mind – he yet never saw the true harmony of economic laws, nor realized how from this one great fundamental wrong flow want and misery, and vice and shame. Else he could never had written this sentence: 'The land of Ireland, the land of every country, belongs to the people of that country. The individuals called landowners have no right in morality and justice to anything but the rent, or compensation for its salable value.'

In the name of the Prophet – figs! If the land of any country belong to the people of that country, what right, in morality and justice, have the individuals called landowners to the rent? If the land belong to the people, why in the name of morality and justice should the people pay its salable value for their own?

Herbert Spencer says: 'Had we to deal with the parties who originally robbed the human race of its heritage, we might make short work of the matter.' Why not make short work of the matter anyhow? For this robbery is not like the robbery of a horse or a sum of money, that ceases with the act. It is a fresh and continuous robbery, that goes on every day and every hour. It is not from the produce of the past that rent is drawn; it is from the produce of the present. It is a toll levied upon labor constantly and continuously. Every blow of the hammer, every stroke of the pick, every thrust of the shuttle, every throb of the steam engine, pays it tribute. It levies upon the earnings of the men who, deep under

ground, risk their lives, and of those who over white surges hang to reeling masts; it claims the just reward of the capitalist and the fruits of the inventor's patient effort; it takes little children from play and from school, and compels them to work before their bones are hard or their muscles are firm; it robs the shivering of warmth; the hungry, of food; the sick, of medicine; the anxious, of peace. it debases, and embrutes, and embitters. It crowds families of eight and ten into a single squalid room; it herds like swine agricultural gangs of boys and girls; it fills the gin palace and groggery with those who have no comfort in their homes; it makes lads who might be useful men candidates for prisons and penitentiaries; it fills brothels with girls who might have known the pure joy of motherhood; it sends greed and all evil passions prowling through society as a hard winter drives the wolves to the abodes of men; it darkens faith in the human soul, and across the reflection of a just and merciful Creator draws the veil of a hard, and blind, and cruel fate!

It is not merely a robbery in the past; it is a robbery in the present – a robbery that deprives of their birthright the infants that are now coming into the world! Why should we hesitate about making short work of such a system? Because I was robbed yesterday, and the day before, and the day before that, is it any reason that I should suffer myself to be robbed today and tomorrow? any reason that I should conclude that the robber has acquired a vested right to rob me?

If the land belong to the people, why continue to permit landowners to take the rent, or compensate them in any manner for the loss of rent? Consider what rent is. It does not arise spontaneously from land; it is due to nothing that the landowners have done. It represents a value created by the whole community. Let the landholders have, if you please, all that the possession of the land would give them in the absence of the rest of the community. But rent, the creation of the whole community, necessarily belongs to the whole community.

Try the case of the landholders by the maxims of the common law by which the rights of man and man are determined. The common law we are told is the perfection of reason, and certainly the landowners cannot complain of its decision, for it has been built up by and for landowners. Now what does the law allow to the innocent possessor when the land for which he paid his money is adjudged rightfully to belong to another? Nothing at all. That he purchased in good faith gives him no right or claim whatever. The law does not concern itself with the 'intricate question of compensation' to the innocent purchaser. The law does not say, as John Stuart Mill says: 'The land belongs to A, therefore B who has thought himself the owner has no right to anything but the rent, or compensation for its salable value.' For that would be indeed like a famous fugitive slave case decision in which the Court was said to have given the law to the North and the Nigger to the South. The law simply says: 'The land belongs to A, let the sheriff put him in possession!' It gives the innocent purchaser of a wrongful title no claim, it allows him no compensation. And not only this, it takes from him all the improvements that he has in good faith made upon the land. You may have paid a high price for land, making every exertion to see that the title is good; you may have held it in undisturbed possession for years without thought or hint of an adverse claimant; made it fruitful by your toil or erected upon it a costly building of greater value than the land itself, or a modest home in which you hope, surrounded by the fig trees you have planted and the vines you have dressed, to pass your declining days; yet if Quirk, Gammon & Snap can mouse out a technical flow in your parchments or hunt up some forgotten heir who never dreamed of his rights, not merely the land, but all your improvements, may be taken away from you. And not merely that. According to the common law, when you have surrendered the land and given up your improvements, you may be called upon to account for the profits you derived from the land during the time you had it.

Now if we apply to this case of The People *vs.* The Landowners the same maxims of justice that have been formulated by landowners into law, and are applied every day in English and American courts to disputes between man and man, we shall not only not think of giving the landholders any compensation for the land, but shall take all the improvements and whatever else they may have as well.

But I do not propose, and I do not suppose that any one else will propose, to go so far. It is sufficient if the people resume the ownership of the land. Let the landowners retain their improvements and personal property in secure possession.

And in this measure of justice would be no oppression, no injury to any class. The great cause of the present unequal distribution of wealth, with the suffering, degradation, and waste that it entails, would be swept away. Even landholders would share in the general gain. The gain of even the large landholders would be a real one. The gain of the small landholders would be enormous. For in welcoming Justice, men welcome the handmaid of Love. Peace and Plenty follow in her train, bringing their good gifts, not to some, but to all.

How true this is, we shall hereafter see.

If in this chapter I have spoken of justice and expediency as if justice were one thing and expediency another, it has been merely to meet the objections of those who so talk. In justice is the highest and truest expediency.

We have traced the want and suffering that everywhere prevail among the working classes, the recurring paroxysms of industrial depression, the scarcity of employment, the stagnation of capital, the tendency of wages to the starvation point, that exhibit themselves more and more strongly as material progress goes on, to the fact that the land on which and from which all must live is made the exclusive property of some.

We have seen that there is no possible remedy for these evils but the abolition of their cause; we have seen that private property in land has no warrant in justice, but stands condemned as the denial of natural right – a subversion of the law of nature that as social development goes on must condemn the masses of men to a slavery the hardest and most degrading.

We have weighed every objection, and seen that neither on the ground of equity or expediency is there anything to deter us from making land common property by confiscating rent.

But a question of method remains. How shall we do it?

We should satisfy the law of justice, we should meet all economic requirements, by at one stroke abolishing all private titles, declaring all land public property, and letting it out to the highest bidders in lots to suit, under such conditions as would sacredly guard the private right to improvements.

Thus we should secure, in a more complex state of society, the same equality of rights that in a ruder state were secured by equal partitions of the soil, and by giving the use of the land to whoever could procure the most from it, we should secure the greatest production.

Such a plan, instead of being a wild, impracticable vagary, has (with the exception that he suggests compensation to the present holders of land – undoubtedly a careless concession which he upon reflection would reconsider) been indorsed by no less eminent a thinker than Herbert Spencer, who says of it:

Such a doctrine is consistent with the highest state of civilization; may be carried out without involving a community of goods, and need cause no very serious revolution in existing arrangements. The change required would simply be a change of landlords. Separate ownership would merge into the joint-stock ownership of the public. Instead of

being in the possession of individuals, the country would be held by the great corporate body – society. Instead of leasing his acres from an isolated proprietor, the farmer would lease them from the nation. Instead of paying his rent to the agent of Sir John or his Grace, he would pay it to an agent or deputy agent of the community. Stewards would be public officials instead of private ones, and tenancy the only land tenure. A state of things so ordered would be in perfect harmony with the moral law. Under it all men would be equally landlords, all men would be alike free to become tenants . . . Clearly, therefore, on such a system, the earth might be enclosed, occupied and cultivated, in entire subordination to the law of equal freedom.

But such a plan, though perfectly feasible, does not seem to me the best. Or rather I propose to accomplish the same thing in a simpler, easier, and quieter way, than that of formally confiscating all the land and formally letting it out to the highest bidders.

To do that would involve a needless shock to present customs and habits of thought – which is to be avoided.

To do that would involve a needless extension of governmental machinery – which is to be avoided.

It is an axiom of statesmanship, which the successful founders of tyranny have understood and acted upon – that great changes can best be brought about under old forms. We, who would be free men, should heed the same truth. It is the natural method. When nature would make a higher type, she takes a lower one and develops it. This, also, is the law of social growth. Let us work by it. With the current we may glide fast and far. Against it, it is hard pulling and slow progress.

I do not propose either to purchase or to confiscate private property in land. The first would be unjust; the second, needless. Let the individuals who now hold it still retain, if they want to, possession of what they are pleased to call their land. Let them continue to call it their land. Let them buy and sell, and bequeath and devise it. We may safely leave them the shell, if we take the kernel. It is not necessary to confiscate land; it is only necessary to confiscate rent.

Nor to take rent for public uses is it necessary that the State should bother with the letting of lands, and assume the chances of the favoritism, collusion, and corruption this might involve. It is not necessary that any new machinery should be created. The machinery already exists. Instead of extending it, all we have to do is to simplify and reduce it. By leaving to landowners a percentage of rent which would probably be much less than the cost and loss involved in attempting to rent lands through State agency, and by making use of this existing machinery, we may, without jar or shock, assert the common right to land by taking rent for public uses.

We already take some rent in taxation. We have only to make some changes in our modes of taxation to take it all.

What I, therefore, propose, as the simple yet sovereign remedy, which will raise wages, increase the earnings of capital, extirpate pauperism, abolish poverty, give remunerative employment to whoever wishes it, afford free scope to human powers, lessen crime, elevate morals, and taste, and intelligence, purify government and carry civilization to yet nobler heights, is — to appropriate rent by taxation.

In this way the State may become the universal landlord without calling herself so, and without assuming a single new function. In form, the ownership of land would remain just as now. No owner of land need be dispossessed, and no restriction need be placed upon the amount of land any one could hold. For, rent being taken by the State in taxes, land, no matter in whose name it stood, or in what parcels it was held, would be really common property, and every member of the community would participate in the advantages of its ownership.

Now, insomuch as the taxation of rent, or land values, must necessarily be increased just as

we abolish other taxes, we may put the proposition into practical form by proposing –

To abolish all taxation save that upon land values.

As we have seen, the value of land is at the beginning of society nothing, but as society develops by the increase of population and the advance of the arts, it becomes greater and greater. In every civilized country, even the newest, the value of the land taken as a whole is sufficient to bear the entire expenses of government. In the better developed countries it is much more sufficient. Hence it will not be enough merely to place all taxes upon the value of land. It will be necessary, where rent exceeds the present governmental revenues, commensurately to increase the amount demanded in taxation, and to continue this increase as society progresses and rent advances. But this is so natural and easy a matter, that it may be considered as involved, or at least understood, in the proposition to put all taxes on the value of land. That is the first step upon which the practical struggle must be made. When the hare is once caught and killed, cooking him will follow as a matter of course. When the common right to land is so far appreciated and all taxes are abolished save those which fall upon rent, there is no danger of much more than is necessary to induce them to collect the public revenues being left to individual landholders.

Experience has taught me (for I have been for some years endeavoring to popularize this proposition) that wherever the idea of concentrating all taxation upon land values finds lodgment sufficient to induce consideration, it invariably makes way, but there are few of the classes most to be benefited by it, who at first, or even for a long time afterward, see its full significance and power. It is difficult for workingmen to get over the idea that there is a real antagonism between capital and labor. It is difficult for small farmers and homestead owners to get over the idea that to pull all taxes on the value of land would be unduly to tax them. It is difficult for both classes to get over the idea that to exempt capital from taxation would be to make the rich richer, and the poor poorer. These ideas spring from confused thought. But behind ignorance and prejudice there is a powerful interest, which has hitherto dominated literature, education, and opinion. A great wrong always dies hard, and the great wrong which in every civilized country condemns the masses of men to poverty and want, will not die without a bitter struggle.

I do not think the idea of which I speak can be entertained by the reader who has followed me thus far; but inasmuch as any popular discussion must deal with the concrete, rather than the abstract, let me ask him to follow me somewhat further, that we may try the remedy I have proposed by the accepted canons of taxation. In doing so, many incidental bearings may be seen that otherwise might escape notice . . .

But the influences which thus stepped in to modify the extortive power of landownership, and which may still be seen on English estates where the landlord and his family deem it their duty to send medicines and comforts to the sick and infirm, and to look after the well-being of their cottagers, just as the southern planter was accustomed to look after his Negroes, are lost in the more refined and less obvious form which serfdom assumes in the more complicated processes of modern production, which separates so widely and by so many intermediate gradations the individual whose labor is appropriated from him who appropriates it, and makes the relations between the members of the two classes not direct and particular, but indirect and general. In modern society, competition has free play to force from the laborer the very utmost he can give, and with what terrific force it is acting may be seen in the condition of the lowest class in the centres of wealth and industry. That the condition of this lowest class is not yet more general, is to be attributed to the great extent of fertile land which has hitherto been open on this continent, and which has not merely afforded an escape for the increasing population of the older sections of the Union, but has greatly relieved the pressure in

Europe – in one country, Ireland, the emigration having been so great as actually to reduce the population. This avenue of relief cannot last forever. It is already fast closing up, and as it closes, the pressure must become harder and harder.

It is not without reason that the wise crow in the Ramayana, the crow Bushanda, 'who has lived in every part of the universe and knows all events from the beginnings of time,' declares that, though contempt of worldly advantages is necessary to supreme felicity, yet the keenest pain possible is inflicted by extreme poverty. The poverty to which in advancing civilization great masses of men are condemned, is not the freedom from distraction and temptation which sages have sought and philosophers have praised; it is a degrading and embruting slavery, that cramps the higher nature, dulls the finer feelings, and drives men by its pain to acts which the brutes would refuse. It is into this helpless, hopeless poverty, that crushes manhood and destroys womanhood, that robs even childhood of its innocence and joy, that the working classes are being driven by a force which acts upon them like a resistless and unpitying machine. The Boston collar manufacturer who pays his girls two cents an hour may commiserate their condition, but he, as they, is governed by the law of competition, and cannot pay more and carry on his business, or exchange is not governed by sentiment. And so, through all intermediate gradations, up to those who receive the earnings of labor without return, in the rent of land, it is the inexorable laws of supply and demand, a power with which the individual can no more quarrel or dispute than with the winds and the tides, that seem to press down the lower classes into the slavery of want.

But in reality, the cause is that which always has and always must result in slavery – the monopolization by some of what nature has designed for all.

Our boasted freedom necessarily involves slavery, so long as we recognize private property in land. Until that is abolished, Declarations of

Independence and Acts of Emancipation are in vain. So long as one man can claim the exclusive ownership of the land from which other men must live, slavery will exist, and as material progress goes on, must grow and deepen!

This – and in previous chapters of this book we have traced the process, step by step – is what is going on in the civilized world today. Private ownership of land is the nether millstone. Material progress is the upper millstone. Between them, with an increasing pressure, the working classes are being ground.

Chapter 26

David Schmidtz

THE INSTITUTION OF PROPERTY

David Schmidtz (1955–   ) is a professor of philosophy and economics at the University of Arizona, and the director of their program in the Philosophy of Freedom. In this essay, Schmidtz tackles the problem of how the original appropriation of unowned resources such as land can be justified, and argues that part of the justification can be found in the way in which property changes the zero-sum game of the Tragedy of the Commons into the positive-sum game of a system that allows for free exchange.

The term 'property rights' is used to refer to a bundle of rights that could include rights to sell, lend, bequeath, and so on. In what follows, I use the phrase to refer primarily to the right of owners to exclude non-owners. Private owners have the right to exclude non-owners, but the right to exclude is a feature of property rights in general rather than the defining feature of private ownership in particular. The National Park Service claims a right to exclude. Communes claim a right to exclude nonmembers. This essay does not settle which kind or which mix of public and private property institutions is best. Instead, it asks how we could justify *any* institution that recognizes a right to exclude.

1. Original Appropriation: The Problem

The right to exclude presents a philosophical problem, though. Consider how full-blooded rights differ from mere liberties. If I am at liberty to plant a garden, that means my planting a garden is permitted. That leaves open the possibility of you being at liberty to interfere with my gardening as you see fit. Thus, mere liberties are not full-blooded rights. When I stake a claim to a piece of land, though, I claim to be changing other people's liberties – canceling them somehow – so that other people no longer are at liberty to use the land without my permission. To say I have a right to the land is to say I have a right to exclude.

From where could such rights have come? There must have been a time when no one had a right to exclude. Everyone had liberties regarding the land, but not rights. (Perhaps this does not seem obvious, but if no one owns the land, no one has a right to exclude. If no one has a right to exclude, everyone has liberties.) How, then, did we get from each person having a liberty to someone having an exclusive right to the land? What justifies original appropriation, that is, staking a claim to previously unowned resources?

To justify a claim to unowned land, people need not make as strong a case as would be needed to justify confiscating land already owned by someone else. Specifically, since there is no prior owner in original appropriation cases, there is no one from whom one can or needs to get consent. What, then, must a person do? Locke's idea seems to have been that any residual (perhaps need-based) communal claim to the land could be met if a person could appropriate it without prejudice to other people, in other words, if a person could leave "enough and as good" for others. This so-called Lockean Proviso can be interpreted in many ways, but an adequate interpretation will note that this is its point: to license claims that can be made without making other people worse off. In the language of modern environmental economics, we might read it as a call for sustainable use.

We also should consider whether the "others" who are to be left with enough and as good include not just people currently on the scene but latecomers as well, including people not yet born. John Sanders asks, "What possible argument could at the same time require that the present generation have scruples about leaving enough and as good for one another, while shrugging off such concern for future generations?" Most theorists accept the more demanding interpretation. It fits better with Locke's idea that the preservation of humankind (which includes future generations) is the ultimate criterion by which any use of resources is assessed. Aside from that, we have a more compelling defense of an appropriation (especially in environmental terms) when we can argue that there was enough left over not just for contemporaries but also for generations to come.

Of course, when we justify original appropriation, we do not in the process justify expropriation. Some say institutions that license expropriation make people better off; I think our histories of violent expropriation are ongoing tragedies for us all. Capitalist regimes have tainted histories. Communist regimes have tainted histories. Indigenous peoples have tainted histories. Europeans took land from native American tribes, and before that, those

tribes took the same land from other tribes. We may regard those expropriations as the history of markets or governments or Christianity or tribalism or simply as the history of the human race. It makes little difference. This essay discusses the history of property institutions, not because their history can justify them, but rather because their history shows how some of them enable people to make themselves and the people around them better off without destroying their environment. Among such institutions are those that license original appropriation (and not expropriation).

2. Original Appropriation: A Solution

Private property's philosophical critics often have claimed that justifying original appropriation is the key to justifying private property, frequently offering a version of Locke's Proviso as the standard of justification. Part of the Proviso's attraction for such critics was that it seemingly could not be met. Even today, philosophers generally conclude that the Proviso is, at least in the case of land appropriation, logically impossible to satisfy, and thus that (private) property in land cannot possibly be justified along Lockean lines.

The way Judith Thomson puts it, if "the first labor-mixer must literally leave as much and as good for others who come along later, then no one can come to own anything, for there are only finitely many things in the world so that every taking leaves less for others". To say the least, Thomson is not alone:

"We leave enough and as good for others only when what we take is not scarce" (Fried).

"The Lockean Proviso, in the contemporary world of overpopulation and scarce resources, can almost never be met" (Held).

"Every acquisition worsens the lot of others – and worsens their lot in relevant ways" (Bogart).

"The condition that there be enough and as good left for others could not of course be literally satisfied by any system of private property rights" (Sartorius).

"If the 'enough and as good' clause were a necessary condition on appropriation, it would follow that, in these circumstances, the only legitimate course for the inhabitants would be death by starvation . . . since *no* appropriation would leave enough and as good in common for others" (Waldron).

And so on. If we take something out of the cookie jar, we *must* be leaving less for others. This appears self-evident. It has to be right.

2.1. Appropriation is not a Zero-Sum Game

But it is not right. First, it is by no means impossible – certainly not logically impossible – for a taking to leave as much for others. Surely we can at least imagine a logically possible world of magic cookie jars in which, every time you take out one cookie, more and better cookies take its place.

Second, the logically possible world I just imagined is the sort of world we actually live in. Philosophers writing about original appropriation tend to speak as if people who arrive first are luckier than those who come later. The truth is, first appropriators begin the process of resource creation; latecomers get most of the benefits. Consider America's first permanent English settlement, the Jamestown colony of 1607. (Or, if you prefer, imagine the lifestyles of people crossing the Bering Strait from Asia twelve thousand years ago.) Was their situation better than ours? How so? Was it that they never worried about being overcharged for car repairs? They never awoke in the middle of the night to the sound of noisy refrigerators, leaky faucets, or flushing toilets? They never had to change a light bulb? They never agonized over the choice of long-distance telephone companies?

Philosophers are taught to say, in effect, that original appropriators got the good stuff for free. We have to pay for ugly leftovers. But in truth, original appropriation benefits latecomers far more than it benefits original appropriators. Original appropriation is a cornucopia of wealth, but mainly for latecomers. The people who got here first never dreamt of things we latecomers take for granted. The poorest among us have life expectancies exceeding theirs by several decades. This is not political theory. It is not economic rhetoric. It is fact.

Original appropriation diminishes the stock of what can be originally appropriated, at least in the case of land, but that is not the same thing as diminishing the stock of what can be owned. On the contrary, in taking control of resources and thereby removing those particular resources from the stock of goods that can be acquired by originally appropriation, people typically generate massive increases in the stock of goods that can be acquired by trade. The lesson is that appropriation typically is not a zero-sum game. It normally is a positive sum game. As Locke himself stressed, it creates the possibility of mutual benefit on a massive scale. It creates the possibility of society as a cooperative venture.

The argument is not merely that enough is produced in appropriation's aftermath to compensate latecomers who lost out in the race to appropriate. The argument is that the bare fact of being an original appropriator is not the prize. The prize is prosperity, and latecomers win big, courtesy of those who got here first. If anyone had a right to be compensated, it would be the first appropriators.

2.2. The Commons Before Appropriation is not Zero-Sum Either

The second point is that the commons before appropriation is not a zero-sum game either. Typically it is a negative sum game. Let me tell two stories. The first comes from the coral reefs of the Philippine and Tongan Islands. People once fished those reefs with lures and traps, but have recently caught on to a technique called bleach-fishing, which involves dumping bleach into the reefs. Fish cannot breathe sodium hypochlorite. Suffocated, they float to the surface where they are easy to collect.

The problem is, the coral itself is composed of living animals. The coral suffocates along with the fish, and the dead reef is no longer a viable habitat. (Another technique, blast-fishing, involves dynamiting the reefs. The concussion produces an easy harvest of stunned fish and dead coral.) You may say people ought to be more responsible. They ought to preserve the reefs for their children.

That would miss the point, which is that individual fishermen lack the option of saving the coral for their children. Individual fishermen obviously have the option of not destroying it themselves, but what happens if they elect not to destroy it? What they want is for the reef to be left for their children; what is actually happening is that the reef is left for the next blast-fisher down the line. If a fisherman wants to have anything at all to give his children, he must act quickly, destroying the reef and grabbing the fish himself. It does no good to tell fishermen to take responsibility. They are taking responsibility – for their children. Existing institutional arrangements do not empower them to take responsibility in a way that would save the reef.

Under the circumstances, they are at liberty to not destroy the reef themselves, but they are not at liberty to do what is necessary to save the reef for their children. To save the reef for their children, fishermen must have the power to restrict access to the reef. They must claim a right to exclude blast-fishers. Whether they stake that claim as individuals or as a group is secondary, so long as they actually succeed in restricting access. But one way or another, they must claim and effectively exercise a right to restrict access.

The second story comes from the Cayman Islands. The Atlantic Green Turtle has long been prized as a source of meat and eggs. The turtles were a commonly held resource and were being harvested in an unsustainable way. In 1968, when by some estimates there were as few as three to five thousand left in the wild, a group of entrepreneurs and concerned scientists created Cayman Turtle Farm and began raising and selling captive-bred sea turtles. In the wild, as few as one tenth of one percent of wild hatchlings survive to adulthood. Most are seized by predators before they can crawl from nest to sea. Cayman Farm, though, boosted the survival rate of captive-bred animals to well over fifty percent. At the peak of operations, they were rearing in excess of a hundred thousand turtles. They were releasing one percent of their hatchlings into the wild at the age of ten months, an age at which hatchlings had a decent chance of surviving to maturity.

In 1973, commerce in Atlantic Green Turtles was restricted by CITES (the Convention on International Trade in Endangered Species) and, in the United States, by the Fish and Wildlife Service, the Department of Commerce, and the Department of the Interior. Under the newly created Endangered Species Act, the U.S. classified the Atlantic Green Turtle as an endangered species, but Cayman Farm's business was unaffected, at first, because regulations pertaining to commerce in Atlantic Green Turtles exempted commerce in captive-bred animals. In 1978, however, the regulations were published in their final form, and although exemptions were granted for trade in captive-bred animals of other species, no exemption was made for trade in turtles. The company could no longer do business in the U.S. Even worse, the company no longer could ship its products through American ports, so it no longer had access via Miami to world markets. The Farm exists today only to serve the population of the Cayman Islands themselves.

What do these stories tell us? The first tells us we do not need to justify failing to preserve the commons in its pristine, original, unappropriated form, because preserving the commons in pristine original form is not an option. The commons is not a time capsule. Leaving our environment in the commons is not like putting our environment in a time capsule as a legacy for future generations. In some cases, putting resources in a time capsule might be a good idea. However, the second story reminds us: there are ways to take what we find in the commons and preserve it − to put it in a time capsule − but before we can put something in a time capsule, we have to appropriate it.

2.3. Justifying the Game

Note a difference between justifying institutions that regulate appropriation and justifying particular acts of appropriation. Think of original appropriation as a game and of particular acts of appropriation as moves within the game. Even if the game is justified, a given move within the game may have nothing to recommend it. Indeed, we could say (for argument's sake) that any act of appropriation will seem arbitrary when viewed in isolation, and some will seem unconscionable. Even so, there can be compelling reasons to have an institutional framework that recognizes property claims on the basis of moves that would carry no weight in an institutional vacuum. Common law implicitly acknowledges morally weighty reasons for not requiring original appropriators to supply morally weighty reasons for their appropriations. Carol Rose argues that a rule of first possession, when the world is notified in an unambiguous way, induces discovery (and future productive activity) and minimizes disputes over discovered objects. Particular acts of appropriation are justified not because they carry moral weight but because they are permitted moves within a game that carries moral weight.

Needless to say, the cornucopia of wealth generated by the appropriation and subsequent mobilization of resources is not an unambiguous benefit. The commerce made possible by original appropriation creates pollution, and other negative externalities as well. (I will return to this point.) Further, there may be people who attach no value to the increases in life expectancy and other benefits that accompany the appropriation of resources for productive use. Some people may prefer a steady-state system that indefinitely supports their lifestyles as hunter-gatherers, untainted by the shoes and tents and safety matches of Western culture. If original appropriation forces such people to participate in a culture they want no part of, then from their viewpoint, the game does more harm than good.

Here are two things to keep in mind, though. First, as I said, the commons is not a time capsule. It does not preserve the status quo. For all kinds of reasons, quality of life could drop after appropriation. However, pressures that drive waves of people to appropriate are a lot more likely to compromise quality of life when those waves wash over an unregulated commons. In an unregulated commons, those who conserve pay the costs but do not get the benefits of conservation, while overusers get the benefits but do not pay the costs of overuse. Therefore, an unregulated commons is a prescription for overuse, not for conservation.

Second, the option of living the life of a hunter-gatherer has not entirely disappeared. It is not a comfortable life. It never was. But it remains an option. There are places in northern Canada and elsewhere where people can and do live that way. As a bonus, those who opt to live as hunter-gatherers retain the option of participating in western culture on a drop-in basis during medical emergencies, to trade for supplies, and so on. Obviously, someone might respond, "Even if the hunter-gatherer life is an option now, that option is disappearing as expanding populations equipped with advancing technologies claim the land for other purposes." Well, probably so. What does that prove? It proves that, in the world as it is, if hunter-gatherers want their children to have the option of living as hunter-gatherers, then they need to stake a claim to the territory on which they intend to preserve that option. They need to argue that they, as rightful owners, have a right to regulate access to it. If they want a steady-state civilization, they need to be aware that they will not find it in an unregulated commons. They need to argue that they have a right to exclude oil companies, for example, which would love to be able to treat northern Canada as an unregulated commons.

When someone says appropriation does not leave enough and as good for others, the reply should be "compared to what?" Compared to the commons as it was? As it is? As it will be? Often, in fact, leaving resources in the commons does not leave enough and as good for others. The Lockean Proviso, far from forbidding appropriation of resources from the commons, actually requires appropriation under conditions of scarcity. Moreover, the more scarce a resource is, the more urgently the Proviso requires that it be removed from the negative sum game that is the unregulated commons. Again, when the burden of common use exceeds the resource's ability to renew itself, the Proviso comes to require, not merely permit, people to appropriate and regulate access to the resource. Even in an unregulated commons, some fishermen will practice self-restraint, but something has to happen to incline the group to practice self-restraint in cases where it already has shown it has no such inclination in an unregulated commons.

Removing goods from the commons stimulates increases in the stock of what can be owned and limits losses that occur in tragic commons. Appropriation replaces a negative sum with a positive sum game. Therein lies a justification for social structures enshrining a right to remove resources from the unregulated commons: when resources become scarce, we need to remove them if we want them to be there for our children. Or anyone else's.

3. What Kind of Property Institution Is Implied?

I have defended appropriation of, and subsequent regulation of access to, scarce resources as a way of preserving (and creating) resources for the future. When resources are abundant, the Lockean Proviso permits appropriation; when resources are scarce, the Proviso requires appropriation. It is possible to appropriate without prejudice to future generations. Indeed, when resources are scarce, it is leaving them in the commons that is prejudicial to future generations.

Private property enables people (and gives them an incentive) to take responsibility for conserving scarce resources. It preserves resources under a wide variety of circumstances. It is the preeminent vehicle for turning negative sum commons into positive sum property regimes. However, it is not the only way. Evidently, it is not always the best way, either. Public property is ubiquitous, and it is not only rapacious governments and mad ideologues who create it. Sometimes it evolves spontaneously as a response to real problems, enabling people to remove a resource from an unregulated commons and collectively take responsibility for its management. The following sections discuss research by Martin Bailey, Harold Demsetz, Robert Ellickson, and Carol Rose, showing how various property institutions help to ensure that enough and as good is left for future generations.

3.1. The Unregulated Commons

An unregulated commons need not be a disaster. An unregulated commons will work well enough so long as the level of use remains within the land's carrying capacity. However, as use nears carrying capacity, there will be pressure to shift to a more exclusive regime. As an example of an unregulated commons evolving into something else as increasing traffic begins to exceed carrying capacity, consider Harold Demsetz's account of how property institutions evolved among indigenous tribes of the Labrador peninsula. As Demsetz tells the story, the region's people had, for generations, treated the land as an open-access commons. The human population was small. There was plenty to eat. Thus, the pattern of exploitation was within the land's carrying capacity. The resource maintained itself. In that situation, the Proviso, as interpreted above, was satisfied. Original appropriation would have been permissible, other things equal, but it was not required.

With the advent of the fur trade, though, the scale of hunting and trapping activity increased sharply. The population of game animals began to dwindle. The unregulated commons had worked for a while, but now the tribes were facing a classic tragedy. The benefits of exploiting the resource were internalized but the costs were not, and the arrangement was no longer viable. Clans began to mark out family plots. The game animals in question were small animals like beaver and otter that tend not to migrate from one plot to another. Thus, marking out plots of land effectively privatized small game as well as the land itself. In sum, the tribes converted the commons in nonmigratory fur-bearing game to family parcels when the fur trade began to spur a rising demand that exceeded the land's carrying capacity. When demand began to exceed carrying capacity, that was when the Proviso came not only to permit but to require original appropriation.

One other nuance of the privatization of fur-bearing game: although the fur was privatized, the meat was not. There was still plenty of meat to go around, so tribal law allowed trespass on another clan's land to hunt for meat. Trespassers could kill a beaver and take the meat, but had to leave the pelt displayed in a prominent place to signal that they had eaten and had respected the clan's right to the pelt. The new customs went to the heart of the matter, privatizing what had to be privatized, leaving intact liberties that people had always enjoyed with respect to other resources where unrestricted access had not yet become a problem.

3.2. *The Communal Alternative*

We can contrast the unregulated or open-access commons with communes. A commune is a restricted-access commons. In a commune, property is owned by the group rather than by individual members. People as a group claim and exercise a right to exclude. Typically, communes draw a sharp distinction between members and nonmembers, and regulate access accordingly. Public property tends to restrict access by time of day or year. Some activities are permitted; others are prohibited.

Ellickson believes a broad campaign to abolish either private property or public and communal property would be ludicrous. Each kind of property serves social welfare in its own way. Likewise, every ownership regime has its own externality problems. Communal management leads to overconsumption and to shirking on maintenance and improvements, because people receive only a fraction of the value of their labor, and bear only a fraction of the costs of their consumption. To minimize these disincentives, a commune must intensively monitor people's production and consumption activities.

In practice, communal regimes can lead to indiscriminate dumping of wastes, ranging from piles of unwashed dishes to ecological disasters that threaten whole continents. Privately managed parcels also can lead to indiscriminate dumping of wastes and to various other uses that ignore spillover effects on neighbors. One advantage of private property is that owners can buy each other out and reshuffle their holdings in such a way as to minimize the extent to which their activities bother each other. But it does not always work out so nicely, and the reshuffling itself can be a waste. There are transaction costs. Thus, one plausible social goal would be to have a system that combines private and public property in a way that reduces the sum of transaction costs and the cost of externalities.

4. Local versus Remote Externalities

Is it generally best to convert an unregulated commons to smaller private parcels or to manage it as a commune with power to exclude non-members? It depends on what kind of activities people tend to engage in. Ellickson separates activities into three categories: small (like cultivating a tomato plant), medium (like damming part of a river to create a pond for ducks), and large (like using an industrial smokestack to disperse noxious fumes). The distinction is not meant to be sharp. As one might expect, it is a matter of degree. It concerns the relative size of the area over which externalities are worth worrying about. The effects of small events are confined to one's own property. Medium events affect people in the immediate neighborhood. Their external effects are localized. Large events affect people who are more remote.

Ellickson says private regimes are clearly superior as methods for minimizing the costs of small and medium events. Small events are not much of a problem for private regimes. When land is parceled out, the effects of small events are internalized. Neighbors do not care much when we pick tomatoes on our own land; they care a great deal when we pick tomatoes on the communal plot. In the former case, we are minding our own business; in the latter, we are minding theirs.

In contrast, the effects of medium events tend to spill over onto one's neighbors, and thus can be a source of friction. Nevertheless, privatization has the advantage of limiting the number of people having to be consulted about how to deal with the externality, which reduces transaction costs. Instead of consulting the entire community of communal owners, each at liberty with respect to the affected area, one consults a handful of people who own parcels in the immediate area of the medium event. A further virtue of privatization is that disputes arising from medium events tend to be left in the hands of people in the immediate vicinity, who tend to have a better understanding of local conditions and thus are in a better position to devise resolutions without harmful unintended consequences. They are in a better position to foresee the costs and benefits of a medium event.

When it comes to large events, though, there is no easy way to say which mix of private and public property is best. Large events involve far-flung externalities among people who do not have face-to-face relationships. The difficulties in detecting such externalities, tracing them to their source, and holding people accountable for them are difficulties for any kind of property regime. It is no easy task to devise institutions that encourage pulp mills to take responsibility for their actions while simultaneously encouraging people downstream to take responsibility for their welfare, and thus to avoid being harmed by large-scale negative externalities. Ellickson says there is no general answer to the question of which regime best deals with them.

A large event will fall into one of two categories. Releasing toxic wastes into the atmosphere, for example, may violate existing legal rights or community norms. Or, such laws or norms may not yet be in place. Most of the problems arise when existing customs or laws fail to settle who (in effect) has the right of way. That is not a problem with parceling land per se but rather with the fact that key resources like air and waterways remain in a largely unregulated commons.

So, privatization exists in different degrees and takes different forms. Different forms have different incentive properties. Simply parceling out land or sea is not always enough to stabilize possession of resources that make land or sea valuable in the first place. Suppose, for example, that fish are known to migrate from one parcel to another. In that case, owners have an incentive to grab as many fish as they can whenever the school passes through their own territory. Thus, simply dividing fishing grounds into parcels may not be enough to put fishermen in a position collectively to avoid exceeding sustainable yields. It depends on the extent to which the sought-after fish migrate from one parcel to another, and on conventions that are continuously evolving to help neighbors deal with the inadequacy of their fences (or other ways of marking off territory).

Clearly, then, not all forms of privatization are equally good at internalizing externalities. Privatization per se is not a panacea, and not all forms of privatization are equal. There are obvious difficulties with how private property regimes handle large events. The nature and extent of the difficulties depend on details. So, for purposes of comparison, Ellickson looked at how communal regimes handle large events.

5. Jamestown and Other Communes

The Jamestown Colony is North America's first permanent English settlement. It begins in 1607 as a commune, sponsored by London-based Virginia Company. Land is held and managed collectively. The colony's charter guarantees to each settler an equal share of the collective product regardless of the amount of work personally contributed. Of the original group of one hundred and four settlers, two thirds die of starvation and disease before their first winter. New shiploads replenish the population, but the winter of 1609 cuts the population from five hundred to sixty. In 1611, visiting Governor Thomas Dale finds living skeletons bowling in the streets, waiting for someone else to plant the crops. Their main food source consists of wild animals such as turtles and raccoons, which settlers hunt and eat by dark of night before neighbors can demand equal shares. In 1614, Governor Dale has seen enough. He assigns three-acre plots to individual settlers, which reportedly increases productivity seven-fold. The colony converts the rest of its land holdings to private parcels in 1619.

Why go communal in the first place? Are there advantages to communal regimes? One advantage is obvious. Communal regimes can help people spread risks under conditions where risks are substantial and where alternative risk-spreading mechanisms, like insurance, are unavailable. But as communities build up capital reserves to the point where they can offer insurance, they tend to privatize, for insurance lets them secure a measure of risk-spreading without having to endure the externalities that afflict a communal regime.

A communal regime might also be an effective response to economies of scale in large-scale public works that are crucial in getting a community started. To build a fort, man its walls, dig wells, and so on, a communal economy is an obvious choice as a way of mobilizing the teams of workers needed to execute these urgent tasks. But again, as these tasks are completed and community welfare increasingly comes to depend on small events, the communal regime gives way to private parcels. At Jamestown, Plymouth, the Amana colonies, and Salt Lake, formerly communal settlers "understandably would switch to private land tenure, the system that most cheaply induces individuals to undertake small and medium events that are socially useful" (Ellickson). (The legend of Salt Lake says the sudden improvement in the fortunes of once-starving Mormons occurred in 1848 when God sent sea gulls to save them from plagues of locusts, at the same time as they coincidentally were switching to private plots. Similarly, the Jamestown tragedy sometimes is attributed to harsh natural conditions, as if those conditions suddenly changed in 1614, multiplying productivity seven-fold while Governor Dale coincidentally was cutting the land into parcels.)

Of course, the tendency toward decentralized and individualized forms of management is only a (strong) tendency and, in any case, there are tradeoffs. For example, what would be a small event on a larger parcel becomes a medium event under more crowded conditions. Loud music is an innocuous small event on a ranch but an irritating medium event in an apartment complex. Changes in technology or population density affect the scope or incidence of externalities. The historical trend, though, is that as people become aware of and concerned about a medium or large event, they seek ways of reducing the extent to which the event's cost is externalized. Social evolution is partly a process of perceiving new externalities and devising institutions to internalize them.

Historically, the benefits of communal management have not been enough to keep communes together indefinitely. Perhaps the most enduring and successful communes in human memory are the agricultural settlements of the Hutterites, dating in Europe back to the sixteenth century. There are now around twenty-eight thousand people living in such communities. Hutterites believe in a fairly strict sharing of assets. They forbid the possession of radio or television sets, to give one example of how strictly they control contact with the outside world.

Ellickson says Hutterite communities have three special things going for them:

1. A population cap: when a settlement reaches a population of one hundred and twenty, a portion of the community must leave to start a new community. The cap helps them retain a close-knit society;
2. Communal dining and worship: people congregate several times a day, which facilitates a rapid exchange of information about individual behavior and a ready avenue for supplying feedback to those whose behavior deviates from the norm;
3. A ban on birth control: the average woman bears nine children, which more than offsets the trickle of emigration.

We might add that Hutterite culture and education leave people ill-prepared to live in anything other than a Hutterite society, which surely accounts in part for the low emigration rate.

Ellickson discusses other examples of communal property regimes. But the most pervasive example of communal ownership in America, Ellickson says, is the family household. American suburbia consists of family communes nested within a network of open-access roadways. Family homes tacitly recognize limits to how far we can go in converting common holdings to individual parcels. Consider your living room. You could fully privatize, having one household member own it while others pay user fees. The fees could be used to pay family members or outside help to keep it clean. In some respects, it would be better that way. The average communal living room today, for example, is notably subject to overgrazing and shirking on maintenance. Yet we put up with it. No one charges user fees to household members. Seeing the living room degraded by communal use may be irritating, but it is better than treating it as one person's private domain.

Some institutions succeed while embodying a form of ownership that is essentially collective. History indicates, though, that members of successful communes internalize the rewards that come with that collective responsibility. In particular, they reserve the right to exclude nonmembers. A successful commune does not run itself as an open-access commons.

6. Governance by Custom

Many commons (such as our living rooms) are regulated by custom rather than by government, so saying there is a role for common property and saying there is a role for government management of common property are two different things. As Ellickson notes, "Group ownership does not necessarily imply government ownership, of course. The sorry environmental records of federal land agencies and Communist regimes are a sharp reminder that governments are often particularly inept managers of large tracts." Carol Rose tells of how, in the nineteenth century, public property was thought to be owned by society at large. The idea of public property often was taken to imply no particular role for government beyond whatever enforcement role is implied by private property. Society's right to such property was held to precede and supersede any claim by government. Rose says, "Implicit in these older doctrines is the notion that, even if a property should be open to the public, it does not follow that public rights should necessarily vest in an active governmental manager". Sometimes, rights were understood to be held by an "unorganized public" rather than by a "governmentally organized public."

Along the same lines, open-field agricultural practices of medieval times gave peasants exclusive cropping rights to scattered thin strips of arable land in each of the village fields. The strips were private only during the growing season, after which the land reverted to the commons for the duration of the grazing season. Thus, ownership of parcels was usufructuary in the sense that once the harvest was in, ownership reverted to the common herdsmen without negotiation or formal transfer. The farmer had an exclusive claim to the land only so long as he was using it for the purpose of bringing in a harvest. The scattering of strips was a means of diversification, reducing the risk of being ruined by small or medium events: small fires, pest infestations, etc.. The post-harvest commons in grazing land exploited economies of scale in fencing and tending a herd.

According to Martin Bailey, the pattern observed by Rose and Ellickson also was common among aboriginal tribes. That is, tribes that practiced agriculture treated the land as private during the growing season, and often treated it as a commons after the crops were in. Hunter-gatherer societies did not practice agriculture, but they too tended to leave the land in the commons during the summer when game was plentiful. It was during the winter, when food was most scarce, that they privatized. The rule among hunter-gatherers is that where group hunting's advantages are considerable, that factor dominates. But in the winter, small game is relatively more abundant, less migratory, and evenly spread. There was no "feast or famine" pattern of the sort one expects to see with big-game hunting. Rather, families tended to gather enough during the course of the day to get themselves through the day, day after day, with little to spare.

Even though this pattern corroborates my own general thesis, I confess to being a bit surprised. I might have predicted that it would be during the harshest part of the year that families would band together and throw everything into the common pot in order to pull through. Not so. It was when the land was nearest its carrying capacity that they recognized the imperative to privatize.

Customary use of medieval commons was hedged with restrictions limiting depletion of resources. Custom prohibited activities inconsistent with the land's ability to recover. In particular, the custom of "stinting" allowed the villagers to own livestock only in proportion to the relative size of their (growing season) land holdings. Governance by custom enabled people to avoid commons tragedies.

Custom is a form of management unlike exclusive ownership by either individuals or governments. Custom is a self-managing system for according property rights. For example, custom governs the kind of rights-claims you establish by taking a place in line at a supermarket checkout counter. Rose believes common concerns often are best handled by decentralized, piecemeal, and self-managing customs that tend to arise as needed at the local level. So, to the previous section's conclusion that a successful commune does not run itself as an open-access commons, we can add that a successful commune does not entrust its governance to a distant bureaucracy.

7. The Hutterite Secret

I argued that the original appropriation of (and subsequent regulation of access to) scarce resources is justifiable as a mechanism for preserving opportunities for future generations. There are various means of exclusive control, though. Some internalize externalities better than others, and how well they do so depends on the context. My argument does not presume there is one form of exclusive control that uniquely serves this purpose. Which form is best depends on what kind of activities are most prevalent in a community at any given time. It also depends on the extent to which public ownership implies control by a distant bureaucracy rather than by local custom.

As mentioned earlier, I have heard people say Jamestown failed because it faced harsh natural conditions. But communal (and noncommunal) settlements typically face harsh natural conditions. Jamestown had to deal with summer in Virginia. Hutterites dealt with winter on the Canadian prairie. It is revealing, not misleading, to compare Jamestown to settlements that faced harsher conditions more successfully. It also is fair to compare the two Jamestowns: the one before and the one immediately following Governor Dale's mandated privatization. What distinguished the first Jamestown from the second was not the harshness of its natural setting but rather the thoroughness with which it prevented people from internalizing externalities.

Sociologist Michael Hechter considers group solidarity to be a function of (a) the extent to which members depend on the group and (b) the extent to which the group can monitor and enforce compliance with expectations that members will contribute to the group rather than free ride upon it. On this analysis, it is unsurprising that Hutterite communal society has been successful. Members are extremely dependent, for their upbringing leaves them unprepared to live in a non-Hutterite culture. Monitoring is intense. Feedback is immediate. But if that is the secret of Hutterite success, why did Jamestown fail? They too were extremely dependent on each other. They too had nowhere else to go. Monitoring was equally unproblematic. Everyone knew who was planting crops (no one) and who was bowling (everyone). What was the problem?

The problem lay in the guarantee embedded in the Jamestown colony's charter. Jamestown's charter entitled people to an equal share regardless of personal contribution, which is to say it took steps to ensure that individual workers would be maximally alienated from the fruits of their labors. The charter ensured that workers would think of their work as disappearing into an open-access commons.

Robert Goodin says, "Working within the constraints set by natural scarcity, the greatest practical obstacle to achieving as much justice as resources permit is, and always has been, the supposition that each of us should cultivate his own garden." However, Jamestown's charter did not suppose each of us should cultivate his own garden. It supposed the opposite. Colonists abided by the charter, and even while they suffered, people in other colonies were tending their own gardens, and thriving.

We should applaud institutions that encourage people to care for each other. But telling people they are required to tend someone else's garden rather than their own does not encourage people to care for each other. It does the opposite. It encourages spite. The people of Jamestown reached the point where they would rather die, bowling in the street, than tend the gardens of their free-riding neighbors, and die they did.

Chapter 27

G. A. Cohen

MARX AND LOCKE ON LAND AND LABOUR

G.A. Cohen (1941–   ) is a professor of social and political theory at Oxford, best known for his explication and defense of Marxist theory from the perspective of analytical philosophy. In this essay, Cohen defends what he calls 'partial egalitarianism'—the thesis which holds that people own themselves but that non-human resources are to be distributed in an egalitarian manner. He defends this thesis against the Lockean claim that since labor is responsible for almost all the value yielded by land, justice does not demand that we rectify inequalities of wealth and condition which result simply from the choices people make about what to do with what they legitimately own.

1. Within political philosophy, we can distinguish three views about the powers of nature and the powers of people. The views differ according as they do or do not encourage an egalitarian approach to the substances and capacities of nature on the one hand, and to the powers of people to modify nature on the other.

There are, first, those who defend an egalitarian approach to both natural resources and human labour. They argue that talented people are merely lucky to be so, and that, to counter the unjustly unequalizing influence of that luck, not only what nature produces but also the product of the powers of people should be distributed according to principles of equality (of, perhaps, in the two cases, appropriately different kinds). John Rawls and Ronald Dworkin are leading exponents of this position.

Others, however, such as Robert Nozick, oppose egalitarianism with respect to both human and non-human productive capacity.

Nozick claims that, to avoid the endorsement of slavery which he thinks implicit in an egalitarian attitude to people's powers, each person must control his own powers and their products. He holds, moreover, that people exercise their powers legitimately when they gather to themselves virtually unrestricted amounts of unowned natural resources. That legitimate gathering justifies a skewed distribution of natural resources, the inequality of which is increased by the fact that Nozick's individuals are entitled not only to what they have themselves taken, but also to the takings of others which come to them by way of trade or gift.

It is possible, finally, to attempt an intermediate course, in which a Nozickian principle of self-ownership is conjoined with an egalitarian regime over the resources of nature only. And in my own recent work, I have been examining that third approach, which I shall here call *partial egalitarianism*, to contrast it with the comprehensive egalitarianism of Rawls and Dworkin on the one hand, and the comprehensive anti-egalitarianism of Nozick on the other. The Rawls/Dworkin and Nozick theories are, of course, sharply conflicting, but they are alike in the important respect that neither distinguishes, so fundamentally as partial egalitarianism does, between the moral status of people's claims to natural resources and the moral status of their claims to their own powers. The first two approaches assimilate the issues of rights over people and rights over nature, though they do so in opposite directions. Nozick endows people's claims to acquired natural resources with the moral quality which belongs, more plausibly, to people's claims over themselves, and Rawls and Dworkin treat personal productivity as subject to egalitarian principles of distribution which they also apply, but less controversially, to the distribution of external wherewithal. The position I have been examining is an intermediate one, since it follows Nozick, and rejects Rawls and Dworkin, in its affirmation (or, at least, non-denial) of self-ownership, but it follows Rawls and Dworkin, and rejects Nozick, in subjecting the distribution of non-human resources to egalitarian appraisal. I want to see how far one can go, in the direction of some sort of final equality of condition, on the basis of an egalitarianism of external resources which concedes each person's sovereignty over himself, on any view of what equality of condition is, be it equality of income, or of utility, or of well-being (if that is different from utility), or of need satisfaction (if that is different from each of those), or of something else again.

My interest in partial egalitarianism reflects a left-wing political sympathy. It is good strategy for a socialist to postpone engagement against the attractive idea that each individual should decide what is to be done with his own person and powers. Leftists should proceed, initially, as partial egalitarianism does, by rejecting only that part of right-wing thinking which is relatively easy to reject, namely, its cavalier way with external resources, which so readily become, in

right-wing thinking, unequal private property. In the end, socialists will have to place some limits on people's claims to self-ownership, since they will not otherwise be able to secure as much equality of condition as they believe to be justified. But I believe that they can move far further in the direction of equality of condition from a merely partial egalitarian starting point than many seem to think. For many suppose that the first thing socialists must do is deny self-ownership, and that the debate between left and right is primarily about the rights individuals have over themselves, against the claims of other people. That way of posing the key political question is too kind to the right: it leaves the right's weak side out of consideration.

2. In this essay I expound and criticize a pair of arguments, which derive from John Locke's *Second Treatise of Government*, and which threaten to undermine the hope that some support for equality of condition might come from an egalitarianism of worldly resources alone. But, before I turn to Locke, I want to describe an anomaly in Marxist views about distributive justice, which must be removed if Marxists are to avert the threat of Locke's arguments.

As everybody knows, Marxists believe in the labour theory of value, or, at any rate, fully orthodox Marxists believe in it, and they are the Marxists about whom I shall speak here. Such Marxists believe that the value of commodities is entirely due to the labour required for their production. And, because of their allegiance to the labour theory, Marxists must assert, and they do in fact assert, that the raw worldly resources to which labour is applied neither possess value, since labour did not create them, nor themselves create value, since they are not themselves labour. Marxists maintain, moreover, that profit on capital comes from exploitation of labour. Capitalists exploit workers when they appropriate part of the value which only the labour of workers can produce.

Yet when Marxists indicate how workers

come to be exploited by capitalists, as opposed to what that exploitation consists in, they suddenly assign extreme importance to natural resources, as I now proceed to explain.

Slaves are exploited because they do not own their labour power, and serfs are exploited because they do not own all of it, but wage-workers, who do own their labour power, are exploited only because they own no means of production. They must therefore sell their labour power to capitalists, on adverse terms. Now most means of production are not raw natural resources, but products of labour, such as tools, machines, and already worked, or, at least, extracted, materials. But, since means of production which are not themselves natural resources are the product, in the end, of natural resources and labour power, it must, ultimately, be some selection of facts about labour power and resource endowments which accounts for workers' vulnerability to exploitation.

Now Marx is emphatic that the answer to the question, how workers come to be exploited, lies in facts about natural resources alone. His commitment to that answer shows up in his discussion of what he called 'the secret of primitive accumulation', which reveals how exploiting capital came into being. Marx disparages the apologetic story in which it was a result of the industry and saving of a 'diligent, intelligent, and, above all, frugal elite'. If that account were true, then a provident use of self-owned labour power, in the context of an initial equality of external resources, would have created capital. But, according to Marx, the truth is that capital came into being when and because exploitable labour did, as a consequence of the resource dispossession of pre-capitalist peasants. 'The expropriation of the . . . peasant from the soil was the basis of the whole process'. Soil, however, is a natural resource, and it follows that, according to Marx, it was a critical loss of natural resources that generated the proletariat. (To be sure, only virgin soil is a natural resource in the strict sense required in this lecture, but it was not because his soil was cultivated that the peasant was exposed to exploitation when it was taken from him.)

It might be objected that, even if lack of land brought the proletariat into being, what they now signally lack are not rude resources but the means of production characteristic of established capitalism. And it is indeed true that, were they provided with those means, then exploitation would cease. But it does not follow that they need those advanced means to escape the necessity of contracting with capitalists. In Marx's account, they sell their labour power to capitalists because otherwise they die, and, if they need existing means of production to live well, a ruder resource provision might nevertheless suffice for them to avoid starvation. It is perhaps for this reason that Marx wrote, in a sentence whose topic was 'present-day' capitalism, and not its origin, that 'the monopoly of land is even the basis of the monopoly of capital'.

But the objector could argue that the growth of population which capitalist productivity made possible means that there is no longer enough land per person for each to survive on the basis, initially, of raw resources alone. Yet, even if that is true, it is of questionable relevance in a discussion of the implications of Marx's account of the basis of exploitation. It is, moreover, a controversial claim, when, as might be thought appropriate, the land endowment of the whole planet is taken into account. But suppose that it is both true and relevant that contemporary workers would, because of their numbers, need relatively sophisticated means of production to escape exploitation. Then why did their forbears not furnish them with them? Not, of course, because they lacked the labour power to produce them, but because they, in turn, lacked means of production, having been furnished with none by their forbears, who were similarly deprived: and so on, backwards in time. By reiterating that impeccably Marxist explanation of each proletarian generation's lack of means of production we arrive at an original loss of natural resources as the ultimate cause of the exploitability of today's proletariat.

Now there is at least an apparent tension here, between the importance imputed to the distribution of worldly resources in the Marxist diagnosis of the cause of exploitation, and the total unimportance of worldly resources in the Marxist account of the source of value. If raw worldly resources do not create or possess value, why should it matter that workers were deprived of them?

3. The Marxist diagnosis of the origin of exploitation is congenial to a redistributive egalitarian policy. But the claim with which it is uneasily conjoined, to wit, that labour is the sole source of value, can be made to serve inegalitarian ends, and such are the ends which, we shall find, something like a labour theory of value is made to serve by John Locke.

To see how the falsehood of the proposition that labour creates value might be encouraging from an egalitarian point of view, let us imagine that nature offered all its resources to us in the form of final consumption goods which there was no need to alter by labour. Suppose, that is, that anything physical which anybody wanted came from nature as a very ripe apple does when it falls from the tree on to a hungry person's lap. Under those benign conditions, labour would not be creating any value, and an equal distribution of worldly resources would tend to foster the final equality of condition which Marxists favour. But in the real world the things we desire depend, in part, for their desirable qualities on labour. Hence, given that people are differentially good at labouring, we have here the makings of a justification of inequality of reward and circumstance, under which more redounds to the more productive and their beneficiaries. Inequality of condition is harder to defend on the hypothesis that, or to the extent that, labour is *not* responsible for the value of commodities. In virtue of the comparative appeal of the self-ownership thesis, which endorses the naturally unequal distribu-

tion of personal powers, and the comparative lack of appeal of a similarly unequal distribution of natural resources and energy, the claim people make to the fruits of their labour is the strongest possible basis for inequality of distribution.

There is, then, a danger of discrepancy between Marxism's egalitarianism and Marxism's deprecation of the role of non-labour inputs in the formation of value. To sustain their egalitarianism, orthodox Marxists must distinguish their position from a Locke-like one which asserts both the pre-eminent place of labour in value creation and the labourer's right to his labour and hence to its products.

There are, in principle, two ways out of this dilemma. The first is to reduce the significance of labour in the account of value creation. But that means giving up the labour theory of value, and, therefore, extinguishing orthodox Marxism. The other, and seemingly more eligible, way out is to deny the labourer's claim to his product. This path seems more open, but two obstacles lie upon it. The first is that, if Marxists deny that the worker has a right to his product, they must then explain why they nevertheless think he counts as exploited, yet they do not usually offer any such alternative explanation. And the second obstacle is that Marxists are, for political reasons, reluctant forthrightly to deny the principle of self-ownership, since they would lose allies if they did so. One expression of that reluctance is the Marxist attachment to the diagnosis of the cause of exploitation which I described in the last section. When Marxists trace exploitation to the producers' dispossession of worldly resources, they account for it without denying self-ownership, and they thereby attract left-liberal support to the anti-capitalist cause. But if I am right, Marxists can retain their distinctive account of value creation, and yet be egalitarians, only if they assert more difference between themselves and left-wing liberals than they have found it convenient to do.

4. But now I must deal with an objection which

informed partisans of Marxist economics would be eager to press. They would complain that, in the foregoing discussion, I rode roughshod over a crucial distinction, the distinction, namely, between (what Marxists call) *exchange-value* and *use-value*. The first, exchange-value, is the power of a thing to exchange against other things on the market, the measure of its power to do so being given by the number of things of any other kind for which it will exchange. And exchange-value is different from use-value, which is the power of a thing to satisfy human desire, whether directly or indirectly. A thing satisfies desire indirectly when, for example, it is used to produce another thing which satisfies desire directly, in the sense that, to satisfy desire, that other thing need only be consumed. The term 'use-value' denotes, moreover, not only such a power, but also anything that has such a power, for it is a Marxian verbal convention that whatever *has* a use-value *is* a use-value. Hence anything which contributes to the satisfaction of desire is a use-value, and so, for example, a tract of fertile land both has and is a use-value, since it may be used to produce a use-valuable crop.

Now the Marxist critic would remind me that the labour theory of value is a theory of exchange-value only. The theory does not pretend to explain why a commodity has the amount of use-value it does, but only why it exchanges against a certain number of other use-values on the market. The labour theory's answer to that question is that market exchange ratios are, in the final analysis, a function of the amounts of labour required to produce commodities. And while Marx did say that labour alone creates exchange-value, he amply acknowledged that land, or nature, contributes to use-value, and he was contemptuous of socialists who denied that truth. He criticized the German socialists for opening their Gotha Programme of 1874 with the declaration that 'labour is the source of all wealth and all culture', and admonished them that 'nature is just as much the source of use-values as labour' is. Labour alone

produces exchange-value, but nothing has exchange-value unless it has use-value, and, since natural resources are needed to produce use-value, they are a presupposition of the creation of exchange-value, even though they do not themselves have or create any. Thereby, so my Marxist critic would conclude, the seeming tension of which I spoke earlier is dissipated. The worker's lack of worldly resources sets the scene for his exploitation, even though exploitation is expropriation of exchange-value, and worldly resources neither possess nor create exchange-value. One can affirm both that labour is the source of all (exchange-)value and that inequality of natural resources is fateful and unjustified. Consequently, one can affirm the labour theory of value but also protest against the resource dispossession from which workers suffer. That answers the question at the end of section 2. And the dilemma constructed at the end of section 3 may also, now, be avoided. One can affirm the labour theory of value and yet call for egalitarian redistribution, without denying the principle of self-ownership, by emphasizing the importance of natural resources in the generation of use-value.

5. But this solution to the problems for orthodox Marxism raised in sections 2 and 3 will not work: the reminder that the labour theory is a theory of exchange-value is of no avail in the present context. For, as I have argued elsewhere, the notion that labour creates exchange-value carries ideological weight only because it is confused with the distinct claim that Marxists officially deny, namely, that labour is the sole creator of the use-valuable product itself. It is only because Marxists (and also their opponents) conflate those two ideas that they are able to suppose that the labour theory of value is a suitable basis for raising a charge of exploitation against capitalists.

To see how the conflation arises, notice, to begin with, that sentences like 'labour creates exchange-value' provide a merely metaphorical rendering of the labour theory of value. What the labour theory literally says is that the exchange-value of a commodity varies directly and uniformly with the amount of labour time required to produce commodities of its kind under currently standard conditions of production, and inversely and uniformly with the amount of labour time standardly required to produce commodities of other kinds. That statement does not imply that labour creates anything. It is the amounts of labour time that would now be required to produce things, a certain set of counterfactual magnitudes, and not any actual sweating toil, which accounts for how much exchange-value things have, if the labour theory of value is true. The past history of a commodity, and, hence, how much labour was spent on it, or even whether any labour was spent on it, have strictly nothing to do with how much exchange-value it has. A commodity has a lot of exchange-value if a lot of labour would be required to replicate it, even if the commodity fell from the sky and therefore has no labour 'embodied' in it at all.

What was required in the past, and still more what happened in the past—these facts are irrelevant to how much exchange-value a commodity has, if the labour theory of value is true. But they are not epistemically irrelevant. For, since technical conditions change relatively slowly, the labour time required to produce something in the recent past is usually a good guide to the labour time required to produce it now. Typical past actual labour time is, moreover, the best guide to how much labour time was necessary in the past. Thereby what did occur, the labour actually spent, becomes a good index of what is now required, and, therefore, a good index of the exchange-value of the commodity. It does not follow that, in any sense of 'creates', it creates the exchange-value of the commodity.

The metaphor widely used to convey the labour theory of value makes people think the theory says that workers create something, and, since the most obvious candidate for something

created by workers is the physical product, the labour theory of value is, in the end, confused with the idea that the workers create the product itself. It is, moreover, only because of that confusion that the labour theory attracts ideological interest. It has none when it is clearly and distinctly conceived. For real ideological interest lies in claims about the creation of the use-valuable thing in which exchange-value inheres.

To see that this is so, suppose, by way of thought-experiment, that something other than counterfactual labour 'creates' exchange-value, in the very sense in which, in the labour theory, counterfactual labour 'creates' it. (I place scare-quotes around 'creates' in contexts where its use is, at best, metaphorical.) Imagine, in particular, that the magnitude of every commodity's exchange-value is wholly determined by the extent and intensity of desire for it, and that we can therefore say that desire, not labour, 'creates' exchange-value. But imagine, too, that labour creates the product itself, out of in all senses worthless raw materials, or—the product being a pure service—out of none. Do we now lose our inclination (supposing, of course, that a belief in the labour theory of value induced one in us) to sympathize with the labourer's claim to the product, and, hence, to its exchange-value, even though we are no longer supposing that labour 'creates' that exchange-value? I do not think we do. The worker continues to look exploited if he creates the exchange-valuable thing and does not get all the exchange-value of the thing he creates. What matters, ideologically, is what creates that thing, or so transforms it that it has (more) exchange-value, not what makes things of its sort have the amount of exchange-value they do, which is what the labour theory of value is really supposed to explain.

If I am right, the labour theory fulfils its ideological function only when it is mistaken for a theory that labour alone creates the product itself. But the latter theory is both false and hard to reconcile with the extreme importance (see earlier) assigned to non-labour resources in the

Marxian diagnosis of what enables capitalists to exploit workers. It is because wordly resources *do* contribute to the creation of the product that they enjoy the importance they have in that diagnosis. The distinction between 'creating' exchange-value and creating the use-valuable product therefore provides no escape from the dilemma in which I sought to place orthodox Marxists at the end of section 3.

6. Recall that the third approach to distributive justice, partial egalitarianism (see earlier), does not restrict people's rights in their own powers, nor, therefore, in the fruits of the exercise of those powers. It follows that the third approach will not enable much movement in the direction of equality of condition if one can say that the things people want are largely the product of human labour, as opposed to of non-human resources. And that, to turn now to Locke, is precisely what he says. He claims that labour is responsible for virtually all of the use-value of what human beings want or need, while natural resources are responsible for virtually none of it.

Some typical embodiments of Locke's claim:

. . . labour makes the far greatest part of the value of things we enjoy in this world. And the ground which produces the materials is scarce to be reckoned in as any, or at most but a very small, part of it . . .

'Tis labour, then, which puts the greatest part of value upon land, without which it would scarcely be worth anything . . . Nature and the earth furnished only the most worthless materials, as in themselves.

Uncultivated land creates virtually no value, and, Locke infers, it therefore possesses virtually no value. It is 'scarcely . . . worth anything', since it 'furnishe[s] the most worthless materials' only.

Locke repeatedly emphasizes the claims that labour creates almost all of the value of things and that natural resources have almost no value.

Clearly, then, he thought something pretty important followed from them. But it is not so clear what he thought the important conclusion was. I shall presently describe two conclusions which might be thought to follow from Locke's contrast between the contributions of land and labour. Each conclusion has been attributed to him by commentators. I shall not try to say which of them he really drew himself, partly because my philosophical interest in Locke is not so historical as that, but also because, when I come to criticize Locke, I shall focus, for the most part, on his premiss that labour creates virtually all value, and what plainly was his argument for it, rather than what, not equally plainly, his inference from it was.

One conclusion which Locke has been thought to draw from the premiss that labour creates virtually all of the value of things is that no one should object very strongly to currently existing inequality, since it largely descends from people's exercise of their self-owned powers and subsequent disposal of what they created by using them. And the other conclusion is that the original formation of private property in unowned external things was justified by the fact that those things were nearly valueless before their labouring appropriators envalued them: appropriators gathered nothing worth mentioning when they established exclusive control over tracts of natural resources.

So we find in Locke, or attributed to Locke, a pair of arguments, with a common premiss. The common premiss is that labour is responsible for virtually all the value of what we use and consume. The conclusion of one argument, which I shall call the value/appropriation argument, is that a person who labours on unowned natural resources becomes, thereby, their legitimate owner. And the conclusion of the other argument, here called the value/inequality argument, is that inequality in distribution is justified, since, or to the extent that, it reflects unequal value-creating applications of labour. I am sure that Locke wanted to draw one or other of these conclusions, or both of them, or conclusions similar to them, from his premiss that labour creates nearly all value, since it is otherwise impossible to explain the importance which he attached to that premiss.

The common premiss of the value/appropriation and value/inequality arguments should not be identified with another, and more famous, Lockean claim. That different claim is that, when one labours on something, one mixes one's labour with it, thereby placing within it something one owns. Locke uses the labour mixture claim as a premiss to justify the original formation of private property out of what nobody privately owns. By mixing what he owns, to wit, his labour, with something unowned, the labouring appropriator becomes the legitimate owner of the resulting mixture, since he alone has any right to any of it.

Let us call that the 'labour mixture argument'. Note now that the labour mixture argument is different from the value/appropriation argument, whose conclusion it shares. The value argument for legitimate appropriation has a different rationale from the argument for labour mixture, although many (and sometimes, perhaps, Locke) are prone to confuse the two. It is easy to confuse them, since it is (at least standardly) by labouring on something that you enhance its value, and perhaps your action on it should count as labour only if it does enhance its value. Nevertheless, in the logic of the labour mixture argument, it is labour itself, and not value-creation, which justifies the claim to private property. If you own what you laboured on because your own labour is in it, then you do not own it because you have enhanced its value, even if what deserves to be called 'labour' necessarily creates value. And, for the value/appropriation argument, it is the conferring of value as such, not the labour by which it is conferred, that is essential. If you magically enhanced something's value without labouring, but, say, by wishing that it were more valuable, then you would be entitled to whatever the value argument justifies

you in having, even though you had not performed any labour.

Locke's principal labour mixture paragraphs in Chap. V of his *Second Treatise of Government* do not, in my view, invoke the consideration that labour enhances the value of that to which it is applied. And Karl Olivecrona may be right that when, in later paragraphs of the chapter, Locke does bring value enhancement to the fore, he is not there trying to defend the initial appropriation of private property, but, instead, advancing the differently concluding value/inequality argument. He is purporting to justify the extensive inequality of goods that obtains now, when original appropriation has long since ceased. The justification he offers is that almost all of present inequality is due not to any unequal initial appropriating but to the labour which followed after initial appropriation. Locke is prepared to concede that untouched natural things have some little value, but he urges that at least 90 per cent and (probably 99 per cent) of the value of things which have been transformed by labour is due to that transforming labour, so that, unless you would rob people of what they produced, or of what they rightfully received, directly, or at the end of a chain of transfers, from labouring producers, you cannot object to the greater part of the inequality that now prevails.

I shall show, in a moment, first, that Locke provides inadequate support for the premiss of the value arguments; second, that that premiss is indefensible; and, third, that, even if it were true, it would not sustain the conclusions drawn from it. But, before offering those criticisms, I must first clarify what the value-creation premiss says, and why Locke was so confident that it was true.

7. Locke's premiss is often described as a rough statement of what, since Marx, has been known as the labour theory of value. That is misleading, since the value which Locke says is (nearly all) due to labour is not the value Marx says labour created. Locke's topic is use-value, not exchange-value. Suppose you own a quantity

of wheat. Then the use-value you own is measured by the number of bushels of wheat you have, or, more abstractly, by the amount of life and enjoyment, or of utility, those bushels will afford, whereas their exchange-value is measured by the quantity of other commodities they will fetch on the market. And use-value and exchange-value can vary independently of each other: the self-same quantity of wheat, with the self-same use-value, will undergo a change in exchange-value as market conditions change, and different quantities of wheat, and hence of use-value, will, under appropriately different market conditions, possess the same exchange-value.

If you read Locke with this distinction in mind, I think you will agree that his labour-praising premiss praises labour as the source of use-, not exchange-, value. Consider, for example, these excerpts from II: 37:

> . . . the provisions serving to the support of human life produced by one acre of enclosed and cultivated land are (to speak much within compass) ten times more than those which are yielded by an acre of land of an equal richness lying waste in common . . . I have here rated the improved land very low, in making its product but as ten to one, when it is much nearer a hundred to one.

Hence land without labour is, as we saw, 'scarcely . . . worth anything'. But the increase in its value which is here assigned to the action of labour is an increase in its use-value. For Locke's figures have to do with the comparative physical yields, or use-values, which virgin and cultivated land produce, not with what virgin and cultivated land would respectively fetch on the market.

Notice, now, how Locke determines the contribution of labour to use-value. He does so by comparing the yield of the land with and without labour, his tool of comparison being what I shall call 'the subtraction criterion'. It operates as follows: you subtract what the land yields without labour from what it yields with it, and then you form the fraction got by putting the result of that subtraction over what the land yields with labour. The resulting fraction, to wit,

$$\frac{\text{Amount land yields with labour} - \text{amount it yields without it}}{\text{Amount land yields with labour}}$$

is supposed to indicate the proportion of use-value which is due to labour, with the rest, consequently, being due to land. I shall later criticize this procedure for gauging comparative contributions to use-value creation, but, for the moment, just note what it is, and that it has nothing to do with exchange-value. Land which produces one-tenth without labour of what it would it would produce with it is not consequently going to fetch, on the market, one-tenth in its virgin state of what it would fetch if it were cultivated.

Since Locke's *explanandum* is use-value, his is not the *explanandum* of the Marxian labour theory, exchange-value. But the *explanans* in Locke's theory is also not the same as the labour-theoretical *explanans*, since, in the labour theory, exchange-value is a positive linear function of labour time, and labour time plays no comparable role in Locke's theory. And that is because the amount of a thing's use-value could not conceivably be imagined to co-vary in a simple way with the labour time required to produce it, even by someone who thought that its use-value was entirely due to labour. As Karl Marx saw, Locke's *explanans* is 'concrete labour', which is to say labour considered in its concrete form of ploughing, sowing, and so forth, not, as Marx put it, labour 'as a quantum'.

To see how labour times play no essential role in Locke's theory, suppose that every piece of land within a given economy is of the same fertility, and that an economy-wide deterioration in fertility, affecting every piece equally, now supervenes. Both before and after the deterioration one acre of the land would yield one bushel of corn per day without labour and a maximum of ten with it, but three hours a day was required to make it yield its maximum ten bushels when the land was good and six hours after it has deteriorated. Then the yield of the cultivated land would not have more value for Locke in stage two than it had in stage one, and that is because the use-value of its yield would have remained the same, even though, on labour-theoretical premisses, its exchange-value would, *ceteris paribus*, have risen.

A simple proof that Locke's is not a labour theory of value in the Marxian sense is that he says only that *almost* all of the value of the product is due to labour. But that point aside, he was not a Marxian labour theorist, for the two reasons rehearsed above.

The second of those reasons was that Locke's *explanans* of value is not the amount of labour time required to produce the product. Yet he does emphasize how prodigious is the amount of labour that goes into elementary consumption goods, reminding us that

> 'tis not barely the ploughman's pains, the reaper's and thresher's toil, and the baker's sweat, is to be counted into the bread we eat; the labour of those who broke the oxen, who dug and wrought the iron and stones, who felled and framed the timber employed about the plough, mill, oven, or any other utensils, which are a vast number, requisite to the corn, from its being seed to be sown to its being made bread, must all be charged on the account of labour, and received as an effect of that. Nature and the earth furnished only the almost worthless materials as in themselves.

Still, the extensive labour catalogued here is not here measured in the relevant Marxian way, as a quantity of undifferentiated labour time with which exchange-value might be thought to vary. Locke's point is rather that a great deal of variously concrete labour is needed to get consumable bread from an almost worthless natural starting point. It is, moreover, not entirely clear how Locke's catalogue is supposed to serve his own purpose, which is to affirm that labour is the source of (almost all) use-value. For his reason for saying that unworked materials are worthless would apply even if only very little labour were needed to transform them into something worthwhile. The application of the subtraction procedure for determining labour's contribution requires no information about the amount of labour, in any sense, that has been spent. (A speculation about Locke's motive for nevertheless emphasizing labour's amount is offered in the following section.)

Finally, a footnote about Marx. As I remarked earlier, he saw that Locke was not propounding a labour theory of exchange-value. But the passage in which Marx expresses that insight is also interesting for another reason. Having observed that, for Locke, 'labour gives things almost all their value', Marx then added this partly curious gloss:

> *value* here is equivalent to use-value, and labour is taken as concrete labour, not as a quantum; but the measuring of exchange-value by labour is in reality based on the fact that the labourer creates use-value.

The curious part follows the semi-colon. Almost certainly, Marx is there stating something he believes to be true, rather than merely something he believes Locke thought true. But then Marx's statement is curious, for how could he think labour's creation of use-value was the basis for 'the measuring of exchange-value by labour' (alone) when, as he knew (see earlier), land too creates use-value? A Marxist might reply that creating use-value is but a necessary condition of a factor's being a measure of exchange-value. But then what further relevant condition does labour, and not also land, satisfy? To answer that question, one must say more than merely: that it is labour.

8. My main criticism of Locke's value arguments is an objection to the basis on which he asserts their premiss, which is the premiss that labour is responsible for almost all of what the land yields. He establishes that premiss on the basis of his subtraction criterion.

Consider a piece of cultivated land which yields ten times as much crop as it did before it was cultivated. Is it true, for the reason Locke gave, and with the sense he attached to the following statement, that labour is responsible for 90 per cent of the crop of the cultivated land? In its intended sense, the statement contrasts the contribution of labour with that of the land itself, which here would be 10 per cent of the crop: the point of the statement is to deprecate the contribution of land itself to use-value.

In my view, the desired statement is not true in the required contrastive sense for the reason Locke gave, since that reason, to wit, Locke's subtraction criterion, is unacceptable. One ground for saying that it is unacceptable is that it has intuitively unacceptable consequences. Another ground is that it generates a logical contradiction.

To see that the subtraction criterion has intuitively unacceptable consequences, suppose that only one hour a year of labour is required to draw a hundred bushels of wheat per year from a field which produces only a single bushel a year spontaneously. Or, to take a more realistic example, suppose that just one hour of digging creates a well which yields a thousand gallons of water a year, where before there was only a measly annual ten-gallon trickle. It would surely be wrong to infer, from the fact that the digging *raised* the water yield from ten to a thousand gallons, that the digging is responsible for 99 per cent of the water yielded by, and, hence, of the use-value produced by, the dug land, while the land itself is responsible for only one per cent of it.

As Locke recognized, land frequently produces consumables without any labour having been applied to it. Contrast the hide of a cow, which produces no shoes, and not merely very few, when no tanning and cutting and shaping of it goes on. Must we therefore say that land which is, spontaneously, modestly productive, makes some small contribution to the use-value of the bread baked from its wheat, whereas cowhide makes none to the use-value of shoes? Or that land which, spontaneously, produces a bit of wheat, but no apples, makes a small contribution to use-value if it is used to produce (more) wheat, but none if it is used to produce apples? These contrasts are absurd, but they are forced upon us by Locke's subtraction criterion.

Locke's criterion fails because the *difference* application of a factor makes to output, its marginal contribution, cannot be treated as its contribution to that output *by contrast* with the contribution of other factors. But it is just such a contrast that Locke needs, so that he can upvalue the contribution of labour and devalue the contribution of land. He needs, in other words, to pass from the unexceptionable premiss of the following argument to its invalidly derived conclusion. It will often be true that

1.   The application of labour makes virgin land produce ten times what it did before.

But it does not follow that, in such a case,

2.   Labour produces 90 per cent of the product of applying it to virgin land.

No one can think such an argument valid once he gets its premiss and conclusion distinguished from each other in his mind, but that sometimes takes effort, since many sentences can be used to express either the premiss or the conclusion, and thereby the argument can acquire an appearance of validity. One might think (2) follows from (1) because one inattentively uses such a sentence as 'the additional output of 90 per cent is due to labour' to express now (1) and now (2).

Some claim that the fallacy exposed above is too simple to attribute to a thinker of Locke's stature. They say that I have not captured the intuitive power of his reply to the egalitarian, which is that the goods the latter would redistribute are so largely due to labour that redistribution of them would violate rightful claims in them. But I think the intuitive power of that reply depends entirely on its ambiguity. It is true in sense (1), but polemically interesting only in sense (2). Unless we represent Locke as confusing (1) and (2), or as unjustifiably inferring (2) from (1), we cannot explain why he lays so much emphasis on (1). (1) serves no labour-praising and land-diminishing polemical purpose when (2) is neither derived from it nor confused with it.

I said that Locke's criterion for determining relative contributions to use-value not only has unintuitive consequences, but also leads to a contradiction. On that criterion, if a piece of land is cropless without labour, but yields a crop with it, then labour is responsible for all of that crop, and land is responsible for none of it. But though the land is entirely cropless without labour, it is equally true that the labour, the ploughing and harrowing and so on, would yield no crop on infertile land. The value of the following fraction, is, consequently, 100 per cent:

$$\frac{\text{Amount labour yields with land} - \text{amount it yields without it}}{\text{Amount labour yields with land}}$$

Then, on a natural generalization of Locke's procedure, we should have to add conclusions (5) and (6) to (3) and (4), which are the ones he draws:

3. Labour is responsible for all of the crop.
4. Land is responsible for none of the crop.
5. Land is responsible for all of the crop.
6. Labour is responsible for none of the crop.

This set of sentences fails to award the palm to labour. But, beyond that, it also entails a manifest contradiction. For even if (3) and (5) are somehow consistent with each other, (3) and (6) (and (4) and (5)) are certainly not. If there exists a defensible criterion for assigning relative contributions to output of labour on the one hand and the original properties of the soil on the other, then it is not Locke's.

For my part, I doubt that there exists such a criterion, and I must therefore distinguish what some economists might think would supply such a criterion from the sort of criterion I doubt exists. Economists call the problem of rewarding co-operating factors of production *the value allocation problem*. An early solution to that problem was provided by Lloyd Shapley. He laid down seemingly plausible axiomatic constraints on any solution, and he proved that the only procedure consistent with them was to allocate to each factor the average of its marginal contributions in all possible orders in which the factors might be combined with one another.

Now the reason why I nevertheless say that there is no criterion which should replace Locke's unacceptable one is that, while Locke seeks, in the end, to answer something like the Shapley allocation question, his criterion is, immediately, not of how to allocate portions of what is produced to factors, in the sense of rewarding them, but of how to diagnose what different factors contribute to the product (in order, on that basis, to do some appropriate rewarding). In short, Locke goes from (i) facts about marginal contributions, to (ii) claims about comparative physical contributions, to (iii) conclusions about rewards. His argument says, roughly, that since land without labour produces hardly anything, and land with labour produces an enormous amount, labour contributes vastly more to output than land does, and labour, should, accordingly, be appropriately rewarded. There is nothing in Shapley which corresponds to the second stage of this argument. He proceeds directly, by dint of his axioms, from (i) to (iii), thereby, unlike Locke, refraining from answering what may be a pseudo-question. I am confident that Locke affirms (ii), since he starts with (i) and ends with (iii), and I do not see how he could otherwise think he has traversed the distance between them. He certainly did not anticipate Shapley's axioms, which have, by the way, distinctly non-Lockean distributional consequences.

To conclude. If J. R. Ewing, or Donna Krebs, produces a well yielding one thousand barrels of oil a day after five minutes' excavation, then we cannot infer, on the Lockean ground that no oil comes without digging, that his or her labour, *as opposed to the land*, is responsible for all of that oil. The conclusion is unavailable, not only because it is absurd so to praise so mere a whiff of labour, but also because, by the same Lockean token, labour is responsible for *none* of the oil, since a digger on oil-less land produces no oil: the digger cannot be both responsible for all of the oil and responsible for none of it.

9. So Locke's defence of his premiss, that labour is responsible for nearly all the use-value of things, is unacceptable. And the premiss is, moreover, indefensible, even if my suspicion that it answers a pseudo-question is unfounded.

I say that it is indefensible for two reasons. The first is that I do not see how one might try to defend it other than on Locke's unacceptable basis: what else could lead one to think that it is true? But my second reason for saying that it is indefensible is more positive. If Locke is right, then land in general has nearly no use-value. Well, consider some land which Locke would regard as particularly friendly to his case, because it yields nothing without labour, though very much with it. One could not say of such land that it has virtually no use-value, let alone, as Locke's criterion would have it, none at all. One could not say that, precisely because the land yields so much *with* labour. Its use-value cannot be considered trivial, since it has a prodigious power to satisfy human desire, in

virtue of how it reacts when labour is applied to it.

10. But even if we were to accept Locke's indefensible—and, perhaps, meaningless—premiss, we should still be able to resist the conclusions he is supposed to have derived from it, which are that original appropriation and/or currently existing inequality are justified. For even if land never produced anything without labour, so that, Locke here being assumed to be right, labour was responsible for all the use-value drawn from the land, the land-owner would not thereby be justified in taking all of the land's fruit, on the supposition that he or relevantly connected predecessors had performed all the labour on it. For that inference ignores the consideration that not everyone might have had an equivalent opportunity to labour on land, because there was no land left to labour on, or because the land left to labour on was less good than what the more fortunate laboured on. It is generally thought that, when Locke advanced his labour mixture argument (see earlier), he made it a condition of the power of labour to create title in land that the labourer leave 'enough and as good' land for others to labour on. To cope with the consideration just mentioned, something similar would have to be added to the value creation premiss, in both of its uses. But then both of the arguments based on it would fail, since enough and as good has not in fact been left for others.

To that complaint of opportunity denied, Robert Nozick has responded that no grievance results, since the landless are no worse off than they would have been had the appropriated land remained unowned. But in focusing only on how the landless in a fully appropriated world would have fared in a wholly unappropriated one, Nozick suppresses other pertinent questions, such as how they would have fared had they, or their forbears, had the opportunity to do some appropriating, and his response therefore fails to allay the grievance here envisaged.

This is the right place to comment on a brilliant Lockean argument for private property, which exploits labour's creative powers in a different way from the arguments discussed above. I mean Locke's contention that the improving cultivator

> who appropriates land to himself by his labour does not lessen but increase the common stock of mankind . . . he that encloses land, and has a greater plenty of the conveniences of life from ten acres than he could have had from a hundred left to nature, may truly be said to give ninety acres to mankind: for his labour now supplies him with provisions out of ten acres, which were but the product of a hundred lying in common.

This argument has the virtue that it requires no claim that the cultivator is responsible for 90 per cent of what he draws from nature. The cultivator's gift to 'the common stock' is not, I think, the surplus provision he produces on his own ten acres, all of which he might himself consume, but the bounty of nature on the ninety acres he is able to vacate for the use of the rest of mankind, because of his productivity on the ten he privatizes. And the argument does justify private property, at any rate if people own their own powers and therefore owe no fruit of them to others, since, on that assumption, this privatizer only benefits the rest of mankind when he retires to his own plot: they now have an additional ninety acres to reap the fruit of. But the argument justifies private property only as long as appropriation generates an expanding common for the privately unendowed to forage on, and it therefore fails to justify actual private property in the real and fully appropriated world. To justify private property in a fully appropriated world in which some own none, something like Nozick's move would be needed, but that move, as I have said, fails.

11. I expressed uncertainty (see section 6) about what conclusion(s) Locke hoped to draw from his premiss that labour creates (nearly all) value, but I also expressed confidence that he thought something important followed from it in favour of private property and/or inequality. I believe, moreover, that he thought what followed favoured private property and/or inequality both in the pre-governmental state of nature and in society under government. James Tully's interpretation of Chap. V of the *Second Treatise* would, if correct, create difficulty for that understanding of Locke, and I shall therefore criticize his interpretation here.

According to Tully, Locke does not seek to justify property which is truly private, either in the state of nature or under government. What God gives to men in common undergoes what Tully calls 'individuation', but not full privatization. And one reason why Tully's Locke refuses to endorse fully private property is that the latter's entitlements would militate against the welfare of the community. But both (a) Tully's attribution to Locke of welfarist intentions, and (b) his denial that individuated property is private seem to me to depend on misuses of Locke's texts.

(a) Some of the material offered by Tully in defence of the first thesis gives it no support whatever. He refers to II: 39 in support of his statement that 'it is the duty of governments to organize the community's possessions and strength for the public good', but nothing in II: 39 bears on that issue. He cites II: 50 to show that the community's laws must 'confine the possession of land' so that everyone can enjoy it, whereas all II: 50 says to the point is that 'in governments the laws regulate the right of property, and the possession of land is determined by positive constitutions'. And he invokes II: 135 in justification of the amazing claim, about which II: 135 says nothing, that, for Locke, 'government is required to constitute a new order of social relations which will bring the actions of men once again in line with God's intentions'.

Tully thinks the actions of men fell out of line with God's intentions in the state of nature, when the introduction of money disrupted naturally ordered relations by facilitating a development of inequality which would have been impossible or unlikely before money appeared. Yet it is not, as Tully groundlessly says, the wealthy themselves who—for Tully's Locke, unjustifiably—'claim to be entitled to their enlarged possessions' in the texts he cites, but John Locke who presents that claim for them. According to Locke, the accumulator of monetary wealth 'invade(s) not the right of others', since 'the exceeding of the bounds of his just property' lies not 'in the largeness of his possession', but in 'the perishing of anything uselessly in it' (II: 46), and money does not perish.

In the *First Treatise* (I: 42) Locke imposes on those who have more than they need a duty to give to those who are in want, and we might reasonably imagine that a Lockean government would enforce that duty (although it is interesting that Locke does not actually say that it would). But there is little reference to a duty of charity in the *Second Treatise*, notwithstanding Tully's straining efforts to show the contrary, some of which I now expose.

Citing II: 37, Tully says:

if a case of need arises then, *ipso facto*, one man's individual right is overridden by another's claim, and the goods become his property. By failing to hand over the goods, the proprietor invades the share now belonging to the needy and is liable to punishment.

This twists what II: 37 says. It says nothing about needy people. It does say that if a man takes more than he can use, so that some of it spoils, then he invades 'his neighbour's share', but he invades it *whether or not his neighbour is needy*. It is not as though a person is allowed to keep fruit which he cannot use unless and until 'a case of need arises'. Rather, he is not supposed to have it at all. He has no presumptive right to it

which someone else's need might, as in I: 42, override.

The duty of charity laid down in I: 42 might be called a duty of the abundantly endowed to *preserve* others, but I have not found a duty to preserve others, in that sense, imposed on the well endowed, or on anyone else, in the *Second Treatise*. Hence I do not agree with Tully when he cites II: 6 in support of 'a natural duty of each man to preserve himself, and, *ceteris paribus*, others'. In fact, II: 6 forbids people to harm others, or to deprive them of what they have produced for themselves, but it does not, as Tully's gloss on it suggests, lay down that, having succeeded in preserving himself, a person is obliged to set about working for the preservation of others, should such activity now be necessary and possible. Note that not even I: 42 obliges a person to labour for the sake of anyone else's preservation.

Tully quotes from II: 149 in further supposed support of this 'natural duty to engage in the end-directed activity of preserving man', but no duty of the individual to preserve anyone but himself is mentioned in II: 149. And when Tully points to II: 11, in which Locke speaks of 'the right he [man] has of preserving all mankind', he refrains from mentioning that the said right is here exercised solely in preventing or deterring others from killing people. Locke is grounding a right to punish aggressors against oneself and others, not addressing himself to need and to the preservation of needy people.

I remarked that not even the *First Treatise* says that the duty of charity is to be enforced by government. Nor do I agree that it 'attributes to Filmer the theory that property in land is independent of social functions and admonishes that it is the "most specious thing"'. For the thing Locke here calls 'most specious' is the idea that if one man (e.g. Adam) were the legitimate proprietor of the whole world, he would have a consequent right to starve everyone else into submission to him. It hardly follows that Locke would think it similarly specious to deny social functions to property where it was distributed with less extravagant inequity.

Tully also cites the *Essays on the Law of Nature* to support his claim that Locke 'finds a theory of property which is not conditional on the performance of social functions an "absurdity" '. But what Locke there declares to be an 'absurdity' is not some theory of property, but a theory of morally correct motivation according to which

> it would be unlawful for a man to renounce his own rights or to impart benefits to another without a definite hope of reward . . . to grant or give anything to a friend, incur expenses on his behalf, or in any other manner do him a favour out of pure kindness.

Locke is denying that 'the rightness of a course of action be derived from expediency', not affirming that property rights are conditional on social service. He urges that, if it were wrong for a man to act against his own selfish interest, then, absurdly, it would be wrong for him to 'renounce his own rights' for the sake of a friend. Locke's words imply that property rights include, as one might expect, the right not to give away what one owns (on which a kind man will not always insist). Hence, far from sustaining Tully's eccentric interpretation, the *Essays* passage actually contradicts it.

(b) So much against Tully's attribution to Locke of welfarist intentions. I turn to the connected issue distinguished earlier, to wit, Tully's denial that the legitimate 'individuation' of what God gives to men in common amounts to the formation of private property.

According to Tully, what most commentators have thought was private property in Locke is, in fact, 'exclusive property within positive community'. The individuation of the world 'does not dissolve, but merely realises property in common'. This is supposed to be demonstrated by II: 26, in which, comments Tully, an 'agent with an exclusive right still remains "a tenant in common" '.

But that comment is a misuse of II: 26. The agent in II:26 is an Indian who has established an exclusive right in some fruit or venison. The fruit did belong to mankind in common, but, once the Indian has appropriated it, it no longer does: the common property in the fruit is entirely 'dissolved'. What he remains 'a tenant in common of' is the land itself, over no part of which, however, does he have any exclusive right, and Locke's point in II: 26 is that private property is so unavoidable that even a tenant in common must privatize the fruit of the common to get any benefit from it. The individuation of land itself arises only later, at II: 32, where Locke says 'it is plain, that property in that too is acquired' as property is acquired in venison and fruit: with full private right. The idea that individuation 'does not dissolve, but merely realises property in common' is entirely without foundation.

Continuing his advocacy of 'exclusive property within positive community', Tully makes curious and unjustified use of paragraphs 28 and 35 of the *Second Treatise*:

> Locke is quite explicit in saying that his model is the English Common. 'We see in Commons, which remain so by compact, that 'tis the taking any part of what is common, and removing it out of the state nature leaves it in, which begins the property; without which the common is of no use' (2.28. cf. 2.35).

Now, as II: 35 makes clear, a common by compact is, by contrast with a common in the state of nature, one whose parts may not be privatized: the compact is an agreement that the land will remain held in common. All that one can privatize here is the fruit of the common, not the land itself, and Locke's point in II: 28 is that *even* when the land is held in common by compact, something must be privatized for it to be of any use. So II: 28 supports the idea that individuation 'realises property in common' just as little as the Indian example in II: 26 does.

Tully's 'cf. 2.35' is, moreover, hard to construe. II: 35 adverts to the impossibility of privatizing the land of a 'common by compact', but points out that 'it is quite otherwise' for commons lacking in legislated status. Where the common is natural you can take land, but you thereby cancel common ownership of the part you take. Where the common is by compact, you can take only fruit, thereby dissolving the common ownership of that fruit. The formula favoured by Tully, of 'exclusive property within positive community' is in no case satisfied, and I do not understand why he refers us to II: 35.

12. In my old-fashioned perception of Locke, he holds that men enter political community in order to secure their lives and their possessions, both of which are at risk in the state of nature. Now it is obviously, because necessarily, the very lives which they had in the state of nature, and not, *per impossibile*, some freshly distributed ones, which come under communal protection once men enter political society. And I believe, with most commentators, and against Tully, that, although it is not equally necessary, it is equally true that, for Locke, the possessions men enjoy in society are, initially, the very possessions which belonged to them in the state of nature, and which they had aimed to make more safe: they do not enter community in order to have some or other secure possessions, but in order to secure the possessions they already precariously enjoyed. In the paragraphs bearing on this issue Locke's language does not distinguish between preservation of life and preservation of property in the way it would if there were not between the two preservations the similarity on which I am here insisting.

In Tully's different view of Locke, once government is established, 'all the possessions a man has in the state of nature . . . become possessions of the community', which determines the members' use of them. But Tully's interpretation confuses possession, or ownership, with political rule. When people join the community, they submit *themselves* to its rule, and, as Locke makes plain (II: 120), they must, on pain of contradiction, submit their property to its rule too. But it no more follows from the community's rule over a person's possessions that they now 'belong to the community' than it does from its rule over him that he belongs to it in the relevant parallel sense of being its slave. The community does not own his goods any more than it owns his person. To be sure, it enacts and enforces rules of criminal and civil law, to which his property and person are subject. One may therefore say, as Locke does, that it 'regulates' (II: 50, 139) property, but it hardly follows that 'the *distribution* of property' is 'in the hands of government'. Its distribution is, temporally speaking, pre-politically grounded, and, speaking in terms of justifying principle, sub-politically grounded. That is why II: 138 emphasizes—on Tully's account, unintelligibly—that the legislature 'cannot take from any man any part of his property without his own consent': if the legislature distributed property in the first place, it could surely redistribute it, when circumstances have changed, on whatever basis underlay the original distribution.

When Locke writes that men, 'by compact and agreement, settled the property which labour and industry began' (II: 45), the natural reading of his words is that it was the very property which each compactor had gathered as a result of his own labour (or that of relevantly connected others) which was now to be 'settled': it was rendered secure, by being placed within a political framework. On Tully's alternative reading, the pre-politically well-endowed would, improbably, have agreed to a dispossession which reduced them to equal standing with the pre-politically indigent. Commenting on II: 45, he tells us that, for Locke, 'property in political society is a creation of that society', but there is no warrant there, or elsewhere, for this assertion, or for Tully's extravagant conclusion that 'community ownership of all possessions is the logical consequence of the premisses of Locke's theory in the *Two Treatises*'. It is no more entailed by Locke's premisses than community ownership of individuals is.

13. For political reasons, I want to emphasize the contribution of non-human resources to human life and enjoyment. Nothing positive about the size of that contribution emerges from the present lecture. But I think I have shown that Locke's claim that its size is small cannot be sustained.

2c. DISTRIBUTIVE JUSTICE

THERE JUST AREN'T ENOUGH good things to go around. Land, money, health care, opportunities, education and romantic partners (to name just a few) are all limited in the sense that demand for them will always exceed supply. How, then, should we determine who gets what? This is the basic question of distributive justice.

Generally, philosophers attempt to answer this question by appealing to some more basic value. A just distribution, one might say, is one that promotes freedom. Or, another might claim, perhaps a just distribution is one that in some way respects people as equals. We will look at both of these values in more detail in subsequent essays. In this section, our concern will be with the concept of distributive justice more generally, rather than its relation to one particular value.

In fact, part of the task of this section will be to examine the legitimacy of the very subject of distributive justice itself. For, the concept is one which has come under severe criticism from certain libertarian theorists such as Robert Nozick and Friedrich Hayek. Such theorists argue that the notion of distributive justice is appropriate only when there is some *agent* making a choice about how to distribute certain goods. A parent, for instance, who allocates allowance money among her children, or a teacher who assigns grades to the various students in her class. But in a market economy, such theorists argue, there is no single agent responsible for the distribution of goods among persons. Who gets what is a result of a complicated series of decisions by many, many different decision-makers whose choices cannot be captured in any single principle. Parents give money and other gifts to their children out of love and obligation, bosses give raises to workers as a reward for merit or as an incentive for future performance, consumers give money to Routledge in exchange for stimulating books on political philosophy, etc. The point is that as long as individuals are free to do what they want with their possessions—including transfer some of those possessions to others—there can be no guarantee that the overall results of their decisions will conform to any single principle of just distribution, nor can it be said that the distribution resulted from the application of some single principle.

Nozick thus argues that the only meaningful sense in which we can talk about the justice of a distribution is as an essentially *historical* matter—the justice of a distribution is a function of the way in which that distribution comes about, and not in the value it promotes or the pattern in which it falls. Distributions are just if they arise as a result of people acting justly, and since Nozick believes that voluntary "capitalist acts between consenting adults" are just, then any distribution which results from a series of such capitalist acts is itself just.

In one sense, this sort of move avoids some potential difficulties for the libertarian. Rawls, in an earlier chapter, argued that individuals in a market economy (or elsewhere) cannot be said to deserve their wealth, since they did nothing to deserve the social or natural endowments of which that wealth was a product. Other critics of capitalism have argued that markets often fail to reward those with the greatest talent, or that they tend to promote material inequality, or fail to meet people's basic needs. But Nozick's position is, in a sense, immune to these sorts of criticisms. For his position is not that markets are good because they give people what they need, deserve, or merit. His position is that they are good because they allow people to do what they choose with what they own. That some people will choose to do things that do not promote equality, merit, or whatever, is not an embarrassment to the theory—it is, rather, the virtually inevitable result of allowing people to act freely.

Still, adopting this position requires the libertarian to bite a fairly sizable bullet. For, as the readings by Ehrenreich, Ackerman, and Nielsen forcefully argue, we care deeply about values like just desert and equality and are inclined to view it as a failure of a social system if it creates distributions which fail to realize them. Barbara Ehrenreich's experience as a low-wage worker in *Nickel and Dimed*, for instance, recalls Marx's critique of capitalism in its illustration of the ways in which markets seem to promote the freedom of some only at the expense of others. Low-skill workers seem forced to spend the greater part of their day engaged in grueling, unpleasant, and sometimes demeaning work in order to make enough money to provide for their basic needs. Their freedom appears to be curtailed both in the concrete sense that they are told what to wear, what to do, how to speak and so on, and in the more general sense that the economic system is set up so that they *must* accept these more concrete limitations on their freedom in order to make ends meet. Can a market system which is indifferent to, and arguably promotes, such inequalities of power really be justified?

Similarly, Ackerman demonstrates how a purely historical principle of distributive justice can seem both arbitrary and incompatible with a society in which individuals regard each other with mutual respect. To the extent that wealth in a capitalist society is based upon who stumbled upon a resource or an idea first, or who happened to be born with a talent for throwing a ball through a hoop in a society that happened to value that peculiar skill, that wealth seems morally arbitrary. How can such an individual whose wealth is in so many ways the product of luck look their fellow citizens in the eye and claim a strong moral entitlement to that wealth? What reasons can be given for allowing the distribution of wealth to be based on such seemingly arbitrary factors? And if no reason can be given, then how can the social system which produces that distribution claim legitimate moral authority as opposed to mere brute force?

Moral theorists have long argued that utilitarianism is inadequate as a moral philosophy because in its single-minded concern with maximizing *total* utility, it utterly neglects the issue of how that utility is distributed among separate persons. A utilitarian seems committed to saying that enslaving a minority of the population would be morally permissible (indeed, required!) if it created greater overall utility than allowing everyone freedom. But most of us share Rawls' intuition that justice guarantees each individual a certain kind of inviolability—there are certain things that you can't do to me no matter *how* much you, or society as a whole for that matter, would benefit.

Showing that capitalism is a just social system, then, will require more than simply showing that it creates a great amount of wealth *in the aggregate*. Like utility, we care not just about how much wealth is created, but how that wealth is distributed among separate persons. And this means that we need to settle on moral principles to distinguish just from unjust distributions. It is to that task that the essays in this section are devoted.

Further Reading

Cohen, G. A. (1997). Where the Action is: On the Site of Distributive Justice. *Philosophy and Public Affairs, 26*(1), 3–30.

Feinberg, J. (1963). Justice and Personal Desert. In C. J. Friedrich and J. W. Chapman (Eds), *Nomos VI, Justice,* 69–97. New York: Atherton Press.

Goodin, R. E. (1995). *Utilitarianism as a Public Philosophy.* Cambridge: Cambridge University Press.

Hayek, F. A. (1976). *Law, Legislation and Liberty, Vol. 2: The Mirage of Social Justice.* London: Routledge & Kegan Paul.

Lamont, J. (1994). The Concept of Desert in Distributive Justice. *Philosophical Quarterly, 44*(174), 45–64.

Miller, D. (1976). *Social Justice.* Oxford: Oxford University Press.

Miller, D. (1999). *Principles of Social Justice.* Cambridge, MA: Harvard University Press.

Nozick, R. (1974). *Anarchy, State, and Utopia.* New York: Basic Books.

Rawls, J. (1971). *A Theory of Justice* (1st ed.). Cambridge, MA: Belknap Press.

Roemer, J. E. (1996). *Theories of Distributive Justice.* Cambridge, MA: Harvard University Press.

Sen, A., & Williams, B. (1982). *Utilitarianism and Beyond.* Cambridge: Cambridge University Press.

Chapter 28

Barbara Ehrenreich

NICKEL AND DIMED

Barbara Ehrenreich (1941–   ) is an American writer and political activist. These excerpts are drawn from her book *Nickel and Dimed* (2001), in which she recorded her experiences trying to live as a low-wage worker in modern America.

Introduction: Getting Ready

The idea that led to this book arose in comparatively sumptuous circumstances. Lewis Lapham, the editor of *Harper's*, had taken me out for a $30 lunch at some understated French country-style place to discuss future articles I might write for his magazine. I had the salmon and field greens, I think, and was pitching him some ideas having to do with pop culture when the conversation drifted to one of my more familiar themes—poverty. How does anyone live on the wages available to the unskilled? How, in particular, we wondered, were the roughly four million women about to be booted into the labor market by welfare reform going to make it on $6 or $7 an hour? Then I said something that I have since had many opportunities to regret: "Someone ought to do the old-fashioned kind of journalism—you know, go out there and try it for themselves." I meant someone much younger than myself, some hungry neophyte journalist with time on her hands. But Lapham got this crazy-looking half smile on his face and ended life as I knew it, for long stretches at least, with the single word "*You*."

The last time anyone had urged me to forsake my normal life for a run-of-the-mill low-paid job had been in the seventies, when dozens, perhaps hundreds, of sixties radicals started going into the factories to "proletarianize" themselves and organize the working class in the process. Not this girl. I felt sorry for the parents who had paid college tuition for these blue-collar wannabes and sorry, too, for the people they intended to uplift. In my own family, the low-wage way of life had never been many degrees of separation away; it was close enough, in any case, to make me treasure the gloriously autonomous, if not always well-paid, writing life. My sister has been through one low-paid job after another—phone company business rep, factory worker, receptionist—constantly struggling against what she calls "the hopelessness of being a wage slave." My husband and companion of seventeen years was a $4.50-an-hour warehouse worker when I fell in with him, escaping eventually and with huge relief to become an organizer for the Teamsters. My father had been a copper miner; uncles and grandfathers worked in the mines or for the Union Pacific. So to me, sitting at a desk all day was not only a privilege but a duty: something I owed to all those people in my life, living and dead, who'd had so much more to say than anyone ever got to hear.

Adding to my misgivings, certain family members kept reminding me unhelpfully that I could do this project, after a fashion, without ever leaving my study. I could just pay myself a typical entry-level wage for eight hours a day, charge myself for room and board plus some plausible expenses like gas, and total up the numbers after a month. With the prevailing wages running at $6–$7 an hour in my town and rents at $400 a month or more, the numbers might, it seemed to me, just barely work out all right. But if the question was whether a single mother leaving welfare could survive without government assistance in the form of food stamps, Medicaid, and housing and child care subsidies, the answer was well known before I ever left the comforts of home. According to the National Coalition for the Homeless, in 1998— the year I started this project—it took, on average nationwide, an hourly wage of $8.89 to afford a one-bedroom apartment, and the Preamble Center for Public Policy was estimating that the odds against a typical welfare recipient's landing a job at such a "living wage" were about 97 to 1. Why should I bother to confirm these unpleasant facts? As the time when I could no longer avoid the assignment approached, I began to feel a little like the elderly man I once knew who used a calculator to balance his checkbook and then went back and checked the results by redoing each sum by hand.

In the end, the only way to overcome my hesitation was by thinking of myself as a scientist, which is, in fact, what I was educated to be. I have a Ph.D. in biology, and I didn't get it by sitting at a desk and fiddling with numbers. In that line of business, you can think all you want, but sooner or later you have to get to the bench and plunge into the everyday chaos of nature, where surprises lurk in the most mundane measurements. Maybe when I got into the project, I would discover some hidden economies in the world of the low-wage worker. After all, if almost 30 percent of the workforce toils for $8 an hour or less, as the Washington-based Economic Policy Institute reported in 1998, they may have found some tricks as yet unknown to me. Maybe I would even be able to detect in myself the bracing psychological effects of getting out of the house, as promised by the wonks who brought us welfare reform. Or, on the other hand, maybe there would be unexpected costs— physical, financial, emotional—to throw off all my calculations. The only way to find out was to get out there and get my hands dirty.

In the spirit of science, I first decided on certain rules and parameters. Rule one, obviously enough, was that I could not, in my search for jobs, fall back on any skills derived from my education or usual work—not that there were a lot of want ads for essayists anyway. Two, I had to take the highest-paying job that was offered me and do my best to hold it; no Marxist rants or sneaking off to read novels in the ladies' room. Three, I had to take the cheapest accommodations I could find, at least the cheapest that offered an acceptable level of safety and privacy, though my standards in this regard were hazy and, as it turned out, prone to deterioration over time. [. . .]

Scrubbing in Maine

I am rested and ready for anything when I arrive at The Maids' office suite Monday at 7:30 A.M. I know nothing about cleaning services like this one, which, according to the brochure I am given, has over three hundred franchises nationwide, and most of what I know about domestics in general comes from nineteenth-century British novels and *Upstairs, Downstairs*.[1] Prophetically enough, I caught a rerun of that very show on PBS over the weekend and was struck by how terribly correct the servants looked in their black-and-white uniforms and how much wiser they were than their callow, egotistical masters. We too have uniforms, though they are more oafish than dignified—ill-fitting and in an overloud combination of kelly-green pants and a blinding sunflower-yellow polo shirt. And, as is explained in writing and over the next day and a half of training, we too have a special code of decorum. No smoking anywhere, or at least not within fifteen minutes of arrival at a house. No drinking, eating, or gum chewing in a house. No cursing in a house, even if the owner is not present, and—perhaps to keep us in practice—no obscenities even in the office. So this is Downstairs, is my chirpy first thought. But I have no idea, of course, just how far down these stairs will take me.

Forty minutes go by before anyone acknowledges my presence with more than a harried nod. During this time the other employees arrive, about twenty of them, already glowing in their uniforms, and breakfast on the free coffee, bagels, and doughnuts The Maids kindly provides for us. All but one of the others are female, with an average age I would guess in the late twenties, though the range seems to go from prom-fresh to well into the Medicare years. There is a pleasant sort of bustle as people get their breakfasts and fill plastic buckets with rags and bottles of cleaning fluids, but surprisingly little conversation outside of a few references to what people ate (pizza) and drank (Jell-O shots are mentioned) over the weekend. Since the room in which we gather contains only two folding chairs, both of them occupied, the other new girl and I sit cross-legged on the floor, silent and alert, while the regulars get sorted into teams of three or four and dispatched to the day's list of houses. One of the women explains to me that teams do not necessarily return to the same houses week after week, nor do you have any guarantee of being on the same team from one day to the next. This, I suppose, is one of the advantages of a corporate cleaning service to its customers: there are no sticky and possibly guilt-ridden relationships involved, because the customers communicate almost entirely with Tammy, the office manager, or with Ted, the franchise owner and our boss.[2] The advantage to

the cleaning person is harder to determine, since the pay compares so poorly to what an independent cleaner is likely to earn—up to $15 an hour, I've heard. While I wait in the inner room, where the phone is and Tammy has her desk, to be issued a uniform, I hear her tell a potential customer on the phone that The Maids charges $25 per person-hour. The company gets $25 and we get $6.65 for each hour we work? I think I must have misheard, but a few minutes later I hear her say the same thing to another inquirer. So the only advantage of working here as opposed to freelancing is that you don't need a clientele or even a car. You can arrive straight from welfare or, in my case, the bus station—fresh off the boat.[3]

At last, after all the other employees have sped off in the company's eye-catching green-and-yellow cars, I am led into a tiny closet-sized room off the inner office to learn my trade via videotape. The manager at another maid service where I'd applied had told me she didn't like to hire people who had done cleaning before because they were resistant to learning the company's system, so I prepare to empty my mind of all prior housecleaning experience. There are four tapes—dusting, bathrooms, kitchen, and vacuuming—each starring an attractive, possibly Hispanic young woman who moves about serenely in obedience to the male voiceover: For vacuuming, begin in the master bedroom; when dusting, begin with the room directly off the kitchen. When you enter a room, mentally divide it into sections no wider than your reach. Begin in the section to your left and, within each section, move from left to right and top to bottom. This way nothing is ever overlooked.

I like *Dusting* best, for its undeniable logic and a certain kind of austere beauty. When you enter a house, you spray a white rag with Windex and place it in the left pocket of your green apron. Another rag, sprayed with disinfectant, goes into the middle pocket, and a yellow rag bearing wood polish in the right-hand pocket. A dry rag, for buffing surfaces, occupies the right-hand pocket of your slacks. Shiny surfaces get Wind-exed, wood gets wood polish, and everything else is wiped dust-free with disinfectant. Every now and then Ted pops in to watch with me, pausing the video to underscore a particularly dramatic moment: "See how she's working around the vase? That's an accident waiting to happen." If Ted himself were in a video, it would have to be a cartoon, because the only features sketched onto his pudgy face are brown button-like eyes and a tiny pug nose; his belly, encased in a polo shirt, overhangs the waistline of his shorts. "You know, all this was figured out with a stopwatch," he tells me with something like pride. When the video warns against oversoaking our rags with cleaning fluids, he pauses it to tell me there's a danger in undersoaking too, especially if it's going to slow me down. "Cleaning fluids are less expensive than your time." It's good to know that *something* is cheaper than my time, or that in the hierarchy of the company's values I rank above Windex.

Vacuuming is the most disturbing video, actually a double feature beginning with an introduction to the special backpack vacuum we are to use. Yes, the vacuum cleaner actually straps onto your back, a chubby fellow who introduces himself as its inventor explains. He suits up, pulling the straps tight across and under his chest and then says proudly into the camera: "See, I *am* the vacuum cleaner." It weighs only ten pounds, he claims, although, as I soon find out, with the attachments dangling from the strap around your waist, the total is probably more like fourteen. What about my petulant and much-pampered lower back? The inventor returns to the theme of human/machine merger: when properly strapped in, we too will be vacuum cleaners, constrained only by the cord that attaches us to an electrical outlet, and vacuum cleaners don't have back-aches. Somehow all this information exhausts me, and I watch the second video, which explains the actual procedures for vacuuming, with the detached interest of a cineast. Could the model maid be an actual maid

and the model home someone's actual dwelling? And who are these people whose idea of decorating is matched pictures of mallard ducks in flight and whose house is perfectly characterless and pristine even before the model maid sets to work?

At first I find the videos on kitchens and bathrooms baffling, and it takes me several minutes to realize why: there is no *water*, or almost no water, involved. I was taught to clean by my mother, a compulsive housekeeper who employed water so hot you needed rubber gloves to get into it and in such Niagara-like quantities that most microbes were probably crushed by the force of it before the soap suds had a chance to rupture their cell walls. But germs are never mentioned in the videos provided by The Maids. Our antagonists exist entirely in the visible world—soap scum, dust, counter crud, dog hair, stains, and smears—and are to be attacked by damp rag or, in hardcore cases, by Dobie (the brand of plastic scouring pad we use). We scrub only to remove impurities that might be detectable to a customer by hand or by eye; otherwise our only job is to wipe. Nothing is said about the possibility of transporting bacteria, by rag or by hand, from bathroom to kitchen or even from one house to the next. It is the "cosmetic touches" that the videos emphasize and that Ted, when he wanders back into the room, continually directs my eye to. Fluff up all throw pillows and arrange them symmetrically. Brighten up stainless steel sinks with baby oil. Leave all spice jars, shampoos, etc., with their labels facing outward. Comb out the fringes of Persian carpets with a pick. Use the vacuum cleaner to create a special, fernlike pattern in the carpets. The loose ends of toilet paper and paper towel rolls have to be given a special fold (the same one you'll find in hotel bathrooms). "Messes" of loose paper, clothing, or toys are to be stacked into "neat messes." Finally, the house is to be sprayed with the cleaning service's signature floral-scented air freshner, which will signal to the owners, the moment they return home, that, yes, their house has been "cleaned."[4]

After a day's training I am judged fit to go out with a team, where I soon discover that life is nothing like the movies, at least not if the movie is *Dusting*. For one thing, compared with our actual pace, the training videos were all in slow motion. We do not walk to the cars with our buckets full of cleaning fluids and utensils in the morning, we run, and when we pull up to a house, we run with our buckets to the door. Liza, a good-natured woman in her thirties who is my first team leader, explains that we are given only so many minutes per house, ranging from under sixty for a 1½-bathroom apartment to two hundred or more for a multibathroom "first timer." I'd like to know why anybody worries about Ted's time limits if we're being paid by the hour but hesitate to display anything that might be interpreted as attitude. As we get to each house, Liza assigns our tasks, and I cross my fingers to ward off bathrooms and vacuuming. Even dusting, though, gets aerobic under pressure, and after about an hour of it—reaching to get door tops, crawling along floors to wipe baseboards, standing on my bucket to attack the higher shelves—I wouldn't mind sitting down with a tall glass of water. But as soon as you complete your assigned task, you report to the team leader to be assigned to help someone else. Once or twice, when the normal process of evaporation is deemed too slow, I am assigned to dry a scrubbed floor by putting rags under my feet and skating around on it. Usually, by the time I get out to the car and am dumping the dirty water used on floors and wringing out rags, the rest of the team is already in the car with the motor running. Liza assures me that they've never left anyone behind at a house, not even, presumably, a very new person whom nobody knows.

In my interview, I had been promised a thirty-minute lunch break, but this turns out to be a five-minute pit stop at a convenience store, if that. I bring my own sandwich—the same turkey breast and cheese every day—as do a couple of the others; the rest eat convenience store fare, a bagel or doughnut salvaged from our free breakfast, or nothing at all. The two older married women I'm teamed up with eat best—sandwiches and fruit. Among the younger women, lunch consists of a slice of pizza, a "pizza pocket" (a roll of dough surrounding some pizza sauce), or a small bag of chips. Bear in mind we are not office workers, sitting around idling at the basal metabolic rate. A poster on the wall in the office cheerily displays the number of calories burned per minute at our various tasks, ranging from about 3.5 for dusting to 7 for vacuuming. If you assume an average of 5 calories per minute in a seven-hour day (eight hours minus time for travel between houses), you need to be taking in 2,100 calories in addition to the resting minimum of, say, 900 or so. I get pushy with Rosalie, who is new like me and fresh from high school in a rural northern part of the state, about the meagerness of her lunches, which consist solely of Doritos—a half bag from the day before or a freshly purchased small-sized bag. She just didn't have anything in the house, she says (though she lives with her boyfriend and his mother), and she certainly doesn't have any money to buy lunch, as I find out when I offer to fetch her a soda from a Quik Mart and she has to admit she doesn't have eighty-nine cents. I treat her to the soda, wishing I could force her, mommylike, to take milk instead. So how does she hold up for an eight- or even nine-hour day? "Well," she concedes, "I get dizzy sometimes."

How poor are they, my coworkers? The fact that anyone is working this job at all can be taken as prima facie evidence of some kind of desperation or at least a history of mistakes and disappointments, but it's not for me to ask. In the prison movies that provide me with a mental guide to comportment, the new guy doesn't go around shaking hands and asking, "Hi there, what are you in for?" So I listen, in the cars and when we're assembled in the office, and learn, first, that no one seems to be homeless. Almost everyone is embedded in extended families or families artificially extended with housemates. People talk about visiting grandparents in the hospital or sending birthday cards to a niece's husband; single mothers live with their own mothers or share apartments with a coworker or boyfriend. Pauline, the oldest of us, owns her own home, but she sleeps on the living room sofa, while her four grown children and three grandchildren fill up the bedrooms.[5]

But although no one, apparently, is sleeping in a car, there are signs, even at the beginning, of real difficulty if not actual misery. Half-smoked cigarettes are returned to the pack. There are discussions about who will come up with fifty cents for a toll and whether Ted can be counted on for prompt reimbursement. One of my teammates gets frantic about a painfully impacted wisdom tooth and keeps making calls from our houses to try to locate a source of free dental care. When my—or, I should say, Liza's—team discovers there is not a single Dobie in our buckets, I suggest that we stop at a convenience store and buy one rather than drive all the way back to the office. But it turns out I haven't brought any money with me and we cannot put together $2 between the four of us.

The Friday of my first week at The Maids is unnaturally hot for Maine in early September—95 degrees, according to the digital time-and-temperature displays offered by banks that we pass. I'm teamed up with the sad-faced Rosalie and our leader, Maddy, whose sullenness, under the circumstances, is almost a relief after Liza's relentless good cheer. Liza, I've learned, is the highest-ranking cleaner, a sort of supervisor really, and said to be something of a snitch, but Maddy, a single mom of maybe twenty-seven or so, has worked for only three months and broods about her child care problems. Her boyfriend's sister, she tells me on the drive to our first house, watches her eighteen-month-old for $50 a week, which is a stretch on The Maids' pay, plus she doesn't entirely trust the sister, but a real day care center could be as much as $90 a week.

After polishing off the first house, no problem, we grab "lunch"—Doritos for Rosalie and a bag of Pepperidge Farm Goldfish for Maddy—and head out into the exurbs for what our instruction sheet warns is a five-bathroom spread and a first-timer to boot. Still, the size of the place makes us pause for a moment, buckets in hand, before searching out an appropriately humble entrance.[6] It sits there like a beached ocean liner, the prow cutting through swells of green turf, windows without number. "Well, well," Maddy says, reading the owner's name from our instruction sheet, "Mrs. W. and her big-ass house. I hope she's going to give us lunch."

Mrs. W. is not in fact happy to see us, grimacing with exasperation when the black nanny ushers us into the family room or sunroom or den or whatever kind of specialized space she is sitting in. After all, she already has the nanny, a cooklike person, and a crew of men doing some sort of finishing touches on the construction to supervise. No, she doesn't want to take us around the house, because she already explained everything to the office on the phone, but Maddy stands there, with Rosalie and me behind her, until she relents. We are to move everything on all surfaces, she instructs during the tour, and get underneath and be sure to do every bit of the several miles, I calculate, of baseboards. And be mindful of the baby, who's napping and can't have cleaning fluids of any kind near her.

Then I am let loose to dust. In a situation like this, where I don't even know how to name the various kinds of rooms, The Maids' special system turns out to be a lifesaver. All I have to do is keep moving from left to right, within rooms and between rooms, trying to identify landmarks so I don't accidentally do a room or a hallway twice. Dusters get the most complete biographical overview, due to the necessity of lifting each object and tchotchke individually, and I learn that Mrs. W. is an alumna of an important women's college, now occupying herself by monitoring her investments and the baby's bowel movements. I find special charts for this latter purpose, with spaces for time of day, most recent fluid intake, consistency, and color. In the master bedroom, I dust a whole shelf of books on pregnancy, breastfeeding, the first six months, the first year, the first two years—and I wonder what the child care-deprived Maddy makes of all this. Maybe there's been some secret division of the world's women into breeders and drones, and those at the maid level are no longer supposed to be reproducing at all. Maybe this is why our office manager, Tammy, who was once a maid herself, wears inch-long fake nails and tarty little outfits—to show she's advanced to the breeder caste and can't be sent out to clean anymore.

It is hotter inside than out, un-air-conditioned for the benefit of the baby, I suppose, but I do all right until I encounter the banks of glass doors that line the side and back of the ground floor. Each one has to be Windexed, wiped, and buffed—inside and out, top to bottom, left to right, until it's as streakless and invisible as a material substance can be. Outside, I can see the construction guys knocking back Gatorade, but the rule is that no fluid or food item can touch a maid's lips when she's inside a house. Now, sweat, even in unseemly quantities, is nothing new to me. I live in a subtropical area where even the inactive can expect to be moist nine months out of the year. I work out, too, in my normal life and take a certain macho pride in the Vs of sweat that form on my T-shirt after ten minutes or more on the StairMaster. But in normal life fluids lost are immediately replaced. Everyone in yuppie-land—airports, for example—looks like a nursing baby these days, inseparable from their plastic bottles of water. Here, however, I sweat without replacement or pause, not in individual drops but in continuous sheets of fluid soaking through my polo shirt, pouring down the backs of my legs. The eyeliner I put on in the morning—vain twit that I am—has long since streaked down onto my cheeks, and I could wring my braid out if I wanted to. Working my way through the living room(s), I wonder if Mrs.

W. will ever have occasion to realize that every single doodad and objet through which she expresses her unique, individual self is, from another vantage point, only an obstacle between some thirsty person and a glass of water.

When I can find no more surfaces to wipe and have finally exhausted the supply of rooms, Maddy assigns me to do the kitchen floor. OK, except that Mrs. W. is in the kitchen, so I have to go down on my hands and knees practically at her feet. No, we don't have sponge mops like the one I use in my own house; the hands-and-knees approach is a definite selling point for corporate cleaning services like The Maids. "We clean floors the old-fashioned way—on our hands and knees" (emphasis added), the brochure for a competing firm boasts. In fact, whatever advantages there may be to the hands-and-knees approach—you're closer to your work, of course, and less likely to miss a grimy patch—are undermined by the artificial drought imposed by The Maids' cleaning system. We are instructed to use less than half a small bucket of lukewarm water for a kitchen and all adjacent scrubbable floors (breakfast nooks and other dining areas), meaning that within a few minutes we are doing nothing more than redistributing the dirt evenly around the floor. There are occasional customer complaints about the cleanliness of our floors—for example, from a man who wiped up a spill on his freshly "cleaned" floor only to find the paper towel he employed for this purpose had turned gray. A mop and a full bucket of hot soapy water would not only get a floor cleaner but would be a lot more dignified for the person who does the cleaning. But it is this primal posture of submission—and of what is ultimately anal accessibility—that seems to gratify the consumers of maid services.[7]

I don't know, but Mrs. W.'s floor is hard—stone, I think, or at least a stonelike substance—and we have no knee pads with us today. I had thought in my middle-class innocence that knee pads were one of Monica Lewinsky's prurient fantasies, but no, they actually exist, and they're usually a standard part of our equipment. So here I am on my knees, working my way around the room like some fanatical penitent crawling through the stations of the cross, when I realize that Mrs. W. is staring at me fixedly—so fixedly that I am gripped for a moment by the wild possibility that I may have once given a lecture at her alma mater and she's trying to figure out where she's seen me before. If I were recognized, would I be fired? Would she at least be inspired to offer me a drink of water? Because I have decided that if water is actually offered, I'm taking it, rules or no rules, and if word of this infraction gets back to Ted, I'll just say I thought it would be rude to refuse. Not to worry, though. She's just watching that I don't leave out some stray square inch, and when I rise painfully to my feet again, blinking through the sweat, she says, "Could you just scrub the floor in the entryway while you're at it?"

I rush home to the Blue Haven at the end of the day, pull down the blinds for privacy, strip off my uniform in the kitchen—the bathroom being too small for both a person and her discarded clothes—and stand in the shower for a good ten minutes, thinking all this water is *mine*. I have paid for it, in fact, I have earned it. I have gotten through a week at The Maids without mishap, injury, or insurrection. My back feels fine, meaning I'm not feeling it at all; even my wrists, damaged by carpal tunnel syndrome years ago, are issuing no complaints. Coworkers warned me that the first time they donned the backpack vacuum they felt faint, but not me. I am strong and I am, more than that, good. Did I toss my bucket of filthy water onto Mrs. W.'s casual white summer outfit? No. Did I take the wand of my vacuum cleaner and smash someone's Chinese porcelain statues or Hummel figurines? Not once. I was at all times cheerful, energetic, helpful, and as competent as a new hire can be expected to be. If I can do one week, I can do another, and might as well, since there's never been a moment for job-hunting. The 3:30 quitting time turns out to be a myth; often we don't

return to the office until 4:30 or 5:00. And what did I think? That I was going to go out to interviews in my soaked and stinky postwork condition? I decide to reward myself with a sunset walk on Old Orchard Beach.

On account of the heat, there are still a few actual bathers on the beach, but I am content to sit in shorts and T-shirt and watch the ocean pummel the sand. When the sun goes down I walk back into the town to find my car and am amazed to hear a sound I associate with cities like New York and Berlin. There's a couple of Peruvian musicians playing in the little grassy island in the street near the pier, and maybe fifty people—locals and vacationers—have gathered around, offering their bland end-of-summer faces to the sound. I edge my way through the crowd and find a seat where I can see the musicians up close—the beautiful young guitarist and the taller man playing the flute. What are they doing in this rinky-dink blue-collar resort, and what does the audience make of this surprise visit from the dark-skinned South? The melody the flute lays out over the percussion is both utterly strange and completely familiar, as if it had been imprinted in the minds of my own peasant ancestors centuries ago and forgotten until this very moment. Everyone else seems to be as transfixed as I am. The musicians wink and smile at each other as they play, and I see then that they are the secret emissaries of a worldwide lower-class conspiracy to snatch joy out of degradation and filth. When the song ends, I give them a dollar, the equivalent of about ten minutes of sweat.

The superwoman mood does not last. For one thing, while the muscles and joints are doing just fine, the skin has decided to rebel. At first I think the itchy pink bumps on my arms and legs must be poison ivy picked up at a lockout. Sometimes an owner forgets we are coming or forgets to leave a key under the mat or changes his or her mind about the service without thinking to notify Ted. This is not, for us, an occasion for joy like a snow day for the grade-school crowd, because Ted blames us for his customers' fecklessness. When owners forget we are coming, he explains at one of our morning send-off meetings, it "means something," like that they're dissatisfied and too passive-aggressive to tell us. Once, when I am with Pauline as my team leader, she calls Ted to report a lockout and his response, she reports ruefully, is, "Don't do this to me." So before we give up and declare a place a lockout, we search like cat burglars for alternative points of entry, which can mean trampling through overgrowth to peer into windows and test all the doors. I haven't seen any poison ivy, but who knows what other members of the poison family (oak, sumac, etc.) lurk in the flora of Maine?

Or maybe the cleaning fluids are at fault, except that then the rash should have begun on my hands. After two days of minor irritation, a full-scale epidermal breakdown is under way. I cover myself with anti-itch cream from Rite Aid but can manage to sleep only for an hour and a half at a time before the torment resumes. I wake up realizing I can work but probably shouldn't, if only because I look like a leper. Ted doesn't have much sympathy for illness, though; one of our morning meetings was on the subject of "working through it." Somebody, and he wasn't going to name names, he told us, was out with a migraine. "Now if I get a migraine I just pop two Excedrins and get on with my life. That's what you have to do—work through it." So it's in the spirit of a scientific experiment that I present myself at the office, wondering if my speckled and inflamed appearance will be enough to get me sent home. Certainly I wouldn't want anyone who looks like me handling my children's toys or bars of bathroom soap. But no problem. Must be a latex allergy, is Ted's diagnosis. Just stay out of the latex gloves we use for particularly nasty work; he'll give me another kind to wear.

I should, if I were going to stay in character, find an emergency room after work and try to cop a little charitable care. But it's too much. The itching gets so bad at night that I have mini-

tantrums, waving my arms and stamping my feet to keep from scratching or bawling. So I fall back on the support net-works of my real-life social class, call the dermatologist I know in Key West, and bludgeon him into prescribing something sight unseen. The whole episode—including anti-itch cream, prednisone, prednisone cream, and Benadryl to get through the nights—eats up $30. It's still unseasonably hot, and I often get to look out on someone's azure pool while I vacuum or scrub, frantic with suppressed itching. Even the rash-free are affected by the juxtaposition of terrible heat and cool, inaccessible water. In the car on one of the hottest days, after cleaning a place with pool, pool house, and gazebo, Rosalie and Maddy and I obsess about immersion in all imaginable forms—salt water versus fresh, lakes versus pools, surf versus smooth, glasslike surfaces. We can't even wash our hands in the houses, at least not after the sinks have been dried and buffed, and when I do manage to get a wash in before the sinks are off-limits, there's always some filthy last-minute job like squeezing out the rags used on floors once we get out of a house. Maybe I picked up some bug at a house or maybe it's the disinfectant I squirt on my hands, straight from the bottle, in an attempt at cleanliness. Three days into the rash, I make another trip to Old Orchard Beach and wade into the water with my clothes on (I didn't think to bring a bathing suit from Key West to Maine), trying to pretend that it's an accident when a wave washes over me and that I'm not just some pathetic street person using the beach as a bathtub.

There's something else working against my mood of muscular elation. I had been gloating internally about my ability to keep up with, and sometimes outwork, women twenty or thirty years younger than myself, but it turns out this comparative advantage says less about me than it does about them. Ours is a physical bond, to the extent that we bond at all. One person's infirmity can be a teammate's extra burden; there's a constant traffic in herbal and over-the-counter solutions to pain. If I don't know how my co-workers survive on their wages or what they make of our hellish condition, I do know about their back pains and cramps and arthritic attacks. Lori and Pauline are excused from vacuuming on account of their backs, which means you dread being assigned to a team with them. Helen has a bum foot, which Ted, in explaining her absence one day, blames on the cheap, ill-fitting shoes that, he implies, she perversely chooses to wear. Marge's arthritis makes scrubbing a torture; another woman has to see a physical therapist for her rotator cuff. When Rosalie tells me that she got her shoulder problem picking blueberries as a "kid"—she still is one in my eyes, of course—I flash on a scene from my own childhood, of wandering through fields on an intense July day, grabbing berries by the handful as I go. But when Rosalie was a kid she worked in the blueberry fields of northern Maine, and the damage to her shoulder is an occupational injury.

So ours is a world of pain—managed by Excedrin and Advil, compensated for with cigarettes and, in one or two cases and then only on weekends, with booze. Do the owners have any idea of the misery that goes into rendering their homes motel-perfect? Would they be bothered if they did know, or would they take a sadistic pride in what they have purchased—boasting to dinner guests, for example, that their floors are cleaned only with the purest of fresh human tears? In one of my few exchanges with an owner, a pert muscular woman whose desk reveals that she works part-time as a personal trainer, I am vacuuming and she notices the sweat. "That's a real workout, isn't it?" she observes, not unkindly, and actually offers me a glass of water, the only such offer I ever encounter. Flouting the rule against the ingestion of anything while inside a house, I take it, leaving an inch undrunk to avoid the awkwardness of a possible refill offer. "I tell all my clients," the trainer informs me, " 'If you want to be fit, just fire your cleaning lady and do it yourself.' " "Ho ho," is all I say, since we're not just chatting in

the gym together and I can't explain that this form of exercise is totally asymmetrical, brutally repetitive, and as likely to destroy the musculo-skeletal structure as to strengthen it.

Self-restraint becomes more of a challenge when the owner of a million-dollar condo (that's my guess anyway, because it has three floors and a wide-angle view of the fabled rock-bound coast) who is (according to a framed photograph on the wall) an acquaintance of the real Barbara Bush takes me into the master bathroom to explain the difficulties she's been having with the shower stall. Seems its marble walls have been "bleeding" onto the brass fixtures, and can I scrub the grouting extra hard? That's not your marble bleeding, I want to tell her, it's the world-wide working class—the people who quarried the marble, wove your Persian rugs until they went blind, harvested the apples in your lovely fall-themed dining room center-piece, smelted the steel for the nails, drove the trucks, put up this building, and now bend and squat and sweat to clean it.

Not that I, even in my more histrionic moments, imagine that I am a member of that oppressed working class. My very ability to work tirelessly hour after hour is a product of decades of better-than-average medical care, a high-protein diet, and workouts in gyms that charge $400 or $500 a year. If I am now a productive fake member of the working class, it's because I haven't been working, in any hard physical sense, long enough to have ruined my body. But I will say this for myself: I have never employed a cleaning person or service (except, on two occasions, to prepare my house for a short-term tenant) even though various partners and husbands have badgered me over the years to do so. When I could have used one, when the kids were little, I couldn't afford it; and later, when I could afford it, I still found the idea repugnant. Partly this comes from having a mother who believed that a self-cleaned house was the hallmark of womanly virtue. Partly it's because my own normal work is sedentary, so that the housework

I do—in dabs of fifteen minutes here and thirty minutes there—functions as a break. But mostly I rejected the idea, even after all my upper-middle-class friends had, guiltily and as covertly as possible, hired help for themselves, because this is just not the kind of relationship I want to have with another human being.[8] [. . .]

Evaluation

But if it's hard for workers to obey the laws of economics by examining their options and moving on to better jobs, why don't more of them take a stand where they are—demanding better wages and work conditions, either individually or as a group? This is a huge question, probably the subject of many a dissertation in the field of industrial psychology, and here I can only comment on the things I observed. One of these was the co-optative power of management, illustrated by such euphemisms as *associate* and *team member*. At The Maids, the boss—who, as the only male in our midst, exerted a creepy, paternalistic kind of power—had managed to convince some of my coworkers that he was struggling against difficult odds and deserving of their unstinting forbearance. Wal-Mart has a number of more impersonal and probably more effective ways of getting its workers to feel like "associates." There was the profit-sharing plan, with Wal-Mart's stock price posted daily in a prominent spot near the break room. There was the company's much-heralded patriotism, evidenced in the banners over the shopping floor urging workers and customers to contribute to the construction of a World War II veterans' memorial (Sam Walton having been one of them). There were "associate" meetings that served as pep rallies, complete with the Wal-Mart cheer: "Gimme a 'W,'" etc.

The chance to identify with a powerful and wealthy entity—the company or the boss—is only the carrot. There is also a stick. What surprised and offended me most about the low-wage workplace (and yes, here all my middle-class privilege is on full display) was the extent to which one is required to surrender one's basic civil rights and—what boils down to the same thing—self-respect. I learned this at the very beginning of my stint as a waitress, when I was warned that my purse could be searched by management at any time. I wasn't carrying stolen salt shakers or anything else of a compromising nature, but still, there's something about the prospect of a purse search that makes a woman feel a few buttons short of fully dressed. After work, I called around and found that this practice is entirely legal: if the purse is on the boss's property—which of course it was—the boss has the right to examine its contents.

Drug testing is another routine indignity. Civil libertarians see it as a violation of our Fourth Amendment freedom from "unreasonable search"; most jobholders and applicants find it simply embarrassing. In some testing protocols, the employee has to strip to her underwear and pee into a cup in the presence of an aide or technician. Mercifully, I got to keep my clothes on and shut the toilet stall door behind me, but even so, urination is a private act and it is degrading to have to perform it at the command of some powerful other. I would add pre-employment personality tests to the list of demeaning intrusions, or at least much of their usual content. Maybe the hypothetical types of questions can be justified—whether you would steal if an opportunity arose or turn in a thieving coworker and so on—but not questions about your "moods of self-pity," whether you are a loner or believe you are usually misunderstood. It is unsettling, at the very least, to give a stranger access to things, like your self-doubts and your urine, that are otherwise shared only in medical or therapeutic situations.

There are other, more direct ways of keeping low-wage employees in their place. Rules against "gossip," or even "talking," make it hard to air your grievances to peers or—should you be so daring—to enlist other workers in a group effort to bring about change, through a union organizing drive, for example. Those who do step out of line often face little unexplained punishments, such as having their schedules or their work assignments unilaterally changed. Or you may be fired; those low-wage workers who work without union contracts, which is the great majority of them, work "at will," meaning at the will of the employer, and are subject to dismissal without explanation. The AFL-CIO estimates that ten thousand workers a year are fired for participating in union organizing drives, and since it is illegal to fire people for union activity, I suspect that these firings are usually justified in terms of unrelated minor infractions. Wal-Mart employees who have bucked the company—by getting involved in a unionization drive or by suing the company for failing to pay overtime—have been fired for breaking the company rule against using profanity.

So if low-wage workers do not always behave in an economically rational way, that is, as free agents within a capitalist democracy, it is because they dwell in a place that is neither free nor in any way democratic. When you enter the low-wage workplace—and many of the medium-wage workplaces as well—you check your civil liberties at the door, leave America and all it supposedly stands for behind, and learn to zip your lips for the duration of the shift. The consequences of this routine surrender go beyond the issues of wages and poverty. We can hardly pride ourselves on being the world's preeminent democracy, after all, if large numbers of citizens spend half their waking hours in what amounts, in plain terms, to a dictatorship.

Any dictatorship takes a psychological toll on its subjects. If you are treated as an untrustworthy person—a potential slacker, drug addict, or thief—you may begin to feel less trustworthy yourself. If you are constantly reminded of your lowly position in the social hierarchy, whether by individual managers or by a plethora of impersonal rules, you begin to accept that unfortunate status. To draw for a moment from an entirely different corner of my life, that part of me still attached to the biological

sciences, there is ample evidence that animals—rats and monkeys, for example—that are forced into a subordinate status within their social systems adapt their brain chemistry accordingly, becoming "depressed" in humanlike ways. Their behavior is anxious and withdrawn; the level of serotonin (the neurotransmitter boosted by some antidepressants) declines in their brains. And—what is especially relevant here—they avoid fighting even in self-defense.

Humans are, of course, vastly more complicated; even in situations of extreme subordination, we can pump up our self-esteem with thoughts of our families, our religion, our hopes for the future. But as much as any other social animal, and more so than many, we depend for our self-image on the humans immediately around us—to the point of altering our perceptions of the world so as to fit in with theirs. My guess is that the indignities imposed on so many low-wage workers—the drug tests, the constant surveillance, being "reamed out" by managers—are part of what keeps wages low. If you're made to feel unworthy enough, you may come to think that what you're paid is what you are actually worth.

It is hard to imagine any other function for workplace authoritarianism. Managers may truly believe that, without their unremitting efforts, all work would quickly grind to a halt. That is not my impression. While I encountered some cynics and plenty of people who had learned to budget their energy, I never met an actual slacker or, for that matter, a drug addict or thief. On the contrary, I was amazed and sometimes saddened by the pride people took in jobs that rewarded them so meagerly, either in wages or in recognition. Often, in fact, these people experienced management as an obstacle to getting the job done as it should be done. Waitresses chafed at managers' stinginess toward the customers; housecleaners resented the time constraints that sometimes made them cut corners; retail workers wanted the floor to be beautiful, not cluttered with excess stock as management required. Left to themselves, they devised systems of cooperation and work sharing; when there was a crisis, they rose to it. In fact, it was often hard to see what the function of management was, other than to exact obeisance.

There seems to be a vicious cycle at work here, making ours not just an economy but a culture of extreme inequality. Corporate decision makers, and even some two-bit entrepreneurs like my boss at The Maids, occupy an economic position miles above that of the underpaid people whose labor they depend on. For reasons that have more to do with class—and often racial—prejudice than with actual experience, they tend to fear and distrust the category of people from which they recruit their workers. Hence the perceived need for repressive management and intrusive measures like drug and personality testing. But these things cost money—$20,000 or more a year for a manager, $100 a pop for a drug test, and so on—and the high cost of repression results in ever more pressure to hold wages down. The larger society seems to be caught up in a similar cycle: cutting public services for the poor, which are sometimes referred to collectively as the "social wage," while investing ever more heavily in prisons and cops. And in the larger society, too, the cost of repression becomes another factor weighing against the expansion or restoration of needed services. It is a tragic cycle, condemning us to ever deeper inequality, and in the long run, almost no one benefits but the agents of repression themselves.

But whatever keeps wages low—and I'm sure my comments have barely scratched the surface—the result is that many people earn far less than they need to live on. How much is that? The Economic Policy Institute recently reviewed dozens of studies of what constitutes a "living wage" and came up with an average figure of $30,000 a year for a family of one adult and two children, which amounts to a wage of $14 an hour. This is not the very minimum such a family could live on; the budget includes health insurance, a telephone, and child care at a licensed center, for example, which are well beyond the reach of millions. But it does not include restaurant meals, video rentals, Internet access, wine and liquor, cigarettes and lottery tickets, or even very much meat. The shocking thing is that the majority of American workers, about 60 percent, earn less than $14 an hour. Many of them get by by teaming up with another wage earner, a spouse or grown child. Some draw on government help in the form of food stamps, housing vouchers, the earned income tax credit, or—for those coming off welfare in relatively generous states—subsidized child care. But others—single mothers for example—have nothing but their own wages to live on, no matter how many mouths there are to feed.

Employers will look at that $30,000 figure, which is over twice what they currently pay entry-level workers, and see nothing but bankruptcy ahead. Indeed, it is probably impossible for the private sector to provide everyone with an adequate standard of living through wages, or even wages plus benefits, alone: too much of what we need, such as reliable child care, is just too expensive, even for middle-class families. Most civilized nations compensate for the inadequacy of wages by providing relatively generous public services such as health insurance, free or subsidized child care, subsidized housing, and effective public transportation. But the United States, for all its wealth, leaves its citizens to fend for themselves—facing market-based rents, for example, on their wages alone. For millions of Americans, that $10—or even $8 or $6—hourly wage is all there is.

It is common, among the nonpoor, to think of poverty as a sustainable condition—austere, perhaps, but they get by somehow, don't they? They are "always with us." What is harder for the nonpoor to see is poverty as acute distress: The lunch that consists of Doritos or hot dog rolls, leading to faintness before the end of the shift. The "home" that is also a car or a van. The illness or injury that must be "worked through," with gritted teeth, because there's no sick pay or health insurance and the loss of one day's pay will mean no groceries for the next. These experiences are not part of a sustainable lifestyle, even a lifestyle of chronic deprivation and relentless low-level punishment. They are, by almost any standard of subsistence, emergency situations. And that is how we should see the poverty of so many millions of low-wage Americans—as a state of emergency.

Notes

1 Nationwide and even international cleaning services like Merry Maids, Molly Maids, and The Maids International, all of which have arisen since the seventies, now control 20–25 percent of the housecleaning business. In a 1997 article about Merry Maids, *Franchise Times* reported tersely that "category is booming, niche is hot too, as Americans look to outsource work even at home" ("72 Merry Maids," *Franchise Times*, December 1997). Not all cleaning services do well, with a high rate of failure among the informal, mom-and-pop services, like the one I applied to by phone that did not even require a cursory interview—all I had to do was show up at seven the next morning. The "boom" is concentrated among the national and international chains—outfits like Merry Maids, Molly Maids, Mini Maids, Maid Brigade, and The Maids International—all named, curiously enough, to highlight the more antique aspects of the industry, although the "maid" may occasionally be male. Merry Maids claimed to be growing at 15–20 percent a year in 1996, while spokesmen for Molly Maids and The Maids International each told me in interviews conducted after I left Maine that their firms' sales are growing by 25 percent a year.

2 The maids' wages, their Social Security taxes, their green cards, backaches, and child care problems—all these are the sole concern of the company, meaning the local franchise owner. If there are complaints on either side, they are addressed to the franchise owner; the customer and the actual workers need never interact. Since the franchise owner is usually a middle-class white person, cleaning services are the ideal solution for anyone still sensitive enough to find the traditional employer-maid relationship morally vexing.

3 I don't know what proportion of my fellow workers at The Maids in Portland had been on welfare, but the owner of The Maids' franchise in Andover, Massachusetts, told me in a phone interview that half his employees are former welfare recipients and that they are as reliable as anyone else.

4 When I described the methods employed by The Maids to housecleaning expert Cheryl Mendelson, author of *Home Comforts*, she was incredulous. A rag moistened with disinfectant will not get a countertop clean, she told me, because most disinfectants are inactivated by contact with organic matter—i.e., dirt—so their effectiveness declines with each swipe of the rag. What you need is a detergent and hot water, followed by a rinse. As for floors, she judged the amount of water we used—one half of a small bucket, which was never any warmer than room temperature—to be grossly inadequate, and, in fact, the water I wiped around on floors was often an unsavory gray. I also ran The Maids' cleaning methods by Don Aslett, author of numerous books on cleaning techniques and self-styled "number one cleaner in America." He was hesitant to criticize The Maids directly, perhaps because he is, or told me he is, a frequent speaker at conventions of cleaning service franchise holders, but he did tell me how he would clean a countertop. First, spray it thoroughly with an all-purpose cleaner, then let it sit for three to four minutes of "kill time," and finally wipe dry with a clean cloth. Merely wiping the surface with a damp cloth, he said, just spreads the dirt around. But the point at The Maids, apparently, is not to clean so much as to create the appearance of *having been cleaned*, not to sanitize but to create a kind of stage setting for family life. And the stage setting Americans seem to prefer is sterile only in the metaphorical sense, like a motel room or the fake interiors in which soap operas and sitcoms take place.

5 The women I worked with were all white and, with one exception, Anglo, as are the plurality of housecleaners in America, or at least those known to the Bureau of Labor Statistics. Of the "private household cleaners and servants" it managed to locate in 1998, the BLS reports that 36.8 percent were Hispanic, 15.8 percent black, and 2.7 percent "other." How-

ever, the association between housecleaning and minority status is well established in the psyches of the white employing class. When my daughter, Rosa, was introduced to the father of a wealthy Harvard classmate, he ventured that she must have been named for a favorite maid. And Audre Lorde reported an experience she had in 1967: "I wheel my two-year-old daughter in a shopping cart through a supermarket . . . and a little white girl riding past in her mother's cart calls out excitedly, 'Oh look, Mommy, a baby maid' " (quoted in Mary Romero, *Maid in the U.S.A.: Perspectives on Gender* [New York: Routledge, 1992], p. 72). But the composition of the household workforce is hardly fixed and has changed with the life chances of the different ethnic groups. In the late nineteenth century, Irish and German immigrants served the urban upper and middle classes, then left for the factories as soon as they could. Black women replaced them, accounting for 60 percent of all domestics in the 1940s, and dominated the field until other occupations began to open up to them. Similarly, West Coast maids were disproportionately Japanese American until that group too found more congenial options (see Phyllis Palmer, *Domesticity and Dirt: Housewives and Domestic Servants in the United States, 1920–1945* [Temple University Press, 1989], pp. 12–13). Today, the color of the hand that pushes the sponge varies from region to region: Chicanas in the Southwest, Caribbeans in New York, native Hawaiians in Hawaii, native whites, many of recent rural extraction, in the Midwest and, of course, Maine.

6 For the affluent, houses have been swelling with no apparent limit. The square footage of new homes increased by 39 percent between 1971 and 1996, to include "family rooms," home entertainment rooms, home offices, bedrooms, and often a bathroom for each family member ("Détente in the Housework Wars," *Toronto Star*, November 20, 1999). By the second quarter of 1999, 17 percent of new homes were larger than three thousand square feet, which is usually considered the size threshold for household help, or the point at which a house becomes unmanageable to the people who live in it ("Molding Loyal Pamperers for the Newly Rich," *New York Times*, October 24, 1999).

7 In *Home Comforts: The Art and Science of Keeping House* (Scribner, 1999), Cheryl Mendelson writes, "Never ask hired housecleaners to clean your floors on their hands and knees; the request is likely to be regarded as degrading" (p. 501).

8 In 1999, somewhere between 14 and 18 percent of households employed an outsider to do the cleaning and the numbers are rising dramatically. Mediamark Research reports a 53 percent increase, between 1995 and 1999, in the number of households using a hired cleaner or service once a month or more, and Maritz Marketing finds that 30 percent of the people who hired help in 1999 had done so for the first time that year.

Managers of the new corporate cleaning services, such as the one I worked for, attribute their success not only to the influx of women into the workforce but to the tensions over housework that arose in its wake. When the trend toward hiring out was just beginning to take off, in 1988, the owner of a Merry Maids franchise in Arlington, Massachusetts, told the *Christian Science Monitor*, "I kid some women. I say, 'We even save marriages. In this new eighties period you expect more from the male partner, but very often you don't get the cooperation you would like to have. The alternative is to pay somebody to come in' " ("Ambushed by Dust Bunnies," *Christian Science Monitor*, April 4, 1988). Another Merry Maids franchise owner has learned to capitalize more directly on housework-related spats; he closes 30–35 percent of his sales by making follow-up calls Saturdays between 9:00 and 11:00 A.M.—which is "prime time for arguing over the fact that the house is a mess" ("Homes Harbor Dirty Secrets," *Chicago Tribune*, May 5, 1994).

Chapter 29

Robert Nozick

THE ENTITLEMENT THEORY OF JUSTICE

Robert Nozick (1938–2002) was a professor of philosophy at Harvard University for almost his entire professional career. He wrote widely in such areas as epistemology and decision theory, but his best-known work is *Anarchy, State, and Utopia* (1974), a book-length exploration of libertarian political theory. In this excerpt, Nozick sets forth his "entitlement theory" of justice, which holds that the justice of a distribution of wealth is entirely determined by the historical way in which it came about. Non-historical, patterned principles, Nozick argues, require continual interference in people's liberty to maintain.

Distributive Justice

The minimal state is the most extensive state that can be justified. Any state more extensive violates people's rights. Yet many persons have put forth reasons purporting to justify a more extensive state. It is impossible within the compass of this book to examine all the reasons that have been put forth. Therefore, I shall focus upon those generally acknowledged to be most weighty and influential, to see precisely wherein they fail. In this essay we consider the claim that a more extensive state is justified, because necessary (or the best instrument) to achieve distributive justice. . . .

The term "distributive justice" is not a neutral one. Hearing the term "distribution," most people presume that some thing or mechanism uses some principle or criterion to give out a supply of things. Into this process of distributing shares some error may have crept. So it is an open question, at least, whether redistribution should take place; whether we should do again what has already been done once, though poorly. However, we are not in the position of children who have been given portions of pie by someone who now makes last minute adjustments to rectify careless cutting. There is no *central* distribution, no person or group entitled to control all the resources, jointly deciding how they are to be doled out. What each person gets, he gets from others who give to him in exchange for something, or as a gift. In a free society, diverse persons control different resources, and new holdings arise out of the voluntary exchanges and actions of persons. There is no more a distributing or distribution of shares than there is a distributing of mates in a society in which persons choose whom they shall marry. The total result is the product of many individual decisions which the different individuals involved are entitled to make. Some uses of the term "distribution," it is true, do not imply a previous distributing appropriately judged by some criterion (for example, "probability distribution"); neverthe-less, despite the term "distributive justice," it would be best to use a terminology that clearly is neutral. We shall speak of people's holdings; a principle of justice in holdings describes (part of) what justice tells us (requires) about hold-ings. I shall state first what I take to be the correct view about justice in holdings, and then turn to the discussion of alternate views.

The Entitlement Theory

The subject of justice in holdings consists of three major topics. The first is the *original acquisition of holdings*, the appropriation of unheld things. This includes the issues of how unheld things may come to be held, the process, or pro-cesses, by which unheld things may come to be held, the things that may come to be held by these processes, the extent of what comes to be held by a particular process, and so on. We shall refer to the complicated truth about this topic, which we shall not formulate here, as the prin-ciple of justice in acquisition. The second topic concerns the *transfer of holdings* from one person to another. By what processes may a person transfer holdings to another? How may a person acquire a holding from another who holds it? Under this topic come general descriptions of voluntary exchange, and gift and (on the other hand) fraud, as well as reference to particular con-ventional details fixed upon in a given society. The complicated truth about this subject (with placeholders for conventional details) we shall call the principle of justice in transfer. (And we shall suppose it also includes principles govern-ing how a person may divest himself of a hold-ing, passing it into an unheld state.)

If the world were wholly just, the following inductive definition would exhaustively cover the subject of justice in holdings.

1. A person who acquires a holding in accordance with the principle of justice in acquisition is entitled to that holding.

2. A person who acquires a holding in accordance with the principle of justice in transfer, from someone else entitled to the holding, is entitled to the holding.
3. No one is entitled to a holding except by (repeated) applications of 1 and 2.

The complete principle of distributive justice would say simply that a distribution is just if everyone is entitled to the holdings they possess under the distribution.

A distribution is just if it arises from another just distribution by legitimate means. The legit-imate means of moving from one distribution to another are specified by the principle of justice in transfer. The legitimate first "moves" are specified by the principle of justice in acquisi-tion. Whatever arises from a just situation by just steps is itself just. The means of change specified by the principle of justice in transfer preserve justice. As correct rules of inference are truth-preserving, and any conclusion deduced via repeated application of such rules from only true premisses is itself true, so the means of transition from one situation to another specified by the principle of justice in transfer are justice-preserving, and any situation actually arising from repeated transitions in accordance with the principle from a just situation is itself just. The parallel between justice-preserving transform-ations and truth-preserving transformations illuminates where it fails as well as where it holds. That a conclusion could have been deduced by truth-preserving means from prem-isses that are true suffices to show its truth. That from a just situation a situation *could* have arisen via justice-preserving means does *not* suffice to show its justice. The fact that a thief's victims voluntarily *could* have presented him with gifts does not entitle the thief to his ill-gotten gains. Justice in holdings is historical; it depends upon what actually has happened. We shall return to this point later.

Not all actual situations are generated in accordance with the two principles of justice in holdings: the principle of justice in acquisition and the principle of justice in transfer. Some people steal from others, or defraud them, or enslave them, seizing their product and preventing them from living as they choose, or forcibly exclude others from competing in exchanges. None of these are permissible modes of transition from one situation to another. And some persons acquire holdings by means not sanctioned by the principle of justice in acquisition. The existence of past injustice (previous violations of the first two principles of justice in holdings) raises the third major topic under justice in holdings: the rectification of injustice in holdings. If past injustice has shaped present holdings in various ways, some identifiable and some not, what now, if anything, ought to be done to rectify these injustices? What obligations do the performers of injustice have toward those whose position is worse than it would have been had the injustice not been done? Or, than it would have been had compensation been paid promptly? How, if at all, do things change if the beneficiaries and those made worse off are not the direct parties in the act of injustice, but, for example, their descendants? Is an injustice done to someone whose holding was itself based upon an unrectified injustice? How far back must one go in wiping clean the historical slate of injustices? What may victims of injustice permissibly do in order to rectify the injustices being done to them, including the many injustices done by persons acting through their government? I do not know of a thorough or theoretically sophisticated treatment of such issues. Idealizing greatly, let us suppose theoretical investigation will produce a principle of rectification. This principle uses historical information about previous situations and injustices done in them (as defined by the first two principles of justice and rights against interference), and information about the actual course of events that flowed from these injustices, until the present, and it yields a description (or descriptions) of holdings in the society. The principle of rectification presumably will make use of its best estimate of subjunctive information about what would have occurred (or a probability distribution over what might have occurred, using the expected value) if the injustice had not taken place. If the actual description of holdings turns out not to be one of the descriptions yielded by the principle, then one of the descriptions yielded must be realized.

The general outlines of the theory of justice in holdings are that the holdings of a person are just if he is entitled to them by the principles of justice in acquisition and transfer, or by the principle of rectification of injustice (as specified by the first two principles). If each person's holdings are just, then the total set (distribution) of holdings is just. To turn these general outlines into a specific theory we would have to specify the details of each of the three principles of justice in holdings: the principle of acquisition of holdings, the principle of transfer of holdings, and the principle of rectification of violations of the first two principles. I shall not attempt that task here.

Historical Principles and End-Result Principles

The general outlines of the entitlement theory illuminate the nature and defects of other conceptions of distributive justice. The entitlement theory of justice in distribution is *historical*; whether a distribution is just depends upon how it came about. In contrast, *current time-slice principles* of justice hold that the justice of a distribution is determined by how things are distributed (who has what) as judged by some *structural* principle(s) of just distribution. A utilitarian who judges between any two distributions by seeing which has the greater sum of utility and, if the sums tie, applies some fixed equality criterion to choose the more equal distribution, would hold a current time-slice principle of justice. As would someone who had a fixed schedule of trade-offs between the sum of happiness and equality. According to a current time-slice principle, all that needs to be looked at, in judging the justice of a distribution, is who ends up with what; in comparing any two distributions one need look only at the matrix presenting the distributions. No further information need be fed into a principle of justice. It is a consequence of such principles of justice that any two structurally identical distributions are equally just. (Two distributions are structurally identical if they present the same profile, but perhaps have different persons occupying the particular slots. My having ten and your having five, and my having five and your having ten are structurally identical distributions.) Welfare economics is the theory of current time-slice principles of justice. The subject is conceived as operating on matrices representing only current information about distribution. This, as well as some of the usual conditions (for example, the choice of distribution is invariant under relabeling of columns), guarantees that welfare economics will be a current time-slice theory, with all of its inadequacies.

Most persons do not accept current time-slice principles as constituting the whole story about distributive shares. They think it relevant in assessing the justice of a situation to consider not only the distribution it embodies, but also how that distribution came about. If some persons are in prison for murder or war crimes, we do not say that to assess the justice of the distribution in the society we must look only at what this person has, and that person has, and that person has, . . . at the current time. We think it relevant to ask whether someone did something so that he *deserved* to be punished, deserved to have a lower share. Most will agree to the relevance of further information with regard to punishments and penalties. Consider also desired things. One traditional socialist view is that workers are entitled to the product and full fruits of their labor; they have earned it; a distribution is unjust if it does not give the workers what they are entitled to.

Such entitlements are based upon some past history. No socialist holding this view would find it comforting to be told that because the actual distribution A happens to coincide structurally with the one he desires D, A therefore is no less just than D; it differs only in that the "parasitic" owners of capital receive under A what the workers are entitled to under D, and the workers receive under A what the owners are entitled to under D, namely very little. This socialist rightly, in my view, holds onto the notions of earning, producing, entitlement, desert, and so forth, and he rejects current time-slice principles that look only to the structure of the resulting set of holdings. (The set of holdings resulting from what? Isn't it implausible that how holdings are produced and come to exist has no effect at all on who should hold what?) His mistake lies in his view of what entitlements arise out of what sorts of productive processes.

We construe the position we discuss too narrowly by speaking of *current* time-slice principles. Nothing is changed if structural principles operate upon a time sequence of current time-slice profiles and, for example, give someone more now to counterbalance the less he has had earlier. A utilitarian or an egalitarian or any mixture of the two over time will inherit the difficulties of his more myopic comrades. He is not helped by the fact that *some* of the information others consider relevant in assessing a distribution is reflected, unrecoverably, in past matrices. Henceforth, we shall refer to such unhistorical principles of distributive justice, including the current time-slice principles, as *end-result principles* or *end-state principles*.

In contrast to end-result principles of justice, *historical principles* of justice hold that past circumstances or actions of people can create differential entitlements or differential deserts to things. An injustice can be worked by moving from one distribution to another structurally identical one, for the second, in profile the same, may violate people's entitlements or deserts; it may not fit the actual history.

Patterning

The entitlement principles of justice in holdings that we have sketched are historical principles of justice. To better understand their precise character, we shall distinguish them from another subclass of the historical principles. Consider, as an example, the principle of distribution according to moral merit. This principle requires that total distributive shares vary directly with moral merit; no person should have a greater share than anyone whose moral merit is greater. (If moral merit could be not merely ordered but measured on an interval or ratio scale, stronger principles could be formulated.) Or consider the principle that results by substituting "usefulness to society" for "moral merit" in the previous principle. Or instead of "distribute according to moral merit," or "distribute according to usefulness to society," we might consider "distribute according to the weighted sum of moral merit, usefulness to society, and need," with the weights of the different dimensions equal. Let us call a principle of distribution *patterned* if it specifies that a distribution is to vary along with some natural dimension, weighted sum of natural dimensions, or lexicographic ordering of natural dimensions. And let us say a distribution is patterned if it accords with some patterned principle. (I speak of natural dimensions, admittedly without a general criterion for them, because for any set of holdings some artificial dimensions can be gimmicked up to vary along with the distribution of the set.) The principle of distribution in accordance with moral merit is a patterned historical principle, which specifies a patterned distribution. "Distribute according to I.Q." is a patterned principle that looks to information not contained in distributional matrices. It is not historical, however, in that it does not look to any past actions creating differential entitlements to evaluate a distribution; it requires only distributional matrices whose columns are labeled by I.Q. scores. The distribution in a society, however, may be composed of such simple patterned distributions, without itself being simply patterned. Different sectors may operate different patterns, or some combination of patterns may operate in different proportions across a society. A distribution composed in this manner, from a small number of patterned distributions, we also shall term "patterned." And we extend the use of "pattern" to include the overall designs put forth by combinations of end-state principles.

Almost every suggested principle of distributive justice is patterned: to each according to his moral merit, or needs, or marginal product, or how hard he tries, or the weighted sum of the foregoing, and so on. The principle of entitlement we have sketched is *not* patterned. There is no one natural dimension or weighted sum or combination of a small number of natural dimensions that yields the distributions generated in accordance with the principle of entitlement. The set of holdings that results when some persons receive their marginal products, others win at gambling, others receive a share of their mate's income, others receive gifts from foundations, others receive interest on loans, others receive gifts from admirers, other receive returns on investment, others make for themselves much of what they have, others find things, and so on, will not be patterned. Heavy strands of patterns will run through it; significant portions of the variance in holdings will be accounted for by pattern-variables. If most people most of the time choose to transfer some of their entitlements to others only in exchange for something from them, then a large part of what many people hold will vary with what they held that others wanted. More details are provided by the theory of marginal productivity. But gifts to relatives, charitable donations, bequests to children, and the like, are not best conceived, in the first instance, in this manner. Ignoring the strands of pattern, let us suppose for the moment that a distribution actually arrived at by the operation of the principle of entitlement is random with respect to any pattern. Though the resulting set of holdings will be unpatterned, it will not be incomprehensible, for it can be seen as arising from the operation of a small number of principles. These principles specify how an initial distribution may arise (the principle of acquisition of holdings) and how distributions may be transformed into others (the principle of transfer of holdings). The process whereby the set of holdings is generated will be intelligible, though the set of holdings itself that results from this process will be unpatterned.

The writings of F. A. Hayek focus less than is usually done upon what patterning distributive justice requires. Hayek argues that we cannot know enough about each person's situation to distribute to each according to his moral merit (but would justice demand we do so if we did have this knowledge?); and he goes on to say, "our objection is against all attempts to impress upon society a deliberately chosen pattern of distribution, whether it be an order of equality or of inequality." However, Hayek concludes that in a free society there will be distribution in accordance with value rather than moral merit; that is, in accordance with the perceived value of a person's actions and services to others. Despite his rejection of a patterned conception of distributive justice, Hayek himself suggests a pattern he thinks justifiable: distribution in accordance with the perceived benefits given to others, leaving room for the complaint that a free society does not realize exactly this pattern. Stating this patterned strand of a free capitalist society more precisely, we get "To each according to how much he benefits others who have the resources for benefiting those who benefit them." This will seem arbitrary unless some acceptable initial set of holdings is specified, or unless it is held that the operation of the system over time washes out any significant effects from the initial set of holdings. As an example of the latter, if almost anyone would have bought a car from Henry Ford, the supposition that it was an arbitrary matter who held the money then (and so bought) would not place Henry Ford's earnings

under a cloud. In any event, his coming to hold it is not arbitrary. Distribution according to benefits to others is a major patterned strand in a free capitalist society, as Hayek correctly points out, but it is only a strand and does not constitute the whole pattern of a system of entitlements (namely, inheritance, gifts for arbitrary reasons, charity, and so on) or a standard that one should insist a society fit. Will people tolerate for long a system yielding distributions that they believe are unpatterned? No doubt people will not long accept a distribution they believe is unjust. People want their society to be and to look just. But must the look of justice reside in a resulting pattern rather than in the underlying generating principles? We are in no position to conclude that the inhabitants of a society embodying an entitlement conception of justice in holdings will find it unacceptable. Still, it must be granted that were people's reasons for transferring some of their holdings to others always irrational or arbitrary, we would find this disturbing. (Suppose people always determined what holdings they would transfer, and to whom, by using a random device.) We feel more comfortable upholding the justice of an entitlement system if most of the transfers under it are done for reasons. This does not mean necessarily that all deserve what holdings they receive. It means only that there is a purpose or point to someone's transferring a holding to one person rather than to another; that usually we can see what the transferrer thinks he's gaining, what cause he thinks he's serving, what goals he thinks he's helping to achieve, and so forth. Since in a capitalist society people often transfer holdings to others in accordance with how much they perceive these others benefiting them, the fabric constituted by the individual transactions and transfers is largely reasonable and intelligible. (Gifts to loved ones, bequests to children, charity to the needy also are nonarbitrary components of the fabric.) In stressing the large strand of distribution in accordance with benefit to others, Hayek shows the point of many transfers, and so shows that the system of transfer of entitlements is not just spinning its gears aimlessly. The system of entitlements is defensible when constituted by the individual aims of individual transactions. No overarching aim is needed, no distributional pattern is required.

To think that the task of a theory of distributive justice is to fill in the blank in "to each according to his _____" is to be predisposed to search for a pattern; and the separate treatment of "from each according to his _____" treats production and distribution as two separate and independent issues. On an entitlement view these are *not* two separate questions. Whoever makes something, having bought or contracted for all other held resources used in the process (transferring some of his holdings for these cooperating factors), is entitled to it. The situation is *not* one of something's getting made, and there being an open question of who is to get it. Things come into the world already attached to people having entitlements over them. From the point of view of the historical entitlement conception of justice in holdings, those who start afresh to complete "to each according to his _____" treat objects as if they appeared from nowhere, out of nothing. A complete theory of justice might cover this limit case as well; perhaps here is a use for the usual conceptions of distributive justice.

So entrenched are maxims of the usual form that perhaps we should present the entitlement conception as a competitor. Ignoring acquisition and rectification, we might say:

> From each according to what he chooses to do, to each according to what he makes for himself (perhaps with the contracted aid of others) and what others choose to do for him and choose to give him of what they've been given previously (under this maxim) and haven't yet expended or transferred.

This, the discerning reader will have noticed, has its defects as a slogan. So as a summary and great simplification (and not as a maxim with any independent meaning) we have:

> *From each as they choose, to each as they are chosen.*

How Liberty Upsets Patterns

It is not clear how those holding alternative conceptions of distributive justice can reject the entitlement conception of justice in holdings. For suppose a distribution favored by one of these non-entitlement conceptions is realized. Let us suppose it is your favorite one and let us call this distribution D_1; perhaps everyone has an equal share, perhaps shares vary in accordance with some dimension you treasure. Now suppose that Wilt Chamberlain is greatly in demand by basketball teams, being a great gate attraction. (Also suppose contracts run only for a year, with players being free agents.) He signs the following sort of contract with a team: In each home game, twenty-five cents from the price of each ticket of admission goes to him. (We ignore the question of whether he is "gouging" the owners, letting them look out for themselves.) The season starts, and people cheerfully attend his team's games; they buy their tickets, each time dropping a separate twenty-five cents of their admission price into a special box with Chamberlain's name on it. They are excited about seeing him play; it is worth the total admission price to them. Let us suppose that in one season one million persons attend his home games, and Wilt Chamberlain winds up with $250,000, a much larger sum than the average income and larger even than anyone else has. Is he entitled to this income? Is this new distribution D_2, unjust? If so, why? There is *no* question about whether each of the people was entitled to the control over the resources they held in D_1; because that was the distribution (your favorite) that (for the purposes of argument) we assumed was acceptable. Each of these persons *chose* to give twenty-five cents of their money to Chamberlain. They could have spent it on going to the movies, or on candy bars, or on copies of *Dissent* magazine, or of *Montly Review*. But they all, at least one million of them, converged on giving it to Wilt Chamberlain in exchange for watching him play basketball. If D_1 was a just distribution, and people voluntarily moved from it to D_2, transferring parts of their shares they were given under D_1 (what was it for if not to do something with?), isn't D_2 also just? If the people were entitled to dispose of the resources to which they were entitled (under D_1), didn't this include their being entitled to give it to, or exchange it with, Wilt Chamberlain? Can anyone else complain on grounds of justice? Each other person already has his legitimate share under D_1. Under D_1, there is nothing that anyone has that anyone else has a claim of justice against. After someone transfers something to Wilt Chamberlain, third parties still have their legitimate shares; their shares are not changed. By what process could such a transfer among two persons give rise to a legitimate claim of distributive justice on a portion of what was transferred, by a third party who had no claim of justice on any holding of the others *before* the transfer? To cut off objections irrelevant here, we might imagine the exchanges occurring in a socialist society, after hours. After playing whatever basketball he does in his daily work, or doing whatever other daily work he does, Wilt Chamberlain decides to put in *overtime* to earn additional money. (First his work quota is set; he works time over that.) Or imagine it is a skilled juggler people like to see, who puts on shows after hours.

Why might someone work overtime in a society in which it is assumed their needs are satisfied? Perhaps because they care about things other than needs. I like to write in books that I read, and to have easy access to books for browsing at odd hours. It would be very pleasant and convenient to have the resources of Widener Library in my back yard. No society, I assume, will provide such resources close to each person who would like them as part of his regular allotment (under D_1). Thus, persons either must

do without some extra things that they want, or be allowed to do something extra to get some of these things. On what basis could the inequalities that would eventuate be forbidden? Notice also that small factories would spring up in a socialist society, unless forbidden. I melt down some of my personal possessions (under D_1) and build a machine out of the material. I offer you, and others, a philosophy lecture once a week in exchange for your cranking the handle on my machine, whose products I exchange for yet other things, and so on. (The raw materials used by the machine are given to me by others who possess them under D_1, in exchange for hearing lectures.) Each person might participate to gain things over and above their allotment under D_1. Some persons even might want to leave their job in socialist industry and work full time in this private sector. I shall say something more about these issues in the next chapter. Here I wish merely to note how private property even in means of production would occur in a socialist society that did not forbid people to use as they wished some of the resources they are given under the socialist distribution D_1. The socialist society would have to forbid capitalist acts between consenting adults.

The general point illustrated by the Wilt Chamberlain example and the example of the entrepreneur in a socialist society is that no end-state principle or distributional patterned principle of justice can be continuously realized without continuous interference with people's lives. Any favored pattern would be transformed into one unfavored by the principle, by people choosing to act in various ways; for example, by people exchanging goods and services with other people, or giving things to other people, things the transferrers are entitled to under the favored distributional pattern. To maintain a pattern one must either continually interfere to stop people from transferring resources as they wish to, or continually (or periodically) interfere to take from some persons resources that others for some reason chose to transfer to them. (But if some time limit is to be set on how long people may keep resources others voluntarily transfer to them, why let them keep these resources for *any* period of time? Why not have immediate confiscation?) It might be objected that all persons voluntarily will choose to refrain from actions which would upset the pattern. This presupposes unrealistically (1) that all will most want to maintain the pattern (are those who don't, to be "reeducated" or forced to undergo "self-criticism"?), (2) that each can gather enough information about his own actions and the ongoing activities of others to discover which of his actions will upset the pattern, and (3) that diverse and far-flung persons can coordinate their actions to dovetail into the pattern. Compare the manner in which the market is neutral among persons' desires, as it reflects and transmits widely scattered information via prices, and coordinates persons' activities.

It puts things perhaps a bit too strongly to say that every patterned (or end-state) principle is liable to be thwarted by the voluntary actions of the individual parties transferring some of their shares they receive under the principle. For perhaps some *very* weak patterns are not so thwarted. Any distributional pattern with any egalitarian component is overturnable by the voluntary actions of individual persons over time; as is every patterned condition with sufficient content so as actually to have been proposed as presenting the central core of distributive justice. Still, given the possibility that some weak conditions or patterns may not be unstable in this way, it would be better to formulate an explicit description of the kind of interesting and contentful patterns under discussion, and to prove a theorem about their instability. Since the weaker the patterning, the more likely it is that the entitlement system itself satisfies it, a plausible conjecture is that any patterning either is unstable or is satisfied by the entitlement system. [. . .]

Redistribution and Property Rights

Apparently, patterned principles allow people to choose to expend upon themselves, but not upon others, those resources they are entitled to (or rather, receive) under some favored distributional pattern D_1. For if each of several persons chooses to expend some of his D_1 resources upon one other person, then that other person will receive more than his D_1 share, disturbing the favored distributional pattern. Maintaining a distributional pattern is individualism with a vengeance! Patterned distributional principles do not give people what entitlement principles do, only better distributed. For they do not give the right to choose what to do with what one has; they do not give the right to choose to pursue an end involving (intrinsically, or as a means) the enhancement of another's position. To such views, families are disturbing; for within a family occur transfers that upset the favored distributional pattern. Either families themselves become units to which distribution takes place, the column occupiers (on what rationale?), or loving behavior is forbidden. We should note in passing the ambivalent position of radicals toward the family. Its loving relationships are seen as a model to be emulated and extended across the whole society, at the same time that it is denounced as a suffocating institution to be broken and condemned as a focus of parochial concerns that interfere with achieving radical goals. Need we say that it is not appropriate to enforce across the wider society the relationships of love and care appropriate within a family, relationships which are voluntarily undertaken?[1] Incidentally, love is an interesting instance of another relationship that is historical, in that (like justice) it depends upon what actually occurred. An adult may come to love another because of the other's characteristics; but it is the other person, and not the characteristics, that is loved. The love is not transferrable to someone else with the same characteristics, even to one who "scores" higher for these characteristics.

And the love endures through changes of the characteristics that gave rise to it. One loves the particular person one actually encountered. Why love is historical, attaching to persons in this way and not to characteristics, is an interesting and puzzling question.

Proponents of patterned principles of distributive justice focus upon criteria for determining who is to receive holdings; they consider the reasons for which someone should have something, and also the total picture of holdings. Whether or not it is better to give than to receive, proponents of patterned principles ignore giving altogether. In considering the distribution of goods, income, and so forth, their theories are theories of recipient justice; they completely ignore any right a person might have to give something to someone. Even in exchanges where each party is simultaneously giver and recipient, patterned principles of justice focus only upon the recipient role and its supposed rights. Thus discussions tend to focus on whether people (should) have a right to inherit, rather than on whether people (should) have a right to bequeath or on whether persons who have a right to hold also have a right to choose that others hold in their place. I lack a good explanation of why the usual theories of distributive justice are so recipient oriented; ignoring givers and transferrers and their rights is of a piece with ignoring producers and their entitlements. But why is it *all* ignored?

Patterned principles of distributive justice necessitate redistributive activities. The likelihood is small that any actual freely-arrived-at set of holdings fits a given pattern; and the likelihood is nil that it will continue to fit the pattern as people exchange and give. From the point of view of an entitlement theory, redistribution is a serious matter indeed, involving, as it does, the violation of people's rights. (An exception is those takings that fall under the principle of the rectification of injustices.) From other points of view, also, it is serious.

Taxation of earnings from labor is on a par with forced labor. Some persons find this claim obviously true: taking the earnings of n hours labor is like taking n hours from the person; it is like forcing the person to work n hours for another's purpose. Others find the claim absurd. But even these, if they object to forced labor, would oppose forcing unemployed hippies to work for the benefit of the needy. And they would also object to forcing each person to work five extra hours each week for the benefit of the needy. But a system that takes five hours' wages in taxes does not seem to them like one that forces someone to work five hours, since it offers the person forced a wider range of choice in activities than does taxation in kind with the particular labor specified. (But we can imagine a gradation of systems of forced labor, from one that specifies a particular activity, to one that gives a choice among two activities, to . . .; and so on up.) Furthermore, people envisage a system with something like a proportional tax on everything above the amount necessary for basic needs. Some think this does not force someone to work extra hours, since there is no fixed number of extra hours he is forced to work, and since he can avoid the tax entirely by earning only enough to cover his basic needs. This is a very uncharacteristic view of forcing for those who *also* think people are forced to do something *whenever* the alternatives they face are considerably worse. However, *neither* view is correct. The fact that others intentionally intervene, in violation of a side constraint against aggression, to threaten force to limit the alternatives, in this case to paying taxes or (presumably the worse alternative) bare subsistence, makes the taxation system one of forced labor and distinguishes it from other cases of limited choices which are not forcings.

The man who chooses to work longer to gain an income more than sufficient for his basic needs prefers some extra goods or services to the leisure and activities he could perform during the possible nonworking hours; whereas the man who chooses not to work the extra time prefers the leisure activities to the extra goods or services he could acquire by working more. Given this, if it would be illegitimate for a tax system to seize some of a man's leisure (forced labor) for the purpose of serving the needy, how can it be legitimate for a tax system to seize some of a man's goods for that purpose? Why should we treat the man whose happiness requires certain material goods or services differently from the man whose preferences and desires make such goods unnecessary for his happiness? Why should the man who prefers seeing a movie (and who has to earn money for a ticket) be open to the required call to aid the needy, while the person who prefers looking at a sunset (and hence need earn no extra money) is not? Indeed, isn't it surprising that redistributionists choose to ignore the man whose pleasures are so easily attainable without extra labor, while adding yet another burden to the poor unfortunate who must work for his pleasures? If anything, one would have expected the reverse. Why is the person with the nonmaterial or nonconsumption desire allowed to proceed unimpeded to his most favored feasible alternative, whereas the man whose pleasures or desires involve material things and who must work for extra money (thereby serving whomever considers his activities valuable enough to pay him) is constrained in what he can realize? Perhaps there is no difference in principle. And perhaps some think the answer concerns merely administrative convenience. (These questions and issues will not disturb those who think that forced labor to serve the needy or to realize some favored end-state pattern is acceptable.) In a fuller discussion we would have (and want) to extend our argument to include interest, entrepreneurial profits, and so on. Those who doubt that this extension can be carried through, and who draw the line here at taxation of income from labor, will have to state rather complicated patterned *historical* principles of distributive justice, since end-state principles would not distinguish *sources* of income in any way. It is enough for now to get

away from end-state principles and to make clear how various patterned principles are dependent upon particular views about the sources or the illegitimacy or the lesser legitimacy of profits, interest, and so on; which particular views may well be mistaken.

What sort of right over others does a legally institutionalized end-state pattern give one? The central core of the notion of a property right in X, relative to which other parts of the notion are to be explained, is the right to determine what shall be done with X; the right to choose which of the constrained set of options concerning X shall be realized or attempted. The constraints are set by other principles or laws operating in the society; in our theory, by the Lockean rights people possess (under the minimal state). My property rights in my knife allow me to leave it where I will, but not in your chest. I may choose which of the acceptable options involving the knife is to be realized. This notion of property helps us to understand why earlier theorists spoke of people as having property in themselves and their labor. They viewed each person as having a right to decide what would become of himself and what he would do, and as having a right to reap the benefits of what he did.

This right of selecting the alternative to be realized from the constrained set of alternatives may be held by an *individual* or by a *group* with some procedure for reaching a joint decision; or the right may be passed back and forth, so that one year I decide what's to become of X, and the next year you do (with the alternative of destruction, perhaps, being excluded). Or, during the same time period, some types of decisions about X may be made by me, and others by you. And so on. We lack an adequate, fruitful, analytical apparatus for classifying the *types* of constraints on the set of options among which choices are to be made, and the *types* of ways decision powers can be held, divided, and amalgamated. A *theory* of property would, among other things, contain such a classification of constraints and decision modes, and from a small number of principles would follow a host of interesting statements about the *consequences* and effects of certain combinations of constraints and modes of decision.

When end-result principles of distributive justice are built into the legal structure of a society, they (as do most patterned principles) give each citizen an enforceable claim to some portion of the total social product; that is, to some portion of the sum total of the individually and jointly made products. This total product is produced by individuals laboring, using means of production others have saved to bring into existence, by people organizing production or creating means to produce new things or things in a new way. It is on this batch of individual activities that patterned distributional principles give each individual an enforceable claim. Each person has a claim to the activities and the products of other persons, independently of whether the other persons enter into particular relationships that give rise to these claims, and independently of whether they voluntarily take these claims upon themselves, in charity or in exchange for something.

Whether it is done through taxation on wages or on wages over a certain amount, or through seizure of profits, or through there being a big *social pot* so that it's not clear what's coming from where and what's going where, patterned principles of distributive justice involve appropriating the actions of other persons. Seizing the results of someone's labor is equivalent to seizing hours from him and directing him to carry on various activities. If people force you to do certain work, or unrewarded work, for a certain period of time, they decide what you are to do and what purposes your work is to serve apart from your decisions. This process whereby they take this decision from you makes them a *part-owner* of you; it gives them a property right in you. Just as having such partial control and power of decision, by right, over an animal or inanimate object would be to have a property right in it.

End-state and most patterned principles of distributive justice institute (partial) ownership by others of people and their actions and labor. These principles involve a shift from the classical liberals' notion of self-ownership to a notion of (partial) property rights in *other* people.

Considerations such as these confront end-state and other patterned conceptions of justice with the question of whether the actions necessary to achieve the selected pattern don't themselves violate moral side constraints. Any view holding that there are moral side constraints on actions, that not all moral considerations can be built into end states that are to be achieved, must face the possibility that some of its goals are not achievable by any morally permissible available means. An entitlement theorist will face such conflicts in a society that deviates from the principles of justice for the generation of holdings, if and only if the only actions available to realize the principles themselves violate some moral constraints. Since deviation from the first two principles of justice (in acquisition and transfer) will involve other persons' direct and aggressive intervention to violate rights, and since moral constraints will not exclude defensive or retributive action in such cases, the entitlement theorist's problem rarely will be pressing. And whatever difficulties he has in applying the principle of rectification to persons who did not themselves violate the first two principles are difficulties in balancing the conflicting considerations so as correctly to formulate the complex principle of rectification itself; he will not violate moral side constraints by applying the principle. Proponents of patterned conceptions of justice, however, often will face head-on clashes (and poignant ones if they cherish each party to the clash) between moral side constraints on how individuals may be treated and their patterned conception of justice that presents an end state or other pattern that *must* be realized.

May a person emigrate from a nation that has institutionalized some end-state or patterned distributional principle? For some principles (for example, Hayek's) emigration presents no theoretical problem. But for others it is a tricky matter. Consider a nation having a compulsory scheme of minimal social provision to aid the neediest (or one organized so as to maximize the position of the worst-off group); no one may opt out of participating in it. (None may say, "Don't compel me to contribute to others and don't provide for me via this compulsory mechanism if I am in need.") Everyone above a certain level is forced to contribute to aid the needy. But if emigration from the country were allowed, anyone could choose to move to another country that did not have compulsory social provision but otherwise was (as much as possible) identical. In such a case, the person's only motive for leaving would be to avoid participating in the compulsory scheme of social provision. And if he does leave, the needy in his initial country will receive no (compelled) help from him. What rationale yields the result that the person be permitted to emigrate, yet forbidden to stay and opt out of the compulsory scheme of social provision? If providing for the needy is of overriding importance, this does militate against allowing internal opting out; but it also speaks against allowing external emigration. (Would it also support, to some extent, the kidnapping of persons living in a place without compulsory social provision, who could be forced to make a contribution to the needy in your community?) Perhaps the crucial compon-

ent of the position that allows emigration solely to avoid certain arrangements, while not allowing anyone internally to opt out of them, is a concern for fraternal feelings within the country. "We don't want anyone here who doesn't contribute, who doesn't care enough about the others to contribute." That concern, in this case, would have to be tied to the view that forced aiding tends to produce fraternal feelings between the aided and the aider (or perhaps merely to the view that the knowledge that someone or other voluntarily is not aiding produces unfraternal feelings).

Note

1   One indication of the stringency of Rawls' difference principle is its inappropriateness as a governing principle even within a family of individuals who love one another. Should a family devote its resources to maximizing the position of its least well off and least talented child, holding back the other children or using resources for their education and development only if they will follow a policy through their lifetimes of maximizing the position of their least fortunate sibling? Surely not. How then can this even be considered as the appropriate policy for enforcement in the wider society? (I discuss elsewhere what I think would be Rawls' reply: that some principles apply at the macro level which do not apply to micro-situations.)

Chapter 30

F. A. Hayek

THE ATAVISM OF SOCIAL JUSTICE

Friedrich Hayek (1899–1992) was an Austrian economist and social theorist, and winner of the Nobel prize in economics in 1974. He is best known for his work on the knowledge-generating function of a free-market price system, but also produced very influential work in jurisprudence and cognitive science. In this essay (published in 1976), Hayek criticizes the notion of 'social justice' as a doctrine appropriate to the small primitive groups of our distant ancestral past, but not to a society governed by abstract rules.

1

To discover the meaning of what is called 'social justice' has been one of my chief preoccupations for more than 10 years. I have failed in this endeavour – or, rather, have reached the conclusion that, with reference to a society of free men, the phrase has no meaning whatever. The search for the reason why the word has nevertheless for something like a century dominated political discussion, and has everywhere been successfully used to advance claims of particular groups for a larger share in the good things of life, remains, however, a very interesting one. It is this question with which I shall here chiefly concern myself.

But I must at first briefly explain, as I attempt to demonstrate at length in volume 2 of my *Law, Legislation and Liberty*, about to be published, why I have come to regard 'social justice' as nothing more than an empty formula, conventionally used to assert that a particular claim is justified without giving any reason. Indeed that volume,

which bears the sub-title. *The Mirage of Social Justice*, is mainly intended to convince intellectuals that the concept of 'social justice', which they are so fond of using, is intellectually disreputable. Some of course have already tumbled to this; but with the unfortunate result that, since 'social' justice is the only kind of justice they have ever thought of, they have been led to the conclusion that all uses of the term justice have no meaningful content. I have therefore been forced to show in the same book that rules of just individual conduct are as indispensable to the preservation of a peaceful society of free men as endeavours to realise 'social' justice are incompatible with it.

The term 'social justice' is today generally used as a synonym of what used to be called 'distributive justice'. The latter term perhaps gives a somewhat better idea of what can be meant by it, and at the same time shows why it can have no application to the results of a market economy: there can be no distributive justice where no one distributes. Justice has meaning only as a rule of human conduct, and no conceivable rules for the conduct of individuals supplying each other with goods and services in a market economy would produce a distribution which could be meaningfully described as just or unjust. Individuals might conduct themselves as justly as possible, but as the results for separate individuals would be neither intended nor foreseeable by others, the resulting state of affairs could neither be called just nor unjust.

The complete emptiness of the phrase 'social justice' shows itself in the fact that no agreement exists about what social justice requires in particular instances; also that there is no known test by which to decide who is right if people differ, and that no preconceived scheme of distribution could be effectively devised in a society whose individuals are free, in the sense of being allowed to use their own knowledge for their own purposes. Indeed, individual moral responsibility for one's actions is incompatible with the realisation of any such desired overall pattern of distribution.

A little inquiry shows that, though a great many people are dissatisfied with the existing pattern of distribution, none of them has really any clear idea of what pattern he would regard as just. All that we find are intuitive assessments of individual cases as unjust. No one has yet found even a single general rule from which we could derive what is 'socially just' in all particular instances that would fall under it – except the rule of 'equal pay for equal work'. Free competition, precluding all that regard for merit or need and the like, on which demands for social justice are based, tends to enforce the equal pay rule.

2

The reason why most people continue firmly to believe in 'social justice', even after they discover that they do not really know what the phrase means, is that they think if almost everyone else believes in it, there must be something in the phrase. The ground for this almost universal acceptance of a belief, the significance of which people do not understand, is that we have all inherited from an earlier different type of society, in which man existed very much longer than in the present one, some now deeply ingrained instincts which are inapplicable to our present civilisation. In fact, man emerged from primitive society when in certain conditions increasing numbers succeeded by disregarding those very principles which had held the old groups together.

We must not forget that before the last 10,000 years, during which man has developed agriculture, towns and ultimately the 'Great Society', he existed for at least a hundred times as long in small food-sharing hunting bands of 50 or so, with a strict order of dominance within the defended common territory of the band. The needs of this ancient primitive kind of society determined much of the moral feelings which still govern us, and which we approve in others. It was a grouping in which, at least for all males, the common pursuit of a perceived physical common object under the direction of the alpha male was as much a condition of its continued existence as the assignment of different shares in the prey to the different members according to their importance for the survival of the band. It is more than probable that many of the moral feelings then acquired have not merely been culturally transmitted by teaching or imitation, but have become innate or genetically determined.

But not all that is natural to us in this sense is therefore necessarily in different circumstances good or beneficial for the propagation of the species. In its primitive form the little band indeed did possess what is still attractive to so many people: a unitary purpose, or a common hierarchy of ends, and a deliberate sharing of means according to a common view of individual merits. These foundations of its coherence, however, also imposed limits on the possible development of this form of society. The events to which the group could adapt itself, and the opportunities it could take advantage of, were only those of which its members were directly aware. Even worse, the individual could do little of which others did not approve. It is a delusion to think of the individual in primitive society as free. There was no natural liberty for a social animal, while freedom is an artifact of civilisation. The individual had in the group no recognised domain of independent action; even the head of the band could expect obedience, support and understanding of his signals only for conventional activities. So long as each must serve that common order of rank for all needs, which present-day socialists dream of, there can be no free experimentation by the individual.

3

The great advance which made possible the development of civilisation and ultimately of the Open Society was the gradual substitution of abstract rules of conduct for specific obligatory ends, and with it the playing of a game for acting in concert under common indicators, thus fostering a spontaneous order. The great gain attained by this was that it made possible a procedure through which all relevant information widely dispersed was made available to ever-increasing numbers of men in the form of the symbols which we call market prices. But it also meant that the incidence of the results on different persons and groups no longer satisfied the age-old instincts.

It has been suggested more than once that the theory explaining the working of the market be called catallactics from the classical Greek word for bartering or exchanging – katalattein. I have fallen somewhat in love with this word since discovering that in ancient Greek, in addition to 'exchanging', it also meant 'to admit into the community' and 'to change from enemy into friend'. I have therefore proposed that we call the game of the market, by which we can induce the stranger to welcome and serve us, the 'game of catallaxy'.

The market process indeed corresponds fully to the definition of a game which we find in The Oxford English Dictionary. It is 'a contest played according to rules and decided by superior skill, strength or good fortune'. It is in this respect both a game of skill as well as a game of chance. Above all, it is a game which serves to elicit from each player the highest worthwhile contribution to the common pool from which each will win an uncertain share.

The game was probably started by men who had left the shelter and obligations of their own tribe to gain from serving the needs of others they did not know personally. When the early neolithic traders took boatloads of flint axes from Britain across the Channel to barter them against amber and probably also, even then, jars of wine, their aim was no longer to serve the needs of known people, but to make the largest gain. Precisely because they were interested only in who would offer the best price for their products, they reached persons wholly unknown to them, whose standard of life they thereby enhanced much more than they could have that of their neighbours by handing the axes to those who no doubt could also have made good use of them.

4

As the abstract signal-price thus took the place of the needs of known fellows as the goal towards which men's efforts were directed, entirely new possibilities for the utilisation of resources opened up – but this also required wholly different moral attitudes to encourage their exploitation. The change occurred largely at the new urban centres of trade and handicrafts, which grew up at ports or the crossroads of trade routes, where men who had escaped from the discipline of tribal morals established commercial communities and gradually developed the new rules of the game of catallaxy.

The necessity to be brief forces me here somewhat to over-simplify and to employ familiar terms where they are not quite appropriate.

When I pass from the morals of the hunting band in which man spent most of his history, to the morals which made possible the market order of the open society, I am jumping over a long intermediate stage, much shorter than man's life in the small band, but still of much greater length than the urban and commercial society has enjoyed yet, and important because from it date those codifications of ethics which became embodied in the teaching of the mono-theistic religions. It is the period of man's life in tribal society. In many ways it represents a transitional stage between the concrete order of the primitive face-to-face society, in which all the members knew each other and served common particular ends, and the open and abstract society, in which an order results from individuals observing the same abstract rules of the game while using their own knowledge in the pursuit of their own ends.

While our emotions are still governed by the instincts appropriate to the success of the small hunting band, our verbal tradition is dominated by duties to the 'neighbour', the fellow mem-ber of the tribe, and still regarding the alien largely as beyond the pale of moral obligation.

In a society in which individual aims were necessarily different, based on specialised know-ledge, and efforts came to be directed towards future exchange of products with yet unknown partners, common rules of conduct increasingly took the place of particular common ends as the foundations of social order and peace. The inter-action of individuals became a game, because what was required from each individual was observation of the rules, not concern for a par-ticular result, other than to win support for himself and his family. The rules which grad-ually developed, because they made this game most effective, were essentially those of the law of property and contract. These rules in turn made possible the progressive division of labour, and that mutual adjustment of indepen-dent efforts, which a functioning division of labour demands.

5

The full significance of this division of labour is often not appreciated, because most people think of it – partly because of the classical illustration given by Adam Smith – as a designed intra-mural arrangement in which different individuals contribute the successive steps in a planned process for shaping certain products. In fact, however, co-ordination by the market of the endeavours of different enterprises in supplying the raw materials, tools and semi-finished prod-ucts which the turning out of the final commod-ity requires, is probably much more important than the organised collaboration of numerous specialist workers.

It is in a great measure this inter-firm division of labour, or specialisation, on which the achieve-ment of the competitive market depends, and which that market makes possible. Prices the producer finds on the market at once tell him what to produce and what means to use in producing it. From such market signals he knows that he can expect to sell at prices cover-ing his outlays, and that he will not use up more resources than are necessary for the purpose. His selfish striving for gain makes him do, and enables him to do, precisely what he ought to do in order to improve the chances of any member of his society, taken at random, as much as pos-sible – but *only* if the prices he can get are deter-mined solely by market forces and not by the coercive powers of government. Only prices determined on the free market will bring it about that demand equals supply. But not only this. Free market prices also ensure that all of a society's dispersed knowledge will be taken into account and used.

The game of the market led to the growth and prosperity of communities who played it because it improved the chances for all. This was made possible because remuneration for the services of individuals depended on object-ive facts, all of which no one could know, and not on someone's opinions about what they ought to have. But it also meant that while skill and industry would improve each individual's chances, they could not guarantee him a specified income; and that the impersonal process which used all that dispersed knowledge set the signals of prices so as to tell people what to do, but without regard to needs or merits. Yet the ordering and productivity enhancing function of prices, and particularly the prices of services, depends on their informing people where they will find their most effective place in the overall pattern of activities – the place in which they are likely to make the greatest contribution to aggregate output. If, therefore, we regard *that* rule of remuneration as just which contributes as much as possible to increasing the chances of any member of the community picked out at random, we ought to regard the remunerations determined by a free market as the just ones.

6

But they are inevitably very different from the relative remunerations which assisted the organisation of the different type of society in which our species lived so much longer, and which therefore still governs the feelings which guide us. This point has become exceedingly important since prices ceased to be accepted as due to unknown circumstances, and governments came to believe they could determine prices with beneficial effects. When governments started to falsify the market price signals, whose appropriateness they had no means of judging (governments as little as anyone else possessing all the information precipitated in prices), in the hope of thereby giving benefits to groups claimed to be particularly deserving, things inevitably started to go wrong. Not only the efficient use of resources, but, what is worse, also the prospects of being able to buy or sell as expected through demand equalling supply were thereby greatly diminished.

It may be difficult to understand, but I believe

there can be no doubt about it, that we are led to utilise more relevant information when our remuneration is made to depend indirectly on circumstances we do not know. It is thus that, in the language of modern cybernetics, the feedback mechanism secures the maintenance of a self-generating order. It was this which Adam Smith saw and described as the operation of the 'invisible hand' – to be ridiculed for 200 years by uncomprehending scoffers. It is indeed *because* the game of catallaxy disregards human conceptions of what is due to each, and rewards according to success in playing the game under the same formal rules, that it produces a more efficient allocation of resources than any design could achieve. I feel that in any game that is played because it improves the prospects of all beyond those which we know how to provide by any other arrangements, the result must be accepted as fair, so long as all obey the same rules and no one cheats. If they accept their winnings from the game, it is cheating for individuals or groups to invoke the powers of government to divert the flow of good things in their favour – whatever we may do outside this game of the market to provide a decent minimum for those for whom the game did not supply it. It is not a valid objection to such a game, the outcome of which depends partly on skill and particular individual circumstances and partly on pure chance, that the initial prospects for different individuals, although they are all improved by playing that game, are very far from being the same. The answer to such an objection is precisely that one of the purposes of the game is to make the fullest possible use of the inevitably different skills, knowledge and environment of different individuals. Among the greatest assets which a society can use in this manner for increasing the pool from which the earnings of individuals are drawn, are the different moral, intellectual and material gifts parents can pass on to their children – and often will acquire, create or preserve only in order to be able to pass them on to their children.

7

The result of this game of catallaxy, therefore, will necessarily be that many have much more than their fellows think they deserve, and even more will have much less than their fellows think they ought to have. It is not surprising that many people should wish to correct this by some authoritative act of redistribution. The trouble is that the aggregate product which they think is available for distribution exists only *because* returns for the different efforts are held out by the market with little regard to deserts or needs, and are needed to attract the owners of particular information, material means and personal skills to the points where at each moment they can make the greatest contribution. Those who prefer the quiet of an assured contractual income to the necessity of taking risks to exploit everchanging opportunities feel at a disadvantage compared with possessors of large incomes, which result from continual redisposition of resources.

High actual gains of the successful ones, whether this success is deserved or accidental, are an essential element for guiding resources to where they will make the largest contribution to the pool from which all draw their share. We should not have as much to share if *that* income of an individual were not treated as *just*, the prospects of which induced him to make the largest contribution to the pool. Incredibly high incomes may thus sometimes be just. What is more important, scope for achieving such incomes may be the necessary condition for the less enterprising, lucky, or clever to get the regular income on which they count.

The inequality, which so many people resent, however, has not only been the underlying condition for producing the relatively high incomes which most people in the West now enjoy. Some people seem to believe that a lowering of this general level of incomes – or at least a slowing down of its rate of increase – would not be too high a price for what they feel would be a juster distribution. But there is an even greater obstacle

to such ambitions today. As a result of playing the game of catallaxy, which pays so little attention to justice but does so much to increase output, the population of the world has been able to increase so much, without the income of most people increasing very much, that we can maintain it, and the further increases in population which are irrevocably on the way, only if we make the fullest possible use of that game which elicits the highest contributions to productivity.

8

If people in general do not appreciate what they owe to catallaxy and how far they are even dependent on it for their very existence, and if they often bitterly resent what they regard as its injustice, this is so because they have never designed it and therefore do not understand it. The game rests on a method of providing benefits for others in which the individual will accomplish most if, within the conventional rules, he pursues solely his own interests – which need not be selfish in the ordinary sense of the word, but are in any case his own.

The moral attitude which this order demands not only of the entrepreneur but of all those, curiously called 'self-employed', who have constantly to choose the directions of their efforts, if they are to confer the greatest benefit on their fellows, is that they compete honestly according to the rules of the game, guided only by the abstract signals of prices and giving no preferences because of their sympathies or views on the merits or needs of those with whom they deal. It would mean not merely a personal loss, but a failure in their duty to the public, to employ a less efficient instead of a more efficient person, to spare an incompetent competitor, or to favour particular users of their product.

The gradually spreading new liberal morals, which the Open or Great Society demanded, required above all that the same rules of conduct should apply to one's relation to all other members of society – except for natural ties to the members of one's family. This extension of old moral rules to wider circles, most people, and particularly the intellectuals, welcome as moral progress. But they apparently did not realise, and violently resented when they discovered it, that the equality of rules applicable to one's relationship to all other men necessarily implied not only that new obligations were extended to people who formerly had no such claims, but also that old obligations which were recognised to some people but could not be extended to all others had to disappear.

It was this unavoidable attenuation of the content of our obligations, which necessarily accompanied their extension, that people with strongly ingrained moral emotions resented. Yet these are kinds of obligations which are essential to the cohesion of the small group but which are irreconcilable with the order, the productivity, and the peace of a great society of free men. They are all those demands which under the name of 'social justice' assert a moral claim on government that it give us what it can take by force from those who in the game of catallaxy have been more successful than we have been. Such an artificial alteration of the relative attractiveness of the different directions of productive efforts can only be counter-productive.

If expected remunerations no longer tell people where their endeavours will make the greatest contribution to the total product, an efficient use of resources becomes impossible. Where the size of the social product, and no longer their contributions to it, gives individuals and groups a moral claim to a certain share of that product, the claims of what deserve really to be described as 'free riders' become an unbearable drag on the economy.

9

I am told that there are still communities in Africa in which able young men, anxious to adopt modern commercial methods, find it impossible thereby to improve their position, because tribal customs demand that they share the products of their greater industry, skill or luck with all their kin. An increased income of such a man would merely mean that he had to share it with an ever-increasing number of claimants. He can, therefore, never rise substantially above the average level of his tribe.

The chief adverse effect of 'social justice' in our society is that it prevents individuals from achieving what they could achieve – through the means for further investment being taken from them. It is also the application of an incongruous principle to a civilisation whose productivity is high, *because* incomes are very unequally divided and thereby the use of scarce resources is directed and limited to where they bring the highest return. Thanks to this unequal distribution the poor get in a competitive market economy more than they would get in a centrally directed system.

All this is the outcome of the, as yet merely imperfect, victory of the obligatory abstract rule of individual conduct over the common particular end as the method of social co-ordination – the development which has made both the open society and individual freedom possible, but which the socialists now want to reverse. Socialists have the support of inherited instincts, while maintenance of the new wealth which creates the new ambitions requires an acquired discipline which the non-domesticated barbarians in our midst, who call themselves 'alienated', refuse to accept although they still claim all its benefits.

10

Let me, before I conclude, briefly meet an objection which is bound to be raised because it rests on a very widespread misunderstanding. My argument, that in a process of cultural selection we have built better than we understood, and that what we call our intelligence has been shaped concurrently with our institutions by a process of trial and error, is certain to be met by an outcry of 'social Darwinism'. But such a cheap way of disposing of my argument by labelling it would rest on an error. It is true that during the latter part of the last century some social scientists, under the influence of Darwin, placed an excessive stress on the importance of natural selection of the most able individuals in free competition. I do not wish to underrate the importance of this, but it is not the main benefit we derive from competitive selection. This is the competitive selection of cultural institutions, for the discovery of which we did not need Darwin, but the growing understanding of which in fields like law and language rather helped Darwin to his biological theories. My problem is not genetic evolution of innate qualities, but cultural evolution through learning – which indeed leads sometimes to conflicts with near-animal natural instincts. Nevertheless, it is still true that civilisation grew not by the prevailing of that which man thought would be most successful, but by the growth of that which turned out to be so, and which, precisely because he did not understand it, led man beyond what he could ever have conceived.

Chapter 31

Bruce A. Ackerman

ON GETTING WHAT WE DON'T DESERVE

Bruce A. Ackerman (1943–   ) is a scholar of constitutional law and a professor at Yale Law School. In this essay, Ackerman challenges the view articulated by Charles Fried (but also adhered to by Nozick and Hayek), that people can unproblematically come to have rights to things that they do not deserve. This view, Ackerman argues, seems to violate the principle that rational individuals living in community with each other should be able to justify themselves to others. To claim a right over some object without being able to so justify it, Ackerman claims, is to fail to treat one's fellow human beings with sufficient respect.

I hope to persuade Charles Fried to think again about his developing views on distributive justice. Since I live at a certain remove from Cambridge, the best I can offer is a hypothetical dialogue with an imaginary person whose views seem, to me at least, of a Friedian inspiration.

My central question deals with the way Fried establishes his rights to things he candidly concedes he does not deserve. To present my problems, I shall begin with a simpler case than those – involving kidneys and talents – that Fried makes central to his discussion. Rather than starting with these rather special goods, I find it clarifying to focus first on more garden variety commodities – which, to emphasize their character, I shall call apples.

Imagine, then, that two bodily creatures, You and I, come upon a couple of apples left by a gardener who has no further use for them. Sitting down to our frugal repast, I am about to ask You to pass an apple in my direction when, much to my surprise, both apples suddenly disappear into your mouth. The dialogue proceeds:

I: Say, why shouldn't I have gotten one of those apples?

You: Why do you ask? Has my eating them made things really tough for you?

I: What are you asking for: a blow-by-blow sob story in exchange for the chance at an apple?

You: Nothing so demeaning. Indeed, I really don't need to know very much about you before determining whether I will help you out. I shall simply compare your present apple holdings with those purchased by unskilled workers – taking into account, of course, the proletariat's unfortunate tendency to stuff themselves with apples beyond real need. If this study shows that your holdings have fallen below a decent minimum, then I'd be happy to help you out.

I: A curious beneficence this, whose exercise depends upon the selfish consumption choices of unskilled workers – people who have never even considered my situation.

You: Don't jump to conclusions. We may well reach a point at which you, and your particular life, become important. For if your holdings have fallen below the level of decency, I will need to know at least one thing about you.

I: And what might that be?

You: Isn't it obvious? I can't assess my sympathy for your predicament until you tell me what use you will make of the apples I provide.

I: I must confess that my own sympathies are shaped differently.

You: How so? Suppose an impoverished neighbor of yours were suffering from acute appendicitis. Sympathizing with his predicament, you give him the money necessary for an emergency operation. Wouldn't you feel betrayed if he spent the money on something else? Even if the something-else were quite fine in its own right – say, piano lessons for his kids?

I: Yes. But I find my own sympathies are not exhausted by dramatic misfortunes suddenly visited upon unsuspecting individuals, in the manner of acute appendicitis.

      I can also sympathize with people who are fated by society to live under undramatic conditions of grinding poverty, dehumanizing employment, social stigma. And I think it meanspirited to reach out to such people with "aid" that smothers them, yet again, in a host of bureaucratic rules and procedures.

      Indeed, worse than mean-spirited – bureaucratized paternalism can often exacerbate the quiet desperation that makes a special claim upon my sympathies in the first place.

You: I shall have to think about this. But in the meantime, I would appreciate an answer to my question – what *would* you do with the apple, anyway?

I: If you must know, I would use it to reenact my own version of Adam's Fall. I can see it now: one bite of the apple and I am transformed. Its work done, the apple falls silently from my lips. Crushed by despair, I sit alone in dumb recognition of forbidden knowledge.

You: How melodramatic. Are you really sure it's necessary to waste a good apple that way, after only one bite?

I: That's the way I choose to write the script.

You: Well, I hardly wish to criticize the authority of the author. But I must say that the whole scene strikes me as a bit much.

      Not that there aren't lots of ways to use an apple. I'd be perfectly sympathetic to apple juice; entirely understanding of apple sauce.

      But to waste a perfectly good apple after only one bite. I'm a liberal fellow, but I simply can't afford to subsidize any odd-ball activity that suits your fancy.

I: Which leads me back to my original question.

You: How so? I had rather thought our conversation at an end. It's quite plain that you'll survive well enough without this apple eating ritual of yours; and so I fail to see the point of giving you any of my apples.

      We must, after all, impose limits on the claims of benevolence. Otherwise, we will all find ourselves lost in the primeval communitarian ooze.

I: I quite agree. And that's precisely why I refuse to base my claim on your sympathy, but on my rights. I want to know why you think you had the right to eat two apples when I got none?

You: Ho hum. Quite frankly, I've gotten bored with all this egalitarian rhetoric – it has, you know, gotten us into such a mess.

I: I did not intend my question rhetorically. Perhaps you *can* give me a reason why you think you were entitled to both the apples.

But until you do so, there is something far more important than an apple at stake in our dispute.

You: And what might that be?

I: Our social identity as rational persons.

You: More melodrama, surely.

I: Not at all. Perhaps angels can reason with one another without the mediation of language. But so far as human beings go, the best way to recognize each other's rights as rational creatures is by asking and answering each other's questions. If you fail to dignify my question about the apples with a good faith effort at an answer, you deal with me as you would a brute. From what you have said thus far, I suspect that this prospect should give you pause.

You: But don't you see that these apples are part of *me* now? Indeed, as we speak, they are entering my kidneys. And I can hardly think of a more intimate part of me than that.

I: But the apples could have ended up in my kidneys. The only reason they didn't is your prior possession of them. Are you saying that the fellow who gets there first is always entitled to the apples?

You: Suppose I said Yes? After all, why shouldn't a person be entitled to take advantage of the accidents that fall her way? Isn't that what liberty is all about?

I: No. The only liberty worthy of a community of rational persons is a liberty each is ready and willing to justify in a conversation with his fellow questioners.

To ground rights on first possession is at war with this ideal.

You: How so?

I: Perhaps a thought experiment will clarify. Suppose I had not been so slow to raise the question of legitimacy in this garden of ours.

Suppose, instead, that I had begun this conversation before you had popped the apples into your mouth. Then, surely, you would not have had the right to appropriate the apples without responding to my question.

You: At least if I wished to present myself to you as a rational person making a serious effort to dignify your questions with answers. And despite my sometime praise of accident, I do hope to remain loyal to something like the ideal of rational liberty you invoke.

I: Well, then: if you would have been obliged to pause if I had asked my question before you grabbed the apples, why should our dialogic situation be any different merely because you acted before I had the chance to ask?

You: Are you suggesting that I was making a pig of myself?

I deny the implication. A couple of apples is poor enough dinner as it is. I merely saw my opportunity and seized it – in the good old American way.

I: I'm not asking you to spend your life in suspended animation, anxiously waiting for somebody to question your rights. There is more – much more – to life than talk about legitimacy.

And yet I do think that your grab at the apples did exhibit a certain sort of thoughtlessness. There I was, after all, standing right before you. Did you really think I'd stand mute while you gained possession of things that you recognize you don't deserve any more than I do?

You: But, after all, this is precisely what happens in everyday life. In the world outside our garden, I am surrounded by have-nots. Yet I do not remember any of them approaching me in the way you have done. All I seem to get in the real world is passive indifference, sullen silence, sporadic violence. Could life really be any different?

I: We have all been hardened by life beyond

the garden. But, for the moment at least, we are in a place where the question of legitimacy may be asked without threatening the real world's fragile stability, its uncertain civility. Surely here, if anywhere, it would be wrong to allow your pre-dialogic exercise of power to transform our dialogic situation. The mere fact that you grabbed first shouldn't allow you to ignore my question of legitimacy. Unless you try to justify your power play, you forfeit your claim upon me to recognize you as a rational person, rather than a powerful brute.

You: But this view leads to an absurdly abstract and ahistorical starting point for a discussion of social justice. In the real world, almost everything *has* been reduced to possession. How can we possibly ignore this basic fact?

I: I'm not asking you to ignore it. I'm asking you to justify the place you occupy within the world of possessions. And to do this, it is not enough to point out that you grabbed something before I did. Instead, you must explain why you think first possessors are more entitled to worldly goods than those who come later on. Do you imagine, for example, that your quick grab at the apples is evidence of your moral superiority? If so, at least you will have given my question the dignity of an answer.

You: Stop putting words in my mouth. I have no intention of impugning your claim to equal respect as a morally autonomous being. I merely insist that you recognize that the world is no garden. In the real world, apples simply aren't allowed to fall from trees before an entire system of rights is *already* impressed upon them. Rather than view the world from your ahistorical perspective, we must accept the fact that a system of rights has already attached to things, and begin the conversation about rights on this solid foundation.

I: Rights do not attach to things in the way that apples attach to trees. The only claims of right recognizable in a rational community are those that can be made intelligible in an ongoing conversation between creatures trying to make sense of the predicaments of power.

If your holding of material goods is rightful, the only way to establish this is to come forward with reasons that explain why you are more entitled to "your" possessions than I am. If you recognize this conversational burden in our garden, I fail to see why you should get off the conversational hook in the real world merely because you've grabbed the trees from which the apples fall, and not merely the apples themselves.

You: And I don't suppose you'd be much impressed if I told you that I got the trees from my parents – who told me, in turn, that they had rightful possession?

I: What else would you expect parents to say? But were they right?

You: Do you find the very idea repugnant?

I: Not at all. If you choose to bring your parents' rights into the conversation, I am perfectly willing to listen.

I only object if you use your ancestors as a way of deflecting my question of legitimacy without answering it. Rather than making your conversational burden easier, setting up your ancestors' rights makes your job more difficult. Not only must you explain why you rightfully got your possessions from your parents, you must also explain why you think they established their claims rightfully against my parents, to speak only of one rival pair of contenders.

You: But once begun, where will this process of rationalization come to an end? If I am obliged to justify my initial material holdings, am I also obliged to justify my talents? Surely I deserve one no more than the other. Is even my spare kidney secure?

I: Let's put your kidneys to one side for a while, and focus on your right to your talents.

You: Not forgetting, I trust, the short step by which I travel from my talents to yet another basic right: my right to a market return on my talents!

I: Indeed, it would be best to begin with this short step — since the move from talent to market reward in fact requires three rather long strides.

Talent isn't enough to make money on a market. Most obviously, a talented person needs education before his abilities can command a market price. And why should you have gotten the training rather than I? An answer to this question serves as a first step in the process of dialogic legitimation.

No less obviously, even the most perfect market — of the kind dreamt up by neo-classical economists — establishes a system of competitive power relations whose legitimacy is hardly self-evident. The dialogic burden becomes far heavier, moreover, once we leave our garden to encounter real-world markets far removed from neo-classical fantasy. In a real-world market system, each of us finds himself burdened by a whole series of market imperfections, informational disadvantages, transactional rigidities. While all of us have to deal with these inconveniences, some are crushed by transactional burdens in their effort to organize economic relations with potential users of their services. How, then, are those favored by real-world markets to answer for their superior transactional positions when called to account by their disadvantaged competitors?

And when this question is answered, a final one remains: the reward my talents will fetch on the market is a function, among other things, of the initial wealth available to those who are bidding for my services. If the initial distribution cannot be justified dialogically, this failure casts a shadow on each and every effort by the talented to appropriate the fruits of their labors.

You: But my talents are an essential part of me!

I: Who can deny it? I merely ask you to reflect upon the fact that talent is never a sufficient condition for economic success. If, then, you wish to move from talent to its just reward, you will have to legitimate all the other power structures that permit you to transform your labor into economically valuable product.

If you fail in this, you have no right to analogize egalitarian taxation to the physical appropriation of talent that occurs, say, in chattel slavery. Instead, you will be obliged to recognize that you cannot explain why you are entitled to a full market reward for your labors; and so cannot justifiably protest when some of these rewards are taxed away by a political community that insists upon the dialogic legitimation of power.

You: A sobering prospect. But I must confess to a certain satisfaction at your failure to make my rite of dialogic passage yet more perilous.

I: How so?

You: Although you ask me to justify the material, transactional, and educational advantages I have — perhaps too thoughtlessly — appropriated, you have not placed a similar burden of justification on me so far as my inborn capacities are concerned. At least here, then, we may call a halt to dialogue and recognize — no questions asked — that my body is rightfully mine.

I: Well, at the very least, I need to change my argumentative strategy. Thus far, I have simply been generalizing from our original encounter in the garden: just as you helped yourself to the apples, so too have

you appropriated other material possessions, educational opportunities, transactional advantages. Just as your grab at the
apples should not transform our dialogic
situation with regard to my rights, so too it
should not change the conversational
ground rules regulating the other advantages you have appropriated.

But when it comes to our own bodies,
the very concept of appropriation breaks
down. Unless we are to begin speaking
from the spirit world, it makes no sense to
talk as if we had "grabbed" our bodies.
Rather than arguing that your "appropriation" of your body has permitted you to
transform our dialogic situation, I must
concede that your bodily existence is an
indispensable precondition for my talking
to you in the familiar way.

You: It is possible, I suppose, to evade this difficulty by continuing the conversation in
the Rawlsian manner, distancing ourselves
from our particular bodies by means of a
veil of ignorance. The veil permits us to
keep talking to one another on the understanding that we are bodily creatures; and
yet our ignorance allows us to speak as if
our inborn capacities were proper objects
for redistribution.

But much as I admire the man, I lose my
way when I try to follow him. A person
stripped of an understanding of my inborn
particularities isn't *me*; and I hereby declare
myself free of any contractual obligations
such an alien creature might find it rational
to make on my behalf.

I: No dispute there. I do not aim for dialogue
at the cost of such radical self-effacement.
I hope, instead, to reach a conversational
understanding with you that can peacefully coexist with our awareness of the
countless particularities that make each of
us unique individuals.

You: So we can proceed at once to claim our
right to our inborn talents?

I: Not so fast. Once we free ourselves from
the veil of ignorance, a new conversational framework appears to view – one
that allows us to talk about our rightful
talents without cutting ourselves off from
our bodies in the search for social justice.

You: What on earth do you have in mind?

I: The simple biology of sexual reproduction. The stork didn't bring you, after all.
The reason you and I have the talents we
have has something to do with the way
our parents made use of their powers of
procreation.

You: But all our parents did was make the best
of their sexual opportunities and let the
natural genetic lottery do the rest.

I: An increasingly misleading picture of the
reproductive situation. Not only can parents determine how many children they
will have; they increasingly have power to
shape their offsprings' genetic inheritance.

Against this background, talk of a "natural" lottery in genes loses its grip upon
social reality. As the reproductive process
becomes transparently subject to self-
conscious control, parents have only two
choices: either they may try to justify
the use they make of their reproductive
powers – both to one another and to their
children; or they may proceed with genetic
engineering in the manner of brutes, only
now of vastly greater potency.

You: I hardly know which road is the more
perilous. Why not put strict limits on
the whole business before it gets out of
control?

I: I think you are right, though I am hardly
optimistic about the prospects for such
deliberate self-restraint.

But let us suppose that we took your
advice, and a handicapped person later
sought to hold us accountable for some
of the consequences of our decision. If
genetic manipulation had been allowed,
he argues, some grave disability of his

might have been ameliorated, even eliminated. Why, then, is it fair for him to bear the burden of our decision to limit genetic engineering for the greater good of humanity?

You: But surely every genetic difference should not qualify for relief. Such a notion would destroy all human diversity.

I: I agree. What is required is a theory of genetic justice which authorizes parents to generate a genetically diverse population without denying the possibility that parents may abuse their proliferating powers of genetic manipulation.

But we are not now in search of an adequate theory. I only aim to convince you to reject a view that places the natural lottery in genes beyond all questioning. It is the story of the apple once again, this time in a technocratic variant. Once parents appropriate the power to manipulate genes, they cannot immunize themselves from questioning – if they hope to gain social recognition as rational members of a common political community.

You: I must think more about this. Yet, even now, I can see that, whatever your point is worth, it cannot undermine my central claim. For surely you cannot, in fairness, hold me responsible for decisions made before I was born. If anyone violated your rights, it was our parents, not I. Complain to them if you like, but let me enjoy my talents in peace.

I: I do not hold you directly responsible for our parents' decisions; merely for taking advantage of the present opportunities generated by the past use of their procreative powers. Imagine, say, that your grab at the apples would not have been so successful if you had confronted a competitor who is not afflicted, as I am, by a crippling birth disability. In such a case, your success in grabbing the apples is causally related to our elders' decision to

impose heavy genetic burdens upon me – a decision I say is illegitimate. Unless you explain why you think they were justified in heaping genetic disabilities upon me, you yourself must recognize that, by eating the apples, you are reaping the fruits of injustice.

You: But how am I to distinguish those rare cases in which my success depends upon your unfair genetic handicap, from the many more in which my success is entirely untainted?

I: I do not insist upon such a microscopic, case-by-case, examination. It will be enough if my genetic disadvantages are taken into account as we talk about the just design of other fundamental power structures that define our worldly situation – notably those regulating our respective educations, transactional facilities, and initial material endowments. If, considered as a whole, the entire power system aims to ameliorate your illegitimate genetic advantages, we shall have at least achieved a rough kind of dialogic justice.

You: And if, instead, the facts turn out otherwise?

I: You must recognize yourself as the beneficiary of systematic injustice.

You: And how to discharge this debt you say I owe?

I: Not so easily. For the benefits you have received are not of a kind that can be readily shucked off. You owe your very sense of yourself as an efficacious, choosing creature to the support you have received from the prevailing system of wealth, education, and exchange – systems that have utterly failed me.

You: So what do you expect from me? Sacrifice everything I have made of myself in a vain effort to make things up to you?

I: Nobody ever promised you life in a liberal Garden of Eden – once you have eaten the apples, you must answer my question of legitimacy and follow the dialogue wherever it leads.

You: But if we have learned anything from the twentieth century, it is the danger of fanatic self-immolation in the cause of social justice. Even if we gave our all to yet another revolution, I do not think your rights would, in the end, be greatly enhanced.

I: Nor do I. Rather than some final solution to the question of legitimacy, the best we may hope for is a slow, painful, and imperfect effort to build a world that is equal to our dignity as rational beings.

You: You reassure me.

I: Not too much, I hope. For I do not mean you to relapse into the state of self-content with which you began this conversation. When I first raised my question of legitimacy, you treated me as if I were some hapless victim of fate, worthy at most of your condescending benevolence. Instead of continuing to patronize me, it is past time for you to take me and my questions seriously, and work with me toward a legitimate solution of our predicament.

How, then, can you justify your grab at the apples?

Chapter 32

Kai Nielsen

A MORAL CASE FOR SOCIALISM

Kai Nielsen (1926–   ) is a professor of philosophy at Concordia University who has written widely on metaphilosophy, ethics, and political philosophy. This essay presents Nielsen's case for the moral superiority of socialism to capitalism. Socialism, Nielsen argues, better promotes well-being, rights, autonomy, equality and justice.

I

In North America socialism gets a bad press. It is under criticism for its alleged economic inefficiency and for its moral and human inadequacy. I want here to address the latter issue. Looking at capitalism and socialism, I want to consider, against the grain of our culture, what kind of moral case can be made for socialism.

The first thing to do, given the extensive, and, I would add, inexcusably extensive, confusions about this, is to say what socialism and capitalism are. That done I will then, appealing to a cluster of values which are basic in our culture, concerning which there is a considerable and indeed a reflective consensus, examine how capitalism and socialism fare with respect to these values. Given that people generally, at least in Western societies, would want it to be the case that these values have a stable exemplification in our social lives, it is appropriate to ask the question: which of these social systems is more likely stably to exemplify them? I shall argue, facing the gamut of a careful comparison in the light of these values, that, everything considered, socialism comes out better than capitalism. And this, if

right, would give us good reason for believing that socialism is preferable – indeed morally preferable – to capitalism if it also turns out to be a feasible socio-economic system.

What, then, are socialism and capitalism? Put most succinctly, capitalism requires the existence of private *productive* property (private ownership of the means of production) while socialism works toward its abolition. What is essential for socialism is public ownership and control of the means of production and public ownership means just what it says: *ownership by the public.* Under capitalism there is a domain of private property rights in the means of production which are not subject to political determination. That is, even where the political domain is a democratic one, they are not subject to determination by the public; only an individual or a set of individuals who own that property can make the final determination of what is to be done with that property. These individuals make that determination and not citizens at large, as under socialism. In fully developed socialism, by contrast, there is, with respect to productive property, no domain which is not subject to political determination by the public, namely by the citizenry at large. Thus, where this public ownership and control is genuine, and not a mask for control by an elite of state bureaucrats, it will mean genuine popular and democratic control over productive property. What socialism is *not* is *state* ownership in the absence of, at the very least, popular sovereignty, i.e., genuine popular control over the state apparatus including any economic functions it might have.

The property that is owned in common under socialism is the means of existence – the productive property in the society. Socialism does not proscribe the ownership of private personal property, such as houses, cars, television sets and the like. It only proscribes the private ownership of the means of production.

The above characterizations catch the minimal core of socialism and capitalism, what used to be called the essence of those concepts. But beyond these core features, it is well, in helping us to make our comparison, to see some other important features which characteristically go with capitalism and socialism. Minimally, capitalism is private ownership of the means of production but it is also, at least characteristically, a social system in which a class of capitalists owns and controls the means of production and hires workers who, owning little or no means of production, sell their labor-power to some capitalist or other for a wage. This means that a capitalist society will be a class society in which there will be two principal classes: capitalists and workers. Socialism by contrast is a social system in which every able-bodied person is, was or will be a worker. These workers commonly own and control the means of production (this is the characteristic form of public ownership). Thus in socialism we have, in a perfectly literal sense, a classless society for there is no division between human beings along class lines.

There are both pure and impure forms of capitalism and socialism. The pure form of capitalism is competitive capitalism, the capitalism that Milton Friedman would tell us is the real capitalism while, he would add, the impure form is monopoly or corporate capitalism. Similarly the pure form of socialism is democratic socialism, with firm workers' control of the means of production and an industrial as well as a political democracy, while the impure form is state bureaucratic socialism.

Now it is a noteworthy fact that, to understate it, actually existing capitalisms and actually existing socialisms tend to be the impure forms. Many partisans of capitalism lament the fact that the actually existing capitalisms overwhelmingly tend to be forms of corporate capitalism where the state massively intervenes in the running of the economy. It is unclear whether anything like a fully competitive capitalism actually exists – perhaps Hong Kong approximates it – and it is also unclear whether many of the actual players in the major capitalist societies (the existing capitalists and their managers) want or even expect that it is possible to have laissez-faire capitalism again (if indeed we ever had it). Some capitalist societies are further down the corporate road than other societies, but they are all forms of corporate, perhaps in some instances even monopoly, capitalism. Competitive capitalism seems to be more of a libertarian dream than a sociological reality or even something desired by many informed and tough-minded members of the capitalist class. Socialism has had a similar fate. Its historical exemplifications tend to be of the impure forms, namely the bureaucratic state socialisms. Yugoslavia is perhaps to socialism what Hong Kong is to capitalism. It is a candidate for what might count as an exemplification, or at least a near approximation, of the pure form.

This paucity of exemplifications of pure forms of either capitalism or socialism raises the question of whether the pure forms are at best unstable social systems and at worse merely utopian ideals. I shall not try directly to settle that issue here. What I shall do instead is to compare *models* with *models*. In asking about the moral case for socialism, I shall compare forms that a not inconsiderable number of the theoretical protagonists of each take to be pure forms but which are still, they believe, historically feasible. But I will also be concerned to ask whether these models – these *pure* forms – can reasonably be expected to come to have a home. If they are not historically feasible models, then, even if we can make a good theoretical moral case for them, we will have hardly provided a good moral case for socialism or capitalism. To avoid bad utopianism we must be talking about forms which could be on the historical agenda. (I plainly here do not take "bad utopianism" to be pleonastic.)

II

Setting aside for the time being the feasibility question, let us compare the pure forms of capitalism and socialism – that is to say, competitive capitalism and democratic socialism – as to how they stand with respect to sustaining and furthering the values of freedom and autonomy, equality, justice, rights and democracy. My argument shall be that socialism comes out better with respect to those values.

Let us first look at freedom and autonomy. An autonomous person is a person who is able to set her ends for herself and in optimal circumstances is able to pursue those ends. But freedom does not only mean being autonomous; it also means the absence of unjustified political and social interference in the pursuit of one's ends. Some might even say that it is just the absence of interference with one's ends. Still it is self-direction – autonomy – not non-interference which is *intrinsically* desirable. Non-interference is only valuable where it is an aid to our being able to do what we want and where we are sufficiently autonomous to have some control over our wants.

How do capitalism and socialism fare in providing the social conditions which will help or impede the flourishing of autonomy? Which model society would make for the greater flourishing of autonomy? My argument is (a) that democratic socialism makes it possible for more people to be more fully autonomous than would

be autonomous under capitalism; and (b) that democratic socialism also interferes less in people's exercise of their autonomy than any form of capitalism. All societies limit liberty by interfering with people doing what they want to do in some ways, but the restrictions are more extensive, deeper and more undermining of autonomy in capitalism than in democratic socialism. Where there is private ownership of productive property, which, remember, is private ownership of the means of life, it cannot help but be the case that a few (the owning and controlling capitalist class) will have, along with the managers beholden to them, except in periods of revolutionary turmoil, a firm control, indeed a domination, over the vast majority of people in the society. The capitalist class with the help of their managers determines whether workers (taken now as individuals) can work, how they work, on what they work, the conditions under which they work and what is done with what they produce (where they are producers) and what use is made of their skills and the like. As we move to welfare state capitalism – a compromise still favoring capital which emerged out of long and bitter class struggles – the state places some restrictions on some of these powers of capital. Hours, working conditions and the like are controlled in certain ways. Yet whether workers work and continue to work, how they work and on what, what is done with what they produce, and the rationale for their work are not determined by the workers themselves but by the owners of capital and their managers; this means a very considerable limitation on the autonomy and freedom of workers. Since workers are the great majority, such socio-economic relations place a very considerable limitation on human freedom and indeed on the very most important freedom that people have, namely their being able to live in a self-directed manner, when compared with the industrial democracy of democratic socialism. Under capitalist arrangements it simply cannot fail to be the case that a very large number of people will lose control over a very central set of facets of their lives, namely central aspects of their work and indeed in many instances, over their very chance to be able to work.

Socialism would indeed prohibit capitalist acts between consenting adults; the capitalist class would lose its freedom to buy and sell and to control the labor market. There should be no blinking at the fact that socialist social relations would impose some limitations on freedom, for there is, and indeed can be, no society without norms and some sanctions. In any society you like there will be some things you are at liberty to do and some things that you may not do. However, democratic socialism must bring with it an industrial democracy where workers by various democratic procedures would determine how they are to work, on what they are to work, the hours of their work, under what conditions they are to work (insofar as this is alterable by human effort at all), what they will produce and how much, and what is to be done with what they produce. Since, instead of there being "private ownership of the means of production," there is in a genuinely socialist society "public ownership of the means of production," the means of life are owned by everyone and thus each person has a *right* to work: she has, that is, a right to the means of life. It is no longer the private preserve of an individual owner of capital but it is owned in common by us all. This means that each of us has an equal right to the means of life. Members of the capitalist class would have a few of their liberties restricted, but these are linked with owning and controlling capital and are not the important civil and political liberties that we all rightly cherish. Moreover, the limitation of the capitalist liberties to buy and sell and the like would make for a more extensive liberty for many, many more people.

One cannot respond to the above by saying that workers are free to leave the working class and become capitalists or at least petty bourgeoisie. They may indeed all in theory, taken *individually*, be free to leave the working class, but

if many in fact try to leave the exits will very quickly become blocked. Individuals are only free on the condition that the great mass of people, taken collectively, are not. We could not have capitalism without a working class and the working class is not free within the capitalist system to cease being wage laborers. We cannot all be capitalists. A people's capitalism is nonsense. Though a petty commodity production system (the family farm writ large) is a logical possibility, it is hardly a stable empirical possibility and, what is most important for the present discussion, such a system would not be a capitalist system. Under capitalism, most of us, if we are to find any work at all, will just have to sell (or *perhaps* "rent" is the better word) our labor-power as a commodity. Whether you sell or rent your labor power or, where it is provided, you go on welfare, you will not have much control over areas very crucial to your life. If these are the only feasible alternatives facing the working class, working class autonomy is very limited indeed. But these are the only alternatives under capitalism.

Capitalist acts between consenting adults, if they become sufficiently widespread, lead to severe imbalances in power. These imbalances in power tend to undermine autonomy by creating differentials in wealth and control between workers and capitalists. Such imbalances are the name of the game for capitalism. Even if we (perversely I believe) call a system of petty commodity production capitalism, we still must say that such a socio-economic system is inherently unstable. Certain individuals would win out in this exchanging of commodities and in fairly quick order it would lead to a class system and the imbalances of power – the domination of the many by the few – that I take to be definitive of capitalism. By abolishing capitalist acts between consenting adults, then (but leaving personal property and civil and political liberties untouched), socialism protects more extensive freedoms for more people and in far more important areas of their lives.

III

So democratic socialism does better regarding the value that epitomizes capitalist pride (*hubris*, would, I think, be a better term), namely autonomy. It also does better, I shall now argue, than capitalism with respect to another of our basic values, namely democracy. Since this is almost a corollary of what I have said about autonomy I can afford to be briefer. In capitalist societies, democracy must simply be *political* democracy. There can in the nature of the case be no genuine or thorough workplace democracy. When we enter the sphere of production, capitalists and not workers own, and therefore at least ultimately control, the means of production. While capitalism, as in some workplaces in West Germany and Sweden, sometimes can be pressured into allowing an ameliorative measure of worker control, once ownership rights are given up, we no longer have private productive property but public productive property (and in that way social ownership): capitalism is given up and we have socialism. However, where worker control is restricted to a few firms, we do not yet have socialism. What makes a system socialist or capitalist depends on what happens across the whole society, not just in isolated firms. Moreover, managers can become very important within capitalist firms, but as long as ownership, including the ability to close the place down and liquidate the business, rests in the hands of capitalists we can have no genuine workplace democracy. Socialism, in its pure form, carries with it, in a way capitalism in any form cannot, workplace democracy. (That some of the existing socialisms are anything but pure does not belie this.)

Similarly, whatever may be said of existing socialisms or at least of some existing socialisms, it is not the case that there is anything in the very idea of socialism that militates against political as well as industrial democracy. Socialists are indeed justly suspicious of some of the tricks played by parliamentary democracy in bourgeois countries, aware of its not infrequent hypocrisy and the limitations of its stress on purely legal and formal political rights and liberties. Socialists are also, without at all wishing to throw the baby out with the bath water, rightly suspicious of any simple reliance on majority rule, unsupplemented by other democratic procedures and safeguards. But there is nothing in socialist theory that would set it against political democracy and the protection of political and civil rights; indeed there is much in socialism that favors them, namely its stress on both autonomy and equality.

The fact that political democracy came into being and achieved stability within capitalist societies may prove something about conditions necessary for its coming into being, but it says nothing about capitalism being necessary for sustaining it. In Chile, South Africa and Nazi Germany, indeed, capitalism has flourished without the protection of civil and political rights or anything like a respect for the democratic tradition. There is nothing structural in socialism that would prevent it from continuing those democratic traditions or cherishing those political and civil rights. That something came about under certain conditions does not establish that these conditions are necessary for its continued existence. That men initially took an interest in chess does not establish that women cannot quite naturally take an interest in it as well. When capitalist societies with long-flourishing democratic traditions move to socialism there is no reason at all to believe that they will not continue to be democratic. (Where societies previously had no democratic tradition or only a very weak one, matters are more problematic.)

IV

I now want to turn to a third basic value, equality. In societies across the political spectrum, *moral* equality (the belief that everyone's life matters equally) is an accepted value. Or, to be somewhat cynical about the matter, at least lip service is paid to it. But even this lip service is the compliment that vice pays to virtue. That is to say, such a belief is a deeply held considered conviction in modernized societies, though it has not been at all times and is not today a value held in all societies. This is most evident concerning moral equality.

While this value is genuinely held by the vast majority of people in capitalist societies, it can hardly be an effective or functional working norm where there is such a diminishment of autonomy as we have seen obtains unavoidably in such societies. Self-respect is deeply threatened where so many people lack effective control over their own lives, where there are structures of domination, where there is alienated labor, where great power differentials and differences in wealth make for very different (and often very bleak) life chances. For not inconsiderable numbers, in fact, it is difficult to maintain self-respect under such conditions unless they are actively struggling against the system. And, given present conditions, fighting the system, particularly in societies such as the United States, may well be felt to be a hopeless task. Under such conditions any real equality of opportunity is out of the question. And the circumstances are such, in spite of what is often said about these states, that equality of condition is an even more remote possibility. But without at least some of these things moral equality cannot even be approximated. Indeed, even to speak of it sounds like an obscene joke given the social realities of our lives.

Although under welfare-state capitalism some of the worst inequalities of capitalism are ameliorated, workers still lack effective control over their work, with repercussions in political and public life as well. Differentials of wealth cannot but give rise to differentials in power and control in politics, in the media, in education, in the direction of social life and in what options get seriously debated. The life chances of workers and those not even lucky enough to be workers

(whose ranks are growing and will continue to grow under capitalism) are impoverished compared to the life chances of members of the capitalist class and its docile professional support stratum.

None of these equality-undermining features would obtain under democratic socialism. Such societies would, for starters, be classless, eliminating the power and control differentials that go with the class system of capitalism. In addition to political democracy, industrial democracy and all the egalitarian and participatory control that goes with that would, in turn, reinforce moral equality. Indeed it would make it possible where before it was impossible. There would be a commitment under democratic socialism to attaining or at least approximating, as far as it is feasible, equality of condition; and this, where approximated, would help make for real equality of opportunity, making equal life chances something less utopian than it must be under capitalism.

In fine, the very things, as we have seen, that make for greater autonomy under socialism than under capitalism, would, in being more equally distributed, make for greater equality of condition, greater equality of opportunity and greater moral equality in a democratic socialist society than in a capitalist one. These values are values commonly shared by both capitalistically inclined people and those who are socialistically inclined. What the former do not see is that in modern industrial societies, democratic socialism can better deliver these goods than even progressive capitalism.

There is, without doubt, legitimate worry about bureaucratic control under socialism. But that is a worry under any historically feasible capitalism as well, and it is anything but clear that state bureaucracies are worse than great corporate bureaucracies. Indeed, if socialist bureaucrats were, as the socialist system requires, really committed to production for needs and to achieving equality of condition, they might, bad as they are, be the lesser of two evils. But in any event democratic socialism is not bureaucratic state socialism, and there is no structural reason to believe that it must – if it arises in a society with skilled workers committed to democracy – give rise to bureaucratic state socialism. There will, inescapably, be some bureaucracy, but in a democratic socialist society it must and indeed will be controlled. This is not merely a matter of optimism about the will of socialists, for there are more mechanisms for democratic control of bureaucracy within a democratic socialism that is both a political and an industrial democracy, than there can be under even the most benign capitalist democracies – democracies which for structural reasons can never be industrial democracies. If, all that notwithstanding, bureaucratic creepage is inescapable in modern societies, then that is just as much a problem for capitalism as for socialism.

The underlying rationale for production under capitalism is profit and capital accumulation. Capitalism is indeed a marvelous engine for building up the productive forces (though clearly at the expense of considerations of equality and autonomy). We might look on it, going back to earlier historical times, as something like a forced march to develop the productive forces. But now that the productive forces in advanced capitalist societies are wondrously developed, we are in a position to direct them to far more humane and more equitable uses under a socio-economic system whose rationale for production is to meet human needs (the needs of everyone as far as this is possible). This egalitarian thrust, together with the socialists' commitment to attaining, as far as that is possible, equality of condition, makes it clear that socialism will produce more equality than capitalism.

V

In talking about autonomy, democracy and equality, we have, in effect, already been talking about justice. A society or set of institutions that does better in these respects than another society will be a more just society than the other society.

Fairness is a less fancy name for justice. If we compare two societies and the first is more democratic than the second; there is more autonomy in the first society than in the second; there are more nearly equal life chances in the first society than in the second and thus greater equality of opportunity; if, without sacrifice of autonomy, there is more equality of condition in the first society than in the second; and if there is more moral equality in the first society than in the second, then we cannot but conclude that the first society is a society with more fairness than the second and, thus, that it is the more just society. But this is exactly how socialism comes out vis-à-vis even the best form of capitalism.

A society which undermines autonomy, heels in democracy (where democracy is not violating rights), makes equality impossible to achieve and violates rights cannot be a just society. If, as I contend, that is what capitalism does, and cannot help doing, then a capitalist society cannot be a just society. Democratic socialism, by contrast, does not need to do any of those things, and we can predict that it would not, for there are no structural imperatives in democratic socialism to do so and there are deep sentiments in that tradition urging us not to do so. I do not for a moment deny that there are similar sentiments for autonomy and democracy in capitalist societies, but the logic of capitalism, the underlying structures of capitalist societies – even the best of capitalist societies – frustrate the realization of the states of affairs at which those sympathies aim. A radical democrat with a commitment to human rights, to human autonomy and moral equality and fair equality of opportunity ought to be a democratic socialist and a firm opponent of capitalism – even a capitalism with a human face.

2d. FREEDOM

MOST POLITICAL PHILOSOPHERS AGREE that freedom is an important value, and that protecting or promoting this value is one of the chief tasks of governments. But what exactly *is* freedom, and what governmental policies are truly consistent with it? The answers to these questions are of crucial importance for political philosophy.

Suppose you've always wanted to climb Mt. Shasta in California. You have the equipment, you've read the books, and you've even hired yourself a guide. Your boss has given you the time off from work, and no one is stopping you from fulfilling your dream. The only problem is that you suffer from a crippling acrophobia—the thought of standing on a high, exposed mountainside leaves you unable to take a single step. Are you free to climb the mountain, or not?

In a sense, of course, you are. There is no law against your climbing the mountain, and no person or external obstacle is standing in the way of your doing so. But then again, *something* is standing in your way. Even if you truly and fully want to climb the mountain, your disease prevents you from doing so. And what difference does it make to you whether what stops you from doing what you want is a disease or a person with a gun telling you "no"?

The problem is that we have two different senses of freedom. One sense—which has been called *negative freedom*—characterizes freedom as the lack of external obstacles, especially those caused by other human beings. The other sense of freedom is generally referred to as *positive freedom*, and has more to do with being able to act in accordance with one's rational and/or autonomous desires.

To say that one values freedom, then, is not enough to give a clear indication of the kind of governmental policies one would support. One must also say what *kind* of freedom one values. For one who values freedom in the negative sense, all that is generally required of governments is to get out of the way—"*laissez faire et laissez passez; le monde va de lui même.*"[1] Governments can enhance individuals' freedom by preventing them from forcibly interfering with each other through laws against robbery, assault and the like. But apart from that, government activity should be severely constrained lest government *itself* become an impediment to liberty by restricting what people can say or read, what they can trade on the market, or what they can do with their bodies or property. This classical liberal emphasis on the importance of negative freedom is to be found both in John Stuart Mill's defense of the "harm principle" as the sole standard for legitimate interference with individual liberty, and in Isaiah Berlin's insistence on the importance of negative liberty, and the dangers of tyranny inherent in its confusion with positive liberty.

But many have found classical liberalism's exclusive focus on negative freedom to be unsatisfying. Consider Anatole France's quip that, "The law, in its majestic equality, forbids rich and poor alike to sleep under bridges, beg in the streets or steal bread." His point, of course, is that the rich and poor only enjoy the same freedoms under the law in a *formal* sense. Sure, the law doesn't forbid the rich from sleeping under bridges, any more than it forbids the poor from dining on caviar and champagne. But the fact that the law doesn't forbid these things is not really what matters. What matters is the *substantive* freedom that people actually enjoy—the activities that they are actually free in a positive sense to engage in. An exclusive focus on negative liberty not only obscures the inequality of formal liberty between rich and poor, but exacerbates that inequality by condemning redistributive transfers of wealth and limits on economic power as violations of the only kind of freedom that really matters.

It was precisely this sort of concern that led Franklin Delano Roosevelt to include "freedom from want" in his "Four Freedoms" speech. Roosevelt gave this speech at a time when the U.S. Supreme Court was striking down numerous economic regulations as unconstitutional on the grounds that they violated freedom of contract. In the famous 1905 case *Lochner v. New York*, for instance, the Court struck down as unconstitutional a New York law limiting the number of hours a baker could work per week, on the grounds that the number of hours worked per week was properly a matter to be decided on by an agreement between a worker and their employer. For Roosevelt and others in the progressive movement, this insistence on defending the (negative) liberty of contract merely privileged the economically powerful at the expense of the (positive) liberty of the economically disadvantaged to work reasonable hours in a safe environment for a fair wage. Freedom from want, Roosevelt thought, should be considered a basic human right along with freedom of speech, and not a privilege of the well-off.

A similar line of reasoning, though taken to a more extreme conclusion, can be found in George Fitzhugh's *Cannibals All!* For Fitzhugh, negative liberty was of so little intrinsic value that even *slavery* could be justified on the grounds that, in his opinion, it increased the positive liberty of American blacks. Freedom from slavery, for Fitzhugh, meant little more than being doomed to "wage slavery," a kind of despotism which was even worse than that practiced in the South, he thought, insofar as capitalists do not even pretend to be any under obligation to care for the well-being of their workers. Fitzhugh's is an extreme argument which brings racist assumptions to a repugnant conclusion, but his critique of capitalism was an important precursor to the American discovery of Marx, and his argument challenges us to think hard about what sorts of liberty we value, and the tradeoffs we are willing to accept for it.

Our widespread agreement on the value of freedom, then, masks a tremendous disagreement regarding the *meaning* of freedom, regarding the comparative value of different types of freedom, and regarding the comparative value of freedom and other distinct values. It is to these difficult questions that the readings in this section are addressed.

Note

1 "Leave things alone, let them pass; the world runs by itself," a saying attributed to the eighteenth-century French economist and head of the Physiocrats, Vincent de Gournay.

Further Reading

Carter, I. (2004). *A Measure of Freedom*. Oxford: Oxford University Press.

Cohen, G. A. (1995). *Self-ownership, Freedom, and Equality*. Cambridge; New York [Paris, France]: Cambridge University Press; Maison des sciences de l'homme.

Constant, B. (1988). The Liberty of the Ancients Compared with That of the Moderns. In B. Fontana (Ed.), *Constant: Political Writings* (pp. 309–328). New York: Cambridge University Press.

Green, T. H. (2006). Liberal Legislation and Freedom of Contract. In D. Miller (Ed.), *The Liberty Reader* (pp. 21–32). Boulder, CO: Paradigm Publishers.

Hayek, F. A. (1944). *The Road to Serfdom*. Chicago: University of Chicago Press.

Hayek, F. A. (1960). *The Constitution of Liberty*. Chicago: University of Chicago Press.

MacCallum, G. (2006). Negative and Positive Freedom. In D. Miller (Ed.), *The Liberty Reader* (pp. 100–122). Boulder, CO: Paradigm Publishers.

Mack, E., & Gaus, G. (2004). Classical Liberalism and Libertarianism: The Liberty Tradition. In G. Gaus & C. Kukathas (Eds.), *Handbook of Political Theory* (pp. 115–130). London: Sage.

McMahon, C. (2005). The Indeterminacy of Republican Policy. *Philosophy and Public Affairs, 33,* 67–93.

Nozick, R. (1974). *Anarchy, State, and Utopia*. New York: Basic Books.

O'Neill, O. (2000). *Bounds of Justice*. Cambridge: Cambridge University Press.

Pettit, P. (2006). The Republican Ideal of Freedom. In D. Miller (Ed.), *The Liberty Reader* (pp. 223–243). Boulder, CO: Paradigm Publishers.

Plato (2004). *The Republic* (C. D. C. Reeve, Trans.). Indianapolis: Hackett.

Rousseau, J.-J. (2002). The Social Contract. In S. Dunn (Ed.), *The Social Contract and the First and Second Discourses*. New Haven, CT: Yale University Press.

Skinner, Q. (2006). A Third Concept of Liberty. In D. Miller (Ed.), *The Liberty Reader* (pp. 243–254). Boulder, CO: Paradigm Publishers.

Taylor, C. (2006). What's Wrong with Negative Liberty? In D. Miller (Ed.), *The Liberty Reader* (pp. 141–162). Boulder, CO: Paradigm Publishers.

Wertheimer, A. (2006). *Coercion*. Princeton, NJ: Princeton University Press.

Chapter 33

John Stuart Mill

ON LIBERTY

John Stuart Mill (1806–1873) was a British philosopher and, with Jeremy Bentham, one of the most historically influential proponents of the moral philosophy known as utilitarianism. In these excerpts from his enormously influential *On Liberty* (1859), Mill sets forth his 'harm principle' – the claim that the only legitimate grounds for interfering with an individual's liberty is to prevent harm to others – and explains the way in which a consistent recognition of that principle would severely limit the authority of society over the individual.

The subject of this Essay is not the so-called Liberty of the Will, so unfortunately opposed to the misnamed doctrine of Philosphical Necessity; but Civil, or Social Liberty: the nature and limits of the power which can be legitimately exercised by society over the individual. A question seldom stated, and hardly ever discussed, in general terms, but which profoundly influences the practical controversies of the age by its latent presence, and is likely soon to make itself recognised as the vital question of the future. It is so far from being new, that, in a certain sense, it has divided mankind, almost from the remotest ages; but in the stage of progress into which the more civilised portions of the species have now entered, it presents itself under new conditions, and requires a different and more fundamental treatment.

The struggle between Liberty and Authority is the most conspicuous feature in the portions of history with which we are earliest familiar, particularly in that of Greece, Rome, and England. But in old times this contest was between subjects, or some classes of subjects, and the Government. By liberty, was meant protection against the tyranny of the political rulers. The rulers were conceived (except in some of the popular governments of Greece) as in a necessarily antagonistic position to the people whom they ruled. They consisted of a governing One, or a governing tribe or caste, who derived their authority from inheritance or conquest, who, at all events, did not hold it at the pleasure of the governed, and whose supremacy men did not venture, perhaps did not desire, to contest, whatever precautions might be taken against its oppressive exercise. Their power was regarded as necessary, but also as highly dangerous; as a weapon which they would attempt to use against their subjects, no less than against external enemies. To prevent the weaker members of the community from being preyed upon by innumerable vultures, it was needful that there should be an animal of prey stronger than the rest, commissioned to keep them down. But as the king of the vultures would be no less bent upon preying on the flock than any of the minor harpies, it was indispensable to be in a perpetual attitude of defence against his beak and claws. The aim, therefore, of patriots was to set limits to the power which the ruler should be suffered to exercise over the community; and this limitation was what they meant by liberty. It was attempted in two ways. First, by obtaining a recognition of certain immunities, called political liberties or rights, which it was to be regarded as a breach of duty in the ruler to infringe, and which, if he did infringe, specific resistance, or general rebellion, was held to be justifiable. A second, and generally a later expedient, was the establishment of constitutional checks, by which the consent of the community, or of a body of some sort, supposed to represent its interests, was made a necessary condition to some of the more important acts of the governing power. To the first of these modes of limitation, the ruling power, in most European countries, was compelled, more or less, to submit. It was not so with the second; and, to attain this, or when already in some degree possessed, to attain it more completely, became everywhere the principal object of the lovers of liberty. And so long as mankind were content to combat one enemy by another, and to be ruled by a master, on condition of being guaranteed more or less efficaciously against his tyranny, they did not carry their aspirations beyond this point.

A time, however, came, in the progress of human affairs, when men ceased to think it a necessity of nature that their governors should be an independent power, opposed in interest to themselves. It appeared to them much better that the various magistrates of the State should be their tenants or delegates, revocable at their pleasure. In that way alone, it seemed, could they have complete security that the powers of government would never be abused to their disadvantage. By degrees this new demand for elective and temporary rulers became the prominent object of the exertions of the popular party, wherever any such party existed; and

superseded, to a considerable extent, the previous efforts to limit the power of rulers. As the struggle proceeded for making the ruling power emanate from the periodical choice of the ruled, some persons began to think that too much importance had been attached to the limitation of the power itself. *That* (it might seem) was a resource against rulers whose interests were habitually opposed to those of the people. What was now wanted was, that the rulers should be identified with the people; that their interest and will should be the interest and will of the nation. The nation did not need to be protected against its own will. There was no fear of its tyrannising over itself. Let the rulers be effectually responsible to it, promptly removable by it, and it could afford to trust them with power of which it could itself dictate the use to be made. Their power was but the nation's own power, concentrated, and in a form convenient for exercise. This mode of thought, or rather perhaps of feeling, was common among the last generation of European liberalism, in the Continental section of which it still apparently predominates. Those who admit any limit to what a government may do, except in the case of such governments as they think ought not to exist, stand out as brilliant exceptions among the political thinkers of the Continent. A similar tone of sentiment might by this time have been prevalent in our own country, if the circumstances which for a time encouraged it, had continued unaltered.

But, in political and philosophical theories, as well as in persons, success discloses faults and infirmities which failure might have concealed from observation. The notion, that the people have no need to limit their power over themselves, might seem axiomatic, when popular government was a thing only dreamed about, or read of as having existed at some distant period of the past. Neither was that notion necessarily disturbed by such temporary aberrations as those of the French Revolution, the worst of which were the work of an usurping few, and which, in any case, belonged, not to the permanent working of popular institutions, but to a sudden and convulsive outbreak against monarchical and aristocratic despotism. In time, however, a democratic republic came to occupy a large portion of the earth's surface, and made itself felt as one of the most powerful members of the community of nations; and elective and responsible government became subject to the observations and criticisms which wait upon a great existing fact. It was now perceived that such phrases as 'self-government', and 'the power of the people over themselves', do not express the true state of the case. The 'people' who exercise the power are not always the same people with those over whom it is exercised; and the 'self-government' spoken of is not the government of each by himself, but of each by all the rest. The will of the people, moreover, practically means the will of the most numerous or the most active part of the people; the majority, or those who succeed in making themselves accepted as the majority; the people, consequently, may desire to oppress a part of their number; and precautions are as much needed against this as against any other abuse of power. The limitation, therefore, of the power of government over individuals loses none of its importance when the holders of power are regularly accountable to the community, that is, to the strongest party therein. This view of things, recommending itself equally to the intelligence of thinkers and to the inclination of those important classes in European society to whose real or supposed interests democracy is adverse, has had no difficulty in establishing itself; and in political speculations 'the tyranny of the majority' is now generally included among the evils against which society requires to be on its guard.

Like other tyrannies, the tyranny of the majority was at first, and is still vulgarly, held in dread, chiefly as operating through the acts of the public authorities. But reflecting persons perceived that when society is itself the tyrant – society collectively, over the separate individuals who compose it – its means of tyrannising are not restricted to the acts which it may do by the hands of its political functionaries. Society can and does execute its own mandates: and if it issues wrong mandates instead of right, or any mandates at all in things with which it ought not to meddle, it practises a social tyranny more formidable than many kinds of political oppression, since, though not usually upheld by such extreme penalties, it leaves fewer means of escape, penetrating much more deeply into the details of life, and enslaving the soul itself. Protection, therefore, against the tyranny of the magistrate is not enough: there needs protection also against the tyranny of the prevailing opinion and feeling; against the tendency of society to impose, by other means than civil penalties, its own ideas and practices as rules of conduct on those who dissent from them; to fetter the development, and, if possible, prevent the formation, of any individuality not in harmony with its ways, and compel all characters to fashion themselves upon the model of its own. There is a limit to the legitimate interference of collective opinion with individual independence: and to find that limit, and maintain it against encroachment, is as indispensable to a good condition of human affairs, as protection against political despotism.

But though this proposition is not likely to be contested in general terms, the practical question, where to place the limit – how to make the fitting adjustment between individual independence and social control – is a subject on which nearly everything remains to be done. All that makes existence valuable to any one, depends on the enforcement of restraints upon the actions of other people. Some rules of conduct, therefore, must be imposed, by law in the first place, and by opinion on many things which are not fit subjects for the operation of law. What these rules should be, is the principal question of human affairs; but if we except a few of the most obvious cases, it is one of those which least progress has been made in resolving. [. . .]

The object of this Essay is to assert one very simple principle, as entitled to govern absolutely the dealings of society with the individual in the way of compulsion and control, whether the means used be physical force in the form of legal penalties, or the moral coercion of public opinion. That principle is, that the sole end for which mankind are warranted, individually or collectively, in interfering with the liberty of action of any of their number, is self-protection. That the only purpose for which power can be rightfully exercised over any member of a civilised community, against his will, is to prevent harm to others. His own good, either physical or moral, is not a sufficient warrant. He cannot rightfully be compelled to do or forbear because it will be better for him to do so, because it will make him happier, because, in the opinions of others, to do so would be wise, or even right. These are good reasons for remonstrating with him, or reasoning with him, or persuading him, or entreating him, but not for compelling him, or visiting him with any evil in case he do otherwise. To justify that, the conduct from which it is desired to deter him, must be calculated to produce evil to some one else. The only part of the conduct of any one, for which he is amenable to society, is that which concerns others. In the part which merely concerns himself, his independence is, of right, absolute. Over himself, over his own body and mind, the individual is sovereign.

It is, perhaps, hardly necessary to say that this doctrine is meant to apply only to human beings in the maturity of their faculties. We are not speaking of children, or of young persons below the age which the law may fix as that of manhood or womanhood. Those who are still in a state to require being taken care of by others, must be protected against their own actions as well as against external injury. For the same reason, we may leave out of consideration those backward states of society in which the race itself may be considered as in its nonage. The early difficulties in the way of spontaneous progress are so great, that there is seldom any choice of means for overcoming them; and a ruler full of the spirit of improvement is warranted in the use of any expedients that will attain an end, perhaps otherwise unattainable. Despotism is a legitimate mode of government in dealing with barbarians, provided the end be their improvement, and the means justified by actually effecting that end. Liberty, as a principle, has no application to any state of things anterior to the time when mankind have become capable of being improved by free and equal discussion. Until then, there is nothing for them but implicit obedience to an Akbar or a Charlemagne, if they are so fortunate as to find one. But as soon as mankind have attained the capacity of being guided to their own improvement by conviction or persuasion (a period long since reached in all nations with whom we need here concern ourselves), compulsion, either in the direct form or in that of pains and penalties for non-compliance, is no longer admissible as a means to their own good, and justifiable only for the security of others.

It is proper to state that I forego any advantage which could be derived to my argument from the idea of abstract right, as a thing independent of utility. I regard utility as the ultimate appeal on all ethical questions; but it must be utility in the largest sense, grounded on the permanent interests of man as a progressive being. Those interests, I contend, authorise the subjection of individual spontaneity to external control, only in respect to those actions of each, which concern the interest of other people. If any one does an act hurtful to others, there is a *primâ facie* case for punishing him, by law, or, where legal penalties are not safely applicable, by general disapprobation. There are also many positive acts for the benefit of others, which he may rightfully be compelled to perform; such as, to give evidence in a court of justice; to bear his fair share in the common defence, or in any other joint work necessary to the interest of the society of which he enjoys the protection; and to perform certain acts of individual beneficence, such as saving a fellow-creature's life, or interposing to protect the defenceless against ill-usage, things which whenever it is obviously a man's duty to do, he may rightfully be made responsible to society for not doing. A person may cause evil to others not only by his actions but by his inaction, and in either case he is justly accountable to them for the injury. The latter case, it is true, requires a much more cautious exercise of compulsion than the former. To make any one answerable for doing evil to others, is the rule; to make him answerable for not preventing evil, is, comparatively speaking, the exception. Yet there are many cases clear enough and grave enough to justify that exception. In all things which regard the external relations of the individual, he is *de jure* amenable to those whose interests are concerned, and if need be, to society as their protector. There are often good reasons for not holding him to the responsibility; but these reasons must arise from the special expediencies of the case: either because it is a kind of case in which he is on the whole likely to act better, when left to his own discretion, than when controlled in any way in which society have it in their power to control him; or because the attempt to exercise control would produce other evils, greater than those which it would prevent. When such reasons as these preclude the enforcement of responsibility, the conscience of the agent himself should step into the vacant judgment seat, and protect those interests of others which have no external protection; judging himself all the more rigidly, because the case does not admit of his being made accountable to the judgment of his fellow-creatures.

But there is a sphere of action in which society, as distinguished from the individual, has, if any, only an indirect interest; comprehending all that portion of a person's life and conduct which affects only himself, or if it also affects others, only with their free, voluntary, and undeceived consent and participation. When I say only himself, I mean directly, and in the first instance: for whatever affects himself, may affect others through himself; and the objection which may be grounded on this contingency, will receive consideration in the sequel. This, then, is the appropriate region of human liberty. It comprises, first, the inward domain of consciousness; demanding liberty of conscience, in the most comprehensive sense; liberty of thought and feeling; absolute freedom of opinion and sentiment on all subjects, practical or speculative, scientific, moral, or theological. The liberty of expressing and publishing opinions may seem to fall under a different principle, since it belongs to that part of the conduct of an individual which concerns other people; but, being almost of as much importance as the liberty of thought itself, and resting in great part on the same reasons, is practically inseparable from it. Secondly, the principle requires liberty of tastes and pursuits; of framing the plan of our life to suit our own character; of doing as we like, subject to such consequences as may follow: without impediment from our fellow-creatures, so long as what we do does not harm them, even though they should think our conduct foolish, perverse, or wrong. Thirdly, from this liberty of each individual, follows the liberty, within the same limits, of combination among individuals; freedom to unite, for any purpose not involving harm to others: the persons combining being supposed to be of full age, and not forced or deceived.

No society in which these liberties are not, on the whole, respected, is free, whatever may be its form of government; and none is completely free in which they do not exist absolute and unqualified. The only freedom which deserves the name, is that of pursuing our own good in our own way, so long as we do not attempt to deprive others of theirs, or impede their efforts to obtain it. Each is the proper guardian of his own health, whether bodily, or mental and spiritual. Mankind are greater gainers by suffering each other to live as seems good to themselves, than by compelling each to live as seems good to the rest.

Though this doctrine is anything but new, and, to some persons, may have the air of a truism, there is no doctrine which stands more directly opposed to the general tendency of existing opinion and practice. [. . .]

Apart from the peculiar tenets of individual thinkers, there is also in the world at large an increasing inclination to stretch unduly the powers of society over the individual, both by the force of opinion and even by that of legislation: and as the tendency of all the changes taking place in the world is to strengthen society, and diminish the power of the individual, this encroachment is not one of the evils which tend spontaneously to disappear, but, on the contrary, to grow more and more formidable. The disposition of mankind, whether as rulers or as fellow-citizens, to impose their own opinions and inclinations as a rule of conduct on others, is so energetically supported by some of the best and by some of the worst feelings incident to human nature, that it is hardly ever kept under restraint by anything but want of power; and as the power is not declining, but growing, unless a strong barrier of moral conviction can be raised against the mischief, we must expect, in the present circumstances of the world, to see it increase. [. . .]

Of the Liberty of Thought and Discussion

We have now recognised the necessity of the mental well-being of mankind (on which all their other well-being depends) of freedom of opinion, and freedom of the expression of opinion, on four distinct grounds; which we will now briefly recapitulate.

First, if any opinion is compelled to silence, that opinion may, for aught we can certainly know, be true. To deny this is to assume our own infallibility.

Secondly, though the silenced opinion be an error, it may, and very commonly does, contain a portion of truth; and since the general or prevailing opinion on any subject is rarely or never the whole truth, it is only by the collision of adverse opinions that the remainder of the truth has any chance of being supplied.

Thirdly, even if the received opinion be not only true, but the whole truth; unless it is suffered to be, and actually is, vigorously and earnestly contested, it will, by most of those who receive it, be held in the manner of a prejudice, with little comprehension or feeling of its rational grounds. And not only this, but, fourthly, the meaning of the doctrine itself will be in danger of being lost, or enfeebled, and deprived of its vital effect on the character and conduct: the dogma becoming a mere formal profession, inefficacious for good, but cumbering the ground, and preventing the growth of any real and heartfelt conviction, from reason or personal experience. [. . .]

Of the Limits to the Authority of Society Over the Individual

What, then, is the rightful limit to the sovereignty of the individual over himself? Where does the authority of society begin? How much of human life should be assigned to individuality, and how much to society?

Each will receive its proper share, if each has that which more particularly concerns it. To individuality should belong the part of life in which it is chiefly the individual that is interested; to society, the part which chiefly interests society.

Though society is not founded on a contract, and though no good purpose is answered by inventing a contract in order to deduce social obligations from it, every one who receives the protection of society owes a return for the benefit, and the fact of living in society renders it indispensable that each should be bound to observe a certain line of conduct towards the rest. This conduct consists first, in not injuring the interests of one another; or rather certain interests, which, either by express legal provision or by tacit understanding, ought to be considered as rights; and secondly, in each person's bearing his share (to be fixed on some equitable principle) of the labours and sacrifices incurred for defending the society or its members from injury and molestation. These conditions society is justified in enforcing at all costs to those who endeavour to withhold fulfilment. Nor is this all that society may do. The acts of an individual may be hurtful to others, or wanting in due consideration for their welfare, without going the length of violating any of their constituted rights. The offender may then be justly punished by opinion, though not by law. As soon as any part of a person's conduct affects prejudicially the interests of others, society has jurisdiction over it, and the question whether the general welfare will or will not be promoted by interfering with it, becomes open to discussion. But there is no room for entertaining any such question when a person's conduct affects the interests of no persons besides himself, or needs not affect them unless they like (all the persons concerned being of full age, and the ordinary amount of understanding). In all such cases there should be perfect freedom, legal and social, to do the action and stand the consequences.

It would be a great misunderstanding of this doctrine to suppose that it is one of selfish indifference, which pretends that human beings have no business with each other's conduct in life, and that they should not concern themselves about the well-doing or well-being of one another, unless their own interest is involved. Instead of any diminution, there is need of a great increase of disinterested exertion to promote the good of others. But disinterested benevolence can find other instruments to persuade people to their good, than whips and scourges, either of the literal or the metaphorical sort. I am the last person to undervalue the self-regarding virtues; they are only second in importance, if even second, to the social. It is equally the business of education to cultivate both. But even education works by conviction and persuasion as well as by compulsion, and it

is by the former only that, when the period of education is past, the self-regarding virtues should be inculcated. Human beings owe to each other help to distinguish the better from the worse, and encouragement to choose the former and avoid the latter. They should be for ever stimulating each other to increased exercise of their higher faculties, and increased direction of their feelings and aims towards wise instead of foolish, elevating instead of degrading, objects and contemplations. But neither one person, nor any number of persons, is warranted in saying to another human creature of ripe years, that he shall not do with his life for his own benefit what he chooses to do with it. He is the person most interested in his own well-being: the interest which any other person, except in cases of strong personal attachment, can have in it, is trifling, compared with that which he himself has; the interest which society has in him individually (except as to his conduct to others) is fractional, and altogether indirect: while, with respect to his own feelings and circumstances, the most ordinary man or woman has means of knowledge immeasurably surpassing those that can be possessed by any one else. The interference of society to overrule his judgment and purposes in what only regards himself, must be grounded on general presumptions: which may be altogether wrong, and even if right, are as likely as not to be misapplied to individual cases, by persons no better acquainted with the circumstances of such cases than those are who look at them merely from without. In this department, therefore, of human affairs, Individuality has its proper field of action. In the conduct of human beings towards one another, it is necessary that general rules should for the most part be observed, in order that people may know what they have to expect; but in each person's own concerns, his individual spontaneity is entitled to free exercise. Considerations to aid his judgment, exhortations to strengthen his will, may be offered to him, even obtruded on him, by others; but he himself is the final judge. All errors which he is likely to commit against advice and warning, are far outweighed by the evil of allowing others to constrain him to what they deem his good.

I do not mean that the feelings with which a person is regarded by others, ought not to be in any way affected by his self-regarding qualities or deficiencies. This is neither possible nor desirable. If he is eminent in any of the qualities which conduce to his own good, he is, so far, a proper object of admiration. He is so much the nearer to the ideal perfection of human nature. If he is grossly deficient in those qualities, a sentiment the opposite of admiration will follow. There is a degree of folly, and a degree of what may be called (though the phrase is not unobjectionable) lowness or depravation of taste, which, though it cannot justify doing harm to the person who manifests it, renders him necessarily and properly a subject of distaste, or, in extreme cases, even of contempt: a person could not have the opposite qualities in due strength without entertaining these feelings. Though doing no wrong to any one, a person may so act as to compel us to judge him, and feel to him, as a fool, or as a being of an inferior order: and since this judgment and feeling are a fact which he would prefer to avoid, it is doing him a service to warn him of it beforehand, as of any other disagreeable consequence to which he exposes himself. It would be well, indeed, if this good office were much more freely rendered than the common notions of politeness at present permit, and if one person could honestly point out to another that he thinks him in fault, without being considered unmannerly or presuming. We have a right, also, in various ways, to act upon our unfavourable opinion of any one, not to the oppression of his individuality, but in the exercise of ours. We are not bound, for example, to seek his society; we have a right to avoid it (though not to parade the avoidance), for we have a right to choose the society most acceptable to us. We have a right, and it may be our duty, to caution others against him, if we think his example or conversation likely to have a pernicious effect on those with whom he associates. We may give others a preference over him in optional good offices, except those which tend to his improvement. In these various modes a person may suffer very severe penalties at the hand of others, for faults which directly concern only himself; but he suffers these penalties only in so far as they are the natural, and, as it were, the spontaneous consequences of the faults themselves, not because they are purposely inflicted on him for the sake of punishment. A person who shows rashness, obstinacy, self-conceit – who cannot live within moderate means – who cannot restrain himself from hurtful indulgences – who pursues animal pleasures at the expense of those of feeling and intellect – must expect to be lowered in the opinion of others, and to have a less share of their favourable sentiments; but of this he has no right to complain, unless he has merited their favour by special excellence in his social relations, and has thus established a title to their good offices, which is not affected by his demerits towards himself.

What I contend for is, that the inconveniences which are strictly inseparable from the unfavourable judgment of others, are the only ones to which a person should ever be subjected for that portion of his conduct and character which concerns his own good, but which does not affect the interests of others in their relations with him. Acts injurious to others require a totally different treatment. Encroachment on their rights; infliction on them of any loss or damage not justified by his own rights; falsehood or duplicity in dealing with them; unfair or ungenerous use of advantages over them; even selfish abstinence from defending them against injury – these are fit objects of moral reprobation, and, in grave cases, of moral retribution and punishment. And not only these acts, but the dispositions which lead to them, are properly immoral, and fit subjects of disapprobation which may rise to abhorrence. Cruelty of disposition; malice and ill-nature; that most anti-social and odious of all passions, envy; dissimulation and insincerity; irascibility on insufficient cause, and resentment disproportioned to the provocation; the love of domineering over others; the desire to engross more than one's share of advantages (the πλεονεξια of the Greeks); the pride which derives gratification from the abasement of others; the egotism which thinks self and its concerns more important than everything else, and decides all doubtful questions in its own favour; – these are moral vices, and constitute a bad and odious moral character: unlike the self-regarding faults previously mentioned, which are not properly immoralities, and to whatever pitch they may be carried, do not constitute wickedness. They may be proofs of any amount of folly, or want of personal dignity and self-respect; but they are only a subject of moral reprobation when they involve a breach of duty to others, for whose sake the individual is bound to have care for himself. What are called duties to ourselves are not socially obligatory, unless circumstances render them at the same time duties to others. The term duty to oneself, when it means anything more than prudence, means self-respect or self-development; and for none of these is any one accountable to his fellow creatures, because for none of them is it for the good of mankind that he be held accountable to them.

The distinction between the loss of consideration which a person may rightly incur by defect of prudence or of personal dignity, and the reprobation which is due to him for an offence against the rights of others, is not a merely nominal distinction. It makes a vast difference both in our feelings and in our conduct towards him, whether he displeases us in things in which we think we have a right to control him, or in things in which we know that we have not. If he displeases us, we may express our distaste, and we may stand aloof from a person as well as from a thing that displeases us; but we shall not therefore feel called on to make his life uncomfortable. We shall reflect that he already bears, or will bear, the whole penalty of his error; if he spoils

his life by mismanagement, we shall not, for that reason, desire to spoil it still further: instead of wishing to punish him, we shall rather endeavour to alleviate his punishment, by showing him how he may avoid or cure the evils his conduct tends to bring upon him. He may be to us an object of pity, perhaps of dislike, but not of anger or resentment; we shall not treat him like an enemy of society: the worst we shall think ourselves justified in doing is leaving him to himself, if we do not interfere benevolently by showing interest or concern for him. It is far otherwise if he has infringed the rules necessary for the protection of his fellow-creatures, individually or collectively. The evil consequences of his acts do not then fall on himself, but on others; and society, as the protector of all its members, must retaliate on him; must inflict pain on him for the express purpose of punishment, and must take care that it be sufficiently severe. In the one case, he is an offender at our bar, and we are called on not only to sit in judgment on him, but, in one shape or another, to execute our own sentence: in the other case, it is not our part to inflict any suffering on him, except what may incidentally follow from our using the same liberty in the regulation of our own affairs, which we allow to him in his.

The distinction here pointed out between the part of a person's life which concerns only himself, and that which concerns others, many persons will refuse to admit. How (it may be asked) can any part of the conduct of a member of society be a matter of indifference to the other members? No person is an entirely isolated being; it is impossible for a person to do anything seriously or permanently hurtful to himself, without mischief reaching at least to his near connections, and often far beyond them. If he injures his property, he does harm to those who directly or indirectly derived support from it, and usually diminishes, by a greater or less amount, the general resources of the community. If he deteriorates his bodily or mental faculties, he not only brings evil upon all who depended on him for any portion of their happiness, but disqualifies himself for rendering the services which he owes to his fellow-creatures generally; perhaps becomes a burthen on their affection or benevolence; and if such conduct were very frequent, hardly any offence that is committed would detract more from the general sum of good. Finally, if by his vices or follies a person does no direct harm to others, he is nevertheless (it may be said) injurious by his example; and ought to be compelled to control himself, for the sake of those whom the sight or knowledge of his conduct might corrupt or mislead.

And even (it will be added) if the consequences of misconduct could be confined to the vicious or thoughtless individual, ought society to abandon to their own guidance those who are manifestly unfit for it? If protection against themselves is confessedly due to children and persons under age, is not society equally bound to afford it to persons of mature years who are equally incapable of self-government? If gambling, or drunkenness, or incontinence, or incontinence, or idleness, or uncleanliness, are as injurious to happiness, and as great a hindrance to improvement, as many or most of the acts prohibited by law, why (it may be asked) should not law, so far as is consistent with practicability and social convenience, endeavour to repress these also? And as a supplement to the unavoidable imperfections of law, ought not opinion at least to organise a powerful police against these vices, and visit rigidly with social penalties those who are known to practise them? There is no question here (it may be said) about restricting individuality, or impeding the trial of new and original experiments in living. The only things it is sought to prevent are things which have been tried and condemned from the beginning of the world until now; things which experience has shown not to be useful or suitable to any person's individuality. There must be some length of time and amount of experience, after which a moral or prudential truth may be regarded as

established: and it is merely desired to prevent generation after generation from falling over the same precipice which has been fatal to their predecessors.

I fully admit that the mischief which a person does to himself may seriously affect, both through their sympathies and their interests, those nearly connected with him, and in a minor degree, society at large. When, by conduct of this sort, a person is led to violate a distinct and assignable obligation to any other person or persons, the case is taken out of the self-regarding class, and becomes amenable to moral disapprobation in the proper sense of the term. If, for example, a man, through intemperance or extravagance, becomes unable to pay his debts, or, having undertaken the moral responsibility of a family, becomes from the same cause incapable of supporting or educating them, he is deservedly reprobated, and might be justly punished; but it is for the breach of duty to his family or creditors, not for the extravagance. If the resources which ought to have been devoted to them, had been diverted from them for the most prudent investment, the moral culpability would have been the same. George Barnwell murdered his uncle to get money for his mistress, but if he had done it to set himself up in business, he would equally have been hanged. Again, in the frequent case of a man who causes grief to his family by addiction to bad habits, he deserves reproach for his unkindness or ingratitude; but so he may for cultivating habits not in themselves vicious, if they are painful to those with whom he passes his life, or who from personal ties are dependent on him for their comfort. Whoever fails in the consideration generally due to the interests and feelings of others, not being compelled by some more imperative duty, or justified by allowable self-preference, is a subject of moral disapprobation for that failure, but not for the cause of it, nor for the errors, merely personal to himself, which may have remotely led to it. In like manner, when a person disables himself, by conduct purely self-regarding, from the performance of some definite duty incumbent on him to the public, he is guilty of a social offence. No person ought to be punished simply for being drunk; but a soldier or a policeman should be punished for being drunk on duty. Whenever, in short, there is a definite damage, or a definite risk of damage, either to an individual or to the public, the case is taken out of the province of liberty, and placed in that of morality or law.

But with regard to the merely contingent, or, as it may be called, constructive injury which a person causes to society, by conduct which neither violates any specific duty to the public, nor occasions perceptible hurt to any assignable individual except himself; the inconvenience is one which society can afford to bear, for the sake of the greater good of human freedom. If grown persons are to be punished for not taking proper care of themselves, I would rather it were for their own sake, than under pretence of preventing them from impairing their capacity of rendering to society benefits which society does not pretend it has a right to exact. [. . .]

But the strongest of all the arguments against the interference of the public with purely personal conduct, is that when it does interfere, the odds are that it interferes wrongly, and in the wrong place. On questions of social morality, of duty to others, the opinion of the public, that is, of an over-ruling majority, though often wrong, is likely to be still oftener right; because on such questions they are only required to judge of their own interests; of the manner in which some mode of conduct, if allowed to be practised, would affect themselves. But the opinion of a similar majority, imposed as a law on the minority, on questions of self-regarding conduct, is quite as likely to be wrong as right; for in these cases public opinion means, at the best, some people's opinion of what is good or bad for other people; while very often it does not even mean that; the public, with the most perfect indifference, passing over the pleasure or convenience of those whose conduct they censure, and considering only their own preference. There are many who consider as an injury to themselves any conduct which they have a distaste for, and resent it as an outrage to their feelings; as a religious bigot, when charged with disregarding the religious feelings of others, has been known to retort that they disregard his feelings, by persisting in their abominable worship or creed. But there is no parity between the feeling of a person for his own opinion, and the feeling of another who is offended at his holding it; no more than between the desire of a thief to take a purse, and the desire of the right owner to keep it. And a person's taste is as much his own peculiar concern as his opinion or his purse. It is easy for any one to imagine an ideal public, which leaves the freedom and choice of individuals in all uncertain matters undisturbed, and only requires them to abstain from modes of conduct which universal experience has condemned. But where has there been seen a public which set any such limit to its censorship? or when does the public trouble itself about universal experience? In its interferences with personal conduct it is seldom thinking of anything but the enormity of acting or feeling differently from itself; and this standard of judgment, thinly disguised, is held up to mankind as the dictate of religion and philosophy, by nine-tenths of all moralists and speculative writers. These teach that things are right because they are right; because we feel them to be so. They tell us to search in our own minds and hearts for laws of conduct binding on ourselves and on all others. What can the poor public do but apply these instructions, and make their own personal feelings of good and evil, if they are tolerably unanimous in them, obligatory on all the world?

The evil here pointed out is not one which exists only in theory; and it may perhaps be expected that I should specify the instances in which the public of this age and country improperly invests its own preferences with the character of moral laws. I am not writing an essay on the aberrations of existing moral feeling. That is too weighty a subject to be discussed parenthetically, and by way of illustration. Yet examples are necessary, to show that the principle I maintain is of serious and practical moment, and that I am not endeavouring to erect a barrier against imaginary evils. And it is not difficult to show, by abundant instances, that to extend the bounds of what may be called moral police, until it encroaches on the most unquestionably legitimate liberty of the individual, is one of the most universal of all human propensities.

As a first instance, consider the antipathies which men cherish on no better grounds than that persons whose religious opinions are different from theirs, do not practise their religious observances, especially their religious abstinences. To cite a rather trivial example, nothing in the creed or practice of Christians does more to envenom the hatred of Mahomedans against them, than the fact of their eating pork. There are few acts which Christians and Europeans regard with more unaffected disgust, than Mussulmans regard this particular mode of satisfying hunger. It is, in the first place, an offence against their religion; but this circumstance by no means explains either the degree or the kind of their repugnance; for wine also is forbidden by their religion, and to partake of it is by all Mussulmans accounted wrong, but not disgusting. Their aversion to the flesh of the 'unclean beast' is, on the contrary, of that peculiar character, resembling an instinctive antipathy, which the idea of uncleanness, when once it thoroughly sinks into the feelings, seems always to excite even in those whose personal habits are anything but scrupulously cleanly, and of which the sentiment of religious impurity, so intense in the Hindoos, is a remarkable example. Suppose now that in a people, of whom the majority were Mussulmans, that majority should insist upon not permitting pork to be eaten within the limits of the country. This would be nothing new in Mahomedan countries. Would it be a legitimate exercise of the moral authority of public opin-

ion? and if not, why not? The practice is really revolting to such a public. They also sincerely think that it is forbidden and abhorred by the Deity. Neither could the prohibition be censured as religious persecution. It might be religious in its origin, but it would not be persecution for religion, since nobody's religion makes it a duty to eat pork. The only tenable ground of condemnation would be, that with the personal tastes and self-regarding concerns of individuals the public has no business to interfere.

To come somewhat nearer home: the majority of Spaniards consider it a gross impiety, offensive in the highest degree to the Supreme Being, to worship him in any other manner than the Roman Catholic; and no other public worship is lawful on Spanish soil. The people of all Southern Europe look upon a married clergy as not only irreligious, but unchaste, indecent, gross, disgusting. What do Protestants think of these perfectly sincere feelings, and of the attempt to enforce them against non-Catholics? Yet, if mankind are justified in interfering with each other's liberty in things which do not concern the interests of others, on what principle is it possible consistently to exclude these cases? or who can blame people for desiring to suppress what they regard as a scandal in the sight of God and man? No stronger case can be shown for prohibiting anything which is regarded as a personal immorality, than is made out for suppressing these practices in the eyes of those who regard them as impieties; and unless we are willing to adopt the logic of persecutors, and to say that we may persecute others because we are right, and that they must not persecute us because they are wrong, we must beware of admitting a principle of which we should resent as a gross injustice the application to ourselves.

The preceding instances may be objected to, although unreasonably, as drawn from contingencies impossible among us: opinion, in this country, not being likely to enforce abstinence from meats, or to interfere with people for worshipping, and for either marrying or not marrying, according to their creed or inclination. The next example, however, shall be taken from an interference with liberty which we have by no means passed all danger of. Wherever the Puritans have been sufficiently powerful, as in New England, and in Great Britain at the time of the Commonwealth, they have endeavoured, with considerable success, to put down all public, and nearly all private, amusements: especially music, dancing, public games, or other assemblages for purposes of diversion, and the theatre. There are still in this country large bodies of persons by whose notions of morality and religion these recreations are condemned; and those persons belonging chiefly to the middle class, who are the ascendant power in the present social and political condition of the kingdom, it is by no means impossible that persons of these sentiments may at some time or other command a majority in Parliament. How will the remaining portion of the community like to have the amusements that shall be permitted to them regulated by the religious and moral sentiments of the stricter Calvinists and Methodists? Would they not, with considerable peremptoriness, desire these intrusively pious members of society to mind their own business? This is precisely what should be said to every government and every public, who have the pretension that no person shall enjoy any pleasure which they think wrong. But if the principle of the pretension be admitted, no one can reasonably object to its being acted on in the sense of the majority, or other preponderating power in the country; and all persons must be ready to conform to the idea of a Christian commonwealth, as understood by the early settlers in New England, if a religious profession similar to theirs should ever succeed in regaining its lost ground, as religions supposed to be declining have so often been known to do.

To imagine another contingency, perhaps more likely to be realised than the one last mentioned. There is confessedly a strong tendency in the modern world towards a democratic constitution of society, accompanied or not by popular political institutions. It is affirmed that in the country where this tendency is most completely realised – where both society and the government are most democratic – the United States – the feeling of the majority, to whom any appearance of a more showy or costly style of living than they can hope to rival is disagreeable, operates as a tolerably effectual sumptuary law, and that in many parts of the Union it is really difficult for a person possessing a very large income, to find any mode of spending it, which will not incur popular disapprobation. Though such statements as these are doubtless much exaggerated as a representation of existing facts, the state of things they describe is not only a conceivable and possible, but a probable result of democratic feeling, combined with the notion that the public has a right to a veto on the manner in which individuals shall spend their incomes. We have only further to suppose a considerable diffusion of Socialist opinions, and it may become infamous in the eyes of the majority to possess more property than some very small amount, or any income not earned by manual labour. Opinions similar in principle to these, already prevail widely among the artisan class, and weigh oppressively on those who are amenable to the opinion chiefly of that class, namely, its own members. It is known that the bad workmen who form the majority of the operatives in many branches of industry, are decidedly of opinion that bad workmen ought to receive the same wages as good, and that no one ought to be allowed, through piecework or otherwise to earn by superior skill or industry more than others can without it. And they employ a moral police, which occasionally becomes a physical one, to deter skilful workmen from receiving, and employers from giving, a larger remuneration for a more useful service. If the public have any jurisdiction over private concerns, I cannot see that these people are in fault, or that any individual's particular public can be blamed for asserting the same authority over his individual conduct, which the general public asserts over people in general.

But, without dwelling on supposititious cases, there are, in our own day, gross usurpations upon the liberty of private life actually practised, and still greater ones threatened with some expectation of success, and opinions propounded which assert an unlimited right in the public not only to prohibit by law everything which it thinks wrong, but in order to get at what it thinks wrong, to prohibit any number of things which it admits to be innocent.

Under the name of preventing intemperance, the people of one English colony, and of nearly half the United States, have been interdicted by law from making any use whatever of fermented drinks, except for medical purposes: for prohibition of their sale is in fact, as it is intended to be, prohibition of their use. And though the impracticability of executing the law has caused its repeal in several of the States which had adopted it, including the one from which it derives its name, an attempt has notwithstanding been commenced, and is prosecuted with considerable zeal by many of the professed philanthropists, to agitate for a similar law in this country. The association, or 'Alliance' as it terms itself, which has been formed for this purpose, has acquired some notoriety through the publicity given to a correspondence between its Secretary and one of the very few English public men who hold that a politician's opinions ought to be founded on principles. Lord Stanley's share in this correspondence is calculated to strengthen the hopes already built on him, by those who know how rare such qualities as are manifested in some of his public appearances, unhappily are among those who figure in political life. The organ of the Alliance, who would 'deeply deplore the recognition of any principle which could be wrested to justify bigotry and persecution', undertakes to point out the 'broad and impassable barrier' which divides such principles from those of the association. 'All matters relating to thought, opinion, conscience,

appear to me', he says, 'to be without the sphere of legislation; all pertaining to social act, habit, relation, subject only to a discretionary power vested in the State itself, and not in the individual, to be within it.' No mention is made of a third class, different from either of these, viz. acts and habits which are not social, but individual; although it is to this class, surely, that the act of drinking fermented liquors belongs. Selling fermented liquors, however, is trading, and trading is a social act. But the infringement complained of is not on the liberty of the seller, but on that of the buyer and consumer; since the State might just as well forbid him to drink wine, as purposely make it impossible for him to obtain it. The Secretary, however, says, 'I claim, as a citizen, a right to legislate whenever my social rights are invaded by the social act of another.' And now for the definition of these 'social rights'. 'If anything invades my social rights, certainly the traffic in strong drink does. It destroys my primary right of security, by constantly creating and stimulating social disorder. It invades my right of equality, by deriving a profit from the creation of a misery I am taxed to support. It impedes my right to free moral and intellectual development, by surrounding my path with dangers, and by weakening and demoralising society, from which I have a right to claim mutual aid and intercourse.' A theory of 'social rights', the like of which probably never before found its way into distinct language: being nothing short of this – that it is the absolute social right of every individual, that every other individual shall act in every respect exactly as he ought; that whosoever fails thereof in the smallest particular, violates my social right, and entitles me to demand from the legislature the removal of the grievance. So monstrous a principle is far more dangerous than any single interference with liberty; there is no violation of liberty which it would not justify; it acknowledges no right to any freedom whatever, except perhaps to that of holding opinions in secret, without ever disclosing them: for, the moment an opinion which I consider noxious passes any one's lips, it invades all the 'social rights' attributed to me by the Alliance. The doctrine ascribes to all mankind a vested interest in each other's moral, intellectual, and even physical perfection, to be defined by each claimant according to his own standard.

Another important example of illegitimate interference with the rightful liberty of the individual, not simply threatened, but long since carried into triumphant effect, is Sabbatarian legislation. Without doubt, abstinence on one day in the week, so far as the exigencies of life permit, from the usual daily occupation, though in no respect religiously binding on any except Jews, is a highly beneficial custom. And inasmuch as this custom cannot be observed without a general consent to that effect among the industrious classes, therefore, in so far as some persons by working may impose the same necessity on others, it may be allowable and right that the law should guarantee to each the observance by others of the custom, by suspending the greater operations of industry on a particular day. But this justification, grounded on the direct interest which others have in each individual's observance of the practice, does not apply to the self-chosen occupations in which a person may think fit to employ his leisure; nor does it hold good, in the smallest degree, for legal restrictions of amusements. It is true that the amusement of some is the day's work of others; but the pleasure, not to say the useful recreation, of many, is worth the labour of a few, provided the occupation is freely chosen, and can be freely resigned. The operatives are perfectly right in thinking that if all worked on Saturday, seven days' work would have to be given for six days' wages: but so long as the great mass of employments are suspended, the small number who for the enjoyment of others must still work, obtain a proportional increase of earnings; and they are not obliged to follow those occupations, if they prefer leisure to emolument. If a further remedy is sought, it might be found in the establishment

by custom of a holiday on some other day of the week for those particular classes of persons. The only ground, therefore, on which restrictions on Sunday amusements can be defended, must be that they are religiously wrong; a motive of legislation which never can be too earnestly protested against. 'Deorum injuriæ Diis curæ'. It remains to be proved that society or any of its officers holds a commission from on high to avenge any supposed offence to Omnipotence, which is not also a wrong to our fellow creatures. The notion that it is one man's duty that another should be religious, was the foundation of all the religious persecutions ever perpetrated, and if admitted, would fully justify them. Though the feeling which breaks out in the repeated attempts to stop railway travelling on Sunday, in the resistance to the opening of Museums, and the like, has not the cruelty of the old persecutors, the state of mind indicated by it is fundamentally the same. It is a determination not to tolerate others in doing what is permitted by their religion, because it is not permitted by the persecutor's religion. It is a belief that God not only abominates the act of the misbeliever, but will not hold us guiltless if we leave him unmolested.

I cannot refrain from adding to these examples of the little account commonly made of human liberty, the language of downright persecution which breaks out from the press of this country, whenever it feels called on to notice the remarkable phenomenon of Mormonism. Much might be said on the unexpected and instructive fact, that an alleged new revelation, and a religion founded on it, the product of palpable imposture, not even supported by the *prestige* of extraordinary qualities in its founder, is believed by hundreds of thousands, and has been made the foundation of a society, in the age of newspapers, railways, and the electric telegraph. What here concerns us is, that this religion, like other and better religions, has its martyrs; that its prophet and founder was, for his teaching, put to death by a mob; that others of its adherents lost their lives by the same lawless violence; that they were forcibly expelled, in a body, from the country in which they first grew up; while, now that they have been chased into a solitary recess in the midst of a desert, many in this country openly declare that it would be right (only that it is not convenient) to send an expedition against them, and compel them by force to conform to the opinions of other people. The article of the Mormonite doctrine which is the chief provocative to the antipathy which thus breaks through the ordinary restraints of religious tolerance, is its sanction of polygamy; which, though permitted to Mahomedans, and Hindoos, and Chinese, seems to excite unquenchable animosity when practised by persons who speak English, and profess to be a kind of Christians. No one has a deeper disapprobation that I have of this Mormon institution; both for other reasons, and because, far from being in any way countenanced by the principle of liberty, it is a direct infraction of that principle, being a mere rivetting of the chains of one-half of the community, and an emancipation of the other from reciprocity of obligation towards them. Still, it must be remembered that this religion is as much voluntary on the part of the women concerned in it, and who may be deemed the sufferers by it, as is the case with any form of the marriage institution; and however surprising this fact may appear, it has its explanation in the common ideas and customs of the world, which teaching women to think marriage the one thing needful, make it intelligible that many a woman should prefer being one of several wives, to not being a wife at all. Other countries are not asked to recognise such unions, or release any portion of their inhabitants from their own laws on the score of Mormonite opinions. But when the dissentients have conceded to the hostile sentiments of others, far more than could justly be demanded; when they have left the countries to which their doctrines were unacceptable, and

established themselves in a remote corner of the earth, which they have been the first to render habitable to human beings; it is difficult to see on what principles but those of tyranny they can be prevented from living there under what laws they please, provided they commit no aggression on other nations, and allow perfect freedom of departure to those who are dissatisfied with their ways. A recent writer, in some respects of considerable merit, proposes (to use his own words) not a crusade, but a *civilizade*, against this polygamous community, to put an end to what seems to him a retrograde step in civilisation. It also appears so to me, but I am not aware that any community has a right to force another to be civilised. So long as the sufferers by the bad law do not invoke assistance from other communities, I cannot admit that persons entirely unconnected with them ought to step in and require that a condition of things with which all who are directly interested appear to be satisfied, should be put an end to because it is a scandal to persons some thousands of miles distant, who have no part or concern in it. Let them send missionaries, if they please, to preach against it; and let them, by any fair means (of which silencing the teachers is not one), oppose the progress of similar doctrines among their own people. If civilisation has got the better of barbarism when barbarism had the world to itself, it is too much to profess to be afraid lest barbarism, after having been fairly got under, should revive and conquer civilisation. A civilisation that can thus succumb to its vanquished enemy, must first have become so degenerate, that neither its appointed priests and teachers, nor anybody else, has the capacity, or will take the trouble, to stand up for it. If this be so, the sooner such a civilisation receives notice to quit, the better. It can only go on from bad to worse, until destroyed and regenerated (like the Western Empire) by energetic barbarians.

Chapter 34

Isaiah Berlin

TWO CONCEPTS OF LIBERTY

Sir Isaiah Berlin (1909–1997) was a political philosopher at Oxford University, known for his defense of value pluralism and individual liberty. In this essay, Berlin introduces the distinction between negative and positive liberty, and argues that the latter concept is ripe for abuse at the hands of tyrants. Because there is no single correct way of judging the relative importance of competing plural values, Berlin argues, a great deal of individual freedom is necessary so that each person may choose a life embodying those values of his or her own choosing.

I

To coerce a man is to deprive him of freedom – freedom from what? Almost every moralist in human history has praised freedom. Like happiness and goodness, like nature and reality, it is a term whose meaning is so porous that there is little interpretation that it seems able to resist. I do not propose to discuss either the history of this protean word or the more than two hundred senses of it recorded by historians of ideas. I propose to examine no more than two of these senses – but they are central ones, with a great deal of human history behind them, and, I dare say, still to come. The first of these political senses of freedom or liberty (I shall use both words to mean the same), which (following much precedent) I shall call the 'negative' sense, is involved in the answer to the question 'What is the area within which the subject – a person or group of persons – is or should be left to do or be what he is able to do or be, without interference by other persons?' The second, which I shall call the 'positive' sense, is involved in the answer to the question 'What, or who, is the source of control or interference that can determine someone to do, or be, this rather than that?' The two questions are clearly different, even though the answers to them may overlap.

The Notion of Negative Freedom

I am normally said to be free to the degree to which no man or body of men interferes with my activity. Political liberty in this sense is simply the area within which a man can act unobstructed by others. If I am prevented by others from doing what I could otherwise do, I am to that degree unfree; and if this area is contracted by other men beyond a certain minimum, I can be described as being coerced, or, it may be, enslaved. Coercion is not, however, a term that covers every form of inability. If I say that I am unable to jump more than ten feet in the air, or cannot read because I am blind, or cannot understand the darker pages of Hegel, it would be eccentric to say that I am to that degree enslaved or coerced. Coercion implies the deliberate interference of other human beings within the area in which I could otherwise act. You lack political liberty or freedom only if you are prevented from attaining a goal by human beings. Mere incapacity to attain a goal is not lack of political freedom. This is brought out by the use of such modern expressions as 'economic freedom' and its counterpart, 'economic slavery'. It is argued, very plausibly, that if a man is too poor to afford something on which there is no legal ban – a loaf of bread, a journey round the world, recourse to the law courts – he is as little free to have it as he would be if it were forbidden him by law. If my poverty were a kind of disease which prevented me from buying bread, or paying for the journey round the world or getting my case heard, as lameness prevents me from running, this inability would not naturally be described as a lack of freedom, least of all political freedom. It is only because I believe that my inability to get a given thing is due to the fact that other human beings have made arrangements whereby I am, whereas others are not, prevented from having enough money with which to pay for it, that I think myself a victim of coercion or slavery. In other words, this use of the term depends on a particular social and economic theory about the causes of my poverty or weakness. If my lack of material means is due to my lack of mental or physical capacity, then I begin to speak of being deprived of freedom (and not simply about poverty) only if I accept the theory. If, in addition, I believe that I am being kept in want by a specific arrangement which I consider unjust or unfair, I speak of economic slavery or oppression. The nature of things does not madden us, only ill will does, said Rousseau. The criterion of oppression is the part that I believe to be played by other human beings, directly or indirectly, with or without the intention of doing so, in frustrating my wishes. By being free in this sense I mean not being interfered with by others. The wider the area of non-interference the wider my freedom.

This is what the classical English political philosophers meant when they used this word. They disagreed about how wide the area could or should be. They supposed that it could not, as things were, be unlimited, because if it were, it would entail a state in which all men could boundlessly interfere with all other men; and this kind of 'natural' freedom would lead to social chaos in which men's minimum needs would not be satisfied; or else the liberties of the weak would be suppressed by the strong. Because they perceived that human purposes and activities do not automatically harmonise with one another, and because (whatever their official doctrines) they put high value on other goals, such as justice, or happiness, or culture, or security, or varying degrees of equality, they were prepared to curtail freedom in the interests of other values and, indeed, of freedom itself. For, without this, it was impossible to create the kind of association that they thought desirable. Consequently, it is assumed by these thinkers that the area of men's free action must be limited by law. But equally it is assumed, especially by such libertarians as Locke and Mill in England, and Constant and Tocqueville in France, that there ought to exist a certain minimum area of personal freedom which must on no account be violated; for if it is overstepped, the individual will find himself in an area too narrow for even that minimum development of his natural faculties which alone makes it possible to pursue, and even to conceive, the various ends which men hold good or right or sacred. It follows that a frontier must be drawn between the area of private life and that of public authority. Where it is to be drawn is a matter of argument, indeed of haggling. Men are largely interdependent, and no man's activity is so completely private as never to obstruct the lives of others in any way. 'Freedom for the pike is death for the minnows'; the liberty of some must depend on the restraint of others. Freedom for an Oxford don, others have been known to add, is a very different thing from freedom for an Egyptian peasant.

This proposition derives its force from something that is both true and important, but the phrase itself remains a piece of political claptrap. It is true that to offer political rights, or safeguards against intervention by the State, to men who are half-naked, illiterate, underfed and diseased is to mock their condition; they need medical help or education before they can understand, or make use of, an increase in their freedom. What is freedom to those who cannot make use of it? Without adequate conditions for the use of freedom, what is the value of freedom? First things come first: there are situations in which – to use a saying satirically attributed to the nihilists by Dostoevsky – boots are superior to Pushkin; individual freedom is not everyone's primary need. For freedom is not the mere absence of frustration of whatever kind; this would inflate the meaning of the word until it meant too much or too little. The Egyptian peasant needs clothes or medicine before, and more than, personal liberty, but the minimum freedom that he needs today, and the greater degree of freedom that he may need tomorrow, is not some species of freedom peculiar to him, but identical with that of professors, artists and millionaires.

What troubles the consciences of Western liberals is, I think, the belief, not that the freedom that men seek differs according to their social or economic conditions, but that the minority who possess it have gained it by exploiting, or, at least, averting their gaze from, the vast majority who do not. They believe, with good reason, that if individual liberty is an ultimate end for human beings, none should be deprived of it by others; least of all that some should enjoy it at the expense of others. Equality of liberty; not to treat others as I should not wish them to treat me; repayment of my debt to those who alone have made possible my liberty or prosperity or enlightenment; justice, in its simplest and most universal sense – these are the foundations of liberal morality. Liberty is not the only goal of men. I can, like the Russian critic Belinsky, say that if others are to be deprived of it – if my brothers are to remain in poverty, squalor and chains – then I do not want it for myself, I reject it with both hands and infinitely prefer to share their fate. But nothing is gained by a confusion of terms. To avoid glaring inequality or widespread misery I am ready to sacrifice some, or all, of my freedom: I may do so willingly and freely; but it is freedom that I am giving up for the sake of justice or equality or the love of my fellow men. I should be guilt-stricken, and rightly so, if I were not, in some circumstances, ready to make this sacrifice. But a sacrifice is not an increase in what is being sacrificed, namely freedom, however great the moral need or the compensation for it. Everything is what it is: liberty is liberty, not equality or fairness or justice or culture, or human happiness or a quiet conscience. If the liberty of myself or my class or nation depends on the misery of a number of other human beings, the system which promotes this is unjust and immoral. But if I curtail or lose my freedom in order to lessen the shame of such inequality, and do not thereby materially increase the individual liberty of others, an absolute loss of liberty occurs. This may be compensated for by a gain in justice or in happiness or in peace, but the loss remains, and it is a confusion of values to say that although my 'liberal', individual freedom may go by the board, some other kind of freedom – 'social' or 'economic' – is increased. Yet it remains true that the freedom of some must at times be curtailed to secure the freedom of others. Upon what principle should this be done? If freedom is a sacred, untouchable value, there can be no such principle. One or other of these conflicting rules or principles must, at any rate in practice, yield: not always for reasons which can be clearly stated, let alone generalised into rules or universal maxims. Still, a practical compromise has to be found.

Philosophers with an optimistic view of human nature and a belief in the possibility of harmonising human interests, such as Locke or Adam Smith or, in some moods, Mill, believed that social harmony and progress were compatible with reserving a large area for private life over which neither the State nor any other authority must be allowed to trespass. Hobbes, and those who agreed with him, especially conservative or reactionary thinkers, argued that if men were to be prevented from destroying one another and making social life a jungle or a wilderness, greater safeguards must be instituted to keep them in their places; he wished correspondingly to increase the area of centralised control and decrease that of the individual. But both sides agreed that some portion of human existence must remain independent of the sphere of social control. To invade that preserve, however small, would be despotism. The most eloquent of all defenders of freedom and privacy, Benjamin Constant, who had not forgotten the Jacobin dictatorship, declared that at the very least the liberty of religion, opinion, expression, property must be guaranteed against arbitrary invasion. Jefferson, Burke, Paine, Mill compiled different catalogues of individual liberties, but the argument for keeping authority at bay is always substantially the same. We must preserve a minimum area of personal freedom if we are not to 'degrade or deny our nature'. We cannot remain absolutely free, and must give up some of our liberty to preserve the rest. But total self-surrender is self-defeating. What then must the minimum be? That which a man cannot give up without offending against the essence of his human nature. What is this essence? What are the standards which it entails? This has been, and perhaps always will be, a matter of infinite debate. But whatever the principle in terms of which the area of non-interference is to be drawn, whether it is that of natural law or natural rights, or of utility, or the pronouncements of a categorical imperative, or the sanctity of the social contract, or any other concept with which men have sought to clarify and justify their convictions, liberty in this sense means liberty from;

absence of interference beyond the shifting, but always recognisable, frontier. 'The only freedom which deserves the name, is that of pursuing our own good in our own way,' said the most celebrated of its champions. If this is so, is compulsion ever justified? Mill had no doubt that it was. Since justice demands that all individuals be entitled to a minimum of freedom, all other individuals were of necessity to be restrained, if need be by force, from depriving anyone of it. Indeed, the whole function of law was the prevention of just such collisions: the State was reduced to what Lassalle contemptuously described as the functions of a night-watchman or traffic policeman.

What made the protection of individual liberty so sacred to Mill? In his famous essay he declares that, unless the individual is left to live as he wishes in 'the part [of his conduct] which merely concerns himself', civilisation cannot advance; the truth will not, for lack of a free market in ideas, come to light; there will be no scope for spontaneity, originality, genius, for mental energy, for moral courage. Society will be crushed by the weight of 'collective mediocrity'. Whatever is rich and diversified will be crushed by the weight of custom, by men's constant tendency to conformity, which breeds only 'withered' capacities, 'pinched and hidebound', 'cramped and dwarfed' human beings. 'Pagan self-assertion' is as worthy as 'Christian self-denial'. 'All errors which [a man] is likely to commit against advice and warning, are far outweighed by the evil of allowing others to constrain him to what they deem his good.' The defence of liberty consists in the 'negative' goal of warding off interference. To threaten a man with persecution unless he submits to a life in which he exercises no choices of his goals; to block before him every door but one, no matter how noble the prospect upon which it opens, or how benevolent the motives of those who arrange this, is to sin against the truth that he is a man, a being with a life of his own to live. This is liberty as it has been conceived by liberals in the modern world from the days of Erasmus (some would say of Occam) to our own. Every plea for civil liberties and individual rights, every protest against exploitation and humiliation, against the encroachment of public authority, or the mass hypnosis of custom or organised propaganda, springs from this individualistic, and much disputed, conception of man.

Three facts about this position may be noted. In the first place Mill confuses two distinct notions. One is that all coercion is, in so far as it frustrates human desires, bad as such, although it may have to be applied to prevent other, greater evils; while non-interference, which is the opposite of coercion, is good as such, although it is not the only good. This is the 'negative' conception of liberty in its classical form. The other is that men should seek to discover the truth, or to develop a certain type of character of which Mill approved – critical, original, imaginative, independent, non-conforming to the point of eccentricity, and so on – and that truth can be found, and such character can be bred, only in conditions of freedom. Both these are liberal views, but they are not identical, and the connection between them is, at best, empirical. No one would argue that truth or freedom of self-expression could flourish where dogma crushes all thought. But the evidence of history tends to show (as, indeed, was argued by James Stephen in his formidable attack on Mill in his *Liberty, Equality, Fraternity*) that integrity, love of truth and fiery individualism grow at least as often in severely disciplined communities, among, for example, the puritan Calvinists of Scotland or New England, or under military discipline, as in more tolerant or indifferent societies; and if this is so, Mill's argument for liberty as a necessary condition for the growth of human genius falls to the ground. If his two goals proved incompatible, Mill would be faced with a cruel dilemma, quite apart from the further difficulties created by the inconsistency of his doctrines with strict utilitarianism, even in his own humane version of it.

In the second place, the doctrine is comparatively modern. There seems to be scarcely any discussion of individual liberty as a conscious political ideal (as opposed to its actual existence) in the ancient world. Condorcet had already remarked that the notion of individual rights was absent from the legal conceptions of the Romans and Greeks; this seems to hold equally of the Jewish, Chinese and all other ancient civilisations that have since come to light. The domination of this ideal has been the exception rather than the rule, even in the recent history of the West. Nor has liberty in this sense often formed a rallying cry for the great masses of mankind. The desire not to be impinged upon, to be left to oneself, has been a mark of high civilisation on the part of both individuals and communities. The sense of privacy itself, of the area of personal relationships as something sacred in its own right, derives from a conception of freedom which, for all its religious roots, is scarcely older, in its developed state, than the Renaissance or the Reformation. Yet its decline would mark the death of a civilisation, of an entire moral outlook.

The third characteristic of this notion of liberty is of greater importance. It is that liberty in this sense is not incompatible with some kinds of autocracy, or at any rate with the absence of self-government. Liberty in this sense is principally concerned with the area of control, not with its source. Just as a democracy may, in fact, deprive the individual citizen of a great many liberties which he might have in some other form of society, so it is perfectly conceivable that a liberal-minded despot would allow his subjects a large measure of personal freedom. The despot who leaves his subjects a wide area of liberty may be unjust, or encourage the wildest inequalities, care little for order, or virtue, or knowledge; but provided he does not curb their liberty, or at least curbs it less than many other regimes, he meets with Mill's specification.

Freedom in this sense is not, at any rate logically, connected with democracy or self-government. Self-government may, on the whole, provide a better guarantee of the preservation of civil liberties than other regimes, and has been defended as such by libertarians. But there is no necessary connection between individual liberty and democratic rule. The answer to the question 'Who governs me?' is logically distinct from the question 'How far does government interfere with me?' It is in this difference that the great contrast between the two concepts of negative and positive liberty, in the end, consists. For the 'positive' sense of liberty comes to light if we try to answer the question, not 'What am I free to do or be?', but 'By whom am I ruled?' or 'Who is to say what I am, and what I am not, to be or do?' The connection between democracy and individual liberty is a good deal more tenuous than it seemed to many advocates of both. The desire to be governed by myself, or at any rate to participate in the process by which my life is to be controlled, may be as deep a wish as that for a free area for action, and perhaps historically older. But it is not a desire for the same thing. So different is it, indeed, as to have led in the end to the great clash of ideologies that dominates our world. For it is this, the 'positive' conception of liberty, not freedom from, but freedom to – to lead one prescribed from of life – which the adherents of the 'negative' notion represent as being, at times, no better than a specious disguise for brutal tyranny.

II

The Notion of Positive Freedom

The 'positive' sense of the world 'liberty' derives from the wish on the part of the individual to be his own master. I wish my life and decisions to depend on myself, not on external forces of whatever kind. I wish to be the instrument of my own, not of other men's, acts of will. I wish to be a subject, not an object; to be moved by reasons, by conscious purposes, which are my own, not by causes which affect me, as it were,

from outside. I wish to be somebody, not nobody; a doer – deciding, not being decided for, self-directed and not acted upon by external nature or by other men as if I were a thing, or an animal, or a slave incapable of playing a human role, that is, of conceiving goals and policies of my own and realising them. This is at least part of what I mean when I say that I am rational, and that it is my reason that distinguishes me as a human being from the rest of the world. I wish, above all, to be conscious of myself as a thinking, willing, active being, bearing responsibility for my choices and able to explain them by reference to my own ideas and purposes. I feel free to the degree that I believe this to be true, and enslaved to the degree that I am made to realise that it is not.

The freedom which consists in being one's own master, and the freedom which consists in not being prevented from choosing as I do by other men, may, on the face of it, seem concepts at no great logical distance from each other – no more than negative and positive ways of saying much the same thing. Yet the 'positive' and 'negative' notions of freedom historically developed in divergent directions, not always by logically reputable steps, until, in the end, they came into direct conflict with each other.

One way of making this clear is in terms of the independent momentum which the, initially perhaps quite harmless, metaphor of self-mastery acquired. 'I am my own master'; 'I am slave to no man'; but may I not (as Platonists or Hegelians tend to say) be a slave to nature? Or to my own 'unbridled' passions? Are these not so many species of the identical genus 'slave' – some political or legal, others moral or spiritual? Have not men had the experience of liberating themselves from spiritual slavery, or slavery to nature, and do they not in the course of it become aware, on the one hand, of a self which dominates, and, on the other, of something in them which is brought to heel? This dominant self is then variously identified with reason, with my 'higher nature', with the self which calculates and aims at what will satisfy it in the long run, with my 'real', or 'ideal', or 'autonomous' self, or with my self 'at its best'; which is then contrasted with irrational impulse, uncontrolled desires, my 'lower' nature, the pursuit of immediate pleasures, my 'empirical' or 'heteronomous' self, swept by every gust of desire and passion, needing to be rigidly disciplined if it is ever to rise to the full height of its 'real' nature. Presently the two selves may be represented as divided by an even larger gap; the real self may be conceived as something wider than the individual (as the term is normally understood), as a social 'whole' of which the individual is an element or aspect: a tribe, a race, a Church, a State, the great society of the living and the dead and the yet unborn. This entity is then identified as being the 'true' self which, by imposing its collective, or 'organic', single will upon its recalcitrant 'members', achieves its own, and therefore their, 'higher' freedom. The perils of using organic metaphors to justify the coercion of some men by others in order to raise them to a 'higher' level of freedom have often been pointed out. But what gives such plausibility as it has to this kind of language is that we recognise that it is possible, and at times justifiable, to coerce men in the name of some goal (let us say, justice or public health) which they would, if they were more enlightened, themselves pursue, but do not, because they are blind or ignorant or corrupt. This renders it easy for me to conceive of myself as coercing others for their own sake, in their, not my, interest. I am then claiming that I know what they truly need better than they know it themselves. What, at most this entails is that they would not resist me if they were rational and as wise as I and understood their interests as I do. But I may go on to claim a good deal more than this. I may declare that they are actually aiming at what in their benighted state they consciously resist, because there exists within them an occult entity – their latent rational will, or their 'true' purpose – and that this entity, although it is belied by all that they overtly feel and do and say, is their 'real' self, of which the poor empirical self in space and time may know nothing or little; and that this inner spirit is the only self that deserves to have its wishes taken into account. One I take this view, I am in a position to ignore the actual wishes of men or societies, to bully, oppress, torture them in the name, and on behalf, of their 'real' selves, in the secure knowledge that whatever is the true goal of man (happiness, performance of duty, wisdom, a just society, self-fulfilment) must be identical with his freedom – the free choice of his 'true', albeit often submerged and inarticulate, self.

This paradox has been often exposed. It is one thing to say that I know what is good for X, while he himself does not; and even to ignore his wishes for its – and his – sake; and a very different one to say that he has *eo ipso* chosen it, not indeed consciously, not as he seems in everyday life, but in his role as a rational self which his empirical self may not know – the 'real' self which discerns the good, and cannot help choosing it once it is revealed. This monstrous impersonation, which consists in equating what X would choose if he were something he is not, or at least not yet, with what X actually seeks and chooses, is at the heart of all political theories of self-realisation. It is one thing to say that I may be coerced for my own good, which I am too blind to see: this may, on occasion, be for my benefit; indeed it may enlarge the scope of my liberty. It is another to say that if it is my good, then I am not being coerced, for I have willed it, whether I know this or not, and am free (or 'truly' free) even while my poor earthly body and foolish mind bitterly reject it, and struggle with the greatest desperation against those who seek, however benevolently, to impose it.

This magical transformation, or sleight of hand (for which William James so justly mocked the Hegelians), can no doubt be perpetrated just as easily with the 'negative' concept of freedom, where the self that should not be interfered with is no longer the individual with his actual wishes and needs as they are normally conceived, but the 'real' man within, identified with the pursuit of some ideal purpose not dreamed of by his empirical self. And, as in the case of the 'positively' free self, this entity may be inflated into some super-personal entity – a State, a class, a nation, or the march of history itself, regarded as a more 'real' subject of attributes than the empirical self. But the 'positive' conception of freedom as self-mastery, with its suggestion of a man divided against himself, has in fact, and as a matter of history, of doctrine and of practice, lent itself more easily to this splitting of personality into two: the transcendent, dominant controller, and the empirical bundle of desires and passions to be disciplined and brought to heel. It is this historical fact that has been influential. This demonstrates (if demonstration of so obvious a truth is needed) that conceptions of freedom directly derive from views of what constitutes a self, a person, a man. Enough manipulation of the definition of man, and freedom can be made to mean whatever the manipulator wishes. Recent history has made it only too clear that the issue is not merely academic.

The consequences of distinguishing between two selves will become even clearer if one considers the two major forms which the desire to be self-directed – directed by one's 'true' self – has historically taken: the first, that of self-abnegation in order to attain independence; the second, that of self-realisation, or total self-identification with a specific principle or ideal in order to attain the selfsame end.

III

The Retreat to the Inner Citadel

I am the possessor of reason and will; I conceive ends and I desire to pursue them; but if I am prevented from attaining them I no longer feel master of the situation. I may be prevented by the laws of nature, or by accidents, or the activities of men, or the effect, often undesigned, of human institutions. These forces may be too much for me. What am I to do to avoid being crushed by them? I must liberate myself from desires that I know I cannot realise. I wish to be master of my kingdom, but my frontiers are long and insecure, therefore I contract them in order to reduce or eliminate the vulnerable area. I begin by desiring happiness, or power, or knowledge, or the attainment of some specific object. But I cannot command them. I choose to avoid defeat and waste, and therefore decide to strive for nothing that I cannot be sure to obtain. I determine myself not to desire what is unattainable. The tyrant threatens me with the destruction of my property, with imprisonment, with the exile or death of those I love. But if I no longer feel attached to property, no longer care whether or not I am in prison, if I have killed within myself my natural affections, then he cannot bend me to his will, for all that is left of myself is no longer subject to empirical fears or desires. It is as if I had performed a strategic retreat into an inner citadel – my reason, my soul, my 'noumenal' self – which, do what they may, neither external blind force, nor human malice, can touch. I have withdrawn into myself; there, and there alone, I am secure. It is as if I were to say: 'I have a wound in my leg. There are two methods of freeing myself from pain. One is to heal the wound. But if the cure is too difficult or uncertain, there is another method. I can get rid of the wound by cutting off my leg. If I train myself to want nothing to which the possession of my leg is indispensable, I shall not feel the lack of it.' This is the traditional self-emancipation of ascetics and quietists, of stoics or Buddhist sages, men of various religions or of none, who have fled the world, and escaped the yoke of society or public opinion, by some process of deliberate self-transformation that enables them to care no longer for any of its values, to remain, isolated and independent, on its edges, no longer vulnerable to its weapons. All political isolationism, all economic autarky, every form of autonomy, has in it some element of this attitude. I eliminate the obstacles in my path by abandoning the path; I retreat into my own sect, my own planned economy, my own deliberately insulated territory, where no voices from outside need be listened to, and no external forces can have effect. This is a form of the search for security; but it has also been called the search for personal or national freedom or independence.

From this doctrine, as it applies to individuals, it is no very great distance to the conceptions of those who, like Kant, identify freedom not indeed with the elimination of desires, but with resistance to them, and control over them. I identify myself with the controller and escape the slavery of the controlled. I am free because, and in so far as, I am autonomous. I obey laws, but I have imposed them on, or found them in, my own uncoerced self. Freedom is obedience, but, in Rousseau's words, 'obedience to a law which we prescribe to ourselves', and no man can enslave himself. Heteronomy is dependence on outside factors, liability to be a plaything of the external world that I cannot myself fully control, and which *pro tanto* controls and 'enslaves' me. I am free only to the degree to which my person is 'fettered' by nothing that obeys forces over which I have no control; I cannot control the laws of nature; my free activity must therefore, *ex hypothesi*, be lifted above the empirical world of causality. This is not the place in which to discuss the validity of this ancient and famous doctrine; I only wish to remark that the related notions of freedom as resistance to (or escape from) unrealisable desire, and as independence of the sphere of causality, have played a central role in politics no less than in ethics.

For if the essence of men is that they are autonomous beings – authors of values, of ends in themselves, the ultimate authority of which consists precisely in the fact that they are willed freely – then nothing is worse than to treat them as if they were not autonomous, but natural objects, played on by causal influences, creatures at the mercy of external stimuli, whose choices can be manipulated by their rulers, whether by threats of force or offers of rewards. To treat men in this way is to treat them as if they were not self-determined. 'Nobody may compel me to be happy in his own way,' said Kant. Paternalism is 'the greatest despotism imaginable'. This is so because it is to treat men as if they were not free, but human material for me, the benevolent reformer, to mould in accordance with my own, not their, freely adopted purpose. This is, of course, precisely the policy that the early utilitarians recommended. Helvétius (and Bentham) believed not in resisting, but in using, men's tendency to be slaves to their passions; they wished to dangle rewards and punishments before men – the acutest possible form of heteronomy – if by this means the 'slaves' might be made happier. But to manipulate men, to propel them towards goals which you – the social reformer – see, but they may not, is to deny their human essence, to treat them as objects without wills of their own, and therefore to degrade them. That is why to lie to men, or to deceive them, that is, to use them as means for my, not their own, independently conceived ends, even if it is for their own benefit, is, in effect, to treat them as subhuman, to behave as if their ends are less ultimate and sacred than my own. In the name of what can I ever be justified in forcing men to do what they have not willed or consented to? Only in the name of some value higher than themselves. But if, as Kant held, all values are made so by the free acts of men, and called values only so far as they are this, there is no value higher than the individual. Therefore to do this is to coerce men in the name of something less ultimate than themselves – to bend them to my will, or to someone else's particular craving for (his or their) happiness or expediency or security or convenience. I am aiming at something desired (from whatever motive, no matter how noble) by me or my group, to which I am using other men as means. But this is a contradiction of what I know men to be, namely ends in themselves. All forms of tampering with human beings, getting at them, shaping them against their will to your own pattern, all thought-control and conditioning, is, therefore, a denial of that in men which makes them men and their values ultimate.

Kant's free individual is a transcendent being, beyond the realm of natural causality. But in its empirical form – in which the notion of man is that of ordinary life – this doctrine was the heart of liberal humanism, both moral and political, that was deeply influenced both by Kant and by Rousseau in the eighteenth century. In its a priori version it is a form of secularised Protestant individualism, in which the place of God is taken by the conception of the rational life, and the place of the individual soul which strains towards union with him is replaced by the conception of the individual, endowed with reason, straining to be governed by reason and reason alone, and to depend upon nothing that might deflect or delude him by engaging his irrational nature. Autonomy, not heteronomy: to act and not to be acted upon. The notion of slavery to the passions is – for those who think in these terms – more than a metaphor. To rid myself of fear, or love, or the desire to conform is to liberate myself from the despotism of something which I cannot control. Sophocles, whom Plato reports as saying that old age alone has liberated him from the passion of love – the yoke of a cruel master – is reporting an experience as real as that of liberation from a human tyrant or slave owner. The psychological experience of observing myself yielding to some 'lower' impulse, acting from a motive that I dislike, or of doing something which at the very moment of doing I may detest, and reflecting later that I was 'not myself', or 'not in control of myself', when I did it, belongs to this way of thinking and speaking. I identify myself with my critical and rational moments. The consequences of my acts cannot matter, for they are not in my control; only my motives are. This is the creed of the solitary thinker who has defied the world and emancipated himself from the chains of men and things. In this form the doctrine may seem

primarily an ethical creed, and scarcely political at all; nevertheless its political implications are clear, and it enters into the tradition of liberal individualism at least as deeply as the 'negative' concept of freedom.

It is perhaps worth remarking that in its individualistic form the concept of the rational sage who has escaped into the inner fortress of his true self seems to arise when the external world has proved exceptionally arid, cruel or unjust. 'He is truly free', said Rousseau, 'who desires what he can perform, and does what he desire' in a world where a man seeking happiness or justice or freedom (in whatever sense) can do little, because he finds too many avenues of action blocked to him, the temptation to withdraw into himself may become irresistible. It may have been so in Greece, where the Stoic ideal cannot be wholly unconnected with the fall of the independent democracies before centralised Macedonian autocracy. It was so in Rome, for analogous reasons, after the end of the Republic. It arose in Germany in the seventeenth century, during the period of the deepest national degradation of the German States that followed the Thirty Years War, when the character of public life, particularly in the small principalities, forced those who prized the dignity of human life, not for the first or last time, into a kind of inner emigration. The doctrine that maintains that what I cannot have I must teach myself not to desire, that a desire eliminated, or successfully resisted, is as good as a desire satisfied, is a sublime, but, it seems to me, unmistakable, form of the doctrine of sour grapes: what I cannot be sure of, I cannot truly want.

This makes it clear why the definition of negative liberty as the ability to do what one wishes – which is, in effect, the definition adopted by Mill – will not do. If I find that I am able to do little or nothing of what I wish, I need only contract or extinguish my wishes, and I am made free. If the tyrant (or 'hidden persuader') manages to condition his subjects (or customers) into losing their original wishes and embracing ('internalising') the form of life he has invented for them, he will, on this definition, have succeeded in liberating them. He will, no doubt, have made them *feel* free – as Epictetus feels freer than his master (and the proverbial good man is said to feel happy on the rack). But what he has created is the very antithesis of political freedom.

Ascetic self-denial may be a source of integrity or serenity and spiritual strength, but it is difficult to see how it can be called an enlargement of liberty. If I save myself from an adversary by retreating indoors and locking every entrance and exit, I may remain freer than if I had been captured by him, but am I freer than if I had defeated or captured him? If I go too far, contract myself into too small a space, I shall suffocate and die. The logical culmination of the process of destroying everything through which I can possibly be wounded is suicide. While I exist in the natural world, I can never be wholly secure. Total liberation in this sense (as Schopenhauer correctly perceived) is conferred only by death.

I find myself in a world in which I meet with obstacles to my will. Those who are wedded to the 'negative' concept of freedom may perhaps be forgiven if they think that self-abnegation is not the only method of overcoming obstacles; that it is also possible to do so by removing them: in the case of non-human objects, by physical action; in the case of human resistance, by force or persuasion, as when I induce somebody to make room for me in his carriage, or conquer a country which threatens the interests of my own. Such acts may be unjust, they may involve violence, cruelty, the enslavement of others, but it can scarcely be denied that thereby the agent is able in the most literal sense to increase his own freedom. It is an irony of history that this truth is repudiated by some of those who practise it most forcibly, men who, even while they conquer power and freedom of action, reject the 'negative' concept of it in favour of its 'positive' counterpart. Their view

rules over half our world; let us see upon what metaphysical foundation it rests.

IV

Self-Realisation

The only true method of attaining freedom, we are told, is by the use of critical reason, the understanding of what is necessary and what is contingent. If I am a schoolboy, all but the simplest truths of mathematics obtrude themselves as obstacles to the free functioning of my mind, as theorems whose necessity I do not understand; they are pronounced to be true by some external authority, and present themselves to me as foreign bodies which I am expected mechanically to absorb into my system. But when I understand the functions of the symbols, the axioms, the formation and transformation rules – the logic whereby the conclusions are obtained – and grasp that these things cannot be otherwise, because they appear to follow from the laws that govern the processes of my own reason, then mathematical truths no longer obtrude themselves as external entities forced upon me which I must receive whether I want to or not, but as something which I now freely will in the course of the natural functioning of my own rational activity. For the mathematician, the proof of these theorems is part of the free exercise of his natural reasoning capacity. For the musician, after he has assimilated the pattern of the composer's score, and has made the composer's ends his own, the playing of the music is not obedience to external laws, a compulsion and a barrier to liberty, but a free, unimpeded exercise. The player is not bound to the score as an ox to the plough, or a factory worker to the machine. He has absorbed the score into his own system, has, by understanding it, identified it with himself, has changed it from an impediment to free activity into an element in that activity itself.

What applies to music or mathematics must,

we are told, in principle apply to all other obstacles which present themselves as so many lumps of external stuff blocking free self-development. That is the programme of enlightened rationalism from Spinoza to the latest (at times unconscious) disciples of Hegel. *Sapere aude.* What you know, that of which you understand the necessity – the rational necessity – you cannot, while remaining rational, want to be otherwise. For to want something to be other than what it must be is, given the premises – the necessities that govern the world – to be *pro tanto* either ignorant or irrational. Passions, prejudices, fears, neuroses spring from ignorance, and take the form of myths and illusions. To be ruled by myths, whether they spring from the vivid imaginations of unscrupulous charlatans who deceive us in order to exploit us, or from psychological or sociological causes, is a form of heteronomy, of being dominated by outside factors in a direction not necessarily willed by the agent. The scientific determinists of the eighteenth century supposed that the study of the sciences of nature, and the creation of sciences of society on the same model, would make the operation of such causes transparently clear, and thus enable individuals to recognise their own part in the working of a rational world, frustrating only when misunderstood. Knowledge liberates, as Epicurus taught long ago, by automatically eliminating irrational fears and desires.

Herder, Hegel and Marx substituted their own vitalistic models of social life for the older, mechanical, ones, but believed, no less than their opponents, that to understand the world is to be freed. They merely differed from them in stressing the part played by change and growth in what made human beings human. Social life could not be understood by an analogy drawn from mathematics or physics. One must also understand history, that is, the peculiar laws of continuous growth, whether by 'dialectical' conflict or otherwise, that govern individuals and groups in their interplay with each other and with nature. Not to grasp this is, according to

these thinkers, to fall into a particular kind of error, namely the belief that human nature is static, that its essential properties are the same everywhere and at all times, that it is governed by unvarying natural laws, whether they are conceived in theological or materialistic terms, which entails the fallacious corollary that a wise lawgiver can, in principle, create a perfectly harmonious society at any time by appropriate education and legislation, because rational men, in all ages and countries, must always demand the same unaltering satisfactions of the same unaltering basic needs. Hegel believed that his contemporaries (and indeed all his predecessors) misunderstood the nature of institutions because they did not understand the laws – the rationally intelligible laws, since they spring from the operation of reason – that create and alter institutions and transform human character and human action. Marx and his disciples maintained that the path of human beings was obstructed not only by natural forces, or the imperfections of their own characters, but, even more, by the workings of their own social institutions, which they had originally created (not always consciously) for certain purposes, but whose functioning they systematically came to misconceive, in practice even more than in theory, and which thereupon became obstacles to their creators' progress. Marx offered social and economic hypotheses to account for the inevitability of such misunderstanding, in particular of the illusion that such man-made arrangements were independent forces, as inescapable as the laws of nature. As instances of such pseudo-objective forces, he pointed to the laws of supply and demand, or the institution of property, or the eternal division of society into rich and poor, or owners and workers, as so many unaltering human categories. Not until we had reached a stage at which the spells of these illusions could be broken, that is, until enough men reached a social stage that alone enabled them to understand that these laws and institutions were themselves the work of human minds and hands, historically needed in their day, and later mistaken for inexorable, objective powers, could the old world be destroyed, and more adequate and liberating social machinery substituted.

We are enslaved by despots – institutions or beliefs or neuroses – which can be removed only by being analysed and understood. We are imprisoned by evil spirits which we have ourselves – albeit not consciously – created, and can exorcise them only by becoming conscious and acting appropriately: indeed, for Marx understanding is appropriate action. I am free if, and only if, I plan my life in accordance with my own will; plans entail rules; a rule does not oppress me or enslave me if I impose it on myself consciously, or accept it freely, having understood it, whether it was invented by me or by others, provided that it is rational, that is to say, conforms to the necessities of things. To understand why things must be as they must be is to will them to be so. Knowledge liberates not by offering us more open possibilities amongst which we can make our choice, but by preserving us from the frustration of attempting the impossible. To want necessary laws to be other than they are is to be prey to an irrational desire – a desire that what must be X should also be not-X. To go further, and believe these laws to be other than what they necessarily are, is to be insane. That is the metaphysical heart of rationalism. The notion of liberty contained in it is not the 'negative' conception of a field (ideally) without obstacles, a vacuum in which nothing obstructs me, but the notion of self-direction or self-control. I can do what I will with my own. I am a rational being; whatever I can demonstrate to myself as being necessary, as incapable of being otherwise in a rational society – that is, in a society directed by rational minds, towards goals such as a rational being would have – I cannot, being rational, wish to sweep out of my way. I assimilate it into my substance as I do the laws of logic, of mathematics, of physics, the rules of art, the principles that govern everything of which I understand, and therefore will, the rational purpose, by which I can never be thwarted, since I cannot want it to be other than it is.

This is the positive doctrine of liberation by reason. Socialised forms of it, widely disparate and opposed to each other as they are, are at the heart of many of the nationalist, Communist, authoritarian, and totalitarian creeds of our day. It may, in the course of its evolution, have wandered far from its rationalist moorings. Nevertheless, it is this freedom that, in democracies and in dictatorships, is argued about, and fought for, in many parts of the earth today. Without attempting to trace the historical evolution of this idea, I should like to comment on some of its vicissitudes.

V

The Temple of Sarastro

Those who believed in freedom as rational self-direction were bound, sooner or later, to consider how this was to be applied not merely to a man's inner life, but to his relations with other members of his society. Even the most individualistic among them – and Rousseau, Kant and Fichte certainly began as individualists – came at some point to ask themselves whether a rational life not only for the individual, but also for society, was possible, and if so, how it was to be achieved. I wish to be free to live as my rational will (my 'real self') commands, but so must others be. How am I to avoid collisions with their wills? Where is the frontier that lies between my (rationally determined) rights and the identical rights of others? For if I am rational, I cannot deny that what is right for me must, for the same reasons, be right for others who are rational like me. A rational (or free) State would be a State governed by such laws as all rational men would freely accept; that is to say, such laws as they would themselves have enacted had they been asked what, as rational beings, they demanded; hence the frontiers would be such as all rational men would consider to be the right frontiers for rational beings.

But who, in fact, was to determine what these frontiers were? Thinkers of this type argued that if moral and political problems were genuine – as surely they were – they must in principle be soluble; that is to say, there must exist one and only one true solution to any problem. All truths could in principle be discovered by any rational thinker, and demonstrated so clearly that all other rational men could not but accept them; indeed, this was already to a large extent the case in the new natural sciences. On this assumption the problem of political liberty was soluble by establishing a just order that would give to each man all the freedom to which a rational being was entitled. My claim to unfettered freedom can prima facie at times not be reconciled with your equally unqualified claim; but the rational solution of one problem cannot collide with the equally true solution of another, for two truths cannot logically be incompatible; therefore a just order must in principle be discoverable – an order of which the rules make possible correct solutions to all possible problems that could arise in it. This ideal, harmonious state of affairs was sometimes imagined as a Garden of Eden before the Fall of Man, an Eden from which we were expelled, but for which we were still filled with longing; or as a golden age still before us, in which men, having become rational, will no longer be 'other-directed', nor 'alienate' or frustrate one another. In existing societies justice and equality are ideals which still call for some measure of coercion, because the premature lifting of social controls might lead to the oppression of the weaker and the stupider by the stronger or abler or more energetic and unscrupulous. But it is only irrationality on the part of men (according to this doctrine) that leads them to wish to oppress or exploit or humiliate one another. Rational men will respect the principle of reason in each other, and lack all desire to fight or dominate one another. The desire to dominate is itself a symptom of irrationality, and can be explained and cured by rational methods. Spinoza offers one kind of explanation and remedy, Hegel another, Marx a third. Some of these theories may perhaps, to some degree, supplement each other, others are not combinable. But they all assume that in a society of perfectly rational beings the lust for domination over men will be absent or ineffective. The existence of, or cravings for, oppression will be the first symptom that the true solution to the problems of social life has not been reached.

This can be put in another way. Freedom is self-mastery, the elimination of obstacles to my will, whatever these obstacles may be – the resistance of nature, of my ungoverned passions, of irrational institutions, of the opposing wills or behaviour of others. Nature I can, at least in principle, always mould by technical means, and shape to my will. But how am I to treat recalcitrant human beings? I must, if I can, impose my will on them too, 'mould' them to my pattern, cast parts for them in my play. But will this not mean that I alone am free, while they are slaves? They will be so if my plan has nothing to do with their wishes or values, only with my own. But if my plan is fully rational, it will allow for the full development of their 'true' natures, the realisation of their capacities for rational decisions, for 'making the best of themselves' – as a part of the realisation of my own 'true' self. All true solutions to all genuine problems must be compatible: more than this, they must fit into a single whole; for this is what is meant by calling them all rational and the universe harmonious. Each man has his specific character, abilities, aspirations, ends. If I grasp both what these ends and natures are, and how they all relate to one another, I can, at least in principle, if I have the knowledge and the strength, satisfy them all, so long as the nature and the purposes in question are rational. Rationality is knowing things and people for what they are: I must not use stones to make violins, nor try to make born violin-players play flutes. If the universe is governed by reason, then there will be no need for coercion; a correctly planned life for all will coincide with full freedom – the freedom of rational self-direction – for all. This will be so if, and only if, the plan is the true plan – the one unique pattern which alone fulfils the claims of reason. Its laws will be the rules which reason prescribes: they will only seem irksome to those whose reason is dormant, who do not understand the true 'needs' of their own 'real' selves. So long as each player recognises and plays the part set him by reason – the faculty that understands his true nature and discerns his true ends – there can be no conflict. Each man will be a liberated, self-directed actor in the cosmic drama. Thus Spinoza tells us that children, although they are coerced, are not slaves, because they obey orders given in their own interests, and that the subject of a true commonwealth is no slave, because the common interests must include his own. Similarly, Locke says 'Where there is no law there is no freedom', because rational law is a direction to a man's 'proper interests' or 'general good'; and adds that since law of this kind is what 'hedges us in only from bogs and precipices' it 'ill deserves the name of confinement', and speaks of desires to escape from it as being irrational, forms of 'licence', as 'brutish', and so on. Montesquieu, forgetting his liberal moments, speaks of political liberty as being not permission to do what we want, or even what the law allows, but only 'the power of doing what we ought to will', which Kant virtually repeats. Burke proclaims the individual's 'right' to be restrained in his own interest, because 'the presumed consent of every rational creature is in unison with the predisposed order of things'.

The common assumption of these thinkers (and of many a schoolman before them and Jacobin and Communist after them) is that the rational ends of our 'true' natures must coincide, or be made to coincide, however violently our poor, ignorant, desire-ridden, passionate, empirical selves may cry out against this process.

Freedom is not freedom to do what is irrational, or stupid, or wrong. To force empirical selves into the right pattern is no tyranny, but liberation. Rousseau tells me that if I freely surrender all the parts of my life to society, I create an entity which, because it has been built by an equality of sacrifice of all its members, cannot wish to hurt any one of them; in such a society, we are informed, it can be in nobody's interest to damage anyone else. 'In giving myself to all, I give myself to none', and get back as much as I lose, with enough new force to preserve my new gains. Kant tells us that when 'the individual has entirely abandoned his wild, lawless freedom, to find it again, unimpaired, in a state of dependence according to law', that alone is true freedom, 'for this dependence is the work of my own will acting as a lawgiver'. Liberty, so far from being incompatible with authority, becomes virtually identical with it. This is the thought and language of all the declarations of the rights of man in the eighteenth century, and of all those who look upon society as a design constructed according to the rational laws of the wise lawgiver, or of nature, or of history, or of the Supreme Being. Bentham, almost alone, doggedly went on repeating that the business of laws was not to liberate but to restrain: every law is an infraction of liberty – even if such infraction leads to an increase of the sum of liberty.

If the underlying assumptions had been correct – if the method of solving social problems resembled the way in which solutions to the problems of the natural sciences are found, and if reason were what rationalists said that it was – all this would perhaps follow. In the ideal case, liberty coincides with law: autonomy with authority. A law which forbids me to do what I could not, as a sane being, conceivably wish to do is not a restraint of my freedom. In the ideal society, composed of wholly responsible beings, rules, because I should scarcely be conscious of them, would gradually wither away. Only one social movement was bold enough to render this assumption quite explicit and accept its consequences – that of the Anarchists. But all forms of liberalism founded on a rationalist metaphysics are less or more watered-down versions of this creed.

In due course, the thinkers who bent their energies to the solution of the problem on these lines came to be faced with the question of how in practice men were to be made rational in this way. Clearly they must be educated. For the uneducated are irrational, heteronomous, and need to be coerced, if only to make life tolerable for the rational if they are to live in the same society and not be compelled to withdraw to a desert or some Olympian height. But the uneducated cannot be expected to understand or co-operate with the purposes of their educators. Education, says Fichte, must inevitably work in such a way that 'you will later recognise the reasons for what I am doing now'. Children cannot be expected to understand why they are compelled to go to school, nor the ignorant – that is, for the moment, the majority of mankind – why they are made to obey the laws that will presently make them rational. 'Compulsion is also a kind of education.' You learn the great virtue of obedience to superior persons. If you cannot understand your own interests as a rational being, I cannot be expected to consult you, or abide by your wishes, in the course of making you rational. I must, in the end, force you to be protected against smallpox, even though you may not wish it. Even Mill is prepared to say that I may forcibly prevent a man from crossing a bridge if there is not time to warn him that it is about to collapse, for I know, or am justified in assuming, that he cannot wish to fall into the water. Fichte knows what the uneducated German of his time wishes to be or do better than he can possibly know this for himself. The sage knows you better than you know yourself, for you are the victim of your passions, a slave living a heteronomous life, purblind, unable to understand your true goals. You want to be a human being. It is the aim of the State to satisfy your wish. 'Compulsion is justi-fied by education for future insight.' The reason within me, if it is to triumph, must eliminate and suppress my 'lower' instincts, my passions and desires, which render me a slave; similarly (the fatal transition from individual to social concepts is almost imperceptible) the higher elements in society – the better educated, the more rational, those who 'possess the highest insight of their time and people' – may exercise compulsion to rationalise the irrational section of society. For – so Hegel, Bradley, Bosanquet have often assured us – by obeying the rational man we obey ourselves: not indeed as we are, sunk in our ignorance and our passions, weak creatures afflicted by diseases that need a healer, wards who require a guardian, but as we could be if we were rational; as we could be even now, if only we would listen to the rational element which is, *ex hypothesi*, within every human being who deserves the name.

The philosophers of 'Objective Reason', from the tough, rigidly centralised, 'organic' State of Fichte, to the mild and humane liberalism of T. H. Green, certainly supposed themselves to be fulfilling, and not resisting, the rational demands which, however inchoate, were to be found in the breast of every sentient being.

But I may reject such democratic optimism, and turning away from the teleological determinism of the Hegelians towards some more voluntarist philosophy, conceive the idea of imposing on my society – for its own betterment – a plan of my own, which in my rational wisdom I have elaborated; and which, unless I act on my own, perhaps against the permanent wishes of the vast majority of my fellow citizens, may never come to fruition at all. Or, abandoning the concept of reason altogether, I may conceive myself as an inspired artist, who moulds men into patterns in the light of his unique vision, as painters combine colours or composers sounds; humanity is the raw material upon which I impose my creative will; even though men suffer and die in the process, they are lifted by it to a height to which they could never have risen without my coercive – but creative – violation of their lives. This is the argument used by every dictator, inquisitor and bully who seeks some moral, or even aesthetic, justification for his conduct. I must do for men (or with them) what they cannot do for themselves, and I cannot ask their permission or consent, because they are in no condition to know what is best for them; indeed, what they will permit and accept may mean a life of contemptible mediocrity, or perhaps even their ruin and suicide. Let me quote from the true progenitor of the heroic doctrine, Fichte, once again: 'No one has . . . rights against reason.' 'Man is afraid of subordinating his subjectivity to the laws of reason. He prefers tradition or arbitrariness.' Nevertheless, subordinated he must be. Fichte puts forward the claims of what he called reason; Napoleon, or Carlyle, or romantic authoritarians may worship other values, and see in their establishment by force the only path to 'true' freedom.

The same attitude was pointedly expressed by August Comte, who asked why, if we do not allow free thinking in chemistry or biology, we should allow it in morals or politics. Why indeed? If it makes sense to speak of political truths – assertions of social ends which all men, because they are men, must, once they are discovered, agree to be such; and if, as Comte believed, scientific method will in due course reveal them; then what case is there for freedom of opinion or action – at least as an end in itself, and not merely as a stimulating intellectual climate – either for individuals or for groups? Why should any conduct be tolerated that is not authorised by appropriate experts? Comte put bluntly what had been implicit in the rationalist theory of politics from its ancient Greek beginnings. There can, in principle, be only one correct way of life; the wise lead it spontaneously, that is why they are called wise. The unwise must be dragged towards it by all the social means in the power of the wise; for why should demonstrable error be suffered to survive and breed?

The immature and untutored must be made to say to themselves: 'Only the truth liberates, and the only way in which I can learn the truth is by doing blindly today what you, who know it, order me, or coerce me, to do, in the certain knowledge that only thus will I arrive at your clear vision, and be free like you.'

We have wandered indeed from our liberal beginnings. This argument, employed by Fichte in his latest phase, and after him by other defenders of authority, from Victorian schoolmasters and colonial administrators to the latest nationalist or Communist dictator, is precisely what the Stoic and Kantian morality protests against most bitterly in the name of the reason of the free individual following his own inner light. In this way the rationalist argument, with its assumption of the single true solution, has led by steps which, if not logically valid, are historically and psychologically intelligible from an ethical doctrine of individual responsibility and individual self-perfection to an authoritarian State obedient to the directives of an élite of Platonic guardians.

What can have led to so strange a reversal – the transformation of Kant's severe individualism into something close to a pure totalitarian doctrine on the part of thinkers some of whom claimed to be his disciples? This question is not of merely historical interest, for not a few contemporary liberals have gone through the same peculiar evolution. It is true that Kant insisted, following Rousseau, that a capacity for rational self-direction belonged to all men; that there could be no experts in moral matters, since morality was a matter not of specialised knowledge (as the Utilitarians and *philosophes* had maintained), but of the correct use of a universal human faculty; and consequently that what made men free was not acting in certain self-improving ways, which they could be coerced to do, but knowing why they ought to do so, which nobody could do for, or on behalf of, anyone else. But even Kant, when he came to deal with political issues, conceded that no law, provided that it was such that I should, if I were asked, approve it as a rational being, could possibly deprive me of any portion of my rational freedom. With this the door was opened wide to the rule of experts. I cannot consult all men about all enactments all the time. The government cannot be a continuous plebiscite. Moreover, some men are not as well attuned to the voice of their own reason as others: some seem singularly deaf. If I am a legislator or a ruler, I must assume that if the law I impose is rational (and I can consult only my own reason) it will automatically be approved by all the members of my society so far as they are rational beings. For if they disapprove, they must, *pro tanto*, be irrational; then they will need to be repressed by reason: whether their own or mine cannot matter, for the pronouncements of reason must be the same in all minds. I issue my orders and, if you resist, take it upon myself to repress the irrational element in you which opposes reason. My task would be easier if you repressed it in yourself; I try to educate you to do so. But I am responsible for public welfare, I cannot wait until all men are wholly rational. Kant may protest that the essence of the subject's freedom is that he, and he alone, has given himself the order to obey. But this is a counsel of perfection. If you fail to discipline yourself, I must do so for you; and you cannot complain of lack of freedom, for the fact that Kant's rational judge has sent you to prison is evidence that you have not listened to your own inner reason, that, like a child, a savage, an idiot, you are either not ripe for self-direction, or permanently incapable of it.

If this leads to despotism, albeit by the best or the wisest – to Sarastro's temple in *The Magic Flute* – but still despotism, which turns out to be identical with freedom, can it be that there is something amiss in the premises of the argument? That the basic assumptions are themselves somewhere at fault? Let me state them once more; first, that all men have one true purpose, and one only, that of rational self-direction; second, that the ends of all rational beings must of

necessity fit into a single universal, harmonious pattern, which some men may be able to discern more clearly than others; third, that all conflict, and consequently all tragedy, is due solely to the clash of reason with the irrational or the insufficiently rational – the immature and undeveloped elements in life, whether individual or communal – and that such clashes are, in principle, avoidable, and for wholly rational beings impossible; finally, that when all men have been made rational, they will obey the rational laws of their own natures, which are one and the same in them all, and so be at once wholly law-abiding and wholly free. Can it be that Socrates and the creators of the central Western tradition in ethics and politics who followed him have been mistaken, for more than two millennia, that virtue is not knowledge, nor freedom identical with either? That despite the fact that it rules the lives of more men than ever before in its long history, not one of the basic assumptions of this famous view is demonstrable, or, perhaps, even true?

VI

The Search for Status

[. . .] No doubt every interpretation of the word 'liberty', however unusual, must include a minimum of what I have called 'negative' liberty. There must be an area within which I am not frustrated. No society literally suppresses all the liberties of its members; a being who is prevented by others from doing anything at all on his own is not a moral agent at all, and could not either legally or morally be regarded as a human being, even if a physiologist or a biologist, or even a psychologist, felt inclined to classify him as a man. But the fathers of liberalism – Mill and Constant – want more than this minimum: they demand a maximum degree of non-interference compatible with the minimum demands of social life. It seems unlikely that this extreme demand for liberty has ever been made by any but a small minority of highly civilised and self-conscious human beings. The bulk of humanity has certainly at most times been prepared to sacrifice this to other goals: security, status, prosperity, power, virtue, rewards in the next world; or justice, equality, fraternity, and many other values which appear wholly, or in part, incompatible with the attainment of the greatest degree of individual liberty, and certainly do not need it as a precondition for their own realisation. It is not a demand for *Lebensraum* for each individual that has stimulated the rebellions and wars of liberation for which men have been ready to die in the past, or, indeed, in the present. Men who have fought for freedom have commonly fought for the right to be governed by themselves or their representatives – sternly governed, if need be, like the Spartans, with little individual liberty, but in a manner which allowed them to participate, or at any rate to believe that they were participating, in the legislation and administration of their collective lives. And men who have made revolutions have, as often as not, meant by liberty no more than the conquest of power and authority by a given sect of believers in a doctrine, or by a class, or by some other social group, old or new. Their victories certainly frustrated those whom they ousted, and sometimes repressed, enslaved or exterminated vast numbers of human beings. Yet such revolutionaries have usually felt it necessary to argue that, despite this, they represented the party of liberty, or 'true' liberty, by claiming universality for their ideal, which the 'real selves' of even those who resisted them were also alleged to be seeking, although they were held to have lost the way to the goal, or to have mistaken the goal itself owing to some moral or spiritual blindness. All this has little to do with Mill's notion of liberty as limited only by the danger of doing harm to others. It is the non-recognition of this psychological and political fact (which lurks behind the apparent ambiguity of the term 'liberty') that has, perhaps, blinded some contemporary liberals to the world in which they live. Their plea is clear, their cause is just. But they do not allow for the variety of basic human needs. Nor yet for the ingenuity with which men can prove to their own satisfaction that the road to one ideal also leads to its contrary. [. . .]

VIII

The One and the Many

One belief, more than any other, is responsible for the slaughter of individuals on the altars of the great historical ideals – justice or progress or the happiness of future generations, or the sacred mission or emancipation of a nation or race or class, or even liberty itself, which demands the sacrifice of individuals for the freedom of society. This is the belief that somewhere, in the past or in the future, in divine revelation or in the mind of an individual thinker, in the pronouncements of history or science, or in the simple heart of an uncorrupted good man, there is a final solution. This ancient faith rests on the conviction that all the positive values in which men have believed must, in the end, be compatible, and perhaps even entail one another. 'Nature binds truth, happiness and virtue together by an indissoluble chain,' said one of the best men who ever lived, and spoke in similar terms of liberty, equality and justice.

But is this true? It is a commonplace that neither political equality nor efficient organisation nor social justice is compatible with more than a modicum of individual liberty, and certainly not with unrestricted *laissez-faire*; that justice and generosity, public and private loyalties, the demands of genius and the claims of society can conflict violently with each other. And it is no great way from that to the generalisation that not all good things are compatible, still less all the ideals of mankind. But somewhere, we shall be told, and in some way, it must be possible for all these values to live together, for unless this is so, the universe is not a cosmos, not a harmony; unless this is so, conflicts of values may be an intrinsic, irremovable element in human life. To admit that the fulfilment of some of our ideals may in principle make the fulfilment of others impossible is to say that the notion of total human fulfilment is a formal contradiction, a metaphysical chimera. For every rationalist metaphysician, from Plato to the last disciples of Hegel or Marx, this abandonment of the notion of a final harmony in which all riddles are solved, all contradictions reconciled, is a piece of crude empiricism, abdication before brute facts, intolerable bankruptcy of reason before things as they are, failure to explain and to justify, to reduce everything to a system, which 'reason' indignantly rejects.

But if we are not armed with an a priori guarantee of the proposition that a total harmony of true values is somewhere to be found – perhaps in some ideal realm the characteristics of which we can, in our finite state, not so much as conceive – we must fall back on the ordinary resources of empirical observation and ordinary human knowledge. And these certainly give us no warrant for supposing (or even understanding what would be meant by saying) that all good things, or all bad things for that matter, are reconcilable with each other. The world that we encounter in ordinary experience is one in which we are faced with choices between ends equally ultimate, and claims equally absolute, the realisation of some of which must inevitably involve the sacrifice of others. Indeed, it is because this is their situation that men place such immense value upon the freedom to choose; for if they had assurance that in some perfect state, realisable by men on earth, no ends pursued by them would ever be in conflict, the necessity and agony of choice would disappear, and with it the central importance of the freedom to choose. Any method of bringing this final state nearer would then seem fully justified, no matter how much freedom were sacrificed to forward its advance.

It is, I have no doubt, some such dogmatic certainty that has been responsible for the deep, serene, unshakeable conviction in the minds of some of the most merciless tyrants and persecutors in history that what they did was fully justified by its purpose. I do not say that the ideal of self-perfection – whether for individuals or nations or Churches or classes – is to be condemned in itself, or that the language which was used in its defence was in all cases the result of a confused or fraudulent use of words, or of moral or intellectual perversity. Indeed, I have tried to show that it is the notion of freedom in its 'positive' sense that is at the heart of the demands for national or social self-direction which animate the most powerful and morally just public movements of our time, and that not to recognise this is to misunderstand the most vital facts and ideas of our age. But equally it seems to me that the belief that some single formula can in principle be found whereby all the diverse ends of men can be harmoniously realised is demonstrably false. If, as I believe, the ends of men are many, and not all of them are in principle compatible with each other, then the possibility of conflict – and of tragedy – can never wholly be eliminated from human life, either personal or social. The necessity of choosing between absolute claims is then an inescapable characteristic of the human condition. This gives its value to freedom as Acton conceived of it – as an end in itself, and not as a temporary need, arising out of our confused notions and irrational and disordered lives, a predicament which a panacea could one day put right.

I do not wish to say that individual freedom is, even in the most liberal societies, the sole, or even the dominant, criterion of social action. We compel children to be educated, and we forbid public executions. These are certainly curbs to freedom. We justify them on the ground that ignorance, or a barbarian upbringing, or cruel pleasures and excitements are worse for us than the amount of restraint needed to repress them. This judgement in turn depends on how we determine good and evil, that is to say, on our moral, religious, intellectual, economic and aesthetic values; which are, in their turn, bound up with our conception of man, and of the basic demands of his nature. In other words, our solution of such problems is based on our vision, by which we are consciously or unconsciously guided, of what constitutes a fulfilled human life, as contrasted with Mill's 'cramped and dwarfed', 'pinched and hide-bound' natures. To protest against the laws governing censorship or personal morals as intolerable infringements of personal liberty presupposes a belief that the activities which such laws forbid are fundamental needs of men as men, in a good (or, indeed, any) society. To defend such laws is to hold that these needs are not essential, or that they cannot be satisfied without sacrificing other values which come higher – satisfy deeper needs – than individual freedom, determined by some standard that is not merely subjective, a standard for which some objective status – empirical or a priori – is claimed.

The extent of a man's, or a people's, liberty to choose to live as he or they desire must be weighed against the claims of many other values, of which equality, or justice, or happiness, or security, or public order are perhaps the most obvious examples. For this reason, it cannot be unlimited. We are rightly reminded by R. H. Tawney that the liberty of the strong, whether their strength is physical or economic, must be restrained. This maxim claims respect, not as a consequence of some a priori rule, whereby the respect for the liberty of one man logically entails respect for the liberty of others like him; but simply because respect for the principles of justice, or shame at gross inequality of treatment, is as basic in men as the desire for liberty. That we cannot have everything is a necessary, not a contingent, truth. Burke's plea for the constant need to compensate, to reconcile, to balance; Mill's plea for novel 'experiments in living' with their permanent possibility of error – the knowledge that it is not merely in practice but in principle impossible to reach clear-cut and certain answers, even in an ideal world of wholly good and rational men and wholly clear ideas – may madden those who seek for final solutions and single, all-embracing systems, guaranteed to

be eternal. Nevertheless, it is a conclusion that cannot be escaped by those who, with Kant, have learnt the truth that 'Out of the crooked timber of humanity no straight thing was ever made.'

There is little need to stress the fact that monism, and faith in a single criterion, have always proved a deep source of satisfaction both to the intellect and to the emotions. Whether the standard of judgement derives from the vision of some future perfection, as in the minds of the *philosophes* in the eighteenth century and their technocratic successors in our own day, or is rooted in the past – *la terre et les morts* – as maintained by German historicists or French theocrats, or neo-Conservatives in English-speaking countries, it is bound, provided it is inflexible enough, to encounter some unforeseen and unforeseeable human development, which it will not fit; and will then be used to justify the a priori barbarities of Procrustes – the vivisection of actual human societies into some fixed pattern dictated by our fallible understanding of a largely imaginary past or a wholly imaginary future. To preserve our absolute categories or ideals at the expense of human lives offends equally against the principles of science and of history; it is an attitude found in equal measure on the right and left wings in our days, and is not reconcilable with the principles accepted by those who respect the facts.

Pluralism, with the measure of 'negative' liberty that it entails, seems to me a truer and more humane ideal than the goals of those who seek in the great disciplined, authoritarian structures the ideal of 'positive' self-mastery by classes, or peoples, or the whole of mankind. It is truer, because it does, at least, recognise the fact that human goals are many, not all of them commensurable, and in perpetual rivalry with one another. To assume that all values can be graded on one scale, so that it is a mere matter of inspection to determine the highest, seems to me to falsify our knowledge that men are free agents, to represent moral decision as an operation which a slide-rule could, in principle, perform. To say that in some ultimate, all-reconciling yet realisable synthesis duty is interest, or individual freedom is pure democracy or an authoritarian State, is to throw a metaphysical blanket over either self-deceit or deliberate hypocrisy. It is more humane because it does not (as the system-builders do) deprive men, in the name of some remote, or incoherent, ideal, of much that they have found to be indispensable to their life as unpredictably self-transforming human beings. In the end, men choose between ultimate values; they choose as they do because their life and thought are determined by fundamental moral categories and concepts that are, at any rate over large stretches of time and space, and whatever their ultimate origins, a part of their being and thought and sense of their own identity; part of what makes them human.

It may be that the ideal of freedom to choose ends without claiming eternal validity for them, and the pluralism of values connected with this, is only the late fruit of our declining capitalist civilisation: an ideal which remote ages and primitive societies have not recognised, and one which posterity will regard with curiosity, even sympathy, but little comprehension. This may be so; but no sceptical conclusions seem to me to follow. Principles are not less sacred because their duration cannot be guaranteed. Indeed, the very desire for guarantees that our values are eternal and secure in some objective heaven is perhaps only a craving for the certainties of childhood or the absolute values of our primitive past. 'To realise the relative validity of one's convictions', said an admirable writer of our time, 'and yet stand for them unflinchingly is what distinguishes a civilised man from a barbarian.' To demand more than this is perhaps a deep and incurable metaphysical need; but to allow such a need to determine one's practice is a symptom of an equally deep, and more dangerous, moral and political immaturity.

Chapter 35

Franklin Delano Roosevelt

THE FOUR FREEDOMS
Annual Message to Congress, January 6, 1941

Franklin Delano Roosevelt (F.D.R.) (1882–1945) was the thirty-second president of the United States, famous for his "New Deal" which sought to relieve the economic depression of the country through a variety of government and social programs. In this excerpt from one of his more famous speeches (1941), Roosevelt draws a connection between the classical freedoms of the American founding (freedom of speech and religion) and other freedoms which would later become hallmarks of twentieth-century American liberalism (freedom from want and from fear).

In the future days, which we seek to make secure, we look forward to a world founded upon four essential human freedoms.

The first is freedom of speech and expression—everywhere in the world.

The second is freedom of every person to worship God in his own way—everywhere in the world.

The third is freedom from want—which, translated into world terms, means economic understandings which will secure to every nation a healthy peacetime life for its inhabitants—everywhere in the world.

The fourth is freedom from fear—which, translated into world terms, means a world-wide reduction of armaments to such a point and in such a thorough fashion that no nation will be in a position to commit an act of physical aggression against any neighbor—anywhere in the world.

That is no vision of a distant millennium. It is a definite basis for a kind of world attainable in our own time and generation. That kind of world is the very antithesis of the so-called new order of tyranny which the dictators seek to create with the crash of a bomb.

To that new order we oppose the greater conception—the moral order. A good society is able to face schemes of world domination and foreign revolutions alike without fear.

Since the beginning of our American history, we have been engaged in change—in a perpetual peaceful revolution—a revolution which goes on steadily, quietly adjusting itself to changing conditions—without the concentration camp or the quick-lime in the ditch. The world order which we seek is the cooperation of free countries, working together in a friendly, civilized society.

This nation has placed its destiny in the hands and heads and hearts of its millions of free men and women; and its faith in freedom under the guidance of God. Freedom means the supremacy of human rights everywhere. Our support goes to those who struggle to gain those rights or keep them. Our strength is our unity of purpose. To that high concept there can be no end save victory.

Chapter 36

George Fitzhugh

CAPITALISM AS SLAVERY

George Fitzhugh (1806–1881) was an American social theorist and notorious defender of slavery. These excerpts are drawn from his most famous book, *Cannibals All! Or Slaves Without Masters* (1857). In that book, Fitzhugh criticizes capitalism as a kind of wage-slavery in which the poor suffer all the evils of despotism with none of the beneficent oversight that, in Fitzhugh's mind, the system of Southern slavery provided. As a result, he argues, working men in the North are actually less free than slaves in the South.

The Universal Trade

We are all, North and South, engaged in the White Slave Trade, and he who succeeds best is esteemed most respectable. It is far more cruel than the Black Slave Trade, because it exacts more of its slaves, and neither protects nor governs them. We boast that it exacts more when we say, "that the profits made from employing free labor are greater than those from slave labor." The profits, made from free labor, are the amount of the products of such labor, which the employer, by means of the command which capital or skill gives him, takes away, exacts, or "exploitates" from the free laborer. The profits of slave labor are that portion of the products of such labor which the power of the master enables him to appropriate. These profits are less, because the master allows the slave to retain a larger share of the results of his own labor than do the employers of free labor. But we not only boast that the White Slave Trade is more exacting and fraudulent (in fact, though not in intention) than Black Slavery; but we also boast that it is more cruel, in leaving the laborer to take care of himself and family out of the pittance which skill or capital have allowed him to retain. When the day's labor is ended, he is free, but is overburdened with the cares of family and household, which make his freedom an empty and delusive mockery. But his employer is really free, and may enjoy the profits made by others' labor, without a care, or a trouble, as to their well-being. The negro slave is free, too, when the labors of the day are over, and free in mind as well as body; for the master provides food, raiment, house, fuel, and everything else necessary to the physical well-being of himself and family. The master's labors commence just when the slave's end. No wonder men should prefer white slavery to capital, to negro slavery, since it is more profitable, and is free from all the cares and labors of black slave-holding.

Now, reader, if you wish to know yourself – to "descant on your own deformity" – read on. But if you would cherish self-conceit, self-esteem, or self-appreciation, throw down our book; for we will dispel illusions which have promoted your happiness, and show you that what you have considered and practiced as virtue is little better than moral Cannibalism. But you will find yourself in numerous and respectable company; for all good and respectable people are "Cannibals all" who do not labor, or who are successfully trying to live without labor, on the unrequited labor of other people: – Whilst low, bad, and disreputable people, are those who labor to support themselves, and to support said respectable people besides. Throwing the negro slaves out of the account, and society is divided in Christendom into four classes: the rich, or independent respectable people, who live well and labor not at all, the professional and skillful respectable people, who do a little light work, for enormous wages; the poor hard-working people, who support everybody, and starve themselves; and the poor thieves, swindlers, and sturdy beggars, who live like gentlemen, without labor, on the labor of other people. The gentlemen exploitate, which being done on a large scale and requiring a great many victims, is highly respectable – whilst the rogues and beggars take so little from others that they fare little better than those who labor.

But, reader, we do not wish to fire into the flock. "Thou art the man!" You are a Cannibal! and if a successful one, pride yourself on the number of your victims quite as much as any Fiji chieftain, who breakfasts, dines, and sups on human flesh – and your conscience smites you, if you have failed to succeed, quite as much as his, when he returns from an unsuccessful foray.

Probably, you are a lawyer, or a merchant, or a doctor, who has made by your business fifty thousand dollars, and retired to live on your capital. But, mark! not to spend your capital. That would be vulgar, disreputable, criminal. That would be, to live by your own labor; for your capital is your amassed labor. That would be to do as common working men do; for they take the pittance which their employers leave them to live

on. They live by labor; for they exchange the results of their own labor for the products of other people's labor. It is, no doubt, an honest, vulgar way of living, but not at all a respectable way. The respectable way of living is to make other people work for you, and to pay them nothing for so doing – and to have no concern about them after their work is done. Hence, white slave-holding is much more respectable than negro slavery – for the master works nearly as hard for the negro as he for the master. But you, my virtuous, respectable reader, exact three thousand dollars per annum from white labor (for your income is the product of white labor) and make not one cent of return in any form. You retain your capital, and never labor, and yet live in luxury on the labor of others. Capital commands labor, as the master does the slave. Neither pays for labor; but the master permits the slave to retain a larger allowance from the proceeds of his own labor, and hence "free labor is cheaper than slave labor." You, with the command over labor which your capital gives you, are a slave owner – a master, without the obligations of a master. They who work for you, who create your income, are slaves, without the rights of slaves. Slaves without a master! Whilst you were engaged in amassing your capital, in seeking to become independent, you were in the White Slave Trade. To become independent is to be able to make other people support you, without being obliged to labor for them. Now, what man in society is not seeking to attain this situation? He who attains it is a slave owner, in the worst sense. He who is in pursuit of it is engaged in the slave trade. You, reader, belong to the one or other class. The men without property, in free society, are theoretically in a worse condition than slaves. Practically, their condition corresponds with this theory, as history and statistics everywhere demonstrate. The capitalists, in free society, live in ten times the luxury and show that Southern masters do, because the slaves to capital work harder and cost less than negro slaves.

The negro slaves of the South are the happiest, and, in some sense, the freest people in the world. The children and the aged and infirm work not at all, and yet have all the comforts and necessaries of life provided for them. They enjoy liberty, because they are oppressed neither by care nor labor. The women do little hard work, and are protected from the despotism of their husbands by their masters. The negro men and stout boys work, on the average, in good weather, not more than nine hours a day. The balance of their time is spent in perfect abandon. Besides, they have their Sabbaths and holidays. White men, with so much of license and liberty, would die of ennui; but negroes luxuriate in corporeal and mental repose. With their faces upturned to the sun, they can sleep at any hour; and quiet sleep is the greatest of human enjoyments. "Blessed be the man who invented sleep." 'Tis happiness in itself – and results from contentment with the present, and confident assurance of the future. We do not know whether free laborers ever sleep. They are fools to do so; for, whilst they sleep, the wily and watchful capitalist is devising means to ensnare and exploitate them. The free laborer must work or starve. He is more of a slave than the negro, because he works longer and harder for less allowance than the slave, and has no holiday, because the cares of life with him begin when its labors end. He has no liberty, and not a single right. We know, 'tis often said, air and water are common property, which all have equal right to participate and enjoy; but this is utterly false. The appropriation of the lands carries with it the appropriation of all on or above the lands, *usque ad cœlum, aut ad inferos*. A man cannot breathe the air without a place to breathe it from, and all places are appropriated. All water is private property "to the middle of the stream," except the ocean, and that is not fit to drink.

Free laborers have not a thousandth part of the rights and liberties of negro slaves. Indeed, they have not a single liberty, unless it be the right or liberty to die. But the reader may think that he

and other capitalists and employers are freer than negro slaves. Your capital would soon vanish, if you dared indulge in the liberty and abandon of negroes. You hold your wealth and position by the tenure of constant watchfulness, care, and circumspection. You never labor; but you are never free.

Where a few own the soil, they have unlimited power over the balance of society, until domestic slavery comes in to compel them to permit this balance of society to draw a sufficient and comfortable living from *terra mater*. Free society asserts the right of a few to the earth – slavery maintains that it belongs, in different degrees, to all.

But, reader, well may you follow the slave trade. It is the only trade worth following, and slaves the only property worth owning. All other is worthless, a mere *caput mortuum*, except in so far as it vests the owner with the power to command the labors of others – to enslave them. Give you a palace, ten thousand acres of land, sumptuous clothes, equipage, and every other luxury; and with your artificial wants you are poorer than Robinson Crusoe, or the lowest working man, if you have no slaves to capital, or domestic slaves. Your capital will not bring you an income of a cent, nor supply one of your wants, without labor. Labor is indispensable to give value to property, and if you owned every thing else, and did not own labor, you would be poor. But fifty thousand dollars means, and is, fifty thousand dollars worth of slaves. You can command, without touching on that capital, three thousand dollars' worth of labor per annum. You could do no more were you to buy slaves with it, and then you would be cumbered with the cares of governing and providing for them. You are a slaveholder now, to the amount of fifty thousand dollars, with all the advantages, and none of the cares and responsibilities of a master.

"Property in man" is what all are struggling to obtain. Why should they not be obliged to take care of man, their property, as they do of their horses and their hounds, their cattle and their sheep. Now, under the delusive name of liberty, you work him "from morn to dewy eve" – from infancy to old age – then turn him out to starve. You treat your horses and hounds better. Capital is a cruel master. The free slave trade, the commonest, yet the cruellest of trades. [. . .]

False Philosophy of the Age

The moral philosophy of our age (which term we use generically to include Politics, Ethics, and Economy, domestic and national) is deduced from the existing relations of men to each other in free society, and attempts to explain, to justify, to generalize and regulate those relations. If that system of society be wrong, and its relations false, the philosophy resulting from it must partake of its error and falsity. On the other hand, if our current philosophy be true, slavery must be wrong, because that philosophy is at war with slavery. No successful defence of slavery can be made, till we succeed in refuting or invalidating the principles on which free society rests for support or defence. The world, however, is sick of its philosophy; and the Socialists have left it not a leg to stand on. In fact, it is, in all its ramifications, a mere expansion and application of Political Economy – and Political Economy may be summed up in the phrase, "Laissez Faire," or "Let Alone." A system of unmitigated selfishness pervades and distinguishes all departments of ethical, political, and economic science. The philosophy is partially true, because selfishness, as a rule of action and guide of conduct, is necessary to the existence of man, and of all other animals. But it should not be, with man especially, the only rule and guide; for he is, by nature, eminently social and gregarious. His wants, his weakness, his appetites, his affections compel him to look without, and beyond self, in order to sustain self. The eagle and the owl, the lion and the tiger are not gregarious, but solitary and self-supporting. They practice political economy because 'tis adapted to their natures. But men and beavers, herds, bees, and

ants require a different philosophy, another guide of conduct. The Bible (independent of its authority) is [by] far man's best guide, even in this world. Next to it, we would place Aristotle. But all books written four hundred or more years ago, are apt to yield useful instruction, whilst those written since that time will generally mislead. We mean, of course, books on moral science. We should not be far out in saying that no book on physics written more than four hundred years ago is worth reading, and none on morals written within that time. [. . .]

The World is Too Little Governed

> Whether with reason or with instinct blest,
> All enjoy that power that suits them best;
> Order is Heaven's first law, and this confessed,
> Some are, and must be greater than the rest –
> More rich, more wise; but who infers from
>   hence
> That such are happier, shocks all common
>   sense.
> Heaven to mankind impartial, we confess,
> If all are equal in their happiness;
> But mutual wants this happiness increase,
> All nature's difference, keeps all nature's
>   peace:
> Condition, circumstance, is not the thing;
> Bliss is the same, in subject, or in king!
>
> POPE.

Mobs, secret associations, insurance companies, and social and communistic experiments are striking features and characteristics of our day, outside of slave society. They are all attempting to supply the defects of regular governments, which have carried the Let Alone practice so far that one-third of mankind are let alone to indulge in such criminal immoralities as they please, and another third to starve. Mobs (*vide* California) supply the deficiencies of a defective police, and insurance companies and voluntary unions and associations afford that security and protection which government, under the lead of political economy, has ceased to render.

A lady remarked to us, a few days since, "that society was like an army, in which the inferior officers were as necessary as the commander-in-chief. Demoralization and insubordination ensue if you dispense with sergeants and corporals in an army, and the same effects result from dispensing with guardians, masters, and heads of families in society." We don't know whether she included the ladies in her ideas of the heads of families; protesting against such construction of her language, we accept and thank her for her illustration. Rev'd Nehemiah Adams has a similar thought in his admirable work, *A South-side View of Slavery*, which we regret is not before us. On some public occasion in Charleston, he was struck with the good order and absence of all dissipation, and very naively asked where was their mob. He was informed that "they were at work." He immediately perceived that slavery was an admirable police institution, and moralizes very wisely on the occasion. Slavery is an indispensable police institution – especially so to check the cruelty and tyranny of vicious and depraved husbands and parents. Husbands and parents have, in theory and practice, a power over their subjects more despotic than kings; and the ignorant and vicious exercise their power more oppressively than kings. Every man is not fit to be king, yet all must have wives and children. Put a master over them to check their power, and we need not resort to the unnatural remedies of woman's rights, limited marriages, voluntary divorces, and free love, as proposed by the abolitionists.

Mr. Carlyle says, "Among practical men the idea prevails that government can do nothing but 'keep the peace.' They say all higher tasks are unsafe for it, impossible for it, and, in fine, not necessary for it or for us. Truly, it is high time that same beautiful notion of No-Government should take itself away. The world is daily rushing towards wreck whilst it lasts. If your government is to be a constituted anarchy, what issue can it have? Our own interest in such government is, that it would be kind enough to cease and go its way before the inevitable wreck." [. . .]

We agree with Mr. Jefferson that all men have natural and inalienable rights. To violate or disregard such rights, is to oppose the designs and plans of Providence, and cannot "come to good." The order and subordination observable in the physical, animal, and human world show that some are formed for higher, others for lower stations – the few to command, the many to obey. We conclude that about nineteen out of every twenty individuals have "a natural and inalienable right" to be taken care of and protected, to have guardians, trustees, husbands, or masters; in other words, they have a natural and inalienable right to be slaves. The one in twenty are as clearly born or educated or some way fitted for command and liberty. Not to make them rulers or masters is as great a violation of natural right as not to make slaves of the mass. A very little individuality is useful and necessary to society – much of it begets discord, chaos and anarchy.

Liberty and Slavery

It seems to us that the vain attempts to define liberty in theory, or to secure its enjoyment in practice, proceed from the fact that man is naturally a social and gregarious animal, subject, not by contract or agreement, as Locke and his followers assume, but by birth and nature, to those restrictions of liberty which are expedient or necessary to secure the good of the human hive, to which he may belong. There is no such thing as *natural human* liberty, because it is unnatural for man to live alone and without the pale and government of society. Birds and beasts of prey, who are not gregarious, are naturally free. Bees and herds are naturally subjects or slaves of society. Such is the theory of Aristotle, promulged more than two thousand years ago, generally considered true for two thousand years, and destined, we hope, soon again to be accepted as the only true theory of government and society.

Modern social reformers, except Mr. Carlyle, proceeding upon the theory of Locke, which is the opposite of Aristotle, propose to dissolve and disintegrate society, falsely supposing that they thereby follow nature. There is not a human tie that binds man to man that they do not propose to cut "sheer asunder." 'Tis true, after their work of destruction is finished, they see the necessity of society; but instead of that natural and historical society, which has usually existed in the world, with its gradations of rank and power, its families, and its slaves, they propose wholly to disregard the natural relations of mankind, and profanely to build up states, like Fourierite Phalansteries, or Mormon and Oneida villages, where religion shall be banished, and in which property, wife and children shall be held somewhat in common. These social establishments, under a self-elected despotism like that of Joe Smith, or Brigham Young, become patriarchal, and succeed so long as such despotism lasts. That is, when the association loses the character intended by its founders, and acquires a despotic head like other family associations, it works well, because it works naturally. But this success can only be temporary; for nothing but the strong rule of a Cromwell or Joe Smith can keep a society together that wants the elements of cohesion in the natural ties that bind man to man; and Cromwells and Joe Smiths are not to be found every day.

'Tis an historical fact that this family association, this patriarchal government, for purposes of defence against enemies from without, gradually merges into larger associations of men under a common government or ruler. This latter is the almost universal and, we may thence infer, natural and normal condition of civilized man. In this state of society there is no liberty for the masses. Liberty has been exchanged by nature for security.

What is falsely called Free Society is a very recent invention. It proposes to make the weak, ignorant, and poor, free, by turning them loose in a world owned exclusively by the few (whom nature and education have made strong, and whom property has made stronger) to get a living. In the fanciful state of nature, where property is unappropriated, the strong have no weapons but superior physical and mental power with which to oppress the weak. Their power of oppression is increased a thousand fold when they become the exclusive owners of the earth and all the things thereon. They are masters without the obligations of masters, and the poor are slaves without the rights of slaves.

It is generally conceded, even by abolitionists, that the serfs of Europe were liberated because the multitude of laborers and their competition as freemen to get employment, had rendered free labor cheaper than slave labor. But, strange to say, few seem to have seen that this is in fact asserting that they were less free after emancipation than before. Their obligation to labor was increased; for they were compelled to labor more than before to obtain a livelihood, else their free labor would not have been cheaper than their labor as slaves. They lost something in liberty, and everything in rights – for emancipation liberated or released the masters from all their burdens, cares, and liabilities, whilst it increased both the labors and the cares of the liberated serf. In our chapter on the Decay of English Liberty, we show that the whole struggle in England has been to oppress the working man, pull down the powers, privileges, and prerogatives of the throne, the nobility, and the church, and to elevate the property-holding class. The extracts from the *Era* and *Northern Churchman*, in another chapter, will further elucidate this subject. We promised to confirm our doctrine of the illusory and undefinable character of liberty and slavery, by extracts from standard authors.

PALEY on Civil Liberty:

To do what we will, is natural liberty: to do

what we will, consistently with the interest of the community to which we belong, is civil liberty; that is to say, the only liberty to be desired in a state of civil society.

I should wish, no doubt, to be allowed to act, in every instance, as I pleased; but I reflect, that the rest also of mankind would then do the same; in which state of universal independence and self-direction, I should meet with so many checks and obstacles to my own will, from the interference and opposition of other men's, that not only my happiness, but my liberty, would be less than whilst the whole community were subject to the dominion of equal laws.

The boasted liberty of a state of nature exists only in a state of solitude. In every kind and degree of union and intercourse with his species, it is possible that the liberty of the individual may be augmented by the very laws which restrain it; because he may gain more from the limitation of other men's freedom than he suffers by the diminution of his own. Natural liberty is the right of common upon a waste; civil liberty is the safe, exclusive, unmolested enjoyment of a cultivated enclosure.

The definitions which have been framed of civil liberty, and which have become the subject of much unnecessary altercation, are most of them adapted to this idea. Thus, one political writer makes the essence of the subject's liberty to consist in his being governed by no laws but those to which he hath actually consented; another is satisfied with an indirect and virtual consent; another, again, places civil liberty in the separation of the legislative and executive offices of government; another in the being governed by *law*; that is, by known, preconstituted, inflexible rules of action and adjudication; a fifth, in the exclusive right of the people to tax themselves by their own representatives; a sixth, in freedom and purity of elections of representatives; a seventh, in the control which the

democratic part of the constitution possesses over the military establishment.

MONTESQUIEU on Liberty:

There is no word that has admitted of more various significations, and has made more different impressions on human minds, than that of *liberty*. Some have taken it for a faculty of deposing a person on whom they had conferred a tyrannical authority; others, for the power of choosing a person whom they are obliged to obey; others, for the right of bearing arms, and of being thereby enabled to use violence; others, for the privilege of being governed by a native of their own country, or by their own laws. A certain nation for a long time thought that liberty consisted in the privilege of wearing a long beard.

Some have annexed this name to one form of government, in exclusion of others; those who had a republican taste applied it to this government; those who like a monarchical state, gave it to monarchies. Thus, they all have applied the name of liberty to the government most conformable to their own customs and inclinations; and as in a republic, people have not so constant and so present a view of the institutions they complain of, and likewise as the laws there seem to speak more, and the executors of the laws least, it is generally attributed to republics, and denied to monarchies. In fine, as in democracies, the people seem to do very near whatever they please, liberty has been placed in this sort of government, and the power of the people has been confounded with their liberty.

It is true, that in democracies the people seem to do what they please; but political liberty does not consist in an unrestrained freedom. In governments, that is, in societies directed by laws, liberty can consist only in the power of doing what we ought to will, and in not being constrained to do what we ought not to will.

We must have continually present to our minds the difference between independence and liberty. Liberty is a right of doing whatever the laws permit; and if a citizen could do what they forbid, he would no longer be possessed of liberty, because all his fellow citizens would have the same power.

BLACKSTONE on Liberty:

The absolute right of man, considered as a free agent, endowed with discernment to know good from evil, and with power of choosing those measures which appear to him to be most desirable, are usually summed up in one general appellation, and denominated the natural liberty of mankind.

This national liberty consists properly in a power of acting as one thinks fit, without any restraint or control, unless by the law of nature; being a right inherent in us by birth, and one of the gifts of God to man at his creation, when he endued him with the faculty of free will. But every man, when he enters into society, gives up a part of his natural liberty, as the price of so valuable a purchase; and, in consideration of receiving the advantages of mutual commerce, obliges himself to conform to those laws which the community has thought proper to establish. And this species of legal obedience and conformity is infinitely more desirable than that wild and savage liberty which is sacrificed to obtain it. For, no man that considers a moment would wish to retain the absolute, uncontrolled power of doing what he pleases; the consequence of which is, that every other man would also have the same power; and then there would be no security to individuals in any of the enjoyments of life. Political, therefore, or civil liberty, which is that of a member of society, is no other than natural liberty, so far restrained by human laws (and no farther) as is necessary and expedient for the general advantage of the public. Hence, we may collect that the law, which restrains a man from doing mischief to his fellow citizens, though it diminishes the natural, increases the civil liberty of mankind; but that every wanton and causeless restraint of the will of the subject, whether practiced by a monarch, a nobility, or a popular assembly, is a degree of tyranny: nay, that even laws themselves, whether made with or without our consent, if they regulate and constrain our conduct in matters of mere indifference, without any good end in view, are regulations destructive of liberty; whereas, if any public advantage can arise from observing such precepts, the control of our private inclinations, in one or two particular points, will conduce to preserve our general freedom in others of more importance, by supporting that state of society which can alone secure our independence. Thus the statute of King Edward IV, which forbade the fine gentlemen of those times (under the degree of a lord) to wear pikes upon their shoes or boots of more than two inches in length, was a law that savored of oppression; because, however ridiculous the fashion then in use might appear, the restraining it by pecuniary penalties, could serve no purpose of common utility. But the statute of King Charles II, which prescribes a thing seemingly as indifferent (a dress for the dead, who are all ordered to be buried in woollen), is a law consistent with public liberty; for it encourages the staple trade, on which, in great measure, depends the universal good of the nation. So that laws, when prudently framed, are by no means subversive, but rather introductive of liberty; for (as Mr. Locke has well observed) where there is no law, there is no freedom. But then, on the other hand, that constitution or frame of government – that system of laws, is alone calculated to maintain civil liberty, which leaves the subject entire master of his own conduct, except in those points wherein the public good requires some direction or restraint.

The idea and practice of this political or civil liberty, flourish in their highest vigor in those kingdoms where it falls little short of perfection, and can only be lost or destroyed by the folly or demerits of its owner: the legislature, and of course the laws of England, being peculiarly adapted to the preservation of this inestimable blessing even in the meanest subject.

Very different from the modern constitutions of other States on the continent of Europe, and from the genius of the imperial law, which, in general, are calculated to vest an arbitrary and despotic power of controlling the actions of the subject, in the prince or in a few grandees. And this spirit of liberty is so deeply implanted in our constitution, and rooted even in our very soil, that a slave, or a negro, the moment he lands in England, falls under the protection of the laws, and so far becomes a freeman, though the master's right to his service may possibly still continue.

Next to personal security, the law of England regards, asserts and preserves the personal liberty of individuals. This personal liberty consists in the power of locomotion, of changing situation, or removing one's person to whatever place one's inclinations may direct, without imprisonment or restraint, unless by due course of law. Concerning which, we may make the same observations as upon the preceding article; that it is a right strictly natural; that the laws of England have never abridged it without sufficient cause; and, that in this kingdom, it can never be abridged at the mere discretion of the magistrate, without the explicit permission of the laws.

Now, let the reader examine and study these definitions of Liberty by Paley, Montesquieu, and Blackstone, and he will see that they are in pursuit of an *ignis fatuus* that eludes their grasp. He will see more, that their liberty is a mere modification of slavery. That each of them proposes that degree of restraint, restriction, and control that will redound to the general good. That each is in pursuit of good government, not liberty. Government presupposes that liberty is surrendered as the price of security. The degree of government must depend on the moral and intellectual condition of those to be governed. Take, for instance, Blackstone's definition of civil liberty, and our negro slaves enjoy liberty, because the restrictions on their free will and free agency not only redound to public good, but are really necessary to the protection and government of themselves. We mean to involve ourselves in no such absurdities. Negroes, according to Blackstone, Paley, and Montesquieu, although slaves, are free, because their liberty is only so far restricted as the public interest and their own good require. Our theory is that they are not free, because God and nature, and the general good and their own good, intended them for slaves. They enjoy all the rights calculated to promote their own interests, or the public good. They are, at the South, well governed and well protected. These are the aims of all social institutions, and of all governments. There can be no liberty where there is government; but there may be security for good government. This the slave has in the selfish interest of the master and in his domestic affection. The free laborer has no such securities. It is the interest of employers to kill them off as fast as possible; and they never fail to do it.

We do not mean to say that the negro slave enjoys liberty. But we do say that he is well and properly governed, so as best to promote his own good and that of society. We do mean to say further that what we have quoted from these great authors is all fudge and nonsense. Liberty is unattainable; and if attainable, not desirable. [. . .]

Government a Thing of Force, Not of Consent

We do not agree with the authors of the Declaration of Independence, that governments "derive their just powers from the consent of the governed." The women, the children, the negroes, and but few of the non-property holders were consulted, or consented to the Revolution, or the governments that ensued from its success. As to these, the new governments were self-elected despotisms, and the governing class self-elected despots. Those governments originated in force, and have been continued by force. All governments must originate in force, and be continued by force. The very term, government, implies that it is carried on against the consent of the governed. Fathers do not derive their authority, as heads of families, from the consent of wife and children, nor do they govern their families by their consent. They never take the vote of the family as to the labors to be performed, the moneys to be expended, or as to anything else. Masters dare not take the vote of slaves as to their government. If they did, constant holiday, dissipation, and extravagance would be the result. Captains of ships are not appointed by the consent of the crew, and never take their vote, even in "doubling Cape Horn." If they did, the crew would generally vote to get drunk, and the ship would never weather the cape. Not even in the most democratic countries are soldiers governed by their consent, nor is their vote taken on the eve of battle. They have some how lost (or never had) the "inalienable rights of life, liberty, and the pursuit of happiness", and, whether Americans or Russians, are forced into battle without and often against their consent. The ancient republics were governed by a small class of adult male citizens who assumed and exercised the government without the consent of the governed. The South is governed just as those ancient republics were. In the county in which we live, there are eighteen thousand souls, and only twelve hundred voters. But we twelve hundred, the governors, never asked and never intend to ask the consent of the sixteen thousand eight hundred whom we govern. Were we to do so, we should soon have an "organized anarchy." The governments of Europe could not exist a week without the positive force of standing armies.

They are all governments of force, not of consent. Even in our North, the women, children, and free negroes, constitute four-fifths of the population; and they are all governed without their consent. But they mean to correct this gross and glaring iniquity at the North. They hold that all men women, and negroes, and smart children are equals, and entitled to equal rights. The widows and free negroes begin to vote in some of those States, and they will have to let all colors and sexes and ages vote soon, or give up the glorious principles of human equality and universal emancipation.

The experiment which they will make, we fear, is absurd in theory, and the symptoms of approaching anarchy and agrarianism among them leave no doubt that its practical operation will be no better than its theory. Anti-rentism, "vote-myself-a-farm-ism," and all the other Isms, are but the spattering drops that precede a social deluge.

Abolition ultimates in "Consent Government"; Consent Government in Anarchy, Free Love, Agrarianism, &c., &c., and "Self-elected Despotism" winds up the play.

If the interests of the governors, or governing class, be not conservative, they certainly will not conserve institutions injurious to their interests. There never was and never can be an old society, in which the immediate interests of a majority of human souls do not conflict with all established order, all right of property, and all existing institutions. Immediate interest is all the mass look to; and they would be sure to revolutionize government, as often as the situation of the majority was worse than that of the minority. Divide all property to-day, and a year hence the inequalities of property would provoke a re-division. [. . .]

There are three kinds of force that occur to us will sustain a government. First, "inside necessity," such as slavery, that occasions a few to usurp power, and to hold it forcibly, without consulting the many; secondly, the force of foreign pressure or aggression, which combines men and States together for common defence; and thirdly, the inherent force of a prescriptive or usurpative government, which sustains itself by standing armies. Such are all the governments of Western Europe. Not one of them could exist forty-eight hours, but for the standing armies. These standing armies became necessary and grew up as slavery disappeared. The old Barons kept the Canaille, the Proletariat, the Sans Culottes, the Nomadic Beggars in order by lashing their backs and supplying their wants. They must be fed and kept at work. Modern society tries to effect this (but in vain) by moral suasion and standing armies. Riots, mobs, strikes, and revolutions are daily occurring. The mass of mankind cannot be governed by Law. More of despotic discretion, and less of Law, is what the world wants. We take our leave by saying "THERE IS TOO MUCH OF LAW AND TOO LITTLE OF GOVERNMENT IN THIS WORLD."

Physical force, not moral suasion, governs the world. The negro sees the driver's lash, becomes accustomed to obedient cheerful industry, and is not aware that the lash is the force that impels him. The free citizen fulfills *con amore*, his round of social, political, and domestic duties, and never dreams that the Law, with its fines and jails, penitentiaries and halters, or Public Opinion, with its ostracism, its mobs, and its tar and feathers, help to keep him revolving in his orbit. Yet, remove these physical forces, and how many good citizens would shoot, like firey comets, from their spheres, and disturb society with their eccentricities and their crimes.

Government is the life of a nation, and as no one can forsee the various future circumstances of social, any more than of individual life, it is absurd to define on paper, at the birth of either the nation or individual, what they shall do and what not do. Broad construction of constitutions is as good as no constitution, for it leaves the nation to adapt itself to circumstances; but strict construction will destroy any nation, for action is necessary to national conservation, and constitution-makers cannot foresee what action will be necessary. If individual or social life were passed in mere passivity, constitutions might answer. Not in a changing and active world. Louisiana, Florida, and Texas would have been denied to the South under strict construction, and she would have been ruined. A constitution, strictly construed, is absolutely inconsistent with permanent national existence.

2e. EQUALITY

THERE IS A SENSE IN WHICH any moral theory whatsoever must presuppose equality as a fundamental value. Morality is, after all, largely about justifying the ways in which we treat one another. And in justifying our actions, the assumption is that we will treat like cases alike. If, for instance, someone were to claim that *his* interests deserved greater consideration in some context than yours, you would naturally want to know *why*. And the answer you would expect him to give would involve him pointing to some feature of his person or situation that justifies that greater consideration, *and that would justify a similarly greater consideration for anyone else* who possessed that same feature. If he cannot or is unwilling to point to such a feature—if he is simply demanding greater consideration *just because*—then he is arguably not making a *moral* argument at all. He is simply being a bully.

Equality, then, is arguably an inescapable commitment of our moral thinking. And for good reason. After all, as both Hobbes and Locke recognized, there doesn't seem to be any sense in which some persons are naturally superior to all others in the sense that their interests are worthy of greater respect than the rest of ours—at least in general. Particular occasions may call for unequal treatment—as when we pay an employee who does superior work more than another. But those occasions stand in need of special justification. Equality is often the default position, and any departures from it stand in need of justification.

Why, then, do our political institutions tolerate so much inequality? To be sure, things are not as bad as they used to be. The feudal system in which some persons are born to the aristocracy and some to the peasantry—social classes that are virtually inescapable and which largely determine the rights and responsibilities of those who live in them—has largely been eliminated from the face of the planet. And in most developed countries, formal discrimination against women, religious, and ethnic minorities has greatly diminished. But even countries which proclaim fidelity to the ideal of "equality before the law" still tolerate tremendous inequalities in income, wealth, access to education and health care, and other important goods. Given the central role of equality in moral thought, it might seem as though these outcomes must be morally objectionable. Are they? And if so, what should be done about it?

Surprisingly, very few contemporary philosophers—even those who are very politically liberal—advocate strict equality in the distribution of resources. The reason is that strict egalitarianism of this sort faces several serious problems—problems that will be brought out in the readings in this section.

The first problem is what has come to be known as the "leveling down objection," and is presented in fictional form in the short story by Kurt Vonnegut (skip this paragraph if you haven't read it yet!). Generally we think that the way to correct inequality is to give the person who has less of a good more of it. But, strictly speaking, this is not necessary. One who valued equality above all else could also achieve her goal by taking goods away from the person who has more. Even if nothing is done with the goods—they are simply destroyed—the resulting distribution will be superior in terms of equality. To many, however, the idea that the resulting distribution could be better all-things-considered is absurd. Take a situation where initially A has 100 units of a good and B has 75, and 25 units of A's goods are seized and burned. Who is better off as a result of our doing this? Not A, who has lost 25 units of his good. But not B, either—for B is just as well off (in terms of possession of the good in question) as he was before. How, then, can the overall distribution be better if there is no person *for whom* it is better? The only plausible way in which the situation can be described as an improvement for any person is that B doesn't have to feel upset about A's greater holdings anymore. But do we really want a theory of justice that takes *envy* as a legitimate ground for making social change?

The second problem, developed in the essay by Harry Frankfurt, can be seen as drawing on insights gleaned from the first. What the leveling down objection appears to show us is that how much we have *relative* to other people is sometimes secondary in importance—or perhaps not important at all—compared to how much we have in absolute terms. A society in which A has 100 units of a good and B has 85 is a society of greater inequality than one in which A has 10 and B has 9, but is also a world in which both A and B are much, much better off. Should we nevertheless conclude that the society with greater inequality is a *worse* society? It depends. In the real world, our concern about inequality often gets mixed up with our concern about other things. Part of the reason that global inequality is troubling (see part 3b, below), for example, is that many people in the world stand in desperate need of help while others live lives of luxury. But is what is troubling about this situation the fact that some people have *more* than others? Or is it that some people don't have *enough* to live decent lives, and that others who could help are failing to do so? The fact that inequality of material resources among a nation composed exclusively of multi-billionaires would not be troubling suggests that often our real moral concern is to see that people have *sufficient* resources, not that they have *equal* resources.

The fourth problem is developed in this section by Richard Arneson, and is one which many people intuitively have with strict egalitarian proposals. The objection is that at least sometimes, people are *responsible* for having less than others because of the choices they make, and in such cases the claim that they have a moral claim to be brought back up to a level of equality with others seems implausible. A prudent person who works hard and saves *deserves* to wind up with more money, we think, than a profligate person who lives fast and works little. But still, even if some inequalities are the result of voluntary choice, clearly not all are. I did nothing to deserve being born to a middle-class family in one of the wealthiest nations on earth; people born with severe mental retardation did nothing to deserve their condition, etc. For Arneson, then, egalitarianism demands not equality of outcome but equality of opportunity— rectifying those inequalities which are a result of brute luck, but allowing those which are the result of voluntary choice.

Ultimately, then, we may wish to conclude with David Schmidtz that the kind of egalitarianism required by morality is equal *treatment*, not necessarily equal *shares* of resources. Schmidtz argues that the circumstances in which treating others as equals requires distributing things equally are severely limited. If resources fell to the earth like manna from heaven, with no one having a greater claim upon them than anyone else, then equal distribution would be a natural solution. But in the real world, most goods are already "attached" in some way to some person or group of persons. And to view goods over which others already claim ownership as up for (re-)distribution in the same way that manna from heaven would be is not to treat those owners with respect, nor would be likely to create a society where people are secure in their plans and welcoming of newcomers.

Still, significant differences remain between the authors in this section. Instantiating Arneson's equality of opportunity for welfare, for instance, would require a great deal more redistribution than the kind of equal respect that Schmidtz counsels. And puzzles remain regarding just how exactly key concepts such as a "sufficient" amount of resources are to be understood. Egalitarianism, though problematic in its details, is far from dead as a philosophical agenda.

Further Reading

Anderson, E. (1999). What is the Point of Equality? *Ethics, 109*, 287–337.

Arneson, R. (1997). Egalitarianism and the Undeserving Poor. *Journal of Political Philosophy, 5*, 327–350.

Cohen, G. A. (1993). Equality of What? On Welfare, Goods, and Capabilities. In M. Nussbaum, and Amartya Sen (Eds.), *The Quality of Life*: Oxford: Oxford University Press.

Cohen, G. A. (1995). *Self-ownership, Freedom, and Equality*. Cambridge; New York [Paris, France]: Cambridge University Press: Maison des sciences de l'homme.

Daniels, N. (1990). Equality of What: Welfare, Resources or Capabilities? *Philosophy and Phenomenological Research, 50*, 273–306.

Dworkin, R. (1981a). What Is Equality? Part I, Equality of Welfare. *Philosophy and Public Affairs, 10*, 185–246.

Dworkin, R. (1981b). What Is Equality? Part 2: Equality of Resources. *Philosophy and Public Affairs, 10*, 283–345.

Nagel, T. (1997). Equality and Priority. *Ratio, 10*, 202–221.

Parfit, D. (1998). Equality and Priority. In A. Mason (Ed.), *Ideals of Equality*. Oxford: Blackwell.

Scanlon, T. M. (1996). The Diversity of Objections to Inequality. In M. Clayton and A. Williams (Eds.), *The Ideal of Equality*. Basingstoke: Palgrave Macmillan.

Sen, A. (1987). Equality of What. In S. M. Mcmurrin (Ed.), *Liberty, Equality, and Law*, pp. 137–162. Salt Lake City: University of Utah Press.

Temkin, L. (1993). *Inequality*. Oxford: Oxford University Press.

Chapter 37

Jean-Jacques Rousseau

DISCOURSE ON THE ORIGINS OF INEQUALITY

Jean-Jacques Rousseau (1712–1778), was a philosopher of the French Enlightenment who was influential both on Kant's development of his ethical theory and on the French Revolution. In these excerpts from his *Discourse on Inequality* (1754), Rousseau distinguishes between what he calls "natural" and "political" inequality, and argues that the latter is produced and reinforced by the structures of civil society, and in no way reflects anything natural or innate in humankind.

It is of man that I have to speak; and the question I am investigating shows me that it is to men that I must address myself: for questions of this sort are not asked by those who are afraid to honour truth. I shall then confidently uphold the cause of humanity before the wise men who invite me to do so, and shall not be dissatisfied if I acquit myself in a manner worthy of my subject and of my judges.

I conceive that there are two kinds of inequality among the human species; one, which I call natural or physical, because it is established by nature, and consists in a difference of age, health, bodily strength, and the qualities of the mind or of the soul: and another, which may be called moral or political inequality, because it depends on a kind of convention, and is established, or at least authorised by the consent of men. This latter consists of the different privileges, which some men enjoy to the prejudice of others; such as that of being more rich, more honoured, more powerful or even in a position to exact obedience.

It is useless to ask what is the source of natural inequality, because that question is answered by the simple definition of the word. Again, it is still more useless to inquire whether there is any essential connection between the two inequalities; for this would be only asking, in other words, whether those who command are necessarily better than those who obey, and if strength of body or of mind, wisdom or virtue are always found in particular individuals, in proportion to their power or wealth: a question fit perhaps to be discussed by slaves in the hearing of their masters, but highly unbecoming to reasonable and free men in search of the truth.

The subject of the present discourse, therefore, is more precisely this. To mark, in the progress of things, the moment at which right took the place of violence and nature became subject to law, and to explain by what sequence of miracles the strong came to submit to serve the weak, and the people to purchase imaginary repose at the expense of real felicity. [. . .]

The First Part

If we strip this being, thus constituted, of all the supernatural gifts he may have received, and all the artificial faculties he can have acquired only by a long process; if we consider him, in a word, just as he must have come from the hands of nature, we behold in him an animal weaker than some, and less agile than others; but, taking him all round, the most advantageously organised of any. I see him satisfying his hunger at the first oak, and slaking his thirst at the first brook; finding his bed at the foot of the tree which afforded him a repast; and, with that, all his wants supplied.

While the earth was left to its natural fertility and covered with immense forests, whose trees were never mutilated by the axe, it would present on every side both sustenance and shelter for every species of animal. Men, dispersed up and down among the rest, would observe and imitate their industry, and thus attain even to the instinct of the beasts, with the advantage that, whereas every species of brutes was confined to one particular instinct, man, who perhaps has not any one peculiar to himself, would appropriate them all, and live upon most of those different foods which other animals shared among themselves; and thus would find his subsistence much more easily than any of the rest.

Accustomed from their infancy to the inclemencies of the weather and the rigour of the seasons, inured to fatigue, and forced, naked and unarmed, to defend themselves and their prey from other ferocious animals, or to escape them by flight, men would acquire a robust and almost unalterable constitution. The children, bringing with them into the world the excellent constitution of their parents, and fortifying it by the very exercises which first produced it, would thus acquire all the vigour of which the human frame is capable. Nature in this case treats them exactly as Sparta treated the children of her citizens: those who come well formed into the world she renders strong and robust, and all the rest she destroys; differing in this respect from our modern communities, in which the State, by making children a burden to their parents, kills them indiscriminately before they are born.

The body of a savage man being the only instrument he understands, he uses it for various purposes, of which ours, for want of practice, are incapable: for our industry deprives us of that force and agility, which necessity obliges him to acquire. If he had had an axe, would he have been able with his naked arm to break so large a branch from a tree? If he had had a sling, would he have been able to throw a stone with so great velocity? If he had had a ladder, would he have been so nimble in climbing a tree? If he had had a horse, would he have been himself so swift of foot? Give civilised man time to gather all his machines about him, and he will no doubt easily beat the savage; but if you would see a still more unequal contest, set them together naked and unarmed, and you will soon see the advantage of having all our forces constantly at our disposal, of being always prepared for every event, and of carrying one's self, as it were, perpetually whole and entire about one.

Hobbes contends that man is naturally intrepid, and is intent only upon attacking and fighting. Another illustrious philosopher holds the opposite, and Cumberland and Puffendorf also affirm that nothing is more timid and fearful than man in the state of nature; that he is always in a tremble, and ready to fly at the least noise or the slightest movement. This may be true of things he does not know; and I do not doubt his being terrified by every novelty that presents itself, when he neither knows the physical good or evil he may expect from it, nor can make a comparison between his own strength and the dangers he is about to encounter. Such circumstances, however, rarely occur in a state of nature, in which all things proceed in a uniform manner, and the face of the earth is not subject to those sudden and continual changes which arise from the passions and caprices of bodies of men living together. But savage man, living dispersed among other animals, and finding himself betimes in a situation to measure his strength with theirs, soon comes to compare himself with them; and, perceiving that he surpasses them more in adroitness than they surpass him in strength, learns to be no longer afraid of them. Set a bear, or a wolf, against a robust, agile, and resolute savage, as they all are, armed with stones and a good cudgel, and you will see that the danger will be at least on both sides, and that, after a few trials of this kind, wild beasts, which are not fond of attacking each other, will not be at all ready to attack man, whom they will have found to be as wild and ferocious as themselves. With regard to such animals as have really more strength than man has adroitness, he is in the same situation as all weaker animals, which notwithstanding are still able to subsist; except indeed that he has the advantage that, being equally swift of foot, and finding an almost certain place of refuge in every tree, he is at liberty to take or leave it at every encounter, and thus to fight or fly, as he chooses. Add to this that it does not appear that any animal naturally makes war on man, except in case of self-defence or excessive hunger, or betrays any of those violent antipathies, which seem to indicate that one species is intended by nature for the food of another. [. . .]

With respect to sickness, I shall not repeat the vain and false declamations which most healthy people pronounce against medicine; but I shall ask if any solid observations have been made from which it may be justly concluded that, in the countries where the art of medicine is most neglected, the mean duration of man's life is less than in those where it is most cultivated. How indeed can this be the case, if we bring on ourselves more diseases than medicine can furnish remedies? The great inequality in manner of living, the extreme idleness of some, and the excessive labour of others, the easiness of exciting and gratifying our sensual appetites, the too exquisite foods of the wealthy which overheat and fill them with indigestion, and, on the other hand,

the unwholesome food of the poor, often, bad as it is, insufficient for their needs, which induces them, when opportunity offers, to eat voraciously and overcharge their stomachs; all these, together with sitting up late, and excesses of every kind, immoderate transports of every passion, fatigue, mental exhaustion, the innumerable pains and anxieties inseparable from every condition of life, by which the mind of man is incessantly tormented; these are too fatal proofs that the greater part of our ills are of our own making, and that we might have avoided them nearly all by adhering to that simple, uniform and solitary manner of life which nature prescribed. If she destined man to be healthy, I venture to declare that a state of reflection is a state contrary to nature, and that a thinking man is a depraved animal. When we think of the good constitution of the savages, at least of those whom we have not ruined with our spirituous liquors, and reflect that they are troubled with hardly any disorders, save wounds and old age, we are tempted to believe that, in following the history of civil society, we shall be telling also that of human sickness. Such, at least, was the opinion of Plato, who inferred from certain remedies prescribed, or approved, by Podalirius and Machaon at the siege of Troy, that several sicknesses which these remedies gave rise to in his time, were not then known to mankind: and Celsus tells us that diet, which is now so necessary, was first invented by Hippocrates.

Being subject therefore to so few causes of sickness, man, in the state of nature, can have no need of remedies, and still less of physicians: nor is the human race in this respect worse off than other animals, and it is easy to learn from hunters whether they meet with many infirm animals in the course of the chase. It is certain they frequently meet with such as carry the marks of having been considerably wounded, with many that have had bones or even limbs broken, yet have been healed without any other surgical assistance than that of time, or any other regimen than that of their ordinary life. At the same time their cures seem not to have been less perfect, for their not having been tortured by incisions, poisoned with drugs, or wasted by fasting. In short, however useful medicine, properly administered, may be among us, it is certain that, if the savage, when he is sick and left to himself, has nothing to hope but from nature, he has, on the other hand, nothing to fear but from his disease; which renders his situation often preferable to our own.

We should beware, therefore, of confounding the savage man with the men we have daily before our eyes. Nature treats all the animals left to her care with a predilection that seems to show how jealous she is of that right. The horse, the cat, the bull, and even the ass are generally of greater stature, and always more robust, and have more vigour, strength and courage, when they run wild in the forests than when bred in the stall. By becoming domesticated, they lose half these advantages; and it seems as if all our care to feed and treat them well serves only to deprave them. It is thus with man also: as he becomes sociable and a slave, he grows weak, timid and servile; his effeminate way of life totally enervates his strength and courage. To this it may be added that there is still a greater difference between savage and civilised man, than between wild and tame beasts: for men and brutes having been treated alike by nature, the several conveniences in which men indulge themselves still more than they do their beasts, are so many additional causes of their deeper degeneracy. [...]

Hitherto I have considered merely the physical man; let us now take a view of him on his metaphysical and moral side.

I see nothing in any animal but an ingenious machine, to which nature hath given senses to wind itself up, and to guard itself, to a certain degree, against anything that might tend to disorder or destroy it. I perceive exactly the same things in the human machine, with this difference, that in the operations of the brute, nature is the sole agent, whereas man has some share in his own operations, in his character as a free agent. The one chooses and refuses by instinct, the other from an act of free-will: hence the brute cannot deviate from the rule prescribed to it, even when it would be advantageous for it to do so; and, on the contrary, man frequently deviates from such rules to his own prejudice. Thus a pigeon would be starved to death by the side of a dish of the choicest meats, and a cat on a heap of fruit or grain; though it is certain that either might find nourishment in the foods which it thus rejects with disdain, did it think of trying them. Hence it is that dissolute men run into excesses which bring on fevers and death; because the mind depraves the senses, and the will continues to speak when nature is silent.

Every animal has ideas, since it has senses; it even combines those ideas in a certain degree; and it is only in degree that man differs, in this respect, from the brute. Some philosophers have even maintained that there is a greater difference between one man and another than between some men and some beasts. It is not, therefore, so much the understanding that constitutes the specific difference between the man and the brute, as the human quality of free-agency. Nature lays her commands on every animal, and the brute obeys her voice. Man receives the same impulsion, but at the same time knows himself at liberty to acquiesce or resist: and it is particularly in his consciousness of this liberty that the spirituality of his soul is displayed. For physics may explain, in some measure, the mechanism of the senses and the formation of ideas; but in the power of willing or rather of choosing, and in the feeling of this power, nothing is to be found but acts which are purely spiritual and wholly inexplicable by the laws of mechanism.

However, even if the difficulties attending all these questions should still leave room for difference in this respect between men and brutes, there is another very specific quality which distinguishes them, and which will admit of no dispute. This is the faculty of self-improvement, which, by the help of circumstances, gradually develops all the rest of our faculties, and is inherent in the species as in the individual: whereas a brute is, at the end of a few months, all he will ever be during his whole life, and his species, at the end of a thousand years, exactly what it was the first year of that thousand. Why is man alone liable to grow into a dotard? Is it not because he returns, in this, to his primitive state; and that, while the brute, which has acquired nothing and has therefore nothing to lose, still retains the force of instinct, man, who loses, by age or accident, all that his *perfectibility* had enabled him to gain, falls by this means lower than the brutes themselves? It would be melancholy, were we forced to admit that this distinctive and almost unlimited faculty is the source of all human misfortunes; that it is this which, in time, draws man out of his original state, in which he would have spent his days insensibly in peace and innocence; that it is this faculty, which, successively producing in different ages his discoveries and his errors, his vices and his virtues, makes him at length a tyrant both over himself and over nature. It would be shocking to be obliged to regard as a benefactor the man who first suggested to the Oroonoko Indians the use of the boards they apply to the temples of their children, which secure to them some part at least of their imbecility and original happiness.

Savage man, left by nature solely to the direction of instinct, or rather indemnified for what he may lack by faculties capable at first of supplying its place, and afterwards of raising him much above it, must accordingly begin with purely animal functions: thus seeing and feeling must be his first condition, which would be common to him and all other animals. To will, and not to will, to desire and to fear, must be the first, and almost the only operations of his soul, till new circumstances occasion new developments of his faculties.

Whatever moralists may hold, the human understanding is greatly indebted to the passions, which, it is universally allowed, are also much indebted to the understanding. It is by the activity of the passions that our reason is improved; for we desire knowledge only because we wish to enjoy; and it is impossible to conceive any reason why a person who has neither fears nor desires should give himself the trouble of reasoning. The passions, again, originate in our wants, and their progress depends on that of our knowledge; for we cannot desire or fear anything, except from the idea we have of it, or from the simple impulse of nature. Now savage man, being destitute of every species of intelligence, can have no passions save those of the latter kind: his desires never go beyond his physical wants. The only goods he recognises in the universe are food, a female, and sleep: the only evils he fears are pain and hunger. I say pain, and not death: for no animal can know what it is to die; the knowledge of death and its terrors being one of the first acquisitions made by man in departing from an animal state. [. . .]

But be the origin of language and society what they may, it may be at least inferred, from the little care which nature has taken to unite mankind by mutual wants, and to facilitate the use of speech, that she has contributed little to make them sociable, and has put little of her own into all they have done to create such bonds of union. It is in fact impossible to conceive why, in a state of nature, one man should stand more in need of the assistance of another, than a monkey or a wolf of the assistance of another of its kind: or, granting that he did, what motives could induce that other to assist him; or, even then, by what means they could agree about the conditions. I know it is incessantly repeated that man would in such a state have been the most miserable of creatures; and indeed, if it be true, as I think I have proved, that he must have lived many ages, before he could have either desire or an opportunity of emerging from it, this would only be an accusation against nature, and not against the being which she had thus unhappily constituted. But as I understand the word *miserable*, it either has no meaning at all, or else signifies only a painful privation of something, or a state of suffering either in body or soul. I should be glad to have explained to me, what kind of misery a free being, whose heart is at ease and whose body is in health, can possibly suffer. I would ask also, whether a social or a natural life is most likely to become insupportable to those who enjoy it. We see around us hardly a creature in civil society, who does not lament his existence: we even see many deprive themselves of as much of it as they can, and laws human and divine together can hardly put a stop to the disorder. I ask, if it was ever known that a savage took it into his head, when at liberty, to complain of life or to make away with himself. Let us therefore judge, with less vanity, on which side the real misery is found. On the other hand, nothing could be more unhappy than savage man, dazzled by science, tormented by his passions, and reasoning about a state different from his own. It appears that Providence most wisely determined that the faculties, which he potentially possessed, should develop themselves only as occasion offered to exercise them, in order that they might not be superfluous or perplexing to him, by appearing before their time, nor slow and useless when the need for them arose. In instinct alone, he had all he required for living in the state of nature; and with a developed understanding he has only just enough to support life in society.

It appears, at first view, that men in a state of nature, having no moral relations or determinate obligations one with another, could not be either good or bad, virtuous or vicious; unless we take these terms in a physical sense, and call, in an individual, those qualities vices which may be injurious to his preservation, and those virtues which contribute to it; in which case, he would have to be accounted most virtuous, who put least check on the pure impulses of nature. But without deviating from the ordinary sense of the words, it will be proper to suspend the judgment we might be led to form on such a state, and be on our guard against our prejudices, till we have weighed the matter in the scales of impartiality, and seen whether virtues or vices preponderate

among civilised men; and whether their virtues do them more good than their vices do harm; till we have discovered, whether the progress of the sciences sufficiently indemnifies them for the mischiefs they do one another, in proportion as they are better informed of the good they ought to do; or whether they would not be, on the whole, in a much happier condition if they had nothing to fear or to hope from any one, than as they are, subjected to universal dependence, and obliged to take everything from those who engage to give them nothing in return.

Above all, let us not conclude, with Hobbes, that because man has no idea of goodness, he must be naturally wicked; that he is vicious because he does not know virtue; that he always refuses to do his fellow-creatures services which he does not think they have a right to demand; or that by virtue of the right he truly claims to everything he needs, he foolishly imagines himself the sole proprietor of the whole universe. Hobbes had seen clearly the defects of all the modern definitions of natural right: but the consequences which he deduces from his own show that he understands it in an equally false sense. In reasoning on the principles he lays down, he ought to have said that the state of nature, being that in which the care for our own preservation is the least prejudicial to that of others, was consequently the best calculated to promote peace, and the most suitable for mankind. He does say the exact opposite, in consequence of having improperly admitted, as a part of savage man's care for self-preservation, the gratification of a multitude of passions which are the work of society, and have made laws necessary. A bad man, he says, is a robust child. But it remains to be proved whether man in a state of nature is this robust child: and, should we grant that he is, what would he infer? Why truly, that if this man, when robust and strong, were dependent on others as he is when feeble, there is no extravagance he would not be guilty of; that he would beat his mother when she was too slow in giving him her breast; that he would strangle one of his younger brothers, if he should be troublesome to him, or bite the arm of another, if he put him to any inconvenience. But that man in the state of nature is both strong and dependent involves two contrary suppositions. Man is weak when he is dependent, and is his own master before he comes to be strong. Hobbes did not reflect that the same cause, which prevents a savage from making use of his reason, as our jurists hold, prevents him also from abusing his faculties, as Hobbes himself allows: so that it may be justly said that savages are not bad merely because they do not know what it is to be good: for it is neither the development of the understanding nor the restraint of law that hinders them from doing ill; but the peacefulness of their passions, and their ignorance of vice: *tanto plus in illis proficit vitiorum ignoratio, quam in his cognitio virtutis.*

There is another principle which has escaped Hobbes; which, having been bestowed on mankind, to moderate, on certain occasions, the impetuosity of egoism, or, before its birth, the desire of self-preservation, tempers the ardour with which he pursues his own welfare, by an innate repugnance at seeing a fellow-creature suffer. I think I need not fear contradiction in holding man to be possessed of the only natural virtue, which could not be denied him by the most violent detractor of human virtue. I am speaking of compassion, which is a disposition suitable to creatures so weak and subject to so many evils as we certainly are: by so much the more universal and useful to mankind, as it comes before any kind of reflection; and at the same time so natural, that the very brutes themselves sometimes give evident proofs of it. [. . .]

It is reason that engenders self-respect, and reflection that confirms it: it is reason which turns man's mind back upon itself, and divides him from everything that could disturb or afflict him. It is philosophy that isolates him, and bids him say, at sight of the misfortunes of others: "Perish if you will, I am secure." Nothing but such general evils as threaten the whole community can disturb the tranquil sleep of the philosopher, or tear him from his bed. A murder may with impunity be committed under his window; he has only to put his hands to his ears and argue a little with himself, to prevent nature, which is shocked within him, from identifying itself with the unfortunate sufferer. Uncivilised man has not this admirable talent; and for want of reason and wisdom, is always foolishly ready to obey the first promptings of humanity. It is the populace that flocks together at riots and street-brawls, while the wise man prudently makes off. It is the mob and the market-women, who part the combatants, and hinder gentle-folks from cutting one another's throats.

It is then certain that compassion is a natural feeling, which, by moderating the violence of love of self in each individual, contributes to the preservation of the whole species. It is this compassion that hurries us without reflection to the relief of those who are in distress: it is this which in a state of nature supplies the place of laws, morals and virtues, with the advantage that none are tempted to disobey its gentle voice: it is this which will always prevent a sturdy savage from robbing a weak child or a feeble old man of the sustenance they may have with pain and difficulty acquired, if he sees a possibility of providing for himself by other means: it is this which, instead of inculcating that sublime maxim of rational justice. *Do to others as you would have them do unto you,* inspires all men with that other maxim of natural goodness, much less perfect indeed, but perhaps more useful; *Do good to yourself with as little evil as possible to others.* In a word, it is rather in this natural feeling than in any subtle arguments that we must look for the cause of that repugnance, which every man would experience in doing evil, even independently of the maxims of education. Although it might belong to Socrates and other minds of the like craft to acquire virtue by reason, the human race would long since have ceased to be, had its preservation depended only on the reasonings of the individuals composing it. [. . .]

The Second Part

The first man who, having enclosed a piece of ground, bethought himself of saying *This is mine,* and found people simple enough to believe him, was the real founder of civil society. From how many crimes, wars and murders, from how many horrors and misfortunes might not any one have saved mankind, by pulling up the stakes, or filling up the ditch, and crying to his fellows, "Beware of listening to this impostor; you are undone if you once forget that the fruits of the earth belong to us all, and the earth itself to nobody." But there is great probability that things had then already come to such a pitch, that they could no longer continue as they were; for the idea of property depends on many prior ideas, which could only be acquired successively, and cannot have been formed all at once in the human mind. Mankind must have made very considerable progress, and acquired considerable knowledge and industry which they must also have transmitted and increased from age to age, before they arrived at this last point of the state of nature. Let us then go farther back, and endeavour to unify under a single point of view that slow succession of events and discoveries in the most natural order.

Man's first feeling was that of his own existence, and his first care that of self-preservation. The produce of the earth furnished him with all he needed, and instinct told him how to use it. Hunger and other appetites made him at various times experience various modes of existence; and among these was one which urged him to propagate his species—a blind propensity that, having nothing to do with the heart, produced a merely animal act. The want once gratified, the two sexes knew each other no more; and even the offspring was nothing to its mother, as soon as it could do without her.

Such was the condition of infant man; the life of an animal limited at first to mere sensations, and hardly profiting by the gifts nature bestowed on him, much less capable of entertaining a thought of forcing anything from her. But difficulties soon presented themselves, and it became necessary to learn how to surmount them: the height of the trees, which prevented him from gathering their fruits, the competition of other animals desirous of the same fruits, and the ferocity of those who needed them for their own preservation, all obliged him to apply himself to bodily exercises. He had to be active, swift of foot, and vigorous in fight. Natural weapons, stones and sticks, were easily found: he learnt to surmount the obstacles of nature, to contend in case of necessity with other animals, and to dispute for the means of subsistence even with other men, or to indemnify himself for what he was forced to give up to a stronger.

In proportion as the human race grew more numerous, men's cares increased. The difference of soils, climates and seasons, must have introduced some differences into their manner of living. Barren years, long and sharp winters, scorching summers which parched the fruits of the earth, must have demanded a new industry. On the seashore and the banks of rivers, they invented the hook and line, and became fishermen and eaters of fish. In the forests they made bows and arrows, and became huntsmen and warriors. In cold countries they clothed themselves with the skins of the beasts they had slain. The lightning, a volcano, or some lucky chance acquainted them with fire, a new resource against the rigours of winter: they next learned how to preserve this element, then how to reproduce it, and finally how to prepare with it the flesh of animals which before they had eaten raw.

This repeated relevance of various beings to himself, and one to another, would naturally give rise in the human mind to the perceptions of certain relations between them. Thus the relations which we denote by the terms, great, small, strong, weak, swift, slow, fearful, bold, and the like, almost insensibly compared at need, must have at length produced in him a kind of reflection, or rather a mechanical prudence, which would indicate to him the precautions most necessary to his security.

The new intelligence which resulted from this development increased his superiority over other animals, by making him sensible of it. He would now endeavour, therefore, to ensnare them, would play them a thousand tricks, and though many of them might surpass him in swiftness or in strength, would in time become the master of some and the scourge of others. Thus, the first time he looked into himself, he felt the first emotion of pride; and, at a time when he scarce knew how to distinguish the different orders of beings, by looking upon his species as of the highest order, he prepared the way for assuming pre-eminence as an individual.

Other men, it is true, were not then to him what they now are to us, and he had no greater intercourse with them than with other animals; yet they were not neglected in his observations. The conformities, which he would in time discover between them, and between himself and his female, led him to judge of others which were not then perceptible; and finding that they all behaved as he himself would have done in like circumstances, he naturally inferred that their manner of thinking and acting was altogether in conformity with his own. This important truth, once deeply impressed on his mind, must have induced him, from an intuitive feeling more certain and much more rapid than any kind of reasoning, to pursue the rules of conduct, which he had best observe towards them, for his own security and advantage.

Taught by experience that the love of well-being is the sole motive of human actions, he found himself in a position to distinguish the few cases, in which mutual interest might justify him in relying upon the assistance of his fellows; and also the still fewer cases in which a conflict of interests might give cause to suspect them. In the former case, he joined in the same herd with them, or at most in some kind of loose association, that laid no restraint on its members, and lasted no longer than the transitory occasion that

formed it. In the latter case, every one sought his own private advantage, either by open force, if he thought himself strong enough, or by address and cunning, if he felt himself the weaker.

In this manner, men may have insensibly acquired some gross ideas of mutual undertakings, and of the advantages of fulfilling them: that is, just so far as their present and apparent interest was concerned: for they were perfect strangers to foresight, and were so far from troubling themselves about the distant future, that they hardly thought of the morrow. If a deer was to be taken, every one saw that, in order to succeed, he must abide faithfully by his post: but if a hare happened to come within the reach of any one of them, it is not to be doubted that he pursued it without scruple, and, having seized his prey, cared very little, if by so doing he caused his companions to miss theirs. [. . .]

Everything now begins to change its aspect. Men, who have up to now been roving in the woods, by taking to a more settled manner of life, come gradually together, form separate bodies, and at length in every country arises a distinct nation, united in character and manners, not by regulations or laws, but by uniformity of life and food, and the common influence of climate. Permanent neighbourhood could not fail to produce, in time, some connection between different families. Among young people of opposite sexes, living in neighbouring huts, the transient commerce required by nature soon led, through mutual intercourse, to another kind not less agreeable, and more permanent. Men began now to take the difference between objects into account, and to make comparisons; they acquired imperceptibly the ideas of beauty and merit, which soon gave rise to feelings of preference. In consequence of seeing each other often, they could not do without seeing each other constantly. A tender and pleasant feeling insinuated itself into their souls, and the least opposition turned it into an impetuous fury: with love arose jealousy; discord triumphed, and human blood was sacrificed to the gentlest of all passions.

As ideas and feelings succeeded one another, and heart and head were brought into play, men continued to lay aside their original wildness; their private connections became every day more intimate as their limits extended. They accustomed themselves to assemble before their huts round a large tree; singing and dancing, the true offspring of love and leisure, became the amusement, or rather the occupation, of men and women thus assembled together with nothing else to do. Each one began to consider the rest, and to wish to be considered in turn; and thus a value came to be attached to public esteem. Whoever sang or danced best, whoever was the handsomest, the strongest, the most dexterous, or the most eloquent, came to be of most consideration; and this was the first step towards inequality, and at the same time towards vice. From these first distinctions arose on the one side vanity and contempt and on the other shame and envy: and the fermentation caused by these new leavens ended by producing combinations fatal to innocence and happiness.

As soon as men began to value one another, and the idea of consideration had got a footing in the mind, every one put in his claim to it, and it became impossible to refuse it to any with impunity. Hence arose the first obligations of civility even among savages; and every intended injury became an affront; because, besides the hurt which might result from it, the party injured was certain to find in it a contempt for his person, which was often more insupportable than the hurt itself.

Thus, as every man punished the contempt shown him by others, in proportion to his opinion of himself, revenge became terrible, and men bloody and cruel. This is precisely the state reached by most of the savage nations known to us: and it is for want of having made a proper distinction in our ideas, and see how very far they already are from the state of nature, that so many writers have hastily concluded that man is naturally cruel, and requires civil institutions to make him more mild; whereas nothing is more gentle than man in his primitive state, as he is placed by nature at an equal distance from the stupidity of brutes, and the fatal ingenuity of civilised man. Equally confined by instinct and reason to the sole care of guarding himself against the mischiefs which threaten him, he is restrained by natural compassion from doing any injury to others, and is not led to do such a thing even in return for injuries received. For, according to the axiom of the wise Locke, *There can be no injury, where there is no property.* [. . .]

In this state of affairs, equality might have been sustained, had the talents of individuals been equal, and had, for example, the use of iron and the consumption of commodities always exactly balanced each other; but, as there was nothing to preserve this balance, it was soon disturbed; the strongest did most work; the most skilful turned his labour to best account; the most ingenious devised methods of diminishing his labour: the husbandman wanted more iron, or the smith more corn, and, while both laboured equally, the one gained a great deal by his work, while the other could hardly support himself. Thus natural inequality unfolds itself insensibly with that of combination, and the difference between men, developed by their different circumstances, becomes more sensible and permanent in its effects, and begins to have an influence, in the same proportion, over the lot of individuals. [. . .]

Behold then all human faculties developed, memory and imagination in full play, egoism interested, reason active, and the mind almost at the highest point of its perfection. Behold all the natural qualities in action, the rank and condition of every man assigned him; not merely his share of property and his power to serve or injure others, but also his wit, beauty, strength or skill, merit or talents: and these being the only qualities capable of commanding respect, it soon became necessary to possess or to affect them.

It now became the interest of men to appear what they really were not. To be and to seem became two totally different things; and from this distinction sprang insolent pomp and cheating trickery, with all the numerous vices that go in their train. On the other hand, free and independent as men were before, they were now, in consequence of a multiplicity of new wants, brought into subjection, as it were, to all nature, and particularly to one another; and each became in some degree a slave even in becoming the master of other men: if rich, they stood in need of the services of others; if poor, of their assistance; and even a middle condition did not enable them to do without one another. Man must now, therefore, have been perpetually employed in getting others to interest themselves in his lot, and in making them, apparently at least, if not really, find their advantage in promoting his own. Thus he must have been sly and artful in his behaviour to some, and imperious and cruel to others; being under a kind of necessity to ill-use all the persons of whom he stood in need, when he could not frighten them into compliance, and did not judge it his interest to be useful to them. Insatiable ambition, the thirst of raising their respective fortunes, not so much from real want as from the desire to surpass others, inspired all men with a vile propensity to injure one another, and with a secret jealousy, which is the more dangerous, as it puts on the mask of benevolence, to carry its point with greater security. In a word, there arose rivalry and competition on the one hand, and conflicting interests on the other, together with a secret desire on both of profiting at the expense of others. All these evils were the first effects of property, and the inseparable attendants of growing inequality. [. . .]

I have endeavoured to trace the origin and progress of inequality, and the institution and abuse of political societies, as far as these are capable of being deduced from the nature of man merely by the light of reason, and independently of those sacred dogmas which give the sanction of divine right to sovereign authority. It follows from this survey that, as there is hardly any inequality in the state of nature, all the inequality which now prevails owes its strength and growth to the development of our faculties and the advance of the human mind, and becomes at last permanent and legitimate by the establishment of property and laws. Secondly, it follows that moral inequality, authorised by positive right alone, clashes with natural right, whenever it is not proportionate to physical inequality; a distinction which sufficiently determines what we ought to think of that species of inequality which prevails in all civilised, countries; since it is plainly contrary to the law of nature, however defined, that children should command old men, fools wise men, and that the privileged few should gorge themselves with superfluities, while the starving multitude are in want of the bare necessities of life.

Chapter 38

Harry Frankfurt

EQUALITY AS A MORAL IDEAL

Harry Frankfurt (1929–   ) is a professor emeritus of philosophy at Princeton University, and has written widely on free will, philosophy of mind, and moral philosophy. The essay reproduced here (published in 1987) argues against strict economic egalitarianism in favor of the position that each individual should be guaranteed access to *sufficient* external resources. If everyone has *enough* resources, Frankfurt argues, it is of no moral significance that some might have more than others.

First man: "How are your children?"
Second man: "Compared to what?"

I

Economic egalitarianism is, as I shall construe it, the doctrine that it is desirable for everyone to have the same amounts of income and of wealth (for short, "money"). Hardly anyone would deny that there are situations in which it makes sense to tolerate deviations from this standard. It goes without saying, after all, that preventing or correcting such deviations may involve costs which—whether measured in economic terms or in terms of noneconomic considerations—are by any reasonable measure unacceptable. Nonetheless, many people believe that economic equality has considerable moral value in itself. For this reason they often urge that efforts to approach the egalitarian ideal should be accorded—with all due consideration for the possible effects of such efforts in obstructing or in conducing to the achievement of other goods—a significant priority.

In my opinion, this is a mistake. Economic equality is not, as such, of particular moral importance. With respect to the distribution of economic assets, what *is* important from the point of view of morality is not that everyone should have *the same* but that each should have *enough*. If everyone had enough, it would be of no moral consequence whether some had more than others. I shall refer to this alternative to egalitarianism—namely, that what is morally important with respect to money is for everyone to have enough—as "the doctrine of sufficiency."

The fact that economic equality is not in its own right a morally compelling social ideal is in no way, of course, a reason for regarding it as undesirable. My claim that equality in itself lacks moral importance does not entail that equality is to be avoided. Indeed, there may well be good reasons for governments or for individuals to deal with problems of economic distribution in accordance with an egalitarian standard and to be concerned more with attempting to increase the extent to which people are economically equal than with efforts to regulate directly the extent to which the amounts of money people have are enough. Even if equality is not as such morally important, a commitment to an egalitarian social policy may be indispensable to promoting the enjoyment of significant goods besides equality or to avoiding their impairment. Moreover, it might turn out that the most feasible approach to the achievement of sufficiency would be the pursuit of equality.

But despite the fact that an egalitarian distribution would not necessarily be objectionable, the error of believing that there are powerful moral reasons for caring about equality is far from innocuous. In fact, this belief tends to do significant harm. It is often argued as an objection to egalitarianism that there is a dangerous conflict between equality and liberty: if people are left to themselves, inequalities of income and wealth inevitably arise, and therefore an egalitarian distribution of money can be achieved and maintained only at the cost of repression. Whatever may be the merit of this argument concerning the relationship between equality and liberty, economic egalitarianism engenders another conflict which is of even more fundamental moral significance.

To the extent that people are preoccupied with equality for its own sake, their readiness to be satisfied with any particular level of income or wealth is guided not by their own interests and needs but just by the magnitude of the economic benefits that are at the disposal of others. In this way egalitarianism distracts people from measuring the requirements to which their individual natures and their personal circumstances give rise. It encourages them instead to insist upon a level of economic support that is determined by a calculation in which the particular features of their own lives are irrelevant. How sizable the economic assets of others are has nothing much to do, after all, with what kind of person

someone is. A concern for economic equality, construed as desirable in itself, tends to divert a person's attention away from endeavoring to discover—within his experience of himself and of his life—what he himself really cares about and what will actually satisfy him, although this is the most basic and the most decisive task upon which an intelligent selection of economic goals depends. Exaggerating the moral importance of economic equality is harmful, in other words, because it is alienating.

To be sure, the circumstances of others may reveal interesting possibilities and provide data for useful judgments concerning what is normal or typical. Someone who is attempting to reach a confident and realistic appreciation of what to seek for himself may well find this helpful. It is not only in suggestive and preliminary ways like these, moreover, that the situations of other people may be pertinent to someone's efforts to decide what economic demands it is reasonable or important for him to make. The amount of money he needs may depend in a more direct way on the amounts others have. Money may bring power or prestige or other competitive advantages. A determination of how much money would be enough cannot intelligently be made by someone who is concerned with such things except on the basis of an estimate of the resources available to those with whose competition it may be necessary for him to contend. What is important from this point of view, however, is not the comparison of levels of affluence as such. The measurement of inequality is important only as it pertains contingently to other interests.

The mistaken belief that economic equality is important in itself leads people to detach the problem of formulating their economic ambitions from the problem of understanding what is most fundamentally significant to them. It influences them to take too seriously, as though it were a matter of great moral concern, a question that is inherently rather insignificant and not directly to the point, namely, how their economic status compares with the economic status of others. In this way the doctrine of equality contributes to the moral disorientation and shallowness of our time.

The prevalence of egalitarian thought is harmful in another respect as well. It not only tends to divert attention from considerations of greater moral importance than equality. It also diverts attention from the difficult but quite fundamental philosophical problems of understanding just what these considerations are and of elaborating, in appropriately comprehensive and perspicuous detail, a conceptual apparatus which would facilitate their exploration. Calculating the size of an equal share is plainly much easier than determining how much a person needs in order to have enough. In addition, the very concept of having an equal share is itself considerably more patent and accessible than the concept of having enough. It is far from self-evident, needless to say, precisely what the doctrine of sufficiency means and what applying it entails. But this is hardly a good reason for neglecting the doctrine or for adopting an incorrect doctrine in preference to it. Among my primary purposes in this essay is to suggest the importance of systematic inquiry into the analytical and theoretical issues raised by the concept of having enough, the importance of which egalitarianism has masked.

II

There are a number of ways of attempting to establish the thesis that economic equality is important. Sometimes it is urged that the prevalence of fraternal relationships among the members of a society is a desirable goal and that equality is indispensable to it. Or it may be maintained that inequalities in the distribution of economic benefits are to be avoided because they lead invariably to undesirable discrepancies of other kinds—for example, in social status, in political influence, or in the abilities of people to make effective use of their various opportunities

and entitlements. In both of these arguments, economic equality is endorsed because of its supposed importance in creating or preserving certain noneconomic conditions. Such considerations may well provide convincing reasons for recommending equality as a desirable social good or even for preferring egalitarianism as a policy over the alternatives to it. But both arguments construe equality as valuable derivatively, in virtue of its contingent connections to other things. In neither argument is there an attribution to equality of any unequivocally inherent moral value.

A rather different kind of argument for economic equality, which comes closer to construing the value of equality as independent of contingencies, is based upon the principle of diminishing marginal utility. According to this argument, equality is desirable because an egalitarian distribution of economic assets maximizes their aggregate utility. The argument presupposes: (a) for each individual the utility of money invariably diminishes at the margin and (b) with respect to money, or with respect to the things money can buy, the utility functions of all individuals are the same. In other words, the utility provided by or derivable from an nth dollar is the same for everyone, and it is less than the utility for anyone of dollar $(n - 1)$. Unless b were true, a rich man might obtain greater utility than a poor man from an extra dollar. In that case an egalitarian distribution of economic goods would not maximize aggregate utility even if a were true. But given both a and b, it follows that a marginal dollar always brings less utility to a rich person than to one who is less rich. And this entails that total utility must increase when inequality is reduced by giving a dollar to someone poorer than the person from whom it is taken.

In fact, however, both a and b are false. Suppose it is conceded, for the sake of the argument, that the maximization of aggregate utility is in its own right a morally important social goal. Even so, it cannot legitimately be inferred that an egalitarian distribution of money must therefore have similar moral importance. For in virtue of the falsity of *a* and *b*, the argument linking economic equality to the maximization of aggregate utility is unsound.

So far as concerns *b*, it is evident that the utility functions for money of different individuals are not even approximately alike. Some people suffer from physical, mental, or emotional weaknesses or incapacities that limit the satisfactions they are able to obtain. Moreover, even apart from the effects of specific disabilities, some people simply enjoy things more than other people do. Everyone knows that there are, at any given level of expenditure, large differences in the quantities of utility that different spenders derive.

So far as concerns *a*, there are good reasons against expecting any consistent diminution in the marginal utility of money. The fact that the marginal utilities of certain goods do indeed tend to diminish is not a principle of reason. It is a psychological generalization, which is accounted for by such considerations as that people often tend after a time to become satiated with what they have been consuming and that the senses characteristically lose their freshness after repetitive stimulation. It is common knowledge that experiences of many kinds become increasingly routine and unrewarding as they are repeated.

It is questionable, however, whether this provides any reason at all for expecting a diminution in the marginal utility of *money*—that is, of anything that functions as a generic instrument of exchange. Even if the utility of everything money can buy were inevitably to diminish at the margin, the utility of money itself might nonetheless exhibit a different pattern. It is quite possible that money would be exempt from the phenomenon of unrelenting marginal decline because of its limitlessly protean versatility. As Blum and Kalven explain: "In . . . analysing the question whether money has a declining utility it is . . . important to put to one side all

analogies to the observation that particular commodities have a declining utility to their users. There is no need here to enter into the debate whether it is useful or necessary, in economic theory, to assume that commodities have a declining utility. Money is infinitely versatile. And even if all the things money can buy are subject to a law of diminishing utility, it does not follow that money itself is." From the supposition that a person tends to lose more and more interest in what he is consuming as his consumption of it increases, it plainly cannot be inferred that he must also tend to lose interest in consumption itself or in the money that makes consumption possible. For there may always remain for him, no matter how tired he has become of what he has been doing, untried goods to be bought and fresh new pleasures to be enjoyed.

There are in any event many things of which people do not, from the very outset, immediately begin to tire. From certain goods, they actually derive more utility after sustained consumption than they derive at first. This is the situation whenever appreciating or enjoying or otherwise benefiting from something depends upon repeated trials, which serve as a kind of "warming up" process: for instance, when relatively little significant gratification is obtained from the item or experience in question until the individual has acquired a special taste for it, has become addicted to it, or has begun in some other way to relate or respond to it profitably. [. . .]

IV

The preceding discussion has established that an egalitarian distribution may fail to maximize aggregate utility. It can also easily be shown that, in virtue of the incidence of utility thresholds, there are conditions under which an egalitarian distribution actually minimizes aggregate utility. Thus, suppose that there is enough of a certain resource (e.g., food or medicine) to enable some but not all members of a population to survive. Let us say that the size of the population is ten, that a person needs at least five units of the resource in question to live, and that forty units are available. If any members of this population are to survive, some must have more than others. An equal distribution, which gives each person four units, leads to the worst possible outcome, namely, everyone dies. Surely in this case it would be morally grotesque to insist upon equality! Nor would it be reasonable to maintain that, under the conditions specified, it is justifiable for some to be better off only when this is in the interests of the worst off. If the available resources are used to save eight people, the justification for doing this is manifestly not that it somehow benefits the two members of the population who are left to die.

An egalitarian distribution will almost certainly produce a net loss of aggregate utility whenever it entails that fewer individuals than otherwise will have, with respect to some necessity, enough to sustain life—in other words, whenever it requires a larger number of individuals to be below the threshold of survival. Of course, a loss of utility may also occur even when the circumstances involve a threshold that does not separate life and death. Allocating resources equally will reduce aggregate utility whenever it requires a number of individuals to be kept below *any* utility threshold without ensuring a compensating move above some threshold by a suitable number of others.

Under conditions of scarcity, then, an egalitarian distribution may be morally unacceptable. Another response to scarcity is to distribute the available resources in such a way that as many people as possible have enough or, in other words, to maximize the incidence of sufficiency. This alternative is especially compelling when the amount of a scarce resource that constitutes enough coincides with the amount that is indispensable for avoiding some catastrophic harm—as in the example just considered, where falling below the threshold of enough food or

enough medicine means death. But now suppose that there are available, in this example, not just forty units of the vital resource but forty-one. Then maximizing the incidence of sufficiency by providing enough for each of eight people leaves one unit unallocated. What should be done with this extra unit?

It has been shown above that it is a mistake to maintain that *where some people have less than enough, no one should have more than anyone else.* When resources are scarce, so that it is impossible for everyone to have enough, an egalitarian distribution may lead to disaster. Now there is another claim that might be made here, which may appear to be quite plausible but which is also mistaken: *where some people have less than enough, no one should have more than enough.* If this claim were correct, then—in the example at hand—the extra unit should go to one of the two people who have nothing. But one additional unit of the resource in question will not improve the condition of a person who has none. By hypothesis, that person will die even with the additional unit. What he needs is not one unit but five. It cannot be taken for granted that a person who has a certain amount of a vital resource is necessarily better off than a person who has a lesser amount, for the larger amount may still be too small to serve any useful purpose. Having the larger amount may even make a person worse off. Thus it is conceivable that while a dose of five units of some medication is therapeutic, a dose of one unit is not better than none but actually toxic. And while a person with one unit of food may live a bit longer than someone with no food whatever, perhaps it is worse to prolong the process of starvation for a short time than to terminate quickly the agony of starving to death.

The claim that no one should have more than enough while anyone has less than enough derives its plausibility, in part, from a presumption that is itself plausible but that is nonetheless false: to wit, giving resources to people who have less of them than enough necessarily means giving resources to people who need them and, therefore, making those people better off. It is indeed reasonable to assign a higher priority to improving the condition of those who are in need than to improving the condition of those who are not in need. But giving additional resources to people who have less than enough of those resources, and who are accordingly in need, may not actually improve the condition of these people at all. Those below a utility threshold are not necessarily benefited by additional resources that move them closer to the threshold. What is crucial for them is to attain the threshold. Merely moving closer to it either may fail to help them or may be disadvantageous.

By no means do I wish to suggest, of course, that it is never or only rarely beneficial for those below a utility threshold to move closer to it. Certainly it may be beneficial, either because it increases the likelihood that the threshold ultimately will be attained or because, quite apart from the significance of the threshold, additional resources provide important increments of utility. After all, a collector may enjoy expanding his collection even if he knows that he has no chance of ever completing it. My point is only that additional resources do not necessarily benefit those who have less than enough. The additions may be too little to make any difference. It may be morally quite acceptable, accordingly, for some to have more than enough of a certain resource even while others have less than enough of it.

V

Quite often, advocacy of egalitarianism is based less upon an argument than upon a purported moral intuition: economic inequality, considered as such, just seems wrong. It strikes many people as unmistakably apparent that, taken simply in itself, the enjoyment by some of greater economic benefits than are enjoyed by others is morally offensive. I suspect, however, that in many cases those who profess to have this intuition concerning manifestations of inequal-

ity are actually responding not to the inequality but to another feature of the situations they are confronting. What I believe they find intuitively to be morally objectionable, in the types of situations characteristically cited as instances of economic inequality, is not the fact that some of the individuals in those situations have *less* money than others but the fact that those with less have *too little*.

When we consider people who are substantially worse off than ourselves, we do very commonly find that we are morally disturbed by their circumstances. What directly touches us in cases of this kind, however, is not a quantitative discrepancy but a qualitative condition—not the fact that the economic resources of those who are worse off are *smaller in magnitude* than ours but the different fact that these people are so *poor*. Mere differences in the amounts of money people have are not in themselves distressing. We tend to be quite unmoved, after all, by inequalities between the well-to-do and the rich; our awareness that the former are substantially worse off than the latter does not disturb us morally at all. And if we believe of some person that his life is richly fulfilling, that he himself is genuinely content with his economic situation, and that he suffers no resentments or sorrows which more money could assuage, we are not ordinarily much interested—from a moral point of view—in the question of how the amount of money he has compares with the amounts possessed by others. Economic discrepancies in cases of these sorts do not impress us in the least as matters of significant moral concern. The fact that some people have much less than others is morally undisturbing when it is clear that they have plenty.

It seems clear that egalitarianism and the doctrine of sufficiency are logically independent: considerations that support the one cannot be presumed to provide support also for the other. Yet proponents of egalitarianism frequently suppose that they have offered grounds for their position when in fact what they have offered is pertinent as support only for the doctrine of sufficiency. Thus they often, in attempting to gain acceptance for egalitarianism, call attention to disparities between the conditions of life characteristic of the rich and those characteristic of the poor. Now it is undeniable that contemplating such disparities does often elicit a conviction that it would be morally desirable to redistribute the available resources so as to improve the circumstances of the poor. And, of course, that would bring about a greater degree of economic equality. But the indisputability of the moral appeal of improving the condition of the poor by allocating to them resources taken from those who are well off does not even tend to show that egalitarianism is, as a moral ideal, similarly indisputable. To show of poverty that it is compellingly undesirable does nothing whatsoever to show the same of inequality. For what makes someone poor in the morally relevant sense—in which poverty is understood as a condition from which we naturally recoil—is not that his economic assets are simply of lesser magnitude than those of others.

A typical example of this confusion is provided by Ronald Dworkin. Dworkin characterizes the ideal of economic equality as requiring that "no citizen has less than an equal share of the community's resources just in order that others may have more of what he lacks." But in support of his claim that the United States now falls short of this ideal, he refers to circumstances that are not primarily evidence of inequality but of poverty: "It is, I think, apparent that the United States falls far short now [of the ideal of equality]. A substantial minority of Americans are chronically unemployed or earn wages below any realistic 'poverty line' or are handicapped in various ways or burdened with special needs; and most of these people would do the work necessary to earn a decent living if they had the opportunity and capacity." What mainly concerns Dworkin—what he actually considers to be morally important—is manifestly not that our society permits a situation in which a

substantial minority of Americans have *smaller shares* than others of the resources which he apparently presumes should be available for all. His concern is, rather, that the members of this minority *do not earn decent livings*.

The force of Dworkin's complaint does not derive from the allegation that our society fails to provide some individuals with as much as others but from a quite different allegation, namely, our society fails to provide each individual with "the opportunity to develop and lead a life he can regard as valuable both to himself and to [the community]." Dworkin is dismayed most fundamentally not by evidence that the United States permits economic inequality but by evidence that it fails to ensure that everyone has enough to lead "a life of choice and value"— in other words, that it fails to fulfill for all the ideal of sufficiency. What bothers him most immediately is not that certain quantitative relationships are widespread but that certain qualitative conditions prevail. He cares principally about the value of people's lives, but he mistakenly represents himself as caring principally about the relative magnitudes of their economic assets.

My suggestion that situations involving inequality are morally disturbing only to the extent that they violate the ideal of sufficiency is confirmed, it seems to me, by familiar discrepancies between the principles egalitarians profess and the way in which they commonly conduct their own lives. My point here is not that some egalitarians hypocritically accept high incomes and special opportunities for which, according to the moral theories they profess, there is no justification. It is that many egalitarians (including many academic proponents of the doctrine) are not truly concerned whether they are as well off economically as other people are. They believe that they themselves have roughly enough money for what is important to them, and they are therefore not terribly preoccupied with the fact that some people are considerably richer than they. Indeed, many egalitarians would consider it rather shabby or even reprehensible to care, with respect to their own lives, about economic comparisons of that sort. And, notwithstanding the implications of the doctrines to which they urge adherence, they would be appalled if their children grew up with such preoccupations.

VI

The fundamental error of egalitarianism lies in supposing that it is morally important whether one person has less than another regardless of how much either of them has. This error is due in part to the false assumption that someone who is economically worse off has more important unsatisfied needs than someone who is better off. In fact the morally significant needs of both individuals may be fully satisfied or equally unsatisfied. Whether one person has more money than another is a wholly extrinsic matter. It has to do with a relationship between the respective economic assets of the two people, which is not only independent of the amounts of their assets and of the amounts of satisfaction they can derive from them but also independent of the attitudes of these people toward those levels of assets and of satisfaction. The economic comparison implies nothing concerning whether either of the people compared has any morally important unsatisfied needs at all nor concerning whether either is content with what he has.

This defect in egalitarianism appears plainly in Thomas Nagel's development of the doctrine. According to Nagel: "The essential feature of an egalitarian priority system is that it counts improvements to the welfare of the worse off as more urgent than improvements to the welfare of the better off. . . . What makes a system egalitarian is the priority it gives to the claims of those . . . at the bottom . . . Each individual with a more urgent claim has priority . . . over each individual with a less urgent claim." And in discussing Rawls's Difference Principle, which

he endorses, Nagel says: the Difference Principle "establishes an order of priority among needs and gives preference to the most urgent." But the preference actually assigned by the Difference Principle is not in favor of those whose needs are most urgent; it is in favor of those who are identified as worst off. It is a mere assumption, which Nagel makes without providing any grounds for it whatever, that the worst off individuals have urgent needs. In most societies the people who are economically at the bottom are indeed extremely poor, and they do, as a matter of fact, have urgent needs. But this relationship between low economic status and urgent need is wholly contingent. It can be established only on the basis of empirical data. There is no necessary conceptual connection between a person's relative economic position and whether he has needs of any degree of urgency.

It is possible for those who are worse off not to have more urgent needs or claims than those who are better off because it is possible for them to have no urgent needs or claims at all. The notion of "urgency" has to do with what is *important*. Trivial needs or interests, which have no significant bearing upon the quality of a person's life or upon his readiness to be content with it, cannot properly be construed as being urgent to any degree whatever or as supporting the sort of morally demanding claims to which genuine urgency gives rise. From the fact that a person is at the bottom of some economic order, moreover, it cannot even be inferred that he has *any* unsatisfied needs or claims. After all, it is possible for conditions at the bottom to be quite good; the fact that they are the worst does not in itself entail that they are bad or that they are in any way incompatible with richly fulfilling and enjoyable lives.

Nagel maintains that what underlies the appeal of equality is an "ideal of acceptability to each individual." On his account, this ideal entails that a reasonable person should consider deviations from equality to be acceptable only if they are in his interest in the sense that he would be worse off without them. But a reasonable person might well regard an unequal distribution as entirely acceptable even though he did not presume that any other distribution would benefit him less. For he might believe that the unequal distribution provided him with quite enough, and he might reasonably be unequivocally content with that, with no concern for the possibility that some other arrangement would provide him with more. It is gratuitous to assume that every reasonable person must be seeking to maximize the benefits he can obtain, in a sense requiring that he be endlessly interested in or open to improving his life. A certain deviation from equality might not be in someone's interest because it might be that he would in fact be better off without it. But as long as it does not *conflict* with his interest, by obstructing his opportunity to lead the sort of life that it is important for him to lead, the deviation from equality may be quite acceptable. To be wholly satisfied with a certain state of affairs, a reasonable person need not suppose that there is no other available state of affairs in which he would be better off.

Nagel illustrates his thesis concerning the moral appeal of equality by considering a family with two children, one of whom is "normal and quite happy" while the other "suffers from a painful handicap." If this family were to move to the city the handicapped child would benefit from medical and educational opportunities that are unavailable in the suburbs, but the healthy child would have less fun. If the family were to move to the suburbs, on the other hand, the handicapped child would be deprived but the healthy child would enjoy himself more. Nagel stipulates that the gain to the healthy child in moving to the suburbs would be greater than the gain to the handicapped child in moving to the city: in the city the healthy child would find life positively disagreeable, while the handicapped child would not become happy "but only less miserable."

Given these conditions, the egalitarian decision is to move to the city; for "it is more urgent to benefit the [handicapped] child even though the benefit we can give him is less than the benefit we can give the [healthy] child." Nagel explains that this judgment concerning the greater urgency of benefiting the handicapped child "depends on the worse off position of the [handicapped] child. An improvement in his situation is more important than an equal or somewhat greater improvement in the situation of the [normal] child." But it seems to me that Nagel's analysis of this matter is flawed by an error similar to the one that I attributed above to Dworkin. The fact that it is preferable to help the handicapped child is not due, as Nagel asserts, to the fact that this child is worse off than the other. It is due to the fact that this child, and not the other, suffers from a painful handicap. The handicapped child's claim is important because his condition is *bad*—significantly undesirable—and not merely because he is *less well off* than his sibling.

This does not imply, of course, that Nagel's evaluation of what the family should do is wrong. Rejecting egalitarianism certainly does not mean maintaining that it is always mandatory simply to maximize benefits and that therefore the family should move to the suburbs because the normal child would gain more from that than the handicapped child would gain from a move to the city. However, the most cogent basis for Nagel's judgment in favor of the handicapped child has nothing to do with the alleged urgency of providing people with as much as others. It pertain rather to the urgency of the needs of people who do not have enough.

VII

What does it mean, in the present context, for a person to have enough? One thing it might mean is that any more would be too much: a larger amount would make the person's life unpleasant, or it would be harmful or in some other way unwelcome. This is often what people have in mind when they say such things as "I've had enough!" or "Enough of that!" The idea conveyed by statements like these is that *a limit has been reached*, beyond which it is not desirable to proceed. On the other hand, the assertion that a person has enough may entail only that *a certain requirement or standard has been met*, with no implication that a larger quantity would be bad. This is often what a person intends when he says something like "That should be enough." Statements such as this one characterize the indicated amount as sufficient while leaving open the possibility that a larger amount might also be acceptable.

In the doctrine of sufficiency the use of the notion of "enough" pertains to *meeting a standard* rather than to *reaching a limit*. To say that a person has enough money means that he is content, or that it is reasonable for him to be content, with having no more money than he has. And to say this is, in turn, to say something like the following: the person does not (or cannot reasonably) regard whatever (if anything) is unsatisfying or distressing about his life as due to his having too little money. In other words, if a person is (or ought reasonably to be) content with the amount of money he has, then insofar as he is or has reason to be unhappy with the way his life is going, he does not (or cannot reasonably) suppose that money would—either as a sufficient or as a necessary condition—enable him to become (or to have reason to be) significantly less unhappy with it.

It is essential to understand that having enough money differs from merely having enough to get along or enough to make life marginally tolerable. People are not generally content with living on the brink. The point of the doctrine of sufficiency is not that the only morally important distributional consideration with respect to money is whether people have enough to avoid economic misery. A person who might naturally and appropriately be said to have just barely enough does not, by the standard

invoked in the doctrine of sufficiency, have enough at all.

There are two distinct kinds of circumstances in which the amount of money a person has is enough—that is, in which more money will not enable him to become significantly less unhappy. On the one hand, it may be that the person is suffering no substantial distress or dissatisfaction with his life. On the other hand, it may be that although the person is unhappy about how his life is going, the difficulties that account for his unhappiness would not be alleviated by more money. Circumstances of this second kind obtain when what is wrong with the person's life has to do with noneconomic goods such as love, a sense that life is meaningful, satisfaction with one's own character, and so on. These are goods that money cannot buy; moreover, they are goods for which none of the things money can buy are even approximately adequate substitutes. Sometimes, to be sure, noneconomic goods are obtainable or enjoyable only (or more easily) by someone who has a certain amount of money. But the person who is distressed with his life while content with his economic situation may already have that much money.

It is possible that someone who is content with the amount of money he has might also be content with an even larger amount of money. Since having enough money does not mean being at a limit beyond which more money would necessarily be undesirable, it would be a mistake to assume that for a person who already has enough the marginal utility of money must be either negative or zero. Although this person is by hypothesis not distressed about his life in virtue of any lack of things which more money would enable him to obtain, nonetheless it remains possible that he would enjoy having some of those things. They would not make him less unhappy, nor would they in any way alter his attitude toward his life or the degree of his contentment with it, but they might bring him pleasure. If that is so, then his life would in this respect be better with more money than without it. The marginal utility for him of money would accordingly remain positive.

To say that a person is content with the amount of money he has does not entail, then, that there would be no point whatever in his having more. Thus someone with enough money might be quite *willing* to accept incremental economic benefits. He might in fact be *pleased* to receive them. Indeed, from the supposition that a person is content with the amount of money he has it cannot even be inferred that he would not *prefer* to have more. And it is even possible that he would actually be prepared to *sacrifice* certain things that he values (e.g., a certain amount of leisure) for the sake of more money.

But how can all this be compatible with saying that the person is content with what he has? What *does* contentment with a given amount of money preclude, if it does not preclude being willing or being pleased or preferring to have more money or even being ready to make sacrifices for more? It precludes his having an *active interest* in getting more. A contented person regards having more money as *inessential* to his being satisfied with his life. The fact that he is content is quite consistent with his recognizing that his economic circumstances could be improved and that his life might as a consequence become better than it is. But this possibility is not important to him. He is simply not much interested in being better off, so far as money goes, than he is. His attention and interest are not vividly engaged by the benefits which would be available to him if he had more money. He is just not very responsive to their appeal. They do not arouse in him any particularly eager or restless concern, although he acknowledges that he would enjoy additional benefits if they were provided to him.

In any event, let us suppose that the level of satisfaction that his present economic circumstances enable him to attain is high enough to meet his expectations of life. This is not fundamentally a matter of how much utility or satisfaction his various activities and experiences provide. Rather, it is most decisively a matter of his attitude toward being provided with that much. The satisfying experiences a person has are one thing. Whether he is satisfied that his life includes just those satisfactions is another. Although it is possible that other feasible circumstances would provide him with greater amounts of satisfaction, it may be that he is wholly satisfied with the amounts of satisfaction that he now enjoys. Even if he knows that he could obtain a greater quantity of satisfaction overall, he does not experience the uneasiness or the ambition that would incline him to seek it. Some people feel that their lives are good enough, and it is not important to them whether their lives are as good as possible.

The fact that a person lacks an active interest in getting something does not mean, of course, that he prefers not to have it. This is why the contented person may without any incoherence accept or welcome improvements in his situation and why he may even be prepared to incur minor costs in order to improve it. The fact that he is contented means only that the possibility of improving his situation is not *important* to him. It only implies, in other words, that he does not resent his circumstances, that he is not anxious or determined to improve them, and that he does not go out of his way or take any significant initiatives to make them better.

It may seem that there can be no reasonable basis for accepting less satisfaction when one could have more, that therefore rationality itself entails maximizing, and, hence, that a person who refuses to maximize the quantity of satisfaction in his life is not being rational. Such a person cannot, of course, offer it as his reason for declining to pursue greater satisfaction that the costs of this pursuit are too high; for if that were his reason then, clearly, he would be attempting to maximize satisfaction after all. But what other good reason could he possibly have for passing up an opportunity for more satisfaction? In fact, he may have a very good reason for this: namely, *that he is satisfied with the amount of satisfaction he already has.* Being satisfied with the way things are is unmistakably an excellent reason for having no great interest in changing them. A person who is indeed satisfied with his life as it is can hardly be criticized, accordingly, on the grounds that he has no good reason for declining to make it better.

He might still be open to criticism on the grounds that he *should not* be satisfied—that it is somehow unreasonable, or unseemly, or in some other mode wrong for him to be satisfied with less satisfaction than he could have. On what basis, however, could *this* criticism be justified? Is there some decisive reason for insisting that a person ought to be so hard to satisfy? Suppose that a man deeply and happily loves a woman who is altogether worthy. We do not ordinarily criticize the man in such a case just because we think he might have done even better. Moreover, our sense that it would be inappropriate to criticize him for that reason need not be due simply to a belief that holding out for a more desirable or worthier woman might end up costing him more than it would be worth. Rather, it may reflect our recognition that the desire to be happy or content or satisfied with life is a desire for a satisfactory amount of satisfaction and is not inherently tantamount to a desire that the quantity of satisfaction be maximized.

Being satisfied with a certain state of affairs is not equivalent to preferring it to all others. If a person is faced with a choice between less and more of something desirable, then no doubt it would be irrational for him to prefer less to more. But a person may be satisfied without having made any such comparisons at all. Nor is it necessarily irrational or unreasonable for a person to omit or to decline to make comparisons between his own state of affairs and possible alternatives. This is not only because making comparisons may be too costly. It is also because if someone is satisfied with the way

things are, he may have no motive to consider how else they might be.

Contentment may be a function of excessive dullness or diffidence. The fact that a person is free both of resentment and of ambition may be due to his having a slavish character or to his vitality being muffled by a kind of negligent lassitude. It is possible for someone to be content merely, as it were, by default. But a person who is content with resources providing less utility than he could have may not be irresponsible or indolent or deficient in imagination. On the contrary, his decision to be content with those resources—in other words, to adopt an attitude of willing acceptance toward the fact that he has just that much—may be based upon a conscientiously intelligent and penetrating evaluation of the circumstances of his life.

It is not essential for such an evaluation to include an *extrinsic* comparison of the person's circumstances with alternatives to which he might plausibly aspire, as it would have to do if contentment were reasonable only when based upon a judgment that the enjoyment of possible benefits has been maximized. If someone is less interested in whether his circumstances enable him to live as well as possible than in whether they enable him to live satisfyingly, he may appropriately devote his evaluation entirely to an *intrinsic* appraisal of his life. Then he may recognize that his circumstances do not lead him to be resentful or regretful or drawn to change and that, on the basis of his understanding of himself and of what is important to him, he accedes approvingly to his actual readiness to be content with the way things are. The situation in that case is not so much that he rejects the possibility of improving his circumstances because he thinks there is nothing genuinely to be gained by attempting to improve them. It is rather that this possibility, however feasible it may be, fails as a matter of fact to excite his active attention or to command from him any lively interest.

Chapter 39

Kurt Vonnegut

HARRISON BERGERON

Kurt Vonnegut (1922–2007) was a prolific novelist and writer of short stories, whose works often blended social satire, science fiction, and dark humor. This story, taken from his *Welcome to the Monkey House* (1968) tells the story of a future society in which a certain kind of equality has been realized—and is ruthlessly enforced by the state.

The year was 2081, and everybody was finally equal. They weren't only equal before God and the law. They were equal every which way. Nobody was smarter than anybody else. Nobody was better looking than anybody else. Nobody was stronger or quicker than anybody else. All this equality was due to the 211th, 212th, and 213th Amendments to the Constitution, and to the unceasing vigilance of agents of the United States Handicapper General.

Some things about living still weren't quite right, though. April, for instance, still drove people crazy by not being springtime. And it was in that clammy month that the H-G men took George and Hazel Bergeron's fourteen-year-old son, Harrison, away.

It was tragic, all right, but George and Hazel couldn't think about it very hard. Hazel had a perfectly average intelligence, which meant she couldn't think about anything except in short bursts. And George, while his intelligence was way above normal, had a little mental handicap radio in his ear. He was required by law to wear it at all times. It was tuned to a government transmitter. Every twenty seconds or so, the transmitter would send out some sharp noise to keep people like George from taking unfair advantage of their brains.

George and Hazel were watching television. There were tears on Hazel's cheeks, but she'd forgotten for the moment what they were about.

On the television screen were ballerinas.

A buzzer sounded in George's head. His thoughts fled in panic, like bandits from a burglar alarm.

"That was a real pretty dance, that dance they just did," said Hazel.

"Huh?" said George.

"That dance—it was nice," said Hazel.

"Yup," said George. He tried to think a little about the ballerinas. They weren't really very good—no better than anybody else would have been, anyway. They were burdened with sash-weights and bags of birdshot, and their faces were masked, so that no one, seeing a free and graceful gesture or a pretty face, would feel like something the cat drug in. George was toying with the vague notion that maybe dancers shouldn't be handicapped. But he didn't get very far with it before another noise in his ear radio scattered his thoughts.

George winced. So did two out of the eight ballerinas.

Hazel saw him wince. Having no mental handicap herself, she had to ask George what the latest sound had been.

"Sounded like somebody hitting a milk bottle with a ball peen hammer," said George.

"I'd think it would be real interesting, hearing all the different sounds," said Hazel, a little envious. "All the things they think up."

"Um," said George.

"Only, if I was Handicapper General, you know what I would do?" said Hazel. Hazel, as a matter of fact, bore a strong resemblance to the Handicapper General, a woman named Diana Moon Glampers. "If I was Diana Moon Glampers," said Hazel, "I'd have chimes on Sunday—just chimes. Kind of in honor of religion."

"I could think, if it was just chimes," said George.

"Well—maybe make 'em real loud," said Hazel. "I think I'd make a good Handicapper General."

"Good as anybody else," said George.

"Who knows better'n I do what normal is?" said Hazel.

"Right," said George. He began to think glimmeringly about his abnormal son who was now in jail, about Harrison, but a twenty-one-gun salute in his head stopped that.

"Boy!" said Hazel, "that was a doozy, wasn't it?"

It was such a doozy that George was white and trembling, and tears stood on the rims of his red eyes. Two of the eight ballerinas had collapsed to the studio floor, were holding their temples.

"All of a sudden you look so tired," said Hazel. "Why don't you stretch out on the sofa, so's you can rest your handicap bag on the pillows, honeybunch." She was referring to the forty-seven pounds of birdshot in a canvas bag, which was padlocked around George's neck.

"Go on and rest the bag for a little while," she said. "I don't care if you're not equal to me for a while."

George weighed the bag with his hands. "I don't mind it," he said. "I don't notice it any more. It's just a part of me."

"You been so tired lately—kind of wore out," said Hazel. "If there was just some way we could make a little hole in the bottom of the bag, and just take out a few of them lead balls. Just a few."

"Two years in prison and two thousand dollars fine for every ball I took out," said George. "I don't call that a bargain."

"If you could just take a few out when you came home from work," said Hazel. "I mean—you don't compete with anybody around here. You just set around."

"If I tried to get away with it," said George, "then other people'd get away with it—and pretty soon we'd be right back to the dark ages again, with everybody competing against everybody else. You wouldn't like that, would you?"

"I'd hate it," said Hazel.

"There you are," said George. "The minute people start cheating on laws, what do you think happens to society?"

If Hazel hadn't been able to come up with an answer to this question, George couldn't have supplied one. A siren was going off in his head.

"Reckon it'd fall all apart," said Hazel.

"What would?" said George blankly.

"Society," said Hazel uncertainly. "Wasn't that what you just said?"

"Who knows?" said George.

The television program was suddenly interrupted for a news bulletin. It wasn't clear at first as to what the bulletin was about, since the announcer, like all announcers, had a serious speech impediment. For about half a minute, and in a state of high excitement, the announcer tried to say, "Ladies and gentlemen—"

He finally gave up, handed the bulletin to a ballerina to read.

"That's all right—" Hazel said of the announcer, "he tried. That's the big thing. He tried to do the best he could with what God gave him. He should get a nice raise for trying so hard."

"Ladies and gentlemen—" said the ballerina, reading the bulletin. She must have been extraordinarily beautiful, because the mask she wore was hideous. And it was easy to see that she was the strongest and most graceful of all the dancers, for her handicap bags were as big as those worn by two-hundred-pound men.

And she had to apologize at once for her voice, which was a very unfair voice for a woman to use. Her voice was a warm, luminous, timeless melody. "Excuse me—" she said, and she began again, making her voice absolutely uncompetitive.

"Harrison Bergeron, age fourteen," she said in a grackle squawk, "has just escaped from jail, where he was held on suspicion of plotting to overthrow the government. He is a genius and an athlete, is under-handicapped, and should be regarded as extremely dangerous."

A police photograph of Harrison Bergeron was flashed on the screen-upside down, then sideways, upside down again, then right side up. The picture showed the full length of Harrison against a background calibrated in feet and inches. He was exactly seven feet tall.

The rest of Harrison's appearance was Halloween and hardware. Nobody had ever born heavier handicaps. He had outgrown hindrances faster than the H-G men could think them up. Instead of a little ear radio for a mental handicap, he wore a tremendous pair of earphones, and spectacles with thick wavy lenses. The spectacles were intended to make him not only half blind, but to give him whanging headaches besides.

Scrap metal was hung all over him. Ordinarily, there was a certain symmetry, a military neatness to the handicaps issued to strong people, but Harrison looked like a walking junkyard. In the race of life, Harrison carried three hundred pounds.

And to offset his good looks, the H-G men required that he wear at all times a red rubber ball for a nose, keep his eyebrows shaved off, and cover his even white teeth with black caps at snaggle-tooth random.

"If you see this boy," said the ballerina, "do not—I repeat, do not—try to reason with him."

There was the shriek of a door being torn from its hinges.

Screams and barking cries of consternation came from the television set. The photograph of Harrison Bergeron on the screen jumped again and again, as though dancing to the tune of an earthquake.

George Bergeron correctly identified the earthquake, and well he might have—for many was the time his own home had danced to the same crashing tune. "My God—" said George, "that must be Harrison!"

The realization was blasted from his mind instantly by the sound of an automobile collision in his head.

When George could open his eyes again, the photograph of Harrison was gone. A living, breathing Harrison filled the screen.

Clanking, clownish, and huge, Harrison stood in the center of the studio. The knob of the uprooted studio door was still in his hand. Ballerinas, technicians, musicians, and announcers cowered on their knees before him, expecting to die.

"I am the Emperor!" cried Harrison. "Do you hear? I am the Emperor! Everybody must do what I say at once!" He stamped his foot and the studio shook.

"Even as I stand here—" he bellowed, "crippled, hobbled, sickened—I am a greater ruler than any man who ever lived! Now watch me become what I *can* become!"

Harrison tore the straps of his handicap harness like wet tissue paper, tore straps guaranteed to support five thousand pounds.

Harrison's scrap-iron handicaps crashed to the floor.

Harrison thrust his thumbs under the bar of the padlock that secured his head harness. The bar snapped like celery. Harrison smashed his headphones and spectacles against the wall.

He flung away his rubber-ball nose, revealed a man that would have awed Thor, the god of thunder.

"I shall now select my Empress!" he said, looking down on the cowering people. "Let the first woman who dares rise to her feet claim her mate and her throne!"

A moment passed, and then a ballerina arose, swaying like a willow.

Harrison plucked the mental handicap from her ear, snapped off her physical handicaps with marvelous delicacy. Last of all, he removed her mask.

She was blindingly beautiful.

"Now——" said Harrison, taking her hand, "shall we show the people the meaning of the word dance? Music!" he commanded.

The musicians scrambled back into their chairs, and Harrison stripped them of their handicaps, too. "Play your best," he told them, "and I'll make you barons and dukes and earls."

The music began. It was normal at first—cheap, silly, false. But Harrison snatched two musicians from their chairs, waved them like batons as he sang the music as he wanted it played. He slammed them back into their chairs.

The music began again and was much improved.

Harrison and his Empress merely listened to the music for a while—listened gravely, as though synchronizing their heartbeats with it.

They shifted their weights to their toes.

Harrison placed his big hands on the girl's tiny waist, letting her sense the weightlessness that would soon be hers.

And then, in an explosion of joy and grace, into the air they sprang!

Not only were the laws of the land abandoned, but the law of gravity and the laws of motion as well.

They reeled, whirled, swiveled, flounced, capered, gamboled, and spun.

They leaped like deer on the moon.

The studio ceiling was thirty feet high, but each leap brought the dancers nearer to it.

It became their obvious intention to kiss the ceiling.

They kissed it.

And then, neutralizing gravity with love and pure will, they remained suspended in air inches below the ceiling, and they kissed each other for a long, long time.

It was then that Diana Moon Glampers, the Handicapper General, came into the studio with a double-barreled ten-gauge shotgun. She fired twice, and the Emperor and the Empress were dead before they hit the floor.

Diana Moon Glampers loaded the gun again. She aimed it at the musicians and told them they had ten seconds to get their handicaps back on.

It was then that the Bergerons' television tube burned out.

Hazel turned to comment about the blackout to George. But George had gone out into the kitchen for a can of beer.

George came back in with the beer, paused while a handicap signal shook him up. And then he sat down again. "You been crying?" he said to Hazel.

"Yup," she said.

"What about?" he said.

"I forget," she said. "Something real sad on television."

"What was it?" he said.

"It's all kind of mixed up in my mind," said Hazel.

"Forget sad things," said George.

"I always do," said Hazel.

"That's my girl," said George. He winced. There was the sound of a rivetting gun in his head.

"Gee—I could tell that one was a doozy," said Hazel.

"You can say that again," said George.

"Gee—" said Hazel, "I could tell that one was a doozy."

Chapter 40

Richard J. Arneson

EQUALITY AND EQUAL OPPORTUNITY FOR WELFARE

Richard Arneson (1945–   ) is a professor of philosophy at the University of California, San Diego, who has written widely in political philosophy and ethics, especially on consequentialism and egalitarianism. This essay (published in 1989) surveys various forms that a morally defensible egalitarianism could take, and winds up advocating a view called "equality of opportunity for welfare" on the grounds that such a view minimizes the extent to which individuals' fates are governed by brute luck, but nevertheless holds them responsible for those outcomes which are the products of their voluntary choices.

Insofar as we care for equality as a distributive ideal, what is it exactly that we prize? Many persons are troubled by the gap between the living standards of rich people and poor people in modern societies or by the gap between the average standard of living in rich societies and that prevalent in poor societies. To some extent at any rate it is the gap itself that is troublesome, not just the low absolute level of the standard of living of the poor. But it is not easy to decide what measure of the "standard of living" it is appropriate to employ to give content to the ideal of distributive equality. Recent discussions by John Rawls and Ronald Dworkin have debated the merits of versions of equality of welfare and equality of resources taken as interpretations of the egalitarian ideal. In this paper I shall argue that the idea of equal opportunity for welfare is the best interpretation of the ideal of distributive equality.

Consider a distributive agency that has at its disposal a stock of goods that individuals want to own and use. We need not assume that each good is useful for every person, just that each good is useful for someone. Each good is homogeneous in quality and can be divided as finely as you choose. The problem to be considered is: How to divide the goods in order to meet an appropriate standard of equality. This discussion assumes that some goods are legitimately available for distribution in this fashion, hence that the entitlements and deserts of individuals do not predetermine the proper ownership of all resources. No argument is provided for this assumption, so in this sense my article is addressed to egalitarians, not their opponents.

I. Equality of Resources

The norm of equality of resources stipulates that to achieve equality the agency ought to give everybody a share of goods that is exactly identical to everyone else's and that exhausts all available resources to be distributed. A straightforward objection to equality of resources so understood is that if Smith and Jones have similar tastes and abilities except that Smith has a severe physical handicap remediable with the help of expensive crutches, then if the two are accorded equal resources, Smith must spend the bulk of his resources on crutches whereas Jones can use his resource share to fulfill his aims to a far greater extent. It seems forced to claim that any notion of equality of condition that is worth caring about prevails between Smith and Jones in this case.

At least two responses to this objection are worth noting. One, pursued by Dworkin, is that in the example the cut between the individual and the resources at his disposal was made at the wrong place. Smith's defective legs and Jones's healthy legs should be considered among their resources, so that only if Smith is assigned a gadget that renders his legs fully serviceable in addition to a resource share that is otherwise identical with Jones's can we say that equality of resources prevails. The example then suggests that an equality of resources ethic should count personal talents among the resources to be distributed. This line of response swiftly encounters difficulties. It is impossible for a distributive agency to supply educational and technological aid that will offset inborn differences of talent so that all persons are blessed with the same talents. Nor is it obvious how much compensation is owed to those who are disadvantaged by low talent. The worth to individuals of their talents varies depending on the nature of their life plans. An heroic resolution of this difficulty is to assign every individual an equal share of ownership of everybody's talents in the distribution of resources. Under this procedure each of the N persons in society begins adult life owning a tradeable 1/N share of everybody's talents. We can regard this share as amounting to ownership of a block of time during which the owner can dictate how the partially owned person is to deploy his talent. Dworkin himself has noticed a flaw in this proposal, which he has aptly named

"the slavery of the talented." The flaw is that under this equal distribution of talent scheme the person with high talent is put at a disadvantage relative to her low-talent fellows. If we assume that each person strongly wants liberty in the sense of ownership over his own time (that is, ownership over his own body for his entire lifetime), the high-talent person finds that his taste for liberty is very expensive, as his time is socially valuable and very much in demand, whereas the low-talent person finds that his taste for liberty is cheap, as his time is less valuable and less in demand. Under this version of equality of resources, if two persons are identical in all respects except that one is more talented than the other, the more talented will find she is far less able to achieve her life plan than her less talented counterpart. Again, once its implications are exhibited, equality of resources appears an unattractive interpretation of the ideal of equality.

A second response asserts that given an equal distribution of resources, persons should be held responsible for forming and perhaps reforming their own preferences, in the light of their resource share and their personal characteristics and likely circumstances. The level of overall preference satisfaction that each person attains is then a matter of individual responsibility, not a social problem. That I have nil singing talent is a given, but that I have developed an aspiration to become a professional opera singer and have formed my life around this ambition is a further development that was to some extent within my control and for which I must bear responsibility.

The difficulty with this response is that even if it is accepted it falls short of defending equality of resources. Surely social and biological factors influence preference formation, so if we can properly be held responsible only for what lies within our control, then we can at most be held to be partially responsible for our preferences. For instance, it would be wildly implausible to claim that a person without the use of his legs should be held responsible for developing a full set of aims and values toward the satisfaction of which leglessness is no hindrance. Acceptance of the claim that we are sometimes to an extent responsible for our preferences leaves the initial objection against equality of resources fully intact. For if we are sometimes responsible we are sometimes not responsible.

The claim that "we are responsible for our preferences" is ambiguous. It could mean that our preferences have developed to their present state due to factors that lay entirely within our control. Alternatively, it could mean that our present preferences, even if they have arisen through processes largely beyond our power to control, are now within our control in the sense that we could now undertake actions, at greater or lesser cost, that would change our preferences in ways that we can foresee. If responsibility for preferences on the first construal held true, this would indeed defeat the presumption that our resource share should be augmented because it satisfies our preferences to a lesser extent than the resource shares of others permit them to satisfy their preferences. However, on the first construal, the claim that we are responsible for our preferences is certainly always false. But on the second, weaker construal, the claim that we are responsible for our preferences is compatible with the claim that an appropriate norm of equal distribution should compensate people for their hard-to-satisfy preferences at least up to the point at which by taking appropriate adaptive measures now, people could reach the same preference satisfaction level as others.

The defense of equality of resources by appeal to the claim that persons are responsible for their preferences admits of yet another interpretation. Without claiming that people have caused their preferences to become what they are or that people could cause their preferences to change, we might hold that people can take responsibility for their fundamental preferences in the sense of identifying with them and regarding these preferences as their own, not as alien intrusions on the self. T. M. Scanlon has suggested the example of religious preferences in this spirit. That a person was raised in one religious tradition rather than another may predictably affect his lifetime expectation of preference satisfaction. Yet we would regard it as absurd to insist upon compensation in the name of distributive equality for having been raised fundamentalist Protestant rather than atheist or Catholic (a matter that of course does not lie within the individual's power to control). Provided that a fair (equal) distribution of the resources of religious liberty is maintained, the amount of utility that individuals can expect from their religious upbringings is "specifically not an object of public policy."

The example of compensation for religious preferences is complex, and I will return to it in section II below. Here it suffices to note that even if in some cases we do deem it inappropriate to insist on such compensation in the name of equality, it does not follow that equality of resources is an adequate rendering of the egalitarian ideal. Differences among people including sometimes differences in their upbringing may render resource equality nugatory. For example, a person raised in a closed fundamentalist community such as the Amish who then loses his faith and moves to the city may feel at a loss as to how to satisfy ordinary secular preferences, so that equal treatment of this rube and city sophisticates may require extra compensation for the rube beyond resource equality. Had the person's fundamental values not altered, such compensation would not be in order. I am not proposing compensation as a feasible government policy, merely pointing out that the fact that people might in some cases regard it as crass to ask for indemnification of their satisfaction-reducing upbringing does not show that in principle it makes sense for people to assume responsibility (act as though they were responsible) for what does not lie within their control. Any policy that attempted to ameliorate these discrepancies would predictably inflict wounds on innocent parents and guardians far out of proportion to any gain that could be realized for the norm of distributive equality. So even if we all agree that in such cases a policy of compensation is inappropriate, all things considered, it does not follow that so far as distributive equality is concerned (one among the several values we cherish), compensation should not be forthcoming.

Finally, it is far from clear why assuming responsibility for one's preferences and values in the sense of affirming them and identifying them as essential to one's self precludes demanding or accepting compensation for these preferences in the name of distributive equality. Suppose the government has accepted an obligation to subsidize the members of two native tribes who are badly off, low in welfare. The two tribes happen to be identical except that one is strongly committed to traditional religious ceremonies involving a psychedelic made from the peyote cactus while the other tribe is similarly committed to its traditional rituals involving an alcoholic drink made from a different cactus. If the market price of the psychedelic should suddenly rise dramatically while the price of the cactus drink stays cheap, members of the first tribe might well claim that equity requires an increase in their subsidy to compensate for the greatly increased price of the wherewithal for their ceremonies. Advancing such a claim, so far as I can see, is fully compatible with continuing to affirm and identify with one's preferences and in this sense to take personal responsibility for them.

In practise, many laws and other public policies differentiate roughly between preferences that we think are deeply entrenched in people, alterable if at all only at great personal cost, and very widespread in the population, versus preferences that for most of us are alterable at moderate cost should we choose to try to change them and thinly and erratically spread throughout the population. Laws and public policies commonly take account of the former and ignore the latter. For example, the law caters to people's deeply felt aversion to public nudity but does not cater to people's aversion to the sight of tastelessly dressed strollers in public spaces. Of course, current American laws and policies are not designed to achieve any strongly egalitarian ideal, whether resource-based or not. But in appealing to common sense as embodied in current practises in order to determine what sort of equality we care about insofar as we do care about equality, one would go badly astray in claiming support in these practises for the contention that equality of resources captures the ideal of equality. We need to search further.

II. Equality of Welfare

According to equality of welfare, goods are distributed equally among a group of persons to the degree that the distribution brings it about that each person enjoys the same welfare. (The norm thus presupposes the possibility of cardinal interpersonal welfare comparisons.) The considerations mentioned seven paragraphs back already dispose of the idea that the distributive equality worth caring about is equality of welfare. To bring this point home more must be said to clarify what "welfare" means in this context.

I take welfare to be preference satisfaction. The more an individual's preferences are satisfied, as weighted by their importance to that very individual, the higher her welfare. The preferences that figure in the calculation of a person's welfare are limited to self-interested preferences—what the individual prefers insofar as she seeks her own advantage. One may prefer something for its own sake or as a means to further ends; this discussion is confined to preferences of the former sort.

The preferences that most plausibly serve as the measure of the individual's welfare are hypothetical preferences. Consider this familiar account: The extent to which a person's life goes well is the degree to which his ideally considered preferences are satisfied. My ideally considered preferences are those I would have if I were to engage in thoroughgoing deliberation about my preferences with full pertinent information, in a calm mood, while thinking clearly and making no reasoning errors. (We can also call these ideally considered preferences "rational preferences.")

To avoid a difficulty, we should think of the full information that is pertinent to ideally considered preferences as split into two stages corresponding to "first-best" and "second-best" rational preferences. At the first stage one is imagined to be considering full information relevant to choice on the assumption that the results of this ideal deliberation process can costlessly correct one's actual preferences. At the second stage one is imagined to be considering also information regarding (a) one's actual resistance to advice regarding the rationality of one's preferences, (b) the costs of an educational program that would break down this resistance, and (c) the likelihood that anything approaching this educational program will actually be implemented in one's lifetime. What it is reasonable to prefer is then refigured in the light of these costs. For example, suppose that low-life preferences for cheap thrills have a large place in my actual conception of the good, but no place in my first-best rational preferences. But suppose it is certain that these low-life preferences are firmly fixed in my character. Then my second-best preferences are those I would have if I were to deliberate in ideal fashion about my preferences in the light of full knowledge about my actual preferences and their resistance to change. If you are giving me a birthday present, and your sole goal is to advance my welfare as much as possible, you are probably advised to give me, say, a bottle of jug wine rather than a volume of Shelley's poetry even though it is the poetry experience that would satisfy my first-best rational preference.

On this understanding of welfare, equality of welfare is a poor ideal. Individuals can arrive at different welfare levels due to choices they make for which they alone should be held responsible. A simple example would be to imagine two persons of identical tastes and abilities who are assigned equal resources by an agency charged to maintain distributive equality. The two then voluntarily engage in highstakes gambling, from which one emerges rich (with high expectation of welfare) and the other poor (with low welfare expectation). For another example, consider two persons similarly situated, so they could attain identical welfare levels with the same effort, but one chooses to pursue personal welfare zealously while the other pursues an aspirational preference (e.g., saving the whales), and so attains lesser fulfillment of self-interested preferences. In a third example, one person may voluntarily cultivate an expensive preference (not cognitively superior to the preference it supplants), while another person does not. In all three examples it would be inappropriate to insist upon equality of welfare when welfare inequality arises through the voluntary choice of the person who gets lesser welfare. Notice that in all three examples as described, there need be no grounds for finding fault with any aims or actions of any of the individuals mentioned. No imperative of practical reason commands us to devote our lives to the maximal pursuit of (self-interested) preference satisfaction. Divergence from equality of welfare arising in these ways need not signal any fault imputable to individuals or to "society" understood as responsible for maintaining distributive equality.

This line of thought suggests taking equal opportunity for welfare to be the appropriate norm of distributive equality.

In the light of the foregoing discussion, consider again the example of compensation for one's religious upbringing regarded as affecting one's lifetime preference satisfaction expectation. This example is urged as a reductio ad absurdum of the norm of equality of welfare, which may seem to yield the counterintuitive implication that such differences do constitute legitimate grounds for redistributing people's resource shares, in the name of distributive equality. As I mentioned, the example is tricky; we should not allow it to stampede us toward resource-based construals of distributive equality. Two comments on the example indicate something of its trickiness.

First, if a person changes her values in the light of deliberation that bring her closer to the ideal of deliberative rationality, we should credit the person's conviction that satisfying the new values counts for more than satisfying the old ones, now discarded. The old values should be counted at a discount due to their presumed greater distance from deliberative rationality. So if I was a Buddhist, then become a Hindu, and correctly regard the new religious preference as cognitively superior to the old, it is not the case that a straight equality of welfare standard must register my welfare as declining even if my new religious values are less easily achievable than the ones they supplant.

Secondly, the example might motivate acceptance of equal opportunity for welfare over straight equality of welfare rather than rejection of subjectivist conceptions of equality altogether. If equal opportunity for welfare obtains between Smith and Jones, and Jones subsequently undergoes religious conversion that lowers his welfare prospects, it may be that we will take Jones's conversion either to be a voluntarily chosen act or a prudentially negligent act for which he should be held responsible. (Consider the norm: Other things equal, it is bad if some people are worse off than others through no voluntary choice or fault of their own.) This train of thought also motivates an examination of equal opportunity for welfare.

III. Equal Opportunity for Welfare

An opportunity is a chance of getting a good if one seeks it. For equal opportunity for welfare to obtain among a number of persons, each must face an array of options that is equivalent to every other person's in terms of the prospects for preference satisfaction it offers. The preferences involved in this calculation are ideally considered secondbest preferences (where these differ from first-best preferences). Think of two persons entering their majority and facing various life choices, each action one might choose being associated with its possible outcomes. In the simplest case, imagine that we know the probability of each outcome conditional on the agent's choice of an action that might lead to it. Given that one or another choice is made and one or another outcome realized, the agent would then face another array of choices, then another, and so on. We construct a decision tree that gives an individual's possible complete life-histories. We then add up the preference satisfaction expectation for each possible life history. In doing this we take into account the preferences that people have regarding being confronted with the particular range of options given at each decision point. Equal opportunity for welfare obtains among persons when all of them face equivalent decision trees—the expected value of each person's best (= most prudent) choice of options, second-best, . . . nth-best is the same. The opportunities persons encounter are ranked by the prospects for welfare they afford.

The criterion for equal opportunity for welfare stated above is incomplete. People might face an equivalent array of options, as above, yet differ in their awareness of these options, their ability to choose reasonably among them, and the strength of character that enables a person to persist in carrying out a chosen option. Further conditions are needed. We can summarize these conditions by stipulating that a number of persons face *effectively* equivalent options just in case one of the following is true: (1) the options are equivalent and the persons are on a par in their ability to "negotiate" these options, or (2) the options are nonequivalent in such a way as to counterbalance exactly any inequalities in people's negotiating abilities, or (3) the options are equivalent and any inequalities in people's negotiating abilities are due to causes for which it is proper to hold the individuals themselves personally responsible. Equal opportunity for welfare obtains when all persons face effectively equivalent arrays of options.

Whether or not two persons enjoy equal opportunity for welfare at a time depends only on whether they face effectively equivalent arrays of options at that time. Suppose that Smith and Jones share equal opportunity for welfare on Monday, but on Tuesday Smith voluntarily chooses or negligently behaves so that from then on Jones has greater welfare opportunities. We may say that in an extended sense people share equal opportunity for welfare just in case there is some time at which their opportunities are equal and if any inequalities in their opportunities at later times are due to their voluntary choice or differentially negligent behavior for which they are rightly deemed personally responsible.

When persons enjoy equal opportunity for welfare in the extended sense, any actual inequality of welfare in the positions they reach is due to factors that lie within each individual's control. Thus, any such inequality will be non-problematic from the standpoint of distributive equality. The norm of equal opportunity for welfare is distinct from equality of welfare only if some version of soft determinism or indeterminism is correct. If hard determinism is true, the two interpretations of equality come to the same.

In actual political life under modern conditions, distributive agencies will be staggeringly ignorant of the facts that would have to be known in order to pinpoint what level of opportunity for welfare different persons have had. To some extent it is technically unfeasible or even physically impossible to collect the needed information, and to some extent we do not trust governments with the authority to collect the needed information, due to worries that such authority, will be subject to abuse. Nonetheless, I suppose that the idea is clear in principle, and that in practise it is often feasible to make reliable rough-and-ready judgments to the effect that some people face very grim prospects for welfare compared to what others enjoy.

In comparing the merits of a Rawlsian conception of distributive equality as equal shares of primary goods and a Dworkinian conception of equality of resources with the norm of equality of opportunity for welfare, we run into the problem that in the real world, with imperfect information available to citizens and policy-makers, and imperfect willingness on the part of citizens and officials to carry out conscientiously whatever norm is chosen, the practical implications of these conflicting principles may be hard to discern, and may not diverge much in practise. Familiar information-gathering and information-using problems will make us unwilling to authorize government agencies to determine people's distributive shares on the basis of their preference satisfaction prospects, which will often be unknowable for all practical purposes. We may insist that governments have regard to primary good share equality or resource equality as rough proxies for the welfarist equality that we are unable to calculate. To test our allegiance to the rival doctrines of equality we may need to consider real or hypothetical examples of situations in which we do have good information regarding welfare prospects and opportunities for welfare, and consider whether this information affects our judgments as to what counts as egalitarian policy. We also need to consider cases in which we gain new evidence that a particular resource-based standard is a much more inaccurate proxy for welfare equality than we might have thought, and much less accurate than another standard now available. Indifference to these considerations would mark allegiance to a resourcist interpretation of distributive equality in principle, not merely as a handy rough-and-ready approximation.

IV. Straight Equality Versus Equal Opportunity; Welfare Versus Resources

The discussion to this point has explored two independent distinctions: (1) straight equality versus equal opportunity and (2) welfare versus resources as the appropriate basis for measuring distributive shares. Hence there are four positions to consider. On the issue of whether an egalitarian should regard welfare or resources as the appropriate standard of distributive equality, it is important to compare like with like, rather than, for instance, just to compare equal opportunity for resources with straight equality of welfare. (In my opinion Ronald Dworkin's otherwise magisterial treatment of the issue in his two-part discussion of "What Is Equality?" is marred by a failure to bring these four distinct positions clearly into focus.)

The argument for equal opportunity rather than straight equality is simply that it is morally fitting to hold individuals responsible for the foreseeable consequences of their voluntary choices, and in particular for that portion of these consequences that involves their own achievement of welfare or gain or loss of resources. If accepted, this, argument leaves it entirely open whether we as egalitarians ought to support equal opportunity for welfare or equal opportunity for resources.

For equal opportunity for resources to obtain among a number of persons, the range of lotteries with resources as prizes available to each of them must be effectively the same. The range of lotteries available to two persons is effectively the same whenever it is the case that, for any lottery the first can gain access to, there is an identical lottery that the second person can gain access to by comparable effort. (So if Smith can gain access to a lucrative lottery by walking across the street, and Jones cannot gain a similar lottery except by a long hard trek across a desert, to this extent their opportunities for resources are unequal.) We may say that equal opportunity for resources in an extended sense obtains among a number of persons just in case there is a time at which their opportunities are equal and any later inequalities in the resource opportunities they face are due to voluntary choices or differentially negligent behavior on their part

for which they are rightly deemed personally responsible.

I would not claim that the interpretation of equal opportunity for resources presented here is the only plausible construal of the concept. However, on any plausible construal, the norm of equal opportunity for resources is vulnerable to the "slavery of the talented" problem that proved troublesome for equality of resources. Supposing that personal talents should be included among the resources to be distributed (for reasons given in section I), we find that moving from a regime of equality of resources to a regime that enforces equal opportunity for resources does not change the fact that a resource-based approach causes the person of high talent to be predictably and (it would seem) unfairly worse off in welfare prospects than her counterpart with lesser talent. If opportunities for resources are equally distributed among more and less talented persons, then each person regardless of her native talent endowment will have comparable access to identical lotteries for resources that include time slices of the labor power of all persons. Each person's expected ownership of talent, should he seek it, will be the same. Other things equal, if all persons strongly desire personal liberty or initial ownership of one's own lifetime labor power, this good will turn out to be a luxury commodity for the talented, and a cheap bargain for the untalented.

A possible objection to the foregoing reasoning is that it relies on a vaguely specified idea of how to measure resource shares that is shown to be dubious by the very fact that it leads back to the slavery of the talented problem. Perhaps by taking personal liberty as a separate resource this result can be avoided. But waiving any other difficulties with this objection, we note that the assumption that any measure of resource equality must be unacceptable if applying it leads to unacceptable results for the distribution of welfare amounts to smuggling in a welfarist standard by the back door.

Notice that the welfare distribution implications of equal opportunity for resources will count as intuitively unacceptable only on the assumption that people cannot be deemed to have chosen voluntarily the preferences that are frustrated or satisfied by the talent pooling that a resourcist interpretation of equal opportunity enforces. Of course it is strictly nonvoluntary that one is born with a particular body and cannot be separated from it, so if others hold ownership rights in one's labor power one's individual liberty is thereby curtailed. But in principle one's self-interested preferences could be concerned no more with what happens to one's own body than with what happens to the bodies of others. To the extent that you have strong self-interested hankerings that your neighbors try their hand at, say, farming, and less intense desires regarding the occupations you yourself pursue, to that extent the fact that under talent pooling your own labor power is a luxury commodity will not adversely affect your welfare. As an empirical matter, I submit that it is just false to hold that in modern society whether any given individual does or does not care about retaining her own personal liberty is due to that person's voluntarily choosing one or the other preference. The expensive preference of the talented person for personal liberty cannot be assimilated to the class of expensive preferences that people might voluntarily cultivate. On plausible empirical assumptions, equal opportunity for welfare will often find tastes compensable, including the talented person's taste for the personal liberty to command her own labor power. Being born with high talent cannot then be a curse under equal opportunity for welfare (it cannot be a blessing either).

V. Sen's Capabilities Approach

The equal opportunity for welfare construal of equality that I am espousing is similar to a "capabilities" approach recently defended by Amartya Sen. I shall now briefly sketch and endorse Sen's criticisms of Rawls's primary social goods standard and indicate a residual welfarist disagreement with Sen.

Rawls's primary social goods proposal recommends that society should be concerned with the distribution of certain basic social resources, so his position is a variant of a resource-based understanding of how to measure people's standard of living. Sen holds that the distribution of resources should be evaluated in terms of its contribution to individual capabilities to function in various ways deemed to be objectively important or valuable. That is, what counts is not the food one gets, but the contribution it can make to one's nutritional needs, not the educational expenditures lavished, but the contribution they make to one's knowledge and cognitive skills. Sen objects to taking primary social goods measurements to be fundamental on the ground that persons vary enormously from one another in the rates at which they transform primary social goods into capabilities to function in key ways. Surely we care about resource shares because we care what people are enabled to be and do with their resource shares, and insofar as we care about equality it is the latter that should be our concern.

So far, I agree. Moreover, Sen identifies a person's well-being with the doings and beings or "functionings" that he achieves, and distinguishes these functionings from the person's capabilities to function or "well-being freedom." Equality of capability is then a notion within the family of equality of opportunity views, a family that also includes the idea of equal opportunity for welfare that I have been attempting to defend. So I agree with Sen to a large extent.

But given that there are indefinitely many kinds of things that persons can do or become, how are we supposed to sum an individual's various capability scores into an overall index? If we cannot construct such an index, then it would seem that equality of capability cannot qualify as a candidate conception of distributive equality. The indexing problem that is known to plague Rawls's primary goods proposal also afflicts Sen's capabilities approach.

Sen is aware of the indexing problem and untroubled by it. The grand theme of his lectures on "Well-being, Agency and Freedom" is informational value pluralism: We should incorporate in our principles all moral information that is relevant to the choice of actions and policies even if that information complicates the articulation of principles and precludes attainment of a set of principles that completely orders the available alternative actions in any possible set of circumstances. "Incompleteness is not an embarrassment," Sen declares. I agree that principles of decision should not ignore morally pertinent matters but I doubt that the full set of my functioning capabilities does matter for the assessment of my position. Whether or not my capabilities include the capability to trek to the South Pole, eat a meal at the most expensive restaurant in Omsk, scratch my neighbor's dog at the precise moment of its daily maximal itch, matters not one bit to me, because I neither have nor have the slightest reason to anticipate I ever will have any desire to do any of these and myriad other things. Presumably only a small subset of my functioning capabilities matter for moral assessment, but which ones?

We may doubt whether there are any objectively decidable grounds by which the value of a person's capabilities can be judged apart from the person's (ideally considered) preferences regarding those capabilities. On what ground do we hold that it is valuable for a person to have a capability that she herself values at naught with full deliberative rationality? If a person's having a capability is deemed valuable on grounds independent of the person's own preferences in the matter, the excess valuation would seem to presuppose the adequacy of an as yet unspecified perfectionist doctrine the like of which has certainly not yet been defended and in my opinion is indefensible. In the absence of such a defense of perfectionism, equal opportunity for welfare

looks to be an attractive interpretation of distributive equality.

Postscript (1995)

My 1989 essay contains an unclear presentation of the norm of equal opportunity for welfare and hence might convey the impression to the reader that the idea is inherently confused. It is not. For the sake of clarity it might be of use to restate the idea in several stages.

Roughly, we can say that equal opportunity for welfare obtains among a group of persons at a time just in case the highest level of expected welfare that each person could gain if she were to behave with perfect prudence is the same for all persons. But it would be implausible for the norm of equal opportunity for welfare to require that people have equal opportunity throughout their lives, because people who are initially equally favorably situated can make choices that result in some having diminished opportunities for welfare compared to the opportunities enjoyed by the rest. The intuitive idea that lies behind the equal opportunity norm is that each individual makes choices that affect her life prospects, and it is morally legitimate that each should bear the consequences of her choices, at least when society has provided a fair menu of options from which to choose. So the equal opportunity norm may provisionally be formulated so: equal opportunity for welfare obtains among a group of persons just in case at the onset of adulthood each person can choose among a set of life strategies, and if the person chooses prudently from this set, her expected welfare over the course of her life is the same as everyone else's.

One further refinement is needed to capture the equal opportunity norm. Two people may have equal opportunity as defined above even though their abilities to make use of these opportunities efficiently to advance their welfare are quite different. For example, suppose that in order to choose prudently one must carry out a mathematical calculation. One person can do it easily, a second cannot do it, a third can do it only with great difficulty, or with acute discomfort. In order to carry out the prudent choice, one must resist a certain temptation, and again we may imagine that people differ markedly in their native "choice-following" talents. I will say that *true equal opportunity for welfare* obtains among a number of persons when society compensates and adjusts for individuals' different abilities to negotiate options, so that if from the onset of adulthood each person behaved as prudently as could reasonably be expected in the light of her choice-making and choice-following abilities, she would have the same expected welfare over the course of her life as anyone else.

Society might compensate for differential choice-making and choice-following ability by providing extra resources to those with lesser abilities. Such compensation can take many forms besides provision of money. Guardrails and warning signs in front of obvious cliff edges at national parks provide no benefit to alert and prudently cautious park visitors but may prevent some injuries to the dull-witted, inattentive, and negligent. Compulsory government programs that require savings for old age tend to equalize opportunities for welfare among myopic and far-sightedly prudent citizens. In some cases paternalistic restrictions of liberty such as bans on dangerous recreational drugs serve a similar function. Since there are various dimensions of personal decision-making talent, and given the difficulty of separating a person's native endowment of prudential talent from the part of a person's present disposition to prudence that is due to her own hard-earned efforts at character transformation for which she should be given credit, it may be unclear what constitutes the level of prudent conduct that it is reasonable to expect of someone. In the simplest case, imagine that individuals differ only in their native willpower, so that individuals who make equal good faith efforts to be prudent may via unequal

willpower end up behaving with different degrees of prudence. In this case compensation and adjustment produce equal opportunity for welfare when it is the case that if each person made good faith efforts to be prudent, all would have equal expected welfare.

In 1989 I wrote that when people enjoy equal opportunity for welfare as characterized just above, "any actual inequality of welfare in the positions they reach is due to factors that lie within each individual's control." But this is obviously false. Equality of opportunity for welfare obtains between Smith and Jones if their expected welfare given reasonably prudent conduct is the same. Facing these equal prospects, Smith and Jones may make exactly the demanded reasonably prudent choices, yet one enjoys better luck, and Smith ends up leading a miserable existence, while Jones lives well. Equal prospects prior to choice are compatible with unequal welfare as individuals lead their lives that comes about through sheer brute luck. (A lightning bolt strikes Smith and misses Jones, who is standing next to her.) Hence equal opportunity for welfare can obtain among a group of persons even though it also turns out to be the case that some of these persons are worse off than others through no fault or voluntary choice of their own.

This discussion suggests an alternate ideal of equal opportunity, call it *equal opportunity for welfare in the strict sense*. Strict equal opportunity obtains among a number of people just in case at the onset of adulthood they face option sets such that if each behaves as prudently as could reasonably be expected, all will attain the same level of welfare over the course of their lives. When strict equal opportunity obtains, no one is worse off than others through no fault or voluntary choice of her own.

Which version of the equal opportunity for welfare norm is ethically more appealing? This is a tricky matter. One might object to strict equal opportunity on the ground that it is violated if two individuals have identical initial prospects and identical tastes and abilities, then engage voluntarily in high-stakes gambling, a game of sheer chance, from which one emerges with high welfare prospects and the other with low welfare prospects. Even though strict equal opportunity is violated here, one might argue that in the morally relevant sense, these two individuals did have equal opportunities for welfare, because the eventual differences in their welfare prospects came about only through a process that both mutually agreed to undergo under conditions of full information against a background of equal initial prospects.

On the other hand, equal opportunity as I characterized it in 1989 (what I am calling here *true equal opportunity for welfare*) can be fully satisfied in circumstances in which some people become worse off than others through processes that entirely bypass their own choice. This difficulty is described three paragraphs back. A vivid illustration of the possibility is provided by an example suggested by Brian Barry: Imagine that in a class-stratified capitalist society marked by great inequalities in life prospects social science researchers discover that for many years nurses in hospitals have been conspiring to switch babies randomly just after birth so that at birth each person faces equal lifetime prospects of welfare, which resolve into very unequal prospects as soon as the nurses' lottery is concluded and you are placed either with a poor family or a rich family. After discovering this odd fact, would we then say that we had thought the society was terribly unjust, but now we see that since everyone had initially equal prospects, the society was just in its distributive practices after all? The inegalitarian society adjusted by the nurses' conspiracy seems to me far from just in its distributive practices, but more nearly just than an otherwise similar society minus the nurses' conspiracy. The implication of this story does not carry over in a completely smooth way to a society regulated by the norm of what I am calling "true" equal opportunity for welfare, because of the wrinkle about requiring equal prospects at

the onset of adulthood. But it would be easy to invent a similar story about true equal opportunity for welfare that shows it vulnerable to Barry's criticism. As mentioned above, the point is that in a society in which the norm of true equal opportunity for welfare is perfectly satisfied, it may yet be the case that some people end up worse off than others through no fault or voluntary choices of their own. The ethical imperative of undoing the effects of unchosen luck on the quality of human lives is only incompletely satisfied in a society that fully satisfies true equal opportunity for welfare.

Up to this point I have been engaged in an intramural dispute among rival versions of equal opportunity for welfare. This family of equal opportunity for welfare norms has been subjected to attack, and the question arises to what extent the criticisms discredit the norm.

One criticism charges that the ideal of equal opportunity for welfare is utopian. We could not actually design and operate a society that would fulfill it. This criticism inflicts no significant damage. The ideal that everyone in the world should enjoy good health and longevity is also utopian, but this does not gainsay the desirability of the state of affairs posited as ideal. If a goal is worthwhile but unattainable, but we can approach it to greater or lesser extent, then a utopian ideal may dictate the eminently practical imperative that we ought to act so that we come as close to achieving the goal as is feasible.

A more significant worry is that given that some unfortunate persons could not be fully compensated for bad luck in their genetic endowments by any means, a serious attempt to attain equal life prospects for all would involve channeling all available resources to a few extremely unfortunate individuals, leaving these resource basin individuals still very badly off and the rest of the human race scarcely better off. The world being as it is, the average level of human welfare prospects would plummet if we tried to make welfare prospects as close to equal for all as possible. This point indicates that the norm of equal opportunity for welfare is one value among other values and that in practice many of these values conflict, so that more of one value means less of the others, and it is arguable that no single value should be given unqualified priority. At least, no version of the value of distributive equality is a likely candidate for the role of the single fundamental value to which all other values are to be subordinated. Any norm of equality, including equal opportunity for welfare, competes with other values and should sometimes lose the competition. My aim in my 1989 essay was not to gauge how important distributive equality is as it competes with other values, but to provide a plausible interpretation of the norm of distributive equality.

Some objections against equal opportunity for welfare are really objections against subjectivist conceptions of welfare. Consider Tiny Tim, the cripple in Charles Dickens's story *A Christmas Carol*. Being extremely cheerful and prone to appreciate small blessings, Tiny Tim can attain a high level of welfare construed as satisfaction despite his grave handicap and poverty. Yet we may judge he is one of society's unfortunates, entitled to compensation to offset his imposed poverty and physical disability. If equal opportunity for welfare cannot ratify this judgment, so much the worse for this ideal (so runs the objection).

In this example there is an implicit appeal to objectivist convictions about human welfare or well-being. We believe that there are some goods that are important constituents of a good human life, and that if one lacks too many of these constitutive elements one does not enjoy a good life, whatever one's level of preference satisfaction. With respect to this worry, my 1989 essay could have been more clear by stating that the conception of welfare I employed in formulating the equal opportunity norm is an objectivist conception—one according to which the measure of the welfare level that a person reaches is not fixed by that very individual's actual beliefs, desires,

and values. After all, the individual could be dead wrong about these matters. At any rate, the issue of whether an objectivist or a subjectivist conception of welfare is more adequate does not impugn the ideal of equal opportunity for welfare as such. This is merely an issue about how best to interpret the ideal.

A more direct challenge to equal opportunity for welfare challenges the normative plausibility of any conception of distributive equality. Perhaps distributive justice is not concerned with equality at all, beyond the formal equality that requires that whatever the rules in place, they should be applied equally and impartially to all persons within their jurisdiction. Insofar as we are committed to distributive justice, perhaps instead of trying to make everyone's condition the same in any sense we should be trying to make the condition of the worst-off person in society as favorable as it can be made. Or perhaps justice requires arranging social practices so that each person is kept above some minimally acceptable threshold of well-being and beyond this floor, human well-being in the aggregate is maximized. Or, to mention an alternative that strikes me as plausible, perhaps justice requires that practices be set so as to maximize some function of aggregate human well-being that gives extra weight to improving the welfare of those who are badly off and that also gives extra weight to securing improvements for more deserving individuals. To suggest a quite different line, perhaps justice is simply refraining from violating anyone's individual rights understood in a neo-Lockean fashion. None of the ideas of social justice just mentioned include any distributive equality requirement—that all persons' conditions be kept equally desirable. The issues raised here are delicate, complex, tangled, and fundamental. I would note only that the issue of the moral weight of the value of distributive equality is independent of the issue of how best to interpret the ideal of distributive equality. My 1989 essay explores the latter issue.

Chapter 41

David Schmidtz

EQUAL RESPECT AND EQUAL SHARES

David Schmidtz (1955–) is a professor of philosophy and economics at the University of Arizona, and the director of their program in the Philosophy of Freedom. In this essay (published in 2002), Schmidtz examines the nature of a morally attractive egalitarianism, and argues that while equality in terms of equal respect for and equal treatment of all persons is desirable, it does not, except in a narrow range of cases, entail equal distribution of resources.

I. Introduction

We are all equal, sort of. We are not equal in terms of our physical or mental capacities. Morally speaking, we are not all equally good. Evidently, if we are equal, it is not in virtue of our actual characteristics, but despite them. Our equality is of a political rather than metaphysical nature. We do not expect people to be the same, but we expect differences to have no bearing on how people ought to be treated as citizens. Or when differences do matter, we expect that they will not matter in the sense of being a basis for class distinction. We admire tenacity, talent, and so on, but do not take such features to entitle their bearers to be treated as "upper class." Neither are people who are relatively lacking in these features obliged to tolerate being treated as "lower class." As a society, we have made moral progress. Such progress consists in part of progress toward political and cultural equality.

Have we also made progress toward *economic* equality? If so, does that likewise count as moral progress? Some people have more than others. Some earn more than others. Do these things matter? In two ways, they could. First, we may care about differences in wealth and income on humanitarian grounds; that is, we may worry about some people having less not because less is less but because less sometimes is not enough. Second, we may care on grounds of justice; that is, we may think people would not have less if some injustice had not been done.

What provokes such concerns? One provocation is conceptual: philosophical thought experiments, and so on. We imagine how the world would be in some idealized hypothetical situation, and then ask whether departures from the ideal are unjust, and if so, how they might be redressed. A second provocation is empirical: statistical reports on income inequality, and so on. Statistics paint a picture of how the world actually is, and how unequal it is. We are left wondering whether such inequality is acceptable, and if not, what to do about it.

This essay examines these two provocations. In response to concerns of a conceptual nature,

Section II offers a limited defense of distribution according to a principle of "equal shares," explaining how and why even nonegalitarians can and should respect egalitarian concerns and make room for them even in otherwise nonegalitarian theories of justice. As Section III notes, though, "equal shares" is only one way of expressing egalitarian concern. The connection between equal treatment and justice may be essential, but the connection between equal treatment and equal shares is not. Sections IV and V reflect on why the rule of first possession limits attempts to distribute according to principles (not only egalitarian principles) of justice. Finally, in response to empirical concerns, Section VI examines recent studies of income distribution in the United States.

Undoubtedly, egalitarians will think I have not made *enough* room for egalitarian concern. After all, if an egalitarian is someone who thinks many economic goods should be distributed equally, and redistributed as often as needed so that shares remain equal, then at the end of the day, I am not an egalitarian. I am, however, a kind of pluralist. Justice is about giving people their due; if we are not talking about what people are due, then we are not talking about justice. On the other hand, what people are due is a complex, multifaceted, context-sensitive matter. There is a place for equal shares.

II. On Behalf of Equal Shares

Political theorist Bruce Ackerman's essay "On Getting What We Don't Deserve" is a short, engaging dialogue that captures the essence of egalitarian concern about the justice of differences in wealth and income. Ackerman imagines you and he are in a garden. As Ackerman tells the story, you see two apples on a tree and swallow them in one gulp while an amazed Ackerman looks on. Ackerman then asks you, as one human being to another, shouldn't I have gotten one of those apples?

Should he? If so, why? Why only one? What grounds our admittedly compelling intuition that Ackerman should have gotten one—exactly one—of those apples? Notably, Ackerman explicitly rejects the idea that his claim to an apple is based on need, signaling that his primary concern is not humanitarian. Instead, Ackerman's view is that the point of getting one apple is that one apple would have been an equal share. Equal shares is a moral default. Morally speaking, distribution by equal shares is what we automatically go to if we cannot justify anything else. As Ackerman sees it, to give Ackerman an equal share is to treat him with respect. In Ackerman's garden, at least, to say he does not command an equal share is to say he does not command respect.

Is Ackerman right? Looking at the question dispassionately, there are several things to say on behalf of equal shares as an allocation rule, even if we reject Ackerman's presumption in favor of it. In Ackerman's garden, equal shares has the virtue of not requiring further debate about who gets the bigger share. No one has reason to envy anyone else's share. When we arrive all at once, equal shares is a cooperative, mutually advantageous, mutually respectful departure from the status quo (in which none of us yet has a share of the good to be distributed). In short, equal shares is easy. We call it "splitting the difference," and often it is a pleasant way of solving our distributional problem. In the process, we not only solve the problem, but offer each other a kind of salute. In Ackerman's garden, it is an obvious way to divide things and get on with our lives—with no hard feelings at worst, and at best with a sense of having been honored by honorable people.

These ideas may not be equality's foundation, but they are among equality's virtues. Crucially, even nonegalitarians can appreciate that they are virtues. Thus, while critics may say Ackerman is assuming the egalitarianism for which he is supposed to be arguing, the virtues just mentioned beg no questions. Even from nonegalitarian perspectives, then, there is something to be said for equal shares. Therefore, whatever conception of justice we ultimately entertain, we can agree there is a place in a just society for dividing certain goods into equal shares. In particular, when we arrive at the bargaining table more or less at the same time, for the purpose of dividing goods to which no one has made a prior claim, we are in a situation where equal shares is a way of achieving a just distribution.

It may not be the only way. For example, we could flesh out the thought experiment in such a way as to make bargainers' unequal needs more salient than their equality as citizens. But it is one way.

III. An Egalitarian Critique of Equal Shares

Yet there are times when following the equal-shares principle—paying people the same wage, say—would fail to show others equal respect. Suppose an employer routinely expects more work, or more competent work, from one employee than from another, but sees no reason to pay them differently. In such cases, the problem is not raw wage differentials so much as a lack of proportion in the relations between contribution and compensation. The lack of proportion is one kind of unequal treatment. And unequal treatment, and the lack of respect it signals, is what people resent.

Children often are jealous when comparing their shares to those of their siblings—or, a bit more precisely, when comparing shares doled out by their parents. Why? Because being given a lesser share by their parents signals to them that they are held in lower esteem. They tend to feel differently about having less than their richest neighbor, because so long as no one is deliberately assigning them smaller shares, no one is sending a signal of unequal esteem. Here, too, the problem is departures from equal respect rather than from equal shares. Equal shares is not the same as equal respect, and is not always compatible with it. "Unequal pay for equal work" is offensive, but so is "equal pay for unequal work."

Intuitively, we all believe some people deserve more than others. This belief, though, is ambiguous. If I have better opportunities than you do, and as a result acquire more than you do, do I deserve more? Egalitarians will say no. The ambiguity is this: I do not deserve "more than you do" *under this description* because there never was a fair competition between us to determine which of us deserves more. Therefore, I do not deserve to have a central distributor maintain any particular ratio between your reward and mine. Nevertheless, notice what this leaves open. I may well deserve X while you deserve Y, on the basis of my working hard for X and your working hard for Y as we live our separate lives, with nothing in this story even suggesting that X = Y. Therefore, even if we were right to suppose that a central distributor would have no basis for judging us to be of unequal merit, and thus could be denounced for deliberately assigning unequal shares, we could still be wrong to infer that the shares we respectively deserve are equal.

Accordingly, there is a difference between unequal treatment and unequal shares. Unequal treatment presupposes treatment; unequal shares do not. If we are being *treated* unequally, then there is someone whom we can ask to justify treating us unequally. It would make sense for an egalitarian such as Ackerman to insist on this. Moreover, in Ackerman's garden, your grabbing both apples arguably is a token of unequal treatment. But what if Ackerman arrives several years after you have grabbed both apples and turned the garden into an orchard? Nonsimultaneous arrival complicates the case, making it harder to see the grab as a token of treatment at all, unequal or otherwise. Suffice it to say, we can be committed to denouncing unequal treatment without being committed to denouncing every unequal outcome as if it were a result of unequal treatment. Ackerman presumes the moral default (in a very general way) is equal shares. Even if, as seems likely, Ackerman is wrong, this is no reason to give up on the idea that the moral default is equal *treatment*.

A. Equal Worth and Equal Treatment

Suppose we have a certain moral worth that is not affected by our choices. That is, although we may live in a morally heroic way or a morally depraved way, how we live makes no difference as far as this moral worth is concerned: there is nothing we can do to make ourselves more or less worthy. If this were true, then we might all, as it happens, be of equal worth.

Now suppose instead that along certain dimensions our moral worth can be affected by our choices. In certain respects, that is, some of our choices make us more or less worthy. In this case, if in certain respects our choices affect our worth over time, it is unlikely that there will ever be a time when we are all of equal worth in those respects.

None of this is a threat to egalitarianism, because only a caricature of egalitarianism would presume that all of us are equally worthy along all dimensions. Instead, part of the point of the liberal ideal of political equality is to foster conditions under which we will tend to make choices that augment rather than diminish our worth along dimensions where worth depends on choice. Liberal political equality is not premised on the false hope that under ideal conditions, we all turn out to be equally worthy. It presupposes only a classically liberal optimism regarding the kind of society that results from putting people (all people, so far as this is realistically feasible) in a position to choose worthy ways of life.

B. Equality and Oppression

Humanitarianism is concerned with how people fare. Egalitarianism is concerned with how people fare relative to each other. So says philosopher Larry Temkin. Humanitarians, he says,

favor equality *solely* as a means to helping the worse off, and given the choice between redistribution from the better off to the worse off, and identical gains for the worse off with equal, or even greater, gains for the better off, they would see no reason to favor the former over the latter. . . . But such people are not egalitarians in my sense if their concerns would be satisfied by a system in which the poor had access to quality care, but the rich had even greater access to much better care.

Accordingly, what distinguishes egalitarianism from humanitarianism is that a humanitarian would never compromise the care offered to the poor merely to greatly worsen the care offered to the rich, whereas an egalitarian at least sometimes would. Temkin, himself an egalitarian, says the problem with humanitarianism is that it is not concerned with equality. In Temkin's words, "As a plausible analysis of what the egalitarian really cares about, . . . humanitarianism is a nonstarter."

Philosopher Elizabeth Anderson responds, "Those on the left have no less reason than conservatives and libertarians to be disturbed by recent trends in academic egalitarian thought." Academic egalitarians, she thinks, have lost sight of why equality matters. Thus, she criticizes philosopher Richard Arneson for saying, "The concern of distributive justice is to compensate individuals for misfortune. . . . Distributive justice stipulates that the lucky should transfer some or all of their gains due to luck to the unlucky." Along with Arneson, Anderson classifies Gerald Cohen and John Roemer as welfare egalitarians. She contrasts this group with those who advocate equalizing resources rather than welfare, such as Ronald Dworkin, Eric Rakowski, and Philippe Van Parijs. Despite differences between these thinkers, what their works collectively show, Anderson says, is that "[r]ecent egalitarian writing has come to be dominated by the view that the fundamental aim of equality is to compensate people for undeserved bad luck."

Anderson, though, thinks that "[t]he proper negative aim of egalitarian justice is not to eliminate the impact of brute luck from human affairs, but to end oppression." Egalitarianism's proper aim, she claims, is to enable us "to live together in a democratic community, as opposed to a hierarchical one."

Anderson says that "democratic equality's principles of distribution neither presume to tell people how to use their opportunities nor attempt to judge how responsible people are for choices that lead to unfortunate outcomes. Instead, it avoids bankruptcy at the hands of the imprudent by limiting the range of goods provided collectively and expecting individuals to take personal responsibility for the other goods in their possession." In contrast, Anderson argues, academic egalitarianism gains some undeserved credibility because we assume anything calling itself egalitarian must also be humanitarian. But although she is an egalitarian herself, Anderson says we cannot assume this connection. Moreover, the academic egalitarian's reasons for granting aid are disrespectful. When redistribution's purpose is to make up for someone's being less capable than others (due to bad luck in the natural lottery), the result in practice is that "[p]eople lay claim to the resources of egalitarian redistribution in virtue of their inferiority to others, not in virtue of their equality to others." Political equality has no such consequence. In the nineteenth century, when women began to present themselves as having a right to vote, they were presenting themselves not as needy inferiors but as autonomous equals—not as having a right to equal shares but as having a right to equal treatment.

We can draw two conclusions from all this. First, egalitarianism cannot afford to define itself by contrast with humanitarianism. No conception of justice can afford that. Second, egalitarians and nonegalitarians can agree that a kind of political equality is called for even when equal shares as a distributive principle is not. Thus, to the conclusion that a pluralistic theory of justice can make some room for equal shares, we can add that a pluralistic theory can make room for a second kind of equality as well, a specifically political kind.

C. Equality and Meritocracy

Very roughly, a regime is meritocratic to the extent that people are judged on the merits of their performance. A pure meritocracy is hard to imagine, but any regime is bound to have meritocratic elements. A corporation is meritocratic insofar as it ties promotions to performance, and departs from meritocracy insofar as it ties promotions to seniority. A society is meritocratic insofar as, within it, people are paid what their work is worth. In short, in meritocracies, rewards track performance. The important point is that rewards actually track performance; it is neither necessary nor sufficient that anyone *intends* for them to do so. A corporation's culture of meritocracy is often partially a product of deliberate design, but a corporation (or especially, a whole society) can be meritocratic in some ways without anyone deciding it ought to be.

The idea of meritocracy is vague, to be sure, yet precise enough for academic egalitarians to see conflict between equality and meritocracy. Thus, philosopher Norman Daniels says that claims of merit derive from considerations of efficiency and cannot support stronger notions of desert. Furthermore, regarding job placement, "the meritocrat is committed, given his concern for productivity, to distributing at least some goods, the jobs themselves, in accordance with a morally arbitrary distribution of abilities and traits." Daniels concludes, "Unfortunately, many proponents of meritocracy have been so concerned with combating the lesser evil of non-meritocratic job placement that they have left unchallenged the greater evil of highly inegalitarian reward schedules. One suspects that an elitist infatuation for such reward schedules lurks behind their ardor for meritocratic job placement."

Daniels's view exemplifies what Anderson calls academic egalitarianism, but liberalism also has an older, nonacademic tradition within which equal respect and meritocracy go hand in hand. We see people as commanding equal respect qua citizens or human beings, but not as commanding equal respect respect in every respect. Egalitarians and nonegalitarians alike appreciate that genuine respect has meritocratic elements, and thus to some extent tracks how people distinguish themselves as they develop their differing potentials in different ways.

Daniels says the "abilities and traits" that individuate people are "morally arbitrary," but I say that if we care about what people contribute to our society, then traits that enable people to contribute are not arbitrary. Those traits make people who they are and define what people aspire to be, at least in societies that respect those traits. We encourage people to work hard and contribute to society by truly respecting people who work hard, not by insisting that hard work is morally arbitrary while conceding a need to fake respect in hope of conditioning people to work harder. Incentive structures work better when we see them not merely as incentive structures but also as structures that recognize merit.

For practical purposes, certain kinds of egalitarian and meritocratic elements often go together. As a broad empirical generalization, wherever we find a substantial degree of political equality, we also find a substantial degree of economic meritocracy. Far from being antithetical, the two ideas are symbiotic. A central facet of the traditional liberal ideal of equal opportunity is a call for removing arbitrary political or cultural barriers to economic mobility. After the fact, we need not and do not attach the same value to what people produce. (Obviously, people themselves are not indifferent to whether their plans pan out one way rather than another. If our inventions work, we attach more value to them than we would have if they had

not, and we expect the market to do likewise.) Before the fact, though, traditional liberals want people—all people—to be as free as possible to pursue their dreams. That is to say, the equal-opportunity element of liberal tradition placed the emphasis on improving opportunities, not equalizing them. The ideal of "equal pay for equal work," within the tradition from which that ideal emerged, has more in common with the ideal of meritocracy, and with the kind of equal respect built into the concept of meritocracy, than with equal shares per se.

In passing, note that meritocracy is not a synonym for market society. Meritocrats could say the marketplace's meritocratic tendencies are too weak; great talent too often goes unrecognized and unrewarded. Egalitarians could say such tendencies are too strong; Daniels seems to worry that rewards for satisfying millions of customers are larger than they should be. Underlying both complaints is the more fundamental fact that markets react to performance only in the form in which said performance is *brought to market*. So long as Emily Dickinson kept her poetry secret, the marketplace had no opinion about its merits. The marketplace tends to reward a particular kind of performance—namely, wealth-creating performance—and tends to reward that kind of performance in a particular way—namely, with wealth, or sometimes with fame and glory. Markets create time and space within which people can afford hobbies; they can write poetry, if that is what pleases them, without having to worry about whether that particular activity is putting dinner on the table. But the marketplace generally does not judge, and does not reward, what people do with the space they reserve for nonmarket activities.

Let me stress that my remarks about the consistency of, and even synergy between, equality and meritocracy are offered in defense of the proposition that there is room within a pluralistic conception of justice for elements of egalitarianism. If, contrary to fact, it really were true that we had to make a choice between equality and meritocracy, it would be like choosing between egalitarianism and humanitarianism. When egalitarianism allows itself to be contrasted with humanitarianism, it begins to look monstrous. It likewise would be monstrous to reject a system not because it fails to recognize and reward merit, but precisely because it succeeds.

D. Pure Distribution is Rare

In the real world, almost nothing we do is purely distributive. To take from one and give to another does not only alter a distribution. It also alters the degree to which products are controlled by their producers. To redistribute under real-world conditions, we must alienate producers from their products. This alienation was identified as a problem by Marx, and ought to be regarded as a problem from any perspective.

In a world bound to depart systematically from egalitarian ideals, egalitarian philosophy can encourage these alienated and alienating attitudes, although egalitarian philosophy is not unique in this respect. As noted by Anderson, academic egalitarians tend to see luck as a moral problem. A purist meritocrat, though, would agree, saying success should not be mere luck, but ought to be earned. So, if meritocratic ideals had the actual effect of encouraging feelings of alienation in a world bound to depart systematically from meritocratic ideals, that would be regrettable. The general point here is that even when an uncompromisingly radical philosophy is attractive on its face, the psychological baggage that goes with it need not be. A theory of justice can deafen us to the cost of alienating producers from their product. It deafens us by telling us what we want to hear: that the product should be distributed in accordance with our dream, not the producers'.

Defenders of redistribution sometimes try to justify ignoring this cost. A familiar move is

to deny that people are producers. On this account, natural endowments produce. Characters produce. Persons do not. A person's character "depends in large part upon fortunate family and social circumstances for which he can claim no credit," and therefore, at least theoretically, there is a form of respect we can have for people even while giving them no credit for the effort and talent they bring to the table.

So the story goes. One basic problem with it is that the form of respect it posits is not the kind that brings producers to the table, and therefore that form of respect is, from any perspective, deficient. It is not the kind of respect that human beings value; it is not the kind that makes societies work.

Anderson notes, as many have noted, that egalitarians "regard the economy as a system of cooperative, joint production," in contrast with "the more familiar image of self-sufficient Robinson Crusoes, producing everything all by themselves until the point of trade." She goes on to say that we ought to "regard every product of the economy as jointly produced by everyone working together." By way of response, we all understand that Anderson's article is the product of a system of cooperative, joint production. We all know she did not produce it by herself. Yet we also understand that it is her article, and we would be furious were we to learn that Ackerman had walked into her office one day and said, "Shouldn't I get half of that article?" We do not start "from scratch." Rather, we build upon work already done. We weave our contribution into an existing fabric of contributions. We contribute at the margin (as an economist would put it) to the system of cooperative production, and, within limits, we are seen as owning our contributions, however humble they may be. This is why people continue to contribute, and this in turn is why we continue to have a system of cooperative production.

The most crucial point, perhaps, is that there is something necessarily and laudably ahistorical about simply respecting the abilities that people bring to the table. We need not always dig around for evidence (or worse, stipulate) that people are products of nature and nurture and therefore ineligible for moral credit. Neither must we think of our trading partners as Robinson Crusoes. Often, we simply give them credit, and often simply giving them credit is the essence of treating them as persons rather than as mere confluences of historical forces.

When we do choose to reflect on the historical background of any particular ongoing enterprise, it is appropriate to feel grateful to Thomas Edison and all those people who actually did help to make the current enterprise possible. It would be inappropriate (that is, disrespectful to people like Edison) to feel similarly grateful to people who did not actually do anything to help make the current enterprise possible. (To my mind, one of the most perfectly incredible facts about political philosophy is that, given the premise that thousands of people contribute to the tide of progress that puts individuals in a position to do what they do, we go on to debate whether the appropriate response is to honor those who did contribute or to take their money and give it to those who did not.) When particular people literally contribute to joint projects, they ought to feel grateful to each other and collectively proud of their joint achievement. However, they need not feign agnosticism about the specifics of each partner's contribution in cases where (as it usually works) they are keenly aware of the nature and value of what particular partners have contributed.

Of course, there is much to be said for acknowledging how lucky we are to live within this particular "system of cooperative, joint production" and for respecting what makes it work. My point is only (and my guess is that Anderson would agree) that the room we make for these attitudes must leave room for acknowledging complementary considerations: the kind that bring producers to the table, and the kind involved in treating individual flesh-and-blood workers with genuine respect.

IV. Equal Shares Versus First Possession

In Section II, I attributed to Ackerman the view that "equal shares" is a moral default, the distribution rule we automatically go to if we cannot justify anything else. Needles to say, that is not how we actually do it. For various resources in the real world, the principle we go to if we cannot justify anything else is one invoking first possession. If you walk into the cafeteria carrying two apples, we do not begin to discuss how to allocate them. If the apples are in your hand, their allocation normally is not our business.

Ackerman, though, rejects the rule of first possession. He says that "the only liberty worthy of a community of rational persons is a liberty each is ready and willing to justify in conversation with his fellow questioners. To ground rights on first possession is at war with this ideal." But if this is so, why is first possession ubiquitous? In Ackerman's garden, we are offended when you grab both apples. Why is the real world so different—so different that if Ackerman were to walk up to you in the cafeteria and say, "Shouldn't I get half of your lunch?" we would be offended by Ackerman's behavior, not yours?

Evidently, there is some difficulty in generalizing from Ackerman's thought experiment. Why? The main reason why Ackerman's point does not generalize is that in the real world we do not begin life by dividing a sack of apples that somehow, on its own, made its way to the bargaining table. Instead, we start with resources that some people have helped to produce and others have not, resources already possessed and in use by some people as others arrive on the scene. Contractarian frameworks like Ackerman's depict everyone as getting to the bargaining table at the same time; it is of fundamental moral importance that the world is not like that.

In a world where virtually everything at the table is there because someone brought it to the table, it is easy for equal respect and equal shares to come apart. In a world like that—a world like ours—to respect people is to acknowledge what they bring to the table, to respect the talent and effort manifest in what they bring, and to respect the hopes and dreams that lead them to bring what they do. But to respect them in this way is to respect their contributions as *theirs*.

A. Respect in a World of Nonsimultaneous Arrival

Why do property regimes around the world and throughout history consistently operate on a principle of first possession rather than one of equal shares? The reason, I suppose, starts with the fact that in the real world people arrive at different times. When people arrive at different times, equal shares no longer has the intuitive salience it had in the case of simultaneous arrival. When someone has gotten there first and is peacefully trying to put his or her discovery to use, trying to grab a piece of the action, even if only an equal piece, is not a peaceful act. It is not a respectful act. If Ackerman were to enter a corner grocery and begin discussing how to allocate whatever he can find in the cash register, as if the shopkeeper were merely another party to the discussion, he would not be treating the shopkeeper with respect. Here is a thought experiment: in a world where Ackerman was not obliged to respect prior possession, how long would shops remain open for business?

Academic lawyer Carol Rose says that a legal rule that confers the status of owner upon the first person unambiguously taking possession of a given object induces discovery. By inducing discovery, the rule induces future productive activity. A second virtue of such a rule is that it minimizes disputes over discovered objects. In short, it enables shopkeepers to make a living in peace.

Recall Ackerman's previous claim: "[T]he only liberty worthy of a community of rational persons is a liberty each is ready and willing to justify in conversation with his fellow questioners. To ground rights on first possession

is at war with this ideal." Simply dismissing the other side as at war with the ideal of rational conversation, as Ackerman does here, is itself at war with the ideal of rational conversation. The truth, for millennia, has been that failing to respect prior possession is the stuff of war in an absolutely literal way. Moreover, the central place of prior possession is not a cultural artifact. Virtually any animal capable of locomotion understands at some level that if you ignore the claim of an animal that got there first, you are not treating it with respect.

B. Xenophobia

An overlooked virtue of first possession is that it lets us live together without having to view newcomers as a threat, whereas a rule of equal shares does not. If we were to regard every newcomer as having a claim to an equal share of our holdings, the arrival of newcomers would be inherently threatening. Imagine another thought experiment: A town has one hundred people. Each has a lot that is one hundred feet wide. Every time someone new shows up, we redraw property lines. Each lot shrinks by the amount needed to make room for the new person's equal share. Question: how friendly will this town be? Even now, in our world, people who see the world in zero-sum terms tend to despise immigrants. The point is not that xenophobia has moral weight, of course, but rather that it is real, a variable we want to minimize if we can. Recognizing first possession helps, compared to redistributing according to an equal-shares principle. To say the least, it would not help to tell people that newly arriving immigrants have a right to an equal share. At first, members of the community would clamor for a wall to stop people from getting in. Eventually, the point of the wall would be to stop people from getting out.

Likewise, apropos Ackerman's assertion that a liberty is worthy only if we are each ready and willing to justify it in conversation, imagine a world in which the title to your property was perpetually contingent on your ability to defeat all challengers in debate. In any remotely successful community, quite a lot of the structure of daily life literally goes without saying and needs no argument; this enables people to take quite a lot for granted and allows them to pour their energy into production rather than self-defense, verbal or otherwise.

The central role played by prior possession in any viable culture, across human history, is a problem for egalitarianism, although not uniquely for egalitarianism. Meritocracy is equally in a position of having to defer somewhat to a norm of respecting prior possession. A viable culture is a web of positive-sum games, but a game is positive-sum only if players are willing to take what they have as their starting point and carry on from there. A viable conception of justice takes this (along with other prerequisites of positive-sum games) as its starting point.

V. The Zero-Sum Perspective

The obvious moral problem with first possession, of course, is that those who arrive later do not get an equal share. Is that fair? It depends. Exactly how bad is it to be a latecomer? Egalitarian thought experiments such as Ackerman's are zero-sum games. In such models, first possession leaves latecomers with nothing. When you, the first appropriator, grab both apples (or even one, for that matter), you leave less for Ackerman or anyone else who comes along later. Your grab is a preface to pure consumption. Thus, as philosopher Hillel Steiner has noted, in the same way that first-comers would see newcomers as a threat under an equal-shares regime, newcomers would see first-comers as a threat under a regime of first possession. Or at least, newcomers would see first-comers as a threat if it really were true that in a first-possession regime it is better to arrive early than late.

But this is not true. One central fact about a regime of first possession is that over time,

as a rule, it is far better to arrive late than early. It would be unusual to meet people in a developed nation who are not substantially more wealthy than their grandparents were at a comparable age. We have unprecedented wealth today precisely because our ancestors got here first, cleared the land, and began the laborious process of turning society into a vast network of cooperative ventures for mutual advantage. In the real world, original appropriation typically is a preface to production, and then to mutually advantageous commerce with widely dispersed benefits. It is not a zero-sum game. First possessors pay the price of converting resources to productive use. Latecomers reap the benefits. We occasionally should remind ourselves that in the race to appropriate, the chance to be a first appropriator is not the prize. The prize is prosperity, and latecomers win big, courtesy of the toil of those who got there first.

So, when someone asks why entrepreneurs should get to keep the whole value of what they produce, the answer is that they don't. To some people, this will seem obvious. Yet there are some who really do see the world in zero-sum terms. To them, when you grab an apple in Ackerman's garden and start planting apple seeds, it is analytic that no one else will ever benefit from all those future harvests.

A. Structural Unemployment

The zero-sum perspective is most tempting when viewing the labor market. Thus, philosopher Robert Goodin can say, "If there are a thousand people looking for work and only one job, one can get work only on condition that the remainder do not. That one person succeeds in getting a job, far from proving that all could, actually precludes others from doing so." Goodin admits labor markets are not really like that, yet he does not retract the claim. Citing philosopher G. A. Cohen, Goodin says, "Marxian economics provides reasons for believing that precisely that is true of the proletarian in any capitalist economy." That is, "If the structure of the situation is such that one can succeed only on condition that not all do, then the freedom of the one is perfectly consistent with the 'unfreedom' of the many." This is what has come to be called "structural" unemployment.

Some will see Goodin as stating a necessary truth: when two people apply for the same job, it is as if there were only one apple in Ackerman's garden. Others will say that in developed economies, the salient ratio is not (or not only) the number of jobs per *job-seeker* but the number of jobs per *month*. The former ratio leads people to misinterpret the supply of jobs as a stock rather than as a flow. If the unemployment rate is 10 percent, that does not mean one-tenth of the population is doomed to unemployment. For many, what it means is that their number is called less often than it would be if the rate were lower—unless there is genuine structural unemployment, as in countries where, for example, women are legally or culturally barred from working. But what creates structural unemployment is structure, not the rate of flow in the labor market.

B. Markets are not Auctions

If society were a zero-sum game, then the only way for some to have more would be for others to have less. When we see society as actually like this, we are tempted to believe the argument that when some people have more dollars, they bid up prices of whatever is available for purchase, thereby outcompeting cash-poor people and making them worse off. This is an interesting and rhetorically powerful idea. It would even be true in a society where people acquire paper dollars from a central distributor without having done anything to create the stock of wealth for which those paper dollars are supposed to be a receipt. But now contrast this zero-sum picture with a generally more realistic picture of market society. If I acquire more dollars by contributing more goods and services to the economy, then

my participation in the economy is not inflationary. On the contrary, insofar as people give me paper dollars in exchange for goods and services I bring to market, the process by which I acquire dollars has a deflationary impact, for the result of my contribution is that there now are more goods and services in circulation with no corresponding increase in the number of paper dollars in circulation. The net impact of the process by which I amass paper dollars is that *prices fall*, unless the money supply is increased to keep pace with the increased volume of goods and services in circulation.

Many people, though, continue to be swayed (if not downright blinded) by arguments premised on the assumption that for some to have more, others must have less. For some reason, this assumption is unshaken by everyday observation of people acquiring wealth not by subtracting it from a fixed stock, but by adding goods and services to the economy.

C. Sexism

Goodin's odd picture of what it is like to participate in an economy is implicit in arguments of theorists who occasionally propose, as a way of redressing our society's sexist bias, that mothers be paid a wage simply for being mothers. This too begins with an interesting and rhetorically powerful idea: When men go to the factory and women stay home to manage the household, they both work really hard. The men get paid. Why don't the women?

Here is one answer. The problem is not that the market does not recognize *women*, but that it does not recognize what is *not brought to market*. Suppose a farmer raises a crop while his wife raises children. Is it sexist that only the man's labor earns money? To test the hypothesis, imagine a farmer saying to prospective customers, "My wife and I have two things for sale: first, the fact that we are growing a crop, and second, the fact that we are raising six kids." Would prospective customers volunteer to pay the farmer for raising crops, but not for raising children?

If they would, that might suggest a sexist bias. But they would not. Their response would be, "Just show us what you have for sale. If your crop or your day-care services are for sale, we're interested. When your kids have goods of their own for sale, we'll be interested. But if what you want is to be paid to consume your own crop and raise your own kids, then in all seriousness, we have children of our own to feed. By the way, would you be better off if the king took your money to feed our kids and took our money to feed yours? Would your daughters be better off if women were expected to maximize their family's slice of the redistributive pie by having more babies than they otherwise would want? Would that end sexism?"

When people say women should be paid to raise their own children, it is as if a farmer demanded to be paid for raising a crop without actually having brought anything to market. It is to fail to grasp what is involved in exchanging value for value. It is a mistake to criticize markets for failing to commodify children. Commodifying children would be catastrophic for everyone, but especially for women. If we want to keep making progress toward the kind of society in which men and women can flourish as political equals, we need to find another way.

VI. About Empirical Studies

I close with observations about the other major source of provocation mentioned at the outset—namely, empirical studies of income inequality. Although I am a professor of economics by joint appointment, I am at heart a philosopher. I trust conceptual arguments. I do not want to win arguments I do not deserve to win, and when the terrain is conceptual, I trust myself to know where I stand. I do not feel this way about statistics. This section's main purpose is not to settle some empirical issue, but simply to show how easily numbers create false impressions.

For example, studies of income distribution typically separate populations into quintiles according to household income. While each quintile for household income contains 20 percent of all households by definition, as of 1997 the United States's bottom quintile contained only 14.8 percent of individual persons, whereas the top quintile contained 24.3 percent. Households in the bottom quintile averaged 1.9 persons and 0.6 workers, compared to 3.1 persons and 2.1 workers in the top. So, one major source of income inequality among households is that some contain more wage-earners than others. If we look at raw data comparing household incomes in the top and bottom quintiles, we will not see this, and will be misled.

We can be misled in another way when studying changes in household income in a society where the number of wage-earners per household is falling. When the number of wage-earners per household falls, average *household* income can fall even as *individual* incomes rise. If two people live in a typical college-student household today versus three in a household a generation ago, this will show up in our statistics as a fall in the bottom quintile's average income. Yet in such cases, household income falls because the individuals are more wealthy, not less, which is why they now can afford to split the rent with fewer people.

It is easy to dig up a study showing that average wages fell by, say, 9 percent between 1975 and 1997, if that is what we want to hear. If not, it is equally easy to verify that such studies are based upon a discredited way of correcting for inflation (in addition, these studies ignore factors such as the burgeoning of fringe benefits) and that when we use more currently accepted ways of correcting for inflation, the corrected numbers show average wages rising 35 percent between 1975 and 1997. In 1996, a panel of five economists, commissioned by the Senate Finance Committee and chaired by Michael Boskin, concluded that the consumer price index overstates inflation by about 1.1 percent per year (perhaps as little as 0.8 percent; perhaps as much as 1.6 percent). If the figure of 1.1 percent is correct, then "instead of the stagnation recorded in official statistics, a lower inflation measure would mean that *real* median family income grew from 1973 to 1995 by 36 percent."

If there is one thing I would like readers to take away as the message of this section, it would not be a number. It would be the following picture. An income distribution is a bunch of people occupying steps on a staircase. Pessimists use numbers to show that the bottom step is where it always has been. Even worse, they claim, the staircase has begun to stretch. The top now climbs higher than it once did, thereby increasing the gap between the top and bottom steps, that is, between the rich and poor. Optimists use the same numbers to show that people who once stood on the lower steps have moved up. While there are still people at the bottom, many belong to a younger generation whose time to move up is still coming. From a "snapshot" perspective, the picture is one of stagnation, but to people actually living these lives, the staircase is a moving escalator, lifting people to heights that did not exist when their grandparents were children. This perspective—which treats life in the way people actually live it—is a picture of incremental improvement.

I am not asking you to be an optimist. The message, instead, is that the pessimistic perspective is, at very best, only one way of being realistic. At bottom, the profound truth of the matter may be, as philosopher Richard Miller once remarked to me, that there is a place for a Democratic sort of emphasis on complaining about where some of us had to start, and also a place for a Republican sort of emphasis on accepting our starting point as a starting point and making the best of it.

A. Inequality and Age in the United States

Statistics seem to indicate that the rich are getting richer. The income gap between the top quintile and other quintiles has, by some measures, been growing. What does this mean? For the sake of reference, when we divide households into income quintiles, the income cutoffs as of 1999 are as follows:

Lowest quintile: Zero to $17,262
Second quintile: $17,263 to $32,034
Third quintile: $32,035 to $50,851
Fourth quintile: $50,852 to $79,454
Top quintile: $79,455 and up

Household income at the 80th percentile is thus 4.6 times household income at the 20th percentile. Compare this to the median household incomes of different age groups, as of 1999:

$24,031 when the head of the household is under 25
$43,309 when the head of the household is between ages 25 and 34
$54,993 when the head of the household is between ages 35 and 44
$65,303 when the head of the household is between ages 45 and 54
$54,249 when the head of the household is between ages 55 and 64

Like the gaps between the quintiles, gaps between age groups appear to be increasing. Where earnings had once begun to trail off as workers entered their forties, earnings now continue to rise as workers reach their fifties, only then beginning to drop as early retirements start to cut into average earnings. Economist Michael Cox and journalist Robert Alm report that "[i]n 1951, individuals aged 35 to 44 earned 1.6 times as much as those aged 20 to 24, on average. By 1993, the highest paid age group had shifted to the 45 to 54-year-olds, who earned nearly 3.1 times as much as the 20 to 24-year-olds."

The numbers seem to say that the top quintile cannot be characterized as a separate caste of aristocrats. To some extent, the quintiles appear to be constituted by ordinary median people at different ages. So, when we read that median income at the 80th percentile has jumped by 46 percent in real dollar terms between 1967 and 1999, we should entertain the likelihood that for many people living at the 20th percentile, that jump represents increasing opportunity for them, not just for some separate elite. It represents what many reasonably hope to earn as they reach the age when people like them take their turn composing the top quintile. Again, the fact that 45- to 54-year-olds are doing much better today, thereby widening the gaps between income quintiles, appears to be good news for a lot of people, not only for people currently in that age group.

Even if the lowest quintile has not been getting richer over time, this does not mean that the group of people flipping burgers a generation ago is still today stuck flipping burgers. Rather, the implication is that when this year's crop of high school graduates flips burgers for a year, they will get paid roughly what their parents were paid when they were the same age, doing the same things. (What else would we expect?) Again, if today's bottom 20 percent is no richer than the bottom 20 percent was a generation ago, the upshot is that the lowest-paying *jobs* do not pay much more than they ever did, not that the people who once held those jobs still hold them today.

Although the lowest-paying jobs may not pay much more now than they ever did, we know many low-pay workers did not remain low-pay workers. "Individuals in the lowest income quintile in 1975 saw, on average, a $25,322 rise in their real income over the sixteen years from 1975 to 1991. Those in the highest income quintile had a $3,974 increase in real income, on average." How could people who had been in the bottom quintile gain over six times as much as people who had been in the top one? Assuming the numbers indicate something real, my conjecture would be that, again, what we call income quintiles are, to some extent, different

age groups. Over sixteen years, people who had in 1975 made up a large part of the top quintile edged into retirement while younger people who had made up a large part of the bottom quintile in 1975 hit their peak earning years. This is only a conjecture, but it would explain why those who had composed the bottom quintile gained substantially more over sixteen years than those who had composed the top did.

B. *While the Rich get Richer*

Ideally, we want to know two things. First, are people doing better than their parents were doing at the same age? Second, do people do better as they get older? The answer to each of these crucial questions appears to be yes in general, although obviously I do not mean to suggest everyone is doing well. Still, in general, the numbers seem to say that it is not only the already rich who are getting richer. There are many more people *getting* rich. In 1967, only 3.2 percent of U.S. households were making the equivalent of $100,000 in 1999 dollars. By 1999, the number had risen to 12.3 percent. For whites, the increase was from 3.4 to 12.9 percent; for blacks, the increase was from 1.0 to 6.1 percent. So, if we ask why the top quintile made further gains between 1967 and 1999, it apparently would be incorrect to explain the change by saying that a small cadre of people had a lot of money in 1967 and that by 1999 that same cadre had pulled even farther ahead. On the contrary, what seems to explain the burgeoning wealth of the top quintile is that millions upon millions of people joined the ranks of the rich. These people were not rich when they were younger. Their parents were not rich. But they are rich today.

In "America's Rags-to-Riches Myth," journalist Michael M. Weinstein says Americans "cling to the conceit that they have unrivaled opportunity to move up." But the conceit, Weinstein says, is merely that. Yet Weinstein is aware that the U.S. Treasury Department's Office of Tax Analysis found that of people in the bottom income quintile in 1979, 65 percent moved up two or more quintiles by 1988. Eighty-six percent jumped at least one quintile. Are these findings unique? There is room for skepticism, here as elsewhere. But no, the finding is not unique. Using independent data from the Michigan Panel Study of Income Dynamics, Cox and Alm's study tracked a different group occupying the lowest quintile in 1975, and saw 80.3 percent of the group move up two or more quintiles by 1991. Ninety-five percent moved up at least one quintile. Furthermore, 29 percent moved from the bottom quintile to the top quintile between 1975 and 1991. In absolute terms (that is, in terms of income gains in real dollar terms), the improvement is even larger. In absolute terms, 39.2 percent of those in the bottom quintile in 1975 had, by 1991, moved to where the top quintile had been in 1975. Only 2.3 percent remained at a living standard equal to that of 1975's lowest quintile.

These studies do not show us to be a nation of people lifting ourselves out of poverty "by our own bootstraps," though, because not everyone with a low income is from a poor background. Many low-income people are students who receive substantial family support. We should not infer from Cox and Alm's study that family background does not matter. Researchers Daniel McMurrer, Mark Condon, and Isabell Sawhill say:

> Overall, the evidence suggests that the playing field is becoming more level in the United States. Socioeconomic origins today are less important than they used to be. Further, such origins have little or no impact for individuals with a college degree, and the ranks of such individuals continue to increase. This growth in access to higher education represents an important vehicle for expanding opportunity. Still, family background continues to matter. While the playing field may be becoming more level, family factors still significantly shape the economic outcomes of children.

A related issue: we have looked at the upward mobility of individuals, but we find less mobility in studies tracking households. Researchers Greg Duncan, Johanne Boisjoly, and Timothy Smeeding estimate that if we were to look at household rather than individual mobility, we would see that 47 percent of those in the bottom quintile in 1975 were still there in 1991. (Actually, they refer to the bottom quintile as "the poor," which is an increasingly untenable equation as the percentage of households officially in poverty continues to drop.) Twenty percent moved to the distribution's top half, and 6 percent moved to the top quintile.

These numbers suggest household mobility is quite substantial; nevertheless, there apparently is a big difference between individual upward mobility and household upward mobility. Why would that be? Imagine a household with two teenagers, circa 1975. Two studies track this household. One study tracks household members as individuals, and finds that sixteen years later the teenagers' incomes have risen several quintiles. A second study tracking the original household as a household finds that the household lost the summer wages the now-departed teenagers earned while living at home. When the teenagers left home, they disappeared from the second study because the households they went on to form did not exist when the study began in 1975. That is, a longitudinal study tracking 1975 households ignores individuals who grow up, move out, form new households, and move up after 1975. Given the same data, a longitudinal study of circa-1975 households paints a picture of modest progress while a longitudinal study of circa-1975 individuals suggests volcanic upward mobility. Which picture is more realistic?

Duncan et al. do not reveal the basis of their estimates. I have no reason to doubt them, but it is interesting that Duncan et al. mention later in their article that their data set, drawn from the Michigan Panel Study, "is designed to be continuously representative of the nonimmigrant population as a whole." I presume they have reasons for excluding immigrants, yet I would wager that immigrant households are more upwardly mobile than nonimmigrant households. Immigrant and nonimmigrant individuals may not differ much, relatively speaking, since they all start with teenage incomes and then move up. Households, though, are another matter, since if we exclude immigrant households, we are excluding households that are not established but are instead in a position like that of individual teenagers: they have little wealth and little income, for now, but they came here to work and make a major move up as a household. A focus on households already lends itself to an understatement of income mobility, compared to studies that focus on tracking individuals. Excluding immigrant households presumably increases the magnitude of that relative understatement.

Again, I do not mean to say that the study by Duncan et al. is especially flawed. On the contrary, it is not. Like any other study, it is potentially informative, and potentially misleading. It offers not simply numbers, but interpretations of numbers. Any study of income mobility begins with key decisions about what the researchers are looking for. Different studies measure different things, and no one is to blame for that.

Weinstein simply dismisses Cox and Alm's study of individuals on the ground that many people who moved up were people who were students when the study began. Of course students make up a big part of the bottom quintile, and of course they move up, Weinstein says, but so what? "This upward mobility of students hardly answers the enduring question: How many grown-ups are trapped in low-paying jobs?" Weinstein answers his own question by saying, "The answer is, a lot." Oddly, though, the only evidence he offers that "a lot" of grown-ups are trapped is a study of poverty among children. To that study we now turn.

C. Children

In their study, economists Peter Gottschalk and Sheldon Danziger separated children into quintiles according to family income. Their data, Weinstein reports, shows that "[a]bout 6 in 10 of the children in the lowest group—the poorest 20 percent—in the early 1970's were still in the bottom group 10 years later. . . . No conceit about mobility, real or imagined, can excuse that unconscionable fact."

Since Weinstein relies solely on Gottschalk and Danziger, I checked the original study. Gottschalk and Danziger were studying American children that were 5 years old or younger when their ten-year studies began—ten years later, the children were still children. What we appear to have, then, is a cohort of mostly young couples with babies, about 40 percent of whom had moved into higher quintiles ten years later. Is this percentage bad? Out of context, it looks neither bad nor good. Has any society ever done better?

Yes. It turns out at least one society has done better: the United States itself. The figure cited by Weinstein is the result from the first decade of a two-decade study. Weinstein presents the figure from the 1970s (only 43 percent moving up) as an indictment of America today, neglecting to mention that the study's corresponding figure from the 1980s was 51 percent. Although the two figures come from the same table in Gottschalk and Danziger's paper, Weinstein evidently felt the more up-to-date number and the upward trend were not worth mentioning.

A further thought: At the end of the Gottschalk-Danziger studies, the parents of the studied children are (generally) in their early thirties, still ten years away from the time when they become most upwardly mobile. And of course, the kids are still thirty years away from the time when they become most upwardly mobile. So, the Gottschalk-Danziger studies end at a point where I would have predicted it would be too soon for there to be much evidence of upward mobility.

I myself would have been one of those kids they are talking about. I grew up on a farm in Saskatchewan. We sold the farm when I was 11 and moved to the city, where Dad became a janitor and Mom became a cashier in a fabric shop. Even before we left the farm, we had already moved up in absolute terms—we got indoor plumbing when I was about 3 years old—but we would still have been in the bottom quintile. Even after we got a flush toilet, water had to be delivered by truck, and it was so expensive that we flushed the toilet only once a day—and it served a family of eight. Thirty-five years later, my household income is in the top 5 percent of the overall distribution. Had I been part of Gottschalk and Danziger's study, though, Weinstein would have been professing to be outraged by the "unconscionable" fact that when I was 10 years old, I had not yet made my move.

In my case, the problem with childhood poverty was not lack of money. Money was never a problem. Even the toilet was not really a problem. Lack of knowledge was a problem. Lack of educated role models was a problem. (My parents received sixth-grade educations. I did not know what a university was until we moved to the city.) I suspect that the Internet notwithstanding, the big obstacles I faced continue to be big obstacles for poor kids today.

Let us return to the study. As I said, I would have predicted that we would see precious little evidence of upward mobility in a study that ends before subjects reach their mid-teens. But let us take a look. According to Gottschalk and Danziger, among children in bottom-quintile families that received welfare payments in the early 1970s, 2.3 percent were in households that rose beyond the second quintile by the early 1980s. Bottom-quintile children living in single-parent families had a 6.4 percent chance of being in a household that moved beyond the second quintile. Unsurprisingly, one-adult households brought in less income than two-adult households at both points in time, and therefore we find them in the bottom two quintiles. How bad is that? The poverty rate in the United States continues to fall and was most recently measured at 11.8 percent, which means that being in the bottom two quintiles—the bottom 40 percent—is not the synonym for "being poor" that it once was.

If there is a problem here, it appears to have less to do with differences in income and wealth per se and more to do with single parenthood (and I do not pretend to know how to solve that problem). Economist Robert Lerman estimates that half the increase in income inequality observed in the late 1980s and early 1990s was due to an increase in the number of single-parent households. According to Gottschalk and Danziger, there is a big difference between being poor and white and being poor and black: blacks are more likely to stay in the bottom quintile. I am reluctant to quarrel with Gottschalk and Danziger here, and yet, according to their own numbers, the result of their ten-year study begun in 1971 is that "black children had a *higher* chance than white children of escaping poverty if they made the transition from a single-parent family to a 2-parent family by the end of the decade (67.9 versus 42.6 percent)." Looking at results of the second study, begun in 1981, we find the chance of a child escaping poverty (actually, the bottom quintile) upon moving from a single-parent to a two-parent family improving to 87.8 percent for blacks and 57.6 percent for whites.

The numbers seem to say that race is not the problem; again, coming from a single-parent family is the problem. However, in the 1980s, whites were nearly three times as likely as blacks to make that move from single-parent to two-parent families (which represents a closing of what had been a fourfold gap in the 1970s). Furthermore, black children are more likely to be in a single-parent setting in the first place. As of 1998, the percentage of out-of-wedlock births was 21.9 percent for non-Hispanic whites and 69.3 percent for blacks. I trust even hardcore egalitarians will agree that what is bad about these numbers is how high they are, not how unequal they are.

In the 1980s, Gottschalk and Danziger say, the overall probability that a child would escape poverty was higher than it was in the 1970s, although the improvement was not significant. For the record—using their numbers—the chance of escaping poverty improved from 43.2 percent to 51.2 percent. Oddly, when Gottschalk and Danziger say that an eight-point swing is not significant, they do not hasten to clarify what this means. What they do not say is that although the change appears huge, they did not collect enough data to be able to call the improvement *statistically* significant. Uncritical readers such as Weinstein are left to infer that there was no improvement.

Gottschalk and Danziger say that "only one demographic group (children in two parent families) shows a significant decline in the probability of remaining poor." (What a discouraging thought—that we have reached a point where children in two-parent families are "only one demographic group.") Within that group, the chance of escaping poverty improved from 47 percent in the 1970s to 65 percent in the 1980s. Again, there is something so odd here that I am left not knowing what to think: the authors acknowledge the massively improved prospects of "children of two parent families" parenthetically, as if that class were a small anomaly that does not bear on their contention that the probability of escaping poverty has not significantly improved.

Finally, recall that we are talking about the chance of escaping poverty (more accurately, the bottom quintile) before leaving the 10–15 age bracket. If we sought deliberately to design an experiment guaranteed to show no evidence of vertical mobility, we could hardly do better. Yet what Gottschalk and Danziger's numbers say is that nearly two-thirds of poor kids in unbroken homes escape poverty before earning their first paycheck. If Gottschalk and Danziger's numbers are right, then it is fact, not myth: these kids live in a land of opportunity.

Are growing differences in wealth and income a problem? Maybe so, in some respects. Nothing said here proves otherwise. The truly obvious problem, though, is more specific. In general, in the United States, poor people not only can but typically do move up—it is kids from broken homes who have a problem.

D. The Political Problem

One might argue that the problem of inequality is fundamentally caused by a lack of political will to "soak" the rich. We can imagine asking young poor people whether it is to their advantage for us to raise marginal rates on the tax brackets they are hoping to move into. It is possible they will say yes, but it is equally possible that the tax hike would take a bigger bite out of their ambitions than out of rich people's wallets. (This last claim may be very hard to imagine for people who grew up in middle-class homes and never saw working-class life as an option, but a "What's the point?" sentiment was common among people with whom I grew up at a time when marginal tax rates were higher.)

Would "soaking the rich" lead to greater equality? The answer, obviously, is that it depends on how the tax revenues would be distributed. The current U.S. federal budget is 1.7 trillion dollars. If we were to distribute that kind of money among the 14.8 percent of people who make up the poorest 20 percent of American households—roughly forty million people—we would already have enough to give a little over $40,000 to each person. A family of four would receive over $160,000. Of course, nothing remotely like that is happening. Why not? At least a part of the story is that the federal government has other priorities, and always will. We might suspect the problem cannot be solved by giving the government more money. After all, gaps between rich and poor apparently widened in tandem with rising federal budgets.

We can hope that as the rich get richer, more money will trickle down to the poor. We can also hope that as federal budgets grow, money will trickle down to the poor. But the rich have been getting richer, and federal budgets have grown. So, if the trickle down is not working now, perhaps it never will. In particular, as federal budgets grow, we would expect to reach a point (if we have not already done so) where the trickle down would come to a halt, or even reverse itself. The reason is that as budgets grow, it becomes increasingly worthwhile for special interest groups to fight for control of those budgets at the expense of the politically disenfranchised. If unequal concentrations of political power can be thought of as a beast, then government budgets are part of what feeds that beast and gives it reason to live. Although it is beyond the scope of this essay, my guess is that an effective coalescing of will and ability to help people avoid or at least cope with single parenthood and other pressing problems is more likely to occur in those local nongovernmental organizations whose budgets are small enough and whose governance is transparent enough to be less inviting to political opportunists.

VII. Summary

As economist Amartya Sen says, "[E]very normative theory or social arrangement that has at all stood the test of time seems to demand equality of *something*." It is worth adding, though, that by the same token every theory, including egalitarian theories, countenances inequality as well. An egalitarian is a person who embraces one kind of unequal treatment as the price of securing equality of (what he or she considers) a more important kind.

There is a place for equal shares. Paradigmatically, there is a place for the principle of equal shares when we arrive simultaneously at the bargaining table to distribute goods to which no one has any prior claim. It would be a thankless task to try to construct a complete catalog of cases where equal shares is most salient. Suffice it to say that we can ask what the virtues of equal shares would be in a given context, were we to assess the principle without begging the question; that is, were we to assess the principle by reference to moral considerations that do not presuppose the principle. This is how we can try to make room for any given principle of justice within a pluralist theory.

Equal respect is among the most basic of moral desiderata. Equal respect or equal treatment may be analytically built into the concept of justice even if equal shares is not. The idea of giving people their due is the basic concept of justice, not merely a contested conception. And the idea of giving people their due is hard to separate (at least at the most abstract level) from an ideal of equal treatment.

However, it would be a mistake to think that a commitment to treat people with equal respect entails a *general* commitment to make sure they have equal shares. In the marketplace, at least, meritocracy can embody one way of implementing a conception of equal treatment. Historically, "equal pay for equal work" has been seen this way within the liberal tradition.

First possession arguably is not a principle of justice at all, yet it plays a central role in any viable society. It is one of the signposts by which we navigate in a social world. We can question the principle in theory (and in theory it probably is easier to attack than to defend), but we do not and cannot question the principle in our daily practice. We would be lost without it.

Empirically, it can be hard to know what to make of recent income trends. We are barraged by numbers, or by interpretations thereof, and people skilled at gathering numbers are not always so skilled at interpreting them. If I were to do serious empirical work, I would ask why people today generally look forward to standards of living almost beyond the imagination of their ancestors from a century ago. (Life expectancy, for example, has nearly doubled.) I would ask who has been left behind by this burgeoning of real prosperity and why, and what can be done about it. I would not assume that all problems have solutions, nor that all solutions are worth their costs. Optimist that I am, I assume we can do better. Realist that I am, I know we could do worse.

PART 3

Global Justice

3a. IMMIGRATION

DEBATES ABOUT IMMIGRATION POLICY often end up with one side accusing the other of bad faith. Advocates of open immigration accuse those who defend closed borders of being racists, fascists, or both. Those who argue in favor of tighter restrictions on immigration, on the other hand, often see immigrants and their advocates as threats to the survival of the cultural or economic way of life they hold dear. This degeneration into name-calling is unfortunate, however, because it ignores the fact that immigration is a complex and multifaceted moral issue, raising difficult questions to which neither side has entirely satisfying answers. Hopefully, philosophers can do better.

One of the key philosophical issues raised by the immigration debate is the moral significance of national borders. In a sense, the fact that national borders matter at all is surprising. After all, the trend in moral philosophy since its beginning in Greece has been toward a kind of cosmopolitanism—the view that all human beings everywhere are of fundamentally equal moral value, and worthy of equal respect. But if this is the case, why should we think that we have a moral duty to pay taxes to provide for basic necessities and social services for those people who live on one side of an imaginary line, but not for those who live on the other? Or, to put the question somewhat less contentiously, if all persons everywhere are moral equals, then why should we set up political institutions to discharge our moral duties among each other in a way that leaves people with such *unequal* access to the benefits of those institutions?

The case for restrictions on immigration, then, will generally rest on establishing some justification for *nationalism* as opposed to *cosmopolitanism*—establishing, that is, the claim that we are morally justified in being especially concerned about, or giving special treatment to, our co-nationals as opposed to other persons with whom we do not share such a relation.

Surprisingly, the nationalist/cosmopolitan divide does not map well onto the standard left/right political division. Popularly, it is true, those on the political left tend to be in favor of more open immigration while those on the political right oppose it. But the correlation is far from perfect, nor is it clearly supported by the logic of the underlying arguments. Those in the libertarian wing of the political right, for instance, will often favor more open immigration on grounds of individual freedom. If A wants to rent a home from B and work for C, then why should it matter that A is currently a citizen of a different country than B and C? What business does the state have in preventing A from engaging in voluntary labor and housing arrangements with B and C? Furthermore, the same efficiency arguments which support the right's defense of free trade across borders in goods such as cars and services would seem to support the free movement of persons. On the other hand, those on the political left have some reason to oppose free immigration insofar as there is some evidence that increased immigration lowers wages for domestic unskilled labor—a group that the political left is often concerned to protect. Moreover, open immigration can make the maintenance of a generous social welfare state more difficult. It is easier to provide a robust social safety net when (a) the people to whom that safety net is provided are ones with whom you can identify culturally and historically, rather than recent immigrants, and (b) the number of people to whom the safety net is provided (and hence the cost of providing that safety net) is relatively small and stable.

More broadly, the claim that restrictions on immigration are necessary to protect culture, especially a country's *political* culture, is one that should have some traction for theorists anywhere on the ideological spectrum. The point is most salient, of course, for conservatives in the classic sense, who put a premium on the preservation of a nation's traditions and values. But even a libertarian who believes that government should be tightly restricted to the protection of individual rights would have reason to worry if she believed that a large percentage of immigrants would be hostile to that vision of government, and would express that hostility at the voting booth. The same is true for liberals and communitarians who value cultural solidarity as an end in itself or as a means toward the political solidarity of the welfare state. One need not think that these cultural considerations are overridingly important to recognize that they have some importance, and to realize that the various cross-cutting issues involved in the politics of immigration will often make for very strange bedfellows indeed!

But the question of how *much* immigration to allow is not the only question of philosophic interest surrounding this topic. For if we concede that *some* restrictions on immigration are permissible, then we must ask the further question of what *form* those restrictions will take. Specifically, is it morally permissible for a country to give preference to some sorts of immigrants over others? Should the decision of which immigrants to accept be guided by national economic self-interest alone (i.e. which immigrants can do the most good for *us*), or by humanitarian concern (i.e. which immigrants can we do the most good for), or by some mixture of both? What weight should be given to considerations of diversity and non-discrimination in immigration decisions? If selecting immigrants with high economic value adversely affects members of certain racial and ethnic groups, is this a problem? Or is adverse effect nothing to worry about so long as our policy is not *intentionally* discriminatory along racial lines, but only incidentally so in virtue of our concern with legitimate economic issues?

The readings in this section will almost certainly not settle the contentious debate over the morality of immigration policy. That would be too much to ask. What is not too much to ask, I hope, is that readers come away with an appreciation of the strength of the arguments that the other side has to offer in this debate. On this issue, like so many others, there is much room for reasonable disagreement between well-meaning persons.

Further Reading

Blake, M. (2003). Immigration. In R. G. Frey (Ed.), *A Companion to Applied Ethics: Blackwell Companions to Philosophy*, pp. 224–237. Malden, MA: Blackwell Publishing.

Block, W. (1998). A Libertarian Case for Free Immigration. *Journal of Libertarian Studies, 13*(2), 167–186.

Carens, J. H. (2003). Who Should Get In? The Ethics of Immigration Admissions. *Ethics and International Affairs, 17*(1), 95–110.

Cole, P. (2001). *Philosophies of Exclusion: Liberal Political Theory and Immigration*. Edinburgh: Edinburgh University Press.

Dummett, M. (2001). *On Immigration and Refugees*. New York: Routledge.

Hoppe, H.-H. (1998). The Case for Free Trade and Restricted Immigration. *Journal of Libertarian Studies, 13*(2), 221–233.

Hospers, J. (1998). A Libertarian Argument Against Opening Borders. *Journal of Libertarian Studies, 13*(2), 153–165.

Kukathas, C. (2003). Immigration. In H. LaFollette (Ed.), *The Oxford Handbook of Practical Ethics*, pp. 567–590. Oxford: Oxford University Press.

Kymlicka, W. (1996). Social Unity in a Liberal State. *Social Philosophy and Policy, 13*(1), 105–136.

Chapter 42

Chandran Kukathas

THE CASE FOR OPEN IMMIGRATION

Chandran Kukathas (1957–) is a professor of political theory at the London School of Economics, who has written widely on multiculturalism and liberalism. In this essay (published in 2005), Kukathas makes the case for open borders on the grounds of individual freedom and humanity. While he believes that this argument can stand up against existing anti-immigration arguments based on cultural and economic considerations, Kukathas concedes that his position challenges an idea of state sovereignty that is very deeply seated in the modern world.

P eople favor or are opposed to immigration for a variety of reasons. It is therefore difficult to tie views about immigration to ideological positions. While it seems obvious that political conservatives are the most unlikely to defend freedom of movement, and that socialists and liberals (classical and modern) are very likely to favor more open borders, in reality wariness (if not outright hostility) to immigration can be found among all groups. Even libertarian anarchists have advanced reasons to restrict the movement of peoples.

The purpose of this essay is to make a case for greater freedom of movement or, simply, freedom of immigration. Its aim is to defend immigration against critics of all stripes, and also to defend immigration against some of its less enthusiastic friends.

To put a case for free immigration is not easy. Though it may be simple enough to enunciate political principles and stand doggedly by them, in questions of public policy coherence and consistency are merely necessary, but not sufficient,

virtues. The feasibility of any policy proposal is also important, and political theory needs to be alive to this. "How open can borders be?" is an obvious question that it may not be possible to evade. The defense of free immigration offered here is, I hope, sensitive to this requirement. Nonetheless, it is an important part of its purpose to suggest that, in the end, political theory needs also to be suspicious of feasibility considerations, particularly when they lead us to morally troubling conclusions.

Before proceeding to the defense of free immigration, however, it will be important to understand what precisely immigration amounts to, and to recognize the nature of the *problem* of immigration as it exists in the world today. This is the task of the first section of this essay. The second section defines and offers a short defense of free immigration. The three sections that follow then consider various challenges to the principle of free immigration coming from economic, national, and security perspectives, and argue that each challenge can be met. The final section offers some general reflections on the dilemmas of contemporary immigration policy, before restating more forcefully the case for the free movement of peoples.

The Problem of Immigration in the Modern World

More than 100 million people today live outside of the states of which they are citizens. But this figure does not come close to identifying the numbers of people who are moving about from country to country across the globe. Many people move between countries as tourists, businessmen, sportswomen or performers without ever stopping to "live" in a country – let alone with any intention to settle in a foreign land. Global human movement is a fact of life, as it has been for centuries, if not for all of human history. This has always had its own difficulties. But the problem of immigration is a problem of a particular kind, for immigrants are people who aim to stop rather than simply to pass through – though, as we shall see, the definition of "stopping" is not an easy one to establish. The migration of people is a problem in the modern world because that world is a world of states, and states guard (sometimes jealously) the right to determine who may settle within their borders. Immigration may be defined as the movement of a person or persons from one state into another for the purpose of temporary or permanent settlement.

Modern states are reluctant to allow people to enter and settle within their borders at will for a variety of reasons. Security is one important consideration, though different states have different security concerns. The United States at present fears terrorist attacks and has tightened its immigration laws in part because of concerns for the safety of its citizens. China, on the other hand, has different security concerns since its political system does not permit much internal freedom of movement and could not tolerate an uncontrolled influx of foreigners into a

population that harbors dissidents who would challenge the authority of the government. For states such as Israel, security is a prominent concern, but perhaps one no more important than the desire to preserve a certain cultural integrity. A state founded as a Jewish homeland cannot allow immigration to transform it into a multicultural polity.

For modern liberal democratic states, however, there are a number of important reasons why immigration is problematic. These states, including Canada, the United States, Australia, Britain, and several countries in Western Europe, are particularly popular destinations for immigrants, whether because they are refugees seeking safe havens, or simply people looking to improve their prospects of a better life. One important reason why immigration is a problem in these cases is that immigrants impose costs on society even as they bring benefits. While economists tend to agree that the consequences of free movement are generally positive, since competitive labor markets make for a more efficient use of resources, not all nations may benefit immediately from an influx of immigrants. Nor do the burdens of accommodating or adjusting to immigrants fall equally on all within a society – much will depend on who the immigrants are, where they settle, and with whom they end up competing for jobs, real estate, and public facilities. Even if the benefits of immigration outweigh the costs to the nation, those who are adversely affected by an influx of settlers will object; and in liberal democratic states this will translate into electorally significant opposition.

Another important reason why immigration is a problem in liberal democratic states is that these states are, to varying degrees, welfare states. The state in such societies provides a range of benefits, including education, unemployment relief, retirement income, medical care, as well as numerous programs to serve particular interests. Immigrants are potential recipients of these services and benefits, and any state considering the level of immigration it will accept will have to consider how likely immigrants are to consume these benefits, how much they might consume, whether or not they are going to be able to finance the extra costs from the lifetime tax contributions of these immigrants, and what are the short-term implications of accepting immigrants who begin by consuming more in benefits than they pay in taxes. Consequently, such states are reluctant to accept immigrants who are infirm, or too old to contribute enough in taxes in their remaining working lives to cover the costs of medical care and retirement subsidies.

Under these circumstances liberal democratic governments will go to great lengths to limit immigration, though they will face pressures both to admit and refuse entry to applicants seeking to enter their countries. The pressures to admit will come from businesses looking for cheaper labor, from humanitarian groups calling for the admission of refugees, and from families and ethnic communities pressing to have relatives join them from their countries of origin. The pressures to refuse entry will generally come from labor unions, from "nativist" groups, and from conservatives concerned about the cultural and economic impact of settlers, particularly if the settlers are predominantly from ethnically different countries. The lengths to which liberal democratic states might go to discourage immigration is well illustrated by the reaction of the Australian government in August 2001 to the appearance near its coastal waters of a Norwegian merchant vessel, *The Tampa*, bearing refugees rescued at sea. The vessel was denied permission to enter Australian waters and to offload its human cargo, which was shipped to the island of Nauru to prevent the refugees from appealing for asylum in Australia. More recently, the United States responded to the crisis in Haiti in February 2004 by intervening to encourage the departure of President Aristide, and to restore some degree of order, because it feared an exodus of Haitian refugees making their way to Florida.

Immigration is a problem largely because of the nature of the modern state. Most states, and certainly all liberal democratic states, regard their people as "citizens" or "members" of the state. Membership is not standard, and the nature of membership has a substantial bearing on the rights that individuals have within a state. Full membership might amount to citizenship and include the right to vote and stand for public office. (Though it is worth noting that in the United States, for example, even full citizenship does not entitle a member to stand for the office of President if he or she was not born in the country.) "Permanent resident" status might give one the right to work and to change employer at will, and also to draw on health, education, and welfare services, but not provide security against deportation. Status as a "guest-worker" or temporary resident might provide fewer rights still. Modern states restrict immigration because they must manage access to the goods for which immigrants and natives would compete. Modern states are like clubs that are reluctant to accept new members unless they can be assured that they have more to gain by admitting people than they have by keeping them out.

In Defense of Free Immigration

Given that immigrants will compete for goods and resources with natives, why should states open their borders when it is their task to manage affairs within their domains? Does the idea of open immigration not go against the principles of good husbandry?

There are many reasons why borders should be open and the movement of people should be free. But before considering these reasons more closely, it should be admitted that the prospect of states opening their borders completely is a remote one. Even as the European Union expands its membership and facilitates freer movement among its denizens, to take one possible counter-example to this claim, it continues to control entry into Europe − and is feeling the pressure from member states to tighten restrictions on entry from refugees and displaced people. "Open borders" is not a policy option currently being considered by any state. Nonetheless, the case for open borders should be considered, though in the end, as we shall see, it cannot be defended without rethinking the idea of the state.

There are two major reasons for favoring open borders. The first is a principle of freedom, and the second a principle of humanity.

Open borders are consistent with − and on occasion, protect − freedom in a number of ways. First, and most obviously, closed borders restrict freedom of movement. Borders prevent people from moving into territories whose governments forbid them to enter; and to the extent that they cannot enter any other territory, borders confine them within their designated boundaries. This fact is not sufficient to establish that so confining people is indefensible; but if freedom is held to be an important value, then there is at least a case for saying that very weighty reasons are necessary to restrict it.

Several other considerations suggest that such reasons would have to be weighty indeed. First, to keep borders closed would mean to keep out people who would, as a consequence, lost not only the freedom to move but also the freedom they might be seeking in an attempt to flee unjust or tyrannical regimes. The effect of this is to deny people the freedom they would gain by leaving their societies and to diminish the incentive of tyrannical regimes to reform the conditions endured by their captive peoples. Second, closing borders means denying people the freedom to sell their labor, and denying others the freedom to buy it. Good reasons are needed to justify abridging this particular freedom, since to deny someone the liberty to exchange his labor is to deny him a very significant liberty. Third, and more generally, keeping borders closed would mean restricting people's freedom to associate. It would require keeping

apart people who wish to come together whether for love, or friendship, or for the sake of fulfilling important duties, such as caring for children or parents.

Now, to be sure, defenders of restricted immigration do not generally argue that borders should be completely sealed, or that no one should be admitted. Many concede that exceptions should be made for refugees, that some people should be allowed to come into a country to work, and that some provision should be made for admitting people who wish to rejoin their families. Those who want restricted or controlled immigration are not indifferent to freedom. Nonetheless, even those who argue for generous levels of immigration by implication maintain that people should be turned away at the border. This in itself is a limitation of liberty, for which good reasons must be given. In the end, or so I will argue, the reasons that have been offered are not weighty enough to justify restricting freedom even to a limited degree.

The second reason for favoring open borders is a principle of humanity. The great majority of the people of the world live in poverty, and for a significant number of them the most promising way of improving their condition is to move. This would remain true even if efforts to reduce trade barriers were successful, rich countries agreed to invest more in poorer ones, and much greater amounts of aid were made available to the developing world. For even if the general condition of a society were good, the situation of particular individuals would often be poor, and for some of them immigration would offer the best prospect of improving their condition. To say to such people that they are forbidden to cross a border in order to improve their condition is to say to them that it is justified that they be denied the opportunity to get out of poverty, or even destitution. And clearly there are many people who share this plight, for numerous illegal immigrants take substantial risks to move from one country to another − courting not only discomfort and even death by traveling under cover in dangerous conditions, but also punishment at the hands of the authorities if caught.

A principle of humanity suggests that very good reasons must be offered to justify turning the disadvantaged away. It would be bad enough to meet such people with indifference and to deny them positive assistance. It would be even worse to deny them the opportunity to help themselves. To go to the length of denying one's fellow citizens the right to help those who are badly off, whether by employing them or by simply taking them in, seems even more difficult to justify – if, indeed, it is not entirely perverse.

Not all people who look to move are poor or disadvantaged. Nor do all of them care about freedom. But if freedom and humanity are important and weighty values, the prima facie case for open borders is a strong one, since very substantial considerations will have to be adduced to warrant ignoring or repudiating them. I suggest that no such considerations are to be found. But to show this, it is necessary to look more closely at arguments that restrictions of immigration are defensible, and indeed desirable.

Economic Arguments Against Open Borders

It is sometimes argued that there are strong economic arguments for limiting immigration. There are two kinds of concern here. The first is about the impact of migrants on the local market economy: large numbers of people entering a society can change the balance of an economy, driving down wages or pushing up the prices of some goods such as real estate – to the disadvantage of many people in the native population. The second is about the impact of migrants on the cost and availability of goods and services supplied through the state: education, healthcare, welfare, and the publicly funded infrastructure of roads, parks, and other non-excludable goods. Do these concerns warrant closing borders to immigrants?

In the end, the answer must be that they do not. But the reasons why are not as straightforward as might be anticipated. If our concern is the impact of migrants on the local market economy, one argument often advanced by economists is that, on balance, the net impact of immigrants is mildly positive. While immigrants do take jobs that might have gone to locals and drive down wages, while driving up some prices, they also have a positive impact on the economy. Migrants expand the size of the workforce and extend the division of labor, so society gains from the benefits this brings. As new consumers, they expand the size of the domestic market and help to lower prices for many goods. Measuring the precise impact of any cohort of immigrants is difficult; but the overall impact is, at best, positive and, at worst, only mildly negative – even with respect to employment. Moreover, the global effect of migration is positive, as it involves a movement of people from places where they are less productive and often unable to make a living to places where they are both more productive and better off – and in many cases no longer a burden on their societies.

The problem, however, is that whatever the overall impact of migration, particular persons will do badly out of it. An influx of cheap labor may be good for society overall, but bad for those who are put out of work or forced to accept lower wages. It is to these people that the critic of open borders will point to illustrate the economic costs of immigration. Why should they bear the costs? Equally, why should other societies be happy about the brain-drain that is also an aspect of immigration, as skilled people leave their native countries for better opportunities abroad?

While it is true that the burdens and benefits of immigration do not fall evenly or equitably on all members of a host society, open borders are defensible nonetheless for a number of reasons. First, it has to be asked why it must be assumed that locals are entitled to the benefits they enjoy as people who have immediate access to particular markets. As residents or citizens, these people enjoy the rents they secure by virtue of an arrangement that excludes others from entering a particular market. Such arrangements are commonplace in every society, and indeed in the world as a whole. Often those who find a resource to exploit, or a demand which they are particularly able to fulfill, are unable to resist the temptation to ensure that they enjoy the gains to be had in exploiting that resource or fulfilling that demand by preventing others from doing the same. Yet it is unclear that there is any principle that can justify granting to some persons privileged access to such rents. To be sure, many of the most egregious examples of rent-seeking (and rent-protecting) behavior are to be found in the activities of capitalist firms and industries. But this does not make such activity defensible, since it serves simply to protect the well-off from having to share the wealth into which they have tapped with those who would like to secure a little of that same wealth for themselves.

If we are considering labor markets, there is no good reason to exclude outsiders from offering their labor in competition with locals. While it may disadvantage locals to have to compete, it is equally true that outsiders will be disadvantaged if they are forbidden to do so. Also, locals who would benefit from the greater availability of labor would also be disadvantaged by the exclusion of outsiders. To prevent, say, firms from hiring outside labor would be no more justifiable on economic grounds than preventing firms from moving their operations abroad to take advantage of cheaper or more productive labor in other countries.

The same arguments hold if we are considering the case of people who wish to move to a different country to sell not their labor but their wares – perhaps by setting up a business. There is no more a justification for preventing them from doing this than there is for preventing them from trading their goods from abroad.

Restricting access to markets certainly benefits some people, but at the expense of others, and generally to the disadvantage of all. If particular privileges should be accorded to some because of their state membership, the justification cannot be economic in the first of the two senses distinguished.

In the second sense of economic, however, the argument for restricting immigration is not that access to particular markets should be limited, but that the economic benefits dispensed by the state must be limited if economic resources and indeed the social system more generally are to be properly managed. Immigration dulls the edge of good husbandry. For some libertarians, the concern here is that open borders – or even increased immigration – will impose a greater tax burden on existing members of society as the poor and disabled move to states with more generous welfare provisions, as well as subsidized education and healthcare. Indeed, a number of libertarians have argued that until the welfare state is abolished, immigration will have to be tightly controlled in countries like the United States.

Here it would not be enough to point out that, to the extent that immigrants join the workforce, they would also contribute to the revenues of the state through taxes, even as they consume resources dispensed by the state. Open immigration might well encourage people to move with the intention of taking advantage of benefits that exceed their tax contributions. People on low incomes and with children or elderly or infirm dependents would find it advantageous to move to countries with generous public education and healthcare. This could impose a significant additional burden on taxpaying individuals and firms, or pressure a state with fiscal problems to reduce the quality of its services. Immigration is a problem for welfare states – understanding welfare in its broadest sense to include health and education services as well as unemployment relief and disability benefits.

The problem here is a significant one. But it

should be noted that it is not a problem that results from the movement of the rich or able, only one that results from the movement of the poor. The independently wealthy, and the well-off moving into well-paying jobs, will contribute to the state's coffers through direct and indirect taxes, and may well pay for more than they consume. The poor will in all likelihood be net consumers of tax dollars – at least at the outset. An important purpose of closed borders is to keep out the poor.

If the concern is to preserve the integrity of the welfare state, however, the most that could be justified is restricting membership of the welfare system. The movement of people into a country could then be free. Such restricted forms of immigration would still impose serious disadvantages upon poorer people, for whom the attraction of immigration would diminish if they were obliged to fund their own healthcare and pay for the education of their children. Yet for many it would be better than no opportunity to move at all. Certainly, immigration with limited entitlements would be attractive to young and able people with dependents, since the opportunity to work abroad and remit money home might significantly improve all their lives.

Nonetheless, it would not do to be too sanguine about the possibility of such an arrangement. Most states would baulk at the suggestion of such arrangements, and even advocates of open immigration may reject the idea of different classes of membership. Moreover, immigrants paying taxes may feel disgruntled if their taxes do not buy them equal entitlements. In the end, it may be that the existence of the welfare state makes open borders, or even extensive immigration, very difficult – if not imposible. From the perspective of a principle of freedom, or a principle of humanity, I suggest, the standard of open borders should prevail. To defend closed borders a principle of nationality would have to take precedence. We should turn then to look more closely at the argument from nationality.

Nationality and Immigration

Implicit in most arguments for closed borders or restricted immigration is an assumption that the good or well-being of the members of a polity should take precedence – to a significant degree, even if not absolutely – over the good of outsiders. From this perspective, that one of my fellow countrymen is harmed or made worse off is a weighty consideration when assessing any policy, in a way that the impact of that policy on foreigners is not. Defenders of this perspective may disagree about the extent to which the interests of outsiders should be discounted; and indeed some may hold that rich nations owe substantial obligations of justice to the world's poor. But they are agreed that something more is owed to one's own country and its people. And this justifies protecting one's nation from the impact of open or substantial immigration.

Immigration, on this view, may be damaging for a number of different reasons. We have already considered some of the economic consequences of immigration; but there are other problems as well. First, immigration in substantial numbers, even if it takes place over a long period of time, "has the effect of changing the recipient area". The influx of Indian workers in the nineteenth century changed Fiji from an island of Polynesian people to one that is bicultural, just as the movement of Indians and Chinese to Malaya turned that society into a multicultural one. The fear of many people is that immigration will change a society's character, and perhaps undermine or displace an ancient identity. The cultural character of Britain or France cannot remain the same if substantial numbers of people move there from Africa or Asia.

Second, immigration from culturally different people may be damaging to wealthy countries to the extent that their wealth is dependent upon the existence of a political culture, and economic and social institutions, that are especially conducive to wealth-creation. Immigration from people who do not share the same values, and who would not help to sustain the same institutions, may ultimately undermine those institutions. If so, this may be good reason to restrict immigration not only by number but also by culture.

Third, immigration may make it very difficult for a society to develop or sustain a level of social solidarity that is necessary for a state to work well, and particularly for it to uphold principles of social justice. This argument has been developed especially forcefully by David Miller, who suggests that if immigration exceeds the absorptive capacities of a society, the bonds of social solidarity make break down. The nation is a natural reference group when people ask whether or not they are getting a fair share of society's resources. If people have different understandings of what their rights and obligations are and disagree about what they may legitimately claim, it may become impossible to establish and operate appropriate standards of social justice. For all of these reasons, then, open borders cannot be justified. Or so it is argued.

While all of these considerations are weighty, they do not suffice to warrant limitations on freedom of movement. First, while it is true that immigrants do change the character of a place – sometimes dramatically – it is not evident that this is necessarily a bad thing. More to the point, it is difficult to know how much change is desirable, partly because the results will not be known for some time and partly because different people – even in relatively homogeneous societies – want different things. It is perfectly understandable that some people want things to remain the way they have been during their lifetimes. Yet it is no less understandable that others want changes they regard as improvements. The Know-Nothings of nineteenth-century America were completely hostile to Catholic, and especially Irish, immigration; though Irish Americans were all too ready to welcome to the United States even more settlers from Ireland. In the end, our capacity to

shape society or preserve its character may be as limited as our capacity to know how much (or how little) change is really desirable – even if we could agree on what sort of character we would like our societies to have.

It is also worth bearing in mind that many societies have experienced significant cultural or social transformations and not only survived but prospered. The United States in the nineteenth century welcomed immigrants from all over the world, incorporated large parts of what was once Mexico into its territory, overturned a three-century old tradition of slavery and yet began the twentieth century a prosperous and vibrant democracy. Canada and Australia have seen their societies transformed by postwar immigration into multicultural polities, while continuing to enjoy economic growth and social stability. And the European Union continues to expand its membership by admitting states from Eastern Europe – and perhaps, eventually, Turkey – in a way that makes it possible for peoples from diverse ethnic, religious, and political traditions to move freely from one end of the continent to the other, without fearing a loss in prosperity; though there can be no doubt that this development will bring with it significant cultural changes to many of Europe's communities.

Social and cultural change can be effected by large-scale immigration, and its significance should not be discounted. But neither should it be overestimated. Nor should too much weight be given to the possibility that immigration from poor nations to rich ones will undermine the institutions of wealth-creation – though it surely is a possibility. If anything, it is perhaps more likely that immigrants who move to wealthy countries will do so because they want to take advantage of the opportunities it offers, and that they will assimilate by adopting the practices that bring success to the natives. In any case, if our interest is in wealth-creation, it is more likely that this skill will be taught to those who enter a rich country than that it will be exported successfully to some countries that are poor.

The most challenging argument against open immigration, however, is that institutions of social justice can only be built if social solidarity is preserved – and that immigration may undermine that solidarity if it is not appropriately restricted. If we accept that social justice is an important concern, then Miller's analysis and argument are powerful and convincing. The only way to resist them is to question the very idea that the nation-state is the appropriate site for the settlement of questions of distributive justice. And indeed that is what we need to do.

There are a number of reasons why we should be suspicious of the idea that the nation-state is the site of distributive justice, but the most powerful have been advanced by Miller in his own critique of the idea of global social justice. Miller maintains that principles of social justice are always, "as a matter of psychological fact, applied within bounded communities". It is easier for us to make judgments of justice in small communities such as workplaces, but difficult in units larger than nation-states. We make such judgments by comparing ourselves with others. But it is difficult for us to compare ourselves with people who are remote from our own circumstances, such as people in other countries. We can more readily make judgments based on comparisons with people who belong to our own reference group – people with whom we are likely to share some common conceptions of value. When conceptions of the value of a resource differ, it becomes very difficult to establish common standards of distributive justice, since the very question of what counts as a resource to be distributed may be impossible to settle. And when we consider that different communities have conflicting views about how trade-offs should be made, for example, between the consumption of what the earth will produce and the preservation of the natural environment, it would be difficult for one community to demand a share of another's resources on the

basis of its own determination of the "true value" of those resources. Global social justice is difficult to defend.

Yet all the things that make global justice problematic also go to make problematic social justice within the nation-state. Certainly, some nation-states are so large that it is difficult to see how they could really share a single conception of social justice. China and India between them hold more than a third of the world's population, and harbor different languages, religions, and customs. Even the United States, though much smaller, is sufficiently diverse that there are noticeable differences among significant groups about morality and justice – from California, to Utah, to Louisiana. Britain and France are smaller still, but are home to a diversity of religions and ethnicities. If the preservation of a shared ethos or sense of social justice is an important reason to restrict immigration, then, it might be defensible if we are considering small, homogeneous nations such as Iceland or Tahiti. It might also be defensible for a state such as Israel, though it might be more difficult to make this case the more it is a multicultural (or bicultural) state. But in larger states, which are diverse and already have a long history of immigration, the idea of a shared conception of social justice might be too much to hope for. Certainly, the vigorous debates among philosophers about social justice suggest that there is no substantial agreement on this question even among a group as homogeneous as the academy. Miller's point about the nature of social justice is a telling one; but it also tells against his own defense of restricted immigration.

Even if states were plausible sites of social justice, however, there is another issue that has to be raised. Is it right that the preservation of local institutions of social justice take precedence over the humanitarian concerns that make open immigration desirable? As was noted earlier, immigration barriers operate largely to limit the movement of the world's poor. It seems odd to suggest that this can be defended by appeal to the importance of social justice. If the price of social justice is exclusion of the worst-off from the lands that offer the greatest opportunity, this may be a mark against the ideal of social justice.

To be fair, however, it should be acknowledged that defenders of social justice or the primacy of membership generally acknowledge the need to make special provision for the world's poor. In this regard, they suggest that refugees may have a special claim to be allowed to immigrate and resettle to escape persecution. But here a number of problems arise. First, the line distinguishing a refugee and what we might term an "economic migrant" is a very fine one. As it stands, the 1951 United Nations Convention relating to the Status of Refugees adopts a very narrow definition of refugee to include only persons with a well-founded fear of persecution for reasons of race, religion, nationality, membership of a particular social group or political opinion. Those people fleeing war, natural disaster, or famine are, on this definition, not refugees. Second, even on this narrow definition, there are more than 20 million people in the world who count as refugees who have yet to be resettled. The problem these two points pose is that making an exception for refugees requires a very significant increase in immigration – even if the narrow definition of refugee is used. If a more humane definition were adopted – one that recognized as refugees people fleeing war zones, for example – an even greater number of immigrants would have to be accepted. Yet then, if the standard of humanity is the appropriate standard, it is difficult to see why any sharp distinction should be made between the desperate fleeing war and the destitute struggling to make a living.

It would perhaps be too much to hope or expect that states – especially wealthy ones – will readily lower the barriers to the free movement of people. As it stands, the world of states has struggled to relocate the refugees for whom it has acknowledged responsibility. Indeed, it is

sobering to remember that immigration controls were tightened with the invention of the passport during the First World War precisely to control refugee flows. Nonetheless, on this much at least, both the defenders of open borders and the advocates of restrictions can agree: that at present the borders are too securely sealed.

Immigration and Security

One reason for greater restriction of immigration, which clearly has assumed enormous significance in recent times, is the need for security. Can immigration be free in an age of terror?

Security from terrorist attack, it should be noted, is only one kind of security. Even before terror became a serious concern, modern states have been anxious about the security of political systems from foreign threats, and the security of society against international criminal organizations. Smugglers, traffickers in illegal goods (from drugs to rare wildlife to historical artifacts), and slave-traders of various kinds operate across boundaries to violate the laws of host states. Nonetheless, the threat of terror has added significantly to the security concerns of a number of Western states. Does this give us greater reason to restrict immigration, or show that the idea of open borders is simply untenable?

In the end, I suggest that security concerns do not do much to diminish the case for open borders. This is not to say that security concerns are unfounded or should not be addressed. But it is to say that immigration controls are not the key. There are a number of reasons why. First, while it is easy to restrict legal immigration, it is another matter to control illegal immigration. Limiting legal immigration is unlikely to deter either criminals or subversive agents from moving between states. Borders are porous even when they are closed. Second, limiting immigration seldom means limiting the movement of people more generally, since many more people move from one country to another as tourists, or students, or businessmen, or government officials than they do as immigrants intending to settle in a new land. If security is a concern, tourism should be more severely limited in many countries than it presently is. If a person is likely to pose a threat to a country's security, it would be odd to think it acceptable for him to be granted a tourist visa for one, three, or six months. Equally, if a person is considered safe to be awarded a three-month tourist visa, it is hard to see why he should be denied the right to permanent residence on security grounds. It might well be that in times of insecurity greater vigilance is necessary: greater scrutiny of many aspects of the behavior of people – including travelers – may be warranted, just as one would expect the police to establish road blocks and search cars when there is an escaped criminal in the vicinity. It is not evident, however, that this would justify further restrictions on immigration rather than simply greater effort to discover who poses a threat to society, to try avert the threat, and to apprehend the particular persons who are menaces.

There are, however, reasons not to place too much weight on the importance of security, for like all things, the search for security comes with costs of its own. In the case of the search for security through immigration controls, the cost is borne not only in the financial expense that is incurred but also in the impact that controls on immigrants and immigration have on society more generally. Immigration control requires the surveillance of people moving in and out of the country, and to some degree of people moving about within the country. But it is not possible to do this with immigrants or outsiders generally without also placing one's own citizens under surveillance. In dangerous times this may not be avoidable, at least to some degree. But the risks it brings are substantial. Even if the burdens imposed upon citizens and residents are trivial, they may be burdens all the same – and for some more than others. Furthermore, there is always a risk that impositions designed to meet a particular danger will remain in place long after the danger has passed. (Malaysia's Internal Security

Act, which, among other things, sanctions arrest and detention without trial, was passed at the height of the communist insurgency in the 1960s, but remains in place 25 years after the emergency ended.) Liberal democracies, in particular, should be wary of state controls advocated in the name of national security – particularly since the trade-off is a loss of liberty.

Concluding Reflections

Whatever the merits of the case for open borders, it is highly unlikely that we will see an end to immigration controls at any time soon – for reasons that were canvassed at the beginning of this paper. In one important respect, free migration is entirely unfeasible: it is politically untenable.

One reason why it is politically untenable is that most voters in wealthy countries do not favor immigration, particularly by the poor. Another is that states themselves do not favor uncontrolled population movements. In a world order shaped by the Westphalian model of states operating within strict geographical boundaries, and dominated by the imperative to secure the welfare of members, the free movement of peoples is not a strong possibility. The inclination of most people to hold on to the advantages they possess also makes it unlikely that nations will open up their borders to allow others to come and take a greater share of what they control.

Yet if the free movement of peoples is not politically feasible, how can there be a case for open borders? Surely, political theory, in considering issues of public policy, should keep its focus on the world of the possible rather than on impossible ideals.

There is a good deal of truth to this. But there is, nonetheless, good reason for putting the case for open immigration. One important consideration is that many feasibility problems have their roots not in the nature of things but in our way of thinking about them. Many of the reasons open immigration is not possible right now have less to do with the disadvantages it might bring than with an unwarranted concern about its dangers. Even to the extent that the source of the problem for open immigration lies in the nature of things, however, it is worth considering the case for open borders because it forces us to confront the inconsistency between moral ideals and our existing social and political arrangements. One of the reasons why open immigration is not possible is that it is not compatible with the modern welfare state. While one obvious response to this is to say, "so much the worse for open immigration," it is not less possible to ask whether the welfare state is what needs rethinking.

Chapter 43

David Miller

IMMIGRATION: THE CASE FOR LIMITS

David Miller (1946–) is a British professor of social and political theory at Nuffield College, best known for his work on nationalism and social justice. In this essay (published in 2005), Miller argues that existing defenses of a moral right of unlimited immigration fail, and claims that considerations regarding the preservation of culture and regarding the limitation of population growth support the right of states to limit immigration.

I t is not easy to write about immigration from a philosophical perspective – not easy at least if you are writing in a society (and this now includes most societies in the Western world) in which immigration has become a highly charged political issue. Those who speak freely and openly about the issue tend to come from the far Right: they are fascists or racists who believe that it is wrong in principle for their political community to admit immigrants who do not conform to the approved cultural or racial stereotype. Most liberal, conservative, and social democratic politicians support quite strict immigration controls in practice, but they generally refrain from spelling out the justification for such controls, preferring instead to highlight the practical difficulties involved in resettling immigrants, and raising the spectre of a right-wing backlash if too many immigrants are admitted. Why are they so reticent? One reason is that it is not easy to set out the arguments for limiting immigration without at the same time projecting a negative image of those immigrants who have already been admitted, thereby playing

directly into the hands of the far Right ideologues who would like to see such immigrants deprived of their full rights of citizenship and/or repatriated to their countries of origin. Is it possible *both* to argue that every member of the political community, native or immigrant, must be treated as a full citizen, enjoying equal status and the equal respect of his or her fellows, *and* to argue that there are good grounds for setting upper bounds both to the rate and the overall numbers of immigrants who are admitted? Yes, it is, but it requires dexterity, and always carries with it the risk of being misunderstood.

In this essay, I shall explain why nation-states may be justified in imposing restrictive immigration policies if they so choose. The argument is laid out in three stages. First, I canvass three arguments that purport to justify an unlimited right of migration between states and show why each of them fails. Second, I give two reasons, one having to do with culture, the other with population, that can justify states in limiting immigration. Third, I consider whether states nonetheless have a duty to admit a special class of potential immigrants – namely refugees – and also how far they are allowed to pick and choose among the immigrants they do admit. The third section, in other words, lays down some conditions that an ethical immigration policy must meet. But I begin by showing why there is no general right to choose one's country of residence or citizenship.

Can There Be an Unlimited Right of Migration Between States?

Liberal political philosophers who write about migration usually begin from the premise that people should be allowed to choose where in the world to locate themselves unless it can be shown that allowing an unlimited right of migration would have harmful consequences that outweigh the value of freedom of choice. In other words, the central value appealed to is simply freedom itself. Just as I should be free to decide who to marry, what job to take, what religion (if any) to profess, so I should be free to decide whether to live in Nigeria, or France, or the USA. Now these philosophers usually concede that in practice some limits may have to be placed on this freedom – for instance, if high rates of migration would result in social chaos or the breakdown of liberal states that could not accommodate so many migrants without losing their liberal character. In these instances, the exercise of free choice would become self-defeating. But the presumption is that people should be free to choose where to live unless there are strong reasons for restricting their choice.

I want to challenge this presumption. Of course there is always *some* value in people having more options to choose between, in this case options as to where to live, but we usually draw a line between *basic* freedoms that people should have as a matter of right and what we might call *bare* freedoms that do not warrant that kind of protection. It would be good from my point of view if I were free to purchase an Aston Martin tomorrow, but that is not going to count as a morally significant freedom – my desire is not one that imposes any kind of obligation on others to meet it. In order to argue against immigration restrictions, therefore, liberal philosophers must be more than show that there is some value to people in being able to migrate, or that they often *want* to migrate (as indeed they do, in increasing numbers). It needs to be demonstrated that this freedom has the kind of weight or significance that could turn it into a right, and that should therefore prohibit states from pursuing immigration policies that limit freedom of movement.

I shall examine three arguments that have been offered to defend a right to migrate. The first starts with the general right to freedom of movement, and claims that this must include the freedom to move into, and take up residence in, states other than one's own. The second begins with a person's right to *exit* from her current state – a right that is widely recognized in international law – and claims that a right of exit is pointless unless it is matched by a right of entry into other states. The third appeals to international distributive justice. Given the huge inequalities in living standards that currently exist between rich and poor states, it is said, people who live in poor states have a claim of justice that can only be met by allowing them to migrate and take advantage of the opportunities that rich states provide.

The idea of a right to freedom of movement is not in itself objectionable. We are talking here about what are usually called basic rights or human rights, and I shall assume (since there is no space to defend the point) that such rights are justified by pointing to the vital interests that they protect. They correspond to conditions in whose absence human beings cannot live decent lives, no matter what particular values and plans of life they choose to pursue. Being able to move freely in physical space is just such a condition, as we can see by thinking about people whose legs are shackled or who are confined in small spaces. A wider freedom of movement can also be justified by thinking about the interests that it serves instrumentally: if I cannot move about over a fairly wide area, it may be impossible for me to find a job, to practice my religion, or to find a suitable marriage partner. Since these all qualify as vital interests, it is fairly clear that freedom of movement qualifies as a basic human right.

What is less clear, however, is the physical extent of that right, in the sense of how much of the earth's surface I must be able to move to in order to say that I enjoy it. Even in liberal societies that make no attempt to confine people within particular geographical areas, freedom of movement is severely restricted in a number of ways. I cannot, in general, move to places that other people's bodies now occupy (I cannot just push them aside). I cannot move on to private property without the consent of its owner, except perhaps in emergencies or where a special right of access exists – and since most land is privately owned, this means that a large proportion of physical space does not fall within the ambit of a right to free movement. Even access to public space is heavily regulated: there are traffic laws that tell me where and at what speed I may drive my car, parks have opening and closing hours, the police can control my movements up and down the streets, and so forth. These are very familiar observations, but they are worth making simply to highlight how hedged about with qualifications the existing right of free movement in liberal societies actually is. Yet few would argue that because of these limitations, people in these societies are deprived of one of their human rights. Some liberals might argue in favor of expanding the right – for instance, in Britain there has been a protracted campaign to establish a legal right to roam on uncultivated privately owned land such as moors and fells, a right that will finally become effective by 2005. But even the advocates of such a right would be hard-pressed to show that some vital interest was

being injured by the more restrictive property laws that have existed up to now.

The point here is that liberal societies in general offer their members sufficient freedom of movement to protect the interests that the human right to free movement is intended to protect, even though the extent of free movement is very far from absolute. So how could one attempt to show that the right in question must include the right to move to some other country and settle there? What vital interest requires the right to be interpreted in such an extensive way? Contingently, of course, it may be true that moving to another country is the only way for an individual to escape persecution, to find work, to obtain necessary medical care, and so forth. In these circumstances the person concerned may have the right to move, not to any state that she chooses, but to some state where these interests can be protected. But here the right to move serves only as a remedial right: its existence depends on the fact that the person's vital interests cannot be secured in the country where she currently resides. In a world of decent states – states that were able to secure their citizens' basic rights to security, food, work, medical care, and so forth – the right to move across borders could not be justified in this way.

Our present world is not, of course, a world of decent states, and this gives rise to the issue of refugees, which I shall discuss in the final section of this chapter. But if we leave aside for the moment cases where the right to move freely across borders depends upon the right to avoid persecution, starvation, or other threats to basic interests, how might we try to give it a more general rationale? One reason a person may want to migrate is in order to participate in a culture that does not exist in his native land – for instance he wants to work at an occupation for which there is no demand at home, or to join a religious community which, again, is not represented in the country from which he comes. These might be central components in his plan of life, so he will find it very frustrating if he is not able to move. But does this ground a right to free movement across borders? It seems to me that it does not. What a person can legitimately demand access to is an *adequate* range of options to choose between – a reasonable choice of occupation, religion, cultural activities, marriage partners, and so forth. Adequacy here is defined in terms of generic human interests rather than in terms of the interests of any one person in particular – so, for example, a would-be opera singer living in a society which provides for various forms of musical expression, but not for opera, can have an adequate range of options in this area even though the option she most prefers is not available. So long as they adhere to the standards of decency sketched above, all contemporary states are able to provide such an adequate range internally. So although people certainly have an *interest* in being able to migrate internationally, they do not have a basic interest of the kind that would be required to ground a human right. It is more like my interest in having an Aston Martin than my interest in having access to *some* means of physical mobility.

I turn next to the argument that because people have a right to leave the society they currently belong to, they must also have a right to enter other societies, since the first right is practically meaningless unless the second exists – there is no unoccupied space in the world to exit *to*, so unless the right to leave society A is accompanied by the right to enter societies B, C, D, etc., it has no real force.

The right of exit is certainly an important human right, but once again it is worth examining why it has the significance that it does. Its importance is partly instrumental: knowing that their subjects have the right to leave inhibits states from mistreating them in various ways, so it helps to preserve the conditions of what I earlier called "decency." However, even in the case of decent states the right of exist remains important, and that is because by being deprived of exit rights individuals are forced to remain in

association with others whom they may find deeply uncongenial – think of the militant atheist in a society where almost everyone devoutly practices the same religion, or the religious puritan in a society where most people behave like libertines. On the other hand, the right of exit from state A does not appear to entail an unrestricted right to enter any society of the immigrant's choice – indeed, it seems that it can be exercised provided that at least one other society, society B say, is willing to take him in. It might seem that we can generate a general right to migrate by iteration: the person who leaves A for B then has the right to exit from B, which entails that C, at least, must grant him the right to enter, and so forth. But this move fails, because our person's right of exit from A depended on the claim that he might find continued association with the other citizens of A intolerable, and he cannot plausibly continue making the same claim in the case of each society that is willing to take him in. Given the political and cultural diversity of societies in the real world, it is simply unconvincing to argue that only an unlimited choice of which one to join will prevent people being forced into associations that are repugnant to them.

It is also important to stress that there are many rights whose exercise is contingent on finding partners who are willing to cooperate in the exercise, and it may be that the right of exit falls into this category. Take the right to marry as an example. This is a right held against the state to allow people to marry the partners of their choice (and perhaps to provide the legal framework within which marriages can be contracted). It is obviously not a right to have a marriage partner provided – whether any given person can exercise the right depends entirely on whether he is able to find someone willing to marry him, and many people are not so lucky. The right of exist is a right held against a person's current state of residence not to prevent her from leaving the state (and perhaps aiding her in that endeavor by, say, providing a passport). But it does not entail an obligation on any other state to let that person in. Obviously, if no state were ever to grant entry rights to people who were not already its citizens, the right of exit would have no value. But suppose states are generally willing to consider entry applications from people who want to migrate, and that most people would get offers from at least one such state: then the position as far as the right of exit goes is pretty much the same as with the right to marry, where by no means everyone is able to wed the partner they would ideally like to have, but most have the opportunity to marry *someone*.

So once the right of exit is properly understood, it does not entail an unlimited right to migrate to the society of one's choice. But now, finally, in this part of the chapter, I want to consider an argument for migration rights that appeals to distributive justice. It begins from the assumption of the fundamental moral equality of human beings. It then points out that, in the world in which we live, a person's life prospects depend heavily on the society into which she happens to be born, so that the only way to achieve equal opportunities is to allow people to move to the places where they can develop and exercise their talents, through employment and in other ways. In other words, there is something fundamentally unfair about a world in which people are condemned to relative poverty through no fault of their own when others have much greater opportunities, whereas if people were free to live and work wherever they wished, then each person could choose whether to stay in the community that had raised him or to look for a better life elsewhere.

The question we must ask here is whether justice demands equality of opportunity at the global level, as the argument I have just sketched assumes, or whether this principle only applies *inside* societies, among those who are already citizens of the same political community. Note to begin with that embracing the moral equality of all human beings – accepting that every human being is equally an object of moral concern –

does not yet tell us what we are required to do for them as a result of that equality. One answer might be that we should attempt to provide everyone with equal opportunities to pursue their goals in life. But another, equally plausible, answer is that we should play our part in ensuring that their basic rights are respected, where these are understood as rights to a certain minimum level of security, freedom, resources, and so forth – a level adequate to protect their basic interests, as suggested earlier in this chapter. These basic rights can be universally protected and yet some people have greater opportunities than others to pursue certain aims, as a result of living in more affluent or culturally richer societies.

Is it nonetheless unfair if opportunities are unequal in this way? That depends upon what we believe about the *scope* of distributive justice, the kind of justice that involves comparing how well different people are faring by some standard. According to Michael Walzer, "the idea of distributive justice presupposes a bounded world within which distributions take place: a group of people committed to dividing, exchanging, and sharing social goods, first of all among themselves." The main reason that Walzer gives for this view is that the very goods whose distribution is a matter of justice gain their meaning and value within particular political communities. Another relevant consideration is that the stock of goods that is available at any time to be divided up will depend on the past history of the community in question, including decisions about, for example, the economic system under which production will take place. These considerations tell against the view that justice at global level should be understood in terms of the equal distribution, at any moment, of a single good, whether this good is understood as "resources" or "opportunity" or "welfare." The basic rights view avoids these difficulties, because it is plausible to think that whatever the cultural values of a particular society, and whatever its historical record, no human being should be allowed to fall below the minimum level of provision that protects his or her basic interests.

But what if somebody does fall below this threshold? Does this not give him the right to migrate to a place where the minimum level is guaranteed? Perhaps, but it depends on whether the minimum *could* be provided in the political community he belongs to now, or whether that community is so oppressive, or so dysfunctional, that escape is the only option. So here we encounter again the issue of refugees, to be discussed in my final section. Meanwhile, the lesson for other states, confronted with people whose lives are less than decent, is that they have a choice: they must either ensure that the basic rights of such people are protected in the places where they live – by aid, by intervention, or by some other means – or they must help them to move to other communities where their lives will be better. Simply shutting one's borders and doing nothing else is not a morally defensible option here. People everywhere have a right to a decent life. But before jumping to the conclusion that the way to respond to global injustice is to encourage people whose lives are less than decent to migrate elsewhere, we should consider the fact that this policy will do little to help the very poor, who are unlikely to have the resources to move to a richer country. Indeed, a policy of open migration may make such people worse off still, if it allows doctors, engineers, and other professionals to move from economically undeveloped to economically developed societies in search of higher incomes, thereby depriving their countries of origin of vital skills. Equalizing opportunity for the few may diminish opportunities for the many. Persisting global injustice does impose on rich states the obligation to make a serious contribution to the relief of global poverty, but in most instances they should contribute to improving conditions of life on the ground, as it were, rather than bypassing the problem by allowing (inevitably selective) inward migration.

Justifications for Limiting Immigration

I have shown that there is no general right to migrate to the country of one's choice. Does it follow that states have a free hand in choosing who, if anyone, to admit to membership? One might think that it does, using the analogy of a private club. Suppose that the members of a tennis club decide that once the membership roster has reached 100, no new members will be taken in. They do not have to justify this decision to would-be members who are excluded: if they decide that 100 members is enough, that's entirely their prerogative. But notice what makes this argument convincing. First, the benefit that is being denied to new applicants is the (relatively superficial) benefit of being able to play tennis. Second, it's a reasonable assumption that the rejected applicants can join another club, or start one of their own. It would be different if the tennis club occupied the only site within a 50-mile radius that is suitable for laying tennis courts: we might then think that they had some obligation to admit new members up to a reasonable total. In the case of states, the advantages that they deny to would-be immigrants who are refused entry are very substantial; and because states monopolize stretches of territory, and in other ways provide benefits that cannot be replicated elsewhere, the "go and start your own club" response to immigrants is not very plausible.

So in order to show that states are entitled to close their borders to immigrants, we have to do more than show that the latter lack the human right to migrate. Potential immigrants have a *claim* to be let in – if nothing else they usually have a strong *desire* to enter – and so any state that wants to control immigration must have good reasons for doing so. In this section, I shall outline two good reasons that states may have for restricting immigration. One has to do with preserving culture, the other with controlling population. I don't claim that these reasons will apply to every state, but they do apply to many liberal democracies that are currently having to decide how to respond to potentially very large flows of immigrants from less economically developed societies (other states may face larger flows still, but the political issues will be different).

The first reason assumes that the states in question require a common public culture that in part constitutes the political identity of their members, and that serves valuable functions in supporting democracy and other social goals. There is no space here to justify this assumption in any detail, so I must refer the reader to other writings where I have tried to do so. What I want to do here is to consider how the need to protect the public culture bears upon the issue of immigration. In general terms we can say (a) that immigrants will enter with cultural values, including *political* values, that are more or less different from the public culture of the community they enter; (b) that as a result of living in that community, they will absorb some part of the existing public culture, modifying their own values in the process; and (c) that their presence will also change the public culture in various ways – for instance, a society in which an established religion had formed an important part of national identity will typically exhibit greater religious diversity after accepting immigrants, and as a consequence religion will play a less significant part in defining that identity.

Immigration, in other words, is likely to change a society's public culture rather than destroy it. And since public cultures always change over time, as a result of social factors that are quite independent of immigration (participation in the established religion might have been declining in any case), it doesn't on the face of it seem that states have any good reason to restrict immigration on that basis. They might have reason to limit the flow of immigrants, on the grounds that the process of acculturation outlined above may break down if too many come in too quickly. But so long as a viable public culture is maintained, it should not matter that its character changes as a result of taking in people with different cultural values.

What this overlooks, however, is that the public culture of their country is something that people have an interest in controlling: they want to be able to shape the way that their nation develops, including the values that are contained in the public culture. They may not of course succeed: valued cultural features can be eroded by economic and other forces that evade political control. But they may certainly have good reason to try, and in particular to try to maintain cultural continuity over time, so that they can see themselves as the bearers of an identifiable cultural tradition that stretches backward historically. Cultural continuity, it should be stressed, is not the same as cultural rigidity: the most valuable cultures are those that can develop and adapt to new circumstances, including the presence of new subcultures associated with immigrants.

Consider the example of language. In many states today the national language is under pressure from the spread of international languages, especially English. People have an incentive to learn and use one of the international languages for economic and other purposes, and so there is a danger that the national language will wither away over the course of two or three generations. If this were to happen, one of the community's most important distinguishing characteristics would have disappeared, its literature would become inaccessible except in translation, and so forth. So the states in question adopt policies to insure, for instance, that the national language is used in schools and in the media, and that exposure to foreign languages through imports is restricted. What effect would a significant influx of immigrants who did not already speak the national language have in these circumstances? It is likely that their choice of second language would be English, or one of the other international languages. So their presence would increase the incentive among natives to defect from use of the national language in everyday transactions, and make the project of language-preservation harder to carry through. The state has good reason to limit immigration, or at least to differentiate sharply among prospective immigrants between those who speak the national language and those who don't, as the government of Quebec has done in recent years.

Language isn't the only feature to which the argument for cultural continuity applies. There is an internal relationship between a nation's culture and its physical shape – its public and religious buildings, the way its towns and villages are laid out, the pattern of the landscape, and so forth. People feel at home in a place in part because they can see that their surroundings bear the imprint of past generations whose values were recognizably their own. This doesn't rule out cultural change, but again it gives a reason for wanting to stay in control of the process – for teaching children to value their cultural heritage and to regard themselves as having a responsibility to preserve the parts of it that are worth preserving, for example. The "any public culture will do" position ignores this internal connection between the cultural and physical features of the community.

How restrictive an immigration policy this dictates depends on the empirical question of how easy or difficult it is to create a symbiosis between the existing public culture and the new cultural values of the immigrants, and this will vary hugely from case to case (in particular the experience of immigration itself is quite central to the public cultures of some states, but not to others). Most liberal democracies are now multicultural, and this is widely regarded as a source of cultural richness. But the more culturally diverse a society becomes, the greater need it has for a unifying public culture to bind its members together, and this culture has to connect to the history and physical shape of the society in question – it can't be invented from scratch. So a political judgment needs to be made about the scale and type of immigration that will enrich rather than dislocate the existing public culture.

The second reason for states to limit immigration that I want to consider concerns population size. This is a huge, and hugely controversial, topic, and all I can do here is to sketch an argument that links together the issues of immigration and population control. The latter issue really arises at two different levels: global and national. At the global level, there is a concern that the carrying capacity of the earth may be stretched to breaking point if the total number of human beings continues to rise as it has over the last half century or so. At national level, there is a concern about the effect of population growth on quality of life and the natural environment. Let me look at each level in turn.

Although there is disagreement about just how many people the earth can sustain before resource depletion – the availability of water, for example – becomes acute, it would be hard to maintain that there is *no* upper limit. Although projections of population growth over the century ahead indicate a leveling off in the rate of increase, we must also expect – indeed should welcome – increases in the standard of living in the developing world that will mean that resource consumption per capita will also rise significantly. In such a world it is in all our interests that states whose populations are growing rapidly should adopt birth control measures and other policies to restrict the rate of growth, as both China and India have done in past decades. But such states have little or no incentive to adopt such policies if they can "export" their surplus population through international migration, and since the policies in question are usually unpopular, they have a positive incentive not to pursue them. A viable population policy at global level requires each state to be responsible for stabilizing, or even possibly reducing, its population over time, and this is going to be impossible to achieve if there are no restrictions on the movement of people between states.

At national level, the effects of population growth may be less catastrophic, but can still be detrimental to important cultural values. What we think about this issue may be conditioned to some extent by the population density of the state in which we live. Those of us who live in relatively small and crowded states experience daily the way in which the sheer number of our fellow citizens, with their needs for housing, mobility, recreation, and so forth, impacts on the physical environment, so that it becomes harder to enjoy access to open space, to move from place to place without encountering congestion, to preserve important wildlife habitats, and so on. It's true, of course, that the problems arise not simply from population size, but also from a population that wants to live in a certain way – to move around a lot, to have high levels of consumption, and so on – so we could deal with them by collectively changing the way that we live, rather than by restricting or reducing population size. Perhaps we should. But this, it seems to me, is a matter for political decision: members of a territorial community have the right to decide whether to restrict their numbers, or to live in a more ecologically and humanly sound way, or to do neither and bear the costs of a high-consumption, high-mobility lifestyle in a crowded territory. If restricting numbers is part of the solution, then controlling immigration is a natural corollary.

What I have tried to do in this section is to suggest why states may have good reason to limit immigration. I concede that would-be immigrants may have a strong interest in being admitted – a strong economic interest, for example – but in general they have no obligation-conferring right to be admitted, for reasons given in the previous section. On the other side, nation-states have a strong and legitimate interest in determining who comes in and who does not. Without the right to exclude, they could not be what Michael Walzer has called "communities of character": "historically stable, ongoing associations of men and women with some special commitment to one another and some special sense of their common life". It remains now to see what conditions an admis-

sions policy must meet if it is to be ethically justified.

Conditions for an Ethical Immigration Policy

I shall consider two issues. The first is the issue of refugees, usually defined as people who have fled their home country as a result of a well-founded fear of persecution or violence. What obligations do states have to admit persons in that category? The second is the issue of discrimination in admissions policy. If a state decides to admit some immigrants (who are not refugees) but refuses entry to others, what criteria can it legitimately use in making its selection?

As I indicated in the first section of this chapter, people whose basic rights are being threatened or violated in their current place of residence clearly do have the right to move to somewhere that offers them greater security. Prima facie, then, states have an obligation to admit refugees, indeed "refugees" defined more broadly than is often the case to include people who are being deprived of rights to subsistence, basic healthcare, etc. . But this need not involve treating them as long-term immigrants. They may be offered temporary sanctuary in states that are able to protect them, and then be asked to return to their original country of citizenship when the threat has passed. Moreover, rather than encouraging long-distance migration, it may be preferable to establish safety zones for refugees close to their homes and then deal with the cause of the rights-violations directly – whether this means sending in food and medical aid or intervening to remove a genocidal regime from power. There is obviously a danger that the temporary solution becomes semi-permanent, and this is unacceptable because refugees are owed more than the immediate protection of their basic rights – they are owed something like the chance to make a proper life for themselves. But liberals who rightly give a high moral priority to protecting the human rights of vulnerable people are regrettably often unwilling to countenance intervention in states that are plainly violating these rights.

If protection on the ground is not possible, the question then arises which state should take in the refugees. It is natural to see the obligation as shared among all those states that are able to provide refuge, and in an ideal world one might envisage some formal mechanism for distributing refugees among them. However, the difficulties in devising such a scheme are formidable. To obtain agreement from different states about what each state's refugee quota should be, one would presumably need to start with simple and relatively uncontroversial criteria such as population or per capita GNP. But this leaves out of the picture many other factors, such as population density, the overall rate of immigration into each state, cultural factors that make absorption of particular groups of refugees particularly easy or difficult, and so forth – all factors that would differentially affect the willingness of political communities to accept refugees and make agreement on a scheme very unlikely. Furthermore, the proposed quota system pays no attention to the choices of the refugees themselves as to where to apply for sanctuary, unless it is accompanied by a compensatory scheme that allows states that take in more refugees than their quota prescribes to receive financial transfers from states that take in less.

Realistically, therefore, states have to be given considerable autonomy to decide on how to respond to particular asylum applications: besides the refugee's own choice, they are entitled to consider the overall number of applications they face, the demands that temporary or longer-term accommodation of refugees will place on existing citizens, and whether there exists any special link between the refugee and the host community – for instance, similarities of language or culture, or a sense of historical responsibility on the part of the receiving state (which might see itself as somehow implicated among the causes of the crisis that has produced

the refugees). If states are given this autonomy, there can be no guarantee that every bona fide refugee will find a state willing to take him or her in. Here we simply face a clash between two moral intuitions: on the one hand, every refugee is a person with basic human rights that deserve protection; on the other, the responsibility for insuring this is diffused among states in such a way that we cannot say that any particular state S has an obligation to admit refugee R. Each state is at some point entitled to say that it has done enough to cope with the refugee crisis. So the best we can hope for is that informal mechanisms will continue to evolve which make all refugees the *special* responsibility of one state or another.

The second issue is discrimination among migrants who are not refugees. Currently, states do discriminate on a variety of different grounds, effectively selecting the migrants they want to take in. Can this be justified? Well, given that states are entitled to put a ceiling on the numbers of people they take in, for reasons canvassed in the previous section, they need to select somehow, if only by lottery (as the USA began to do in 1995 for certain categories of immigrant). So what grounds can they legitimately use? It seems to me that receiving states are entitled to consider the benefit they would receive from admitting a would-be migrant as well as the strength of the migrant's own claim to move. So it is acceptable to give precedence to people whose cultural values are closer to those of the existing population – for instance, to those who already speak the native language. This is a direct corollary of the argument in the previous section about cultural self-determination. Next in order of priority come those who possess skills and talents that are needed by the receiving community. Their claim is weakened, as suggested earlier, by the likelihood that in taking them in, the receiving state is also depriving their country of origin of a valuable resource (medical expertise, for example). In such cases, the greater the interest the potential host country has in admitting the would-be migrant, the more likely it is that admitting her will make life worse for those she leaves behind. So although it is reasonable for the receiving state to make decisions based on how much the immigrant can be expected to contribute economically if admitted, this criterion should be used with caution. What cannot be defended in any circumstances is discrimination on grounds of race, sex, or, in most instances, religion – religion could be a relevant criterion only where it continues to form an essential part of the public culture, as in the case of the state of Israel.

If nation-states are allowed to decide how many immigrants to admit in the first place, why can't they pick and choose among potential immigrants on whatever grounds they like – admitting only red-haired women if that is what their current membership prefers? I have tried to hold a balance between the interest that migrants have in entering the country they want to live in, and the interest that political communities having in determining their own character. Although the first of these interests is not strong enough to justify a right of migration, it is still substantial, and so the immigrants who are refused entry are owed an explanation. To be told that they belong to the wrong race, or sex (or have hair of the wrong color) is insulting, given that these features do not connect to anything of real significance to the society they want to join. Even tennis clubs are not entitled to discriminate among applicants on grounds such as these.

Let me conclude by underlining the importance of admitting all long-term immigrants to full and equal citizenship in the receiving society (this does not apply to refugees who are admitted temporarily until it is safe to return to their country of origin, but it does apply to refugees as soon as it becomes clear that return is not a realistic option for them). Controls on immigration must be coupled with active policies to insure that immigrants are brought into the political life of the community, and acquire the linguistic and other skills that they require to function as active citizens. In several states immigrants are now encouraged to take citizenship classes leading up to a formal admissions ceremony, and this is a welcome development insofar as it recognizes that becoming a citizen isn't something that just happens spontaneously. Precisely because they aim to be "communities of character," with distinct public cultures to which new immigrants can contribute, democratic states must bring immigrants into political dialogue with natives. What is unacceptable is the emergence of a permanent class of non-citizens, whether these are guest workers, illegal immigrants, or asylum seekers waiting to have their applications adjudicated. The underlying political philosophy which informs this chapter sees democratic states as political communities formed on the basis of equality among their members, and just as this gives such states the right to exclude, it also imposes the obligation to protect the equal status of all those who live within their borders.

3b. GLOBAL DISTRIBUTIVE JUSTICE

WITHIN A COUNTRY LIKE THE UNITED STATES, issues of distributive justice seem pressing enough. Vast inequalities in wealth and income (see part 2e) lead many to argue that some form of coercive redistribution is necessary to achieve justice. But when our focus is expanded from a national level to a global level, the problem seems even more pressing. For, as Thomas Pogge points out in his contribution to this section, not only are inequalities in the global distribution of wealth much more severe than those at the domestic level, but the problem of inequality is compounded by the problem of *absolute* poverty. It is not just that many of the world's poor have *less* than everyone else; it is that they do not have nearly enough to meet even the most basic of their needs.

The extremity of the situation makes for compelling intuitions. Peter Singer, for instance, suggests that those of us in wealthy countries who spend money on luxuries—decaf lattes, movie tickets, designer jeans, etc.—rather than sending that money to relief organizations like OXFAM which could use it to cheaply save the lives of desperate people, are morally on a par with someone who passively watches a child drown in a shallow pond in order to avoid muddying his expensive shoes. We are choosing to satisfy our own trivial desires rather than to save the life of another. In a very real sense, we are murderers—only we commit our murder through inaction, rather than through action.

What would it take for us to avoid being murderers, according to Singer? His answer is simple, yet challenging. We should give away what we have as long as we could prevent something very bad from happening by doing so without giving up anything of comparable significance. What this means in practice, however, is that we are essentially forbidden from spending any money ourselves beyond that necessary for bare survival so long as there are others in the world whose death or extreme suffering we could prevent with that money. And since the prospect of ending world starvation and malnutrition seems remote, this probably means that we will *always* be forbidden from spending money on "luxuries" for ourselves.

Singer is a utilitarian, so the claim that we should give our money away if doing so will create more good than harm comes naturally to him. But one needn't be a utilitarian to agree that when the choice is between allocating one's dollars toward saving a life or having an enjoyable night out at the theatre, the morally required decision is obvious. This is especially so when we cannot take full *responsibility* for our own favorable lot in life, nor can we assign responsibility to those who are less fortunate for theirs. The country into which we are born is entirely a matter of *luck*. And the country into which we are born has a tremendous influence on our life prospects. I have worked hard for my educational and professional accomplishments. But had I been born in Somalia instead of California, twice the amount of hard work would probably not have been sufficient to provide me with half the standard of living to which I am accustomed. Is it fair that some people should starve while others prosper if the difference between the two is caused by nothing more significant than a kind of cosmic lottery? Even worse, what if those in wealthy nations are in some way *causally responsible* for the poverty of those in the developing world, perhaps via military imperialism or economic exploitation?

There are many important philosophical questions about what each of us should do on a personal level to remedy this situation. Are we required, as Singer claims, to sacrifice for the greater good until we have given so much that we are no better off than those we are trying to help? Or are we allowed to spend a sizeable chunk of our money in the pursuit of our own personal hobbies and projects, no matter how insignificant these may be in terms of their contribution to global utility? Does it matter if other people are doing their share to alleviate the problem too? As important as these questions are, the readings in this section will largely bypass them. Since this is a text in *political* philosophy, our main concern will be with how political institutions—not individuals—should respond to the problem of global poverty. Some, like Pogge, call for a radical transformation of the global economic order in order to achieve justice. Others, such as Chandran Kukathas, argue against such transformations on two grounds. First, they argue that there are too many reasonable but divergent standards of justice to impose one particular standard on the entire global order. Since we cannot conclusively establish that, say, the socialist conception of justice is correct as opposed to the libertarian conception, it would be unfair to impose one of these standards through the coercive mechanism of the global order. This objection draws on a line of thinking stemming from Rawls' work in *Political Liberalism,* and coincides to a certain extent with his thinking about issues of global justice in *The Law of Peoples*. The other ground for thinking that it would be unwise to radically transform the global economic order in order to pursue justice is that the institutional mechanisms that would be necessary to achieve global justice would be ripe for abuse, and possibly lead to greater oppression, exploitation, and injustice overall. Note that while the first objection represents a principled, deontological objection to the pursuit of global justice, the second line of argument is essentially consequentialist in nature. One argument says that it would be *disrespectful* to quash reasonable disagreement about justice by imposing one standard on everyone; the other does not deny that there may be some one true standard of justice that it would be in principle permissible to impose on everyone, but claims that in practice the costs of trying to do so would be greater than the benefits.

Between thinkers such as Pogge and Kukathas, however, there is ample room for debate regarding both the substantive content of principles of global justice—what they ultimately require of us—and the best institutional mechanisms to instantiate those principles. The kind of philosophical debate represented in this section will go some distance toward exploring the first question, but the first question can probably not be resolved entirely without addressing the second question, and the second question is more the province of disciplines such as economics and political science. Philosophy has much to say about the issue of global justice, but it can reasonably hope to contribute no more than a part of the overall story.

Further Reading

Beitz, C. R. (1975). Justice and International Relations. *Philosophy and Public Affairs, 4*, 360–389.

Beitz, C. R. (1983). Cosmopolitan Ideals and National Sentiment. *Journal of Philosophy, 80*, 591–599.

Cullity, G. (2006). *The Moral Demands of Affluence.* Oxford: Oxford University Press.

Lomasky, L. E. (2007). Liberalism beyond Borders. *Social Philosophy and Policy, 24*(1), 206–233.

Mollendorf, D. (2002). *Cosmopolitan Justice.* New York: Westview Press.

Murphy, L. (2003). *Moral Demands in Nonideal Theory.* Oxford: Oxford University Press.

Nussbaum, M. (2000). *Women and Human Development: The Capabilities Approach.* Cambridge: Cambridge University Press.

Pogge, T. W. (1994). An Egalitarian Law of Peoples. *Philosophy and Public Affairs, 23*(3), 195–224.

Rawls, J. (1999). *The Law of Peoples.* Cambridge, MA: Harvard University Press.

Scheffler, S. (2003). *Boundaries and Allegiances: Problems of Justice and Responsibility in Liberal Thought.* Oxford: Oxford University Press.

Sen, A. (1999). *Development as Freedom.* New York: Random House.

Teson, F. R. (1995). The Rawlsian Theory of International Law. *Ethics and International Affairs, 9*, 79–99.

Chapter 44

Peter Singer

FAMINE, AFFLUENCE, AND MORALITY

Peter Singer (1946–   ) is an Australian philosopher who is currently the Ira W. DeCamp Professor of Bioethics at Princeton University. His writings in defense of utilitarianism and animal liberation have been tremendously influential. In this essay (published in 1972), Singer argues that individuals living in wealthy countries such as the United States have a strong moral obligation to give away a significant portion of their income to mitigate the devastating effects of poverty in the developing world. Spending money on trivial luxuries for ourselves while others starve is grossly immoral.

As I write this, in November 1971, people are dying in East Bengal from lack of food, shelter, and medical care. The suffering and death that are occurring there now are not inevitable, not unavoidable in any fatalistic sense of the term. Constant poverty, a cyclone, and a civil war have turned at least nine million people into destitute refugees; nevertheless, it is not beyond the capacity of the richer nations to give enough assistance to reduce any further suffering to very small proportions. The decisions and actions of human beings can prevent this kind of suffering. Unfortunately, human beings have not made the necessary decisions. At the individual level, people have, with very few exceptions, not responded to the situation in any significant way. Generally speaking, people have not given large sums to relief funds; they have not written to their parliamentary representatives demanding increased government assistance; they have not demonstrated in the streets, held symbolic fasts, or done anything else directed toward providing the refugees with the means to satisfy their essential needs. At the government level, no government has given the sort of massive aid that would enable the refugees to survive for more than a few days. Britain, for instance, has given rather more than most countries. It has, to date, given £14,750,000. For comparative purposes, Britain's share of the nonrecoverable development costs of the Anglo-French Concorde project is already in excess of £275,000,000, and on present estimates will reach £440,000,000. The implication is that the British government values a supersonic transport more than thirty times as highly as it values the lives of the nine million refugees. Australia is another country which, on a per capita basis, is well up in the "aid to Bengal" table. Australia's aid, however, amounts to less than one-twelfth of the cost of Sydney's new opera house. The total amount given, from all sources, now stands at about £65,000,000. The estimated cost of keeping the refugees alive for one year is £464,000,000. Most of the refugees have now been in the camps for more than six months. The World Bank has said that India needs a minimum of £300,000,000 in assistance from other countries before the end of the year. It seems obvious that assistance on this scale will not be forthcoming. India will be forced to choose between letting the refugees starve or diverting funds from her own development program, which will mean that more of her own people will starve in the future.

These are the essential facts about the present situation in Bengal. So far as it concerns us here, there is nothing unique about this situation except its magnitude. The Bengal emergency is just the latest and most acute of a series of major emergencies in various parts of the world, arising both from natural and from man-made causes. There are also many parts of the world in which people die from malnutrition and lack of food independent of any special emergency. I take Bengal as my example only because it is the present concern, and because the size of the problem has ensured that it has been given adequate publicity. Neither individuals nor governments can claim to be unaware of what is happening there.

What are the moral implications of a situation like this? In what follows, I shall argue that the way people in relatively affluent countries react to a situation like that in Bengal cannot be justified; indeed, the whole way we look at moral issues—our moral conceptual scheme—needs to be altered, and with it, the way of life that has come to be taken for granted in our society.

In arguing for this conclusion I will not, of course, claim to be morally neutral. I shall, however, try to argue for the moral position that I take, so that anyone who accepts certain assumptions, to be made explicit, will, I hope, accept my conclusion.

I begin with the assumption that suffering and death from lack of food, shelter, and medical care are bad. I think most people will agree about this, although one may reach the same view by differ-

ent routes. I shall not argue for this view. People can hold all sorts of eccentric positions, and perhaps from some of them it would not follow that death by starvation is in itself bad. It is difficult, perhaps impossible, to refute such positions, and so for brevity I will henceforth take this assumption as accepted. Those who disagree need read no further.

My next point is this: if it is in our power to prevent something bad from happening, without thereby sacrificing anything of comparable moral importance, we ought, morally, to do it. By "without sacrificing anything of comparable moral importance" I mean without causing anything else comparably bad to happen, or doing something that is wrong in itself, or failing to promote some moral good, comparable in significance to the bad thing that we can prevent. This principle seems almost as uncontroversial as the last one. It requires us only to prevent what is bad, and not to promote what is good, and it requires this of us only when we can do it without sacrificing anything that is, from the moral point of view, comparably important. I could even, as far as the application of my argument to the Bengal emergency is concerned, qualify the point so as to make it: if it is in our power to prevent something very bad from happening, without thereby sacrificing anything morally significant, we ought, morally, to do it. An application of this principle would be as follows: if I am walking past a shallow pond and see a child drowning in it, I ought to wade in and pull the child out. This will mean getting my clothes muddy, but this is insignificant, while the death of the child would presumably be a very bad thing.

The uncontroversial appearance of the principle just stated is deceptive. If it were acted upon, even in its qualified form, our lives, our society, and our world would be fundamentally changed. For the principle takes, firstly, no account of proximity or distance. It makes no moral difference whether the person I can help is a neighbor's child ten yards from me or a

Bengali whose name I shall never know, ten thousand miles away. Secondly, the principle makes no distinction between cases in which I am the only person who could possibly do anything and cases in which I am just one among millions in the same position.

I do not think I need to say much in defense of the refusal to take proximity and distance into account. The fact that a person is physically near to us, so that we have personal contact with him, may make it more likely that we *shall* assist him, but this does not show that we *ought* to help him rather than another who happens to be further away. If we accept any principle of impartiality, universalizability, equality, or whatever, we cannot discriminate against someone merely because he is far away from us (or we are far away from him). Admittedly, it is possible that we are in a better position to judge what needs to be done to help a person near to us than one far away, and perhaps also to provide the assistance we judge to be necessary. If this were the case, it would be a reason for helping those near to us first. This may once have been a justification for being more concerned with the poor in one's own town than with famine victims in India. Unfortunately for those who like to keep their moral responsibilities limited, instant communication and swift transportation have changed the situation. From the moral point of view, the development of the world into a "global village" has made an important, though still unrecognized, difference to our moral situation. Expert observers and supervisors, sent out by famine relief organizations or permanently stationed in famine-prone areas, can direct our aid to a refugee in Bengal almost as effectively as we could get it to someone in our own block. There would seem, therefore, to be no possible justification for discriminating on geographical grounds.

There may be a greater need to defend the second implication of my principle—that the fact that there are millions of other people in the same position, in respect to the Bengali refugees, as I am, does not make the situation significantly different from a situation in which I am the only person who can prevent something very bad from occurring. Again, of course, I admit that there is a psychological difference between the cases; one feels less guilty about doing nothing if one can point to others, similarly placed, who have also done nothing. Yet this can make no real difference to our moral obligations. Should I consider that I am less obliged to pull the drowning child out of the pond if on looking around I see other people, no further away than I am, who have also noticed the child but are doing nothing? One has only to ask this question to see the absurdity of the view that numbers lessen obligation. It is a view that is an ideal excuse for inactivity; unfortunately most of the major evils—poverty, overpopulation, pollution—are problems in which everyone is almost equally involved.

The view that numbers do make a difference can be made plausible if stated in this way: if everyone in circumstances like mine gave £5 to the Bengal Relief Fund, there would be enough to provide food, shelter, and medical care for the refugees; there is no reason why I should give more than anyone else in the same circumstances as I am; therefore I have no obligation to give more than £5. Each premise in this argument is true, and the argument looks sound. It may convince us, unless we notice that it is based on a hypothetical premise, although the conclusion is not stated hypothetically. The argument would be sound if the conclusion were: if everyone in circumstances like mine were to give £5, I would have no obligation to give more than £5. If the conclusion were so stated, however, it would be obvious that the argument has no bearing on a situation in which it is not the case that everyone else gives £5. This, of course, is the actual situation. It is more or less certain that not everyone in circumstances like mine will give £5. So there will not be enough to provide the needed food, shelter, and medical care. Therefore by giving more than £5 I will prevent more suffering than I would if I gave just £5.

It might be thought that this argument has an absurd consequence. Since the situation appears to be that very few people are likely to give substantial amounts, it follows that I and everyone else in similar circumstances ought to give as much as possible, that is, at least up to the point at which by giving more one would begin to cause serious suffering for oneself and one's dependents—perhaps even beyond this point to the point of marginal utility, at which by giving more one would cause oneself and one's dependents as much suffering as one would prevent in Bengal. If everyone does this, however, there will be more than can be used for the benefit of the refugees, and some of the sacrifice will have been unnecessary. Thus, if everyone does what he ought to do, the result will not be as good as it would be if everyone did a little less than he ought to do, or if only some do all that they ought to do.

The paradox here arises only if we assume that the actions in question—sending money to the relief funds—are performed more or less simultaneously, and are also unexpected. For if it is to be expected that everyone is going to contribute something, then clearly each is not obliged to give as much as he would have been obliged to had others not been giving too. And if everyone is not acting more or less simultaneously, then those giving later will know how much more is needed, and will have no obligation to give more than is necessary to reach this amount. To say this is not to deny the principle that people in the same circumstances have the same obligations, but to point out that the fact that others have given, or may be expected to give, is a relevant circumstance: those giving after it has become known that many others are giving and those giving before are not in the same circumstances. So the seemingly absurd consequence of the principle I have put forward can occur only if people are in error about the actual circumstances—that is, if they think they are giving when others are not, but in fact they are giving when others are. The result of every-

one doing what he really ought to do cannot be worse than the result of everyone doing less than he ought to do, although the result of everyone doing what he reasonably believes he ought to do could be.

If my argument so far has been sound, neither our distance from a preventable evil nor the number of other people who, in respect to that evil, are in the same situation as we are, lessens our obligation to mitigate or prevent that evil. I shall therefore take as established the principle I asserted earlier. As I have already said, I need to assert it only in its qualified form: if it is in our power to prevent something very bad from happening, without thereby sacrificing anything else morally significant, we ought, morally, to do it.

The outcome of this argument is that our traditional moral categories are upset. The traditional distinction between duty and charity cannot be drawn, or at least, not in the place we normally draw it. Giving money to the Bengal Relief Fund is regarded as an act of charity in our society. The bodies which collect money are known as "charities." These organizations see themselves in this way—if you send them a check, you will be thanked for your "generosity." Because giving money is regarded as an act of charity, it is not thought that there is anything wrong with not giving. The charitable man may be praised, but the man who is not charitable is not condemned. People do not feel in any way ashamed or guilty about spending money on new clothes or a new car instead of giving it to famine relief. (Indeed, the alternative does not occur to them.) This way of looking at the matter cannot be justified. When we buy new clothes not to keep ourselves warm but to look "well-dressed" we are not providing for any important need. We would not be sacrificing anything significant if we were to continue to wear our old clothes, and give the money to famine relief. By doing so, we would be preventing another person from starving. It follows from what I have said earlier that we ought to give money away, rather than spend it on clothes which we do not need to keep us warm. To do so is not charitable, or generous. Nor is it the kind of act which philosophers and theologians have called "supererogatory"—an act which it would be good to do, but not wrong not to do. On the contrary, we ought to give the money away, and it is wrong not to do so.

I am not maintaining that there are no acts which are charitable, or that there are no acts which it would be good to do but not wrong not to do. It may be possible to redraw the distinction between duty and charity in some other place. All I am arguing here is that the present way of drawing the distinction, which makes it an act of charity for a man living at the level of affluence which most people in the "developed nations" enjoy to give money to save someone else from starvation, cannot be supported. It is beyond the scope of my argument to consider whether the distinction should be redrawn or abolished altogether. There would be many other possible ways of drawing the distinction—for instance, one might decide that it is good to make other people as happy as possible, but not wrong not to do so.

Despite the limited nature of the revision in our moral conceptual scheme which I am proposing, the revision would, given the extent of both affluence and famine in the world today, have radical implications. These implications may lead to further objections, distinct from those I have already considered. I shall discuss two of these.

One objection to the position I have taken might be simply that it is too drastic a revision of our moral scheme. People do not ordinarily judge in the way I have suggested they should. Most people reserve their moral condemnation for those who violate some moral norm, such as the norm against taking another person's property. They do not condemn those who indulge in luxury instead of giving to famine relief. But given that I did not set out to present a morally neutral description of the way people make moral judgments, the way people do in fact

judge has nothing to do with the validity of my conclusion. My conclusion follows from the principle which I advanced earlier, and unless that principle is rejected, or the arguments shown to be unsound, I think the conclusion must stand, however strange it appears.

It might, nevertheless, be interesting to consider why our society, and most other societies, do judge differently from the way I have suggested they should. In a well-known article, J. O. Urmson suggests that the imperatives of duty, which tell us what we must do, as distinct from what it would be good to do but not wrong not to do, function so as to prohibit behavior that is intolerable if men are to live together in society. This may explain the origin and continued existence of the present division between acts of duty and acts of charity. Moral attitudes are shaped by the needs of society, and no doubt society needs people who will observe the rules that make social existence tolerable. From the point of view of a particular society, it is essential to prevent violations of norms against killing, stealing, and so on. It is quite inessential, however, to help people outside one's own society.

If this is an explanation of our common distinction between duty and supererogation, however, it is not a justification of it. The moral point of view requires us to look beyond the interests of our own society. Previously, as I have already mentioned, this may hardly have been feasible, but it is quite feasible now. From the moral point of view, the prevention of the starvation of millions of people outside our society must be considered at least as pressing as the upholding of property norms within our society.

It has been argued by some writers, among them Sidgwick and Urmson, that we need to have a basic moral code which is not too far beyond the capacities of the ordinary man, for otherwise there will be a general breakdown of compliance with the moral code. Crudely stated, this argument suggests that if we tell people that they ought to refrain from murder and give everything they do not really need to famine relief, they will do neither, whereas if we tell them that they ought to refrain from murder and that it is good to give to famine relief but not wrong not to do so, they will at least refrain from murder. The issue here is: Where should we drawn the line between conduct that is required and conduct that is good although not required, so as to get the best possible result? This would seem to be an empirical question, although a very difficult one. One objection to the Sidgwick-Urmson line of argument is that it takes insufficient account of the effect that moral standards can have on the decisions we make. Given a society in which a wealthy man who gives five percent of his income to famine relief is regarded as most generous, it is not surprising that a proposal that we all ought to give away half our incomes will be thought to be absurdly unrealistic. In a society which held that no man should have more than enough while others have less than they need, such a proposal might seem narrow-minded. What it is possible for a man to do and what he is likely to do are both, I think, very greatly influenced by what people around him are doing and expecting him to do. In any case, the possibility that by spreading the idea that we ought to be doing very much more than we are to relieve famine we shall bring about a general breakdown of moral behavior seems remote. If the stakes are an end to widespread starvation, it is worth the risk. Finally, it should be emphasized that these considerations are relevant only to the issue of what we should require from others, and not to what we ourselves ought to do.

The second objection to my attack on the present distinction between duty and charity is one which has from time to time been made against utilitarianism. It follows from some forms of utilitarian theory that we all ought, morally, to be working full time to increase the balance of happiness over misery. The position I have taken here would not lead to this conclusion in all circumstances, for if there were no bad occurrences that we could prevent without sac-

rificing something of comparable moral importance, my argument would have no application. Given the present conditions in many parts of the world, however, it does follow from my argument that we ought, morally, to be working full time to relieve great suffering of the sort that occurs as a result of famine or other disasters. Of course, mitigating circumstances can be adduced—for instance, that if we wear ourselves out through overwork, we shall be less effective than we would otherwise have been. Nevertheless, when all considerations of this sort have been taken into account, the conclusion remains: we ought to be preventing as much suffering as we can without sacrificing something else of comparable moral importance. This conclusion is one which we may be reluctant to face. I cannot see, though, why it should be regarded as a criticism of the position for which I have argued, rather than a criticism of our ordinary standards of behavior. Since most people are self-interested to some degree, very few of us are likely to do everything that we ought to do. It would, however, hardly be honest to take this as evidence that it is not the case that we ought to do it.

It may still be thought that my conclusions are so wildly out of line with what everyone else thinks and has always thought that there must be something wrong with the argument somewhere. In order to show that my conclusions, while certainly contrary to contemporary Western moral standards, would not have seemed so extraordinary at other times and in other places, I would like to quote a passage from a writer not normally thought of as a way-out radical, Thomas Aquinas.

> Now, according to the natural order instituted by divine providence, material goods are provided for the satisfaction of human needs. Therefore the division and appropriation of property, which proceeds from human law, must not hinder the satisfaction of man's necessity from such goods. Equally, whatever a man has in super-abundance is owed, of

natural right, to the poor for their sustenance. So Ambrosius says, and it is also to be found in the *Decretum Gratiani*: "The bread which you withhold belongs to the hungry; the clothing you shut away, to the naked; and the money you bury in the earth is the redemption and freedom of the penniless."

I now want to consider a number of points, more practical than philosophical, which are relevant to the application of the moral conclusion we have reached. These points challenge not the idea that we ought to be doing all we can to prevent starvation, but the idea that giving away a great deal of money is the best means to this end.

It is sometimes said that overseas aid should be a government responsibility, and that therefore one ought not to give to privately run charities. Giving privately, it is said, allows the government and the noncontributing members of society to escape their responsibilities.

This argument seems to assume that the more people there are who give to privately organized famine relief funds, the less likely it is that the government will take over full responsibility for such aid. This assumption is unsupported, and does not strike me as at all plausible. The opposite view—that if no one gives voluntarily, a government will assume that its citizens are uninterested in famine relief and would not wish to be forced into giving aid—seems more plausible. In any case, unless there were a definite probability that by refusing to give one would be helping to bring about massive government assistance, people who do refuse to make voluntary contributions are refusing to prevent a certain amount of suffering without being able to point to any tangible beneficial consequence of their refusal. So the onus of showing how their refusal will bring about government action is on those who refuse to give.

I do not, of course, want to dispute the contention that governments of affluent nations should be giving many times the amount of genuine, no-strings-attached aid that they are giving now. I agree, too, that giving privately is not enough, and that we ought to be campaigning actively for entirely new standards for both public and private contributions to famine relief. Indeed, I would sympathize with someone who thought that campaigning was more important than giving one-self, although I doubt whether preaching what one does not practice would be very effective. Unfortunately, for many people the idea that "it's the government's responsibility" is a reason for not giving which does not appear to entail any political action either.

Another, more serious reason for not giving to famine relief funds is that until there is effective population control, relieving famine merely postpones starvation. If we save the Bengal refugees now, others, perhaps the children of these refugees, will face starvation in a few years' time. In support of this, one may cite the now well-known facts about the population explosion and the relatively limited scope for expanded production.

This point, like the previous one, is an argument against relieving suffering that is happening now, because of a belief about what might happen in the future; it is unlike the previous point in that very good evidence can be adduced in support of this belief about the future. I will not go into the evidence here. I accept that the earth cannot support indefinitely a population rising at the present rate. This certainly poses a problem for anyone who thinks it important to prevent famine. Again, however, one could accept the argument without drawing the conclusion that it absolves one from any obligation to do anything to prevent famine. The conclusion that should be drawn is that the best means of preventing famine, in the long run, is population control. It would then follow from the position reached earlier that one ought to be doing all one can to promote population control (unless one held that all forms of population control were wrong in themselves, or would have significantly bad consequences). Since there are organizations working specifically for population control, one would then support them rather than more orthodox methods of preventing famine.

A third point raised by the conclusion reached earlier relates to the question of just how much we all ought to be giving away. One possibility, which has already been mentioned, is that we ought to give until we reach the level of marginal utility—that is, the level at which, by giving more, I would cause as much suffering to myself or my dependents as I would relieve by my gift. This would mean, of course, that one would reduce oneself to very near the material circumstances of a Bengali refugee. It will be recalled that earlier I put forward both a strong and a moderate version of the principle of preventing bad occurrences. The strong version, which required us to prevent bad things from happening unless in doing so we would be sacrificing something of comparable moral significance, does seem to require reducing ourselves to the level of marginal utility. I should also say that the strong version seems to me to be the correct one. I proposed the more moderate version—that we should prevent bad occurrences unless, to do so, we had to sacrifice something morally significant—only in order to show that even on this surely undeniable principle a great change in our way of life is required. On the more moderate principle, it may not follow that we ought to reduce ourselves to the level of marginal utility, for one might hold that to reduce oneself and one's family to this level is to cause something significantly bad to happen. Whether this is so I shall not discuss, since, as I have said, I can see no good reason for holding the moderate version of the principle rather than the strong version. Even if we accepted the principle only in its moderate form, however, it should be clear that we would have to give away enough to ensure that the consumer society, dependent as it is on people spending on trivia rather than giving to famine relief, would slow down and perhaps disappear entirely. There are several reasons

why this would be desirable in itself. The value and necessity of economic growth are now being questioned not only by conservationists, but by economists as well. There is no doubt, too, that the consumer society has had a distorting effect on the goals and purposes of its members. Yet looking at the matter purely from the point of view of overseas aid, there must be a limit to the extent to which we should deliberately slow down our economy; for it might be the case that if we gave away, say, forty percent of our Gross National Product, we would slow down the economy so much that in absolute terms we would be giving less than if we gave twenty-five percent of the much larger GNP that we would have if we limited our contribution to this smaller percentage.

I mention this only as an indication of the sort of factor that one would have to take into account in working out an ideal. Since Western societies generally consider one percent of the GNP an acceptable level for overseas aid, the matter is entirely academic. Nor does it affect the question of how much an individual should give in a society in which very few are giving substantial amounts.

It is sometimes said, though less often now than it used to be, that philosophers have no special role to play in public affairs, since most public issues depend primarily on an assessment of facts. On questions of fact, it is said, philosophers as such have no special expertise, and so it has been possible to engage in philosophy without committing oneself to any position on major public issues. No doubt there are some issues of social policy and foreign policy about which it can truly be said that a really expert assessment of the facts is required before taking sides or acting, but the issue of famine is surely not one of these. The facts about the existence of suffering are beyond dispute. Nor, I think, is it disputed that we can do something about it, either through orthodox methods of famine relief or through population control or both. This is therefore an issue on which philosophers are competent to take a position. The issue is one which faces everyone who has more money than he needs to support himself and his dependents, or who is in a position to take some sort of political action. These categories must include practically every teacher and student of philosophy in the universities of the Western world. If philosophy is to deal with matters that are relevant to both teachers and students, this is an issue that philosophers should discuss.

Discussion, though, is not enough. What is the point of relating philosophy to public (and personal) affairs if we do not take our conclusions seriously? In this instance, taking our conclusion seriously means acting upon it. The philosopher will not find it any easier than anyone else to alter his attitudes and way of life to the extent that, if I am right, is involved in doing everything that we ought to be doing. At the very least, though, one can make a start. The philosopher who does so will have to sacrifice some of the benefits of the consumer society, but he can find compensation in the satisfaction of a way of life in which theory and practice, if not yet in harmony, are at least coming together.

Chapter 45

Thomas Pogge

WORLD POVERTY AND HUMAN RIGHTS

Thomas Pogge (1953–   ) is a professor of philosophy and international affairs at Yale University, widely known for his writings on global justice and health care. The following article is a revised version of an essay which first appeared in a symposium on his book, *World Poverty and Human Rights*. In it, he puts forward some data about the problem of world poverty, and argues that this poverty is a harm imposed on the developing world by the developed world. It is therefore a harm for which those in the developed world bear moral responsibility.

Despite a high and growing global average income, billions of human beings are still condemned to lifelong severe poverty, with all its attendant evils of low life expectancy, social exclusion, ill health, illiteracy, dependency, and effective enslavement. The annual death toll from poverty-related causes is around 18 million, or one-third of all human deaths, which adds up to approximately 360 million deaths since the end of the Cold War.[1]

This problem is hardly unsolvable, in spite of its magnitude. In 2004, the 2.5 billion people counted as living below the World Bank's more generous $2 per day international poverty line—though constituting 39 percent of the world's population—accounted for only about 1 percent of the global product, and would have needed only 0.7 percent more to escape poverty so defined.[2] By contrast, the high-income countries, with one billion citizens, had about 80 percent of the global product.[3] With our average per capita income some 200 times greater than that of the poor (at market exchange rates), we could eradicate severe poverty worldwide if we chose to try—in fact, we could have eradicated it decades ago.

Citizens of the rich countries are, however, conditioned to downplay the severity and persistence of world poverty and to think of it as an occasion for minor charitable assistance. Thanks in part to the rationalizations dispensed by our economists, most of us believe that severe poverty and its persistence are due exclusively to local causes. Few realize that severe poverty is an ongoing harm we inflict upon the global poor. If more of us understood the true magnitude of the problem of poverty and our causal involvement in it, we might do what is necessary to eradicate it.

That world poverty is an ongoing harm *we* inflict seems completely incredible to most citizens of the affluent countries. We call it tragic that the basic human rights of so many remain unfulfilled, and are willing to admit that we should do more to help. But it is unthinkable to us that we are actively responsible for this catastrophe. If we were, then we, civilized and sophisticated denizens of the developed countries, would be guilty of the largest crime against humanity ever committed, the death toll of which exceeds, every three years, that of World War II with concentration camps and gulags included. What could be more preposterous?

But think about the unthinkable for a moment. Are there steps the affluent countries could take to reduce severe poverty abroad? It seems very likely that there are, given the enormous inequalities in income and wealth already mentioned. The common assumption, however, is that reducing severe poverty abroad at the expense of our own affluence would be generous on our part, not something we owe, and that our failure to do this is thus at most a lack of generosity that does not make us morally responsible for the continued deprivation of the poor.

I deny this popular assumption. I deny that the one billion citizens of the affluent countries are morally entitled to their 80 percent of the global product in the face of much larger numbers of people mired in severe poverty. Is this denial really so preposterous that one need not consider the arguments in its support? Does not the radical inequality between our wealth and their dire need at least put the burden on us to show why we should be morally entitled to so much while they have so little? In *World Poverty and Human Rights*,[4] I dispute the popular assumption by showing that the usual ways of justifying our great advantage fail. My argument poses three mutually independent challenges.

Actual History

Many believe that the radical inequality we face can be justified by reference to how it evolved, for example through differences in diligence, culture, and social institutions, soil, climate, or fortune. I challenge this sort of justification by invoking the common and very violent history through which the present radical inequality

accumulated. Much of it was built up in the colonial era, when today's affluent countries ruled today's poor regions of the world: trading their people like cattle, destroying their political institutions and cultures, taking their lands and natural resources, and forcing products and customs upon them. I recount these historical facts specifically for readers who believe that even the most radical inequality is morally justifiable if it evolved in a benign way. Such readers disagree about the conditions a historical process must meet for it to justify such vast inequalities in life chances. But I can bypass these disagreements because the actual historical crimes were so horrendous, diverse, and consequential that no historical entitlement conception could credibly support the view that our common history was sufficiently benign to justify today's huge inequality in starting places.

Challenges such as this are often dismissed with the lazy response that we cannot be held responsible for what others did long ago. This response is true but irrelevant. We indeed cannot inherit responsibility for our forefathers' sins. But how then can we plausibly claim the fruits of their sins? How can we have been entitled to the great head start our countries enjoyed going into the postcolonial period, which has allowed us to dominate and shape the world? And how can we be entitled to the huge advantages over the global poor we consequently enjoy from birth? The historical path from which our exceptional affluence arose greatly weakens our moral claim to it—certainly in the face of those whom the same historical process has delivered into conditions of acute deprivation. They, the global poor, have a much stronger moral claim to that 1 percent of the global product they may need to meet their basic needs than we affluent have to take 80 rather than 79 percent for ourselves. Thus, I write, "A morally deeply tarnished history should not be allowed to result in *radical inequality*" (p. 209).

Fictional Histories

Since my first challenge addressed adherents of historical entitlement conceptions of justice, it may leave others unmoved. These others may believe that it is permissible to uphold any economic distribution, no matter how skewed, if merely it *could* have come about on a morally acceptable path. They insist that we are entitled to keep and defend what we possess, even at the cost of millions of deaths each year, unless there is conclusive proof that, without the horrors of the European conquests, severe poverty worldwide would be substantially less today.

Now, *any* distribution, however unequal, *could* be the outcome of a sequence of voluntary bets or gambles. Appeal to such a fictional history would "justify" anything and would thus be wholly implausible. John Locke does much better, holding that a fictional history can justify the status quo only if the changes in holdings and social rules it involves are ones that all participants could have rationally agreed to. He also holds that in a state of nature persons would be entitled to a proportional share of the world's natural resources. Whoever deprives others of "enough and as good"—either through unilateral appropriations or through institutional arrangements, such as a radically unequal property regime—harms them in violation of a *negative* duty. For Locke, the justice of any institutional order thus depends on whether the worst-off under it are at least as well off as people would be in a state of nature with a proportional resource share.[5] This baseline is imprecise, to be sure, but it suffices for my second challenge: however one may want to imagine a state of nature among human beings on this planet, one could not realistically conceive it as involving suffering and early deaths on the scale we are witnessing today. Only a thoroughly organized state of civilization can produce such horrendous misery and sustain an enduring poverty death toll of 18 million annually. The existing distribution is then morally unacceptable on

Lockean grounds insofar as, I point out, "the better-off enjoy significant advantages in the use of a single natural resource base from whose benefits the worse-off are largely, and without compensation, excluded" (p. 208).

The attempt to justify today's coercively upheld radical inequality by appeal to some morally acceptable *fictional* historical process that *might* have led to it thus fails as well. On Locke's permissive account, a small elite may appropriate all of the huge cooperative surplus produced by modern social organization. But this elite must not enlarge its share even further by reducing the poor *below* the state-of-nature baseline in order to capture *more* than the entire cooperative surplus. The citizens and governments of the affluent states are violating this negative duty when we, in collaboration with the ruling cliques of many poor countries, coercively exclude the global poor from a proportional resource share and any equivalent substitute.

Present Global Institutional Arrangements

A third way of thinking about the justice of a radical inequality involves reflection on the institutional rules that sustain it. Using this approach, one can justify an economic order and the distribution it reproduces (irrespective of historical considerations) by comparing them to feasible alternative institutional schemes and the distributional profiles they would produce. Many broadly consequentialist and contractualist conceptions of justice exemplify this approach. They differ in how they characterize the relevant affected parties (groups, persons, time slices of persons, and so on), in the metric they employ for measuring how well off such parties are (in terms of social primary goods, capabilities, welfare, and so forth), and in how they aggregate such well-being information into one overall assessment (for example, by averaging, or in some egalitarian, prioritarian, or sufficientarian way). These conceptions consequently disagree about how economic institutions should best be shaped under modern conditions. But I can bypass such disagreements insofar as these conceptions agree that an economic order is unjust when it—like the systems of serfdom and forced labor prevailing in feudal Russia or France—foreseeably and avoidably gives rise to massive and severe human rights deficits. My third challenge, addressed to adherents of broadly consequentialist and contractualist conceptions of justice, is that we are preserving our great economic advantages by imposing a global economic order that is unjust in view of the massive and avoidable deprivations it foreseeably reproduces: "There is a shared institutional order that is shaped by the better-off and imposed on the worse-off," I contend. "This institutional order is implicated in the reproduction of radical inequality in that there is a feasible institutional alternative under which such severe and extensive poverty would not persist. . . . The radical inequality cannot be traced to extra-social factors (such as genetic handicaps or natural disasters) which, as such, affect different human beings differentially" (p. 205).

Three Notions of Harm

These three challenges converge on the conclusion that the global poor have a compelling moral claim to some of our affluence and that we, by denying them what they are morally entitled to and urgently need, are actively contributing to their deprivations. Still, these challenges are addressed to different audiences and thus appeal to diverse and mutually inconsistent moral conceptions.

They also deploy different notions of harm. In most ordinary contexts, the word "harm" is understood in a historical sense, either diachronically or subjunctively: someone is harmed when she is rendered worse off than she was at some earlier time, or than she would have been had some earlier arrangements continued undisturbed. My first two challenges conceive

harm in this ordinary way, and then conceive justice, at least partly, in terms of harm: we are behaving unjustly toward the global poor by imposing on them the lasting effects of historical crimes, or by holding them below any credible state-of-nature baseline. But my third challenge does not conceive justice and injustice in terms of an independently specified notion of harm. Rather, it relates the concepts of *harm* and *justice* in the opposite way, conceiving harm in terms of an independently specified conception of social justice: we are *harming* the global poor if and insofar as we collaborate in imposing an *unjust* global institutional order upon them. And this institutional order is definitely unjust if and insofar as it foreseeably perpetuates large-scale human rights deficits that would be reasonably avoidable through feasible institutional modifications.[6]

The third challenge is empirically more demanding than the other two. It requires me to substantiate three claims: Global institutional arrangements are causally implicated in the reproduction of massive severe poverty. Governments of our affluent countries bear primary responsibility for these global institutional arrangements and can foresee their detrimental effects. And many citizens of these affluent countries bear responsibility for the global institutional arrangements their governments have negotiated in their names.

Two Main Innovations

In defending the claims underlying my three challenges, my view on these more empirical matters is as oddly perpendicular to the usual empirical debates as my diagnosis of our moral relation to world poverty is to the usual moral debates.

The usual *moral* debates concern the stringency of our moral duties to help the poor abroad. Most of us believe that these duties are rather feeble, meaning that it isn't very wrong of us to give no help at all. Against this popular view, some (Peter Singer, Henry Shue, Peter

Unger) have argued that our positive duties are quite stringent and quite demanding; and others (such as Liam Murphy) have defended an intermediate view according to which our positive duties, insofar as they are quite stringent, are not very demanding. Leaving this whole debate to one side, I focus on what it ignores: our moral duties not to harm. We do, of course, have positive duties to rescue people from life-threatening poverty. But it can be misleading to focus on them when more stringent negative duties are also in play: duties not to expose people to life-threatening poverty and duties to shield them from harms for which we would be actively responsible.

The usual *empirical* debates concern how developing countries should design their economic institutions and policies in order to reduce severe poverty within their borders. The received wisdom (often pointing to Hong Kong and, lately, China) is that they should opt for free and open markets with a minimum in taxes and regulations so as to attract investment and to stimulate growth. But some influential economists call for extensive government investment in education, health care, and infrastructure (as illustrated by the example of the Indian state of Kerala), or for some protectionist measures to "incubate" fledgling niche industries until they become internationally competitive (as illustrated by South Korea's growth spurt). Leaving these debates to one side, I focus once more on what is typically ignored: the role that the design of the *global* institutional order plays in the persistence of severe poverty.

Thanks to the inattention of our economists, many believe that the existing global institutional order plays no role in the persistence of severe poverty, but rather that national differences are the key factors. Such "explanatory nationalism" (pp. 145 ff.) appears justified by the dramatic performance differentials among developing countries, with poverty rapidly disappearing in some and increasing in others. Cases of the latter kind usually display plenty of incompetence, corruption, and oppression by ruling elites, which seem to give us all the explanation we need to understand why severe poverty persists there.

But consider this analogy. Suppose there are great performance differentials among the students in a class, with some improving greatly while many others learn little or nothing. And suppose the latter students do not do their readings and skip many classes. Such performance differentials surely show that local, student-specific factors play a role in explaining academic success. But they decidedly *fail* to show that global factors (the quality of teaching, textbooks, classroom, and so forth) play no such role. For example, it remains possible that the teacher is uninspiring, and thereby dampens the performance of all students. And it remains possible that poor attendance and preparation arise from the teacher's efforts failing to engage the interests of many students or from his sexist comments de-motivating half his class. Analogues to these three possibilities obtain with regard to global institutional arrangements. Its design may be—and actually is, I argue—highly unfavorable for the poor and very supportive of corrupt and dictatorial government, especially in the resource-rich poor countries.

Once we break free from explanatory nationalism, global factors relevant to the persistence of severe poverty are easy to find. In the negotiations, establishing the WTO, the affluent countries insisted on continued and asymmetrical protections of their markets through tariffs, quotas, anti-dumping duties, export credits, and huge subsidies to domestic producers. Such protectionism provides a compelling illustration of the hypocrisy of the rich states who insist and command that their own exports be received with open markets (pp. 20–23). And it greatly impairs export opportunities for the very poorest countries and regions. If the rich countries scrapped their protectionist barriers against imports from poor countries, the populations of the latter would benefit greatly: hundreds of millions would escape unemployment, wage levels would rise substantially, and incoming export revenues would be higher by hundreds of billions of dollars each year.

The same rich states also insist that their intellectual property rights—ever-expanding in scope and duration—must be vigorously enforced in the poor countries. Music and software, production processes, words, seeds, biological species, and medicines—for all these, and more, rents must be paid to the corporations of the rich countries as a condition for (still multiply restricted) access to their markets. Millions would be saved from diseases and death if generic producers could freely manufacture and market life-saving medicines in the poor countries (pp. 222–61).

While charging billions for their intellectual property, the rich countries pay nothing for the externalities they impose through their vastly disproportionate contributions to global pollution and resource depletion. The global poor benefit least, if at all, from polluting activities, and also are least able to protect themselves from the impact such pollution has on their health and on their natural environment (such as flooding due to rising sea levels). It is true, of course, that we pay for the vast quantities of natural resources we import. But such payments cannot make up for the price effects of our inordinate consumption, which restrict the consumption possibilities of the global poor as well as the development possibilities of the poorer countries and regions (in comparison to the opportunities our countries could take advantage of at a comparable stage of economic development).

More important, the payments we make for resource imports go to the rulers (and affluent elites) of the resource-rich countries, with no concern about whether they are democratically elected or at least minimally attentive to the needs of the people whose resources they sell. It is on the basis of effective power alone that we recognize any such ruler as entitled to sell us the resources of "his" country and to borrow, to undertake treaty commitments, and to buy arms in its name. These international resource, borrowing, treaty, and arms privileges we extend to such rulers are highly advantageous to them, providing them with the money and arms they need to stay in power—often with great brutality and negligible popular support. These privileges are also quite convenient to us, securing our resource imports from poor countries irrespective of who may rule them and how badly. But these privileges have devastating effects on the global poor by enabling corrupt rulers to oppress them, to exclude them from the benefits of their countries' natural resources, and to saddle them with huge debts and onerous treaty obligations. By substantially augmenting the perks of governmental power, these same privileges also greatly strengthen the incentives to attempt to take power by force, thereby fostering coups, civil wars, and interstate wars in the poor countries and regions—especially in Africa, which has many desperately poor but resource-rich countries, where the resource sector constitutes a large part of the gross domestic product.

Reflection on the popular view that severe poverty persists in many poor countries because they govern themselves so poorly shows, then, that it is evidence not for but against explanatory nationalism. The populations of most of the countries in which severe poverty persists or increases do not "govern themselves" poorly, but *are* very poorly governed, and much against their will. They are helplessly exposed to such "government" because the rich states recognize their rulers as entitled to rule on the basis of effective power alone. We pay these rulers for their people's resources, often advancing them large sums against the collateral of future exports, and we eagerly sell them the weapons on which their continued rule all too often depends. Yes, severe poverty is fueled by local misrule. But such local misrule is fueled, in turn, by global rules that we impose and from which we benefit greatly.

Once this causal nexus between our global institutional order and the persistence of severe poverty is better understood, the injustice of that order, and of our imposition of it, becomes visible: "What entitles a small global elite—the citizens of the rich countries *and* the holders of political and economic power in the resource-rich developing countries—to enforce a global property scheme under which we may claim the world's natural resources for ourselves and can distribute these among ourselves on mutually agreeable terms?" I ask. "How, for instance, can our ever so free and fair agreements with tyrants give us property rights in crude oil, thereby dispossessing the local population and the rest of humankind?" (p. 148).

Notes

1 World Health Organization, *World Health Report 2004* (Geneva: WHO, 2004), Annex Table 2, pp. 120–25; available at www.who.int/whr/2004.

2 This estimate is based on the latest (2004) poverty statistics provided by the World Bank (econ.worldbank.org/povcalnet, accessed May 18, 2008). The $2 per day poverty line is defined in terms of a monthly consumption expenditure equivalent to the purchasing power that $65.48 had in the US in 1993. To count as poor by this standard in the US today, one would need to have to live on less than $98 per person per month (www.bls.gov/cpi, accessed May 18, 2008). The headcount figure provided, 46.75, gives the percentage of poor within the developing-country population which, in 2004, was 5,358.85 million. The poverty gap figure provided, 19.31, gives the average shortfall from the poverty line in percent. Because this shortfall is zero for the non-poor, the average shortfall among the poor is the ratio of poverty gap divided by headcount. So the average poor person lives 41.3 percent below the poverty line. For all poor people together, this works out to an annual shortfall (poverty gap) of about $300 billion (converted at market exchange rates). For an explanation of this rough estimate, see Thomas Pogge: *World Poverty and Human Rights: Cosmopolitan Responsibilities and Reforms*, second edition (Cambridge: Polity Press, 2008), pp. 2–3 and 103, with notes. For a methodological critique of the World Bank's poverty statistics, see Thomas Pogge, "The First UN Millennium Development Goal: A Cause for Celebration?," *Journal of Human Development* 5, no. 3 (2004), as well as Sanjay Reddy and Thomas Pogge "How Not to Count the Poor," forthcoming in Sudhir Anand, Paul Segal and Joseph Stiglitz, eds.: *Debates in the Measurement of Global Poverty* (Oxford: Oxford University Press 2009), also available at www.socialanalysis.org (accessed May 18, 2008).

3 World Bank, *World Development Report 2006* (New York: Oxford University Press, 2005), p. 293.

4 Op. cit. (note 2). All in-text citation references will be to this book.

5 For a fuller reading of Locke's argument, see Pogge, *World Poverty and Human Rights*, ch. 5.

6 One might say that the existing global order is not unjust if the only feasible institutional modifications that could substantially reduce the offensive deprivations would be extremely costly in terms of culture, say, or the natural environment. I preempt such objections by inserting the word "reasonably." Broadly consequentialist and contractualist conceptions of justice agree that an institutional order that foreseeably gives rise to massive severe deprivations is unjust if there are feasible institutional modifications that foreseeably would greatly reduce these deprivations without adding other harms of comparable magnitude.

Chapter 46

Chandran Kukathas

THE MIRAGE OF GLOBAL JUSTICE

Chandran Kukathas (1957–   ) is a professor of political theory at the London School of Economics who has written widely on multiculturalism and liberalism. In this essay, Kukathas argues that the international order should not be radically reformed in order to better pursue global justice. Creating international institutions with the power to impose justice on the global order also creates institutions that are capable of doing great harm. Rather than designing institutions with the goal of securing justice, our concern should be to design them with the goal of limiting their power.

I. Introduction

Theories of global justice address two main issues. First, what would a just distribution of benefits and burdens across the world look like? Second, what sorts of institutions would be required to secure such a just distribution? Many other related questions inevitably arise when these problems are addressed. Perhaps the most notable is how to establish such institutions given the diversity of sovereign nations and the fact of global inequalities of wealth and power. For many, these questions are urgent because we live in a world in which millions live in desperate poverty. They are salient not only because many people enjoy great wealth but also because the disparity in riches may itself be the product of unjust global institutions. On this view, it might be said, justice is the first virtue of global institutions. Institutions, no matter how efficient and well-arranged, must be reformed or abolished if they are unjust.

For some theories, however, the issue of global justice has a wider scope. The protection of human rights generally, it is argued, is a matter of justice. Just institutions would ensure not only that the distribution of benefits and burdens was morally justifiable but also that people were secure against the predations of despots and warlords. The security of people's individual liberties and political rights is also a matter of justice. To establish global justice requires institutions that secure human rights broadly understood.

The thesis of this essay is that the political pursuit of global justice is not a worthy goal, and that our aims in establishing international legal and political institutions should be more modest. Its primary argument is that the pursuit of justice in the international order is dangerous to the extent that it requires the establishment of powerful supranational agencies, or legitimizes greater and more frequent exercises of political, economic, and military power by strong states or coalitions. The primary concern in the establishment and design of all legal and political institutions should be not to secure justice but to limit power. It is a mistake to think that a distinction can be drawn between power created to do good and power created to do evil, or that we are capable of devising institutions that can honor the distinction.

The essay is organized in the following way. In Section II, I articulate a conception of global order in which justice has a limited part. In Section III, I advance the main reasons why our concern for justice should be limited. In Section IV, I consider some important objections to this viewpoint, particularly those advanced by such contemporary political philosophers as Allen Buchanan and Thomas Pogge, who contend that justice should be a central concern of global economic and legal institutions. In Section V, I offer replies to these criticisms, and in Section VI, I offer some general conclusions.

II. Justice and Global Order

There are two primary positions taken in contemporary political theory on global justice. The first asserts that justice, and in particular, social justice, is something that cannot be attained globally but can be pursued successfully only by the nation-state. The most influential statement of this view is offered by John Rawls in *The Law of Peoples*, though there have been other notable defenders of this position who have presented independent or complementary reasons for it. David Miller, for example, has presented a case for limiting the scope of distributive justice; and Michael Walzer has argued that justice cannot be a global ideal but only a local one, tied as it must be to local understandings. The second position on global justice repudiates the first, insisting that there are standards of justice that should properly be regarded as globally significant. Principles of justice that hold within the nation-state should also hold, *mutatis mutandis*, across or among states. To put the matter in another way, if individuals have basic rights in virtue of their humanity, then these are rights they hold as against the whole world; and responsibility for upholding them falls upon the world as a whole rather than upon the nations in which they happen to reside. Such views have been defended most recently by philosophers such as Allen Buchanan and Thomas Pogge, though others, such as Henry Shue and Peter Singer, have been arguing for some time that considerations of justice should inform the foreign policies of wealthy nations to a much greater degree than such considerations do at present.

A particularly sharp statement of this second position is put forward by Darrel Moellendorf in criticism of Rawls, and in defense of cosmopolitan justice. Rawls, he observes, conceives of the international order as one in which toleration is extended even to regimes that are "unreasonable, intolerant, [and] oppressive" by the standards of Rawls's own doctrine as developed in his *Political Liberalism*. But to be tolerant of such regimes, Moellendorf suggests, is to be tolerant of unjust actions or oppressive cultural practices when there are no good reasons for being so. "In fact, just as institutionalizing an arrangement that permitted individuals to be unjust could be seen as being complicit in the injustice, so institutionalizing principles of international conduct that licensed oppression could be seen as being complicit in the oppression." On this view, if there are good reasons to pursue or uphold justice within the nation-state, those reasons also support upholding justice across the globe.

My thesis in this essay is that justice should not be pursued globally. The position defended here differs from those of Rawls, Walzer, and Miller, however, because it also rejects the idea that justice is something that should be pursued within the nation-state. It acknowledges that the advocates of global or cosmopolitan justice have a point in demanding consistency from those who argue for justice at home but are prepared to tolerate injustice abroad. But it also acknowledges the force of the arguments of those who are skeptical about global justice, and who consider the pursuit of justice on that scale implausible.

Justice, it should be noted, may be understood in many different ways. At its broadest, justice could be said to be the subject of any general account of how people should live. On this view, Plato's *Republic* gives us an account of justice no less than does Marx's theory of communism—even if Marx regards "justice" as a bourgeois virtue that has no place in post-capitalist society. A narrower view of justice sees it as concerning the proper distribution of benefits and burdens in society. Justice is a characteristic of the rules or the institutions that determine the entitlements people have, individually or as groups, to parts of the material world, and to the services of others. A theory of justice would offer an account of what people are entitled to under the rules of justice, and also what measures may be taken by an appropriately constituted authority to ensure that justice is upheld. A narrower view still regards justice as a matter of the application of rules rather than a matter of the rightness or "fairness" of the rules. Justice, in this sense, may be served if the law is consistently applied, even if the law is systematically unfair.

My concern in this essay is with justice in the second of these three senses. That is to say, my concern is with social or distributive justice. Theories of distributive justice are numerous, ranging from the Nozickian view that a just distribution is any distribution that is the outcome of just acquisition and just transfer of resources, to socialist views that regard all resources as collectively owned and properly allocated according to need, to views associated with particular religious or cultural traditions. Islamic conceptions of distributive justice, for example, allow for private property, but impose particular constraints on its use. Different views of distributive justice may also be shaped by particular views about the status of persons, what constitutes a violation of persons or their

property, and what forms of punishment are justified. Ideas about what justice requires are at least as numerous as the different communities that are to be found in a diverse society (such as the United States), though the differences among some of them are more trivial than the differences among others. Christians have much in common in their thinking about justice; yet while some think that distributive justice requires ensuring that all women have access to medical services to terminate unwanted pregnancies, others think that justice can require no such thing, since abortion is morally wrong.

On this understanding of justice, it is something that would be difficult to pursue in a society marked by a diversity of opinions and a variety of communities, since there would be many views about what justice demands. Any commitment to accommodating a diversity of ways of life would make it difficult to advocate a single standard of social or distributive justice. I suggest that it is neither possible nor desirable to pursue justice in this sense within a single nation-state. Consequently, we should not pursue social or distributive justice at the global level.

To put the issue schematically, there are four possible positions available on the question of whether justice (or social justice) should be pursued at home and abroad. (See Figure 46.1.) Position A suggests that social justice should be pursued at home and abroad; B that it should be pursued at home but not abroad; C that it should be pursued abroad but not at home; and D that it should be pursued neither at home nor abroad. Position C is perhaps the view least likely to find a representative, though it is not unusual for some political leaders to argue for global (re)distributive justice, while insisting on the importance of national sovereignty, and their own immunity from international criticism. This position has been expressed in a number of international declarations, such as the 1993 Bangkok Declaration. In this essay, I defend position D against A, B, and C. (F. A. Hayek has

	Social justice abroad	No social justice abroad
Social justice at home	A: Pogge, Moellendorf	B: Rawls, Walzer, Miller
No social justice at home	C: Bangkok Declaration	D: Hayek, Kukathas

Figure 46.1 Four positions on the pursuit of social justice.

also defended position D, insisting that social justice cannot be pursued at home or abroad since the very idea is incoherent.)

In my view, then, the international global order should, like domestic or national societies, properly be conceived as a network of independent jurisdictions bound not by any shared (or imposed) understanding of justice but simply by a commitment to mutual toleration. The most important imperative in the international order is to avoid war. International institutions, including international organizations (such as the United Nations) and international regimes (such as that established by the 1951 Refugee Convention) may be useful if they help to keep the peace, and if they define mutually acceptable conventions by which problems common to global society might be peacefully addressed.

This view might appear to be a defense of a Westphalian model of international order, one that is dominated by sovereign states recognized as the subjects of international law. The Peace of Westphalia, which in 1648 brought an end to the Eighty Years' War between Spain and the Netherlands, and to the German phase of the Thirty Years' War, greatly weakened the power of the Holy Roman Empire. It confirmed the 1555 Peace of Augsburg, which had granted Lutherans religious toleration in the Holy Roman Empire, and it extended toleration to the Calvinists. In recognizing the territorial sovereignty of member states, it is often asserted, the Peace of Westphalia also established the

principle *cuius regio eius religio*: that the religion of the head of state would be the religion of the people within that domain. This is not quite accurate, since the articles of peace required states to tolerate religious minorities. The authority of the Holy Roman Empire was dramatically reduced, however, and the sovereign power of some three hundred princes was increased. The modern world order could be said to operate on the Westphalian model in as much as it is a world of states, since European colonialism—and, more particularly, decolonization—brought states into being right across the globe. By the provisions of the Peace of Westphalia, princes eventually became absolute sovereigns in their own dominions, immune to the interventions of the Holy Roman Emperor. In the modern world, independence and immunity against foreign intervention are central aspects of state sovereignty.

At least to a limited extent, it is the Westphalian model that is commended in this essay. The virtue of the Westphalian ideal is that it divides power, recognizing as it does the diversity of claims of political authority, and that it appreciates the importance of avoiding war. Its weakness is that it strengthens the hand of the state, allowing it to act with immunity within its borders—even when its behavior is imprudent, unjust, or, at the extreme, barbaric. But if it is undesirable that there be any authority with power that can be so abused, it is even less desirable that such power be extended in scope to cover more and more domains—to create empires or a world government. Better to have many petty tyrants than a few great ones.

There are, of course, other reasons to be skeptical about the Westphalian model. In the 350 years and more since the Treaty of Westphalia was signed, not just Europe but the world has seen countless wars in which millions have died. Moreover, particularly in the twentieth century, the numbers killed in war have been dwarfed by the hundreds of millions killed by their own governments. The state is a difficult institution to defend even with mild enthusiasm. Nonetheless, the Westphalian model may have something to commend it if only because some of the alternatives being advocated are so unattractive. One alternative is to establish a more powerful force able to deal with the problem of bad states. A second alternative is to develop international institutions that will authorize systematic intervention in the affairs of bad states by other states or coalitions of states—so that good states will reform bad ones. The Westphalian model is preferable to either of these. Further decentralization may be preferable to a world of sovereign states; but a world of independent states is still better than a world of states subordinated to a greater power—whether the global Leviathan is a single body or an assembly of states.

This view does not assume that states must be regarded as economically self-sufficient units, or as culturally and politically undifferentiated entities, capable of relating to one another only as bargainers pursuing their own advantage. In freer political systems, cities and provinces, as well as other forms of association, will also be internationally significant political actors. Agreements will be reached between many different forms of associations besides states. States themselves may relinquish aspects of their sovereignty when they sign treaties or enter into conventions that bind them and limit what they may do even within their own borders. Signing the Kyoto Agreement on global warming (and then ratifying it) would limit a state's freedom to make

laws that violated the agreement's provisions on acceptable greenhouse gas emissions. Being party to the 1951 convention on the treatment of refugees restricts a state's ability to turn people away from its borders if they come seeking asylum, for signing the agreement meant signing away elements of state sovereignty. A world of sovereign states need not be a world in which all political relations exist only between undifferentiated polities unaffected by international ties or international obligations.

Despite these ties, however, ours is not a world united by shared moral convictions or a common idea of justice. The virtue of the Westphalian model of a world of sovereign states that emerged in the seventeenth and eighteenth centuries was that it was able to secure peace in the face of religious disagreement. The virtue of this model in the twenty-first century is that it might preserve peace in the face of ethical diversity. One way of describing this model of global order is as an archipelago of interdependent jurisdictions not subject to any common power, existing under norms of mutual toleration. Justice has no significant part to play in accounting for such an order.

III. Reasons for the Limited Role of Justice

The primary reason for limiting the role of justice in international affairs is that understandings of justice are diverse and contentious. A secondary reason is that the pursuit of justice threatens to do little more than enhance the influence of the dominant states, and of the elites that guide them, while taking us further away from self-rule. We should consider these reasons more closely.

To begin with the primary reason, though justice is a value or an ideal that is universally recognized, it is also one whose content is widely disputed. It is disputed in several different and important ways. First, there is widespread disagreement about what are the fundamental requirements of justice. This disagreement is clearly in evidence among philosophers and scholars, who have disputed the merits of liberal, socialist, libertarian, utilitarian, Marxian, and other principles of distributive justice. However, even among people more generally, there are disagreements: for one thing, the various political parties in most Western democracies favor different standards of social justice, and appeal to different concerns or attitudes found in their electorates. Moreover, while the political parties may try to win office by appealing to the median voter, the fact remains that there are also voters at the extremes. It is also worth noting that often there is a significant gap between the attitudes of party elites and the masses within the party on a host of issues—including justice.

Second, there is disagreement about issues of justice because there is disagreement about questions of value. Some people may value a resource because they regard it as having spiritual significance, while others may look at the same resource and see it as a potential source of material wealth. Thus, for example, some Aboriginal peoples have been reluctant to exploit the mineral wealth on lands they hold sacred, while their fellow citizens have argued that not exploiting these resources deprives others of the income that might be generated for everyone. Similarly, the issue of whether to permit oil exploration in wilderness areas brings out the conflict between those who attach greater value to the preservation of natural beauty or endangered ecosystems and those who see the need for energy as more pressing. Even those who agree on principles of justice in distribution may disagree on what should be distributed and how it should be valued.

There is a further complication here. Often it is difficult to say just what is the value of the resources a particular society or community may have, since questions of value can only be settled against the range of background conditions that give things worth. Oil was not an asset but a liability when discovered in the days before there

was any demand for petroleum. Today, uranium would be of little value to a society unable to exploit it, and soil suitable for cultivating vines would not be prized in a society of teetotalers. Even if value could be established here, however, there is also the problem of determining how different values are to be traded off. Some communities may prefer to trade off higher incomes from uranium sales for untouched wilderness and rural enterprise. Some communities may prefer to trade off future income by consuming their resources more rapidly now—opting for development rather than conservation. Some communities will simply have more children than others, and this will affect the distribution of resources. This can have a bearing on justice to the extent that these choices affect the overall distribution of resources not only within but also among different communities. Clearly, however, different communities will favor different conceptions of justice, since not every conception of justice will support the values of every community.

Third, a problem arises because different communities or societies have different understandings of property. This means not only that there are different understandings of what ownership means—what rights and duties come with possession of different kinds of things owned—but also that there are different understandings of how ownership may be transferred and to whom. Laws of inheritance vary from society to society, sometimes considerably.

Fourth, there may be disagreements about justice to the extent that there are more general ethical disagreements among people. For example, to the extent that people disagree about the morality of abortion or assisted suicide, they may also disagree about whether to subsidize pregnancy termination and related forms of medical care or to subsidize adoption—or whether to subsidize anything at all. But there are also other matters on which people disagree that have a bearing on justice. Different religions, communities, and societies have varying attitudes on the definition of childhood and the responsibilities of children and parents. They differ on what they recognize as marriage and what they consider the proper grounds for divorce. At the extreme, there are differences among people as to what constitutes harm to or violation of persons. Most people would consider female genital mutilation an unjustifiable violation of a child's body, but some communities consider it not just acceptable but a duty of responsible parents in their societies.

In the face of this great diversity of views about justice, and about morality more generally, how can justice be pursued across a variety of communities with different views about what justice demands? This is a problem not just for international society but also for domestic societies, particularly if a society is large and internally diverse. Countries such as India, China, Russia, Brazil, Indonesia, and the United States contain numerous communities with different languages, religions, customs, and ethical traditions. Under such circumstances, the most a society can reasonably pursue is the establishment of a framework or set of norms that might accommodate ethical disagreement, allowing different traditions to coexist.

An alternative view, however, is that even in the face of diversity and ethical disagreement, it is nonetheless important to pursue justice, at least to ensure that some standards of universal significance prevail. This is vital in the international realm no less than in domestic societies. This requires establishing international institutions, governed by universal ethical standards, aimed at promoting justice and ensuring that the actions of states and communities alike are governed by standards of justice. It means rejecting "moral minimalism" in favor of developing institutions governed by robust ethical standards that apply across international borders. But this view has to be rejected if ethical diversity is to be taken seriously.

This brings us to the secondary reason for limiting the role of justice in international affairs. If there are substantial differences over questions of justice, then trying to establish institutions whose purpose is to serve justice can produce either of two outcomes. First, it can lead to the creation of institutions of justice on which there is general agreement, but only because the understanding of "justice" is diluted or broadened to secure agreement among the different parties. Or, second, it can lead to the dominant powers establishing their own preferred understandings of justice, and running the institutions created according to their own ethical convictions—not to mention their interests. Most likely, we will see some combination of these two outcomes, which means that we will see some kind of rule by elites in the name of something they agree to call "justice."

The establishment in 1998 of the International Criminal Court (ICC) provides an illustration of the problematic role of elites in the establishment of institutions of international justice. The impetus to create the court came from the failed attempts to prosecute General Augusto Pinochet in Britain and in Spain for crimes, including torture, illegal detention, causing the disappearance of persons, and murder, alleged to have been committed while he was president of Chile. The ICC, it was hoped, would help resolve the problem of determining the legal jurisdiction in which such charges could be brought against persons accused of war crimes or crimes against humanity. After several years of preparation and five weeks of negotiation in Rome, the ICC was established on July 17, 1998, but not before the provisions of the statute governing its operation, and the definitions of crime that it would work with, were suitably modified to placate the convictions and interests of various parties. Thus, for example, the definition of crimes against humanity brought protests for references to gender persecution (from some Islamic states) and to enforced sterilization (from China). Syria and a number of Arab states insisted that the list of crimes compiled to illustrate the prohibition on attacks on civilian populations would be acceptable provided it only applied in cases of interstate conflict. Israel objected to Article 8 (section viii), which included in the definition of a war crime "the transfer directly or indirectly by an Occupying Power of parts of its own civilian population into the territory it occupies," arguing that this provision was aimed at its policies on Jewish settlements on the West Bank.

The United States also had serious objections to the Rome Statute, worrying that the war crimes provisions could be used by its enemies to prosecute its soldiers serving abroad. Along with many other states, it expressed a concern over granting any proposed court the sole power to determine what constituted an act of aggression, particularly since this would contravene the authority of the United Nations Security Council. Since the United States is a permanent member of the Security Council, with a right of veto over its resolutions, the U.S. took a much less favorable view of such an outcome than did India, which would like to be but is not a permanent member. In the end, however, the final statute incorporated provisions ensuring the sovereign rights of states, and enabling the court to operate only at the invitation of states or of the Security Council—though even then, a number of states, including the United States, Russia, China, and all the states of the Middle East except Jordan, declined to become members of the ICC.

In the end, an institution established to deal with criminal justice was shaped as much by the interests of important powers as by any concern for justice. The more general point this leads to is that international political institutions, like many domestic ones, are shaped by the interests and attitudes of elites. Unlike many local political institutions, however, the elites in question are a long way removed from the people who are ultimately governed by them.

To extend responsibility for justice to international institutions is to detract from self-government. This point was recognized in 1863 by Lord Acton in his analysis of the implications of the development of the nation-state itself and its usurpation of the powers of local jurisdictions. True republicanism, he argued, "is the principle of self-government in the whole and in all the parts." In an extensive country, he continued, self-government could only prevail in a confederacy, "so that a large republic not founded on the federal principle must result in the government of a single city, like Rome and Paris." A great democracy, he concluded, "must either sacrifice self-government to unity, or preserve it by federalism."

To try to establish a single standard of social justice even within a single country is a dubious undertaking. If a standard is agreed to by different communities, with different ethical traditions, that standard will be a weak one that reflects the compromises made to secure agreement rather than anything resembling justice. If the standard of justice is imposed by the more powerful, however, self-government will be sacrificed—without there being any assurance that the standards imposed have anything to do with justice rather than the interests of the dominant powers. This point holds even more strongly for international institutions. Powerful nations or coalitions will always find it advantageous to use the language of justice to defend the arrangements they establish. But this does not mean that justice is what they will pursue or defend.

We should be wary, then, of proposals to take action or devise institutions to secure international or global justice. The chances are that such proposals will simply serve the interests of elites, and will not secure justice even to the extent that we agree on what justice amounts to. More worryingly, however, appeals to justice, particularly when institutionalized, may simply serve as a cover or pretext for intervention in the affairs of people unwilling to accept ethical standards other than their own. At worst, such appeals may serve as pretexts for war. To the extent that it is important that we consider establishing international institutions to address matters of global concern, our priority should be not working out what justice requires and how it might be pursued but how to ensure that the power of global institutions, or the power that might be exerted through them, is kept limited. In the international domain, no less than in the domestic realm, the main political problem is how to keep power in check, not how to devise mechanisms to do good.

What this position implies is that in the international realm we should be concerned not to establish institutions that facilitate intervention in the affairs of other societies but to secure norms of toleration. A further implication of this outlook must also be recognized. If toleration is to take priority over justice, this means that injustice will have to be tolerated. This may be difficult if the perceived injustice is great. Nonetheless, toleration means nonintervention even in cases of injustice. For this reason, many hold either that toleration must be redefined so that justice establishes its limits, or that toleration must be subordinated to justice—perhaps to the extent that toleration simply becomes irrelevant as a substantial moral consideration. The position defended here is that toleration takes precedence over justice.

It is important, however, to make clear what is not an implication of my view. The argument advanced here is not the one offered by Rawls in *The Law of Peoples*, which seeks to make a case not merely for nonintervention but also for respecting nonliberal peoples and states if they come up to certain minimal standards of morality. I am not suggesting that we should think about the world as constituted by "peoples," or that we need to address the issue of whether or not certain societies deserve our respect. Nor, however, am I suggesting that states or state sovereignty are worthy of respect for other reasons such as those advanced by Martha Nussbaum in her critique of Rawls. For Nussbaum, "we ought to respect the state" since the state is "morally important because it is an expression of human choice and autonomy," because it "expresses the desire of human beings to live under laws they give to themselves." My position makes no such assumption about the nature of the state; indeed, it is entirely skeptical about the state's moral credentials.

It is also important to note that my view denies the significance of a distinction sometimes drawn between "not tolerating" and "intervening." The philosopher Kok-Chor Tan, for example, argues that a global theory of justice based on comprehensive liberal ideas "does not face the tension between tolerating nonliberal societies and protecting individual liberty—it simply does not tolerate nonliberal societies." But not tolerating, Tan insists, does not mean intervening. Indeed, there is a very strong presumption against intervening, especially with military force, even on behalf of oppressed peoples. Liberal states, he thinks, may take a whole range of other actions short of armed intervention, including public criticism and condemnation of nonliberal states. Comprehensive liberals "can deploy state (i.e., publicly shared) resources to question and even criticize some nonliberal group practices without actually criminalizing or enacting legislation against them." Much the same kind of view is advanced by Nussbaum, who makes a distinction between the justification and the implementation of moral standards. We may think that the standards of a nation are defective, but this does not mean that it would be right "to intervene, either militarily or through economic and political sanctions, simply in order to implement better human rights protections"—in most cases, "diplomatic pressures and persuasion seem more fitting than any sort of coercion."

The problem with relying on this distinction (between "not tolerating" and "intervening") to diminish the likelihood of being drawn down the path of intervention is that it does not recognize the significance of the presumption against intervention in the affairs of people in other states or communities. The reason for rejecting justice in favor of toleration is precisely that this stance makes clear that nonintervention is the default position. It is intervention, particularly if it is to involve coercion or violence, that requires justification. Tan and Nussbaum, in different ways, want to assert the primacy of justice or substantive standards of morality; but in insisting that such standards may only be enforced in very rare cases, they, in effect, concede the priority of the principle of nonintervention or toleration over justice. In the case of Tan's claim that criticism without intervention or enforcement is not toleration, the use of the word "toleration" seems odd to the extent that it makes even criticism an act of intolerance. It surely makes more sense to say that we are intolerant not when we reject or criticize another's views but when we try to impose our own through the exercise of force rather than through persuasive reasoning.

IV. Arguments for Global Justice

The main targets of this essay's criticism, then, are those who defend global justice as an ideal that should inform the establishment of international institutions, and would form the basis for collective action to enforce standards of morality across the world. The literature advancing the case for global justice is substantial. Rather than try to address it as a whole, the remainder of this essay will focus on arguments developed by two philosophers, Allen Buchanan and Thomas Pogge. Both reject the view advanced by Rawls and others that justice should be pursued only within the confines of the nation-state: Buchanan emphasizes the importance of protecting human rights as an imperative of the natural duty of justice, and Pogge emphasizes the importance of reforming the global basic structure to end world poverty. I will consider these arguments in turn, beginning with Buchanan's.

According to Buchanan, justice must be the primary moral goal of international law. He rejects the idea that peace should be the main goal of the international system, and that the

ideals of peace and justice are in conflict. He writes:

> [I]t is wrong to assume that justice and peace are somehow *essentially* in conflict. On the contrary, justice largely subsumes peace. Justice requires the prohibition of wars of aggression (understood as morally unjustifiable attacks as opposed to justified wars of self-defense or of humanitarian intervention) because wars of aggression inherently violate human rights. To that extent the pursuit of justice is the pursuit of peace.

He adds that "protecting some of the most important human rights is securing peace."

This view, Buchanan insists, is not as extreme as might be thought. It does not deny that justice may sometimes conflict with peace—though, for the most part, this will be the case in the period of transition from very unjust to more just conditions. Furthermore, he concedes that the principle "Let there be justice, though the world perish" is not defensible. A commitment to justice cannot require allowing considerations of justice to trump all other moral considerations in every instance, for not all injustices are equally serious. The protection of basic human rights should be the primary goal of the international system, but this is entirely compatible with the fact that justice is not all that matters. Nonetheless, "the protection of basic human rights is the core of justice, and the *raison d'être* for political power."

There are two arguments that Buchanan offers for the conclusion that justice is a morally obligatory goal of international law. The first is that there is a global basic structure of institutions through which people across the globe relate and that this basic structure can be assessed for its justice. If justice is, as Rawls asserted, the first virtue of social institutions, then "justice is a morally imperative institutional goal," in the global as well as in the domestic sphere. Here Buchanan endorses Thomas Pogge's contention that the global basic structure is a human creation, and that to accept it uncritically would be to support massive injustices. The second argument is that there is a "Natural Duty of Justice" that requires everyone to contribute to ensuring that all persons have access to just institutions, and that this implies that "justice is a morally obligatory goal of international law." This duty flows from a "Moral Equality Principle"; and equal consideration of persons requires that we help to ensure that they have access to institutions that protect their basic rights. We have a duty not simply not to harm but to help, even at substantial cost to ourselves.

With this outlook comes a particular view of the state and its ethical basis. Buchanan rejects what he calls the "discretionary association" view, according to which the state is nothing more than a discretionary association for the mutual advantage of its citizens—designed to further their interests. On this view, "the state is not even in part an instrument for moral progress." This view is, in the end, entirely incompatible with the Natural Duty of Justice.

The view Buchanan defends is one he describes as "moderate cosmopolitanism." It recognizes that we have moral obligations beyond our own borders, but without going to the extreme of suggesting that all our particular obligations are simply derived from our obligations to humanity more broadly. Equally, he insists, it is not a view that, in rejecting the discretionary association conception, suggests that governments may simply use the resources of the state to pursue global justice as they choose. Indeed, the state is, at least in part, "a resource for global, not just local, progress toward justice." But its officials must be properly authorized, ideally by democratic processes, to carry out their fiduciary obligations. What is very clearly rejected, however, is the idea that the national interest is the supreme value that should guide the conduct of foreign policy. This would be entirely inconsistent with a view that gives an important place to human rights.

Central to Buchanan's argument is the claim that there are basic human rights, and that there is "an expanding global culture of human rights that exhibits a broad consensus on the idea that justice requires respect for the inherent dignity of all persons." In this regard, he rejects the contention that there is widespread moral disagreement, and the idea that no global moral consensus can emerge. The evidence, in his view, points the other way. Thus, he rejects arguments, such as those offered by political philosopher Michael Walzer, that the world is marked by "deep distributive pluralism"; or that societies ought to be able to develop their own principles of justice. Buchanan also rejects as a reason for minimizing the role of distributive justice in the development of international law the idea that the international system lacks the institutional capacity to determine the requirements for, and to enforce, distributive justice. Our aim, he thinks, should be to develop that capacity.

Buchanan argues not only for theoretical innovation but also for practical reform of the international legal order. Two aspects of his argument merit special mention. First, he makes clear that it is necessary to develop "a more permissive law regarding humanitarian intervention," for "liberalizing the international law of humanitarian intervention is likely to be a necessary condition for achieving" other reforms. Second, Buchanan rejects the idea of relying on the development of customary law, or working through established authorities like the United Nations, to establish appropriate conventions, arguing that a serious commitment to the international rule of law may require deliberate effort, by a coalition of like-minded (and right-minded) countries, to establish new rules of international law—illegally, if necessary. He makes this plain when he writes:

[C]onsider again the proposal for a treaty-based, rule-governed intervention regime whose members would be restricted to the most democratic, human-rights respecting states. To the extent that it authorizes humanitarian interventions in the absence of Security Council authorization, such a regime would violate existing international law. But it would embody, rather than repudiate, a commitment to the rule of law in the normatively rich sense.

In fact, Buchanan insists that being "willing to act illegally to make a very unjust system more just need not be inconsistent with a commitment to justice through law; it may indeed be required by it."

Buchanan's concern is to present a case for the creation or reform of basic international institutions in order to bring about a more just world. Such reforms would bring about justice by protecting or enforcing individual rights. Despite some significant philosophical differences between their approaches, Buchanan's concerns are shared by Thomas Pogge, who also calls for reform of the basic structure of international society, but whose writings on global justice have focused on the problem of world poverty and human rights rather than on international law.

For Pogge, the interdependence of persons in a world order makes it essential that we look at justice in global rather than local terms. Institutional interconnections across the planet, he argues, "render obsolete the idea that countries can peacefully agree to disagree about justice, each committing itself to a conception of justice appropriate to its history, culture, population size and density, natural environment, geopolitical context, and stage of development." In the modern world, people's lives are profoundly affected by global rules of governance, trade, and diplomacy; and about such institutions we cannot agree to disagree, since they can only be structured one way—not differently in each country. If they are to be justified to all persons in all parts of the world, "then we must aspire to a *single, universal* criterion of justice which all persons and peoples can accept as the basis for

moral judgments about the global order." This acceptance is vitally important, for it matters that a society's institutional order be endorsed by those to whom the order applies. This is why "we should try to formulate the universal criterion of justice so that it can gain universal acceptance."

Despite his emphasis on universalism, Pogge is aware of its shortcomings and has some sympathy for the contextualist ethics defended by philosopher David Miller. Pogge's most serious criticisms of contextualism, however, are reserved for John Rawls, whom he charges with offering a theory that fails to justify applying quite different fundamental principles to national and international institutional schemes. For example, Pogge argues, Rawls rejects the difference principle as a requirement of global justice on the ground that it is unacceptable for one people to bear the costs of decisions made by another—decisions on national birth-rates, for instance—but Rawls does not explain "why this ground should not analogously disqualify the difference principle for national societies as well," since one province or township may have to bear the costs of decisions made by another. To the extent that Rawls argues that his theory, and the difference principle in particular, can only apply to a closed society or a self-contained system, Pogge also points out, it is hard to see why it should not apply to the world if it can apply to the United States, which is neither closed nor self-contained. If the objection is that principles of justice must be acceptable to the people who live under them, as they are not in other parts of the world, Pogge replies that the same holds true for the United States, where the difference principle is not one that commands agreement—even, one might add, among liberal political philosophers. If there are reasons why the standards of justice that apply domestically cannot be applied internationally, Pogge argues, Rawls has not supplied them.

For Pogge, there are compelling reasons why justice is an issue that has to be addressed globally. First, it is clear that many people live lives of desperate poverty and enormous suffering, even as others, particularly in the countries of the developed West, enjoy great affluence. Second, an important cause of this suffering—and affluence—is the system of global institutions that protects the wealth of some while prolonging the poverty of others. Third, to the extent that global institutions are capable of being reformed but have not been improved, those who benefit from those institutions must bear responsibility for the condition of those who suffer under them. In the world today, Pogge maintains, the affluent benefit from a system that sustains radical inequality such that they enjoy significant advantages in the use of a single natural resource base—the earth—from whose benefits the worst-off are excluded without compensation. This system itself emerged out of a historical process that was pervaded by massive, grievous wrongs.

As a first step toward justice, Pogge proposes the establishment of a Global Resources Dividend (GRD)—a fund created by payments made by all states, to be used to eradicate poverty—"to ensure that all human beings can meet their own basic needs with dignity." With the help of "economists and international lawyers," Pogge suggests, it may be possible to design a scheme that disburses funds to the poor—if necessary, directly rather than through their governments—and provides governments with incentives to rule better. "A good government brings enhanced prosperity through GRD support and thereby generates more popular support which in turn makes it safer from coup attempts." Such a scheme would not only make available funds owed to the world's poor, but also encourage the governments of developing countries to pursue much-needed reforms. "Combined with suitable disbursement rules, the GRD can stimulate a peaceful international competition in effective poverty eradication."

Like Buchanan, Pogge defends what amounts to a moderate cosmopolitanism. What both philosophers share is a conviction that justice is a global issue, though both want to give particularism some due. Both thus make what they regard as moderate proposals for reforming global institutions. Neither thinks that a proper respect for human dignity or moral principle warrants anything less.

V. Against Global Justice

There can be no doubt that we live in a world in which many people suffer poverty and oppression, or that where one is born has a greater bearing on one's prospects in life than, say, one's talents or character. A modern variant of the ancient Chinese curse might well run, "May you live in an interesting country." There is surely a case for helping the destitute, opening our borders to those looking to make a better life, and welcoming those who are trying to escape oppressive regimes. This does not mean, however, that there is a case for seeking the mirage of global justice, and the problems with the theories advanced by Buchanan and Pogge help to bring this out. Both set out to show that universal justice is desirable, and that it may be better secured across the world by the reform or creation of institutions authorized and empowered to do so. Yet the outcome of their philosophical effort is, in effect, a justification of rule by elites, guided by (and unchecked by anything other than) a commitment to a view of justice. We should be skeptical of these efforts, for they promise only elite rule, not justice.

One important reason for this is that political institutions cannot secure justice, particularly when they cover large areas of territory and a great number and diversity of people. The most they can secure is peace as people agree to abide by common laws and the rule of common authorities. There are two reasons why justice is not a likely outcome. First, given the nature of politics, the institutions or rules that are adopted will reflect not the demands of justice but the balance of power. Second, the likelihood of agreement on justice diminishes with the increasing size of the polity: any agreement reached will be a compromise, assented to in the end in order to bring negotiation to a close. To say this is not to take refuge in skepticism about justice. One might remain convinced that one view of justice is true and still recognize that political institutions are incapable of securing it, or that securing it is no part of their purpose.

Allen Buchanan takes a different view in arguing that justice subsumes peace, and that the best way to secure peace is to secure justice by protecting human rights. But this seems straightforwardly implausible. If two parties to a dispute disagree about justice but one is successful in having his view of justice prevail, there is no reason to think that this will produce peace between them. If peace is produced because one is able to persuade the other that his view of justice really is correct, it is agreement that produces peace, not the justice of the agreed-upon view. Peace would be the outcome even if the agreed-upon view of justice was wrong. If agreement were the outcome simply of the stronger party's being able to enforce his view of justice, the resulting peace would hardly be the product of justice, simply of power.

Consider as an illustration what is perhaps the most intractable of all problems in contemporary international politics: the dispute over Palestine. It would be simplifying matters considerably even to assert that there were only two sides to this conflict. We can say, however, that there are a number of issues in play: the legitimacy of the very existence of Israel; the proper boundaries of the Israeli state (whether they should be defined by the 1947 U.N. determination, or the war at the founding of the state, or the 1967 war, or the view of the present Israeli state, or some other set of considerations altogether); the right of return, if any, of Palestinian refugees; the status of Jewish settlers and their settlements on the West Bank; and the rights of Palestinians or Arabs living or working in Israel. It is safe to say that there is agreement neither among Israelis nor

among Palestinians about what justice demands, let alone agreement between the government of Israel and the various groups, including the Palestinian Authority, who claim to speak on behalf of all Palestinians. To suggest that the path to peace in this land is to establish justice by protecting human rights seems utterly implausible given the unlikelihood that those who lose by the establishment of what is alleged to be justice will simply accept the outcome with good grace—even if the judgment were offered by Solomon himself. Buchanan suggests that justice requires the prohibition of wars of aggression "understood as morally unjustified attacks as opposed to justified wars of self-defense or of humanitarian intervention." Yet each of the warring parties in the Holy Land believes others to be the aggressors and sees itself as acting in self-defense. If we must wait for this disagreement over justice to be settled before there can be peace, we will be waiting for a long time. If there is any plausible route to peace, it must surely involve most parties' recognizing and accepting that they will not obtain justice in the sense of receiving the full measure of what they regard as their due, but being willing to take less than justice in the interests of peace. This would surely be easier to take than being forced to accept that what one receives is all that one is justly entitled to.

Buchanan, however, suggests that "progress towards justice is especially likely to require illegal acts if the system's imperfections include serious barriers to expeditious, legally permissible reform," and recommends the creation of a "rule-governed intervention regime," its membership restricted to the "most democratic, human rights-respecting states," to authorize intervention in regimes that violate human rights. For him, current norms of nonintervention are too robust and are an obstacle to the establishment of justice. But it is difficult to know what to make of this call for human rights-respecting states to take matters into their own hands in the name of justice. To the extent that his point is simply that illegal acts are sometimes morally justified, it is hard to disagree. It is also fair to say that those acting illegally may well be truly committed to the rule of law, in the way that, say, Martin Luther King or Gandhi were in their acts of civil disobedience. But what would this mean, say, for international society confronted by the knowledge of these past acts of civil disobedience and their suppression by the American and British governments? The norm in international law is that other states not intervene in such cases, even when accusations of human rights violations are very serious. Buchanan's proposal is that a coalition of right-thinking nations should not simply intervene in such cases, but should get together, rewrite international law, authorize themselves to act, and then claim to be acting lawfully—understanding law "in the normatively rich way."

This is a troubling view, but it is important to understand what lies behind it. Buchanan's concern is that existing international norms (and in particular, the structure of the United Nations) make it difficult to pursue justice or morality. Human rights abuses go unaddressed. Reform, he thinks, is necessary to make it more possible for human rights to be protected. What is troubling about this view is that it assumes or asserts that a world in which such constraints on intervention are removed or weakened will be a better world, presumably because the just are freer to act. Yet it would also leave the unjust freer to act. If the recommendation is that right-thinking states should combine when necessary, restructure patterns of international authority by establishing treaties, and then authorize themselves to act in the name of justice, this looks like a general invitation to all states to so act. No state thinks it is not right-thinking, and most even claim to recognize human rights—and indeed are signatories to the major human rights agreements, including the Universal Declaration of Human Rights (1948).

Buchanan's theory, in the end, requires that we accept either one of two views, the first one implausible and the second unattractive. The first view is that there is a level of consensus in the international order that would make it possible for global institutions to be restructured by concerted action of the kind he recommends. In fact, however, there is no such consensus—or at least, not yet. Now, Buchanan is aware of this argument, but he questions the claim that there is no consensus and suggests that the implication of denying the existence of consensus is a denial of the legitimacy of the international system as a whole. The Universal Declaration of Human Rights, he points out, "as well as other central human rights conventions, explicitly endorses the idea that the inherent dignity of free and equal individuals entitles them to be treated in certain ways—and this sounds very much like a widely shared, core conception of justice." This, he thinks, throws into question the whole "moral minimalist" perspective. Yet the most such agreements reveal is the existence of elite consensus, and a limited consensus at that. The reasons why some countries might sign on to important declarations may have less to do with acceptance (by the elites of those states) of the expressed moral principles than with the political advantages of joining. Even after declarations have been endorsed, however, there is no reason to think that the elites, or populations, of different countries interpret them in the same way. When the U.N. Human Rights Committee protested that Iran's Islamic Penal Code, which required the amputation of four fingers of the right hand for a first conviction for theft, and flogging for consuming alcohol, violated article 7 of the International Covenant on Civil and Political Rights (ICCPR), the Iranian government insisted that it was upholding not violating the covenant. Article 7 prohibits "cruel, inhuman or degrading treatment or punishment," but Iran, as a signatory to the ICCPR, insisted that it took the strictures of article 7 very seriously, while interpreting it in a way consistent with its own social norms. If there is an international moral consensus, it is weaker than Buchanan suggests.

He is quite right to say that we should not assume that a consensus will never emerge; but until it does, we should operate on the assumption that it does not yet exist.

The second view is that a minority of states should pursue the task of engaging in the restructuring of global institutions. The objection to this is not simply that any such effort would fail without the major powers, such as the United States and the European Union, going along with it, though Buchanan thinks there is much to be said for trying to engage in such restructuring without the United States, which is "widely regarded—and not without reason—as an international scoff-law." The problem is that the claim is that international law, and more specifically, a "liberal-democratic intervention regime," should be created by a self-selected elite. This elite, led, in Buchanan's ideal scenario, by the European Union, would admit only those countries with "decent" human rights records and those that meet the minimum criteria for democracy. It would establish an alternative international organization that would have "a stronger claim to legitimacy than a state-majoritarian UN entity such as the General Assembly"; after all, "[i]f the goal is to protect human rights, then who would be better qualified than a coalition of states that have the best records for doing so?" Yet even if the self-selected members of this regime should be satisfied that they are the best standard-bearers for human rights, why would, or should, anyone else accept this assertion, or accord this group any moral or legal standing simply because it claims to have the best human rights record?

It is difficult to see how Buchanan's proposal here amounts to much more than a recommendation that like-minded states who believe in human rights should set out to collude and enforce, whenever possible, their own conception of justice. If this is so, it does not look like an improvement on the norm that Buchanan is looking to undermine: international customary law. The disadvantage of customary law is that it changes slowly and is not a tool that may readily be used to right serious wrongs. It depends on the development of consensus, mostly among states, and does nothing to enhance the capacity of international agencies to intervene in the affairs of tyrannical regimes. Its advantage, however, is precisely that it does make intervention, and the resort to arms, more difficult.

More generally, whatever the weaknesses of the Westphalian system, it does have some important virtues. In a world of unequal power, a norm of nonintervention, even if upheld by a convention recognizing states as sovereign powers, checks the capacity of stronger states to enforce their wills. For weaker states, sovereignty is an important asset, particularly if it can be deployed with effect against stronger states whose assertions of the common purposes of states in international society can easily be self-serving and to the detriment of lesser polities. As the theorist of international relations Hedley Bull noted, "If a right of intervention is proclaimed for the purpose of enforcing standards of conduct, and yet no consensus exists in the international community governing its use, then the door is open to interventions by particular states using such a right as a pretext."

In the end, the world is more diverse than Buchanan's theory is prepared to admit. We live in an international society that is pluralist rather than solidarist. Until there is in fact greater moral agreement, any attempt to restructure the international order in accordance with principles of justice risks sanctioning the enforcement of international norms that serve the interests of powerful states, without doing much to serve the interests of weaker states or their members. In any case, we should be wary of setting up institutions of international justice intended to protect the weak, because more powerful agents are often better able to exploit the resources these institutions provide. This is not a decisive consideration; but it is an important, cautionary one, nonetheless.

This consideration calls into question the

claims Buchanan makes on behalf of the Natural Duty of Justice. The Natural Duty of Justice is "the limited moral obligation to contribute to ensuring that all persons have access to just institutions." Showing proper concern and respect for all persons, in Buchanan's view, requires doing what is necessary, within the limits of what can reasonably be expected of anyone, to ensure that those persons have access to the institutions needed to protect individual rights. Thus, "conscientiously acting on the Natural Duty of Justice means supporting institutional efforts to secure justice for all." In part, the problem with this is that the very idea that the Natural Duty of Justice requires acting to ensure that others have access to institutions is not as plausible as Buchanan suggests. Here he draws on Kant's idea that there is a duty to leave the state of nature to enter a juridical condition. But all that really follows from our having a duty of justice is that we must fulfill our obligations to act justly. If some people wish to establish institutions to govern themselves in order better to secure justice, there is no duty for us to take part. But even if there were a duty to support institutional efforts to secure justice for all, that would give us no reason to think that we should support *any* institutional efforts that are undertaken. Indeed, one might be well advised to take a skeptical attitude toward most claims made in defense of developing institutions—particularly when the claims are that such institutions will serve justice, rather than the interests of those creating them.

These considerations also tell against Pogge's arguments in defense of establishing an international regime to secure global economic justice. There is no question that large numbers of people live in poverty. Even on very modest assumptions about what constitutes poverty (say, an income of less than US $1.50 a day), nearly a sixth of humanity is poor. The moral imperative to address this problem is a strong one. Yet this does not mean that our obligation is to restructure the international system. There are a number of steps that can surely be taken unilaterally by individuals and governments with complete justification. First, it may be incumbent on those who are well off to act unilaterally to contribute more to relief of the poor and destitute. Since relief is often better supplied by collective action, it may be morally better to act through international agencies, such as Community Aid Abroad or Oxfam, to do so. Second, the governments of various states can act unilaterally to reform their own economic policies, opening their borders to trade, ceasing to subsidize domestic industries, admitting greater numbers of refugees and immigrants, particularly from the ranks of the poor, and ceasing to finance regimes that are corrupt, inefficient, or oppressive—indeed, ceasing to finance other governments altogether. Free trade does not, at least in principle, require a World Trade Organization, or formal international agreements. Third, international federations such as the European Union can themselves act unilaterally to eliminate practices, including their agricultural policies, that harm the world's poor.

Now it might be argued that these recommendations are not enough: first, because private unilateral action is not going to do very much good, and second, because it is simply politically naive to think that states will take unilateral action to open their borders to foreign goods and people. In the first instance, it is probably true that private charity will not be sufficient to make a substantial impact on global poverty. Other changes are necessary. Yet, second, if there is no possibility of states and international federations taking unilateral action to cease their harmful trade and immigration policies, there is surely little reason to think that more ambitious reforms of global economic structures are possible. What hope is there of a Global Resources Dividend in a world of butter mountains, wine lakes, and billion-dollar subsidies to grow rice in deserts, or sugar in the wilderness?

Pogge is looking for solutions that involve reform on a global scale, using mechanisms that will do justice by making possible large transfers of funds from rich to poor societies. In his view, justice requires such transfers to reduce the inequality that exists between the rich and the poor. The question is, who is to establish what justice demands, and how are we to ensure that justice is properly served? Pogge's answer is that these questions will be settled by states, or elites within them, who will enlist experts—economists and lawyers—to devise suitable schemes to raise and distribute funds. Whatever practical problems this may involve, two difficulties stand out. First, the GRD sets out to solve a problem of global distribution by creating yet another political institution. Yet given that the existing political institutions have struggled to address the problem of taking care of the world's poor, what reason is there to think that creating another layer of intervention will help in any way? Past experience suggests that all the problems that beset other institutions, from the nation-state itself to the agencies of the United Nations, would simply reappear. In particular, if a fund were created making available for redistribution tens of billions of dollars, it is hard to see how there could not be another scramble for a slice of the largesse, with the spoils going to those who know best how to manipulate the system. Even if the outcome of this was a greater share of the world's wealth going to the poor, it is not clear that this would be desirable if it means that poor nations put their energies not into learning how to develop and manage their productive assets but into perfecting the art of securing aid money.

Second, establishing institutions of global distributive justice in this way once again means entrenching the power of the world's elites: those powerful states who would supply the funds and control their disbursement, with the help of elites in developing countries. The assumption here is that good will and sound institutional design will overcome the major difficulties and enable us to get closer to eliminating global inequality and securing justice. Past experience, however, suggests only that it will take us closer to global political inequality.

VI. Conclusion

The fact of global poverty and the prevalence of oppressive regimes have provoked the call for attention to the problem of global injustice. The aim of this essay has not been to deny the existence of poverty or oppression; its aim has been to seek the appropriate response to these conditions. The main thesis it advances is that the solution does not lie in establishing or expanding political powers to address these problems. This promises neither to establish an acceptable understanding of justice, nor to do much more than provide another opportunity for political elites to pursue their own particular ends. However, it should also be made clear what is not being suggested here.

First, this is not a defense of realism in international politics. In Buchanan's account, realism recommends that states be guided at all times by a concern for their national interests. As a moral theory, this has little to commend it. The argument here is not that states should pursue their own interests but that we should not look for ways of increasing the power of political elites in the expectation that they will do anything but pursue their own interests. Contrary to what Buchanan and others suggest, the state and other political institutions are not instruments of moral progress. We should be more thoroughly cynical about political power, for justice is not its *raison d'être*.

Second, this is not a rejection of the importance of international law. What is rejected, however, is the idea that global justice demands sweeping reforms of international institutions, and the establishment of new structures.

Third, the argument here is not a rejection of cosmopolitanism, even though it criticizes the work of modest cosmopolitans such as

Buchanan and Pogge. The main assumption of the essay in this regard is that the development of cosmopolitanism should not be the product of political reform. It may well be that there will be a convergence across the globe on common moral standards in the years to come. Unless that happens, however, we cannot even begin to think in terms of global justice.

3c. SECESSION

MOST OF US PROBABLY ENJOY A REASONABLY happy relationship with our state. Like any relationship, it involves some give and take. For our part, we pay taxes and sometimes put up with rules and regulations that we find burdensome, stupid, or even morally offensive. And in return, the state provides us with protection from domestic and international violence, provides us with roads and other public goods, a legal system within which to arrange contracts and settle disputes, and so on. Usually, for all our complaining, we view the relationship as worth maintaining—or at least not worth the trouble of formally ending. But sometimes problems in the relationship become so severe, or our alternative options so attractive, that some form of dissolution appears to be our best option. In such cases, we may wish to consider the option of political "divorce."

The normal means by which individuals exercise this option, of course, is emigration. If they become dissatisfied with their state, they simply pack up their belongings and leave to look for a new home elsewhere. But this, we should note, is a rather burdensome method of exiting a relationship. For in emigrating, one removes oneself from not just one's government, but from one's friends, one's land, and often one's history, language, and culture. And these things will very often be of tremendous value to the émigré. We might very well ask, then, why people should be forced to make this trade-off. Why should they not be able to leave their government without having to leave their land and everything else they care about? Why assume that in political divorce, it is the government that always gets to keep the house?

Herbert Spencer argues that we should not, in fact, make this assumption. For Spencer, this conclusion was based on what he called the "law of equal freedom," which holds that "every man has freedom to do all that he wills, provided he infringes not the equal freedom of any other man." Since ending one's relationship with the state does not infringe upon the freedom of others, according to Spencer, any individual or group of individuals has the right to do so at will. The state is never anything more than an agent of the people, and ending our relationship with it is no different in principle from, say, firing our lawyer. We are simply telling the state that we do not wish to subscribe to its protective services any longer, and hence that we will no longer be paying for them. In doing so, we need not give up our home, our culture, or our friends. We simply give up the right to have the state protect us in our enjoyment of these things.

In contemporary terminology, what Spencer was arguing for was an individual right of secession. We can define secession as the act of a group within the territory of a state of breaking off relations with the old state and creating a new state to rule over that territory. In theory, as Spencer's argument demonstrates, the size of the "group" *could* be one. But real world secession movements almost always consist of groups united by some cultural, linguistic, religious, or other commonality. The Quebecois in Canada, the Kurds in Turkey, Iraq, and Iran, and the FAC in Angola, to name but a few current movements, all seek some sovereignty over some territory that is currently claimed by another state. There is even a group called "Californians for Independence," which seeks to create a Californian Republic independent from the United States.

One of the main practical differences between emigration and secession, of course, is that the former is much less costly to the state. A state can afford to give up a few persons without much setback to its interests. But losing territory is another matter entirely. Most states, then, actively resist secessionist movements—through their law, by influencing public opinion and, when necessary, by force.

One of the chief philosophical issues regarding secession, then, is under what circumstances individuals or groups have a right to secede without the consent of the original political unit, and when the original states are obligated to let them go. Spencer, as we saw, seems to believe that the answer to both these questions is "always." But others have argued that the situation is more complicated. If individuals or groups could secede at will, for instance, would it not become extremely difficult for governments to perform many of their essential functions? The right to secession could, if frequently exercised, very well end up leaving the map of a country's sovereignty looking like a piece of Swiss cheese. With its authority so fragmented, how could a country run an effective highway system? How could it provide for national defense ("if you launch a missile at *this* guy's house, that's OK, but if it hits *that* guy's house, we're at war!")? And what if we disagree with Spencer that the only relevant moral considerations are the ways in which our actions impinge upon the (negative) liberty of others? Suppose, for instance, that the wealthiest 1% of Americans decided to secede and form their own country so that they could get out of their obligation of paying for public schools, health care, etc., for the less fortunate? Should the state stop them from leaving in the name of distributive justice? Of course, if distributive justice is sufficient to block the moral claim to secede, then we must ask whether it is also therefore sufficient to block a moral claim to emigrate.

These are difficult questions, and the readings in this section will only scratch their surface. What should be clear, however, is that the issue of secession raises questions of political authority, freedom, and justice that are fundamental to political philosophy, and demonstrates in an especially vivid way that these questions are of the utmost practical importance hundreds of years after Locke, Hobbes and others first raised them.

Further Reading

Buchanan, A. (1991). *Secession: The Legitimacy of Political Divorce from Fort Sumter to Lithuania and Quebec*. Boulder, CO: Westview Press.

Copp, D. (1998). International Law and Morality in the Theory of Secession. *Journal of Ethics, 2*(3), 219–245.

Corlett, J. A. (1998). The Morality and Constitutionality of Secession. *Journal of Social Philosophy, 29*(3), 120–128.

Gordon, D. (2002). *Secession, State, and Liberty*. New Brunswick, NJ: Transaction Publishers.

Kymlicka, W. (2000). Federalism and Secession: At Home and Abroad. *Canadian Journal of Law and Jurisprudence, 13*(2), 207–224.

Miller, D. (1995). *On Nationality*. New York: Clarendon Press.

Wellman, C. (2005). *A Theory of Secession: The Case for Political Self-Determination*. Cambridge: Cambridge University Press.

Chapter 47

Herbert Spencer

THE RIGHT TO IGNORE THE STATE

Herbert Spencer (1820–1903) was an English philosopher, political theorist, and sociologist, widely known for his integration of evolutionary theory into his social thought, and for coining the phrase "survival of the fittest." In this essay from his book *Social Statics* (1851), Spencer argues that it is an implication of the law of equal freedom—the principle that each person may do what he wills so long as he does not infringe on the equal freedom of others—that any person may choose to break off relations with his state at any time and for any reason.

1. As a corollary to the proposition that all institutions must be subordinated to the law of equal freedom, we cannot choose but admit the right of the citizen to adopt a condition of voluntary outlawry. If every man has freedom to do all that he wills, provided he infringes not the equal freedom of any other man, then he is free to drop connection with the state—to relinquish its protection and to refuse paying toward its support. It is self-evident that in so behaving he in no way trenches upon the liberty of others, for his position is a passive one, and while passive he cannot become an aggressor. It is equally self-evident that he cannot be compelled to continue one of a political corporation without a breach of the moral law, seeing that citizenship involves payment of taxes; and the taking away of a man's property against his will is an infringement of his rights. Government being simply an agent employed in common by a number of individuals to secure to them certain advantages, the very nature of the connection implies that it is for each to say whether he will employ such an agent or not. If any one of them determines to ignore this mutual-safety confederation, nothing can be said except that he loses all claim to its good offices and exposes himself to the danger of maltreatment—a thing he is quite at liberty to do if he likes. He cannot be coerced into political combination without a breach of the law of equal freedom; he can withdraw from it without committing any such breach, and he has therefore a right so to withdraw.

2. "No human laws are of any validity if contrary to the law of nature; and such of them as are valid derive all their force and all their authority mediately or immediately from this original." Thus writes Blackstone, to whom let all honor be given for having so far outseen the ideas of his time and, indeed, we may say of our time. A good antidote, this, for those political superstitions which so widely prevail. A good check upon that sentiment of power worship which still misleads us by magnifying the prerogatives of constitutional governments as it once did

those of monarchs. Let men learn that a legislature is not "our God upon earth," though, by
the authority they ascribe to it and the things
they expect from it, they would seem to think it
is. Let them learn rather that it is an institution
serving a purely temporary purpose, whose
power, when not stolen, is at the best borrowed.

Nay, indeed, have we not seen that government is essentially immoral? Is it not the offspring of evil, bearing about it all the marks of its
parentage? Does it not exist because crime exists?
Is it not strong—or, as we say, despotic—when
crime is great? Is there not more liberty—that is,
less government—as crime diminishes? And
must not government cease when crime ceases,
for very lack of object on which to perform its
function? Not only does magisterial power exist
because of evil, but it exist by evil. Violence is
employed to maintain it, and all violence
involves criminality. Soldiers, policemen, and
jailers; swords, batons, and fetters are instruments for inflicting pain; and all inflection of
pain is in the abstract wrong. The state employs
evil weapons to subjugate evil and is alike con-
taminated by the objects with which it deals and
the means by which it works. Morality cannot
recognize it, for morality, being simply a statement of the perfect law, can give no countenance
to anything growing out of, and living by,
breaches of that law. Wherefore, legislative
authority can never be ethical—must always be
conventional merely.

Hence, there is a certain inconsistency in the
attempt to determine the right position, structure, and conduct of a government by appeal to
the first principles of rectitude. For, as just
pointed out, the acts of an institution which is in
both nature and origin imperfect cannot be
made to square with the perfect law. All that we
can do is to ascertain, firstly, in what attitude a
legislature must stand to the community to avoid
being by its mere existence an embodied wrong;
secondly, in what manner it must be constituted
so as to exhibit the least incongruity with the
moral law; and thirdly, to what sphere its actions

must be limited to prevent it from multiplying
those breaches of equity it is set up to prevent.

The first condition to be conformed to before
a legislature can be established without violating
the law of equal freedom is the acknowledgment
of the right now under discussion—the right to
ignore the state.

3. Upholders of pure despotism may fitly believe
state control to be unlimited and unconditional.
They who assert that men are made for governments and not governments for men may consistently hold that no one can remove himself
beyond the pale of political organization. But
they who maintain that the people are the only
legitimate source of power—that legislative
authority is not original, but deputed—cannot
deny the right to ignore the state without
entangling themselves in an absurdity.

For, if legislative authority is deputed, it follows that those from whom it proceeds are the
masters of those on whom it is conferred; it
follows further that as masters they confer the
said authority voluntarily; and this implies that
they may give or withhold it as they please. To
call that deputed which is wrenched from men,
whether they will or not, is nonsense. But what is
here true of all collectively is equally true of each
separately. As a government can rightly act for
the people only when empowered by them, so
also can it rightly act for the individual only
when empowered by him. If A, B, and C debate
whether they shall employ an agent to perform
for them a certain service, and if while A and B
agree to do so C dissents, C cannot equitably be
made a party to the agreement in spite of himself. And this must be equally true of thirty as of
three; and if of thirty, why not of three hundred,
or three thousand, or three million?

4. Of the political superstitions lately alluded to,
none is so universally diffused as the notion that
majorities are omnipotent. Under the impression that the preservation of order will ever
require power to be wielded by some party, the

moral sense of our time feels that such power cannot rightly be conferred on any but the largest moiety of society. It interprets literally the saying that "the voice of the people is the voice of God," and, transferring to the one the sacredness attached to the other, it concludes that from the will of the people—that is, of the majority—there can be no appeal. Yet is this belief entirely erroneous.

Suppose, for the sake of argument, that, struck by some Malthusian panic, a legislature duly representing public opinion were to enact that all children born during the next ten years should be drowned. Does anyone think such an enactment would be warrantable? If not, there is evidently a limit to the power of a majority. Suppose, again, that of two races living together—Celts and Saxons, for example—the most numerous determined to make the others their slaves. Would the authority of the greatest number be in such case valid? If not, there is something to which its authority must be subordinate. Suppose, once more, that all men having incomes under £50 a year were to resolve upon reducing every income above that amount to their own standard, and appropriating the excess for public purposes. Could their resolution be justified? If not, it must be a third time confessed that there is a law to which the popular voice must defer. What, then, is that law, if not the law of pure equity—the law of equal freedom? These restraints, which all would put to the will of the majority, are exactly the restraints set up by that law. We deny the right of a majority to murder, to enslave, or to rob, simply because murder, enslaving, and robbery are violations of that law—violations too gross to be overlooked. But if great violations of it are wrong, so also are smaller ones. If the will of the many cannot supersede the first principle of morality in these cases, neither can it in any. So that, however insignificant the minority, and however trifling the proposed trespass against their rights, no such trespass is permissible.

When we have made our constitution purely democratic, thinks to himself the earnest reformer, we shall have brought government into harmony with absolute justice. Such a faith, though perhaps needful for the age, is a very erroneous one. By no process can coercion be made equitable. The freest form of government is only the least objectional form. The rule of the many by the few we call tyranny; the rule of the few by the many is tyranny also, only of a less intense kind. "You shall do as we will, and not as you will," is in either case the declaration; and if the hundred make it to the ninety-nine, instead of the ninety-nine to the hundred, it is only a fraction less immoral. Of two such parties, whichever fulfills this declaration necessarily breaks the law of equal freedom: the only difference being that by the one it is broken in the persons of ninety-nine, while by the other it is broken in the persons of a hundred. And the merit of the democratic form of government consists solely in this, that it trespasses against the smallest number.

The very existence of majorities and minorities is indicative of an immoral state. The man whose character harmonizes with the moral law, we found to be one who can obtain complete happiness without diminishing the happiness of his fellows. But the enactment of public arrangements by vote implies a society consisting of men otherwise constituted—implies that the desires of some cannot be satisfied without sacrificing the desires of others—implies that in the pursuit of their happiness the majority inflict a certain amount of unhappiness on the minority—implies, therefore, organic immorality. Thus, from another point of view, we again perceive that even in its most equitable form it is impossible for government to dissociate itself from evil; and further, that unless the right to ignore the state is recognized, its acts must be essentially criminal.

5. That a man is free to abandon the benefits and throw off the burdens of citizenship may indeed be inferred from the admissions of existing authorities and of current opinion. Unprepared as they probably are for so extreme a doctrine as the one here maintained, the radicals of our day yet unwittingly profess their belief in a maxim which obviously embodies this doctrine. Do we not continually hear them quote Blackstone's assertion that "no subject of England can be constrained to pay any aids or taxes even for the defence of the realm or the support of government, but such as are imposed by his own consent, or that of his representative in parliament?" And what does this mean? It means, say they, that every man should have a vote. True, but it means much more. If there is any sense in words it is a distinct enunciation of the very right now contended for. In affirming that a man may not be taxed unless he has directly or indirectly given his consent, it affirms that he may refuse to be so taxed; and to refuse to be taxed is to cut all connection with the state. Perhaps it will be said that this consent is not a specific, but a general one, and that the citizen is understood to have assented to everything his representative may do when he voted for him. But suppose he did not vote for him, and on the contrary did all in his power to get elected someone holding opposite views—what then? The reply will probably be that, by taking part in such an election, he tacitly agreed to abide by the decision of the majority. And how if he did not vote at all? Why, then he cannot justly complain of any tax, seeing that he made no protest against its imposition. So, curiously enough, it seems that he gave his consent in whatever way he acted— whether he said yes, whether he said no, or whether he remained neuter! A rather awkward doctrine, this. Here stands an unfortunate citizen who is asked if he will pay money for a certain proffered advantage; and whether he employs the only means of expressing his refusal or does not employ it, we are told that he practically agrees, if only the number of others who agree is greater than the number of those who dissent. And thus we are introduced to the novel principle that A's consent to a thing is not determined by what A says, but by what B may happen to say!

It is for those who quote Blackstone to choose between this absurdity and the doctrine above set forth. Either his maxim implies the right to ignore the state, or it is sheer nonsense.

6. There is a strange heterogeneity in our political faiths. Systems that have had their day and are beginning here and there to let the daylight through are patched with modern notions utterly unlike in quality and color; and men gravely display these systems, wear them, and walk about in them, quite unconscious of their grotesqueness. This transition state of ours, partaking as it does equally of the past and the future, breeds hybrid theories exhibiting the oddest union of bygone despotism and coming freedom. Here are types of the old organization curiously disguised by germs of the new, peculiarities showing adaptation to a preceding state modified by rudiments that prophesy of something to come, making altogether so chaotic a mixture of relationships that there is no saying to what class these births of the age should be referred.

As ideas must of necessity bear the stamp of the time, it is useless to lament the contentment with which these incongruous beliefs are held. Otherwise it would seem unfortunate that men do not pursue to the end the trains of reasoning which have led to these partial modifications. In the present case, for example, consistency would force them to admit that, on other points besides the one just noticed, they hold opinions and use arguments in which the right to ignore the state is involved.

For what is the meaning of Dissent? The time was when a man's faith and his mode of worship were as much determinable by law as his secular acts; and, according to provisions extant in our statute book, are so still. Thanks to the growth of a Protestant spirit, however, we have ignored the state in this matter—wholly in theory, and partly in practice. But how have we done so? By assuming an attitude which, if consistently maintained, implies a right to ignore the state entirely. Observe the positions of the two parties. "This is your creed," says the legislator; "you must believe and openly profess what is here set down for you." "I shall not do anything of the kind," answers the nonconformist; "I will go to prison rather." "Your religious ordinances," pursues the legislator, "shall be such as we have prescribed. You shall attend the churches we have endowed and adopt the ceremonies used in them." "Nothing shall induce me to do so," is the reply; "I altogether deny your power to dictate to me in such matters, and mean to resist to the uttermost." "Lastly," adds the legislator, "we shall require you to pay such sums of money toward the support of these religious institutions as we may see fit to ask." "Not a farthing will you have from me," exclaims our sturdy Independent; "even did I believe in the doctrines of your church (which I do not), I should still rebel against your interference; and if you take my property, it shall be by force and under protest."

What now does this proceeding amount to when regarded in the abstract? It amounts to an assertion by the individual of the right to exercise one of his faculties—the religious sentiment—without let or hindrance, and with no limit save that set up by the equal claims of others. And what is meant by ignoring the state? Simply an assertion of the right similarly to exercise all the faculties. The one is just an expansion of the other—rests on the same footing with the other—must stand or fall with the other. Men do indeed speak of civil and religious liberty as different things: but the distinction is quite arbitrary. They are parts of the same whole and cannot philosophically be separated.

"Yes, they can," interposes an objector; "assertion of the one is imperative as being a religious duty. The liberty to worship God in the way that seems to him right is a liberty without which a man cannot fulfill what he believes to be Divine commands, and therefore conscience requires him to maintain it." True enough; but

how if the same can be asserted of all other liberty? How if maintenance of this also turns out to be a matter of conscience? Have we not seen that human happiness is the Divine will—that only by exercising our faculties is this happiness obtainable—and that it is impossible to exercise them without freedom? And if this freedom for the exercise of faculties is a condition without which the Divine will cannot be fulfilled, the preservation of it is, by our objector's own showing, a duty. Or, in other words, it appears not only that the maintenance of liberty of action may be a point of conscience, but that it ought to be one. And thus we are clearly shown that the claims to ignore the state in religious and in secular matters are in essence identical.

The other reason commonly assigned for nonconformity admits of similar treatment. Besides resisting state dictation in the abstract, the dissenter resists it from disapprobation of the doctrines taught. No legislative injunction will make him adopt what he considers an erroneous belief; and, bearing in mind his duty toward his fellow men, he refuses to help through the medium of his purse in disseminating this erroneous belief. The position is perfectly intelligible. But it is one which either commits its adherents to civil nonconformity also, or leaves them in a dilemma. For why do they refuse to be instrumental in spreading error? Because error is adverse to human happiness. And on what ground is any piece of secular legislation disapproved? For the same reason—because thought adverse to human happiness. How, then, can it be shown that the state ought to be resisted in the one case and not in the other? Will anyone deliberately assert that if a government demands money from us to aid in *teaching* what we think will produce evil we ought to refuse it, but that if the money is for the purpose of *doing* what we think will produce evil we ought not to refuse it? Yet such is the hopeful proposition which those have to maintain who recognize the right to ignore the state in religious matters but deny it in civil matters.

7. The substance of this chapter once more reminds us of the incongruity between a perfect law and an imperfect state. The practicability of the principle here laid down varies directly as social morality. In a thoroughly vicious community its admission would be productive of anarchy. In a completely virtuous one its admission will be both innocuous and inevitable. Progress toward a condition of social health—a condition, that is, in which the remedial measures of legislation will no longer be needed—is progress toward a condition in which those remedial measures will be cast aside and the authority prescribing them disregarded. The two changes are of necessity co-ordinate. That moral sense whose supremacy will make society harmonious and government unnecessary is the same moral sense which will then make each man assert his freedom even to the extent of ignoring the state—is the same moral sense which, by deterring the majority from coercing the minority, will eventually render government impossible. And as what are merely different manifestations of the same sentiment must bear a constant ratio to each other, the tendency to repudiate governments will increase only at the same rate that governments become needless.

Let not any be alarmed, therefore, at the promulgation of the foregoing doctrine. There are many changes yet to be passed through before it can begin to exercise much influence. Probably a long time will elapse before the right to ignore the state will be generally admitted, even in theory. It will be still longer before it receives legislative recognition. And even then there will be plenty of checks upon the premature exercise of it. A sharp experience will sufficiently instruct those who may too soon abandon legal protection. While, in the majority of men, there is such a love of tried arrangements and so great a dread of experiments that they will probably not act upon this right until long after it is safe to do so.

Chapter 48

Allen Buchanan

SECESSION AND NATIONALISM

Allen Buchanan (1948–   ) is a professor of philosophy and public policy studies at Duke University who is well known for his work in political philosophy, bioethics, and the philosophy of international law. In this essay (published in 1993), Buchanan discusses the nature of secession and autonomy movements, and surveys the philosophical arguments for and against the moral legitimacy of secession.

Secession, Autonomy and the Modern State

From Croatia to Azerbaijan to Quebec, secessionist movements are breaking states apart. In some cases, as with Lithuania, a formerly subordinate unit seeks to become and remain a fully sovereign state in its own right. In others, such as Ukraine, one of the first exercises of new-found sovereignty is to forge ties with other units to create new forms of political association – ties which immediately limit the sovereignty of their components. These momentous events call into question not only the legitimacy of particular states and their boundaries, but also the nature of sovereignty and the purposes of political association.

Less publicized and less dramatic movements for greater self-determination of groups within the framework of existing states are also becoming pervasive. The indigenous peoples' rights movement, pursued with vigour in the United Nations and other arenas of international law, embraces Indians in North, Central and South America, Southeast Asian Hill Tribes, the Saami (Lapps) in a number of countries touched by the Arctic Circle, and Native Hawaiians, among others. Self-determination movements among Flemings in Belgium and Scots in the United Kingdom appear to be building as well. In most of these cases the groups in question do not seek full sovereignty, but rather greater autonomy through the achievement of limited rights of self-government as distinct subunits within the state.

The proper analysis of the concept of sovereignty is, of course, a matter of dispute. However, the root idea is that of a supreme authority – one whose powers are unrestricted by those of other entities. It is useful to distinguish between *internal* and *external* sovereignty. Internal sovereignty is the state's supremacy with respect to all affairs within its borders. External sovereignty is the state's supremacy with respect to its relations with other political units beyond its borders; in particular, its right to the integrity of its territory, and to control crossings of its borders, as well as the right to enter as an independent party into economic agreements or military alliances or treaties with other states.

No state enjoys literally unrestricted external

sovereignty. International law imposes a number of restrictions on every state's dealings with other states, the most fundamental of which is that each is to recognize the others' territorial integrity. In addition, virtually all modern states acknowledge (in principle if not in practice) that their internal sovereignty is limited by *individual rights*, in particular the human rights recognized in international law.

Autonomy movements seek to impose further limitations on internal sovereignty through the recognition of various *group rights*. These include not only so-called minority cultural rights, such as the right to speak one's own language or to wear cultural dress, but also collective property rights for the group, rights of internal self-government, and in some cases rights to participate in joint decision-making concerning the development and exploitation of resources in the area occupied by the group.

Autonomy movements may appear to be less radical than outright bids for secession. After all, what they demand is not the dismemberment of the state into two or more new states, but only a reallocation of certain powers within the state. This appearance, however, is misleading. If a state recognizes substantial powers of self-determination for groups within its borders, it thereby acknowledges limits on its own sovereignty. And if the modern state is defined as a political authority which (credibly) claims full sovereignty over the entire area within its borders, then a state that recognizes rights of self-determination for minorities within its borders thereby transforms itself into something less than a fully sovereign state. (For example, American Indian law in conferring significant powers of self-government upon Indian tribes, uses the term 'Indian Nation', and is increasing regarded as approaching the status of international law.)

Thus, secession movements only threaten the myth of the permanence of the state; autonomy movements assault the concept of state sovereignty itself. Successful and frequent secession would certainly shatter the international order; but it would not challenge the basic conceptual framework that has governed international law for over 300 years, since the rise of the modern state. What is fundamental to that framework is the assumption that international law concerns relations among sovereign states. If successful, autonomy movements within existing states may make the case of sovereign states the exception rather than the rule.

Even though secession is in this sense a phenomenon which the traditional framework of international law and relations can in principle accommodate, it is the most extreme and radical response to the problems of group conflict within the state. For this reason, a consideration of the case for and against secession puts the moral issues of group conflict in bold relief. In what follows, we will explore the morality of secession, while bearing in mind that it is only the most extreme point on a continuum of phenomena involving the struggles of groups within existing political units to gain greater autonomy.

Nationalism and the Justification of Secession

Some see the spate of secessionist movements now appearing around the globe as the expression of an unpredicted and profoundly disturbing resurgence of *nationalism*, which many rightly regard as one of the most dangerous phenomena of the modern era. And indeed one of the most familiar and stirring justifications offered for secession appeals to *the right of self-determination for 'peoples'*, interpreted such that it is equivalent to what is sometimes called the *normative nationalist principle*. It is also one of the least plausible justifications.

The normative nationalist principle states that every 'people' is entitled to its own state, that is, that political and cultural (or ethnic) boundaries must coincide. In other words, according to the normative nationalist principle, the right of self-determination is to be understood in a very strong way, as requiring complete political independence – that is, full sovereignty.

An immediate difficulty, of course, is the meaning of 'peoples'. Presumably a 'people' is a distinct ethnic group, the identifying marks of which are a common language, shared tradition and a common culture. Each of these criteria has its own difficulties. The question of what count as different dialects of the same language, as opposed to two or more distinct languages, raises complex theoretical and metatheoretical issues in linguistics. The histories of many groups exhibit frequent discontinuities, infusion of new cultural elements from outside, and alternating degrees of assimilation to and separation from other groups.

More disturbingly, if 'people' is interpreted broadly enough, then the normative nationalist principle denies the legitimacy of any state containing more than one cultural group (unless all 'peoples' within it freely waive their rights to their own states). Yet cultural pluralism is often taken to be a distinguishing feature of the modern state, or at least of the modern liberal state. Moreover, if the number of ethnic or cultural groups or peoples is not fixed but may increase, then the normative nationalist principle is a recipe for limitless political fragmentation.

Nor is this all. Even aside from the instability and economic costs of the repeated fragmentation which it endorses, there is a more serious objection to the normative nationalist principle, forcefully formulated by Ernest Gellner.

To put it in the simplest terms: there is a very large number of potential nations on earth. Our planet also contains room for a certain number of independent or autonomous political units. On any reasonable calculation, the former number (of potential nations) is probably much, much larger than that of possible viable states. If this argument or calculation is correct, not all nationalisms can be satisfied, at any rate not at the same time. The satisfaction of some spells the frustration

of others. This argument is furthered and immeasurably strengthened by the fact that very many of the potential nations of this world live, or until recently have lived, not in compact territorial units but intermixed with each other in complex patterns. It follows that a territorial political unit can only become ethnically homogenous, in such cases if it either kills, or expels, or assimilates all non-nationals.

With arch understatement, Gellner concludes that the unwillingness of people to suffer such fates 'may make the implementation of the nationalist principle difficult'. Thus, to say that the normative nationalist principle must be rejected because it is too *impractical or economically costly* would be grossly misleading. It ought to be abandoned because the *moral costs*, of even attempting to implement it would be prohibitive.

It is important to see that this criticism of the principle of self-determination is decisive *only* against the strong version of that principle that makes it equivalent to the normative nationalist principle, which states that each people (or ethnic group) is to have its own fully sovereign state. For the objection focuses on the unacceptable implications of granting a right of self-determination to all 'peoples' *on the assumption that self-determination means complete political independence, that is, full sovereignty.*

However, as we have already suggested, the notion of self-determination is vague or, rather, multiply ambiguous, inasmuch as there are numerous forms and a range of degrees of political independence or autonomy that a group might attain. Instead of asserting an ambiguous *right* to self-determination, it might be better to acknowledge that many if not most groups have a *legitimate interest* in self-determination and that this interest can best be served in different circumstances by a range of more specific rights or combinations of rights, including a number of distinct group rights to varying forms and degrees of political autonomy, with the right to secede being only the most extreme of these.

I have argued elsewhere that there is a moral right to secede, though it is a highly qualified, limited right. It is not a right which all 'peoples' or ethnic or cultural groups have simply by virtue of their being distinct groups. Instead, only those groups whose predicament satisfies the conditions laid out in any of several sound justifications for secession have this right. In this sense the right to secede, as I conceive it, is not a general right of groups, but rather a special or selective right that obtains only under certain conditions.

Among the strongest justifications that can be given for the claim that a group has a right to secede under certain circumstances are (1) the argument from the rectification of past unjust takings: (2) the self-defence argument; and (3) the argument from discriminatory redistribution. Since secession involves the taking of territory, not just the severing of bonds of political obligation, each prosecession argument must be construed as including the establishment of a valid claim to the territory on the part of the seceding group.

plausible, of course, in situation in which the people attempting to secede are literally the same people who held legitimate title to the territory at the time of the unjust annexation, or at least are the indisputable descendants of those people (their legitimate political heirs, so to speak). But matters are considerably more complex if the seceding group is not closely or clearly related to the group whose territory was unjustly taken, or if the group that was wrongly dispossessed did not itself have clear, unambiguous title to it. But at least in the paradigm case, the argument from rectificatory justice is a convincing argument for a moral right to secede. The right of the Baltic Republics to secede from the Soviet Union, which forcibly and unjustly annexed them in 1940, is well supported by this first justification.

It is one thing to say that a group has the right to secede because in so doing they will simply be reclaiming what was unjustly taken from them. The *terms* of secession are another question. In some cases secession will adversely affect individuals who had no part in the unjust acquisition of the territory. Whether, or under what conditions, they are owed compensation or other special consideration is a complex matter.

Rectifying Past Unjust Takings

This first justification is the simplest and most intuitively appealing argument for secession. It has obvious application to many actual secessionist movements, including some of those which completed the dissolution of the Soviet Union. The claim is that a region has a right to secede if it was unjustly incorporated into the larger unit from which its members seek to separate.

The argument's power stems from the assumption that secession is simply the reappropriation, by the legitimate owner, of stolen property. The right to secede, under these circumstances, is just the right to reclaim what is one's own. This simple interpretation is most

The Self-Defence Argument

The common law, common-sense morality and the great majority of ethical systems, religious and secular, acknowledge a right of self-defence against an aggressor who threatens lethal force. For good reason this is not thought to be an unlimited right. Among the more obvious restrictions on it are (1) that only that degree of force necessary to avert the threat be used, and (2) that the attack against which one defends oneself not be provoked by one's own actions. If such restrictions are acknowledged, the assertion that there is a right of self-defence is highly plausible. Each of these restrictions is pertinent to the right of groups to defend themselves. There are two quite different types of situations in which a group might invoke the right of self-defence to justify secession.

In the first, a group wishes to secede from a state in order to protect its members from extermination by that state itself. Under such conditions the group may either attempt to overthrow the government, that is, to engage in revolution; or, if strategy requires it, the group may secede in order to organize a defensible territory, forcibly appropriating the needed territory from the aggressor, creating the political and military machinery required for its survival, and seeking recognition and aid from other sovereign states and international bodies. Whatever moral title to the seceding territory the aggressor state previously held is invalidated by the gross injustice of its genocidal efforts. Or, at the very least, we can say that whatever legitimate claims to the seceding territory the state had are outweighed by the claims of its innocent victims. We may think of the aggressor's right to the territory, in the former case, as dissolving in the acid of his own iniquities, and, in the latter, as being pushed down in the scales of the balance by the greater weight of the victim's right of self-defence. Whether we say that the evil state's right to territory is invalidated (and disappears entirely) or merely is outweighed, it is clear enough that in these circumstances its claim to the territory should not be an insurmountable bar to the victim group's seceding, if this is the only way to avoid its wrongful destruction. Unfortunately, this type of case is far from fanciful. One of the strongest arguments for recognizing an independent Kurdish state, for example, is that only this status, with the control over territory it includes, will ensure the survival of this group in the face of genocidal threats from Turkey, Iran and Iraq.

There is a second situation in which secessionists might invoke the right of self-defence, but in a more controversial manner. They could argue that in order to defend itself against a lethal aggressor a group may secede from a state that is not itself that aggressor. This amounts to

the claim that the need to defend itself against genocide can *generate* a claim to territory of sufficient moral weight to override the claims of those who until now held valid title to it and who, unlike the aggressor in the first version of the argument, have not forfeited their claim to it by lethal aggression.

Suppose the year is 1939. Germany has inaugurated a policy of genocide against the Jews. Jewish pleas to the democracies for protection have fallen on deaf ears (in part because the Jews are not regarded as a *nation* – nationhood carrying a strong presumption of territory, which they do not possess). Leaders of Jewish populations in Germany, Eastern Europe and the Soviet Union agree that the only hope for the survival of their people is to create a Jewish state, a sovereign territory to serve as a last refuge for European Jewry. Suppose further that the logical choice for its location – the only choice with the prospect of any success in saving large numbers of Jews – is a portion of Poland. Polish Jews, who are not being protected from the Nazis by the government of Poland, therefore occupy a portion of Poland and invite other Jews to join them there in a Jewish sanctuary state. They do not expel non-Jewish Poles who already reside in that area but, instead, treat them as equal citizens. (From 1941 until 1945 something like this actually occurred on a smaller scale. Jewish partisans, who proved to be heroic and ferocious fighters, occupied and defended an area in the forests of Poland, in effect creating their own mini-state, for purposes of defending themselves and others from annihilation by the Germans.)

The force of this second application of the self-defence argument derives in part from the assumption that the Polish Jews who create the sanctuary state *are not being protected by their own state, Poland.* The idea is that *a state's authority over territory is based at least in part in its providing protection to all its citizens* – and that its retaining that authority is conditional on its continuing to do so. In the circumstances described, the Polish state is not providing protection to its Jewish citizens, and this fact voids the state's title to the territory in question. The Jews may rightly claim the territory, if doing so is necessary for their protection against extermination.

Escaping Discriminatory Redistribution

The idea here is that a group may secede if this is the only way for them to escape discriminatory redistribution. Discriminatory redistribution, also called regional exploitation and internal colonization, occurs whenever the state implements economic policies that systematically work to the disadvantage of some groups, while benefiting others, in morally arbitrary ways. A clear example of discriminatory redistribution would be the state imposing higher taxes on one group while spending less on it, or placing economic restrictions on one region, without any sound moral justification for this unequal treatment.

Charges of discriminatory redistribution abound in actual secessionist movements. Indeed, it would be hard to find cases in which this charge does not play a central role in justifications for secession, even though other reasons are often given as well. Here are only a few illustrations:

1. American Southerners complained that the federal tariff laws were discriminatory in intent and effect – that they served to foster the growth of infant industries in the North by protecting them from European and especially British competition, at the expense of the South's import-dependent economy. The Southern statesman John C. Calhoun and others argued that the amount of money the South was contributing to the federal government, once the effects of the tariff were taken into account, far exceeded what that region was receiving from it.
2. Basque secessionists have noted that the percentage of total tax revenues in Spain paid by those in their region is more than three times the percentage of state expenditures there (a popular Basque protest song expresses this point vividly, saying that 'the cow of the state has its mouth in the Basque country but its udder elsewhere').
3. Biafra, which unsuccessfully attempted to become independent from Nigeria in 1967, while containing only 22 per cent of the Nigerian population, contributed 38 per cent of total revenues, and received back from the government only 14 per cent of those revenues.
4. Secessionists in the Baltic Republics and in Soviet Central Asia protested that the government in Moscow for many years implemented economic policies that benefited the rest of the country at the expense of staggering environmental damage in their regions. To support this allegation of discriminatory redistribution, they cited reports of abnormally high rates of birth defects in Estonia, Latvia and Lithuania, apparently due to chemical pollutants from the heavy industry which Soviet economic policy concentrated there, and contamination of ground water in Central Asia due to massive use of pesticides and herbicides at the order of planners in Moscow whose goal it was to make that area a major cotton producer.

An implicit premise of the argument from discriminatory redistribution is that *failure to satisfy this fundamental condition of non-discrimination voids the state's claim to the territory in which the victims reside*, whereas the fact that they have no other recourse to avoid this fundamental injustice *gives them a valid title to it*. This premiss forges the needed connection between the grounds for seceding (discriminatory redistribution) and the territorial claim that every sound justification for secession must include (since secession involves the taking of territory). One good reason for accepting this premiss is that it explains our intuitions about the justifiability of secession in certain central and relatively uncontroversial cases.

In other words, unless this premiss is acceptable, the argument from discriminatory redistribution is not sound; and unless the argument from discriminatory redistribution is sound, it is hard to see how secession is justifiable in certain cases in which there is widespread agreement that it is justified. Consider, for example, the secession of the thirteen American Colonies from the British Empire. (Strictly speaking this was secession, not revolution. The aim of the American colonists was not to overthrow the British government, but only to remove a part of the North American territory from the Empire.) The chief justification for American independence was discriminatory redistribution: Britain's mercantilist policies systematically worked to the disadvantage of the colonies for the benefit of the mother country. Lacking representation in the British Parliament, the colonists reasonably concluded that this injustice would persist. It seems, then, that if the American 'Revolution' was justified, then there are cases in which the state's persistence in the injustice of discriminatory redistribution, together with the lack of alternatives to secession for remedying it, *generates* a valid claim to territory on the part of the secessionists.

The force of the argument from discriminatory redistribution does not rest solely, however, on brute moral intuitions about particular cases such as that of American independence. We can *explain* our responses to such cases by a simple but powerful principle: the legitimacy of the state – including its rightful jurisdiction over territory – depends upon its providing a framework for co-operation that does not systematically discriminate against any group.

The self-defence argument and the argument from discriminatory redistribution share an underlying assumption, namely, that the justification for a state's control over territory is at least in part *functional*. Generally speaking, what entitles a state to exercise exclusive jurisdiction ('territorial sovereignty') over a territory is the state's provision of a regime that enforces basic rights in a nondiscriminatory way. If the state fails to fulfil these legitimating jurisdictional functions with respect to a group, and if there is no other way for the group to protect itself from the ensuing injustices, then it can rightfully claim the jurisdictional authority for itself.

Attempts to justify secession on grounds of discriminatory redistribution are more complicated than might first appear. The mere fact that there is a net flow of revenue out of one region does not show that discriminatory redistribution is occurring. Instead, the state may simply be implementing policies designed to satisfy the demands of *distributive justice*. (Theories of distributive justice attempt to formulate and defend principles that specify the proper distribution of the burdens and benefits of social co-operation.) The problem is that distributive justice is a highly controversial matter and that different theories will yield different and in some cases directly opposing assessments of distributive patterns across regions of a country. A policy which redistributes wealth from one region to others may be a case of discriminatory redistribution according to one theory of distributive justice, but a case of just redistribution according to another. Even if there is fairly widespread agreement that the better-off owe *something* to the worse-off, there can be and is disagreement as to *how much* is owed. To this extent, the theory of secession is derivative upon the theory of distributive justice and subject to its uncertainties.

Justifications for Forcible Resistance to Secession

An adequate moral theory of secession must consider not only arguments to justify secession but justifications for resisting it as well. Here I will concentrate on only two of the more influential and plausible of the latter.

Avoiding Anarchy

From Lincoln to Gorbachev, leaders of states have opposed secession, warning that recognition of a right to secede would result in chaos. The *reductio ad absurdum* of the right to secede is the prospect of the most extreme anarchy: not every man's home his castle; rather, every man's yard his country. Even if political fragmentation stops short of this, recognition of a right to secede is likely to produce more fragmentation than is tolerable.

This argument would be much more plausible if recognizing a right to secede meant recognizing an *unlimited* right to secede. But as we have argued, the right to secede is a special or selective right that exists only when one or more of a limited set of justifying conditions is satisfied; it is not a general right of all peoples. Nor, as we have also seen, can it reasonably be understood to be included in or derivable from an alleged right of all peoples to self-determination. At most, the threat of anarchy could create a rebuttable presumption against secession, so that secessionists would, generally speaking, have to make a case for seceding.

The theory of the right to secede sketched above can be seen as including such a presumption: a sound justification for secession is to include a justification for the secessionists' claim to the territory. In a sense, this requirement constitutes a presumption in favour of the status quo and to that extent addresses the worry about anarchy. And since, as I have also noted, secession involves not only the severing of bonds of political obligation but also the taking of territory, this requirement seems reasonable.

Some might argue that by requiring secessionists to offer grounds for their claim to the territory, the theory proposed here stacks the deck against them. Especially from the standpoint of liberal political philosophy, which prizes liberty and self-determination, why should there not be a presumption that secession is justified, or at the very least, why should not secessionists and anti-secessionists start out on level ground in the process of justification?

There are, I believe, two sound reasons for a presumption that secessionists must make a case for taking the territory. First, a moral theory of secession should be viewed as a branch of *institutional ethics*. One relevant consideration for evaluating proposed principles for institutional ethics is the consequences of their general acceptance. So long as it is recognized that the presumption against secession can be rebutted by any of the arguments stated above in favour of a right to secede, such a presumption seems superior to the alternatives. Given the gravity of secession – and the predictable and unpredictable disruptions and violence which it may produce – legitimate interests in the stability of the international order speak in favour of the presumption.

Another consideration in favour of assigning the burden of argument where I have is that such a presumption – which gives some weight to the status quo – is much more likely to contribute to general acceptance of a right to secede in the international community. Other things being equal, a moral theory which is more likely to gain acceptance is to be preferred, especially if it is a theory of how institutions, in this case, the institutions of international law and diplomacy, ought to operate. It is often remarked that the one principle of international law that has gained almost universal acceptance is a strong presumption against violations of the territorial integrity of existing states. Requiring that secessionists be able to justify secession and in such a way as to establish their claim to the territory in question, serves to give appropriate weight to this fundamental principle, while at the same time recognizing that the state's claim to control over its territory is not absolute and can be overridden under certain conditions.

Avoiding Strategic Bargaining That Undermines Majority Rule

It could be argued that if the right to secede is recognized, then a minority may use the threat of secession to undermine majority rule. In conditions in which the majority views secession a prohibitive cost, a group's threat to secede can function as a veto over the majority's decisions. Consideration of this risk might lead one to conclude that the only adequate way to protect democracy is to refuse to acknowledge a right to secede.

However, as we have seen, there can be compelling justifications for secession under certain conditions. Accordingly, a more appropriate response than denying the right to secede is to devise constitutional mechanisms or processes of international law that give some weight both to legitimate interests in secession and to the equally legitimate interest in preserving the integrity of majority rule (and in political stability). The most obvious way to do this would be to allow secession under certain circumstances, but to minimize the risk of strategic bargaining with the threat of secession by erecting inconvenient but surmountable procedural hurdles to secession. For example a constitution might recognize a right to secede, but require a strong majority – say three-quarters – of those in the potentially seceding area to endorse secession in a referendum. This type of hurdle is the analogue of an obstacle to constitutional amendment which the US Constitution's Amendment Clause itself establishes: any proposed amendment must receive a two-thirds vote in Congress and be ratified by three-quarters of the states.

The purpose of allowing amendment while erecting these two strong (that is, non-simple) majority requirements is to strike an appropriate balance between two legitimate interests: the interest in providing flexibility for needed change and the interest in securing stability. Similarly, the point of erecting inconvenient but surmountable barriers to secession (either in a constitution or in international law) would be not to make secession impossible but to avoid making it too easy. A second approach would be to levy special exit costs, a secession tax. Once these possibilities are recognized, the objection that acknowledgment of a right to secede necessarily undermines democracy is seen to be less than compelling.

Secession and the Problem of Group Conflict in the Modern State

Secession is only the most extreme – and in some cases the least desirable – response to problems of group conflict. A comprehensive moral theory of international relations would include an account of the scope and limits of the right to secede; but it would also formulate and support principles to guide the establishment of a wider range of rights of self-determination. Such a theory, if it gained wide acceptance, would undoubtedly produce fundamental changes in our conceptions of the state, of sovereignty, and of the basic categories of international law.

3d. WAR, HUMANITARIANISM, AND TORTURE

GLOBALIZATION IS THE PROCESS WHEREBY technological and political barriers to the movement of good, services, ideas, and people across borders are dismantled. The same process that makes it easier to move these things between countries, however, also makes it easier to export violence. Countries with the right technology can strike at each other from around the world, rendering geographical distance a much less significant barrier to aggression. And with increased technology including biological and chemical weapons, the capability of aggression has devolved down to the individual level. Acts of war are no longer the sole province of states.

What does this imply for the ways in which philosophers ought to think about war and similar phenomena? There is a rich tradition of philosophical theorizing running back through Grotius and Aquinas, most of which deals with questions about the conditions under which one state may legitimately go to war with another (a topic known as *jus ad bellum*), and the kinds of things that may legitimately be done within the context of a just war (*jus in bello*). This tradition still has a good many adherents, and has recently expanded to deal with some of the questions that have been neglected by the tradition, or that have only recently arisen as a result of technological or other developments. A number of theorists, for instance, now write about the issue of *jus post bellum*, which deals with the ending of wars and the transition back to peace.

Moreover, although the just war tradition has long endorsed the idea that the only just wars are those fought defensively, there is less consensus than ever on exactly what constitutes a "defensive" war. If one has reliable intelligence that a foreign power is planning to attack your territory (or citizens?), is this a sufficient provocation to allow you to use violence to stop it? How reliable does the intelligence have to be, and how imminent must the threat be in order to justify violence as opposed to, say, further diplomatic measures? Moreover, and this is an issue that Fernando Tesón will address in this section, must a state be fighting in defense of *its own citizens* in order to be justified, or can states legitimately go to war to protect the citizens of another state? Perhaps the target state is deliberately murdering its own citizens, as was the case in Hitler's Germany. Or perhaps it is just recklessly incompetent and causing its citizens to starve needlessly, as appears to be the case in Mugabe's Zimbabwe. Traditionally, the idea that a state is *sovereign* over its own territory has stood as a virtually insurmountable barrier to other states forcefully intervening within their country for humanitarian purposes. But as political theorists began during the twentieth century to stress the importance of individual rights over state rights, this barrier has begun to crumble.

The fact that states no longer possess a monopoly on acts of war might be thought to undermine Randolph Bourne's thesis that "war is the health of the state." If individuals and small groups of individuals can now wage wars or at least engage in war-like acts, then perhaps states can no longer use war as a tool of self-aggrandizement? But we should not jump to this conclusion so quickly. The fact that acts of war may now be carried out by small groups makes the potential threat of war much greater, and quite possibly more difficult to detect. In such a situation, the state can claim for itself a tremendous amount of power in the name of providing for the security of its citizens. Witness the political climate in the United States in the wake of September 11, 2001, where it appears that government (and citizens) have been quite willing to sacrifice individual privacy and liberties for the promise of greater security. The more widespread and dangerous the threat of violence becomes, the greater becomes the state's ability to enlarge itself in the name of protecting its citizens.

And the more citizens become willing to allow their state to do for the sake of providing that security. For instance, even though torture is prohibited by the U.N. Declaration of Human Rights (see chapter 12 of this book) and other national agreements, it nevertheless has been defended as a tool for fighting international terrorism by both academics and actual government leaders—a resurgence in acceptability reflected in the popular culture in movies and television shows like *24*. What has happened is not that people have changed their minds about the various ways in which torture can be degrading and cruel. Rather, the thought is that the "stakes have gone up," and that we can therefore no longer afford to be as fastidious in refraining from such degrading and cruel acts as we once hoped to be. Terrorists are hard to detect, the consequences of their terrorist acts can be devastating, and law enforcement, it is thought, needs to take advantage of every possible tool to combat this menace. So while it might be unfortunate that we find ourselves in a situation where torture is our best option, we must nevertheless balance the moral costs involved in torturing against the moral costs involved in *not* torturing—costs which may be measured in terms of thousands of innocent lives.

This, at any rate, is the argument. It is an argument with obvious roots in the consequentialist analysis of moral problems. But it is one which even rights theorists must grapple with seriously. After all, if there is a right against torture, is it really plausible to suppose that it is an *absolute* right, one that may not be breached no matter how serious the costs of respecting it may be? Ticking time bomb scenarios are meant to challenge this assumption by asking what we would do if torture were the only way to obtain the location of a bomb set to go off soon and claim many innocent lives. And as far as thought experiments go, they are quite powerful in challenging our absolutist thinking on the moral status of torture. David Luban, though, in his essay in this section, raises serious questions about the implications of hypothetical thought experiments for real world policy. The kinds of assumptions we need to make about the efficacy of torture, our certainty about what the intended victim of torture really knows, and our ability to successfully weigh the costs and benefits of torture on a case-by-case basis, for instance, are assumptions that will almost never be jointly satisfied in the real world.

Still, it's hard to rule out any policy absolutely, including torture, on purely consequentialist grounds. If the moral standard is to do *whatever* produces the best consequences, then it seems like we must be open to the possibility that in *some* circumstances the situation will be such that the benefits of torture outweigh the costs. And unfortunately, the problem doesn't get any easier for deontological, rights-based theorists. For the more absolutist a theory of rights is in prohibiting acts like torture no matter what the cost, the more reason it seems we have to doubt whether that theory of rights is one to which we wish to subscribe.

The twentieth century was witness to some of the bloodiest and most destructive wars in human history. Now, at the dawn of the twenty-first century we face two risks. The first is that the upward trend in the destructiveness of war will continue as weapons become more destructive and easier for small unstable groups to utilize. The second is that the powers that we give to the state (or that are seized by the state) to combat this threat will be irrevocable and ultimately destructive of human liberty and well-being. The disease of war is deadly, but the cure of a state powerful enough to protect us might end up being even worse.

Further Reading

Allhoff, Fritz (2003). Terrorism and Torture. *International Journal of Applied Philosophy, 17*(1), 105–18.

Anscombe, G. E. M. (1981). "War and Murder" and "Mr. Truman's Degree." In *Ethics, Religion and Politics: Collected Philosophical Papers, V3*. Minneapolis: University of Minnesota Press.

Aquinas, "On War."

Augustine, *The City of God*, Book XIX.

Kemp, Kenneth W. (1988). Just-War Theory: A Reconceptualization. *Public Affairs Quarterly, 2*(2), 57–74.

Luban, David (1980) Just War and Human Rights. *Philosophy and Public Affairs 9*(2), 160–181.

Nagel, T. (1972). War and Massacre. *Philosophy and Public Affairs, 1*, 123–144.

Narveson, Jan (1965). Pacifism: A Philosophical Analysis. *Ethics, 75*(4), 259–271.

Ramsey, Paul (1968). *The Just War*. New York: Charles Scribner's Sons.

Shue, Henry (1978). Torture. *Philosophy and Public Affairs, 7*, 124–143.

Waldron, Jeremy (2005). Torture and Positive Law: Jurisprudence for the White House. *Columbia Law Review, 105*(6), 1681–1750.

Walzer, Michael (2000). *Just and Unjust Wars: A Moral Argument with Historical Illustrations* (3rd ed.). New York: Basic Books.

Walzer, Michael (2004). *Arguing About War*. New Haven, CT: Yale University Press.

Chapter 49

Randolph Bourne

WAR IS THE HEALTH OF THE STATE

Randolph Bourne (1886–1918) was a progressive social theorist best known for his opposition to American militarism in general and World War I in particular. In this essay (published in 1918), Bourne draws a distinction between State and government, and argues that war is the ultimate source of power and authority for the former. War weakens the individual and puts her into a state of subservience while at the same time imbuing the State with an almost mystical authority.

To most Americans of the classes which consider themselves significant the war brought a sense of the sanctity of the State which, if they had had time to think about it, would have seemed a sudden and surprising alteration in their habits of thought. In times of peace, we usually ignore the State in favor of partisan political controversies, or personal struggles for office, or the pursuit of party policies. It is the Government rather than the State with which the politically minded are concerned. The state is reduced to a shadowy emblem which comes to consciousness only on occasions of patriotic holiday.

Government is obviously composed of common and unsanctified men, and is thus a legitimate object of criticism and even contempt. If your own party is in power, things may be assumed to be moving safely enough; but if the opposition is in, then clearly all safety and honor have fled the State. Yet you do not put it to yourself in quite that way. What you think is only that there are rascals to be turned out of a very practical machinery of offices and functions which you take for granted. When we say that Americans are lawless, we usually mean that they are less conscious than other peoples of the august majesty of the institution of the State as it stands behind the objective government of men and laws which we see. In a republic the men who hold office are indistinguishable from the mass. Very few of them possess the slightest personal dignity with which they could endow their political role; even if they ever thought of such a thing. And they have no class distinction to give them glamour. In a Republic the Government is obeyed grumblingly, because it has no bedazzlements or sanctities to gild it. If you are a good old-fashioned democrat, you rejoice at this fact, you glory in the plainness of a system where every citizen has become a king. If you are more sophisticated you bemoan the passing of dignity and honor from affairs of State. But in practice, the democrat does not in the least treat his elected citizen with the respect due to a king, nor does the sophisticated citizen pay tribute to the dignity even when he finds it. The republican State has almost no trappings to appeal to the common man's emotions. What it has are of military origin, and in an unmilitary era such as we have passed through since the Civil War, even military trappings have been scarcely seen. In such an era the sense of the State almost fades out of the consciousness of men.

With the shock of war, however, the State comes into its own again. The Government, with no mandate from the people, without consultation of the people, conducts all the negotiations, the backing and filling, the menaces and explanations, which slowly bring it into collision with some other Government, and gently and irresistibly slides the country into war. For the benefit of proud and haughty citizens, it is fortified with a list of the intolerable insults which have been hurled toward us by the other nations; for the benefit of the liberal and beneficent, it has a convincing set of moral purposes which our going to war will achieve; for the ambitious and aggressive classes, it can gently whisper of a bigger role in the destiny of the world. The result is that, even in those countries where the business of declaring war is theoretically in the hands of representatives of the people, no legislature has ever been known to decline the request of an Executive, which has conducted all foreign affairs in utter privacy and irresponsibility, that it order the nation into battle. Good democrats are wont to feel the crucial difference between a State in which the popular Parliament or Congress declares war, and the State in which an absolute monarch or ruling class declares war. But, put to the stern pragmatic test, the difference is not striking. In the freest of republics as well as in the most tyrannical of empires, all foreign policy, the diplomatic negotiations which produce or forestall war, are equally the private property of the Executive part of the Government, and are equally exposed to no check whatever from popular bodies, or the people voting as a mass themselves.

The moment war is declared, however, the mass of the people, through some spiritual alchemy, become convinced that they have willed and executed the deed themselves. They then, with the exception of a few malcontents, proceed to allow themselves to be regimented, coerced, deranged in all the environments of their lives, and turned into a solid manufactory of destruction toward whatever other people may have, in the appointed scheme of things, come within the range of the Government's disapprobation. The citizen throws off his contempt and indifference to Government, identifies himself with its purposes, revives all his military memories and symbols, and the State once more walks, an august presence, through the imaginations of men. Patriotism becomes the dominant feeling, and produces immediately that intense and hopeless confusion between the relations which the individual bears and should bear toward the society of which he is a part.

The patriot loses all sense of the distinction between State, nation, and government. In our quieter moments, the Nation or Country forms the basic idea of society. We think vaguely of a loose population spreading over a certain geographical portion of the earth's surface, speaking a common language, and living in a homogeneous civilization. Our idea of Country concerns itself with the non-political aspects of a people, its ways of living, its personal traits, its literature and art, its characteristic attitudes toward life. We are Americans because we live in a certain bounded territory, because our ancestors have carried on a great enterprise of pioneering and colonization, because we live in certain kinds of communities which have a certain look and express their aspirations in certain ways. We can see that our civilization is different from contiguous civilizations like the Indian and Mexican. The institutions of our country form a certain network which affects us vitally and intrigues our thoughts in a way that these other civilizations do not. We are a part of Country, for better or for worse. We have arrived in it through the operation of physiological laws, and not in any way through our own choice. By the time we have reached what are called years of discretion, its influences have molded our habits, our values, our ways of thinking, so that however aware we may become, we never really lost the stamp of our civilization, or could be mistaken for the child of any other country. Our feeling for our fellow countrymen is one of similarity or of mere acquaintance. We may be intensely proud of and congenial to our particular network of civilization, or we may detest most of its qualities and rage at its defects. This does not alter the fact that we are inextricably bound up in it. The Country, as an inescapable group into which we are born, and which makes us its particular kind of a citizen of the world, seems to be a fundamental fact of our consciousness, an irreducible minimum of social feeling.

Now this feeling for country is essentially noncompetitive; we think of our own people merely as living on the earth's surface along with other groups, pleasant or objectionable as they may be, but fundamentally as sharing the earth with them. In our simple conception of country there is no more feeling of rivalry with other peoples than there is in our feeling for our family. Our interest turns within rather than without, is intensive and not belligerent. We grow up and our imaginations gradually stake out the world we live in, they need no greater conscious satisfaction for their gregarious impulses than this sense of a great mass of people to whom we are more or less attuned, and in whose institutions we are functioning. The feeling for country would be an uninflatable maximum were it not for the ideas of State and Government which are associated with it. Country is a concept of peace, of tolerance, of living and letting live. But State is essentially a concept of power, of competition; it signifies a group in its aggressive aspects. And we have the misfortune of being born not only into a country but into a State, and as we grow up we learn to mingle the two feelings into a hopeless confusion.

The State is the country acting as a political unit, it is the group acting as a repository of force, determiner of law, arbiter of justice. Inter-

national politics is a "power politics" because it is a relation of States and that is what States infallibly and calamitously are, huge aggregations of human and industrial force that may be hurled against each other in war. When a country acts as a whole in relation to another country, or in imposing laws on its own inhabitants, or in coercing or punishing individuals or minorities, it is acting as a State. The history of America as a country is quite different from that of America as a State. In one case it is the drama of the pioneering conquest of the land, of the growth of wealth and the ways in which it was used, of the enterprise of education, and the carrying out of spiritual ideals, of the struggle of economic classes. But as a State, its history is that of playing a part in the world, making war, obstructing international trade, preventing itself from being split to pieces, punishing those citizens whom society agrees are offensive, and collecting money to pay for all. . . .

Government on the other hand is synonymous with neither State nor Nation. It is the machinery by which the nation, organized as a State, carries out its State functions. Government is a framework of the administration of laws, and the carrying out of the public force. Government is the idea of the State put into practical operation in the hands of definite, concrete, fallible men. It is the visible sign of the invisible grace. It is the word made flesh. And it has necessarily the limitations inherent in all practicality. Government is the only form in which we can envisage the State, but it is by no means identical with it. That the State is a mystical conception is something that must never be forgotten. Its glamour and its significance linger behind the framework of Government and direct its activities.

Wartime brings the ideal of the State out into very clear relief, and reveals attitudes and tendencies that were hidden. In times of peace the sense of the State flags in a republic that is not militarized. For war is essentially the health of the State. The ideal of the State is that within its territory its power and influence should be universal. As the Church is the medium for the spiritual salvation of men, so the State is thought of as the medium for his political salvation. Its idealism is a rich blood flowing to all the members of the body politic. And it is precisely in war that the urgency for union seems greatest, and the necessity for universality seems most unquestioned. The State is the organization of the herd to act offensively or defensively against another herd similarly organized. The more terrifying the occasion for defense, the closer will become the organization and the more coercive the influence upon each member of the herd. War sends the current of purpose and activity flowing down to the lowest level of the herd, and to its most remote branches. All the activities of society are linked together as fast as possible to this central purpose of making a military offensive or a military defense, and the State becomes what in peacetimes it has vainly struggled to become—the inexorable arbiter and determinant of men's business and attitudes and opinions. The slack is taken up, the crosscurrents fade out, and the nation moves lumberingly and slowly, but with ever accelerated speed and integration, toward the great end, toward the "peacefulness of being at war," of which L. P. Jacks has so unforgettably spoken.

The classes which are able to play an active and not merely a passive role in the organization for war get a tremendous liberation of activity and energy. Individuals are jolted out of their old routine, many of them are given new positions of responsibility, new techniques must be learned. Wearing home ties are broken and women who would have remained attached with infantile bonds are liberated for service overseas. A vast sense of rejuvenescence pervades the significant classes, a sense of new importance in the world. Old national ideals are taken out, readapted to the purpose and used as universal touchstones, or molds into which all thought is poured. Every individual citizen who in peacetimes had no function to perform by which he could imagine himself an expression or living

fragment of the State becomes an active amateur agent of the Government in reporting spies and disloyalists, in raising Government funds, or in propagating such measures as are considered necessary by officialdom. Minority opinion, which in times of peace, was only irritating and could not be dealt with by law unless it was conjoined with actual crime, becomes, with the outbreak of war, a case for outlawry. Criticism of the State, objections to war, lukewarm opinions concerning the necessity or the beauty of conscription, are made subject to ferocious penalties, far exceeding in severity those affixed to actual pragmatic crimes. Public opinion, as expressed in the newspapers, and the pulpits and the schools, becomes one solid block. "Loyalty," or rather war orthodoxy, becomes the sole test for all professions, techniques, occupations. Particularly is this true in the sphere of the intellectual life. There the smallest taint is held to spread over the whole soul, so that a professor of physics is *ipso facto* disqualified to teach physics or to hold honorable place in a university—the republic of learning—if he is at all unsound on the war. Even mere association with persons thus tainted is considered to disqualify a teacher. Anything pertaining to the enemy becomes taboo. His books are suppressed wherever possible, his language is forbidden. His artistic products are considered to convey in the subtlest spiritual way taints of vast poison to the soul that permits itself to enjoy them. So enemy music is suppressed, and energetic measures of opprobrium taken against those whose artistic consciences are not ready to perform such an act of self-sacrifice. The rage for loyal conformity works impartially, and often in diametric opposition to other orthodoxies and traditional conformities, or even ideals. The triumphant orthodoxy of the State is shown at its apex perhaps when Christian preachers lose their pulpits for taking in more or less literal terms the Sermon on the Mount, and Christian zealots are sent to prison for twenty years for distributing tracts which argue that war is unscriptural.

War is the health of the State. It automatically sets in motion throughout society those irresistible forces for uniformity, for passionate cooperation with the Government in coercing into obedience the minority groups and individuals which lack the larger herd sense. The machinery of government sets and enforces the drastic penalties; the minorities are either intimidated into silence, or brought slowly around by a subtle process of persuasion which may seem to them really to be converting them. Of course, the ideal of perfect loyalty, perfect uniformity is never really attained. The classes upon whom the amateur work of coercion falls are unwearied in their zeal, but often their agitation instead of converting, merely serves to stiffen their resistance. Minorities are rendered sullen, and some intellectual opinion bitter and satirical. But in general, the nation in wartime attains a uniformity of feeling, a hierarchy of values culminating at the undisputed apex of the State ideal, which could not possibly be produced through any other agency than war. Loyalty—or mystic devotion to the State—becomes the major imagined human value. Other values, such as artistic creation, knowledge, reason, beauty, the enhancement of life, are instantly and almost unanimously sacrificed, and the significant classes who have constituted themselves the amateur agents of the State are engaged not only in sacrificing these values for themselves but in coercing all other persons into sacrificing them.

War—or at least modern war waged by a democratic republic against a powerful enemy—seems to achieve for a nation almost all that the most inflamed political idealist could desire. Citizens are no longer indifferent to their Government, but each cell of the body politic is brimming with life and activity. We are at last on the way to full realization of that collective community in which each individual somehow contains the virtue of the whole. In a nation at war, every citizen identifies himself with the whole, and feels immensely strengthened in that identification. The purpose and desire of the collective community live in each person who throws himself wholeheartedly into the cause of war. The impeding distinction between society and the individual is almost blotted out. At war, the individual becomes almost identical with his society. He achieves a superb self-assurance, an intuition of the rightness of all his ideas and emotions, so that in the suppression of opponents or heretics he is invincibly strong; he feels behind him all the power of the collective community. The individual as social being in war seems to have achieved almost his apotheosis. Not for any religious impulse could the American nation have been expected to show such devotion *en masse*, such sacrifice and labor. Certainly not for any secular good, such as universal education or the subjugation of nature, would it have poured forth its treasure and its life, or would it have permitted such stern coercive measures to be taken against it, such as conscripting its money and its men. But for the sake of a war of offensive self-defense, undertaken to support a difficult cause to the slogan of "democracy," it would reach the highest level ever known of collective effort.

For these secular goods, connected with the enhancement of life, the education of man and the use of the intelligence to realize reason and beauty in the nation's communal living, are alien to our traditional ideal of the State. The State is intimately connected with war, for it is the organization of the collective community when it acts in a political manner, and to act in a political manner towards a rival group has meant, throughout all history—war.

There is nothing invidious in the use of the term "herd" in connection with the State. It is merely an attempt to reduce closer to first principles the nature of this institution in the shadow of which we all live, move, and have our being. Ethnologists are generally agreed that human society made its first appearance as the human pack and not as a collection of individuals or of couples. The herd is in fact the original unit, and only as it was differentiated did personal individuality develop. All the most primitive surviving tribes of men are shown to live in a very complex but very rigid social organization where opportunity for individuation is scarcely given. These tribes remain strictly organized herds, and the difference between them and the modern State is one of degree of sophistication and variety of organization, and not of kind.

Psychologists recognize the gregarious impulse as one of the strongest primitive pulls which keeps together the herds of the different species of higher animals. Mankind is no exception. Our pugnacious evolutionary history has prevented the impulse from ever dying out. This gregarious impulse is the tendency to imitate, to conform, to coalesce together, and is most powerful when the herd believes itself threatened with attack. Animals crowd together for protection, and men become most conscious of their collectivity at the threat of war. Consciousness of collectivity brings confidence and a feeling of massed strength, which in turn arouses pugnacity and the battle is on. In civilized man, the gregarious impulse acts not only to produce concerted action for defense, but also to produce identity of opinion. Since thought is a form of behavior, the gregarious impulse floods up into its realms and demands that sense of uniform thought which wartime produces so successfully. And it is in this flooding of the conscious life of society that gregariousness works its havoc.

For just as in modern societies the sex instinct is enormously oversupplied for the requirements of human propagation, so the gregarious impulse is enormously oversupplied for the work of protection which it is called upon to perform. It would be quite enough if we were gregarious enough to enjoy the companionship of others, to be able to cooperate with them, and to feel a slight malaise at solitude. Unfortunately, however, this impulse is not content with these reasonable and healthful demands, but insists that like-mindedness shall prevail everywhere, in all departments of life. So that all human progress, all novelty, and nonconformity, must be carried against the resistance of this tyrannical herd instinct which drives the individual into obedience and conformity with the majority. Even in the most modern and enlightened societies this impulse shows little sign of abating. As it is driven by inexorable economic demand out of the sphere of utility, it seems to fasten itself ever more fiercely in the realm of feeling and opinion, so that conformity comes to be a thing aggressively desired and demanded.

The gregarious impulse keeps its hold all the more virulently because when the group is in motion or is taking any positive action, this feeling of being with and supported by the collective herd very greatly feeds that will to power, the nourishment of which the individual organism so constantly demands. You feel powerful by conforming, and you feel forlorn and helpless if you are out of the crowd. While even if you do not get any access of power by thinking and feeling just as everybody else in your group does, you get at least the warm feeling of obedience, the soothing irresponsibility of protection.

Joining as it does to these very vigorous tendencies of the individual—the pleasure in power and the pleasure in obedience—this gregarious impulse becomes irresistible in society. War stimulates it to the highest possible degree, sending the influences of its mysterious herd-current with its inflations of power and obedience to the farthest reaches of the society, to every individual and little group that can possibly be affected. And it is these impulses which the State—the organization of the entire herd, the entire collectivity—is founded on and makes use of.

There is, of course, in the feeling toward the State a large element of pure filial mysticism. The sense of insecurity, the desire for protection, sends one's desire back to the father and mother, with whom is associated the earliest feelings of protection. It is not for nothing that one's State is still thought of as Father or Motherland, that one's relation toward it is conceived in terms of family affection. The war has shown that nowhere under the shock of danger have these primitive childlike attitudes failed to assert themselves again, as much in this country as anywhere. If we have not the intense Father-sense of the German who worships his Vater-land, at least in Uncle Sam we have a symbol of protecting, kindly authority, and in the many Mother-posters of the Red Cross, we see how easily in the more tender functions of war ser-vice, the ruling organization is conceived in fam-ily terms. A people at war have become in the most literal sense obedient, respectful, trustful children again, full of that naïve faith in the all-wisdom and all-power of the adult who takes care of them, imposes his mild but neces-sary rule upon them and in whom they lost their responsibility and anxieties. In this recrudescence of the child, there is great com-fort, and a certain influx of power. On most people the strain of being an independent adult weighs heavily, and upon none more than those members of the significant classes who have had bequeathed to them or have assumed the responsibilities of governing. The State provides the convenientest of symbols under which these classes can retain all the actual pragmatic satisfac-tion of governing, but can rid themselves of the psychic burden of adulthood. They continue to direct industry and government and all the institutions of society pretty much as before, but in their own conscious eyes and in the eyes of the general public, they are turned from their selfish and predatory ways, and have become loyal servants of society, or something greater than they—the State. The man who moves from the direction of a large business in New York to a post in the war management industrial service in Washington does not apparently alter very much his power or his administrative technique. But psychically, what a transfiguration has occurred! His is now not only the power but the glory! And his sense of satisfaction is directly proportional not to the genuine amount of personal sacrifice that may be involved in the change but to the

extent to which he retains his industrial preroga-tives and sense of command.

From members of this class a certain insuper-able indignation arises if the change from private enterprise to State service involves any real loss of power and personal privilege. If there is to be pragmatic sacrifice, let it be, they feel, on the field of honor, in the traditionally acclaimed deaths by battle, in that detour to suicide, as Nietzsche calls war. The State in wartime sup-plies satisfaction for this very real craving, but its chief value is the opportunity it gives for this regression to infantile attitudes. In your reaction to an imagined attack on your country or an insult to its government, you draw closer to the herd for protection, you conform in word and deed, and you insist vehemently that everybody else shall think, speak, and act together. And you fix your adoring gaze upon the State, with a truly filial look, as upon the Father of the flock, the quasi-personal symbol of the strength of the herd, and the leader and determinant of your definite action and ideas.

The members of the working classes, that por-tion at least which does not identify itself with the significant classes and seek to imitate it and rise to it, are notoriously less affected by the symbolism of the State, or, in other words, are less patriotic than the significant classes. For theirs is neither the power nor the glory. The State in wartime does not offer them the opportunity to regress, for, never having acquired social adulthood, they cannot lose it. If they have been drilled and regimented, as by the industrial regime of the last century, they go out docilely enough to do battle for their State, but they are almost entirely without that filial sense and even without that herd-intellect sense which operates so powerfully among their "betters." They live habitually in an industrial serfdom, by which, though nominally free, they are in prac-tice as a class bound to a system of machine-production the implements of which they do not own, and in the distribution of whose product they have not the slightest voice, except what they can occasionally exert by a veiled intimidation which draws slightly more of the product in their direction. From such serfdom, military conscription is not so great a change. But into the military enterprise they go, not with those hurrahs of the significant classes whose instincts war so powerfully feeds, but with the same apathy with which they enter and continue in the industrial enterprise.

From this point of view, war can be called almost an upper-class sport. The novel interests and excitements it provides, the inflations of power, the satisfaction it gives to those very tenacious human impulses—gregariousness and parent-regression—endow it with all the qualities of a luxurious collective game which is felt intensely just in proportion to the sense of significant rule the person has in the class division of his society. A country at war—particularly our own country at war—does not act as a purely homogeneous herd. The significant classes have all the herd-feeling in all its primitive intensity, but there are barriers, or at least differentials of intensity, so that this feeling does not flow freely without impediment throughout the entire nation. A modern country represents a long historical and social process of disaggregation of the herd. The nation at peace is not a group, it is a network of myriads of groups representing the cooperation and similar feeling of men on all sorts of planes and in all sorts of human interests and enterprises. In every modern industrial country, there are parallel planes of economic classes with divergent attitudes and institutions and interests—bourgeois and proletariat, with their many subdivisions according to power and function, and even their interweaving, such as those more highly skilled workers who habitually identify themselves with the owning and the significant classes and strive to raise themselves to the bourgeois level, imitating their cultural standards and manners. Then there are religious groups with a certain definite, though weakening sense of kinship, and there are the powerful ethnic groups which behave almost as cultural colonies in the New World, clinging tenaciously to language and historical tradition, though their herdishness is usually founded on cultural rather than State symbols. There are even certain vague sectional groupings. All these small sects, political parties, classes, levels, interests, may act as foci for herd-feelings. They intersect and interweave, and the same person may be a member of several different groups lying at different planes. Different occasions will set off his herd-feeling in one direction or another. In a religious crisis he will be intensely conscious of the necessity that his sect (or sub-herd) may prevail; in a political campaign, that his party shall triumph.

To the spread of herd-feeling, therefore, all these smaller herds offer resistance. To the spread of that herd-feeling which arises from the threat of war, and which would normally involve the entire nation, the only groups which make serious resistance are those, of course, which continue to identify themselves with the other nation from which they or their parents have come. In times of peace they are for all practical purposes citizens of their new country. They keep alive their ethnic traditions more as a luxury than anything. Indeed these traditions tend rapidly to die out except where they connect with some still unresolved nationalistic cause abroad, with some struggle for freedom, or some irredentism. If they are consciously opposed by a too invidious policy of Americanism, they tend to be strengthened. And in time of war, these ethnic elements which have any traditional connection with the enemy, even though most of the individuals may have little real sympathy with the enemy's cause, are naturally lukewarm to the herd-feeling of the nation which goes back to State traditions in which they have no share. But to the natives inbued with State-feeling, any such resistance or apathy is intolerable. This herd-feeling, this newly awakened consciousness of the State, demands universality. The leaders of the significant classes, who feel most intensely this State compulsion, demand a

100 per cent Americanism, among 100 per cent of the population. The State is a jealous God and will brook no rivals. Its sovereignty must pervade every one, and all feeling must be run into the stereotyped forms of romantic patriotic militarism which is the traditional expression of the State herd-feeling.

Thus arises conflict within the State. War becomes almost a sport between the hunters and the hunted. The pursuit of enemies within outweighs in psychic attractiveness the assault on the enemy without. The whole terrific force of the State is brought to bear against the heretics. The nation boils with a slow insistent fever. A white terrorism is carried on by the Government against pacifists, socialists, enemy aliens, and a milder unofficial persecution against all persons or movements that can be imagined as connected with the enemy. War, which should be the health of the State, unifies all the bourgeois elements and the common people, and outlaws the rest. The revolutionary proletariat shows more resistance to this unification, is, as we have seen, psychically out of the current. Its vanguard, as the I.W.W., is remorselessly pursued, in spite of the proof that it is a sympton, not a cause, and its persecution increases the disaffection of labor and intensifies the friction instead of lessening it.

But the emotions that play around the defense of the State do not take into consideration the pragmatic results. A nation at war, led by its significant classes, is engaged in liberating certain of its impulses which have had all too little exercise in the past. It is getting certain satisfactions, and the actual conduct of the war or the condition of the country are really incidental to the enjoyment of new forms of virtue and power and aggressiveness. If it could be shown conclusively that the persecution of slightly disaffected elements actually increased enormously the difficulties of production and the organization of the war technique, it would be found that public policy would scarcely change. The significant classes must have their pleasure in hunting down and chastizing everything that they feel instinct-

ively to be not imbued with the current State enthusiasm, though the State itself be actually impeded in its efforts to carry out those objects for which they are passionately contending. The best proof of this is that with a pursuit of plotters that has continued with ceaseless vigilance ever since the beginning of the war in Europe, the concrete crimes unearthed and punished have been fewer than those prosecutions for the mere crime of opinion or the expression of sentiments critical of the State or the national policy. The punishment for opinion has been far more ferocious and unintermittent than the punishment of pragmatic crime. Unimpeachable Anglo-Saxon Americans who were freer of pacifist or socialist utterance than the State-obsessed ruling public opinion, received heavier penalties and even greater opprobrium, in many instances, than the definitely hostile German plotter. A public opinion which, almost without protest, accepts as just, adequate, beautiful, deserved, and in fitting harmony with ideals of liberty and freedom of speech, a sentence of twenty years in prison for mere utterances, no matter what they may be, shows itself to be suffering from a kind of social derangement of values, a sort of social neurosis, that deserves analysis and comprehension.

On our entrance into the war, there were many persons who predicted exactly this derangement of values, who feared lest democracy suffer more at home from an America at war than could be gained for democracy abroad. That fear has been amply justified. The question whether the American nation would act like an enlightened democracy going to war for the sake of high ideals, or like a State-obsessed herd, has been decisively answered. The record is written and cannot be erased. History will decide whether the terrorization of opinion and the regimentation of life were justified under the most idealistic of democratic administrations. It will see that when the American nation had ostensibly a chance to conduct a gallant war, with scrupulous regard to the safety of democratic values at home, it chose rather to adopt all the most obnoxious and coercive techniques of the enemy and of the other countries at war, and to rival in intimidation and ferocity of punishment the worst governmental systems of the age. For its former unconsciousness and disrespect of the State ideal, the nation apparently paid the penalty in a violent swing to the other extreme. It acted so exactly like a herd in its irrational coercion of minorities that there is no artificiality in interpreting the progress of the war in terms of the herd psychology. It unwittingly brought out into the strongest relief the true characteristics of the State and its intimate alliance with war. It provided for the enemies of war and the critics of the State the most telling arguments possible. The new passion for the State ideal unwittingly set in motion and encouraged forces that threaten very materially to reform the State. It has shown those who are really determined to end war that the problem is not the mere simple one of finishing a war that will end war.

For war is a complicated way in which a nation acts, and it acts so out of a spiritual compulsion which pushes it on, perhaps against all its interests, all its real desires, and all its real sense of values. It is States that make wars and not nations, and the very thought and almost necessity of war is bound up with the ideal of the State. Not for centuries have nations made war; in fact the only historical example of nations making war is the great barbarian invasions into southern Europe, the invasions of Russia from the East, and perhaps the sweep of Islam through northern Africa into Europe after Mohammed's death. And the motivations for such wars were either the restless expansion of migratory tribes or the flame of religious fanaticism. Perhaps these great movements could scarcely be called wars at all, for war implies an organized people drilled and led; in fact, it necessitates the State. Ever since Europe has had any such organization, such huge conflicts between nations—nations, that is, as cultural groups—have been unthink-

able. It is preposterous to assume that for centuries in Europe there would have been any possibility of a people *en masse*, (with their own leaders, and not with the leaders of their duly constituted State), rising up and overflowing their borders in a war raid upon a neighboring people. The wars of the Revolutionary armies of France were clearly in defense of an imperiled freedom, and, moreover, they were clearly directed not against other peoples, but against the autocratic governments that were combining to crush the Revolution. There is no instance in history of a genuinely national war. There are instances of national defenses, among primitive civilizations such as the Balkan peoples, against intolerable invasion by neighboring despots or oppression. But war, as such, cannot occur except in a system of competing States, which have relations with each other through the channels of diplomacy.

War is a function of this system of States, and could not occur except in such a system. Nations organized for internal administration, nations organized as a federation of free communities, nations organized in any way except that of a political centralization of a dynasty, or the reformed descendant of a dynasty, could not possibly make war upon each other. They would not only have no motive for conflict, but they would be unable to muster the concentrated force to make war effective. There might be all sorts of amateur marauding, there might be guerrilla expeditions of group against group, but there could not be that terrible war *en masse* of the national State, that exploitation of the nation in the interests of the State, that abuse of the national life and resource in the frenzied mutual suicide, which is modern war.

It cannot be too firmly realized that war is a function of States and not of nations, indeed that it is the chief function of States. War is a very artificial thing. It is not the naïve spontaneous outburst of herd pugnacity; it is no more primary than is formal religion. War cannot exist without a military establishment, and a military establishment cannot exist without a

State organization. War has an immemorial tradition and heredity only because the State has a long tradition and heredity. But they are inseparably and functionally joined. We cannot crusade against war without crusading implicitly against the State. And we cannot expect, or take measures to ensure, that this war is a war to end war, unless at the same time we take measures to end the State in its traditional form. The State is not the nation, and the State can be modified and even abolished in its present form, without harming the nation. On the contrary, with the passing of the dominance of the State, the genuine life-enhancing forces of the nation will be liberated. If the State's chief function is war, then the State must suck out of the nation a large part of its energy for its purely sterile purposes of defense and aggression. It devotes to waste or to actual destruction as much as it can of the vitality of the nation. No one will deny that war is a vast complex of life-destroying and life-crippling forces. If the State's chief function is war, then it is chiefly concerned with coordinating and developing the powers and techniques which makes for destruction. And this means not only the actual and potential destruction of the enemy, but of the nation at home as well. For the very existence of a State in a system of States means that the nation lies always under a risk of war and invasion, and the calling away of energy into military pursuits means a crippling of the productive and life-enhancing processes of the national life.

All this organization of death-dealing energy and technique is not a natural but a very sophisticated process. Particularly in modern nations, but also all through the course of modern European history, it could never exist without the State. For it meets the demands of no other institution, it follows the desires of no religious, industrial, political group. If the demand for military organization and a military establishment seems to come not from the officers of the State but from the public, it is only that it comes from the State-obsessed portion of the public, those groups which feel most keenly the State ideal. And in this country we have had evidence all too indubitable how powerless the pacifically minded officers of State may be in the face of a State obsession of the significant classes. If a powerful section of the significant classes feels more intensely the attitudes of the State, then they will most infallibly mold the Government in time to their wishes, bring it back to act as the embodiment of the State which it pretends to be. In every country we have seen groups that were more loyal than the king—more patriotic than the Government—the Ulsterites in Great Britain, the Junkers in Prussia, L'Action Française in France, our patrioteers in America. These groups exist to keep the steering wheel of the State straight, and they prevent the nation from ever veering very far from the State ideal.

Militarism expresses the desires and satisfies the major impulse only of this class. The other classes, left to themselves, have too many necessities and interests and ambitions, to concern themselves with so expensive and destructive a game. But the State-obsessed group is either able to get control of the machinery of the State or to intimidate those in control, so that it is able through use of the collective force to regiment the other grudging and reluctant classes into a military program. State idealism percolates down through the strata of society; capturing groups and individuals just in proportion to the prestige of this dominant class. So that we have the herd actually strung along between two extremes, the militaristic patriots at one end, who are scarcely distinguishable in attitude and animus from the most reactionary Bourbons of an Empire, and unskilled labor groups, which entirely lack the State sense. But the State acts as a whole, and the class that controls governmental machinery can swing the effective action of the herd as a whole. The herd is not actually a whole, emotionally. But by an ingenious mixture of cajolery, agitation, intimidation, the herd is licked into shape, into an effective mechanical unity, if not into a spiritual whole. Men are told simultaneously that they will enter the military establishment of their own volition, as their splendid sacrifice for their country's welfare, and that if they do not enter they will be hunted down and punished with the most horrid penalties; and under a most indescribable confusion of democratic pride and personal fear they submit to the destruction of their livelihood if not their lives, in a way that would formerly have seemed to them so obnoxious as to be incredible.

In this great herd machinery, dissent is like sand in the bearings. The State ideal is primarily a sort of blind animal push toward military unity. Any difference with that unity turns the whole vast impulse toward crushing it. Dissent is speedily outlawed, and the Government, backed by the significant classes and those who in every locality, however small, identify themselves with them, proceeds against the outlaws, regardless of their value to the other institutions of the nation, or to the effect their persecution may have on public opinion. The herd becomes divided into the hunters and the hunted, and war enterprise becomes not only a technical game but a sport as well.

It must never be forgotten that nations do not declare war on each other, nor in the strictest sense is it nations that fight each other. Much has been said to the effect that modern wars are wars of whole peoples and not of dynasties. Because the entire nation is regimented and the whole resources of the country are levied on for war, this does not mean that it is the country *qua* country which is fighting. It is the country organized as a State that is fighting, and only as a State would it possibly fight. So literally it is States which make war on each other and not peoples. Governments are the agents of States, and it is Governments which declare war on each other, acting truest to form in the interests of the great State ideal they represent. There is no case known in modern times of the people being consulted in the initiation of a war. The present demand for "democratic control" of foreign policy indicates

how completely, even in the most democratic of modern nations, foreign policy has been the secret private possession of the executive branch of the Government.

However representative of the people Parliaments and Congresses may be in all that concerns the internal administration of a country's political affairs, in international relations it has never been possible to maintain that the popular body acted except as a wholly mechanical ratifier of the Executive's will. The formality by which Parliaments and Congresses declare war is the merest technicality. Before such a declaration can take place, the country will have been brought to the very brink of war by the foreign policy of the Executive. A long series of steps on the downward path, each one more fatally committing the unsuspecting country to a warlike course of action, will have been taken without either the people or its representatives being consulted or expressing its feeling. When the declaration of war is finally demanded by the Executive, the Parliament or Congress could not refuse it without reversing the course of history, without repudiating what has been representing itself in the eyes of the other States as the symbol and interpreter of the nation's will and animus. To repudiate an Executive at that time would be to publish to the entire world the evidence that the country had been grossly deceived by its own Government, that the country with an almost criminal carelessness had allowed its Government to commit it to gigantic national enterprises in which it had no heart. In such a crisis, even a Parliament, which in the most democratic States represents the common man and not the significant classes who most strongly cherish the State ideal, will cheerfully sustain the foreign policy which it understands even less than it would care for if it understood, and will vote almost unanimously for an incalculable war, in which the nation may be brought well nigh to ruin. That is why the referendum which was advocated by some people as a test of American sentiment in entering the war was considered even by thoughtful democrats to be something subtly improper. The die had been cast. Popular whim could only derange and bungle monstrously the majestic march of State policy in its new crusade for the peace of the world. The irresistible State ideal got hold of the bowels of men. Whereas up to this time, it had been irreproachable to be neutral in word and deed, for the foreign policy of the State had so decided it, henceforth it became the most arrant crime to remain neutral. The Middle West, which had been soddenly pacifistic in our days of neutrality, became in a few months just as soddenly bellicose, and in its zeal for witch-burnings and its scent for enemies within gave precedence to no section of the country. The herd mind followed faithfully the State mind and, the agitation for a referendum being soon forgotten, the country fell into the universal conclusion that, since its Congress had formally declared the war, the nation itself had in the most solemn and universal way devised and brought on the entire affair. Oppression of minorities became justified on the plea that the latter were perversely resisting the rationally constructed and solemnly declared will of a majority of the nation. The herd coalescence of opinion which became inevitable the moment the State had set flowing the war attitudes became interpreted as a prewar popular decision, and disinclination to bow to the herd was treated as a monstrously antisocial act. So that the State, which had vigorously resisted the idea of a referendum and clung tenaciously and, of course, with entire success to its autocratic and absolute control of foreign policy, had the pleasure of seeing the country, within a few months, given over to the retrospective impression that a genuine referendum had taken place. When once a country has lapped up these State attitudes, its memory fades; it conceives itself not as merely accepting, but of having itself willed, the whole policy and technique of war. The significant classes, with their trailing satellites, identify themselves with the State, so that what the state, through the agency of the Government, has willed, this majority conceives itself to have willed.

All of which goes to show that the State represents all the autocratic, arbitrary, coercive, belligerent forces within a social group, it is a sort of complexus of everything most distasteful to the modern free creative spirit, the feeling for life, liberty, and the pursuit of happiness. War is the health of the State. Only when the State is at war does the modern society function with that unity of sentiment, simple uncritical patriotic devotion, cooperation of services, which have always been the ideal of the State lover. With the ravages of democratic ideas, however, the modern republic cannot go to war under the old conceptions of autocracy and death-dealing belligerency. If a successful animus for war requires a renaissance of State ideals, they can only come back under democratic forms, under this retrospective conviction of democratic control of foreign policy, democratic desire for war, and particularly of this identification of the democracy with the State. How unregenerate the ancient State may be, however, is indicated by the laws against sedition, and by the Government's unreformed attitude on foreign policy. One of the first demands of the more farseeing democrats in the democracies of the Alliance was that secret diplomacy must go. The war was seen to have been made possible by a web of secret agreements between States, alliances that were made by Governments without the shadow of popular support or even popular knowledge, and vague, half-understood commitments that scarcely reached the stage of a treaty or agreement, but which proved binding in the event. Certainly, said these democratic thinkers, war can scarcely be avoided unless this poisonous underground system of secret diplomacy is destroyed, this system by which a nation's power, wealth, and manhood may be signed away like a blank check to an allied nation to be cashed in at some future crisis. Agreements which are to affect the lives of whole peoples must be made between peoples and not by Governments, or at least by their representatives in the full glare of publicity and criticism.

Such a demand for "democratic control of foreign policy" seemed axiomatic. Even if the country had been swung into war by steps taken secretly and announced to the public only after they had been consummated, it was felt that the attitude of the American State toward foreign policy was only a relic of the bad old days and must be superseded in the new order. The American President himself, the liberal hope of the world, had demanded, in the eyes of the world, open diplomacy, agreements freely and openly arrived at. Did this mean a genuine transference of power in this most crucial of State functions from Government to people? Not at all. When the question recently came to a challenge in Congress, and the implications of open discussion were somewhat specifically discussed, and the desirabilities frankly commended, the President let his disapproval be known in no uncertain way. No one ever accused Mr. Wilson of not being a State idealist, and whenever democratic aspirations swung ideals too far out of the State orbit, he could be counted on to react vigorously. Here was a clear case of conflict between democratic idealism and the very crux of the concept of the State. However unthinkingly he might have been led on to encourage open diplomacy in his liberalizing program, when its implication was made vivid to him, he betrayed how mere a tool the idea had been in his mind to accentuate America's redeeming role. Not in any sense as a serious pragmatic technique had he thought of a genuinely open diplomacy. And how could he? For the last stronghold of State power is foreign policy. It is in foreign policy that the State acts most concentratedly as the organized herd, acts with fullest sense of aggressive-power, acts with freest arbitrariness. In foreign policy, the State is most itself. States, with reference to each other, may be said to be in a continual state of latent war. The "armed truce," a phrase so familiar before 1914, was an accurate description of the normal relation of States when they are not at war. Indeed, it is not too much to say that the normal relation of States is war. Diplomacy is a disguised war, in which States seek to gain by barter and intrigue, by the cleverness of wits, the objectives which they would have to gain more clumsily by means of war. Diplomacy is used while the States are recuperating from conflicts in which they have exhausted themselves. It is the wheedling and the bargaining of the worn-out bullies as they rise from the ground and slowly restore their strength to begin fighting again. If diplomacy had been a moral equivalent for war, a higher stage in human progress, an inestimable means of making words prevail instead of blows, militarism would have broken down and given place to it. But since it is a mere temporary substitute, a mere appearance of war's energy under another form, a surrogate effect is almost exactly proportioned to the armed force behind it. When it fails, the recourse is immediate to the military technique whose thinly veiled arm it has been. A diplomacy that was the agency of popular democratic forces in their non-State manifestations would be no diplomacy at all. It would be no better than the Railway or Education commissions that are sent from one country to another with rational constructive purpose. The State, acting as a diplomatic-military ideal, is eternally at war. Just as it must act arbitrarily and autocratically in time of war, it must act in time of peace in this particular role where it acts as a unit. Unified control is necessarily autocratic control. Democratic control of foreign policy is therefore a contradiction in terms. Open discussion destroys swiftness and certainty of action. The giant State is paralyzed. Mr. Wilson retains his full ideal of the State at the same time that he desires to eliminate war. He wishes to make the world safe for democracy as well as safe for diplomacy. When the two are in conflict, his clear political insight, his idealism of the State, tells him that it is the naïve democratic values that must be sacrificed. The world must primarily be made safe for diplomacy. The State must not be diminished.

What is the State essentially? The more closely we examine it, the more mystical and personal it becomes. On the Nation we can put our hand as a definite social group, with attitudes and qualities exact enough to mean something. On the Government we can put our hand as a certain organization of ruling functions, the machinery of lawmaking and law-enforcing. The Administration is a recognizable group of political functionaries, temporarily in charge of the government. But the State stands as an idea behind them all, eternal, sanctified, and from it Government and Administration conceive themselves to have the breath of life. Even the nation, especially in times of war—or at least, its significant classes—considers that it derives its authority and its purpose from the idea of the State. Nation and State are scarcely differentiated, and the concrete, practical, apparent facts are sunk in the symbol. We reverence not our country but the flag. We may criticize ever so severely our country, but we are disrespectful to the flag at our peril. It is the flag and the uniform that make men's heart beat high and fill them with noble emotions, not the thought of and pious hopes for America as a free and enlightened nation.

It cannot be said that the object of emotion is the same, because the flag is the symbol of the nation, so that in reverencing the American flag we are reverencing the nation. For the flag is not a symbol of the country as a cultural group, following certain ideals of life, but solely a symbol of the political State, inseparable from its prestige and expansion. The flag is most intimately connected with military achievement, military memory. It represents the country not in it intensive life, but in its far-flung challenge to the world. The flag is primarily the banner of war; it is allied with patriotic anthem and holiday. It recalls old martial memories. A nation's patriotic history is solely the history of its wars, that is, of the State in its health and glorious functioning. So in responding to the appeal of the flag, we are responding to the appeal of the State, to the symbol of the herd organized as an offensive and defensive body, conscious of its prowess and its mystical herd strength.

Even those authorities in the present Administration, to whom has been granted autocratic control over opinion, feel, though they are scarcely able to philosophize over, this distinction. It has been authoritatively declared that the horrid penalties against seditious opinion must not be construed as inhibiting legitimate, that is, partisan criticism of the Administration. A distinction is made between the Administration and the Government. It is quite accurately suggested by this attitude that the Administration is a temporary band of partisan politicians in charge of the machinery of Government, carrying out the mystical policies of State. The manner in which they operate this machinery may be freely discussed and objected to by their political opponents. The Governmental machinery may also be legitimately altered, in case of necessity. What may not be discussed or criticized is the mystical policy itself or the motives of the State in inaugurating such a policy. The President, it is true, has made certain partisan distinctions between candidates for office on the ground of support or nonsupport of the Administration, but what he means was really support or nonsupport of the State policy as faithfully carried out by the Administration. Certain of the Administration measures were devised directly to increase the health of the State, such as the Conscription and the Espionage laws. Others were concerned merely with the machinery. To oppose the first was to oppose the State and was therefore not tolerable. To oppose the second was to oppose fallible human judgment, and was therefore, though to be depreciated, not to be wholly interpreted as political suicide.

The distinction between Government and State, however, has not been so carefully observed. In time of war it is natural that Government as the seat of authority should be confused with the State or the mystic source of authority. You cannot very well injure a mystical idea which is the State, but you can very well interfere with the processes of Government. So that the two become identified in the public mind, and any contempt for or opposition to the workings of the machinery of Government is considered equivalent to contempt for the sacred State. The State, it is felt, is being injured in its faithful surrogate, and public emotion rallies passionately to defend it. It even makes any criticism of the form of Government a crime.

The inextricable union of militarism and the State is beautifully shown by those laws which emphasize interference with the Army and Navy as the most culpable of seditious crimes. Pragmatically, a case of capitalistic sabotage, or a strike in war industry would seem to be far more dangerous to the successful prosecution of the war than the isolated and ineffectual efforts of an individual to prevent recruiting. But in the tradition of the State ideal, such industrial interference with national policy is not identified as a crime against the State. It may be grumbled against; it may be seen quite rationally as an impediment of the utmost gravity. But it is not felt in those obscure seats of the herd mind which dictate the identity of crime and fix their proportional punishments. Army and Navy, however, are the very arms of the State; in them flows its most precious lifeblood. To paralyze them is to touch the very State itself. And the majesty of the State is so sacred that even to attempt such a paralysis is a crime equal to a successful strike. The will is deemed sufficient. Even though the individual in his effort to impede recruiting should utterly and lamentably fail, he shall be in no wise spared. Let the wrath of the State descend upon him for his impiety! Even if he does not try any overt action, but merely utters sentiments that may incidentally in the most indirect way cause someone to refrain from enlisting, he is guilty. The guardians of the State do not ask whether any pragmatic effect flowed out of this evil will or desire. It is enough that the will is present. Fifteen or twenty years in prison is not deemed too much for such sacrilege.

Such attitudes and such laws, which affront every principle of human reason, are no accident, nor are they the result of hysteria caused by the war. They are considered just, proper, beautiful by all the classes which have the State ideal, and they express only an extreme of health and vigor in the reaction of the State to its nonfriends.

Such attitudes are inevitable as arising from the devotees of the State. For the State is a personal as well as a mystical symbol, and it can only be understood by tracing its historical origin. The modern State is not the rational and intelligent product of modern men desiring to live harmoniously together with security of life, property, and opinion. It is not an organization which has been devised as pragmatic means to a desired social end. All the idealism with which we have been instructed to endow the State is the fruit of our retrospective imaginations. What it does for us in the way of security and benefit of life, it does incidentally as a by-product and development of its original functions, and not because at any time men or classes in the full possession of their insight and intelligence have desired that it be so. It is very important that we should occasionally lift the incorrigible veil of that *ex post facto* idealism by which we throw a glamor of rationalization over what is, and pretend in the ecstasies of social conceit that we have personally invented and set up for the glory of God and man the hoary institutions which we see around us. Things are what they are, and come down to us with all their thick encrustations of error and malevolence. Political philosophy can delight us with fantasy and convince us who need illusion to live that the actual is a fair and approximate copy—full of failings, of course, but approximately sound and sincere— of that ideal society which we can imagine ourselves as creating. From this it is a step to the tacit assumption that we have somehow had a hand in its creation and are responsible for its maintenance and sanctity.

Nothing is more obvious, however, than that every one of us comes into society as into something in whose creation we had not the slightest hand. We have not even the advantage, like those little unborn souls in *The Blue Bird*, of consciousness before we take up our careers on earth. By the time we find ourselves here we are caught in a network of customs and attitudes, the major directions of our desires and interests have been stamped on our minds, and by the time we have emerged from tutelage and reached the years of discretion when we might conceivably throw our influence to the reshaping of social institutions, most of us have been so molded into the society and class we live in that we are scarcely aware of any distinction between ourselves as judging, desiring individuals and our social environment. We have been kneaded so successfully that we approve of what our society approves, desire what our society desires, and add to the group our own passionate inertia against change, against the effort of reason, and the adventure of beauty.

Every one of us, without exception, is born into a society that is given, just as the fauna and flora of our environment are given. Society and its institutions are, to the individual who enters it, as much naturalistic phenomena as is the weather itself. There is, therefore, no natural sanctity in the State any more than there is in the weather. We may bow down before it, just as our ancestors bowed before the sun and moon, but it is only because something in us unregenerate finds satisfaction in such an attitude, not because there is anything inherently reverential in the institution worshiped. Once the State has begun to function, and a large class finds its interest and its expression of power in maintaining the State, this ruling class may compel obedience from any uninterested minority. The State thus becomes an instrument by which the power of the whole herd is wielded for the benefit of a class. The rulers soon learn to capitalize the reverence which the State produces in the majority, and turn it into a general resistance toward a lessening of their privileges. The sanctity of the State becomes identified with the sanctity of the ruling class, and the latter are permitted to remain in power under the impression that in obeying and serving them, we are obeying and serving society, the nation, the great collectivity of all of us.

Chapter 50

Fernando R. Tesón

THE LIBERAL CASE FOR HUMANITARIAN INTERVENTION

Fernando Tesón (1950–   ) is a professor of law at Florida State University who has written widely on the philosophy of law and international justice. In this essay, he defends humanitarian intervention on the grounds that the major purpose of states is to protect and secure human rights. Governments that seriously violate those rights cannot call upon the international order for protection, and states that opt to protect the citizens of these unjust states are not acting wrongly, at least when their interventions meet certain conditions.

Introduction

In this chapter I argue that humanitarian intervention is morally justified in appropriate cases. The argument centrally rests on a standard assumption of liberal political philosophy: a major purpose of states and governments is to protect and secure human rights, that is, rights that all persons have by virtue of personhood alone. Governments and others in power who seriously violate those rights undermine the one reason that justifies their political power, and thus should not be protected by international law. A corollary of the argument is that, to the extent that state sovereignty is a value, it is an instrumental, not an intrinsic, value. Sovereignty serves valuable human ends, and those who grossly assault them should not be allowed to shield themselves behind the sovereignty principle. Tyranny and anarchy cause the moral collapse of sovereignty.

I supplement this argument with further moral assumptions. The fact that persons are

right-holders has normative consequences for others. We all have (1) the obligation to *respect* those rights; (2) the obligation to *promote* such respect for all persons; (3) depending on the circumstances, the obligation to *rescue* victims of tyranny or anarchy, if we can do so at a reasonable cost to ourselves. The obligation in (3) analytically entails, under appropriate circumstances, the *right* to rescue such victims – the right of humanitarian intervention. Because human rights are rights held by individuals by virtue of their personhood, they are independent of history, culture, or national borders.

I define permissible humanitarian intervention as the *proportionate international use or threat of military force, undertaken in principle by a liberal government or alliance, aimed at ending tyranny or anarchy, welcomed by the victims, and consistent with the doctrine of double effect.*

I present the argument in the next section. In subsequent sections I consider and reject possible objections: the relativist objection; the argument that humanitarian intervention violates communal integrity or some similar moral status of national borders; the view that governments should refrain from intervening out of respect for international law; and the view that humanitarian intervention undermines global stability. A further section addresses the difficult question of the moral status of acts and omissions. I discuss the conceptual structure of the liberal argument and respond to the objection that humanitarian intervention is wrong because it causes the deaths of innocent persons. I also evaluate the moral status of the failure to intervene and conclude that, depending on the circumstances, it can be morally culpable. I then examine the internal legitimacy of humanitarian intervention. I conclude with a few critical reflections about the non-intervention doctrine.

The liberal argument for humanitarian intervention has two components. The first is the quite obvious judgment that the exercise of governmental tyranny and the behavior that typically takes place in situations of extreme anarchy are serious forms of injustice towards persons. The second is the judgment that, subject to important constraints, external intervention is (at least) morally permissible to end that injustice. I suggest below that the first part of the argument is uncontroversial. For the most part, critics of humanitarian intervention do not disagree with the judgment that the situations that (according to interventionists) call for intervention are morally abhorrent. The situations that trigger humanitarian intervention are acts such as crimes against humanity, serious war crimes, mass murder, genocide, widespread torture, and the Hobbesian state of nature (war of all against all) caused by the collapse of social order. Rather, the disagreement between supporters and opponents of humanitarian intervention concerns the second part of the argument: interventionists claim that foreigners may help stop the injustices; non-interventionists claim they may not. The related claims from political and moral philosophy that I make (that sovereignty is dependent on justice and that we have a right to assist victims of injustice) concern this second part of

the argument. If a situation is morally abhorrent (as non-interventionists, I expect, will concede) then neither the sanctity of national borders nor a general prohibition against war should by themselves preclude humanitarian intervention.

This discussion concerns *forcible* intervention to protect human rights. I address here the use and the threat of military force (what I have elsewhere called hard intervention) for humanitarian purposes. However, the justification for the international protection of human rights is best analyzed as part of a continuum of international behavior. Most of the reasons that justify humanitarian intervention are extensions of the general reasons that justify interference with agents in order to help victims of their unjust behavior. Interference and intervention in other societies to protect human rights are special cases of our duty to assist victims of injustice. However, many people disagree that humanitarian intervention is part of a continuum: they treat war as a special case of violence, as a unique case, and not simply as a more violent and destructive form of human behavior that can nonetheless be sometimes justified. They do not regard war as part of a continuum of state action; and do not agree with Clausewitz that war is the continuation of politics (*politik*) by other means. Intuitively, there is something particularly terrible, or awesome, about war. It is the ultimate form of human violence. That is why many people who are committed to human rights nonetheless oppose humanitarian intervention. To them, war is a crime, the most hideous form of destruction of human life, and so it cannot be right to support war, even for the benign purpose of saving people's lives. Good liberals should not support war in any of its forms.

I am, of course, in sympathy with that view. Who would not be? If there is an obvious proposition in international ethics, it has to be that war is a terrible thing. Yet the deeply ingrained view that war is always immoral regardless of cause is mistaken. Sometimes it is morally permissible to fight; occasionally, fighting is even mandatory. The uncritical opposition to all wars begs the question about the justification of violence generally. Proponents of humanitarian intervention simply argue that humanitarian intervention in some instances (rare ones, to be sure) is morally justified, while agreeing of course that war is generally a bad thing. But it is worth emphasizing here that critics of humanitarian intervention are not pacifists. They support the use of force in self-defense and (generally) in performance of actions duly authorized by the Security Council. So their hostility to humanitarian intervention cannot be grounded on a general rejection of war. Part of the task of this chapter is to examine those other reasons.

The Liberal Argument

As I indicated, the liberal case for humanitarian intervention relies on principles of political and moral philosophy. Political philosophy addresses the justification of political power, and hence the justification of the state. Most liberal accounts of the state rely on social contract theory of some kind to explain and justify the state. Here I follow a Kantian account of the state. States are justified as institutions created by ethical agents, that is, by autonomous persons. The liberal state centrally includes a constitution that defines the powers of governments in a manner consistent with respect for individual autonomy. This Kantian conception of the state is the liberal solution to the dilemmas of anarchy and tyranny. Anarchy and tyranny are the two extremes in a continuum of political coercion. Anarchy is the complete absence of social order, which inevitably leads to a Hobbesian war of all against all. The exigencies of survival compel persons in the state of nature to lead a brutal existence marked by massive assaults on human dignity. This is a case of too little government, as it were. At the other extreme, the perpetration of tyranny is not simply an obvious assault on the dignity of persons: it is a betrayal of the very purpose for which government exists. It is a case of abuse of

government – of too much government, as it were. Humanitarian intervention is one tool to help move the quantum of political freedom in the continuum of political coercion to the Kantian center of that continuum away, on the one hand, from the extreme lack of order (anarchy), and, on the other, from governmental suppression of individual freedom (tyranny). Anarchical conditions prevent persons, by reason of the total collapse of social order, from conducting meaningful life in common or pursuing individual plans of life. Tyrannical conditions (the misuse of social coercion) prevent the victims, by the overuse of state coercion, from pursuing their autonomous projects. If human beings are denied basic human rights and are, for that reason, deprived of their capacity to pursue their autonomous projects, then others have a prima facie duty to help them. The serious violation of fundamental civil and political rights generates obligations on others. Outsiders (foreign persons, governments, international organizations) have a duty not only to respect those rights themselves but also to help ensure that governments respect them. Like justified revolutions, interventions are sometimes needed to secure a modicum of individual autonomy and dignity. Persons trapped in such situations deserve to be rescued, and sometimes the rescue can only be accomplished by force. We have a general duty to assist persons in grave danger if we can do it at reasonable cost to ourselves. If this is true, we have, by definition, a right to do so. The right to intervene thus stems from a general duty to assist victims of grievous injustice. I do not think that the critic of humanitarian intervention necessarily disagrees with this in a general sense. Rather, his opposition to humanitarian intervention relies on the supposed moral significance of state sovereignty and national borders.

There has been considerable debate about whether or not the concept of a legitimate state requires a thick liberal account. David Copp and John Rawls, among others, have argued that it does not. They claim, in only slightly different ways, that legitimacy is unrelated to the duty of obedience, and that liberals generally must respect non-liberal states that fulfill some minimal functions. They want to say that there is a layer of legitimacy (presumably banning foreign intervention) stemming from the fact that the government in question fulfills those functions. This is true even if the government does not fare well under liberal principles and thus cannot legitimately command the citizens' allegiance.

That discussion, important as it is for other purposes, is largely irrelevant to the present question. The argument in this chapter is concerned with the conditions for the legitimacy of forcible humanitarian intervention, not with the related but distinct question of which states and governments are members in good standing of the international community. These authors seem at times to conflate these two issues. The collapse of state legitimacy is a necessary but not a sufficient condition of humanitarian intervention. The issue of the justification of humanitarian intervention, therefore, is narrower than the general issue of how liberal governments should treat non-liberal regimes. It is perfectly possible to say (*contra* Rawls and Copp) that a non-liberal government should *not* be treated as a member in good standing of the international community while acknowledging (with Rawls and Copp) that it would be wrong to intervene in those states to force liberal reforms. The situations that qualify for forcible intervention are best described as "beyond the pale" situations. Only outlaw regimes (to use Rawls's terminology) are morally vulnerable to humanitarian intervention. Because I differ with these writers on the question of legitimacy of non-liberal (but not "beyond the pale") regimes, I believe that *non-forcible* interference to increase human rights observance in those societies is morally justified – a view they reject. All regimes that are morally vulnerable to humanitarian intervention are of course illegitimate, but the reverse is not true. For many reasons, it may be wrong to intervene by force in many regimes that are

objectionable from a liberal standpoint. Humanitarian intervention is reserved for the more serious cases – those that I have defined as tyranny and anarchy. Again, the illegitimacy of the government is a necessary, not a sufficient, condition for the permissibility of humanitarian intervention.

But if this is correct, it does require amending my original argument. It is no longer possible to ground the legitimacy of humanitarian intervention *solely* on the question of the moral legitimacy of the regime, because there are many cases where the collapse of political legitimacy will not be enough to justify intervention. Still, there are several consequences to the finding of illegitimacy. First, intervention against legitimate regimes is always banned. Second, it may well be that in a particular case it would be wrong to intervene, but the reason will never be the need to respect the *sovereignty* of the target state. Third, the liberal conception of state legitimacy will guide the correct behavior by the intervenor. He must abide by the general duty to promote, create, or restore institutions and practices under which the dignity of persons will be preserved.

I indicated that critics of humanitarian intervention are not pacifists. They object to this kind of war, a war to protect human rights. They do not object to wars, say, in defense of territory. This position is somewhat anomalous because it requires separate justifications for different kinds of wars. In contrast, the liberal argument offers a unified justification of war. War is justified if, and only if, it is in defense of persons and complies with the requirements of proportionality and the doctrine of double effect. Take the use of force in self-defense. What can possibly be its moral justification? Very plausibly, this: that the aggressor is assaulting the rights of persons in the state that is attacked. The government of the attacked state, then, has a right to muster the resources of the state to defend its citizens' lives and property against the aggressor. The defense of states is justified *qua* defense of persons. There is no defense of the *state* as such that is not parasitic on the rights and interests of individuals. If this is correct, any moral distinction between self-defense and humanitarian intervention, that is, any judgment that self-defense is justified while humanitarian intervention is not, has to rely on something above and beyond the general rationale of defense of persons.

The Relativist Objection

Some object to the very project of using liberal political theory to address humanitarian intervention – or indeed any international question. The argument goes something like this. The world is ideologically and culturally too diverse to apply any one philosophy to a problem that concerns all persons in the globe. Because many people reject liberal principles, attempts to use liberal philosophy are unduly biased. One would have to draw on different ethical traditions in order to analyze international problems. The outcome of liberal analysis might be good for someone who already accepts liberal principles, but not for those who do not. In other words, it might be necessary to do some comparative ethics before addressing these problems in order to identify which, if any, is the content of a global "overlapping consensus."

I have a general answer and a specific answer to this criticism of the liberal case for humanitarian intervention. I have never been able to see merit in relativism as a general philosophical view. If, say, our philosophical judgment that all persons have rights is sound, then it is universally sound. It does not really matter if the *historical origin* of that judgment is Western or something else. Those who object to liberal principles on the grounds that they are Western commit the genetic fallacy. They confuse the problem of the *origin* of a political theory with the problem of its *justification*. The truth (moral or empirical) of a proposition is logically independent of its origin. The liberal can concede that the views he defends are Western, and still maintain that they are the better views.

Another way of putting this is that the effort to find a justification for the exercise of political power is not an effort to *describe* the way Westerners think. Philosophical analysis is critical and normative, not descriptive. Of course, liberal views may be right or wrong, but they cannot possibly be right for some and wrong for others. Conversely, if *illiberal* views of politics are correct, then that has to be shown by rational argument, not by merely recognizing that some people, or other people, or many people, believe in them. To be sure, any philosophical justification of political power relies on assumptions, and critics may challenge the liberal justification of political power by challenging the assumptions. But that, of course, is philosophical argument. Perhaps the illiberal assumptions are as plausible as the liberal ones, but that will not be because, say, many people in illiberal societies believe in them. If many persons endorse liberal assumptions and many other people endorse inconsistent illiberal assumptions, both sides cannot be right. Liberal analysis must assume that liberal assumptions (such as the importance of individual autonomy) are the better ones, universally. The liberal conception I defend is thus cosmopolitan, and as such rejects attempts at locating political morality in overlapping consensus, or other forms of majority validation. It rejects arguments *ad populum*.

Second, that objection does not seem to reach the first part of the argument: that the situations that warrant intervention – tyranny and anarchy – are morally abhorrent forms of political injustice. I believe that all reasonable religious and ethical theories converge in the judgment that those situations (mass murder, widespread torture, crimes against humanity, serious war crimes) are morally abhorrent. We are not dealing here with differences in conceptions of the good, or with various ways to realize human and collective excellence, or with the place of religion, civic deliberation, or free markets in political life. We are confronting governments that perpetrate atrocities against people, and situations of anarchy and breakdown of social order of such magnitude that no reasonable ethical or political theory could reasonably condone them. And, of course, if there are political theories that condone those situations, too bad for them: they cease to be reasonable or plausible. I do not believe, however, that the critic of humanitarian intervention wants to rely on a moral theory that justifies grievous human rights violations. I hope that I do not need deep studies in comparative ethics and religion to say that under any religious or ethical system the kind of situation that warrants humanitarian intervention is morally intolerable. For example, I doubt that someone who endorses religious or political doctrines that advance communal values and reject liberal reliancè on individual autonomy will treat the extreme examples of tyranny or anarchy that warrant humanitarian intervention as morally tolerable or justified.

On the other hand, the *second* part of the argument requires a reliance on conceptions about the justification of states, governments, and borders. As indicated above, I want to say that certain situations are morally abhorrent under any plausible ethical theory, *and* that those situations sometimes justify humanitarian intervention under a liberal conception of politics. Someone may agree with the first proposition but not with the second. He might agree that the situations are morally abhorrent but maintain that humanitarian intervention is still not justified: it is not for foreigners to remedy those wrongs. These other theories might hold particular views about the sanctity of borders, or about the moral centrality of communities, or about the moral relevance of distinctions between nationals and foreigners. Here again, all I can do is offer arguments to reject those views in favor of a more cosmopolitan approach. My point is rather this: to the objection that supporting humanitarian intervention presupposes a (biased) liberal commitment to human rights, the liberal can respond, "But surely you're not saying that under your (non-liberal) view these atrocities are justified.

Whatever it is that you value, it cannot be this." The non-liberal critic can then make the following move: "I agree that this is morally abhorrent under my non-liberal principles as well, but those same principles, unlike yours, bar foreign interventions." Thus, noninterventionist views of international ethics attempt to *sever* (unconvincingly, I contend) domestic from international legitimacy. But if the non-liberal agrees that the situation is abhorrent, then the liberal interventionist cannot be biased because he thinks just that. The non-liberal needs reasons beyond his skepticism about rights and autonomy in order to question the legitimacy of humanitarian intervention in cases where he would agree with the liberal that the situation is morally abhorrent. He needs a theory of sovereignty under which foreigners are morally precluded from saving victims of extreme injustice.

The Moral Relevance of National Borders: Communal Integrity

If the non-interventionist accepts that tyranny and anarchy are morally abhorrent, he might resort to theses of international ethics that place decisive value on sovereignty and national borders. Consider the following case. The provincial government in a federal state is committing atrocities against an ethnic group. Moreover, the provincial army is prepared to resist the federal army, so that a civil war will take place if the federal government tries to stop the massacre. Non-interventionists (like everyone else) will no doubt regret that a civil war will erupt, but surely will not object in principle to the *internal* intervention by federal troops aimed at stopping the massacre. In fact, they will likely praise the intervention.

Yet they will object if those same troops cross an *international* border to stop similar atrocities committed by a sovereign government in a neighboring state. For them, national borders mysteriously operate a *change in the description of the* act of humanitarian rescue: it is no longer humanitarian rescue, but war. (Why aren't massive human rights violations also called war, for example a war of the government against its people? Is it because usually part of the population is an accomplice in the perpetration?) The argument for this distinction has to rely on the moral significance of national borders as a corollary of the principle of sovereignty. But national borders can hardly have moral significance *in this context*. For one thing, national borders are the serendipitous result of past violence and other kinds of morally objectionable or irrelevant historical facts. More generally, a great deal of suffering and injustice in the world derives from the exaggerated importance that people assign to national borders. From ethnic cleansing to discrimination against immigrants, from prohibitions to speak foreign languages to trade protections that only benefit special interests, the ideas of nation, state, and borders have been consistently used to justify all kinds of harm to persons.

In spite of all that, there are surely reasons for respecting national borders, at least as long as one believes that a world of separate states is a desirable thing. Those reasons are, in my view, two, and neither invalidates humanitarian intervention in appropriate cases. The first and most important has to do with the legitimacy of the social contract, as it were. Kant famously wrote, "No state having an independent existence, whether it be small or great, may be acquired by another state through inheritance, exchange, purchase, or gift." The idea here is that a state that is somehow the result of the free consent by autonomous individuals in civil society must be respected. Violating those borders would amount, then, to treating the state and its citizens "as things." This is the liberal premise defended here, that the sovereignty of the state and the inviolability of its borders are parasitic on the legitimacy of the social contract, and thus sovereignty and borders, too, serve the liberal ends of respecting freedom and human rights. Where half the population of the state is

murdering the other half, or where the government is committing massive atrocities against its own citizens, national borders have lost most of their moral strength. At the very least, they are morally impotent to contain foreign acts aimed at stopping the massacres.

Michael Walzer offers the best-known defense of the moral aptitude of national borders to ban humanitarian intervention. According to Walzer, there is a crucial distinction between domestic and international legitimacy. A government may be illegitimate internally, but that does not mean that foreign armies are entitled to intervene to restore legitimacy. Walzer claims that in most cases there is enough "fit" between people and government to make injustice a purely domestic matter from which foreigners are excluded. Only the citizens themselves may overthrow their tyrant. It is only when the lack of fit is *radically* apparent, says Walzer, that intervention can be allowed. That will only occur in cases of genocide, enslavement, or mass deportation. He supports this thesis by communal considerations: nations have histories and loyalties that define their political process, and that process should be protected as such, even if some of its outcomes are repulsive to liberal philosophers. Walzer calls this "communal integrity."

As a preliminary matter, Walzer (unlike other non-interventionists) allows humanitarian intervention in important classes of cases. Yet his rationale for not allowing humanitarian intervention in other cases of tyranny and anarchy is, I believe, deeply wrong. By pointing out that dictators come from the society itself, from its families and neighborhoods, Walzer insinuates that tyranny and anarchy come naturally, as it were; that in some sense the victims are responsible for the horrors they suffer. It also presupposes that there is something morally valuable ("self-determination") in the fortuitous balance of existing political forces in a society. But political processes are not valuable per se. Their value depends on their being minimally consistent with the imperative to respect persons.

It is even grotesque to describe the kinds of cases that warrant humanitarian intervention as "processes of self-determination" and suggest, as Walzer does, that unless there is genocide, there is a necessary fit between government and people. David Luban put it best: "The government fits the people the way the sole of a boot fits a human face: After a while the patterns of indentation fit with uncanny precision."

Having said that, there is a kernel of truth in a possible reading of Walzer's argument, best put by John Stuart Mill. Mill argued that humanitarian intervention is always wrong because freedom has no value unless the victims themselves fight for their liberation. People cannot really be free if foreigners do the fighting for them. While this argument is problematic (why isn't freedom valuable if someone else helps us achieve it?), it does make an important point. Citizens of the state ruled by a tyrant (or victimized by warlords in a failed state) have a responsibility to help put an end to their plight. The intervenor has a right to expect their reasonable cooperation in putting an end to tyranny, in shouldering the moral and material costs of intervention, and in building democratic institutions. It is their government, their society. Foreign efforts to help them depend on their cooperation and willingness to build or restore those institutions.

One corollary of Mill's point is the requirement that the victims of tyranny or anarchy welcome the intervention. Walzer and other critics of humanitarian intervention say that in most cases the victims do not really want to be liberated by foreigners, that they would rather put up with their tyrants than see their homeland invaded. This is a view influenced by communitarianism. Communitarians contend that persons not only have liberty interests: they also, and more importantly, have communal interests, those that define their membership in a group or community – their social identity. Indeed, for communitarians, liberty interests are parasitic on communal interests or values. On this view, the average citizen in any country (including those

ruled by tyrannical regimes) will be wounded in his self-respect if foreigners intervene, even if it is for a good purpose, because such intervention strikes at the heart of his social identity. The corollary seems to be that the average citizen in an oppressive regime *prefers* to remain oppressed than to be freed by foreigners.

I believe that while this situation is empirically possible, it is highly unlikely to occur. For one thing, there is no valid community interest of the citizen who *collaborates* with the abusers. In a society afflicted by tyranny there is a group (sometimes the minority, sometimes the majority) that benefits from the government's persecution of others. These are the rent-seekers of the worst kind, those who capture the machine of horror for their own purposes. To describe this as "community interest" is grotesque. It is also wrong to presume that victims oppose liberating intervention. I would think that the evidence supports the opposite presumption: that victims of serious oppression will welcome rather than oppose outside help. This was seemingly the case in the interventions in Grenada, Iraq, Rwanda, Haiti, and Kosovo, among others.

The only persons whose consent deserves consideration are those who oppose both the regime *and* foreign intervention for moral reasons. They might say that the regime is murderous but that foreign invasion of their homeland is unacceptable, even if undertaken for the purpose of ending the ongoing killings. Should their refusal be decisive? Should prospective intervenors treat the veto by political and civic leaders who oppose the regime as a decisive reason for not intervening? I do not think so, for the following reason: I very much doubt that you can cite *your* communal interests validly to oppose aid to *me*, when I am strapped to the torture chamber, even if you are not complicitous. Only I (the torture victim) can waive my right to seek aid; only my consent counts for that purpose. So, to summarize: in a tyrannical regime the population can be divided into the following groups: the victims; the accomplices and collaborators; and the bystanders. The last group can in turn be subdivided into those who support the regime and those who oppose it. Of these groups, only the first, the victims, have (arguably) a right to refuse aid. The accomplices and bystanders who support the regime are excluded for obvious reasons. Their opposition to intervention does not count. And the bystanders who oppose the regime cannot validly refuse foreign aid on behalf of the victims.

Democratic leaders must make sure before intervening that they have the support of the very persons they want to assist, the victims. Yet the view (suggested by Walzer) that a *majority* of the population must support the intervention is wrong, because the majority may be complicitous in the human rights violations. Suppose the government of a multi-ethnic state tries to exterminate a minority ethnic group. Let us further assume that a history of ethnic animosity leads the majority group to support the genocide. Humanitarian intervention is justified even if the majority of the population of the state opposes it. An intervenor must abide by the duty to restore the rights of persons threatened by tyranny or anarchy. Whether or not these goals will be advanced cannot be decided by simply taking opinion polls in the population of the tyrannical or anarchical society.

Another reason to respect national borders is that they may help secure the stability of social interaction, that is, the mutual expectations of individuals who interact within and across demarcations of political jurisdictions. The reasons for having national borders, then, are analogous to the reasons for respecting the demarcations of property rights. Property owners should be allowed to exclude trespassers because that facilitates the internalization of externalities and thus maximizes the efficiency in the use of resources. Similarly, it might be argued that states must be allowed to exclude

foreign "trespassers" who attempt to free ride on the cooperative efforts of the citizens of the state. Giving the state exclusive jurisdiction over its territory maximizes global gains, just as giving farmers exclusive property rights over their land maximizes aggregate wealth. These efficiency considerations become particularly relevant in the aftermath of the intervention. Successful intervenors, unlike internal victors, have little incentive to treat the target country as something that is theirs – they lack long-term property rights over the territory. Likewise, internal victors (such as the current ruling group in Afghanistan) in an intervention have a greater incentive to restore the political fabric of their society than do external victors. These reasons point to the need to assign *some* instrumental importance to national borders and counsel prudence on the part of the intervenor. Consequentialist considerations are also crucial for planning the post-intervention stage in order to achieve lasting success in terms of the moral values that justified the intervention.

However, these considerations do not exclude the legitimacy of humanitarian intervention, because the kinds of situations that warrant intervention are of such gravity that they cannot possibly be trumped by the pragmatic considerations just discussed. The protection of national borders is necessary, under this argument, to preserve the glue that binds international society, and as such re-emerges in the post-intervention phase. Yet allowing the atrocities to continue is a much worse dissolver of that glue than the infringement of borders.

I conclude, then, that the right of humanitarian intervention in appropriate cases is unaffected by the existence of national borders. The latter owe their importance to considerations of justice and efficiency. Where these values are grossly assaulted by tyranny and anarchy, invoking the sanctity of borders to protect tyranny and anarchy is, on reflection, self-defeating.

The Argument From International Law

This chapter is mostly concerned with the moral–political defense of humanitarian intervention. However, I want to consider a popular argument against humanitarian intervention frequently offered by international lawyers. Humanitarian intervention is objectionable, they claim, because states have an obligation to abide by international law. Governments who intervene by force violate a central tenet of the international legal system. This argument, of course, locates the obligation to obey the law outside international law itself: there is a moral reason to comply with international law even where doing so leads sometimes to undesirable or even immoral outcomes.

This argument is fatally flawed. First, it rests on a highly dubious premise. The view that international law (conceived as anchored in the practice of states) prohibits humanitarian intervention depends upon a reading of state practice informed by state-oriented values. Critics of humanitarian intervention have complained that supporters of the doctrine engage in a subjective, value-oriented analysis of custom and treaty. On their view, objective analysis yields instead an unequivocal verdict against humanitarian intervention. Again, this is not the place for legal debates, but I will say this much: state practice is at the very least ambivalent on the question of humanitarian intervention, so any interpretation of that practice (for or against) has to rely on extra-legal values. There is no such thing as a "state practice" that mechanically yields a legal rule. Diplomatic history has to be interpreted in the light of our moral and empirical assumptions about the purposes of international law. If this is correct, the positivist rejection of humanitarian intervention is far from objective, notwithstanding the claims of international lawyers to the contrary. It is informed by a set of values that privileges the preservation of governments and political regimes over the protection of human rights. The contrast is not between "subjective" interventionist legal analysis and "objective" non-interventionist legal analysis, but between international lawyers who uphold human values and international lawyers who uphold state values. Non-interventionists delude themselves when they accuse interventionists of bias. They have their own bias. Part of their problem is their mistaken belief that legal analysis is conceptually autonomous and that political philosophy and other forms of normative analysis have no place in legal reasoning. In reality, what many international lawyers do is smuggle their statist bias under the guise of autonomous legal analysis. The critic of humanitarian intervention will fare much better if he deals with the applicable moral arguments for and against humanitarian intervention rather than hiding behind the supposed conceptual autonomy of legal reasoning.

There is another answer to this objection. No one disputes that international law prohibits the use of force generally. Yet the kinds of cases that warrant humanitarian intervention disclose *other* serious violations of international law: genocide, crimes against humanity, and so on. The typical situation where we consider intervening is not one where we are contemplating violating international law as opposed to not violating international law. These are cases where whatever we do we will end up tolerating a violation of *some* fundamental rule of international law. Either we intervene and put an end to the massacres, in which case we apparently violate the general prohibition of war, or we abstain from intervening, in which case we tolerate the violation by other states of the general prohibition of gross human rights abuses. The maxim "other things being equal, states must obey international law" can hardly mean "other things being equal, states must obey international law even if doing so allows an ongoing, equally egregious violation of international law." The obligation to abide by international law, then, does not help the non-interventionist. His position now depends either on a dubious judgment that an international war is always worse than tyranny or anarchy, or on an equally dubious distinction between acts and omissions.

The decisive reason for solving this conflict of principles in favor of allowing humanitarian intervention in appropriate cases stems from the realization that the value of sovereignty is problematic unless it is understood as an *instrumental* good, that is, as a means to other more fundamental ends. The gross violation of human rights is not only an obvious assault on the dignity of persons, *but a betrayal of the principle of sovereignty itself*. The non-interventionist faces a dilemma here. Either he believes that state sovereignty is intrinsically valuable, or he concedes that sovereignty is instrumental to the realization of other human values. If the former, he has to say that the prohibition of intervention has nothing to do with respecting persons, in which case he is forced to invoke unappealing (and wholly discredited) organicist conceptions of the state. If the latter, he has to demonstrate that the human values served by sovereignty in the long term justify allowing the massacres to continue now – a daunting task.

Readers unpersuaded by my jurisprudential stance will still claim that law and morality are separate and that a positivist reading of international law prohibits humanitarian intervention. Even so, this chapter may be of some use to them: they may take the argument here as a *de lege ferenda* proposal, that is, a proposal for reforming international law. Someone who thinks that a positivist reading of international law prohibits humanitarian intervention yet also thinks the moral argument in this chapter is correct must conclude that international law is morally objectionable and should join in the effort to reform it.

A sovereign state is an institution created by men and women to protect themselves against injustice, and to facilitate mutually beneficial social co-operation. The non-interventionist cannot locate his priority of sovereignty in anything that is *internal* to the target state in these kinds of cases. Therefore, the argument against humanitarian intervention must rely on the importance of sovereignty for ends that are *external* to the target state. To these arguments I now turn.

The Objection From Global Stability

One important objection to humanitarian intervention relies on the need to preserve world order. The idea here is not that there is anything morally important *internally* about the sovereignty of the state. What is important instead is to preserve the stability of the *system of states* in the long run. Humanitarian intervention undermines that stability both by the very act of intervening, and by creating a dangerous precedent that lends itself to abuse by aggressive states. The use of the doctrine of humanitarian intervention rationale by even well-intentioned governments will contribute to generalized chaos, and an unjust order is preferable to chaos. Injustices should be remedied in ways that do not undermine the stability of the state system, that is, by "peaceful" means. The avoidance of conflict is a prerequisite for world order.

This objection to humanitarian intervention is unconvincing. First, it is open to an important moral rejoinder. Assuming for the sake of argument that the state system is worth preserving, it is highly problematic to use the victims of tyranny and anarchy for that purpose. The non-interventionist argument has a decidedly theological flavor. It is analogous to the response of the religious believer to the complaint that God allows things like the Holocaust to happen. The believer claims that God allows the Holocaust because He has a higher purpose that we, as finite beings, cannot possibly grasp. Similarly, the non-interventionist claims that there is a higher global purpose that justifies not interfering with tyranny and anarchy. In this case, however, that higher purpose is not inscrutable: we are told it is the preservation of the state system. I am unconvinced by the believer's response (what higher end can an omnipotent Being possibly have to allow the Holocaust?) Yet while I am willing to give God the benefit of the doubt, that benefit does not extend to academics. The claim seems to me morally unappealing, because whatever the merits of the state system, its preservation cannot surely be achieved at that kind of human cost. It is not even clear that "the preservation of the state system" is much more than a euphemism for the arch-conservative view that incumbent governments and the status quo should be preserved regardless of their value to actual human beings.

The second answer to the argument is the same as I gave in the discussion of the relevance of national borders. Tyranny and anarchy are at least as likely to generate instability and chaos as interventions — perhaps even including in the calculation the harm caused by non-humanitarian interventions. The argument from the stability of world order ignores this crucial fact. The reason for this strange neglect is theoretical: statism treats states as the only relevant units in international relations and ignores what happens between states. This is the anthropomorphic view of the state that has caused so much harm to persons and confusion in international thinking. As long as there is "order" within states, the non-interventionist thinks that he can safely ignore what happens within them. I do not need to cite here the overwhelming evidence about the causal relation between internal upheaval and international instability. In the face of that evidence, one who is concerned with long-term stability should rationally support a general prohibition of aggressive war *and* a system for protection of human rights that includes a properly limited right of humanitarian intervention.

Finally, the empirical claim that a rule allowing humanitarian intervention will trigger unjustified interventions and will thus threaten world order is implausible. The claim can now be tested, because there have been a number of humanitarian interventions since 1990 or so.

The non-interventionist argument, as I understand it, is that allowing these humanitarian interventions will encourage governments and other international actors to over-intervene, often with spurious motives. Governments, it is argued, will find it easier to intervene for selfish motives because they can rely on precedent and offer self-serving humanitarian justifications. But this, quite simply, has not happened. It is true that the end of the Cold War has caused, alongside the spread of democracy and free markets, political instability in certain regions. Yet this had nothing to do with the occurrence of more humanitarian interventions, but rather with ethnic rivalries and similar factors. (Perhaps if we had had a clearly defined and institutionalized rule allowing humanitarian intervention we might have been able to prevent, through deterrence, some of the horrific things that happened in those ethnic conflicts.) I do not think it can be seriously claimed that the interventions in Somalia, Rwanda, Haiti, and Kosovo have shaken the world order beyond recognition. On the contrary, those interventions have improved things on the whole. And when interventions have failed, that merely means that tyranny and anarchy have continued unchecked. Failed humanitarian interventions have not made matters worse. There is an obvious reason why humanitarian interventions are unlikely to produce the chaos that non-interventionists fear: intervention is very costly, so governments have a considerable disincentive to undertake *any* intervention. Acting in Kosovo was very costly to NATO — if only in economic terms. In addition, the right of humanitarian intervention can be suitably designed to prevent escalation, perhaps allowing intervention when such risk is minimal. Furthermore, if the system of states breaks down because there are many humanitarian interventions (by definition prompted by tyranny and anarchy) perhaps this collapse is a desirable thing. Just as the surrender of sovereignty by individuals to states need not involve the elimination of their moral autonomy, so the surrender of sovereignty by states to an international *liberal* authority should not necessarily result in universal tyranny. The death of a state is never bad in itself (think of the demise of the Soviet Union or East Germany). Only the deaths of its citizens.

Acts, Omissions, and the Rights of the Innocent

Tyranny or anarchy is a necessary but not a sufficient condition of the legitimacy of humanitarian intervention. As in all moral matters, we have competing reasons of various kinds to guide behavior. It might well be that in a particular case humanitarian intervention in a state would be wrong notwithstanding the fact that the government of that state is itself guilty of serious human rights violations. Sometimes we cannot right the wrong even if it is justified for us to do so. Sometimes intervening is unacceptably costly to us, the intervenor. And sometimes righting a wrong entails harming persons in objectionable ways; that is, in ways and to an extent that would be at least as objectionable as the wrongs we are intending to remedy.

The moral dilemmas of intervention are not well captured by distinctions between deontological and consequentialist approaches to humanitarian intervention, for several reasons. First, philosophical defenses of humanitarian intervention will necessarily combine deontological and consequentialist elements. The liberal case for humanitarian intervention, for instance, contains both deontological elements (a principled commitment to human rights) and consequentialist ones (the requirement that interventions cause more good than harm). Second, military action, including humanitarian intervention, will almost always violate the rights of innocent persons, so under a strict deontological view the intervenor will presumably never be justified, even if his purpose is to protect human rights, and even if it is certain that such will be the result of the intervention. This is because the intervention will violate the rights of innocents. The objection, then, is that, even if successful, the humanitarian intervention would have used innocent persons as a means to an end – something prohibited by a strict deontological approach. There is an interesting paradox here: the liberal argument for humanitarian intervention is rights-based, and as such it has a strong deontological flavor, yet at the same time the liberal interventionist is countenancing the deaths of innocents in apparent violation of deontological constraints.

The reply to this objection is that the strict deontological approach is misguided here. If it were sound, no war or revolution would ever be justified, because the just warriors almost always would have to kill innocents. For example, under that view the Allies would have had no justification to respond to Germany's aggression in World War II, because such response would have resulted (as it did) in the deaths of many innocent persons (such as German children). The strict deontological approach leads to counterintuitive results – at least as far as international politics are concerned.

The liberal argument for humanitarian intervention has a somewhat different conceptual structure. Justified intervention aims to *maximize* human rights observance, but the intervenor is constrained by *the doctrine of double effect*. Thus, humanitarian intervention cannot be simply grounded in what Nozick has called "utilitarianism of rights," because this may conceivably allow the deliberate targeting of innocent persons if conducive to realizing the humanitarian objective. This is prohibited by the doctrine of double effect. According to this doctrine, an act in which innocents are killed is only legitimate when three conditions are satisfied:

1. The act has good consequences – such as the killing of enemy soldiers in a just war;
2. The actor's intentions are good, that is, he aims to achieve the good consequences. Any bad consequences – such as the killing

of non-combatants – are not intended; and

3. The act's good consequences – such as the killing of enemy soldiers – outweigh its bad consequences – such as the killing of non-combatants. This is called the doctrine of proportionality.

The doctrine of double effect thus distinguishes between actions with intended bad consequences and actions with unintended bad consequences. The former give rise to moral blameworthiness. The latter may, depending on the circumstances, be excused. Thus proportionate collateral harm caused by a humanitarian intervention, where the goal is to rescue victims of tyranny or anarchy, may, depending on the circumstances, be morally excusable. So on the one hand, humanitarian intervention is not an action conceptually structured, from the standpoint of the agent, as deontologically pure behavior where the agent (the intervenor) is absolutely constrained to respect the rights of everybody. It is instead an action intended to *maximize* universal respect for human rights but morally constrained by the prohibition of *deliberately* targeting innocent persons. The proportionate *collateral* deaths of innocent persons, while indirectly caused by the intervenor, do not necessarily condemn the intervention as immoral. The argument for humanitarian intervention is located midway between strict deontological approaches and consequentialist ones like utilitarianism. The latter directs agents to intervene whenever they maximize the good in terms of the general welfare (often conceived in terms of human lives). The former would forbid intervention that would result in violations of the rights of innocents – even intervention that will certainly maximize universal rights observance. Instead, humanitarian intervention understood as a morally constrained form of help to others accepts that sometimes causing harm to innocent persons is justified as long as one does not will such harm in order to achieve, not a greater

general welfare, but a goal that is normatively compelling under appropriate principles of morality. The doctrine rejects, as deontological doctrines do, undifferentiated calculations of costs and benefits where justice (as a goal of the intervention) would be just one indicator of good aggregate consequences among many others.

The goal of saving lives and restoring human rights and justice is compelling enough to authorize humanitarian intervention even at the cost of innocent lives. It is not simply that the intervenor is improving the world in a general sense. In typical cases, the intervenor is not just saving lives – although this goal is, indeed, normatively compelling. He is helping to restore justice and rights, the purpose of all justified political institutions – most prominently the state. The goal of restoring human rights and justice thus is more than simply helping people, although of course if it is achieved people will be helped. The goal of restoring minimally just institutions and practices is *normatively privileged* regardless of the advancement of the general welfare. For example, humanitarian *aid* is of course desirable, but it only temporarily relieves some of the symptoms of anarchy and tyranny. Building and restoring democratic, rights-respecting institutions, if successful, not only means doing the right thing for that society: it also addresses a central cause of the problem. In that sense the justification of humanitarian intervention is both deontological and utilitarian. That is why the loss of lives is not the only indicator of the legitimacy of humanitarian intervention.

This conceptual understanding of humanitarian intervention as an action aimed at maximizing respect for human rights yet constrained by the doctrine of double effect prompts the examination of two related issues. One is the permissibility of killing innocent persons in an (otherwise justified) humanitarian intervention. The other is the moral status of the *failure* to intervene. Interventionists have to explain why the (inevitable) deaths of innocents that occur in any humanitarian intervention are morally justified. After all, such persons do not voluntarily surrender their right to life. Therefore, knowingly causing their deaths is morally problematic, even for a benign purpose. Conversely, non-interventionists have to explain why the *failure* to intervene is justified in cases where a potential intervenor can prevent or end a massacre or similar event at reasonable cost. The two issues are related. As a preliminary matter, the critic of humanitarian intervention needs to say more than that he condemns violence generally. If his opposition to humanitarian intervention is part of his general condemnation of political violence, then presumably he must weigh the moral costs of allowing the massacres against the moral cost of intervening. The scale may tip for or against intervention, but a categorical non-interventionist position cannot be justified by a general abhorrence of violence, since the non-interventionist is taking a position that permits the perpetration of the atrocities. It is hard to see why opponents of humanitarian intervention rarely mention *that* violence while invoking their general condemnation of war. To the charge that failure to intervene may be morally culpable, the non-interventionist replies by making a moral distinction between acts and omissions. He claims that those who intervene will *cause* the bad results (deaths of innocents, destruction), whereas those who do not intervene *do not cause* the atrocities (the tyrant does). That position is part of a general view that killing is morally worse than letting die. The argument goes something like this. A government that fails to intervene to stop atrocities in another country (assuming it can do so at reasonable cost to itself) is simply *letting innocent people die*. If that government decides instead to intervene, it will *kill some innocent people* for sure. Because killing is morally worse than letting die, humanitarian intervention should therefore be prohibited.

The question of the moral status of actions and omissions has been extensively discussed in philosophy, but not to my knowledge in international relations or international law. Some of the conclusions that can be drawn from the philosophy literature are relevant here. It seems that it is justified *sometimes* to cause the deaths of some persons in order to save a greater number, even if one rejects a purely utilitarian approach. In other words, killing some to save others does not always amount to *using* the former to save the latter. It seems that we need to know *how* persons are killed and saved, as well as ascertain the nature of the relationship between the greater good and the lesser evil. One solution is along ideal consent lines: the action is justified if all of the persons involved in the event, that is, those who would be sacrificed and those who would be saved (not knowing whether or not they would have been one or the other), would have agreed in advance that the action would have been appropriate.

Now let us recast the problem in terms of humanitarian intervention. The government that intervenes knows that some innocent persons will (regrettably) die if it intervenes to save the many victims of tyranny or anarchy. Let us stipulate that the intervention will indirectly cause one-fifth of the innocent casualties that the tyrant will cause. I suggest that the case for the permissibility of humanitarian intervention is *more compelling* than the standard case for the permissibility of killing one person to save five. In the former, those who intervene to stop human rights abuses attempt to *remedy an injustice*. In the latter sort of cases there is no ongoing injustice. Rather, the problem is how to reconcile (1) our intuition that we cannot kill an innocent person in order to save five persons with (2) our intuition that sometimes we are justified in doing so, and (3) our further conviction that the explanation of (2) cannot simply be that it is always justified to kill some people to save more lives (as shown by compelling counterexamples). But in the humanitarian intervention situation, it is not simply a question of saving more than those who are killed by the intervention: as we saw, the intervenor attempts to restore human rights and justice. So if we think that it is sometimes permissible to allow the deaths of innocent persons in order to save others in case where the beneficiaries suffer no injustice, *a fortiori* it should be permissible to allow (regrettably) the deaths of innocent persons in cases where the agent is attempting to rescue persons from ongoing and serious acts of injustice. As I indicated above, in the typical humanitarian intervention case the situation to be redressed is *normatively qualified* as gross injustice; it is not merely a question of numbers. A crucial related requirement, of course, is that the intervenor avoid as much as possible collateral deaths and damage, and that, where those collateral deaths are unavoidable, the intervenor abide by the doctrine of double effect. Under these doctrines, the just warrior should never *intend* the deaths of innocents. He should centrally intend the restoration of human rights. If, in doing so, he collaterally causes the reasonably proportionate deaths of some innocent persons, the warrior can, depending on the circumstances, be excused for having done so.

Plausibly, humanitarian intervention meets the test of ideal consent as well. Citizens of a state would ideally agree that humanitarian intervention should be allowed for those extreme cases of injustice even at the cost of the deaths of some innocents, and even if some of those citizens will inevitably be those persons. The parties might agree to humanitarian intervention either by application of John Rawls's *maximin* principle or by a stronger assumption about the parties' public-spirited commitment to political justice and human rights, or by a combination of both. This test should not be confused with a similar test of hypothetical consent that we could employ to determine whether or not ideal *global* contractors would agree to an international legal *principle* allowing for humanitarian intervention. I believe the result of that mental experiment is positive as well. In summary, rational persons *within a state* will agree, I believe, to allow humanitarian intervention, not knowing what place they will have in that society. These parties know the state to which they belong. And rational *global* parties who *do not* know what state they belong to will likewise agree to a general rule allowing humanitarian intervention in appropriate cases. No rational person will agree to a blanket sovereignty principle banning intervention because they may end up trapped as victims of tyranny or anarchy.

What about the possible non-interventionist's claim that failure to intervene cannot be culpable? Even if correct, this would not be an argument against humanitarian intervention, but only in favor of the *permissibility of abstaining* from intervening. If the foregoing conclusions are correct, the supporter of humanitarian intervention has met the objection that intervention is wrong because it is a positive act that results in the deaths of innocents. At the very least, the foreigner who abides by the doctrine of double effect is not morally precluded from acting by the fact that his behavior may result in the deaths of innocent persons. He is morally permitted to act.

But more importantly, it is difficult to maintain a coherent and intuitively acceptable moral distinction between acts and omissions in many cases. The foreigner who refrains from intervening to stop atrocities may be negligent or culpable in some cases. Whatever the philosophical differences between acts and omissions, the agent who refuses to intervene is responsible for not having done things he could have done to stop the atrocities. Even if there is a valid distinction between act and omission, all that it proves is that the actor who refuses to intervene to stop atrocities is not as morally blameworthy as the perpetrator himself. But this fact does not exonerate this actor from the quite distinct charge of having failed to help others.

Consider the genocide committed in Srebrenica in July 1995. Bosnian Serb forces overran the Bosnian town before the eyes of 300 Dutch peacekeepers. The Bosnian Serb forces captured between 7,000 and 8,000 defenseless men and boys and killed almost all of them. The

International Criminal Tribunal for the Former Yugoslavia properly decided that this was genocide, and sentenced the field commander, Radislav Krstic, to forty-six years in prison. This is considered one of the worst atrocities committed in any European conflict since World War II. The shock we felt in the face of such evil has perhaps obscured another shocking fact. The area was supposed to be a protected United Nations enclave. However, General Bernard Janvier of France, the overall United Nations commander for Bosnia at the time, ignored repeated warnings by the peacekeepers and vetoed, until the very last minute, NATO air strikes requested by them. He could have saved those 7,000 victims, but chose not to act. Now let us assume that General Janvier is an educated officer of the French Army. Very likely he took international law classes as part of his instruction. If so, very likely he was told that humanitarian intervention is prohibited by international law, by the same people who argue for that proposition today in France and elsewhere. We can say that he is guilty of omission, because he could have acted, and he had the necessary authority and ability to understand the gravity of the situation. To borrow a famous phrase used in Nuremberg, he was capable of moral choice. General Janvier's blameworthiness is not the same as Krstic's, of course, but he is still morally culpable.

Yet we must also blame, I believe, the moral poverty of the principle of non-intervention. Sometimes, those who believe in wrong ideas can cause great harm when they implement them. It is not too farfetched to imagine that General Janvier was implementing his belief in the principle of non-intervention. If interventionists have to explain Somalia, non-interventionists have to explain Srebrenica.

The condemnation of war is part of the condemnation of political violence generally, and thus it should include the condemnation of internal atrocities. The moral issue is not: are we prepared to fight a war, with all the bad consequences we know all wars involve? The question is: should we act to stop the internal atrocities, knowing that there will be serious moral costs? Simply put, the non-interventionist has the burden of explaining why the killings that occur across borders are morally distinguishable from the killings that occur within them. As we saw, he has not met that burden.

The Internal Legitimacy of Humanitarian Intervention

There is a seldom-discussed yet centrally important aspect of humanitarian intervention: how can a liberal government justify humanitarian intervention to its own citizens? Under some liberal justifications of the state, humanitarian intervention is problematic. For example, a liberal might claim that the state is justified as a mere instrument for solving certain inefficiencies that occur in the state of nature (such as those created by the private punishment of wrongs). The state, on this view, would be a mere tool for advancing its citizens' interest. This is what Allen Buchanan calls the "discretionary association" view of the state. Under this view, the government does not have authority to engage the collective resources of the state in a humanitarian intervention because it does not owe any duties to foreigners. The government would be violating its fiduciary duty. Buchanan, rightly in my view, rejects this position and argues for the existence of a natural duty to "contribute to the inclusion of all persons in just arrangements." The discretionary association view endorses a world in which states act properly when they pay no attention to oppression elsewhere, as long as they discharge their fiduciary duty towards their own citizens (Buchanan calls this the "Swiss model"). Such a world is undesirable, so, Buchanan concludes, states should properly be seen also as instruments of justice, and can and should be used to promote human rights in other societies as long as this is done at a reasonable cost.

Buchanan's point is important because it

removes a preliminary philosophical objection to cosmopolitan, pro-human rights, foreign policy. In order to assess the validity of humanitarian intervention, however, the argument needs to be supplemented by considerations related to the legitimacy of the use of military resources. Buchanan correctly shows that citizens and their governments have an obligation to promote human rights in a general way. For example, citizens must accept that their tax dollars may be used to contribute to the organizations of free elections in foreign countries, or to foreign aid given for democratic purposes, or to the financing of international human rights courts and other liberal international institutions. They can accept – indeed demand – that their government adopt pro-human rights positions in international organizations. But this is consistent with the citizens' opposition to the government using force for humanitarian purposes. A state that promotes human rights generally yet refuses to use military force to stop atrocities departs from the Swiss model. Yet the issue of whether or not it is permissible or mandatory for a liberal government to send military forces to end anarchy or tyranny abroad remains intact.

To see this clearly, consider libertarian arguments against humanitarian intervention. According to them, governments do not have the right to compel citizens to fight for the freedom of foreigners. This argument differs, on the one hand, from the one given by international lawyers and some realists, and, on the other, from Buchanan's argument. Unlike lawyers and some realists, libertarians do not believe in the principle of sovereignty and despise tyranny much as liberal interventionists do. For libertarians (as for liberal interventionists), despotic regimes lack legitimacy and are thus not protected by any sovereignty principle. However, libertarians believe that a government cannot legitimately force its own citizens to fight for someone else's freedom. This argument has a strong and a weak version. The strong version is that the government can never coerce people into fighting wars,

even wars in the defense of the person's own society. Persons retain an absolute control over their choices to use violence in self-defense. For libertarians, aggressive force is morally banned, and one legitimate function of the state is to control aggressive violence. But the use of force to repel aggression (defensive force) is not banned: it is morally permitted. If the use of force is morally permitted, not obligatory, then the victim of an attack retains the power to decide whether he will fight for his life, property, or freedom. Others (the government especially) cannot make those choices for him, and especially cannot coerce him into combat. If this is true with respect to force used in one's own defense, it is true *a fortiori* of coercion for the purpose of forcing someone to fight in defense of her fellow citizens, and even more *a fortiori* of coercion to force someone to defend foreigners. In short: the strong libertarian argument contends that a state is worth defending only if citizens rise spontaneously against the aggressor. Those who choose not to fight are within their rights and should be left alone.

The weak version of the libertarian argument holds that coercion to force people to fight in defense of their own state, their fellow citizens (self-defense), is justified, but coercion to force people to fight in defense of the freedom of foreigners is not. This weaker version may rely on the public goods argument. National defense is a public good. If people are allowed to choose individually whether they should contribute to repelling an aggression they will be tempted to free ride on the defense efforts of others. There is market failure with respect to national defense: everyone wants to repel the aggressor, but they hope others will risk their lives to do so. Because everyone reasons in the same way, the public good (defense) is under-produced and the state succumbs to the aggressor. This version of the libertarian argument, then, accepts the government's role in defending the state. It rejects, however, the legitimacy of humanitarian intervention, perhaps because it does not regard foreigners as participants in a cooperative enterprise (as fellow citizens would be) and thus the public goods problem does not even arise. And the government in a libertarian state surely does not have a mandate to protect the rights of persons other than its own citizens. Both versions of the libertarian critique of humanitarian intervention are consistent with accepting Buchanan's view: libertarians may consistently concede that the government has a prima facie obligation peacefully to promote universal human rights as part of their natural duty of justice, yet claim that the government may not force people *to fight* in order to save foreigners from tyranny.

Libertarians rightly draw our attention to the exaggerated claims that government makes on our freedoms and resources. It is easy for someone who thinks that "something must be done" about, say, the victims in Kosovo, to send *others* to risk their lives to do it. Because of that, libertarians have given a powerful cautionary warning against conscription for fighting foreign wars. What was wrong with Vietnam, on that view, is not that it was an unjust war (an uncertain assertion, perhaps) but that the government was forcing unwilling persons to fight for the freedoms of others. This is an important question of political philosophy: what is the proper role of a liberal government with respect to military efforts? Under what conditions can a liberal government force citizens to fight? The answers to these questions are independent of the answer to the question of the place of sovereignty as a bar to intervention. The questions, however, should be addressed as important questions of democratic theory, and they have a direct bearing on humanitarian intervention. If libertarians are right, humanitarian intervention is wrong, not because dictators are or should be protected by international law, but because governments cannot validly force people to fight in foreign wars.

A possible reply to the libertarian argument is that the duty to assist victims of injustice in other societies raises (as self-defense does) problems of collective action. Just as a government can give a public goods argument to justify coercing its citizens into fighting for national defense, so could a government conceivably give a public goods argument to justify coercing its own citizens to fight for the freedom of foreigners. The argument would go as follows. Humanitarian intervention is risky, so individuals in a liberal society who think it is right to intervene in a neighboring country to end tyranny or anarchy might nonetheless expect that others will make the effort. They free ride on the courage of others. And if enough people think this way, the public good (rescuing foreigners from tyranny or anarchy) is under-produced. Assuming the existence of a natural duty to justice, the power of the government to draft soldiers for humanitarian intervention is necessary in order to block opportunistic moves *ex post*.

I think that the public goods argument justifies humanitarian intervention with the important qualification that the government must send *voluntary soldiers* before resorting to conscription. This is because the public goods argument depends on the assumption that the good in question is demanded by a sufficient number of people. Because the demand for national defense is likely to be strong, conscription is needed to eliminate free riders. But, while humanitarian intervention is also a public good in the sense that it allows for opportunistic moves *ex post* (people who would agree *ex ante* to intervene will refuse to fight once the veil of ignorance is lifted), it is not certain that demand for humanitarian intervention will be as strong as demand for national defense. There will be genuine objectors who are not, by definition, opportunistic agents. Therefore, a liberal argument must balance respect for these genuine dissenters with the need to implement the natural duty of justice. In other words, the duty that liberal governments have to promote global human rights is not absolute: it must cohere with other important moral–political considerations, such as the need to respect non-opportunistic exercises of individual autonomy. A way to do this is to resort to voluntary armed forces.

The libertarian cannot oppose the use of a voluntary army. Voluntary soldiers have validly consented to fight in cases where the legitimate government believes there is (a morally) sufficient reason (apart from consent) to fight. The libertarian would have to say that the government is misreading the contract: perhaps the contract contains an implicit clause under which the person inducted into the armed forces only consented to fight in self-defense. I doubt those contracts can reasonably be construed that way. Rather, the draftee has plausibly delegated to the government the right to choose for him whether a war is worth fighting.

Some people might object to this view, saying that consent is tainted, that draftees come from the poorer segments of society and cannot foresee the multifarious ways in which they can be used and manipulated by the powerful party, the government. But whatever the merits of this view, it cannot be held by a libertarian, who insists that revealed consent be honored even if the terms of the contract are otherwise objectionable. The unconscionability objection may be available to someone who objects to humanitarian intervention for other reasons, but not to the libertarian. I am skeptical about the merits of the unconscionability argument anyway, for a number of reasons. First, if one is going to uphold the validity of draft contracts one cannot plausibly read into them an implicit clause that devolves on the draftee the power to pick and choose among the wars he wants to fight. This would of course frustrate the very idea of voluntary draft, because the temptation not to fight when the occasion arises is too strong. But more important, I believe that the draftee can reasonably expect that he will be sent to fight for worthy causes, and whether or not a humanitarian intervention is a worthy cause is an open question to be decided on its merits, not on the dubious grounds that the draftee could not

plausibly foresee that such occasion (the need to save foreigners from tyranny or anarchy) could arise. Another way of putting this is that the notion of unconscionability is parasitic on the merits of the intended enforcement of the contract. To say that forcing an enlisted member of the armed forces to fight to save Kosovars from genocide is unconscionable is to *decide* that it is outrageous, that the cause does not warrant fighting. But this is surely an independent question to be decided on its merits.

The doctrine of humanitarian intervention simply holds that sometimes such wars are justified. It seems natural to say that enlisted persons have agreed to let the government decide when those wars are justified.

I conclude this section by rejecting the libertarian position insofar as it overlooks the public good argument for humanitarian intervention. I accept, however, an amendment inspired by the libertarian insight: when a government decides to intervene for humanitarian reasons, it must use the standing armed forces first, then call for volunteers, and only as a last resort enact a general draft.

Concluding Comment

Non-interventionism is a doctrine of the past. It feeds on illiberal intellectual traditions (relativism, communitarianism, nationalism, and statism) that are objectionable for various reasons and that, where implemented, have caused grievous harm to persons. Neither the assumptions nor the consequences of non-interventionism are defensible from a liberal standpoint. The very structure of the non-interventionist argument belies the spurious pedigree of the doctrine. We are supposed to outlaw humanitarian intervention because that is what most governments say we should do. But, of course, those who wield or seek power over their fellow citizens (incumbent governments and would-be rulers) have an obvious incentive to support non-intervention. We know that governments (even the better ones) will think about international law and institutions with their priorities in mind, that is, presupposing and affirming state values. But we like to think that we are not victims of such a perverse structure of incentives. We have the choice to think about international law and institutions with human values in mind. Non-interventionists deceptively present their doctrine as one that protects communal values and self-government, yet even a cursory look at history unmasks non-intervention as the one doctrine whose origin, design, and effect is to protect established political power and render persons defenseless against the worst forms of human evil. The principle of non-intervention denies victims of tyranny and anarchy the possibility of appealing to people other than their tormentors. It condemns them to fight unaided or die. Rescuing others will always be onerous, but if we deny the moral duty and legal right to do so, we deny not only the centrality of justice in political affairs, but also the common humanity that binds us all.

Chapter 51

David Luban

LIBERALISM, TORTURE, AND THE TICKING BOMB

David Luban (1949–   ) is a professor of law and philosophy at Georgetown University who has written on just war theory, international human rights, and moral responsibility within complex organizations. In this essay (published in 2005), Luban examines the argument that torture might be permissible in certain "ticking time bomb" cases. He criticizes this argument as an "intellectual fraud" that ignores the institutional context in which real world torture takes place.

Introduction

Torture used to be incompatible with American values. Our Bill of Rights forbids cruel and unusual punishment, and that has come to include all forms of corporal punishment except prison and death by methods purported to be painless. Americans and our government have historically condemned states that torture; we have granted asylum or refuge to those who fear it. The Senate ratified the Convention Against Torture, Congress enacted anti-torture legislation, and judicial opinions spoke of "the dastardly and totally inhuman act of torture."

Then came September 11. Less than one week later, a feature story reported that a quiz in a university ethics class "gave four choices for the proper U.S. response to the terrorist attacks: A.) execute the perpetrators on sight; B.) bring them back for trial in the United States; C.) subject the perpetrators to an international tribunal; or D.) torture and interrogate those involved." Most students chose A and D—execute them on sight and torture them. Six weeks after September 11,

the press reported that frustrated FBI interrogators were considering harsh interrogation tactics; a few weeks after that, the *New York Times* reported that torture had become a topic of conversation "in bars, on commuter trains, and at dinner tables." By mid-November 2001, the *Christian Science Monitor* found that thirty-two percent of surveyed Americans favored torturing terror suspects. Alan Dershowitz reported in 2002 that "[d]uring numerous public appearances since September 11, 2001, I have asked audiences for a show of hands as to how many would support the use of nonlethal torture in a ticking-bomb case. Virtually every hand is raised." American abhorrence to torture now appears to have extraordinarily shallow roots.

To an important extent, one's stance on torture runs independent of progressive or conservative ideology. Alan Dershowitz suggests that torture should be regulated by a judicial warrant requirement. Liberal Senator Charles Schumer has publicly rejected the idea "that torture should never, ever be used." He argues that most U.S. senators would back torture to find out where a ticking time bomb is planted. By contrast, William Safire, a self-described "conservative . . . and card-carrying hard-liner[]," expresses revulsion at "phony-tough" pro-torture arguments, and forthrightly labels torture "barbarism." Examples like these illustrate how vital it is to avoid a simple left-right reductionism. For the most part, American conservatives belong no less than progressives to liberal culture, broadly understood. Henceforth, when I speak of "liberalism," I mean it in the broad sense used by political philosophers from John Stuart Mill on, a sense that includes conservatives as well as progressives, so long as they believe in limited government and the importance of human dignity and individual rights.

My aim in this Essay is threefold. First, in Parts I and II, I will examine the place of torture within liberalism. I hope to demonstrate that there are reasons that liberals find torture peculiarly abhorrent to their political outlook—but also reasons why liberal revulsion toward torture may be only skin deep. On its surface, iberal reverence for individual rights makes torture morally unacceptable; at a deeper level, the same liberal ideas seemingly can justify interrogational torture in the face of danger. These ideas allow us to construct a liberal ideology of torture, by which liberals reassure themselves that essential interrogational torture is detached from its illiberal roots. The liberal ideology of torture is expressed perfectly in so-called "ticking-bomb hypotheticals" designed to show that even perfectly compassionate liberals (like Senator Schumer) might justify torture to find the ticking bomb.

Second, I will criticize the liberal ideology of torture and suggest that ticking-bomb stories are built on a set of assumptions that amount to intellectual fraud (Parts III and IV). Ticking-bomb stories depict torture as an emergency exception, but use intuitions based on the exceptional case to justify institutionalized practices and procedures of torture. In short, the ticking bomb begins by denying that torture belongs

to liberal culture, and ends by constructing a torture culture.

My third aim in the Essay is to illustrate these dialectical adventures of the liberal ideology of torture through a case study of the executive-branch lawyers who solicited or wrote memoranda justifying some cases of official brutality (Part V). The result, I believe, will be a perfect example of how a secretive torture culture emerges from the liberal ideology of torture—a disquieting illustration of how liberalism deals with the unpleasant question of torture.

I. Putting Cruelty First

Unhappily, torture is as old as human history. Montaigne once wrote, "[n]ature herself, I fear, attaches to man some instinct for inhumanity." That sounds right. Most children at some point entertain sadistic fantasies, and many act them out. Infantile sadism may actually be an essential stage in the process of differentiating self from other and acquiring physical agency in the external world: "I can pinch and I feel nothing, but *you* or *she* or *the cat* yelps in pain; I am not you or her or the cat; and it's fun making you or her or the cat notice me." Causing pain in others allows the child to learn that some of the objects around him are subjects with feelings of their own, and in this way, bouts of infantile sadism may be essential to developing adult empathy. But, while infantile sadism may be essential for human development, eventually torture fantasies must be repressed. To be sure, sadism persists in some people's erotic lives. But apart from consensual bedroom behavior, liberal societies condemn torture as a serious and depraved form of battery.

Yet the modern liberal's revulsion toward torture is unusual. As Nietzsche and Foucault remind us, through most of human history there was no taboo on torture in military and juridical contexts, and so no need to repress the infantile sadism that nature has bequeathed us. Indeed, Judith Shklar notes a remarkable fact, namely that cruelty did not seem to figure in classical moral thought as an important vice: "[O]ne looks in vain for a Platonic dialogue on cruelty. Aristotle discusses only pathological bestiality, not cruelty. Cruelty is not one of the seven deadly sins. . . . The many manifestations of cupidity seem, to Saint Augustine, more important than cruelty." It is only in relatively modern times, Shklar thinks, that we have come to "put cruelty first"—that is, regard it as the most vicious of all vices. She thinks that Montaigne and Montesquieu, both of them proto-liberals, were the first political philosophers to think this way; and, more generally, she holds that "hating cruelty, and putting it first [among vices], remain a powerful part of the liberal consciousness." Shklar also observes that putting cruelty first, as liberals do, incurs genuine moral costs: "It makes political action difficult beyond endurance, may cloud our judgment, and may reduce us to a debilitating misanthropy. . . ."

Perhaps these difficulties account for the ease with which we abandoned our reluctance to torture in the aftermath of 9/11. But I believe there are indeed reasons why torture and cruelty are particularly incompatible with liberalism. And, as I hope to show, one way this incompatibility manifests itself is through arguments designed to show that torturing terrorists for information is not done out of cruelty.

II. The Five Aims of Torture

What makes torture, the deliberate infliction of suffering and pain, especially abhorrent to liberals? This may seem like a bizarre question, because the answer seems self-evident: making people suffer is a horrible thing. Pain hurts and bad pain hurts badly. But let me pose the question in different terms. Realistically, the abuses of detainees at Abu Ghraib, Baghram, and Guantanamo pale by comparison with the death, maiming, and suffering in collateral damage during the Afghan and Iraq wars. Bombs crush limbs and burn people's faces off; nothing even

remotely as horrifying has been reported in American prisoner abuse cases. Yet as much as we may regret or in some cases decry the wartime suffering of innocents, we do not seem to regard it with the special abhorrence that we do torture. This seems hypocritical and irrational, almost fetishistic, and it raises the question of what makes torture more illiberal than bombing and killing. The answer lies in the relationship between torturer and victim. The self-conscious aim of torture is to turn its victim into someone who is isolated, over-whelmed, terrorized, and humiliated. Torture aims to strip away from its victim all the qualities of human dignity that liberalism prizes. The torturer inflicts pain one-on-one, deliberately, up close and personal, in order to break the spirit of the victim—in other words, to tyrannize and dominate the victim. The relationship between them becomes a perverse parody of friendship and intimacy: intimacy transformed into its inverse image, where the torturer focuses on the victim's body with the intensity of a lover, except that every bit of that focus is bent to causing pain and tyrannizing the victim's spirit.

I am arguing that torture is a microcosm, raised to the highest level of intensity, of the tyrannical political relationships that liberalism hates the most. I have said that torture isolates and privatizes. Pain forcibly severs our concentration on anything outside of us; it collapses our horizon to our own body and the damage we feel in it. Even much milder sensations of prolonged discomfort can distract us so much that it becomes impossible to pay attention to anything else, as anyone knows who has had to go to the bathroom in a situation where it cannot be done. Ludwig Wittgenstein wrote that the world of the happy is different from the world of the unhappy, and this is not simply a figure of speech when we suffer severe pain. The world of the man or woman in great pain is a world without relationships or engagements, a world without an exterior. It is a world reduced to a point, a world that makes no sense and in which the human soul finds no home and no repose.

And torture terrorizes. The body in pain winces; it trembles. The muscles themselves register fear. This is rooted in pain's biological function of impelling us in the most urgent way possible to escape from the source of pain—for that impulse is indistinguishable from panic. U.S. interrogators have reportedly used the technique of "waterboarding" to break the will of detainees. Waterboarding involves immersing the victim's face in water or wrapping it in a wet towel to induce drowning sensations. As anyone who has ever come close to drowning or suffocating knows, the oxygen-starved brain sends panic signals that overwhelm everything else. You can experience suffocation-panic for yourself right now by fully exhaling and then holding your breath for thirty seconds.

And torture humiliates. It makes the victim scream and beg; the terror makes him lose control of his bowels and bladder. The essence of cruelty is inflicting pain for the purpose of lording it over someone—we sometimes say "breaking" them—and the mechanism of cruelty is making the victim the audience of your own mastery. Cruelty always aims at humiliation. One curious feature of legal procedure in both ancient Greece and Rome was a rule "that slaves were permitted to [testify in a court of law] only under torture." Sir Moses Finley's plausible explanation is that the rule served to mark off the absolute difference in status between slaves and even the lowliest freemen. The torture rule reinforces the message that slaves are absolutely subjugated. Humiliation occurs when I am low and you are high and you insist on it.

Victor's Pleasure

The predominant setting for torture has always been military victory. The victor captures the enemy and tortures him. I recently saw some spectacular Mayan murals depicting defeated enemies from a rival city-state having their fingernails torn out before being executed in a ritual reenactment of the battle.

Underneath whatever religious significance that attaches to torturing the vanquished, the victor tortures captives for the simplest of motives: to relive the victory, to demonstrate the absoluteness of his mastery, to rub the loser's face in it, and to humiliate the loser by making him scream and beg. For the victorious warrior, it's fun; it's entertainment. It prolongs the rush of victory. Montaigne denounced what he called "the uttermost point that cruelty can attain," namely torture "for the sole purpose of enjoying the pleasing spectacle of the pitiful gestures and movements, the lamentable groans and cries, of a man dying in anguish." Even if the torturer's motives do not reach that level of cruelty, the victim's humiliation and subjugation are undeniable.

Already we can see why liberals abhor torture. Liberalism incorporates a vision of engaged, active human beings possessing an inherent dignity regardless of their social station. The victim of torture is in every respect the opposite of this vision. The torture victim is isolated and reduced instead of engaged and enlarged, terrified instead of active, humiliated instead of dignified. And, in the paradigm case of torture, the victor's torment of defeated captives, liberals perceive the living embodiment of their worst nightmare: tyrannical rulers who take their pleasure from the degradation of those unfortunate enough to be subject to their will.

There are at least four other historically significant reasons for torture besides victor's cruelty (the paradigm case), and as we shall see, all but one of them is fundamentally inimical to liberalism.

Terror

First, there is torture for the purpose of terrorizing people into submission. Dictators from Hitler to Pinochet to Saddam Hussein tortured their political prisoners so that their enemies, knowing that they might face a fate far worse than death, would be afraid to oppose them.

Genghis Khan's conquests were made easier because his reputation for cruelty against those who opposed him led cities to surrender without a fight. Terror is a force-magnifier that permits a relatively small number of police to subdue a far larger population than they could if would-be rebels were confident that they would be treated humanely upon capture. But of course, a practice that exists to make it easier to subdue and tyrannize people is fundamentally hostile to liberals' political philosophy.

Punishment

Second, until the last two centuries, torture was used as a form of criminal punishment. It was torture as a form of punishment that drew Montaigne's condemnation, and it is noteworthy that the Eighth Amendment to the U.S. Constitution prohibits cruel and unusual *punishments*, rather than cruelty more generally. Beccaria condemns punishments that are more cruel than is absolutely necessary to deter crime, arguing on classical-liberal grounds that people in the state of nature will surrender only the smallest quantum of liberty necessary to secure society: "The aggregate of these smallest possible portions of individual liberty constitutes the right to punish; everything beyond that is an abuse and not justice, a fact but scarcely a right." Beccaria makes it clear that torture would turn society into "a herd of slaves who constantly exchange timid cruelties with one another." Such punishments, he adds, "would also be contrary to justice and to the nature of the social contract itself," presumably because turning society into a herd of slaves undermines the liberal understanding of the ends of society. Beccaria was widely read in America during the founding era.

Foucault argues that the abolition of punitive torture had little to do with increased humanitarianism. Instead, it had to do with a change in the distribution of crime in Western Europe. As the West grew more prosperous, property crimes eclipsed crimes of passion as a social problem.

This led to calls for a milder but more certain system of punishments. The trouble with torture is that when the punishment is so awful, the temptation to mercy becomes too great. Imprisonment, out of sight and out of mind, replaced the public spectacle of torment.

Be that as it may, it seems equally clear that punitive torture had no place in liberal polities. Torture, as Foucault explains, was a symbolic assertion of the absolute sovereign whose personal prerogatives had been affronted by crime. It was a ritual of royal dominance and royal revenge, acted out in public spectacle to shock and awe the multitude. With the growth of liberal democracy, the ideology of popular sovereignty deflated the purpose of punitive torture: if the people rule, then the responsibility of torture would fall on the people, and the need for a spectacle of suffering by which the people could impress themselves seemed pointless.

Extracting Confessions

Curiously, when Beccaria writes explicitly about the subject of torture, he does not mention torture as punishment. Rather, he polemicizes against judicial torture in order to extract confessions from criminal suspects. This is the third historically significant use of torture, distinct from punishment, even though judges administer both. The French language has different words for them: *le supplice*, torture as punishment, and *la question*, torture to extract confessions. As John Langbein observes, pre-modern legal rules required either multiple eyewitnesses or confessions for criminal convictions. At first glance, these were important rights of the accused, but they had the perverse effect of legitimating judicial torture in order to make convictions possible. But once it was accepted that the criminal justice system could base guilty verdicts on various types of evidence that rationally establish facts, rather than insisting on the ritual of confession, then the need for torture to secure convictions vanished. Furthermore, the only crimes for which the primary evidence is the perpetrator's own words are crimes of heretical or seditious belief—and liberalism rejects the criminalization of belief.

Intelligence Gathering

These, then, are the four illiberal motives for torture: victor's pleasure, terror, punishment, and extracting confessions. That leaves only one rationale for torture that might conceivably be acceptable to a liberal: torture as a technique of intelligence gathering from captives who will not talk. This may seem indistinguishable from torture to extract confessions, because both practices couple torture with interrogation. The crucial difference lies in the fact that the confession is backward-looking, in that it aims to document and ratify the past for purposes of retribution, while intelligence gathering is forward-looking because it aims to gain information to forestall future evils like terrorist attacks.

It is striking, and in obvious ways reassuring, that this is the only rationale for torture that liberal political culture admits could even possibly be legitimate. To speak in a somewhat perverse and paradoxical way, liberalism's insistence on limited governments that exercise their power only for instrumental and pragmatic purposes creates the possibility of seeing torture as a civilized, not an atavistic, practice, provided that its sole purpose is preventing future harms. Rejecting torture as victor's spoils, as terror, as punishment, and as a device to force confession drastically limits the amount of torture that a liberal society might conceivably accept. But more importantly, the liberal rationale for torture as intelligence gathering in gravely dangerous situations transforms and rationalizes the motivation for torture. Now, for the first time, it becomes possible to think of torture as a last resort of men and women who are profoundly reluctant to torture. And in that way, liberals can for the first time think of torture dissociated from cruelty—torture authorized and adminis-tered by decent human beings who abhor what circumstances force them to do. Torture to gather intelligence and save lives seems almost heroic. For the first time, we can think of kindly torturers rather than tyrants.

I shall be arguing shortly that this way of thinking represents a dangerous delusion. But before abandoning the subject of how torture "became civilized," it is important to note one other dimension in which torture has become less cruel.

Readers of Foucault's *Discipline and Punish* will probably never forget its nauseating opening pages, in which Foucault describes in loving detail the gruesome death by torture of the man who assaulted Louis XV. Foucault aims to shock, of course, and he certainly succeeded with me: I closed the book and would not open it again for twenty years. There is a vast difference, however, between the ancient world of torture, with its appalling mutilations, its roastings and flayings, and the tortures that liberals might accept: sleep deprivation, prolonged standing in stress positions, extremes of heat and cold, bright lights and loud music—what some refer to as "torture lite."

I do not mean to diminish how horrible these experiences are, nor do I mean to suggest that American interrogators never go further than torture lite. Waterboarding, withholding of pain medication from wounded captives, putting lit cigarettes in their ears, rape, and beatings all go much further. At least five, and maybe more than twenty captives have been beaten to death by American interrogators. My point is rather that liberals generally draw the line at forms of torture that maim the victim's body. This, like the limitation of torture to intelligence gathering, marks an undeniable moderation in torture, the world's most immoderate practice. It's almost enough to persuade us that torture lite is not torture at all, or at least that it isn't cruel enough to make liberals wince, at least not when the stakes are sufficiently high. Indeed, they may even deny that it is torture.

Let me summarize this part of my argument. Liberals, I have said, rank cruelty first among vices—not because liberals are more compassionate than anyone else, but because of the close connection between cruelty and tyranny. Torture is the living manifestation of cruelty, and the peculiar horror of torture within liberalism arises from the fact that torture is tyranny in microcosm, at its highest level of intensity. The history of torture reinforces this horror because torture has always been bound up with military conquest, regal punishment, dictatorial terror, forced confessions, and the repression of dissident belief—a veritable catalogue of the evils of absolutist government that liberalism abhors. For all these reasons, it should hardly surprise us that liberals wish to ban torture absolutely—a wish that became legislative reality in the Torture Convention's insistence that nothing can justify torture.

But what about torture as intelligence gathering, torture to forestall greater evils? I suspect that throughout history this has been the least common motivation for torture, and thus the one most readily overlooked. And yet it alone bears no essential connection with tyranny. This is not to say that the torture victim experiences it as any less terrifying, humiliating, or tyrannical. The victim, after all, undergoes abject domination by the torturer. But it will dawn on reluctant liberals that the torturer's goal of forestalling greater evils is one that liberals share. It seems like a rational motivation, far removed from cruelty and power-lust. In fact, the liberal may for the first time find it possible to view torture from the torturer's point of view rather than the victim's.

Thus, even though absolute prohibition remains liberalism's primary teaching about torture, and the basic liberal stance is empathy for the torture victim, a more permissive stance remains an unspoken possibility, the Achilles' heel of absolute prohibitions. As long as the intelligence needs of a liberal society are slight, this possibility within liberalism remains dormant, perhaps even unnoticed. But when a catastrophe like 9/11 happens, liberals may cautiously conclude that, in the words of a well-known *Newsweek* article, it is "Time to Think About Torture."

But the pressure of liberalism will compel them to think about it in a highly stylized and artificial way, what I will call the "liberal ideology of torture." The liberal ideology insists that the sole purpose of torture must be intelligence gathering to prevent a catastrophe; that torture is necessary to prevent the catastrophe; that torturing is the exception, not the rule, so that it has nothing to do with state tyranny; that those who inflict the torture are motivated solely by the looming catastrophe, with no tincture of cruelty; that torture in such circumstances is, in fact, little more than self-defense; and that, because of the associations of torture with the horrors of yesteryear, perhaps one should not even call harsh interrogation "torture."

And the liberal ideology will crystallize all of these ideas in a single, mesmerizing example: the ticking time bomb.

III. The Ticking Bomb

Suppose the bomb is planted somewhere in the crowded heart of an American city, and you have custody of the man who planted it. He won't talk. Surely, the hypothetical suggests, we shouldn't be too squeamish to torture the information out of him and save hundreds of lives. Consequences count, and abstract moral prohibitions must yield to the calculus of consequences.

Everyone argues the pros and cons of torture through the ticking time bomb. Senator Schumer and Professor Dershowitz, the Israeli Supreme Court and indeed every journalist devoting a think-piece to the unpleasant question of torture, begins with the ticking time bomb and ends there as well. The Schlesinger Report on Abu Ghraib notes that "[f]or the U.S., most cases for permitting harsh treatment of detainees on moral grounds begin with variants of the 'ticking time-bomb' scenario." At this point in my argument, I mean to disarm the ticking time bomb and argue that it is the wrong thing to think about. If so, then the liberal ideology of torture begins to unravel.

But before beginning these arguments, I want to pause and ask why this jejune example has become the alpha and omega of our thinking about torture. I believe the answer is this: The ticking time bomb is proffered against liberals who believe in an absolute prohibition against torture. The idea is to force the liberal prohibitionist to admit that yes, even he or even she would agree to torture in at least this one situation. Once the prohibitionist admits that, then she has conceded that her opposition to torture is not based on principle. Now that the prohibitionist has admitted that her moral principles can be breached, all that is left is haggling about the price. No longer can the prohibitionist claim the moral high ground; no longer can she put the burden of proof on her opponent. She is down in the mud with them, and the only question left is how much further down she will go. Dialectically, getting the prohibitionist to address the ticking time bomb is like getting the vegetarian to eat just one little oyster because it has no nervous system. Once she does that—*gotcha!*

The ticking time-bomb scenario serves a second rhetorical goal, one that is equally important to the proponent of torture. It makes us see the torturer in a different light—one of the essential points in the liberal ideology of torture because it is the way that liberals can reconcile themselves to torture even while continuing to "put cruelty first." Now, he is not a cruel man or a sadistic man or a coarse, insensitive brutish man. The torture is instead a conscientious public servant, heroic the way that New York firefighters were heroic, willing to do desperate things only because the plight is so desperate and so many innocent lives are weighing on the public servant's conscience. The time bomb clinches the

great divorce between torture and cruelty; it placates liberals, who put cruelty first.

Wittgenstein once wrote that confusion arises when we become bewitched by a picture. He meant that it's easy to get seduced by simplistic examples that look compelling but actually misrepresent the world in which we live. If the subject is the morality of torture, philosophical confusions can have life-or-death consequences. I believe the ticking time bomb is the picture that bewitches us.

I don't mean that the time-bomb scenario is completely unreal. To take a real-life counterpart: in 1995, an al Qaeda plot to bomb eleven U.S. airliners and assassinate the Pope was thwarted by information tortured out of a Pakistani bombmaker by the Philippine police. According to journalists Marites Dañguilan Vitug and Glenda M. Gloria, the police had received word of possible threats against the Pope. They went to work. "For weeks, agents hit him with a chair and a long piece of wood, forced water into his mouth, and crushed lighted cigarettes into his private parts. . . . His ribs were almost totally broken that his captors were surprised that he survived. . . ." Grisly, to be sure—but if they hadn't done it, thousands of innocent travelers might have died horrible deaths.

But look at the example one more time. The Philippine agents were surprised he survived—in other words, they came close to torturing him to death *before* he talked. And they tortured him *for weeks*, during which time they didn't know about any specific al Qaeda plot. What if he too didn't know? Or what if there had been no al Qaeda plot? Then they would have tortured him for weeks, possibly tortured him to death, for nothing. For all they knew at the time, that is exactly what they were doing. You cannot use the argument that preventing the al Qaeda attack justified the decision to torture, because *at the moment the decision was made* no one knew about the al Qaeda attack.

The ticking-bomb scenario cheats its way around these difficulties by stipulating that the bomb is there, ticking away, and that officials know it and know they have the man who planted it. Those conditions will seldom be met. Let us try some more realistic hypotheticals and the questions they raise:

1. The authorities know there may be a bomb plot in the offing, and they have captured a man who may know something about it, but may not. Torture him? How much? For weeks? For months? The chances are considerable that you are torturing a man with nothing to tell you. If he doesn't talk, does that mean it's time to stop, or time to ramp up the level of torture? How likely does it have to be that he knows something important? Fifty-fifty? Thirty-seventy? Will one out of a hundred suffice to land him on the waterboard?

2. Do you really want to make the torture decision by running the numbers? A one-percent chance of saving a thousand lives yields ten statistical lives. Does that mean that you can torture up to nine people on a one-percent chance of finding crucial information?

3. The authorities think that one out of a group of fifty captives in Guantanamo might know where Osama bin Laden is hiding, but they do not know which captive. Torture them all? That is: Do you torture forty-nine captives with nothing to tell you on the uncertain chance of capturing bin Laden?

4. For that matter, would capturing Osama bin Laden demonstrably save a single human life? The Bush administration has downplayed the importance of capturing bin Laden because American strategy has succeeded in marginalizing him. Maybe capturing him would save lives, but how certain do you have to be? Or does it not matter whether torture is intended to save human lives from a specific threat, as long as it furthers some goal in the War on Terror? This last question is especially important once we realize that the interrogation of al Qaeda suspects will almost never be employed to find out where the ticking bomb is hidden. Instead, interrogation is a more general fishing expedition for

any intelligence that might be used to help "unwind" the terrorist organization. Now one might reply that al Qaeda is itself the ticking time bomb, so that unwinding the organization meets the formal conditions of the ticking-bomb hypothetical. This is equivalent to asserting that any intelligence that promotes victory in the War on Terror justifies torture, precisely because we understand that the enemy in the War on Terror aims to kill American civilians. Presumably, on this argument, Japan would have been justified in torturing American captives in World War II on the chance of finding intelligence that would help them shoot down the Enola Gay; I assume that a ticking-bomb hard-liner will not flinch from this conclusion. But at this point, we verge on declaring all military threats and adversaries that menace American civilians to be ticking bombs whose defeat justifies torture. The limitation of torture to emergency exceptions, implicit in the ticking-bomb story, now threatens to unravel, making torture a legitimate instrument of military policy. And then the question becomes inevitable: Why not torture in pursuit of any worthwhile goal?

5. Indeed, if you are willing to torture forty-nine innocent people to get information from the one who has it, why stop there? If suspects will not break under torture, why not torture their loved ones in front of them? They are no more innocent than the forty-nine you have already shown you are prepared to torture. In fact, if only the numbers matter, torturing loved ones is almost a no-brainer if you think it will work. Of course, you won't know until you try whether torturing his child will break the suspect. But that just changes the odds; it does not alter the argument.

The point of the examples is that in a world of uncertainty and imperfect knowledge, the ticking-bomb scenario should not form the point of reference. The ticking bomb is the picture that bewitches us. The real debate is not between one guilty man's pain and hundreds of innocent lives. It is the debate between the certainty of anguish and the mere possibility of learning something vital and saving lives. And, above all, it is the question about whether a responsible citizen must unblinkingly think the unthinkable and accept that the morality of torture should be decided purely by totaling up costs and benefits. Once you accept that only the numbers count, then anything, no matter how gruesome, becomes possible. "Consequentialist rationality," as Bernard Williams notes sardonically, "will have something to say even on the difference between massacring seven million, and massacring seven million and one."

I am inclined to think that the path of wisdom instead lies in Holocaust survivor David Rousset's famous caution that normal human beings do *not* know that everything is possible. As Williams says, "there are certain situations so monstrous that the idea that the processes of moral rationality could yield an answer in them is insane" and "to spend time thinking what one would decide if one were in such a situation is also insane, if not merely frivolous."

IV. Torture as a Practice

There is a second, insidious, error built into the ticking-bomb hypothetical. It assumes a single, ad hoc decision about whether to torture, by officials who ordinarily would do no such thing except in a desperate emergency. But in the real world of interrogations, decisions are not made one-off. The real world is a world of policies, guidelines, and directives. It is a world of *practices*, not of ad hoc emergency measures. Therefore, any responsible discussion of torture must address the practice of torture, not the ticking-bomb hypothetical. I am not saying anything original here; other writers have made exactly this point. But somehow, we always manage to forget this and circle back to the ticking time bomb. Its rhetorical power has made it indispensable to the sensitive liberal soul, and we would much rather talk about the ticking bomb than about torture as an organized social practice.

Treating torture as a practice rather than as a desperate improvisation in an emergency means changing the subject from the ticking bomb to other issues like these: Should we create a professional cadre of trained torturers? That means a group of interrogators who know the techniques, who learn to overcome their instinctive revulsion against causing physical pain, and who acquire the legendary surgeon's arrogance about their own infallibility. It has happened before. Medieval executioners were schooled in the arts of agony as part of the trade: how to break men on the wheel, how to rack them, and even how to surreptitiously strangle them as an act of mercy without the bloodthirsty crowd catching on. In Louis XVI's Paris, torture was a hereditary family trade whose tricks were passed on from father to son. Who will teach torture techniques now? Should universities create an undergraduate course in torture? Or should the subject be offered only in police and military academies? Do we want federal grants for research to devise new and better techniques? Patents issued on high-tech torture devices? Companies competing to manufacture them? Trade conventions in Las Vegas? Should there be a medical subspecialty of torture doctors, who ensure that captives do not die before they talk? The questions amount to this: Do we really want to create a torture culture and the kind of people who inhabit it? The ticking time bomb distracts us from the real issue, which is not about emergencies, but about the normalization of torture.

Perhaps the solution is to keep the practice of torture secret in order to avoid the moral corruption that comes from creating a public culture of torture. But this so-called "solution" does not reject the normalization of torture. It accepts it, but layers on top of it the normalization of state secrecy. The result would be a shadow culture of torturers and those who train and support them, operating outside the public eye and accountable only to other insiders of the torture culture.

Just as importantly: Who guarantees that case-hardened torturers, inured to levels of violence and pain that would make ordinary people vomit at the sight, will know where to draw the line on when torture should be used? They rarely have in the past. They didn't in Algeria. They didn't in Israel, where in 1999, the Israeli Supreme Court backpedaled from an earlier consent to torture lite because the interrogators were running amok and torturing two-thirds of their Palestinian captives. In the Argentinian Dirty War, the tortures began because terrorist cells had a policy of fleeing when one of their members had disappeared for forty-eight hours, leaving authorities two days to wring the information out of the captive. Mark Osiel, who has studied the Argentinean military in the Dirty War, reports that many of the torturers initially had qualms about what they were doing, until their priests reassured them that they were fighting God's fight. By the end of the Dirty War, the qualms were gone, and, as John Simpson and Jana Bennett report, hardened young officers were placing bets on who could kidnap the prettiest girl to rape and torture. Escalation is the rule, not the aberration.

There are two fundamental reasons for this: one rooted in the nature of bureaucracy and the other in social psychology. The liberal ideology of torture presupposes a torturer impelled by the desire to stop a looming catastrophe, not by cruelty. Implicitly, this image presumes that the interrogator and the decisionmaker are the same person. But the defining fact about real organizations is the division of labor. The person who decides whether this prisoner presents a genuine ticking-bomb case is not the interrogator. The decision about what counts as a ticking-bomb case—one where torture is the lesser evil—depends on complex value judgments, and these are made further up the chain of command. The interrogator simply executes decisions made elsewhere.

Interrogators do not inhabit a world of loving kindness, or of equal concern and respect for all human beings. Interrogating resistant prisoners non-violently and non-abusively still requires a relationship that in any other context would be morally abhorrent. It requires tricking information out of the subject, and the interrogator does this by setting up elaborate scenarios to disorient the subject and propel him into an alternative reality. The subject must be deceived into thinking that his high-value intelligence has already been revealed by someone else, so that it is no longer of any value. He must be fooled into thinking that his friends have betrayed him or that the interrogator is his friend. The interrogator disrupts his sense of time and place, disorients him with sessions that never take place at predictable times or intervals, and manipulates his emotions. The very names of interrogation techniques show this: "Emotional Love," "Emotional Hate," "Fear Up Harsh," "Fear Up Mild," "Reduced Fear," "Pride and Ego Up," "Pride and Ego Down," "Futility." The interrogator may set up a scenario to make the subject think he is in the clutches of a much-feared secret police organization from a different country ("False Flag"). Every bit of the subject's environment is fair game for manipulation and deception, as the interrogator aims to create the total lie that gets the subject talking.

Let me be clear that I am not objecting to these deceptions. None of these practices rises to the level of abuse or torture lite, let alone torture heavy, and surely tricking the subject into talking is legitimate if the goals of the interrogation are legitimate. But what I have described is a relationship of totalitarian mind-control more profound than the world of Orwell's 1984. The interrogator is like Descartes' Evil Deceiver, and the subject lives in a false reality reminiscent of The Matrix. The liberal fiction that interrogation can be done by people who are neither cruel nor tyrannical runs aground on the fact that regardless of the interrogator's character off the job, on the job, every fiber of his concentration is devoted to dominating the mind of the subject.

Only one thing prevents this from turning into abuse and torture, and that is a clear set of bright-line rules, drummed into the interrogator with the intensity of a religious indoctrination, complete with warnings of fire and brimstone. American interrogator Chris Mackey reports that warnings about the dire consequences of violating the Geneva Conventions "were repeated so often that by the end of our time at [training school] the three syllables 'Leaven-worth' were ringing in our ears."

But what happens when the line is breached? When, as in Afghanistan, the interrogator gets mixed messages about whether Geneva applies, or hears rumors of ghost detainees, of high-value captives held for years of interrogation in the top-secret facility known as "Hotel California," located in some nation somewhere? Or when the interrogator observes around him the move from deception to abuse, from abuse to torture lite, from torture lite to beatings and waterboarding? Without clear lines, the tyranny innate in the interrogator's job has nothing to hold it in check. Perhaps someone, somewhere in the chain of command, is wringing hands over whether this interrogation qualifies as a ticking-bomb case; but the interrogator knows only that the rules of the road have changed and the posted speed limits no longer apply. The liberal fiction of the conscientious interrogator overlooks a division of moral labor in which the person with the fastidious conscience and the person doing the interrogation are not the same.

The fiction must presume, therefore, that the interrogator operates only under the strictest supervision, in a chain of command where his every move gets vetted and controlled by the superiors who are actually doing the deliberating. The trouble is that this assumption flies in the face of everything that we know about how organizations work. The basic rule in every bureaucratic organization is that operational details and the guilty knowledge that goes with them get pushed down the chain of command as far as possible. As sociologist Robert Jackall explains,

> [i]t is characteristic . . . that details are pushed down and credit is pulled up. Superiors do not like to give detailed instructions to subordinates. . . . [O]ne of the privileges of authority is the divestment of humdrum intricacies. . . . Perhaps more important, pushing details down protects the privilege of authority to declare that a mistake has been made. . . . Moreover, pushing down details relieves superiors of the burden of too much knowledge, particularly guilty knowledge.

We saw this phenomenon at Abu Ghraib, where military intelligence officers gave military police vague orders like: " 'Loosen this guy up for us;' 'Make sure he has a bad night.' 'Make sure he gets the treatment.' " Suppose that the eighteen-year-old guard interprets "[m]ake sure he has a bad night" to mean, simply, "keep him awake all night." How do you do that without physical abuse? Furthermore, personnel at Abu Ghraib witnessed far harsher treatment of prisoners by "other governmental agencies" (OGA), a euphemism for the Central Intelligence Agency. They saw OGA spirit away the dead body of an interrogation subject, and allegedly witnessed a contract employee rape a youthful prisoner. When that is what you see, abuses like those in the Abu Ghraib photos will not look outrageous. Outrageous compared with what?

This brings me to the point of social psychology. Simply stated, it is this: we judge right and wrong against the baseline of whatever we have come to consider "normal" behavior, and if the norm shifts in the direction of violence, we will come to tolerate and accept violence as a normal response. The psychological mechanisms for this re-normalization have been studied for more than half a century, and by now they are reasonably well understood. Rather than detour into psychological theory, however, I will illustrate the point with the most salient example—one that seems so obviously applicable to Abu Ghraib that the Schlesinger Commission discussed it at length in an appendix to its report. This is the famous Stanford Prison Experiment. Male volunteers were divided randomly into two groups who would simulate the guards and inmates in a mock prison. Within a matter of days, the inmates began acting like actual prison inmates—depressed, enraged, and anxious. And the guards began to abuse the inmates to such an alarming degree that the researchers had to halt the two-week experiment after just seven days. In the words of the experimenters:

> The use of power was self-aggrandising and self-perpetuating. The guard power, derived initially from an arbitrary label, was intensified whenever there was any perceived threat by the prisoners and this new level subsequently became the baseline from which further hostility and harassment would begin-. . . . [T]he absolute level of aggression as well as the more subtle and "creative" forms of aggression manifested, increased in a spiralling function.

It took only five days before a guard, who prior to the experiment described himself as a pacifist, was forcing greasy sausages down the throat of a prisoner who refused to eat; and in less than a week, the guards were placing bags over prisoners' heads, making them strip, and sexually humiliating them in ways reminiscent of Abu Ghraib.

My conclusion is very simple. Abu Ghraib is the fully predictable image of what a torture culture looks like. Abu Ghraib is not a few bad apples—it is the apple tree. And you cannot reasonably expect that interrogators in a torture culture will be the fastidious and well-meaning torturers that the liberal ideology fantasizes.

This is why Alan Dershowitz has argued that judges, not torturers, should oversee the permission to torture, which in his view must be regulated by warrants. The irony is that Jay S. Bybee, who signed the Justice Department's highly permissive torture memo, is now a federal judge. Politicians pick judges, and if the politicians accept torture, the judges will as well. Once we create a torture culture, only the naive would suppose that judges will provide a safeguard. Judges do not fight their culture—they reflect it.

For all these reasons, the ticking-bomb scenario is an intellectual fraud. In its place, we must address the real questions about torture—questions about uncertainty, questions about the morality of consequences, and questions about what it does to a culture and the torturers themselves to introduce the practice. Once we do so, I suspect that few Americans will be willing to accept that everything is possible.

V. The Construction of a Torture Culture: The Torture Lawyers of Washington

A skeptic might respond that my dire warnings about a torture culture are exaggerated, overwrought, and (above all) hypothetical. Would that it were so. As a coda to the argument I have presented, I wish to offer a case study of a torture culture constructed under our noses in Washington. I am referring to the group of lawyers in President George W. Bush's administration who wrote the highly-permissive secret memoranda that came close to legitimizing torture for interrogation purposes. These lawyers illustrate as graphically as any group how quickly and easily a secret culture of torture supporters can emerge even in the heart of a liberal culture. They illustrate as well how readily the liberal ideology of torture transforms into something far removed from liberalism.

By now, the background is well known, but it may be worthwhile to recapitulate briefly. There were, in reality, over a dozen memoranda pertaining to the status and treatment of detainees circulated between the White House, the Department of Defense, the State Department, and the Justice Department. The most controversial, though, emerged from the Office of Legal Counsel in the Justice Department ("OLC"). Two OLC memos, written in early 2002, concluded that the Geneva Conventions do not cover al Qaeda or Taliban captives. These set the stage for President Bush's February 7, 2002, memo affirming that conclusion, and asserting that prisoners would be treated consistently with Geneva "to the extent appropriate and consistent with military necessity"—a large loop-hole for intelligence-gathering. In effect, the President, relying on the OLC, proclaimed that if military necessity requires it, Geneva is gone.

Six months later, OLC tendered another memo, this one on the question of whether harsh interrogation tactics violate U.S. obligations under the Torture Convention and its implementing statutes. This memo, drafted in part by Professor John Yoo and signed by OLC head Jay S. Bybee, reached a series of startling conclusions: that the infliction of pain rises to the level of torture only if the pain is as severe as that accompanying "death, organ failure, or serious impairment of body functions;" that the infliction of psychological pain rises to the level of torture only if the interrogator specifically intended it to cause "lasting . . . damage" such as posttraumatic stress disorder; that it would be unconstitutional to apply anti-torture laws to interrogations authorized by the President in the War on Terror; and that, "under the current circumstances, necessity or self-defense may justify interrogation methods that might violate" the criminal prohibition on torture.

The Bybee Memo proved to be enormously influential. In January 2003, Defense Secretary Donald Rumsfeld formed a working group on interrogation techniques, which produced its own report in April. Significantly, the working-group report was based substantially on the Bybee Memo, and in fact, incorporated portions of it verbatim. The working-group report, in turn, influenced policy on interrogation tactics. Two months after the Bybee Memorandum, a Defense Department lawyer, Lieutenant Colonel Diane Beaver, produced a memo of her own that legitimized harsh interrogational tactics, including "[t]he use of a wet towel to induce the misperception of suffocation," provided that there is a legitimate national security objective.

None of these memoranda and reports were produced in a vacuum. The Bybee Memorandum "was vetted by a larger number of officials, including lawyers at the National Security Council, the White House counsel's office, and Vice President Cheney's office." Apparently, then-White House counsel Alberto Gonzales requested the memorandum. And the Department of Defense working group was formed after the head of an Army interrogation team requested permission to escalate to harsher tactics.

Once they were leaked, the OLC memoranda proved to be incredibly controversial, not only because of their conclusions, but because of a near consensus that the legal analysis in the Bybee Memo was bizarre. The memo argued that because a health-care statute lists severe pain as a possible symptom of a medical emergency, only pain equivalent to that accompanying medical emergencies is severe. It attempted to show that while the necessity defense applies to torture, it need not apply to life-saving abortions. It also argued that Congress had defined torture so as to permit its use when necessary, even though Congress categorically forbade torture regardless of its purpose. And it argued that the President has authority to order torture regardless of the statutory prohibition, without bothering to so much as raise the question whether this runs contrary to the Take Care Clause of the Constitution. It is hard not to agree with Peter Brooks's blunt assessment: the Bybee Memo "offers a remarkable example of textual interpretation run amok—less 'lawyering as usual' than the work of some bizarre literary deconstructionist." Unsurprisingly, in the wake of the Abu Ghraib scandal, the Justice Department repudiated the Bybee Memo. Indeed, former OLC lawyers from past Republican administrations criticized the memo, and Ruth Wedgwood, perhaps the most prominent academic defender of Bush Administration legal positions in the War on Terror, denounced the Bybee Memo in a blistering Wall Street Journal op-ed, which she co-authored with former CIA Director R. James Woolsey. Shortly before Alberto Gonzales faced confirmation hearings as Attorney General, the OLC issued a new torture memorandum (the "Levin Memorandum"), repudiating and replacing the Bybee Memo. It was posted unannounced on the Department of Justice's website, on December 30, 2004.

What should we make of this? Not much, some might say. The Justice Department has disowned the Bybee Memo, Mr. Bybee has been promoted out of the OLC to the federal appellate bench, and Professor Yoo, the principal author of the Bybee Memo, has left government service. One way to understand the Bybee Memo is that it represents an odd moment when several stars and planets fell into an unusual alignment and the moonshine threw the OLC into a peculiarly aggressive mood. Now, however, the OLC has officially rescinded the Bybee Memo and replaced it with a document that begins with a ringing affirmation of U.S. opposition to torture.

But the lawyers' torture culture is not just the OLC in an isolated period of time, now past. It would be a dramatic mistake to suppose that the Justice Department has abandoned its views merely because it has disowned the Bybee Memo. Although the Levin Memo condemns torture and repudiates the Bybee Memo's narrow definition of "severe pain," a careful reading shows that it does not broaden it substantially. Stunningly, all its illustrative examples amples of "the nature of the extreme conduct that falls within the statutory definition" of torture are on the upper end of the scale of barbarism. They include, for example, "severe beatings to the genitals, head, and other parts of the body with metal pipes, brass knuckles, batons, a baseball bat, and various other items; removal of teeth with pliers . . . cutting off . . . fingers, pulling out . . . fingernails" and similar atrocities. Levin includes no hint that torture lite, or even torture medium, are prohibited by the statute. The Levin Memo's analysis of "severe mental pain" differs from that of the Bybee Memo in that it no longer suggests that the term encompasses only psychological damage that lasts for months or even years. Again, however, its illustrative examples all involve damage that lasted for years. Nor does Levin criticize the Bybee Memo's analyses of self-defense or necessity; it simply declines to discuss defenses. Similarly, it leaves open the question of whether the President can authorize torture, declaring evasively that because this President opposes torture, any discussion of the limits of his authority is unnecessary. The Levin Memo does acknowledge that techniques causing "severe physical suffering" count as torture even if they do not cause "severe physical pain"—and that may rule out some stress positions that the Bybee Memo permits. But apart from this one change, the Levin Memo represents the minimum possible cosmetic emendation of the Bybee Memo. It retracts only the arguments that journalists had jumped on (the "organ failure" definition of torture and the excessive emphasis Bybee placed on the specific intent requirement), retains a conception of torture as atrocity fully in line with the liberal ideology, and evades the questions of criminal defenses and Presidential authority to authorize torture.

Indeed, the OLC prepared other opinions, never released or leaked, which addressed specific interrogation techniques—and the Levin Memo leaves these untouched. In December 2004, the Bush administration fought off restrictions (passed by a ninety-six to two Senate vote) which "would have explicitly extended to intelligence officers a prohibition against torture or inhumane treatment, and would have required the C.I.A. as well as the Pentagon to report to

Congress about the methods they were using." When asked why the administration resisted these restrictions, both Alberto Gonzales and Condaleezza Rice replied that it was to deny protection to people who are not entitled to it. Neither finished the sentence: "not entitled to protection from torture or inhumane treatment."

One major loophole that the torture lawyers exploit is the distinction drawn in the Torture Convention between torture and "cruel, inhuman, or degrading" ("CID") treatment. The Convention bans both, but U.S.-implementing legislation criminalized only torture, not CID. Mr. Gonzales told the U.S. Senate in his written answers to questions that cruel, inhuman, and degrading treatment of detainees is forbidden to interrogators only within U.S. territory. The legal basis for this opinion was another piece of loop-hole lawyering on a par with the Bybee Memo. When the United States ratified the Torture Convention, it attached a reservation interpreting "cruel, inhuman, and degrading" treatment to mean treatment violative of the Fifth, Eighth, or Fourteenth Amendments. Because these amendments do not apply extraterritorially, Mr. Gonzales argued, the prohibition on CID does not bind U.S. interrogators abroad. Clearly, however, the Senate's reservation was referring to the substantive standards in the three amendments, not their jurisdictional scope. To read it as Mr. Gonzales does would attribute to the Senate the remarkably absurd proposition that *by definition*, nothing U.S. interrogators do abroad could ever be cruel, inhuman, or degrading.

It goes on. In March 2004, the OLC prepared a draft memorandum loopholing the Geneva Convention's prohibition on removing captives from the country of their capture and authorizing brief transfers of Iraqi captives out of Iraq for interrogation. In early 2005, there were new revelations that the United States engages in "extraordinary renditions"—sending suspects for interrogation to states that engage in torture. Reportedly, secret legal opinions justify

extraordinary renditions, which may violate the Torture Convention. In one well-known case, Maher Arar, a Canadian citizen of Syrian birth, was detained while transferring from one flight to another in New York City and sent to Syria, where he was tortured for a year. He is currently suing the U.S. government, which has moved to dismiss his suit on remarkable grounds, asserting that the facts needed to litigate his case are U.S. state secrets, and therefore he has no case. In another well-known case, Omar Abu Ali, a U.S. citizen of Saudi descent, was allegedly snatched by Saudi agents from his university classroom in Saudi Arabia, tortured, and detained for a year and a half at U.S. request. When his parents filed for habeas corpus, the government offered no rebuttal of their allegations, instead arguing that the court lacks jurisdiction, and grounding the government's action in the President's foreign affairs power (not even his commander-in-chief power).

In April 2005, the circle beginning with the Abu Ghraib scandal closed, as a military investigation of alleged abuses at Guantanamo concluded that several of the humiliating techniques that drew shocked responses at Abu Ghraib—techniques such as sexually humiliating detainees, forcing them to wear women's underwear on their heads, leading them around on leashes, and forcing them to do dog tricks—are not illegal, and indeed have been authorized all along by Army Field Manual 34–52, the standard U.S. Army doctrine regarding interrogation. Along with this creative and unprecedented interpretation of Army doctrine, the report "found no evidence of torture or inhumane treatment at [Guantanamo]." Apparently, the Army no longer regards many of the Abu Ghraib techniques as "inhumane."

Conclusion

The only reasonable inference to draw from these recent efforts by the government to defend its actions is that the torture culture is still firmly in place, notwithstanding official condemnation of torture. Indeed, given that lawyers at the highest levels of government continue to loophole the laws against torture as energetically as ever, more than half a year after the Abu Ghraib revelations, the only reasonable inference to draw is *that the United States government is currently engaging in brutal and humiliating interrogations*. At most, torture has given way to CID. The persistence of interrogational brutality should surprise no one, because the liberal ideology of torture fully legitimizes it. The memos illustrate the ease with which arguments that pretend that torture can exist in liberal society, but only as an exception, quickly lead to erecting a torture culture, a network of institutions and practices that regularize the exception and make it standard operating procedure.

For this reason, the liberal ideology of torture, which assumes that torture can be neatly confined to exceptional ticking-bomb cases and surgically severed from cruelty and tyranny, represents a dangerous delusion. It becomes more dangerous still coupled with an endless war on terror, a permanent emergency in which the White House eagerly insists that its emergency powers rise above the limiting power of statutes and treaties. Claims to long-term emergency powers that entail the power to torture should send chills through liberals of the right as well as the left, and no one should still think that liberal torture has nothing to do with tyranny.

Glossary

Anarchism—As a philosophic doctrine, anarchism is the view that no state is justified; that all purported political authority is illegitimate.

Communitarianism—Refers to a family of political theories united by their rejection of liberalism's universalism and individualism, and their stress upon the importance of the social nature of the individual and political life in general.

Consequentialism—The moral doctrine that the consequences of an action (or policy) are the only criteria for its rightness or wrongness. Opposed to deontology.

Cosmopolitanism—The idea that all human beings, regardless of their political affiliation, belong to a common moral community. Cosmopolitans often believe that all individuals have the same basic moral status, and tend to downplay the importance or desirability of national political institutions. Opposed to nationalism.

Deontology—Refers to a family of moral theories that trace their roots to Immanuel Kant. Deontologists believe that morality is a matter of fulfilling duties and/or respecting rights, even when the effect of remaining committed to this principle are less than optimific. Opposed to consequentialism.

Difference Principle—The more widely discussed of Rawls' two principles of justice, this principle holds that social and economic equalities are to be tolerated only if the effect of allowing them is to benefit the least well-off members of society.

Distributive Justice—That area of philosophy concerned with the moral principles that ought to govern the allocation of benefits and burdens amongst individuals and groups.

Externalities—An economic term that refers to costs or benefits of an activity that are borne by persons not directly party to that activity. Negative (costly) externalities are often thought of as a market failure and a justification for corrective action by government.

Liberalism—Philosophically, liberalism refers not just to "left-wing" political positions, as it does in contemporary American politics, but to all political positions that share a commitment to the idea that political institutions are to be morally assessed by their effects on individuals, that are committed to the value of individual liberty, and that tend to favor (relatively) restricted government in order to secure this liberty.

Libertarianism—The doctrine that no more (or not much more) than a minimal state—one that provides police, military, and a court system—is morally legitimate; that government should be restricted to the protection of individual negative liberty; and that most functions currently provided by the state should be left to the market mechanism or other voluntary methods of provision.

Nationalism—The view that nations and national identity are deeply important values that ought to be protected by social norms and political institutions. This position bears some affinity with communitarianism and is most directly opposed to cosmopolitanism.

Natural Law—Natural law theorists trace their roots to St. Thomas Aquinas, and hold that there are objective moral truths that hold simply in virtue of human nature and the nature of the human world, and that these truths indicate a natural human good. Often, but not necessarily, these moral truths are held to derive their authority from God.

Natural Rights—The view that human beings have rights independent of and prior to the existence of government, and that these rights constrain the ways in which governments may legitimately treat individuals. Often connected with the natural law tradition, though the natural rights tradition tends to be less strictly tied with religious views.

Negative Liberty—Negative liberty is freedom from certain sorts of interference by others. Libertarians believe that negative liberty is the only sort of liberty we have, or that it is the only sort of liberty that may be politically enforced. Contrasted with positive liberty. One might have negative liberty to do something without actually being *able* to do it.

Negative Rights—Negative rights are claims against others that they refrain from engaging in certain types of activity. Libertarians believe that negative rights are the only sorts of rights we have, or that they are the only sorts of rights that may be politically enforced. Contrasted with positive rights.

Political Authority—That which renders a government morally legitimate—which justifies it in ruling over a population, exercising coercion upon them, and claiming a monopoly on the use of force.

Positive Liberty—A more nebulous concept than its cousin, negative liberty, positive liberty refers variously to the power to do what one desires (or might desire) to do, to realize one's true self, or to do what one morally ought to do. Having the positive liberty to do something may require more than non-interference from others.

Positive Rights—Claims against others which require them to perform some positive act for one's benefit, and not merely that they refrain from interfering. Rights to a state-provided education or to poverty-relief are examples of positive rights.

Prisoner's Dilemma—A model of certain types of human interaction drawn from game theory. In the standard two-person Prisoner's Dilemma, each player has an incentive to defect against the other, even though mutual defection leaves both players worse off than they would have been with mutual cooperation.

Prioritarianism—The view that in matters of distributive justice, priority ought to be given to meeting the needs/desires of the least well-off.

Public Good—In economic terms, a public good is one which has the characteristics of non-rivalry (one person's consumption does not diminish the amount available for others) and non-excludability (it is impossible to exclude people from consuming the good). Because of these characteristics, rational and self-interested individuals will not choose to pay for public goods but to free-ride on the contributions of others, and markets will therefore tend to under-supply them. The provision of public goods such as clean air and national defense has been thought to be one of the chief justifications of government.

Social Contract—An agreement, sometimes thought to be a real historical event but more often hypothetical and heuristic in nature, by which individuals in the state of nature agree to the formation of government.

State of Nature—A state of affairs in which individuals are not subject to the authority of any government.

Utilitarianism—The moral view that holds that happiness/pleasure is the only intrinsic good, and that right actions are those that produce the greatest possible amount of happiness.

Index

Ackerman, Bruce 116, 121, 340, 399, 496–8, 501–5

Aggression 36–37, 39, 42–45, 62, 162–4, 191, 367, 414, 437, 449, 572, 574, 578, 599, 605, 619, 638, 643, 659

Alienation 56–7, 59–60, 62–4, 319, 377, 392, 428, 467, 501,

Anarchism 36–45, 684

Anarchy 84, 133, 140, 443, 448, 594, 602, 626–6

Appropriation 241, 243–244, 281–2, 287–9, 297–8, 301, 308–14, 318, 326–7, 332–3, 359, 384, 441, 504, 554, 560, 598

Aquinas, Thomas 554, 605, 665

Arbitrariness 34, 36, 43, 57, 128–9, 167, 190, 197, 206, 210–13, 217, 224, 312, 340, 363, 418, 431, 447, 499, 500, 593, 580, 621–2, 659

Arneson, Richard 452–3, 482, 498

Aristotle 49, 56, 104, 201, 220, 442–4, 649

Arrow, Kenneth 277–8

Authority, political 3–5, 20, 55, 57–8, 67, 71–7, 80, 103, 106–7, 111–3, 118–21, 130, 232, 399, 404, 448, 465, 488, 522, 567–8, 589–91, 595–601, 623–4, 638, 642

Autonomy 101, 107, 167, 196, 221, 343, 382, 387, 389–93, 395, 421–3, 429, 489, 542, 573, 595–8, 628, 630–2, 635, 637, 645

Basic structure of society 98, 194, 195, 197, 205–9, 211–3, 215, 574–6

Benevolence 37, 92, 148–9, 151, 169, 173–5, 185, 191, 197, 216, 270, 380, 386, 402, 405, 407–8, 418, 421, 423, 465

Bentham, Jeremy 108, 123, 132, 178, 192, 203, 205–6, 423, 429

Blackstone, William 114, 447, 589, 592

Borders, national 129, 517–8, 521–38, 562, 568–9, 571, 575, 577, 581, 595–6, 605, 618, 626–8, 631–2, 634, 637, 642

Buchanan, Allen 566, 574–83, 595, 642–4

Buchanan, James 107, 270

Capitalism 36, 79, 84, 231–2, 322, 340–1, 407–13, 396

Chamberlain, Wilt 364–5

Charity 13, 149, 185, 268, 334, 363, 369, 552–4, 581

Children 9, 50, 55–7, 73, 75, 130, 152, 166, 170, 173, 177, 241, 245, 247–8, 251, 285–6, 302, 311–13, 317, 339, 348, 351, 355, 358, 362–3, 370, 375, 384, 402, 408, 429–30, 434, 441, 443–4, 448, 456, 459, 465, 473–4, 497, 505–507, 509–12, 514, 516–17, 520, 555, 570–1, 591, 615, 638, 648

Citizenship 61, 99, 127, 194, 206–7, 223, 523, 533–4, 541, 543, 589, 591

Class, social 106, 167, 210, 213, 254, 351, 451

Coase, Ronald 264–5

Coercion 36–8, 40–1, 43–4, 83, 85, 402, 415–16, 419, 421, 428–9, 573–4, 591, 613, 618, 628, 643

Cohen, G.A. 320, 498, 504

Commerce 76, 176, 236, 238–9, 245–6, 288, 292, 311–2, 446, 463, 504

Common Good 44, 49, 63, 103, 117, 138, 146, 205, 224–6

Compensation 159, 189, 299, 301–4, 360, 417, 483–6, 492, 494, 497, 557, 560, 577, 598

Competition 9, 14, 41, 49, 83, 87, 88, 187, 238–40, 242, 246, 258–9, 265–6, 272, 306, 372, 378, 444, 462, 465, 467, 494, 497, 526, 577, 600, 611

Conflict 24–5, 68, 82, 91–100, 103–7, 111–2, 119, 134, 139, 185, 189–90, 194–5, 203, 205, 235, 255, 266, 271, 274–5, 282, 294, 321, 369, 378, 417, 420, 426, 429, 432–4, 448, 463, 465, 467, 474, 488, 494, 489, 529, 570, 572, 574, 578, 596, 603, 617–18, 622, 636–7, 642

Conquest 8, 45, 58, 72–4, 81, 239, 243, 399, 433, 560, 611, 651, 653

Consent 3–5, 17, 19, 48–50, 52–4, 63, 67, 69, 71–77, 106, 116, 129, 161, 188–9, 199, 204, 206–7, 286–9, 291–2, 297, 309, 336, 339, 365, 390, 400, 403, 413, 423, 429, 431, 445–8, 455, 535, 586 592, 632–3, 640–1, 645, 657; tacit 4, 52, 53–4, 75–7, 288, 292–3, 582

Consequentialism 119, 166, 231, 282, 482, 546, 560–1, 606, 634, 638–9, 656, 664

Conservatism 119, 134–40, 271, 276, 418, 435, 448, 498, 518, 521, 523, 533, 617, 647–8

Constant, Benjamin 416, 418, 432

Constitution 11, 53, 66, 69, 74, 90, 93–4, 97–105, 107, 114, 118, 121, 128, 133, 136–7, 141, 143, 196, 220, 227, 238, 255, 260–1, 270, 293, 333, 396, 400, 411, 445–7, 449, 478, 589, 583, 603, 628, 51, 660

Contract, social 3–5, 59–61, 63, 98, 114, 195, 418, 628, 632, 651, 666

Contractualism 106–9, 114–5, 560–1

Cooperation 20–39, 82, 130, 194–7, 200–3, 206, 211, 213–15, 223–4, 249, 310, 355, 357, 364, 437, 496, 501–2, 504, 560, 613, 616, 621, 633–4

Custom 45, 66, 170, 177, 223, 304, 314–15, 317–19, 357, 413–4, 418, 445, 529, 559, 571, 575, 580, 625, 635

Decentralization 226, 316, 318, 569, 618

Democracy 5, 84, 90–1, 93–105, 106–9, 111, 113, 115–121, 131, 134, 139, 209, 211, 226–7, 247–8, 252–5, 267–9, 272, 276–80, 354, 387–93, 401, 411, 419–20, 424, 427, 430, 436, 445, 448, 499, 507, 522–3, 528, 531, 533, 539–40, 543, 563, 570, 572, 575, 578, 580, 591, 599, 603, 609–10, 613, 617–18, 620–22, 633–4, 637, 639, 643–4, 651

Deontology 107–10, 119, 204, 282, 546–7, 638–9, 664

Desert, moral 81, 150–1, 157, 160, 182, 192, 202, 213–14, 224, 241, 281, 340, 361, 376, 414, 482, 499

Difference principle 99, 209, 211–14, 217, 223–5, 370, 473, 576, 664

Dignity 17, 49, 127–8, 130, 142–6, 155, 158, 232, 260, 353, 382, 386, 407, 424, 575, 577, 579, 609, 628–9, 636, 648–50

Disagreement 4–5, 90–105, 107, 110–12, 119, 121, 135, 396, 518, 520, 546, 549, 569–71, 575, 578, 601, 627

Discount/discounting 23–4, 140, 487, 527

Discrimination 128, 130, 144, 199, 295, 451, 518, 541–3, 600, 632

Distributive Justice 167, 192, 263, 268, 283, 321, 326, 339–41, 358–69, 371, 379, 494, 498, 529, 534, 537, 545–7, 566–7, 570, 575, 582, 586, 601, 664

Dworkin, Ronald 125, 132, 320–1, 472, 474, 482–3, 488–9, 598

Education 71, 105, 125, 128, 130, 143, 156, 170, 171, 177, 187, 188, 210, 212, 245, 247, 255, 263, 264, 280, 337, 370, 383–5, 392, 405, 417, 426, 430, 444, 474, 483, 486, 490, 509, 511, 522–3, 525–7, 562, 611, 613, 622

Efficiency 38, 40–1, 43–4, 81, 83, 118, 136, 142, 161, 190, 194, 202, 206, 209–12, 217, 224, 262–8, 269–76, 279–80, 301, 375–7, 387, 433, 491, 499, 522, 565, 581, 634, 642

Egalitarianism 92, 117, 212–14, 321–6, 331, 361, 366, 380, 383, 392–3, 451–3, 466–74, 482, 484–5, 488–9, 493, 495–501, 504, 512–13, 560

Ellickson, Robert 313–18

Equality 8, 13–14, 63–5, 68, 70, 72, 94, 97–9, 115–16, 119–21, 128, 132–3, 141–3, 145–6, 166–7, 183, 192, 195–200, 203, 206–12, 217, 251, 263, 271, 280, 321–6, 360–1, 363, 377, 389, 391–3, 412, 416–17, 428–9, 433, 435, 448, 451–3, 464, 466–77, 478, 482–94, 495–501, 512–13, 517, 543, 551, 575

Equilibrium 199, 267–8

Exploitation 22, 27–8, 32, 34–5, 78, 237, 239, 243, 245–6, 252, 274, 313, 321–4, 373, 419, 439–41, 546, 596, 600, 618

Expression, freedom of 95, 101, 109, 114, 127, 129, 132–3, 137–8, 141–6, 206, 227, 404, 418–19, 437, 617

Externality 264–6, 268, 312, 314–19, 563, 634

Fairness 41–2, 58, 73, 76, 91, 93, 95–9, 104, 106–7, 118, 120–1, 128, 143, 156, 167, 187, 195–217, 219, 224, 227, 249, 251, 279, 292, 300, 375, 385, 393, 402, 406, 414, 416–17, 478, 480, 484, 489, 491, 497, 504, 528, 537, 546, 564, 567

Family 55–6, 73, 90, 127, 129–30, 170–1, 182, 211, 214, 225, 237, 241, 245, 280, 302, 306, 314, 317–18, 348, 354–7, 366, 370, 377, 408, 439, 443–4, 448, 463, 474, 493, 501, 506–7, 509–12, 523–4, 556, 611, 615, 632

First possession 281–3, 308–14, 318, 327, 332, 381, 496, 502–4, 513

Fraud 10, 74, 159, 189, 359–60, 434, 439

Free market 36, 38–9, 41–5, 209–10, 262–3, 265, 275, 374–5, 418, 630, 637

Freedom 13, 17, 19, 52, 75, 76, 95, 98, 99, 101, 109, 114, 127–31, 142–3, 145, 178, 189, 191, 194, 203–4, 206, 208, 220–1, 237, 243–6, 253–5, 277, 282–3, 297, 304, 306, 339–40, 353, 373, 377, 389–90, 395–6, 403–5, 409, 412, 414, 415–436, 437–8, 439, 445–6, 490–1, 505, 517, 521–2, 524–5, 527–8, 534–5, 537, 555, 569, 585–6, 589–594, 616–18, 632–3, 643–4

Friedman, Milton 252, 276, 388

Gauthier, David 107–8

General Will 60–1, 63–5, 67–70

Glampers, Diana Moon 479, 481

God 11, 14–16, 19, 50, 56, 66–7, 116, 134, 142, 151–2, 285–8, 290, 294–5, 297, 302 316, 333–5, 410, 413–4, 437–8, 446–7, 478, 480–1, 590–1, 593, 617, 624, 636–7, 657

Grotius 56–9, 605

Hayek, Friedrich 270, 339, 363, 369, 567
Hobbes, Thomas 3–4, 20, 56, 80, 91, 151, 418, 451, 456 460–1, 627–8
Human nature 4, 15, 44, 66, 74, 91–2, 148, 170, 173, 221, 404, 406, 417–18, 426
Hume, David 4, 92, 166, 205–6
Hypothetical contract 4–5, 195–6, 200, 207, 215, 641

Impartiality 41, 44, 166, 182–3, 192, 460, 551
Incentives 20, 22, 88, 114, 265–7, 270, 274, 282, 313–5, 339, 500, 524, 539–40, 563, 577, 634, 637, 645–6
Individualism 366, 419, 424, 431
Inequality 63, 99, 115–16, 120, 167, 183, 190, 192, 197, 204, 206–9, 211–12, 217, 223, 251–3, 271, 280, 293, 320, 323, 326–7, 332–4, 340, 355, 363, 365, 376, 392, 396, 417, 419, 435, 448, 451–3, 455, 457, 459, 461, 463–5, 467–8, 471–2, 486–9, 492–3, 495, 506–7, 511–14, 545, 559–61, 565, 577, 582
Inheritance 54, 247, 363, 384, 399, 570, 632
Invisible Hand 231–2, 270, 375

Jefferson, Thomas 84, 123, 226, 418, 443
Justice 3–4, 10–11, 13–14, 18–19, 48–9, 61, 64–6, 72, 74, 76, 82, 92–3, 99–102, 104, 107, 127, 142, 153, 165–7, 169, 171–7, 178–93, 194–218, 219–20, 222–6, 255, 263, 268, 280, 283, 294–307, 319, 320–1, 326, 339–41, 358–69, 371–3, 375–7, 379, 382, 384–6, 387, 389, 393, 402, 410, 416–18, 421, 424, 428, 433, 435, 452, 461, 494–501, 504, 513, 527–30, 533–4, 537–8, 545–6, 560–1, 564, 565–83, 591, 598–601, 611, 627–8, 630–2, 634, 636, 639–42, 644, 646, 651

Kant, Immanuel 108, 142, 148, 150, 161–2, 166–7, 186, 195, 216, 220–3, 423–4, 427, 429, 431–2, 435, 581, 628, 632

Labor 8, 62, 83, 150, 169–70, 183, 190, 231–2, 236–45, 247–54, 257, 259–61, 263, 281–3, 286–93, 295–8, 300–2, 305–6, 309, 314, 319, 320–37, 343, 355–6, 361, 367–9, 374, 383, 388, 390, 392, 405, 411, 413, 439–41, 444, 447–8, 457, 464, 489–90, 504–5, 517–18, 522–6, 561, 613, 617, 619, 657–8
Law of Nature 4, 10, 13–17, 19, 47, 49, 52, 64, 73, 245, 286–7, 289, 298, 304, 335, 395, 422–3, 426, 446, 465, 589
Legislation 66–7, 98, 114, 117, 133, 141, 254, 257, 265–6, 275, 404, 412–13, 426, 433, 573, 593–4, 647, 662
Legitimacy 3–5, 37–9, 44–5, 55–8, 62–3, 65, 78–81, 91, 95, 98, 103–4, 160, 163, 180, 182, 188–9, 213, 281, 297, 310, 320, 326–7, 334–5, 339–40, 359, 365, 368, 381–3, 385–6, 392, 395, 399, 401–2, 410, 413, 452, 465, 468, 482, 486, 491, 518, 528, 536, 541–2, 578–80, 590, 595, 597–9, 601–3, 605, 609, 623, 627–9, 631–2, 634, 638–9, 642–3, 645, 651–2, 655, 657, 660

Liberalism 106, 109–12, 114–17, 119–21, 134–6, 138, 145–6, 159, 167, 209–11, 219–20, 223–7, 255, 257, 260, 323, 369, 376, 380, 385, 395, 400, 417–19, 424, 429–34, 451, 498, 500, 513, 518, 521–3, 531, 533–35, 539–41, 566, 570, 573, 575–6, 580, 597, 602, 610, 622, 626–32, 638, 642–45, 648–53, 655, 657, 659, 661, 663
Libertarianism 45, 11, 125, 162–3, 223, 253, 282–3, 339–40, 353, 388, 416, 420, 498, 517–18, 521, 526, 546, 570, 643–5
Liberty 4, 8, 10, 14, 16–18, 46–8, 52–4, 55–9, 61, 64–5, 69–70, 72, 74, 95, 98–9, 101, 123, 128, 137, 153, 173, 176, 181–2, 195, 202–4, 206–11, 217, 219–20, 227, 246, 290, 308, 311, 315, 364, 371, 373, 381, 389–90, 395–6, 399–404, 407, 409–14, 415–21, 424–5, 427–9, 432–3, 435, 441–8, 457–8, 460, 467, 483, 489–90, 492, 502–4, 531, 573, 586, 589–90, 593, 602, 607, 617, 621, 633, 651
Locke, John 3–4, 112, 195, 205–6, 282, 309–10, 313, 321, 323, 326–37, 360, 368, 390, 416, 418, 424, 429, 443–4, 446, 451, 464, 494, 560

Majoritarian 93–97, 580
Market 37–39, 41–5, 78, 83, 209–10, 224, 226, 232, 236–7, 239, 246, 258, 259, 262–8, 270–2, 274–5, 277, 279–80, 300–1, 309, 311, 318, 324, 328, 339–40, 343, 355, 366, 371–7, 383, 390, 395, 418, 485, 500, 504–6, 513, 522, 525–6, 558, 562–3, 630, 637, 643
Market Failure 232, 263–8, 643
Marx, Karl 92, 146, 232, 263, 321–4, 326–9, 340, 344, 396, 426–8, 434, 501, 504, 567, 570
Military 74, 78–9, 82, 84, 86–8, 254, 300, 419, 445, 480, 546, 565, 573, 595, 599, 610, 612, 616, 618–20, 622–3, 626–7, 638, 643–4, 648, 650, 653, 655–8, 660, 662
Mill, John Stuart 99, 103, 115–17, 121, 166, 220, 223, 231, 300–1, 303, 395, 416, 418–19, 424, 430, 432–3, 435, 633, 648
Miller, David 528–9, 566, 576
Minimum Wage 231, 243, 276
Money 3, 5, 37, 44, 68, 86, 123, 135, 150, 156, 162, 231, 237, 244, 257, 259–60, 271–2, 276, 301–3, 334, 339–40, 347–8, 355, 363–5, 368, 380, 383, 408, 416, 448, 452, 466–9, 471–3, 475–6, 492, 502, 505–6, 508, 511–13, 527, 545–6, 549, 552–3, 555, 557, 563, 582, 592–3, 600, 611, 613
Monopoly 36–8, 41, 43–4, 80, 82–4, 150–2, 159, 161, 247, 265–6, 322, 388, 605
Montesquieu 66, 294, 429, 447, 649
Mutual Benefit 23, 13, 32, 108, 194, 197, 310, 504, 575, 636

Nagel, Thomas 473–4
Nationality 129, 167, 242, 246, 527, 530
Needs, basic 99, 157, 340, 367, 426, 559, 577

Negative liberty 395–6, 415, 424, 432, 435, 586
Nietzsche, Friedrich 116, 201, 615, 648
Nock, Albert Jay 37
Nozick, Robert 125, 231, 282–3, 320–1, 332–3, 339–40, 567, 638

Obedience 4, 53, 55–7, 61, 72–7, 112, 133–4, 136–8, 140, 146, 149, 152–3, 181–2, 189, 191, 287, 345, 373, 402, 423, 425, 430, 446, 455, 579, 613–14, 625, 629
Obligation 4, 13, 46, 48, 52, 54, 56–60, 71–7, 128, 134, 136, 149–52, 172, 174–6, 182, 184–5, 187, 190–3, 196, 205, 225, 227, 339, 360, 373–4, 377, 384, 396, 404, 408, 414, 440, 444, 460, 464, 485, 527–8, 534, 537–8, 541–3, 551–2, 555, 563, 569, 575, 581, 586, 598, 602, 626, 628, 635, 643–4, 660
Opportunity 37, 85, 99, 106, 167, 171, 176, 207, 209–12, 217, 232, 263, 266, 271, 276, 293, 332, 353, 381, 392–3, 452–3, 457, 459, 472, 474, 476, 482–3, 485–94, 500, 508–9, 512, 524–5, 527, 530, 537–8, 582, 614–15
Original Appropriation see First Possession
Original Position 167, 195–200, 203–4, 206, 209, 211, 214–17, 222–3, 226
Ownership 83, 151, 154, 250–1, 281–2, 295–9, 301, 303–7, 308, 314, 317–21, 323–4, 336–7, 369, 387, 387–91, 453, 482–3, 489–90, 570

Pacifism 43, 617, 621, 628–9, 659
Pareto Efficiency 263, 267, 269
Paternalism 163, 353, 380, 423, 592
Peace 7, 10, 12, 13–14, 18, 38–9, 46–50, 52, 58, 68, 72, 76, 82–3, 87–88, 96, 127, 129–30, 172–4, 176–7, 191, 226, 254, 295, 302–3, 371, 374, 377, 384–5, 417, 437, 442–3, 459–61, 503, 568–9, 574, 576–8, 605, 609, 611–12, 616, 621–2, 636, 641–2, 644
Plato 66, 165, 420, 424, 431, 434, 457, 567, 649
Pogge, Thomas 545–6, 566, 574, 576–7, 581–3
Positive liberty 395–6, 420
Poverty 102, 144, 249, 252, 297, 300, 305–6, 343, 354–6, 380, 416–7, 472, 494, 509–12, 524, 537–8, 545–6, 549, 551, 558–64, 565, 574, 576–7, 581–2, 642
Procedure 5, 23, 40, 42, 90, 93–101, 103–5, 106–7, 112–21, 130, 137, 145, 161, 198, 208, 210, 214, 225–7, 229, 328–9, 331, 346, 368, 373, 380, 390–1, 483, 603, 648, 650, 663
Profit 58, 67, 83–5, 202, 257–60, 265–6, 270, 274–5, 280, 291, 303, 321, 353, 368–9, 393, 412, 439, 462, 465, 469
Proletariat 235–6, 239–43, 245–8, 254, 322–3, 343, 379, 449, 504, 616–17
Property 14, 19, 36–9, 42–3, 45, 54, 58, 61–2, 72, 76–7, 84, 109–10, 124–5, 128–9, 144–6, 151, 172, 174–7, 179, 181, 190, 206, 210, 237–9, 241 243–5, 247–9, 252, 255, 275, 281–3, 285–93, 294–7, 299–300, 303–6, 308–10, 312–18, 321, 326–7, 333–6, 353, 365,

366, 368–9374, 387–91, 395, 407, 411, 418, 422, 426, 440–1, 444, 448, 462, 464–5, 513–15, 535, 553–4, 560, 563–4, 567, 570, 589, 593, 596, 598, 610, 624, 629, 634, 643, 651
Protection 36–9, 44, 49, 54, 72, 78–81, 83–88, 104, 117, 128–31, 133, 137, 139, 145, 152, 159–61, 183, 190, 202, 265, 267, 290, 336, 391, 399, 401–4, 407–8, 418, 443, 447, 518, 534, 541–2, 562, 565, 573–4, 585, 589, 594, 599–600, 614–15, 627, 632, 634–5, 637, 661–2
Public Good 58, 62, 68, 84, 99, 107, 232, 264, 268, 270–1, 333, 446–7, 585, 643–5
Punishment 10, 14–16, 19, 21–22, 24, 27, 29–30, 45, 48, 92, 123, 128, 134, 138, 165–6, 182, 184, 187–9, 191–2, 334, 354, 356, 361, 406–7, 423, 525, 567, 579, 617–18, 624, 642, 647, 651–3

Rationality 16, 19, 21, 50, 53, 106, 109–11, 119–21, 161, 167, 180, 186–7, 192, 195–204, 206–7, 211, 214–17, 221, 225, 232, 265, 273–4, 279, 287, 354, 363, 381–2, 384–6, 395, 404, 420–1, 424–32, 434–5, 461, 476–7, 486–7, 491, 502–3, 560, 618, 621, 622, 624, 630, 637, 641, 649, 651, 653, 656
Rawls, John 98–100, 107–9, 165–7, 220, 222–4, 231, 320–1, 339–40, 370, 384, 473, 482, 488, 490–1, 546, 566, 573–4, 576, 628–9, 641
Reasonable 5, 8, 11, 15–17, 47–8, 93–5, 98–99, 101–2, 104, 106–11, 113–18, 120–1, 130, 140–1, 191, 196–200, 204, 208, 213–14, 218, 222, 277, 353, 363, 396, 455, 466–7, 470–1, 473–7, 486, 492, 518, 536, 538, 543, 546, 566, 597, 602, 614, 626, 628, 630–1, 633, 640, 642, 662
Reciprocity 197, 213, 414
Redistribution 110–11, 159, 224, 263, 267–8, 269, 271, 280, 294, 323–4, 331, 336, 349, 358, 366–8, 376, 384, 396, 453, 472, 486, 496, 498–9, 501, 503, 506, 545, 582, 598, 600–1
Reflective Equilibrium 199
Religion 37, 68, 86, 101, 114, 123, 128–30, 134–5, 143–4, 152, 167, 196, 199, 237, 241, 246, 255, 354, 374, 409–11, 413–14, 418–19, 422, 434, 444, 451, 479, 484–7, 528–30, 534–6, 539–40, 543, 567–71, 586, 593, 598, 613, 616, 618–19, 630–1, 636, 650, 658
Respect 62, 93–95, 97–98, 104, 127–8, 130–1, 132, 134–6, 138, 140, 142, 144, 146, 150, 152, 155, 158, 162, 166, 181, 204–6, 217, 221, 223, 282–3, 340, 353, 382, 391–2, 407, 428, 435, 453, 461, 464, 496–7, 500–3, 513, 517, 533, 573, 575, 577, 581, 595, 609, 626–9, 632–4, 639, 644–5, 657
Retaliation 24, 27, 35, 44, 80, 159, 186–7
Revolution 44, 82, 87, 241–3, 246–8, 304, 386, 400, 437, 448, 599, 601, 618, 638
Rights, legal 63, 123–4, 133, 136–7, 157, 181–2, 185, 210, 315, 535, 646 moral 94, 123–4, 132–41, 143, 157, 182, 185, 533, 598

Rousseau, Jean-Jacques 3, 195, 248, 416, 423–4, 427, 429, 431

Rule of Law 95, 127, 206, 575–6, 579

Scarcity 92, 102, 156, 171, 174, 303, 313, 319, 470

Self-defense 43, 159, 163, 186, 188, 191, 354, 457, 504, 574, 578, 598–9, 601, 613, 628–30, 643–5, 653, 660–1

Self-interest 21, 41, 83, 91–2, 103, 106, 115, 165, 173, 177, 187, 232, 237, 270, 485–6, 490, 518, 554

Self-ownership 282, 320–1, 323–4, 369

Sen, Amartya 490–1, 513

Sidgwick, Henry 200, 203, 205–6, 262, 553–4

Singer, Peter 120, 545–6, 561, 566

Slavery 17, 44, 55–8, 61, 69, 124, 128, 166, 183, 190, 193, 207, 235–6, 239, 242, 248, 253, 295, 297, 299–301, 303–4, 306–7, 320, 322, 336, 343, 360, 383, 396, 415–16, 420, 423–5, 427–30, 433, 439–49, 455, 458, 465, 483, 489, 528, 530, 558, 591, 632, 650–1

Smith, Adam 231–2, 270, 374–5, 418

Social Contract 3–5, 60–1, 65, 78, 114, 195, 418, 628, 632, 651

Social Justice 100, 195, 198–9, 214, 371–2, 377, 382, 384, 386, 433, 494, 528–30, 561, 566–8, 570, 572

Socialism 115, 252, 255, 387–393

Sovereignty 13, 62–66, 69, 72, 128, 254, 269, 321, 388, 404, 567–9, 573, 580, 586, 595–7, 601, 603, 617, 626–9, 631–2, 636–8, 641, 643–4, 651

Spencer, Herbert 300, 302, 304, 585–6

State of nature 3–5, 13–19, 20, 52–4, 58–9, 61–2, 66, 173–4, 177, 195, 205–6, 287, 333–6, 444–5, 456–7, 459–62, 464–5, 560–1, 581, 627–8, 642, 651

Talent 189, 209–13, 204, 320, 340, 370, 379, 382–5, 461, 464, 483, 489–90, 492, 495, 500–1, 503, 537, 542, 577

Taxation 36–7, 44, 77, 81, 83–6, 88, 115, 136, 151, 190, 198, 231, 236, 238, 247, 254–5, 258–61, 263–4, 267, 271–3, 276, 280, 283, 300, 305–6, 355–6, 367–9, 383, 412, 445, 508, 512, 517, 523, 526–7, 562, 585, 589, 592, 600, 603, 643

Teleology 107–10, 119, 201, 204, 220, 222, 430

Territory 36, 62, 69, 79–81, 85–6, 88, 99, 113, 128, 290, 312, 315, 372, 423, 524, 528, 538, 541, 572, 577, 585–6, 595, 598–602, 605, 610–11, 629, 634, 662

Torture 128, 163, 352, 421, 458, 571, 606–7, 627, 630, 633, 647–663

Tradition 47, 102, 108, 195, 198–9, 205, 209, 222–3, 226, 232, 247, 357, 361, 374, 391, 393, 422, 424, 431–2, 484–5, 500, 513, 518, 528, 539, 552, 567, 571–2, 596–7, 605, 612–13, 615–17, 619, 624, 630, 645

Tullock, Gordon 107, 270, 279–80

Tyranny 67, 127, 193, 304, 395, 399–401, 414, 420, 429, 437, 443, 446, 591, 626–46, 653, 658, 663

Unanimity 43, 49, 59, 68–70, 216–17, 278, 409, 613, 620

Utilitarianism 108, 123, 138, 144–5, 160, 166, 178, 186, 190 193, 197, 200, 203–6, 216, 220, 223–4, 282, 340, 360–1, 399, 419, 423, 431, 545, 549, 554, 570, 638–40

Utility 72, 75, 137–8, 166, 178–81, 183, 187–8, 190–3, 196–7, 201, 203, 205, 209, 223, 260, 300, 321, 328, 340–1, 360 402, 418, 446, 468–71, 475–7, 484, 546, 552, 556, 614, 657

Veil of Ignorance 100, 195, 198–9, 214–17, 226, 384, 444

Violence 9, 11, 14–18, 37, 47, 67, 71, 73–4, 79–85, 87, 103, 139, 141, 144–5, 163, 171, 173–5, 281, 381, 413, 425, 445, 455, 461, 541, 574, 585, 590, 602, 605–6, 627–8, 632, 640, 642–3, 657–8

Virtue 90, 104, 105, 121, 148, 165, 169, 171, 173–7, 179, 185, 192–3, 194, 219, 220, 222, 226, 245, 272, 315, 333, 352, 392, 405, 419, 430, 432–3, 440, 455, 459–61, 496, 503, 513, 521, 565, 567–9, 574, 580, 594, 617

Voluntariness 7, 11, 37, 39–41, 47, 51, 55, 69, 71–75, 88, 165, 182, 189, 192, 196, 223, 225, 232, 242, 277, 292, 339, 358–9, 365–6, 369–70, 403, 414, 430, 442–3, 452, 482, 486–90, 492–3, 517, 555, 560, 589–90, 540, 544–5

Voting 59–60, 64–5, 67–70, 94–97, 115–18, 120–1, 123, 130, 137, 141, 206, 261, 271–80, 448, 499, 518, 523, 531, 570, 591–2, 603, 610, 620, 661

Walzer, Michael 537, 541, 566, 575, 632–4

War 4, 7, 9–11, 15, 17–19, 44, 46–50, 54, 57–8, 72, 75, 78–82, 84–89, 137, 139–40, 143–4, 174, 227, 239, 242, 373, 381, 424, 433, 457, 462, 503, 530, 549, 558–9, 563, 568–9, 571–2, 574, 578, 586, 605–7, 609–25, 627–32, 635–8, 642–45, 649, 655, 657, 660–1, 663

Wealth 103, 167, 196–9, 202, 207, 210–11, 217, 231, 239, 242, 248–9, 251, 267, 270–1, 280, 282, 296–9, 300–1, 303, 306, 310, 312, 324, 334, 339–41, 353, 355, 357, 377, 383, 385, 390, 392, 396, 441, 451–2, 455, 457, 466–7, 495–6, 500, 504–6, 508, 510–12, 526–8, 530–1, 545–6, 554, 559, 555–6, 570, 577, 582, 586, 601, 611, 621, 634

Welfare 44, 83, 109–10, 131, 136, 146, 161, 165, 194, 197–8, 200–1, 203–4, 212, 214, 217, 219, 223, 226–7, 267, 270, 275–7, 280, 314–16, 333, 343–5, 355–6, 361, 389–90, 392, 405, 432, 453, 461, 473, 482, 485–94, 498, 511, 518, 522–3, 525–7, 531–2, 537, 560, 620, 639

Well-being 57, 68, 71, 130, 166–7, 172, 175, 179, 190, 197, 200, 208, 213, 269, 306, 321, 387, 396, 404–5, 439, 490–1, 494, 527, 560, 607